# McDougal, Littell
# Literature

## Blue Level

**David W. Foote**
Evanston Township High School
Evanston, Illinois

**Brenda Pierce Perkins**
Lake Forest High School
Lake Forest, Illinois

McDougal, Littell & Company
Evanston, Illinois
New York   Sacramento

# Consultants

**Joseph F. Dutton,** English Department Head, Columbus East High School, Columbus, Indiana

**Harvey S. Farr,** Elk Grove High School, Elk Grove, California

**Betty Niles,** English Department Head, Northwest High School, Indianapolis, Indiana

**Jack A. Pelletier,** English Department Head, La Sierra High School, Carmichael, California

**Frances M. Russell,** Director of English, Winchester Public Schools, Winchester, Massachusetts

**Robert Squires,** English Department Head, Oneonta High School, Oneonta, New York

**Acknowledgments**

The Atlantic Monthly: For "Gaston, A Story" by William Saroyan; copyright © 1962, by The Atlantic Monthly Company, Boston, Mass. Patricia Ayers: For "Forever" and "Metaphor," from *It Doesn't Always Have To Rhyme* by Eve Merriam, published by Atheneum; copyright © 1964 by Eve Merriam, reprinted by permission of the author. Robert Bly: For "Driving to Town Late To Mail a *continued on page 850*

ISBN: 0–88343–268–4

# Contents

# Special Features of This Text

## High-Quality Selections

- The **McDougal, Littell Literature Series** offers exceptionally high-quality selections—both traditional and contemporary.
- The selections have appeal to a broad range of student interests and abilities.

## Clear, Consistent Organization

- Each book is organized into units. Each unit deals with a literary type.
- Each unit follows a consistent organization:

  **Unit Opener**—The fine art evokes images that reflect the unifying idea of the unit.

  **Introduction to the Unit**—This page prepares the student for the literary type or thematic idea to be covered in the unit.

  **The Selections and Study Questions**—Each selection is followed by its own set of study questions and skills.

  **Unit Review**—Each unit ends with a unit review that synthesizes similarities, differences, and relationships among the ideas in the selections.

## Sustained Study of Literary Types

- The series provides an exceptionally comprehensive study of literary types: the short story, nonfiction, poetry, drama, the novel. The sustained exploration of each literary type gives students a strong grasp of the possibilities of the genre.
- Literary types have been subdivided into elements that provide the focus of study of each genre, as follows:

  **The Short Story**—Setting, Character, Plot, Theme, Point of View

  **Nonfiction**—Autobiography, Biography, Nature, Social Commentary

  **Poetry**—Rhythm and Rhyme, Form and Meaning, Speaker and Tone, Imagery, Figures of Speech, Idea

  **Drama**

  **The Novel**

## Carefully Formulated Study Questions

- In-depth study questions develop the following skills:

  **Getting at Meaning**—These study questions help students uncover the deeper meanings of a work of literature.

  **Developing Skills in Reading Literature**—These questions introduce and reinforce literary terms and techniques that guide the students in learning how to read and understand literature.

  **Developing Vocabulary**—These exercises provide for the study, analysis, and improvement of vocabulary.

  **Developing Writing Skills**—These exercises provide continuing guided opportunities for writing in all forms, including creative writing.

MAN AND WOMAN IN A LARGE ROOM, 1957. *Richard Diebenkorn.*
*Hirshhorn Museum and Sculpture Garden, Smithsonian Institution.*

# Unit 1

# The Short Story

INTERIOR OF A RESTAURANT, 1887. *Vincent Van Gogh.*
*Collection: State Museum Kröller-Müller, Otterlo, The Netherlands.*

# Introduction to the Unit

Fiction is literature created in the imagination of a writer. Often inspired by actual situations, fiction may be anchored in historical or contemporary reality; however, a work of fiction also may be an unfettered flight of fantasy.

The subjects available to the writer of fiction are practically unlimited. In this unit, writers deal with subjects as diverse as life in the twenty-first century, the marriage of a seventeen-year-old pioneer, the rise and fall of a cowardly dragon slayer, the insect-resident of a peach stone, and the odyssey of a lonely crow.

Some writers of fiction treat subjects lightly, having as a purpose the entertainment of the reader. Other writers criticize, interpret, and comment on behavior and situations in order to deepen reader understanding of the human experience.

The short story is one type of fiction. Unlike longer forms of fiction, the short story develops a few characters, in a limited setting, with a narrow range of action. Five elements of the short story are explored in this unit: setting, character, plot, point of view, and theme. Setting refers to where and when the action of a story takes place. Characters are the individuals who participate in the action. Characters are both unique and symbolic; they are interesting in themselves and also provide insights into human behavior. The plot of a story is the structure of events. The events are related by a narrator who maintains a certain point of view. As a story unfolds, the theme, or message of the writer, emerges.

As you study the short stories in this unit, you will consider these elements separately, paying particular attention to those that dominate each story. Keep in mind, though, that in every story all five elements interact. A change in character, for example, helps to convey theme. A setting might trigger events in the plot. By examining the special blend of elements in a story, the reader can perceive the writer's intentions and can appreciate the skill with which they have been carried out.

# Setting

OLD FRIENDS. *Winslow Homer.*
*Worcester Art Museum, Worcester, Massachusetts.*

# Searching for Summer   *Joan Aiken*

Lily wore yellow on her wedding day. In the 'eighties people put a lot of faith in omens, and believed that if a bride's dress was yellow, her married life would be blessed with a bit of sunshine.

It was years since the bombs had been banned, but still the cloud never lifted. Whitish gray, day after day, sometimes darkening to a weeping slate-color, or, at the end of an evening, turning to smoky copper, the sky endlessly, secretively brooded.

Old people began their stories with the classic, fairy-tale opening: "Long, long ago, when I was a liddle 'un, in the days when the sky was blue . . ." and children, listening, chuckled among themselves at the absurd thought, because, *blue,* imagine it! How could the sky ever have been *blue?* You might as well say, "In the days when the grass was pink."

Stars, rainbows, and all other such heavenly sideshows had been permanently withdrawn, and if the radio announced that there was a blink of sunshine in such and such a place, where the cloud belt had thinned for half an hour, cars and buses would pour in that direction for days in an unavailing search for warmth and light.

After the wedding, when all the relations were standing on the church porch, with Lily shivering prettily in her buttercup nylon, her father prodded the dour and withered grass on a grave—although it was August the leaves were hardly out yet—and said, "Well, Tom, what are you aiming to do now, eh?"

"Going to find a bit of sun and have our honeymoon in it," said Tom. There was a general laugh from the wedding party.

"Don't get sunburned," shrilled Aunt Nancy.

"Better start off Bournemouth[1] way. Paper said they had a half hour of sun last Wednesday week," Uncle Arthur weighed in heavily.

"We'll come back brown as—as this grass," said Tom, and ignoring the good-natured teasing from their respective families, the two young people mounted on their scooter, which stood ready at the churchyard wall, and chugged away in a shower of golden confetti. When they were out of sight, and the yellow paper had subsided on the gray and gritty road, the Whitemores and the Hoskinses strolled off, sighing, to eat wedding cake and drink currant wine; and old Mrs. Hoskins spoiled everyone's pleasure by bursting into tears as she thought of her own wedding day when everything was so different.

Meanwhile Tom and Lily buzzed on hopefully across the gray countryside, with Lily's veil like a gilt banner floating behind. It was chilly going for her in her wedding things, but the sight of a bride was supposed to bring good luck, and so she stuck it out, although her fingers were blue to the knuckles. Every now and then they switched on their portable radio and listened to the forecast. Inverness had seen the sun for ten minutes yesterday, and Southend[2] for five minutes this morning, but that was all.

"Both those places are a long way from here," said Tom cheerfully. "All the more

---

1. **Bournemouth** (bôrn' məth): a seaside resort in south-central England.
2. **Inverness** (in' vər nes') . . . **Southend-on-Sea:** two other resort cities in the British Isles.

reason we'd find a nice bit of sunshine in these parts somewhere. We'll keep on going south. Keep your eyes peeled, Lil, and tell me if you see a blink of sun on those hills ahead."

But they came to the hills and passed them, and a new range shouldered up ahead and then slid away behind, and still there was no flicker or patch of sunshine to be seen anywhere in the gray, winter-ridden landscape. Lily began to get discouraged, so they stopped for a cup of tea at a drive-in.

"Seen the sun lately, mate?" Tom asked the proprietor.

He laughed shortly. "Notice any buses or trucks around here? Last time I saw the sun was two years ago September; came out just in time for the wife's birthday."

"It's stars I'd like to see," Lily said, looking wistfully at her dust-colored tea. "Ever so pretty they must be."

"Well, better be getting on I suppose," said Tom, but he had lost some of his bounce and confidence. Every place they passed through looked nastier than the last, partly on account of the dismal light, partly because people had given up bothering to take a pride in their boroughs. And then, just as they were entering a village called Molesworth, the dimmest, drabbest, most insignificant huddle of houses they had come to yet, the engine coughed and died on them.

"Can't see what's wrong," said Tom, after a prolonged and gloomy survey.

"Oh, Tom!" Lily was almost crying. "What'll we do?"

"Have to stop here for the night, s'pose." Tom was short-tempered with frustration. "Look, there's a garage just up the road. We can push the bike there, and they'll tell us if there's a pub where we can stay. It's nearly six anyway."

They had taken the bike to the garage, and the man there was just telling them that the only pub in the village was the Rising Sun, where Mr. Noakes might be able to give them

a bed, when a bus pulled up in front of the petrol pumps.

"Look," the garage owner said, "there's Mr. Noakes just getting out of the bus now. Sid!" he called.

But Mr. Noakes was not able to come to them at once. Two old people were climbing slowly out of the bus ahead of him: a blind man with a white stick, and a withered, frail old lady in a black satin dress and hat. "Careful now, George," she was saying, "mind ee be careful with my son, William."

"I'm being careful, Mrs. Hatching," the conductor said patiently, as he almost lifted the unsteady old pair off the bus platform. The driver had stopped his engine, and everyone on the bus was taking a mild and sympathetic interest, except for Mr. Noakes just behind who was cursing irritably at the delay. When the two old people were on the narrow pavement, the conductor saw that they were going to have trouble with a bicycle that was propped against the curb just ahead of them; he picked it up and stood holding it until they had passed the line of petrol pumps and were going slowly off along a path across the fields. Then, grinning, he put it back, jumped hurriedly into the bus, and rang his bell.

"Old nuisances," Mr. Noakes said furiously. "Wasting public time. Every week that palaver goes on, taking the old man to Midwick Hospital Out Patients and back again. I know what I'd do with 'em. Put to sleep, that sort ought to be."

Mr. Noakes was a repulsive-looking individual, but when he heard that Tom and Lily wanted a room for the night, he changed completely and gave them a leer that was full of false goodwill. He was a big, red-faced man with wet, full lips, bulging pale-gray bloodshot eyes, and a crop of stiff greasy black hair. He wore tennis shoes. "Honeymooners, eh?" he said, looking sentimentally at Lily's pale prettiness. They followed Mr. Noakes glumly up the street to the Rising Sun.

While they were eating their baked beans, Mr. Noakes stood over their table grimacing at them. Lily unwisely confided to him that they were looking for a bit of sunshine. Mr. Noakes's laughter nearly shook down the ramshackle building.

"Sunshine! That's a good 'un! Hear that, Mother?" he bawled to his wife. "They're looking for a bit of sunshine. Heh-heh-heh-heh-heh-heh! Why," he said, banging on the table till the baked beans leaped about, "if I could find a bit of sunshine near here, permanent bit that is, dja know what I'd do?"

The young people looked at him inquiringly across the bread and margarine.

"Lido,[3] trailer-site, country club, holiday camp—you wouldn't know the place. Land around here is dirt cheap, I'd buy up the lot. Nothing but woods. I'd advertise—I'd have people flocking to this little dump from all over the country. But what a hope, what a hope, eh? Well, feeling better? Enjoyed your tea? Ready for bed?

Avoiding one another's eyes, Tom and Lily stood up.

"I—I'd like to go for a bit of a walk first, Tom," Lily said in a small voice. "Look, I picked up that old lady's bag on the pavement. I didn't notice it till we'd done talking to Mr. Noakes, and by then she was out of sight. Should we take it back to her?"

"Good idea," said Tom, pouncing on the suggestion with relief. "Do you know where she lives, Mr. Noakes?"

"Who, old Ma Hatching? Sure I know. She lives in the wood. But you don't want to go taking her bag back, not this time o' the evening you don't. Let her worry. She'll come asking for it in the morning."

"She walked so slowly," said Lily, holding the bag gently in her hands. It was very old, made of black velvet on two ring-handles, and embroidered with beaded roses. "I think we ought to take it to her, don't you Tom?"

"Oh, very well, very well, have it your own way," Mr. Noakes said, winking at Tom. "Take that path by the garage. You can't go wrong. I've never been there meself, but they live somewhere in that wood back o' the village. You'll find it soon enough."

They found the path soon enough, but not the cottage. Under the lowering sky they walked forward endlessly among trees that carried only tiny and rudimentary leaves, wizened and poverty stricken. Lily was still wearing her wedding sandals, which had begun to blister her. She held onto Tom's arm, biting her lip with the pain, and he looked down miserably at her bent brown head; everything had turned out so differently from what he had planned.

By the time they reached the cottage, Lily could hardly bear to put her left foot to the ground, and Tom was gentling her along. "It can't be much farther now, and they'll be sure to have a bandage. I'll tie it up, and you can have a sit-down. Maybe they'll give us a cup of tea. We could borrow an old pair of socks or something. . . ." Hardly noticing the cottage garden, beyond a vague impression of rows of runner beans, they made for the clematis-grown porch and knocked. There was a brass lion's head on the door, carefully polished.

"Eh, me dear!" It was the old lady, old Mrs. Hatching, who opened the door, and her exclamation was a long-drawn gasp of pleasure and astonishment. "Eh, me dear! 'Tis the pretty bride. See'd ye s'arternoon when we was coming home from hospital."

"Who be?" shouted a voice from inside.

"Come in, come in, me dears. My son William'll be glad to hear company; he can't see, poor soul, nor has this thirty year, ah, and a pretty sight he's losing this minute——"

"We brought back your bag," Tom said, putting it in her hands, "and we wondered if

---

3. **lido** (lē' dō): *British:* a public open-air swimming pool.

you'd have a bit of plaster[4] you could kindly let us have. My wife's hurt her foot——"

My wife. Even in the midst of Mrs. Hatching's voluble welcome the strangeness of these words struck the two young people, and they fell quiet, each of them, pondering, while Mrs. Hatching thanked and commiserated, all in a breath, and asked them to take a seat on the sofa and fetched a basin of water from the scullery; and William from his seat in the chimney corner demanded to know what it was all about.

"Wot be doing? Wot be doing, Mother?"

" 'Tis a bride, all in's finery," she shrilled back at him, "an's blistered her foot, poor heart." Keeping up a running commentary for William's benefit, she bound up the foot, every now and then exclaiming to herself in wonder over the fineness of Lily's wedding dress, which lay in yellow nylon swathes around the chair. "There, me dear. Now us'll have a cup of tea, eh? Proper thirsty you'm fare to be, walking all the way to here this hot day."

Hot day? Tom and Lily stared at each other and then around the room. Then it was true, it was not their imagination, that a great, dusty golden square of sunshine lay on the fireplace wall, where the brass pendulum of the clock at every swing blinked into sudden brilliance? That the blazing geraniums on the windowsill housed a drove of murmuring bees? That, through the window the gleam of linen hung in the sun to whiten suddenly dazzled their eyes?

"The sun? Is it really the sun?" Tom said, almost doubtfully.

"And why not?" Mrs. Hatching demanded. "How else'll beans set, tell me that? Fine thing if sun were to stop shining." Chuckling to herself she set out a Crown Derby tea set, gorgeously colored in red and gold, and a baking of saffron buns. Then she sat down and, drinking her own tea, began to question the two of them about where they had come from, where they were going. The tea was tawny and hot and sweet; the clock's tick was like a bird chirping; every now and then a log settled in the grate. Lily looked sleepily around the little room, so rich and peaceful, and thought, I wish we were staying here. I wish we needn't go back to that horrible pub. . . . She leaned against Tom's comforting arm.

"Look at the sky," she whispered to him. "Out there between the geraniums. Blue!"

"And ee'll come up and see my spare bedroom, won't ee now?" Mrs. Hatching said, breaking off the thread of her questions—which indeed was not a thread, but merely a savoring of her pleasure and astonishment at this unlooked-for visit—"Bide here, why don't ee? Mid as well. The lil un's fair wore out. Us'll do for ee better 'n rangy old Noakes, proper old scoundrel 'e be. Won't us, William?"

"Ah," William said appreciatively. "I'll sing ee some o' my songs."

A sight of the spare room settled any doubts. The great white bed, huge as a prairie, built up with layer upon solid layer of mattress, blanket, and quilt, almost filled the little shadowy room in which it stood. Brass rails shone in the green dimness. "Isn't it quiet," Lily whispered. Mrs. Hatching, silent for the moment, stood looking at them proudly, her bright eyes slowly moving from face to face. Once her hand fondled, as if it might have been a baby's downy head, the yellow brass knob.

And so, almost without any words, the matter was decided.

Three days later they remembered that they must go to the village and collect the scooter which must, surely, be mended by now.

They had been helping old William pick a

---

4. **plaster:** *British:* adhesive tape.

basketful of beans. Tom had taken his shirt off, and the sun gleamed on his brown back; Lily was wearing an old cotton print which Mrs. Hatching, with much chuckling, had shortened to fit her.

It was amazing how deftly, in spite of his blindness, William moved among the beans, feeling through the rough, rustling leaves for the stiffness of concealed pods. He found twice as many as Tom and Lily, but then they, even on the third day, were still stopping every other minute to exclaim over the blueness of the sky. At night they sat on the back doorstep while Mrs. Hatching clucked inside as she dished the supper, "Star-struck ee'll be! Come along in, do-ee, before soup's cold. Stars niver run away yet as I do know."

"Can we get anything for you in the village?" Lily asked, but Mrs. Hatching shook her head.

"Baker's bread and suchlike's no use but to cripple thee's innardses wi' colic. I been living here these eighty year wi'out troubling doctors, and I'm not faring to begin now." She waved to them and stood watching as they walked into the wood, thin and frail beyond belief, but wiry, indomitable, her black eyes full of zest. Then she turned to scream menacingly at a couple of pullets who had strayed and were scratching among the potatoes.

Almost at once they noticed, as they followed the path, that the sky was clouded over.

"It *is* only there on that one spot," Lily said in wonder. "All the time. And they've never even noticed that the sun doesn't shine in other places."

"That's how it must have been all over the world, once," Tom said.

At the garage they found their scooter ready and waiting. They were about to start back when they ran into Mr. Noakes.

"Well, well, well, well, *well!*" he shouted, glaring at them with ferocious good humor.

"How many wells make a river, eh? And where did you slip off to? Here's me and the missus was just going to tell the police to have the rivers dragged. But hullo, hullo, what's this? Brown, eh? Suntan? Scrumptious," he said, looking meltingly at Lily and giving her another tremendous pinch. "Where'd you get it, eh? That wasn't all got in half an hour, *I* know. Come on, this means money to you and me, tell us the big secret. Remember what I said; land around these parts is dirt cheap."

Tom and Lily looked at each other in horror. They thought of the cottage, the bees humming among the runner beans, the sunlight glinting in the red-and-gold teacups. At night, when they had lain in the huge, sagging bed, stars had shone through the window, and the whole wood was as quiet as the inside of a shell.

"Oh, we've been miles from here," Tom lied hurriedly. "We ran into a friend, and he took us right away beyond Brinsley." And as Mr. Noakes still looked suspicious and unsatisfied, he did the only thing possible. "We're going back there now," he said; "the sunbathing's grand." And opening the throttle he let the scooter go. They waved at Mr. Noakes and chugged off toward the gray hills that lay to the north.

"My wedding dress," Lily said sadly. "It's on our bed."

They wondered how long Mrs. Hatching would keep tea hot for them, who would eat all the pastries.

"Never mind, you won't need it again," Tom comforted her.

At least, he thought, they had left the golden place undisturbed. Mr. Noakes never went into the wood. And they had done what they intended; they had found the sun. Now they, too, would be able to tell their grandchildren, when beginning a story, "Long, long ago, when we were young, in the days when the sky was blue. . . ."

GRAY AND GOLD, 1942. John Rogers Cox.
The Cleveland Museum of Art. Purchase, Mr. and Mrs. William H. Marlatt Fund.

## Getting at Meaning

1. People believe in the omen of a yellow bridal dress; children laugh at the idea of a blue sky; and Tom hopes to return from his honeymoon "brown as grass." What does this information at the beginning of the story reveal about the environment?

2. Lily wears her flimsy yellow wedding dress, even though she is cold. Why? What does this reveal about her character?

3. When Lily and Tom stop for tea, Tom asks, "Seen the sun lately, mate?" The proprietor responds, "Notice any buses or trucks around here?" What do buses and trucks have to do with the sun?

4. What does the reaction of Mr. Noakes to Mrs. Hatching and her son reveal about his character? Describe the change in his personality when he learns that Tom and Lily want a room for the night.

5. Why don't Tom and Lily immediately notice the details of Mrs. Hatching's sun-filled world? How do they react when they do notice them?

6. Contrast the attitudes of Mrs. Hatching and Mr. Noakes toward Tom and Lily as guests.

7. Why do Tom and Lily hide the truth from Noakes?

8. Reread the opening paragraph of the story. Does the omen of a yellow bridal dress work for Lily? What happens to the bridal dress at the end of the story? What does this mean in terms of Lily and Tom's future life?

## Developing Skills in Reading Literature

1. **Fiction.** The term *fiction* describes literature that is created in the imagination of a writer. Although fiction can feature actual people, places, and events, a work of fiction considered in its entirety is imaginative rather than factual.

The short story is one kind of fiction. In this short story, which elements are purely imaginary? Which are realistic? Are the realistic elements necessarily factual? Explain.

2. **Setting.** Setting is the time and place in which the action of a story occurs. The writer of this story tells the reader that the story takes place in the "eighties." Which "eighties"? How do you know?

The writer creates two distinct environments, both of which are crucial to the development of the story. Find words and phrases that describe the cloudy, gray environment that dominates the beginning of the story. How does this environment affect Tom and Lily? Now find words and phrases that describe the sunny environment at the cottage. How are Tom and Lily altered by this environment?

3. **Conflict.** The conflict in a story is the struggle between two opposing forces. In this story, the opposing forces are the attitudes represented by Mr. Noakes and those represented by Tom, Lily, and the Hatchings. What do Mr. Noakes's plans for a holiday camp reveal about his views on the value of sunshine? What impact would his plans have upon the Hatchings' world? How is the conflict resolved?

## Developing Writing Skills

1. **Describing a Place.** Imagine that you are saying to your own grandchildren, "Long, long ago, when I was young, . . ." Complete this sentence so that it makes a statement about a place where you have been very happy. Then describe the place in one paragraph. Use vivid adjectives and many specific details so that your readers will "see" the place as you see it.

2. **Description: Creating a Dominant Impression.** The writer of this story uses specific details to create two distinct worlds, each with its own atmosphere. In one world, the sky is a "weeping slate-color"; even the tea is "dust-colored." In the Hatchings' world, polished brass "blinked into sudden brilliance" and the tea is "tawny and hot and sweet."

Write two paragraphs, each describing a familiar scene. In the first paragraph, use specific details to show the scene as it appears at a particular time of day, during a certain season of the year, or in the midst of unique weather conditions. In the second paragraph, use appropriate details to show the same scene under different conditions. For example, if your first paragraph describes a city street on a sunny day, your second paragraph might describe the same street in a snowstorm.

# The Tradition  *Algernon Blackwood*

The noises outside the little flat at first were very disconcerting after living in the country. They made sleep difficult. At the cottage in Sussex[1] where the family had lived, night brought deep, comfortable silence, unless the wind was high, when the pine trees round the duck-pond made a sound like surf, or, if the gale was from the southwest, the orchard roared a bit unpleasantly.

But in London it was very different; sleep was easier in the daytime than at night. For, after nightfall, the rumble of the traffic became spasmodic instead of continuous; the motor-horns startled like warnings of alarm; after comparative silence the furious rushing of a taxicab touched the nerves. From dinner till eleven o'clock the streets subsided gradually; then came the army from theatres, parties, and late dinners, hurrying home to bed. The motor-horns during this hour were lively and incessant, like bugles of a regiment moving into battle. The parents rarely retired until this attack was over. If quick about it, sleep was possible then before the flying of the night-birds—an uncertain squadron—screamed half the street awake again. But, these finally disposed of, a delightful hush settled down upon the neighborhood, profounder far than any peace of the countryside. The deep rumble of the produce wagons, coming in to the big London markets from the farms—generally about three A.M.—held no disturbing quality.

But sometimes in the stillness of very early morning, when streets were empty and pavements all deserted, there was a sound of another kind that was startling and unwelcome.

For it was ominous. It came with a clattering violence that made nerves quiver and forced the heart to pause and listen. A strange resonance was in it, a volume of sound, moreover, that was hardly justified by its cause. For it was hoofs. A horse swept hurrying up the deserted street, and was close upon the building in a moment. It was audible suddenly, no gradual approach from a distance, but as though it turned a corner from soft ground that muffled the hoofs, on to the echoing, hard paving that emphasized the dreadful clatter. Nor did it die away again when once the house was reached. It ceased as abruptly as it came. The hoofs did not go away.

It was the mother who heard them first, and drew her husband's attention to their disagreeable quality.

"It is the mail-vans, dear," he answered. "They go at four A.M. to catch the early trains into the country."

She looked up sharply, as though something in his tone surprised her.

"But there's no sound of wheels," she said. And then, as he did not reply, she added gravely, "You have heard it too, John. I can tell."

"I have," he said. "I have heard it—twice."

And they looked at one another searchingly, each trying to read the other's mind. She did not question him; he did not propose writing to complain in a newspaper; both understood something that neither of them quite believed.

"I heard it first," she then said softly, "the

night before Jack got the fever. And, as I listened, I heard him crying. But when I went in to see he was asleep. The noise stopped just outside the building." There was a shadow in her eyes as she said this, and a hush crept in between her words. "I did not hear it *go*." She said this almost beneath her breath.

He looked a moment at the ground; then, coming towards her, he took her in his arms and kissed her. And she clung very tightly to him.

"Sometimes," he said in a quiet voice, "a mounted policeman passes down the street, I think."

"It is a horse," she answered. But whether it was a question or mere corroboration he did not ask, for at that moment the doctor arrived, and the question of little Jack's health became the paramount matter of immediate interest. The great man's verdict was uncommonly disquieting.

All that night they sat up in the sick room. It was strangely still, as though by one accord the traffic avoided the house where a little boy hung between life and death. The motor-horns even had a muffled sound, and heavy drays and wagons used the side streets; there were fewer taxicabs about, or else they flew by noiselessly. Yet no straw was down; the expense prohibited that. And towards morning, very early, the mother decided to watch alone. She had been a trained nurse before her marriage, accustomed when she was younger to long vigils. "You go down, dear, and get a little sleep," she urged in a whisper. "He's quiet now. At five o'clock I'll come for you to take my place."

"You'll fetch me at once," he whispered, "if——" then hesitated as though breath failed him. A moment he stood there staring from her face to the bed. "If you hear anything," he finished. She nodded, and he went downstairs to his study, not to his bedroom. He left the door ajar. He sat in darkness, listening. Mother, he knew, was listening, too, beside the bed. His heart was very full, for he did not believe the boy could live till morning. The picture of the room was all the time before his eyes—the shaded lamp, the table with the medicines, the little wasted figure beneath the blankets, and mother close beside it, listening. He sat alert, ready to fly upstairs at the smallest cry.

But no sound broke the stillness; the entire neighborhood was silent; all London slept. He heard the clock strike three in the dining-room at the end of the corridor. It was still enough for that. There was not even the heavy rumble of a single produce wagon, though usually they passed about this time on their way to Smithfield and Covent Garden markets. He waited, far too anxious to close his eyes. . . . At four o'clock he would go up and relieve her vigil. Four, he knew, was the time when life sinks to its lowest ebb. . . . Then, in the middle of his reflections, thought stopped dead, and it seemed his heart stopped too.

Far away, but coming nearer with extraordinary rapidity, a sharp, clear sound broke out of the surrounding stillness—a horse's hoofs. At first it was so distant that it might have been almost on the high roads of the country, but the amazing speed with which it came closer, and the sudden increase of the beating sound was such, that by the time he turned his head it seemed to have entered the street outside. It was within a hundred yards of the building. The next second it was before the very door. And something in him blanched. He knew a moment's complete paralysis. The abrupt cessation of the heavy clatter was strangest of all. It came like lightning, it struck, it paused. It did not go away again. Yet the sound of it was still beating in his ears as he dashed upstairs three steps at a time. It seemed in the house as well, on the stairs behind him, in the little passage-way, *inside the very bedroom.* It was an appalling

sound. Yet he entered a room that was quiet, orderly, and calm. It was silent. Beside the bed his wife sat, holding Jack's hand and stroking it. She was soothing him; her face was very peaceful. No sound but her gentle whisper was audible.

He controlled himself by a tremendous effort, but his face betrayed his consternation and distress. "Hush," she said beneath her breath, "he's sleeping much more calmly now. The crisis, bless God, is over, I do believe. I dared not leave him."

He saw in a moment that she was right, and an untellable relief passed over him. He sat down beside her, very cold, yet perspiring with heat.

"You heard——?" he asked after a pause.

"Nothing," she replied quickly, "except his pitiful, wild words when the delirium was on him. It's passed. It lasted but a moment, or I'd have called you."

He stared closely into her tired eyes. "And his words?" he asked in a whisper. Whereupon she told him quietly that the little chap had sat up with wide-opened eyes and talked excitedly about a "great, great horse" he heard, but that was not "coming for him." "He laughed and said he would not go with it because he 'was not ready yet.' Some scrap of talk he had overheard from us," she added, "when we discussed the traffic once. . . ."

"But *you* heard nothing?" he repeated almost impatiently.

No, she had heard nothing. After all, then, he *had* dozed a moment in his chair. . . .

Four weeks later Jack, entirely convalescent, was playing a restricted game of hide-and-seek with his sister in the flat. It was really a forbidden joy, owing to noise and risk of breakages, but he had unusual privileges after his grave illness. It was dusk. The lamps in the street were being lit. "Quietly, remember; your mother's resting in her room," were the father's orders. She had just returned from a week by the sea, recuperating from the strain of nursing for so many nights. The traffic rolled and boomed along the streets below.

"Jack! Do come on and hide. It's your turn. I hid last."

But the boy was standing spellbound by the window, staring hard at something on the pavement. Sybil called and tugged in vain. Tears threatened. Jack would not budge. He declared he saw something.

"Oh, you're always seeing something. I wish you'd go and hide. It's only because you can't think of a good place, really."

"Look!" he cried in a voice of wonder. And as he said it his father rose quickly from his chair before the fire.

"Look!" the child repeated with delight and excitement. "It's a great, great horse. And it's perfectly white all over." His sister joined him at the window. "Where? Where? I can't see it. Oh, *do* show me!"

Their father was standing close behind them now. "I heard it," he was whispering, but so low the children did not notice him. His face was very pale.

"Straight in front of our door, stupid! Can't you see it? Oh, I do wish it had come for me. It's *such* a beauty!" And he clapped his hands with pleasure and excitement. "Quick, quick! I can hear it. It's going away again!"

But, while the children stood half squabbling by the window, their father leaned over a sofa in the adjoining room above a figure whose heart in sleep had quietly stopped its beating. The great, great horse had come. But this time he had not only heard its wonderful arrival. He had also heard it go. It seemed he heard the awful hoofs beat down the sky, far, far away, and very swiftly, dying into silence, finally up among the stars.

**Getting at Meaning**

1. What is the difference between the night noises in the country and in London? Where is it easier to sleep? Why?

2. What is the ominous noise occasionally heard late at night? What is unusual about this noise?

3. When does the mother first hear the strange noise?

4. Why are Jack's parents so concerned about him? What does each parent do during the night following the doctor's visit? What does each one hear during the night?

5. While Jack and his sister are playing, what does Jack see in front of the door? Describe his reaction to this sight.

6. For whom has the white horse come? What does the father hear this time that he has not heard earlier?

## Developing Skills in Reading Literature

1. **Setting.** At the beginning of this story, the narrator contrasts two settings, country and city. What characteristics of city life make it seem threatening? Motor-horns are described as "bugles of a regiment moving into battle." Find other examples of military terminology in the beginning of the story. What effect does the use of this terminology have on the reader?

2. **Suspense.** Suspense is the build-up of tension in a story that makes the reader continue reading. In this story, the opening description of setting creates tension. Then, the introduction of the ominous noise adds to the suspense. As the story progresses, how do the following events add to the suspense?

Jack's parents discuss the strange noise.
Jack becomes gravely ill.
The mother hears a horse the night before Jack's illness, and the father during his illness.
Jack sees a horse on the pavement while playing with his sister.

3. **Foreshadowing.** Foreshadowing is a clue or hint of some future event in a story. Although the reader is led to believe that Jack's health is in danger, the boy does not die. What clues are given during the story that prepare the reader for the mother's death? When answering this question, consider the member of the family who first hears the horse, the mother's profession, what each parent hears the night of Jack's illness, and the words spoken by Jack during his delirium.

## Developing Vocabulary

1. **Getting Word Meaning from Context.** Read the following sentences, and try to guess the meaning of each italicized word. Then look up each word in the Glossary and write its correct definition. Use the word in an original sentence that demonstrates its meaning.

a. After nightfall, the rumble of the traffic became *spasmodic* instead of continuous.

b. A strange *resonance* was in it, a volume of sound, moreover, that was hardly justified by its cause.

c. The question of little Jack's health became the *paramount* matter of immediate interest.

d. He controlled himself by a tremendous effort, but his face betrayed his *consternation* and distress.

e. She heard nothing except his pitiful, wild words when the *delirium* was on him.

2. **Prefixes.** A prefix is one or more syllables placed in front of a root word to change the meaning of the root. One of the most common negative prefixes is *un-*. *Un-* can mean "not" as in *unafraid* or "the opposite of" as in *untie*.

Skim the story up to the line, "All that night they sat up in the sick room." (p. 12) Find four words that begin with the prefix *un-*. Define each word in terms of the prefix. For example, *unnatural* means "not natural." Then locate the word *untellable* on p. 13. Define this word in terms of the prefix *un-*.

## Developing Writing Skills

**Explaining an Idea.** This story recalls the old belief that the appearance of a great white horse signals a death. Select a similar superstitious belief or a widely practiced holiday tradition; for example, the belief in the connection between black cats and bad luck or the practice of trick or treating on Halloween. Write a paragraph in which you describe the belief or superstition; then explain its origin, using the information in encyclopedias and other reference books as the basis for your discussion.

# The Magic Shop    *H. G. Wells*

**I** had seen the Magic Shop from afar several times. I had passed it once or twice, a shop window of alluring little objects, magic balls, magic hens, wonderful cones, ventriloquist dolls, the material of the basket trick, packs of cards that *looked* all right, and all that sort of thing, but never had I thought of going in until one day, almost without warning, Gip hauled me by my finger right up to the window, and so conducted himself that there was nothing for it but to take him in. I had not thought the place was there, to tell the truth—a modest-sized frontage in Regent Street,[1] between the picture shop and the place where the chicks run about just out of patent incubators—but there it was sure enough. I had fancied it was down nearer the Circus, or round the corner in Oxford Street, or even in Holborn; always over the way and a little inaccessible it had been, with something of the mirage in its position; but here it was now quite indisputably, and the fat end of Gip's pointing finger made a noise upon the glass.

"If I was rich," said Gip, dabbing a finger at the Disappearing Egg, "I'd buy myself that. And that"—which was The Crying Baby, Very Human—"and that," which was a mystery, and called, so a neat card asserted, "Buy One and Astonish Your Friends."

"Anything," said Gip, "will disappear under one of those cones. I have read about it in a book.

"And there, dadda, is the Vanishing Halfpenny—only they've put it this way up so's we can't see how it's done."

Gip, dear boy, inherits his mother's breeding, and he did not propose to enter the shop or worry in any way; only, you know, quite unconsciously, he lugged my finger doorward, and he made his interest clear.

"That," he said, and pointed to the Magic Bottle.

"If you had that?" I said; at which promising inquiry he looked up with a sudden radiance.

"I could show it to Jessie," he said, thoughtful as ever of others.

"It's less than a hundred days to your birthday, Gibbles," I said, and laid my hand on the door-handle.

Gip made no answer, but his grip tightened on my finger, and so we came into the shop.

It was no common shop this; it was a magic shop, and all the prancing precedence Gip would have taken in the matter of mere toys was wanting. He left the burden of the conversation to me.

It was a little, narrow shop, not very well lit, and the doorbell pinged again with a plaintive note as we closed it behind us. For a moment or so we were alone and could glance about us. There was a tiger in *papier-mâché* on the glass case that covered the low counter—a grave, kind-eyed tiger that waggled his head in a methodical manner. There were several crystal spheres, a china hand holding magic cards, a stock of magic fish-bowls in various sizes, and an immodest

---

1. **Regent Street:** a street in London. The Circus, Oxford, and Holborn also refer to London street areas.

magic bat that shamelessly displayed its springs. On the floor were magic mirrors; one to draw you out long and thin, one to swell your head and vanish your legs, and one to make you short and fat like a draught; and while we were laughing at these the shopman, as I suppose, came in.

At any rate, there he was behind the counter—a curious, sallow, dark man, with one ear larger than the other and a chin like the toecap of a boot.

"What can we have the pleasure?" he said, spreading his long magic fingers on the glass case; and so with a start we were aware of him.

"I want," I said, "to buy my little boy a few simple tricks."

"Legerdemain?"[2] he asked. "Mechanical? Domestic?"

"Anything amusing?" said I.

"Um!" said the shopman, and scratched his head for a moment as if thinking. Then, quite distinctly, he drew from his head a glass ball. "Something in this way?" he said, and held it out.

The action was unexpected. I had seen the trick done at entertainments endless times before—it's part of the common stock of conjurers—but I had not expected it here. "That's good," I said, with a laugh.

"Isn't it?" said the shopman.

Gip stretched out his disengaged hand to take this object and found merely a blank palm.

"It's in your pocket," said the shopman, and there it was!

"How much will that be?" I asked.

"We make no charge for glass balls," said the shopman politely. "We get them"—he picked one out of his elbow as he spoke—"free." He produced another from the back of his neck, and laid it beside its predecessor on the counter. Gip regarded his glass ball sagely, then directed a look of inquiry at the two on the counter, and finally brought his

round-eyed scrutiny to the shopman, who smiled. "You may have those two," said the shopman, "and, if you *don't* mind one from my mouth. *So!*"

Gip counselled me mutely for a moment, and then in a profound silence put away the four balls, resumed my reassuring finger, and nerved himself for the next event.

"We get all our smaller tricks in that way," the shopman remarked.

I laughed in the manner of one who subscribes to a jest. "Instead of going to the wholesale shop," I said. "Of course, it's cheaper."

"In a way," the shopman said. "Though we pay in the end. But not so heavily—as people suppose. . . . Our larger tricks, and our daily provisions, and all the other things we want, we get out of that hat. . . . And you know, sir, if you'll excuse my saying it, there *isn't* a wholesale shop, not for Genuine Magic goods, sir. I don't know if you noticed our inscription—the Genuine Magic Shop." He drew a business card from his cheek and handed it to me. "Genuine," he said, with his finger on the word, and added, "There is absolutely no deception, sir."

He seemed to be carrying out the joke pretty thoroughly, I thought.

He turned to Gip with smile of remarkable affability. "You, you know, are the Right Sort of Boy."

I was surprised at his knowing that, because, in the interests of discipline, we keep it rather a secret even at home; but Gip received it in unflinching silence, keeping a steadfast eye on him.

"It's only the Right Sort of Boy gets through that doorway."

And, as if by way of illustration, there came a rattling at the door, and a squeaking little voice could be faintly heard. "Nyar! I *warn* 'a go in there, dadda, I WARN 'a go in

---

2. **legerdemain** (lej′ ər di mān′): sleight of hand tricks.

there. Ny-a-a-ah!" and then the accents of a downtrodden parent, urging consolations and propitiations. "It's locked, Edward," he said.

"But it isn't," said I.

"It is, sir," said the shopman, "always—for that sort of child," and as he spoke we had a glimpse of the other youngster, a little, white face, pallid from sweet-eating and over-sapid food, and distorted by evil passions, a ruthless little egotist, pawing at the enchanted pane. "It's no good, sir," said the shopman, as I moved, with my natural helpfulness, doorward, and presently the spoilt child was carried off howling.

"How do you manage that?" I said, breathing a little more freely.

"Magic!" said the shopman, with a careless wave of the hand, and behold! sparks of colored fire flew out of his fingers and vanished into the shadows of the shop.

"You were saying," he said, addressing himself to Gip, "before you came in, that you would like one of our 'Buy One and Astonish your Friends' boxes?"

Gip, after a gallant effort, said "Yes."

"It's in your pocket."

And leaning over the counter—he really had an extraordinary long body—this amazing person produced the article in the customary conjurer's manner. "Paper," he said, and took a sheet out of the empty hat with the springs; "string," and behold his mouth was a string box, from which he drew an unending thread, which when he had tied his parcel he bit off—and, it seemed to me, swallowed the ball of string. And then he lit a candle at the nose of one of the ventriloquist's dummies, stuck one of his fingers (which had become sealing-wax red) into the flame, and so sealed the parcel. "Then there was the Disappearing Egg," he remarked, and produced one from within my coat-breast and packed it, and also The Crying Baby, Very Human. I handed each parcel to Gip as

it was ready, and he clasped them to his chest.

He said very little, but his eyes were eloquent; the clutch of his arms was eloquent. He was the playground of unspeakable emotions. These, you know, were *real* Magics.

Then, with a start, I discovered something moving about in my hat—something soft and jumpy. I whipped it off, and a ruffled pigeon—no doubt a confederate—dropped out and ran on the counter, and went, I fancy, into a cardboard box behind the *papier-mâché* tiger.

"Tut, tut!" said the shopman, dexterously relieving me of my headdress; "careless bird, and—as I live—nesting!"

He shook my hat, and shook out into his extended hand, two or three eggs, a large marble, a watch, about half a dozen of the inevitable glass balls, and then crumpled, crinkled paper, more and more and more, talking all the time of the way in which people neglect to brush their hats *inside* as well as out—politely, of course, but with a certain personal application. "All sorts of things accumulate, sir. . . . Not *you*, of course, in particular. . . . Nearly every customer. . . . Astonishing what they carry about with them. . . ." The crumpled paper rose and billowed on the counter more and more and more, until he was nearly hidden from us, until he was altogether hidden, and still his voice went on and on. "We none of us know what the fair semblance of a human being may conceal, sir. Are we all then no better than brushed exteriors, whited sepulchres——"

His voice stopped—exactly like when you hit a neighbor's gramophone with a well-aimed brick, the same instant silence—and the rustle of the paper stopped, and everything was still. . . .

"Have you done with my hat?" I said, after an interval.

There was no answer.

I stared at Gip, and Gip stared at me, and

there were our distortions in the magic mirrors, looking very rum,[3] and grave, and quiet. . . .

"I think we'll go now," I said. "Will you tell me how much all this comes to? . . .

"I say," I said, on a rather louder note, "I want the bill; and my hat, please."

It might have been a sniff from behind the paper pile. . . .

"Let's look behind the counter, Gip," I said. "He's making fun of us."

I led Gip round the head-wagging tiger, and what do you think there was behind the counter? No one at all! Only my hat on the floor, and a common conjurer's lop-eared white rabbit lost in meditation, and looking as stupid and crumpled as only a conjurer's rabbit can do. I resumed my hat, and the rabbit lolloped a lollop or so out of my way.

"Dadda!" said Gip, in a guilty whisper.

"What is it, Gip?" said I.

"I *do* like this shop, dadda."

"So should I," I said to myself, "if the counter wouldn't suddenly extend itself to shut one off from the door." But I didn't call Gip's attention to that. "Pussy!" he said, with a hand out to the rabbit as it came lolloping past us. "Pussy, do Gip a magic!" and his eyes followed it as it squeezed through a door I had certainly not remarked a moment before. Then this door opened wider, and the man with one ear larger than the other appeared again. He was smiling still, but his eye met mine with something between amusement and defiance. "You'd like to see our show-room, sir," he said, with an innocent suavity. Gip tugged my finger forward. I glanced at the counter and met the shopman's eye again. I was beginning to think the magic just a little too genuine. "We haven't *very* much time," I said. But somehow we were inside the showroom before I could finish that.

"All goods of the same quality," said the shopman, rubbing his flexible hands together,

"and that is the Best. Nothing in the place that isn't genuine Magic, and warranted thoroughly rum. Excuse me, sir!"

I felt him pull at something that clung to my coatsleeve, and then I saw he held a little, wriggling red demon by the tail—the little creature bit and fought and tried to get at his hand—and in a moment he tossed it carelessly behind a counter. No doubt the thing was only an image of twisted indiarubber, but for the moment——! And his gesture was exactly that of a man who handles some petty biting bit of vermin. I glanced at Gip, but Gip was looking at a magic rockinghorse. I was glad he hadn't seen the thing. "I say," I said, in an undertone, and indicating Gip and the red demon with my eyes, "you haven't many things like *that* about, have you?"

"None of ours! Probably brought it with you," said the shopman—also in an undertone, and with a more dazzling smile than ever. "Astonishing what people *will* carry about with them unawares!" And then to Gip, "Do you see anything you fancy here?"

There were many things that Gip fancied there.

He turned to this astonishing tradesman with mingled confidence and respect. "Is that a Magic Sword?" he said.

"A Magic Toy Sword. It neither bends, breaks, nor cuts the fingers. It renders the bearer invincible in battle against any one under eighteen. Half a crown to seven and sixpence, according to size. These panoplies[4] on cards are for juvenile knights-errant and very useful—shield of safety, sandals of swiftness, helmet of invisibility."

"Oh, dadda!" gasped Gip.

I tried to find out what they cost, but the shopman did not heed me. He had got Gip now; he had got him away from my finger;

---

3. **rum:** *British slang:* odd, strange.
4. **panoplies** (pan' ə plēz): armor for wandering knights.

he had embarked upon the exposition of all his confounded stock, and nothing was going to stop him. Presently I saw with a qualm of distrust and something very like jealousy that Gip had hold of this person's finger as usually he has hold of mine. No doubt the fellow was interesting, I thought, and had an interestingly faked lot of stuff, really *good* faked stuff, still——

I wandered after them, saying very little, but keeping an eye on this prestidigital[5] fellow. After all, Gip was enjoying it. And no doubt when the time came to go we should be able to go quite easily.

It was a long, rambling place, that showroom, a gallery broken up by stands and stalls and pillars, with archways leading off to other departments, in which the queerest-looking assistants loafed and stared at one, and with perplexing mirrors and curtains. So perplexing, indeed, were these that I was presently unable to make out the door by which we had come.

The shopman showed Gip magic trains that ran without steam or clockwork, just as you set the signals, and then some very, very valuable boxes of soldiers that all came alive directly you took off the lid and said—— I myself haven't a very quick ear, and it was a tongue-twisting sound, but Gip—he has his mother's ear—got it in no time. "Bravo!" said the shopman, putting the men back into the box unceremoniously and handing it to Gip. "Now," said the shopman, and in a moment Gip had made them all alive again.

"You'll take that box?" asked the shopman.

"We'll take that box," said I, "unless you charge its full value. In which case it would need a Trust Magnate——"

"Dear heart! *No!*" and the shopman swept the little men back again, shut the lid, waved the box in the air, and there it was, in brown paper, tied up and—*with Gip's full name and address on the paper!*

The shopman laughed at my amazement.

"This is the genuine magic," he said. "The real thing."

"It's a little too genuine for my taste," I said again.

After that he fell to showing Gip tricks, odd tricks, and still odder the way they were done. He explained them, he turned them inside out, and there was the dear little chap nodding his busy bit of a head in the sagest manner.

I did not attend as well as I might. "Hey, presto!" said the Magic Shopman, and then would come the clear, small "Hey, presto!" of the boy. But I was distracted by other things. It was being borne in upon me just how tremendously rum this place was; it was, so to speak, inundated by a sense of rumness. There was something a little rum about the fixtures even, about the ceiling, about the floor, about the casually distributed chairs. I had a queer feeling that whenever I wasn't looking at them straight they went askew, and moved about, and played a noiseless puss-in-the-corner[6] behind my back. And the cornice had a serpentine design with masks—masks altogether too expressive for proper plaster.

Then abruptly my attention was caught by one of the odd-looking assistants. He was some way off and evidently unaware of my presence—I saw a sort of three-quarter length of him over a pile of toys and through an arch—and, you know, he was leaning against a pillar in an idle sort of way, doing the most horrid things with his features! The particular horrid thing he did was with his nose. He did it just as though he was idle and wanted to amuse himself. First of all it was a short, blobby nose, and then suddenly he shot it

---

5. **prestidigital** (pres′ tə dij′ i təl): skillful in the execution of sleight of hand tricks.

6. **puss-in-the-corner:** a children's game in which all players but one occupy corners of a room and exchange places at a signal, the one without a corner trying to get one.

out like a telescope, and then out it flew and became thinner and thinner until it was like a long, red flexible whip. Like a thing in a nightmare it was! He flourished it about and flung it forth as a fly-fisher flings his line.

My instant thought was that Gip mustn't see him. I turned about, and there was Gip quite preoccupied with the shopman, and thinking no evil. They were whispering together and looking at me. Gip was standing on a little stool, and the shopman was holding a sort of big drum in his hand.

"Hide and seek, dadda!" cried Gip. "You're He!"

And before I could do anything to prevent it, the shopman had clapped the big drum over him.

I saw what was up directly. "Take that off," I cried, "this instant! You'll frighten the boy. Take it off!"

The shopman with the unequal ears did so without a word, and held the big cylinder towards me to show its emptiness. And the little stool was vacant! In that instant my boy had utterly disappeared! . . .

You know, perhaps, that sinister something that comes like a hand out of the unseen and grips your heart about. You know it takes your common self away and leaves you tense and deliberate, neither slow nor hasty, neither angry nor afraid. So it was with me.

I came up to this grinning shopman and kicked his stool aside.

"Stop this folly!" I said. "Where is my boy?"

"You see," he said, still displaying the drum's interior, "there is no deception——"

I put out my hand to grip him, and he eluded me by a dexterous movement. I snatched again, and he turned from me and pushed open a door to escape. "Stop!" I said, and he laughed, receding. I leapt after him— into utter darkness.

*Thud!*

"Lor' bless my 'eart! I didn't see you coming, sir!"

I was in Regent Street, and I had collided with a decent-looking working man; and a yard away, perhaps, and looking a little perplexed with himself, was Gip. There was some sort of apology, and then Gip had turned and come to me with a bright little smile, as though for a moment he had missed me.

And he was carrying four parcels in his arm!

He secured immediate possession of my finger.

For the second I was rather at a loss. I stared round to see the door of the Magic Shop, and, behold, it was not there! There was no door, no shop, nothing, only the common pilaster between the shop where they sell pictures and the window with the chicks! . . .

I did the only thing possible in that mental tumult; I walked straight to the curbstone and held up my umbrella for a cab.

"'Ansoms,"[7] said Gip, in a note of culminating exultation.

I helped him in, recalled my address with an effort, and got in also. Something unusual proclaimed itself in my tailcoat pocket, and I felt and discovered a glass ball. With a petulant expression I flung it into the street.

Gip said nothing.

For a space neither of us spoke.

"Dadda!" said Gip, at last, "that *was* a proper shop!"

I came round with that to the problem of just how the whole thing had seemed to him. He looked completely undamaged—so far, good. He was neither scared nor unhinged; he was simply tremendously satisfied with the afternoon's entertainment and there in his arms were the four parcels.

---

7. **'ansom:** hansom (han' səm): two-wheeled covered carriage with the driver's seat above and behind.

Confound it! What could be in them?

"Um!" I said. "Little boys can't go to shops like that every day."

He received this with his usual stoicism, and I decided not to pursue the subject. After all, I thought, the thing wasn't so very bad.

But it was only when we opened the parcels that I really began to be reassured. Three of them contained boxes of soldiers, quite ordinary lead soldiers, but of so good a quality as to make Gip altogether forget that originally these parcels had been Magic Tricks of the only genuine sort; and the fourth contained a kitten, a little living white kitten, in excellent health and appetite and temper.

I saw this unpacking with a sort of provisional relief. I hung about in the nursery for quite an unconscionable time. . . .

That happened six months ago. And now I am beginning to believe it is all right. The kitten had only the magic natural to all kittens, and the soldiers seemed as steady a company as any colonel could desire. And Gip——?

The intelligent parent will understand that I have to go cautiously with Gip.

But I went so far as this one day. I said, "How would you like your soldiers to come alive, Gip, and march about by themselves?"

"Mine do," said Gip. "I just have to say a word I know before I open the lid."

"Then they march about alone?"

"Oh, *quite*, dadda. I shouldn't like them if they didn't do that."

I displayed no unbecoming surprise, and since then I have taken occasion to drop in upon him once or twice, unannounced, when the soldiers were about; but so far I have never discovered them performing in anything like a magical manner. . . .

It's so difficult to tell.

There's also a question of finance. I have an incurable habit of paying bills. I have been up and down Regent Street several times looking for that shop. I am inclined to think, indeed, that in that matter honor is satisfied, and that, since Gip's name and address are known to them, I may very well leave it to these people, whoever they may be, to send in their bill in their own time.

## Getting at Meaning

1. Why hasn't the narrator visited the magic shop before?

2. What does the shopman mean when he calls Gip the "Right Sort of Boy"? Why is the little boy who can't get inside the shop *not* the "Right Sort"?

3. The shopman seems to know what Gip and his father were saying outside the shop. What does this add to the reader's understanding of the real magic in the shop?

4. The lop-eared white rabbit squeezes through a door, and a moment later the shopman with one ear larger than the other enters through the same door. What is the writer suggesting about the identity of the rabbit?

5. What does the narrator mean when he says, "I was beginning to think the magic just a little too genuine"?

6. What fascinates Gip in the showroom? What fascinates his father in the same room? Why do they notice different items?

7. Why does Gip's father become jealous of the shopman? When and why does he fear the shopman?

8. What finally reassures Gip's father about the magic shop experience? Is he certain about his final conclusion? Why or why not?

## Developing Skills in Reading Literature

1. **Setting.** Reread the first four paragraphs of the story. What is strange about the location of the magic shop? What items are displayed in the shop window? How are these items different from those displayed for Gip in the shop and then in the showroom? What purpose does the gradual change in setting serve?

2. **Mood.** The mood of a story is the atmosphere or feeling it creates in the reader. The writer of this story gradually develops an eerie, questioning mood, as the narrator and his son move from outside the shop, into the shop, then into the showroom. Find several examples of dialogue and events that help to create the mood of the story. Pay particular attention to the items noticed only by Gip's father. What effect do the descriptions of these items have upon the mood of the story?

3. **Narrator and Point of View.** If three people share the same experience and each one later retells the story, three distinct versions of the experience will be related. Each person will tell the story as he or she experienced it, from a unique point of view. When the pronouns *I* and *we* are used, the story is said to be told in the first person. This story is told from the point of view of Gip's father. What details are included that would not be noted if Gip were the narrator? What is revealed about Gip's father as a parent?

## Developing Vocabulary

**Using a Glossary.** Look up the following italicized words in the Glossary and write their definitions. Then reread the sentences, substituting a synonym for each word.

1. ". . . a shop window of *alluring* little objects, magic balls, magic hens, wonderful cones, . . ."

2. ". . . the doorbell pinged again with a *plaintive* note as we closed it behind us."

3. "He turned to Gip with a smile of remarkable *affability*."

4. " 'You'd like to see our showroom, sir,' he said, with an innocent *suavity*."

5. ". . . and there was the dear little chap nodding his busy bit of a head in the *sagest* manner."

6. ". . . he eluded me by a *dexterous* movement."

## Developing Writing Skills

**Telling the Same Story from a Different Point of View.** Gip's experience in the magic shop is quite different from his father's. However, the reader does not learn specific details about Gip's reactions and feelings. In one paragraph, retell a portion of the story from Gip's point of view. Use first-person narration, but remember that this time the "I" in the story is Gip. Be sure to reveal Gip's thoughts and feelings about the shopman and his merchandise.

# There Will Come Soft Rains   *Ray Bradbury*

In the living room the voice-clock sang, *Tick-tock, seven o'clock, time to get up, time to get up, seven o'clock!* as if it were afraid that nobody would. The morning house lay empty. The clock ticked on, repeating and repeating its sounds into the emptiness. *Seven-nine, breakfast time, seven-nine!*

In the kitchen the breakfast stove gave a hissing sigh and ejected from its warm interior eight pieces of perfectly browned toast, eight eggs sunnyside up, sixteen slices of bacon, two coffees, and two cool glasses of milk.

"Today is August 4, 2026," said a second voice from the kitchen ceiling, "in the city of Allendale, California." It repeated the date three times for memory's sake. "Today is Mr. Featherstone's birthday. Today is the anniversary of Tilita's marriage. Insurance is payable, as are the water, gas, and light bills."

Somewhere in the walls, relays clicked, memory tapes glided under electric eyes.

*Eight-one, tick-tock, eight-one o'clock, off to school, off to work, run, run, eight-one!* But no doors slammed, no carpets took the soft tread of rubber heels. It was raining outside. The weather box on the front door sang quietly: "Rain, rain, go away; rubbers, raincoats for today . . ." And the rain tapped on the empty house, echoing.

Outside, the garage chimed and lifted its door to reveal the waiting car. After a long wait the door swung down again.

At eight-thirty the eggs were shriveled and the toast was like stone. An aluminum wedge scraped them into the sink, where hot water whirled them down a metal throat that digested and flushed them away to the distant sea. The dirty dishes were dropped into a hot washer and emerged twinkling dry.

*Nine-fifteen,* sang the clock, *time to clean.*

Out of warrens in the wall, tiny robot mice darted. The rooms were acrawl with the small cleaning animals, all rubber and metal. They thudded against chairs, whirling their mustached runners, kneading the rug nap, sucking gently at hidden dust. Then, like mysterious invaders, they popped into their burrows. Their pink electric eyes faded. The house was clean.

*Ten o'clock.* The sun came out from behind the rain. The house stood alone in a city of rubble and ashes. This was the one house left standing. At night the ruined city gave off a radioactive glow which could be seen for miles.

*Ten-fifteen.* The garden sprinklers whirled up in golden founts, filling the soft morning air with scatterings of brightness. The water pelted windowpanes, running down the charred west side where the house had been burned evenly free of its white paint. The entire west face of the house was black, save for five places. Here the silhouette in paint of a man mowing a lawn. Here, as in a photograph, a woman bent to pick flowers. Still farther over, their images burned on wood in one titanic instant, a small boy, hands flung into the air; higher up, the image of a thrown ball, and opposite him a girl, hands raised to catch a ball which never came down.

The five spots of paint—the man, the woman, the children, the ball—remained. The rest was a thin charcoaled layer.

The gentle sprinkler rain filled the garden with falling light.

Until this day, how well the house had kept its peace. How carefully it had inquired, "Who goes there? What's the password?" and, getting no answer from lonely foxes and whining cats, it had shut up its windows and drawn shades in a preoccupation with self-protection that bordered on a mechanical paranoia.

It quivered at each sound, the house did. If a sparrow brushed a window, the shade snapped up. The bird, startled, flew off! No, not even a bird must touch the house!

The house was an altar with ten thousand attendants, big, small, servicing, attending, in choirs. But the gods had gone away, and the ritual of the religion continued senselessly, uselessly.

*Twelve noon.*

A dog whined, shivering, on the front porch.

The front door recognized the dog voice and opened. The dog, once huge and fleshy, but now gone to bone and covered with sores, moved in and through the house, tracking mud. Behind it whirred angry mice, angry at having to pick up mud, angry at inconvenience.

For not a leaf fragment blew under the door but what the wall panels flipped open and the copper scrap rats flashed swiftly out. The offending dust, hair, or paper, seized in miniature steel jaws, was raced back to the burrows. There, down tubes which fed into the cellar, it was dropped into the sighing vent of an incinerator which sat like evil Baal[1] in a dark corner.

The dog ran upstairs, hysterically yelping to each door, at last realizing, as the house realized, that only silence was here.

It sniffed the air and scratched the kitchen door. Behind the door, the stove was making pancakes that filled the house with a rich baked odor and the scent of maple syrup.

The dog frothed at the mouth, lying at the door, sniffing, its eyes turned to fire. It ran wildly in circles, biting at its tail, spun in a frenzy, and died. It lay in the parlor for an hour.

*Two o'clock,* sang a voice.

Delicately sensing decay at last, the regiments of mice hummed out as softly as blown gray leaves in an electrical wind.

*Two-fifteen.*

The dog was gone.

In the cellar, the incinerator glowed suddenly and a whirl of sparks leaped up the chimney.

*Two thirty-five.*

Bridge tables sprouted from patio walls. Playing cards fluttered onto pads in a shower of pips. Drinks manifested on an oaken bench with egg-salad sandwiches. Music played.

But the tables were silent and the cards untouched.

At four o'clock the tables folded like great butterflies back through the paneled walls.

*Four-thirty.*

The nursery walls glowed.

Animals took shape: yellow giraffes, blue lions, pink antelopes, lilac panthers cavorting in crystal substance. The walls were glass. They looked out upon color and fantasy. Hidden films clocked through well-oiled sprockets, and the walls lived. The nursery floor was woven to resemble a crisp, cereal meadow. Over this ran aluminum roaches and iron crickets, and in the hot still air butterflies of delicate red tissue wavered among the sharp aroma of animal spoors! There was the sound like a great matted yellow hive of bees within a dark bellows, the lazy bumble of a purring lion. And there was the patter of okapi feet and the murmur of a fresh jungle rain, like other hoofs, falling upon the summer-starched grass. Now the walls dissolved into distances of parched

---

1. **Baal** (bā′ əl): a false god or idol.

weed, mile on mile, and warm endless sky. The animals drew away into thorn brakes and water holes.

It was the children's hour.

*Five o'clock.* The bath filled with clear hot water.

*Six, seven, eight o'clock.* The dinner dishes manipulated like magic tricks, and in the study a *click.* In the metal stand opposite the hearth where a fire now blazed up warmly, a cigar popped out, half an inch of soft gray ash on it, smoking, waiting.

*Nine o'clock.* The beds warmed their hidden circuits, for nights were cool here.

*Nine-five.* A voice spoke from the study ceiling:

"Mrs. McClellan, which poem would you like this evening?"

The house was silent.

The voice said at last, "Since you express no preference, I shall select a poem at random." Quiet music rose to back the voice. "Sara Teasdale. As I recall, your favorite. . . .

There will come soft rains and the smell of
     the ground,
And swallows circling with their shimmer-
     ing sound;

And frogs in the pools singing at night,
And wild plum trees in tremulous white;

Robins will wear their feathery fire,
Whistling their whims on a low fence-wire;

And not one will know of the war, not one
Will care at last when it is done.

Not one would mind, neither bird nor tree,
If mankind perished utterly;

And Spring herself, when she woke at dawn
Would scarcely know that we were gone."

The fire burned on the stone hearth, and the cigar fell away into a mound of quiet ash on its tray. The empty chairs faced each other between the silent walls, and the music played.

At ten o'clock the house began to die.

The wind blew. A falling tree bough crashed through the kitchen window. Cleaning solvent, bottled, shattered over the stove. The room was ablaze in an instant!

"Fire!" screamed a voice. The house lights flashed, water pumps shot water from the ceilings. But the solvent spread on the linoleum, licking, eating, under the kitchen door, while the voices took it up in chorus: "Fire, fire, fire!"

The house tried to save itself. Doors sprang tightly shut, but the windows were broken by the heat and the wind blew and sucked upon the fire.

The house gave ground as the fire in ten billion angry sparks moved with flaming ease from room to room and then up the stairs. While scurrying water rats squeaked from the walls, pistoled their water, and ran for more. And the wall sprays let down showers of mechanical rain.

But too late. Somewhere, sighing, a pump shrugged to a stop. The quenching rain ceased. The reserve water supply which had filled baths and washed dishes for many quiet days was gone.

The fire crackled up the stairs. It fed upon Picassos and Matisses[2] in the upper halls, like delicacies, baking off the oily flesh, tenderly crisping the canvases into black shavings.

Now the fire lay in beds, stood in windows, changed the colors of drapes!

And then, reinforcements.

From attic trapdoors, blind robot faces peered down with faucet mouths gushing green chemical.

The fire backed off, as even an elephant must at the sight of a dead snake. Now there were twenty snakes whipping over the floor, killing the fire with a clear cold venom of green froth.

---

2. **Picassos and Matisses** (pi kä′ sō, mä tēs′): works by the modern painters Pablo Picasso and Henri Matisse.

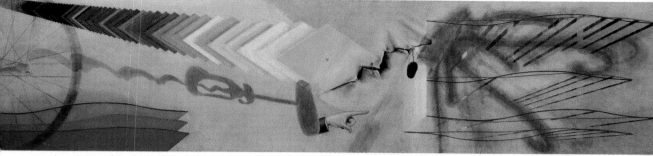

TU M', 1918. *Marcel Duchamp. Yale University Art Gallery. Gift from the Estate of Katherine A. Dreier to the Collection Societé Anonyme.*

But the fire was clever. It had sent flame outside the house, up through the attic to the pumps there. An explosion! The attic brain which directed the pumps was shattered into bronze shrapnel on the beams.

The fire rushed back into every closet and felt the clothes hung there.

The house shuddered, oak bone on bone, its bared skeleton cringing from the heat, its wire, its nerves revealed as if a surgeon had torn the skin off to let the red veins and capillaries quiver in the scalded air. Help, help; Fire! Run, run! Heat snapped mirrors like the first brittle winter ice. And the voices wailed Fire, fire, run, run, like a tragic nursery rhyme, a dozen voices, high, low, like children dying in a forest, alone, alone. And the voices fading as the wires popped their sheathings like hot chestnuts. One, two, three, four, five voices died.

In the nursery the jungle burned. Blue lions roared, purple giraffes bounded off. The panthers ran in circles, changing color, and ten million animals, running before the fire, vanished off toward a distant steaming river. . . .

Ten more voices died. In the last instant under the fire avalanche, other choruses, oblivious, could be heard announcing the time, playing music, cutting the lawn by remote-control mower, or setting an umbrella frantically out and in the slamming and opening front door, a thousand things happening, like a clock shop when each clock strikes the hour insanely before or after the other, a scene of maniac confusion, yet unity; singing, screaming, a few last cleaning mice darting bravely out to carry the horrid ashes away! And one voice, with sublime disregard for the situation, read poetry aloud in the fiery study, until all the film spools burned, until all the wires withered and the circuits cracked.

The fire burst the house and let it slam flat down, puffing out skirts of spark and smoke.

In the kitchen, an instant before the rain of fire and timber, the stove could be seen making breakfasts at a psychopathic rate, ten dozen eggs, six loaves of toast, twenty dozen bacon strips, which, eaten by fire, started the stove working again, hysterically hissing!

The crash. The attic smashing into kitchen and parlor. The parlor into cellar, cellar into sub-cellar. Deep freeze, armchair, film tapes, circuits, beds, and all like skeletons thrown in a cluttered mound deep under.

Smoke and silence. A great quantity of smoke.

Dawn showed faintly in the east. Among the ruins, one wall stood alone. Within the wall, a last voice said, over and over again and again, even as the sun rose to shine upon the heaped rubble and steam:

"Today is August 5, 2026, today is August 5, 2026, today is . . ."

## Getting at Meaning

1. In the opening paragraphs of the story, what unusual qualities and abilities of the house are described? What indicates that the house is unoccupied?

2. Describe the city in which the house is located. What are the five spots of paint on the side of the house? What caused them?

3. What do the dog's condition and death indicate about the presence of human beings in this environment?

4. What do the preparations for a bridge game, the mural on the nursery wall, and the reading of the poem indicate about the quality of the lives led by the former inhabitants of the house?

5. What finally destroys the house? How does the destruction begin? How does the house react?

## Developing Skills in Reading Literature

1. **Personification.** The giving of human qualities to an object, animal, or idea is called personification. In this story, the setting—a house in the twenty-first century—takes on the role of a major character and is thus personified. The narrator, for example, says that the house sings and sighs and that it has voices and eyes. As the story progresses, the personification of the house develops; the door recognizes the dog, the cleaning mice become angry, and the house notices the pervading silence. What do these new comparisons add to the initial description of the house? In death, the house is compared to a human being who suffers a nervous breakdown. Find specific examples in the story to illustrate this final personification.

2. **Simile.** A simile is a figure of speech in which two things that do not appear to be similar are compared. A simile always includes the words *like* or *as*. The sentence "Heat snapped mirrors like the first brittle winter ice" is an example of a simile. Find ten other similes in the story and write them out, giving the page number on which each example appears.

3. **Theme.** Theme is the main idea or message that the writer attempts to convey through a story.

The writer of this story states that "The house was an altar . . . but the gods had gone away. . . ." What might he be saying about the relationship between human beings and their accomplishments? Then, the writer uses a poem to comment on the situation in the story. What might he be saying through this poem about the relationship between human beings and nature? Finally, through carefully detailed descriptions of the house in its final hours, the writer develops a comparison between the house and a person experiencing a nervous breakdown. What might he be implying about the condition of human beings in the twenty-first century?

## Developing Vocabulary

**Using Precise Verbs.** The verbs in this story create precise images of the action: eggs *shrivel*, hot water *whirls*, mice *dart*, wires *pop*. Find at least five other examples of strong, precise verbs. Then use each in a sentence of your own that demonstrates the meaning of the verb.

## Developing Writing Skills

**Supporting an Opinion.** What do you think the year 2026 will bring? Is your image of the future similar to or different from that of the writer? Write a paragraph in which you accept or reject the writer's concept of the future. Give reasons to support your position.

# A White Heron     *Sarah Orne Jewett*

The woods were already filled with shadows one June evening, just before eight o'clock, though a bright sunset still glimmered faintly among the trunks of the trees. A little girl was driving home her cow, a plodding, dilatory, provoking creature in her behavior, but a valued companion for all that. They were going away from the western light, and striking deep into the dark woods, but their feet were familiar with the path, and it was no matter whether their eyes could see it or not.

There was hardly a night the summer through when the old cow could be found waiting at the pasture bars; on the contrary, it was her greatest pleasure to hide herself away among the high huckleberry bushes, and though she wore a loud bell she had made the discovery that if one stood perfectly still it would not ring. So Sylvia had to hunt for her until she found her, and call Co'! Co'! with never an answering Moo, until her childish patience was quite spent. If the creature had not given good milk and plenty of it, the case would have seemed very different to her owners. Besides, Sylvia had all the time there was, and very little use to make of it. Sometimes in pleasant weather it was a consolation to look upon the cow's pranks as an intelligent attempt to play hide and seek, and as the child had no playmates she lent herself to this amusement with a good deal of zest. Though this chase had been so long that the wary animal herself had given an unusual signal of her whereabouts, Sylvia had only laughed when she came upon Mistress Moolly at the swamp-side, and urged her affectionately homeward with a twig of birch leaves. The old cow was not inclined to wander farther, she even turned in the right direction for once as they left the pasture, and stepped along the road at a good pace. She was quite ready to be milked now, and seldom stopped to browse. Sylvia wondered what her grandmother would say because they were so late. It was a great while since she had left home at half past five o'clock, but everybody knew the difficulty of making this errand a short one. Mrs. Tilley had chased the hornéd torment too many summer evenings herself to blame any one else for lingering, and was only thankful as she waited that she had Sylvia, nowadays, to give such valuable assistance. The good woman suspected that Sylvia loitered occasionally on her own account; there never was such a child for straying about out-of-doors since the world was made! Everybody said that it was a good change for a little maid who had tried to grow for eight years in a crowded manufacturing town, but, as for Sylvia herself, it seemed as if she never had been alive at all before she came to live at the farm. She thought often with wistful compassion of a wretched dry geranium that belonged to a town neighbor.

" 'Afraid of folks,' " old Mrs. Tilley said to herself, with a smile, after she had made the unlikely choice of Sylvia from her daughter's houseful of children, and was returning to the farm. " 'Afraid of folks,' they said! I guess she won't be troubled so great with 'em up to the old place!" When they reached the door of the lonely house and stopped to unlock it, and the cat came to purr loudly, and rub against them, a deserted pussy, indeed, but fat with young robins, Sylvia whispered that this was a beautiful place to live in, and she never should wish to go home.

The companions followed the shady wood-road, the cow taking slow steps, and the child very fast ones. The cow stopped long at the brook to drink, as if the pasture were not half a swamp, and Sylvia stood still and waited, letting her bare feet cool themselves in the shoal water, while the great twilight moths struck softly against her. She waded on through the brook as the cow moved away, and listened to the thrushes with a heart that beat fast with pleasure. There was a stirring in the great boughs overhead. They were full of little birds and beasts that seemed to be wide-a-wake, and going about their world, or else saying goodnight to each other in sleepy twitters. Sylvia herself felt sleepy as she walked along. However, it was not much far-ther to the house, and the air was soft and sweet. She was not often in the woods so late as this, and it made her feel as if she were a part of the gray shadows and the moving leaves. She was just thinking how long it seemed since she first came to the farm a year ago, and wondering if everything went on in the noisy town just the same as when she was there; the thought of the great red-faced boy who used to chase and frighten her made her hurry along the path to escape from the shadow of the trees.

Suddenly this little woods-girl is horror-stricken to hear a clear whistle not very far away. Not a bird's whistle, which would have a sort of friendliness, but a boy's whistle, de-termined, and somewhat aggressive. Sylvia left the cow to whatever sad fate might await her, and stepped discreetly aside into the bushes, but she was just too late. The enemy had discovered her, and called out in a very cheerful and persuasive tone, "Halloa, little girl, how far is it to the road?" and trembling Sylvia answered almost inaudibly, "A good ways."

She did not dare to look boldly at the tall young man, who carried a gun over his shoulder, but she came out of her bush and again followed the cow, while he walked alongside.

"I have been hunting for some birds," the stranger said kindly, "and I have lost my way, and need a friend very much. Don't be afraid," he added gallantly. "Speak up and tell me what your name is, and whether you think I can spend the night at your house and go out gunning early in the morning."

Sylvia was more alarmed than before. Would not her grandmother consider her much to blame? But who could have foreseen such an accident as this? It did not appear to be her fault, and she hung her head as if the stem of it were broken, but managed to answer "Sylvy," with much effort when her companion again asked her name.

Mrs. Tilley was standing in the doorway when the trio came into view. The cow gave a loud moo by way of explanation.

"Yes, you'd better speak up for yourself, you old trial! Where'd she tuck herself away this time, Sylvy?" Sylvia kept an awed si-lence; she knew by instinct that her grand-mother did not comprehend the gravity of the situation. She must be mistaking the stranger for one of the farmer-lads of the region.

The young man stood his gun beside the door, and dropped a heavy game-bag beside it, then he bade Mrs. Tilley good-evening, and repeated his wayfarer's story, and asked if he could have a night's lodging.

"Put me anywhere you like," he said. "I must be off early in the morning, before day; but I am very hungry, indeed. You can give me some milk at any rate, that's plain."

"Dear sakes, yes," responded the hostess, whose long-slumbering hospitality seemed to be easily awakened. "You might fare better if you went out on the main road a mile or so, but you're welcome to what we've got. I'll milk right off, and you make yourself at home. You can sleep on husks or feathers," she proffered graciously. "I raised them all myself. There's good pasturing for geese just below here towards the ma'sh.[1] Now step round and set a plate for the gentleman, Sylvy!" And Sylvia promptly stepped. She was glad to have something to do, and she was hungry herself.

It was a surprise to find so clean and comfortable a little dwelling in this New England wilderness. The young man had known the horrors of its most primitive housekeeping, and the dreary squalor of that level of society which does not rebel at the companionship of hens. This was the best thrift of an old-fashioned farmstead, though on such a small scale that it seemed like a hermitage. He listened eagerly to the old woman's quaint talk, he watched Sylvia's pale face and shining gray eyes with ever growing enthusiasm, and insisted that this was the best supper he had eaten for a month; then, afterward, the new-made friends sat down in the doorway together while the moon came up.

Soon it would be berry-time, and Sylvia was a great help at picking. The cow was a good milker, though a plaguy thing to keep track of, the hostess gossiped frankly, adding presently that she had buried four children, so that Sylvia's mother, and a son (who might be dead) in California were all the children she had left. "Dan, my boy, was a great hand to go gunning," she explained sadly. "I never wanted for pa'tridges or gray squer'ls while he was to home. He's been a great wand'rer, I expect, and he's no hand to write letters. There, I don't blame him. I'd ha' seen the world myself if it had been so I could.

"Sylvia takes after him," the grandmother continued affectionately, after a minute's pause. "There ain't a foot o' ground she don't

know her way over, and the wild creatur's counts her one o' themselves. Squer'ls she'll tame to come an' feed right out o' her hands, and all sorts o' birds. Last winter she got the jay-birds to bangeing here, and I believe she'd 'a' scanted herself of her own meals to have plenty to throw out amongst 'em, if I hadn't kep' watch. Anything but crows, I tell her, I'm willin' to help support—though Dan he went an' tamed one o' them that did seem to have reason same as folks. It was round here a good spell after he went away. Dan an' his father they didn't hitch—but he never held up his head ag'in after Dan had dared him an' gone off."

The guest did not notice this hint of family sorrows in his eager interest in something else.

"So Sylvy knows all about birds, does she?" he exclaimed, as he looked round at the little girl who sat, very demure but increasingly sleepy, in the moonlight. "I am making a collection of birds myself. I have been at it ever since I was a boy." (Mrs. Tilley smiled.) "There are two or three very rare ones I have been hunting for these five years. I mean to get them on my own ground if they can be found."

"Do you cage 'em up?" asked Mrs. Tilley doubtfully, in response to this enthusiastic announcement.

"Oh, no, they're stuffed and preserved, dozens and dozens of them," said the ornithologist, "and I have shot or snared every one myself. I caught a glimpse of a white heron three miles from here on Saturday, and I have followed it in this direction. They have never been found in this district at all. The little white heron, it is," and he turned again to look at Sylvia with the hope of discovering that the rare bird was one of her acquaintances.

---

1. **ma'sh:** marsh, a swamp or low-lying wetland.

But Sylvia was watching a hop-toad in the narrow footpath.

"You would know the heron if you saw it," the stranger continued eagerly. "A queer, tall white bird with soft feathers and long thin legs. And it would have a nest perhaps in the top of a high tree, made of sticks, something like a hawk's nest."

Sylvia's heart gave a wild beat; she knew that strange white bird, and had once stolen softly near where it stood in some bright green swamp grass, away over at the other side of the woods. There was an open place where the sunshine always seemed strangely yellow and hot, where tall, nodding rushes grew, and her grandmother had warned her that she might sink in the soft black mud underneath and never be heard of more. Not far beyond were the salt marshes and beyond those was the sea, the sea which Sylvia wondered and dreamed about, but never had looked upon, though its great voice could often be heard above the noise of the woods on stormy nights.

"I can't think of anything I should like so much as to find that heron's nest," the handsome stranger was saying. "I would give ten dollars to anybody who could show it to me," he added desperately, "and I mean to spend my whole vacation hunting for it if need be.

Perhaps it was only migrating, or had been chased out of its region by some bird of prey."

Mrs. Tilley gave amazed attention to all this, but Sylvia still watched the toad, not divining, as she might have done at some calmer time, that the creature wished to get to its hole under the doorstep, and was much hindered by the unusual spectators at that hour of the evening. No amount of thought, that night, could decide how many wished-for treasures the ten dollars, so lightly spoken of, would buy.

The next day the young sportsman hovered about the woods, and Sylvia kept him company, having lost her first fear of the friendly lad, who proved to be most kind and sympathetic. He told her many things about the birds and what they knew and where they lived and what they did with themselves. And he gave her a jack-knife, which she thought as great a treasure as if she were a desert-islander. All day long he did not once make her troubled or afraid except when he brought down some unsuspecting singing creature from its bough. Sylvia would have liked him vastly better without his gun; she could not understand why he killed the very birds he seemed to like so much. But as the day waned, Sylvia still watched the young man with loving admiration. She had never seen anybody so charming and delightful; the woman's heart, asleep in the child, was vaguely thrilled by a dream of love. Some premonition of that great power stirred and swayed these young foresters who traversed the solemn woodlands with soft-footed silent care. They stopped to listen to a bird's song; they pressed forward again eagerly, parting the branches—speaking to each other rarely and in whispers; the young man going first and Sylvia following, fascinated, a few steps behind, with her gray eyes dark with excitement.

She grieved because the longed-for white heron was elusive, but she did not lead the guest, she only followed, and there was no such thing as speaking first. The sound of her own unquestioned voice would have terrified her—it was hard enough to answer yes or no when there was need of that. At last evening began to fall, and they drove the cow home together, and Sylvia smiled with pleasure when they came to the place where she heard the whistle and was afraid only the night before.

Half a mile from home, at the farther edge of the woods, where the land was highest, a great pine-tree stood, the last of its generation. Whether it was left for a boundary mark, or for what reason, no one could say; the woodchoppers who had felled its mates were dead and gone long ago, and a whole forest of sturdy trees, pines and oaks and maples, had grown again. But the stately head of this old pine towered above them all and made a landmark for sea and shore miles and miles away. Sylvia knew it well. She had always believed that whoever climbed to the top of it could see the ocean; and the little girl had often laid her hand on the great rough trunk and looked up wistfully at those dark boughs that the wind always stirred, no matter how hot and still the air might be below. Now she thought of the tree with a new excitement, for why, if one climbed it at break of day, could not one see all the world, and easily discover whence the white heron flew, and mark the place, and find the hidden nest?

What a spirit of adventure, what wild ambition! What fancied triumph and delight and glory for the later morning when she could make known the secret! It was almost too real and too great for the childish heart to bear.

All night the door of the little house stood open, and the whippoorwills came and sang upon the very step. The young sportsman and his old hostess were sound asleep, but Sylvia's great design kept her broad awake and watching. She forgot to think of sleep. The short summer night seemed as long as the winter darkness, and at last when the whippoorwills ceased, and she was afraid the morning would after all come too soon, she stole out of the house and followed the pasture path through the woods, hastening toward the open ground beyond, listening with a sense of comfort and companionship to the drowsy twitter of a half-awakened bird, whose perch she had jarred in passing. Alas, if the great wave of human interest that flooded for the first time this dull little life should sweep away the satisfactions of an existence heart to heart with nature and the dumb life of the forest!

There was the huge tree asleep yet in the paling moonlight; and small and hopeful, Sylvia began with utmost bravery to mount to the top of it, with tingling, eager blood coursing the channels of her whole frame, with her bare feet and fingers that pinched and held like bird's claws to the monstrous ladder reaching up, up, almost to the sky itself. First she must mount the white oak tree that grew alongside, where she was almost lost among the dark branches and the green leaves heavy and wet with dew; a bird fluttered off its nest, and a red squirrel ran to and fro and scolded pettishly at the harmless housebreaker. Sylvia felt her way easily. She had often climbed there, and knew that higher still one of the oak's upper branches chafed against the pine trunk, just where its lower boughs were set close together. There, when she made the dangerous pass from one tree to the other, the great enterprise would really begin.

She crept out along the swaying oak limb at last, and took the daring step across into the old pine-tree. The way was harder than she thought, she must reach far and hold fast, the sharp dry twigs caught and held her and scratched her like angry talons, the pitch made her thin little fingers clumsy and stiff as she went round and round the tree's great stem, higher and higher upward. The sparrows and robins in the woods below were beginning to wake and twitter to the dawn, yet it seemed much lighter there aloft in the pine-tree, and the child knew that she must hurry if her project were to be of any use.

The tree seemed to lengthen itself out as she went up, and to reach farther and farther upward. It was like a great main-mast to the voyaging earth; it must truly have been amazed that morning through all its ponderous frame as it felt this determined spark of human spirit creeping and climbing from higher branch to branch. Who knows how steadily the least twigs held themselves to advantage this light, weak creature on her way! The old pine must have loved its new dependent. More than all the hawks, and bats, and moths, and even the sweet-voiced thrushes, was the brave, beating heart of the solitary gray-eyed child. And the tree stood still and held away the winds that June morning while the dawn grew bright in the east.

Sylvia's face was like a pale star, if one had seen it from the ground, when the last thorny bough was past, and she stood trembling and tired but wholly triumphant, high in the tree-top. Yes, there was the sea with the dawning sun making a golden dazzle over it, and toward that glorious east flew two hawks with slow-moving pinions. How low they looked in the air from that height when before one had only seen them far up, and dark against the blue sky. Their gray feathers were as soft as moths; they seemed only a little way from the tree, and Sylvia felt as if she too could go flying away among the clouds. Westward, the woodlands and farms reached miles and miles into the distance; here and there were church steeples, and white villages; truly it was a vast and awesome world.

The birds sang louder and louder. At last

the sun came up, bewilderingly bright. Sylvia could see the white sails of ships out at sea, and the clouds that were purple and rose-colored and yellow at first began to fade away. Where was the white heron's nest in the sea of green branches, and was this wonderful sight and pageant of the world the only reward for having climbed to such a giddy height? Now look down again, Sylvia, where the green marsh is set among the shining birches and dark hemlocks; there where you saw the white heron once you will see him again; look, look! a white spot of him like a single floating feather comes up from the dead hemlock and grows larger, and rises, and comes close at last, and goes by the landmark pine with steady sweep of wing and outstretched slender neck and crested head. And wait! wait! do not move a foot or a finger, little girl; do not send an arrow of light and consciousness from your two eager eyes, for the heron has perched on a pine bough not far beyond yours, and cries back to his mate on the nest, and plumes his feathers for the new day!

The child gives a long sigh a minute later when a company of shouting cat-birds comes also to the tree, and vexed by their fluttering and lawlessness the solemn heron goes away. She knows his secret now, the wild, light, slender bird that floats and wavers, and goes back like an arrow presently to his home in the green world beneath. Then Sylvia, well satisfied, makes her perilous way down again, not daring to look far below the branch she stands on, ready to cry sometimes because her fingers ache and her lamed feet slip. Wondering over and over again what the stranger would say to her, and what he would think when she told him how to find his way straight to the heron's nest.

"Sylvy, Sylvy!" called the busy old grandmother again and again, but nobody answered; and the small husk bed was empty,

and Sylvia had disappeared.

The guest waked from a dream, and remembering his day's pleasure hurried to dress himself that it might sooner begin. He was sure from the way the shy little girl looked once or twice yesterday that she had at least seen the white heron, and now she must really be persuaded to tell. Here she comes now, paler than ever, and her worn old frock is torn and tattered, and smeared with pine pitch. The grandmother and the sportsman stand in the door together and question her, and the splendid moment has come to speak of the dead hemlock-tree by the green marsh.

But Sylvia does not speak after all, though the old grandmother fretfully rebukes her, and the young man's kind, appealing eyes are looking straight into her own. He can make them rich with money; he has promised it, and they are poor now. He is so well worth making happy, and he waits to hear the story she can tell.

No, she must keep silence! What is it that suddenly forbids her and makes her dumb? Has she been nine years growing, and now, when the great world for the first time puts out a hand to her, must she thrust it aside for a bird's sake? The murmur of the pine's green branches is in her ears, she remembers how the white heron came flying through the golden air and how they watched the sea and the morning together, and Sylvia cannot speak; she cannot tell the heron's secret and give its life away.

Dear loyalty, that suffered a sharp pang as the guest went away disappointed later in the day, that could have served and followed him and loved him as a dog loves! Many a night Sylvia heard the echo of his whistle haunting the pasture path as she came home with the loitering cow. She forgot even her sorrow at the sharp report of his gun and the piteous sight of thrushes and sparrows dropping silent to the ground, their songs hushed and their pretty feathers stained and wet with blood. Were the birds better friends than their hunter might have been—who can tell? Whatever treasures were lost to her, wood-lands and summer-time, remember! Bring your gifts and graces and tell your secrets to this lonely country child!

## Getting at Meaning

1. Why does Sylvia prefer living in the country with her grandmother to living in town?

2. Sylvia's grandmother is told that Sylvia is "afraid of folks." How does Sylvia's reaction to meeting the stranger illustrate this view of her?

3. The stranger does not notice the "hint of family sorrows" in the grandmother's conversation. What does this indicate about his character? How is he different from Sylvia, who is so sensitive to her surroundings?

4. Why does the stranger become interested in Sylvia? What does he do with the birds he captures? What particular bird does he now seek? What does he offer to anyone who helps him find it?

5. How does Sylvia's attitude toward the stranger change? What doesn't she understand about him?

6. How does Sylvia discover the white heron's secret nest? What else does Sylvia discover at the same time?

7. Why doesn't Sylvia tell the stranger of her discovery?

## Developing Skills in Reading Literature

1. **Setting.** In this story, setting and character are closely related. What is Sylvia's attitude toward the forest and its inhabitants? Why is her attitude important to the story? How does the writer stress the importance of this relationship? Notice the gradual development of Sylvia's character in terms of her relationship to the forest. For instance, at the beginning of the story, Sylvia remembers a dry geranium that belonged to a neighbor in town. Why is this detail important? Near the end of the story, Sylvia has an experience in a pine tree. How is she changed by the experience?

2. **Conflict.** The conflict in a story may be both internal and external. External conflict is a struggle between the main character and other characters or outside forces. Internal conflict is a struggle within the main character and usually concerns values or moral decisions. Describe both the internal and the external conflicts in this story and explain how the resolution of one conflict leads to the resolution of the other.

3. **Symbol.** A symbol is a person, object, place, or idea that suggests a meaning beyond itself. In this story, the white heron has symbolic meaning for two characters. What does the bird symbolize for the stranger? for Sylvia?

## Developing Writing Skills

**Describing a Place.** Sylvia's favorite place is the woods surrounding her grandmother's home. This place seems real to the reader due to the writer's use of descriptive details. Choose a place that you enjoy, and describe it in a five-paragraph composition. Use specific details and indicate how you feel when you are in this setting.

# By the Waters of Babylon

*Stephen Vincent Benét*

The north and the west and the south are good hunting ground, but it is forbidden to go east. It is forbidden to go to any of the Dead Places except to search for metal, and then he who touches the metal must be a priest or the son of a priest. Afterwards, both the man and the metal must be purified. These are the rules and the laws; they are well made. It is forbidden to cross the great river and look upon the place that was the Place of the Gods—this is most strictly forbidden. We do not even say its name though we know its name. It is there that spirits live, and demons—it is there that there are the ashes of the Great Burning. These things are forbidden—they have been forbidden since the beginning of time.

My father is a priest; I am the son of a priest. I have been in the Dead Places near us, with my father—at first, I was afraid. When my father went into the house to search for the metal, I stood by the door and my heart felt small and weak. It was a dead man's house, a spirit house. It did not have the smell of man, though there were old bones in a corner. But it is not fitting that a priest's son should show fear. I looked at the bones in the shadow and kept my voice still.

Then my father came out with the metal —a good, strong piece. He looked at me with both eyes but I had not run away. He gave me the metal to hold—I took it and did not die. So he knew that I was truly his son and would be a priest in my time. That was when I was very young—nevertheless, my brothers would not have done it, though they are good hunters. After that, they gave me the good piece of meat and the warm corner by the fire. My father watched over me—he was glad that I should be a priest. But when I boasted or wept without a reason, he punished me more strictly than my brothers. That was right.

After a time, I myself was allowed to go into the dead houses and search for metal. So I learned the ways of those houses—and if I saw bones, I was no longer afraid. The bones are light and old—sometimes they will fall into dust if you touch them. But that is a great sin.

I was taught the chants and the spells—I was taught how to stop the running of blood from a wound and many secrets. A priest must know many secrets—that was what my father said. If the hunters think we do all things by chants and spells, they may believe so—it does not hurt them. I was taught how to read in the old books and how to make the old writings—that was hard and took a long time. My knowledge made me happy— it was like a fire in my heart. Most of all, I liked to hear of the Old Days and the stories of the gods. I asked myself many questions that I could not answer, but it was good to ask them. At night, I would lie awake and listen to the wind—it seemed to me that it was the voice of the gods as they flew through the air.

We are not ignorant like the Forest People —our women spin wool on the wheel; our priests wear a white robe. We do not eat grubs from the tree; we have not forgotten the old writings, although they are hard to understand. Nevertheless, my knowledge and my lack of knowledge burned in me—I wished to know more. When I was a man at last, I came to my father and said, "It is time for me to go on my journey. Give me your leave."

He looked at me for a long time, stroking his beard; then he said at last, "Yes. It is time." That night, in the house of the priesthood, I asked for and received purification. My body hurt, but my spirit was a cool stone. It was my father himself who questioned me about my dreams.

He bade me look into the smoke of the fire and see—I saw and told what I saw. It was what I have always seen—a river, and, beyond it, a great Dead Place and in it the gods walking. I have always thought about that. His eyes were stern when I told him—he was no longer my father but a priest. He said, "This is a strong dream."

"It is mine," I said, while the smoke waved and my head felt light. They were singing the Star song in the outer chamber, and it was like the buzzing of bees in my head.

He asked me how the gods were dressed, and I told him how they were dressed. We know how they were dressed from the book, but I saw them as if they were before me. When I had finished, he threw the sticks three times and studied them as they fell.

"This is a very strong dream," he said. "It may eat you up."

"I am not afraid," I said and looked at him with both eyes. My voice sounded thin in my ears, but that was because of the smoke.

He touched me on the breast and the forehead. He gave me the bow and the three arrows.

"Take them," he said. "It is forbidden to travel east. It is forbidden to cross the river. It is forbidden to go to the Place of the Gods. All these things are forbidden."

"All these things are forbidden," I said, but it was my voice that spoke and not my spirit. He looked at me again.

"My son," he said. "Once I had young dreams. If your dreams do not eat you up, you may be a great priest. If they eat you, you are still my son. Now go on your journey."

I went fasting, as is the law. My body hurt but not my heart. When the dawn came, I was out of sight of the village. I prayed and purified myself, waiting for a sign. The sign was an eagle. It flew east.

Sometimes signs are sent by bad spirits. I waited again on the flat rock, fasting, taking no food. I was very still—I could feel the sky above me and the earth beneath. I waited till the sun was beginning to sink. Then three deer passed in the valley, going east—they did not wind me or see me. There was a white fawn with them—a very great sign.

I followed them, at a distance, waiting for what would happen. My heart was troubled about going east, yet I knew that I must go. My head hummed with my fasting—I did not even see the panther spring upon the white fawn. But, before I knew it, the bow was in my hand. I shouted and the panther lifted his head from the fawn. It is not easy to kill a panther with one arrow, but the arrow went through his eye and into his brain. He died as he tried to spring—he rolled over, tearing at the ground. Then I knew I was meant to go east—I knew that was my journey. When the night came, I made my fire and roasted meat.

It is eight suns' journey to the east, and a man passes by many Dead Places. The Forest People are afraid of them, but I am not. Once I made my fire on the edge of a Dead Place at night and, next morning, in the dead house, I found a good knife, little rusted. That was small to what came afterward, but it made my heart feel big. Always when I looked for game, it was in front of my arrow, and twice I passed hunting parties of the Forest People without their knowing. So I knew my magic was strong and my journey clean, in spite of the law.

Toward the setting of the eighth sun, I

came to the banks of the great river. It was half-a-day's journey after I had left the god-road—we do not use the god-roads now for they are falling apart into great blocks of stone, and the forest is safer going. A long way off, I had seen the water through trees, but the trees were thick. At last, I came out upon an open place at the top of a cliff. There was the great river below, like a giant in the sun. It is very long, very wide. It could eat all the streams we know and still be thirsty. Its name is Ou-dis-sun, the Sacred, the Long. No man of my tribe had seen it, not even my father, the priest. It was magic and I prayed.

Then I raised my eyes and looked south. It was there, the Place of the Gods.

How can I tell what it was like—you do not know. It was there, in the red light, and they were too big to be houses. It was there with the red light upon it, mighty and ruined. I knew that in another moment the gods would see me. I covered my eyes with my hands and crept back into the forest.

Surely, that was enough to do, and live. Surely it was enough to spend the night upon the cliff. The Forest People themselves do not come near. Yet, all through the night, I knew that I should have to cross the river and walk in the places of the gods, although the gods ate me up. My magic did not help me at all, and yet there was a fire in my bowels, a fire in my mind. When the sun rose, I thought, "My journey has been clean. Now I will go home from my journey." But, even as I thought so, I knew I could not. If I went to the Place of the Gods, I would surely die, but, if I did not go, I could never be at peace with my spirit again. It is better to lose one's life than one's spirit, if one is a priest and the son of a priest.

Nevertheless, as I made the raft, the tears ran out of my eyes. The Forest People could have killed me without fight, if they had come upon me then, but they did not come. When the raft was made, I said the sayings for the dead and painted myself for death. My heart was cold as a frog and my knees like water, but the burning in my mind would not let me have peace. As I pushed the raft from the shore, I began my death song—I had the right. It was a fine song.

"I am John, son of John," I sang. "My people
   are the Hill People. They are the men.
I go into the Dead Places but I am not slain.
I take the metal from the Dead Places but I
   am not blasted.
I travel upon the god-roads and am not
   afraid. E-yah! I have killed the panther,
   I have killed the fawn!
E-yah! I have come to the great river. No
   man has come there before.
It is forbidden to go east, but I have gone,
   forbidden to go on the great river, but I
   am there.
Open your hearts, you spirits, and hear my
   song.
Now I go to the Place of the Gods, I shall not
   return.
My body is painted for death and my limbs
   weak, but my heart is big as I go to the
   Place of the Gods!"

All the same, when I came to the Place of Gods, I was afraid, afraid. The current of the great river is very strong—it gripped my raft with its hands. That was magic, for the river itself is wide and calm. I could feel evil spirits about me, in the bright morning; I could feel their breath on my neck as I was swept down the stream. Never have I been so much alone —I tried to think of my knowledge, but it was a squirrel's heap of winter nuts. There was no strength in my knowledge any more, and I felt small and naked as a new-hatched bird—alone upon the great river, the servant of the gods.

Yet, after a while, my eyes were opened and I saw. I saw both banks of the river—I saw that once there had been god-roads across it, though now they were broken and fallen like broken vines. Very great they were, and wonderful and broken—broken in the time of the Great Burning when the fire fell out of the sky. And always the current took me nearer to the Place of the Gods, and the huge ruins rose before my eyes.

I do not know the customs of rivers—we are the People of the Hills. I tried to guide my raft with the pole but it spun around. I thought the river meant to take me past the Place of the Gods and out into the Bitter Water of the legends. I grew angry then—my heart felt strong. I said aloud, "I am a priest and the son of a priest!" The gods heard me—they showed me how to paddle with the pole on one side of the raft. The current changed itself—I drew near to the Place of the Gods.

When I was very near, my raft struck and turned over. I can swim in our lakes—I swam to the shore. There was a great spike of rusted metal sticking out into the river—I hauled myself up upon it and sat there, panting. I had saved my bow and two arrows and the knife I found in the Dead Place but that was all. My raft went whirling downstream toward the Bitter Water. I looked after it, and thought if it had trod me under, at least I would be safely dead. Nevertheless, when I had dried my bowstring and re-strung it, I walked forward to the Place of the Gods.

It felt like ground underfoot; it did not burn me. It is not true what some of the tales say, that the ground there burns forever, for I have been there. Here and there were the marks and stains of the Great Burning, on the ruins, that is true. But they were old marks and old stains. It is not true either, what some of our priests say, that it is an island covered with fogs and enchantments. It is not. It is a great Dead Place—greater than any Dead Place we know. Everywhere in it there are god-roads, though most are cracked and broken. Everywhere there are the ruins of the high towers of the gods.

How shall I tell what I saw? I went care-fully, my strung bow in my hand, my skin ready for danger. There should have been the wailings of spirits and the shrieks of demons, but there were not. It was very silent and sunny where I had landed—the wind and the rain and the birds that drop seeds had done their work—the grass grew in the cracks of the broken stone. It is a fair island—no wonder the gods built there. If I had come there, a god, I also would have built.

How shall I tell what I saw? The towers are not all broken—here and there one still stands, like a great tree in a forest, and the birds nest high. But the towers themselves look blind, for the gods are gone. I saw a fish-hawk, catching fish in the river. I saw a little dance of white butterflies over a great heap of broken stones and columns. I went there and looked about me—there was a carved stone with cut-letters, broken in half. I can read letters but I could not understand these. They said UBTREAS. There was also the shattered image of a man or a god. It had been made of white stone and he wore his hair tied back like a woman's. His name was ASHING, as I read on the cracked half of a stone. I thought it wise to pray to ASHING, though I do not know that god.

How shall I tell what I saw? There was no smell of man left, on stone or metal. Nor were there many trees in that wilderness of stone. There are many pigeons, nesting and dropping in the towers—the gods must have loved them, or, perhaps, they used them for sacrifices. There are wild cats that roam the god-roads, green-eyed, unafraid of man. At night they wail like demons, but they are not demons. The wild dogs are more dangerous, for they hunt in a pack, but them I did not meet till later. Everywhere there are the carved stones, carved with magical numbers or words.

I went North—I did not try to hide my-self. When a god or a demon saw me, then I would die, but meanwhile I was no longer afraid. My hunger for knowledge burned in me—there was so much that I could not understand. After awhile, I knew that my belly was hungry. I could have hunted for my meat, but I did not hunt. It is known that the gods did not hunt as we do—they got their food from enchanted boxes and jars. Sometimes these are still found in the Dead Places—once, when I was a child and foolish, I opened such a jar and tasted it and found the food sweet. But my father found out and punished me for it strictly, for, often that food is death. Now, though, I had long gone past what was forbidden, and I entered the likeliest towers, looking for the food of the gods.

I found it at last in the ruins of a great temple in the mid-city. A mighty temple it must have been, for the roof was painted like the sky at night with its stars—that much I could see, though the colors were faint and dim. It went down into great caves and tunnels—perhaps they kept their slaves there. But when I started to climb down, I heard the squeaking of rats, so I did not go—rats are unclean, and there must have been many tribes of them, from the squeaking. But near there, I found food, in the heart of a ruin, behind a door that still opened. I ate only the fruits from the jars—they had a very sweet taste. There was drink, too, in bottles of glass—the drink of the gods was strong and made my head swim. After I had eaten and drunk, I slept on the top of a stone, my bow at my side.

When I woke, the sun was low. Looking down from where I lay, I saw a dog sitting on his haunches. His tongue was hanging out of his mouth; he looked as if he were laughing. He was a big dog, with a gray-brown coat, as big as a wolf. I sprang up and shouted at him but he did not move—he just sat there as if he were laughing. I did not like that. When I reached for a stone to throw, he moved swiftly out of the way of the stone. He was

not afraid of me; he looked at me as if I were meat. No doubt I could have killed him with an arrow, but I did not know if there were others. Moreover, night was falling.

I looked about me—not far away there was a great, broken god-road, leading North. The towers were high enough, but not so high, and while many of the dead-houses were wrecked, there were some that stood. I went toward this god-road, keeping to the heights of the ruins, while the dog followed. When I had reached the god-road, I saw that there were others behind him. If I had slept later, they would have come upon me asleep and torn out my throat. As it was, they were sure enough of me; they did not hurry. When I went into the dead-house, they kept watch at the entrance—doubtless they thought they would have a fine hunt. But a dog cannot open a door, and I knew, from the books, that the gods did not like to live on the ground but on high.

I had just found a door I could open when the dogs decided to rush. Ha! They were surprised when I shut the door in their faces—it was a good door, of strong metal. I could hear their foolish baying beyond it, but I did not stop to answer them. I was in darkness—I found stairs and climbed. There were many stairs, turning around till my head was dizzy. At the top was another door—I found the knob and opened it. I was in a long, small chamber—on one side of it was a bronze door that could not be opened, for it had no handle. Perhaps there was a magic word to open it, but I did not have the word. I turned to the door in the opposite side of the wall. The lock of it was broken and I opened it and went in.

Within, there was a place of great riches. The god who lived there must have been a powerful god. The first room was a small ante-room—I waited there for some time, telling the spirits of the place that I came in peace and not as a robber. When it seemed to me that they had had time to hear me, I went on. Ah, what riches! Few, even, of the windows had been broken—it was all as it had been. The great windows that looked over the city had not been broken at all though they were dusty and streaked with many years. There were coverings on the floors, the colors not greatly faded, and the chairs were soft and deep. There were pictures upon the walls, very strange, very wonderful—I remember one of a bunch of flowers in a jar—if you came close to it, you could see nothing but bits of color, but if you stood away from it, the flowers might have been picked yesterday. It made my heart feel strange to look at this picture—and to look at the figure of a bird, in some hard clay, on a table and see it so like our birds. Everywhere there were books and writings, many in tongues that I could not read. The god who lived there must have been a wise god and full of knowledge. I felt I had right there, as I sought knowledge also.

Nevertheless, it was strange. There was a washing-place but no water—perhaps the gods washed in air. There was a cooking-place but no wood, and though there was a machine to cook food, there was no place to put fire in it. Nor were there candles or lamps —there were things that looked like lamps but they had neither oil nor wick. All these things were magic, but I touched them and lived—the magic had gone out of them. Let me tell one thing to show. In the washing-place, a thing said "Hot" but it was not hot to the touch—another thing said "Cold" but it was not cold. This must have been a strong magic, but the magic was gone. I do not understand—they had ways—I wish that I knew.

It was close and dry and dusty in their house of the gods. I have said the magic was gone, but that is not true—it had gone from the magic things, but it had not gone from the place. I felt the spirits about me, weighing upon me. Nor had I ever slept in a Dead Place before—and yet, tonight, I must sleep there. When I thought of it, my tongue felt dry in my throat, in spite of my wish for knowledge. Almost I would have gone down again and faced the dogs, but I did not.

I had not gone through all the rooms when the darkness fell. When it fell, I went back to the big room looking over the city and made fire. There was a place to make fire and a box with wood in it, though I do not think they cooked there. I wrapped myself in a floor-covering and slept in front of the fire—I was very tired.

Now I tell what is very strong magic. I woke in the midst of the night. When I woke, the fire had gone out and I was cold. It seemed to me that all around me there were whisperings and voices. I closed my eyes to shut them out. Some will say that I slept again, but I do not think that I slept. I could feel the spirits drawing my spirit out of my body as a fish is drawn on a line.

Why should I lie about it? I am a priest and the son of a priest. If there are spirits, as they say, in the small Dead Places near us, what spirits must there not be in that great Place of the Gods? And would not they wish to speak? After such long years? I know that I felt myself drawn as a fish is drawn on a line. I had stepped out of my body—I could see my body asleep in front of the cold fire, but it was not I. I was drawn to look out upon the city of the gods.

It should have been dark, for it was night, but it was not dark. Everywhere there were lights—lines of light—circles and blurs of light—ten thousand torches would not have been the same. The sky itself was alight— you could barely see the stars for the glow in the sky. I thought to myself "This is strong magic," and trembled. There was a roaring in my ears like the rushing of rivers. Then my eyes grew used to the light and my ears to the sound. I knew that I was seeing the city as it had been when the gods were alive.

That was a sight indeed—yes, that was a sight: I could not have seen it in the body—my body would have died. Everywhere went the gods, on foot and in chariots—there were gods beyond number and counting and their chariots blocked the streets. They had turned night to day for their pleasure—they did not sleep with the sun. The noise of their coming and going was the noise of many waters. It was magic what they could do—it was magic what they did.

I looked out of another window—the great vines of their bridges were mended and the god-roads went East and West. Restless, restless, were the gods and always in motion! They burrowed tunnels under rivers—they flew in the air. With unbelievable tools they did giant works—no part of the earth was safe from them, for, if they wished for a thing, they summoned it from the other side of the world. And always, they labored and rested, as they feasted and made love, there was a drum in their ears—the pulse of the giant city, beating and beating like a man's heart.

Were they happy? What is happiness to the gods? They were great, they were mighty, they were wonderful and terrible. As I looked upon them and their magic, I felt like a child —but a little more, it seemed to me, and they would pull down the moon from the sky. I saw them with wisdom beyond wisdom and knowledge beyond knowledge. And yet not all they did was well done—even I could see that—and yet their wisdom could not but grow until all was peace.

Then I saw their fate come upon them and that was terrible past speech. It came upon them as they walked the streets of their city. I have been in the fights with the Forest People—I have seen men die. But this was not like that. When gods war with gods, they use weapons we do not know. It was fire falling out of the sky and a mist that poisoned. It was the time of the Great Burning and the Destruction. They ran about like ants in the streets of their city—poor gods, poor gods! Then the towers began to fall. A few escaped —yes, a few. The legends tell it. But, even after the city became a Dead Place, for many years the poison was still in the ground. I saw it happen, I saw the last of them die. It was darkness over the broken city, and I wept.

All this, I saw. I saw it as I have told it, though not in the body. When I woke in the morning, I was hungry, but I did not think first of my hunger, for my heart was perplexed and confused. I knew the reason for the Dead Places, but I did not see why it had happened. It seemed to me it should not have happened, with all the magic they had. I went through the house looking for an answer. There was so much in the house I could not understand—and yet I am a priest and the son of a priest. It was like being on one side of the great river, at night, with no light to show the way.

Then I saw the dead god. He was sitting in his chair, by the window, in a room I had not entered before and, for the first moment, I thought that he was alive. Then I saw the skin on the back of his hand—it was like dry leather. The room was shut, hot and dry —no doubt that had kept him as he was. At first I was afraid to approach him—then the fear left me. He was sitting looking out over the city—he was dressed in the clothes of the gods. His age was neither young nor old—I could not tell his age. But there was wisdom in his face and great sadness. You could see that he would have not run away. He had sat at his window, watching his city die—then he himself had died. But it is better to lose one's life than one's spirit—and you could see from the face that his spirit had not been lost. I knew, that, if I touched him, he would

fall into dust—and yet, there was something unconquered in the face.

That is all of my story, for then I knew he was a man—I knew then that they had been men, neither gods nor demons. It is a great knowledge, hard to tell and believe. They were men—they went a dark road, but they were men. I had no fear after that—I had no fear going home, though twice I fought off the dogs, and once I was hunted for two days by the Forest People. When I saw my father again, I prayed and was purified. He touched my lips and my breast; he said, "You went away a boy. You come back a man and a priest." I said, "Father, they were men! I have been in the Place of the Gods and seen it! Now slay me, if it is the law—but still I know they were men."

He looked at me out of both eyes. He said, "The law is not always the same shape—you have done what you have done. I could not have done it in my time, but you come after me. Tell!"

I told and he listened. After that, I wished to tell all the people but he showed me otherwise. He said, "Truth is a hard deer to hunt.

If you eat too much truth at once, you may die of the truth. It was not idly that our fathers forbade the Dead Places." He was right—it is better the truth should come little by little. I have·learned that, being a priest. Perhaps, in the old days, they ate knowledge too fast.

Nevertheless, we make a beginning. It is not for the metal alone we go to the Dead Places now—there are the books and the writings. They are hard to learn. And the magic tools are broken—but we can look at them and wonder. At least, we make a beginning. And, when I am chief priest we shall go beyond the great river. We shall go to the Place of the Gods—the place newyork—not one man but a company. We shall look for the images of the gods and find the god ASHING and the others—the gods Lincoln and Biltmore[1] and Moses. But they were men who built the city, not gods or demons. They were men. I remember the dead man's face. They were men who were here before us. We must build again.

---

1. **Biltmore:** a famous hotel.

## Getting at Meaning

1. Who may go to the Dead Places? Why do they go?

2. How does John's father know that John will be a priest? What is John's opinion of his people's religion? How do you know?

3. John is proud of his people's accomplishments; he says, "We are not ignorant like the Forest People. . . ." What information in the story supports this statement? What information shows that John's people are primitive?

4. During John's journey east, he encounters broken god-roads and describes buildings that are "too big to be houses." What do these descriptions plus earlier descriptions of the metal found in the Dead Places reveal about civilization before the Great Burning?

5. When John arrives in the Place of the Gods, which of the tales that he has been told prove to be false? As he explores further, which items continue to confuse John? Identify these items and explain their functions.

6. During the night, John has a vision. How do the sights and activities he views differ from his experiences in his own village? How does John explain the difference? Why does John's vision make him sad?

7. What does John's discovery of the dead god reveal to him?


## Developing Skills in Reading Literature

1. **Setting.** The writer of this story presents detailed descriptions of two distinct worlds, the world of John's people and the world of the gods. Identify the unique characteristics of each world. What is the relationship between the two worlds?

2. **Character.** Gradually, throughout the story, John increases his understanding of his surroundings. Beginning with his experiences in his village, continuing through his travels, and concluding with his exploration of "newyork," cite incidents from the story that show how John matures in his attitudes.

3. **Point of View.** In this first-person narrative, John is both the narrator and a character within the story. John's ability to interpret his experiences is limited by his own ignorance. At what point in the story did you as a reader recognize and understand the setting, even though John as yet did not? What does John's limited point of view add to the story?

4. **Conflict.** The external conflicts in this story involve John's desires, the laws of his society, and the dangers that may prevent his fulfilling his desires. What internal conflicts does John experience during the story? How does he resolve these conflicts?

5. **Theme.** What ideas about human beings today might the writer be suggesting through John's comment, "Perhaps, in the old days, they ate knowledge too fast"?


## Developing Writing Skills

**Analyzing a Character.** At first, John is presented as a person who has much to fear in life, but who also seeks knowledge. By the end of the story, he has the confidence to say, "We must build again." Choose one of John's experiences, and in one paragraph, explain how the experience helped him to mature and to gain confidence. Begin your paragraph with a topic sentence that describes what John gained from the experience. Then describe the experience and explain its effect upon John.

# Character

RUBY GREEN SINGING. *James Chapin.*
*Norton Gallery and School of Art. West Palm Beach, Florida.*

# The Wooing of Ariadne     *Harry Mark Petrakis*

I knew from the begining she must accept my love—put aside foolish female protestations. It is the distinction of the male to be the aggressor and the cloak of the female to lend grace to the pursuit. Aha! I am wise to these wiles.

I first saw Ariadne at a dance given by the Spartan[1] brotherhood in the Legion Hall on Laramie Street. The usual assemblage of prune-faced and banana-bodied women smelling of virtuous anemia. They were an outrage to a man such as myself.

Then I saw her! A tall, stately woman, perhaps in her early thirties. She had firm and slender arms bare to the shoulders and a graceful neck. Her hair was black and thick and piled in a great bun at the back of her head. That grand abundance of hair attracted me at once. This modern aberration women have of chopping their hair close to the scalp and leaving it in fantastic disarray I find revolting.

I went at once to my friend Vasili, the baker, and asked him who she was.

"Ariadne Langos," he said. "Her father is Janco Langos, the grocer."

"Is she engaged or married?"

"No," he said slyly. "They say she frightens off the young men. They say she is very spirited."

"Excellent," I said and marveled at my good fortune in finding her unpledged. "Introduce me at once."

"Marko," Vasili said with some apprehension. "Do not commit anything rash."

I pushed the little man forward. "Do not worry, little friend," I said. "I am a man suddenly possessed by a vision. I must meet her at once."

We walked together across the dance floor to where my beloved stood. The closer we came the more impressive she was. She towered over the insignificant apple-core women around her. He eyes, dark and thoughtful, seemed to be restlessly searching the room.

Be patient, my dove! Marko is coming.

"Miss Ariadne," Vasili said. "This is Mr. Marko Palamas. He desires to have the honor of your acquaintance."

She looked at me for a long and piercing moment. I imagined her gauging my mighty strength by the width of my shoulders and the circumference of my arms. I felt the tips of my mustache bristle with pleasure. Finally she nodded with the barest minimum of courtesy. I was not discouraged.

"Miss Ariadne," I said, "may I have the pleasure of this dance?"

She stared at me again with her fiery eyes. I could imagine more timid men shriveling before her fierce gaze. My heart flamed at the passion her rigid exterior concealed.

"I think not," she said.

"Don't you dance?"

Vasili gasped beside me. An old prune-face standing nearby clucked her toothless gums.

"Yes, I dance," Ariadne said coolly. "I do not wish to dance with you."

"Why?" I asked courteously.

"I do not think you heard me," she said.

---

1. **Spartan** (spär′ t'n): pertaining to the ancient Greek city-state of Sparta.

"I do not wish to dance with you."

Oh, the sly and lovely darling. Her subterfuge so apparent. Trying to conceal her pleasure at my interest.

"Why?" I asked again.

"I am not sure," she said. "It could be your appearance, which bears considerable resemblance to a gorilla, or your manner, which would suggest closer alliance to a pig."

"Now that you have met my family," I said engagingly, "let us dance."

"Not now," she said, and her voice rose. "Not this dance or the one after. Not tonight or tomorrow night or next month or next year. Is that clear?"

Sweet, sweet Ariadne. Ancient and eternal game of retreat and pursuit. My pulse beat more quickly.

Vasili pulled at my sleeve. He was my friend, but without the courage of a goat. I shook him off and spoke to Ariadne.

"There is a joy like fire that consumes a man's heart when he first sets eyes on his beloved," I said. "This I felt when I first saw you." My voice trembled under a mighty passion. "I swear before God from this moment that I love you."

She stared shocked out of her deep dark eyes and, beside her, old prune-face staggered as if she had been kicked. Then my beloved did something that proved indisputably that her passion was as intense as mine.

She doubled up her fist and struck me in the eye. A stout blow for a woman that brought a haze to my vision, but I shook my head and moved a step closer.

"I would not care," I said, "if you struck out both my eyes. I would cherish the memory of your beauty forever."

By this time the music had stopped, and the dancers formed a circle of idiot faces about us. I paid them no attention and ignored Vasili, who kept whining and pulling at my sleeve.

"You are crazy!" she said. "You must be mad! Remove yourself from my presence or I will tear out both your eyes and your tongue besides!"

You see! Another woman would have cried, or been frightened into silence. But my Ariadne, worthy and venerable, hurled her spirit into my teeth.

"I would like to call on your father tomorrow," I said. From the assembled dancers who watched there rose a few vagrant whispers and some rude laughter. I stared at them carefully and they hushed at once. My temper and strength of arm were well known.

Ariadne did not speak again, but in a magnificent spirit stamped from the floor. The music began, and men and women began again to dance. I permitted Vasili to pull me to a corner.

"You are insane!" he said. He wrung his withered fingers in anguish. "You assaulted her like a Turk! Her relatives will cut out your heart!"

"My intentions were honorable," I said. "I saw her and loved her and told her so." At this point I struck my fist against my chest. Poor Vasili jumped.

"But you do not court a woman that way," he said.

"*You* don't, my anemic friend," I said. "Nor do the rest of these sheep. But I court a woman that way!"

He looked to heaven and helplessly shook his head. I waved goodbye and started for my hat and coat.

"Where are you going?" he asked.

"To prepare for tomorrow," I said. "In the morning I will speak to her father."

I left the hall and in the street felt the night wind cold on my flushed cheeks. My blood was inflamed. The memory of her loveliness fed fuel to the fire. For the first time I understood with a terrible clarity the driven heroes of the past performing mighty deeds in love.

GREEK VASE (detail), Fifth Century B. C. Kithara Player. The Metropolitan Museum of Art, Fletcher Fund, 1956.

Paris[2] stealing Helen in passion, and Menelaus[3] pursuing with a great fleet. In that moment, if I knew the whole world would be plunged into conflict, I would have followed Ariadne to Hades.[4]

I went to my rooms above my tavern. I could not sleep. All night I tossed in restless frenzy. I touched my eye that she had struck with her spirited hand.

*Ariadne! Ariadne!* my soul cried out.

In the morning I bathed and dressed carefully. I confirmed the address of Langos, the grocer, and started to his store. It was a bright cold November morning, but I walked with spring in my step.

When I opened the door of the Langos grocery, a tiny bell rang shrilly. I stepped into the store piled with fruits and vegetables and smelling of cabbages and greens.

A stooped little old man with white bushy hair and owlish eyes came toward me. He looked as if his veins contained vegetable juice instead of blood, and if he were, in truth, the father of my beloved, I marveled

---

2. **Paris:** in Greek mythology, the prince of Troy whose kidnapping of Helen started the Trojan War.
3. **Menelaus** (men' ə lā' əs): in Greek mythology, the husband of Helen and king of Sparta.
4. **Hades** (hā' dēz): in Greek mythology, the kingdom of the dead.

at how he could have produced such a paragon of women.

"Are you Mr. Langos?"

"I am," he said, and he came closer. "I am."

"I met your daughter last night," I said. "Did she mention I was going to call?"

He shook his head somberly.

"My daughter mentioned you," he said. "In thirty years I have never seen her in such a state of agitation. She was possessed."

"The effect on me was the same," I said. "We met for the first time last night, and I fell passionately in love."

"Incredible," the old man said.

"You wish to know something about me," I said. "My name is Marko Palamas. I am a Spartan emigrated to this country eleven years ago. I am forty-one years old. I have been a wrestler and a sailor and fought with the resistance movement in Greece in the war. For this service I was decorated by the king. I own a small but profitable tavern on Dart Street. I attend church regularly. I love your daughter."

As I finished he stepped back and bumped a rack of fruit. An orange rolled off to the floor. I bent and retrieved it to hand it to him, and he cringed as if he thought I might bounce it off his old head.

"She is a bad-tempered girl," he said. "Stubborn, impatient, and spoiled. She has been the cause of considerable concern to me. All the eligible young men have been driven away by her temper and disposition."

"Poor girl," I said. "Subjected to the courting of calves and goats."

The old man blinked his owlish eyes. The front door opened and a battleship of a woman sailed in.

"Three pounds of tomatoes, Mr. Langos," she said. "I am in a hurry. Please to give me good ones. Last week two spoiled before I had a chance to put them into Demetri's salad."

"I am very sorry," Mr. Langos said. He turned to me. "Excuse me, Mr. Poulmas."

"Palamas," I said. "Marko Palamas."

He nodded nervously. He went to wait on the battleship, and I spent a moment examining the store. Neat and small. I would not imagine he did more than hold his own. In the rear of the store there were stairs leading to what appeared to be an apartment above. My heart beat faster.

When he had bagged the tomatoes and given change, he returned to me and said, "She is also a terrible cook. She cannot fry an egg without burning it." His voice shook with woe. "She cannot make pilaf or lamb with squash." He paused. "You like pilaf and lamb with squash?"

"Certainly."

"You see?" he said in triumph. "She is useless in the kitchen. She is thirty years old, and I am resigned she will remain an old maid. In a way I am glad because I know she would drive some poor man to drink."

"Do not deride her to discourage me," I said. "You need have no fear that I will mistreat her or cause her unhappiness. When she is married to me she will cease being a problem to you." I paused. "It is true that I am not pretty by the foppish standards that prevail today. But I am a man. I wrestled Zahundos and pinned him two straight falls in Baltimore. A giant of a man. Afterward he conceded he had met his master. This from Zahundos was a mighty compliment."

"I am sure," the old man said without enthusiasm. "I am sure."

He looked toward the front door as if hoping for another customer.

"Is your daughter upstairs?"

He looked startled and tugged at his apron. "Yes," he said. "I don't know. Maybe she has gone out."

"May I speak to her? Would you kindly tell her I wish to speak with her."

"You are making a mistake," the old man said. "A terrible mistake."

"No mistake," I said firmly.

The old man shuffled toward the stairs. He climbed them slowly. At the top he paused and turned the knob of the door. He rattled it again.

"It is locked," he called down. "It has never been locked before. She has locked the door."

"Knock," I said. "Knock to let her know I am here."

"I think she knows," the old man said. "I think she knows."

He knocked gently.

"Knock harder," I suggested. "Perhaps she does not hear."

"I think she hears," the old man said. "I think she hears."

"Knock again," I said. "Shall I come up and knock for you?"

"No, no," the old man said quickly. He gave the door a sound kick. Then he groaned as if he might have hurt his foot.

"She does not answer," he said in a quavering voice. "I am very sorry she does not answer."

"The coy darling," I said and laughed. "If that is her game." I started for the front door of the store.

I went out and stood on the sidewalk before the store. Above the grocery were the front windows of their apartment. I cupped my hands about my mouth.

"Ariadne!" I shouted. "Ariadne!"

The old man came out of the door running disjointedly. He looked frantically down the street.

"Are you mad?" he asked shrilly. "You will cause a riot. The police will come. You must be mad!"

"Ariadne!" I shouted. "Beloved!"

A window slammed open, and the face of Ariadne appeared above me. Her dark hair tumbled about her ears.

"Go away!" she shrieked. "Will you go away!"

"Ariadne," I said loudly. "I have come as I promised. I have spoken to your father. I wish to call on you."

"Go away!" she shrieked. "Madman! Imbecile! Go away!"

By this time a small group of people had assembled around the store and were watching curiously. The old man stood wringing his hands and uttering what sounded like small groans.

"Ariadne," I said. "I wish to call on you. Stop this nonsense and let me in."

She pushed farther out the window and showed me her teeth.

"Be careful, beloved," I said. "You might fall."

She drew her head in quickly, and I turned then to the assembled crowd.

"A misunderstanding," I said. "Please move on."

Suddenly old Mr. Langos shrieked. A moment later something broke on the sidewalk a foot from where I stood. A vase or a plate. I looked up, and Ariadne was preparing to hurl what appeared to be a water pitcher.

"Ariadne!" I shouted. "Stop that!"

The water pitcher landed closer than the vase, and fragments of glass struck my shoes. The crowd scattered, and the old man raised his hands and wailed to heaven.

Ariadne slammed down the window.

The crowd moved in again a little closer, and somewhere among them I heard laughter. I fixed them with a cold stare and waited for some one of them to say something offensive. I would have tossed him around like a sardine, but they slowly dispersed and moved on. In another moment the old man and I were alone.

I followed him into the store. He walked an awkward dance of agitation. He shut the door and peered out through the glass.

"A disgrace," he wailed. "A disgrace. The whole street will know by nightfall. A disgrace."

"A girl of heroic spirit," I said. "Will you speak to her for me? Assure her of the sincerity of my feelings. Tell her I pledge eternal love and devotion."

The old man sat down on an orange crate and weakly made his cross.

"I had hoped to see her myself," I said. "But if you promise to speak to her, I will return this evening."

"That soon?" the old man said.

"If I stayed now," I said, "it would be sooner."

"This evening," the old man said and shook his head in resignation. "This evening."

I went to my tavern for a while and set up the glasses for the evening trade. I made arrangements for Pavlakis to tend bar in my place. Afterward I sat alone in my apartment and read a little majestic Pindar[5] to ease the agitation of my heart.

Once in the mountains of Greece when I fought with the guerrillas in the last year of the great war, I suffered a wound from which it seemed I would die. For days, high fever raged in my body. My friends brought a priest at night secretly from one of the captive villages to read the last rites. I accepted the coming of death and was grateful for many things. For the gentleness and wisdom of my old grandfather, the loyalty of my companions in war, the years I sailed between the wild ports of the seven seas, and the strength that flowed to me from the Spartan earth. For one thing only did I weep when it seemed I would leave life, that I had never set ablaze the world with a burning song of passion for one woman. Women I had known, but I had been denied mighty love for one woman. For that I wept.

In Ariadne I swore before God I had found my woman. I knew by the storm-lashed hurricane that swept within my body. A woman whose majesty was in harmony with the earth, who would be faithful and beloved to me as Penelope[6] had been to Ulysses.

That evening near seven I returned to the grocery. Deep twilight had fallen across the street, and the lights in the window of the store had been dimmed. The apples and oranges and pears had been covered with brown paper for the night.

I tried the door and found it locked. I knocked on the glass, and a moment later the old man came shuffling out of the shadows and let me in.

"Good evening, Mr. Langos."

He muttered some greeting in answer. "Ariadne is not here," he said. "She is at the church. Father Marlas wishes to speak with you."

"A fine young priest," I said. "Let us go at once."

I waited on the sidewalk while the old man locked the store. We started the short walk to the church.

"A clear and ringing night," I said. "Does it not make you feel the wonder and glory of being alive?"

The old man uttered what sounded like a groan, but a truck passed on the street at that moment and I could not be sure.

At the church we entered by a side door leading to the office of Father Marlas. I knocked on the door, and when he called to us to enter we walked in.

Young Father Marlas was sitting at his desk in his black cassock and with his black goatee trim and imposing beneath his clean-shaven cheeks. Beside the desk, in a dark blue dress sat Ariadne, looking somber and beautiful. A bald-headed, big-nosed old man with flint and fire in his eyes sat in a chair beside her.

---

5. **Pindar** (pin′ dər): a Greek poet who lived from 522–443 B.C.
6. **Penelope** (pə nel′ ə pē): in Greek mythology, the wife of Ulysses, the king of Ithaca, who waited faithfully for his return.

"Good evening, Marko," Father Marlas said and smiled.

"Good evening, Father," I said.

"Mr. Langos and his daughter you have met," he said, and he cleared his throat. "This is Uncle Paul Langos."

"Good evening, Uncle Paul," I said. He glared at me and did not answer. I smiled warmly at Ariadne in greeting, but she was watching the priest.

"Sit down," Father Marlas said.

I sat down across from Ariadne, and old Mr. Langos took a chair beside Uncle Paul. In this way we were arrayed in battle order as if we were opposing armies.

A long silence prevailed during which Father Marlas cleared his throat several times. I observed Ariadne closely. There were grace and poise even in the way her slim-fingered hands rested in her lap. She was a dark and lovely flower, and my pulse beat more quickly at her nearness.

"Marko," Father Marlas said finally. "Marko, I have known you well for the three years since I assumed duties in this parish. You are most regular in your devotions and very generous at the time of the Christmas and Easter offerings. Therefore, I find it hard to believe this complaint against you."

"My family are not liars!" Uncle Paul said, and he had a voice like hunks of dry, hard cheese being grated.

"Of course not," Father Marlas said quickly. He smiled benevolently at Ariadne. "I only mean to say—"

"Tell him to stay away from my niece," Uncle Paul burst out.

"Excuse me, Uncle Paul," I said very politely. "Will you kindly keep out of what is not your business?"

Uncle Paul looked shocked. "Not my business?" He looked from Ariadne to Father Marlas and then to his brother. "Not my business?"

"This matter concerns Ariadne and me," I said. "With outside interference it becomes more difficult."

"Not my business!" Uncle Paul said. He couldn't seem to get that through his head.

"Marko," Father Marlas said, and his composure was slightly shaken. "The family feels you are forcing your attention upon this girl. They are concerned."

"I understand, Father," I said. "It is natural for them to be concerned. I respect their concern. It is also natural for me to speak of love to a woman I have chosen for my wife."

"Not my business!" Uncle Paul said again, and shook his head violently.

"My daughter does not wish to become your wife," Mr. Langos said in a squeaky voice.

"That is for your daughter to say," I said courteously.

Ariadne made a sound in her throat, and we all looked at her. Her eyes were deep and cold, and she spoke slowly and carefully as if weighing each word on a scale in her father's grocery.

"I would not marry this madman if he were one of the Twelve Apostles," she said.

"See!" Mr. Langos said in triumph.

"Not my business!" Uncle Paul snarled.

"Marko," Father Marlas said. "Try to understand."

"We will call the police!" Uncle Paul raised his voice. "Put this hoodlum under a bond!"

"Please!" Father Marlas said. "Please!"

"Today he stood on the street outside the store," Mr. Langos said excitedly. "He made me a laughingstock."

"If I were a younger man," Uncle Paul growled, "I would settle this without the police. Zi-ip!" He drew a callused finger violently across his throat.

"Please," Father Marlas said.

"A disgrace!" Mr. Langos said.

"An outrage!" Uncle Paul said.

"He must leave Ariadne alone!" Mr. Langos said.

"We will call the police!" Uncle Paul said.

"Silence!" Father Marlas said loudly.

With everything suddenly quiet he turned to me. His tone softened.

"Marko," he said and he seemed to be pleading a little. "Marko, you must understand."

Suddenly a great bitterness assailed me, and anger at myself, and a terrible sadness that flowed like night through my body because I could not make them understand.

"Father," I said quietly, "I am not a fool. I am Marko Palamas and once I pinned the mighty Zahundos in Baltimore. But this battle, more important to me by far, I have lost. That which has not the grace of God is better far in silence."

I turned to leave and it would have ended there.

"Hoodlum!" Uncle Paul said. "It is time you were silent!"

I swear in that moment if he had been a younger man I would have flung him to the dome of the church. Instead I turned and spoke to them all in fire and fury.

"Listen," I said. "I feel no shame for the violence of my feelings. I am a man bred of the Spartan earth and my emotions are violent. Let those who squeak of life feel shame. Nor do I feel shame because I saw this flower and loved her. Or because I spoke at once of my love."

No one moved or made a sound.

"We live in a dark age," I said. "An age where men say one thing and mean another. A time of dwarfs afraid of life. The days are gone when mighty Pindar sang his radiant blossoms of song. When the noble passions of men set ablaze cities, and the heroic deeds of men rang like thunder to every corner of the earth."

I spoke my final words to Ariadne. "I saw you and loved you," I said gently. "I told you

of my love. This is my way—the only way I know. If this way has proved offensive to you, I apologize to you alone. But understand clearly that for none of this do I feel shame."

I turned then and started to the door. I felt my heart weeping as if waves were breaking within my body.

"Marko Palamas," Ariadne said. I turned slowly. I looked at her. For the first time the warmth I was sure dwelt in her body radiated within the circles of her face. For the first time she did not look at me with her eyes like glaciers.

"Marko Palamas," she said, and there was a strange moving softness in the way she spoke my name. "You may call on me tomorrow."

Uncle Paul shot out of his chair. "She is mad too!" he shouted. "He has bewitched her!"

"A disgrace!" Mr. Langos said.

"Call the police!" Uncle Paul shouted. "I'll show him if it's my business!"

"My poor daughter!" Mr. Langos wailed.

"Turk!" Uncle Paul shouted. "Robber!"

"Please!" Father Marlas said. "Please!"

I ignored them all. In that winged and zestful moment I had eyes only for my beloved, for Ariadne, blossom of my heart and black-eyed flower of my soul!

## Getting at Meaning

1. What does Marko mean when he says that it is the "cloak of the female to lend grace to the pursuit"? Who or what is being pursued? What clues to the character of Marko are provided in the opening paragraph of the story?

2. Why is Marko not discouraged by Ariadne's words and actions? What game does he think that she is playing?

3. Is Ariadne playing a game with Marko? Why does she change her mind and invite him to call?

4. Mr. Langos says that Ariadne returned from the dance "possessed." Of what is she possessed? Marko replies, "The effect on me was the same." Of what is he possessed?

5. When Marko openly declares his love, people react with shock. Why? What is unusual about Marko's approach to wooing Ariadne?

6. Marko is forty-one years old. He has lived a full life. How do his age and experience make his behavior more understandable?

7. In Father Marlas's office, Marko finally admits defeat. Why?

8. In his final speech, Marko expresses anger that "We live in a dark age . . . an age where men say one thing and mean another." Does Marko believe that Ariadne says one thing and means another? Is he angry with her for her behavior? What does this contradiction reveal about Marko's view of women?

## Developing Skills in Reading Literature

1. **Protagonist; Antagonist.** The central character in a story is called the protagonist. Who is the protagonist in this story? If the protagonist is pitted against an important opponent, the opponent is called the antagonist. Who is the antagonist in this story?

2. **Conflict.** In this story, the central conflict arises from the struggle between the protagonist and the antagonist. Describe the struggle.

3. **Characterization.** One way that a writer develops a character is by describing the character's reactions to situations and to other characters. How would you expect a person to react to being called a gorilla and a pig? to being struck in the eye? How does Marko react? What does Marko's reaction reveal about his character?

## Developing Vocabulary

**Finding the Appropriate Meaning.** The writer uses the words *spirit* and *spirited* to describe Ariadne. Find at least four examples of this usage in the story. Then look up the word *spirit* in a dictionary and select the appropriate meaning for this word as it is used in your examples.

## Developing Writing Skills

1. **Writing Dialogue.** What will happen when Marko calls on Ariadne? Imagine the scene as Marko enters the grocery store, asks for Ariadne, and then goes upstairs to meet her. Now, write the dialogue for this scene in play form. Make sure that the words spoken by the characters are appropriate to their personalities.

2. **Supporting an Opinion.** Some readers might think that Marko is a self-centered and conceited man who tries to get what he wants no matter what stands in his way. Others might feel that Marko is simply a determined man who has finally found something that he has always wanted and that he does not wish to lose. Which view do you take? Write one paragraph in which you state your opinion of Marko, and then support your view with details from the story.

# Blues Ain't No Mockin' Bird

*Toni Cade Bambara*

The puddle had frozen over, and me and Cathy went stompin in it. The twins from next door, Tyrone and Terry, were swingin so high out of sight we forgot we were waitin our turn on the tire. Cathy jumped up and came down hard on her heels and started tap-dancin. And the frozen patch splinterin every which way underneath kinda spooky. "Looks like a plastic spider web," she said. "A sort of weird spider, I guess, with many mental problems." But really it looked like the crystal paperweight Granny kept in the parlor. She was on the back porch, Granny was, making the cakes drunk. The old ladle dripping rum into the Christmas tins, like it used to drip maple syrup into the pails when we lived in the Judson's woods, like it poured cider into the vats when we were on the Cooper place, like it used to scoop buttermilk and soft cheese when we lived at the dairy.

"Go tell that man we ain't a bunch of trees."

"Ma'am?"

"I said to tell that man to get away from here with that camera." Me and Cathy look over toward the meadow where the men with the station wagon'd been roamin around all mornin. The tall man with a huge camera lassoed to his shoulder was buzzin our way.

"They're makin movie pictures," yelled Tyrone, stiffenin his legs and twistin so the tire'd come down slow so they could see.

"They're makin movie pictures," sang out Terry.

"That boy don't never have anything original to say," say Cathy grown-up.

By the time the man with the camera had cut across our neighbor's yard, the twins were out of the trees swingin low and Granny was onto the steps, the screen door bammin soft and scratchy against her palms. "We thought we'd get a shot or two of the house and everything and then—"

"Good mornin," Granny cut him off. And smiled that smile.

"Good mornin," he said, head all down the way Bingo does when you yell at him about the bones on the kitchen floor. "Nice place you got here, aunty. We thought we'd take a—"

"Did you?" said Granny with her eyebrows. Cathy pulled up her socks and giggled.

"Nice things here," said the man, buzzin his camera over the yard. The pecan barrels, the sled, me and Cathy, the flowers, the printed stones along the driveway, the trees, the twins, the toolshed.

"I don't know about the thing, the it, and the stuff," said Granny, still talkin with her eyebrows. "Just people here is what I tend to consider."

Camera man stopped buzzin. Cathy giggled into her collar.

"Mornin, ladies," a new man said. He had come up behind us when we weren't lookin. "And gents," discoverin the twins givin him a nasty look. "We're filmin for the county," he said with a smile. "Mind if we shoot a bit around here?"

"I do indeed," said Granny with no smile. Smilin man was smiling up a storm. So was Cathy. But he didn't seem to have another word to say, so he and the camera man backed on out of the yard, but you could hear the camera buzzin still. "Suppose you just shut that machine off," said Granny real low through her teeth, and took a step down off the porch and then another.

"Now, aunty," Camera said, pointin the thing straight at her.

"Your mama and I are not related."

Smilin man got his notebook out and a chewed-up pencil. "Listen," he said movin back into our yard, "we'd like to have a statement from you . . . for the film. We're filmin for the county, see. Part of the food stamp campaign. You know about the food stamps?"

Granny said nuthin.

"Maybe there's somethin you want to say for the film. I see you grow your own vegetables," he smiled real nice. "If more folks did that, see, there'd be no need—"

Granny wasn't sayin nuthin. So they backed on out, buzzin at our clothesline and the twins' bicycles, then back on down to the meadow. The twins were danglin in the tire, lookin at Granny. Me and Cathy were waitin, too, cause Granny always got something to say. She teaches steady with no let-up. "I was on this bridge one time," she started off. "Was a crowd cause this man was goin to jump, you understand. And a minister was there and the police and some other folks. His woman was there, too."

"What was they doin?" asked Tyrone.

"Tryin to talk him out of it was what they was doin. The minister talkin about how it was a mortal sin, suicide. His woman takin bites out of her own hand and not even knowin it, so nervous and cryin and talkin fast."

"So what happened?" asked Tyrone.

"So here comes . . . this person . . . with a camera, takin pictures of the man and the minister and the woman. Takin pictures of the man in his misery about to jump, cause life so bad and people been messin with him so bad. This person takin up the whole roll of film practically. But savin a few, of course."

"Of course," said Cathy, hatin the person. Me standin there wonderin how Cathy knew it was "of course" when I didn't and it was *my* grandmother.

After a while Tyrone say, "Did he jump?"

"Yeh, did he jump?" say Terry all eager.

And Granny just stared at the twins till their faces swallow up the eager and they don't even care any more about the man jumpin. Then she goes back onto the porch and lets the screen door go for itself. I'm lookin to Cathy to finish the story cause she knows Granny's whole story before me even. Like she knew how come we move so much and Cathy ain't but a third cousin we picked up on the way last Thanksgivin visitin. But she knew it was on account of people drivin Granny crazy till she'd get up in the night and start packin. Mumblin and packin and wakin everybody up sayin, "Let's get off away from here before I kill me somebody." Like people wouldn't pay her for things like they said they would. Or Mr. Judson bringin us boxes of old clothes and raggedy magazines. Or Mrs. Cooper comin in our kitchen and touchin everything and sayin how clean it all was. Granny going crazy, and Granddaddy Cain pullin her off the people, sayin, "Now, now, Cora." But next day loadin up the truck, with rocks all in his jaw, madder than Granny in the first place.

"I read a story once," said Cathy soundin like Granny teacher. "About this lady Goldilocks who barged into a house that wasn't even hers. And not invited, you understand. Messed over the people's groceries and broke up the people's furniture. Had the nerve to sleep in the folks' bed."

"Then what happened?" asked Tyrone.

"What they do, the folks, when they come in to all this mess?"

"Did they make her pay for it?" asked Terry, makin a fist. "I'd've made her pay me."

I didn't even ask. I could see Cathy actress was very likely to just walk away and leave us in mystery about this story which I heard was about some bears.

"Did they throw her out?" asked Tyrone, like his father sounds when he's bein extra nasty-plus to the washin-machine man.

"Woulda," said Terry. "I woulda gone up-side her head with my fist and—"

"You woulda done whatcha always do—go cry to Mama, you big baby," said Tyrone. So naturally Terry starts hittin on Tyrone, and next thing you know they tumblin out the tire and rollin on the ground. But Granny didn't say a thing or send the twins home or step out on the steps to tell us about how we can't afford to be fightin amongst ourselves. She didn't say nuthin. So I get into the tire to take my turn. And I could see her leanin up against the pantry table, starin at the cakes she was puttin up for the Christmas sale, mumblin real low and grumpy and holdin her forehead like it wanted to fall off and mess up the rum cakes.

Behind me I hear before I can see Grand-daddy Cain comin through the woods in his field boots. Then I twist around to see the shiny black oilskin cuttin through what little left there was of yellows, reds, and oranges. His great white head not quite round cause of this bloody thing high on his shoulder, like he was wearin a cap on sideways. He takes the shortcut through the pecan grove, and the sound of twigs snapping overhead and underfoot travels clear and cold all the way up to us. And here comes Smilin and Camera up behind him like they was goin to do somethin. Folks like to go for him some-times. Cathy say it's because he's so tall and quiet and like a king. And people just can't

stand it. But Smilin and Camera don't hit him in the head or nuthin. They just buzz on him as he stalks by with the chicken hawk slung over his shoulder, squawkin, drippin red down the back of the oilskin. He passes the porch and stops a second for Granny to see he's caught the hawk at last, but she's just starin and mumblin, and not at the hawk. So he nails the bird to the toolshed door, the hammerin crackin through the ear-drums. And the bird flappin himself to death and droolin down the door to paint the gravel in the driveway red, then brown, then black. And the two men movin up on tiptoe like they was invisible or we were blind, one.

"Get them persons out of my flower bed, Mister Cain," says Granny moanin real low like at a funeral.

"How come your grandmother calls her husband 'Mister Cain' all the time?" Tyrone whispers all loud and noisy and from the city and don't know no better. Like his mama, Miss Myrtle, tell us never mind the formality as if we had no better breeding than to call her Myrtle, plain. And then this awful thing —a giant hawk—come wailin up over the meadow, flyin low and tilted and screamin, zigzaggin through the pecan grove, breakin branches and hollerin, snappin past the clothesline, flyin every which way, flyin into things reckless with crazy.

"He's come to claim his mate," say Cathy fast, and ducks down. We all fall quick and flat into the gravel driveway, stones scrapin my face. I squinch my eyes open again at the hawk on the door, tryin to fly up out of her death like it was just a sack flown into by mistake. Her body holdin her there on that nail, though. The mate beatin the air over-head and clutchin for hair, for heads, for landin space.

The camera man duckin and bendin and runnin and fallin, jigglin the camera and scared. And Smilin jumpin up and down swipin at the huge bird, tryin to bring the hawk down with just his raggedy ole cap. Granddaddy Cain straight up and silent, watchin the circles of the hawk, then aimin the hammer off his wrist. The giant bird fallin, silent and slow. Then here comes Camera and Smilin all big and bad now that the awful screechin thing is on its back and broken, here they come. And Granddaddy Cain looks up at them like it was the first time noticin, but not payin them too much mind cause he's listenin, we all listenin, to that low groanin music comin from the porch. And we figure any minute, somethin in my back tells me any minute now, Granny gonna bust through that screen with somethin in her hand and murder on her mind. So Granddaddy say above the buzzin, but quiet, "Good day, gentlemen." Just like that. Like he'd invited them in to play cards and they'd stayed too long and all the sandwiches were gone and Reverend Webb was droppin by and it was time to go.

They didn't know what to do. But like Cathy say, folks can't stand Granddaddy tall and silent and like a king. They can't neither. The smile the men smilin is pullin the mouth back and showin the teeth. Lookin like the wolf man, both of them. Then Granddaddy holds his hand out—this huge hand I used to sit in when I was a baby and he'd carry me through the house to my mother like I was a gift on a tray. Like he used to on the trains. They called the other men just waiters. But they spoke of Granddaddy separate and said, The Waiter. And said he had engines in his feet and motors in his hands and couldn't no train throw him off and couldn't nobody turn him round. They were big enough for motors, his hands were. He held that one hand out all still and it gettin to be not at all a hand but a person in itself.

"He wants you to hand him the camera," Smilin whispers to Camera, tiltin his head to talk secret like they was in the jungle or somethin and come upon a native that don't speak the language. The men start untyin the straps, and they put the camera into that great hand speckled with the hawk's blood all black and crackly now. And the hand don't even drop with the weight, just the fingers move, curl up around the machine. But Granddaddy lookin straight at the men. They lookin at each other and everywhere but at Granddaddy's face.

"We filmin for the county, see," say Smilin. "We puttin together a movie for the food stamp program . . . filmin all around these parts. Uhh, filmin for the county."

"Can I have my camera back?" say the tall man with no machine on his shoulder, but still keepin it high like the camera was still there or needed to be. "Please, sir."

Then Granddaddy's other hand flies up like a sudden and gentle bird, slaps down fast on top of the camera and lifts off half like it was a calabash cut for sharing.

"Hey," Camera jumps forward. He gathers up the parts into his chest and everything unrollin and fallin all over. "Whatcha tryin to do? You'll ruin the film." He looks down into his chest of metal reels and things like he's protectin a kitten from the cold.

"You standin in the misses' flower bed," say Granddaddy. "This is our own place."

The two men look at him, then at each other, then back at the mess in the camera man's chest, and they just back off. One sayin over and over all the way down to the meadow, "Watch it, Bruno. Keep ya fingers off the film." Then Granddaddy picks up the hammer and jams it into the oilskin pocket, scrapes his boots, and goes into the house. And you can hear the squish of his boots headin through the house. And you can see the funny shadow he throws from the parlor window onto the ground by the string-bean patch. The hammer draggin the pocket of the oilskin out so Granddaddy looked even wider. Granny was hummin now—high, not low and grumbly. And she was doing the cakes again, you could smell the molasses from the rum.

"There's this story I'm goin to write one day," say Cathy dreamer. "About the proper use of the hammer."

"Can I be in it?" Tyrone say with his hand up like it was a matter of first come, first served.

"Perhaps," say Cathy, climbin onto the tire to pump us up. "If you there and ready."

## Getting at Meaning

1. What does the passage that describes Granny's ladle reveal about the family's recent history?

2. What does the man with the camera capture on film? Why is Granny so offended by the actions of the cameraman and his companion?

3. Who is the villain in Granny's story about the attempted suicide? Why?

4. When Granny stares at the twins ". . . till their faces swallow up the eager . . ." what is she trying to teach them?

5. Cathy describes Granddaddy Cain as ". . . tall and quiet and like a king." How does his behavior with the film makers and with the hawks prove that Cathy's description is appropriate?

## Developing Skills in Reading Literature

1. **Character.** The characters in this story evidence marked differences in age and experience. Tyrone and Terry demonstrate their youth and immaturity several times. They are impressed that the men are making "movie pictures"; they easily begin to fight when "naturally Terry starts hittin on Tyrone." How do they show their immaturity and lack of perception in response to Granny's story about the attempted suicide? In contrast, Cathy and the narrator seem older than the twins. What does the author imply or reveal about the narrator and Cathy to make them seem older?

Granny and Granddaddy Cain are not only older than the other characters, but also are wiser. What understandings and values does Granny try to impart to the children? How does Granddaddy Cain manage to get rid of the film makers? What do his actions imply about his past experiences?

2. **Characterization.** One way that the writer develops the individual characters in this story is through physical description. For example, when Granny first greets the film makers, she "smiled that smile." How else does Granny express herself physically? How does the writer use physical details to develop the characters of Granddaddy Cain and "smilin man"?

3. **Structure.** The structure of a short story is the arrangement of the events within the story. One event leads to or prepares for another in an attempt to create a certain effect. Why are the relatively late entrance of Granddaddy Cain and the episode with the hawk appropriately placed? What would be lost if these events occurred earlier in the story?

4. **Stereotype.** In literature, a stereotype is a standardized, conventional character who conforms to a fixed idea of how a certain type of person, or animal, looks or acts. What stereotype does the man with the camera have in mind when he says to Granny, "Now, aunty"? What opinion of this stereotype and of the man with the camera does Granny reveal when she responds, "Your mamma and I are not related"?

## Developing Writing Skills

**Creating a Dominant Impression.** Cathy summarizes her impression of Granddaddy Cain when she describes him as ". . . so tall and quiet and like a king." Choose someone whom you know well. What is the dominant impression that this person creates? Write one paragraph that begins with a brief description of this impression. Then develop the paragraph with examples that illustrate your topic sentence.

# A Visit to Grandmother

*William Melvin Kelley*

Chig knew something was wrong the instant his father kissed her. He had always known his father to be the warmest of men, a man so kind that when people ventured timidly into his office, it took only a few words from him to make them relax, and even laugh. Doctor Charles Dunford cared about people.

But when he had bent to kiss the old lady's black face, something new and almost ugly had come into his eyes: fear, uncertainty, sadness, and perhaps even hatred.

Ten days before in New York, Chig's father had decided suddenly he wanted to go to Nashville to attend his college class reunion, twenty years out. Both Chig's brother and sister, Peter and Connie, were packing for camp and besides were too young for such an affair. But Chig was seventeen, had nothing to do that summer, and his father asked if he would like to go along. His father had given him additional reasons: "All my running buddies got their diplomas and were snapped up by them crafty young gals, and had kids within a year—now all those kids, some of them gals, are your age."

The reunion had lasted a week. As they packed for home, his father, in a far too off-hand way, had suggested they visit Chig's grandmother. "We this close. We might as well drop in on her and my brothers."

So, instead of going north, they had gone farther south, had just entered her house. And Chig had a suspicion now that the reunion had been only an excuse to drive south, that his father had been heading to this house all the time.

His father had never talked much about his family, with the exception of his brother, GL, who seemed part con man, part practical joker, and part Don Juan; he had spoken of GL with the kind of indulgence he would have shown a cute, but ill-behaved and potentially dangerous, five-year-old.

Chig's father had left home when he was fifteen. When asked why, he would answer, "I wanted to go to school. They didn't have a black high school at home, so I went up to Knoxville and lived with a cousin and went to school."

They had been met at the door by Aunt Rose, GL's wife, and ushered into the living room. The old lady had looked up from her seat by the window. Aunt Rose stood between the visitors.

The old lady eyed his father. "Rose, who that? Rose?" She squinted. She looked like a doll, made of black straw, the wrinkles in her face running in one direction like the head of a broom. Her hair was white and coarse and grew out straight from her head. Her eyes were brown—the whites, too, seemed light brown—and were hidden behind thick glasses, which remained somehow on a tiny nose. "That Hiram?" That was another of his father's brothers. "No, it ain't Hiram; too big for Hiram." She turned then to Chig. "Now that man, he look like Eleanor, Charles's wife, but Charles wouldn't never send my grandson to see me. I never even hear from Charles." She stopped again.

"It Charles, Mama. That who it is." Aunt Rose, between them, led them closer. "It Charles come all the way from New York to see you, and brung little Charles with him."

The old lady stared up at them. "Charles? Rose, that really Charles?" She turned away, and reached for a handkerchief in the pocket of her clean, ironed, flowered housecoat, and wiped her eyes. "God have mercy. Charles." She spread her arms up to him, and he bent down and kissed her cheek. That was when Chig saw his face, grimacing. She hugged him; Chig watched the muscles in her arms as they tightened around his father's neck. She half rose out of her chair. "How are you, son?"

Chig could not hear his father's answer.

She let him go, and fell back into her chair, grabbing the arms. Her hands were as dark as the wood, and seemed to become part of it. "Now, who that standing there? Who that man?"

"That's one of your grandsons, Mama." His father's voice cracked. "Charles Dunford, junior. You saw him once, when he was a baby, in Chicago. He's grown now."

"I can see that, boy!" She looked at Chig squarely. "Come here, son, and kiss me once." He did. "What they call you? Charles too?"

"No, ma'am, they call me Chig."

She smiled. She had all her teeth, but they were too perfect to be her own. "That's good. Can't have two boys answering to Charles in the same house. Won't nobody at all come. So you that little boy. You don't remember me, do you. I used to take you to church in Chicago, and you'd get up and hop in time to

PORTRAIT OF A FARMER'S WIFE, 1951. Robert Gwathmey. Hirshhorn Museum and Sculpture Garden, Smithsonian Institution.

the music. You studying to be a preacher?"

"No, ma'am. I don't think so. I might be a lawyer."

"You'll be an honest one, won't you?"

"I'll try."

"Trying ain't enough! You be honest, you hear? Promise me. You be honest like your daddy."

"All right. I promise."

"Good. Rose, where's GL at? Where's that thief? He gone again?"

"I don't know, Mama." Aunt Rose looked embarrassed. "He say he was going by the store. He'll be back."

"Well, then where's Hiram? You call up those boys, and get them over here—now! You got enough to eat? Let me go see." She started to get up. Chig reached out his hand. She shook him off. "What they tell you about me, Chig? They tell you I'm all laid up? Don't believe it. They don't know nothing about old ladies. When I want help, I'll let you know. Only time I'll need help getting anywheres is when I dies and they lift me into the ground."

She was standing now, her back and shoulders straight. She came only to Chig's chest. She squinted up at him. "You eat much? Your daddy ate like two men."

"Yes, ma'am."

"That's good. That means you ain't nervous. Your mama, she ain't nervous. I remember that. In Chicago, she'd sit down by a window all afternoon and never say nothing, just knit." She smiled. "Let me see what we got to eat."

"I'll do that, Mama." Aunt Rose spoke softly. "You haven't seen Charles in a long time. You sit and talk."

The old lady squinted at her. "You can do the cooking if you promise it ain't because you think I can't."

Aunt Rose chuckled. "I know you can do it, Mama."

"All right. I'll just sit and talk a spell." She sat again and arranged her skirt around her short legs.

Chig did most of the talking, told all about himself before she asked. His father only spoke when he was spoken to, and then, only one word at a time, as if by coming back home, he had become a small boy again, sitting in the parlor while his mother spoke with her guests.

When Uncle Hiram and Mae, his wife, came they sat down to eat. Chig did not have to ask about Uncle GL's absence; Aunt Rose volunteered an explanation: "Can't never tell where the man is at. One Thursday morning he left here and next thing we knew, he was calling from Chicago, saying he went up to see Joe Louis fight. He'll be here though; he ain't as young and footloose as he used to be." Chig's father had mentioned driving down that GL was about five years older than he was, nearly fifty.

Uncle Hiram was somewhat smaller than Chig's father; his short-cropped kinky hair was half gray, half black. One spot, just off his forehead, was totally white. Later, Chig found out it had been that way since he was twenty. Mae (Chig could not bring himself to call her Aunt) was a good deal younger than Hiram, pretty enough so that Chig would have looked at her twice on the street. She was a honey-colored woman, with long eye lashes. She was wearing a white sheath.

At dinner, Chig and his father sat on one side, opposite Uncle Hiram and Mae; his grandmother and Aunt Rose sat at the ends. The food was good; there was a lot and Chig ate a lot. All through the meal, they talked about the family as it had been thirty years before, and particularly about the young GL. Mae and Chig asked questions; the old lady answered; Aunt Rose directed the discussion, steering the old lady onto the best stories;

Chig's father laughed from time to time; Uncle Hiram ate.

"Why don't you tell them about the horse, Mama?" Aunt Rose, over Chig's weak protest, was spooning mashed potatoes onto his plate. "There now, Chig."

"I'm trying to think." The old lady was holding her fork halfway to her mouth, looking at them over her glasses. "Oh, you talking about that crazy horse GL brung home that time."

"That's right, Mama." Aunt Rose nodded and slid another slice of white meat on Chig's plate.

Mae started to giggle. "Oh, I've heard this. This is funny, Chig."

The old lady put down her fork and began. Well, GL went out of the house one day with an old, no-good chair I wanted him to take over to the church for a bazaar, and he met up with this man who'd just brung in some horses from out West. Now, I reckon you can expect one swindler to be in every town, but you don't rightly think there'll be two; and God forbid they should ever meet—but they did, GL and his chair, this man and his horses. Well, I wished I'd-a been there; there must-a been some mighty high-powered talking going on. That man with his horses, he told GL them horses was half-Arab, half-Indian, and GL told that man the chair was an antique he'd stole from some rich white folks. So they swapped. Well, I was a-looking out the window and seen GL dragging this animal to the house. It looked pretty gentle and its eyes was most closed and its feet was shuffling.

"GL, where'd you get that thing?" I says.

"I swapped him for that old chair, Mama," he says. "And made myself a bargain. This is even better than Papa's horse."

Well, I'm a-looking at this horse and noticing how he be looking more and more wide awake every minute, sort of warming up like a teakettle until, I swears to you, that horse is blowing steam out its nose.

"Come on, Mama," GL says, "come on and I'll take you for a ride." Now George, my husband, God rest his tired soul, he'd brung home this white folks' buggy which had a busted wheel and fixed it and was to take it back that day and GL says: "Come on, Mama, we'll use this fine buggy and take us a ride."

"GL," I says, "no, we ain't. Them white folks'll burn us alive if we use their buggy. You just take that horse right on back." You see, I was sure that boy'd come by that animal ungainly.

"Mama, I can't take him back," GL says.

"Why not?" I says.

"Because I don't rightly know where that man is at," GL says.

"Oh," I says. "Well, then I reckon we stuck with it." And I turned around to go back into the house because it was getting late, near dinner time, and I was cooking for ten.

"Mama," GL says to my back. "Mama, ain't you coming for a ride with me?"

"Go on, boy. You ain't getting me inside kicking range of that animal." I was eying that beast and it was boiling hotter all the time. I reckon maybe that man had drugged it. "That horse is wild, GL," I says.

"No, he ain't. He ain't. That man say he is buggy and saddle broke and as sweet as the inside of a apple."

My oldest girl, Essie, had-a come out on the porch and she says, "Go on, Mama. I'll cook. You ain't been out the house in weeks."

"Sure, come on, Mama," GL says. "There ain't nothing to be fidgety about. This horse is gentle as a rose petal." And just then that animal snorts so hard it sets up a little dust storm around its feet.

"Yes, Mama," Essie says, "you can see he gentle." Well, I looked at Essie and then at that horse because I didn't think we could be looking at the same animal. I should-a figured how Essie's eyes ain't never been so good.

"Come on, Mama," GL says.

"All right," I says. So I stood on the porch and watched GL hitching that horse up to the white folks' buggy. For a while there, the animal was pretty quiet, pawing a little, but not much. And I was feeling a little better about riding with GL behind that crazy-looking horse. I could see how GL was happy I was going with him. He was scurrying around that animal buckling buckles and strapping straps, all the time smiling, and that made me feel good.

Then he was finished, and I must say, that horse looked mighty fine hitched to that buggy and I knew anybody what climbed up there would look pretty good too. GL came around and stood at the bottom of the steps, and took off his hat and bowed and said, "Madam," and reached out his hand to me and I was feeling real elegant like a fine lady. He helped me up to the seat and then got up beside me and we moved out down our alley. And I remember how black folks come out on their porches and shook their heads, saying, "Lord now, will you look at Eva Dunford, the fine lady! Don't she look good sitting up there!" And I pretended not to hear and sat up straight and proud.

We rode on through the center of town, up Market Street, and all the way out where Hiram is living now, which in them days was all woods, there not being even a farm in sight and that's when that horse must-a first realized he weren't at all broke or tame or maybe thought he was back out West again, and started to gallop.

"GL," I says, "now you ain't joking with your mama, is you? Because if you is, I'll strap you purple if I live through this."

Well, GL was pulling on the reins with all his meager strength, and yelling, "Whoa, you. Say now, whoa!" He turned to me just long enough to say, "I ain't fooling with you, Mama. Honest!"

I reckon that animal weren't too satisfied with the road, because it made a sharp right turn just then, down into a gulley and struck out across a hilly meadow. "Mama," GL yells. "Mama, do something!"

I didn't know what to do, but I figured I had to do something so I stood up, hopped down onto the horse's back and pulled it to a stop. Don't ask me how I did that; I reckon it was that I was a mother and my baby asked me to do something, is all.

"Well, we walked that animal all the way home; sometimes I had to club it over the nose with my fist to make it come, but we made it, GL and me. You remember how tired we was, Charles?"

"I wasn't here at the time." Chig turned to his father and found his face completely blank, without even a trace of a smile or a laugh.

"Well, of course you was, son. That happened in . . . in . . . it was a hot summer that year and—"

"I left here in June of that year. You wrote me about it."

The old lady stared past Chig at him. They all turned to him; Uncle Hiram looked up from his plate.

"Then you don't remember how we all laughed?"

"No, I don't, Mama. And I probably wouldn't have laughed. I don't think it was funny." They were staring into each other's eyes.

"Why not, Charles?"

"Because in the first place, the horse was gained by fraud. And in the second place, both of you might have been seriously injured or even killed." He broke off their stare and spoke to himself more than to any of them, "And if I'd done it, you would've beaten me good for it."

"Pardon?" The old lady had not heard him; only Chig had heard.

Chig's father sat up straight as if preparing to debate. "I said that if I had done it, if I had done just exactly what GL did, you would have beaten me good for it, Mama." He was looking at her again.

"Why you say that, son?" She was leaning toward him.

"Don't you know? Tell the truth. It can't hurt me now." His voice cracked, but only once. "If GL and I did something wrong, you'd beat me first and then be too tired to beat him. At dinner, he'd always get seconds and I wouldn't. You'd do things with him, like ride in that buggy; but if I wanted you to do something with me, you were always too busy." He paused and considered whether to say what he finally did say. "I cried when I left here. Nobody loved me, Mama. I cried all the way up to Knoxville. That was the last time I ever cried in my life."

"Oh, Charles." She started to get up, to come around the table to him.

He stopped her. "It's too late."

"But you don't understand."

"What don't I understand? I understood then; I understand now."

Tears now traveled down the lines in her face, but when she spoke, her voice was clear. "I thought you knew. I had ten children. I had to give all of them what they needed most." She nodded. "I paid more mind to GL. I had to. GL could-a ended up swinging if I hadn't. But you was smarter. You was more growed up than GL when you was five and he was ten, and I tried to show you that by letting you do what you wanted to do."

"That's not true, Mama. You know it. GL was light-skinned and had good hair and looked almost white and you loved him for that."

"Charles, no. No, son. I didn't love any one of you more than any other."

"That can't be true." His father was standing now, his fists clenched tight. "Admit it, Mama . . . please!" Chig looked at him, shocked; the man was actually crying.

"It may not-a been right what I done, but I ain't no liar." Chig knew she did not really understand what had happened, what he wanted of her. "I'm not lying to you, Charles."

Chig's father had gone pale. He spoke very softly. "You're about thirty years too late, Mama." He bolted from the table. Silverware and dishes rang and jumped. Chig heard him hurrying up to their room.

They sat in silence for awhile and then heard a key in the front door. A man with a new, lacquered straw hat came in. He was wearing brown and white two-tone shoes with very pointed toes and a white summer suit. "Say now! Man! I heard my brother was in town. Where he at? Where that rascal?"

He stood in the doorway, smiling broadly, an engaging, open, friendly smile, the innocent smile of a five-year-old.

## Getting at Meaning

1. Chig suspects that the college reunion is only an excuse to drive south and that his father has really been heading for grandmother's home all along. Why does his father want to return home? What does he hope to accomplish?

2. When Charles kisses his mother, Chig sees "fear, uncertainty, sadness, and perhaps even hatred" in his father's eyes. What does Charles fear? Why might he feel uncertain and sad? Who or what does he hate?

3. What is the attitude of Charles toward GL? Is this attitude similar to or different from his mother's attitude toward GL?

4. Grandmother says to Chig, "You be honest like your daddy." Then she immediately says, "Rose, where's GL at? Where's that thief?" What does this reveal about her feelings for her two sons?

5. What does grandmother mean when she says that GL could have ended up swinging? How did she try to prevent this?

6. In the final lines of the story, GL is described as smiling "the innocent smile of a five-year-old." How does this description support grandmother's explanation of why she paid more attention to GL?

## Developing Skills in Reading Literature

1. **Characterization.** One way that a writer develops a character is through the comments of other characters. Even though GL doesn't appear until the end of the story, the reader learns a great deal about him from the members of his family. Identify four or five character traits possessed by GL, and explain how these traits are revealed by the other characters in the course of the story.

2. **Character.** A minor character generally is presented with little detail. Such a character can be described in a single sentence. Identify three minor characters in this story. Sum up what you know about each character in one sentence.

A main character usually is a complex and many-sided individual. Like people in real life, it is difficult to describe such a character in a few sentences. Main characters are central to a story and are in-

volved in the main conflict. Identify three main characters in this story.

3. **Third-Person Narration.** When a narrator outside the story tells the tale, the narrative technique is called third-person narration. In third-person narration, the narrator refers to the characters as *he, she,* and *they.*

Frequently, third-person narration is omniscient; the narrator is all-knowing and can see into the minds of all the characters.

This story is told from the third-person omniscient point of view. The point of view, however, is limited. The writer reveals only the thoughts and feelings of one character rather than of all the characters. Who is this one character? Is this character well developed or relatively undeveloped? Explain.

## Developing Vocabulary

**Understanding Dialect.** Although Charles occasionally uses the rural Southern dialect of his family, his speech is quite different from the speech of his mother and brothers. Does his language sound more formal or more informal than the rest of his family? Find several examples to support your answer. What influences in Charles's life have changed his language patterns?

## Developing Writing Skills

**Writing an Explanation.** It has been over thirty years since Charles left home, yet this is the first time that his family has understood his reasons for leaving. In a five-paragraph composition, explain the importance of discussing problems as a family. In the introduction, explain why it is important for families to discuss problems. In the three developmental paragraphs, explain what Charles's family does discuss, what they avoid discussing, and what problems have resulted from lack of communication. In the conclusion, give an example from your own family that illustrates either the negative results of not discussing a problem openly or the positive results of talking about a problem.

# The Heyday of the Blood    *Dorothy Canfield*

The older professor looked up at the assistant, fumbling fretfully with a pile of papers. "Farrar, what's the *matter* with you lately?" he said sharply.

The younger man started, "Why . . . why . . ." the brusqueness of the other's manner shocked him suddenly into confession. "I've lost my nerve, Professor Mallory, that's what's the matter with me. I'm frightened to death," he said melodramatically.

"What *of?*" asked Mallory, with a little challenge in his tone.

The flood-gates were open. The younger man burst out in exclamations, waving his thin, nervous, knotted fingers, his face twitching as he spoke. "Of myself . . . no, not myself, but my body! I'm not well . . . I'm getting worse all the time. The doctors don't make out what is the matter . . . I don't sleep . . . I worry . . . I forget things, I take no interest in life . . . the doctors intimate a nervous breakdown ahead of me . . . and yet I rest . . . I rest . . . more than I can afford to! I never go out. Every evening I'm in bed by nine o'clock. I take no part in college life beyond my work, for fear of the nervous strain. I've refused to take charge of that summer-school in New York, you know, that would be such an opportunity for me . . . if I could only sleep! But though I never do anything exciting in the evening . . . heavens! what nights I have. Black hours of seeing myself in a sanitarium, dependent on my brother! I never . . . why, I'm in hell . . . that's what's the matter with me, a perfect hell of ignoble terror!"

He sat silent, his drawn face turned to the window. The older man looked at him specu-latively. When he spoke it was with a cheerful, casual quality in his voice that made the other look up at him surprised.

"You don't suppose those great friends of yours, the nerve specialists, would object to my telling you a story, do you? It's very quiet and unexciting. You're not too busy?"

"Busy! I've forgotten the meaning of the word! I don't dare to be!"

"Very well, then; I mean to carry you back to the stony little farm in the Green Mountains, where I had the extreme good luck to be born and raised. You've heard me speak of Hillsboro; and the story is all about my great-grandfather, who came to live with us when I was a little boy."

"Your great-grandfather?" said the other incredulously. "People don't remember their great-grandfathers!"

"Oh, yes, they do, in Vermont. There was my father on one farm, and my grandfather on another, without a thought that he was no longer young, and there was 'gran'ther' as we called him, eighty-eight years old and just persuaded to settle back, let his descendants take care of him, and consent to be an old man. He had been in the War of 1812—think of that, you mushroom!—and had lost an arm and a good deal of his health there. He had lately begun to get a pension of twelve dollars a month, so that for an old man he was quite independent financially, as poor Vermont farmers look at things; and he was a most extraordinary character, so that his arrival in our family was quite an event.

"He took precedence at once of the oldest man in the township, who was only eighty-four and not very bright. I can remember

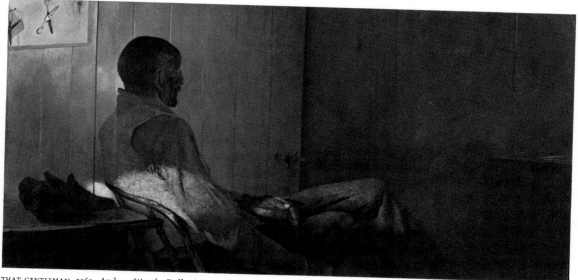

THAT GENTLEMAN, 1960. *Andrew Wyeth. Dallas Museum of Fine Arts. Dallas Art Association Purchase.*

bragging at school about Gran'ther Pendleton, who'd be eighty-nine come next Woodchuck day, and could see to read without glasses. He had been ailing all his life, ever since the fever he took in the war. He used to remark triumphantly that he had now outlived six doctors who had each given him but a year to live; 'and the seventh is going downhill fast, so I hear!' This last was his never-failing answer to the attempts of my conscientious mother and anxious, dutiful father to check the old man's reckless indifference to any of the rules of hygiene.

"They were good disciplinarians with their children, and this naughty old man, who would give his weak stomach frightful attacks of indigestion by stealing out to the pantry and devouring a whole mince pie because he had been refused two pieces at the table—this rebellious, unreasonable, whimsical old madcap was an electric element in our quiet, orderly life. He insisted on going to every picnic and church sociable, where he ate recklessly of all the indigestible dainties he could lay his hands on, stood in drafts, tired himself to the verge of fainting away by playing games with the children, and returned home, exhausted, animated, and quite ready to pay the price of a day in bed, groaning and screaming out with pain as heartily and unaffectedly as he had laughed with the pretty girls the evening before.

"The climax came, however, in the middle of August, when he announced his desire to go to the county fair, held some fourteen miles down the valley from our farm. Father never dared to let gran'ther go anywhere without himself accompanying the old man, but he was perfectly sincere in saying that it was not because he could not spare a day from the haying that he refused pointblank to consider it. The doctor who had been taking care of gran'ther since he came to live with us said that it would be crazy to think of such a thing. He added that the wonder was that gran'ther lived at all, for his heart was all wrong, his asthma was enough to kill a young man, and he had no digestion; in short, if father wished to kill his old grandfather, there was no surer way than to drive fourteen miles in the heat of August to the noisy excitement of a county fair.

"So father for once said 'No,' in the tone that we children had come to recognize as final. Gran'ther grimly tied a knot in his empty sleeve—a curious, enigmatic mode of his to express strong emotion—put his one hand on his cane, and his chin on his hand, and withdrew himself into that incalculable distance from the life about him where very old people spend so many hours.

"He did not emerge from this until one morning toward the middle of fair-week, when all the rest of the family were away—father and the bigger boys on the far-off upland meadows haying, and mother and the girls off blackberrying. I was too little to be of any help, so I had been left to wait on gran'ther, and to set out our lunch of bread and milk and huckleberries. We had not been alone half an hour when gran'ther sent me to extract, from under the mattress of his bed, the wallet in which he kept his pension money. There was six dollars and forty-three cents—he counted it over carefully, sticking out his tongue like a schoolboy doing a sum; and when he had finished he began to laugh and snap his fingers and sing out in his high, cracked old voice:

" 'We're goin' to go a skylarkin'! Little Jo Mallory is going to the county fair with his Gran'ther Pendleton, an' he's goin' to have more fun than ever was in the world, and he——'

" 'But gran'ther, father said we mustn't!' I protested, horrified.

" 'But I say we *shall!* I was your gre't-gran'ther long before he was your feyther, and anyway I'm here and he's not—so, *march!* Out to the barn!'

"He took me by the collar, and, executing a shuffling fandango of triumph, he pushed me ahead of him to the stable, where old white Peggy, the only horse left at home, looked at us amazed.

" 'But it'll be twenty-eight miles, and Peg's never driven over eight!' I cried, my old-established world of rules and orders reeling before my eyes.

" 'Eight—and—twenty-eight!
But I—am—*eighty*-eight!'

"Gran'ther improvised a sort of whooping chant of scorn as he pulled the harness from the peg. 'It'll do her good to drink some pink lemonade—old Peggy! An' if she gits tired comin' home, I'll git out and carry her part way myself!'

"His adventurous spirit was irresistible. I made no further objection, and we hitched up together, I standing on a chair to fix the check-rein, and gran'ther doing wonders with his one hand. Then, just as we were—gran'ther in a hickory shirt, and with an old hat flapping over his wizened face, I bare-legged, in ragged old clothes—so we drove out of the grassy yard, down the steep, stony hill that led to the main valley road, and along the hot, white turnpike, deep with the dust that had been stirred up by the teams on their way to the fair. Gran'ther sniffed the air jubilantly, and exchanged hilarious greetings with the people who constantly overtook old Peg's jogging trot. Between times he regaled me with spicy stories of the hundreds of thousands—they seemed no less numerous to me then—of county fairs he had attended in his youth. He was horrified to find that I had never been even to one.

" 'Why, Joey, how old be ye? 'Most eight, ain't it? When I was your age I had run away and been to two fairs an' a hangin'.'

" 'But didn't they lick you when you got home?' I asked shudderingly.

" 'You *bet* they did!' cried gran'ther with gusto.

"I felt the world changing into an infinitely larger place with every word he said.

" 'Now, this is somethin' *like!*' he exclaimed, as we drew near to Granville and fell into a procession of wagons all filled with country people in their best clothes, who looked with friendly curiosity at the little, shriveled cripple, his face shining with perspiring animation; and at the little boy beside him, his bare feet dangling high above the floor of the battered buckboard, overcome with the responsibility of driving a horse for the first time in his life, and filled with such a flood of new emotions and ideas that he must have been quite pale."

Professor Mallory leaned back and laughed aloud at the vision he had been evoking—laughed with so joyous a relish in his reminiscences that the drawn, impatient face of his listener relaxed a little. He drew a long breath; he even smiled a little absently.

"Oh, that was a day!" went on the professor, still laughing and wiping his eyes. "Never will I have such another! At the entrance to the grounds gran'ther stopped me while he solemnly untied the knot in his empty sleeve. I don't know what kind of hairbrained vow he had tied up in it, but with the little ceremony disappeared every trace of restraint, and we plunged head over ears into the saturnalia of delights that was an old-time county fair.

"People had little cash in those days, and gran'ther's six dollars and forty-three cents lasted like the widow's cruse of oil. We went to see the fat lady, who, if she was really as big as she looked to me then, must have weighed at least a ton. My admiration for gran'ther's daredevil qualities rose to infinity when he entered into free-and-easy talk with her, about how much she ate, and could she raise her arms enough to do up her own hair, and how many yards of velvet it took to make her gorgeous, gold-trimmed robe. She laughed a great deal at us, but she was evidently touched by his human interest, for she confided to him that it was not velvet at all, but furniture covering; and when we went away she pressed on us a bag of peanuts. She said

she had more peanuts than she could eat—a state of unbridled opulence which fitted in for me with all the other superlatives of that day.

"We saw the dog-faced boy, whom we did not like at all; gran'ther expressing, with a candidly outspoken cynicism, his belief that 'them whiskers were glued to him.' We wandered about the stock exhibit, gazing at the monstrous oxen, and hanging over the railings where the prize pigs lived to scratch their backs. In order to miss nothing, we even conscientiously passed through the Woman's Building, where we were very much bored by the serried ranks of preserve jars.

" 'Sufferin' Hezekiah!' cried gran'ther irritably. 'Who cares how gooseberry jel *looks*. If they'd give a felly a taste, now——'

"This reminded him that we were hungry, and we went to a restaurant under a tent, where, after taking stock of the wealth that yet remained of gran'ther's hoard, he ordered the most expensive things on the bill of fare."

Professor Mallory suddenly laughed out again. "Perhaps in heaven, but certainly not until then, shall I ever taste anything so ambrosial as that fried chicken and coffee ice-cream! I have not lived in vain that I have such a memory back of me!"

This time the younger man laughed with the narrator, settling back in his chair as the professor went on:

"After lunch we rode on the merry-go-round, both of us, gran'ther clinging desperately with his hand to his red camel's wooden hump, and crying out shrilly to me to be sure and not lose his cane. The merry-go-round had just come in at that time, and gran'ther had never experienced it before. After the first giddy flight we retired to a lemonade-stand to exchange impressions, and finding that we both alike had fallen completely under the spell of the new sensation, gran'ther said that we 'sh'd keep on a-ridin' till we'd had enough! King Solomon couldn't tell when we'd ever git a chance again!' So we returned to the charge, and rode and rode and rode, through blinding clouds of happy excitement, so it seems to me now, such as I was never to know again. The sweat was pouring off from us, and we had tried all the different animals on the machine before we could tear ourselves away to follow the crowd to the race-track.

"We took reserved seats, which cost a quarter apiece, instead of the unshaded ten-cent benches, and gran'ther began at once to pour out to me a flood of horse-talk and knowing race-track aphorisms, which finally made a young fellow sitting next to us laugh superciliously. Gran'ther turned on him heatedly.

" 'I bet-che fifty cents I pick the winner in the next race!' he said sportily.

" 'Done!' said the other, still laughing.

"Gran'ther picked a big black mare, who came in almost last, but he did not flinch. As he paid over the half-dollar he said, 'Every-body's likely to make mistakes about *some* things; King Solomon was a fool in the head about women-folks! I bet-che a dollar I pick the winner in *this* race!' and 'Done!' said the disagreeable young man, still laughing. I gasped, for I knew we had only eighty-seven cents left, but gran'ther shot me a command to silence out of the corner of his eyes, and announced that he bet on the sorrel gelding.

"If I live to be a hundred and break the bank at Monte Carlo three times a week," said Mallory, shaking his head reminiscently, "I could not know a tenth part of the frantic excitement of that race or of the mad tri-umph when our horse won. Gran'ther cast his hat upon the ground, screaming like a steam-calliope with exultation as the sorrel swept past the judges' stand ahead of all the others, and I jumped up and down in an agony of delight which was almost more than my little body could hold.

"After that we went away, feeling that the world could hold nothing more glorious. It was five o'clock, and we decided to start back. We paid for Peggy's dinner out of the dollar we had won on the race—I say 'we,' for by that time we were welded into one organism—and we still had a dollar and a quarter left. 'While ye're about it, always go the whole hog!' said gran'ther, and we spent twenty minutes in laying out that money in trinkets for all the folks at home. Then, dusty, penniless, laden with bundles, we be-stowed our exhausted bodies and our uplifted hearts in the old buckboard, and turned Peg's head toward the mountains. We did not talk much during that drive, and though I thought at the time only of the carnival of joy we had left, I can now recall every detail of the trip—how the sun sank behind Indian Mountain, a peak I had known before only through dis-tant views; then, as we journeyed on, how the stars came out above Hemlock Mountain —our own home mountain behind our house, and later, how the fireflies filled the darkening meadows along the river below us, so that we seemed to be floating between the steady stars of heaven and their dancing, twinkling reflection in the valley.

"Gran'ther's dauntless spirit still sur-rounded me. I put out of mind doubts of our reception at home, and lost myself in delight-ful ruminatings on the splendors of the day. At first, every once in a while, gran'ther made a brief remark, such as, ' 'Twas the hind-quarters of the sorrel I bet on. He was the only one in the hull kit and bilin' of 'em that his quarters didn't fall away'; or, 'You needn't tell *me* that them Siamese twins ain't un-pinned every night as separate as you and me!' But later on, as the damp evening air began to bring on his asthma, he subsided into silence, broken only by great gasping coughs.

"These were heard by the anxious, heart-sick watchers at home, and, as old Peg stum-bled wearily up the hill, father came running down to meet us. 'Where you be'n?' he demanded, his face pale and stern in the light of his lantern. 'We be'n to the county fair!' croaked gran'ther with a last flare of triumph, and fell over sideways against me. Old Peg stopped short, hanging her head as if she, too, were at the limit of her strength. I was frightfully tired myself, and frozen with terror of what father would say. Gran'ther's collapse was the last straw. I began to cry loudly, but father ignored my distress with an indifference which cut me to the heart. He lifted gran'ther out of the buckboard, carrying the unconscious little old body into the house, without a glance backward at me. But when I crawled down to the ground, sobbing and digging my fists into my eyes, I felt mother's arms close around me.

" 'Oh, poor, naughty little Joey!' she said. 'Mother's bad, dear little boy!' "

Professor Mallory stopped short.

"Perhaps that's something else I'll know again in heaven," he said soberly, and waited a moment before he went on. "Well, that was the end of our day. I was so worn out that I fell asleep over my supper, in spite of the excitement in the house about sending for a doctor for gran'ther, who was, so one of my awe-struck sisters told me, having some kind of 'fits.' Mother must have put me to bed, for the next thing I remember, she was shaking me by the shoulder and saying, 'Wake up, Joey. Your great-grandfather wants to speak to you. He's been suffering terribly all night, and the doctor think's he's dying.'

"I followed her into gran'ther's room, where the family was assembled about the bed. Gran'ther lay drawn up in a ball, groaning so dreadfully that I felt a chill like cold water at the roots of my hair; but a moment or two after I came in, all at once he gave a great sigh and relaxed, stretching out his legs and laying his arms down on the coverlid. He looked at me and attempted a smile.

" 'Well, it was wuth it, warn't it, Joey?' he said gallantly, and closed his eyes peacefully to sleep."

"Did he die?" asked the younger professor, leaning forward eagerly.

"Die? Gran'ther Pendleton? Not much! He came tottering down to breakfast the next morning, as white as an old ghost, with no voice left, his legs trembling under him, but he kept the whole family an hour and a half at the table, telling them in a loud whisper all about the fair, until father said really he would have to take us to the one next year. Afterward he sat out on the porch watching old Peg graze around the yard. I thought he was in one of his absent-minded fits, but when I came out, he called me to him, and, setting his lips to my ear, he whispered:

" ' 'An' the seventh is a-goin' down-hill fast, so I hear!' He chuckled to himself over this for some time, wagging his head feebly, and then he said: 'I tell ye, Joey, I've lived a long time, and I've larned a lot about the way folks is made. The trouble with most of 'em is, they're 'fraid-cats! As Jeroboam Warner used to say—he was in the same regiment with me in 1812—the only way to manage this business of livin' is to give a whoop and let her rip! If ye just about half-live, ye just the same as half-die; and if ye spend yer time half-dyin', some day ye turn in and die all over, without rightly meanin' to at all— just a kind o' bad habit ye've got yerself inter.' Gran'ther fell into a meditative silence for a moment. 'Jeroboam, he said that the evenin' before the battle of Lundy's Lane, and he got killed the next day. Some live, and some die; but folks that live all over die happy, anyhow! Now I tell you what's my motto, an' what I've lived to be eighty-eight on——' "

Professor Mallory stood up and, towering over the younger man, struck one hand into the other as he cried, "This was the motto he told me: 'Live while you live, and then die and be done with it!' "

## Getting at Meaning

1. What type of life does Professor Mallory's assistant lead? What does the contrast between the assistant and "gran'ther" Pendleton add to the story?

2. The assistant remarks, "People don't remember their great-grandfathers!" What does this statement reveal about how the world has changed since Professor Mallory was a little boy?

3. Although Professor Mallory's parents disciplined their children well, they could not control gran'ther. Why not?

4. What is gran'ther's reaction to the verdict that he cannot go to the county fair? What approach does he take to convince the narrator, Little Jo Mallory, to go to the fair? What does this contrasting behavior reveal about gran'ther's understanding of people?

5. Why does young Mallory feel that his world expands during the drive to the fair?

6. How do the experiences at the fair show that gran'ther not only believes in but also lives by the motto, "Live while you live, and then die and be done with it"?

7. Why does Professor Mallory tell his assistant the story about gran'ther? Describe the gradual changes in the assistant's behavior as Professor Mallory tells the story.

## Developing Skills in Reading Literature

1. **Characterization.** One way that a writer develops a character is by presenting the reactions of others to that character. In this story, young Jo Mallory experiences a variety of reactions to his gran'ther. Initially he is horrified by gran'ther's proposal to travel fourteen miles to the fair. Following their triumphant experience at the races, he says ". . . by that time we were welded into one organism. . . ." Specifically, which aspects of gran'ther's character cause this change in attitude? Professor Mallory's assistant also reacts to the character of gran'ther Pendleton. What do the assistant's reactions reveal about the strength of gran'ther as a character?

2. **Setting and Character.** Often, certain qualities of a character are revealed when the character interacts with the setting of a story. For example, gran'ther's insatiable curiosity and zest for life are brought out when he enters into "free-and-easy talk" with the fat lady. What else is revealed about gran'ther's character as he encounters the various delights offered by the county fair: the dog-faced boy, the preserve jars, the merry-go-round, and the horse race?

3. **Title.** The word *heyday* refers to a period of great success or popularity, a person's prime. Why is the title "The Heyday of the Blood" appropriate to this story?

## Developing Vocabulary

**Suffixes.** A suffix is one or more syllables placed at the end of a root word to form a new word. Some adjective suffixes mean exactly what they say. For example, the suffix *-able* means "able"; the suffix *-like* means "like."

Examine the meaning of the italicized word in each of these sentences. Then write a definition for the word.

After their experience at the fair, Young Mallory and gran'ther were dusty, *penniless,* and laden with bundles.

Professor Mallory responded to his assistant with a *cheerful,* casual quality in his voice.

Now, write five original sentences, each containing a word with a suffix that means what it says.

## Developing Writing Skills

**Writing About an Incident.** Professor Mallory obviously still finds pleasure in recalling his trip to the county fair with gran'ther. Choose an incident from your childhood that you cherish as a special memory. Write one paragraph in which you describe the event, providing details to make the experience real and vivid for your readers.

# Act of a Hero    *Hugh Garner*

George Ellsworth drove slowly along the small town's main street, waving occasionally to people he knew on the sidewalks.

The winter morning was cold and brisk, and the tires of his stakebody truck crunched on the snow. Now and then he hunched his long frame above the wheel as he shifted his position on the seat. Above his smooth thirty-year-old face his ski-cap was pushed back to release a few locks of taffy-colored hair, which hung on his forehead like a boy's.

While his truck was being loaded with flour at the mill, he had stepped across the street for a coffee, and now he felt warm and at peace with the world. If nothing delayed him, he could drop off his load at the freight sheds and be back home in time for an early lunch.

He left the business blocks of Main Street behind him and rolled down the hill to the residential section of town. As he approached the public school, he glanced in its direction; several small children spilled from the front door of the school into the street. He slowed his truck, hoping to catch a glimpse of his own youngsters, Barry and Sandra, when they emerged too for what he thought must be morning recess.

When he drew abreast of the school, a larger group of youngsters shot from the doorway and tumbled down the front steps into the snow. They picked themselves up and ran around in frenzied circles, shouting and pointing to the doorway, from which a steady stream of pupils and teachers were hurrying. Now he noticed, for the first time, that none of them were wearing their outer clothing, despite the cold. The reason became apparent immediately as a heavy red-tipped cloud of smoke burst from a window at the side of the building. He twisted the wheel and pulled the truck into the curb.

As he ran across the sidewalk, he met Mr. Manning, the principal. "Children trapped!" Manning pointed without halting his headlong rush. "Got to phone—firemen—across the street!"

George felt his body slump as if it was suddenly drained of blood. He shoved his way through the screaming crowd of children, trying to spot the faces of his own son and daughter. As he stumbled about, unable to see them, his fear grew to panic, and he began shouting their names above the hubbub about him.

Now and then, youngsters, singly or in hand-holding pairs, groped their way through the doorway, wiping their eyes and screaming with fright, before rushing down the front steps into the crowd. These children were much younger than the ones he had first seen running from the building, and George remembered with horror that the kindergarten classroom was situated at the rear of the old building. It was the room in which his youngest child, Barry, was a pupil.

Clawing his way through the mob of children he reached the front steps. The front door opened and out of a choking cloud of heavy smoke came the kindergarten teacher, carrying a little girl in her arms. Clinging to her skirts and to each other were four other youngsters, their faces gray and their eyes wide-staring despite the acrid smoke. None of them were his own two children.

He grabbed the young kindergarten teacher by the arm. "Are there any more inside!" he screamed at her.

She nodded, coughing. "I lost some, I'm afraid."

He pulled open the heavy door and ran headlong into the smoke-filled hallway. Ahead of him, showing beneath the billowing clouds of smoke, were two small girls, running across the hallway or corridor from one classroom to another. Farther along, towards the rear of the building, one wall was blazing. There was a sound like the whimpering of wounded dogs.

He peered into the two empty classrooms nearest him, then bent low as he ran along the corridor to another classroom, into which he had seen the two little girls disappear a moment before. This room was almost free of smoke, and the two children were climbing to the top of a radiator so they could reach the catch on a window. They were in no immediate danger from either the flames or smoke, and George knew they would be rescued as soon as they were seen from outside.

He turned from the classroom door and saw that the flames had now scaled the wall and were licking their way across the ceiling. On their trailing edge, large sheets of wallboard were hanging like fiery stalactites, curling and undulating in the intense heat. When he drew closer to the fire the heat engulfed him in a nauseating wave, and turning his head away, he groped for the parka on his sheepskin jacket and pulled it over his head.

In order to reach the rear of the corridor, where he felt certain his own children were trapped, he would have to run the gauntlet of the flames. It flashed through his mind that he had often thought of rescuing a family from a burning house, especially if it was his own. It had seemed such a simple fundamental act of manhood when he had thought of it. Now, facing the painful, stabbing flames that barred his path, and choking on the heavy smoke, he hesitated. From behind the fire came the sobbing cries of the trapped children, their screams muted now by the crackling roar of the nearby flames.

He edged slowly into the burning section of the corridor, but a quick stabbing flame reaching towards his face made him retreat. *I'm a coward!* he realized suddenly through the panic that now closed in on him. *Now, the one time in my life when I need courage, I have none!*

With a coward's clarity he rationalized, *Perhaps my kids have already reached the yard,* excusing his fear and hesitation. There was only the slightest chance of getting through to the children on the other side of the fire, and if he failed it would mean the loss of *his own* life as well as theirs. And it was quite probable that they would be rescued by the firemen through the rear windows of the school.

That morning at breakfast young Barry had asked, "Can I go out in the truck with you this afternoon, Daddy?" God! He took a step towards the fire once again, fighting the cowardly voice of reason that told him to turn and run.

*Can I go out with you this afternoon, Daddy?* Of course! Of course! Now he remembered. The children had stayed home from school today so their mother could take them to the dentist. They weren't in the blazing school at all, but back in the center of town at the dentist's office! Oh, dear God! Suddenly the conflicting fears and hesitations dropped their weight from his heart.

When he once again noticed the fire, his estimation of his chances of getting through it had become impersonal, and now the space between the burning piles of wallboard and wood panelling had narrowed considerably. It would be almost impossible to crawl or run between them without being burned. The sobbing of the trapped children and the noise of the fire were suddenly dimmed in his ears by the rising wail of sirens from the street, showing him that the fire trucks had arrived. He was no longer forced to make a decision, and he backed away from the flames and smoke with hurried stumbling eagerness.

As he hurried back along the corridor, he glanced into the room where he had last seen the two little girls. They were standing on a ledge, silhouetted against the window, and had almost succeeded in opening a space large enough to crawl through.

He had to accomplish something to justify his frightened return to the outside. He ran between the desks and picked both children from the window ledge, and with one beneath each arm hurried out of the room and along the corridor to the front door.

As he emerged from inside the building, there was a loud cheer from the children on the lawn and from the thickening crowd of adults who were approaching the school along the street. Several cars parked along the curbs gave him an accolade with their horns.

He set the two little girls on their feet in the snow, and allowed the teachers and some newly-arrived parents to pump his arm and shout their thanks in his ear. When he remembered the children still trapped at the rear of the building, he shouted the information to a passing fireman.

Much later, after being interviewed briefly by a young man from *The Clarion*, the local paper, he was able to drag himself away from

the admiring crowd that now surrounded him. The fire was out, and the trapped children in the kindergarten class had all been rescued by the firemen. The schoolchildren had been formed into classes, and the only casualty was a small boy who had been overcome by smoke.

As George climbed into his truck he heard the principal shout, "Now, children, let's give three cheers and a tiger for Mr. Ellsworth!" With the children's cheers echoing like a mockery behind him, he stepped on the gas and pushed the truck as fast as he could away from the school.

He took his time unloading the flour at his destination, and drove as slowly as he could on the way home. When he arrived at his house in the late afternoon, the kitchen table was set, and his smiling wife and children came to the back door to meet him.

After making himself ready for supper, he sat down at the table and glanced up into the beaming face of his wife. She pointed in front of him at the open newspaper propped against the sugar bowl. There was a photograph of himself coming down the school steps with the two little girls under his arms, and a headline over the story of the fire that read, THE ACT OF A HERO. He swept the paper from the table to the floor.

"Are you mad, Daddy?" Sandra asked, in open-mouthed wonder.

He stared down at his plate, unable to face his wife and children.

"Why are you mad, Daddy?" his daughter asked again.

It was an unanswerable question. It was a question he would be unable to answer for the rest of his life.

## Getting at Meaning

1. At the end of the story, why is George angry? What has he done that makes him feel shame? Would George feel the same way if no one had seen him enter and leave the burning school? Explain.

2. George had often thought about rescuing a family from a fire. How is the real situation different from his idealized vision?

3. Why doesn't George want to leave the building empty-handed? How might he have felt later if he had left empty-handed? Explain.

## Developing Skills in Reading Literature

**Conflict.** Internal conflict usually occurs when a character is struggling with emotions or moral decisions. Describe the internal conflict in this story.

## Developing Vocabulary

**Word Origins.** George realizes "he would have to run the gauntlet of the flames" to get to the trapped children. Look up *gauntlet* in a dictionary. Study the etymology, or origin, of the word. What language did *gauntlet* originally come from? What did it mean in this language? What does the word mean as it is used in this story?

## Developing Writing Skills

**Writing About an Incident.** Think of a time when you received credit that you did not deserve or a time when you did not receive the credit you did deserve. Describe the incident in detail and the feelings that resulted from the incident.

# Early Marriage     *Conrad Richter*

For two days the leathery face of Asa Putman had been a document in cipher to anyone who could read the code. Since Saturday but one traveler had passed his solitary post, a speck of adobe and picket corrals lost on the vast, sandy stretch of the Santa Ana plain.[1] Far as the eye could see from his doorway, the rutted El Paso trail, unfenced, gutterless, innocent of grading, gravel, culverts, or telephone poles, imprinted only by iron tires, the hoofs of horses and oxen, sheep and cattle, and the paw of the loping lobo wolf, lay with dust unraised.

Ordinarily, there were freighters with cracking whips and trailers rumbling on behind. Army trains to and from the forts set up their tents for the night beyond the springs. The private coaches of Santa Fe and Colorado merchants, of cattle kings and Government officials, stopped long enough for the Putman children to admire the ladies, the magnificent woodwork, and the luxurious cushions inside. Trail herds of gaunt red steers bawled for the water in the earthen tank, and pairs and companies of horsemen rode up and down.

But since Saturday not even a solitary buckboard from the far settlements in the Cedar country had called for supplies or letters. Only a girl from the Blue Mesa had ridden in for her and her neighbors' mail. She had eaten dinner with the Putmans, refused to stay overnight and started her long ride home.

A stranger from the East would have spoken about the stillness, the deadly waiting, and asked uneasily why Uncle Gideon hadn't come as promised. But in the Putman household it was not mentioned.

Asa deliberately busied himself about the post, filling the bin beneath the counter with navy beans and green coffee, leafing through the packet of letters in the drawer, and making a long rite out of feeding the occupants of the picket corrals—four horses of which were fresh for the next stage.

Rife, just turned fifteen, carried water and gathered cow chips in an old hide dragged by a rope to his saddle horn. Ignacita, the Mexican housekeeper, spat sharply on her heavy irons in the torrid kitchen and kept glancing over her shoulder and out of the open door and windows.

And Nancy Belle, going on seventeen, packed and repacked the high, iron-bound trunk that her father had bought for her at Santa Fe and sang softly to herself in the way that women sang fifty and sixty years ago.

Saturday she was being married at Gunstock, two hundred miles away—five days' journey in a wagon, four in a saddle or buckboard.

For six months she had thought of little else. The almanac fell apart at June as naturally as her mother's Bible did at the Twenty-third Psalm. So often had she run her finger down the page that anyone might tell from the worn line of type the very day she and Stephen Dewee would be man and wife. The Dewees lived four hundred miles west across the territory in the Beaverhead country. She

---

1. **Santa Ana plain:** an area in the New Mexico territory, now in central New Mexico.

and Stephen were taking a mountain ranch near his people, and for the wedding they had compromised on Gunstock, nearly equidistant from both families and convenient to friends scattered up and down the Rio Grande.[2]

She had lighted a candle in the dusk, when a figure appeared reluctantly in her doorway. Asa Putman had never been at ease in his daughter's bedroom. A tall, rawhide man in an unbuttoned, sagging vest, he was visibly embarrassed by any furnishings that suggested refinement. Invariably he kept his hat on in the house. He had it on now, a flat top and a flat brim, not so much like the Western hats you see now. Nancy Belle knew that her mother's people had never forgiven him for bringing his young wife and their two small children to this lonely post, at the mercy of outlaws and the worse Apaches.

Tonight she could see that something bothered him. He gave her a sidewise glance, so sharp and characteristic.

"I don't expect, Nancy Belle, you could put off your weddin'?"

The girl stood quietly gazing at him with a face like the tintype[3] of her mother. But under her sedate gray dress, with tight waist and full skirts to the instep, she had frozen. She looked much older than her years. Her air of gentlefolk and her wide-apart gray eyes came from her mother. But the chin, tipped up with resolute fearlessness, was her father's.

"No, papa!" Her two clear words held all the steady insistence of the desert.

"I figured how you'd feel," he nodded, avoiding her eyes. "I just wanted to put it up to you. I'd 'a' covered the *jornada*[4] on foot to be on time at my own weddin', but I didn't have to count on Gideon to hold me up."

"Are you telling me, papa, that you can't go to Gunstock tomorrow?" Her voice remained quiet, but a coldness had seized her. Of all the people she had visualized at her wedding, the one next to Stephen she could

least spare was the tall, grave figure of her father.

"I reckon I kind of can't, Nancy Belle," he said soberly. "Rife could tend to the stage all right and do the feedin'. But they's men come to this post no boy can handle." He shifted his position. "I figured once on closin' up the post till I got back. But the stage is comin' and the mail. And the freighters count on me for feed and grub. Then I got to protect my own property and the mail and freight for the Cedar country that's in the storage room."

"I know," Nancy Belle said steadily. "I can get to Gunstock all right."

Far back in her father's assaying eyes, she fancied she saw a glint of pride.

"You're pretty nigh a woman now, Nancy Belle. And Rife's a good slice of a man. It's a straight trail to the Rio Grande, once you turn at the old post. Both you and Rife's been over it before. Of course, I'd like to be at the weddin', but the boy can tell me about it." He went to the window. "Rife!" he called.

Nancy Belle's brother came in presently. A slight boy, with his father's blue eyes, he seldom made a fuss over anything, even when he shot a stray duck on the tank or when they braked down the last cedar hill into Santa Fe with all the open doors of the plaza shops in sight. And when his father told him now, he showed neither enthusiasm nor regret—merely straightened.

"Sure. I can take you, Nancy Belle," he said.

Something pulled under his sister's tight basque.[5] She remembered the long miles they would have in the wagon, the camps at lonely places, the ugly shadow ever hovering over the outposts of this frontier country,

---

2. **Rio Grande** (rē′ ō grand′): a river in the southwest United States, flowing through New Mexico.
3. **tintype** (tin′ tīp): a photograph made directly on a tin or iron plate.
4. *jornada* (hôr nä′ dä) *Spanish:* journey.
5. **basque** (bask): a woman's close-fitting bodice.

and the blight that, since Saturday, seemed to have fallen on the trail. Her eyes swam. Now, at the last minute, she yielded.

"If you'll let me ride, papa, I'll wait another day for Uncle Gideon," she promised.

Her father's eyes moved to the ruffled red calico curtains at the shadeless windows.

"I don't hardly count on Gideon comin' any more, Nancy Belle. Besides, it's too long in the saddle to Gunstock—especially for a girl to get married. You'd be plumb wore out, and you wouldn't have your trunk. You couldn't get dressed for your weddin'."

He turned thoughtfully and went out, Rife close behind. Nancy Belle could hear her father's tones, slow and grave, coming from near one of the picket corrals.

It was too far to catch the words; but when they came in, she saw that her brother's features looked a little pale under the tan.

"You better get some sleep, Nancy Belle," her father said. "You and Rife are startin' before daylight. If Gideon comes, I'll ride after."

They had scarcely gone from the room when Ignacita came in from the kitchen, her black eyes glittering over a pile of freshly starched white in her arms.

"Nancy Belle, *chinita!*"[6] she whispered, plucking at the girl's sleeve. "You don't say to your *papacito* I talk to you! I have promise I don't scare you. But I can't see you go so far in the wildness alone, *pobrecita!*[7] Sometimes people go safe from one place to the other, oh, *si!*[8] But sometimes, *chinita,* they don't come back! You have not the oldness like Ignacita. Ay, I tell you these old eyes have see men and women quartered from a tree like sheep or maybe tied over a stove like I don't have the words to say to you."

Nancy Belle did not answer except to lay, one by one, the ironed pieces in her trunk—a bride's muslin underwear trimmed with red and blue feather stitching; long petticoats stiffly flounced with ruffles, and nightgowns long in the sleeve and high in the neck, with ruffles at wrist and throat. The Mexican woman went on hoarsely. The girl folded away her winter's cashmere dress, buttoned up the front and with a white fichu. She unwrapped and wrapped again in crumpled white tissue the red slippers the old gentleman on the stage had sent her as a wedding present from Philadelphia.

When Ignacita had left, she opened her keepsake box covered with colored shells. The mirror on the inside lid turned back a face as calm as the little golden clouds that hung of an evening over the east to catch the desert sunset. But after she had undressed and put on her nightdress, for a long time she was aware of the soft pound of her heart faintly swaying the bed on its rawhide springs.

At the first sound of Ignacita's hand on the kitchen stove, Nancy Belle sprang out of bed. She dressed on the brown pool of burro skin, the only carpet on her adobe floor. Through the west window she could see the morning star burning like a brilliant candle. It hung, she told herself, over Gunstock and the Beaverhead, where Stephen, at this moment, in their new log ranch house, lay thinking about her.

They ate in the kitchen by lamplight. She had never been so conscious of every detail— the great white cups and saucers, the familiar steel knives, the homy smell of the scorched paper lamp-shade, the unreadable eyes of her father, Rife, and Ignacita.

Asa Putman himself carried out the trunk. There was already hay in the wagon, a gunny sack of oats, food in a canned-tomato box and utensils in another, a water-keg, bed roll tied in a wagon sheet, an ax, a bridle, and her own side-saddle, made to order over a man's

---

6. **chinita** (chē nē′ tä) *Spanish:* little girl.
7. **pobrecita** (pō brä sē′ tä) *Spanish:* poor little thing.
8. **si** (sē) *Spanish:* yes.

tree. Her eyes caught the gleam of a rifle leaning up against the seat in the lantern-light. Tethered to the rear of the wagon stood her saddle mare, Fancy, with pricked-up ears. She was going along to their new ranch home. Nancy Belle felt that she was still among intimate things, but outside the little circle of light lay darkness and the unknown.

When she said goodbye to her father, he kissed her—something he had not done for years.

"You haven't changed your mind, Nancy Belle?" he asked.

She climbed quickly up over the wheel to the spring seat of the wagon before he might see that she was crying. Rife swung up like a monkey on the other side and pushed the rifle into the crevice behind the seat cushion. The lines tautened and the wagon lurched.

"*Dios*[9] go with you safe to your husband, Nancy Belle!" she heard Ignacita cry after her.

The morning star had set. They moved into a world of silent blackness. Nancy Belle could not see how the horses remained on the trail. When she looked back, the only light in all these square miles of black, unfriendly earth was the yellow window of her father's post.

It was almost a vision, golden and far away, like all beautiful things. She didn't trust herself to look again.

Two hours later the wagon was a lonely speck of boat rocking in an illimitable sage-green sea beneath the sun. The canvas wagon sheet fastened over the bows was a kind of sail, and eastward the sandy water did not stop rolling till it washed up at the foot of the faintly blue ramparts of the distant Espiritu Range.

Just before they turned west on the cross trail to the Rio Grande, a heavy wagon with a yoke of oxen in front and a cow behind toiled round the crumbling adobe walls of the old, abandoned post house. A bearded man and a thin woman with a white face sat on the seat. She held a baby in her arms, and three black-eyed children peered from under the wagon sheet.

The bearded man saluted and stopped his willing team. Rife did likewise. The woman spoke first. Her tongue was swift and slightly acid.

"You better turn around and follow us if you want to save your hair!" she called. "Yesterday a sheepherder told us he saw—"

A sharp word from the bearded man caused her to relapse into sullen silence. He asked Rife where he might be going, then climbed down to the trail and said he wanted to talk to him a little. The boy followed reluctantly behind his wagon. Nancy Belle could hear the bearded man's tones coming slow and grave like her father's, while the woman made silent and horribly expressive lip language.

Rife came back, walking stiffly. The bearded man climbed up beside the woman.

"They got to go on," he told her in a low tone, then saluted with his whip. "Good luck, boy! And you, miss!"

Rife raised his whip in stiff acknowledgment. The wagons creaked apart. Nancy Belle saw in front of her the trail to the Rio Grande, little more than a pair of wheel tracks, that lost itself on the lonely plain. Rife seemed relieved that she did not ask what the bearded man had said. But it was enough for her not to be able to forget the woman's fearful signs and mouthings and the horror in the curious eyes of the staring children.

Sister and brother talked very little. Nancy Belle saw her brother's eyes keep sweeping the country, scanning the horizons. Bunches of bear grass that might have been feathers pinioned his blue gaze, and clumps of cane cactus that seemed to hold pointing gun barrels. At arroyos[10] thick with chamiso and

---

9. **Dios** (dē ōs) *Spanish:* God.
10. **arroyo** (ə roi' ō) *Spanish:* a dry gully.

Apache plume she could see his feet tighten on the footboard. Once he pulled out the rifle, but it was only a herd of antelopes moving across the desert page.

They camped for the night when the sun was still high. Nancy Belle asked no questions as the boy drove far off the trail into a grassy *cañada*.[11] She sang softly to herself as she fried the salt side bacon and put the black coffeepot to boil.

Rife hobbled Anton Chico and the Bar X horse and staked out Fancy close to the wagon.

She pretended not to notice when, before dark, he poured earth on the fire till not a spark or wisp of smoke remained. Out of one eye she watched him climb the side of the *cañada* and stand long minutes sweeping the country from the ridge, a slight, tense figure against the sullen glow of the sunset.

"It's all right," he said when he came down. "You can go to bed."

"What's all right?" she asked him.

"The horses," he said, turning away, and Nancy Belle felt a stab of pain that so soon this boy must bear a man's responsibilities and tell a man's lies.

She prayed silently on her blankets spread on the hay in the wagon box, and lay down with her head on the side-saddle, her unread Testament in her hand. She heard Rife unroll his camp bed on the ground beneath the wagon. It was all very strange and hushed without her father. Just to feel the Testament in her hand helped to calm her and to remember the day at the post when she had first met Stephen.

Her father had never let her come in contact with the men of the trail. Always, at the first sign of dust cloud on the horizon, he would tell both children to heap up the chip-box, fill the water-buckets and carry saddles and bridles into the house. But this day Asa Putman and Rife had gone to Fort Sumner.

And to Nancy Belle, Uncle Gideon could seldom say no.

It had been a very hot day. She had been sitting in the shade of the earthen bank of the tank, moving her bare feet in the cool water, watching the ripples in the hot south wind. The leaves of the cottonwoods clashed overhead, and she heard nothing until she looked up, and there was a young man on a blue-gray horse with dust clinging to his hat brim and mustache. His eyes were direct as an eagle's. Firm lines modeled his lean face. But what she noticed most at the time was the little bow tie on his dark shirt.

Instantly she had tucked her bare, wet legs under her red dress. Her face burned with shame, but the young stranger talked to her about her father coolly, as if she, a girl of fifteen, had not been caught barefooted. Then he did what in her mind was a noble thing. When Uncle Gideon came out he magnificently turned his back for her to run into the house and pull on shoes and stockings.

She thought of Stephen constantly next day and the next. She had grown a little used to the journey without her father now—the still, uncertain nights under the wagon sheet, sitting, lying, listening, waiting; the less uncertain days with the sun on the endless spaces; her never-quiet perch on the high spring seat under the slanted bow; the bumps, creaks, and lumberings of the wagon; the sand sifting softly over the red, turning wheels; all afternoon the sun in their faces; ahead the far haze and heat waves in which were still lost Gunstock and the Rio Grande. Almost she had forgotten the bearded man with the oxen and the curious, detached horror in the eyes of his children.

Since morning of the third day their progress had been slower. The trail seemed level, except for the heavy breathing of the horses.

---

11. **cañada** (cä nyä′ dä) *Spanish:* a valley.

But when Nancy Belle glanced back she could see the steady grade they had been climbing. Abruptly, in mid-afternoon, she found that the long, blue Espiritu Range had disappeared, vanished behind a high pine-clad hill which was its southernmost beginning. It was like the lizard that swallowed itself, a very real lizard. At this moment they were climbing over the lizard's tail.

"Cedars!" Rife said briefly, pointing with the whip to dark sprawling growths ahead.

"You breathe deep up here!" Nancy Belle drank in the light air.

Rife took a sniff, but his blue eyes never ceased to scan the high, black-thatched hill under whose frowning cliff they must pass.

"Soon we can see the Gunstock Mountains," Nancy Belle said.

"And Martin Cross's cabin," Rife nodded. "It's the last water to the Rio Grande."

"He's a nice old man," Nancy Belle ventured casually. "It would be nice to camp by his cabin tonight and talk."

The boy inclined his head. After a few moments he started to whistle softly. At the first cedar Nancy Belle leaped off the moving wagon and climbed back with an evergreen branch. The twig, crushed in her hand, smelled like some store in Santa Fe.

They gained the summit. A breeze was sweeping here from the southwest, and the horses freshened. But Rife had suddenly stopped whistling and Nancy Belle's sprig of cedar lay on her lap. The frowning cliff of the pine-clad hill was still there. But Martin Cross's cabin had turned to a desolate mound of ashes. As they stared, a gust of wind sent wisps of smoke scurrying from the mound, and a red eye opened to watch them from the embers. Nancy Belle felt an uncontrollable twitching in the hair roots at the base of her scalp.

Where Martin Cross's eastbound wheel tracks met the trail, Rife reluctantly halted the horses and wet his air-dried lips.

"The water keg's dry, and the horses. If papa was here, he'd drive over."

"I'm the oldest." Nancy Belle found her voice steady. "I'll ride over. There might be something we can do."

The boy rose quickly. His eyes seemed to remember something his father had said.

"You can drive the wagon over if I wave."

He had thrown her the lines and slipped back through the canvas-covered tunnel of wagon box, picking up Fancy's bridle and the rifle. Barebacked he rode toward the smoldering ashes at the foot of that frowning hill. The chestnut mare's tail and mane streamed like something gold in the wind.

When she looked back to the trail, her eyes were pinioned by a light object in the wheel track ahead of the Bar X horse. It was a long gray feather. Instantly she told herself that it had come from some wild turkey Martin Cross had shot, and yet never had air anywhere become so suddenly horrible and choking as in this canyon.

Rife did not signal her to drive over. She saw him come riding back at full speed. The mare was snorting. As he stopped her at the wagon, her chestnut head kept turning back toward what had once been a cabin. Rife slipped the lead rope about her neck and climbed into the seat with the rifle in his hands.

"The water—you wouldn't want it!" he said thickly. His cheeks, she noticed, were the color of yeso.[12]

"Rife"—Nancy Belle touched his arm when she had driven down the canyon— "what did you see at the cabin?"

The boy sat deaf and rigid beside her, eyes staring straight ahead. She saw that his young hands were still tortured around the barrel of his rifle.

Far down on the pitch-dark mesa she stopped the horses in the trail and listened.

---

12. **yeso** (yā′ sō) *Spanish:* gypsum, a white mineral.

There were no stars, not a sound but the flapping of the wagon sheet in the wind and the clank of coffee-pot and water-bucket under the wagon. Half standing on the footboard, she guided the team off the trail in the intense blackness. Her swift hands helped the trembling boy stake out the mare and hobble the team. They did not light a lantern. Rife declined to eat. Nancy Belle chewed a few dry mouthfuls.

The wind came drawing out of the blackness with a great draft. It hissed through the grass, sucked and tore at the wagon sheet, and whistled through the spokes and brake rigging. Rife did not take his bed roll under the wagon tonight. He drew the ends of the wagon sheet together and lay down in the wagon box near his sister. For a long time they were silent. When she heard his heavy breathing, she lifted the rifle from his chest.

The storm grew. Sand began pelting against the canvas and sifted into the wagon box. An invisible cloud of choking dust found its way into eyes, mouth, ears, and lungs. Nancy Belle laid down the rifle a moment to pull a blanket over the face of the boy. He tossed and muttered pitifully, but he slept on.

Magically the rain, when it came, stopped the sand and dust. The girl drank in the clean-washed air. At daylight she slipped out to the ground. The mesa, stretching away in the early light, touched here and there with feathers of mist, would have been beautiful except for a sharp new loneliness. The horses were gone!

At her exclamation, Rife appeared from the wagon box. His shame at having slept through the night was quickly overshadowed by their misfortune.

Together they found where Fancy's stake had been pulled out and dragged. Yards farther on they could tell by Anton Chico's tracks that his hobbles had parted.

Nancy Belle made her brother come back to the wagon and stuff his pockets with cold biscuits and antelope jerky. She said she would have a hot breakfast ready when he returned. The horses, perhaps, were just down in some draw where they had drifted with the wind.

When he had gone with the rifle, she filled the coffee-pot from a clearing water-hole in the nearest arroyo. She fried potatoes and onions in the long-handled skillet. And when he did not come, she set fresh biscuits in the Dutch oven. Each biscuit held a square of salt side bacon in its top, and as it baked, the fat oozed down and incased it in a kind of glazed tastiness.

At noon she thought she heard a shot. Nowhere could she see him on the endless sweep of mesa. By late afternoon she was still alone. She read her Testament and wondered how many women over the world had read it in hours like this. Sitting in the shadow of the wagon, facing the direction in which he had gone, she looked up every few minutes. But all her eyes could find were cloud shadows racing across the lonely face of the mesa. All she could hear were the desolate cries from the unseen lark sparrows.

Darkness, stillness settled down on the empty land. She climbed back into the wagon and sat on the chuck-box, hands rigid on her knees. Again and again she convinced herself that the horses could not have been driven off or she would have seen the drivers' tracks. When wild, sharp barks shattered the stillness and set wires jerking in her limbs, she talked to herself steadily, but a little meaninglessly, of the post—on and on as the darkness was filled with the ringing and counter-ringing of shrill cracked yappings—not long tones like a dog's, but incredibly short syllables rising, rising in a mad eternal scale and discord.

"I wish papa had given me two of the chairs," she repeated. "Mamma said they were post oak from Texas. She said they had got white from scrubbing. I liked the laced rawhide seats with the hair left on. It made them soft to sit on. The seats in the parlor were black. And the ones in the kitchen were red. But I liked the brockle one in my room best."

The insane din around the wagon had become terrific. There were only two or three of the animals, Nancy Belle guessed, but they threw their voices and echoes together to make a score.

"When I was little I liked to go in the storage room," her voice went on, scarcely intelligible to her own ears. "It was dark and cool, and smelled of burlap and kerosene and whisky, and sweetish with brown sugar. I can see the fat sacks of green coffee. And the round tins of kerosene had boards on the side. The flour-sacks were printed 'Rough and Ready' in red letters. Mamma once used to make our underwear out of the sacking. I can smell the salt side bacon in the gunny sacks."

She could tell from the sounds that one of the animals was running insanely back and forth near the wagon tongue. She had never noticed before that they yelped both when breathing in and out. Suddenly came silence. It warned her. Instinctively she felt for the ax.

"Nancy Belle!" a boy's far, anxious voice called from the darkness.

She hallooed and leaned out over the tailboard. Three shadowy forms were coming across the mesa in the starlight. Never had horses looked so good.

"Were you scared?" Rife greeted. "Anything bother you?"

"Nothing," Nancy Belle said. "Just coyotes."

"I had to give Fancy her head after it got dark." He slid wearily to the ground. "She brought us straight back to the wagon."

Nancy Belle had wanted to put her arms around her brother. Now she hugged the mare instead. Rife ate fresh biscuits and a tin plate of cold potatoes. He drank several tin cups of coffee. Nancy Belle had slipped the oats-laden gunny-sack *morrals*[13] over the horses' heads.

"I had to walk halfway to the mountain," Rife said.

"Just help hitch up; then you can sleep all night," she promised.

It rained again heavily toward midnight. Flashes of lightning lit the drenched plain. For minutes at a time, quivering fingers of blue phosphorescence stood on the ears of the toiling horses. At dawn Nancy Belle still held the reins as the mud-splashed wagon crawled through a world bathed in early purple splendor.

Four days they had been crossing a hundred and seventy miles of desolate plain. Now the end waited in sight. To the west lay a land broken and tumbled by a mighty hand. Hill shouldered hill and range peered over

---

13. **morral** (mō räl') *Spanish:* a food bag from which horses eat while traveling.

range, all indescribably violet except where peaks tipped by the unseen sun were far-off flaming towers of copper.

It was a new land, her promised land, Stephen's land, Nancy Belle told herself, where nobody burned cow chips, but snapping cedar and pine; where cold water ran in the wooded canyons, and the eye, weary of one flat circle the horizon round, had endless geometric designs to refresh the retina.

She sang softly as the wagon lumbered to the edge of a long, shallow valley, brown and uninhabited running north and south, and desolate except for a winding ribbon that was white with sky and narrowly bordered with green.

"Rife!" Nancy Belle cried. "The Rio Grande!"

An hour afterwards they pulled out of the sun into the shade of the long cottonwood *bosque*.[14] Nancy Belle wasn't singing now. Where she remembered wide sandbars glistening with sky and tracked by waterfowl, a chocolate-red flood rolled. Where had been the island, tops of tule and scrub willow swung to and fro with the current.

Anton Chico and the Bar X horse stopped of their own accord in the trail, ears pricked forward at the swirling brown wash. While Rife turned the three horses loose to graze, Nancy Belle silently fried bacon and made coffee. When she had washed skillet and tin dishes in the river, the boy had wired the wagon box to the brake rigging. Now he was tying securely one end of his rope to the center of the coupling pole under the wagon. The other end she knew he would fasten to the inadequate upper horn of the side-saddle.

"I wouldn't mind the river if I just had my own saddle," he mourned.

They hitched up the team silently. Rife cinched the side-saddle on Fancy and straddled it, the single stirrup useless to a man. Nancy Belle climbed into the wagon and

14. **bosque** (bōs′ kā) *Spanish:* woods or forest.

picked up the lines. The other bank looked as far away as the Espiritu Range from the post. She wanted to say something to her brother—some last word, in case they didn't make it. But all she did was cluck her tongue to the horses.

Gingerly, one slow foot at a time, the team moved down the trail into the water.

"Give 'em their heads!" Rife called from the right rear.

Nancy Belle held a rein in each hand. The red channel water came to the wagon tongue, covered it, reached the horses' bellies. The team wanted to stop. Nancy Belle swung her whip, a stick tipped with a long rawhide lash. The wagon went on. The collars of both horses kept dipping, but never entirely out of sight. Still barely wading, the slow team reached the firmer footing of the island.

Two-thirds of the river still rolled in front of the wagon. The west bank did not seem to have grown much closer, but the east bank behind them had moved far away. The team had to be whipped into the violent current. The water churned white through the wagon wheels. Suddenly both horses appeared to stumble and drop out of sight. Their heads came up wildly, spray blowing from their nostrils. The muddy water hid their legs, but by their bobbing motions Nancy Belle knew that they were swimming.

"Keep 'em pointed up the river!" Rife shouted.

Already she felt the wagon floating. It swung downstream with the current; then Rife's rope from Fancy's saddle snubbed it. The team was snorting with every breath. The Bar X horse swam high in the water, his withers and part of his back out of the chocolate current. But all she could see of Anton Chico were his nose and ears.

Down between her ankles she saw water in the wagon box. She thought of the hemstitched sheets at the bottom of her trunk, the towels and pillowcases crocheted with shell lace. Her blue velvet corduroy dress was probably wet already, and all the cunning print aprons with dust caps to match. River water couldn't hurt the little yellow creamer, sugar bowl, and covered butter dish that had been her mother's. And the gingham dresses could be washed. What worried her were her wedding dress and the keepsake box, especially the tintypes, one of which was Rife in a child's suit edged with black braid, his brand-new hat on his knee.

An older Rife was shouting something behind her now. She couldn't catch the words. Then she found what it was. The neck and withers of Anton Chico raised suddenly out of the water and both horses were scrambling up the steep bank below the ford. Only quick work with the lines saved the wagon from turning over. Safe and blowing on the high bank, the dripping horses shook themselves like puppies.

Nancy Belle couldn't go on until she had opened the trunk and appraised the damage. Rife unsaddled Fancy and drove on with the refreshed team. Behind his slight back in the wagon box, the girl changed to her blue velvet corduroy, which was hardly wet at all. Then she combed her hair and rolled into a cranny of her trunk the old felt hat that had been too large for her father.

A half-dozen riders met the wagon some miles down the Gunstock Canyon. All of them, Nancy Belle noticed, carried guns. Stephen wore a new white shirt and a gray hat with curled brim she had not seen before. He stood in his stirrups and swung her down in front of him on the saddle, where he kissed her. She had never felt his lips press into such a straight line.

"Papa couldn't come," she said. "So Rife brought me."

She felt Stephen's rigid arm around her.

"We just got in from the Beaverhead ourselves."

"He means they never get any news out in

the Beaverhead or he'd 'a' come further east to meet you!" Uncle Billy Williams put in. He had a lovable, squeaky voice. "The Apaches been breakin' loose again. Funny you didn't hear anything over in your country."

Nancy Belle gave him an inscrutable look with her gray eyes. Uncle Billy pulled out his bandanna and blew his nose.

"They got my old friend Judge Hower and his wife and kid in a buggy on the Upper Espiritu. The man that found what they did to 'em, they say, cried like a baby."

"That's all right, Uncle Billy," Stephen said in a gentle voice.

Nancy Belle glanced at Rife. Her brother's face looked gray, the eyes staring as when he had ridden in the late afternoon sunlight from the smoking ashes of Martin Cross's cabin.

Nearly fifty people, gathered in the big parlor upstairs at the hotel, greeted Nancy Belle. An old man whose young black eyes twinkled out of a bearded face said he was glad to see that she had her "hair on straight." Rife stopped with the trunk before driving to the livery, and Stephen's mother showed Nancy Belle to a room to dress.

The guests stopped talking when she came into the parlor in her white wedding dress.

Her basque came to a point in the front and back. It fitted like a glove. The silk underskirt came to her instep, and the ruffled overskirt to her knees. She had parted her hair from side to side and brushed the bangs down on her forehead. She felt very lightheaded. The wagon still seemed to be jerking under her.

She glimpsed Rife gazing at her, a rapt expression in his reticent blue eyes. She was glad to see that he had brushed his hair. The brass swinging lamp had been lighted and the dark woodwork of the parlor festooned with evergreen branches. White streamers from the wall met in a papier-mâché bell in one corner. She noticed two children peering eagerly from the dark hall.

Stephen came to her, very straight in a long coat and stand-up collar with a black tie. He led her up beneath the papier-mâché bell. In a sibilant churchlike whisper, the Gunstock preacher made sure of her full name. Then he coughed and began the ceremony. He had a deep voice, but Nancy Belle didn't hear all of the service. Her mind kept going back to a tall, grave man in a lonely adobe post on the wide Santa Ana plain. And after she had said, "I do," her lips moved, but she was not praying for Stephen, her husband.

## Getting at Meaning

1. Asa Putman's face reveals a message to anyone "who could read the code." The look on his face, the absence of travelers, and Uncle Gideon's failure to arrive imply what message?

2. When Asa Putman tells Nancy Belle why he cannot attend her wedding, his reasons hint at his real concerns. What does he mean when he says, "But they's men come to this post no boy can handle. . . . I got to protect my own property. . . ."?

3. How does Nancy Belle react to Ignacita's warnings? What does her reaction reveal about her character?

4. Even though Nancy Belle does not speak to the bearded man at the cross trail to the Rio Grande, she experiences a vivid impression of his family's fear. How is this impression created?

5. What is unusual about Rife's behavior during the trip? How do his actions contribute to Nancy Belle's uneasiness?

6. What effect does the discovery of Martin Cross's burned-out cabin have upon Nancy Belle and Rife?

7. When Nancy Belle spends a day and most of a night alone, she carries on a conversation with herself. Why does this behavior reassure her? Despite her meaningless chatter, what makes it evident that she is still alert and cautious?

8. Only the joint efforts of both brother and sister make it possible to cross the flooded Rio Grande. What does each one do to make the crossing successful?

9. When they reach Gunstock Canyon, Uncle Billy Williams seems astonished to see Nancy Belle and Rife. Why?

10. During the wedding ceremony, Nancy Belle's thoughts and prayers are with her father. Why?

### Developing Skills in Reading Literature

1. **Characterization.** One technique of character development is the description of a character's actions. Twice Nancy Belle refuses to delay her wedding even though she knows that she must make a dangerous journey to join her future husband. Later, during the journey, she reveals her courage and determination. Specifically, what actions develop these two aspects of her character?

Another technique of character development is the use of dialogue. This technique is used sparingly in this story. In fact, the members of the Putman family do not voice their major concerns. Three minor characters, however, do speak openly and directly. These characters are Ignacita, the bearded man's wife, and Uncle Billy Williams. What do the words spoken by these characters add to the story? How do their comments affect the reader's view of Nancy Belle?

2. **Third-Person Narration.** As you know, a third-person narrator often is an omniscient narrator who sees into the minds of the characters. In this story, the third-person narrator is omniscient to a limited extent. Only Nancy Belle's thoughts are revealed. What does the reader know about Nancy Belle that Rife does not know and that Uncle Billy Williams would never guess?

3. **Suspense.** The opening description of the lonely outpost sets the scene for the suspense in this story. What do each of the following contribute to the subsequent development of suspense: Ignacita's warnings, the encounter with the bearded man and his family, Rife's behavior on the journey, the discovery of Martin Cross's cabin, the loss of the horses, the night of the coyotes, the Rio Grande crossing?

### Developing Vocabulary

**Word Origins.** Many words that today are considered common English words have their origins in the Spanish language. For instance, the words *adobe* and *corral* were originally Spanish words. Use a dictionary to determine the meanings of the italicized words in the following sentences. Note any changes in spelling that occurred in the transition from Spanish to English.

1. She dressed on the brown pool of *burro* skin, the only carpet on her adobe floor.

2. Never had air anywhere become so suddenly horrible and choking as in this *canyon*.

3. Far down on the pitch-dark *mesa* she stopped the horses.

4. Nancy Belle heard the yapping of the *coyotes*.

### Developing Writing Skills

**Using the Senses in Writing: The Sense of Hearing.** When Nancy Belle spends a night alone, she is especially sensitive to the noises in the forest. Recall an experience that you have had or imagine one in which your sense of hearing was particularly acute. Write one paragraph to describe this experience. Begin with a specific description of one sound. Then develop the paragraph with specific details that will appeal to the reader's sense of hearing.

# Sweet Potato Pie    *Eugenia Collier*

From up here on the fourteenth floor, my brother Charley looks like an insect scurrying among other insects. A deep feeling of love surges through me. Despite the distance, he seems to feel it, for he turns and scans the upper windows, but failing to find me, continues on his way. I watch him moving quickly—gingerly, it seems to me—down Fifth Avenue and around the corner to his shabby taxicab. In a moment he will be heading back uptown.

I turn from the window and flop down on the bed, shoes and all. Perhaps because of what happened this afternoon or maybe just because I see Charley so seldom, my thoughts hover over him like hummingbirds. The cheerful, impersonal tidiness of this room is a world away from Charley's walk-up flat in Harlem and a hundred worlds from the bare, noisy shanty where he and the rest of us spent what there was of childhood. I close my eyes, and side by side I see the Charley of my boyhood and the Charley of this afternoon, as clearly as if I were looking at a split TV screen. Another surge of love, seasoned with gratitude, wells up in me.

As far as I know, Charley never had any childhood at all. The oldest children of sharecroppers never do. Mama and Pa were shadowy figures whose voices I heard vaguely in the morning when sleep was shallow and whom I glimpsed as they left for the field before I was fully awake or as they trudged wearily into the house at night when my lids were irresistibly heavy.

They came into sharp focus only on special occasions. One such occasion was the day when the crops were in and the sharecroppers were paid. In our cabin there was so much excitement in the air that even I, the "baby," responded to it. For weeks we had been running out of things that we could neither grow nor get on credit. On the evening of that day we waited anxiously for our parents' return. Then we would cluster around the rough wooden table—I on Lil's lap or clinging to Charley's neck, little Alberta nervously tugging her plait, Jamie crouched at Mama's elbow, like a panther about to spring, and all seven of us silent for once, waiting. Pa would place the money on the table—gently, for it was made from the sweat of their bodies and from their children's tears. Mama would count it out in little piles, her dark face stern and, I think now, beautiful. Not with the hollow beauty of well modeled features but with the strong radiance of one who has suffered and never yielded.

"This for store bill," she would mutter, making a little pile. "This for c'llection. This for piece o'gingham . . ." and so on, stretching the money as tight over our collective needs as Jamie's outgrown pants were stretched over my bottom. "Well, that's the crop." She would look up at Pa at last. "It'll do." Pa's face would relax, and a general grin flitted from child to child. We would survive, at least for the present.

The other time when my parents were solid entities was at church. On Sundays we would don our threadbare Sunday-go-to-meeting clothes and tramp, along with neighbors similarly attired, to the Tabernacle Baptist Church, the frail edifice of bare boards held together by God knows what, which was all that my parents ever knew of security and future promise.

Being the youngest and therefore the most likely to err, I was plopped between my father and my mother on the long wooden bench. They sat huge and eternal like twin mountains at my sides. I remember my father's still, black profile silhouetted against the sunny window, looking back into dark recesses of time, into some dim antiquity, like an ancient ceremonial mask. My mother's face, usually sternly set, changed with the varying nuances of her emotion, its planes shifting, shaped by the soft highlights of the sanctuary, as she progressed from a subdued "amen" to a loud "Help me, Jesus" wrung from the depths of her gaunt frame.

My early memories of my parents are associated with special occasions. The contours of my everyday were shaped by Lil and Charley, the oldest children, who rode herd on the rest of us while Pa and Mama toiled in fields not their own. Not until years later did I realize that Lil and Charley were little more than children themselves.

Lil had the loudest, screechiest voice in the county. When she yelled, "Boy, you better git yourself in here!" you *got* yourself in there. It was Lil who caught and bathed us, Lil who fed us and sent us to school, Lil who punished us when we needed punishing and comforted us when we needed comforting. If her voice was loud, so was her laughter. When she laughed, everybody laughed. And when Lil sang, everybody listened.

Charley was taller than anybody in the world, including, I was certain, God. From his shoulders, where I spent considerable time in the earliest years, the world had a different perspective. I looked down at tops of heads rather than at the undersides of chins. As I grew older, Charley become more father than brother. Those days return in fragments of splintered memory: Charley's slender dark hands whittling a toy from a chunk of wood, his face thin and intense, brown as the loaves Lil baked when there was flour. Charley's quick fingers guiding a stick of charred kindling over a bit of scrap paper, making a wondrous picture take shape —Jamie's face or Alberta's rag doll or the spare figure of our bony brown dog. Charley's voice low and terrible in the dark, telling ghost stories so delightfully dreadful that later in the night the moan of the wind through the chinks in the wall sent us scurrying to the security of Charley's pallet, Charley's sleeping form.

Some memories are more than fragmentary. I can still feel the *whap* of the wet dish rag across my mouth. Somehow I developed a stutter, which Charley was determined to cure. Someone had told him that an effective cure was to slap the stutterer across the mouth with a sopping wet dish rag. Thereafter whenever I began, "Let's g-g-g--," *whap!* from nowhere would come the ubiquitous rag. Charley would always insist, "I don't want hurt you none, Buddy—" and *whap* again. I don't know when or why I stopped stuttering. But I stopped.

Already laid waste by poverty, we were easy prey for ignorance and superstition, which hunted us like hawks. We sought education feverishly—and, for most of us, futilely, for the sum total of our combined energies was required for mere brute survival. Inevitably each child had to leave school and bear his share of the eternal burden.

Eventually the family's hopes for learning fastened on me, the youngest. I remember—I *think* I remember, for I could not have been more than five—one frigid day Pa huddled on a rickety stool before the coal stove, took me on his knee and studied me gravely. I was a skinny little thing, they tell me, with large, solemn eyes.

"Well, boy," Pa said at last, "if you got to depend on your looks for what you get out'n this world, you just as well lay down right now." His hand was rough from the plow, but gentle as it touched my cheek. "Lucky for you, you got a *mind*. And that's something ain't everybody got. You go to school, boy, get yourself some learning. Make something out'n yourself. Ain't nothing you can't do if you got learning."

Charley was determined that I would break the chain of poverty, that I would "be somebody." As we worked our small vegetable garden in the sun or pulled a bucket of brackish water from the well, Charley would tell me, "You ain gon be no poor farmer, Buddy. You gon be a teacher or maybe a doctor or a lawyer. One thing, bad as you is, you ain gon be no preacher."

I loved school with a desperate passion, which became more intense when I began to realize what a monumental struggle it was for my parents and brothers and sisters to keep me there. The cramped, dingy classroom became a battleground where I was victorious. I stayed on top of my class. With glee I out-read, out-figured, and out-spelled the country boys who mocked my poverty, calling me "the boy with eyes in back of his head"—the "eyes" being the perpetual holes in my hand-me-down pants.

As the years passed, the economic strain was eased enough to make it possible for me to go on to high school. There were fewer mouths to feed, for one thing. Alberta went North to find work at sixteen; Jamie died at twelve.

I finished high school at the head of my class. For Mama and Pa and each of my brothers and sisters, my success was a personal triumph. One by one they came to me the week before commencement bringing crumpled dollar bills and coins long hoarded,

muttering, "Here, Buddy, put this on your gradiation clothes." My graduation suit was the first suit that was all my own.

On graduation night our cabin (less crowded now) was a frantic collage of frayed nerves. I thought Charley would drive me mad.

"Buddy, you ain pressed out them pants right . . . Can't you git a better shine on them shoes? . . . Lord, you done messed up that tie!"

Overwhelmed by the combination of Charley's nerves and my own, I finally exploded. "Man, cut it out!" Abruptly he stopped tugging at my tie, and I was afraid I had hurt his feelings. "It's okay, Charley. Look, you're strangling me. The tie's okay."

Charley relaxed a little and gave a rather sheepish chuckle. "Sure, Buddy." He gave my shoulder a rough joggle. "But you gotta look good. You *somebody*."

My valedictory address was the usual idealistic, sentimental nonsense. I have forgotten what I said that night, but the sight of Mama and Pa and the rest is like a lithograph burned on my memory; Lil, her round face made beautiful by her proud smile; Pa, his head held high, eyes loving and fierce; Mama radiant. Years later when her shriveled hands were finally still, my mind kept coming back to her as she was now. I believe this moment was the apex of her entire life. All of them, even Alberta down from Baltimore—different now, but united with them in her pride. And Charley, on the end of the row, still somehow the protector of them all. Charley, looking as if he were in the presence of something sacred.

As I made my way through the carefully rehearsed speech it was as if part of me were standing outside watching the whole thing— their proud, work-weary faces, myself wearing the suit that was their combined strength and love and hope: Lil with her lovely, low-pitched voice, Charley with the hands of an artist, Pa and Mama with God knows what potential lost with their sweat in the fields. I realized in that moment that I wasn't necessarily the smartest—only the youngest.

And the luckiest. The war came along, and I exchanged three years of my life (including a fair amount of my blood and a great deal of pain) for the GI Bill[1] and a college education. Strange how time can slip by like water flowing through your fingers. One by one the changes came—the old house empty at last, the rest of us scattered; for me, marriage, graduate school, kids, a professorship, and by now a thickening waistline and thinning hair. My mind spins off the years, and I am back to this afternoon and today's Charley— still long and lean, still gentle-eyed, still my greatest fan, and still determined to keep me on the ball.

I didn't tell Charley I would be at a professional meeting in New York and would surely visit; he and Bea would have spent days in fixing up, and I would have had to be company. No, I would drop in on them, take them by surprise before they had a chance to stiffen up. I was eager to see them—it had been so long. Yesterday and this morning were taken up with meetings in the posh Fifth Avenue hotel—a place we could not have dreamed in our boyhood. Late this afternoon I shook lose and headed for Harlem, hoping that Charley still came home for a few hours before his evening run. Leaving the glare and glitter of downtown, I entered the subway that lurks like the dark, inscrutable *id*[2] beneath the surface of the city. When I emerged, I was in Harlem.

Whenever I come to Harlem I feel somehow as if I were coming home—to some mythic ancestral home. The problems are real, the people are real—yet there is some mysterious epic quality about Harlem, as if all Black people began and ended there, as if each had left something of himself. As if in Harlem the very heart of Blackness pulsed its beautiful tortured rhythms. Joining the throngs of people that saunter Lenox Avenue late afternoons, I headed for Charley's apartment. Along the way I savored the panorama of Harlem—women with shopping bags trudging wearily home; little kids flitting saucily through the crowd; groups of adolescent boys striding boldly along—some boisterous, some ominously silent; tables of merchandise spread on the sidewalks with hawkers singing their siren songs of irresistible bargains; a blaring microphone sending forth waves of words to draw passersby into a restless bunch around a slender young man whose eyes have seen Truth; defeated men standing around on street corners or sitting on steps, heads down, hands idle; posters announcing Garvey Day; "Buy Black" stamped on pavements; store windows bright with things African; stores still boarded up, a livid scar from last year's rioting. There was a terrible tension in the air; I thought of how quickly dry timber becomes a roaring fire from a single spark.

I mounted the steps of Charley's building —old and in need of paint, like all the rest— and pushed the button to his apartment. The graffiti on the dirty wall recorded the fantasies of past visitors. Some of it was even a dialogue of sorts. Someone had scrawled, "Call Lola" and a telephone number, followed by a catalog of Lola's friends. Someone else had written, "I called Lola and she is a Dog." Charley's buzzer rang. I pushed open the door and mounted the urine-scented stairs.

"Well, do Jesus—it's Buddy!" roared Charley as I arrived on the third floor. "Bea! Bea! Come here, girl, it's Buddy!" And somehow I

---

1. **GI Bill:** United States government program to help veterans, including education at government expense.
2. ***id:*** in psychoanalysis, the part of the mind associated with instinctual drives and primitive urges.

was simultaneously shaking Charley's hand, getting clapped on the back, and being buried in the fervor of Bea's gigantic hug. They swept me from the hall into their dim apartment.

"Lord, Buddy, what you doing here? Whyn't you tell me you was coming to New York?" His face was so lit up with pleasure that in spite of the inroads of time, he still looked like the Charley of years gone by, excited over a new litter of kittens.

"The place look a mess! Whyn't you let us know?" put in Bea, suddenly distressed.

"Looks fine to me, girl. And so do you!"

And she did. Bea is a fine-looking woman, plump and firm still, with rich brown skin and thick black hair.

"Mary, Lucy, look, Uncle Buddy's here!" Two neat little girls came shyly from the TV. Uncle Buddy was something of a celebrity in this house.

I hugged them heartily, much to their discomfort. "Charley, where you getting all these pretty women?"

We all sat in the warm kitchen, where Bea was preparing dinner. It felt good there.

Beautiful odors mingled in the air. Charley sprawled in a chair near mine, his long arms and legs akimbo. No longer shy, the tinier girl sat on my lap, while her sister darted here and there like a merry little water bug. Bea bustled about, managing to keep up with both the conversation and the cooking.

I told them about the conference I was attending and, knowing it would give them pleasure, I mentioned that I had addressed the group that morning. Charley's eyes glistened.

"You hear that, Bea?" he whispered. "Buddy done spoke in front of all them professors!"

"Sure I hear," Bea answered briskly, stirring something that was making an aromatic steam. "I bet he weren't even scared. I bet them professors learnt something, too."

We all chuckled. "Well anyway," I said, "I hope they did."

We talked about a hundred different things after that—Bea's job in the school cafeteria, my Jess and the kids, our scattered family.

"Seem like we don't git together no more, not since Mama and Pa passed on," said Charley sadly. "I ain't even got a Christmas card from Alberta for three-four year now."

"Well, ain't no two a y'all in the same city. An' everybody scratchin to make ends meet," Bea replied. "Ain't nobody got time to git together."

"Yeah, that's the way it goes, I guess," I said.

"But it sure is good to see you, Buddy. Say, look, Lil told me bout the cash you sent the children last winter when Jake was out of work all that time. She sure preciated it."

"Lord, man, as close as you and Lil stuck to me when I was a kid, I owed her that and more. Say, Bea, did I ever tell you about the time—" and we swung into the usual reminiscences.

They insisted that I stay for dinner. Persuading me was no hard job: fish fried golden,

ham hocks and collard greens, corn bread—if I'd *tried* to leave, my feet wouldn't have taken me. It was good to sit there in Charley's kitchen, my coat and tie flung over a chair, surrounded by soul food and love.

"Say, Buddy, a couple months back I picked up a kid from your school."

"No stuff."

"I axed him did he know you. He say he was in your class last year."

"Did you get his name?"

"No, I didn't ax him that. Man he told me you were the best teacher he had. He said you were one smart cat!"

"He told you that cause you're my brother."

"Your *brother*—I didn't tell him I was your brother. I said you was a old friend of mine."

I put my fork down and leaned over. "What you tell him *that* for?"

Charley explained patiently as he had explained things when I was a child and had missed an obvious truth. "I didn't want your students to know your brother wasn't nothing but a cab driver. You *somebody*."

"You're a nut," I said gently. "You should've told that kid the truth." I wanted to say, I'm proud of you, you've got more on the ball than most people I know, I wouldn't have been anything at all except for you. But he would have been embarrassed.

Bea brought in the dessert—homemade sweet potato pie! "Buddy, I must of knew you were coming! I just had a mind I wanted to make sweet potato pie."

There's nothing in this world I like better than Bea's sweet potato pie! "Lord, girl, how you expect me to eat all that?"

The slice she put before me was outrageously big—and moist and covered with a light, golden crust—I ate it all.

"Bea, I'm gonna have to eat and run," I said at last.

Charley guffawed. "Much as you et, I don't

see how you gonna *walk,* let alone *run.*" He went out to get his cab from the garage several blocks away.

Bea was washing the tiny girl's face. "Wait a minute, Buddy, I'm gon give you the rest of that pie to take with you."

"Great!" I'd eaten all I could hold, but my *spirit* was still hungry for sweet potato pie.

Bea got out some waxed paper and wrapped up the rest of the pie. "That'll do you for a snack tonight." She slipped it into a brown paper bag.

I gave her a long goodbye hug. "Bea, I love you for a lot of things. Your cooking is one of them!" We had a last comfortable laugh together. I kissed the little girls and went outside to wait for Charley, holding the bag of pie reverently.

In a minute Charley's ancient cab limped to the curb. I plopped into the seat next to him, and we headed downtown. Soon we were assailed by the garish lights of New York on a sultry spring night. We chatted as Charley skillfully managed the heavy traffic. I looked at his long hands on the wheel and wondered what they could have done with artists' brushes.

We stopped a bit down the street from my hotel. I invited him in, but he said he had to get on with his evening run. But as I opened the door to get out, he commanded in the old familiar voice, "Buddy, you wait!"

For a moment I thought my coat was torn or something. "What's wrong?"

"What's that you got there?"

I was bewildered. "That? You mean this bag? That's a piece of sweet potato pie Bea fixed for me."

"You ain't going through the lobby of no big hotel carrying no brown paper bag."

"Man, you *crazy!* Of course I'm going— Look, Bea fixed it for me—*That's my pie—*"

Charley's eyes were miserable. "Folks in that hotel don't go through the lobby carrying no brown paper bags. That's *country.*

And you can't neither. You *somebody,* Buddy. You got to be *right.* Now gimme that bag."

"I want that pie, Charley. I've got nothing to prove to anybody—"

I couldn't believe it. But there was no point in arguing. Foolish as it seemed to me, it was important to him.

"You got to look *right,* Buddy. Can't nobody look dignified carrying a brown paper bag."

So finally, thinking how tasty it would have been and how seldom I got a chance to eat anything that good, I handed over my bag of sweet potato pie. If it was that important to him—

I tried not to show my irritation. "Okay, man—take care now." I slammed the door harder than I had intended, walked rapidly to the hotel, and entered the brilliant, crowded lobby.

"That Charley!" I thought. Walking slower now, I crossed the carpeted lobby toward the elevator, still thinking of my lost snack. I had to admit that of all the herd of people who jostled each other in the lobby, not one was carrying a brown paper bag. Or anything but expensive attaché cases or slick packages from exclusive shops. I suppose we all operate according to the symbols that are meaningful to us, and to Charley a brown paper bag symbolizes the humble life he thought I had left. I was *somebody.*

I don't know what made me glance back, but I did. And suddenly the tears of laughter, toil, and love of a lifetime burst around me like fireworks in a night sky.

For there, following a few steps behind, came Charley, proudly carrying a brown paper bag full of sweet potato pie.

## Getting at Meaning

1. Charley and Buddy are closer than brothers. Why? Describe the special relationship they share.

2. What does Buddy mean when he says, "I wasn't necessarily the smartest—only the youngest"? Why haven't his brothers and sisters continued in school? What is the "eternal burden" that each of the older children has to bear?

3. On graduation night, Buddy thinks of his parents and the potential "they lost with their sweat in the fields." What does he mean? What potential does Charley have that he has never been able to realize? Is Charley bitter or angry about this?

4. What does Charley mean when he says that carrying a brown paper bag is "country"?

5. Why has it always been so important to Charley that Buddy succeed?

## Developing Skills in Reading Literature

1. **Protagonist; Antagonist.** Sometimes it is not clear which of two characters in a story is the protagonist. One clue is that the protagonist often changes or develops a new understanding as a result of the action of the story. Who is the protagonist in this story? How does this person change? Who or what is the antagonist? What is the central conflict?

2. **Flashback.** A flashback is an interruption in a story in which a writer inserts a description or a narration of events that happened before the story begins. What is the setting for the beginning and ending of this story? How many flashbacks does the writer include in the body of the story? What information does the reader learn in these flashbacks? How do the flashbacks explain the opening scene of the story?

3. **Symbol.** For Charley, a brown paper bag symbolizes, or stands for, the kind of life that Buddy has left behind. What does Buddy's graduation symbolize for his mother? for the rest of his family? What does the sweet potato pie symbolize for Buddy? for Charley?

## Developing Vocabulary

1. **Words from Greek.** As Buddy walks through Harlem, he hears the *siren songs* of the street vendors selling their products. Look up *siren* in a dictionary. Find the meaning that explains the origin of the word. What is similar about the original meaning and the meaning that applies to the street vendors? Can you explain how the word *siren* came to have its present-day meaning?

2. **Inferring Meaning from Context.** Buddy says that his family was "laid waste" by poverty. (p. 92) Using your knowledge of the context, suggest an appropriate synonym for this phrase.

## Developing Writing Skills

**Using Modifiers in Description.** The writer of this story uses particularly strong modifiers to describe the narrator's parents. For example, the mother has a *"dark, stern* face;" she is beautiful "Not with the *hollow* beauty of *well modeled* features." Choose someone you know well, and write a detailed description of his or her face, using precise modifiers to create a vivid impression in the mind of the reader. Confine your description to one well developed paragraph.

# The Breed of 'Em    *Will James*

**I**f it wasn't that he'd be hard to replace, I'd fire that man, and mighty quick—" Such was the words that came to the chore-man's ears one evening as that feller was busy pumping the milk cows under the big shelter shed.

The San Jacinto[1] ranch foreman was peeved, that much the chore-man could see at a glance, but there was more than that, he was aggravated by the fact that he couldn't do nothing to ease them peeved feelings of his. Here he was, foreman over twenty men and more, he had the privilege of firing any of 'em as he seen fit, but he was satisfied with his men, all excepting *one,* and that one sure made up for the others. He was aching to send him down the road a-talking to himself, but, as he'd said, it'd be hard to replace him, not only hard but near impossible.

He knowed that to keep making good as ranch foreman he had to have good men under him, men that understood their work, and the man he wanted to fire most was the best and steadiest man on the ranch. He needed him, and on that account he had to keep down his feelings, also keep the man that stirred 'em, and that's what hurt.

The foreman started to walk away from under the big shed, on toward the cook house, but he stood in his tracks as he seen the cause of his trouble come into sight and heading for the corrals. At a distance he sized him up with a long look; he took in the curved brim of the big hat, the tall, straight slim built of the man on down to the neat-fitting high-heeled boots; then he turned and walked away talking.

"You'd think he was a king or something, the way he acts."

But if the foreman could of glimpsed into Todd Lander's heart as that cowboy went on toward the corrals, he'd found there just the opposite from high elevating kingly throbs. The cowboy was lonesome, more lonesome than he'd been for many a day, and all because he was by himself and the only one of his kind left on the old San Jacinto holdings.

He'd went to the corrals to see the ponies there and for the company they'd give. He was greeted by snorts as he climbed the corral poles and the wild ones scattered out to bunch on the far side; he'd just run 'em in off the range that day and they was pretty spooky. Todd set on the top pole of the corral and rolled a smoke while his eyes went over the slick rumps and backs of the horses. He savvied them, they fitted into his language.

He watched 'em quite a spell, and his cigarette was over half smoked when the colors of the setting sun on the hills caught his attention; and then he found himself looking at the big range called the San Jacinto Mountains. They fitted into his language too. His dad had told him once, a long time ago, how come them mountains to get that name, but Todd had forgot that now, like he'd forgot many things that was while his dad was alive.

And, as his eyes left the mountains and far-away hills, to roam over the big fields and meadows that now strung out many miles both sides of the San Jacinto ranch, the cow-

---

1. **San Jacinto** (san' jə sin' tō): a city in southern California.

boy thought maybe it was a good thing his dad was gone; he didn't think that the transformation, from open range and cattle to cut up fields of grain and alfalfa, as it was now, would please him.

Todd remembered when his dad was cow foreman of the San Jacinto. The fields he was now looking at was open range land then, and as a kid, by his dad's side, he'd chased his first steer, right on that same land where now tall stems of grain was waving to the breeze.

After his dad had gone, the San Jacinto changed hands, and with the new owner's coming there begin the disfiggering[2] of the big range; the river that run through the land was headed off by a big dam in a tall narrow canyon and the water was divided through irrigating canals, in a way that'd cover thousands of acres. Cowboys drifted away, one by one, as grain fields took the place of range land; the thousands and thousands of cattle that went to make up the big herds of the San Jacinto was gradually sold, and dwindled away till finally there was only a few hundred left. Ranch hands with hob-nailed shoes had took the place of the cowboy with his stirrup-fitting boots, and the cow foreman was replaced by a ranch foreman who was a farming expert and imported from somewheres.

Todd had been the only cowboy to stay, and maybe for no reason much only that this was the only country he knowed. He wasn't the kind that cared to drift much, and when the superintendent, a man who seemed to savvy cowboys, told him that the job of taking charge of the few cattle that was left was his as long as he wanted it, Todd had been pleased; and he'd overlooked the fact that he had to ride through a lane to get to where the cattle was running.

He ranged the cattle along the foothills of the San Jacinto Mountains and above where irrigation could reach. There was only around eight hundred head left and sometimes the herd would accumulate up to a thousand, a nice one-man job if all went well; but sometimes Todd had found himself wishing he was three men instead of one. Even at that, the cowboy smiled through the worst of them times. It was his work, and as a cowboy he done it all as it come, without a whimper.

There was many a raw cold day with a stiff wind blowing when he had to be in the saddle to eighteen and twenty hours at the time. The worst the weather was, the more he had to be out in it, but it was all in the day's riding and with no certain hours nor time to do it in. There was times, of course, along in the summer, when there wasn't so much work, but that was all due to his ability as a cowboy and his understanding of range and cattle. For long stretches, in good weather, he only rode two days out of three and very short hours even during the days he worked.

Them short days' work as they followed one another for a spell is what'd come to be the cause of that rumpus between Todd and the ranch foreman, or the farm boss, as the cowboy called him. The foreman had seen the cowboy ride in early in the afternoon, day after day, and how some days he didn't go out at all; he'd watch him in the blacksmith shop trying to forge out spurs and bits, and to the foreman that sure seemed a waste of company time.

He never stopped to think of the times when the bad weather kept the cowboy in the saddle from early in the morning, with nothing to eat through the day and riding a tired horse, till away after the foreman had hit his bed and went to sleep. He never thought how when the cowboy rode in, even on the short days' rides, that he'd had no lunch hour and no lunch, and that he'd have to wait till night before he had anything to eat: that was a cowboy custom, and a custom

---

2. **disfiggering**: mispronunciation of *disfiguring*, spoiling the appearance of.

that the foreman would of most likely disagreed with mighty strong.

The foreman only noticed the time the cowboy wasn't working during the regular hours; he didn't consider the time he'd worked away past them working-hours, and on that account he begin to fret when some nice day he would find the cowboy doing nothing much, only maybe tinkering around breaking a horse or fixing his saddle.

The day of the clash between the two came when the foreman met the cowboy heading back to the ranch early one afternoon. The rush of the haying season was on; ranch hands was scarce and the foreman was short-handed. When he seen the cowboy that day, it came to him to break the news to the rider, which would be that, after he was through with his work from now on, to hitch up a team to a hay mower and finish up the day in the hay field.

The foreman broke the news all right, but they didn't seem to break well. The cowboy never looked at him and went to rolling a smoke as the foreman talked. His hat brim covered most of his face, and the foreman talked on about making use of his time and so on, till finally the cowboy looked at him from under his hat brim. His lips was near white as he held a match up to his cigarette and lit it.

He eyed the foreman for a spell, then, as though he'd only stopped to roll a smoke, and just that, the cowboy reined his horse to a start and rode away. Somehow the foreman felt glad to see him go.

But as the afternoon wore on toward quitting time, the foreman gradually begin to get peeved; the cowboy and the mowing-machine wasn't showing up very fast. Quitting time came and still no sign of the cowboy on the machine nowheres. Then the foreman got really peeved. He was for firing that man right away, and he would of most likely done it, only it had struck him as he drove in that he didn't want to take the responsibilities of the cattle that cowboy had charge of. The ranch foreman didn't know anything about range and range cattle and cowboys, but, as he'd said to the chore-man that night, if it wasn't that he'd be hard to replace, he'd fire that man, and mighty quick.

As far as Todd was concerned, things was pretty well the same as before between him and the foreman, even from that day. Of course that's not saying much, because, to begin with, the cowboy had never noticed the foreman, not any to speak of. It was the same way with the ranch hands; he never noticed them either, only when they got in front of him. It wasn't that he didn't like 'em. It was just that they was of different breed and not the kind he was used to mixing with; they couldn't talk his language nor of the things he knowed.

To him, they was just part of a crowd, a happy-go-lucky crowd, and when he'd come in late of evenings from some long day's ride and gather with 'em at the big bunk house, he could sort of feel their eyes on him, as he pulled off his chaps, like as if he was something strange. One well meaning ranch hand suggested one night as Todd came in late, that cowboys should form a union and work regular hours the same as anybody.

Todd smiled at him and said, "There can't be no regular hours for us. A cowboy can't quit snowbound or bogged cattle on account of a meal or because it's quitting time."

Todd would lay in his bunk at night and listen to the talk of the men. He'd sometimes compare it with the cowboys' talk and subjects and found it a lot different. The ranch hands seldom ever talked of their work of the day. Instead, it run to something they was plum away from. They'd drift into politics or argue about new mechanical inventions and predict things about this or that. With the cowboys, the work of the day was pretty well gone over by the evening fire, and the talk seldom went away from horses, cattle, ropes, and saddles. There was pride in the work and how each cowboy done it, and where there's pride there's always a little jealousy. That way each man was contesting against the other, each tried to be a better rider, roper, or cowman, and none was of the same standing.

The working hours was never thought of, on account that with them a man could show what he was made of. The kind of horses he rode and how neat he throwed a rope all went for or against him to tell what kind of a hand he was, and it kept him on the jump, because no matter how good he might of been there is always room for improvement in that game, and there could always be somebody that was a little better.

Then in the evening there'd be songs, old trail-herd songs that some used to sing. There was even poetry at times, made right there at the cowcamp. It'd always be about some cowboy and some bad horse, and the whole outfit chipped in or suggested a word to make it up. Then sometimes that poetry would be illustrated too, for it seemed like there'd always been some cowboy around that could draw pretty well.

The talk, the songs and all went with the range—the cattle, horses, and the work. Todd missed that talk and them songs, and sometimes he felt a whole lot like hitting for some cow outfit. There was a big spread just the other side of the San Jacinto Mountains, that he knowed; it was still all open range over there, and it would always be because there was no river to irrigate from; but as was said before, Todd wasn't of the drifting kind much. He knowed his horses here, and his cattle, and his range, and in a way he was satisfied.

The one-sided rumpus he'd had with the foreman didn't bother him none at all. He hadn't expected him to understand range work, and he'd been looking for a break to come sooner or later. Todd had forgot all about that when a month later, while riding through a big pasture, the cowboy seen the foreman driving toward him. Todd noticed that there was more of a pleasant look on his face, as he stopped his team to within talking distance and pointed to a fence with his whip.

"That fence there," says the foreman, "has been tore down by your cattle, and I wish you'd find time to fix it before they get into the grain."

"Not *my* cattle," says Todd, also looking pleasant, "you mean the company's cattle, the same company you're working for, and as for fixing the fence, my dad left Texas on account he was asked to do that once."

The foreman drove away, peeved a second time. Todd sat on his horse, rolled a smoke and smiled. The foreman didn't see that the cattle had broke in from the outside fence which *he* was responsible for and was supposed to keep up; he didn't see that the cowboy would be busy till away after dark to

get the cattle out of the big field and back on the range.

As it was, he drove away, and with intentions to get another man to put in the place of Todd as soon as he could. He'd stood that cowboy long enough, he thought; but he never figgered that another cowboy, to qualify with Todd's job, wasn't apt to be the kind who'd get off his horse and do labor, either. To his way of thinking, any hired help should do as they're asked, and he didn't know that a cowboy, to be that, couldn't be a ranch hand too.

Todd rode on to his work, day after day, the same as usual and plum ignorant of the fact that the foreman was looking for another man to take his place. And as time went on, another thing happened which made the foreman want to fire Todd on the spot and without even considering.

The cowboy was at the ranch that day and topping off a bronk he'd started to break that summer. That pony had been loose for a long time, and with the fat he was packing he'd got ornery and wild. Todd had to start breaking him pretty well all over again, and it was just as that cowboy was bringing that pony to time that it happened. The foreman had seen it all.

The bronk's orneriness had come to the top, and that pony, disappointed that he couldn't buck out from under the leather and cowboy that was on his back, begin to get sort of desperate and to looking for a way out. There was only one and that was the way he came in, through the gate. Of course the gate was closed, but that didn't seem to matter much right then. Head down and bucking in grand style, the horse headed straight for it. There was a crash of timber as the eleven hundred pounds of wiry horseflesh hit it, and Todd, seeing that no timbers was left to knock him off the saddle, stuck to his seat and fanned his pony on out to the open.

It was an hour or so later when he rode back, unsaddled his bronk and turned him loose in the pasture. The foreman noticed by his watch that it was still an hour or more before quitting time, and seeing that Todd never seemed to see the gate his horse had tore down, he thought to head him off and tell him about it.

Todd took on all the foreman had to say and then walked on to where he'd first been headed. Two days went by and the gate was still scattered splinters, with no sign of a new one taking its place. Then the foreman caught up with the cowboy once more.

"When are you going to fix the gate?" he asks, sort of peeved.

"When I hire out as a ranch hand," answers Todd.

For some reason or other the foreman had nothing to say to that. The answer had sort of crippled his tongue and took his breath away. He was mad, so mad that he couldn't say "you're fired," not as much as he wanted to.

He glared at the cowboy for a spell and walked away. He wouldn't have to say anything; he'd just make out a check for his time and get rid of him like he'd so often threatened to. He started to open the door of his office when the purr of a motor attracted his attention and a second later the big car of the superintendent came around the corner of the building and to a stop right in front of the office.

The foreman was glad to see the superintendent at such a good time; he'd tell him all about that cowboy and ask him to pick a man to take his place, a man who was *willing to work*. The foreman opened the office door for the big boss and, doing his best to hold down his feelings, begin to tell his story and all about that cowboy who wouldn't do nothing but ride.

The superintendent listened for a spell and a grin begin to spread on his features; then he held up a hand the same as to say he'd heard enough.

"All the good cowboys that I know are that way," he says; "if they wasn't they wouldn't be cowboys, for that's a deep game all by itself." He kept quiet for a spell and then went on. "I'm afraid it's my fault that you two have tangled and come to disagree, and I am sorry for that too, because you're both mighty fine men and I know you'd both get along fine under ordinary circumstances; and what I should of told you before is this, that Todd Lander is not working under your orders. I couldn't expect you, being you're such a good ranch foreman, to also be a good cow foreman, so I'd kind of figgered for Todd to be his own boss.

"I hope you haven't done anything that would cause him to quit," sort of asked the superintendent.

"Well, if I have," says the foreman, "he sure don't seem to worry about it."

"Good, because I'm satisfied with him, so satisfied I am now buying three thousand head more cattle for him to take charge of. We've got the range and we'd just as well use it. Todd will be our cow foreman, and with the riders he'll be needing I thought of making the Upper Creek ranch his headquarters. This is what I came to see you about, and I wish you'd send a few men up there to fix the corrals and things that need fixing. Of course there's no rush about that, because the cattle I'm buying won't be delivered for some months, but do that whenever you can. In the meantime, don't tell Todd anything about this, because I want to surprise him. I know it'll be *some* surprise."

Well, that sure put a different light on the subject, and as the superintendent drove away, there seemed to be a big aggravating load drop off the foreman's shoulders. There was a pleasant change in his face as he looked around, trying to get sight of the man he'd once been so peeved at, but that man wasn't to be seen nowheres. He looked around the bunk house and most everywheres and couldn't find him, and he was just about to give up the hunt when he heard a crash of timbers that sounded like it come from the corrals.

That sounded like Todd, sure enough. When the foreman got there, he seen where a whole side of the corral had been tore down, and he spotted the cowboy a straddle the same bronk that'd made splinters of the gate a few days before. The pony was tearing the earth and wiping things up in long, high, and crooked jumps toward the open and unfenced.

The foreman stood in his tracks and watched the great and graceful ride that cowboy was putting up. He'd forgot about the corral, and instead he was finding himself wondering how any man could stay on the back of a horse like that, let alone pulling off any fancy didos[3] like that cowboy was doing. He stood still, watching every move of the man and horse, and for the first time, he really admired.

"You'd think he was a king or something," and this time there was no slur attached as the foreman passed the remark.

An hour or so later, when Todd hazed his bronk back to the corrals, he found the foreman there and waiting for him. The cowboy took in the damage his horse had done to the corral, and he figgered that here would be another job that would be put up for him to do and which, as far as he was concerned, would be left undone.

"Looks like we need a new corral," says that cowboy as he twisted his bronk's ear. With the action of a cougar he slid out of his saddle and landed on his spurred heels, out of reach of his bronk's hoofs.

The foreman's eyes popped with wonder at the easy way the cowboy seemed to miss them flying hoofs, and, knowing horses, he also wondered how a man could handle, let alone ride, a horse like that, without having it in a steel-barred cage.

"Queer about this bronk," went on the cowboy as he pulled out the makings to roll a smoke. "He seems to crave for open country the minute I get on him."

Todd had noticed a sort of different look on the foreman's face, when he first rode up. It wasn't the kind he'd ever seen there before, and he wondered about it; but he wondered a heap more when the foreman spoke.

"Well, I won't ask you to fix this, this time," he says, sort of grinning and pointing at the splintered part of the corral, "it wouldn't do me any good to ask you anyway —and what's more, I want to kind of apologize for pestering you like I have, off and on, I——"

"Oh, that's all right," Todd interrupted, smiling back at him, "I didn't mind it."

As the days went by, Todd wondered at what'd come over the foreman; that feller had turned from a glaring cuss to a friendly human, and the cowboy couldn't figger out why; but he had no way of knowing, and so, he quit wondering and accepted his friendship for what it was. Things went smooth from then on and Todd felt a lot more satisfied as he went to his work.

With fall coming on, the easy riding days of summer begin to disappear; there was no more two days' riding and one day's tinkering; there was more branding to be done, big calves to be weaned, and the cattle had to be shoved down off the high mountains before the heavy snows come. The cowboy rode out on a best horse early every morning and came in late every night.

Then, without warning, a howling blizzard struck the land, one of the worst blizzards the country had ever seen, and it'd come a

---

3. **didos** (dī′ dōs): tricks.

month before any heavy snow could be expected. From then on Todd found no time to tinker around. He settled down to tall hard riding, and every morning, the same as though the weather wasn't out of the ordinary, he rode out, faced the blinding storm to the highest peaks of the San Jacintos, and rode the high land for stock that instead of drifting to the foothills with the coming of the storm, had found shelter up there and huddled together while the snow drifted around 'em.

It was hard and ticklish riding up to them cattle, for it seemed like in no time the trails had been covered with fifteen-foot drifts, and the cowboy had to find a way around 'em, often putting his horse up rocky ledges that'd bother a human to climb. Then, the cattle that was left up there, being the wildest, wasn't what a feller would call easy to handle, specially in a country they knowed so well. Often they'd scatter like a bunch of antelope at the sight of the rider, and hightail it any direction excepting the right one.

But no matter how wild they was nor how hard it was to get 'em down, the high country *had* to be cleaned of all the cattle that was there. The feed was all buried under the snow, and on account of the drifts, the cattle would never try to get down themselves; they would of lived on branches and twigs till finally they'd starve to death, *snowbound*.

The cowboy, knowing all that better than anyone else, rode on through the thick of the storm and made every minute count. He knowed that if the storm kept on he'd never be able to get up them mountains, no matter how he schemed or worked; and the thought of the hundred or more cattle that was still to be accounted for kept him going till it was impossible for him to go any more; and when finally he would turn back for the ranch, it was seldom that he was ready to quit, it would be his horse that made him turn back, for as big and powerful as his horse was, each

one he'd ride out would be very tired and ganted up before he'd rein him toward the long trail to the ranch.

The tired horse of that day would then get a good rest, but there was no such a thing for the cowboy. He went on again early the next morning on another fresh horse, faced the stinging snow, broke trails through the drifts and, by good maneuvering, persuaded the snowbound cattle to string out of their white walled prisons and follow the trail his horse had made.

There was times, on account of the snow being too deep, that the cattle wouldn't always follow them trails. The leaders would turn back, time after time, and then the cowboy would have to skirt around, ride his horse through some other place, and make them another trail. All this work went on while the storm howled and the cowboy could only see a few feet in front of him. Sometimes he'd slide his horse into a drift that was a whole lot deeper than he'd thought. The horse would go near out of sight; then the cowboy would get out of the saddle, waller around, and by different schemes get his horse out.

That was mighty hard and muscle-straining work for both man and horse, and not only that, but mighty dangerous, because sometimes them drifts might be hanging over the edge of some ungodly steep place which, on account of the fast-drifting snow, couldn't be seen. A fall at such places meant only one thing, and the story of it would never be told till the thawing winds of the following spring took away the snows.

The storm kept up for many days, and through it all the cowboy kept in the saddle and breaking trails. Often the trail he'd made would be drifted over with fresh snow before he could get whatever snowbound cattle he'd found to follow it; then he'd have to ride ahead and break it over again. Every once in a while as he rode, he kept a-reaching for a handful of snow and rubbing his face with it; but, even at that, the stinging frost had sneaked in and turned one side of his face white and then to a leather brown.

Finally, the storm broke up and the clouds drifted away, but there was still cattle up in them snow-covered mountains and Todd kept riding to get 'em down. He knowed that another storm would be the end of all the stock that was still there, and if there was any left when it come, it sure wouldn't be his fault.

He kept a-riding out early in the morning and riding back on a mighty tired horse late at night. After taking care of his horse and disturbing the Chinese cook for something to eat, he'd hit for the bunk house and a few hours' rest. The fire was died down in there, the place was cold, and all the ranch hands was asleep. They'd still be asleep when the cowboy would get up, get a bite, and get out for another eighteen-hour ride.

After a few more days' hard riding, Todd finally brought down the last of the cattle; all of the herd was accounted for and down to where there was no more danger. That was no more than done when another storm, a good mate to the first one, came to pile on more snow. But there was no dread for Todd in that storm. His cattle was all down in the low country and amongst shelter and feed that'd carry 'em all through any kind of winter.

When, after a few days, that second storm cleared, there was no sign of rocky ledges on the San Jacinto Mountains. They was all covered over and rounded out with many deep feet of hard-packed snow. Todd took a long breath at the sight and sort of smiled. He'd got his cattle down just in time.

But that cowboy wasn't through with his work, and even though his riding wouldn't keep him out for so long for some time to come, he had to be out plenty long enough; and with the short days of daylight that came at that time of the year, it was very seldom that he ever walked in the bunk house till it was night and dark had come.

It was as Todd was riding out for a usual day's circle, one morning, that the ranch foreman spotted him. He stood and watched the cowboy away for a spell and then he spoke to one of the ranch hands near him.

"It's the first time I've seen him in plain daylight for a long time," he remarked. Then after a while he went on, "It's dang queer about that feller. He'll ride horses I wouldn't touch with a forty-foot pole, in all kinds of weather, and for sometimes eighteen hours a day—but," he grinned, "*he won't work.*"

## Getting at Meaning

1. Even though the ranch foreman does not like Todd, he does respect him. How does the reader know this?

2. How has the San Jacinto ranch changed since the days when Todd's father was cow foreman? How have the changes affected Todd?

3. The ranch foreman thinks that Todd is wasting time when he sees Todd forging out spurs and bits, breaking a horse, or fixing his saddle. What is the relationship between these activities and Todd's work? Why can't the foreman understand this relationship?

4. The foreman looks upon Todd as hired help; Todd sees himself as a cowboy. Why does it seem impossible for the two men to communicate? After talking to the superintendent, the foreman's attitude changes. Specifically, what does the superintendent say to cause this change?

5. Even though Todd claims not to have noticed the foreman's attitude, he feels more satisfied about his work after the foreman becomes friendlier. What does this imply about important factors in a person's work situation?

6. Despite the foreman's final comment about the cowboy, how does the reader know that the foreman's understanding and appreciation of Todd's work have increased since the beginning of the story?

## Developing Skills in Reading Literature

1. **Character and Conflict.** The conflict in a story is closely related to the development of character. As a character is aware of, reacts to, and resolves the conflict, the character's ideas and personality become apparent to the reader. In this story, the conflict is the struggle between Todd and the ranch foreman. What does Todd value in life? What appears to be important to the ranch foreman? What does Todd's reaction to the foreman's anger suggest about Todd's personality? Is it probable that the two men would have resolved the conflict without the influence of the superintendent? Why or why not?

2. **Climax.** The climax is the turning point in a story. The action in this story builds toward an angry, hostile confrontation between Todd and the ranch foreman. The confrontation, however, does not take place. What, then, is the climax of the story? If the expected confrontation were the climax, how would the ending of the story be different?

## Developing Vocabulary

**Getting Word Meaning from Context.** Often the meaning of an unfamiliar word becomes clear from the clues in the context surrounding the word. Write a definition for each of the following italicized words, basing the definition on the context of the word.

1. "He wasn't the kind that cared to drift much, and when the superintendent, a man who seemed to *savvy* cowboys, told him that the job of taking charge of the few cattle that was left was his as long as he wanted it, Todd had been pleased. . . ."

2. "There was only around eight hundred head left and sometimes the herd would *accumulate* up to a thousand. . . ."

3. "Even at that, the cowboy smiled through the worst of them times. It was his work, and as a cowboy he done it all as it come, without a *whimper*."

4. "As the days went by, Todd wondered at what'd come over the foreman; that feller had turned from a glaring *cuss* to a friendly human, and the cowboy couldn't figure out why; but he had no way of knowing, and so, he quit wondering and accepted his friendship for what it was."

5. ". . . he didn't think that the *transformation*, from open range and cattle to cut up fields of grain and alfalfa . . . would please him."

## Developing Writing Skills

**Developing an Argument.** Often in a work situation, you must persuade an employer to hire you, to give you a transfer, a promotion, or to retain your services. In order to do this, you must use communication skills that are better than those demonstrated by either Todd or the ranch foreman. To practice your skills, write one paragraph that has as a goal the persuasion of an employer to agree to something you want. Begin the paragraph with a clear statement of your goal. Then develop the paragraph with specific reasons that illustrate why it is to the employer's advantage to grant your request. For instance, if you are trying to persuade someone to hire you, specifically describe the personality traits and the skills that would insure your success on the job.

# Snapshot of a Dog   *James Thurber*

I ran across a dim photograph of him the other day, going through some old things. He's been dead twenty-five years. His name was Rex (my two brothers and I named him when we were in our early teens) and he was a bull terrier. "An American bull terrier," we used to say, proudly; none of your English bulls. He had one brindle[1] eye that sometimes made him look like a clown and sometimes reminded you of a politician with derby hat and cigar. The rest of him was white except for a brindle saddle that always seemed to be slipping off and a brindle stocking on a hind leg. Nevertheless, there was a nobility about him. He was big and muscular and beautifully made. He never lost his dignity even when trying to accomplish the extravagant tasks my brothers and myself used to set for him. One of these was the bringing of a ten-foot wooden rail into the yard through the back gate. We would throw it out into the alley and tell him to go get it. Rex was as powerful as a wrestler, and there were not many things that he couldn't manage somehow to get hold of with his great jaws and lift or drag to wherever he wanted to put them, or wherever we wanted them put. He could catch the rail at the balance and lift it clear of the ground and trot with great confidence toward the gate. Of course, since the gate was only four feet wide or so, he couldn't bring the rail in broadside. He found that out when he got a few terrific jolts, but he wouldn't give up. He finally figured out how to do it, by dragging the rail, holding onto one end, growling. He got a great, wagging satisfaction out of his work. We used to bet kids who had never seen Rex in action that he could catch a baseball thrown as high as they could throw it. He almost never let us down. Rex could hold a baseball with ease in his mouth, in one cheek, as if it were a chew of tobacco.

He was a tremendous fighter, but he never started fights. I don't believe he liked to get into them, despite the fact that he came from a line of fighters. He never went for another dog's throat but for one of its ears (that teaches a dog a lesson), and he would get his grip, close his eyes, and hold on. He could hold on for hours. His longest fight lasted from dusk until almost pitch-dark, one Sunday. It was fought in East Main Street in Columbus with a large, snarly nondescript that belonged to a big black man. When Rex finally got his ear grip, the brief whirlwind of snarling turned to screeching. It was frightening to listen to and to watch. The black man boldly picked the dogs up somehow and began swinging them around his head, and finally let them fly like a hammer in a hammer throw, but although they landed ten feet away with a great plump, Rex still held on.

The two dogs eventually worked their way to the middle of the car tracks, and after a while two or three streetcars were held up by the fight. A motorman tried to pry Rex's jaws open with a switch rod; somebody lighted a fire and made a torch of a stick and held that to Rex's tail, but he paid no attention. In the end, all the residents and storekeepers in the

---

1. **brindle** (brin' d'l): tawny or grayish with spots of another color.

neighborhood were on hand, shouting this, suggesting that. Rex's joy of battle, when battle was joined, was almost tranquil. He had a kind of pleasant expression during fights, not a vicious one, his eyes closed in what would have seemed to be sleep had it not been for the turmoil of the struggle. The Oak Street Fire Department finally had to be sent for—I don't know why nobody thought of it sooner. Five or six pieces of apparatus arrived, followed by a battalion chief. A hose was attached and a powerful stream of water was turned on the dogs. Rex held on for several moments more while the torrent buffeted him about like a log in a freshet. He was a hundred yards away from where the fight started when he finally let go.

The story of that Homeric fight got all around town, and some of our relatives looked upon the incident as a blot on the family name. They insisted that we get rid of Rex, but we were very happy with him, and nobody could have made us give him up. We would have left town with him first, along any road there was to go. It would have been different, perhaps, if he'd ever started fights, or looked for trouble. But he had a gentle disposition. He never bit a person in the ten strenuous years that he lived, nor ever growled at anyone except prowlers. He killed cats, that is true, but quickly and neatly and without especial malice, the way hunters kill certain animals. It was the only thing he did that we could never cure him of doing. He never killed, or even chased, a squirrel. I don't know why. He had his own philosophy about such things. He never ran barking after wagons or automobiles. He didn't seem to see the idea in pursuing something you couldn't catch, or something you couldn't do anything with, even if you did catch it. A wagon was one of the things he couldn't tug along with his mighty jaws, and he knew it. Wagons, therefore, were not a part of his world.

Swimming was his favorite recreation. The first time he ever saw a body of water (Alum Creek), he trotted nervously along the steep bank for a while, fell to barking wildly, and finally plunged in from a height of eight feet or more. I shall always remember that shining, virgin dive. Then he swam upstream and back just for the pleasure of it, like a man. It was fun to see him battle upstream against a stiff current, struggling and growling every foot of the way. He had as much fun in the water as any person I have known. You didn't have to throw a stick in the water to get him to go in. Of course, he would bring back a stick to you if you did throw one in. He would even have brought back a piano if you had thrown one in.

That reminds me of the night, way after midnight, when he went a-roving in the light of the moon and brought back a small chest of drawers that he found somewhere—how far from the house nobody ever knew; since it was Rex, it could easily have been half a mile. There were no drawers in the chest when he got it home, and it wasn't a good one—he hadn't taken it out of anybody's house; it was just an old cheap piece that somebody had abandoned on a trash heap. Still, it was something he wanted, probably because it presented a nice problem in transportation. It tested his mettle. We first knew about his achievement when, deep in the night, we heard him trying to get the chest up onto the porch. It sounded as if two or three people were trying to tear the house down. We came downstairs and turned on the porch light. Rex was on the top step trying to pull the thing up, but it had caught somehow and he was just holding his own. I suppose he would have held his own till dawn if we hadn't helped him. The next day we carted the chest miles away and threw it out. If we had thrown it out in a nearby alley, he would have brought it home again, as a small token of his integrity in such matters.

After all, he had been taught to carry heavy wooden objects about, and he was proud of his prowess.

I am glad Rex never saw a trained police dog jump. He was just an amateur jumper himself, but the most daring and tenacious I have ever seen. He would take on any fence we pointed out to him. Six feet was easy for him, and he could do eight by making a tremendous leap and hauling himself over finally by his paws, grunting and straining; but he lived and died without knowing that twelve- and sixteen-foot walls were too much for him. Frequently, after letting him try to go over one for a while, we would have to carry him home. He would never have given up trying.

There was in his world no such thing as the impossible. Even death couldn't beat him down. He died, it is true, but only, as one of his admirers said, after "straight-arming the death angel" for more than an hour. Late one afternoon he wandered home, too slowly and too uncertainly to be the Rex that had trotted briskly homeward up our avenue for ten years. I think we all knew when he came through the gate that he was dying. He had apparently taken a terrible beating, probably from the owner of some dog that he had got into a fight with. His head and body were scarred. His heavy collar with the teeth marks of many a battle on it was awry; some of the big brass studs in it were sprung loose from the leather. He licked at our hands and, staggering, fell, but got up again. We could see that he was looking for someone. One of his three masters was not home. He did not get home for an hour. During that hour the bull terrier fought against death as he had fought against the cold current of Alum Creek, as he had fought to climb twelve-foot walls. When the person he was waiting for did come through the gate, whistling, ceasing to whistle, Rex walked a few wobbly paces toward him, touched his hand with his muzzle, and fell down again. This time he didn't get up.

## Getting at Meaning

1. What triggers the narrator's reminiscence of Rex? In what way is the entire story a snapshot of this dog?

2. In a fight with another dog, why does Rex choose to go for an ear rather than for the throat? How is this choice related to Rex's desire never to start a fight?

3. Would witnesses to Rex's big fight on the streetcar tracks believe that he has a gentle disposition? What don't they see in Rex that the narrator sees?

4. The first time that Rex sees a body of water he dives right in. What does this act reveal about his character?

5. How is Rex's death similar to his fight on the streetcar tracks?

6. What does the narrator mean when he says that Rex died only after "straight-arming the death angel"?

## Developing Skills in Reading Literature

1. **Characterization.** The main character in this story is a dog. Describe the techniques used by the writer to develop this character.

2. **Stereotype.** Describe briefly the stereotype of a fighting bull dog. In what ways does Rex not conform to this stereotype?

3. **Conflict.** Although this story is a character sketch and as such lacks dramatic conflicts, the story does include some internal and external conflicts. Identify them.

## Developing Vocabulary

**Words from Greek.** The author of the epic poems *The Iliad* and *The Odyssey* is believed to be Homer, who lived in Greece in the eighth century B. C. In his long narrative poems, Homer created heroes of exceptional strength, cunning, and bravery. The great deeds of these heroes were told and retold by succeeding generations.

The writer of "Snapshot of a Dog" refers to Rex's great fight as Homeric. What does he mean? With whom is he comparing Rex? Look up the word *Homeric* in a dictionary, and find the meaning of the word as it is used in this story.

## Developing Writing Skills

**Using Specific Incidents to Reveal Character.** The writer of this story uses events in Rex's life to illustrate specific character traits. For example, the long fight in the street shows his courage and perseverance. Bringing home the chest of drawers shows his strength and determination.

Describe a pet that you have owned or that someone you know has owned. Select three or four incidents that reveal this animal's character traits. Describe these incidents in a five-paragraph composition. In the introduction, identify the pet and tell who owned the pet and for how long. In the second, third, and fourth paragraphs, relate three incidents and explain what character traits they reveal. In the conclusion, either relate an incident that reveals the most important character trait of this pet or describe how this pet died or otherwise left the family.

# Plot

MOTHER AND SON, 1933. *Daniel Garber.*
*Pennsylvania Academy of the Fine Arts. Gift of the artist.*

# The Open Window     *Saki*

**M**y aunt will be down presently, Mr. Nuttel," said a very self-possessed young lady of fifteen; "in the meantime you must try and put up with me."

Framton Nuttel endeavored to say the correct something that should duly flatter the niece of the moment without unduly discounting the aunt that was to come. Privately he doubted more than ever whether these formal visits on a succession of total strangers would do much towards helping the nerve cure which he was supposed to be undergoing.

"I know how it will be," his sister had said when he was preparing to migrate to this rural retreat; "you will bury yourself down there and not speak to a living soul, and your nerves will be worse than ever from moping. I shall just give you letters of introduction to all the people I know there. Some of them, as far as I can remember, were quite nice."

Framton wondered whether Mrs. Sappleton, the lady to whom he was presenting one of the letters of introduction, came into the nice division.

"Do you know many of the people round here?" asked the niece, when she judged that they had had sufficient silent communion.

"Hardly a soul," said Framton. "My sister was staying here, at the rectory, you know, some four years ago, and she gave me letters of introduction to some of the people here."

He made the last statement in a tone of distinct regret.

"Then you know practically nothing about my aunt?" pursued the self-possessed young lady.

"Only her name and address," admitted the caller. He was wondering whether Mrs. Sappleton was in the married or widowed state. An undefinable something about the room seemed to suggest masculine habitation.

"Her great tragedy happened just three years ago," said the child; "that would be since your sister's time."

"Her tragedy?" asked Framton; somehow in this restful country spot tragedies seemed out of place.

"You may wonder why we keep that window wide open on an October afternoon," said the niece, indicating a large French window that opened on to a lawn.

"It is quite warm for the time of the year," said Framton; "but has that window got anything to do with the tragedy?"

"Out through that window, three years ago to a day, her husband and her two young brothers went off for their day's shooting. They never came back. In crossing the moor to their favorite snipe-shooting ground they were all three engulfed by a treacherous piece of bog. It had been that dreadful wet summer, you know, and places that were safe in other years gave way suddenly without warning. Their bodies were never recovered. That was the dreadful part of it." Here the child's voice lost its self-possessed note and became falteringly human. "Poor aunt always thinks that they will come back some day, they and the little brown spaniel that was lost with them, and walk in that window just as they used to do. That is why the window is kept open every evening till it is quite dusk. Poor dear aunt, she has often told me how they went out, her husband with his white waterproof coat over his arm, and Ronnie, her youngest brother, singing 'Bertie, why do you bound?' as he always did to tease her, because she said it got on her nerves. Do you know, sometimes on still, quiet evenings like this, I almost get a creepy feeling that they will all walk in through that window——"

She broke off with a little shudder. It was a relief to Framton when the aunt bustled into the room with a whirl of apologies for being late in making her appearance.

"I hope Vera has been amusing you?" she said.

"She has been very interesting," said Framton.

"I hope you don't mind the open window," said Mrs. Sappleton briskly; "my husband and brothers will be home directly from shooting, and they always come in this way. They've been out for snipe in the marshes today, so they'll make a fine mess over my poor carpets. So like you menfolk, isn't it?"

She rattled on cheerfully about the shooting and the scarcity of birds, and the prospects for duck in the winter. To Framton it was all purely horrible. He made a desperate but only partially successful effort to turn the talk on to a less ghastly topic; he was conscious that his hostess was giving him only a fragment of her attention, and her eyes were constantly straying past him to the open window and the lawn beyond. It was certainly an unfortunate coincidence that he should have paid his visit on this tragic anniversary.

"The doctors agree in ordering me complete rest, an absence of mental excitement, and avoidance of anything in the nature of violent physical exercise," announced Framton, who labored under the tolerably wide-spread delusion that total strangers and chance acquaintances are hungry for the least detail of one's ailments and infirmities, their cause and cure. "On the matter of diet they are not so much in agreement," he continued.

"No?" said Mrs. Sappleton, in a voice which only replaced a yawn at the last moment. Then she suddenly brightened into alert attention—but not to what Framton was saying.

"Here they are at last!" she cried. "Just in time for tea, and don't they look as if they were muddy up to the eyes!"

Framton shivered slightly, and turned towards the niece with a look intended to convey sympathetic comprehension. The child was staring out through the open window with dazed horror in her eyes. In a chill shock of nameless fear Framton swung round in his seat and looked in the same direction.

In the deepening twilight three figures were walking across the lawn towards the window; they all carried guns under their arms, and one of them was additionally burdened with a white coat hung over his shoulders. A tired brown spaniel kept close at their heels. Noiselessly they neared the house, and then a hoarse young voice chanted out of the dusk:

"I said, Bertie, why do you bound?"

Framton grabbed wildly at his stick and hat; the hall door, the gravel drive, and the front gate were dimly noted stages in his headlong retreat. A cyclist coming along the road had to run into the hedge to avoid imminent collision.

"Here we are, my dear," said the bearer of the white mackintosh, coming in through the window; "fairly muddy, but most of it's dry. Who was that who bolted out as we came up?"

"A most extraordinary man, a Mr. Nuttel," said Mrs. Sappleton; "could only talk about his illnesses, and dashed off without a word of goodbye or apology when you arrived. One would think he had seen a ghost."

"I expect it was the spaniel," said the niece calmly; "he told me he had a horror of dogs. He was once hunted into a cemetery somewhere on the banks of the Ganges[1] by a pack of pariah dogs, and had to spend the night in a newly dug grave with the creatures snarling and grinning and foaming just above him. Enough to make anyone lose his nerve."

Romance at short notice was her specialty.

---

1. **the Ganges** (gan' jēz): a river in northern India.

## Getting at Meaning

1. What does Framton think he has seen? What, in fact, has he seen?

2. When does the reader realize that the niece has been lying to Framton?

3. Why is Framton a particularly good candidate for believing the niece's lies?

4. The author repeatedly refers to the niece as "self-possessed." What does this mean? Why is it important that the reader know this about the niece?

5. The niece is a good actress, as well as being a good liar. Give two examples of her convincing acting.

## Developing Skills in Reading Literature

1. **Climax.** In a short story, the climax, or moment when the outcome of the plot suddenly becomes clear, usually occurs near the end of the story. What event is the climax of this story?

2. **Surprise Ending.** A surprise ending is an unexpected twist at the end of a story. Such an ending is said to be ironic because it is not what the reader expects. What ending is the reader led to expect in this story? Find clues early in the story that foreshadow the surprise ending.

3. **Irony.** Irony is the contrast between what is expected and what actually happens. Dramatic irony results from the reader's knowing something that a character does not know. Mrs. Sappleton says that Mr. Nuttel dashed off so fast "one would think he had seen a ghost." Why is this statement ironic?

4. **Character.** What mental image does the name Framton Nuttel create? Is this image consistent with the character as he is presented in the story? Explain your answer.

## Developing Vocabulary

**Finding the Appropriate Meaning.** The last line of the story includes the word *romance*. Look up *romance* in a dictionary and find the meaning for the word as it is used in this story. Then think of a synonym and rewrite the last line of the story, using this synonym.

## Developing Writing Skills

**Combining Narration and Exposition.** Select a television show or a movie that had an unexpected ending. Describe the plot and explain what led you to believe that the story would end a certain way. Then explain how the show ended and what clues, if any, could have warned you of that ending.

Develop this topic in a five-paragraph composition, following this plan:

Paragraph 1: Summary of the plot
Paragraph 2: Description of the expected ending, along with reasons for your expectation
Paragraph 3: Description of the actual ending
Paragraph 4: Identification of clues that hinted at the actual ending
Paragraph 5: Statement of opinion about the effectiveness of surprise endings and about the kinds of stories for which they are most effective

# The Red-Headed League

## *Arthur Conan Doyle*

I had called upon my friend, Mr. Sherlock Holmes, one day in the autumn of last year and found him in deep conversation with a very stout, florid-faced, elderly gentleman with fiery red hair. With an apology for my intrusion, I was about to withdraw when Holmes pulled me abruptly into the room and closed the door behind me.

"You could not possibly have come at a better time, my dear Watson," he said cordially.

"I was afraid that you were engaged."

"So I am. Very much so."

"Then I can wait in the next room."

"Not at all. This gentleman, Mr. Wilson, has been my partner and helper in many of my most successful cases, and I have no doubt that he will be of the utmost use to me in yours also."

The stout gentleman half rose from his chair and gave a bob of greeting, with a quick little questioning glance from his small, fat-encircled eyes.

"Try the settee," said Holmes, relapsing into his armchair and putting his finger-tips together, as was his custom when in judicial moods. "I know, my dear Watson, that you share my love of all that is bizarre and outside the conventions and humdrum routine of everyday life. You have shown your relish for it by the enthusiasm that has prompted you to chronicle, and, if you will excuse my saying so, somewhat to embellish so many of my own little adventures."

"Your cases have indeed been of the greatest interest to me," I observed.

"You will remember that I remarked the other day, just before we went into the very simple problem presented by Miss Mary Sutherland, that for strange effects and extraordinary combinations we must go to life itself, which is always far more daring than any effort of the imagination."

"A proposition that I took the liberty of doubting."

"You did, Doctor, but none the less you must come round to my view, for otherwise I shall keep on piling fact upon fact on you until your reason breaks down under them and acknowledges me to be right. Now, Mr. Jabez Wilson here has been good enough to call upon me this morning, and to begin a narrative that promises to be one of the most singular that I have listened to for some time. You have heard me remark that the strangest things are very often connected not with the larger but with the smaller crimes, and occasionally, indeed, where there is room for doubt whether any positive crime has been committed. As far as I have heard, it is impossible for me to say whether the present case is an instance of crime or not, but the course of events is certainly among the most singular that I have ever listened to. Perhaps, Mr. Wilson, you would have the great kindness to recommence your narrative. I ask you not merely because my friend Dr. Watson has not heard the opening part but also because the peculiar nature of the story makes me eager to have every possible detail from your lips. As a rule, when I have heard some slight indication of the course of events, I am able to guide myself by the thousands of other similar cases that occur to my memory. In the present instance I am forced to admit that the facts are, to the best of my belief, unique."

The portly client puffed out his chest with an appearance of some little pride and pulled a dirty and wrinkled newspaper from the inside pocket of his great-coat. As he glanced down the advertisement column, with his head thrust forward and the paper flattened out upon his knee, I took a good look at the man and endeavored, after the fashion of my companion, to read the indications that might be presented by his dress or appearance.

I did not gain very much, however, by my inspection. Our visitor bore every mark of being an average commonplace British tradesman, obese, pompous, and slow. He wore rather baggy gray shepherd's check trousers, a not over-clean black frock-coat, unbuttoned in the front, and a drab waistcoat with a heavy brassy Albert chain, and a square pierced bit of metal dangling down as an ornament. A frayed top-hat and a faded brown overcoat with a wrinkled velvet collar lay upon a chair beside him. Altogether, look as I would, there was nothing remarkable about the man save his blazing red head, and the expression of extreme chagrin and discontent upon his features.

Sherlock Holmes's quick eye took in my occupation, and he shook his head with a smile as he noticed my questioning glances. "Beyond the obvious facts that he has at some time done manual labor, that he takes snuff, that he is a Freemason,[1] that he has been in China, and that he has done a considerable amount of writing lately, I can deduce nothing else."

Mr. Jabez Wilson started up in his chair, with his forefinger upon the paper, but his eyes upon my companion.

"How, in the name of good fortune, did you know all that, Mr. Holmes?" he asked. "How did you know, for example, that I did manual labor? It's as true as gospel, for I began as a ship's carpenter."

"Your hands, my dear sir. Your right hand is quite a size larger than your left. You have worked with it, and the muscles are more developed."

"Well, the snuff, then, and the Freemasonry?"

"I won't insult your intelligence by telling you how I read that, especially as, rather against the strict rules of your order, you use an arc-and-compass breastpin."

"Ah, of course, I forgot that. But the writing?"

"What else can be indicated by that right cuff so very shiny for five inches, and the left one with the smooth patch near the elbow where you rest it upon the desk?"

"Well, but China?"

"The fish that you have tattooed immediately above your right wrist could have been done only in China. I have made a small study of tattoo marks and have even contributed to the literature on the subject. That trick of staining the fishes' scales a delicate pink is quite peculiar to China. When, in addition, I see a Chinese coin hanging from your watch chain, the matter becomes even more simple."

Mr. Jabez Wilson laughed heavily. "Well, I never!" said he. "I thought at first that you had done something clever, but I see that there was nothing in it, after all."

"I begin to think, Watson," said Holmes, "that I make a mistake in explaining. 'Omne ignotum pro magnifico,'[2] you know, and my poor little reputation, such as it is, will suffer shipwreck if I am so candid. Can you not find the advertisement, Mr. Wilson?"

---

1. **Freemason** (frē′ mās ′n): a member of the Free and Accepted Masons, an international secret society; also called a *Mason*.
2. ***Omne ignotum pro magnifico*** (ôm ne ig nō′ tum prō mag nif′ i kō): *Latin:* Everything unknown is prized greatly.

"Yes, I have got it now," he answered with his thick red finger planted halfway down the column. "Here it is. This is what began it all. You just read it for yourself, sir."

I took the paper from him and read as follows:

To the Red-headed League:

On account of the bequest of the late Ezekiah Hopkins, of Lebanon, Pennsylvania, U.S.A., there is now another vacancy open that entitles a member of the League to a salary of £4 a week for purely nominal services. All red-headed men who are sound in body and mind, and above the age of twenty-one years, are eligible. Apply in person on Monday, at eleven o'clock, to Duncan Ross, at the offices of the League, 7 Pope's Court, Fleet Street.

"What on earth does this mean?" I ejaculated after I had twice read over the extraordinary announcement.

Holmes chuckled and wriggled in his chair, as was his habit when in high spirits. "It is a little off the beaten track, isn't it?" said he. "And now, Mr. Wilson, off you go at scratch and tell us all about yourself, your household, and the effect that this advertisement had upon your fortunes. You will first make a note, Doctor, of the paper and the date."

"It is *The Morning Chronicle* of April 27, 1890. Just two months ago."

"Very good. Now, Mr. Wilson?"

"Well, it is just as I have been telling you, Mr. Sherlock Holmes," said Jabez Wilson, mopping his forehead; "I have a small pawnbroker's business at Coburg Square, near the City. It's not a very large affair, and of late years it has not done more than just give me a living. I used to be able to keep two assistants, but now I keep only one; and I would have a job to pay him but that he is willing to come for half wages so as to learn the business."

"What is the name of this obliging youth?" asked Sherlock Holmes.

"His name is Vincent Spaulding, and he's not such a youth, either. It's hard to say his age. I should not wish a smarter assistant, Mr. Holmes; and I know very well that he could better himself and earn twice what I am able to give him. But, after all, if he is satisfied, why should I put ideas in his head?"

"Why, indeed? You seem most fortunate in having an employee who comes under the full market price. It is not a common experience among employers in this age. I don't know that your assistant is not as remarkable as your advertisement."

"Oh, he has his faults, too," said Mr. Wilson. "Never was such a fellow for photography. Snapping away with a camera when he ought to be improving his mind, and then diving down into the cellar like a rabbit into its hole to develop his pictures. That is his main fault, but on the whole he's a good worker. There's no vice in him."

"He is still with you, I presume?"

"Yes, sir. He and a girl of fourteen, who does a bit of simple cooking and keeps the place clean—that's all I have in the house, for I am a widower and never had any family. We live very quietly, sir, the three of us; and we keep a roof over our heads and pay our debts, if we do nothing more.

"The first thing that put us out was that advertisement. Spaulding, he came down into the office just this day eight weeks, with this very paper in his hand, and he says:

" 'I wish to the Lord, Mr. Wilson, that I was a red-headed man.'

" 'Why that?' I asks.

" 'Why,' says he, 'here's another vacancy in the League of the Red-headed Men. It's worth quite a little fortune to any man who gets it, and I understand that there are more vacancies than there are men, so that the trustees are at their wits' end what to do with the money. If my hair would only change color, here's a nice little crib all ready for me to step into.'

" 'Why, what is it, then?' I asked. You see,

Mr. Holmes, I am a very stay-at-home man, and as my business came to me instead of my having to go to it, I was often weeks on end without putting my foot over the door-mat. In that way I didn't know much of what was going on outside, and I was always glad of a bit of news.

" 'Have you never heard of the League of the Red-headed Men?' he asked with his eyes open.

" 'Never.'

" 'Why, I wonder at that, for you are eligible yourself for one of the vacancies.'

" 'And what are they worth?' I asked.

" 'Oh, merely a couple of hundred a year, but the work is slight, and it need not interfere very much with one's other occupations.'

"Well, you can easily think that that made me prick up my ears, for the business has not been over-good for some years, and an extra couple of hundred would have been very handy.

" 'Tell me all about it,' said I.

" 'Well,' said he, showing me the advertisement, 'you can see for yourself that the League has a vacancy, and there is the address where you should apply for particulars. As far as I can make out, the League was founded by an American millionaire, Ezekiah Hopkins, who was very peculiar in his ways. He was himself red-headed, and he had a great sympathy for all red-headed men; so when he died it was found that he had left his enormous fortune in the hands of trustees, with instructions to apply the interest to the providing of easy berths to men whose hair is of that color. From all I hear it is splendid pay and very little to do.'

" 'But,' said I, 'there would be millions of red-headed men who would apply.'

" 'Not so many as you might think,' he answered. 'You see it is really confined to Londoners, and to grown men. This American had started from London when he was young, and he wanted to do the old town a good turn. Then, again, I have heard it is no use your applying if your hair is light red, or dark red, or anything but real bright, blazing, fiery red. Now, if you cared to apply, Mr. Wilson, you would just walk in; but perhaps it would hardly be worth your while to put yourself out of the way for the sake of a few hundred pounds.'

"Now, it is a fact, gentlemen, as you may see for yourselves, that my hair is of a very full and rich tint, so that it seemed to me that if there was to be any competition in the matter, I stood as good a chance as any man that I had ever met. Vincent Spaulding seemed to know so much about it that I thought he might prove useful, so I just ordered him to put up the shutters for the day and to come right away with me. He was very willing to have a holiday, so we shut the business up and started off for the address that was given us in the advertisement.

"I never hope to see such a sight as that again, Mr. Holmes. From north, south, east, and west every man who had a shade of red in his hair had tramped into the city to answer the advertisement. Fleet Street was choked with red-headed folk, and Pope's Court looked like a coster's orange barrow. I should not have thought there were so many in the whole country as were brought together by that single advertisement. Every shade of color they were—straw, lemon, orange, brick, Irish-setter, liver, clay; but, as Spaulding said, there were not many who had the real, vivid flame-colored tint. When I saw how many were waiting, I would have given it up in despair; but Spaulding would not hear of it. How he did it I could not imagine, but he pushed and pulled and butted until he got me through the crowd, and right up to the steps that led to the office. There was a double stream upon the stair, some going up in hope, and some coming back dejected; but we wedged in as well as we could and soon found ourselves in the office."

"Your experience has been a most entertaining one," remarked Holmes, as his client paused and refreshed his memory with a huge pinch of snuff. "Pray continue your very interesting statement."

"There was nothing in the office but a couple of wooden chairs and a deal table, behind which sat a small man with a head that was even redder than mine. He said a few words to each candidate as he came up, and then he always managed to find some fault in them that would disqualify them. Getting a vacancy did not seem to be such a very easy matter, after all. However, when our turn came the little man was much more favorable to me than to any of the others, and he closed the door as we entered, so that he might have a private word with us.

" 'This is Mr. Jabez Wilson,' said my assistant, 'and he is willing to fill a vacancy in the League.'

" 'And he is admirably suited for it,' the other answered. 'He has every requirement. I cannot recall when I have seen anything so fine.' He took a step backward, cocked his head on one side, and gazed at my hair until I felt quite bashful. Then suddenly he plunged forward, wrung my hand, and congratulated me warmly on my success.

" 'It would be injustice to hesitate,' said he. 'You will, however, I am sure, excuse me for taking an obvious precaution.' With that he seized my hair in both his hands, and tugged until I yelled with the pain. 'There is water in your eyes,' said he as he released me. 'I perceive that all is as it should be. But we have to be careful, for we have twice been deceived by wigs and once by paint. I could tell you tales of cobbler's wax that would disgust you with human nature.' He stepped over to the window and shouted through it at the top of his voice that the vacancy was filled. A groan of disappointment came up from below, and the folk all trooped away in different directions until there was not a red head to be seen except my own and that of the manager.

" 'My name,' said he, 'is Mr. Duncan Ross, and I am myself one of the pensioners upon the fund left by our noble benefactor. Are you a married man, Mr. Wilson? Have you a family?'

"I answered that I had not.

"His face fell immediately.

" 'Dear me!' he said gravely, 'that is very serious indeed! I am sorry to hear you say that. The fund was, of course, for the propagation and spread of the red-heads as well as for their maintenance. It is exceedingly unfortunate that you should be a bachelor.'

"My face lengthened at this, Mr. Holmes, for I thought that I was not to have the vacancy after all; but after thinking it over for a few minutes he said that it would be all right.

" 'In the case of another,' said he, 'the objection might be fatal, but we must stretch a point in favor of a man with such a head of hair as yours. When shall you be able to enter upon your new duties?'

" 'Well, it is a little awkward, for I have a business already,' said I.

" 'Oh, never mind about that, Mr. Wilson!' said Vincent Spaulding. 'I should be able to look after that for you.'

" 'What would be the hours?' I asked.

" 'Ten to two.'

"Now a pawnbroker's business is mostly done of an evening, Mr. Holmes, especially Thursday and Friday evening, which is just before pay day; so it would suit me very well to earn a little in the mornings. Besides, I knew that my assistant was a good man, and that he would see to anything that turned up.

" 'That would suit me very well,' said I. 'And the pay?'

" 'Is £4 a week.'

" 'And the work?'

" 'Is purely nominal.'

" 'What do you call purely nominal?'

" 'Well, you have to be in the office, or at least in the building, the whole time. If you leave, you forfeit your whole position forever. The will is very clear upon that point. You don't comply with the conditions if you budge from the office during that time.'

" 'It's only four hours a day, and I should not think of leaving,' said I.

" 'No excuse will avail,' said Mr. Duncan Ross; 'neither sickness nor business nor anything else. There you must stay, or you lose your billet.'

" 'And the work?'

" 'Is to copy out the Encyclopædia Britannica. There is the first volume of it in that press. You must find your own ink, pens, and blotting-paper, but we provide this table and chair. Will you be ready tomorrow?'

" 'Certainly,' I answered.

" 'Then, goodbye, Mr. Jabez Wilson, and let me congratulate you once more on the important position that you have been fortunate enough to gain.' He bowed me out of the room, and I went home with my assistant, hardly knowing what to say or do, I was so pleased at my own good fortune.

"Well, I thought over the matter all day, and by evening I was in low spirits again; for I had quite persuaded myself that the whole affair must be some great hoax or fraud, though what its object might be I could not imagine. It seemed altogether past belief that anyone could make such a will, or that they would pay such a sum for doing anything so simple as copying out the Encyclopædia Britannica. Vincent Spaulding did what he could to cheer me up, but by bedtime I had reasoned myself out of the whole thing. However, in the morning I determined to have a look at it anyhow, so I bought a penny bottle of ink, and with a quill pen, and seven sheets of foolscap paper, I started off for Pope's Court.

"Well, to my surprise and delight, everything was as right as possible. The table was set out ready for me, and Mr. Duncan Ross was there to see that I got fairly to work. He started me off upon the letter A, and then he left me; but he would drop in from time to time to see that all was right with me. At two o'clock he bade me good-day, complimented me upon the amount that I had written, and locked the door of the office after me.

"This went on day after day, Mr. Holmes, and on Saturday the manager came in and planked down four golden sovereigns for my week's work. It was the same next week, and the same the week after. Every morning I was there at ten, and every afternoon I left at two. By degrees, Mr. Duncan Ross took to coming in only once of a morning, and then, after a time, he did not come in at all. Still, of course, I never dared to leave the room for an instant, for I was not sure when he might come, and the billet was such a good one, and suited me so well, that I would not risk the loss of it.

"Eight weeks passed away like this, and I had written about Abbots and Archery and Armor and Architecture and Attica, and hoped with diligence that I might get on to the B's before very long. It cost me something in foolscap, and I had pretty nearly filled a shelf with my writings. And suddenly the whole business came to an end."

"To an end?"

"Yes, sir. And no later than this morning. I went to my work as usual at ten o'clock, but the door was shut and locked, with a little square cardboard hammered on to the middle of the panel with a tack. Here it is, and you can read for yourself."

He held up a piece of white cardboard about the size of a sheet of note paper. It read in this fashion:

THE RED-HEADED LEAGUE

IS

DISSOLVED.

OCTOBER 9, 1890.

Sherlock Holmes and I surveyed this curt announcement and the rueful face behind it, until the comical side of the affair so completely overtopped every other consideration that we both burst out into a roar of laughter.

"I cannot see that there is anything very funny," cried our client, flushing up to the roots of his flaming head. "If you can do nothing better than laugh at me, I can go elsewhere."

"No, no," cried Holmes, shoving him back into the chair from which he had half risen. "I really wouldn't miss your case for the world. It is most refreshingly unusual. But there is, if you will excuse my saying so, something just a little funny about it. Pray what steps did you take when you found the card upon the door?"

"I was staggered, sir. I did not know what to do. Then I called at the offices round, but none of them seemed to know anything about it. Finally, I went to the landlord, who is an accountant living on the ground floor, and I asked him if he could tell me what had become of the Red-headed League. He said that he had never heard of any such body. Then I asked him who Mr. Duncan Ross was. He answered that the name was new to him.

" 'Well,' said I, 'the gentleman at No. 4.'

" 'What, the red-headed man?'

" 'Yes.'

" 'Oh,' said he, 'his name was William Morris. He was a solicitor and was using my room as a temporary convenience until his new premises were ready. He moved out yesterday.'

" 'Where could I find him?'

" 'Oh, at his new offices. He did tell me the address. Yes, 17 King Edward Street, near St. Paul's.'

"I started off, Mr. Holmes, but when I got to that address it was a manufactory of artificial knee-caps, and no one in it had ever heard of either Mr. William Morris or Mr. Duncan Ross."

"And what did you do then?" asked Holmes.

"I went home to Saxe-Coburg Square, and I took the advice of my assistant. But he could not help me in any way. He could only say that if I waited I should hear by post. But that was not quite good enough, Mr. Holmes. I did not wish to lose such a place without a struggle, so, as I had heard that you were good enough to give advice to poor folks who were in need of it, I came right away to you."

"And you did very wisely," said Holmes. "Your case is an exceedingly remarkable one, and I shall be happy to look into it. From what you have told me I think that it is possible that graver issues hang from it than might at first sight appear."

"Grave enough!" said Mr. Jabez Wilson. "Why, I have lost four pound a week."

"As far as you are personally concerned," remarked Holmes, "I do not see that you have any grievance against this extraordinary league. On the contrary, you are, as I understand, richer by some £30, to say nothing of the minute knowledge that you have gained on every subject that comes under the letter A. You have lost nothing by them."

"No, sir. But I want to find out about them, and who they are, and what their object was in playing this prank—if it was a prank—upon me. It was a pretty expensive joke for them, for it cost them two and thirty pounds."

"We shall endeavor to clear up these points for you. And, first, one or two questions, Mr. Wilson. This assistant of yours who first called your attention to the advertisement—how long had he been with you?"

"About a month then."

"How did he come?"

"In answer to an advertisement."

"Was he the only applicant?"

"No, I had a dozen."

"Why did you pick him?"

"Because he was handy and would come cheap."

"At half-wages, in fact."

"Yes."

"What is he like, this Vincent Spaulding?"

"Small, stout-built, very quick in his ways, no hair on his face, though he's not short of thirty. Has a white splash of acid upon his forehead."

Holmes sat up in his chair in considerable excitement. "I thought as much," said he. "Have you ever observed that his ears are pierced for earrings?"

"Yes, sir. He told me that a gypsy had done it for him when he was a lad."

"Hum!" said Holmes, sinking back in deep thought. "He is still with you?"

"Oh, yes, sir; I have only just left him."

"And has your business been attended to in your absence?"

"Nothing to complain of, sir. There's never very much to do of a morning."

"That will do, Mr. Wilson. I shall be happy to give you an opinion upon the subject in the course of a day or two. Today is Saturday, and I hope that by Monday we may come to a conclusion."

"Well, Watson," said Holmes when our visitor had left us, "what do you make of it all?"

"I make nothing of it," I answered frankly. "It is a most mysterious business."

"As a rule," said Holmes, "the more bizarre a thing is the less mysterious it proves to be. It is your commonplace, featureless crimes that are really puzzling, just as a commonplace face is the most difficult to identify. But I must be prompt over this matter."

"What are you going to do, then?" I asked.

"To smoke," he answered. "It is quite a three-pipe problem, and I beg that you won't speak to me for fifty minutes." He curled himself up in his chair, with his thin knees drawn up to his hawk-like nose, and there he sat with his eyes closed and his black clay pipe thrusting out like the bill of some strange bird. I had come to the conclusion that he had dropped asleep, and indeed was nodding myself, when he suddenly sprang out of his chair with the gesture of a man who has made up his mind and put his pipe down upon the mantelpiece.

"Sarasate[3] plays at the St. James's Hall this afternoon," he remarked. "What do you think, Watson? Could your patients spare you for a few hours?"

"I have nothing to do today. My practice is never very absorbing."

"Then put on your hat and come. I am going through the City first, and we can have some lunch on the way. I observe that there is a good deal of German music on the program, which is rather more to my taste than Italian or French. It is introspective, and I want to introspect. Come along!"

We travelled by the Underground[4] as far as Aldersgate; and a short walk took us to Saxe-Coburg Square, the scene of a singular story that we had listened to in the morning. It was a poky, little, shabby-genteel place, where four lines of dingy two-storied brick houses looked out into a small railed-in enclosure, where a lawn of weedy grass and a few clumps of faded laurel-bushes made a hard fight against a smoke-laden and uncongenial atmosphere. Three gilt balls and a brown board with "JABEZ WILSON" in white letters, upon a corner house, announced the place where our red-headed client carried on his business. Sherlock Holmes stopped in front of it with his head on one side and looked it all over, with his eyes shining brightly between puckered lids. Then he walked slowly up the street, and then down again to the corner, still looking keenly at the houses. Finally he returned to the pawnbroker's, and, having thumped vigorously upon the pavement with his stick two or

three times, he went up to the door and knocked. It was instantly opened by a bright-looking, clean-shaven young fellow, who asked him to step in.

"Thank you," said Holmes, "I only wished to ask you how you would go from here to the Strand."

"Third right, fourth left," answered the assistant promptly, closing the door.

"Smart fellow, that," observed Holmes as we walked away. "He is, in my judgment, the fourth smartest man in London, and for daring I am not sure that he has not a claim to be third. I have known something of him before."

"Evidently," said I, "Mr. Wilson's assistant counts for a good deal in this mystery of the Red-headed League. I am sure that you inquired your way merely in order that you might see him."

"Not him."

"What then?"

"The knees of his trousers."

"And what did you see?"

"What I expected to see."

"Why did you beat the pavement?"

"My dear doctor, this is a time for observation, not for talk. We are spies in an enemy's country. We know something of Saxe-Coburg Square. Let us now explore the parts that lie behind it."

The road in which we found ourselves as we turned round the corner from the retired Saxe-Coburg Square presented as great a contrast to it as the front of a picture does to the back. It was one of the main arteries that conveyed the traffic of the City to the north and west. The roadway was blocked with the immense stream of commerce flowing in a double tide inward and outward, while the

---

3. **Sarasate:** Pablo Martin Meleton Sarasate y Navascuez, a successful Spanish violinist.

4. **Underground:** the British subway system.

footpaths were black with the hurrying swarms of pedestrians. It was difficult to realize as we looked at the line of fine shops and stately business premises that they really abutted on the other side upon the faded and stagnant square that we had just quitted.

"Let me see," said Holmes, standing at the corner and glancing along the line, "I should like just to remember the order of the houses here. It is a hobby of mine to have an exact knowledge of London. There is Mortimer's, the tobacconist, the little newspaper shop, the Coburg branch of the City and Suburban Bank, the Vegetarian Restaurant, and Mc-Farlane's carriage-building depot. That carries us right on to the other block. And now, Doctor, we've done our work, so it's time we had some play. A sandwich and a cup of coffee, and then off to violin-land, where all is sweetness and delicacy and harmony, and there are no red-headed clients to vex us with their conundrums."

My friend was an enthusiastic musician, being himself not only a very capable performer but a composer of no ordinary merit. All the afternoon he sat in the stalls wrapped in the most perfect happiness, gently waving his long, thin fingers in time to the music, while his gently smiling face and his languid dreamy eyes were as unlike those of Holmes, the sleuth-hound, Holmes the relentless, keen-witted, ready-handed criminal agent, as it was possible to conceive. In his singular character the dual nature alternately asserted itself, and his extreme exactness and astuteness represented, as I have often thought, the reaction against the poetic and contemplative mood which occasionally predominated in him. The swing of his nature took him from extreme languor to devouring energy; and, as I knew well, he was never so truly formidable as when, for days on end, he had been lounging in his armchair amid his improvisations and his black-letter editions. Then it was that

the lust of the chase would suddenly come upon him, and that his brilliant reasoning power would rise to the level of intuition, until those who were unacquainted with his methods would look askance at him as on a man whose knowledge was not that of other mortals. When I saw him that afternoon so enwrapped in the music at St. James's Hall, I felt that an evil time might be coming upon those whom he had set himself to hunt down.

"You want to go home, no doubt, Doctor," he remarked as we emerged.

"Yes, it would be as well."

"And I have some business to do that will take some hours. This business at Coburg Square is serious."

"Why serious?"

"A considerable crime is in contemplation. I have every reason to believe that we shall be in time to stop it. But today being Saturday rather complicates matters. I shall want your help tonight."

"At what time?"

"Ten will be early enough."

"I shall be at Baker Street at ten."

"Very well. And, I say, Doctor, there may be some little danger, so kindly put your army revolver in your pocket." He waved his hand, turned on his heel, and disappeared in an instant among the crowd.

I trust that I am not more dense than my neighbors, but I was always oppressed with a sense of my own stupidity in my dealings with Sherlock Holmes. Here I had heard what he had heard, I had seen what he had seen, and yet from his words it was evident that he saw clearly not only what had happened but what was about to happen, while to me the whole business was still confused and grotesque. As I drove home to my house in Kensington, I thought over it all, from the extraordinary story of the red-headed copier of the Encyclopædia down to the visit to Saxe-Coburg Square, and the ominous words with which he had parted from me. What was this nocturnal expedition, and why should I go armed? Where were we going, and what were we to do? I had the hint from Holmes that this smooth-faced pawnbroker's assistant was a formidable man—a man who might play a deep game. I tried to puzzle it out, but gave it up in despair and set the matter aside until night should bring an explanation.

It was a quarter-past nine when I started from home and made my way across the Park, and so through Oxford Street to Baker Street. Two hansoms were standing at the door, and as I entered the passage I heard the sound of voices from above. On entering his room I found Holmes in animated conversation with two men, one of whom I recognized as Peter Jones, the official police agent, while the other was a long, thin, sad-faced man, with a very shiny hat and oppressively respectable frock-coat.

"Ha! our party is complete," said Holmes, buttoning up his pea-jacket and taking his heavy hunting crop from the rack. "Watson, I think you know Mr. Jones, of Scotland Yard? Let me introduce you to Mr. Merryweather, who is to be our companion in to-night's adventure."

"We're hunting in couples again, Doctor, you see," said Jones in his consequential way. "Our friend here is a wonderful man for starting a chase. All he wants is an old dog to help him to do the running down."

"I hope a wild goose may not prove to be the end of our chase," observed Mr. Merryweather gloomily.

"You may place considerable confidence in Mr. Holmes, sir," said the police agent loftily. "He has his own little methods, which are, if he won't mind my saying so, just a little too theoretical and fantastic, but he has the makings of a detective in him. It is not too much to say that once or twice, as in that business of the Sholto murder and the Agra treasure, he has been more nearly correct than the official force."

"Oh, if you say so, Mr. Jones, it is all right," said the stranger with deference. "Still, I confess that I miss my bridge game. It is the first Saturday night for seven-and-twenty years that I have not had my bridge game."

"I think you will find," said Sherlock Holmes, "that you will play for a higher stake tonight than you have ever done yet, and that the play will be more exciting. For you, Mr. Merryweather, the stake will be some £30,000; and for you, Jones, it will be the man upon whom you wish to lay your hands."

"John Clay, the murderer, thief, smasher, and forger. He's a young man, Mr. Merryweather, but he is at the head of his profession, and I would rather have my bracelets on him than on any other criminal in London. He's a remarkable man, is young John Clay. His grandfather was a royal duke, and he himself has been to Eton and Oxford.[5] His brain is as cunning as his fingers, and though we meet signs of him at every turn, we never know where to find the man himself. He'll crack a crib[6] in Scotland one week, and be raising money to build an orphanage in Cornwall the next. I've been on his track for years and have never set eyes on him yet."

"I hope that I may have the pleasure of introducing you tonight. I've had one or two little turns also with Mr. John Clay, and I agree with you that he is at the head of his profession. It is past ten, however, and quite time that we started. If you two will take the first hansom, Watson and I will follow in the second."

Sherlock Holmes was not very communicative during the long drive, and lay back in the cab humming the tunes that he had heard

---

5. **Eton and Oxford** (ēt' 'n, äks' fərd): prestigious British schools.
6. **crib** Informal: a petty theft.

in the afternoon. We rattled through an endless labyrinth of gas-lit streets until we emerged into Farringdon Street.

"We are close there now," my friend remarked. "This fellow Merryweather is a bank director, and personally interested in the matter. I thought it as well to have Jones with us also. He is not a bad fellow, though an absolute imbecile in his profession. He has one positive virtue. He is as brave as a bulldog and as tenacious as a lobster if he gets his claws upon anyone. Here we are, and they are waiting for us."

We had reached the same crowded thoroughfare in which we had found ourselves in the morning. Our cabs were dismissed, and, following the guidance of Mr. Merryweather, we passed down a narrow passage and through a side door, which he opened for us. Within there was a small corridor, which ended in a very massive iron gate. This also was opened, and led down a flight of winding stone steps, which terminated at another formidable gate. Mr. Merryweather stopped to light a lantern, and then conducted us down a dark, earth-smelling passage, and so, after opening a third door, into a huge vault or cellar, which was piled all round with crates and massive boxes.

"You are not very vulnerable from above," Holmes remarked as he held up the lantern and gazed about him.

"Nor from below," said Mr. Merryweather, striking his stick upon the flags that lined the floor. "Why, dear me, it sounds quite hollow!" he remarked, looking up in surprise.

"I must really ask you to be a little more quiet!" said Holmes severely. "You have already imperiled the whole success of our expedition. Might I beg that you would have the goodness to sit down upon one of those boxes, and not to interfere?"

The solemn Mr. Merryweather perched himself upon a crate, with a very injured expression upon his face, while Holmes fell upon his knees upon the floor and, with the lantern and a magnifying lens, began to examine minutely the cracks between the stones. A few seconds sufficed to satisfy him, for he sprang to his feet again and put his glass in his pocket.

"We have at least an hour before us," he remarked, "for they can hardly take any steps until the good pawnbroker is safely in bed. Then they will not lose a minute, for the sooner they do their work the longer time they will have for their escape. We are at present, Doctor—as no doubt you have divined—in the cellar of the City branch of one of the principal London banks. Mr. Merryweather is the chairman of directors, and he will explain to you that there are reasons why the more daring criminals of London should take a considerable interest in this cellar at present."

"It is our French gold," whispered the director. "We have had several warnings that an attempt might be made upon it."

"Your French gold?"

"Yes. We had occasion some months ago to strengthen our resources, and borrowed for that purpose 30,000 napoleons from the Bank of France. It has become known that we have never had occasion to unpack the money, and that it is still lying in our cellar. The crate upon which I sit contains 2,000 napoleons packed between layers of lead foil. Our reserve of bullion is much larger at present than is usually kept in a single branch office, and the directors have had misgivings upon the subject."

"Which were very well justified," observed Holmes. "And now it is time that we arranged our little plans. I expect that within an hour matters will come to a head. In the meantime, Mr. Merryweather, we must put the screen over that dark lantern."

"And sit in the dark?"

"I am afraid so. I had brought a pack of cards in my pocket, and I thought that, as we were a *partie carrée*,[7] you might have your bridge game after all. But I see that the enemy's preparations have gone so far that we cannot risk the presence of a light. And, first of all, we must choose our positions. These are daring men, and though we shall take them at a disadvantage, they may do us some harm unless we are careful. I shall stand behind this crate, and do you conceal yourselves behind those. Then, when I flash a light upon them, close in swiftly. If they fire, Watson, have no compunction about shooting them down."

I placed my revolver, cocked, upon the top of the wooden case behind which I crouched. Holmes shot the slide across the front of his lantern and left us in pitch darkness—such an absolute darkness as I have never before experienced. The smell of hot metal remained to assure us that the light was still there, ready to flash out at a moment's notice. To me, with my nerves worked up to a pitch of expectancy, there was something depressing and subduing in the sudden gloom, and in the cold dank air of the vault.

"They have but one retreat," whispered Holmes. "That is back through the house into Saxe-Coburg Square. I hope that you have done what I asked you, Jones?"

"I have an inspector and two officers waiting at the front door."

"Then we have stopped all the holes. And now we must be silent and wait."

What a time it seemed! From comparing notes afterwards it was but an hour and a quarter, yet it appeared to me that the night must have almost gone, and the dawn be breaking above us. My limbs were weary and stiff, for I feared to change my position; yet my nerves were worked up to the highest pitch of tension, and my hearing was so acute that I could not only hear the gentle breathing of my companions, but I could distinguish the deeper, heavier in-breath of the bulky Jones from the thin, sighing note of the bank director. From my position I could look over the case in the direction of the floor. Suddenly my eyes caught the glint of a light.

At first it was but a lurid spark upon the stone pavement. Then it lengthened out until it became a yellow line, and then, without any warning or sound, a gash seemed to open and a hand appeared; a white, almost womanly hand, which felt about in the center of the little area of light. For a minute or more the hand, with its writhing fingers, protruded out of the floor. Then it was withdrawn as suddenly as it appeared, and all was dark again save the single lurid spark that marked a chink between the stones.

Its disappearance, however, was but momentary. With a rending, tearing sound, one of the broad, white stones turned over upon its side and left a square, gaping hole, through which streamed the light of a lantern. Over the edge there peeped a clean-cut, boyish face, which looked keenly about it, and then, with a hand on either side of the aperture, drew itself shoulder-high and waist-high, until one knee rested upon the edge. In another instant he stood at the side of the hole and was hauling after him a companion, lithe and small like himself, with pale face and a shock of very red hair.

"It's all clear," he whispered. "Have you the chisel and the bags? Great Scott! Jump, Archie, jump, and I'll swing for it!"

Sherlock Holmes had sprung out and seized the intruder by the collar. The other dived down the hole, and I heard the sound of rending cloth as Jones clutched at his skirts. The light flashed upon the barrel of a revolver, but Holmes's hunting crop came

---

7. **partie carrée** (pär tē′ kë rā′) *French*: a party of four.

down on the man's wrist, and the pistol clinked upon the stone floor.

"It's no use, John Clay," said Holmes blandly. "You have no chance at all."

"So I see," the other answered with the utmost coolness. "I fancy that my pal is all right, though I see you have got his coattails."

"There are three men waiting for him at the door," said Holmes.

"Oh, indeed! You seem to have done the thing very completely. I must compliment you."

"And I you," Holmes answered. "Your redheaded idea was very new and effective."

"You'll see your pal again presently," said Jones. "He's quicker at climbing down holes than I am. Just hold out while I fix the derbies."

"I beg that you will not touch me with your filthy hands," remarked our prisoner as the handcuffs clattered upon his wrists. "You may not be aware that I have royal blood in my veins. Have the goodness, also, when you address me always to say 'sir' and 'please.'"

"All right," said Jones with a stare and a snigger. "Well, would you please, sir, march upstairs, where we can get a cab to carry your Highness to the police station?"

"That is better," said John Clay serenely. He made a sweeping bow to the three of us and walked quietly off in the custody of the detective.

"Really, Mr. Holmes," said Mr. Merryweather as we followed them from the cellar, "I do not know how the bank can thank you or repay you. There is no doubt that you have detected and defeated in the most complete manner one of the most determined attempts at bank robbery that have ever come within my experience."

"I have had one or two little scores of my own to settle with Mr. John Clay," said Holmes. "I have been at some small expense over this matter, which I shall expect the bank to refund, but beyond that I am amply repaid by having had an experience that is in many ways unique, and by hearing the very remarkable narrative of the Red-headed League."

"You see, Watson," he explained in the early hours of the morning as we sat over a drink in Baker Street, "it was perfectly obvious from the first that the only possible object of this rather fantastic business of the advertisement of the League, and the copying of the Encyclopædeia, must be to get this not over-bright pawnbroker out of the way for a number of hours every day. It was a curious way of managing it, but, really, it would be difficult to suggest a better. The method was no doubt suggested to Clay's ingenious mind by the color of his accomplice's hair. The £4 a week was a lure that must draw him, and what was it to them, who were playing for thousands? They put in the advertisement, one rogue has the temporary office, the other rogue incites the man to apply for it, and together they manage to secure his absence every morning in the week. From the time that I heard of the assistant having come for half wages, it was obvious to me that he had some strong motive for securing the situation."

"But how could you guess what the motive was?"

"Had there been women in the house, I should have suspected a mere vulgar intrigue. That, however, was out of the question. The man's business was a small one, and there was nothing in his house that could account for such elaborate preparations, and such an expenditure as they were at. It must, then, be something out of the house. What could it be? I thought of the assistant's fondness for photography, and his trick of vanishing into the cellar. The cellar! There was the end of this tangled clue. Then I made inquiries as to this mysterious assistant and found that I had to deal with one of the coolest and most daring criminals in London. He was doing something in the cellar—something that took many hours a day for months on end. What could it be, once more? I could think of nothing save that he was running a tunnel to some other building.

"So far I had got when we went to visit the scene of action. I surprised you by beating upon the pavement with my stick. I was ascertaining whether the cellar stretched out in front or behind. It was not in front. Then I rang the bell, and, as I hoped, the assistant answered it. We have had some skirmishes, but we had never set eyes upon each other before. I hardly looked at his face. His knees were what I wished to see. You must yourself have remarked how worn, wrinkled, and stained they were. They spoke of those hours of burrowing. The only remaining point was what they were burrowing for. I walked round the corner, saw that the City and Suburban Bank abutted on our friend's premises, and felt that I had solved my problem. When you drove home after the concert, I called upon Scotland Yard and upon the chairman of the bank directors, with the result that you have seen."

"And how could you tell that they would make their attempt tonight?" I asked.

"Well, when they closed their League offices, that was a sign that they cared no longer about Mr. Jabez Wilson's presence—in other words, that they had completed their tunnel. But it was essential that they should use it soon, as it might be discovered, or the bullion might be removed. Saturday would suit them better than any other day, as it would give them two days for their escape. For all these reasons I expected them to come tonight."

"You reasoned it out beautifully," I exclaimed in unfeigned admiration. "It is so long a chain, and yet every link rings true."

"It saved me from ennui," he answered, yawning. "Alas! I already feel it closing in upon me. My life is spent in one long effort to escape from the commonplaces of existence. These little problems help me to do so."

"And you are a benefactor of the race," said I.

He shrugged his shoulders. "Well, perhaps, after all, it is of some little use. 'L'homme c'est rien—l'œuvre c'est tout,'[8] as Gustave Flaubert[9] wrote to George Sand."[10]

---

8. **L'homme c'est rien—l'oeuvre c'est tout** (l'ōm' sä ryan' l'ëvr' sä tū') *French:* Man is nothing—work is everything.

9. **Gustave Flaubert** (flō ber'): French novelist.

10. **George Sand:** pen name of French novelist Aurore Lucie Dupin, Baroness Dudevant.

## Getting at Meaning

1. What is Watson's attitude toward Holmes? What does Watson say and do that makes the attitude clear?

2. Although both Holmes and Watson examine Mr. Wilson's appearance, only Holmes develops accurate conclusions about the man. Why? What is the difference between the powers of observation possessed by Holmes and by Watson?

3. Why does Holmes tell Mr. Wilson, "I don't know that your assistant is not as remarkable as your advertisement"? What is the assistant's main fault? How does this fault connect with the assistant's role in the attempted burglary?

4. When Mr. Wilson sees the hundreds of red-headed men waiting in line, he is ready to give up in despair. Why doesn't he?

5. Mr. Duncan Ross seems delighted to meet Mr. Wilson. How does Mr. Ross convince Mr. Wilson that the red-headed league is legitimate?

6. Why does Mr. Ross emphasize that Mr. Wilson must stay in the office during the entire four hours each day?

7. Why did Mr. Ross and John Clay choose Mr. Wilson for their scheme? What aspect of his personality didn't they anticipate?

8. Why is Holmes excited by Mr. Wilson's description of his assistant? What unique physical features does the assistant possess?

9. Following the visit to Saxe-Coburg Square and its surrounding area, why does Watson feel frustrated?

10. Mr. Merryweather enters the adventure late in the story. What purposes are served by including his character in the story?

11. Although Watson is impressed by the solution of the mystery, Holmes does not seem impressed by his own performance. Why not?

## Developing Skills in Reading Literature

1. **Plot.** Plot is the sequence of events that make up a story. The events must be arranged logically, according to an overall plan, with one event leading to or preparing for another. What does Holmes do after Mr. Wilson's visit? Why? During his visit to Saxe-Coburg Square, Holmes gains certain information. What does this information cause him to do? Could the three major events of the story—Wilson's visit to Holmes, the visit to Saxe-Coburg Square, and the night vigil at the bank—be rearranged? Why or why not?

2. **Conflict.** As a reader becomes involved in the conflict of a story, he or she experiences a deepening interest in its outcome. The skill with which a writer develops conflict determines to a great degree the success of a story in capturing and holding the reader's attention. In a mystery story, the conflict is presented as a puzzle that must be solved by a detective. During Mr. Wilson's visit to Baker Street, how does the writer assure the reader that Holmes is equal to the challenge of Mr. Wilson's case? On the other hand, how does the writer communicate the idea that the case is quite challenging?

3. **Narrator.** Dr. Watson is one of literature's most famous narrators. He faithfully describes the events of a case, but he lacks Holmes's keen ability to interpret the events and to draw accurate conclusions. What do Watson's abilities, as well as his limitations, allow the reader to do? What effect does Watson's role as narrator have upon the reader's impression of Holmes? Explain your answers.

## Developing Vocabulary

**Synonyms.** Synonyms are words that have similar meanings. For instance, Mr. Jabez Wilson is described as *stout, portly* and *obese.* Each of these words means "fat." However, each word also has its own particular shade of meaning. Following are three groups of synonyms. Use each word in a sentence, making sure that the sentence highlights the particular shade of meaning possessed by that word.

| | | |
|---|---|---|
| flexible | snicker | aperture |
| lithe | giggle | slit |
| supple | laugh | chink |

# The Cask of Amontillado

*Edgar Allan Poe*

The thousand injuries of Fortunato I had borne as I best could; but when he ventured upon insult, I vowed revenge. You, who so well know the nature of my soul, will not suppose, however, that I gave utterance to a threat. *At length* I would be avenged; this was a point definitively settled—but the very definitiveness with which it was resolved, precluded the idea of risk. I must not only punish, but punish with impunity. A wrong is unredressed when retribution overtakes its redresser. It is equally unredressed when the avenger fails to make himself felt as such to him who has done the wrong.

It must be understood, that neither by word nor deed had I given Fortunato cause to doubt my good will. I continued, as was my wont, to smile in his face, and he did not perceive that my smile *now* was at the thought of his immolation.[1]

He had a weak point—this Fortunato—although in other regards he was a man to be respected and even feared. He prided himself on his connoisseurship in wine. Few Italians have the true virtuoso spirit. For the most part their enthusiasm is adopted to suit the time and opportunity—to practice imposture upon the British and Austrian millionaires. In painting and gemmary Fortunato, like his countrymen, was a quack—but in the matter of old wines he was sincere. In this respect I did not differ from him materially; I was skilful in the Italian vintages myself, and bought largely whenever I could.

It was about dusk, one evening during the supreme madness of the carnival season, that I encountered my friend. He accosted me with excessive warmth, for he had been drinking much. The man wore motley. He had on a tight-fitting parti-striped dress, and his head was surmounted by the conical cap and bells. I was so pleased to see him that I thought I should never have done wringing his hand.

I said to him, "My dear Fortunato, you are luckily met. How remarkably well you are looking today! But I have received a pipe[2] of what passes for Amontillado,[3] and I have my doubts."

"How?" said he. "Amontillado? A pipe? Impossible! And in the middle of the carnival!"

"I have my doubts," I replied; "and I was silly enough to pay the full Amontillado price without consulting you in the matter. You were not to be found, and I was fearful of losing a bargain."

"Amontillado!"

"I have my doubts."

"Amontillado!"

"And I must satisfy them."

"Amontillado!"

"As you are engaged, I am on my way to Luchesi. If any one has a critical turn, it is he. He will tell me——"

---

1. **immolation** (im′ ə lā′ shən): a sacrificial killing.
2. **pipe**: a cask with a capacity of 126 gallons.
3. **Amontillado** (ə män′ tə lä′ dō): a pale dry sherry.

TWILIGHT IN ROME, 1961. William Thon. National Museum of American Art (formerly National Collection of Fine Arts). Smithsonian Institution. Gift of S. C. Johnson & Son, Inc.

"Luchesi cannot tell Amontillado from Sherry."

"And yet some fools will have it that his taste is a match for your own."

"Come, let us go."

"Whither?"

"To your vaults."

"My friend, no; I will not impose upon your good nature. I perceive you have an engagement. Luchesi——"

"I have no engagement;—come."

"My friend, no. It is not the engagement, but the severe cold with which I perceive you are afflicted. The vaults are insufferably damp. They are encrusted with nitre."[4]

"Let us go, nevertheless. The cold is merely nothing. Amontillado! You have been imposed upon. And as for Luchesi, he cannot distinguish Sherry from Amontillado."

Thus speaking, Fortunato possessed himself of my arm. Putting on a mask of black silk, and drawing a *roquelaire*[5] closely about my person, I suffered him to hurry me to my palazzo.

There were no attendants at home; they had absconded to make merry in honor of the time. I had told them that I should not return until the morning, and had given them explicit orders not to stir from the house. These orders were sufficient, I well knew, to insure their immediate disappearance, one and all, as soon as my back was turned.

I took from their sconces two flambeaux,[6] and giving one to Fortunato, bowed him through several suites of rooms to the archway that led into the vaults. I passed down a long and winding staircase, requesting him to be cautious as he followed. We came at

---

4. **nitre** (nīt' ər): a white, gray, or colorless mineral of potassium nitrate.
5. *roquelaire* (räk' ə lôr'): a man's knee-length cloak, popular during the eighteenth and nineteenth centuries.
6. **flambeaux** (flam' bōz'): lighted torches.

length to the foot of the descent, and stood together on the damp ground of the catacombs of the Montresors.

The gait of my friend was unsteady, and the bells upon his cap jingled as he strode.

"The pipe?" said he.

"It is farther on," said I; "but observe the white web-work which gleams from these cavern walls."

He turned toward me, and looked into my eyes with two filmy orbs that distilled the rheum of intoxication.

"Nitre?" he asked, at length.

"Nitre," I replied. "How long have you had that cough?"

"Ugh! ugh! ugh!—ugh! ugh! ugh!—ugh! ugh! ugh!—ugh! ugh! ugh!—ugh! ugh! ugh!"

My poor friend found it impossible to reply for many minutes.

"It is nothing," he said, at last.

"Come," I said, with decision, "we will go back; your health is precious. You are rich, respected, admired, beloved; you are happy, as once I was. You are a man to be missed. For me it is no matter. We will go back; you will be ill, and I cannot be responsible. Besides, there is Luchesi——"

"Enough," he said; "the cough is a mere nothing; it will not kill me. I shall not die of a cough."

"True—true," I replied; "and, indeed, I had no intention of alarming you unnecessarily; but you should use all proper caution. A draught of this Medoc will defend us from the damps."

Here I knocked off the neck of a bottle that I drew from a long row of its fellows that lay upon the mould.

"Drink," I said, presenting him the wine.

He raised it to his lips with a leer. He paused and nodded to me familiarly, while his bells jingled.

"I drink," he said, "to the buried that repose around us."

"And I to your long life."

He again took my arm, and we proceeded.

"These vaults," he said, "are extensive."

"The Montresors," I replied, "were a great and numerous family."

"I forget your arms."

"A huge human foot d'or, in a field azure; the foot crushes a serpent rampant whose fangs are imbedded in the heel."

"And the motto?"

"*Nemo me impune lacessit.*"[7]

"Good!" he said.

The wine sparkled in his eyes and the bells jingled. My own fancy grew warm with the Medoc. We had passed through walls of piled bones, with casks and puncheons intermingling, into the inmost recesses of the catacombs. I paused again, and this time I made bold to seize Fortunato by an arm above the elbow.

"The nitre!" I said; "see, it increases. It hangs like moss upon the vaults. We are below the river's bed. The drops of moisture trickle among the bones. Come, we will go back ere it is too late. Your cough——"

"It is nothing," he said; "let us go on. But first, another draught of the Medoc."

I broke and reached him a flagon of De Grâve. He emptied it at a breath. His eyes flashed with a fierce light. He laughed and threw the bottle upward with a gesticulation I did not understand.

I looked at him in surprise. He repeated the movement—a grotesque one.

"You do not comprehend?" he said.

"Not I," I replied.

"Then you are not of the brotherhood."

"How?"

"You are not of the masons."

"Yes, yes," I said; "yes, yes."

"You? Impossible! A mason?"

"A mason," I replied.

"A sign," he said.

---

7. **Nemo me impune lacessit** (nee′ mō me im pū′ ne la ses′ it) *Latin:* Nobody provokes me without punishment.

"It is this," I answered, producing a trowel from beneath the folds of my *roquelaire*.

"You jest," he exclaimed, recoiling a few paces. "But let us proceed to the Amontillado."

"Be it so," I said, replacing the tool beneath the cloak, and again offering him my arm. He leaned upon it heavily. We continued our route in search of the Amontillado. We passed through a range of low arches, descended, passed on, and descending again, arrived at a deep crypt, in which the foulness of the air caused our flambeaux rather to glow than flame.

At the most remote end of the crypt there appeared another less spacious. Its walls had been lined with human remains, piled to the vault overhead, in the fashion of the great catacombs of Paris. Three sides of this interior crypt were still ornamented in this manner. From the fourth the bones had been thrown down, and lay promiscuously upon the earth, forming at one point a mound of some size. Within the wall thus exposed by the displacing of the bones, we perceived a still interior recess, in depth about four feet, in width three, in height six or seven. It seemed to have been constructed for no especial use within itself, but formed merely the interval between two of the colossal supports of the roof of the catacombs, and was backed by one of their circumscribing walls of solid granite.

It was in vain that Fortunato, uplifting his dull torch, endeavored to pry into the depth of the recess. Its termination the feeble light did not enable us to see.

"Proceed," I said; "herein is the Amontillado. As for Luchesi——"

"He is an ignoramus," interrupted my friend, as he stepped unsteadily forward, while I followed immediately at his heels. In an instant he had reached the extremity of the niche, and finding his progress arrested by the rock, stood stupidly bewildered. A moment more and I had fettered him to the granite. In its surface were two iron staples, distant from each other about two feet, horizontally. From one of these depended a short chain, from the other a padlock. Throwing the links about his waist, it was but the work of a few seconds to secure it. He was too much astounded to resist. Withdrawing the key I stepped back from the recess.

"Pass your hand," I said, "over the wall; you cannot help feeling the nitre. Indeed it is *very* damp. Once more let me *implore* you to return. No? Then I must positively leave you. But I must first render you all the little attentions in my power."

"The Amontillado!" ejaculated my friend, not yet recovered from his astonishment.

"True," I replied; "the Amontillado."

As I said these words I busied myself among the pile of bones of which I have before spoken. Throwing them aside, I soon uncovered a quantity of building stone and mortar. With these materials and with the aid of my trowel, I began vigorously to wall up the entrance of the niche.

I had scarcely laid the first tier of the masonry when I discovered that the intoxication of Fortunato had in a great measure worn off. The earliest indication I had of this was a low moaning cry from the depth of the recess. It was *not* the cry of a drunken man. There was then a long and obstinate silence. I laid the second tier, and the third, and the fourth; and then I heard the furious vibrations of the chain. The noise lasted for several minutes, during which, that I might hearken to it with the more satisfaction, I ceased my labors and sat down upon the bones. When at last the clanking subsided, I resumed the trowel, and finished without interruption the fifth, the sixth, and the seventh tier. The wall was now nearly upon a level with my breast. I again paused, and holding the flambeaux over the mason-work, threw a few feeble rays upon the figure within.

A succession of loud and shrill screams, bursting suddenly from the throat of the chained form, seemed to thrust me violently back. For a brief moment I hesitated—I trembled. Unsheathing my rapier, I began to grope with it about the recess; but the thought of an instant reassured me. I placed my hand upon the solid fabric of the catacombs, and felt satisfied. I reapproached the wall. I replied to the yells of him who clamored. I re-echoed—I aided—I surpassed them in volume and in strength. I did this, and the clamorer grew still.

It was now midnight, and my task was drawing to a close. I had completed the eighth, the ninth, and the tenth tier. I had finished a portion of the last and the eleventh; there remained but a single stone to be fitted and plastered in. I struggled with its weight; I placed it partially in its destined position. But now there came from out the niche a low laugh that erected the hairs upon my head. It was succeeded by a sad voice, which I had difficulty in recognizing as that of the noble Fortunato. The voice said——

"Ha! ha! ha!—he! he!—a very good joke indeed—an excellent jest. We will have many a rich laugh about it at the palazzo—he! he! he!—over our wine—he! he! he!"

"The Amontillado!" I said.

"He! he he!—he! he! he!—yes, the Amontillado. But is it not getting late? Will not they be awaiting us at the palazzo, the Lady Fortunato and the rest? Let us be gone."

"Yes," I said, "let us be gone."

"*For the love of God, Montresor!*"

"Yes," I said, "for the love of God!"

But to these words I hearkened in vain for a reply. I grew impatient. I called aloud,

"Fortunato!"

No answer. I called again,

"Fortunato!"

No answer still. I thrust a torch through the remaining aperture and let it fall within. There came forth in return only a jingling of the bells. My heart grew sick—on account of the dampness of the catacombs. I hastened to make an end of my labor. I forced the last stone into its position; I plastered it up. Against the new masonry I re-erected the old rampart of bones. For the half of a century no mortal has disturbed them. *In pace requiescat!*[8]

---

8. **In pace requiescat** (in pä' che rek wi es' kat) *Latin:* Rest in peace.

## Getting at Meaning

1. Reread the opening paragraph of this story. According to the narrator, what are two requirements of meaningful revenge?

2. What is Fortunato's one weakness? How does Montresor use this weakness for his revenge?

3. Why is carnival season an ideal time for Montresor to carry out his plan?

4. Why is Montresor's family motto appropriate?

5. Why is Montresor carrying a trowel under his cloak?

6. When Fortunato begins to scream, Montresor hesitates and begins to tremble. Of what is Montresor afraid? How does the thickness of the catacomb walls alleviate his fear?

7. Not only does Montresor seek a horrible revenge, he also seems to enjoy it. Beginning with the point at which Montresor starts to build the wall, find two examples that illustrate his enjoyment of the revenge. What do these examples reveal about Montresor's character?

8. In the final paragraph, Montresor calls to Fortunato, but he hears only the jingling of bells. Where are the bells? What has happened to Fortunato? Traditionally, when is a bell rung for a person? Why does Montresor's heart grow sick? Does this feeling last?

9. All the reader knows is that Fortunato insulted Montresor; no other specifics are given. Given Fortunato's behavior around Montresor, do you think that Fortunato realizes that he has insulted Montresor? From what you know about Montresor's character, what kind of insult might this have been?

## Developing Skills in Reading Literature

1. **Rising Action.** Rising action is that section of plot that builds suspense and leads directly to the climax. The rising action usually begins after the writer gives some background information. What background details does the writer give in the opening paragraphs of this story? Where does the rising action begin? To what climax does the action lead?

2. **Irony.** Verbal irony occurs when a character says one thing but means entirely the opposite. Irony of situation occurs when a character or reader expects one thing to happen but something entirely different happens instead. Dramatic irony occurs when the reader is aware of some fact that a character or characters do not know or when a character says something that the reader knows has a meaning of which the character is totally unaware.

Find eight examples of irony in this story. Either quote an ironic statement or describe an ironic situation. For each example, identify the type of irony being used.

3. **Style.** Style is a writer's own unique way of expressing ideas. Word choice and sentence structure are important elements of style. What kinds of words does the writer of this story use? Describe his sentences.

Next, compare the words and sentences used in this story with those in "The Red-Headed League."

Now, choose either "Act of a Hero" or "Snapshot of a Dog" and contrast the words and sentences in the selection you chose with those in "The Cask of Amontillado."

## Developing Vocabulary

**Prefixes.** These are four of the most common prefixes in English:

*in-* or *im-* meaning "not," "in or into," or "very"
*pre-* meaning "before"
*re-* meaning "again" or "back"
*un-* meaning "not" or "opposite of"

Look up the following five words in the Glossary and define them in terms of their prefixes. For example, *preview* means to "see before."

impunity      unredressed
precluded      insufferably
retribution

## Developing Writing Skills

**Explaining an Idea.** Revenge is a powerful motivator. It is one way that human beings handle anger. Are there any other less hostile ways to deal with anger? What are the alternatives to seeking revenge? In one paragraph, explain the actions that a person who has been wronged or insulted might take instead of seeking revenge.

# Test    *Theodore L. Thomas*

Robert Proctor was a good driver for so young a man. The Turnpike curved gently ahead of him, lightly traveled on this cool morning in May. He felt relaxed and alert. Two hours of driving had not yet produced the fatigue that appeared first in the muscles in the base of the neck. The sun was bright, but not glaring, and the air smelled fresh and clean. He breathed it deeply, and blew it out noisily. It was a good day for driving.

He glanced quickly at the slim, gray-haired woman sitting in the front seat with him. Her mouth was curved in a quiet smile. She watched the trees and the fields slip by on her side of the pike. Robert Proctor immediately looked back at the road. He said, "Enjoying it, Mom?"

"Yes, Robert." Her voice was as cool as the morning. "It is very pleasant to sit here. I was thinking of the driving I did for you when you were little. I wonder if you enjoyed it as much as I enjoy this."

He smiled, embarrassed. "Sure I did."

She reached over and patted him gently on the arm, and then turned back to the scenery.

He listened to the smooth purr of the engine. Up ahead he saw a great truck, spouting a geyser of smoke as it sped along the Turnpike. Behind it, not passing it, was a long blue convertible, content to drive in the wake of the truck. Robert Proctor noted the arrangement and filed it in the back of his mind. He was slowly overtaking them, but he would not reach them for another minute or two.

He listened to the purr of the engine, and he was pleased with the sound. He had tuned that engine himself over the objections of the mechanic. The engine idled rough now, but it ran smoothly at high speed. You needed a special feel to do good work on engines, and Robert Proctor knew he had it. No one in the world had a feel like his for the tune of an engine.

It was a good morning for driving, and his mind was filled with good thoughts. He pulled nearly abreast of the blue convertible and began to pass it. His speed was a few miles per hour above the Turnpike limit, but his car was under perfect control. The blue convertible suddenly swung out from behind the truck. It swung out without warning and struck his car near the right front fender, knocking his car to the shoulder on the left side of the Turnpike lane.

Robert Proctor was a good driver, too wise to slam on the brakes. He fought the steering wheel to hold the car on a straight path. The left wheels sank into the soft left shoulder, and the car tugged to pull to the left and cross the island and enter the lanes carrying the cars heading in the opposite direction. He held it; then the wheel struck a rock buried in the soft dirt, and the left front tire blew out. The car slewed, and it was then that his mother began to scream.

The car turned sideways and skidded part of the way out into the other lanes. Robert Proctor fought against the steering wheel to straighten the car, but the drag of the blown tire was too much. The scream rang steadily

THE CRY, 1895. Edward Munch. Courtesy of The Art Institute of Chicago.

in his ears, and even as he strained at the wheel one part of his mind wondered coolly how a scream could so long be sustained without a breath. An oncoming car struck his radiator from the side and spun him viciously, full into the left-hand lanes.

He was flung into his mother's lap, and she was thrown against the right door. It held. With his left hand he reached for the steering wheel and pulled himself erect against the force of the spin. He turned the wheel to the left, and tried to stop the spin and careen out of the lanes of oncoming traffic. His mother was unable to right herself; she lay against the door, her cry rising and falling with the eccentric spin of the car.

The car lost some of its momentum. During one of the spins he twisted the wheel straight, and the car wobblingly stopped spinning and headed down the lane. Before Robert Proctor could turn it off the pike to safety, a car loomed ahead of him, bearing down on him. There was a man at the wheel of that other car, sitting rigid, unable to move, eyes wide and staring and filled with fright. Alongside the man was a girl, her head against the back of the seat, soft curls framing a lovely face, her eyes closed in easy sleep. It was not the fear in the man that reached into Robert Proctor; it was the trusting helplessness in the face of the sleeping girl. The two cars sped closer to each other, and Robert Proctor could not change the direction of his car. The driver of the other car remained frozen at the wheel. At the last moment Robert Proctor sat motionless, staring into the face of the onrushing, sleeping girl, his mother's cry still sounding in his ears. He heard no crash when the two cars collided head-on at a high rate of speed. He felt something push into his stomach, and the world began to go gray. Just before he lost consciousness he heard the scream stop, and he knew then that he had been hearing a single, short-lived scream that had only seemed to drag on and on. There came a painless wrench, and then darkness.

Robert Proctor seemed to be at the bottom of a deep black well. There was a spot of faint light in the far distance, and he could hear the rumble of a distant voice. He tried to pull himself toward the light and the sound, but the effort was too great. He lay still and gathered himself and tried again. The light grew brighter and the voice louder. He tried harder, again, and he drew closer. Then he opened his eyes full and looked at the man sitting in front of him.

"You all right, Son?" asked the man. He wore a blue uniform, and his round, beefy face was familiar.

Robert Proctor tentatively moved his head, and discovered he was seated in a reclining chair, unharmed, and able to move his arms and legs with no trouble. He looked around the room, and he remembered.

The man in the uniform saw the growing intelligence in his eyes and he said, "No harm done, Son. You just took the last part of your driver's test."

Robert Proctor focused his eyes on the man. Though he saw the man clearly, he seemed to see the faint face of the sleeping girl in front of him.

The uniformed man continued to speak. "We put you through an accident under hypnosis—do it to everybody these days before they can get their drivers' licenses. Makes better drivers of them, more careful drivers the rest of their lives. Remember it now? Coming in here and all?"

Robert Proctor nodded, thinking of the sleeping girl. She never would have awakened; she would have passed right from a sweet, temporary sleep into the dark heavy sleep of death, nothing in between. His mother would have been bad enough; after all, she was pretty old. The sleeping girl was downright waste.

The uniformed man was still speaking. "So you're all set now. You pay me the ten dollar fee, and sign this application, and we'll have your license in the mail in a day or two." He did not look up.

Robert Proctor placed a ten dollar bill on the table in front of him, glanced over the application and signed it. He looked up to find two white-uniformed men, standing one on each side of him, and he frowned in annoyance. He started to speak, but the uniformed man spoke first. "Sorry, Son. You failed. You're sick; you need treatment."

The two men lifted Robert Proctor to his feet, and he said, "Take your hands off me. What is this?"

The uniformed man said, "Nobody should want to drive a car after going through what you just went through. It should take months before you can even think of driving again, but you're ready right now. Killing people doesn't bother you. We don't let your kind run around loose in society any more. But don't you worry now, Son. They'll take good care of you, and they'll fix you up." He nodded to the two men, and they began to march Robert Proctor out.

At the door he spoke, and his voice was so urgent the two men paused. Robert Proctor said, "You can't really mean this. I'm still dreaming, aren't I? This is still part of the test, isn't it?"

The uniformed man said, *"How do any of us know?"* And they dragged Robert Proctor out of the door, knees stiff, feet dragging, his rubber heels sliding along the two grooves worn into the floor.

## Getting at Meaning

1. What specific personal information does the reader learn about Robert Proctor in the opening paragraph? How does Robert's attitude toward driving relate to his age?

2. Robert is proud of his ability to tune an engine. How are his pride and the quality of his work related to his youth?

3. Reread the description of the accident from the time that the blue convertible swings into the path of Robert's car until he loses consciousness. Evaluate Robert's performance. Is he a good driver? Explain your answer.

4. After Robert regains consciousness, he has a conversation with a uniformed man. What important new information does the reader gain from this conversation? What seems to be the man's attitude toward Robert?

5. As Robert thinks of his mother and the sleeping girl, what does he reveal about his own personality? What does he seem to value?

6. Why doesn't the uniformed man look up as he asks for Robert's ten dollar fee and signature?

7. Why does Robert fail his driving test?

8. What may have caused the "two grooves worn into the floor?"

## Developing Skills in Reading Literature

1. **Conflict.** The conflict in a story may be presented early in the narrative. What is the conflict implied in the opening sentence, "Robert Proctor was a good driver for so young a man"? How does Robert's attitude toward his mother and toward his ability as a mechanic help to develop this conflict?

2. **Science Fiction.** Science fiction is a type of literature in which the writer uses extrapolation, the imaginative leap from what is to what might be, to create a story. Science fiction stories are often full of surprises, because of sudden twists or unexpected turns in the plot. As you began reading this story, how did you expect the plot to develop? What might have happened to Robert and his mother? What effect does the introduction of the uniformed man have upon the plot? Considering the title and the way the man speaks to Robert, did you assume that Robert had passed his test? What is the final twist in the plot?

3. **Indeterminate Ending.** The plot of a story generally presents a conflict, then develops and resolves it. Occasionally, however, the ending of a story leaves the reader with a question instead of an answer. When Robert asks, "This is still part of the test, isn't it?" he does not receive a definite answer. What do the comment ". . . they'll fix you up" and the reference to the grooves in the floor suggest about Robert's fate?

## Developing Writing Skills

**Using Precise Verbs.** In this story, the writer's use of precise verbs helps to create a vivid experience for the reader. The convertible *swung out;* Robert *fought* the steering wheel, but the car *tugged* to the left. Then the car *slewed* and *skidded.* Even though he tried to *careen* out of the lanes of oncoming traffic, Robert was too late; a car *loomed* ahead of him. Choose an activity in which control of your actions is important; for example, roller-skating, riding a bicycle, playing soccer. Then, write one paragraph in which you describe the activity, using precise verbs to make your description vivid.

# Point of Departure     *Leland Webb*

That summer Mary Dru Conroy was half way between thirteen and fourteen. She had dozed off in the warm weather of childhood and had been roughly awakened into an uncertain climate peopled by dim half strangers. Each day she moved in a mingling of curiosity and dread and dream, looking for her place, her purpose.

She spent much of her time staring out of windows or lying on the sofa and looking up at the ceiling. There were nights when she went to bed immediately after supper and slept until noon of the next day. On other nights her light was on past midnight and in the morning her early-rising father would find her up before him.

"My poor baby," her mother said. "I had planned to teach her to cook, maybe to sew, this summer, but she suddenly seems to have forgotten even how to hold a dust mop."

"I meant to teach her to drive and get her a restricted license for her fourteenth birthday," her father said. "But not now. I'm afraid of those faraway, dreamy eyes."

"I think you ought to take her to a psychiatrist," her older brother said. "Or wait a while longer and we can all go, and get a family rate."

The family had settled down to endure, like a town under siege, when rescue came. Great-aunt Drusilla Conroy sent word from downstate that she had taken a bad fall and dislocated her hip. She needed a member of her family to run errands, to read to her, to talk to her; she had chosen her namesake, Mary Dru. Since there was no precedent of a Conroy's refusing Great-aunt Drusilla, the family prepared to drive down and deliver Mary Dru to her.

But Mary Dru came back into the family suddenly. "No," she said. "I want to go down on the bus by myself."

"That's hardly practical," her father said. "It's much too far for you to go alone at your age."

"And there's a change of buses at Indian Springs," her brother said. "You'd get on the wrong bus."

But her mother had taken a long look at her, and she said, "Oh, I think it may be quite all right." She added, "We must begin somewhere, I suppose."

At the bus station Mary Dru insisted on buying her own ticket and checking her baggage. When her bus was announced, she offered her cheek to her brother and father, then kissed her mother, all with grave formality. She boarded the bus, and from her seat by the window she looked down at them on the platform and smiled as if to encourage them.

"I should have asked the driver to look out for her," her father said. "But she looked so grown-up, I knew she'd get mad." In a moment of baffled helplessness that morning he had given her fifty dollars in private. "Just in case . . ." he had said, not knowing how to finish the sentence.

"Say, that little old Mary Dru's about a bird and a third in stockings and high-heeled shoes," her brother mocked, and marveled at her. . . . The bus was moving and Mary Dru was waving, and then she was gone.

The deputy sheriff saw the boy walking down the road at sunrise and again at mid-morning. He had seen him for the first time yesterday, fifteen miles down the highway. He thought, The kid should be out of the county by noontime; and then he thought, It's nothing to do with me. He was profoundly irritated at himself when he stopped and said, "Get in, bub—I'll ride you to the county line."

The boy got in and shut the door. He sat on the edge of the seat, one hand on the door handle. He looked straight down the road.

"Got a name?" the deputy sheriff asked as the car moved on. "Going somewhere or running from somewhere—which?"

The boy licked his lips quickly but made no other sign that he had heard.

"See you got a tongue even if you haven't learned to use it," the deputy sheriff said. "Saw you when you was thrown off the cabbage truck you rode into the county on. Didn't catch a ride yesterday, did you? Spent the night in the woods, didn't you?"

He judged the boy to be maybe fifteen but ready to swear to sixteen, and tall enough to get away with it. He figured him to be running away—from an orphans' home or a juvenile court order, or maybe just a firetrap in some big city—but running away, not headed for any place in particular. He thought, Beat him with a belt from now until sundown and he'd never say one true, loving word.

"Ain't going to catch a ride today either," he said after a while. "As a gospel fact, you ain't going to catch a ride until you get 100 miles or so down the state. Last week a hitchhiker killed an old man in Boree County, which is the next county down the road a

little ways. They caught the kid who did it, but folks are all jumpy now and scared to death of hitchhiking kids. Inside an hour after you cross the county line, you'll be picked up so that they can send you back where you belong. But they ain't in no hurry, and they'll jail you a spell before they get around to it. So why don't you turn around and head back where you come from?"

He had tried to tell the boy, and that was all a mortal man could do. But you couldn't tell these big city rats anything—they were tough and as dumb as they were tough, and bound and determined to go on and get their hard licks. And it had nothing to do with him—nothing.

At the county line he stopped the car. As the boy moved he said, "Wait up, bub." He fished in his rear pocket, hauled out his billfold, pulled out a five-dollar bill and stuffed it into the boy's shirt pocket. "All right—get out," he said.

And the boy was gone, seeming to go through the door with it still closed. The deputy sheriff closed his eyes and said over and over, "It's no business of mine," and then he heard the sound of feet pounding back down the road. He opened his eyes and looked directly into the boy's pale blue ones.

"Why?" the boy said.

It was a fair question, and one the deputy sheriff intended to ask himself when he got around to it. He looked in the rearview mirror and saw the bus coming and thought, Well, the cavalry always comes just when the Indians make the last attack on the settlement. He jerked his head toward the bus and gave the boy a push away from the window.

"Run!" he said. "Catch it! Ride it clear through Boree County. Don't stand, bub—run!"

The boy turned and ran and threw up his

hand to wave, but the bus went by with a roar. The boy ran after it, not yelling or waving, just running, and the bus went on 1000 yards or more down the road and then stopped. The deputy sheriff had already turned his car around and was headed back down the highway. He saw the boy for the last time in the rearview mirror as he boarded the bus.

Mary Dru had shouted on impulse and conviction—a boy was running down the road to catch the bus, and that was what a bus was for, to stop when people wanted to get on it. She had amazed herself. She had scrambled down the aisle, yelling like a demon, "Stop this bus! There's somebody back there who wants to get on! Stop!" Then she returned to her seat, tremendously embarrassed.

She watched him get on with a mildly proprietary interest. She heard the bus driver ask him where he was going, and the boy didn't answer. She thought, He doesn't have any money, but then she saw the bill in the boy's hand. The driver asked again and ground the gears as he started the bus off with a lurch.

"Far as this will take me," the boy said loudly, shoving the bill at the driver. He turned to find a seat.

"Okay. That'll be Indian Springs," the driver said.

The boy came down the aisle and passed her, and then he came back and sat down beside her. She felt an obscure satisfaction that the only vacant seat was by her. She decided to speak to him. It seemed to her to be her duty; he was her good deed and in a sense she was responsible for him.

"I'm going to Indian Springs too," she said, and smiled.

He looked at her. There was nothing whatever in his look, as though she were not anything he considered worth the trouble of looking at or not looking at.

"Go ahead," he said. "I ain't stopping you."

She had been dismissed. He did not wish her to speak to him and he did not wish to speak to her. This was a reasonable attitude, one she had frequently taken herself. She came to a swift conclusion—she had loathed and despised him on sight. It was a brand-new sensation and she found it exhilarating.

His hair, she thought, is too long . . . and what color are his eyes? He had turned away quickly; she wanted to nudge him and make him turn back. And why did he wear a jacket in the summertime? And what about that scar—how did he get that deep, jagged line across his chin? And why did she care anyway? She dismissed him altogether—and then was appalled by a sudden discovery about him.

He smelled.

The smell was faint but unmistakable, a smell that once had been quite rank. But what did he smell of? She breathed in lightly, to isolate and identify this smell. Finally she got it. She leaned toward him.

"Why do you smell like cabbage?" she asked.

He stiffened and turned toward her slowly. His eyes were blue, a very pale blue. They were uninteresting eyes, but she saw in them that she had reached inside him.

"I hooked a ride on this truck night before last," he said. He spoke rapidly, in low, even tones. "It was loaded down with cabbages. I had to scrooch down under the cabbages so the guy that owned the truck wouldn't see me. Some of them cabbages wasn't in very good shape. Is that what you wanted to know?"

She faltered before the hostility in his look. "I guess so," she said.

"So now you know," he said, and turned away.

She looked again out the window. There was nothing more to say. This clod, this oaf, this *person*, would ride beside her all the way to Indian Springs, silent and smelling of cabbage. Her journey to Great-aunt Drusilla, which she had seen as a voyage in absolute solitude, free of her stifling, narrowing family, was now ruined. Furiously she began to read, heavy with awareness of him sitting by her like some bleak, jagged stone.

Finally she decided she was hungry. Her mother had prepared a picnic lunch for her, ignoring her outraged protest that she could eat in a bus-stop restaurant; the basket lay at her feet. She opened it and found fried chicken and deviled eggs and potato salad and a big slice of chocolate cake and two enormous pickles. She unwrapped the foil from around a piece of chicken, grateful that her mother never paid any attention to her, and began to eat.

Later she remembered that her stomach was the first part of her to react. Far, far ahead of her brain there was a sudden tightening of her stomach muscles that caused her chewing to slow and finally stop. Then she had a feeling of panic that she could not swallow, and her throat contracted violently. He was watching her eat.

Without turning, without a sidelong glance, she knew that he was staring at the half-eaten drumstick in her hand and that he was hungry—he was trembling and shaking with *hunger*. The word was suddenly hideous and enormous in her mind.

Dumbly she pondered what to do. If she turned and invited him to share with her, what would he do? Close his eyes again? Or say something ugly and return back into himself? She knew he would. But he was hungry and he must be fed. Her mind wheeled and circled around the problem of this person, this human being, who had to eat and would not eat.

Finally she gave up thinking, and as soon as she did she knew what to do. She reached down for the basket and placed it on the seat between them. She drew a paper napkin out of the basket and put a piece of chicken on it and put it on his lap. She left the top of the basket open. She then looked out the window and sternly banished every image of the boy from her mind. She set her jaw and willed herself into total insignificance. She was no longer really there; she did not really exist; so what could it possibly matter if somebody ate her food?

When her instinct told her that he had eaten the first piece of chicken, she got out another piece and placed it on his lap. After the second piece she knew he would not be able to stop eating, and she opened her magazine again. It was most important that she read—really read, not just pretend to. She turned to an article on hairdos and surrendered her attention to it.

She had no need to look at him to know that he was crying very quietly. It was all right; he had eaten every scrap of food and now he must cry until he was finished. Until then he was no concern of hers. She was surprised when he spoke.

"Man, I was hungry," he said. "I ain't eat in three, four days."

I ain't eat in three, four days, she thought —I haven't eaten in three or four days. Saying it the way he said it meant he was an uneducated person. It also made him sound hungrier. Instinctively she moved to change the subject before embarrassment set in.

"I'm Mary Drusilla Conroy," she said. "I'm named for a great-aunt. My family, most people, call me Mary Dru, but at school the girls call me Con or Conroy. We have this thing of calling each other by our last names. I can't say I like it so very much, but you know how things get started in a girls' school." Oh, please shut up, she said to herself. Bravely she asked, "What is your name?"

He hesitated. "J. C. Holtzclaw," he said reluctantly. "That's some lousy name, ain't it?"

She considered his name carefully. "Well, it's not handsome," she said, "but it sounds quick and strong and sort of tough. Holtzclaw. I've never heard it before. Conroy's not an unusual name. What does the J. C. stand for?"

"Nothing," he said. "That's all they gave me, just a lousy J and a lousy C that don't stand for nothing."

Who were *they*? She immediately did not like them. What if she had been named M. D. Conroy? She agreed with him. It was a lousy name and there was nothing that could be done about it. . . .

"Oh, no—just think!" she said. "You can pick out your own name. Everyone else is absolutely stuck with the name their parents gave them, but you can have any name you want. Beginning with a J and a C, of course."

She had caught him. "I never thought of that," he said. "I wouldn't ever thought of that. You're not such a dumb kid; you know that?"

"I do not happen to be a kid, dumb or otherwise," she said. "I happen to be fifteen and a half." She was appalled that she was not appalled by her lie.

"Get off your ear," he said. "What's some good names starting with a J and a C?"

"John and James and Joseph and Charles and Calvin and Clifford," she said. "There are lots more, but that's a start. But it would work better if you picked out the name you would like to be called by, like John or Christopher, and then match it up with the other initial."

"John Christopher," he said. "John Christopher Holtzclaw. John C. Holtzclaw." His face darkened. "I don't know. There's probably a law against it."

"That's not so," she said. "People go to court and have their names legally changed all the time, and sometimes their whole names, last names as well as first."

"No, you can't change nothing," he said flatly. "If you get stuck with J. C., you're stuck. It's the way everything is."

"That isn't true," she said. But she was not sure. He might be right. But if so, it was the saddest thing she'd ever heard.

And the conversation, begun so well and promising so much, had ended. He had slipped back inside himself, his face sullen, his eyes half closed. If she spoke to him, he would not answer. She felt cheated, not by him or by herself, but by something larger than both of them. Then he opened his eyes and looked at her.

"Mary Drusilla Conroy," he said carefully, as though committing her name to memory. "Drusilla." His face was very thoughtful. "Silla," he said. His mouth softened at the corners and there was a quick flicker in his eyes. "I'll call you Silla. Where you going, Silla?"

"To Indian Springs," she said. "I change buses there and go on to Fort Wellington. There's no fort there; no one knows why it's called that. Maybe it was named for the Duke of Wellington, or perhaps someone named Wellington founded it. But nobody knows now."

"We can ride to Indian Springs together, then," he said. He spoke in a rush. "That's as far as we can go, but we can go that far."

He looked away from her, tensing violently. She remained perfectly still. He reached down and took her hand in his. He sat back in his seat and looked toward the front of the bus, his face disassociated from his hand holding hers so tightly and then so gently. And then he laid his head back and closed his eyes and went to sleep.

She was taken by surprise, and in a dismay she thought, Oh, please open your eyes—I've forgotten what color they are. And then she was obscurely and enormously pleased and she laid her cheek against the back of her seat. To watch him sleep seemed as inevitable as his going to sleep. He had not eaten, and she had fed him; he had not been sleeping because he had been afraid to close his eyes, but with her hand in his, he was not afraid.

Within and far off, voices spoke.

"Conroy, look at him," the girls at school said. "His clothes are dirty, his face is dirty, his hands are dirty, and he smells of cabbage. Sincerely, Con, you have gone psycho. Indubitably you have."

"Hey, dopey, watch out," her brother said. "Who do you think you are, Florence Nightingale?"

"I don't like the looks of this at all, Dewdrop," her father said. "It seems to me that you've forgotten everything you've ever been taught."

And her mother was silent and watchful and the expression on her face could not be read.

But what color were his eyes? She was ashamed because she could not remember. He was so slender she could almost see his bones through his pale skin, and his hair was all straggly down his neck and he was rather an all-over mess, really, but what color were his eyes? And the way he looked at her—was it bold or shy? Cruel or kind? She liked the way he looked at her and she did not like the way he looked at her, and pondering this she began to doze. And then she roused and said aloud. "Blue!" and she went to sleep.

She awoke as the bus was pulling into the station at Indian Springs. He was awake; his expression was glum. They were no longer holding hands, and she could not evoke her feelings of just before her nap. That they should have slept at all seemed sad and unfair, as though a promise had been made and withdrawn in the same breath.

"I have to wait an hour before the bus leaves for Fort Wellington," she said. "Will you wait with me until it comes?"

He didn't answer until they were off the bus. "Sure," he said. "I ain't in a rush."

"We can talk," she said. "We can become better acquainted."

"Yeah, sure, better acquainted," he said.

He was barely listening to her. He was looking about the small waiting room as though expecting someone. He froze momentarily when he saw a policeman on the sidewalk in front of the station.

"He's not going to bother you," she said. "You haven't done anything wrong, have you?"

He gave her a brief look. "Yeah, I committed a big crime," he said. "I got born."

They saw an empty bench and sat down. She was aware that he turned slightly so that he could see the policeman. She decided to ignore it.

"Okay, let's get acquainted," he said. "Tell me your whole life story, all the exciting parts."

She flushed at the cutting edge in his voice. Why should he want to make her feel small? She looked down at her lap.

"I really haven't had an exciting life up to now," she said quietly. "I've always lived in the same house in the same city; this is the first time I've gone anywhere by myself. My father owns a lumber company—not an awfully big one, but he owns it, anyway. I have an older brother who goes away to college in the fall. I go to a private school for girls. I have several close acquaintances but no real friends. I—"

She stopped, bored by her dreary autobiography. She had a curious feeling that it made no difference what she said or what he said. He was working himself up to something and there was nothing to do but wait until it happened. Abruptly she decided to be bold.

"Tell me about you," she said. "You know —where you come from, where you're going, and what you'll do when you get there. All that, and why. I always like to know why."

She could tell from his eyes that the policeman had moved away from the window. And suddenly she read his intentions in his face.

"I'm going to Miami Beach," he said. "My old man owns nine hundred hotels there, great big ones, but he owns them. He sent me a money order for eleven thousand dollars for traveling money but I blew it all in a crap game. I could've got all the money I needed, of course, from my sister Doris Day or my big brother Mickey Mantle, but what the heck, I figure my old man'll get a charge when I tell him about my exciting adventures. You know, hooking rides, sleeping behind filling stations, and bumming fried chicken from little girls who feel sorry for me."

She felt serene and remote, as though all this were a movie she was seeing for the second time.

"Why don't you get off *your* ear?" she said, and, inspired, added, "Tell me how you got the scar on your chin."

He looked quickly about the half-empty waiting room. He looked again toward the window where the policeman had been. He turned and stared at her, and his expression was exactly the same as it had been just before he seized her hand in his. He licked his lips and she braced herself. She gave only a small start as he snatched her purse from her lap; and as he went across the waiting room toward the side exit, she watched him with only a mild concern that no one else should notice him.

She thought, speaking to her father, to her brother, to her friends, to whomever it might concern—What else could he do but steal my money?

The mood of waking dream persisted until he was out the door, and then she was on her feet and running after him. She saw him as soon as she got outside, and it was no longer a movie full of suspense with the inevitable happy ending. He had got no farther than the street corner. The policeman had come up and was talking to him and reaching for the handbag.

She knew that J. C. was going to run, and when he ran he would be caught, and when he was caught he would go to jail. She kicked off her high heels, picked them up in her hands and ran down to the corner in her stocking feet, shouting as she ran.

"I'm going to kill you, J. C. Holtzclaw, you devil!" she yelled as she came sailing up to the corner. She began to beat him on the shoulder with the heel of one shoe.

"Hold it! Hold it!" the policeman said, and seized her arm. "Now, then, what's going on here? This boy steal your purse, young lady?"

"I never seen her before," J. C. said, but his face was stony with despair.

People were flocking around them. She put her shoes back on quickly. There was no time for her thoughts to catch up with her tongue.

"What are you doing with my purse, then, J. C. Holtzclaw, if you never saw me before?" she said. She turned to the policeman angrily. "Yes, he stole my purse, and he's stolen it in every station we've been in so far. Listen, he's just mad because my father wouldn't trust him with the money or the tickets. But look at him—would you trust him? And if he doesn't get on the next bus to Miami and if I don't get on the bus to Fort Wellington, he's going to be in trouble with my father, that's all, and so am I. Can't you beat him with your club or something and make him behave?"

The policeman thought it wildly unlikely that these kids knew each other, so wildly unlikely that it must be true. In all his long experience he had never encountered a purse snatcher who was known by name to his victim. Somewhere, he thought, there is an otherwise intelligent, levelheaded parent who thought it perfectly sensible to send this child off on a bus journey with the likes of this boy. It made his blood run cold when he contemplated the unbelievable actions of respectable people. And he looked at the girl. He estimated that she could, and would, talk forever, and that it would take nearly all day to find out what really was going on here.

"Honey, if he's supposed to get on the next bus to Miami, he'll be on it," he said. "And you'll be on the Fort Wellington bus. Now, buddy, hand her back her purse. And let's all three of us go back in the bus station and sit until the buses come."

They sat side by side in the bus station. The policeman sat on a bench across from them reading a newspaper. He hardly gave them a glance but managed still to convey the impression of watchfulness.

J. C. was holding her hand; there was nothing he could do about anything as long as the policeman was there.

"Listen," he said. "You think because you gave me a handout that you own me, or something?"

"Oh, shut up," she said. "I didn't give you a handout. I shared my lunch with you. I don't know why you have to be so dumb. You don't want to trust anybody. You're afraid, that's what's wrong with you—do you know that?"

"You got anything else you want to preach about?" he said. "You got some more laws you want to lay down to get me straight?"

"No, you're too dumb to learn," she said. "I want you to tell me how you got the scar on your chin."

"Honest to Pete," he said, and shut his eyes in fury. "Okay—why not? It's a real cute story. You see, my old man's a real jolly kind of a guy who likes to sit in the kitchen at night, sometimes *all* night, and cuss out the world and throw stuff against the kitchen wall. And one night I just happened to come in the kitchen right at the time he heaved a

can. It got me right on the chin. And the funny thing, the real cute part, the can was full. My old man can get pretty jolly sometimes in the kitchen, but that's the only time he ever threw a *full* can."

"And your mother?" she said. "What did she say?"

He opened his eyes and considered her. "It was on Saturday night," he said. "She always came home a little later on Saturday night."

She wanted to press his hand or to cry, or both together, but the bus to Fort Wellington was due and she had to take as many short cuts as possible.

"You know what you ought to do?" she said. "You ought to just leave your family. I mean it. Just go away from them and not ever have anything to do with them at all."

"I guess I'm dumb, like you say," he said. "I got this real way-out idea I *am* running away."

"No, you're not," she said. "You're carrying them around with you all the time. They got on the bus with you and they're sitting here on this bench right now. And it seems to me that you just can't wait until you sit in a kitchen and throw some cans up against the wall yourself."

"Well, I ain't got plans for buying up a lumber company, that's for sure," he said.

"That's right, you *ain't,*" she said. "You think I'm me and you're you because my father owns a little old lumber company and yours doesn't, don't you? But that's not true. I'm something else besides the family I was born into, or what has happened to me, or will ever happen to me—I don't know what I am, but I know that I'm different from anybody else who ever lived. But you, you don't want to be a—a *person,* do you? You'd rather mope along and feel sorry for yourself because that's easier. And that's all I have to say about it, and you can simply go to the devil for all I care."

"Okay, okay, I won't be a bum if you don't

like the idea," he said. "I tell you what—I'll get rich. I'll make about a ton of money and I'll hire some wise joker to educate me, and then when I'm one of these *persons* you keep blowing about, I'll come rolling up the driveway of your house in a swanky convertible and you and me—" He broke off and squeezed her hand. "Oh, kid," he said. "Oh, Silla, what's the use?"

She leaned forward to speak, but the announcer began to call the bus for Fort Wellington.

"Will you kiss me?" she said. "I haven't ever been kissed. Not by anybody that counts. I don't even know what it's like. Please?"

"What kind of a dumb joke is that?" he said angrily, and then he said, "Look, you can't go around asking just any guy you run into . . ."

The kiss was not a long one, nor was it much of a kiss. There was too much trouble in him and too much expectation in her. But when it was over there was no further pretense of striving between them. Awkwardly they got up and moved out to the departure platform.

"Look, I ain't got any money," he said. "Can you give me some money to get a ticket on the bus? Ain't no use to say I'm borrowing. Just give it to me."

"You've got money," she said. "Five ten-dollar bills. I put them in your shirt pocket when you kissed me."

He shook his head. "You know what?" he said. "You'll whip the world. Easy. You got it outnumbered, that's all."

"So will you," she said. "Just don't get back on your high horse when you leave here."

He made a face. "No, I ain't going to whip it," he said. "But I might not let it whip me. I might stand it to a draw."

At her bus he took her hand again. "I wish it was just you and me and nobody else," he said. "Just you and me going place to place.

But it ain't. You got to leave, and me—I don't know what I've got to do. Go on bumming, I guess, until I find a place or learn a way to quit bumming. But that don't make no difference now, you hear? Right now it's eating me up and I can't help it, but it's okay. You believe it?"

"It won't matter, if you don't forget about me," she said. "Because it wouldn't be fair if I remembered you and you forgot about me."

He shook his head and let her hand go, but she clung to his. She reached out with her other hand and touched his face, tracing the scar across his chin. Then she let go of him.

"So long, Silla," he said.

"So long. So long, John Christopher Holtzclaw," she said, and watched his face anxiously.

He frowned and backed away a step. His lips moved, shaping the name—his name? He shrugged and gave her a half smile as if to say, "Maybe—I'll have to wear it for a while to see if it fits me." Then he turned and went back into the bus station.

She watched him go. When he turned toward the ticket counter she saw that his lips were still moving. As she boarded her bus, her lips were moving also.

The policeman was unaware of the tremendous event that had happened under his nose. Because he had said that he would, he stayed in the bus station until the boy got on the Miami bus, and then he returned to his regular duties. Within an hour the boy and girl had become just two kids in an anecdote illustrating the silly, unnecessary side of a policeman's life. He would tell the story two or three times and forget it.

The deputy sheriff would never mention the boy at all; there are some things in this world a man cannot afford to think about and go on living. He had given the boy $5 out of a bitter understanding that no one had ever before given him anything but a curse or a cuff. But he knew that $5 will not buy much in this world, no more than safe passage through Boree County. The world is wide and there are many dark patches in it.

But the girl had done a thing beyond calculation. With one foot still planted in childhood and the other gingerly advancing into womanhood, she had interposed herself between a boy and the world for a brief moment and said, "Leave him alone; he belongs to me." And she shifted the odds against him from a million to zero to a million to one.

The boy rode on to Miami, where nothing and nobody awaited him. He slept most of the way, waking from time to time to stare at the night rushing by outside the window. By the time the bus reached Miami a change had occurred in him, so small it was unnoticed by him. The name John Christopher Holtzclaw fitted him like his skin.

Great-aunt Drusilla Conroy lay in bed like a benign old mountain and laughed and laughed. She laughed about the cabbages and she laughed about the picnic lunch and especially she laughed about the purse-snatching.

Mary Dru found that she did not mind the old woman's laughter; it made a sort of shield behind which her own thoughts and feelings could hide.

"I couldn't very well let him get away with my purse, Aunt Drusilla," she explained. "My bus ticket was in my purse, and I was afraid if the policeman dragged him off to jail, it might be hours before I could get it back."

"Oh, you goose, you," Great-aunt Drusilla said. "I hope you learned a lesson from him."

Mary Dru regarded her aunt with the gravely amused tolerance possible only to the very young when they contemplate the very old. Someday, she thought, she would be as old as Great-aunt Drusilla, and as wise and as foolish, which was just as wise and as foolish as she felt right at this moment in her life. A boy had held her hand; a boy had kissed her. He had not wanted to; he had even been afraid to; but he could not help himself. The cold, dry, meaningless facts of life had been transplanted into some sort of working truth. Instinctively she sensed danger ahead for her, a danger equal to the pleasure and inseparable from it, but nothing to fear if you were brave and honest.

She smiled. "He gave me something to think about," she said. "And I'll bet I gave him something to think about in return."

**Getting at Meaning**

1. Reread the first two paragraphs. What is Mary Dru's problem?

2. Why is the deputy sheriff irritated at himself for giving J.C. a ride? Near the end of the story, the sheriff is mentioned again. The narrator says, "The deputy sheriff would never mention the boy at all; there are some things in this world a man cannot afford to think about and go on living." Why can't the sheriff afford to think about J.C.? What does he imagine will happen to J.C.?

3. When he first sits beside her, Mary Dru asks J.C. why he smells like cabbage, and then looking into his eyes, she sees that "she has reached inside him." What does it mean to reach inside some-

one? Why does Mary Dru's question have such an effect on J.C.?

4. J.C. cries after eating Mary Dru's lunch? Why? How does his crying affect the reader's view of J.C.?

5. Describe the change that comes over J.C. in the bus station. What has caused this change?

6. In what way is J.C. "carrying his parents around with him"?

7. How is J.C. changed by his encounter with Mary Dru? How is Mary Dru changed? Reread the next to the last paragraph of the story. What does the narrator mean by the statement, "The cold, dry, meaningless facts of life had been transplanted into some sort of working truth."? How does this statement help to explain the change in Mary Dru?

## Developing Skills in Reading Literature

1. **Title and Theme.** The title of this story gives the reader a clue to the main idea that the writer is trying to communicate. Explain the significance of the title for Mary Dru and for J.C. What idea does the writer convey in this story?

2. **Exposition.** Exposition consists in passages of prose that provide the reader with the background information necessary for understanding setting, character, and conflict. The exposition in this story is quite long for a short story, and it is presented in two parts. Where does the first part of the exposition end? What information has the reader learned? Where does the second part end? What information has the reader learned?

3. **Metaphor.** A metaphor is an implied comparison. For example, a narrator might describe a cold house by saying, "The house was a refrigerator." This statement implies that the house is cold without stating the fact directly.

Reread the opening paragraph of the story. Think about the metaphor that the writer uses to describe Mary Dru's age. To help you identify this metaphor, complete the following:

Childhood is _____.
Young adulthood is _____.

Write your own metaphors to describe the following:
a stuffy classroom
a dripping ice cream cone
weekends

## Developing Vocabulary

**Slang.** Slang is informal language that changes rapidly; the slang expressions that you use today might sound outdated by next year. List some slang words or expressions that you once used but that you no longer use. Now list several slang words or expressions that you use often.

Rewrite the following slang expressions from the story in your own slang:

1. "Say, that little old Mary Dru's about a bird and a third in stockings and high-heeled shoes."

2. "Get off your ear."

3. "Sincerely, Con, you have gone psycho."

4. "Just don't get back on your high horse when you leave here."

## Developing Writing Skills

1. **Writing Dialogue.** As Mary Dru watches J.C. turn toward the ticket counter, she notices that his lips are moving. As she boards the bus, her lips also are moving. What might J.C. and Mary Dru be mumbling? Write two passages of dialogue, one for Mary Dru and one for J.C. Be sure that the dialogue for each character is appropriate for the character and for that particular moment in the story.

2. **Developing an Argument.** Mary Dru's father does not want her to ride the bus alone. Her mother disagrees. If Mary Dru were your daughter, would you allow her to make this trip alone? Assume that your spouse, husband or wife, disagrees with you. Write one paragraph of persuasion in which you present reasons for your point of view. Keep in mind that the purpose of the paragraph is to convince your spouse that your decision is the correct one.

# Of Missing Persons     *Jack Finney*

*Walk in as though it were an ordinary travel
bureau, the stranger I'd met at a cafeteria had
told me. Ask a few ordinary questions—about
a trip you're planning, a vacation, anything
like that. Then hint about The Folder a little,
but whatever you do, don't mention it directly; wait till he brings it up himself. And
if he doesn't, you might as well forget it. If
you can. Because you'll never see it; you're
not the type, that's all. And if you ask about
it, he'll just look at you as though he doesn't
know what you're talking about.*

I rehearsed it all in my mind, over and
over, but what seems possible at night over
coffee isn't easy to believe on a raw, rainy
day, and I felt like a fool, searching the store
fronts for the street number I'd memorized.
It was noon hour. West 42nd Street, New
York, rainy and windy; and like half the men
around me, I walked with a hand on my hatbrim, wearing an old trench coat, head bent
into the slanting rain, and the world was real
and drab, and this was hopeless.

Anyway, I couldn't help thinking, who am
I to see The Folder, even if there is one?
Name? I said to myself, as though I were already being asked. It's Charley Ewell, and
I'm a young guy who works in a bank; a
teller. I don't like the job; I don't make much
money, and I never will. I've lived in New
York for over three years and haven't many
friends. What the heck, there's really nothing
to say—I see more movies than I want to,
read too many books, and I'm sick of meals

alone in restaurants. I have ordinary abilities,
looks, and thoughts. Does that suit you; do I
qualify?

Now I spotted it, the address in the 200
block, an old, pseudo-modernized office
building, tired, outdated, refusing to admit it
but unable to hide it. New York is full of
them, west of Fifth.

I pushed through the brass-framed glass
doors into the tiny lobby, paved with freshly
mopped, permanently dirty tile. The green-
painted walls were lumpy from old plaster
repairs; in a chrome frame hung a little wall
directory—white-celluloid, easily changed
letters on a black-felt background. There
were some twenty-odd names, and I found
"Acme Travel Bureau" second on the list,
between "A-1 Mimeo" and "Ajax Magic Supplies." I pressed the bell beside the old-style,
open-grille elevator door; it rang high up in
the shaft. There was a long pause, then a
thump, and the heavy chains began rattling
slowly down toward me, and I almost turned
and left—this was insane.

But upstairs the Acme office had divorced
itself from the atmosphere of the building. I
pushed open the pebble-glass door, walked
in, and the big square room was bright and
clean, fluorescent-lighted. Beside the wide
double windows, behind a counter, stood a
tall gray-haired, grave-looking man, a telephone at his ear. He glanced up, nodded to
beckon me in, and I felt my heart pumping—
he fitted the description exactly. "Yes, United
Air Lines," he was saying into the phone.

"Flight"—he glanced at a paper on the glass-topped counter—"seven-oh-three, and I suggest you check in forty minutes early."

Standing before him now, I waited, leaning on the counter, glancing around; he was the man, all right, and yet this was just an ordinary travel agency; big bright posters on the walls, metal floor racks full of folders, printed schedules under the glass on the counter. This is just what it looks like and nothing else, I thought, and again I felt like a fool.

"Can I help you?" Behind the counter the tall gray-haired man was smiling at me, replacing the phone, and suddenly I was terribly nervous.

"Yes." I stalled for time, unbuttoning my raincoat. Then I looked up at him again and said, "I'd like to—get away." You fool, that's too fast, I told myself. Don't rush it! I watched in a kind of panic to see what effect my answer had had, but he didn't flick an eyelash.

"Well, there are a lot of places to go," he said politely. From under the counter he brought out a long, slim folder and laid it on the glass, turning it right side up for me. "Fly to Buenos Aires—Another World!" it said in a double row of pale-green letters across the top.

I looked at it long enough to be polite. It showed a big silvery plane banking over a harbor at night, a moon shining on the water, mountains in the background. Then I just shook my head; I was afraid to talk, afraid I'd say the wrong thing.

"Something quieter, maybe?" He brought out another folder: thick old tree trunks, rising way up out of sight, sunbeams slanting down through them—"The Virgin Forests of Maine, via Boston and Maine Railroad." "Or"—he laid a third folder on the glass—"Bermuda is nice just now." This one said, "Bermuda, Old World in the New."

I decided to risk it. "No," I said, and shook my head. "What I'm really looking for is a permanent place. A new place to live and settle down in." I stared directly into his eyes. "For the rest of my life." Then my nerve failed me, and I tried to think of a way to backtrack.

But he only smiled pleasantly and said, "I don't know why we can't advise you on that." He leaned forward on the counter, resting on his forearms, hands clasped; he had all the time in the world for me, his posture conveyed. "What are you looking for; what do you want?"

I held my breath, then said it. "Escape."

"From what?"

"Well—" Now I hesitated; I'd never put it into words before. "From New York, I'd say. And cities in general. From worry. And fear. And the things I read in my newspapers. From loneliness." And then I couldn't stop, though I knew I was talking too much, the words spilling out. "From never doing what I really want to do or having much fun. From selling my days just to stay alive. From life itself—the way it is today, at least." I looked straight at him and said softly, "From the world."

Now he was frankly staring, his eyes studying my face intently with no pretense of doing anything else, and I knew that in a moment he'd shake his head and say, "Mister, you better get to a doctor." But he didn't. He continued to stare, his eyes examining my forehead now. He was a big man, his gray hair crisp and curling, his lined face very intelligent, very kind; he looked the way ministers should look; he looked the way all fathers should look.

He lowered his gaze to look into my eyes and beyond them; he studied my mouth, my chin, the line of my jaw, and I had the sudden conviction that without any difficulty he was learning a great deal about me, more than I knew myself. Suddenly he smiled and placed both elbows on the counter, one hand grasping the other fist and gently massaging it. "Do you like people? Tell the truth, because I'll know if you aren't."

"Yes. It isn't easy for me to relax though, and be myself, and make friends."

He nodded gravely, accepting that. "Would you say you're a reasonably decent kind of man?"

"I guess so; I think so." I shrugged.

"Why?"

I smiled wryly; this was hard to answer. "Well—at least when I'm not, I'm usually sorry about it."

He grinned at that, and considered it for a moment or so. Then he smiled—deprecatingly, as though he were about to tell a little joke that wasn't too good. "You know," he said casually, "we occasionally get people in here who seem to be looking for pretty much what you are. So just as a sort of little joke—"

I couldn't breathe. This was what I'd been told he would say if he thought I might do.

"—we've worked up a little folder. We've even had it printed. Simply for our own amusement, you understand. And for occasional clients like you. So I'll have to ask you to look at it here if you're interested. It's not the sort of thing we'd care to have generally known."

I could barely whisper, "I'm interested."

He fumbled under the counter, then brought out a long thin folder, the same size and shape as the others, and slid it over the glass toward me.

I looked at it, pulling it closer with a finger tip, almost afraid to touch it. The cover was dark blue, the shade of a night sky, and across the top in white letters it said, "Visit Enchanting Verna!" The blue cover was sprinkled with white dots—stars—and in the lower left corner was a globe, the world, half surrounded by clouds. At the upper right, just under the word *Verna*, was a star larger and brighter than the others; rays shot out from it, like from a star on a Christmas card. Across the bottom of the cover it said, "Romantic Verna, where life is the way it *should* be." There was a little arrow beside the legend, meaning turn the page.

I turned, and the folder was like most travel folders inside—there were pictures and text, only these were about "Verna" instead of Paris, or Rome, or the Bahamas. And it was beautifully printed; the pictures looked real. What I mean is, you've seen color stereopticon pictures? Well, that's what these were like, only better, far better. In one picture you could see dew glistening on the grass, and it looked wet. In another, a tree trunk seemed to curve out of the page, in perfect detail, and it was a shock to touch it and feel smooth paper instead of the rough actuality of bark. Miniature human faces, in a third picture, seemed about to speak, the lips moist and alive, the eyeballs shining, the actual texture of skin right there on paper; and it seemed impossible, as you stared, that the people wouldn't move and speak.

I studied a large picture spreading across the tops of two open pages. It seemed to have been taken from the top of a hill; you saw the land dropping away at your feet far down into a valley, then rising up again, way over on the other side. The slopes of both hills were covered with forest, and the color was beautiful, perfect; there were miles of green, majestic trees, and you knew as you looked that this forest was virgin, almost untouched. Curving through the floor of the valley, far below, ran a stream, blue from the sky in most places; here and there, where the current broke around massive boulders, the water was foaming white; and again it seemed that if you'd only look closely enough you'd be certain to see that stream move and shine in the sun. In clearings beside the stream there were shake-roofed cabins, some of logs, some of brick or adobe. The caption under the picture simply said, "The Colony."

"Fun fooling around with a thing like that," the man behind the counter murmured, nodding at the folder in my hands. "Relieves the monotony. Attractive-looking place, isn't it?"

I could only nod dumbly, lowering my eyes to the picture again because that picture told you even more than just what you saw. I don't know how you knew this, but you realized, staring at that forest-covered valley, that this was very much the way America once looked when it was new. And you knew this was only a part of a whole land of unspoiled, unharmed forests, where every stream ran pure; you were seeing what people, the last of them dead over a century ago, had once looked at in Kentucky and Wisconsin and the old Northwest. And you knew that if you could breathe in that air you'd feel it flow into your lungs sweeter than it's been anywhere on Earth for a hundred and fifty years.

Under that picture was another, of six or eight people on a beach—the shore of a lake, maybe, or the river in the picture above. Two children were squatting on their haunches, dabbling in the water's edge, and in the foreground a half circle of adults were sitting, kneeling, or squatting in comfortable balance on the yellow sand. They were talking, several were smoking, and most of them held half-filled coffee cups; the sun was bright, you knew the air was balmy and that it was morning, just after breakfast. They were smiling, one woman talking, the others listening. One man had half risen from his squatting position to skip a stone out onto the surface of the water.

You knew this; that they were spending twenty minutes or so down on that beach after breakfast before going to work, and you

knew they were friends and that they did this every day. You knew—I tell you, you *knew*—that they liked their work, all of them, whatever it was; that there was no forced hurry or pressure about it. And that—well, that's all, I guess; you just knew that every day after breakfast these families spent a leisurely half-hour sitting and talking, there in the morning sun, down on that wonderful beach.

I'd never seen anything like their faces before. They were ordinary enough in looks, the people in that picture—pleasant, more or less familiar types. Some were young, in their twenties; others were in their thirties; one man and woman seemed around fifty. But the faces of the youngest couple were completely unlined, and it occurred to me then that they had been born there, and that it was a place where no one worried or was ever afraid. The others, the older ones, there were lines in their foreheads, grooves around their mouths, but you felt that the lines were no longer deepening, that they were healed and untroubled scars. And in the faces of the oldest couple was a look of—I'd say it was a look of permanent *relief*. Not one of those faces bore a trace of malice; these people were *happy*. But even more than that, you knew they'd *been* happy, day after day after day for a long, long time, and that they always would be, and they knew it.

I wanted to join them. The most desperate longing roared up in me from the bottom of my soul to *be* there—on that beach, after breakfast, with those people in the sunny morning—and I could hardly stand it. I looked up at the man behind the counter and managed to smile. "This is—very interesting."

"Yes." He smiled back, then shook his head in amusement. "We've had customers so interested, so carried away, that they didn't want to talk about anything else." He laughed. "They actually wanted to know rates, details, everything."

I nodded to show I understood and agreed with them. "And I suppose you've worked out a whole story to go with this?" I glanced at the folder in my hands.

"Oh, yes. What would you like to know?"

"These people," I said softly, and touched the picture of the group on the beach. "What do they do?"

"They work; everyone does." He took a pipe from his pocket. "They simply live their lives doing what they like. Some study. We have, according to our little story," he added, and smiled, "a very fine library. Some of our people farm, some write, some make things with their hands. Most of them raise children, and—well, they work at whatever it is they really want to do."

"And if there isn't anything they really want to do?"

He shook his head. "There is always something for everyone, that he really wants to do. It's just that here there is so rarely time to find out what it is." He brought out a tobacco pouch and, leaning on the counter, began filling his pipe, his eyes level with mine, looking at me gravely. "Life is simple there, and it's serene. In some ways, the good ways, it's like the early pioneering communities here in your country, but without the drudgery that killed people young. There is electricity. There are washing machines, vacuum cleaners, plumbing, modern bathrooms, and modern medicine, very modern. But there are no radios, television, telephones, or automobiles. Distances are small, and people live and work in small communities. They raise or make most of the things they use. Every family builds its own house, with all the help it needs from its neighbors. Their recreation is their own, and there is a great deal of it, but there is no recreation for sale, nothing you buy a ticket to. They have dances, card parties, weddings, christenings, birthday cele-brations, harvest parties. There are swimming and sports of all kinds. There is conversation, a lot of it, plenty of joking and laughter. There is a great deal of visiting and sharing of meals, and each day is well filled and well spent. There are no pressures, economic or social, and life holds few threats. Every man, woman, and child is a happy person." After a moment he smiled. "I'm repeating the text, of course, in our little joke"—he nodded at the folder.

"Of course," I murmured, and looked down at the folder again, turning a page. "Homes in The Colony," said a caption, and there, true and real, were a dozen or so pictures of the interiors of what must have been the cabins I'd seen in the first photograph, or others like them. There were living rooms, kitchens, dens, patios. Many of the homes seemed to be furnished in a kind of Early American style, except that it looked—authentic, as though those rocking chairs, cupboards, tables, and hooked rugs had been made by the people themselves, taking their time and making them well and beautifully. Others of the interiors seemed modern in style; one showed a definite Oriental influence.

All of them had, plainly and unmistakably, one quality in common: You knew as you looked at them that these rooms were *home*, really home, to the people who lived in them. On the wall of one living room, over the stone fireplace, hung a handstitched motto; it said, "There Is No Place Like Home," but the words didn't seem quaint or amusing, they didn't seem old-fashioned, resurrected or copied from a past that was gone. They seemed real; they belonged; those words were nothing more or less than a simple expression of true feeling and fact.

"Who are you?" I lifted my head from the folder to stare into the man's eyes.

He lighted his pipe, taking his time, sucking the match flame down into the bowl, eyes glancing up at me. "It's in the text," he said then, "on the back page. We—that is to say, the people of Verna, the original inhabitants —are people like yourself. Verna is a planet of air, sun, land, and sea, like this one. And of the same approximate temperature. So life evolved there, of course, just about as it has here, though rather earlier: and we are people like you. There are trivial anatomical differences, but nothing important. We read and enjoy your James Thurber, John Clayton, Rabelais, Allen Marple, Hemingway, Grimm, Mark Twain, Alan Nelson. We like your chocolate, which we didn't have, and a great deal of your music, and you'd like many of the things we have. Our thoughts, though, and the great aims and directions of our history and development have been—drastically different from yours." He smiled and blew out a puff of smoke. "Amusing fantasy, isn't it?"

"Yes." I knew I sounded abrupt, and I hadn't stopped to smile; the words were spilling out. "And where is Verna?"

"Light years away, by your measurements."

I was suddenly irritated, I didn't know why. "A little hard to get to, then, wouldn't it be?"

For a moment he looked at me; then he turned to the window beside him. "Come here," he said, and I walked around the counter to stand beside him. "There, off to the left" —he put a hand on my shoulder and pointed with his pipe stem—"are two apartment buildings, built back to back. The entrance to one is on Fifth Avenue, the entrance to the other on Sixth. See them? In the middle of the block; you can just see their roofs."

I nodded, and he said, "A man and his wife live on the fourteenth floor of one of those buildings. A wall of their living room is the back wall of the building. They have friends on the fourteenth floor of the other building, and a wall of *their* living room is the back wall of *their* building. These two couples live, in other words, within two feet of one another, since the back walls actually touch."

The big man smiled. "But when the Robinsons want to visit the Bradens, they walk from their living room to the front door. Then they walk down a long hall to the elevators. They ride fourteen floors down; then, in the street, they must walk around to the next block. And the city blocks there are long; in bad weather they have sometimes actually taken a cab. They walk into the other building, then go on through the lobby, ride up fourteen floors, walk down a hall, ring a bell, and are finally admitted into their friends' living room—only two feet from their own."

The big man turned back to the counter, and I walked around it to the other side again. "All I can tell you," he said then, "is that the way the Robinsons travel is like space travel, the actual physical crossing of those enormous distances." He shrugged. "But if they could only step through those two feet of wall without harming themselves or the wall—well, that is how we 'travel.' We don't cross space, we avoid it." He smiled. "Draw a breath here—and exhale it on Verna."

I said softly, "And that's how they arrived, isn't it? The people in the picture. You took them there." He nodded, and I said, "Why?"

He shrugged. "If you saw a neighbor's house on fire, would you rescue his family if you could? As many as you could, at least?"

"Yes."

"Well—so would we."

"You think it's that bad, then? With us?"

"How does it look to you?"

I thought about the headlines in my morning paper, that morning and every morning. "Not so good."

He just nodded and said, "We can't take you all, can't even take very many. So we've been selecting a few."

"For how long?"

"A long time." He smiled. "One of us was a member of Lincoln's cabinet. But it was not until just before your First World War that we felt we could see what was coming; until then we'd been merely observers. We opened our first agency in Mexico City in nineteen thirteen. Now we have branches in every major city."

"Nineteen thirteen," I murmured, as something caught at my memory. "Mexico. Listen! Did—"

"Yes." He smiled, anticipating my question. "Ambrose Bierce joined us that year, or the next. He lived until nineteen thirty-one, a very old man, and wrote four more books, which we have." He turned back a page in the folder and pointed to a cabin in the first large photograph. "That was his home."

"And what about Judge Crater?"

"Crater?"

"Another famous disappearance; he was a New York judge who simply disappeared some years ago."

"I don't know. We had a judge, I remember, from New York City, some twenty-odd years ago, but I can't recall his name."

I leaned across the counter toward him, my face very close to his, and I nodded. "I like your little joke," I said. "I like it very much, more than I can possibly tell you." Very softly I added, "When does it stop being a joke?"

For a moment he studied me; then he spoke. "Now. If you want it to."

*You've got to decide on the spot,* the middle-aged man at the Lexington Avenue cafeteria had told me, *because you'll never get another chance. I know; I've tried.* Now I stood there thinking; there were people I'd hate never to see again, and a girl I was just getting to know, and this was the world I'd been born in. Then I thought about leaving that room, going back to my job, then back to my room at night. And finally I thought of the deep-green valley in the picture and the little yellow beach in the morning sun. "I'll go," I whispered. "If you'll have me."

He studied my face. "Be sure," he said sharply. "Be certain. We want no one there who won't be happy, and if you have any least doubt, we'd prefer that—"

After a moment the gray-haired man slid open a drawer under the counter and brought out a little rectangle of yellow cardboard. One side was printed, and through the printing ran a band of light green; it looked like a railroad ticket to White Plains or somewhere. The printing said, "Good, when validated, for ONE TRIP TO VERNA. Nontransferable. One-way only."

"Ah—how much?" I said, reaching for my wallet, wondering if he wanted me to pay.

He glanced at my hand on my hip pocket. "All you've got. Including your small change." He smiled. "You won't need it any more, and we can use your currency for operating expenses. Light bills, rent, and so on."

"I don't have much."

"That doesn't matter." From under the counter he brought out a heavy stamping machine, the kind you see in railroad ticket offices. "We once sold a ticket for thirty-seven hundred dollars. And we sold another just like it for six cents." He slid the ticket into the machine, struck the lever with his fist, then handed the ticket to me. On the back, now, was a freshly printed rectangle of purple ink, and within it the words, "Good this day only," followed by the date. I put two five-dollar bills, a one, and seventeen cents in change on the counter. "Take the ticket to the Acme Depot," the gray-haired man said, and, leaning across the counter, began giving me directions for getting there.

It's a tiny hole-in-the-wall, the Acme Depot; you may have seen it—just a little store front on one of the narrow streets west of Broadway. On the window is painted, not very well, "Acme." Inside, the walls and ceiling, under layers of old paint, are covered with the kind of stamped tin you see in the old buildings. There's a worn wooden counter and a few battered chrome-and-imitation-red-leather chairs. There are scores of places like the Acme Depot in that area—little theatre-ticket agencies, obscure bus-line offices, employment agencies. You could pass this one a thousand times and never really see it; and if you live in New York, you probably have.

Behind the counter, when I arrived, a shirt-sleeved man smoking a cigar stump stood working on some papers; four or five people silently waited in the chairs. The man at the counter glanced up as I stepped in, looked down at my hand for my ticket, and when I showed it, nodded at the last vacant chair, and I sat down.

There was a girl beside me, hands folded on her purse. She was pleasant-looking, rather pretty; I thought she might have been a stenographer. Across a narrow little office sat a young black man in work clothes, his wife beside him holding their little girl in her lap. And there was a man of around fifty, his face averted from the rest of us, staring out into the rain at passing pedestrians. He was expensively dressed and wore a gray Homburg hat; he could have been the vice-president of a large bank, I thought, and wondered what his ticket had cost.

Maybe twenty minutes passed, the man behind the counter working on some papers; then a small, battered old bus pulled up at the curb outside, and I heard the hand brake set. The bus was a shabby thing, bought

RAINY NIGHT, 1930. Charles Burchfield. San Diego Museum of Art.

third- or fourth-hand and painted red and white over the old paint, the fenders lumpy from countless pounded-out dents, the tire treads worn almost smooth. On the side, in red letters, it said "Acme," and the driver wore a leather jacket and the kind of worn cloth cap that cab drivers wear. It was precisely the sort of obscure little bus you see around there, ridden always by shabby, tired, silent people, going no one knows where.

It took nearly two hours for the little bus to work south through the traffic, toward the tip of Manhattan, and we all sat, each wrapped in one's own silence and thoughts, staring out the rain-spattered windows; the little girl was asleep. Through the streaking glass beside me I watched drenched people huddled at city bus stops, and saw them rap angrily on the closed doors of buses jammed to capacity, and saw the strained, harassed faces of the drivers. At 14th Street I saw a speeding cab splash a sheet of street-dirty water on a man at the curb, and saw the man's mouth writhe as he cursed. Often our bus stood motionless, the traffic light red, as throngs flowed out into the street from the curb, threading their way around us and the other waiting cars. I saw hundreds of faces, and not once did I see anyone smile.

I dozed; then we were on a glistening black highway somewhere on Long Island. I slept again, and awakened in darkness as we jolted off the highway onto a muddy double-rut road, and I caught a glimpse of a farmhouse, the windows dark. Then the bus slowed, lurched once, and stopped. The hand brake set, the motor died, and we were parked beside what looked like a barn.

It *was* a barn—the driver walked up to it, pulled the big sliding wood door open, its wheels creaking on the rusted old trolley overhead, and stood holding it open as we filed in. Then he released it, stepping inside with us, and the big door slid closed of its own weight. The barn was damp, old, the walls no longer plumb, and it smelled of cattle; there was nothing inside on the packed-dirt floor but a bench of unpainted pine, and the driver indicated it with a beam of a flashlight. "Sit here, please," he said quietly. "Get your tickets ready." Then he moved down the line, punching each of our tickets, and on the floor I caught a momentary glimpse, in the shifting beam of his light, of tiny mounds of countless more round bits of cardboard, like little drifts of yellow confetti. Then he was at the door again, sliding it open just enough to pass through, and for a moment we saw him silhouetted against the night sky. "Good luck," he said. "Just wait where you are." He released the door; it slid closed, snipping off the wavering beam of his flashlight; and a moment later we heard the motor start and the bus lumber away in low gear.

The dark barn was silent now, except for our breathing. Time ticked away, and I felt an urge, presently, to speak to whoever was next to me. But I didn't quite know what to say, and I began to feel embarrassed, a little foolish, and very aware that I was simply sitting in an old and deserted barn. The seconds passed, and I moved my feet restlessly; presently I realized that I was getting cold and chilled. Then suddenly I knew—and my face flushed in violent anger and a terrible shame. We'd been tricked! bilked out of our money by our pathetic will to believe an absurd and fantastic fable and left, now, to sit there as long as we pleased, until we came to our senses finally, like countless others before us, and made our way home as best we could. It was suddenly impossible to understand or even remember how I could have been so gullible, and I was on my feet, stumbling through the dark across the uneven floor, with some notion of getting to a phone and the police. The big barn door was heavier than I'd thought, but I slid it back, took a running step through it, then turned to shout back to the others to come along.

You perhaps have seen how very much you can observe in the fractional instant of a lightning flash—an entire landscape sometimes, every detail etched on your memory, to be seen and studied in your mind for long moments afterwards. As I turned back toward the opened door the inside of that barn came alight. Through every wide crack of its walls and ceiling and through the big dust-coated windows in its side streamed the light of an intensely brilliant blue and sunny sky, and the air pulling into my lungs as I opened my mouth to shout was sweeter than any I had ever tasted in my life. Dimly, through a wide, dust-smeared window of that barn, I looked —for less than the blink of an eye—down into a deep majestic V of forest-covered slope, and I saw, tumbling through it, far below, a tiny stream, blue from the sky, and at that stream's edge between two low roofs a yellow patch of sun-drenched beach. And then, that picture engraved on my mind forever, the heavy door slid shut, my fingernails rasping along the splintery wood in a desperate effort to stop it—and I was standing alone in a cold and rain-swept night.

It took four or five seconds, no longer, fumbling at that door, to heave it open again. But it was four or five seconds too long. The barn was empty, dark. There was nothing inside but a worn pine bench—and, in the flicker of the lighted match in my hand, tiny drifts of what looked like damp confetti on the floor. As my mind had known even as my hands scratched at the outside of that door, there was no one inside now; and I knew where they were—knew they were walking, laughing aloud in a sudden wonderful and eager ecstasy, down into that forest-green valley, toward home.

I work in a bank, in a job I don't like; and I ride to and from it in the subway, reading the daily papers, the news they contain. I live in a rented room, and in the battered dresser under a pile of my folded handkerchiefs is a little rectangle of yellow cardboard. Printed on its face are the words, "Good, when validated, for one trip to Verna," and stamped on the back is a date. But the date is gone, long since, the ticket void, punched in a pattern of tiny holes.

I've been back to the Acme Travel Bureau. The first time the tall gray-haired man walked up to me and laid two five-dollar bills, a one, and seventeen cents in change before me. "You left this on the counter last time you were here," he said gravely. Looking me squarely in the eyes, he added blankly, "I don't know why." Then some customers came in, he turned to greet them, and there was nothing for me to do but leave.

## Getting at Meaning

1. Why is Charley Ewell unhappy with his life? Why does he want to see The Folder?

2. Why is Charley nervous as he talks to the man at the Acme Travel Bureau? What kinds of thoughts run through his mind?

3. Why does the travel agent refer to the Verna folder as a joke?

4. Why is the world pictured in the Verna folder so appealing to Charley?

5. According to the travel agent, life on Verna is simple. Why are commercial entertainments inappropriate to this world?

6. Charley is unexplainably irritated when he learns that Verna is "light years away." What does this reaction reveal about Charley? What does it foreshadow?

7. Why does the travel agent tell the story of the Robinsons and the Bradens?

8. As the travel agent asks him to decide about Verna, Charley remembers the words of the man in the Lexington Avenue cafeteria. What was the man's experience with The Folder and Verna?

9. What impresses Charley during the time that he spends in the Acme Depot and on the trip through Manhattan? What does he notice about his surroundings?

10. Why does Charley feel foolish as he sits in the barn? He says that he has been tricked, but who or what does he really mistrust?

11. Why does Charley keep his outdated ticket to Verna? Why do you think he tells his story?

## Developing Skills in Reading Literature

1. **Conflict.** The conflict in this story is internal, or within the mind of the main character. Why does Charley Ewell want to escape to Verna? Do any external forces prevent his trip? Reread the first three paragraphs of the story. What does he think of himself? How does his opinion of himself cause him to ruin his chances for happiness?

2. **Rising Action.** The rising action of a story develops the conflict. Specifically, what happens to develop Charley's desire to escape to Verna?

Throughout the conversation with the travel agent, how does the writer develop the opposing force, which eventually prevents Charley from satisfying his desire?

3. **Climax.** What is the turning point of this story? Which of the opposing forces triumphs?

4. **Falling Action.** The falling action in a story consists of those events that occur as a result of the turning point. The falling action in this story is described in the last two paragraphs. Why do these paragraphs sound familiar? What effect does Charley's experience have upon his life? How is he similar to the man in the cafeteria?

## Developing Vocabulary

**Context Clue: Definition or Restatement.** Some context clues are quite direct; they define or restate words in the context in which they appear. Determine the meanings of the following italicized words. Then choose five difficult words either from the story or from a dictionary. Write a sentence for each word that includes a definition or restatement of the word.

1. Then he smiled—*deprecatingly,* as though he were about to tell a little joke that wasn't too good.

2. We'd been tricked! *bilked* out of our money.

## Developing Writing Skills

**Combining Description and Exposition.** Charley Ewell clearly and specifically describes what he wants to leave behind; his descriptions of city life and his observations during the bus ride are detailed. Verna, his ideal escape, becomes a vivid image as Charley describes the pictures in The Folder. Write a five-paragraph composition in which you create a setting, a world or environment that represents either what you hate about this world or your idea of an ideal world. Use the first paragraph to present the general characteristics of the world. In paragraphs two through four give detailed descriptions of those characteristics you consider most important. Use your conclusion to express opinions on the world you have described.

# Without Words  *Elliott Merrick*

He came over a knoll and stopped, head back, his rifle in one mitten, his axe in the other. Below him spread the river, ice-locked between the hills. A mile across, the birch bluffs were turning blue in the twilight.

He was not given to poetic fancies, but it touched him always, coming out to the river after days and nights in the spruces to the west, following brooks and isolated chains of lakes that didn't lead anywhere, plowing through willow tangles and up and down the wooded hills. It gave him a feeling of spaciousness, like stepping out of doors to see the broad river again, sweeping out of sight between the hills.

That country behind him, his east trap line where he had been for ten days, was just a cut-up jumble of wilderness, lost, nameless, known only to himself. But the river was the river. This was the road to home, this was the known thread that joined him to other men.

This water that was flowing under the ice would slide past the village sometime, in a month maybe. "It'll get there 'fore I do, anyways," he said aloud. It was nine weeks now since the day the crowd had waved from the wharf, and the double-barrel shotguns split the air in the old time farewell, "Boomboom" . . . and a pause to load . . . "Boom," saying "Goodbye. . . . Luck"; nine weeks since the trappers fired their one answering shot, "Luck." It gave a fellow something to remember way off here where you didn't hear anything much except your own voice.

It would be pretty near three months yet before he'd be home and maybe see Luce, he

was thinking as he scrambled down the bank and legged it along the ice for the house. *This* cabin had a window, and a door with hinges, a good tight roof of birch bark, and within, such luxuries as a sleeping bag, which his tiny log tilts back in the woods had not.

It was nearly dark when he got there, but not too dark to see in the cove the print of strange snowshoes. And by the point where the current flowed fast and the ice was thin, somebody had been chopping a water hole. "Hello!" he called to the cabin.

From the ridge that rose up behind the cabin came a silvery, mocking "hello," and faintly, seconds later, a distant hello from across the river, the echo of the echo. Jan crossed the cove, bent double, studying the tracks. There was three of them, a big pair of snowshoes and two smaller pairs. The smaller snowshoes had been dragging in a stick of firewood from alongshore—the women.

Jan threw off his bag and hurried into the cabin. Nobody made snowshoes of that pattern but Mathieu Su-saka-shish, the Seven Islands Indian. Nobody but Mathieu knew this cabin was here. He and his wife and daughter had come last year and begged a little tea and sugar. Now they were here again with their Indian idea that food belongs to anybody who is hungry. The dirty dogs! Where three fifty-pound bags of flour had been hanging, only two hung now. They had dripped candle grease onto his bunk and left his big meat kettle unwashed. He dove under the bunk and pulled out his food boxes. They'd made off with some of his split peas and a few of his beans, a handful of candles too. They had sliced a big chunk of salt pork neatly down the middle.

In a frenzy of rage he ripped open his fur bag. Every skin was there, and in addition, a black and shining otter skin lay crosswise on his bundles of mink and marten, fox and ermine. He held it up and blew the hair and felt its thickness and its length, stroking its blue-black luster. It was a prize. It would bring forty dollars, perhaps. But the sight of it made him angrier than before.

"So!" he muttered. "Mathieu thinks one miserable skin of fur pays me for my grub, eh?" He lit a candle, and his hand was trembling with rage. From now on he'd be half-hungry all the time, and hunting meat when he ought to be tending the trap line. This was his whole year's earnings, these five months in the bush. And Mathieu thought he could steal the grub that made it possible, did he? He thought he could come every year and fit himself out, likely.

Jan took his rifle and emptied the magazine. It was only one bag of flour—but still, there were men way off here in the country who'd died for lack of a cupful, yes, a spoonful. Slowly he reloaded with the soft-nosed cartridges he had always kept for caribou, heretofore. Would he ever tell anybody, Luce for instance, would he ever be able to forget that somewhere back in the ridges, by some secret little lake that no one knew, he had shot three Indians and stuffed them through the ice? Didn't the Bible say, an eye for an eye and a tooth for a tooth?

Jan had already walked twenty miles to-day. And he was tired with the piled-up weariness of weeks and weeks of that, traveling, traveling to cover and re-cover his two hundred miles of fur paths. With a sigh he set to work; wood to chop, water from the river, a partridge to be stewed and ten cakes of bannock bread to bake in the frying pan.

While the bread was baking he skinned two mink, a marten, four weasels, humming as he did so a song that he was very fond of.

Oh, we've sailed the seven seas from pole
    to pole,
And we've conquered stormy gale and
    stinging foam,
And we've seen the strangest sights of far-
    off lands,
But the best is to see the cheery lights of
    home.

It called up visions of a light in the window, if he should ever have a real home, if, perhaps, Luce did not go away at all.

It was too bad he couldn't just shoot Mathieu, but it would be no use to leave the women to wander around and starve. At the thought of actually squeezing the trigger and seeing them drop, he shuddered.

It was nearly midnight when he stoked up the stove and rolled in on the bunk for the last good sleep he expected to know for awhile. At five o'clock, in the starlight, he was out on the river shore with a candle lantern made of a baking powder can, examining tracks. The polished, shallow trench that their two toboggans had left was so plain a child could have followed it. Mathieu was ahead, taking long steps, hurrying. The two women were behind, hauling their toboggan in double harness, tandem fashion. One of them fell and left the print of her knee going down the bank. Jan smiled as though he had seen it and heard her mutter.

He followed their track across the river to the top of a draw between two bare hills. There in the sunrise he turned and looked back at the ice, sparkling with frost in the soft golden light, spotted with long blue shadows of the hills. As he plunged downhill into the thick country to the north he had an ominous feeling that he was leaving something.

Maybe Mathieu would ambush him; it would be an easy thing to do on a track like this. Would Mathieu guess that he was being tracked?

Jan studied the track, unconsciously noting every detail. Here in this book of the snow he might perhaps read Mathieu's thoughts, even a warning of an ambush. Ah, but Indians were smart in the woods. Did he really think he could out-track an Indian hunter?

"By the Lord Harry, I can have a try," he whispered to himself.

Two mornings ago, he decided it was, that they had passed through here under the firs, across that little brook. Two days were not much of a start for them. They had sleds and he had none. Mathieu had to break trail, while he had their hard frozen track to walk on. They had all their winter gear, their blankets and kettles, their tin stove and tent, traps, trout nets probably. He had nothing but the game-bag on his back, nine cakes of bread, tea and sugar, his rifle and axe, a single blanket. The chances were he could travel twice as fast as they.

He passed their first fire, where they had stopped to boil tea and thrown the leaves on the embers. The tea leaves were frozen stiff.

All day he swung on, parting the boughs where the spruces were thick, slipping through them as effortlessly as a weasel, trotting down all the hills with a tireless shuffle, trotting again where the way was level and open. Once he stopped for ten minutes to sit on a log and munch dry bread, then lit his pipe and swung on. It was frosty, and the edges of his fur cap grew white with his breathing.

Before sunset he had long passed their first night's camp. Through the semi-darkness of early twilight he pressed on, following the hardness of their track more by touch than by sight. In the starlight he made his fire and boiled tea in a ravine by a brook. Here and there a tree snapped with the frost. The brook murmured under the ice. On the western hill a horn owl was hooting.

Every hour he woke with the cold, threw on more wood, turned over and slept again. Once, around three o'clock, he woke and could not sleep. He sat hunched in the blanket looking into the fire thinking what a fool he was. He should be on the trap line, not here. He had not come up the river so far away to waste time chasing Indians around the hills. Already he was hungry and wished he had brought more food.

The wind had risen and was blowing hard. That was bad. He could not feel it here, but the treetops were rocking, and branches now and then rubbed together and spoke with weird, childlike voices.

By half-past four he had boiled and eaten, and was picking his way along the track again. He should have rested another hour, he knew. But he could not rest, though he was tired. He wanted to get it over with. Probably they would not bleed much; it was so cold.

The Indians were still heading northwest. Likely they were bound for the headwaters of streams that flowed into Hudson's Bay.[1] Mathieu would feel safe there. And he would be too. It was much farther than Jan could track him with only three days' grub in the bag.

In the morning he passed their second night's camp. By noontime he had come to the edge of a big, oval marsh that was about six miles wide at its narrowest. On its barren floor were occasional clumps of dead sticks, juniper and fir, no higher than a man's head, the firs rotten and falling, the junipers gaunt and wind-carved. Compared to its bleak, dead savagery the greenwoods' borders seemed sociable and friendly and snug. As the merciless northwest wind had stunted and killed the trees, so it could shrivel and kill a man if it caught him out there in a blizzard.

The trail was dim and wind-scoured on the marsh. A mile out and there was nothing but the dully shining spots the sleds had polished; two miles out and Mathieu was veering off to the east, deviating for the first time from his northwest course.

The marks petered out entirely, heading at the last straight east. Jan stopped and rubbed his forehead. "Mathieu, you're a cute fox, eh?"

If Mathieu was heading northwest the blue notch was the obvious way for him. Then why, in the middle of the marsh, did he swing off for the steep ridges?

Jan trotted about in a circle, slapping his mittens together and pounding the toes that were aching in his moccasins. The drifting snow slid by like sand, rising in little eddies as the wind rose.

He stopped and stood with his back to the wind, leaning against it. "Now look. Mathieu wants to go through the blue notch, but it's too plain. He knows I'd pick up his track there first thing. So he cuts off in the middle of the marsh, thinkin' there'll be no sign of it when I gets here, and he makes a big half a circle. When I gets to the blue draw I can't find ere a sign of him, and I don't know where he's gone.

"I don't, eh? Well, I know he's got to strike the valley of that notch-stream somewheres. Him and his women haulin' sleds can't get

---

1. **Hudson's Bay:** an inland sea in east central Canada.

along in the hills no faster than a fox with a trap on his foot."

Jan picked up his game-bag and trotted off toward the now-invisible notch. If he'd guessed right, all right; if he'd guessed wrong, all right too. What odds! Lord Harry, he was hungry. In all this time he hadn't seen a partridge, though he'd seen plenty of feathers where that devil Mathieu'd shot all there was.

He began to sing a song to rival the sweep of the strong wind. In the wind it was good to sing, the wind drowned sound, sang a song of its own, saved a man from feeling that miles of quiet woods were listening. He roared in a strong baritone.

> Oh, we've sailed the seven seas from pole to pole,
> And we've conquered stormy gale and stinging foam,
> And we've seen the strangest sights of far-off lands,
> But the be-e-e-est is to see the chee-eery lights of ho-o-me.

The drift had obscured the shores now, and he was as though alone in the middle of a white sea, snow above, below, and on all sides. But he did not think of it. The wind was compass enough for him and had been since boyhood.

He clasped his gun and axe in the crook of one elbow, put his curled mitts up around his mouth and imitated a mouth organ, hunching his shoulders and swinging his body, dancing on his snowshoes in the gale. When he got home and the fiddle was squeaking in the schoolhouse and old Si Willetts was callin' out the figures, oh he'd swing his girl like this—and he whirled around with his gun and axe, holding them high in the air and shaking them.

"You! you got no more sense than a porcupine," he said.

At dusk, miles beyond the blue notch, he picked up the Indians' track again. He glowed with the warmth of a hunter's pride; his nostrils quivered and his jaw clenched. Lord Harry, how they had traveled. But he had them now. They'd never get away; they were doomed, unless it snowed.

A mile farther on they had camped, and there he camped too. A few split chunks of wood that they hadn't burned he used. There was still a faint warmth in the depths of their ashes. But something in the low branches of a spruce made him pause. Lashed there, rolled up in a hairy caribouskin were a big trout net and a heavyish iron Dutch oven. So, they were lightening loads were they? They knew they were being tracked then. How did they know?

Jan sat on the fir brush of their tent site and thought about it. They didn't know; they couldn't know. Mathieu was just playing safe, that was all, announcing, if he should be followed, that he was still a-drivin' 'er for all he was worth, bluffing a pursuer, trying to say, "I know I am being followed"—just in case he should be followed. Mathieu would go on for a week, get his women set in a good camp, then circle back, hunting, setting traps in likely places, looking for beaver houses, back to this very tree. Here he'd pick up his stuff, have a look around, and mosey along westward.

"That's what you think, Mathieu."

That night he ate another half a bannock, only half when he could easily have eaten three whole ones. What a fool he was to have traveled so light. If by some mischance he didn't catch them now, he'd be stranded off here with nothing to eat.

Rolled in his blanket and their caribou robe, he had the best sleep yet. It was risky. He had his gun beside him. For why couldn't Mathieu come back tonight as well as in a week? All about was the ring of darkness. Here was the firelight. What a perfect mark to shoot at. Yes, but Mathieu wouldn't shoot him. Why, Mathieu's father used to camp on the shore at Turner's Harbor years ago. Mathieu's cousin used to wrestle with Jan by the hour, and Mathieu himself had been in the foot races they ran on the beach summer afternoons long ago by the blue cool bay. Mathieu knew him all to pieces, even if they didn't meet but once in years and years way off in the country. Mathieu'd steal a little grub, but Mathieu'd never shoot him.

He sat looking into the fire. "Mathieu wouldn't shoot you," he said, "but you'd shoot Mathieu. You wouldn't steal Mathieu's grub, but he'd steal yours." He rocked his head in his hands, bewildered and hating this mental tangle. Life was simple. You went up the river in winter, and you were home by the bay in summer. You had good luck furring, or you didn't. You were hungry once in a while, and you froze your chin, or a cheek or a toe odd times, but what was that? You fell through the thin ice, or you didn't. You lived or you died, and that was all there was to it.

Yes, but it wasn't so simple when people stole your grub. Oh, if only Mathieu hadn't taken a whole bag of flour, he would be so glad for Mathieu. He settled it this way: if Mathieu wants to come along and shoot me tonight, let him, that's good luck for Mathieu; but if Mathieu doesn't, maybe Mathieu will get shot himself tomorrow night.

The stars paled and the east grayed the same as on other mornings. Jan did not set out until there was a little light. It would be so easy for Mathieu to wait hidden by the track.

He walked with his cap on the side, exposing one ear; and when that ear began to freeze, he tilted the cap and uncovered the other. Every mile he stopped and listened, mouth open, holding his breath. Late in the forenoon he came to a small valley thick with willows and boulders. As he examined it, he was conscious from the corner of his eye that a tuft of snow was slipping down the face of a gray boulder on his left. Was somebody behind there? He turned and ran, dodging through the trees. Skirting the end of the willows, he stealthily approached the trail farther on. No, no one had been there. It must have been a willow twig brushing the rock in the breeze. Here were the three prints, just the three prints, Mathieu's almost indistinguishable under the women's and the sled's. The women had given up hauling tandem. They took turns single, and when they changed places Mathieu didn't wait for them. They had to run a little to catch up, poor things. Luce could never have hauled like that.

As he tramped, he got to thinking of the otter skin Mathieu had left. It was funny the way Indian hunters would take food. They'd been hunters for so many ages they thought a bag of flour, like a caribou, was for anybody who needed it. But they wouldn't steal fur. Indians! They were like a necessary evil; they were like children. It would be better if they *did* steal fur and left the grub alone. They could pack food into this height-of-land country as well as anybody else if they wanted to. But they were too lazy. They let the trappers wear themselves to skin and bone struggling up the river in canoes loaded to the gunnels, risking their lives for it in the white rapids, lugging their loads up The Great Bank, a mile long and steeper than the bridge of Satan's own nose, breaking their backs for it across twelve miles of swamps and brooks and slippery rocks on the Grand Portage where the tump-lines pulled their hair out by the roots; and they carried till their eyes turned black and their trembling knees sagged under them. And then—then the Indians came along and helped themselves as though flour were worth no more up here than down on the bay shore.

"They won't help themselves to my grub," said Jan grimly. "Some day I'll come back to my house maybe, and find it cleaned right out. And then what about me, livin' on jays' legs and moss till I fall in the snow and die?"

The sky was growing deeper gray, darkness coming early. The air was chill with a suspicion of dampness. Come a big batch of snow to cover their track and make the walkin' back heavy, right to the knees, no food, he'd be in a fine fix, wouldn't he? He smelled the wind and it smelled like snow. Before dark it began to fall, and at dark he still had not caught them. Must be gettin' weak, he thought ruefully. He'd set some rabbit snares tonight. Or maybe he'd get a partridge. And maybe he wouldn't.

He stood on the shore of a little lake and leaned against a tree, uncertain. What with the new snow and the dark, there was only the barest sign of the track now. By morning it would be gone. What was that sharp smell?

He threw back his head and sniffed. Wood smoke! He had caught them. Let the snow pelt down. Let it snow six feet in the night. He had caught them and they couldn't get away.

Strange, though, that they should camp before the snow got thick. An hour more and they would have been safe. Well, Mathieu had made his last mistake this time.

Over a knoll in a thick clump of firs he built a small fire to boil the kettle. He was ravenous, and weary to the bone. They were camped; they would keep till he got ready for them. And they couldn't smell his smoke with the wind this way.

He ate the last of his bannock, drank four cups of tea and smoked his pipe to the last dregs. Then he left his bag and axe, took his rifle, and stole out across the dark lake. It was black as ink, and the new snow was like cotton wool to muffle his steps. Just back from the far shore he saw their dome-shaped *meetchwop*[2] glimmering. They were burning

a candle in there, one of his own probably.

He crept up closer, on his belly, foot by foot. The two sleds were stuck up against a tree; there was the chopping block, the axe, the chips. Snowshoes were hanging from a limb, the two small pairs. The women inside were baking bread. He could hear the frying pan scrape on the tin stove. They were talking in their soft musical voices, more like a brook under the ice than like human talk. They weren't hardly human anyway. But he could not bring himself to walk into the tent and shoot the women in cold blood. Better get Mathieu first. But where were the big snowshoes? Where was Mathieu? Behind that black tree there with his rifle cocked?

Jan lay silent, scarcely breathing, ears stretched for the slightest sound. But there were only the wind and the falling snow and the women's voices and the scraping pan.

Fifteen minutes, half an hour, he lay thus.

He was freezing; he couldn't lie there all night. Inch by inch he crawled away. Silent as a shadow he went back across the lake. There was danger everywhere now, every time he moved a muscle. He could feel it all around him, feel a prickling in his scalp and a supernatural certainty that as he was stalking Mathieu, Mathieu was stalking him. Cautiously, with long waits, he approached his camp. The fire was out. His fingers touched the game-bag and drew back. Something was there, something that shouldn't be! *Something was wrong.* Chills went up and down his spine. He whirled toward a deeper patch of shadow, knowing with the certainty of panic that gunfire would belch from that shadow and blind him. His eyes roamed round in his head in the darkness and he waited, turned to stone.

There was no sound. Nothing but the soft hiss of the snowflakes drifting down.

Then he smelled it. Bread, new-baked

---

2. **meetchwop** *Indian:* a small tentlike dwelling.

bread, sweet as life to his nostrils. He drew off his mitten and touched the game-bag again. His finger counted them—seven crusty bannock cakes, still warm.

"Mathieu," he whispered to the engulfing darkness. There was no answer. He struck a match and looked at the cakes. He bit one, and shook his head, ashamed. All his muscles sagged, and he slumped into the snow as though it were a bed.

Everything was different now. Noisily he crashed down a big tree for his night's fire. He was sticking up a lean-to by the fireplace, chilled by the night's cold, not by the cold horror of that other unthinkable job. Lord, he'd rather Mathieu plugged him full of holes than to take a sight on Mathieu. It was like waking up from a nightmare. He had half a mind to go across the lake now and ask Mathieu's woman to sew up the tear in his britches and have a good sleep in the Indians' warm tent. How they'd giggle and talk, with their black eyes!

But he was too ashamed. Mathieu was a better man than he was, that was all; more forgiving, smarter in the woods. "I wouldn't forgive him for taking a bag of flour, but he forgives me for tryin' to kill him. All the time the snow's comin' down and he only had to go on a little piece farther tonight to lose me altogether. He knows that, and he knows I was going to shoot him. But he takes a chance and sneaks back to feed me, me that's chasin' him to kill him. Mathieu don't want I should starve goin' back to the river. Mathieu—he don't want us to part unfriendly."

Lord, it beat all. If ever he told this to Luce, she'd say he was the head liar of all the liars on the whole river.

He finished one of the fragrant, tender bread cakes and lay down with his back to the fire. It was a long time since he'd felt so happy. Wonderful strange too, how much he and Mathieu had said to each other without words, way off here, never meeting, eating each other's grub.

Toward morning the snow stopped. Just after sunrise the Indian family broke camp and climbed the hill up from the shore. Jan, watching from the opposite hill across the lake, saw them silhouetted, three dark figures on the bare ridge. He pointed his gun at a treetop and let go greeting. Boomboom. . . . Boom. He saw the two women, startled, duck behind their sled.

But Mathieu stood erect against the brightening sky. He raised his rifle and fired one answering shot.

So they stood for a moment, on opposite hills, with upraised hand. *Goodbye. Luck.*

### Getting at Meaning

1. How does Jan know that it was Mathieu who took his supplies?

2. According to Jan, what is the Indian view of food supplies? How does the Indian view differ from that of the trappers?

3. Jan grows angrier when he sees the otter skin that Mathieu has left behind. Why? Later in the story, Jan describes how the trappers carry in their supplies. Why does this memory increase Jan's anger?

4. As he begins to track the Indians, Jan senses danger, and experiences an ominous feeling that he is leaving something behind. What does he fear that he is leaving? Think about the ending of the story. Does Jan leave anything on the shores of the snow-covered lake? Explain your answer.

5. Jan says to himself, "Mathieu wouldn't shoot you . . . but you'd shoot Mathieu. You wouldn't steal Mathieu's grub, but he'd steal yours." What does this inconsistency reveal about Indians and trappers?

6. When Jan smells the smoke from the Indians' fire, he knows that he has caught them. Has Mathieu made a mistake, as Jan believes? Has Mathieu made any mistakes up to this point?

7. As Jan tastes the fresh bannock cakes that Mathieu has put in his game bag, he realizes that "everything is different." What has changed? Has Jan changed? Mathieu?

8. What have Mathieu and Jan said to each other "without words"?

## Developing Skills in Reading Literature

1. **Falling Action.** The falling action of a story may be as short as one sentence or as long as several pages. What event is the climax of this story? Where does the falling action begin? What insights into character does the reader gain from the falling action?

2. **Flashback.** Writers sometimes provide background information through flashbacks. Where does the writer use flashback in this story? What information do these flashbacks give the reader about Jan? about Mathieu?

3. **Character.** A character in a short story should be consistent from beginning to end. If a character changes, the change should be consistent with what the reader already knows about his or her personality.

Jan undergoes a major change in this story. Is this change consistent with what the reader already knows about him? Skim the story for all references to Jan's plan to kill the Indians. Is he convinced that it is the right thing to do? Can you find any hints in the story that Jan is sympathetic toward the Indians? Support your answers with examples from the story.

## Developing Vocabulary

1. **Latin Roots.** Root words are the basic building blocks of vocabulary. They are the elements from which other words are formed and the base to which prefixes and suffixes are added. Many of the most common root words come from Latin.

Look up the word *portage* in a dictionary. What does the word mean as it is used in this story? Check the etymology in brackets. What is the Latin root of *portage*? Skim the entries around *portage* and find at least four other English words that have the same root. Be careful not to confuse the root of *portage* with the Latin root *porta,* which means "gate."

2. **Words from Indian Languages.** Look up *tumpline* in an unabridged dictionary. What is the definition? What Indian language did this word probably come from?

3. **Understanding Changes in Language.** The original spelling of *gunnel* was *gunwale.* Look up *gunwale* in a dictionary. How is this word pronounced? Why might the spelling have changed?

## Developing Writing Skills

**Using Figures of Speech.** The writer of this story uses similes and metaphors to describe the winter landscapes of the North Woods. For example, "the drifting snow slid by like sand" (simile); the frozen river is "the known thread that joined him to other men" (metaphor); "he was alone in the middle of a white sea" (metaphor).

Select a favorite place and season, such as the beach in summer or a field of grain in fall. Using similes and metaphors, describe the scene in one paragraph.

# The Fifty-First Dragon     *Heywood Broun*

Of all the pupils at the knight school, Gawaine le Cœur-Hardy was among the least promising. He was tall and sturdy, but his instructors soon discovered that he lacked spirit. He would hide in the woods when the jousting class was called, although his companions and members of the faculty sought to appeal to his better nature by shouting to him to come out and break his neck like a man. Even when they told him that the lances were padded, the horses no more than ponies, and the field unusually soft for late autumn, Gawaine refused to grow enthusiastic. The Headmaster and the Assistant Professor of Pleasaunce[1] were discussing the case one spring afternoon, and the Assistant Professor could see no remedy but expulsion.

"No," said the Headmaster, as he looked out at the purple hills that ringed the school, "I think I'll train him to slay dragons."

"He might be killed," objected the Assistant Professor.

"So he might," replied the Headmaster brightly, but he added more soberly, "We must consider the greater good. We are responsible for the formation of this lad's character."

"Are the dragons particularly bad this year?" interrupted the Assistant Professor. This was characteristic. He always seemed restive when the head of the school began to talk ethics and the ideals of the institution.

"I've never known them worse," replied the Headmaster. "Up in the hills to the south last week they killed a number of peasants, two cows, and a prize pig. And if this dry spell

holds, there's no telling when they may start a forest fire simply by breathing around indiscriminately."

"Would any refund on the tuition fee be necessary in case of an accident to young Cœur-Hardy?"

"No," the principal answered, judicially, "that's all covered in the contract. But as a matter of fact he won't be killed. Before I send him up in the hills I'm going to give him a magic word."

"That's a good idea," said the Professor. "Sometimes they work wonders."

From that day on, Gawaine specialized in dragons. His course included both theory and practice. In the morning there were long lectures on the history, anatomy, manners, and customs of dragons. Gawaine did not distinguish himself in these studies. He had a marvelously versatile gift for forgetting things. In the afternoon he showed to better advantage, for then he would go down to the South Meadow and practice with a battle-ax. In this exercise he was truly impressive, for he had enormous strength, as well as speed and grace. He even developed a deceptive display of ferocity. Old alumni say that it was a thrilling sight to see Gawaine charging across the field toward the dummy paper dragon that had been set up for his practice. As he ran, he would brandish his ax and shout "A murrain[2] on thee!" or some other vivid bit of

---

1. **Pleasaunce** (plez′ ′ns) archaic spelling of *pleasance*: pleasure, merriment, or sport.
2. **murrain** (mur′ in) *Archaic:* any pestilence or plague.

campus slang. It never took him more than one stroke to behead the dummy dragon.

Gradually his task was made more difficult. Paper gave way to papier-mâché and finally to wood, but even the toughest of these dummy dragons had no terrors for Gawaine. One sweep of the ax always did the business. There were those who said that when the practice was protracted until dusk and the dragons threw long, fantastic shadows across the meadow, Gawaine did not charge so impetuously nor shout so loudly. It is possible there was malice in this charge. At any rate, the Headmaster decided by the end of June that it was time for the test. Only the night before, a dragon had come close to the school grounds and had eaten some of the lettuce from the garden. The faculty decided that Gawaine was ready. They gave him a diploma and a new battle-ax, and the Headmaster summoned him to a private conference.

"Sit down," said the Headmaster. "Have a cigarette."

Gawaine hesitated.

"Oh, I know it's against the rules," said the Headmaster. "But after all, you have received your preliminary degree. You are no longer a boy. You are a man. Tomorrow you will go out into the world, the great world of achievement."

Gawaine took a cigarette. The Headmaster offered him a match, but he produced one of his own and began to puff away with a dexterity that quite amazed the principal.

"Here you have learned the theories of life," continued the Headmaster, resuming the thread of his discourse, "but after all, life is not a matter of theories. Life is a matter of facts. It calls on the young and the old alike to face these facts, even though they are hard and sometimes unpleasant. Your problem, for example, is to slay dragons."

"They say that those dragons down in the south wood are five hundred feet long," ventured Gawaine, timorously.

"Stuff and nonsense!" said the Headmaster. "The curate saw one last week from the top of Arthur's Hill. The dragon was sunning himself down in the valley. The curate didn't have an opportunity to look at him very long because he felt it was his duty to hurry back to make a report to me. He said the monster, or shall I say, the big lizard?—wasn't an inch over two hundred feet. But the size has nothing at all to do with it. You'll find the big ones even easier than the little ones. They're far slower on their feet and less aggressive, I'm told. Besides, before you go I'm going to equip you in such fashion that you need have no fear of all the dragons in the world."

"I'd like an enchanted cap," said Gawaine.

"What's that?" answered the Headmaster, testily.

"A cap to make me disappear," explained Gawaine.

The Headmaster laughed indulgently. "You mustn't believe all those old wives' stories," he said. "There isn't any such thing. A cap to make you disappear, indeed! What would you do with it? You haven't even appeared yet. Why, my boy, you could walk from here to London, and nobody would so much as look at you. You're nobody. You couldn't be more invisible than that."

Gawaine seemed dangerously close to a relapse into his old habit of whimpering. The Headmaster reassured him. "Don't worry; I'll give you something much better than an enchanted cap. I'm going to give you a magic word. All you have to do is to repeat this magic charm once and no dragon can possibly harm a hair of your head. You can cut off his head at your leisure."

He took a heavy book from the shelf behind his desk and began to run through it. "Sometimes," he said, "the charm is a whole phrase or even a sentence. I might, for instance, give you 'To make the'—No, that might not do. I think a single word would be best for dragons."

"A short word," suggested Gawaine.

"It can't be too short or it wouldn't be potent. There isn't so much hurry as all that. Here's a splendid magic word, 'Rumplesnitz.' Do you think you can learn that?"

Gawaine tried, and in an hour or so he seemed to have the word well in hand. Again and again he interrupted the lesson to inquire, "And if I say 'Rumplesnitz' the dragon can't possibly hurt me?" And always the Headmaster replied, "If you only say 'Rumplesnitz,' you are perfectly safe."

Toward morning Gawaine seemed resigned to his career. At daybreak the Headmaster saw him to the edge of the forest and pointed him to the direction in which he should proceed. About a mile away to the southwest a cloud of steam hovered over an open meadow in the woods, and the Headmaster assured Gawaine that under the steam he would find a dragon. Gawaine went forward slowly. He wondered whether it would be best to approach the dragon on the run as he did in his practice in the South Meadow or to walk slowly toward him, shouting "Rumplesnitz" all the way.

The problem was decided for him. No sooner had he come to the fringe of the meadow than the dragon spied him and began to charge. It was a large dragon, and yet it seemed decidedly aggressive in spite of the Headmaster's statement to the contrary. As the dragon charged, it released huge clouds of hissing steam through its nostrils. It was almost as if a gigantic teapot had gone mad. The dragon came forward so fast, and Gawaine was so frightened that he had time to say "Rumplesnitz" only once. As he said it, he swung his battle-ax and off popped the head of the dragon. Gawaine had to admit that it was even easier to kill a real dragon

than a wooden one if only you said "Rumplesnitz."

Gawaine brought the ears home and a small section of the tail. His schoolmates and the faculty made much of him; but the Headmaster wisely kept him from being spoiled by insisting that he go on with his work. Every clear day Gawaine rose at dawn and went out to kill dragons. The Headmaster kept him at home when it rained, because he said that the woods were damp and unhealthy at such times and that he didn't want the boy to run any needless risks. Few good days passed in which Gawaine failed to get a dragon. On one particularly fortunate day he killed three, a husband and wife and a visiting relative. Gradually he developed a technique. Pupils who sometimes watched him from the hilltops a long way off said that he often allowed the dragon to come within a few feet before he said "Rumplesnitz." He came to say it with a mocking sneer. Occasionally he did stunts. Once when an excursion party from London was watching him, he went into action with his right hand tied behind his back. The dragon's head came off just as easily.

As Gawaine's record of killings mounted higher, the Headmaster found it impossible to keep him completely in hand. He fell into the habit of stealing out at night and engaging in long drinking bouts at the village tavern. It was after such a debauch that he rose a little before dawn one fine August morning and started out after his fiftieth dragon. His head was heavy and his mind sluggish. He was heavy in other respects as well, for he had adopted the somewhat vulgar practice of wearing his medals, ribbons and all, when he went out dragon hunting. The decorations began on his chest and ran all the way down to his abdomen. They must have weighed at least eight pounds.

Gawaine found a dragon in the same

meadow where he had killed the first one. It was a fair-sized dragon, but evidently an old one. Its face was wrinkled, and Gawaine thought he had never seen so hideous a countenance. Much to the lad's disgust, the monster refused to charge, and Gawaine was obliged to walk toward him. He whistled as he went. The dragon regarded him hopelessly, but craftily. Of course it had heard of Gawaine. Even when the lad raised his battle-ax, the dragon made no move. It knew that there was no salvation in the quickest thrust of the head, for it had been informed that this hunter was protected by an enchantment. It merely waited, hoping something would turn up. Gawaine raised the battle-ax and suddenly lowered it again. He had grown very pale, and he trembled violently. The dragon suspected a trick. "What's the matter?" it asked, with false solicitude.

"I've forgotten the magic word," stammered Gawaine.

"What a pity," said the dragon. "So that was the secret. It doesn't seem quite sporting to me, all this magic stuff, you know. Not cricket, as we used to say when I was a little dragon; but after all, that's a matter of opinion."

Gawaine was so helpless with terror that the dragon's confidence rose immeasurably, and it could not resist the temptation to show off a bit.

"Could I possibly be of any assistance?" it asked. "What's the first letter of the magic word?"

"It begins with an r," said Gawaine weakly.

"Let's see," mused the dragon, "that doesn't tell us much, does it? What sort of word is this? Is it an epithet, do you think?"

Gawaine could do no more than nod.

"Why, of course," exclaimed the dragon, " 'reactionary Republicans.' "

Gawaine shook his head.

"Well, then," said the dragon, "we'd better get down to business. Will you surrender?"

With the suggestion of a compromise, Gawaine mustered up enough courage to speak.

"What will you do if I surrender?" he asked.

"Why, I'll eat you," said the dragon.

"And if I don't surrender?"

"I'll eat you just the same."

"Then it doesn't make any difference, does it?" moaned Gawaine.

"It does to me," said the dragon with a smile. "I'd rather you didn't surrender. You'd taste much better if you didn't."

The dragon waited for a long time for Gawaine to ask "Why?" but the boy was too frightened to speak. At last the dragon had to give the explanation without his cue line. "You see," he said, "if you don't surrender you'll taste better because you'll die game."

This was an old and ancient trick of the dragon's. By means of some such quip, he was accustomed to paralyze his victims with laughter and then to destroy them. Gawaine was sufficiently paralyzed as it was, but laughter had no part in his helplessness. With the last word of the joke the dragon drew back his head and struck. In that second there flashed into the mind of Gawaine the magic word "Rumplesnitz," but there was no time to say it. There was time only to strike and, without a word, Gawaine met the onrush of the dragon with a full swing. He put all his back and shoulders into it. The impact was terrific and the head of the dragon flew away almost a hundred yards and landed in a thicket.

Gawaine did not remain frightened very long after the death of the dragon. His mood was one of wonder. He was enormously puzzled. He cut off the ears of the monster almost in a trance. Again and again he thought to himself, "I didn't say 'Rumplesnitz'!" He was sure of that, and yet there was no question that he had killed the dragon. In fact, he had never killed one so utterly. Never before had he driven a head for anything like the same distance. Twenty-five yards was perhaps his best previous record. All the way back to the knight school he kept rumbling about in his mind seeking an explanation for what had occurred. He went to the Headmaster immediately, and after closing the door told him what had happened. "I didn't say Rumplesnitz," he explained with great earnestness.

The Headmaster laughed. "I'm glad you've found out," he said. "It makes you ever so much more of a hero. Don't you see that? Now you know that it was you who killed all these dragons and not that foolish little word Rumplesnitz."

Gawaine frowned. "Then it wasn't a magic word after all?" he asked.

"Of course not," said the Headmaster, "you ought to be too old for such foolishness. There isn't any such thing as a magic word."

"But you told me it was magic," protested Gawaine. "You said it was magic and now you say it isn't."

"It wasn't magic in a literal sense," answered the Headmaster, "but it was much more wonderful than that. The word gave you confidence. It took away your fears. If I hadn't told you that, you might have been killed the very first time. It was your battle-ax did the trick."

Gawaine surprised the Headmaster by his attitude. He was obviously distressed by the explanation. He interrupted a long philosophic and ethical discourse by the Headmaster with, "If I hadn't of hit 'em all mighty hard and fast, any one of 'em might have crushed me like a, like a—" He fumbled for a word.

"Egg shell," suggested the Headmaster.

"Like a egg shell," assented Gawaine, and he said it many times. All through the evening meal people who sat near him heard him muttering, "Like a egg shell, like a egg shell."

The next day was clear, but Gawaine did not get up at dawn. Indeed, it was almost noon when the Headmaster found him cowering in bed, with the clothes pulled over his head. The principal called the Assistant Professor of Pleasaunce, and together they dragged the boy toward the forest.

"He'll be all right as soon as he gets a couple more dragons under his belt," explained the Headmaster.

The Assistant Professor of Pleasaunce agreed. "It would be a shame to stop such a fine run," he said. "Why, counting that one yesterday, he's killed fifty dragons."

They pushed the boy into a thicket above which hung a meager cloud of steam. It was obviously quite a small dragon. But Gawaine did not come back that night or the next. In fact, he never came back. Some weeks afterward, brave spirits from the school explored the thicket, but they could find nothing to remind them of Gawaine except the metal parts of his medals. Even the ribbons had been devoured.

The Headmaster and the Assistant Professor of Pleasaunce agreed that it would be just as well not to tell the school how Gawaine had achieved his record and still less how he came to die. They held that it might have a bad effect on school spirit. Accordingly, Gawaine has lived in the memory of the school as its greatest hero. No visitor succeeds in leaving the building today without seeing a great shield that hangs on the wall of the dining hall. Fifty pairs of dragons' ears are mounted upon the shield, and underneath in gilt letters is "Gawaine le Cœur-Hardy," followed by the simple inscription, "He killed fifty dragons." The record has never been equaled.

## Getting at Meaning

1. Gawaine is the least promising student at the school for knights. What qualities does he lack? Why does the Headmaster choose him to slay dragons?

2. As he practices to become a dragon slayer, what weaknesses and strengths does Gawaine display?

3. Why does Gawaine ask for an enchanted cap? for a short magic word?

4. What does Gawaine's behavior as a dragon slayer reveal about his attitude toward his work? about himself as a person?

5. In the conversation between Gawaine and his fiftieth dragon, the dragon appears to be crafty and tricky. What does Gawaine appear to be?

6. How does the Headmaster react to the boy's discovery that Rumplesnitz is not a magic word? How does Gawaine react? Why are their reactions different?

7. Why is Gawaine killed by his fifty-first dragon?

## Developing Skills in Reading Literature

1. **Conflict.** What are the external conflicts faced by Gawaine in this story? What internal conflict does he face?

2. **Climax.** What is the turning point in this story?

3. **Character and Plot.** As the rising action moves toward the climax, the character of Gawaine develops. The reader forms a clear picture of Gawaine through descriptions of his behavior while slaying dragons and of his actions as a celebrated hero. How is the climax of the story created or affected by the person that Gawaine has become?

4. **Tone.** The tone of a story is the attitude of a writer toward his or her subject. Tone may be serious, sad, humorous, objective, or whatever else the writer chooses. In this story, a young man, who is rather cowardly, becomes a great dragon slayer, but he is killed in the end by his fifty-first dragon. Although the subject is essentially tragic, the pervading tone is amusement. Find five examples of humorous incidents, descriptive passages, and comments made by the characters. Explain how each helps to establish and maintain the tone of the story.

# Theme

**LES BALADINS,** 1905. *Pablo Picasso.*
*Stattsgalerie, Stuttgart.*

# A Day's Wait    *Ernest Hemingway*

He came into the room to shut the windows while we were still in bed, and I saw he looked ill. He was shivering, his face was white, and he walked slowly as though it ached to move.

"What's the matter, Schatz?"

"I've got a headache."

"You better go back to bed."

"No. I'm all right."

"You go to bed. I'll see you when I'm dressed."

But when I came downstairs he was dressed, sitting by the fire, looking a very sick and miserable boy of nine years. When I put my hand on his forehead I knew he had a fever.

"You go up to bed," I said, "you're sick."

"I'm all right," he said.

When the doctor came he took the boy's temperature.

"What is it?" I asked him.

"One hundred and two."

Downstairs, the doctor left three different medicines in different colored capsules with instructions for giving them. One was to bring down the fever, another a purgative, the third to overcome an acid condition. The germs of influenza can exist only in an acid condition, he explained. He seemed to know all about influenza and said there was nothing to worry about if the fever did not go above one hundred and four degrees. This was a light epidemic of flu, and there was no danger if you avoided pneumonia.

Back in the room I wrote down the boy's temperature and made a note of the time to give the various capsules.

"Do you want me to read to you?"

"All right. If you want to," said the boy. His face was very white and there were dark areas under his eyes. He lay still in the bed and seemed very detached from what was going on.

I read aloud from Howard Pyle's *Book of Pirates;* but I could see he was not following what I was reading.

"How do you feel, Schatz?" I asked him.

"Just the same, so far," he said.

I sat at the foot of the bed and read to myself while I waited for it to be time to give another capsule. It would have been natural for him to go to sleep, but when I looked up he was looking at the foot of the bed, looking very strangely.

"Why don't you try to go to sleep? I'll wake you up for the medicine."

"I'd rather stay awake."

After a while he said to me, "You don't have to stay in here with me, Papa, if it bothers you."

"It doesn't bother me."

"No, I mean you don't have to stay if it's going to bother you."

I thought perhaps he was a little light-headed, and after giving him the prescribed capsules at eleven o'clock I went out for a while. It was a bright, cold day, the ground covered with a sleet that had frozen so that it seemed as if all the bare trees, the bushes, the cut brush and all the grass and the bare ground had been varnished with ice. I took the young Irish setter for a little walk up the road and along a frozen creek, but it was difficult to stand or walk on the glassy surface, and the red dog slipped and slithered and I fell twice, hard, once dropping my gun

and having it slide away over the ice.

We flushed a covey of quail under a high clay bank with overhanging brush, and I killed two as they went out of sight over the top of the bank. Some of the covey lit in trees, but most of them scattered into brush piles; and it was necessary to jump on the ice-coated mounds of brush several times before they would flush. Coming out while you were poised unsteadily on the icy, springy brush, they made difficult shooting and I killed two, missed five, and started back pleased to have found a covey close to the house and happy there were so many left to find on another day.

At the house they said the boy had refused to let any one come into the room.

"You can't come in," he said. "You mustn't get what I have."

I went up to him and found him in exactly the position I had left him, white-faced, but with the tops of his cheeks flushed by the fever, staring still, as he had stared, at the foot of the bed.

I took his temperature.

"What is it?"

"Something like a hundred," I said. It was one hundred and two and four-tenths.

"It was a hundred and two," he said.

"Who said so?"

"The doctor."

"Your temperature is all right," I said. "It's nothing to worry about."

"I don't worry," he said, "but I can't keep from thinking."

"Don't think," I said. "Just take it easy."

"I'm taking it easy," he said and looked straight ahead. He was evidently holding tight onto himself about something.

"Take this with water."

"Do you think it will do any good?"

"Of course it will."

I sat down and opened the *Pirate* book and commenced to read, but I could see he was not following, so I stopped.

"About what time do you think I'm going to die?" he asked.

"What?"

"About how long will it be before I die?"

"You aren't going to die. What's the matter with you?"

"Oh, yes, I am. I heard him say a hundred and two."

"People don't die with a fever of one hundred and two. That's a silly way to talk."

"I know they do. At school in France the boys told me you can't live with forty-four degrees. I've got a hundred and two."

He had been waiting to die all day, ever since nine o'clock in the morning.

"You poor Schatz," I said. "Poor old Schatz. It's like miles and kilometers. You aren't going to die. That's a different thermometer. On that thermometer thirty-seven is normal. On this kind it's ninety-eight."

"Are you sure?"

"Absolutely," I said. "It's like miles and kilometers. You know, like how many kilometers we make when we do seventy miles in the car?"

"Oh," he said.

But his gaze at the foot of the bed relaxed slowly. The hold over himself relaxed too, finally, and the next day it was very slack and he cried very easily at little things that were of no importance.

## Getting at Meaning

1. The narrator asks, "What's the matter, Schatz?" Why does Schatz answer, "I've got a headache"?

2. Who hears the doctor report that Schatz's temperature is one hundred and two? Who hears the doctor explain that the fever is nothing to worry about?

3. What is unusual about Schatz's behavior as his father reads to him? How does his father explain this behavior?

4. Despite the icy conditions, Schatz's father is pleased with his hunting. Why?

5. Why had Schatz been "holding tight onto himself"?

6. Why does Schatz cry easily the day after his discovery that he is not going to die?

## Developing Skills in Reading Literature

1. **Theme.** Even if the theme of a story is not direct or obvious, the main idea unifies the story, giving a purpose to the comments and actions of characters and to apparently minor incidents. As he waits to die, why does Schatz stare at the foot of the bed? Why does he seem detached from the activities going on around him? What is he attempting to endure? How does he feel about the future? When the father goes hunting, what difficulties does he experience? How does he feel about his experience? What is his attitude toward the immediate future based upon his hunting experience? Given the contrast in the feelings of these two characters, what might the writer be saying about the effect of future hopes upon current feelings?

2. **First-Person Narration.** Schatz's father is the narrator of this story. Thus, the reader shares his experience and his adult point of view. What is the narrator's attitude toward sickness? How does this attitude affect the way he treats his son? What is the narrator's reaction to his son's belief that he is going to die?

## Developing Writing Skills

**Telling the Same Story from a Different Point of View.** How would this story be different if it were told from Schatz's point of view? Write one paragraph in which Schatz is the first-person narrator. Reveal his thoughts either while his father is talking to the doctor or while his father is hunting.

# Evening Flight   *Don Moser*

It was almost time for the evening flight, and Jeff walked along the Lake Erie beach near the water's edge where the sand was hard, and the late sun threw a long shadow in front of him. A boy of eleven, he walked slowly, hands in his blue jeans' pockets, his new tennis shoes leaving waffle-prints in the wet sand behind him. After a while he looked up and stopped. He saw Black Jack shuffle out of the sand dunes farther up the beach. Black Jack dropped his burlap sack of empty pop bottles on the sand and peered around. He saw Jeff and put his hand over his eyes to shade them from the low sun.

The boy and the old beachcomber stood on the sand looking at each other. Jeff took his hands from his pockets and rubbed them on his jeans. He was frightened. If Ken and Jimmy were with him he would not be afraid, but there was no one at all on the beach, nothing but the gulls curling over the water. Jeff didn't believe the stories he had heard about Black Jack putting children in the burlap sack and carrying them off to his shack down in the marsh. Jeff didn't believe that story or the others Ken's father had told him, but he was still afraid of the old man.

Black Jack kept peering at him from under his hand. Jeff thought, "I won't leave. I want to go to the bridge and see the birds. I'll just stand here and flip stones, and maybe he won't recognize me. If he comes down the beach I can run and I can beat him back to the park, and if he goes up the beach I can wait a while and go on to the bridge."

Jeff picked up a small flat stone from the sand and flipped it out on the water, using only his wrist. The stone sailed flat and bounced off the water and sailed and bounced again and again. The low sun turned the waves bright and silvery, and Jeff couldn't see the stone fly in the glare until it hit and made a splash of spray. He pretended to look for another stone then, watching the beachcomber out of the corner of his eye. He saw Black Jack pick up his sack of bottles again and sling it over his shoulder and go shuffling up the beach.

"He didn't recognize me," Jeff thought. "That's good. I can still go to the bridge now and see the flight."

Jeff stayed by the water's edge until Black Jack had gone farther up the beach, then followed slowly so that he wouldn't catch up. Black Jack moved along, taking his time, looking on the sand for empty soda-pop bottles and things bathers had left during the day. Jeff saw him lean over to pick something from the sand and put it in the burlap sack. "I wish he would hurry," Jeff thought. "I'll miss them if I don't get to the bridge soon."

After a while the old man passed the point where the path to the bridge came out of the dunes onto the beach, and when the boy reached it he ran in among the dunes, not afraid now that Black Jack couldn't see him. He ran along the faint sandy path, dodging twisted driftwood logs until he reached the grass meadow that skirted the marsh. He followed the meadow to the line of willow trees and went down among them, stooping low under the heavy-hanging branches. He parted the branches and came out onto the old wooden footbridge that crossed a neck of the marsh.

Jeff walked onto the bridge and climbed up on the wide handrail and sat on it, swinging his legs over the dark water. "I'm in time," he thought. "They haven't started yet." He looked out across the low dunes to the lake lying like hammered silver in the sun. "The flight won't start until the sun is almost on the water," he thought. He pushed his brown hair back from his eyes and watched the swallows spinning over the marsh, and thought about how he had first found the bridge and watched the evening flight.

Two weeks before, Jeff had moved from the city to the little shore village on the lake. A few evenings ago his new friends, Ken and Jimmy, asked him to go to the beach with them. Jeff's mother didn't want him to go because of the things she had heard about the old man who lived in the marsh and prowled the beach in the evening.

"He's filthy," she said. "I saw him down at Morrow's grocery—he'd brought in a sack of bottles to get the deposit refunds. He's the filthiest thing I've ever seen, and I don't want you to go near that man." But Jeff's father said that he could go if he was careful.

So he and Ken and Jimmy went to the beach, and they saw Black Jack there and teased him. After they ran away from him, they walked along the water's edge looking for stones and shells. Moving ahead, Ken picked up something from the sand, then called for them to come look at it. He held a small piece of driftwood, smoothed and shaped by the waves so that it looked like a knife—like a pirate's dagger. Jeff wanted the dagger, but Ken said that he was going to sand it and paint it silver like a real dagger. And when they walked back down the beach, Ken wore it stuck in his belt, draping his hand carelessly over the hilt.

The next night Jeff went back to the beach to see if he could find another. Ken and Jimmy had gone to the movies, so he went alone. He walked up the beach for a long way, much farther than they had gone the night before, and he watched the sand closely for a piece of driftwood shaped like a dagger, but he found nothing. Then he came upon the faint path leading back through the dunes, and wondering where it led, he followed it to the bridge.

He had sat on the rail, just as now, and then the flight began, with all the world yellow in the sunset and the small birds flying in thousands up the marsh. He watched it until dusk, and he had never seen anything like it before. It was better than African movies, better than circuses, better than anything.

Something dimpled the water of the marsh, and a ring swelled out across the dark smooth surface and rippled against cattail stems. Jeff wondered what had done it. Then a rustling sound came from the willows. Jeff looked at the green band of trees and stiffened.

Black Jack shuffled out of the willows onto the bridge. The burlap sack of bottles clinked as he set it on the footboards. Black Jack peered down the bridge and saw Jeff. "Hello, boy," he said. His voice was hard.

Jeff sat frozen still on the rail and didn't answer. He stared at Black Jack. The old man's face was red, with wrinkles black-lined with dirt. His long gray hair was matted over his ears and hung down from beneath his smashed hat. Red eyes looked out from under thick gray eyebrows. He wore baggy trousers and a dark and greasy suit coat ripped at the shoulder. He had old and calloused hands. Black Jack leaned against the rail and looked down the marsh.

Jeff sat unmoving on the rail. "I wonder if I ought to run?" he thought. But if he ran down to the other end of the bridge he would come out into the marshes, and he was afraid he would get lost or fall into the quicksand Ken said was there. And he couldn't get to the beach end of the bridge without passing Black Jack. He was afraid of the old man, but he didn't want to leave and miss the flight. "Maybe he won't know me," Jeff thought. "I hope he doesn't remember me."

They had teased Black Jack when he came shuffling along the sand looking for bottles. They ran up the beach before him and found some bottles by a burned out campfire. They waited until the old man got almost to them, then they threw the bottles far out into the waves. Jeff wanted to stop them, but Ken ran near the old man and screamed at him, "You're a tramp! You're a dirty tramp!" Then Ken pulled out his slingshot and picked up a pebble from the sand and snapped it away. It hit Black Jack in the shoulder, and he dropped the sack of bottles and started to chase Ken, half running, half shuffling in the soft sand. They all ran then, down the long beach near the water's edge until the old man was just a small black shape behind them.

Suddenly Black Jack stepped away from the bridge rail and pointed out toward the lake.

"Look there," he said.

Jeff looked up. Two specks cracked down over the marsh and flashed high above the bridge. At the east end of the marsh the ducks banked and turned and came back low over the bridge, wings straining against the air, heads out straight on long necks. They slid out across the bright water of the lake into the sun. The boy and the old man shaded their eyes with their hands and watched them until they were gone.

"Them's mallards," Black Jack said.

"I know it," Jeff lied. "Anybody knows mallards."

Black Jack took off his hat and ran his hand through his matted gray hair. Then he looked at Jeff, who was staring at him with wide eyes.

"You ever been here before, boy?"

"Sure, I've been here lots of time. I've been all through these marshes."

It was only the third time he had been there. There was the first night and then last night when he had asked his father to go with him to the bridge. He tried to tell his father about the flight, but his father was reading the paper, and he said he was too tired to walk all that way down the beach. "Why don't you take Kenneth?" his father said. "And you be careful about that old tramp who lives down there in the marsh. I don't want you going near him." Jeff didn't want to take Ken somehow. He didn't think Ken would like the place he had found, but he did take him, finally.

"Hey, boy," Black Jack said, "ain't you one of them kids who was pestering me the other night?" Jeff sat stiffly on the rail and looked at the old man's calloused hands and the big burlap sack curled on the footboards. "Ain't you one of them kids?"

"No. I never bothered you. I've never seen you before."

Black Jack shuffled a few steps closer and peered at the boy with his small red eyes. Jeff gripped the rail and bit down on his lip. "Do you know that tow-headed kid? Ken, his name is."

"No. No, I don't know him."

"Well, that kid's no good. I better not ever get my hands on him. He'll be sorry if I do."

Black Jack rubbed his hands on his dirty trousers and leaned against the rail again.

Jeff relaxed his grip on the rail and sucked in a deep breath. When he had brought Ken to the marsh the night before to show him the flight, Ken stamped on the bridge and shook it and tried to break off a section of the rail, and Jeff began to wish that he had come alone. Later, after the flight began, Jeff looked over at Ken standing spread-legged with his slingshot pulled back the length of his arm. "Hey!" Jeff cried, but the sling snapped and one of the birds dropped from the flock and fell softly onto the water. The small brown bird floated slowly down beneath them with its still wings stretched out on the smooth water and its head turned sideways on the neck, one veiled eye gazing up at them.

"Here," Ken said holding out the sling, "You want to get one?"

"No." Jeff watched the dead bird swing in slow circles on the water. "Don't shoot any more, all right?"

And Ken didn't shoot any more, but the evening was spoiled for Jeff, so this night he had come to the bridge alone.

Black Jack was fumbling in the deep pockets of his old coat. He brought out something wrapped in brown paper. He sloughed the paper off and took out a thick meat sandwich. He broke it in two and held one of the halves toward Jeff. "You want a piece of samwich, boy?"

"No, thank you," Jeff said. "I'm not hungry."

The old man shrugged. He ate one of the halves of the sandwich, stuffing it into his mouth and licking his fingers afterward. Then he took a chunk of the meat from the other half and dropped it into the water below the bridge. The water swirled and splashed and the meat was gone. Jeff stared at the rippling water. Black Jack looked at him and grinned.

"What was it?" Jeff whispered.

"Bass," Black Jack said. "There's big uns in here. Watch now." He broke another piece from the sandwich and dropped it into the water. The swirl and splash again, and the meat was gone. "If you stand right here above 'em," he said, "you can see 'em in the water."

Jeff hesitated, then climbed down from the rail and walked slowly down the bridge. A few feet from the old man he stopped and looked over the rail. His mouth opened in surprise. Two heavy dark shapes coasted in slow circles in the brown water below him. Black Jack dropped another piece of meat. Jeff saw one of the shapes circle near the floating meat, saw the muscle-banded tail snap and the sudden flash and swirl of the strike. Black Jack dropped another piece and this time the other fish struck. Jeff stood on the bottom rail and leaned out to watch the two long shadows cruising in the dark water.

"Hey!" Black Jack said. "You be careful you don't fall in there, boy." He held out the rest of the sandwich toward Jeff. "Here, boy. You want to feed 'em some?"

"No." Jeff stepped down from the rail. "They aren't anything. They're just old fish."

He moved back down the bridge a few feet and leaned against the rail and looked out across the dunes to the lake. The sun almost touched the waves. The light would begin soon, Jeff thought. He wished that Black Jack would leave. If he stayed he would spoil it.

"If you find something really nice," the boy thought, "you want to tell somebody. You want somebody to see it with you and talk about it a little bit afterward. But if you do tell somebody, they either don't come, like my father; or they spoil it, like Ken, so it's better not to tell anybody and just watch it by yourself."

Black Jack scratched himself. "Birds'll start coming up the marsh pretty soon now," he said. "The sun is almost on the water, so they'll start pretty soon, and you never seen so many birds."

"There's not so many," Jeff said. "I've been here lots of times. This place isn't much."

"Well, maybe it's not," the old man said. "I always thought this was a pretty nice place, but I guess there's plenty of places I ain't ever been."

"Why can't he leave and not spoil it?" Jeff

thought. He remembered some of the things that his father and Ken's father had said about Black Jack. Ken's father said that he was a worthless old tramp, and the sheriff should get rid of him because the villagers didn't like to let their children go down to the beach alone with him always prowling around.

Black Jack took a dark old pipe from the pocket of his coat and dipped it full from a cracked leather tobacco pouch. He struck a big wooden match on the rail and lit the pipe. He puffed out smoke, then suddenly pointed down the marsh with his pipestem.

"Here they come, boy. Here come the first of them."

Jeff looked down the marsh and saw a group of specks grow into flying birds and whir in across the water. They passed low on straining wings over the man and the boy on the bridge.

Another flock spun out of the cattails and then another and another. The low sun cut across the marsh, and the world of the marsh turned butter-yellow in the evening light. The north wind came in from the lake and moved in the sweeping branches of the willows and rustled them, and the tall poplars standing down the marsh spun their silver

leaves in the sunset. The flocks of small brown birds came up out of the cattails and up out of the marshland, and they filled the air with the rush of their soft wings and the high, thin sound of their voices. The flocks became larger and joined together and joined again and passed in streaming hundreds above the bridge.

The old man moved down the bridge and leaned against the rail at Jeff's side. The boy looked at him, then looked back to the flight.

"What are they?"

"Red-wings," the old man said. "I call 'em that, but it don't matter much what the name is."

"But they are brown," the boy said. "The wings aren't red at all."

"Them is just the mother birds. The mothers and the young 'uns. The fathers got red on the wings, but they left already. Gone South for the winter. These'll go too, pretty soon now." He pointed into the streaming flocks with his pipestem. "Watch them, boy," he said. "Watch them, how they race the sun."

Jeff looked up again. There were flocks no longer, just a great river of flying birds thrumming up out of the marsh and whirring over the bridge on soft dark wings. Jeff sat on the rail with his legs over the brown water and smelled the strong, rich smell of the old man's pipe, and he saw the swallows cutting and skimming over the smooth water and whisking through the cattail clumps. He watched a pair of teal drop from high against a tower of clouds on fire in sunset and rifle in across the lake and over evening-yellow dunes and all the yellow burlap land of cattails and marsh grasses. And above the lake gulls turned on long, bent wings against the sun and dropped to the glittering waves.

The sun was almost gone behind the edge of the water and the marsh turned from yellow into gray and only the tall poplars glittered yellow and silver down the last seconds of the day. And the rushing stream above him became flocks again, and the flocks grew smaller and smaller as they strained up out of the dusk. The gray line of night moved up the yellow and silver of the poplars and then it reached the top and the yellow and silver were gone and out across the lake the sun was gone and in the air the birds were gone, and the air was empty and quiet.

The boy and the old man on the bridge were silent. The old man drew on his pipe and blew the smoke out into the air; the boy swung his legs and looked down at the water below them.

"I wonder where they all go?" he said.

"To find some place to sleep, some place to spend the night," the old man said. "I don't know where they go, exactly, but I like to watch them here at evening when they fly the marsh. Look there, boy. There's the first bat. You see him?"

Jeff saw the bat spin and turn above the cattails on quick wings. "He's fast," Jeff said. "I didn't know they were so fast. I've never seen one before."

They stayed on the bridge for a while, watching the bat; then the old man knocked out his pipe against the rail.

"Be dark pretty soon, boy. You want to walk back down the beach with me?"

Jeff looked at the old man and hesitated for a moment. Then, "No," he said. "I don't go home along the beach. I go across the bridge and through the marshes. I don't care about the dark anyway."

"All right, boy. If you can find your way. Good night now."

The old man shuffled back down the bridge and picked up his clinking sack of bottles, then went down into the willows and was gone. Jeff sat on the rail with his chin in his hands and looked down at the water. He sat there for a while, and then he climbed down and went off the bridge and through the willows. He crossed the meadow and went in among the dunes. He walked slowly along the path, his hands jammed down in his pockets. When he reached the beach he saw something dark and shiny half buried in the sand. He stopped and kicked at it with his tennis shoe, then reached down and picked it up. He held it in his hand and stood there looking at it for a long time, and then he looked up, and he ran, ran down the long beach in the dusk after the small dark figure ahead of him, holding the bottle to his chest.

## Getting at Meaning

1. Why do the villagers dislike Black Jack? Has Jack harmed anyone? Jeff doesn't believe the stories about Jack, yet he fears the old man. Why?

2. Jeff is fascinated by the mallards, the bass, and the birds, yet he hides his interest from Black Jack. Why? What is Jeff trying to prove?

3. Does Jeff's father appreciate what Jeff has found in the marsh? Explain.

4. How does Ken spoil Jeff's experience at the bridge? Contrast Ken's reaction to the evening flight with Black Jack's. Which view does Jeff share? Does Jeff realize this similarity immediately? Why or why not?

5. Find two examples of Black Jack's concern for Jeff's safety. What effect does this concern have on the reader's view of Black Jack?

6. Why does Jeff chase Black Jack with the bottle? What change has occurred in Jeff?

## Developing Skills in Reading Literature

1. **Theme.** One way to formulate the theme of a story is to think about what happens to the central character, and then to state the importance of that event in terms that apply to all human beings.

Who is the protagonist in this story? What of major importance happens to him? What does the writer want the reader to understand about the reactions of all human beings in similar situations? State the theme of the story in a declarative sentence.

2. **Tone.** What is the writer's attitude toward nature in this story? What adjectives might you use to describe his attitude? Which of these adjectives describe the tone of the story as a whole?

## Developing Vocabulary

**Using Precise Verbs.** This writer uses precise verbs to describe even the most ordinary actions. The boy *dodges* the logs, and *skirts* the marsh. Something *dimples* the water and the surface *ripples*. The mallards *crack down* over the marsh and *flash* above the bridge.

Skim the story and find at least eight more examples of precise verbs. List the examples, along with the page number on which each appears.

## Developing Writing Skills

**Combining Description and Exposition.** Jeff says, "If you find something really nice, . . . you want to tell somebody. . . . But if you do tell somebody they either don't come, . . . or they spoil it. . . ."

Do you agree or disagree? Describe a place that you discovered and then tried to share with someone. Explain whether the sharing was a success or a failure and why. Develop this topic as a five-paragraph composition.

# The Passing    *Durango Mendoza*

Ever since Mama married Miguel we had lived in the country. He had built a tall, single-walled, two-room house on the land of his family above the big bend of Fish Creek, and it stood there, lean and unpainted among the trees back from the road. Even after Mama and I came to live there it remained unpainted. It was built of unfinished sawmill planks and had two stovepipe chimneys sticking through its green roof. Right across the road was the Indian church.

The house stood above a steep, boulder-littered and heavily wooded slope and the creek that ran below. I had developed a swimming hole there, and across the creek on the wooded slopes I played at hunting. It had been almost ten years since we had settled there, and I had already explored the surrounding countryside for miles in winter and summer so that I now usually stayed close to the house. Summer had grown old, and I was becoming restless.

One evening as I played cars with pieces of wood in the dust beside the house, Mama saw the boy coming along the road. She stopped gathering the clothes from the line and took the clothespins from her mouth. I looked after her gaze and beyond. Through the shadows and trees I saw how the road curved and disappeared quickly into the dusk and woods. I looked back to her when she spoke.

"Sonny, there goes Joe Willow," she said. Then she paused and put the shirt she was holding into the basket at her feet. "He sure does work hard. I hope old Jimmy Bear and Fannie appreciate it, those two."

She shook her head and began to gather the rest of the clothes. I sat back on my heels and wondered at the tone of her voice. I had never really noticed Joe Willow before, but I knew the rest of the family from church meetings. And once I had seen where they lived.

It was about a mile beyond the curve, far back from the road and reached by a rutted drive that skirted the Indian graveyard. I knew the graveyard because near it were some pecan trees from which I gathered the nuts each fall. Their house was very old and unpainted. It sat low and gray under a group of large blackjack oaks and within a grassless yard that was pressed closely by the thick, surrounding woods.

Joe Willow's mother, Fannie, was a short, round woman with mottled brown skin and a high, shiny forehead that wrinkled when she laughed. Jimmy Bear was her second husband, and they used to pass our house often on their way to town. They had once driven an old Dodge, but it no longer ran, and it now sat lopsided and windowless among the weeds beside their lane. Jimmy Bear was a skinny man, but he had a round, protruding belly and wore his belt under it so that it looked as if he carried a basketball inside. He had gaps in his teeth and a rough, guttural laugh and walked with a shuffle. Mama told me that Fannie had once had money, but that they had long since used it up.

The next evening when Joe Willow passed the gate, I got up and ran to hang on it as I watched him pass on up the road. The sun, being low and to his back, sent a long finger of shadow ahead of him. I could hear the crunch and whisper of his footsteps between the squeaks of the bucket he carried until they began to fade with the coming of the breeze through the tall grass alongside the road. The bucket creaked faintly and the breeze dropped for a moment.

I called to him.

"Hello, Joe Willow," I said.

In the stillness my voice carried, and he turned, his shadow pointing into the woods, and lifted his hand. He squinted into the sun and smiled. I waved, and he turned back up the road and soon faded against the shadow and trees.

I sat on the gate for a while until a deeper darkness crept from the woods and began to fuse with the trees. I heard the trees begin to sigh and settle down for the night, the lonely cooing of a dove, and from somewhere across the creek the hoot of an owl. Then I hurried back to the house in the new coolness and stood near my mom for a while as she moved about the warm iron cookstove preparing supper.

Almost every evening of August that summer, the young Indian passed along the road in front of our gate. I saw him several times a week as he came up from the bridge, always carrying a small, empty lard bucket whose handle squeaked faintly as he passed by and out of sight. He walked like someone who is used to walking, slowly, without spirit, but with the strength seen in a young workhorse.

Many evenings I swung back and forth on the gate and waited for him to come by. I had no brothers or sisters as yet, but Mama was expecting Miguel's first child before spring. Miguel was my stepfather, and since he said very little to me and because I couldn't be around Mama all the time, I waited for Joe Willow to pass by, although I seldom spoke except to reply to his greetings. Often I didn't even show myself at all and only sat among the grapevines next to the gate until the darkness sent me home.

I remember one of the last times I saw him. It was early in September, and I was sitting on the gate watching the sun caught on the treetops, noticing how the leaves looked like embers across its face as it settled into them, when Joe Willow appeared like a moving post upon the road. I had just gotten down from the gate and sat on the large rock that propped up our mailbox when Miguel called for me to eat supper. Instead, I began to sift sand into little conical piles as I waited. I looked down the road past the young worker to where the sun had fallen behind the trees. It looked trapped. The wind was very soft and smelled of smoke and dust. A few birds chuckled above me in the trees, and the insects of the evening buzzed in the weeds below.

Miguel called again and I looked up.

"Howdy, Joe Willow," I said. "You coming home from work?"

He stopped and grinned.

"That's right," he said. He leaned on the mailbox, and we said nothing for a few moments until he spoke again. "You're Miguel's boy, aren't you?"

"Huh-uh. I belong to Rosa."

"Oh." He squatted down. "You know what? I'm the same way. Everybody calls me Jimmy Bear's boy, but I'm not. He's not my daddy."

We both shifted around and watched where the sun had gone down.

"You see what happens when the sun goes down?" He pointed to the evening star and motioned toward the other stars that had appeared in the east. "When the daddy goes to bed, all the little children come out." His teeth gleamed in the gathering darkness, and I smiled, too.

We had watched the stars for only a moment when Miguel called again.

"You better get on home," Joe Willow said. "That's your daddy calling you."

"I'm Rosa's boy," I said.

"I know," he said, "but you better get on back." He looked up again at the deepening sky and laughed softly. "I'll see you some other time—'Rosa's boy.'"

After September came, I started school and no longer saw Joe Willow pass our gate. One day I asked Mama about him, and she said that he had gone to the free Indian boarding school in the northern part of the state, just south of the Kansas line. It was when winter was just melting into spring, a few weeks after Mama had returned from the hospital with my baby brother, that I remembered him again.

Just before supper Miguel came into the kitchen, stamping the bits of dirty snow from his overshoes.

"Jimmy Bear's boy's been killed by the Santa Fe train at Chillocco," he said. "But they say they ain't sure how it happened." He warmed his hands over the stove and sat down.

I looked at Mama. She said nothing and rocked the baby. On the stove the beans bubbled softly, and their smell filled the room. I watched the lid on the pot jiggle as the steam escaped and I heard the wind rattle gently at the window. Miguel struggled with his overshoes and continued.

"Fannie tol' me a railroad man was down the first thing and said they was willin' to pay." He grunted and shoved the overshoes near the stove. "The funeral's Tuesday," he said.

Mama nodded and handed me the baby and got up to put the food on the table. She touched my head, and we sat down to supper.

At the funeral Joe Willow's family cried, and old Fannie even fainted at the grave site when they started to cover him. Jimmy Bear had to struggle to keep her from falling. The dirt sounded on the wooden vault, and the little houses over the older graves looked gray and damp with the people standing among them. I went over to the pecan trees and kicked among the damp mulch looking for good nuts, but I couldn't find any.

That evening after supper I stepped out onto the back stoop, and the yellow lamplight behind me threw my shadow onto the patches of snow and earth, enclosing it in the rectangle that the doorway formed. I looked up. The spotty clouds looked like bits of melting snow pressed into the darkness, and the stars were out, sprinkled into the stillness beyond. The black trees swayed, and the cold wind was familiar.

Behind me Mama moved around the kitchen, and I heard the chink and gentle clatter of the plates and pans as she put those things away. I shivered. And I knew that soon, as it did every spring, the clouds would come and it would begin to rain, a cold, heavy drizzle, and the land would turn to mud.

## Getting at Meaning

1. What does the narrator mean when he says, "Summer had grown old. . . ."?

2. What does Mama think of Joe Willow? What do her comments imply about the attitudes of his mother and stepfather toward the boy?

3. On the evening when the narrator first greets Joe Willow, he notices Joe Willow's shadow as the young Indian approaches. What else does the narrator notice about the light and shadows that evening? Why does he hurry back to the house and stand near his mother as she prepares supper?

4. What possible explanations does the story offer for the narrator's comment, "He [Joe Willow] walked like someone who is used to walking, slowly, without spirit, but with the strength seen in a young workhorse"?

5. Why does Joe Willow become special or important to the narrator?

6. During one of his last conversations with Joe Willow, the narrator ignores Miguel's call to supper. Why does the narrator ignore Miguel? What do the narrator and Joe Willow have in common?

7. How does Joe Willow die? What is ironic about the reactions of his mother and stepfather to his death?

8. The evening of Joe Willow's funeral, the narrator notices a familiar cold wind and the gentle noises his mother makes in the kitchen. Why does he then shiver? What does his comment about the approaching spring have to do with his shivering?

## Developing Skills in Reading Literature

1. **Character.** The narrator, who is also the main character, undergoes significant changes in the course of this story. In the first three paragraphs, what impression does the writer create about the narrator's age? The night that the narrator ignores Miguel's call to supper, what does he attempt to do in his conversation with Joe Willow? What does the narrator's final observation about spring show about what he has learned since the beginning of the story?

2. **Theme and Title.** Often, the title helps to develop the theme or themes of a story. The title of this story has several meanings. In what ways does Joe Willow pass through the narrator's life? Why are the narrator's experiences with Joe Willow important to him? What does he gain from these experiences? In what sense does the narrator pass from one stage of life to another? What is Joe Willow's final "passing"?

3. **Imagery.** Imagery is the literary term used to describe words and phrases that appeal to one or more of the reader's senses: sight, hearing, taste, touch, and smell. The imagery in this story appeals particularly to the senses of sight and hearing. For example, the narrator describes an old car as "lopsided and windowless"; he recalls the "crunch and whisper" of Joe Willow's footsteps. Find three other examples of images that appeal to the sense of sight and three that appeal to the sense of hearing.

## Developing Vocabulary

**Multiple Meanings of Words.** Often a single word has several different meanings. The meaning the writer intends for the word depends upon its use in context. Write at least two distinct definitions for each of these words: *skirt, fuse, stoop*. Study the use of each word in the following sentences. Then choose the definition for the word as the writer uses it. Refer to a dictionary for help if necessary.

"It was . . . reached by a rutted drive that *skirted* the Indian graveyard."

". . . a deeper darkness crept from the woods and began to *fuse* with the trees."

". . . I stepped out onto the back *stoop*. . . ."

# Gaston    *William Saroyan*

They were to eat peaches, as planned, after her nap, and now she sat across from the man who would have been a total stranger except that he was in fact her father. They had been together again (although she couldn't quite remember when they had been together before) for almost a hundred years now, or was it only since day before yesterday? Anyhow, they were together again, and he was kind of funny. First, he had the biggest mustache she had ever seen on anybody, although to her it was not a mustache at all; it was a lot of red and brown hair under his nose and around the ends of his mouth. Second, he wore a blue-and-white striped jersey instead of a shirt and tie, and no coat. His arms were covered with the same hair, only it was a little lighter and thinner. He wore blue slacks, but no shoes and socks. He was barefoot, and so was she, of course.

He was at home. She was with him in his home in Paris, if you could call it a home. He was very old, especially for a young man—thirty-six, he had told her; and she was six, just up from sleep on a very hot afternoon in August.

That morning, on a little walk in the neighborhood, she had seen peaches in a box outside a small store and she had stopped to look at them, so he had bought a kilo.

Now, the peaches were on a large plate on the card table at which they sat.

There were seven of them, but one of them was flawed. It *looked* as good as the others, almost the size of a tennis ball, nice red fading to light green, but where the stem had been there was now a break that went straight down into the heart of the seed.

He placed the biggest and best-looking peach on the small plate in front of the girl, and then took the flawed peach and began to remove the skin. When he had half the skin off the peach he ate that side, neither of them talking, both of them just being there, and not being excited or anything—no plans, that is.

The man held the half-eaten peach in his fingers and looked down into the cavity, into the open seed. The girl looked, too.

While they were looking, two feelers poked out from the cavity. They were attached to a kind of brown knob-head, which followed the feelers, and then two large legs took a strong grip on the edge of the cavity and hoisted some of the rest of whatever it was out of the seed, and stopped there a moment, as if to look around.

The man studied the seed dweller, and so, of course, did the girl.

The creature paused only a fraction of a second, and then continued to come out of the seed, to walk down the eaten side of the peach to wherever it was going.

The girl had never seen anything like it—a whole big thing made out of brown color, a knob-head, feelers, and a great many legs. It was very active, too. Almost businesslike, you might say. The man placed the peach back on the plate. The creature moved off the peach onto the surface of the white plate. There it came to a thoughtful stop.

"Who is it?" the girl said.

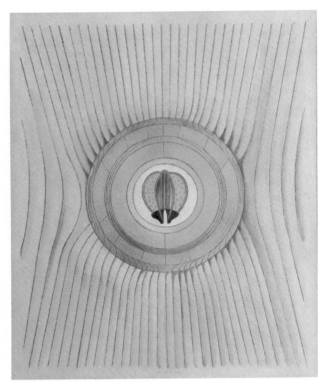

"Gaston."

"Where does he live?"

"Well, he *used* to live in this peach seed, but now that the peach has been harvested and sold, and I have eaten half of it, it looks as if he's out of house and home."

"Aren't you going to squash him?"

"No, of course not, why should I?"

"He's a bug. He's *ugh.*"

"Not at all. He's Gaston the grand boulevardier."

"Everybody hollers when a bug comes out of an apple, but you don't holler or *anything.*"

"Of course not. How would *we* like it if somebody hollered every time we came out of our house?"

"Why *would* they?"

"Precisely. So why should we holler at Gaston?"

"He's not the same as us."

"Well, not exactly, but he's the same as a lot of other occupants of peach seeds. Now, the poor fellow hasn't got a home, and there he is with all that pure design and handsome form, and nowhere to go."

"Handsome?"

"Gaston is just about the handsomest of his kind I've ever seen."

"What's he saying?"

"Well, he's a little confused. Now, inside that house of his he had everything in order. Bed here, porch there, and so forth."

"Show me."

The man picked up the peach, leaving Gaston entirely alone on the white plate. He removed the peeling and ate the rest of the peach.

"Nobody else I know would do that," the girl said. "They'd throw it away."

"I can't imagine why. It's a perfectly good peach."

He opened the seed and placed the two sides not far from Gaston. The girl studied the open halves.

"Is *that* where he lives?"

"It's where he used to live. Gaston is out in the world and on his own now. You can see for yourself how comfortable he was in there. He had everything."

"Now what has he got?"

"Not very much, I'm afraid."

"What's he going to do?"

"What are *we* going to do?"

"Well, we're not going to squash him, that's one thing we're *not* going to do," the girl said.

"What *are* we going to do, then?"

"Put him back?"

"Oh, *that* house is finished."

"Well, he can't live in our house, can he?"

"Not happily."

"Can he live in our house *at all?*"

"Well, he could *try*, I suppose. Don't you want to eat a peach?"

"Only if it's a peach with somebody in the seed."

"Well, see if you can find a peach that has an opening at the top, because if you can, that'll be a peach in which you're likeliest to find somebody."

The girl examined each of the peaches on the big plate.

"They're all shut," she said.

"Well, eat one, then."

"No. I want the same kind that you ate, with somebody in the seed."

"Well, to tell you the truth, the peach I ate would be considered a bad peach, so of course stores don't like to sell them. I was sold that one by mistake, most likely. And so now

Gaston is without a home, and we've got six perfect peaches to eat."

"I don't want a perfect peach. I want a peach with people."

"Well, I'll go out and see if I can find one."

"Where will I go?"

"You'll go with me, unless you'd rather stay. I'll only be five minutes."

"If the phone rings, what shall I say?"

"I don't think it'll ring, but if it does, say hello and see who it is."

"If it's my mother, what shall I say?"

"Tell her I've gone to get you a bad peach, and anything else you want to tell her."

"If she wants me to go back, what shall I say?"

"Say yes if you want to go back."

"Do you want me to?"

"Of course not, but the important thing is what you want, not what I want."

"Why is *that* the important thing?"

"Because I want you to be where you want to be."

"I want to be here."

"I'll be right back."

He put on socks and shoes, and a jacket, and went out. She watched Gaston trying to find out what to do next. Gaston wandered around the plate, but everything seemed wrong and he didn't know what to do or where to go.

The telephone rang and her mother said she was sending the chauffeur to pick her up because there was a little party for somebody's daughter who was also six, and then tomorrow they would fly back to New York.

"Let me speak to your father," she said.

"He's gone to get a peach."

"*One* peach?"

"One with people."

"You haven't been with your father two days and already you *sound* like him."

"There *are* peaches with people in them. I know. I saw one of them come out."

"A *bug?*"

"Not a bug. Gaston."

"*Who?*"

"Gaston the grand something."

"Somebody else gets a peach with a bug in it, and throws it away, but not him. He makes up a lot of foolishness about it."

"It's not foolishness."

"All right, all right, don't get angry at me about a horrible peach bug of some kind."

"Gaston is right here, just outside his broken house, and I'm not angry at you."

"You'll have a lot of fun at the party."

"OK."

"We'll have fun flying back to New York, too."

"OK."

"Are you glad you saw your father?"

"Of course I am."

"Is he funny?"

"Yes."

"Is he crazy?"

"Yes. I mean, no. He just doesn't holler when he sees a bug crawling out of a peach seed or anything. He just looks at it carefully. But it *is* just a bug, isn't it, *really?*"

"That's all it is."

"And we'll *have* to squash it?"

"That's right. I can't wait to see you, darling. These two days have been like two years to me. Goodbye."

The girl watched Gaston on the plate, and she actually didn't like him. He was all *ugh*, as he had been in the first place. He didn't have a home anymore and he was wandering around on the white plate and he was silly and wrong and ridiculous and useless and all sorts of other things. She cried a little, but only inside, because long ago she had decided she didn't like crying because if you ever started to cry it seemed as if there was so much to cry about you almost couldn't stop, and she didn't like that at all. The open halves of the peach seed were wrong, too. They were ugly or something. They weren't clean.

The man bought a kilo of peaches but found no flawed peaches among them, so he bought another kilo at another store, and this time his luck was better, and there were *two* that were flawed. He hurried back to his flat and let himself in.

His daughter was in her room, in her best dress.

"My mother phoned," she said, "and she's sending the chauffeur for me because there's another birthday party."

"Another?"

"I mean, there's *always* a lot of them in New York."

"Will the chauffeur bring you back?"

"No. We're flying back to New York tomorrow."

"Oh."

"I liked being in your house."

"I liked having you here."

"Why do you live here?"

"This is my home."

"It's nice, but it's a lot different from our home."

"Yes, I suppose it is."

"It's kind of like Gaston's house."

"Where *is* Gaston?"

"I squashed him."

"Really? Why?"

"Everybody squashes bugs and worms."

"Oh. Well. I found you a peach."

"I don't want a peach anymore."

"OK."

He got her dressed, and he was packing her stuff when the chauffeur arrived. He went down the three flights of stairs with his daughter and the chauffeur, and in the street he was about to hug the girl when he decided he had better not. They shook hands instead, as if they were strangers.

He watched the huge car drive off, and then he went around the corner where he took his coffee every morning, feeling a little, he thought, like Gaston on the white plate.

## Getting at Meaning

1. How does the appearance of the girl's father differ from that of other men? What does the girl mean when she says, "He was very old, especially for a young man . . ."?

2. How does the father's reaction to Gaston differ from what the girl expects? Does she begin to see Gaston in the same way? How has her father changed her viewpoint?

3. The father refers to Gaston's "pure design" and "handsome form." What do these comments reveal about his life and personality? What might he do for a living? To support your answer, find another reference to the way he looks at his surroundings.

4. How is the mother's lifestyle different from the father's?

5. After talking with her mother, the girl once again sees Gaston as "all *ugh.*" What causes this reversal? Why is this change accomplished so easily?

6. Are the girl and her father any closer at the end of the story than at the beginning? Give examples from the story to support your answer.

## Developing Skills in Reading Literature

1. **Conflict.** What in life is important to the father? What seems to be important to the mother? Whose values does the girl share when she asks her father to find another peach with people? Whose values does she share at the end of the story? Describe the conflict in this story. How is the conflict resolved? Is it an internal or an external conflict?

2. **Character.** Who is the protagonist in this story? Remember, the protagonist is involved in the central conflict and is affected by the resolution of that conflict. Support your answer with examples from the story.

3. **Theme.** The theme of a story is universal; that is, it can apply to all people who share the situation of the story. What does the reader learn about children like the girl in this story? What does the reader learn about parents like the father? What is the theme of the story?

## Developing Vocabulary

**Suffixes.** The girl's father refers to Gaston as the "grand boulevardier." The suffix -*er* (-*ier* in French) means "someone who does something," as in worker or photographer What is a boulevard? Literally, what do you think a boulevardier does? What sort of person would do this? Can you guess at the figurative meaning of the word? Look up *boulevardier* in a French-English dictionary to find out how close you have come to the correct definition. Then list five other words that end with the suffix -*er* meaning "one who does something."

## Developing Writing Skills

**Using Comparisons.** The girl says that her father's house is a lot like Gaston's house. At the end of the story, the father feels a lot like Gaston on the white plate. In a single paragraph, compare the girl's father to Gaston. Use examples from the story to show how the two are alike.

# Prelude     *Albert Halper*

I was coming home from school, carrying my books by a strap, when I passed Gavin's poolroom and saw the big guys hanging around. They were standing in front near the windows, looking across the street. Gavin's has a kind of thick window curtain up to eye level, so all I saw was their heads. The guys were looking at Mrs. Oliver, who lately has started to get talked about. Standing in her window across the street, Mrs. Oliver was doing her nails. Her nice red hair was hanging loose down her back. She certainly is a nice-looking woman. She comes to my father's newspaper stand on the corner and buys five or six movie magazines a week, also the afternoon papers. Once she felt me under the chin, and laughed. My father laughed, too, stamping about in his old worn leather jacket to keep warm. My old man stamps a lot because he has leg pains and he's always complaining about a heavy cold in his head.

When I passed the poolroom one or two guys came out. "Hey, Ike, how's your good-looking sister?" they called, but I didn't turn around. The guys are eighteen or nineteen and haven't ever had a job in their life. "What they need is work," my father is always saying when they bother him too much. "They're not bad; they get that way because there's nothing to do," and he tries to explain the meanness of their ways. But I can't see it like my father. I hate those fellas and I hope every one of them dies under a truck. Every time I come home from school past Lake Street they jab me, and every time my sister Syl comes along they say things. So when one

of them, Fred Gooley, calls, "Hey, Ike, how's your sister?" I don't answer. Besides, Ike isn't my name anyway. It's Harry.

I passed along the sidewalk, keeping close to the curb. Someone threw half an apple but it went over my head. When I went a little farther someone threw a stone. It hit me in the back of the leg and stung me, but it didn't hurt much. I kept a little toward the middle of the sidewalk because I saw a woman coming the other way, and I knew they wouldn't throw.

When I reached the corner under the Elevated,[1] two big new trucks were standing with their motors going, giving my father the latest editions. The drivers threw the papers onto the sidewalk with a nice easy roll so the papers wouldn't get hurt. The papers are bound with that heavy yellow cord that my father saves and sells to the junkyard when he fills up a bag. "All right, Silverstein," a driver called out. "We'll give you a five-star at six," and both trucks drove off.

The drivers are nice fellas, and when they take back the old papers they like to kid my old man. They say, "Hey, you old banker, when are you gonna retire?" or, "Let's roll him, boys, he's got bags of gold in his socks." Of course, they know my old man isn't wealthy and that the bags in the inside of the newsstand hold only copper pennies. But they like to kid him and they know he likes it. Sometimes the guys from Gavin's pitch in,

---

1. **Elevated:** the railway system in Chicago that is raised above the streets.

but the truck drivers would flatten them if they ever got rough with my old man.

I came up to the newsstand and put my school books inside. "Well, Pa," I said, "you can go to Florida now." So my Pa went to "Florida," that is, a chair near the radiator that Nick Pappas lets him use in his restaurant. He has to use Nick's place because our own flat is too far away, almost a quarter-mile off.

While my father was in Nick's place another truck came to a stop. They dropped off a big load of early sport editions and yelled, "Hey, there, Harry, how's the old man?" I checked off the papers, yelling back, "He's okay, he's in Nick's." Then the truck drove away and the two helpers waved.

I stood around, putting the papers on the stand and making a few sales. The first ten minutes after coming home from school and taking care of the newsstand always excites me. Maybe it's the traffic. The trucks and cars pound along like anything, and of course there's the Elevated right up above you that thunders to beat the band. We have our newsstand right up against a big El post, and the stand is a kind of cabin that you enter from the side. But we hardly use it, only in the late morning and around two P.M., when business isn't very rushing. Customers like to see you stand outside over the papers ready for business and not hidden inside where they can't get a look at you at all. Besides, you have to poke your head out and stretch your arm to get the pennies, and kids can swipe magazines from the sides, if you don't watch. So we most always stand outside the newsstand, my father, and me, and my sister. Anyhow, I like it. I like everything about selling papers for my father. The fresh air gets me, and I like to talk to customers and see the rush when people are let out from work. And the way the news trucks bring all the new editions so we can see the latest headlines, like a bank got held up on the South Side on Sixty-third

Street, or the Cubs are winning their tenth straight and have a good chance to cop the pennant, is exciting.

The only thing I don't like is those guys from Gavin's. But since my father went to the police station to complain they don't come around so often. My father went to the station a month ago and said the gang was bothering him, and Mr. Fenway, he's the desk sergeant there, said, "Don't worry any more about it, Mr. Silverstein, we'll take care of it. You're a respectable citizen and tax-payer and you're entitled to protection. We'll take care of it." And the next day they sent over a patrolman who stood around almost two hours. The gang from Gavin's saw him and started to go away, but the cop hollered, "Now listen, don't bother this old fella. If you bother him any I'll have to run some of you in."

And then one of the guys recognized that the cop was Butch, Fred Gooley's cousin. "Listen who's talkin'," he yells back. "Hey, Fred, they got your cousin Butch takin' care of the Yid." They said a lot of other things until the cop got mad and started after them. They ran faster than lightning, separating into alleys. The cop came back empty-handed and said to my father, "It'll blow over, Mr. Silverstein; they won't give you any more trouble." Then he went up the street, turning into Steuben's bar.

Well, all this happened three or four weeks ago, and so far the gang has let us alone. They stopped pulling my sixteen-year-old sister by her sweater, and when they pass the stand going home to supper all they give us is dirty looks. During the last three or four days, however, they passed by and kinda muttered, calling my father a communist banker and me and my sister reds. My father says they really don't mean it, it's the hard times and bad feelings; and they got to put the blame on somebody, so they put the blame on us. It's certain speeches on the radio and the pieces in some of the papers, my father told us. "Something is happening to some of the people and we got to watch our step," he says.

I am standing there hearing the traffic and thinking it over when my little fat old man comes out from Nick's looking like he liked the warm air in Nick's place. My old man's cheeks looked rosy, but his cheeks are that way from high blood pressure and not from good health. "Well, colonel," he says smiling, "I am back on the job." So we stand around, the two of us, taking care of the trade. I hand out change snappy and say thank you after each sale. My old man starts to stamp around in a little while and, though he says nothing, I know he's got pains in his legs again. I look at the weather forecast in all the papers and some of them say flurries of snow and the rest of them say just snow. "Well, Pa," I tell my old man, "maybe I can go skating tomorrow if it gets cold again."

Then I see my sister coming from high school carrying her briefcase and heading this way. Why the heck doesn't she cross over so she won't have to pass the poolroom, I say to myself; why don't she walk on the other side of the street? But that's not like Sylvia; she's a girl with a hot temper, and when she thinks she is right you can't tell her a thing. I knew she wouldn't cross the street and then cross back, because according to her, why, that's giving in. That's telling those hoodlums that you're afraid of their guts. So she doesn't cross over but walks straight on. When she comes by the pool hall, two guys come out and say something to her. She just holds herself tight and goes right on past them both. When she finally comes up, she gives me a poke in the side. "Hello, you mickey mouse, what mark did you get in your algebra exam?" I told her I got A, but the truth is I got a C.

"I'll check up on you later," she says to me. "Pa, if he's lying to us we'll fine him ten years!"

My father started to smile and said, "No, Harry is a good boy; two years is enough."

So we stand around kidding, and pretty soon, because the wind is coming so sharp up the street, my old man has to "go to Florida" for a while once more. He went into Nick's for some "sunshine," he said, but me and Syl could tell he had the pains again. Anyway, when he was gone we didn't say anything for a while. Then Hartman's furniture factory, which lately has been checking out early, let out, and we were busy making sales to the men. They came up the sidewalk, a couple of hundred, all anxious to get home, so we had to work snappy. But Syl is a fast worker. Then we stood waiting for the next rush from the Hillman's cocoa factory up the block to start.

We were standing around when something hit me in the head, a half of a rotten apple. It hurt a little. I turned quick but didn't see anybody, but Syl started yelling. She was pointing to a big El post across the street behind which a guy was hiding.

"Come on, show your face," my sister was saying. "Come on, you hero, show your yellow face!" But the guy sneaked away, keeping the post between. Syl turned to me and her face was boiling. "The rats! It's not enough with all the trouble over in Europe; they have to start it here."

Just then our old man come out of Nick's, and when he saw Syl's face he asked what was the matter.

"Nothing," she says. "Nothing, I'm just thinking."

But my old man saw the half of a rotten apple on the sidewalk, and at first he didn't say anything but I could see he was worried. "We just have to stand it," he said, like he was speaking to himself, "we just have to stand it. If we give up the newsstand, where else can we go?"

"Why do we have to stand it?" I exploded, almost yelling. "Why do we—"

But Mrs. Oliver just then came up to the stand, so I had to wait on her. Besides, she's a good customer, and there's more profit on two or three magazines than from a dozen papers.

"I'll have a copy of *Film Fan*, a copy of *Breezy Stories*, and a copy of *Movie Stars on Parade*," she says. I go and reach for the copies.

"Harry is a nice boy," Mrs. Oliver told my father, patting my arm. "I'm very fond of him."

"Yes, he's not bad," my father answered smiling. "Only he has a hot temper once in a while."

But who wouldn't have one, that's what I wanted to say! Who wouldn't? Here we stand around minding our own business and the guys won't let us alone. I tell you sometimes it almost drives me crazy. We don't hurt anybody and we're trying to make a living, but they're always picking on us and won't let us alone. It's been going on for a couple of years now, and though my old man says it'll pass with the hard times, I know he's worried because he doesn't believe what he says. He reads the papers as soon as he gets them from the delivery trucks, and lately the news about Europe is all headlines and I can see that it makes him sick. My old man has a soft heart, and every time he sees in the papers that something bad in Europe has happened again he seems to grow older, and he stands near the papers kind of small and all alone. I tell you, sometimes it almost drives me crazy. My old man should be down in Florida, where he can get healthy, not in Nick Pappas' "Florida," but down in real Florida where you have to go by train. That's where he should be. Then maybe his legs would be all right, and he wouldn't have that funny color in his cheeks. Since our mother died last year it seems the doctor's treatments don't make him any better, and he has to skip a treatment once in a while because he

says it costs too much. But when he stands there with a customer chuckling, you think he's healthy and hasn't got any worries, and you feel maybe he has a couple thousand in the bank.

And another thing, what did he mean when he said something two days ago when the fellas from Gavin's passed by and threw a stone at the stand? What did he mean, that's what I want to know. Gooley had a paper rolled up with some headlines about Europe on it, and he wiggled it at us and my father looked scared. When they were gone my father said something to me, which I been thinking and thinking about. My Pa said we got to watch our step extra careful now because there's no other place besides this country where we can go. We've always been picked on, he said, but we're up against the last wall now, he told me, and we got to be calm because if they start going after us here there's no other place where we can go. I been thinking and thinking about that, especially the part about the wall. When he said that, his voice sounded funny, and I felt like our newsstand was a kind of island and if that went we'd be under the waves.

"Harry, what are you thinking of?" Mrs. Oliver asked me. "Don't I get any change?" She was laughing.

And then I came down from the clouds and found she had given me two quarters. I gave her a nickel change. She laughed again. "When he looks moody and kind of sore like that, Mr. Silverstein, I think he's cute."

My old man crinkled up his eyes and smiled. "Who can say, Mrs. Oliver. He should only grow up to be a nice young man and a good citizen and a credit to his country. That's all I want."

"I'm sure Harry will." Mrs. Oliver answered, then talked to Syl a while and admired Syl's new sweater and was about to go away. But another half of a rotten apple came over and splashed against the stand.

Some of it splashed against my old man's coat sleeve. Mrs. Oliver turned around and got mad.

"Now you boys leave Mr. Silverstein alone! You've been pestering him long enough! He's a good American citizen who doesn't hurt anybody! You leave him alone!"

"Yah!" yelled Gooley, who ducked behind an El post with two other guys. "Yah! Sez you!"

"You leave him alone!" hollered Mrs. Oliver.

"Aw, go peddle your papers," Gooley answered. "Go run up a rope."

"Don't pay any attention to them," Syl told Mrs. Oliver. "They think they're heroes, but to most people they're just yellow rats."

I could tell by my old man's eyes that he was nervous and wanted to smooth things over, but Syl didn't give him a chance. When she gets started and knows she's in the right not even the Governor of the State could make her keep quiet.

"Don't pay any attention to them," she said in a cutting voice while my old man looked anxious. "When men hide behind Elevated posts and throw rotten apples at women, you know they're not men but just

things that wear pants. In Europe they put brown shirts on them and call them saviors of civilization. Here they haven't got the shirts yet and hang around poolrooms."

Every word cut like a knife, and the guys ducked away. If I or my father would have said it, we would have been nailed with some rotten fruit, but the way Syl has of getting back at those guys makes them feel like yellow dogs. I guess that's why they respect her even though they hate her, and I guess that's why Gooley and one or two of his friends are always trying to get next to her and date her up.

Mrs. Oliver took Syl's side and was about to say something more when Hillman's cocoa factory up the block let out and the men started coming up the street. The 4:45 rush was on and we didn't have time for anything, so Mrs. Oliver left, saying she'd be back when the blue-streak edition of the *News* would arrive. Me and Syl were busy handing out the papers and making change, and our Pa helped us while the men took their papers and hurried for the El. It started to get darker and colder, and the traffic grew heavier along the street.

Then the *Times* truck, which was a little late, roared up and dropped a load we were waiting for. I cut the strings and stacked the papers, and when my father came over and read the first page he suddenly looked scared. In his eyes there was that hunted look I had noticed a couple of days ago. I started to look at the first page of the paper while my old man didn't say a word. Nick came to the window and lit his new neon light and waved to us. Then the light started flashing on and off, flashing on the new headlines. It was all about Austria and how people were fleeing toward the borders and trying to get out of the country before it was too late. My old man grew sick and looked kind of funny and just stood there. Sylvia, who is active in the high-school social science club, began to

read the *Times* out loud and started analyzing the news to us; but our Pa didn't need her analysis and kept standing there kind of small with that hunted look on his face. He looked sick all right. It almost drove me crazy.

"For Pete's sake," I yelled at Syl. "Shut up, shut up!"

Then she saw our Pa's face, looked at me, and didn't say anything more.

In a little while it was after five and Syl had to go home and make supper. "I'll be back in an hour," she told me. "Then Pa can go home and rest a bit and me and you can take care of the stand." I said all right.

After she was gone it seemed kind of lonesome. I couldn't stop thinking about what my father had said about this being our last wall. It got me feeling funny, and I didn't want to read the papers any more. I stood there feeling queer, like me and my old man were standing on a little island and the waves were coming up. There was still a lot of traffic and a few people came up for papers, but from my old man's face I could tell he felt the same as me.

But pretty soon some more editions began coming and we had to check and stack them up. More men came out from factories on Walnut Street, and we were busy making sales. It got colder than ever and my old man began to stamp again. "Go into Nick's, Pa," I told him. "I can handle it out here." But he wouldn't do it because just then another factory let out, and we were swamped for a while. "Hi, there, Silverstein," some of the men called to him, "what's the latest news, you king of the press?" They took the papers, kidding him, and hurried up the stairs to the Elevated, reading all about Austria and going home to eat. My father kept staring at the headlines and couldn't take his eyes off the print where it said that soldiers were pouring across the border and mobs were robbing people they hated and spitting on them and making them go down on their hands and knees to scrub the streets. My old man's eyes grew small, like he had the toothache, and he shook his head like he was sick. "Pa, go into Nick's," I told him. He just stood there, sick over what he read.

Then the guys from Gavin's poolroom began passing the stand on their way home to supper after a day of just killing time. At first they looked as if they wouldn't bother us. One or two of them said something mean to us, but my old man and me didn't answer. If you don't answer hoodlums, my father once told me, sometimes they let you alone.

But then it started. The guys who passed by came back, and one of them said: "Let's have a little fun with the Yids." That's how it began. A couple of them took some magazines from the rack and said they wanted to buy a copy and started reading.

In a flash I realized it was all planned out. My father looked kind of worried but stood quiet. There were about eight or nine of them, all big boys around eighteen and nineteen, and for the first time I got scared. It was just after six o'clock and they had picked a time when the newspaper trucks had delivered the five-star and when all the factories had let out their help and there weren't many people about. Finally one of them smiled at Gooley and said, "Well, this physical culture magazine is mighty instructive, but don't you think we ought to have some of the exercises demonstrated?" Gooley said, "Sure, why not?"

So the first fella pointed to some pictures in the magazine and wanted me to squat on the sidewalk and do the first exercise. I wouldn't do it. My father put his hand on the fella's arm and said, "Please, please." But the guy pushed my father's hand away.

"We're interested in your son, not you. Go on, squat."

"I won't," I told him.

"Go on," he said. "Do the first exercise so that the boys can learn how to keep fit."

"I won't," I said.

"Go on," he said, "do it."

"I won't."

Then he came over to me smiling, but his face looked nasty. "Do it. Do it if you know what's good for you."

"Please, boys," said my Pa. "Please go home and eat and don't make trouble. I don't want to have to call a policeman—"

But before I knew it someone got behind me and tripped me so that I fell on one knee. Then another of them pushed me, trying to make me squat. I shoved someone and then someone hit me, and then I heard someone trying to make them stop. While they held me down on the sidewalk I wiggled and looked up. Mrs. Oliver, who had come for the blue-flash edition, was bawling them out.

"You let him alone! You tramps, you hoodlums, you let him alone!" She came over and tried to help me, but they pushed her away. Then Mrs. Oliver began to yell as two guys twisted my arm and told me to squat.

By this time a few people were passing, and Mrs. Oliver called at them to interfere. But the gang were big fellows and there were eight or nine of them, and the people were afraid.

Then, while they had me down on the sidewalk, Syl came running up the street. When she saw what was happening she began kicking them and yelling and trying to make them let me up. But they didn't pay any attention to her, merely pushing her away.

"Please," my Pa kept saying. "Please let him up; he didn't hurt you. I don't want to call the police—"

Then Syl turned to the people who were watching and yelled at them. "Why don't you help us? What are you standing there for?" But none of them moved. Then Syl began to scream:

"Listen, why don't you help us? Why don't you make them stop picking on us? We're human beings the same as you!"

But the people just stood there, afraid to do a thing. Then while a few guys held me, Gooley and about four others went for the stand, turning it over and mussing and stamping on all the newspapers they could find. Syl started to scratch them, so they hit her; then I broke away to help her, and then they started socking me too. My father tried to reach me, but three guys kept him away. Four guys got me down and started kicking me, and all the time my father was begging them to let me up and Syl was screaming at the people to help. And while I was down, my face was squeezed against some papers on the sidewalk telling about Austria and I guess I went nuts while they kept hitting me, and I kept seeing the headlines against my nose.

Then someone yelled, "Jiggers, the cops!" and they got off of me right away. Nick had looked out of the window and had called the station, and the guys let me up and beat it away fast.

But when the cops came it was too late; the stand was a wreck. The newspapers and magazines were all over the sidewalk, and the rack that holds the *Argosy* and *Western Aces* was all twisted up. My Pa, who looked sicker than ever, stood there crying, and pretty soon I began to bawl. People were standing looking at us like we were some kind of fish, and I just couldn't help it. I started to bawl.

Then the cops came through the crowd and began asking questions right and left. In the end they wanted to take us to the station to enter a complaint, but Syl wouldn't go. She looked at the crowd watching and she said, "What's the use? All those people standing around and none of them would help!" They were standing all the way to the second El post, and when the cops asked for wit-

nesses none of them except Mrs. Oliver offered to give their names. Then Syl looked at Pa and me and saw our faces and turned to the crowd and began to scream.

"In another few years, you wait! Some of you are working people, and they'll be marching through the streets and going after you too! They pick on us Jews because we're weak and haven't any country; but after they get us down they'll go after you! And it'll be your fault; you're all cowards; you're afraid to fight back!"

"Listen," one of the cops told my sister, "are you coming to the station or not? We can't hang around here all evening."

Then Syl broke down and began to bawl as hard as me. "Oh, leave us alone," she told them and began wailing her heart out. "Leave us alone. What good would it do?"

By this time the crowd was bigger, so the cops started telling people to break it up and move on. Nick came out and took my father by the arm into the lunchroom for a drink of hot tea. The people went away slowly and then, as the crowd began to dwindle, it started to snow. When she saw that, Syl started bawling harder than ever and turned her face to me. But I was down on my hands and knees with Mrs. Oliver, trying to save some of the magazines. There was no use going after the newspapers, which were smeared up, torn, and dirty from the gang's feet. But I thought I could save a few, so I picked a couple of them up.

"Oh, leave them be," Syl wept at me. "Leave them be, leave them be!"

## Getting at Meaning

1. Why does the gang from Gavin's pick on the narrator and his family? What is the difference between the way the truck drivers kid Mr. Silverstein and the way the gang kids him?

2. List three reasons why the narrator finds selling papers exciting. What does he dislike about the job?

3. The furniture factory has been closing early. What does this indicate about economic conditions?

4. Why are people looking for someone to blame? What is happening in the country? Why are the Silversteins the targets for the blame?

5. How does the political situation in Europe affect Mr. Silverstein? What does he fear? What does he mean when he says ". . . there's no other place besides this country where we can go."?

6. Syl compares the boys from Gavin's to the men in Europe who put on brown shirts. Who are the brown shirts? In what other ways are the conflicts in Europe and the activities of the gang from the poolroom related?

7. As the gang wrecks the newsstand, a crowd gathers to watch. Why don't these people help the Silversteins? How does Syl react to the crowd's behavior?

8. Why does Syl refuse to report the incident to the police? Is her behavior at the end of the story consistent with what the reader has already learned of her character? What has happened to her?

## Developing Skills in Reading Literature

1. **Conflict.** The Silversteins are involved in two conflicts. One is local; the other is international. Describe these conflicts. Which conflict does the writer want the reader to be most aware of at the end of the story? How do you know?

2. **Title.** The title of this story gives a clue to its theme. What is a prelude? If you are uncertain, look up the word in a dictionary. In what way are the events in this story a prelude? To what are they a prelude?

3. **Theme.** Reread Syl's speech to the crowd beginning with "In another few years, you wait!" (p. 207) Keeping this speech in mind and remembering what you have already learned about conflict and title, write a statement of the theme of this story.

4. **Style.** As you have learned, word choice and sentence structure are two elements of a writer's style. Another element is the particular point of view used by the writer. In this story, a first-person narrator relates the events. Approximately how old is the narrator? How does his language give you a clue to his age? Find four examples from the story to support your answer.

## Developing Vocabulary

**Word Origins.** In this story, the Silversteins are the scapegoats for the gang's anger and frustration. Define the word *scapegoat*, using a dictionary if necessary. Then find a book on word origins and research the origin of *scapegoat*. Be prepared to explain its origin and the story behind its original use.

## Developing Writing Skills

**Explaining an Idea.** The following Declaration of Guilt was signed by Pastor Martin Niemoller at the Council of the Evangelical Church in Germany, October 18, 1945. Read it carefully several times.

> In Germany, the Nazis first came for the Communists, and I didn't speak up because I was not a Communist.
> Then they came for the Jews, and I did not speak up because I was not a Jew.
> Then they came for the Trade Unionists, and I didn't speak up because I wasn't a Trade Unionist.
> Then they came for the Catholics, and I was a Protestant so I didn't speak up.
> Then they came for ME . . . by that time there was no one to speak up for anyone.
> To make sure this doesn't happen again, the injustice to anyone anywhere must be the concern of everyone everywhere.

In a well developed paragraph, explain how this declaration illustrates the theme of the story.

# The Cub    *Lois Dykeman Kleihauer*

One of his first memories was of his father bending down from his great height to sweep him into the air. Up he went, gasping and laughing with delight. He could look down on his mother's upturned face as she watched, laughing with them, and at the thick shock of his father's brown hair and at his white teeth.

Then he would come down, shrieking happily, but he was never afraid, not with his father's hands holding him. No one in the world was as strong, or as wise, as his father.

He remembered a time when his father moved the piano across the room for his mother. He watched while she guided it into its new position, and he saw the difference in their hands as they rested, side by side, upon the gleaming walnut. His mother's hands were white and slim and delicate, his father's large and square and strong.

As he grew, he learned to play bear. When it was time for his father to come home at night, he would lurk behind the kitchen door. When he heard the closing of the garage doors, he would hold his breath and squeeze himself into the crack behind the door. Then he would be quiet.

It was always the same. His father would open the door and stand there, the backs of his long legs beguilingly close. "Where's the boy?"

He would glance at the conspiratorial smile on his mother's face, and then he would leap and grab his father about the knees, and his father would look down and shout, "Hey, what's this? A bear—a young cub!"

Then, no matter how tightly he tried to cling, he was lifted up and perched upon his father's shoulder, and they would march past his mother, and together they would duck their heads beneath the doors.

And then he went to school. And on the playground he learned how to wrestle and shout, how to hold back tears, how to get a half-nelson[1] on the boy who tried to take his football away from him. He came home at night and practiced his new wisdom on his father. Straining and puffing, he tried to pull his father off the lounge chair while his father kept on reading the paper, only glancing up now and then to ask in mild wonderment, "What are you trying to do, boy?"

He would stand and look at his father. "Gee whiz, Dad!" And then he would realize that his father was teasing him, and he would crawl up on his father's lap and pummel him in affectionate frustration.

And still he grew—taller, slimmer, stronger. He was like a young buck, with tiny new horns. He wanted to lock them with any other young buck's, to test them in combat. He measured his biceps with his mother's tape measure. Exultantly, he thrust his arm in front of his father. "Feel that! How's that for muscle?"

His father put his great thumb into the flexed muscle and pressed, and the boy pulled back, protesting, laughing. "Ouch!"

Sometimes they wrestled on the floor together, and his mother moved the chairs

---

1. **half-nelson:** a wrestling hold.

SELF-PORTRAIT, 1929. John Kane. Collection, The Museum of Modern Art, New York. Abby Aldrich Rockefeller Fund.

back. "Be careful, Charles—don't hurt him."

After a while his father would push him aside and sit in his chair, his long legs thrust out before him, and the boy would scramble to his feet, half resentful, half mirthful over the ease with which his father mastered him.

"Doggone it, Dad, someday—" he would say.

He went out for football and track in high school. He surprised even himself now, there was so much more of him. And he could look down on his mother. "Little one," he called her, or "Small fry."

Sometimes he took her wrists and backed her into a chair, while he laughed and she scolded. "I'll—I'll take you across my knee."

"Who will?" he demanded.

"Well—your father still can," she said.

His father—well, that was different.

They still wrestled occasionally, but it distressed his mother. She hovered about them, worrying, unable to comprehend the need for their struggling. It always ended the same way, with boy upon his back, prostrate, and his father grinning down at him. "Give?"

"Give." And he got up, shaking his head.

"I wish you wouldn't," his mother would say, fretting. "There's no point in it. You'll hurt yourselves; don't do it any more."

So for nearly a year they had not wrestled, but he thought about it one night at dinner. He looked at his father closely. It was queer, but his father didn't look nearly as tall or broad-shouldered as he used to. He could even look his father straight in the eyes.

"How much do you weigh, Dad?" he asked.

His father threw him a mild glance.

"About the same; about a hundred and ninety. Why?"

The boy grinned. "Just wondering."

But after a while he went over to his father where he sat reading the paper and took it out of his hands. His father glanced up, his eyes at first questioning and then narrowing to meet the challenge in his son's. "So," he said softly.

"Come on, Dad."

His father took off his coat and began to unbutton his shirt. "You asked for it," he said.

His mother came in from the kitchen, alarmed. "Oh, Charles! Bill! Don't—you'll hurt yourselves!" But they paid no attention to her. They were standing now, their shirts off. They watched each other, intent and purposeful. The boy's teeth gleamed again. They circled for a moment, and then their hands closed upon each other's arms.

They strained against each other, and then the boy went down, taking his father with him. They moved and writhed and turned, in silence seeking an advantage, in silence pressing it to its conclusion. There was the sound of the thumps of their bodies upon the rug and of the quick, hard intake of breath. The boy showed his teeth occasionally in a grimace of pain. His mother stood at one side, both hands pressed against her ears. Occasionally her lips moved, but she did not make a sound.

After a while the boy pinned his father on his back. "Give!" he demanded.

His father said, "Heck no!" And with a great effort he pushed the boy off, and the struggle began again.

But at the end his father lay prostrate, and a look of bewilderment came into his eyes. He struggled desperately against his son's merciless, restraining hands. Finally he lay quiet, only his chest heaving, his breath coming loudly.

The boy said, "Give!"

The man frowned, shaking his head.

Still the boy knelt on him, pinning him down.

"Give!" he said, and tightened his grip. "Give!"

All at once his father began to laugh, silently, his shoulders shaking. The boy felt his mother's fingers tugging fiercely at his shoulder. "Let him up," she said. "Let him up!"

The boy looked down at his father. "Give up?"

His father stopped laughing, but his eyes were still wet. "Okay," he said. "I give."

The boy stood up and reached a hand to his father to help him up, but his mother was before him, putting an arm about his father's shoulders, helping him to rise. They stood together and looked at him, his father grinning gamely, his mother with baffled pain in her eyes.

The boy started to laugh. "I guess I——" He stopped. "Gosh, Dad, I didn't hurt you, did I?"

"Heck, no, I'm all right. Next time. . . ."

"Yeah, maybe next time. . . ."

And his mother did not contradict what they said, for she knew as well as they that there would never be a next time.

For a moment the three of them stood looking at one another, and then, suddenly, blindly, the boy turned. He ran through the door under which he had ducked so many times when he had ridden on his father's shoulders. He went out the kitchen door, behind which he had hidden, waiting to leap out and pounce upon his father's legs.

It was dark outside. He stood on the steps, feeling the air cool against his sweaty body. He stood with lifted head, looking at the stars, and then he could not see them because of the tears that burned his eyes and ran down his cheeks.

## Getting at Meaning

1. In his early memories of his father, what impresses the boy the most?

2. What is the mother's role in the game of bear? What is her attitude toward the game?

3. When the boy first goes to school and then to high school, what obvious changes does he experience? How do these changes affect his relationship with his father? with his mother?

4. Why does the mother become alarmed as the boy and his father continue to wrestle?

5. Why does the boy insist that his father "give" after the boy has successfully pinned him down?

6. What causes the pain in the mother's eyes? Why is the pain "baffled"? Why is the mother so sure that ". . . there would never be a next time"?

7. Why does the boy cry at the end of the story? When he finally beats his father, what does he lose?

## Developing Skills in Reading Literature

1. **Character and Theme.** A writer may develop the theme of a story through the changes experienced by the main character. The theme may be revealed through the lesson that the character learns by the end of the story. As a young child, during the game of bear, what is the boy's attitude toward his father's strength and toward his father? Why does the writer describe the teenaged boy as a "young buck"? At this point, what is the boy's attitude toward his father's strength? Following their final wrestling match, what does the boy realize about his father and about himself? What has he learned that might be expressed as the theme of the story?

2. **Structure.** What device does the writer use to organize the events in this story? In the last two paragraphs, how does the writer make clever use of incidents that occur earlier in the story?

3. **Understatement.** Understatement is the technique of saying less than is actually meant. When using understatements, a writer implies an idea rather than states it directly. At one point in the story, the writer compares the boy to a young buck. How is this same comparison implied in the boy's final wrestling match with his father? Why is the implied comparison appropriate to this incident? How does it help the reader to understand the purpose of the final wrestling match?

## Developing Vocabulary

**Using Precise Verbs.** The action in this story becomes clear and vivid through the writer's use of precise verbs. For example,

As a little child, the boy ". . . would *lurk* behind the kitchen door."

When his father teased him, the boy would ". . . *pummel* him in affectionate frustration."

Find five other examples from the story that illustrate the writer's use of precise verbs.

## Developing Writing Skills

**Narration: Using Chronological Order.** This story begins when the boy is a young child, continues through his early school days, and concludes when he is in high school. Within the framework of chronological order, the writer reveals changes in the boy and in the boy's relationship with his father.

Think about your own childhood and about the attitudes and relationships you once had. Select one of these attitudes or relationships, and write a five-paragraph composition about the changes you experienced as you grew older. Use your first paragraph to introduce the subject and to provide details about your early childhood. Use paragraphs two through four to describe incidents that reveal changes in your views. Organize these paragraphs in chronological order. In the fifth paragraph comment upon your earlier experiences and describe your current feelings.

# The Sentimentality of William Tavener

*Willa Cather*

It takes a strong woman to make any sort of success of living in the West, and Hester undoubtedly was that. When people spoke of William Tavener as the most prosperous farmer in McPherson County, they usually added that his wife was a "good manager." She was an executive woman, quick of tongue and something of an imperatrix.[1] The only reason her husband did not consult her about his business was that she did not wait to be consulted.

It would have been quite impossible for one man, within the limited sphere of human action, to follow all Hester's advice, but in the end William usually acted upon some of her suggestions. When she incessantly denounced the "shiftlessness" of letting a new threshing machine stand unprotected in the open, he eventually built a shed for it. When she sniffed contemptuously at his notion of fencing a hog corral with sod walls, he made a spiritless beginning on the structure— merely to "show his temper," as she put it— but in the end he went off quietly to town and bought enough barbed wire to complete the fence. When the first heavy rains came on, and the pigs rooted down the sod wall and made little paths all over it to facilitate their ascent, he heard his wife relate with relish the story of the little pig that built a mud house, to the minister at the dinner table, and William's gravity never relaxed for an instant. Silence, indeed, was William's refuge and his strength.

William set his boys a wholesome example to respect their mother. People who knew him very well suspected that he even admired her. He was a hard man towards his neighbors, and even towards his sons, grasping, determined, and ambitious.

There was an occasional blue day about the house when William went over the store bills, but he never objected to items relating to his wife's gowns or bonnets. So it came about that many of the foolish, unnecessary little things that Hester bought for the boys, she had charged to her personal account.

One spring night Hester sat in a rocking chair by the sitting room window, darning socks. She rocked violently and sent her long needle vigorously back and forth over her gourd, and it took only a very casual glance to see that she was wrought up over something. William sat on the other side of the table reading his farm paper. If he had noticed his wife's agitation, his calm, clean-shaven face betrayed no sign of concern. He must have noticed the sarcastic turn of her remarks at the supper table, and he must have noticed the moody silence of the older boys as they ate. When supper was but half over little Billy, the youngest, had suddenly pushed back his plate and slipped away from the table, manfully trying to swallow a sob. But William Tavener never heeded ominous forecasts in the domestic horizon, and he

---

1. **imperatrix** (im pe rā' triks): an empress.

never looked for a storm until it broke.

After supper the boys had gone to the pond under the willows in the big cattle corral, to get rid of the dust of plowing. Hester could hear an occasional splash and a laugh ringing clear through the stillness of the night, as she sat by the open window. She sat silent for almost an hour reviewing in her mind many plans of attack. But she was too vigorous a woman to be much of a strategist, and she usually came to her point with directness. At last she cut her thread and suddenly put her darning down, saying emphatically,

"William, I don't think it would hurt you to let the boys go to that circus in town tomorrow."

William continued to read his farm paper, but it was not Hester's custom to wait for an answer. She usually divined his arguments and assailed them one by one before he uttered them.

"You've been short of hands all summer, and you've worked the boys hard, and a man ought to use his own flesh and blood as well as he does his hired hands. We're plenty able to afford it, and it's little enough our boys ever spend. I don't see how you can expect 'em to be steady and hard workin', unless you encourage 'em a little. I never could see much harm in circuses, and our boys have never been to one. Oh, I know Jim Howley's boys get drunk an' carry on when they go, but our boys ain't that sort, an' you know it, William. The animals are real instructive, an' our boys don't get to see much out here on the prairie. It was different where we were raised, but the boys have got no advantages here, an' if you don't take care, they'll grow up to be greenhorns."[2]

Hester paused a moment, and William folded up his paper, but vouchsafed no remark. His sisters in Virginia had often said that only a quiet man like William could ever have lived with Hester Perkins. Secretly, William was rather proud of his wife's "gift of speech," and of the fact that she could talk in prayer meeting as fluently as a man. He confined his own efforts in that line to a brief prayer at Covenant meetings.

Hester shook out another sock and went on.

"Nobody was ever hurt by goin' to a circus. Why, law me! I remember I went to one myself once, when I was little. I had most forgot about it. It was over at Pewtown, an' I remember how I had set my heart on going. I don't think I'd ever forgiven my father if he hadn't taken me, though that red clay road was in a frightful way after the rain. I mind they had an elephant and six poll parrots, an' a Rocky Mountain lion, an' a cage of monkeys, an' two camels. My! but they were a sight to me then!"

Hester dropped the black sock and shook her head and smiled at the recollection. She was not expecting anything from William yet, and she was fairly startled when he said gravely, in much the same tone in which he announced the hymns in prayer meeting:

"No, there was only one camel. The other was a dromedary."

She peered around the lamp and looked at him keenly.

"Why, William, how come you to know?"

William folded his paper and answered with some hesitation, "I was there, too."

Hester's interest flashed up. "Well, I never, William! To think of my finding it out after all these years! Why, you couldn't have been much bigger'n our Billy then. It seems queer I never saw you when you was little, to remember about you. But then you Back Creek folks never have anything to do with us Gap people. But how come you to go? Your father was stricter with you than you are with your boys."

"I reckon I shouldn't 'a gone," he said slowly, "but boys will do foolish things. I had

_____

2. **greenhorn:** an inexperienced person.

done a good deal of fox hunting the winter before, and father let me keep the bounty money. I hired Tom Smith's Tap to weed the corn for me, an' I slipped off unbeknownst to father an' went to the show."

Hester spoke up warmly: "Nonsense, William! It didn't do you no harm, I guess. You was always worked hard enough. It must have been a big sight for a little fellow. That clown must have just tickled you to death."

William crossed his knees and leaned back in his chair.

"I reckon I could tell all that fool's jokes now. Sometimes I can't help thinkin' about 'em in meetin' when the sermon's long. I mind I had on a pair of new boots that hurt me like the mischief, but I forgot all about 'em when that fellow rode the donkey. I recall I had to take them boots off as soon as I got out of sight o' town, and walked home in the mud barefoot."

"O poor little fellow!" Hester ejaculated, drawing her chair nearer and leaning her elbows on the table. "What cruel shoes they did use to make for children. I remember I went up to Back Creek to see the circus wagons go by. They came down from Romney, you know. The circus men stopped at the creek to water the animals, an' the elephant got stubborn an' broke a big limb off the yellow willow tree that grew there by the toll house porch, an' the Scribners were 'fraid as death he'd pull the house down. But this much I saw him do; he waded in the creek an' filled his trunk with water and squirted it in at the window and nearly ruined Ellen Scribner's pink lawn dress that she had just ironed an' laid out on the bed ready to wear to the circus."

"I reckon that must have been a trial to Ellen," chuckled William, "for she was mighty prim in them days."

Hester drew her chair still nearer William's. Since the children had begun growing up, her conversation with her husband had been almost wholly confined to questions of

economy and expense. Their relationship had become purely a business one, like that between landlord and tenant. In her desire to indulge her boys she had unconsciously assumed a defensive and almost hostile attitude towards her husband. No debtor ever haggled with his usurer more doggedly than did Hester with her husband in behalf of her sons. The strategic contest had gone on so long that it had almost crowded out the memory of a closer relationship. This exchange of confidences tonight, when common recollections took them unawares and opened their hearts, had all the miracle of romance. They talked on and on; of old neighbors, of old familiar faces in the valley where they had grown up, of long forgotten incidents of their youth—weddings, picnics, sleighing parties, and baptizings. For years they had talked of nothing else but butter and eggs and the prices of things, and now they had as much to say to each other as people who meet after a long separation.

When the clock struck ten, William rose and went over to his walnut secretary and unlocked it. From his red leather wallet he took out a ten dollar bill and laid it on the table beside Hester.

"Tell the boys not to stay late, an' not to drive the horses hard," he said quietly, and went off to bed.

Hester blew out the lamp and sat still in the dark a long time. She left the bill lying on the table where William had placed it. She had a painful sense of having missed something, or lost something; she felt that somehow the years had cheated her.

The little locust trees that grew by the fence were white with blossoms. Their heavy odor floated in to her on the night wind and recalled a night long ago, when the first whippoorwill of the spring was heard, and the rough, buxom girls of Hawkins Gap had held her laughing and struggling under the locust trees, and searched in her bosom for a lock of her sweetheart's hair, which is supposed to be on every girl's breast when the first whippoorwill sings. Two of those same girls had been her bridesmaids. Hester had been a very happy bride. She rose and went softly into the room where William lay. He was sleeping heavily, but occasionally moved his hand before his face to ward off the flies. Hester went into the parlor and took the piece of mosquito net from the basket of wax apples and pears that her sister had made before she died. One of the boys had brought it all the way from Virginia, packed in a tin pail, since Hester would not risk shipping so precious an ornament by freight. She went back to the bedroom and spread the net over William's head. Then she sat down by the bed and listened to his deep, regular breathing until she heard the boys returning. She went out to meet them and warn them not to waken their father.

"I'll be up early to get your breakfast, boys. Your father says you can go to the show." As she handed the money to the eldest, she felt a sudden throb of allegiance to her husband and said sharply, "And you be careful of that, an' don't waste it. Your father works hard for his money."

The boys looked at each other in astonishment and felt that they had lost a powerful ally.

## Getting at Meaning

1. What is Hester's attitude toward her husband? How does she treat him?

2. How does Hester's attitude toward her sons differ from her attitude toward her husband?

3. Why doesn't William respond immediately to Hester's comment that the boys should be allowed to go to the circus?

4. What is William's attitude toward his wife? How does the reader know what he thinks of her?

5. Why is it surprising that William had been to the circus as a child? What impression did the circus make upon William?

6. In what way have Hester and William been separated for a long time? Why do common recollections offer them the "miracle of romance"?

7. How does Hester's treatment of William and of the boys change by the end of the story?

## Developing Skills in Reading Literature

1. **Theme.** A writer may create a story that has two or more themes. These themes, which generally are related, may be developed in several different ways. One way a writer can bring out a theme is through direct statements by the narrator. For instance, what might the writer be saying about people through the narrator's comment, "She had a painful sense of having missed something, or lost something; she felt that somehow the years had cheated her"?

· Another method that a writer can use to develop a theme is to create a contrast between two characters. What might the writer be saying about marriage through her emphasis on the differences between Hester and William? A writer might also use the title of a story to give the reader a clue to a possible theme. How does the writer of this story use the title to make a comment about people who are similar to William Tavener?

The ideas developed by these three techniques are related. Think about each idea in terms of the entire story. Then create one statement that accounts for all three ideas and that could serve as a statement of theme for the entire story.

2. **Characterization.** Writers may develop characters through the comments made by other characters, through the dialogue spoken by the characters, and through the actions of the characters. How does the writer of this story use each of these techniques in developing the character of Hester Tavener?

3. **Setting.** Where do the Taveners live? During what historical period do you suppose they live? How does the setting influence William's treatment of his sons? Hester's treatment of the boys?

## Developing Vocabulary

**Multiple Meanings of Words.** Using context clues, write a definition for each of the italicized words.

"It would have been quite impossible for one man, within the limited *sphere* of human action, . . ."

". . . he heard his wife relate with *relish* the story of the little pig that built a mud house. . . ."

". . . William rose and went over to his walnut *secretary* and unlocked it."

Next, find in a dictionary, definitions for each word that are different from the one you wrote. Select one of the definitions for each word and use the word in a sentence that illustrates the definition you have chosen.

## Developing Writing Skills

**Writing a Report.** Willa Cather's fiction re-creates the world of the pioneers who settled America's western frontier. Using an encyclopedia, at least one book, and one magazine article, gather information about these prairie settlers. Use the encyclopedia article as a general introduction to the subject. Then, select a specific topic, such as houses, schools, forms of recreation, the difficulties presented by weather or disease, or ethnic backgrounds. After you have narrowed your topic, find specific information in books and magazines. Read your sources carefully and take notes. Using your notes, write a five-paragraph report presenting the information you have found and your own evaluations. Be sure to give credit to your sources.

# Point of View

JOSÉ HERRERA, 1938. *Peter Hurd.*
*Nelson Gallery—Atkins Museum, Kansas City, Missouri.*

# The Scarlet Ibis  *James Hurst*

It was in the clove of seasons, summer was dead but autumn had not yet been born, that the ibis lit in the bleeding tree. The flower garden was stained with rotting brown magnolia petals and ironweeds grew rank amid the purple phlox. The five o'clocks by the chimney still marked time, but the oriole nest in the elm was untenanted and rocked back and forth like an empty cradle. The last graveyard flowers were blooming, and their smell drifted across the cotton field and through every room of our house, speaking softly the names of our dead.

It's strange that all this is still so clear to me, now that that summer has long since fled and time has had its way. A grindstone stands where the bleeding tree stood, just outside the kitchen door, and now if an oriole sings in the elm, its song seems to die up in the leaves, a silvery dust. The flower garden is prim, the house a gleaming white, and the pale fence across the yard stands straight and spruce. But sometimes (like right now), as I sit in the cool, green-draped parlor, the grindstone begins to turn, and time with all its changes is ground away—and I remember Doodle.

Doodle was just about the craziest brother a boy ever had. Of course, he wasn't a crazy crazy like old Miss Leedie, who was in love with President Wilson and wrote him a letter every day, but was a nice crazy, like someone you meet in your dreams. He was born when I was six and was, from the outset, a disappointment. He seemed all head, with a tiny body which was red and shriveled like an old man's. Everybody thought he was going to die —everybody except Aunt Nicey, who had de-livered him. She said he would live because he was born in a caul,[1] and cauls were made from Jesus' nightgown. Daddy had Mr. Heath, the carpenter, build a little mahogany coffin for him. But he didn't die, and when he was three months old, Mama and Daddy decided they might as well name him. They named him William Armstrong, which was like tying a big tail on a small kite. Such a name sounds good only on a tombstone.

I thought myself pretty smart at many things, like holding my breath, running, jumping, or climbing the vines in Old Woman Swamp, and I wanted more than anything else someone to race to Horsehead Landing, someone to box with, and someone to perch with in the top fork of the great pine behind the barn, where across the fields and swamps you could see the sea. I wanted a brother. But Mama, crying, told me that even if William Armstrong lived, he would never do these things with me. He might not, she sobbed, even be "all there." He might, as long as he lived, lie on the rubber sheet in the center of the bed in the front bedroom where the white marquisette curtains billowed out in the afternoon sea breeze, rustling like palmetto fronds.

It was bad enough having an invalid brother, but having one who possibly was not all there was unbearable, so I began to make plans to kill him by smothering him with a pillow. However, one afternoon as I watched him, my head poked between the iron posts of the foot of the bed, he looked

---

1. **caul** (kôl): a membrane sometimes surrounding the head of child at birth.

straight at me and grinned. I skipped through the rooms, down the echoing halls, shouting, "Mama, he smiled. He's all there! He's all there!" and he was.

When he was two, if you laid him on his stomach, he began to try to move himself, straining terribly. The doctor said that with his weak heart this strain would probably kill him, but it didn't. Trembling, he'd push himself up, turning first red, then a soft purple, and finally collapse back onto the bed like an old worn-out doll. I can still see Mama watching him, her hand pressed tight across her mouth, her eyes wide and unblinking. But he learned to crawl (it was his third winter), and we brought him out of the front bedroom, putting him on the rug before the fireplace. For the first time he became one of us.

As long as he lay all the time in bed, we called him William Armstrong, even though it was formal and sounded as if we were referring to one of our ancestors, but with his creeping around on the deerskin rug and beginning to talk, something had to be done about his name. It was I who renamed him. When he crawled, he crawled backwards, as if he were in reverse and couldn't change gears. If you called him, he'd turn around as if he were going in the other direction, then he'd back right up to you to be picked up. Crawling backward made him look like a doodlebug, so I began to call him Doodle, and in time even Mama and Daddy thought it was a better name than William Armstrong. Only Aunt Nicey disagreed. She said caul babies should be treated with special respect since they might turn out to be saints. Renaming my brother was perhaps the kindest thing I ever did for him, because nobody expects much from someone called Doodle.

Although Doodle learned to crawl, he showed no signs of walking, but he wasn't idle. He talked so much that we all quit listening to what he said. It was about this time that Daddy built him a go-cart and I had to pull him around. At first I just paraded him up and down the piazza, but then he started crying to be taken out into the yard, and it ended up by my having to lug him wherever I went. If I so much as picked up my cap, he'd start crying to go with me and Mama would call from wherever she was, "Take Doodle with you."

He was a burden in many ways. The doctor had said that he mustn't get too excited, too hot, too cold, or too tired and that he must always be treated gently. A long list of don'ts went with him, all of which I ignored once we got out of the house. To discourage his coming with me, I'd run with him across the ends of the cotton rows and careen him around corners on two wheels. Sometimes I accidentally turned him over, but he never told Mama. His skin was very sensitive, and he had to wear a big straw hat whenever he went out. When the going got rough and he had to cling to the sides of the go-cart, the hat slipped all the way down over his ears. He was a sight. Finally, I could see I was licked. Doodle was my brother and he was going to cling to me forever, no matter what I did, so I dragged him across the burning cotton field to share with him the only beauty I knew, Old Woman Swamp. I pulled the go-cart through the saw-tooth fern, down into the green dimness where the palmetto fronds whispered by the stream. I lifted him out and set him down in the soft rubber grass beside a tall pine. His eyes were round with wonder as he gazed about him, and his little hands began to stroke the rubber grass. Then he began to cry.

"For heaven's sake, what's the matter?" I asked, annoyed.

"It's so pretty," he said. "So pretty, pretty, pretty."

After that day Doodle and I often went down into Old Woman Swamp. I would gather wildflowers, wild violets, honeysuckle, yellow jasmine, snakeflowers, and water lilies, and with wire grass we'd weave them into necklaces and crowns. We'd bedeck ourselves with our handiwork and loll about thus beautified, beyond the touch of the everyday world. Then when the slanted rays of the sun burned orange in the tops of the pines, we'd drop our jewels into the stream and watch them float away toward the sea.

There is within me (and with sadness I have watched it in others) a knot of cruelty borne by the stream of love, much as our blood sometimes bears the seed of our destruction, and at times I was mean to Doodle. One day I took him up to the barn loft and showed him his casket, telling him how we all had believed he would die. It was covered with a film of Paris green sprinkled to kill the rats, and screech owls had built a nest inside it.

Doodle studied the mahogany box for a long time, then said, "It's not mine."

"It is," I said. "And before I'll help you down from the loft, you're going to have to touch it."

"I won't touch it," he said sullenly.

"Then I'll leave you here by yourself," I threatened, and made as if I were going down.

Doodle was frightened of being left. "Don't go leave me, Brother," he cried, and he leaned toward the coffin. His hand, trembling, reached out, and when he touched the casket he screamed. A screech owl flapped out of the box into our faces, scaring us and covering us with Paris green. Doodle was paralyzed, so I put him on my shoulder and carried him down the ladder, and even when we were outside in the bright sunshine, he clung to me, crying, "Don't leave me. Don't leave me."

When Doodle was five years old, I was embarrassed at having a brother of that age who couldn't walk, so I set out to teach him. We were down in Old Woman Swamp and it was spring and the sick-sweet smell of bay flowers hung everywhere like a mournful song. "I'm going to teach you to walk, Doodle," I said.

He was sitting comfortably on the soft grass, leaning back against the pine. "Why?" he asked.

I hadn't expected such an answer. "So I won't have to haul you around all the time."

"I can't walk, Brother," he said.

"Who says so?" I demanded.

"Mama, the doctor—everybody."

"Oh, you can walk," I said, and I took him by the arms and stood him up. He collapsed onto the grass like a half-empty flour sack. It was as if he had no bones in his little legs.

"Don't hurt me, Brother," he warned.

"Shut up. I'm not going to hurt you. I'm going to teach you to walk." I heaved him up again, and again he collapsed.

This time he did not lift his face up out of the rubber grass. "I just can't do it. Let's make honeysuckle wreaths."

"Oh yes you can, Doodle," I said. "All you got to do is try. Now come on," and I hauled him up once more.

It seemed so hopeless from the beginning that it's a miracle I didn't give up. But all of us must have something or someone to be proud of, and Doodle had become mine. I did not know then that pride is a wonderful, terrible thing, a seed that bears two vines, life and death. Every day that summer we went to the pine beside the stream of Old Woman Swamp, and I put him on his feet at least a hundred times each afternoon. Occasionally I too became discouraged because it didn't seem as if he was trying, and I would say, "Doodle, don't you *want* to learn to walk?"

He'd nod his head, and I'd say, "Well, if you don't keep trying, you'll never learn." Then I'd paint for him a picture of us as old men, white-haired, him with a long white beard and me still pulling him around in the go-cart. This never failed to make him try again.

Finally one day, after many weeks of practicing, he stood alone for a few seconds. When he fell, I grabbed him in my arms and hugged him, our laughter pealing through the swamp like a ringing bell. Now we knew it could be done. Hope no longer hid in the dark palmetto thicket but perched like a cardinal in the lacy toothbrush tree, brilliantly visible. "Yes, yes," I cried, and he cried it too, and the grass beneath us was soft and the smell of the swamp was sweet.

With success so imminent, we decided not to tell anyone until he could actually walk. Each day, barring rain, we sneaked into Old Woman Swamp, and by cotton-picking time Doodle was ready to show what he could do. He still wasn't able to walk far, but we could wait no longer. Keeping a nice secret is very hard to do, like holding your breath. We chose to reveal all on October eighth, Doodle's sixth birthday, and for weeks ahead we mooned around the house, promising everybody a most spectacular surprise. Aunt Nicey said that, after so much talk, if we produced anything less tremendous than the Resurrection, she was going to be disappointed.

At breakfast on our chosen day, when Mama, Daddy, and Aunt Nicey were in the dining room, I brought Doodle to the door in the go-cart just as usual and had them turn their backs, making them cross their hearts and hope to die if they peeked. I helped Doodle up, and when he was standing alone I let them look. There wasn't a sound as Doodle walked slowly across the room and sat down at his place at the table. Then Mama began to cry and ran over to him, hugging him and kissing him. Daddy hugged him too, so I went to Aunt Nicey, who was thanks praying in the doorway, and began to waltz her around. We danced together quite well until she came down on my big toe with her brogans, hurt-ing me so badly I thought I was crippled for life.

Doodle told them it was I who had taught him to walk, so everyone wanted to hug me, and I began to cry.

"What are you crying for?" asked Daddy, but I couldn't answer. They did not know that I did it for myself; that pride, whose slave I was, spoke to me louder than all their voices, and that Doodle walked only because I was ashamed of having a crippled brother.

Within a few months Doodle had learned to walk well and his go-cart was put up in the barn loft (it's still there) beside his little mahogany coffin. Now, when we roamed off together, resting often, we never turned back until our destination had been reached, and to help pass the time, we took up lying. From the beginning Doodle was a terrible liar and he got me in the habit. Had anyone stopped to listen to us, we would have been sent off to Dix Hill.

My lies were scary, involved, and usually pointless, but Doodle's were twice as crazy. People in his stories all had wings and flew wherever they wanted to go. His favorite lie was about a boy named Peter who had a pet peacock with a ten-foot tail. Peter wore a golden robe that glittered so brightly that when he walked through the sunflowers they turned away from the sun to face him. When Peter was ready to go to sleep, the peacock spread his magnificent tail, enfolding the boy gently like a closing go-to-sleep flower, burying him in the gloriously iridescent, rustling vortex. Yes, I must admit it. Doodle could beat me lying.

Doodle and I spent lots of time thinking about our future. We decided that when we were grown we'd live in Old Woman Swamp and pick dog-tongue for a living. Beside the stream, he planned, we'd build us a house of whispering leaves and the swamp birds would be our chickens. All day long (when we weren't gathering dog-tongue) we'd swing through the cypresses on the rope vines, and if it rained we'd huddle beneath an umbrella tree and play stickfrog. Mama and Daddy could come and live with us if they wanted to. He even came up with the idea that he could marry Mama and I could marry Daddy. Of course, I was old enough to know this wouldn't work out, but the picture he painted was so beautiful and serene that all I could do was whisper Yes, yes.

Once I had succeeded in teaching Doodle to walk, I began to believe in my own infallibility, and I prepared a terrific development program for him, unknown to Mama and Daddy, of course. I would teach him to run, to swim, to climb trees, and to fight. He, too, now believed in my infallibility, so we set the deadline for these accomplishments less than a year away, when, it had been decided, Doodle could start to school.

That winter we didn't make much progress, for I was in school and Doodle suffered from one bad cold after another. But when spring came, rich and warm, we raised our sights again. Success lay at the end of summer like a pot of gold, and our campaign got off to a good start. On hot days, Doodle and I went down to Horsehead Landing, and I gave him swimming lessons or showed him how to row a boat. Sometimes we descended into the cool greenness of Old Woman Swamp and climbed the rope vines or boxed scientifically beneath the pine where he had learned to walk. Promise hung about us like the leaves, and wherever we looked, ferns unfurled and birds broke into song.

That summer, the summer of 1918, was blighted. In May and June there was no rain and the crops withered, curled up, then died under the thirsty sun. One morning in July a hurricane came out of the east, tipping over the oaks in the yard and splitting the limbs of the elm trees. That afternoon it roared back out of the west, blew the fallen oaks around, snapping their roots and tearing them out of the earth like a hawk at the entrails of a chicken. Cotton bolls were wrenched from the stalks and lay like green walnuts in the valleys between the rows, while the cornfield leaned over uniformly so that the tassels touched the ground. Doodle and I followed Daddy out into the cotton field, where he stood, shoulders sagging, surveying the ruin. When his chin sank down onto his chest, we were frightened, and Doodle slipped his hand into mine. Suddenly Daddy straightened his shoulders, raised a giant knuckly fist, and with a voice that seemed to rumble out of the earth itself began cursing the weather and the Republican Party. Doodle and I, prodding each other and giggling, went back to the house, knowing that everything would be all right.

And during that summer, strange names were heard through the house: Château Thierry, Amiens, Soissons, and in her blessing at the supper table, Mama once said, "And bless the Pearsons, whose boy Joe was lost at Belleau Wood."

So we came to that clove of seasons. School was only a few weeks away, and Doodle was far behind schedule. He could barely clear the ground when climbing up the rope vines, and his swimming was certainly not passable. We decided to double our efforts, to make that last drive and reach our pot of gold. I made him swim until he turned blue and row until he couldn't lift an oar. Wherever we went, I purposely walked fast, and although he kept up, his face turned red and his eyes became glazed. Once, he could go no further, so he collapsed on the ground and began to cry.

"Aw, come on, Doodle," I urged. "You can do it. Do you want to be different from everybody else when you start school?"

"Does it make any difference?"

"It certainly does," I said. "Now, come on," and I helped him up.

As we slipped through dog days, Doodle began to look feverish, and Mama felt his forehead, asking him if he felt ill. At night he didn't sleep well, and sometimes he had nightmares, crying out until I touched him and said, "Wake up, Doodle. Wake up."

It was Saturday noon, just a few days before school was to start. I should have already admitted defeat, but my pride wouldn't let me. The excitement of our program had now been gone for weeks, but still we kept on with a tired doggedness. It was too late to turn back, for we had both wandered too far into a net of expectations and had left no crumbs behind.

Daddy, Mama, Doodle, and I were seated at the dining-room table having lunch. It was a hot day, with all the windows and doors open in case a breeze should come. In the kitchen Aunt Nicey was humming softly. After a long silence, Daddy spoke. "It's so calm, I wouldn't be surprised if we had a storm this afternoon."

"I haven't heard a rain frog," said Mama, who believed in signs, as she served the bread around the table.

"I did," declared Doodle. "Down in the swamp."

"He didn't," I said contrarily.

"You did, eh?" said Daddy, ignoring my denial.

"I certainly did," Doodle reiterated, scowling at me over the top of his iced-tea glass, and we were quiet again.

Suddenly, from out in the yard, came a strange croaking noise. Doodle stopped eating, with a piece of bread poised ready for his mouth, his eyes popped round like two blue buttons. "What's that?" he whispered.

I jumped up, knocking over my chair, and had reached the door when Mama called, "Pick up the chair, sit down again, and say excuse me."

By the time I had done this, Doodle had excused himself and had slipped out into the yard. He was looking up into the bleeding tree. "It's a great big red bird!" he called.

The bird croaked loudly again, and Mama and Daddy came out into the yard. We shaded our eyes with our hands against the hazy glare of the sun and peered up through the still leaves. On the topmost branch a bird the size of a chicken, with scarlet feathers and long legs, was perched precariously. Its wings hung down loosely, and as we watched, a feather dropped away and floated slowly down through the green leaves.

"It's not even frightened of us," Mama said.

"It looks tired," Daddy added. "Or maybe sick."

Doodle's hands were clasped at his throat, and I had never seen him stand still so long. "What is it?" he asked.

Daddy shook his head. "I don't know, maybe it's—"

At that moment the bird began to flutter, but the wings were uncoordinated, and amid much flapping and a spray of flying feathers, it tumbled down, bumping through the limbs of the bleeding tree and landing at our feet with a thud. Its long, graceful neck jerked twice into an S, then straightened out, and the bird was still. A white veil came over the eyes and the long white beak unhinged. Its legs were crossed and its clawlike feet were delicately curved at rest. Even death did not mar its grace, for it lay on the earth like a broken vase of red flowers, and we stood around it, awed by its exotic beauty.

"It's dead," Mama said.

"What is it?" Doodle repeated.

"Go bring me the bird book," said Daddy.

I ran into the house and brought back the bird book. As we watched, Daddy thumbed through its pages. "It's a scarlet ibis," he said, pointing to a picture. "It lives in the tropics—South America to Florida. A storm must have brought it here."

Sadly, we all looked back at the bird. A

scarlet ibis! How many miles it had traveled to die like this, in *our* yard, beneath the bleeding tree.

"Let's finish lunch," Mama said, nudging us back toward the dining room.

"I'm not hungry," said Doodle, and he knelt down beside the ibis.

"We've got peach cobbler for dessert," Mama tempted from the doorway.

Doodle remained kneeling. "I'm going to bury him."

"Don't you dare touch him," Mama warned. "There's no telling what disease he might have had."

"All right," said Doodle. "I won't."

Daddy, Mama, and I went back to the dining-room table, but we watched Doodle through the open door. He took out a piece of string from his pocket and, without touching the ibis, looped one end around its neck. Slowly, while singing softly *Shall We Gather at the River,* he carried the bird around to the front yard and dug a hole in the flower garden, next to the petunia bed. Now we were watching him through the front window, but he didn't know it. His awkwardness at digging the hole with a shovel whose handle was twice as long as he was made us laugh, and we covered our mouths with our hands so he wouldn't hear.

When Doodle came into the dining room, he found us seriously eating our cobbler. He was pale, and lingered just inside the screen door. "Did you get the scarlet ibis buried?" asked Daddy.

Doodle didn't speak but nodded his head.

"Go wash your hands, and then you can have some peach cobbler," said Mama.

"I'm not hungry," he said.

"Dead birds is bad luck," said Aunt Nicey, poking her head from the kitchen door. "Specially *red* dead birds!"

As soon as I had finished eating, Doodle and I hurried off to Horsehead Landing. Time was short, and Doodle still had a long way to

go if he was going to keep up with the other boys when he started school. The sun, gilded with the yellow cast of autumn, still burned fiercely, but the dark green woods through which we passed were shady and cool. When we reached the landing, Doodle said he was too tired to swim, so we got into a skiff and floated down the creek with the tide. Far off in the marsh a rail was scolding, and over on the beach locusts were singing in the myrtle trees. Doodle did not speak and kept his head turned away, letting one hand trail limply in the water.

After we had drifted a long way, I put the oars in place and made Doodle row back against the tide. Black clouds began to gather in the southwest, and he kept watching them, trying to pull the oars a little faster. When we reached Horsehead Landing, lightning was playing across half the sky and thunder roared out, hiding even the sound of the sea. The sun disappeared and darkness descended, almost like night. Flocks of marsh crows flew by, heading inland to their roosting trees; and two egrets, squawking, arose from the oyster-rock shallows and careened away.

Doodle was both tired and frightened, and when he stepped from the skiff he collapsed onto the mud, sending an armada of fiddler crabs rustling off into the marsh grass. I helped him up, and as he wiped the mud off his trousers, he smiled at me ashamedly. He had failed and we both knew it, so we started back home, racing the storm. We never spoke (What are the words that can solder cracked pride?), but I knew he was watching me, watching for a sign of mercy. The lightning was near now, and from fear he walked so close behind me he kept stepping on my heels. The faster I walked, the faster he walked, so I began to run. The rain was coming, roaring through the pines, and then, like a bursting Roman candle, a gum tree ahead of us was shattered by a bolt of lightning. When the deafening peal of thunder had

died, and in the moment before the rain arrived, I heard Doodle, who had fallen behind, cry out, "Brother, Brother, don't leave me! Don't leave me!"

The knowledge that Doodle's and my plans had come to naught was bitter, and that streak of cruelty within me awakened. I ran as fast as I could, leaving him far behind with a wall of rain dividing us. The drops stung my face like nettles, and the wind flared the wet glistening leaves of the bordering trees. Soon I could hear his voice no more.

I hadn't run too far before I became tired, and the flood of childish spite evanesced as well. I stopped and waited for Doodle. The sound of rain was everywhere, but the wind had died and it fell straight down in parallel paths like ropes hanging from the sky. As I waited, I peered through the downpour, but no one came. Finally I went back and found him huddled beneath a red nightshade bush beside the road. He was sitting on the ground, his face buried in his arms, which were resting on his drawn-up knees. "Let's go, Doodle," I said.

He didn't answer, so I placed my hand on his forehead and lifted his head. Limply, he fell backwards onto the earth. He had been bleeding from the mouth, and his neck and the front of his shirt were stained a brilliant red.

"Doodle! Doodle!" I cried, shaking him, but there was no answer but the ropy rain. He lay very awkwardly, with his head thrown far back, making his vermilion neck appear unusually long and slim. His little legs, bent sharply at the knees, had never before seemed so fragile, so thin.

I began to weep, and the tear-blurred vision in red before me looked very familiar. "Doodle!" I screamed above the pounding storm and threw my body to the earth above his. For a long long time, it seemed forever, I lay there crying, sheltering my fallen scarlet ibis from the heresy of rain.

## Getting at Meaning

1. Who is the narrator of this story? At what time in his life is the story set?

2. In what ways is Doodle a "disappointment," particularly to his brother? Why is Doodle an appropriate name?

3. Although Doodle is not the brother the narrator has hoped for, what do the two boys share as brothers? How do they demonstrate their loyalty to one another?

4. Why does the narrator show Doodle the coffin in the barn? Why does Doodle touch the coffin even though he is reluctant to do so?

5. How does the story demonstrate the truth of the statement that ". . . pride is a wonderful, terrible thing, a seed that bears two vines, life and death"?

6. What do Doodle's favorite lie and his plans for the future reveal about his character?

7. Explain the meaning of the narrator's comment, "It was too late to turn back, for we had both wandered too far into a net of expectations and had left no crumbs behind."

8. Why does the red bird create so much excitement for the family? Why is Doodle particularly attracted to it?

9. Compare Doodle's appearance in death with the appearance of the scarlet ibis.

## Developing Skills in Reading Literature

1. **Point of View.** Approximately how old is the narrator of this story? How have the narrator's feelings about Doodle and about the events related in the story changed since the events took place? How might the story be different if it were told by the narrator at a younger age?

2. **Mood.** Reread the first paragraph of the story. What mood does this paragraph create? Which words in the paragraph are particularly important in developing this mood? Is the mood appropriate to the rest of the story? Why or why not?

3. **Setting.** This story includes detailed descriptions of natural surroundings, particularly of Old Woman Swamp. How does the writer use these descriptions to develop the story? Similarly, how does the writer use time of day, historical time, and time of year to present his ideas?

4. **Simile.** The writer of this story uses similes to create vivid impressions for the reader. For instance, the narrator says that the dead ibis "lay on the earth like a broken vase of red flowers." Find at least five other similes in the story. Be prepared to evaluate the effectiveness of the similes in terms of other elements in the story.

5. **Symbol.** The narrator of this story sees a great similarity between Doodle and the scarlet ibis. For the narrator, what does the scarlet ibis symbolize?

## Developing Vocabulary

**Adjectives.** Precise, vivid adjectives create clear images in the mind of the reader. In this story, the writer uses several adjectives to indicate shades of the color red:

> ". . . a bird . . . with *scarlet* feathers and long legs, was perched precariously."
> ". . . his neck and the front of his shirt were stained a *brilliant* red."
> "He lay very awkwardly . . . making his *vermilion* neck appear unusually long and slim."

Choose a color such as blue, yellow, or green. Write five sentences, each of which includes one or more adjectives to indicate a precise shade of the color.

# Corvus the Crow  *Franklin Russell*

The day's hunting had been a disaster. The merciless wind, blowing without relief, had driven all the creatures deep into shelters in the snow. They crouched under the bark of trees and folded themselves into hollows in dead wood. Corvus the crow, black as midnight as he stalked across great billows of snow, turned over empty, rattling bones. For the moment he mastered the nag of hunger, but he soon had to have food to resist the wind. He knew where to get it: in a sheltered valley to the north, beyond the swamp. A harvest of dried berries awaited him there, but this meant a long flight against the terrible north wind. He disliked the wind almost as much as he hated to be hungry.

He peered through slowly thickening snow and shook snowflakes off his eyes, but he could see no other life in the storm. He already felt a chill beginning in his empty gut. His lean, taut body, all muscle and fatless flesh, did not provide enough fuel to warm him. The heat must come from food. He shook himself and stropped his beak on the branch of a tree. As he bent sideways, he glimpsed something moving. Snow crusted the entrance to a hole in the tree trunk. Inside, packed snow slowly moved outward. Corvus poked at the snow and was astonished to see a mass of exposed dark fur. Something was alive in there. He jabbed at the fur and then leaped backward when the crusted snow exploded as the animal in the hole twitched violently. Corvus turned at the end of his branch and watched as a raccoon, half-awake and irritable, twisted her body

into a new position, jammed her back against the hole, and went back to sleep. Unlike Corvus, she had no need to eat; she was warmed by burning up the fat she had gathered on her body the previous year.

Corvus gave one honking cry and flew to a familiar tree overlooking a pond. Nothing moved except hard grains of wind-driven snow that scampered in quick bursts from one billow to another. The pond thrust its frozen face into the trees in many places, surrounded an island in its center, and disappeared from sight to east and west. In summer, Corvus hunted there, among thriving jungles of cattail and alder. But now the pond seemed dead. He lifted himself off against the searching wind into the highest branches of the tree where, in an old squirrel hole, he had secreted a cache of nuts, bones, pieces of dried meat, and berries. He had spent the earlier part of the winter stuffing the hole with reserve food, but he knew the food cache was empty now. Some forest dweller had found it and cleaned it out days before. He looked down into the gaping hole and felt a long chill in his gut. Below, still visible in the snow, was a large pellet of bones. This he had spat out, as was his custom, after his last feeding.

He closed his eyes for a moment and drifted on wings of memory. He was young, fifteen years ago, when the forest had glowed crimson and a big white structure, a church west of the pond, had burned down to a black scar on the ground. He remembered a farmer's voice, but the clatter of machinery had disappeared into the depths of the years. The farmer's house had burned a year after the church. The red light in the dark trees, the shouts, these he recalled, and then the quiet years afterward when the men and the farm animals had disappeared. Cedars clustered in the abandoned fields. Fruit dropped from the neglected orchard. Rich green grass sprouted from the burned ruins. Overgrown tracks faded. A flood of new trees moved in, sumac and maple, hesitant pine and beech. Hemlocks thrust up graceful, curved heads over the green jungles below. The abandoned fields and orchard grew with populations of creeping mice and grubs and worms and beetles. And Corvus hunted there.

He jerked his eyes open.

The wind fell abruptly to a soft whisper in the treetops and Corvus turned north, sensing a lull that might let him drive rapidly to the food. But a moment later wind engulfed him again, shook a tingling shower of ice from the trees, and roared away in a cloud of white. Corvus shook himself and fluffed out his feathers. The pond was his territory through necessity, not choice. He had been born here. He resembled all other crows in his hatred of owls, his fear of large hawks, his urge to roam widely, but he had suffered crippling injuries at this place of his birth and so had become a watcher at the fringes of the great crow armies of other seasons. His injuries prevented him from keeping up with their urgent group flying. He could not follow them north in the spring, nor fall back south before the onset of winter. He remained defiantly Corvus at the pond, a captive of the place.

He stropped his heavy, wedge-shaped beak on a branch, a beak that could hammer holes in ice or tear red flesh to shreds. It could pick up an egg and carry it, or drill a hole in wood to reach a beetle. It could seize a subterranean worm or pick a single berry. Corvus was one of the balancers of life at the pond; he punished the unwary, hunted those who became too numerous, and scavenged after any disaster. His body was as big as a large hawk's, with broad, flat wings for buoyant flight. His plumage was unrelieved black; legs dull black, eyes gleaming black and keen as an owl's. Corvus, the all-purpose hunter, given neither grace nor beauty, had instead a reasoning brain, memory, and a cool cunning.

The wind fingered deeply into his fluffed-out feathers, and he shivered. Alone, a black mark in this winter infinity of white, he remained a crow to the core of his being. He cried out. No answer. No moment passed without his hoping to hear another crow, without his searching for familiar black bodies pumping along a distant horizon. He expected the summer crows who bred near or at the pond to go south in the fall. In some years, he would be joined by a few crows who had bred in the far north and had come south to winter at the pond. Those were the best winters of all, but they had not come this year.

He must move. He must eat. He had so long outlived a wild crow's lifespan of five or six years that he was not well fitted for prolonged hunger. He flew directly into the wind, eyes stinging with its cold, wings driven by the agony and desperation of his hunger. Pain jabbed at his side. The valley of the dried berries seemed a thousand days' flying away. As he thrashed northward, ghostly crow calls echoed in his head. His wings creaked and swished in the wind, and that was real, though the ghostly cries were not. He imagined the distress cry of a drowning crow that once had brought him wheeling across summer alders and willows, his dark shadow fleeing across grasslands leading into sedges, into cattails, and then over the open water of the pond to rescue a fellow crow trapped in waterweeds. The phantom crow calls faded. He was flying north into a wind that almost froze his heart. He plowed on

through air empty of crows, no sound of them now in fact or in memory.

Corvus was flying toward an uncertain horizon. He had become a creature of boundaries at the pond. He hunted only in places where he felt secure. He was suspicious and wary of everything beyond the boundaries of his territory. Over the years the limits had become fixed. Beyond the southern shore of the pond lay a forest, then a river and a hill. Beyond that hill there were cornfields and the sound of men's guns began. To the west, a winding track wandered through a pine grove to the burned-out house and church and led down into a valley. There, buildings thickened, and more men and guns appeared. The northern limits were dictated by the forest that was mostly too thick for good hunting and rolled away into a far horizon. To the east, swampy land led to a marsh that nourished the earth until it was stopped by the sea. Corvus's territory was a kind of haven from which men had retreated, and so he was protected by laws he did not need to understand.

He climbed a long, unsweeping forest slope. The pain in his side grew. At the top of the ridge, he knew, the force of the wind would redouble. To avoid this he dropped into the bare, rattling trees, and cautiously worked his way forward near the ground. He dropped onto the snow at the peak of the ridge and walked, head hunched back into his feathers.

This ridge was familiar territory, but he rarely went beyond it. Creatures had walked in the snow before him here. He knew how to read footprints. Nearby, the scuff marks of a partridge told of the bird's struggle up a snowbank to reach the tips of shrub leaves partially buried. Further on, the plow marks of hasty deer ran from some invisible pursuer. In front of him, the incomplete signature of a rabbit moved from one thicket to another, leaving foot marks that stopped suddenly, as though the rabbit had taken flight. Corvus, the pain in his side diminishing, had seen rabbits flying before, leaving specks of blood, tufts of hair, and one scream of defeat lurking in the air as the great-horned owl bore them away.

Corvus forced himself onward, touched a ridge of snow with his feet, flew into the white glare of snow at his left wing, flew into wind-whipped granules plucked from the snow blanket. Now, because he had made such an effort to reach the berry valley, he had to eat there to survive the night. The cold was increasing. He had not expected this. Each hour of his winter life was governed by winds and temperatures. Each moment was ruled by thaws that brought insects into the open, or freezes that killed the unwary and weak. When he failed to anticipate these changes, he chanced hunger and death.

Below, in a rift in the trees, he saw snow blasted up in thick billowing white clouds, and he dropped down to the bared earth for signs of victims overwhelmed in previous snowfalls and now uncovered. Nothing. In better times he was usually the first to find an old opossum stricken by the cold or an unlucky wood rat far from his nest. But now he was caught in an emergency, with luck eluding him.

The winding white line of a narrow, frozen river curved through a valley below him. He glided down to the river, guided by memories of frogs asleep in shoreline mud who had been caught in ice and then passed slowly up to the surface. He could hack such victims loose and bear them away with a cry of triumph. But the winding river unrolled empty and dead. He looked in vain for the black marks of springs bubbling out of the ice where the vegetable debris of winter might float: berries and seeds, cocoons and drowned sleepers of the insect legions. A river bank was also the place to find stricken fish that he could pull from the shallows or chop from the ice.

For a second he saw himself floating downstream on an ice floe, crowing his success at a stomach well filled and a winter well beaten.

But that was in another time. Now, he balanced energy and strength against distance and cold. There was no certainty that his flight would ensure survival. The berries might be gone. He often made mistakes. He already had allowed himself to become too reliant on an old dog muskrat frozen in blue ice at one secluded edge of the pond. Two days ago, he had found the muskrat gone. Some sharp-clawed creature had gouged out all of the frozen flesh. At first Corvus had been merely irritated, but as he flew, belly empty, from one hunting failure to another, his hunger reproached him for his laziness in letting himself become dependent on the muskrat.

The river narrowed and twisted under trees, still offering nothing; Corvus turned up toward the crest of another hill. A fire half a dozen years before had stripped away the tree cover, so he dropped to the ground among shrubs. This was a calculated risk. He might meet a fox or a mink or other ground hunter, but the pain of the wind blunted his caution. He walked through the shrubs, took flight, and planed down through the trees on the other side. He sheltered among pines and flew the protected length of a rocky ravine, the bare vertical sides echoing to the hum and rumble of the icy wind. He came to a rock face and was propelled unexpectedly upward, eyes aching, and fell, untidy and frustrated, into a forest roaring with the rage of the north wind.

When Corvus reached the valley of berries, he was exhausted and trembling with cold. He glided down, sharp eyes probing for where the berry plants drooped under a partial covering of snow. He saw the berries set against the snow and fell among them. There, until dusk, he filled his gut with the berries of poison ivy and poison sumac, with ragweed and dried grapes. He found old dogwood berries and pokeberries. He continued to feast, even though night was upon him, and he juggled his fear of the darkness with the comfortable warmth spreading throughout his body. At dusk the hunger pain was gone. He looked up out of the valley into a gloomy sky, odd stars glittering now, the snow gone, and trees bare against all skylines. The wind remained unfriendly.

Suddenly, Corvus felt panic sweep through his body. The darkness, the wind, aloneness, all these were alien and frightening to a crow. He hurled himself up the northern side of the valley. He flew in the firm grip of the wind, flew south at exhilarating speed, flew into the eye of the melting moon. Then, panic fading, he came down toward the black pond with an exultant croak, wings rustling, and landed in his roost in a hemlock. Tomorrow he must pit himself against winter's odds in some new and dangerous way.

For long, ice-chilled days, Corvus existed under the shadow of his escape from death. He relived those moments in the tangle of shrub branches; the great wings spread above him, golden eyes blazing, the cruel beak reaching for him. He remembered the torment of staying motionless, lying on his back, helpless with panic, and unable to move. He remembered the long, terrible wait as the owl scrambled back and forth, trying to find a break in the shrub tangle. Finally, frustrated, he had flown away.

All this had sharpened Corvus's worst fears. He hung back in his refuge at the hemlock and looked fearfully across the pond. Once, when an owl cry sounded near him at night under a full, brilliant moon, he had leaped instinctively from his perch before he was fully awake and hurled himself away.

For an hour, still panic-stricken, he blundered around the pond, reliving the attack of the snowy owl until, exhausted, he fetched up in the shelter of a grove of cedars.

Gradually his fear subsided. His spring cry rang out again. But now, with the sun rising in the eastern sky, a new feeling of anticipation came to him. He stood for hours intently watching the southern horizon beyond the pond. He awaited an arrival. He anticipated crows. They must come here, he knew, even if only to pass through his territory. The crows always came. And so, when he flew, it was with this anticipation swelling inside him. It was an excitement greater even than the feeling for the changing season. Yet perhaps it was the same feeling.

He flew slowly along the upland country north of the pond and faced into a chill north wind that could not quite dispel the new warmth of the sun touching his back. Beeches unrolled beneath him, flanked or mixed with oak and hickories and hemlocks, ancient giants of the past, towering up to meet his eyes. He turned into a shallow valley. An updraft urged him higher, and he passed stately white pines crowding together. He turned east and then south, flying with a reckless lack of objective, his memory feeding him images of crows, crows, crows. He remembered a group of giant willows and their satellite alders near the marsh east of the pond where other crowds were fond of gathering. He turned back toward them, restless and excited. When the marsh opened before him as he topped a ridge, he heard a strange —yet expected—new sound, and his blood quickened.

The marsh grumbled, groaned, and snapped out piercing explosions as it broke up. Corvus's shadow drifted across spreading patches of ice that no longer glittered but shone with a golden glow from melted water upswelling, and spreading out, turning the ice myriad colors under the sun. The change of season was now irresistible; the winter was dead, spring had begun. Corvus heralded it with a series of hooting cries that echoed emptily across the ice wastes.

Then he was overwhelmed by the events of the thaw. At warm midnight he stood wide awake at his roost. His chest and side pained excruciatingly but he ignored them. The forest and pond thundered with the movement of water. The snap and crackle of breaking ice was long buried under the roar of moving water. Creeks filled, hissed, boomed; the pond turned with whirlpools. Corvus, despite his terror of the night, uttered a loud cry as heavy rain began and blotted out his vision of the nearest tree in the gloom. A branch fell and rapped his head. Involuntarily, he launched himself. Caution told him of the dangers but he pushed off into the rain, into the sound of spring, into the blackness of the wet spring night.

Almost immediately his sense of caution returned. He struck a pine branch, brought down showers of water, turned and hit another branch, falling all the time because he was afraid to use his full wing power. Eyes stabbing the darkness, he tried to see where he could land, but darkness rushed upward. Water hissed suddenly close and he tried to halt his fall. But his downthrust feet were caught and he somersaulted and fell backwards, wings spread, and finding himself speeding in a torrent through the night. The main flush of water through the pond took him toward the roaring creek that drained it. Corvus went with it, twisting and turning in the water, helpless and voiceless in his terror.

As he entered the creek channel, he could not see that he was not the only victim of the thaw. Frantic mice were in the dark water with him. Many drowned. He swept past a terrified raccoon clinging for life to a sapling that was too thin for her to climb, barely thick enough to hold her against the flow of the current. Corvus felt himself surging forward, and the roar of water filled the night world. He croaked. He was drowning. He was dying.

When the creek widened and made a turn south toward its meeting with the river, Corvus, now sodden and almost ready to sink under the weight of his wet feathers, was propelled into an eddy of shallower water at the turn. He floated, choking, then realized his swift downstream movement had stopped. He thrashed himself forward, felt gravel underfoot, lunged and lurched, and got himself up onto leaf-strewn earth. Crouched in the undergrowth and panting, he awaited daylight.

The following days banished the memory of winter. Corvus's near-drowning did not slow his entry into the new season. He could accept such dangers and shrug them off. He gorged himself on mice. Thousands of grass nests, built by the mice during the winter and interconnected by tunnels through matted grass, were revealed. The slow and the unwary fell to the walking Corvus. He saw the mortality of winter sleepers. As his feet scrunched in honeycombed ice at the edge of the pond, the rushing waters all around him, he saw snails revealed, some dead, some alive. Life-giving oxygen flushed into the winter waters, and some of the snails stirred, fell from the ice that gripped them, cut new tracks in winter-borne mud. The decayed shells of those who had died fell into the still, murky water; and in one place alone were fifty dead through some miscalculation of the previous fall. But for every one dead, a hundred were alive.

At times Corvus shouted his excitement. The ground softened and caked his feet with mud. From deep subterranean sleeping chambers came millions of earthworms. They were so anxious to escape the earth they crawled great distances, moving through puddles and mud, leaving long slithering tracks at the fringes of the pond. Others, more careful, left one end of their bodies inside their holes, probed around with their mouth ends, and fed on dead leaves. Corvus walked and ate, and walked and flew fat with them inside his body.

In spite of the food and the excitement of the season, Corvus still moved expectantly to a watching place at the curving tip of the hemlock. The pond changed a little each day, each hour, each minute. He looked for crows but saw only a bare horizon. He could not see bulrushes pulsing with life in sunken tangles of roots, or cattails stirring in the mud, or the growth of movement in silent tree trunks and sunken beds. Behind him, a cardinal whistled a piercing first cry of the season. From the far side of the pond, a prophetic voice called out. A redwinged blackbird had arrived.

Corvus pushed himself along into the hazy dusk of late afternoon and saw half a dozen black forms swinging on the dry stems of last summer. The first of the redwings, vagrants or pioneers, shouted spring cries at the unresponsive water. Their arrival sent Corvus winging high like a hawk. He curved across the sky, imploring the southern horizon to reveal another crow. His appeals were desperate, then raging, while all around him, day upon day, a silent and now visible frenzy of growth appeared. Spears of vegetation stabbed up under water. Tinges of grass gathered in sheltered, sunny places. Exuberant pike, possessed by spawning madness, leaped and dashed through the shallows of the pond, bound for the eastern marshlands. Corvus came down from shouting at the clouds to catch wood frogs and leopard frogs and unwary salamanders who were all depositing eggs.

He dashed into early morning haze, and the yellow perch, who had spent all winter scarcely moving in deep hollows in the pond,

## Getting at Meaning

1. Why is Corvus a captive of the pond? In what way is Corvus one of the "balancers of life" at the pond?

2. The narrator says that Corvus has a reasoning brain, memory, and a cool cunning. Give an incident from the story to illustrate each of these traits.

3. Corvus preys upon smaller animals. For whom is Corvus the prey? What other dangers does Corvus face?

4. What does Corvus see and hear in his hallucinations? Besides hunger, what internal struggle brings on these hallucinations?

5. What signs, both internal and external, indicate to Corvus that spring is coming?

6. What pleasures does Corvus rediscover with the return of other crows?

## Developing Skills in Reading Literature

1. **Point of View.** Through whose eyes does the reader view the action of this story? What is unusual about this point of view?

2. **Plot.** What is the major conflict in this story? Is it internal or external? What is the climax? Is the conflict resolved in the falling action? Explain.

3. **Description.** Good description helps the reader to picture a particular scene or character. In this story, the descriptions of nature are especially vivid and appeal strongly to the reader's senses, particularly to the sense of sight.

Go back over the story and select three descriptive sentences that appeal to the sense of sight. Copy the words that help you to see what is being described. Also find examples of sentences that describe how things sound, smell, taste, and feel.

## Developing Vocabulary

1. **Prefixes.** Corvus uses his beak to seize subterranean worms. Look up the word *subterranean* in a dictionary. What is the meaning of the prefix *sub-*? What does the root word mean? Define *subterranean* in terms of its prefix and root. Skim the dictionary for other words with the prefix *sub-*. List five of these words and define them in terms of the prefix.

2. **Conversion.** Notice the use of the word *finger* in the following sentence: "The wind fingered deeply into his feathers." The word *finger,* which is usually a noun, has been used here as a verb. The process of using words as different parts of speech is called conversion. Write five sentences in which nouns that name parts of the body are converted to other parts of speech. For example, "He headed home."

## Developing Writing Skills

1. **Creating a Dominant Impression.** Corvus is so lonely that he is continually looking and listening for another crow. In a single paragraph, describe a time when you were lonely. You need not have been physically alone, for it is possible to be lonely in a crowd. Describe your loneliness in detail, focusing on this one feeling.

2. **Maintaining the Same Point of View.** Reread the opening paragraph of the story. This paragraph and much of the story focus on Corvus's search for food. Narrate the story of another animal's search for food. You may choose a household pet or a wild animal. Tell the story in the third person, from the animal's point of view, using the opening paragraph of "Corvus the Crow" as a model. You may choose to imitate the serious tone of this story or to take a light, humorous tone.

# The Carnival     *Michael W. Fedo*

The chartered bus stopped at the corner of Fourteenth and Squire. Jerry smiled nervously, turned and waved to his mother, who stood weeping a few feet away, and boarded the bus.

He returned the driver's silent nod and settled himself in the only remaining seat—near the front—next to a poorly dressed middle-aged woman.

Jerry tingled with excitement. He glanced around, eager for conversation, but the other passengers were strangely silent. This puzzled Jerry, for he was looking forward with great anticipation to the carnival.

Indeed, he felt fortunate in having won the drawing at school that allowed him to attend the carnival free, as a special guest of the government. In an effort to encourage patronage among young people, the government agency—Populace Control—sponsored drawings and contests for students.

The man and woman seated behind Jerry began talking about carnivals of years gone by—how they used to be very popular with kids, but weren't nearly as exciting as those of today. From the way they spoke, Jerry guessed they had attended many carnivals. He turned around and saw they were about the age of his parents.

How much more interesting than his parents they were, Jerry thought. His parents wouldn't dream of taking in the carnival, and Jerry sometimes wondered what they had to live for.

The couple noticed Jerry staring at them, and he coughed and faced the front. He squirmed in his seat.

The woman next to Jerry nudged him. "You don't look old enough," she said, looking straight ahead.

"I'm sixteen," Jerry responded sharply.

The woman turned toward him. "They never had these when I was sixteen. I wish they had."

"Why?"

The woman ignored him. "I hope today's my day," she sighed. "Oh, let it be today." She blew her nose into a crumpled handkerchief and stared out of the mud-spattered window.

The bus rolled past gray neighborhoods. Silent people on the streets, wearing distant, vacant faces, did not look up as the bus went by.

The bus joggled along with its silent passengers until it came to a stop in a part of town unfamiliar to Jerry.

The driver stood and faced the passengers. "All right, folks," he said. "This is it. Get your I.D. cards ready. The P.C. officer will be boarding in a minute. Those with government passes step to the front."

Jerry got up.

"You got a pass?" the woman next to him asked.

"Yes," Jerry said. "I won it at school."

The woman turned away again, and Jerry

went to the front of the bus, where the Populace Control officer was standing.

"Just a second, boy," he said, as Jerry held out his identification and pass. "I have an announcement to make." The passengers listlessly raised their heads.

"As you know," he began, "some of you may not be making the return trip on this bus."

Jerry wished the officer would hurry. Didn't he know there was a carnival out there? Couldn't he tell that nobody wanted to hear him drone on and on? *Well, hurry up,* Jerry wanted to shout. *Hurry up!*

The man completed his memorized presentation and looked at Jerry, who was chewing his knuckles in impatience. "Take it easy, son," the officer said. "There's plenty of time —plenty of opportunity for everyone."

"Yes, sir," Jerry said.

He leaped from the bus as soon as the officer had punched his pass, and ran to join the clamoring throng at the carnival's main gate.

It was just the way he had pictured it. The bright lights; the scuffling noises of the mass of moving people; the laughter and the shrieks of those who had dared board the death-defying rides.

Jerry's heartbeat quickened as he walked along the midway.

"First time, sonny?" an ancient carny called to him. "Chance your life on this little spin, why doncha?"

Jerry gazed at the large, whirling machine high above his head. "I might later, mister," he said.

"If you're lucky," the carny replied.

Jerry found himself being swept along with the crowd. Ahead of him a police officer was leading a young woman by the arm. She was sobbing and telling the officer she didn't want to leave her husband.

Jerry hardly noticed. He had more important things on his mind. He was attending his first carnival, and he had to make the most of it. He inhaled deeply, then reached into his pocket and tightly clutched his pass.

The crush of the crowd took Jerry several hundred yards south of the main gate. Hundreds of attractions awaited the customers. Jerry sat down on a bench to study a map of the carnival grounds and decide which amusements he wanted to chance.

No sooner had he removed the map from his pocket than two burly men, struggling with something in a large black plastic bag, passed him. They half-dragged their load to a huge pit and tossed it in.

Jerry wandered over to the edge of the pit. It was enormous—a hundred yards square and no telling how deep.

"The odds are one in eight you'll make it, kid," one of the men said with a crooked smile. "One in eight today." Both men laughed and walked away.

Jerry peered into the pit. There seemed to be a mountain of black plastic bags rising from the floor of the abyss. Jerry shuddered briefly, then turned away.

He didn't look back, but sought cheerier sights instead—the flashing neon lights all about him. The spectacle was breathtaking. Jerry had never in his life been so excited. But then he had never known such cause for excitement, either.

He felt in his pocket for his pass and stopped for a drink from a water fountain, then continued along the midway.

The sky was darkening slightly, but Jerry didn't expect rain. The forecast said no rain, and the Weather Control Center was never wrong.

Jerry got into the line of people who wanted to ride on the Thunder Clapper. In front of him stood a young man with glasses. He was sweating profusely, although the temperature was on the cool side.

The young man glanced over his shoulder. "First time?" he asked, nervously rubbing his hands together.

"Yes," Jerry answered.

"Good luck," the man said. "This one's a real killer."

Jerry saw the contraption resting fifty feet ahead. "You ever been on it before?"

The man cleared his throat. "Nope, not this one. But I've gone on a lot of the other ones."

"This is my first ride," Jerry said.

The young man laughed. "You sure picked a good one for a starter."

"I hope so," Jerry said.

The riders grew funereally silent as they came up to the boarding ramp. Jerry took a deep breath. He could feel his pulse in his throat. He stepped onto the ramp and selected a seat next to the young man he had met in the line.

An attendant came over and strapped them both in. The straps covered most of the body and were fastened very tightly. Jerry found breathing difficult.

"That'll hold you, Shorty," the attendant said, as he finished with Jerry. Jerry noticed that the attendant wore thick-soled boots and carried heavy gloves in his back pocket.

An announcement was made, stating that the ride would last only ninety seconds. It was everyone for himself. The announcer then wished the riders good luck, and the motor started.

It rumbled and coughed, then gained momentum as it lifted the apparatus and its occupants into the air. It picked up speed now, and the low rumble became a violent roar.

Jerry felt his stomach knot beneath the straps holding him. He hoped he wasn't going to be sick.

The roar was deafening. Jerry screamed, but no sound seemed to come from his lips.

Lightning cracked all about him, coming so close he thought he could feel its intense heat.

Then suddenly the roar subsided, and the huge metal wheel was gently eased onto its base. The attendant unstrapped Jerry and the young man next to him. The young man didn't move, and two men came over to take him from the seat.

Jerry bounded quickly down the ramp. "I did it! I made it on my first try!" he shrieked, half-stumbling back onto the midway.

A uniformed statistician smiled at Jerry's youthful exuberance, and continued with his work. In the "Departure" column on the paper in front of him, he added another check.

Jerry wanted to shout his success; he wanted to run, but there was no room on the crowded midway.

*What's so tough about this anyway?* Jerry thought. *If you take a positive approach, you'll overcome it.*

He had easily met the challenge of this first ride—the one everybody had said would be the roughest. Well, he had come through, almost without flinching.

The taste of this kind of success was something he had not known before. He felt so exhilarated that he giggled in spite of himself.

He would try his luck again after he had had some food. He walked over to a refreshment stand and bought two hot dogs. "I've just been on the Thunder Clapper," he told the concessionaire.

"That's living pretty dangerously," the man said.

"Is there any other way?" Jerry asked lightly, paying for the food.

He ate rapidly, eager to get back into action. Although he reveled in his achievement, he knew that he could really prove his mettle only by continuing to accept chal-

lenge. As soon as he had swallowed the last bite, he joined a red-haired boy about his own age in the line for the Whirl-Away.

The other boy smiled and told Jerry that this was to be his first ride.

"This is nothing," Jerry told him. "I've just come off the Thunder Clapper."

The red-haired boy's eyes widened with admiration. "I think this will be just as tough," he said, without conviction.

"I doubt it," Jerry scoffed. "But it'll probably help build your confidence."

The thrill-seekers were led to their places by Whirl-Away attendants, and strapped onto the spokes of the machine in upright, standing positions.

Again there was an announcement over the public address system. It was the usual drivel that Jerry hardly heard. The announcer wished the riders good luck, and the engines started.

Jerry was relaxed; a calm smile played over his lips. He settled back, ready to enjoy this new experience to the fullest.

The Whirl-Away began to vibrate, its engines *whooshing* like a great wind storm. The structure throbbed and gained speed until the passengers near the rim were moving at about two hundred miles an hour.

Jerry was thinking of the stories he'd tell his classmates at school tomorrow. How he took on the Thunder Clapper and the Whirl-Away, straight off. "You take the meanest ones first," he would tell them.

The Whirl-Away, spinning at an ever-increasing speed, rose three hundred feet off the ground.

Jerry became aware of a dizzy sensation. Then the sense of motion ceased, and suddenly he was free of movement and sound. He was in the air, hurtling headlong downward. "It isn't fair!" he tried to shout. "They said eight to one—eight to one! . . ."

Men from the pit moved into position with their black plastic bags. But Jerry did not see them; nor was he conscious when he ceased to be—approaching the earth, meeting it face to face at almost the speed of sound.

## Getting at Meaning

1. Describe the difference between Jerry's behavior and that of his mother, the bus driver, and the other passengers on the bus.

2. What might be the function of a government agency named "Populace Control"?

3. Why might the woman seated next to Jerry on the bus wish, "Oh, let it be today"?

4. How does the Populace Control officer annoy Jerry? What do the man's comments imply about the carnival?

5. What is unusual about the behavior of the young woman who is being led away by a police officer?

6. What is inside the black plastic bags in the pit? Does Jerry know what is in these bags? Explain your answer.

7. After his first ride, Jerry passes a uniformed statistician. What is significant about this person's actions? Do they seem significant to Jerry?

8. How does the danger of the carnival make Jerry feel? What does Jerry reveal about himself in his conversation with the red-haired boy?

9. To what do the odds "one in eight" refer? How does Jerry do against these odds?

## Developing Skills in Reading Literature

1. **Point of View.** Of the characters in this story, whose thoughts does the narrator reveal to the reader? What type of narration is used in the story? What does Jerry notice at the carnival? What are the "important things on his mind"? How do Jerry's interests affect the reader's understanding of the events of the story?

2. **Character.** What kind of person is Jerry? What does he want from life? Why does he wonder what his parents have to live for? What do other people in the story notice about Jerry? What does his interaction with other characters reveal about him?

3. **Foreshadowing.** Find five examples in the story of incidents and observations that foreshadow, or hint at, the true nature of the carnival and Jerry's final fate.

## Developing Vocabulary

**Prefixes.** Decide which of the two meanings of the prefix un- — "not" and "the opposite of" —, applies in each of the following italicized words.

"the bus . . . came to a stop in a part of town *unfamiliar* to Jerry."
"The attendant *unstrapped* Jerry. . . ."

Now write five sentences and in each one use a word that begins with the prefix un-. Label each sentence "not" or "opposite" to indicate the meaning of un- illustrated in the sentence.

## Developing Writing Skills

**Analyzing a Character.** The writer of this story presents what Jerry says, what he does, and the reactions of several characters to him. Write a five-paragraph composition in which you analyze the character of Jerry. In the first paragraph, describe your main impression of this character and indicate briefly your reasons for forming this impression. In the next three paragraphs, develop these reasons, using examples from the story to support them. In the fifth paragraph, review your analysis of Jerry and present your final judgment.

# The Snob

*Morley Callaghan*

It was at the book counter in the department store that John Harcourt, the student, caught a glimpse of his father. At first he could not be sure in the crowd that pushed along the aisle, but there was something about the color of the back of the elderly man's neck, something about the faded felt hat, that he knew very well. Harcourt was standing with the girl he loved, buying a book for her. All afternoon he had been talking to her, eagerly, but with an anxious diffidence, as if there still remained in him an innocent wonder that she should be delighted to be with him. From underneath her wide-brimmed straw hat, her face, so fair and beautifully strong with its expression of cool independence, kept turning up to him and sometimes smiled at what he said. That was the way they always talked, never daring to show much full, strong feeling. Harcourt had just bought the book, and had reached into his pocket for the money with a free, ready gesture to make it appear that he was accustomed to buying books for young ladies, when the white-haired man in the faded felt hat, at the other end of the counter, turned half toward him, and Harcourt knew he was standing only a few feet away from his father.

The young man's easy words trailed away and his voice became little more than a whisper, as if he were afraid that everyone in the store might recognize it. There was rising in him a dreadful uneasiness; something very precious that he wanted to hold seemed close to destruction. His father, standing at the end of the bargain counter, was planted squarely on his two feet, turning a book over thoughtfully in his hands. Then he took out his glasses from an old, worn leather case and adjusted them on the end of his nose, looking down over them at the book. His coat was thrown open, two buttons on his vest were undone, his gray hair was too long, and in his rather shabby clothes he looked very much like a working-man, a carpenter perhaps. Such a resentment rose in young Harcourt that he wanted to cry out bitterly, "Why does he dress as if he never owned a decent suit in his life? He doesn't care what the whole world thinks of him. He never did. I've told him a hundred times he ought to wear his good clothes when he goes out. Mother's told him the same thing. He just laughs. And now Grace may see him. Grace will meet him."

So young Harcourt stood still, with his head down, feeling that something very painful was impending. Once he looked anxiously at Grace, who had turned to the bargain counter. Among those people drifting aimlessly by with hot red faces, getting in each other's way, using their elbows but keeping their faces detached and wooden, she looked tall and splendidly alone. She was so sure of herself, her relation to the people in the aisles, the clerks behind the counter, the books on the shelves, and everything around her. Still keeping his head down and moving close, he whispered uneasily, "Let's go and have tea somewhere, Grace."

"In a minute, dear," she said.

"Let's go now."

"In just a minute, dear," she repeated absently.

"There's not a breath of air in here. Let's go now."

"What makes you so impatient?"

"There's nothing but old books on that counter."

"There may be something here I've wanted

all my life," she said, smiling at him brightly and not noticing the uneasiness in his face.

So Harcourt had to move slowly behind her, getting closer to his father all the time. He could feel the space that separated them narrowing. Once he looked up with a vague, sidelong glance. But his father, red-faced and happy, was still reading the book, only now there was a meditative expression on his face, as if something in the book had stirred him and he intended to stay there reading for some time.

Old Harcourt had lots of time to amuse himself, because he was on a pension after working hard all his life. He had sent John to the university and he was eager to have him distinguish himself. Every night when John came home, whether it was early or late, he used to go into his father's and mother's bedroom and turn on the light and talk to them about the interesting things that had happened to him during the day. They listened and shared this new world with him. They both sat up in their night-clothes and, while his mother asked all the questions, his father listened attentively with his head cocked on one side and a smile or a frown on his face. The memory of all this was in John now, and there was also a desperate longing and a pain within him growing harder to bear as he glanced fearfully at his father, but he thought stubbornly, "I can't introduce him. It'll be easier for everybody if he doesn't see us. I'm not ashamed. But it will be easier. It'll be more sensible. It'll only embarrass him to see Grace." By this time he knew he was ashamed, but he felt that his shame was justified, for Grace's father had the smooth, confident manner of a man who had lived all his life among people who were rich and sure of themselves. Often when he had been in Grace's home talking politely to her mother, John had kept on thinking of the plainness of his own home and of his parents' laughing, good-natured untidiness,

and he resolved desperately that he must make Grace's people admire him.

He looked up cautiously, for they were about eight feet away from his father, but at that moment his father, too, looked up and John's glance shifted swiftly far over the aisle, over the counters, seeing nothing. As his father's blue, calm eyes stared steadily over the glasses, there was an instant when their glances might have met. Neither one could have been certain, yet John, as he turned away and began to talk to Grace hurriedly, knew surely that his father had seen him. He knew it by the steady calmness in his father's blue eyes. John's shame grew, and then humiliation sickened him as he waited and did nothing.

His father turned away, going down the aisle, walking erectly in his shabby clothes, his shoulders very straight, never once looking back. His father would walk slowly along the street, he knew, with that meditative expression deepening and becoming grave.

Young Harcourt stood beside Grace, brushing against her soft shoulder, and made faintly aware again of the delicate scent she used. There, so close beside him, she was holding within her everything he wanted to reach out for, only now he felt a sharp hostility that made him sullen and silent.

"You were right, John," she was drawling in her soft voice. "It does get unbearable in here on a hot day. Do let's go now. Have you ever noticed that department stores after a time can make you really hate people?" But she smiled when she spoke, so he might see that she really hated no one.

"You don't like people, do you?" he said sharply.

"People? What people? What do you mean?"

"I mean," he went on irritably, "you don't like the kind of people you bump into here, for example."

"Not especially. Who does? What are you

talking about?"

"Anybody could see you don't," he said recklessly, full of a savage eagerness to hurt her. "I say you don't like simple, honest people, the kind of people you meet all over the city." He blurted the words out as if he wanted to shake her, but he was longing to say, "You wouldn't like my family. Why couldn't I take you home to have dinner with them? You'd turn up your nose at them, because they've no pretensions. As soon as my father saw you, he knew you wouldn't want to meet him. I could tell by the way he turned."

His father was on his way home now, he knew, and that evening at dinner they would meet. His mother and sister would talk rapidly, but his father would say nothing to him, or to anyone. There would only be Harcourt's memory of the level look in the blue eyes, and the knowledge of his father's pain as he walked away.

Grace watched John's gloomy face as they walked through the store, and she knew he was nursing some private rage, and so her own resentment and exasperation kept growing, and she said crisply, "You're entitled to your moods on a hot afternoon, I suppose, but if I feel I don't like it here, then I don't like it. You wanted to go yourself. Who likes to spend very much time in a department store on a hot afternoon? I begin to hate every stupid person that bangs into me, everybody near me. What does that make me?"

"It makes you a snob."

"So I'm a snob now?" she said angrily.

"Certainly you're a snob," he said. They were at the door and going out to the street. As they walked in the sunlight, in the crowd moving slowly down the street, he was groping for words to describe the secret thoughts he had always had about her. "I've always known how you'd feel about people I like who didn't fit into your private world," he said.

"You're a very stupid person," she said. Her face was flushed now, and it was hard for her to express her indignation, so she stared straight ahead as she walked along.

They had never talked in this way, and now they were both quickly eager to hurt each other. With a flow of words, she started to argue with him, then she checked herself and said calmly, "Listen, John, I imagine you're tired of my company. There's no sense in having tea together. I think I'd better leave you right here."

"That's fine," he said. "Good afternoon."

"Goodbye."

"Goodbye."

She started to go, she had gone two paces, but he reached out desperately and held her arm, and he was frightened, and pleading, "Please don't go, Grace."

All the anger and irritation had left him; there was just a desperate anxiety in his voice as he pleaded, "Please forgive me. I've no right to talk to you like that. I don't know why I'm so rude or what's the matter. I'm ridiculous. I'm very, very ridiculous. Please, you must forgive me. Don't leave me."

He had never talked to her so brokenly, and his sincerity, the depth of his feeling, began to stir her. While she listened, feeling all the yearning in him, they seemed to have been brought closer together, by opposing each other, than ever before, and she began to feel almost shy. "I don't know what's the matter. I suppose we're both irritable. It must be the weather," she said. "But I'm not angry, John."

He nodded his head miserably. He longed to tell her that he was sure she would have been charming to his father, but he had never felt so wretched in his life. He held her arm tight, as if he must hold it or what he wanted most in the world would slip away from him; yet he kept thinking, as he would ever think, of his father walking away quietly with his head never turning.

## Getting at Meaning

1. What effect does seeing his father have on John Harcourt?

2. Has John had a good relationship with his father up to this point? Give an example from the story to support your answer.

3. Contrast John's family with Grace's family.

4. Once his father leaves the store, John turns on Grace. Why is John suddenly so eager to hurt Grace?

5. By the end of the story, how have John's relationships with his father and with Grace changed?

6. Just after noticing his father, John fears that something precious is close to destruction. What does he fear will be destroyed? At the end of the story, what precious thing has been destroyed?

7. Who is the snob in this story? Support your answer with details from the selection.

## Developing Skills in Reading Literature

1. **Point of View.** Through whose eyes does the reader view the action of this story? Why is this a particularly effective point of view for the story?

2. **Characterization.** Following are listed three character traits possessed by John Harcourt. Skim the story, and for each trait find a speech by John or a description of him that reveals the trait.

   a. the need to climb socially
   b. the need to make excuses for his own conduct
   c. the need to transfer guilt to other people

3. **Flashback.** Where does the writer use flashback in this story? What information does the flashback give the reader?

4. **Setting.** What is the setting of the story? How does the setting increase the tension among the characters?

## Developing Vocabulary

**Word Origins.** Sometimes it is difficult to determine how a word acquired its present meaning. *Snob* is such a word. Look up *snob* in a dictionary and check the etymology of the word. What did *snob* originally mean? On the basis of this informa-

tion, construct a logical theory for how the word came to mean "a person who tries to associate with those of a higher social status."

Now research the word *snob* in a book on word origins. What other theories can you find about how the meaning of this word evolved?

## Developing Writing Skills

1. **Writing an Explanation.** John Harcourt is afraid to introduce Grace to his father. Instead of facing the situation, he avoids it, causing pain and creating more problems for himself. The inability to deal with difficult situations is a common human problem. In a five-paragraph composition, explain why people avoid problem situations and what happens as a result. In the opening paragraph, state the problem and describe your attitude toward the problem. In the three developmental paragraphs, give examples of situations that were not faced and the resulting consequences. You may draw on your own experiences, those of friends and family, or those of fictional characters such as John Harcourt. In the final paragraph, come to a conclusion about the best way to handle problem situations.

2. **Using the Senses in Writing.** In the following sentence, the italicized words appeal to the reader's senses of touch and smell. "Young Harcourt stood beside Grace, *brushing* against her *soft* shoulder, and made *faintly* aware again of the *delicate scent* she used."

In a single paragraph, describe the experience of standing close to another person in a crowd. The person can be a stranger or someone you know well. In your description, try to appeal to the senses of smell and touch.

# Winter Night    *Kay Boyle*

There is a time of apprehension that begins with the beginning of darkness and to which only the speech of love can lend security. It is there, in abeyance, at the end of every day, not urgent enough to be given the name of fear but rather of concern for how the hours are to be reprieved from fear; and those who have forgotten how it was when they were children can remember nothing of this. It may begin around five o'clock on a winter afternoon, when the light outside is dying in the windows. At that hour, the New York apartment in which Felicia lived was filled with shadows, and the little girl would wait alone in the living room, looking out at the winter-stripped trees that stood black in the Park against the isolated ovals of unclean snow. Now it was January, and the day had been a cold one; the water of the artificial lake was frozen fast, but because of the cold and the coming darkness, the skaters had ceased to move across its surface. The street that lay between the Park and the apartment house was wide, and the two-way streams of cars and buses, some with their head lamps already shining, advanced and halted, halted and poured swiftly on, to the tempo of the traffic signals' altering lights. The time of apprehension had set in, and Felicia, who was seven, stood at the window in the evening and waited before she asked the question. When the signals below changed from red to green again, or when the double-decker bus turned the corner below, she would ask it. The words of it were already there, tenta-

tive in her mouth, when the answer came from the far end of the hall.

"Your mother," said the voice among the sound of kitchen things, "she telephoned up before you came in from school. She won't be back in time for supper. I was to tell you a sitter was coming in from the sitting-parents' place."

Felicia turned back from the window into the obscurity of the living room, and she looked toward the open door and into the hall beyond it, where the light from the kitchen fell in a clear, yellow angle across the wall and onto the strip of carpet. Her hands were cold, and she put them in her jacket pockets as she walked carefully across the living-room rug and stopped at the edge of light.

"Will she be home late?" she said.

For a moment there was the sound of water running in the kitchen, a long way away, and then the sound of the water ceased, and the high, Southern voice went on, "She'll come home when she gets ready to come home. That's all I have to say. If she wants to spend two dollars and fifty cents and ten cents carfare on top of that three or four nights out of the week for a sitting parent to come in here and sit, it's her own business. It certainly ain't nothing to do with you or me. She makes her money, just like the rest of us does. She works all day down there in the office, or whatever it is, just like the rest of us works, and she's entitled to spend her money like she wants to spend it. There's no law in the world against buying your own freedom. Your mother and me, we're just buying our own freedom, that's all we're doing. And we're not doing nobody no harm."

"Do you know who she's having supper with?" said Felicia from the edge of dark. There was one more step to take and then she would be standing in the light that fell on the strip of carpet, but she did not take the step.

"Do I know who she's having supper with?" the voice cried out in what might have been derision, and there was the sound of dishes striking the metal ribs of the drainboard by the sink. "Maybe it's Mr. Van Johnson or Mr. Frank Sinatra, or maybe it's just the Duke of Wincers[1] for the evening. All I know is you're having soft-boiled egg and spinach and applesauce for supper, and you're going to have it quick now because the time is getting away."

The voice from the kitchen had no name. It was as variable as the faces and figures of the women who came and sat in the evenings. Month by month the voice in the kitchen altered to another voice, and the sitting parents were no more than lonely aunts of an evening or two, who sometimes returned and sometimes did not to this apartment in which they had sat before. Nobody stayed anywhere very long any more, Felicia's mother told her. It was part of the time in which you lived, and part of the life of the city, but when the fathers came back, all this would be miraculously changed. Perhaps you would live in a house again, a small one, with fir trees on either side of the short brick walk, and Father would drive up every night from the station just after darkness set in. When Felicia thought of this, she stepped quickly into the clear angle of light, and she left the dark of the living room behind her and ran softly down the hall.

The drop-leaf table stood in the kitchen between the refrigerator and the sink, and

Felicia sat down at the place that was set. The voice at the sink was speaking still, and while Felicia ate, it did not cease to speak until the bell of the front door rang abruptly. The girl walked around the table and went down the hall, wiping her dark palms in her apron, and, from the drop-leaf table, Felicia watched her step from the angle of light into darkness and open the door.

"You put in an early appearance," the girl said, and the woman who had rung the bell came into the hall. The door closed behind her, and the girl showed her into the living room and lit the lamp on the bookcase, and the shadows were suddenly bleached away. But when the girl turned, the woman turned from the living room, too, and followed her, humbly and in silence, to the threshold of the kitchen. "Sometimes they keep me standing around waiting after it's time for me to be getting on home, the sitting parents do," the girl said, and she picked up the last two dishes from the table and put them in the sink. The woman who stood in the doorway was small, and when she undid the white silk scarf from around her head, Felicia saw that her hair was black. She wore it parted in the middle, and it had not been cut but was drawn back loosely into a knot behind her head. She had very clean white gloves on, and her face was pale, and there was a look of sorrow in her soft black eyes. "Sometimes I have to stand out there in the hall with my hat and coat on, waiting for the sitting parents to turn up," the girl said, and as she turned on the water in the sink, the contempt she had for them hung on the kitchen air. "But you're ahead of time," she said, and she held the dishes, first one and then the other, under the flow of steaming water.

The woman in the doorway wore a neat black coat, not a new-looking coat, and it

1. **Duke of Wincers:** mispronunciation of *Duke of Windsor,* a British nobleman.

had no fur on it, but it had a smooth velvet collar and velvet lapels. She did not move or smile, and she gave no sign that she had heard the girl speaking above the sound of water at the sink. She simply stood looking at Felicia, who sat at the table with the milk in her glass not finished yet. "Are you the child?" she said at last, and her voice was low and the pronunciation of the words a little strange.

"Yes, this here's Felicia," the girl said, and the dark hands dried the dishes and put them away. "You drink up your milk quick, now, Felicia, so's I can rinse your glass."

"I will wash the glass," said the woman. "I would like to wash the glass for her," and Felicia sat looking across the table at the face in the doorway that was filled with such unspoken grief. "I will wash the glass for her and clean off the table," the woman was saying quietly. "When the child is finished, she will show me where her night things are."

"The others, they wouldn't do anything like that," the girl said, and she hung the dishcloth over the rack. "They wouldn't put their hand to housework, the sitting parents. That's where they got the name for them," she said.

Whenever the front door closed behind the girl in the evening, it would usually be that the sitting parent who was there would take up a book of fairy stories and read aloud for a while to Felicia, or else would settle herself in the big chair in the living room and begin to tell the words of a story in drowsiness to her, while Felicia took off her clothes in the bedroom, and folded them, and put her pajamas on, and brushed her teeth, and did her hair. But this time that was not the way it happened. Instead, the woman sat down on the other chair at the kitchen table, and she began at once to speak, not of good fairies or bad, or of animals endowed with human speech, but to speak quietly, in spite of the eagerness behind her words, of a thing that seemed of singular importance to her.

"It is strange that I should have been sent here tonight," she said, her eyes moving slowly from feature to feature of Felicia's face, "for you look like a child that I knew once, and this is the anniversary of that child."

"Did she have hair like mine?" Felicia asked quickly, and she did not keep her eyes fixed on the unfinished glass of milk in shyness any more.

"Yes, she did. She had hair like yours," said the woman, and her glance paused for a moment on the locks that fell straight and thick on the shoulders of Felicia's dress. It may have been that she thought to stretch out her hand and touch the ends of Felicia's hair, for her fingers stirred as they lay clasped together on the table, and then they relapsed into passivity again. "But it is not the hair alone, it is the delicacy of your face, too, and your eyes the same, filled with the same spring-lilac color," the woman said, pronouncing the words carefully. "She had little coats of golden fur on her arms and legs," she said, "and when we were closed up there, the lot of us in the cold, I used to make her laugh when I told her that the fur that was so pretty, like a little fawn's skin on her arms, would always help to keep her warm."

"And did it keep her warm?" asked Felicia, and she gave a little jerk of laughter as she looked down at her own legs hanging under the table, with the bare calves thin and covered with a down of hair.

"It did not keep her warm enough," the woman said, and now the mask of grief had come back upon her face. "So we used to take everything we could spare from ourselves, and we would sew them into cloaks and other kinds of garments for her and for the other children."

"Was it a school?" said Felicia when the woman's voice had ceased to speak.

"No," said the woman softly, "it was not a school, but still there were a lot of children there. It was a camp—that was the name the place had; it was a camp. It was a place where they put people until they could decide what was to be done with them." She sat with her hands clasped, silent a moment, looking at Felicia. "That little dress you have on," she said, not saying the words to anybody, scarcely saying them aloud. "Oh, she would have liked that little dress, the little buttons shaped like hearts, and the white collar—"

"I have four school dresses," Felicia said. "I'll show them to you. How many dresses did she have?"

"Well, there, you see, there in the camp," said the woman, "she did not have any dresses except the little skirt and the pullover. That was all she had. She had brought just a handkerchief of her belongings with her, like everybody else—just enough for three days away from home was what they told us, so she did not have enough to last the winter. But she had her ballet slippers," the woman said, and her clasped fingers did not move. "She had brought them because she thought during her three days away from home she would have the time to practice her ballet."

"I've been to the ballet," Felicia said suddenly, and she said it so eagerly that she stuttered a little as the words came out of her mouth. She slipped quickly down from the chair and went around the table to where the woman sat. Then she took one of the woman's hands away from the other that held it fast, and she pulled her toward the door. "Come into the living room and I'll do a pirouette for you," she said, and then she stopped speaking, her eyes halted on the woman's face. "Did she—did the little girl—could she do a pirouette very well?" she said.

"Yes, she could. At first she could," said the woman, and Felicia felt uneasy now as the sound of sorrow in her words. "But after that she was hungry. She was hungry all winter," she said in a low voice. "We were all hungry, but the children were the hungriest. Even now," she said, and her voice went suddenly savage, "when I see milk like that, clean, fresh milk standing in a glass, I want to cry out loud, I want to beat my hands on the table, because it did not have to be!" She had drawn her fingers abruptly away from Felicia now, and Felicia stood before her, cast off, forlorn, alone again in the time of apprehension. "That was three years ago," the woman was saying, and one hand was lifted, as if in weariness, to shade her face. "It was somewhere else, it was in another country," she said, and behind her hand her eyes were turned upon the substance of a world in which Felicia had played no part.

"Did—did the little girl cry when she was hungry?" Felicia asked, and the woman shook her head.

"Sometimes she cried," she said, "but not very much. She was very quiet. One night, when she heard the other children crying, she said to me, 'You know, they are not crying because they want something to eat. They are crying because their mothers have gone away.'"

"Did the mothers have to go out to supper?" Felicia asked, and she watched the woman's face for the answer.

"No," said the woman. She stood up from her chair, and now that she put her hand on the little girl's shoulder, Felicia was taken into the sphere of love and intimacy again. "Shall we go into the other room, and you will do your pirouette for me?" the woman said, and they went from the kitchen and down the strip of carpet on which the clear light fell. In the front room, they paused, hand in hand, in the glow of the shaded lamp, and the woman looked about her, at the books, the low tables with the magazines and ashtrays on them, the vase of roses on the

piano, looking with dark, scarcely seeing eyes at these things that had no reality at all. It was only when she saw the little white clock on the mantelpiece that she gave any sign, and then she said quickly, "What time does your mother put you to bed?"

Felicia waited a moment, and in the interval of waiting, the woman lifted one hand and, as if in reverence, touched Felicia's hair.

"What time did the little girl you knew in the other place go to bed?" Felicia asked.

"Ah, God, I do not know, I do not remember," the woman said.

"Was she your little girl?" said Felicia softly, stubbornly.

"No," said the woman. "She was not mine. At least, at first she was not mine. She had a mother, a real mother, but the mother had to go away."

"Did she come back late?" asked Felicia.

"No, ah, no, she could not come back, she never came back," the woman said, and now she turned, her arm around Felicia's shoulders, and she sat down in the low, soft chair. "Why am I saying all this to you, why am I doing it?" she cried out in grief, and she held Felicia close against her. "I had thought to speak of the anniversary to you, and that was all, and now I am saying these other things to you. Three years ago today, exactly, the little girl became my little girl because her mother went away. That is all there is to it. There is nothing more."

Felicia waited another moment, held close against the woman, and listening to the swift, strong heartbeats in the woman's breast.

"But the mother," she said then, in the small, persistent voice, "did she take a taxi when she went?"

"This is the way it used to happen," said the woman, speaking in hopelessness and bitterness in the softly lighted room. "Every week they used to come into the place where we were and they would read a list of names out. Sometimes it would be the names of children they would read out, and then a little later they would have to go away. And sometimes it would be the grown people's names, the names of the mothers or big sisters, or other women's names. The men were not with us. The fathers were somewhere else, in another place."

"Yes," Felicia said. "I know."

"We had been there only a little while, maybe ten days or maybe not so long," the woman went on, holding Felicia against her still, "when they read the name of the little girl's mother out, and that afternoon they took her away."

"What did the little girl do?" Felicia said.

"She wanted to think up the best way of getting out, so that she could go find her mother," said the woman, "but she could not think of anything good enough until the third or fourth day. And then she tied her ballet slippers up in the handkerchief again, and she went up to the guard standing at the door." The woman's voice was gentle, controlled now. "She asked the guard please to open the door so that she could go out. 'This is Thursday,' she said, 'and every Tuesday and Thursday I have my ballet lessons. If I miss a ballet lesson, they do not count the money off, so my mother would be just paying for nothing, and she cannot afford to pay for nothing. I missed my ballet lesson on Tuesday,' she said to the guard, 'and I must not miss it again today.'"

Felicia lifted her head from the woman's shoulder, and she shook her hair back and looked in question and wonder at the woman's face.

"And did the man let her go?" she said.

"No, he did not. He could not do that," said the woman. "He was a soldier and he had to do what he was told. So every evening after her mother went, I used to brush the little girl's hair for her," the woman went on saying. "And while I brushed it, I used to tell her the stories of the ballets. Sometimes I

would begin with 'Narcissus,'"[2] the woman said, and she parted Felicia's locks with her fingers, "so if you will go and get your brush now, I will tell it while I brush your hair."

"Oh, yes," said Felicia, and she made two whirls as she went quickly to her bedroom. On the way back, she stopped and held onto the piano with the fingers of one hand while she went up on her toes. "Did you see me? Did you see me standing on my toes?" she called to the woman, and the woman sat smiling in love and contentment at her.

"Yes, wonderful, really wonderful," she said. "I am sure I have never seen anyone do it so well." Felicia came spinning toward her, whirling in pirouette after pirouette, and she flung herself down in the chair close to her, with her thin bones pressed against the woman's soft, wide hip. The woman took the silver-backed, monogrammed brush and the tortoise-shell comb in her hands, and now she began to brush Felicia's hair. "We did not have any soap at all and not very much water to wash in, so I never could fix her as nicely and prettily as I wanted to," she said, and the brush stroked regularly, carefully down, caressing the shape of Felicia's head.

"If there wasn't very much water, then how did she do her teeth?" Felicia said.

"She did not do her teeth," said the woman, and she drew the comb through Felicia's hair. "There were not any toothbrushes or toothpaste, or anything like that."

Felicia waited a moment, constructing the unfamiliar scene of it in silence, and then she asked the tentative question.

"Do I have to do my teeth tonight?" she said.

"No," said the woman, and she was thinking of something else, "you do not have to do your teeth."

---

2. **Narcissus** (när sis′ əs): a ballet based on the myth of a beautiful youth who pines away for love of his own reflection in a brook.

"If I am your little girl tonight, can I pretend there isn't enough water to wash?" said Felicia.

"Yes," said the woman, "you can pretend that if you like. You do not have to wash," she said, and the comb passed lightly through Felicia's hair.

"Will you tell me the story of the ballet?" said Felicia, and the rhythm of the brushing was like the soft, slow rocking of sleep.

"Yes," said the woman. "In the first one, the place is a forest glade with little, pale birches growing in it, and they have green veils over their faces and green veils drifting from their fingers, because it is the springtime. There is the music of a flute," said the woman's voice softly, softly, "and creatures of the wood are dancing——"

"But the mother," Felicia said as suddenly as if she had been awaked from sleep. "What did the little girl's mother say when she didn't do her teeth and didn't wash at night?"

"The mother was not there, you remember," said the woman, and the brush moved steadily in her hand. "But she did send one little letter back. Sometimes the people who went away were able to do that. The mother wrote it in a train, standing up in a car that had no seats," she said, and she might have been telling the story of the ballet still, for her voice was gentle and the brush did not falter on Felicia's hair. "There were perhaps a great many other people standing up in the train with her, perhaps all trying to write their little letters on bits of paper they had managed to hide on them, or that they had found in forgotten corners as they traveled. When they had written their letters, then they must try to slip them out through the boards of the car in which they journeyed, standing up," said the woman, "and these letters fell down on the tracks under the train, or they were blown into the fields or onto the country roads, and if it was a kind person who picked them up, he would seal them in envelopes and send them to where they were addressed to go. So a letter came back like this from the little girl's mother," the woman said, and the brush followed the comb, the comb the brush in steady pursuit through Felicia's hair. "It said goodbye to the little girl, and it said please to take care of her. It said, 'Whoever reads this letter in the camp, please take good care of my little girl for me, and please have her tonsils looked at by a doctor if this is possible to do.' "

"And then," said Felicia softly, persistently, "what happened to the little girl?"

"I do not know. I cannot say," the woman said. But now the brush and comb had ceased to move, and in the silence Felicia turned her thin, small body on the chair, and she and the woman suddenly put their arms around each other. "They must all be asleep now, all of them," the woman said, and in the silence that fell on them again, they held each other closer. "They must be quietly asleep somewhere, and not crying all night because they are hungry and because they are cold. For three years I have been saying 'They must all be asleep, and the cold and the hunger and the seasons or night or day or nothing matters to them——' "

It was after midnight when Felicia's mother put her key in the lock of the front door, and pushed it open, and stepped into the hallway. She walked quickly to the living room, and just across the threshold she slipped the three blue foxskins from her shoulders and dropped them, with her little velvet bag, upon the chair. The room was quiet, so quiet that she could hear the sound of breathing in it, and no one spoke to her in greeting as she crossed toward the bedroom door. And then, as startling as a slap across her delicately tinted face, she saw the woman lying sleeping on the divan, and Felicia, in her school dress still, asleep within the woman's arms.

## Getting at Meaning

1. Reread the first paragraph of the story. What is frightening or disquieting about late afternoon? What does the narrator imply about the questions that Felicia is about to ask? Are they unique or repetitions of questions that have been asked before?

2. The servant comments that Felicia's mother is buying her freedom. What does she mean?

3. When does this story take place? How do you know?

4. How is the woman who arrives on this particular evening different from most of the sitting parents? What does Felicia notice about her face?

5. As the woman tells the story of the little girl, several of her comments hint at the source of her sorrow. What does she mean when she says ". . . we were closed up there . . ."? Why didn't the little girl have any clothes besides those she was wearing? Why were the children always hungry? What kind of camp was it?

6. Felicia asks the woman if the mothers had to go to supper, if they came back late, and if they left in taxis. What does she assume about the little girl and her world? How does the woman's reference to the absent fathers confirm Felicia's assumption?

7. What does the story about the little girl and the guard reveal about the child?

8. What does the story of the mother and her letter reveal about the mother?

9. Why does the woman wish to believe that the people she once knew are all asleep?

10. Based upon the few details describing her physical appearance, what impression of Felicia's mother does the writer create? What other evidence from the story supports this impression?

## Developing Skills in Reading Literature

1. **Point of View.** The writer of this story does not reveal directly the thoughts of any characters. Rather, the narrator, who is not a character in the story, functions as an unseen observer of the characters and their actions. Reread the following comments by the narrator, paying particular attention to the italicized words. How does the use of these words affect reader involvement in the story?

". . . the voice cried out in what *might have been* derision. . . ."

". . . she began at once to speak . . . of a thing that *seemed* of singular importance to her."

"It *may have been* that she thought to stretch out her hand and touch the ends of Felicia's hair . . ."?

2. **Setting.** The action of this story begins about five o'clock on a January afternoon. What do the time of day and time of year contribute to the setting? What do the size of the apartment and its lighting add to the setting? How do these elements of setting affect Felicia?

3. **Character.** What is revealed about Felicia when the little girl avoids the lighted areas of the apartment? Why does the thought of her father enable her to step into the light? What does Felicia need? Why does Felicia feel comfortable with her sitting parent? How does the woman's behavior reveal that she has suffered tremendous grief? When the woman first arrives, the writer gives a detailed description of her coat. Contrast this description with the description in the final paragraph of the story. What comment might the writer be making about the two women?

4. **Theme.** Considering the treatment that Felicia receives from her mother and from the nameless servant, what does the writer seem to be implying about the cause of Felicia's uneasiness? What does the woman from the sitting parents' place offer Felicia that she does not appear to receive from the other two women? What might the writer be saying about the needs of children?

## Developing Writing Skills

**Supporting an Opinion.** The servant says of herself and of Felicia's mother, ". . . we're not doing nobody no harm." Do you agree? Write one paragraph in which you either agree or disagree with the servant. Use evidence from the story to support your opinion.

# Unit Review  *The Short Story*

## Understanding the Unit

1. The setting for "By the Waters of Babylon" is a dangerous and mysterious world. The setting for most of "The Heyday of the Blood" is a country fair. In each story, how does the setting develop the main character and help to present the writer's ideas? In which other stories does the setting play an important role? Explain your answer.

2. Which characters in this unit change significantly as a result of their experiences? Which characters appear not to change at all? Using one example of each type of character, explain the writer's purpose in developing the character in this particular way.

3. Which stories in this unit present an external conflict? Which stories focus on internal conflicts? Which stories present conflicts that are left unresolved?

4. "Searching for Summer," "There Will Come Soft Rains," and "By the Waters of Babylon" all have futuristic settings. In what ways are these settings similar? How are they different? How do the writers of these stories view the relationship between human beings and their environment?

5. "A Visit to Grandmother," "Gaston," "The Cub," and "The Snob" explore the relationships between children and their parents. In what ways are the children in these stories similar? What do these characters suggest about the influence that parents may have upon their offspring?

6. In "A White Heron," Sylvia gives up something that she wants, the friendship of the stranger, to protect something that she reveres, the white heron. In which other stories do characters make similar choices? What do these characters gain from their experiences?

7. In "The Scarlet Ibis" and "Of Missing Persons," first-person narrators recall events that occurred earlier in their lives. Which other stories use this type of narration? What does the use of a first-person narrator who reflects upon past events add to each story?

## Writing

1. Several stories in this unit present characters who have specific goals, things for which they are searching or things that they are trying to achieve. In some stories, the goals are reached, bringing the characters happiness and satisfaction. In other stories, the goals are not achieved or fail to bring the characters the joy that they expected.

Choose one of the following stories: "Searching for Summer," "The Wooing of Ariadne," "The Cask of Amontillado," "Of Missing Persons," "The Cub," or "The Carnival." Write a five-paragraph composition in which you describe the goal of the main character and the effect on the character of seeking the goal and of succeeding or failing in the quest. Illustrate your conclusions with evidence from the story.

2. "Blues Ain't No Mockin' Bird," "A Visit to Grandmother," and "The Heyday of the Blood" all feature grandparents as pivotal characters. Using your own recollections and/or those of your parents, write a five-paragraph character sketch of one of your grandparents. Include physical description, analysis of unique speech patterns, favorite sayings, and specific incidents to bring your grandparent to life for the reader.

3. Choose a story—for example, "The Cask of Amontillado," "Without Words," or "Winter Night"—and explain in a five-paragraph composition how the setting, characters, and plot interact to reveal the theme of the story. The introduction should give the title and the author of the story and should identify its theme. The three body paragraphs should discuss the function of setting, characters, and plot in developing the theme. The final paragraph should comment on the effectiveness with which the theme is presented.

# Unit 2

# Nonfiction

# Introduction to the Unit

Nonfiction is literature that is based on facts. Unlike the writer of fiction whose stories spring from the imagination, the writer of nonfiction begins with reality— real people, actual places, and historical events. Three types of nonfiction are included in this unit: autobiography, biography, and essay.

An autobiography is a narrative of events that occurred in the life of the writer. The account of incidents experienced and conflicts overcome reveals the development of the writer's character and personality.

Biography also provides opportunities to learn about people and events. A biography is the story of a person's life written by another person. Some biographies deal with major historical figures. The biography of Harriet Tubman in this unit, for example, paints a portrait of a remarkable woman who helped to shape the history of pre-Civil War America. The subjects of other biographies are people whose lives are interesting less for what they have accomplished than for their creative approach to life or their strength of character in the face of adversity.

The essay is one of the most flexible of literary forms. The word *essay* comes from the French word *essayer*, which means "to try." An essayist literally "tries out" ideas on the reader. In this unit, writers express their thoughts on topics as diverse as the horrors of war, parent-child relationships, and the mystique of the mobile home. In some of the essays, the treatment of subject is serious and formal; in others, it is light and humorous.

The essays in the unit are divided into two sections, essays on nature and essays of social commentary. The essays on nature all focus on the magnetism and power of water. The essays of social commentary all make some point about society and its values.

Although nonfiction is essentially factual, writers of nonfiction use many of the same literary devices as writers of fiction; for example, character development, setting, suspense, and theme. As you read the examples of nonfiction in this unit, watch for these devices, and note how each writer blends imaginative elements with factual information to produce a unique piece of literature.

# Autobiography

# Fair and Circus Days    *Carl Sandburg*

We were between nine and twelve when we took in the Knox County Fair one year after another for three years. We walked the four and a half miles to the fair grounds just outside of Knoxville—Husky Larson, his brother Al, and one or two other boys. The dust lay thick on the road. We walked barefoot, carrying our shoes and putting them on when we came to the fair grounds so we wouldn't get our bare toes stepped on in the crowds. We walked to save the round-trip railroad fare, and after paying twenty-five cents admission, we watched our few nickels.

One nickel went to the man who had the new and amazing Edison Talking Phonograph. Around the machine stood people watching what it did to the faces of those who clapped on the earphones and were listening. Some faces sober and doubting stayed sober and came away saying, "It works, doggone it, you can hear that brass band playing like it was here on the fair grounds." Most faces, however, wore smiles, and came away saying, "It's pretty cute, I tell you. The machine talks like it's human."

We stepped up with our nickels. We plugged our ears with the phone ends. We watched the cylinder on the machine turning. We heard a voice saying this was the Edison Talking Phonograph and that next we would hear a famous brass band playing. We looked at one another and nodded and smiled, "It works! I can hear it! Ain't it the doggonedest thingamajig? I wouldn't believe it if I wasn't hearing it."

We watched the stallions and mares, bulls and cows, boars and sows, cocks and hens— and the judges awarding prizes and blue ribbons. We saw farmers proud of what they had bred and raised. We felt something in the air very different from a circus. Many a farmer and his boy had come to learn. Their work the year round was in trying to make the land and the animals bring bigger crops and more food. They had on their best clothes, but their muscles stood out in little humps and bunches so that their coats hung on them. Their women carried the signs of hard work, some of them taking pride in the jellies and preserves they had entered for showing. The biggest Knox County potato of the year was worth seeing, as also the largest rutabaga.

We didn't have the two bits for grandstand seats to see the horse races. We stood at the board fence next to the grandstand and watched the fastest horses in Knox County— saddle horses, thoroughbreds, pacers and trotters, with drivers in sulkies with high wheels, spokes of wood, and the rims iron. Several of the drivers, like Fred Seacord, we had seen on the streets of Galesburg exercising their horses and getting them used to the sulkies.

There was a "special feature"—"The Only Pacing Dog in the World." Occasionally we had seen Mr. Redfield with his Irish setter on Main Street. And we knew it was no common dog. Now at last we saw Mr. Redfield come out on the track with his horse and sulky. Alongside the right wheel so the grandstand could see him was the Irish setter, handsome with his coat of brown hair gleaming, his gait that of a pacer, the legs in that peculiar continuous sidewise throw. Twice around the half-mile track went the pacing dog. He wasn't as fast as pacing horses but the crowd believed he was the only pacing dog in the world and they cheered him and Mr. Redfield.

That year we caught a ride in a hayrack from the fair grounds to Galesburg. Arriving home we talked most about having heard the first Edison Talking Phonograph in Knox County and having seen the only pacing dog in the world. About the dog Papa merely remarked that it was interesting. That Edison Talking Phonograph, however, giving you a band concert without bringing you the band, that was curious and he said, "Wat will dey tink up next?" When the talking machine later came to a vacant store on Main Street he spent several nickels listening to the new-fangled contraption.

When the circus came to town, we managed to shake out of sleep at four o'clock in the morning, grab a slice of bread and butter, and make a fast walk to the Q yards to watch the unloading in early daylight. A grand clear voice the man had who rode his horse a half-block ahead of the elephants in the parade and cried out, "The elephants are coming, watch your horses!" First to one side of the street and then the other he cried it and those who had skittish horses watched them.

The great P. T. Barnum himself never met my eyes, but on a bright summer morning I did see Mr. Bailey of the firm of Barnum & Bailey in a black swallowtail coat giving orders and running the circus in the big green pasture that soon was subdivided into city lots. And with the other kids who had seen Bailey I joined in saying, "Wasn't he something to look at? And think of it, he's nearly as great a man as Barnum himself!"

After the unloading we went home for a quick breakfast and then a run to the circus grounds, a big pasture at Main and Farnham near the city limits. If we were lucky we got jobs at carrying water for the elephants or lugging to the big tent the boards for the audience to sit on. After three or four hours of this work we were presented with slips of paper that let us in to see the big show in the afternoon. If we hadn't been lucky and if we didn't have the fifty cents for a ticket, we tried to slide under the canvas and crawl to where we could peek through boards and between legs to see the grand march, the acrobats, the trapezists, the clowns, the hippodrome chariot race given before our eyes as it was in the time of Nero in Rome. Once as I was nearly through the canvas a pair of strong hands caught me by the ankles, yanked me out and threw me for a fall, and a voice told me I could get going.

I walked around to the Side Show. There out front as a free show I saw the man with the elastic skin. He would pull it out from his face and neck and it would snap back into place. There I saw the tattooed man with fish, birds, brunette girls, ships, and many other shapes inked deep into his skin—and there too the Oriental Dancing Girl smiling to some giggling farm hands.

The spieler, a man with a thick uncurled mustache, turned to the crowd and let go in a smooth, loud voice: "La-deez and gen-tul-men, beneath yon canvas we have the curi-aw-si-ties and the mon-straw-si-ties—the Wild Man of Borneo, the smallest dwarf ever seen of mankind and the tallest giant that ever came into existence, the most marvelous snake ever brought to your fair city, a man-eating python captured in the darkest jungles of Africa ever penetrated by man. And I would call your particular attention to Jo Jo, the dogfaced boy born forty miles from land and forty miles from sea. The price of admission, la-deez and gen-tul-men, is a dime, ten cents only, the tenth part of a dollar. Buy your tickets now before the big rush comes."

I had a dime and a nickel. With the dime, I bought a ticket. I went in and I saw the Wild

Man of Borneo was a sad little shrimp and his whiskers messy. The Fat Woman, the Dwarf, the Giant seemed to me to be mistakes God had made, that God was absent-minded when he shaped them. I hung around the midget and his wife, watched them sign their names to photographs they sold at ten cents —and they were so pleasant and witty that I saw I had guessed wrong about them and they were having more fun out of life than some of the men in the Q shops.

I stood a long while watching the Giant and noticed he was quiet and satisfied about things. If a smarty asked, "How's the weather up there?" he might lift one eyebrow and let it pass, for he had heard it often enough. Nor did I feel sorry for the python. He may have been a man-eater, but he was sleeping as if he had forgotten whoever it was he had swallowed and digested. After a third or fourth time around, the only one I felt sorry for was the Wild Man of Borneo. He could have been the only lonely creature among all the freaks. The Oriental Dancing Girl certainly was no freak, an average good-looking showgirl, somewhat dark of skin and probably a gypsy.

Later it came over me that at first sight of the freaks I was sad because I was bashful. Except at home and among playmates, it didn't come easy for me to be looked at. I would pass people on the street and when they had gone by, I would wonder if they had turned their heads for another look at me. Walking down a church aisle between hundreds of people, I had a feeling of eyes on me. This was silly, but when you're bashful you have that feeling of eyes following you and boring through you. And there at the side show were these people, the freaks—and the business, the work, of each one of them was to be looked at. Every week, day by day, they sat or stood up to be looked at by thousands of people and they were paid to be looked at. If some one of them was more looked at than any others there was danger of jealousy on

the part of those who didn't get looked at as much as they wished. Only the Wild Man of Borneo and the python seemed to be careless about whether anyone looked at them or not.

I walked out of the side show with my nickel still in my pocket. I passed the cane stand where a man held out rings and spoke like his tongue was oiled, "Only ten cents for a ring and the cane you ring is the cane you get." I stopped where a man was cheerfully calling with no letup, "Lem-o-nade, ice-cold lem-o-nade, a nice cool refreshing drink for a nickel, five cents, the twentieth part of a dollar." I passed by him to hear a laughing voice, "Here's where you get your hot roasted peanuts, those big double-jointed humpbacked peanuts, five a sack." I passed him by and still had my nickel.

Then I came to a man sitting on the ground, a deep-chested man with a face that had quiet on it and wouldn't bawl at you. I noticed he was barefoot. I looked up from his bare feet to see only stumps of arms at his shoulders. Between the first two toes of his right foot he held a card and lifted it toward me and said, "Take it and read it." I read in perfect handwriting, "I can write your name for you on a card for you to keep. The charge is only ten cents." I said, "I would if I had the ten cents. All I've got is a nickel." I took out the nickel and turned my pockets inside out and showed him that besides the nickel there was only a knife, a piece of string, and a buckeye. He took the nickel in his left foot. He put a pen between the first two toes of his right foot and on the card wrote "Charles A. Sandburg," lifted the foot up toward me, and I took the card. It was the prettiest my name had ever been written. His face didn't change. All the time it kept that quiet look that didn't strictly belong with a circus. I was near crying. I said some kind of thanks and picked up my feet and ran.

## Getting at Meaning

1. Why is the Edison Talking Phonograph such a popular attraction?

2. What purpose do the farmers have in coming to the fair? In what way do they seem out of place?

3. What is Sandburg's first reaction to the Side Show freaks? Why does he change his mind about the midgets? the giant? Who is the one freak that he does not change his mind about? Why?

4. According to Sandburg, what is the business of the freaks in the Side Show? Why is it difficult for him to understand their work?

5. Why does the armless man seem out of place in the circus? What is it about this man that brings Sandburg close to tears?

## Developing Skills in Reading Literature

1. **Nonfiction.** Fiction is the product of a writer's imagination and is not necessarily based on fact. Nonfiction, on the other hand, is a true story based on facts. Identify two facts about Sandburg's life that you learn in the opening paragraph of the selection.

2. **Autobiography.** When a person writes about his or her own life, the result is called autobiography. Generally, the writer of an autobiography narrates incidents that are significant or that are the basis for vivid memories. The reader can infer a great deal about the writer's life from these incidents. Consider what you learn from this selection about the environment in which Sandburg grew up. Was it urban or rural? Was his family wealthy or poor? Was his father a native-born American? Support your answers with details from the selection.

3. **Character.** The incidents recalled in an autobiography reveal the character of the writer. Sometimes the reader must infer a character trait; other times the writer comments on a trait directly. What trait is revealed by Sandburg's reaction to the Side Show freaks? How does he present this trait? What trait does his reaction to the armless man reveal? Are the two traits related? Explain.

## Developing Vocabulary

**Greek Roots.** The word *autobiography* is made up of three Greek words: *autos* meaning "self," *bios* meaning "life," and *graphein* meaning "to write." Literally the word means "self life writing."

*Phonograph* contains the Greek roots *phone* meaning "a sound" and *graphein*. Literally, what is a phonograph?

Following is a list of words that contain these common Greek roots. Look up each in a dictionary. Check both the etymology and the definition, and then define the word in terms of its root.

| | |
|---|---|
| automatic | photograph |
| autonomous | telegraph |
| autopsy | graphology |
| biology | telephone |
| biopsy | phonology |
| bionics | phonetic |

## Developing Writing Skills

1. **Using Contrast.** Sandburg says about the fair, "We felt something in the air very different from a circus." Select one or two differences between the fair and the circus described in this selection; then develop these differences into a paragraph of contrast.

2. **Writing About an Incident.** Young Sandburg is fascinated by the Edison Talking Phonograph, which could do something that no one had ever dreamed possible. Relate an incident in which you first experienced a new invention; for example, your first experience with a video game or a microcomputer. Describe the invention and your reactions to it. Did you enjoy the experience? How did other people react? Develop this topic in a five-paragraph composition.

# Joseph    *Peter Abrahams*

*In the strictly segregated society of South Africa, the nonwhites lived in an area called "the location" near the town of Elsburg where the black and "colored" men were allowed to work. Lee's friendship with Joseph, described here, coincides with the warm summer season in South Africa. Both friendship and season contrast with the severe, bleak winter from which the nonwhites were too poor to protect themselves adequately.*

**T**he long winter passed. Slowly, day by day, the world of Elsburg became a warmer place. The cracks in my feet began to heal. The spells of bearable, noonday cold gave way to warmth. The noise of the veld[1] at night became a din. The freezing nights changed, became bearable; changed again, became warm. Warm nights and hot days!

Summer had come, and with its coming the world became a softer, kindlier, more beautiful place. Sunflowers began blooming in people's yards. And people themselves began to relax and laugh. When one evening as I came in with some washing from the line, I heard Uncle Sam's voice raised in laughter and saw him and Aunt Liza playing, I knew the summer had really come. Later that same evening he went into the other room and returned with a guitar. Aunt Liza beamed.

"Open the door?"

Uncle Sam nodded. He played. Soon people from the other houses came, in ones and twos, till our little room was crowded. Some-one sang with his arms on his wife's shoulders, a love song.

> *I'll be your sweetheart,*
> *If you will be mine. . . .*

Summer had come indeed.

In the long summer afternoons, after my day's work, I went down to the river. Sometimes Andries and some of the other children went with me. Often I went alone.

Often, with others or alone, I climbed the short willows with their long drooping branches. The touch of willow leaf on the cheek gives a feeling of cool wonder. Often I jumped from stone to stone on the broad bed of the shallow, clear, fast-flowing river. Sometimes I found little pools of idle water, walled off by stones from the flow. I tickled long-tailed tadpoles in these. The sun on the water touched their bodies with myriad colors. Sometimes I watched the *springhaas*—the wild rabbit of the veld—go leaping across the land, almost faster than my eye could follow. And sometimes I lay on my back on the green grass on the bank of the river and looked up at the distant sky, watching thin, fleecy white clouds form and re-form and trying to associate the shapes with people and things I knew. I loved being alone by the river. It became my special world.

Each day I explored a little more of the river, going further up or downstream, extending the frontiers of my world. One day,

---

1. **veld** (velt): in South Africa, open grassy country.

going further downstream than I had been before, I came upon a boy. He was on the bank on the other side from me. We saw each other at the same time and stared. He was completely naked. He carried two finely carved sticks of equal size and shape, both about his own height. He was not light brown, like the other children of our location, but dark brown, almost black. I moved almost to the edge of the river. He called out in a strange language.

"Hello!" I shouted.

He called out again, and again I could not understand. I searched for a place with stones, then bounded across. I approached him slowly. As I drew near, he gripped his sticks more firmly. I stopped.

He spoke harshly, flung one stick on the ground at my feet, and held the other ready as though to fight.

"Don't want to fight," I said.

I reached down to pick up the stick and return it to him. He took a step forward and raised the one in his hand. I moved back quickly. He stepped back and pointed at the stick on the ground. I shook my head.

"Don't want to fight."

I pushed the stick towards him with my foot, ready to run at the first sign of attack. I showed my new, stubby teeth in a tentative smile. He said something that sounded less aggressive. I nodded, smiling more broadly. He relaxed, picked up the stick, and transferred both to his left hand. He smacked his chest.

"Joseph! Zulu!"

I smacked my own chest.

"Lee. . . ." But I didn't know what I was apart from that.

He held out his hand. We shook. His face lit up in a sunny smile. He said something and pointed downstream. Then he took my arm and led me down.

Far downstream, where the river skirted a hillside, hidden by a cluster of willows, we came on a large, clear pool. Joseph flung his sticks on the ground and dived in. He shot through the water like a tadpole. He went down and came up. He shouted and beckoned me to come in. I undressed and went in more tentatively. Laughing, he pulled me under. I came up gasping and spluttering, my belly filled with water. He smacked me on the back and the water shot out of my mouth in a rush. When he realized I could not swim he became more careful. We spent the afternoon with Joseph teaching me to swim. At home, that evening, I stood beside Aunt Liza's wash-tub.

"Aunt Liza. . . ."

"Yes?"

"What am I?"

"What are you talking about?"

"I met a boy at the river. He said he was Zulu."

She laughed.

"You are colored. There are three kinds of people: white people, colored people, and black people. The white people come first, then the colored people, then the black people."

"Why?"

"Because it is so."

Next day, when I met Joseph, I smacked my chest and said: "Lee colored!"

He clapped his hands and laughed.

Joseph and I spent most of the long summer afternoons together. He learned some Afrikaans from me; I learned some Zulu from him. Our days were full.

There was the river to explore.

There were my swimming lessons, and others.

I learned to fight with sticks, to weave a green hat of young willow wands and leaves, to catch frogs and tadpoles with my hands, to set a trap for the *springhaas,* to make the sounds of the river birds.

There was the hot sun to comfort us. . . .

There was the green grass to dry our bodies. . . .

There was the soft clay with which to build. . . .

There were the locust swarms when the skies turned black and we caught them by the hundreds. . . .

There was the rare taste of crisp, brown baked, salted locusts. . . .

There was the voice of the heaven in the thunderstorms. . . .

There were the voices of two children in laughter, ours. . . .

There were Joseph's tales of black kings who lived in days before the white man. . . .

At home, I said: "Aunt Liza. . . ."

"Yes?"

"Did we have colored kings before the white man?"

"No."

"Then where did we come from? Joseph and his mother come from the black kings who were before the white man."

And laughing, and ruffling my head, she said: "You talk too much. . . . Go'n wash up."

And to Joseph, next day, I said: "We didn't have colored kings before the white man."

And he comforted me and said: "It is of no moment. You are my brother. Now my kings will be your kings. Come, I have promised the mother to bring you home. She awaits you. I will race you to the hill."

From the top of the hill I looked into a long valley where cattle grazed. To the right, on the sloping land, nestled a cluster of mud huts. Round each hut was a wall built of mud.

"That is my home," Joseph pointed.

We veered right and went down to it. From a distance, we saw a woman at the gate of one of the huts.

"There is the mother!" He walked faster.

She was barefooted. She wore a slight skirt that came above her knees. A child was strapped to her back. The upper part of her body was naked except for the cloth across her chest that supported the child. Round her neck, arms, and legs were strings of white beads. As we drew near, I saw that she was young. And her broad, round face was beautiful. Her black eyes were liquid soft. She called out a greeting and smiled. Joseph pushed me forward.

"This is my brother, Lee of the coloreds, little mother."

"Greetings, Mother," I said.

"I greet you, my son," she said softly, a twinkle in her eyes.

"As the man of my house has told you, food awaits. Come."

"See!" Joseph puffed out his chest. To his mother he said, "He would not believe when I told him I was the man in our house."

"He is indeed," she said.

Circling the hut was a raised platform. We sat on this while she brought us the food, salted fried locusts and corn on the cob. She sat nearby and watched us eating.

Christmas came and it was a feast of eating and laughter. I spent half my time at home with Aunt Liza and Uncle Sam and the other half with Joseph and the little mother.

My sixth birthday came. Joseph and the little mother and I celebrated it by the river.

Then, early one morning, just as the first cold touches crept into the morning air, Joseph came to our location.

I was washing up when I heard young voices shouting: "Look at the naked kaffir![2] Lee's kaffir!"

I rushed out. Joseph came gravely to me.

"I come to take leave, my brother. My father has died in the mines so we go back to our land."

He stood straight and stern, not heeding the shouts of the children about. He was a man. This was the burden of his manhood. I

---

2. **kaffir** (kaf′ ər): a member of a Bantu tribe of southeast Africa.

had learned much from him, so I said equally coldly, "I must take leave of the little mother."

"She is a woman. She weeps."

We ran all the way there. . . .

When the little cart had taken them away, I climbed the hill and went down to the river. I carried Joseph's two sticks with me. These were his parting gift to his brother.

"Defend yourself," he had said. "I will make others."

I walked along the river that had been our kingdom. Now it was a desolate place. Joseph had been here with me; now Joseph had gone. Before I realized it, my tears flowed fast. There had been much between us.

So the summer passed. The autumn came. The leaves went brown on the willows by the river. They fluttered to the ground and turned to mold. The long days shortened suddenly. The cold came. Winter had come to torture us again.

## Getting at Meaning

1. How is the winter unbearable? What changes in behavior coincide with the arrival of warmer weather?

2. What is Joseph's initial reaction to Lee? How does Lee convince Joseph that he has no wish to fight?

3. Lee extends the frontiers of his world by exploring the river. How does his relationship with Joseph extend his world even further?

4. What is the difference between Lee's understanding of his heritage and Joseph's? Does this difference matter to the boys? Why, or why not?

5. When Joseph first takes Lee to meet his mother, Joseph expresses pride in his role as the man of the house. After his father's death, how does his role change? Explain your answer.

6. What has Lee lost by the time that winter returns?

## Developing Skills in Reading Literature

1. **Autobiography.** What facts does the writer reveal about himself in this selection? What do his responses to the situations he describes reveal about his personality?

2. **Setting.** Where do the incidents described in this selection take place? What special features of this location influence the development of the action? In what way is time important in this selection?

3. **Character.** Joseph and Lee come from different backgrounds. What facts and qualities does the writer emphasize about Joseph to reveal his friend's uniqueness?

## Developing Writing Skills

**Writing About a Personal Experience.** In this selection, the writer recreates vividly a childhood experience. Think about your own childhood friendships. Write one paragraph in which you describe in detail an experience that you shared with a friend.

# *from* Fifth Chinese Daughter

## *Jade Snow Wong*

Without much enthusiasm, Jade Snow decided upon junior college. Now it was necessary to inform Mama and Daddy. She chose an evening when the family was at dinner. All of them were in their customary places, and Daddy, typically, was in conversation with Older Brother about the factory:

"Blessing, when do you think Lot Number fifty-one twenty-six will be finished? I want to ask for a check from our jobber so that I can have enough cash for next week's payroll."

To which Older Brother replied, "As soon as Mama is through with the seams in Mrs. Lee's and Mrs. Choy's bundles, the women can finish the hems. Another day, probably."

Mama had not been consulted; therefore, she made no comment. Silence descended as the Wongs continued their meal, observing the well learned precept that talk was not permissible while eating.

Jade Snow considered whether to break the silence. Three times she thought over what she had to say, and still found it worth saying. This also was according to family precept.

"Daddy," she said, "I have made up my mind to enter junior college here in San Francisco. I will find a steady job to pay my expenses, and by working in the summers I'll try to save enough money to take me through my last two years at the university."

Then she waited. Everyone went on eating. No one said a word. Apparently no one was interested enough to be curious. But at least no one objected. It was settled.

Junior college was at first disappointing in more ways than one. There was none of the glamor usually associated with college because the institution was so young that it had not yet acquired buildings of its own. Classes were held all over the city, wherever accommodations were available. The first days were very confusing to Jade Snow, especially when she discovered that she must immediately decide upon a college major.

While waiting to register, she thumbed through the catalog in search of a clue. English . . . mathematics . . . chemistry. . . . In the last semester of high school she had found chemistry particularly fascinating; so with a feeling of assurance, she wrote that as her major on the necessary forms and went to a sign-up table.

"I wish to take the lecture and laboratory classes for Chemistry 1A," she informed the gray-haired man who presided there.

He looked at her, a trifle impatiently, she thought.

"Why?"

"Because I like it." To herself she sounded reasonable.

"But you are no longer in high school. Chemistry here is a difficult subject on a university level, planned for those who are majoring in medicine, engineering, or the serious sciences."

Jade Snow set her chin stubbornly. "I still want to take Chemistry 1A."

Sharply he questioned: "What courses in mathematics have you had? What were your grades?"

Finally Jade Snow's annoyance rose to the surface. "Straight A's. But why must you ask? Do you think I would want to take a course

I couldn't pass? Why don't you sign me up and let the instructor be the judge of my ability?"

"Very well," he replied stiffly. "I'll accept you in the class. And for your information, young lady, I am the instructor!"

With this inauspicious start, Jade Snow began her college career.

Of her college courses, Latin was the easiest. This was a surprise, for everyone had told her of its horrors. It was much more logical than French, almost mathematical in its orderliness and precision, and actually a snap after nine years of Chinese.

Chemistry, true to the instructor's promise, was difficult, although the classes were anything but dull. It turned out that he was a very nice person with a keen sense of humor and a gift for enlivening his lectures with stories of his own college days. There were only two girls in a class of more than fifty men—a tense blonde girl from Germany, who always ranked first; and Jade Snow, who usually took second place.

But if Latin was the easiest course and chemistry the most difficult, sociology was the most stimulating. Jade Snow had chosen it without thought, simply to meet a requirement; but that casual decision completely revolutionized her thinking, shattering her Wong-constructed conception of the order of things. This was the way it happened:

After several uneventful weeks during which the class explored the historical origins of the family and examined such terms as *norms, mores, folkways,* there came a day when the instructor stood before them to discuss the relationship of parents and children. It was a day like many others, with the students listening in varying attitudes of interest or indifference. The instructor was speaking casually of ideas to be accepted as standard. Then suddenly upon Jade Snow's astounded ears there fell this statement:

"There was a period in our American history when parents had children for economic reasons, to put them to work as soon as possible, especially to have them help on the farm. But now we no longer regard children in this way. Today we recognize that children are individuals, and that parents can no longer demand their unquestioning obedience. Parents should do their best to understand their children, because young people also have their rights."

The instructor went on talking, but Jade Snow heard no more, for her mind was echoing and re-echoing this startling thought. "Parents can no longer demand unquestioning obedience from their children. They should do their best to understand. Children also have their rights." For the rest of the day, while she was doing her chores at the Simpsons', while she was standing in the streetcar going home, she was busy translating the idea into terms of her own experience.

"My parents demand unquestioning obedience. Older Brother demands unquestioning obedience. By what right? I am an individual besides being a Chinese daughter. I have rights too."

Could it be that Daddy and Mama, although they were living in San Francisco in the year 1938, actually had not left the Chinese world of thirty years ago? Could it be that they were forgetting that Jade Snow would soon become a woman in a new America, not a woman in old China? In short, was it possible that Daddy and Mama could be wrong?

For days Jade Snow gave thought to little but her devastating discovery that her parents might be subject to error. As it was her habit always to act after reaching a conclusion, she wondered what to do about it. Should she tell Daddy and Mama that they needed to change their ways? One moment she thought she should; the next she thought not. At last she decided to overcome her fears in the interests of education and better understanding. She would at least try to open their minds to modern truths. If she succeeded, good! If not, she was prepared to suffer the consequences.

In this spirit of patient martyrdom she waited for an opportunity to speak.

It came, surprisingly, one Saturday. Ordinarily that was a busy day at the Simpsons', a time for entertaining, so that Jade Snow was not free until too late to go anywhere, even had she had a place to go. But on this particular Saturday the Simpsons were away for the weekend, and by three in the afternoon Jade Snow was ready to leave the apartment with unplanned hours ahead of her. She didn't want to spend these rare hours of freedom in any usual way. And she didn't want to spend them alone.

"Shall I call Joe?" she wondered. She had never telephoned to a boy before, and she debated whether it would be too forward. But she felt too happy and carefree to worry much, and she was confident that Joe would not misunderstand.

Even before reporting to Mama that she was home, she ran downstairs to the telephone booth and gave the operator Joe's number. His mother answered and then went to call him while Jade Snow waited in embarrassment.

"Joe." She was suddenly tongue-tied. "Joe, I'm already home."

That wasn't at all what she wanted to say. What did she want to say?

"Hello! Hello!" Joe boomed back. "What's the matter with you! Are you all right?"

"Oh, yes, I'm fine. Only, only . . . well, I'm through working for the day." That was really all she had to say, but now it sounded rather pointless.

"Isn't that wonderful? It must have been unexpected." That was what was nice and different about Joe. He always seemed to know without a lot of words. But because his teasing was never far behind his understanding, he added quickly, "I suppose you're going to study and go to bed early."

Jade Snow was still not used to teasing and didn't know how to take it. With an effort she swallowed her shyness and disappointment. "I thought we might go for a walk . . . that is, if you have nothing else to do . . . if you would care to . . . if. . . ."

Joe laughed. "I'll go you one better. Suppose I take you to a movie. I'll even get all dressed up for you, and you get dressed up too."

Jade Snow was delighted. Her first movie with Joe! What a wonderful day. In happy anticipation she put on her long silk stockings, lipstick, and the nearest thing to a suit she owned—a hand-me-down jacket and a brown skirt she had made herself. Then with a bright ribbon tying back her long black hair she was ready.

Daddy didn't miss a detail of the preparations as she dashed from room to room. He waited until she was finished before he demanded, "Jade Snow, where are you going?"

"I am going out into the street," she answered.

"Did you ask my permission to go out into the street?"

"No, Daddy."

"Do you have your mother's permission to go out into the street?"

"No, Daddy."

A sudden silence from the kitchen indicated that Mama was listening.

Daddy went on. "Where and when did you learn to be so daring as to leave this house without permission of your parents? You did not learn it under my roof."

It was all very familiar. Jade Snow waited, knowing that Daddy had not finished. In a moment he came to the point.

"And with whom are you going out into the street?"

It took all the courage Jade Snow could muster, remembering her new thinking, to say nothing. It was certain that if she told Daddy that she was going out with a boy whom he did not know, without a chaperone, he would be convinced that she would lose her maidenly purity before the evening was over.

"Very well," Daddy said sharply. "If you will not tell me, I forbid you to go! You are now too old to whip."

That was the moment.

Suppressing all anger, and in a manner that would have done credit to her sociology instructor addressing his freshman class, Jade Snow carefully turned on her mentally rehearsed speech.

"That is something you should think more about. Yes, I am too old to whip. I am too old to be treated as a child. I can now think for myself, and you and Mama should not demand unquestioning obedience from me. You should understand me. There was a time in America when parents raised children to make them work, but now the foreigners regard them as individuals with rights of their own. I have worked too, but now I am an individual besides being your fifth daughter."

It was almost certain that Daddy blinked, but after the briefest pause he gathered himself together.

"Where," he demanded, "did you learn such an unfilial theory?"

Mama had come quietly into the room and slipped into a chair to listen.

"From my teacher," Jade Snow answered triumphantly, "who you taught me is supreme after you, and whose judgment I am not to question."

Daddy was feeling pushed. Thoroughly aroused, he shouted: "A little learning has gone to your head! How can you permit a foreigner's theory to put aside the practical experience of the Chinese, who for thousands of years have preserved a most superior family pattern? Confucius[1] had already presented an organized philosophy of manners and conduct when the foreigners were unappreciatively persecuting Christ. Who brought you up? Who clothed you, fed you, sheltered you, nursed you? Do you think you were born aged sixteen? You owe honor to us before you satisfy your personal whims."

Daddy thundered on, while Jade Snow kept silent.

"What would happen to the order of this household if each of you four children started to behave like individuals? Would we have one peaceful moment if your personal desires came before your duty? How could we maintain our self-respect if we, your parents, did not know where you were at night and with whom you were keeping company?"

With difficulty Jade Snow kept herself from being swayed by fear and the old familiar arguments. "You can be bad in the daytime as well as at night," she said defensively. "What could happen after eleven that couldn't happen before?"

Daddy was growing excited. "Do I have to justify my judgment to you? I do not want a daughter of mine to be known as one who walks the streets at night. Have you no thought for our reputations if not for your own? If you start going out with boys, no good man will want to ask you to be his wife. You just do not know as well as we do what is good for you."

Mama fanned Daddy's wrath, "Never having been a mother, you cannot know how much grief it is to bring up a daughter. Of course we will not permit you to run the risk of corrupting your purity before marriage."

"Oh, Mama!" Jade Snow retorted. "This is America, not China. Don't you think I have any judgment? How can you think I would go out with just any man?"

"Men!" Daddy roared. "You don't know a thing about them. I tell you, you can't trust

---

1. **Confucius** (kən fyoo′ shəs): Chinese philosopher and teacher who was born in the sixth century B.C.

any of them."

Now it was Jade Snow who felt pushed. She delivered the balance of her declaration of independence. "Both of you should understand that I am growing up to be a woman in a society greatly different from the one you knew in China. You expect me to work my way through college—which would not have been possible in China. You expect me to exercise judgment in choosing my employers and my jobs and in spending my own money in the American world. Then why can't I choose my friends? Of course independence is not safe. But safety isn't the only consideration. You must give me the freedom to find some answers for myself."

Mama found her tongue first. "You think you are too good for us because you have a little foreign book knowledge."

"You will learn the error of your ways after it is too late," Daddy added darkly.

By this Jade Snow knew that her parents had conceded defeat. Hoping to soften the blow, she tried to explain. "If I am to earn my living, I must learn how to get along with many kinds of people, with foreigners as well as Chinese. I intend to start finding out about them now. You must have confidence that I shall remain true to the spirit of your teachings. I shall bring back to you the new knowledge of whatever I learn."

Daddy and Mama did not accept this offer graciously. "It is as useless for you to tell me such ideas as 'The wind blows across a deaf ear.' You have lost your sense of balance," Daddy told her bluntly. "You are shameless. Your skin is yellow. Your features are forever Chinese. We are content with our proven ways. Do not try to force foreign ideas into my home. Go. You will one day tell us sorrowfully that you have been mistaken."

After that there was no further discussion of the matter. Jade Snow came and went without any questions being asked. In spite of her parents' dark predictions, her new freedom in the choice of companions did not result in a rush of undesirables. As a matter of fact, the boys she met at school were more concerned with copying her lecture notes than with anything else.

As for Joe, he remained someone to walk with and talk with. On the evening of Jade Snow's seventeenth birthday he took her up Telegraph Hill and gave her as a remembrance a sparkling grown-up bracelet with a card that read: "Here's to your making Phi Beta Kappa[2]." And there under the stars he gently tilted her face and gave her her first kiss.

Standing straight and awkward in her full-skirted red cotton dress, Jade Snow was caught by surprise and without words. She felt that something should stir and crash within her, in the way books and the movies described, but nothing did. Could it be that she wasn't in love with Joe, in spite of liking and admiring him? After all, he was twenty-three and probably too old for her anyway.

Still she had been kissed at seventeen, which was cause for rejoicing. Laughing happily, they continued their walk.

But while the open rebellion gave Jade Snow a measure of freedom she had not had before, and an outer show of assurance, she was deeply troubled within. It had been simple to have Daddy and Mama tell her what was right and wrong; it was not simple to decide for herself. No matter how critical she was of them, she could not discard all they stood for and accept as a substitute the philosophy of the foreigners. It took very little thought to discover that the foreign philosophy also was subject to criticism, and that for her there had to be a middle way.

There was good to be gained from both concepts if she could extract and retain her own

---

2. **Phi Beta Kappa** (fī′ bāt′ ə kap′ ə): an honorary society of U.S. college students of high scholastic rank.

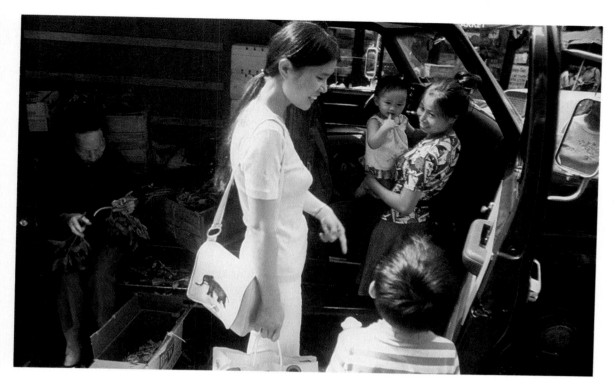

personally applicable combination. She studied her neighbor in class, Stella Green, for clues. Stella had grown up reading Robert Louis Stevenson, learning to swim and play tennis, developing a taste for roast beef, mashed potatoes, sweets, aspirin tablets, and soda pop, and she looked upon her mother and father as friends. But it was very unlikely that she knew where her great-grandfather was born, or whether or not she was related to another strange Green she might chance to meet. Jade Snow had grown up reading Confucius, learning to embroider and cook rice, developing a taste for steamed fish and bean sprouts, tea, and herbs, and she thought of her parents as people to be obeyed. She not only knew where her ancestors were born but where they were buried, and how many chickens and roast pigs should be brought annually to their graves to feast their spirits. She knew all of the branches of the Wong family, the relation to each to the other, and under-

stood why Daddy must help support the distant cousins in China who bore the sole responsibility of carrying on the family heritage by periodic visits to the burial grounds in Fragrant Mountains. She knew that one could purchase in a Chinese stationery store the printed record of her family tree relating their Wong line and other Wong lines back to the original Wong ancestors. In such a scheme the individual counted for little weighed against the family, and after sixteen years it was not easy to sever roots.

There were, alas, no books or advisers to guide Jade Snow in her search for balance between the pull from two cultures. If she chose neither to reject nor accept *in toto*,[3] she must sift both and make her decisions alone. It would not be an easy search. But pride and determination, which Daddy had given her, prevented any thought of turning back. . . .

---

3. **in toto** (in tō′ tō) *Latin:* as a whole.

*from FIFTH CHINESE DAUGHTER*   273

## Getting at Meaning

1. What are the two Wong family precepts regarding talk?

2. Who is the head of the Wong household? Contrast the roles of men and women in this family.

3. How does Jade Snow's sociology instructor shatter her "Wong-constructed conception of the order of things"? Does the instructor realize the impact of his words? Explain.

4. Why is it so devastating for Jade Snow to discover that her parents might be wrong?

5. How might Jade Snow's father react if he found out about her call to Joe? Considering when this selection takes place, why is Jade Snow's call to Joe even more remarkable?

6. Why has Jade Snow's new freedom left her troubled and confused? How is life more difficult now?

7. Jade Snow's father tells her that she has lost her sense of balance. Has she? Explain.

## Developing Skills in Reading Literature

1. **Conflict.** What are the external conflicts in this selection? What are the internal conflicts? How does Jade Snow hope to resolve her inner conflicts?

2. **Character.** Explain what the reader learns about Jade Snow's character from each of the following:

    a. her decision to go to junior college

    b. her insistence on registering for a course in chemistry

    c. her phone call to Joe

    d. her observance of her classmate, Stella Green

3. **Point of View.** What is the point of view of this selection? Considering that the selection is autobiographical, what is unusual about this point of view? Why might the writer have chosen this point of view?

4. **Theme.** In addition to relating incidents, the writer of a nonfiction selection may also try to communicate a major idea or theme. What is the theme of this selection?

## Developing Vocabulary

**Prefixes.** Two of the most common negative prefixes are *in-* (or *im-*) and *un-*. These prefixes appear in this selection in the following words:

| | |
|---|---|
| impatiently | unfilial |
| inauspicious | undesirable |
| indifference | |

Write a conversation in which a teenager asks his or her parents for the use of the family car. Use each of the listed words in the dialogue. Consult a dictionary if you need help. (If you cannot find the word *unfilial,* try looking up *filial.*)

## Developing Writing Skills

1. **Supporting an Opinion.** Jade Snow tells her parents, "Of course independence is not safe. But safety isn't the only consideration." In one well developed paragraph, agree or disagree with this statement. Support your opinion with examples from history, newspaper articles, or the lives of friends and relatives.

2. **Writing Dialogue.** When writing dialogue, skillful writers do not keep repeating "he said" and "she said." Rather, they use more precise verbs to show how the words are spoken. For example, during Jade Snow's argument with her parents, her father *demands, shouts, thunders,* and *roars.*

After each of the following sentences, supply a precise verb.

    a. "I've lost my purse!" she _____.

    b. "Meat loaf, again?" he _____.

    c. "I thought you knew how to drive!" she _____.

    d. "Step right this way," she _____.

    e. "What's the answer to number 3?" he _____.

    f. "Wait 'til he sees what's inside," he _____.

Now write a brief dialogue between two people, using precise verbs instead of the verb *said.*

# *from* **Policewoman**       *Dorothy Uhnak*

The window washer with the light fingers was due in the office sometime that day. He was finishing up the third floor and he always worked Kensington—it was his section. They didn't know exactly when he'd arrive, but I was hoping it would be soon.

Hank had asked why the girls hadn't complained to the man's boss, confront him with the accusation, even press charges, but the old man had insisted that he be caught in the act. Mr. Mac liked action, liked things done right, so there I sat at that crazy little pink typewriter and fooled around with the magic keys. Hank was in an adjoining office—the offices outside the executive suites were linked by airy, lacy white room dividers.

I did a few finger exercises to get the feel of the machine. I could see Hank looking over the sample shoes displayed on the wall-to-ceiling display case, fingering the fragile, needle-heeled high-style things with his large, unaccustomed hands. He held a shoe up to me, grinning. Somebody's secretary, floating past, caught our amusement and froze in my direction, glancing quickly down. I tried to hide my feet but there they were on display under the glass desk. Then she raised her eyes to my face and looked right through me.

They spoke to each other in voices that were carpeted: soft, thick, and expensively trained at one of those how-to-succeed schools that I had learned Mr. Mac insisted upon. He wanted them not only young but of a particular pattern. The only loud voice in the company was Mr. Mac's, and when he

blasted forth on the small pink intercoms placed here and there on shelves about the room, everyone stood stock-still, breathless, until he finished speaking. It seemed he had a technique all his own. Only when he finished the message would he announce the name of the person for whom it was intended. After an hour of these sudden pronouncements, I found myself listening intently, along with the others, as though it might be meant for me. "Those drawings are all smudges and smears and crummy, and I want the whole mess drawn up again. And play down the red edges. Marion!" "I want that showroom in one hundred percent perfect order and no speck of dust showing and those new slippers—the pink ones and the off-green ones in K-13 case—right now. Harold!" It was a little upsetting.

There was no conversation with these girls. I was someone who was just not there. They continued their quiet little gossipy huddles of office talk over drawings of shoes, pictures of shoes clipped from the best magazines— the kind that have a woman's face all over the page, sinking mysteriously into some kind of foggy background, and one word printed neatly in a corner, the name of a firm manufacturing some cosmetic or miraculous rejuvenation lotion. They might have stepped from some similar fog, and with their veiled, mean little glances, have wondered where I had stepped from. They knew I was a policewoman and drew certain inferences from this —probably that I was depraved and jaded from contact with the unspeakables of some remote and barely existent world.

I was wearing a little black dress, my "nothing" dress, with one small gold pin—a little owl Tony had found in the sand at Montauk[1]—that was all grubby and chipped but had "Tiffany—14 k" engraved near the safety catch. He had had it cleaned and polished for me, and that little pin gave me a certain courage even if their rigid poise and rightness were somewhat unnerving. They all had noticed my feet with my unacceptable shoes, just plain black pumps and not expensive, but none of them had even looked at my good little gold owl. I would have lasted about a day in that place. I could feel the delicate wallpaper and antique picture frames —placed around little shelves of silly looking shoes—and the air of arduous refinement strangling me.

The window washer came in from the reception room, wordless, and went directly to his task. As had been prearranged, the girls vaporized soundlessly without any sign of emotion, like a bunch of cardboard dolls floating effortlessly away. Mr. Mac thundered from the walls for his secretary, and she glided over the carpet staring straight ahead, her notebook against her narrow, bony thigh. Hank was handling the shoes again, but he was watching me now, and I knew that he would keep his eyes on me until he received a signal.

I was typing some paragraph from some shoe newspaper, fascinated by the weirdness of the machine. It was typing with a strange power of its own, barely relying on my fingers. My back was to the window, but there was a lovely, wide-framed mirror perched on one of the room dividers that gave me a perfect view of the suspect. I could glance up from my machine easily and observe him. He was smearing a squeegee over the pane of window from outside the building. He hadn't strapped on his safety belt and he seemed to hang by the tip of one finger. I could hear him making grunting noises as he hefted himself inside the window frame and sloshed his arm up and down. I kept my fingers on the keys and they clicked furiously, in a frenzy of noise and activity. He had his back to me, bending over his bucket and rags and equipment, straps and buckles hanging from all sides of him. He ran a dirty gray rag over the back of his neck, then stuffed it into a back pocket. He leaned heavily on the desk alongside of him, rested his hand on the surface of the desk, and without looking behind him, toward me, pocketed the diamond engagement ring that had been left next to the pink telephone.

As I touched my hair, my left hand on the clicking keys of the machine, Hank started for the room. The window washer reached into his shirt pocket, pulled out a cigarette and was placing it between his lips when Hank walked in and caught my nod and motion toward an imaginary pocket on my dress. I don't think Hank realized he was carrying the purple shoe in his left hand. He seemed a little surprised and let it drop to the floor as he took the window washer's arm and stuck his shield in the man's face.

Hank was a tall man, deceptively swift while appearing almost motionless. He had the suspect against a wall, or the latticework that passed for a wall, before I could even stand up.

"Put the bucket down, pal. Police."

Hank had one hand on the man's shoulder, and he jerked his head at the prisoner. "Okay, buddy, take the ring out of your pocket."

The man stared motionless, but there was a whiteness coming over his face. Hank pushed the man's chest. "Take out the cig-

---

1. **Montauk:** Montauk Point, a peak at the easternmost tip of Long Island, New York.

arettes and the ring. C'mon, c'mon, put everything on the desk."

"I got no ring," the man said tensely, his eyes wandering around the room, then back to Hank's face. He bit his lip, seemed to be weighing things, making some decision. "Not me, pal, I'm not your man."

Hank reached roughly into the pocket, tossed the cigarettes on the desk, then fished the ring out and held it before the man's eyes. "This yours?" he asked softly.

Hank motioned to me; the suspect seemed surprised to see me. He hadn't even noticed me. "I'm a policewoman. I saw you take the ring from the desk and put it in your pocket."

The voice of Mr. Mac suddenly boiled into the room, seeming to come from the ceilings and the floors. He had apparently been tuned in on us, and he was howling furiously about what he was going to do to the "bum." In the instant it took us to realize what the sudden sound was, the prisoner shoved Hank into me and lunged across the room. He crashed into the room divider and through the glass doors of the reception room into the hallway. I raced after Hank, grabbing my pocketbook from the desk, and saw Hank catch the glass door on his shoulder, fighting it back open. I heard the commotion on the stairway, a sound of ugly scuffling. Hank was hanging onto the straps that were dangling from the window washer's pants, and the man kicked up with his heavy-booted feet at Hank's legs. The stairway was hard steel, fireproof, and dangerous, with sharp, point-edged steps. Hank had the man by the collar and I managed to grab a loose strap, but he shook me off with an elbow. I hadn't realized what a hugely powerful man he was, with arms and shoulders and back hardened by years of labor. He was a heavy-set man with no scrap of fat on him, and he made thick, grunting sounds. Hank was tall and wiry, but in the scuffling he lost his footing and tum-

bled on the stairs. The three of us fell together, Hank on the bottom, the prisoner on top. I fell clear of the men, pulled along by the strap which had gotten tangled around my wrist. I was clutching my pocketbook as though it were part of me, and I felt no pain even though I was aware of being pulled down the stairs. We all stood up together, still clinging to each other in one way or another, and fell against the brass door that opened onto the lobby of the building.

We exploded into the lobby into the midst of startled office workers on their way to lunch: three grappling, grasping figures. I had lost my shoes somewhere. I felt the cut on my leg. I heard the terrible sounds of blows—he was actually hitting *me*. My face felt the impact of the blow, but I felt no pain, just an awareness of having been struck. There was a terrible tangle of arms and legs; my hair was being pulled, and I felt a hand inside my mouth, roughly scraping the roof of it.

"The gun," Hank gasped, unable to reach his own. "For Pete's sake, Dot, pull the gun."

I let loose my hold of the strap and dug the gun out, dropped my pocketbook somewhere. Hank managed to shove the man against the wall with his shoulder, holding him, leaning against him, trying to hold himself up, and I pointed the gun in the man's face. But I could see that the glazed, pale eyes did not recognize the weapon. It made no impression on him, and his blank transparent expression was genuine.

"Sit still, you, or I'll shoot you!"

He managed a kick at Hank's shinbone. I held the gun flatly in my palm, the finger off the trigger, as I felt myself being shoved halfway across the lobby. I landed against a candy stand, and some face stuck itself in mine, some frantic candy-clerk face, saying words to me, hysterical words: "Lady, please, lady, get off my merchandise. Lady, you're messing up my papers and my magazines." I heard the words and the voice and saw the sickening face, the arms outstretched over the shelves of candy bars and gum, the voice wailing in grief for his magazines and newspapers and nickel and dime merchandise. I saw all the faces all around us, a horrified, fascinated group of faces, openmouthed, wide-eyed, drawing back, yet far too intrigued to move away—watching.

"Call the police!" I said in a thin, far-away, unknown voice. "We're police officers; for Pete's sake, someone make a call!"

Hank and the prisoner were grappling, and the powerful man, using the advantage of his weight and conditioned strength and those murderous dusty boots, delivered a terrific blow and kick at the same time. As Hank held on to him, pulling him down too, I cracked the butt of my gun at the base of his skull as hard as I could. It was a horrible, loud, unimaginable sound, unreal. . . . He gave another lunge at me, and I slipped backward, my feet skidding along the slippery polished floor. I felt myself making contact with something, with someone, and some hands pushed me angrily away. I turned. A woman, standing in back of me, her face outraged, contorted, had pushed me. She was pregnant, I could see that, it registered, but I couldn't understand why she had pushed me. The prisoner and Hank were on the floor, each making motions, reaching for the other. As I moved toward them, some man, some red-faced, tough-faced old man, some skinny wiry old guy in a bank guard's uniform shoved his face at me.

"Cop?" That's all he said. I nodded, and he reached down and gave the window washer a terrific punch in the face, and the prisoner settled down on the floor. Then the man caught Hank's arms and pulled him to a sitting position and pushed his own face at Hank.

"Okay? Okay, officer?"

Hank nodded, not seeing the face before him, just nodding, maybe just trying to shake it off, to focus. He reached for his handcuffs, but the old guy snatched them.

"I'll do it, pal." Quickly, professionally, he slipped the handcuffs on the prisoner, who was reviving, twisting. He cuffed the man's hands behind his back, explaining as he did so, "Six years off the force and I haven't lost the old speed. Heard the commotion. I'm at First National—right in the building. You okay? Seventieth Precinct in Brooklyn last ten years on the job. Hey, you okay?"

I nodded, not looking at him but at the crowd, at the faces that were watching us, watching us, talking about us, pointing at us, at Hank and the prisoner and the bank guard and me. I saw the uniformed cops come in through the revolving doors—four of them, then three more, then a sergeant, a big, fat sergeant with great big cheeks.

The uniformed cops grabbed everyone; the sergeant had my arm. I was still holding my gun. "Policewoman—sergeant—that's my partner, and this man here, he helped us."

The spectators moved a little closer, wanting to hear some more of it. They knew nothing of what was happening. Some woman, some woman from the crowd, whom I had never seen, kept calling to the sergeant, telling him she wanted to talk to someone in charge. She saw his stripes and kept on calling and calling until finally, with a heave of annoyance, he turned to her.

"Lady, what is it? Whassa matter—what d'ya want? C'mon, you men, get these people outta here—show's over—go to lunch." The woman, eyes blazing, pointed at us.

"I was a witness," she said in a high, shrill voice, and everyone came closer for a better look. "I want to know who to talk to here."

"Lady," the sergeant said, in his oldtimer's growl, "whatd'ya want?"

"I want to report an incident of police

brutality," she said indignantly and shaking with rage. "I saw the whole thing: this girl hit that man on the head with a blackjack or a gun or something, and he was on his knees, helpless. Then this man, this bank guard, came and beat him mercilessly, and all the time his hands were handcuffed behind his back."

## Getting at Meaning

1. How does Mr. Mac communicate instructions to his employees?

2. Why does Dot feel out of place in the office?

3. What does the description of the window washer's behavior reveal about Dot's skill as a police officer?

4. Dot's identity as a police officer surprises the window washer. What is there about the window washer that surprises Dot?

5. What causes the simple, routine arrest to escalate beyond the officers' control?

6. What are Dot's feelings as she hits the window washer with her gun?

7. Describe the crowd's reaction to the police officers' struggle. Why doesn't anyone help them? Who finally does help them?

8. At the end of the selection, what part of the witness's account is factually inaccurate?

## Developing Skills in Reading Literature

1. **Autobiography.** As the writer describes one incident in her life, she also reveals her feelings about her identity as a police officer. How does the writer assume that the other employees view her because of her job? What does she think of these people? Later, what do the descriptions of the lobby scene show about people's attitudes toward the police? How does the writer feel about these attitudes?

2. **Setting.** Describe the office that is the setting at the beginning of this account. How is it different from most business offices? How do the employees who work there fit into the atmosphere of the office?

3. **Irony.** What is ironic about the report given by the witness at the end of the selection?

## Developing Vocabulary

**Suffixes.** Adding the suffix -ation or -ment to a verb changes the verb to a noun. Look up each of the following nouns in a dictionary, and write its definition next to the word. Be prepared to identify and to define the verbs to which the suffixes were added.

| | | |
|---|---|---|
| accusation | rejuvenation | conversation |
| amusement | pronouncement | equipment |

## Developing Writing Skills

**Describing a Character.** The writer describes in detail several characters: Hank, the window washer, the bank guard. She does not, however, describe Mr. Mac. What might Mr. Mac look like? How might he react to the window washer's arrest? Write one paragraph in which you use specific details to describe Mr. Mac and his reactions to the incident related in the selection.

# *from* **Act One**    *Moss Hart*

Can success change the human mechanism so completely between one dawn and another? Can it make one feel taller, more alive, handsomer, uncommonly gifted and indomitably secure with the certainty that this is the way life will always be? It can and it does! Only one aspect of that other self remained to spill over into the new. I was once again wolfishly, overpoweringly hungry. It would take at least two more successes to make me lose my appetite, and it is only fair to point out that success can and does accomplish this, too. Everyone but me, however, had eaten during the long wait for the notices, and only that bitter-ender, Joe Hyman, was not too exhausted by this time to declare himself ready to sit through a full meal with me. The others were visibly wilting, and I did not press them to stay. My family had long since gone home on the strength of that first glowing notice in the *Times*—indeed, their own glow must have sped the train halfway to Brooklyn with no help from the subway system at all.

I protested a little during the goodbyes, but I was secretly relieved that the others were going now, too, for a childish reason of my own. It satisfied my sense of drama to complete the full circle of *Once in a Lifetime*[1] alone with Joe Hyman—the circle that had begun with a dinner alone with him before the opening in Atlantic City and would end with this dinner alone with him now after the opening in New York. It is a childish game I have always played and have never been able to resist—a game of arranging life,

whenever possible, in a series of scenes that make perfect first-act or third-act curtains. When it works, and it often does, it lends an extra zest and a keener sense of enjoyment to whatever the occasion may be where my thirst for drama has contrived to make life imitate a good third act. It worked beautifully now.

I cannot recall one word that was exchanged between us, but it must have taken a fairly long time to satisfy my sense of the dramatic entities, for when we came out of the restaurant it was six o'clock in the morning and broad daylight. For the second dawn in a row I peered down the streets of a sleeping city, searching for a taxi. This dawn, however, was going to usher in an historic moment. My last subway ride was behind me. Never again would I descend those dingy steps or hear those turnstiles click off another somber day behind me.

A cab pulled up beside us and Joe Hyman and I silently shook hands. The driver eyed me warily when I gave him a Brooklyn address, and I was conscious, looking at Joe Hyman, of how disreputable I too must look. I looked at him again and burst into laughter. His eyes were red-rimmed with excitement and weariness, his face grimy with a full day-and-night's growth of beard, and his suit looked as though he had slept in it. The driver obviously and quite rightly was wondering if there was enough money between us to

---

1. *Once in a Lifetime:* the comedy by Moss Hart and George Kaufman that became a Broadway hit in 1930.

pay for that long ride, or if we had not already spent every cent in some speakeasy. I took a ten-dollar bill out of my pocket and waved it at him and climbed into the cab. I waved at Joe Hyman through the rear window until the cab turned the corner, and then settled back in the seat, determined that I would not fall asleep. I had no intention of dozing through the first ride to Brooklyn above ground—I intended to enjoy every visible moment of it and I very shortly reaped the reward for staying awake.

No one has ever seen the skyline of the city from Brooklyn Bridge as I saw it that morning with three hit notices under my arm. The face of the city is always invested with grandeur, but grandeur can be chilling. The overpowering symmetry of that skyline can crush the spirit and make the city seem forbidding and impenetrable, but today it seemed to emerge from cold anonymity and grant its acknowledgment and acceptance.

There was no sunlight—it was a gray day and the buildings were half shrouded in mist, but it was a city that would know my name today, a city that had not turned me aside, and a city that I loved. Unexpectedly and without warning, a great wave of feeling for this proud and beautiful city swept over me. We were off the bridge now and driving through the sprawling, ugly area of tenements that stretch interminably over the approaches to each of its boroughs. They are the first in the city to awake, and the long unending rows of drab, identical houses were already stirring with life. Laundry was being strung out to dry along roof tops and fire escapes, men with lunch boxes were coming out of the houses, and children returning from the corner grocery with bottles of milk and loaves of bread were hurrying up the steps and into the doorways.

I stared through the taxi window at a pinch-faced ten-year-old hurrying down the

steps on some morning errand before school, and I thought of myself hurrying down the street on so many gray mornings out of a doorway and a house much the same as this one. My mind jumped backward in time and then whirled forward, like a many-faceted prism—flashing our old neighborhood in front of me, the house, the steps, the candy store—and then shifted to the skyline I had just passed by, the opening last night, and the notices I still hugged tightly under my arm. It was possible in this wonderful city for that nameless little boy—for any of its millions—to have a decent chance to scale the walls and achieve what they wished. Wealth, rank or an imposing name counted for nothing. The only credential the city asked was the boldness to dream. For those who did, it unlocked its gates and its treasures, not caring who they were or where they came from. I watched the boy disappear into a tailor shop, and a surge of shamefaced patriotism overwhelmed me. I might have been watching a victory parade on a flag-draped Fifth Avenue instead of the mean streets of a city slum. A feeling of patriotism, however, is not always limited to the feverish emotions called forth by war. It can sometimes be felt as profoundly and perhaps more truly at a moment such as this.

It had suddenly begun to rain very hard, and in a few minutes I could no longer see much of anything through the windows. All too quickly I made that swift turnabout from patriotism to enlightened self-interest. I closed my eyes and thought about how I would spend the money that would soon start to pour in. To my surprise, affluence did not seem nearly as easy to settle into as I had always imagined it would be. Try as I would, I could not think of how to begin or in what ways I wanted to spend the large sums that would now be mine to command. I could think of little ways to spend it—new suits, new shirts, new ties, new overcoats—but

after that my mind went disappointingly blank. In some ways sudden riches are no easier to live with than poverty. Both demand artistry of a kind, if one or the other is not to leave the mark of a sour and lingering cynicism, and opulence in many ways is harder to manage than penury. It is, however, one of the pleasantest problems with which to drift off to sleep. It is a problem that apparently also induces the deepest and most refreshing kind of sleep. I cheated myself out of the major portion of that first taxi ride by sleeping soundly through the rest of it. The driver had to leave his seat and shake me awake to collect his fare.

I was wide awake again, thoroughly wide awake, and disappointed to find the shades still drawn and the family fast asleep when I unlocked the door and stepped into the apartment. It was, of course, only a little after seven o'clock in the morning, but today was too memorable a day to waste on anything so commonplace as sleep. I was tempted to wake them up at once and show them the other notices, but I went into the kitchen instead and fixed a pot of coffee. I wanted a little more time alone to think about something.

I stood in the doorway of the kitchen while I waited for the water to boil and gazed at the sleeping figure of my brother on the daybed in the dining room, and beyond it at the closed door of the one bedroom where my parents slept. The frayed carpet on the floor was the carpet I had crawled over before I could walk. Each flower in the badly faded and worn design was sharply etched in my mind. Each piece of furniture in the cramped dim room seemed mildewed with a thousand double-edged memories. The ghosts of a thousand leaden meals hovered over the dining-room table. The dust of countless black-hearted days clung to every crevice of the squalid ugly furniture I had known since childhood. To walk out of it forever—not piecemeal, but completely—would give meaning to the wonder of what had happened to me, make success tangible, decisive.

The goal behind the struggle for success is not always one goal, but many—some real, some hidden; some impossible to achieve, even with success piled upon success. The goal differs with each of us in the mysterious and wonderful way each human being is different from any other, in the way each of us is the sum total of the unexpressed longings and desires that strew the seas of childhood and are glimpsed long afterward from a safe distance—a submerged iceberg, only the tip of which is seen.

Whatever dominant force in my nature shaped the blind demands that made it imperative to me to make the theatre my goal, had taken possession of me early, and I was still possessed by it. What fulfillment it held I would know only when I walked resolutely out of one world and into another. I poured myself a cup of coffee, and by the time I had finished it, my mind was made up.

It is always best if one is about to embark on a wild or reckless venture not to discuss it with anybody beforehand. Talk will rob the scheme of its fire and make what seemed mettlesome and daring merely foolhardy. It is easier on everyone concerned to present it as an accomplished fact, turn a deaf ear to argument, and go ahead with it.

I awakened my brother by dumping the papers on the bed for him to read and then called through the bedroom door to my mother and father to get up right away. I gave them barely enough time to read the notices and then plunged. "We're moving into New York today—as soon as you have a cup of coffee—and we're not taking anything with us. We're walking out of here with just the clothes on our backs and nothing else. The coffee's on the stove, so hurry up and get dressed."

My mother stared at me and then spoke quietly, as if a raised voice at this moment might send me further out of my senses. "Where are we going?" she asked logically enough.

"To a hotel," I said, "until we find an apartment and furnish it." There was a stunned silence and before anyone else could speak, I spoke again, not impatiently but as if what I was saying was inarguable. "There's nothing to pack; we just walk out of the door. No," I added in answer to my mother's mute startled look around the room, "not a thing. We leave it all here just as it stands, and close the door. We don't take anything—not even a toothbrush, a bathrobe, pajamas, or nightgown. We buy it all new in New York. We're walking out of here and starting fresh."

My mother walked to the window and pulled up the shades as though she might hear or understand what I was saying better with more light, and then turned helplessly toward my father.

He was the first to recover his breath and his wits. "We just paid two months' rent in advance," he said, as though that solid fact would help me recover my own.

"That gives us the right to let this stuff sit here and rot, or you can give it to the janitor," I replied. "We're walking out of here with just what clothes you put on, and tomorrow we'll get rid of those, too."

This second bit of information created an even more astonished silence than the first. "Don't you understand?" I heard myself shouting. "All I'm asking you to do *now* is—"

"I'm not walking out of here without the pictures," my mother said with great firmness.

It was my turn to be astonished. "What pictures?" I asked.

"*All* the pictures," she replied. "The baby pictures of you and Bernie and the pictures of my father and my sister, and Bernie's diploma and your letters, and all the other pictures and things I've got in the closet in that big box."

I threw my arms around her and kissed her. I had won. It was being accepted as a fact—incomprehensible but settled.

"One suitcase," I ordered. "Put it all into one suitcase, but one suitcase—that's all."

I looked at my brother, who had remained silent through all of this. He handed the papers back to me with a flourish and winked. "Don't you have to give *some* of the money to George Kaufman?" he said.

"Half," I replied. "But my share will be over a thousand dollars a week."

"That'll buy a lot of toothbrushes," he said. "I'm going to get ready." And he climbed out of bed.

My mother and father stared at us as if to make sure we were not indulging in some elaborate joke for their benefit.

"It's true," I said soberly. "It's not a salary. I get a percentage of every dollar that comes into the box office. Don't you understand how it works?"

Obviously, they did not, and I realized somewhat belatedly that it had never occurred to either of them to translate good fortune in the theatre into anything more than what my mother's friends defined as "making a good living." No wonder my proposal had sounded lunatic, but now as the belief came to them that what I had just said might be the literal truth, they were suddenly seized with some of my own excitement. My mother's reaction was a curious one. She burst into a peal of laughter. She had a merry and ringing laugh and it was contagious. My father and I joined in her laughter, though we would have been hard put to tell exactly what we were laughing at. I was reminded of that moment and of her laughter long, long afterward, when I heard someone say, "Nothing makes people laugh like money—the rich get wrinkles from laughing." It was said sardonically, of course, but it is not with-

out an element of truth. Money does generate its own kind of excitement, and its sudden acquisition creates an *ambiance* of gaiety and merriment that it would be nonsense to deny or not to enjoy. It induces, moreover, a momentum of its own. Everything moves with an unaccustomed and almost miraculous speed.

We were all ready to leave in less than an hour, despite the fact that there were more things of heaven and earth in that box in the closet than could be contained in one suitcase. I carried the box, my father and brother each carried a suitcase, and my mother, her victory complete, hugged a brown paper parcel of last-minute treasures that had turned up in an old tin box. We walked out the door and waited in the lobby while my brother hurried out in the rain to try to get a taxi. The rain was pouring down in a great solid sheet now, and gusts of wind were slashing it against the building. I watched it burst savagely against the glass doors of the lobby and was seized by a sudden and irresistible impulse.

"I forgot something," I said shortly. "I'll be right back."

I unlocked the door of the empty apartment and closed and locked it again carefully behind me. I took one quick look around to keep the memory of that room forever verdant and then walked to each window and threw it wide open. The rain whipped in through the windows like a broadside of artillery fire. I watched a large puddle form on the floor and spread darkly over the carpet. The rain streamed across the top and down the legs of the dining-room table and splashed over the sideboard and the china closet. It soaked the armchair and cascaded down the sofa. It peppered the wallpaper with large wet blotches, and the wind sent two lamps crashing to the floor. I kicked them out of my way and walked over to the daybed, which was still dry, and pulled it out into the middle of the room, where a fresh onset of wind and rain immediately drenched it. I looked around me with satisfaction, feeling neither guilty nor foolish. More reasonable gestures have seldom succeeded in giving me half the pleasure this meaningless one did. It was the hallmark, the final signature, of defiance and liberation. Short of arson, I could do no more.

I slammed the door behind me without looking back.

## Getting at Meaning

1. Why does Hart want to have breakfast with Joe Hyman? What need does it fulfill for him?

2. How does the skyline of New York seem different this particular morning? What emotion does the sight evoke?

3. During the taxi ride through the city, Hart experiences a surge of patriotism. Why? How is this patriotism related to his success?

4. According to Hart, why are "sudden riches no easier to live with than poverty"?

5. How is Hart's final action of throwing open the apartment windows similar to his breakfast with Joe Hyman? Is the act a beginning or an ending? Explain.

## Developing Skills in Reading Literature

1. **Symbol.** In this selection what does the subway symbolize for the writer? What do the apartment and its furnishings symbolize? Is the writer aware of the symbolism? Explain.

2. **Character.** What kind of life has the writer led up to this point? What inferences can you draw about his childhood and the family's economic condition? How does this knowledge help to explain the conclusion?

3. **Autobiography.** A skilled autobiographer is honest. He or she does not distort or exaggerate details for effect. Do you think that the writer of this selection is being honest with the reader? Do you think that the ending is an exact account of what happened? Be prepared to support your opinion with details from the story.

## Developing Vocabulary

1. **Antonyms.** Antonyms are words that have opposite, or nearly opposite, meanings. This selection includes the following sentence:

"Opulence in many ways is harder to manage than penury."

*Opulence* and *penury* are antonyms. Look up each word in the Glossary and write the definition.

The following pairs of words also are antonyms. Write one sentence using each pair of words. Check a dictionary if you need help.

squalid — immaculate
affluence — poverty
elaborate — simple
incomprehensible — understandable
mettlesome — foolhardy

2. **Word Origins.** Check the definition for *sardonic* in the Glossary; then research the origin of the word in a book of word origins. Be prepared to explain the history of this word.

## Developing Writing Skills

**Writing About an Incident.** The writer claims, "It is always best if one is about to embark on a wild or reckless venture not to discuss it with anybody beforehand." Think of an incident in your life in which you either followed this advice or wished you had followed it. In one paragraph, relate the incident and explain the results.

# *from* I Know Why the Caged Bird Sings

*Maya Angelou*

**M**y room had all the cheeriness of a dungeon and the appeal of a tomb. It was going to be impossible to stay there, but leaving held no attraction for me, either. The answer came to me with the suddenness of a collision. I would go to work. Mother wouldn't be difficult to convince; after all, in school I was a year ahead of my grade and Mother was a firm believer in self-sufficiency. In fact, she'd be pleased to think that I had that much gumption, that much of her in my character. (She liked to speak of herself as the original "do-it-yourself girl.")

Once I had settled on getting a job, all that remained was to decide which kind of job I was most fitted for. My intellectual pride had kept me from selecting typing, shorthand, or filing as subjects in school, so office work was ruled out. War plants and shipyards demanded birth certificates, and mine would reveal me to be fifteen, and ineligible for work. So the well-paying defense jobs were also out. Women had replaced men on the streetcars as conductors and motormen, and the thought of sailing up and down the hills of San Francisco in a dark-blue uniform, with a money changer at my belt, caught my fancy.

Mother was as easy as I had anticipated. The world was moving so fast, so much money was being made, so many people were dying in Guam,[1] and Germany, that hordes of strangers became good friends overnight. Life was cheap and death entirely free. How could she have the time to think about my academic career?

To her question of what I planned to do, I replied that I would get a job on the streetcars. She rejected the proposal with "They don't accept black people on the streetcars."

I would like to claim an immediate fury that was followed by the noble determination to break the restricting tradition. But the truth is, my first reaction was one of disappointment. I'd pictured myself, dressed in a neat blue serge suit, my money changer swinging jauntily at my waist, and a cheery smile for the passengers that would make their own work day brighter.

From disappointment, I gradually ascended the emotional ladder to haughty indignation, and finally to that state of stubbornness where the mind is locked like the jaws of an enraged bulldog.

I would go to work on the streetcars and wear a blue serge suit. Mother gave me her support with one of her usual terse asides, "That's what you want to do? Then nothing beats a trial but a failure. Give it everything you've got. I've told you many times, 'Can't do is like Don't Care.' Neither of them has a home."

Translated, that meant there is nothing a person can't do, and there should be nothing a human being doesn't care about. It was the most positive encouragement I could have hoped for.

In the offices of the Market Street Railway Company, the receptionist seemed as sur-

---

1. **Guam** (gwäm): an island in the west Pacific, a scene of fighting during World War II.

prised to see me there as I was surprised to find the interior dingy and drab. Somehow I had expected waxed surfaces and carpeted floors. If I had met no resistance, I might have decided against working for such a poor-mouth-looking concern. As it was, I explained that I had come to see about a job. She asked, was I sent by an agency, and when I replied that I was not, she told me they were only accepting applicants from agencies.

The classified pages of the morning papers had listed advertisements for motorettes and conductorettes, and I reminded her of that. She gave me a face full of astonishment that my suspicious nature would not accept.

"I am applying for the job listed in this morning's *Chronicle,* and I'd like to be presented to your personnel manager." While I spoke in supercilious accents, and looked at the room as if I had an oil well in my own backyard, my armpits were being pricked by millions of hot pointed needles. She saw her escape and dived into it.

"He's out. He's out for the day. You might call him tomorrow, and if he's in, I'm sure you can see him." Then she swiveled her chair around on its rusty screws, and with that I was supposed to be dismissed.

"May I ask his name?"

She half turned, acting surprised to find me still there.

"His name? Whose name?"

"Your personnel manager."

We were firmly joined in the hypocrisy to play out the scene.

"The personnel manager? Oh, he's Mr. Cooper, but I'm not sure you'll find him here tomorrow. He's . . . Oh, but you can try."

"Thank you."

"You're welcome."

And I was out of the musty room and into the even mustier lobby. In the street I saw the receptionist and myself going faithfully through paces that were stale with familiarity, although I had never encountered that kind of situation before and, probably, neither had she. We were like actors who, knowing the play by heart, were still able to cry afresh over the old tragedies and laugh spontaneously at the comic situations.

The miserable little encounter had nothing to do with me, the me of me, any more than it had to do with that silly clerk. The incident was a recurring dream concocted years before by whites, and it eternally came back to haunt us all. The secretary and I were like people in a scene where, because of harm done by one ancestor to another, we were bound to duel to the death. Also, because the play must end somewhere.

I went further than forgiving the clerk; I accepted her as a fellow victim of the same puppeteer.

On the streetcar, I put my fare into the box, and the conductorette looked at me with the usual hard eyes of white contempt. "Move into the car, please move on in the car." She patted her money changer.

Her Southern nasal accent sliced my meditation, and I looked deep into my thoughts. All lies, all comfortable lies. The receptionist was not innocent and neither was I. The whole charade we had played out in that waiting room had directly to do with me, black, and her, white.

I wouldn't move into the streetcar but stood on the ledge over the conductor, glaring. My mind shouted so energetically that the announcement made my veins stand out, and my mouth tighten into a prune.

I WOULD HAVE THE JOB. I WOULD BE A CONDUCTORETTE AND SLING A FULL MONEY CHANGER FROM MY BELT. I WOULD.

The next three weeks were a honeycomb of determination with apertures for the days to go in and out. The black organizations to whom I appealed for support bounced me back and forth like a shuttlecock on a badminton court. Why did I insist on that particular job? Openings were going begging that paid nearly twice the money. The minor officials with whom I was able to win an audience thought me mad. Possibly I was.

Downtown San Francisco became alien and cold, and the streets I had loved in a personal familiarity were unknown lanes that twisted with malicious intent. My trips to the streetcar office were of the frequency of a person on salary. The struggle expanded. I was no longer in conflict only with the Market Street Railway but with the marble lobby of the building that housed its offices, and elevators and their operators.

During this period of strain, Mother and I began our first steps on the long path toward mutual adult admiration. She never asked for reports and I didn't offer any details. But every morning she made breakfast, gave me carfare and lunch money, as if I were going to work. She comprehended that in the struggle lies the joy. That I was no glory seeker was obvious to her, and that I had to exhaust every possibility before giving in was also clear.

On my way out of the house one morning she said, "Life is going to give you just what you put in it. Put your whole heart in everything you do, and pray; then you can wait." Another time she reminded me that "God helps those who help themselves." She had a store of aphorisms that she dished out as the occasion demanded. Strangely, as bored as I was with clichés, her inflection gave them something new, and set me thinking for a little while at least. Later, when asked how I got my job, I was never able to say exactly. I only knew that one day, which was tiresomely like all the others before it, I sat in the Railway office, waiting to be interviewed. The receptionist called me to her desk and shuffled a bundle of paper to me. They were job application forms. She said they had to be filled in triplicate. I had little time to wonder if I had won or not, for the standard questions reminded me of the necessity for lying. How old was I? List my previous jobs, starting from the last held and go backward to the first. How much money did I earn, and why did I leave the position? Give two references (not relatives). I kept my face blank (an old art) and wrote quickly the fable of Marguerite Johnson, aged nineteen, former companion and driver for Mrs. Annie Henderson (a White Lady) in Stamps, Arkansas.

I was given blood tests, aptitude tests, and physical coordination tests; then, on a blissful day, I was hired as the first black on the San Francisco streetcars.

Mother gave me the money to have my blue serge suit tailored, and I learned to fill out work cards, operate the money changer and punch transfers. The time crowded together, and at an End of Days I was swinging on the back of the rackety trolley, smiling sweetly and persuading my charges to "step forward in the car, please."

For one whole semester the streetcars and I shimmied up and scooted down the sheer hills of San Francisco. I lost some of my need for the black ghetto's shielding-sponge quality, as I clanged and cleared my way down Market Street, with its honky-tonk homes for homeless sailors, past the quiet retreat of Golden Gate Park, and along closed undwelled-in-looking dwellings of the Sunset District.

My work shifts were split so haphazardly that it was easy to believe that my superiors had chosen them maliciously. Upon mentioning my suspicions to Mother, she said, "Don't you worry about it. You ask for what you want, and you pay for what you get. And I'm going to show you that it ain't no trouble when you pack double."

She stayed awake to drive me out to the car barn at four-thirty in the mornings, or to pick me up when I was relieved just before dawn. Her awareness of life's perils convinced her that while I would be safe on the public conveyances, she "wasn't about to trust a taxi driver with her baby."

When the spring classes began, I resumed my commitment with formal education. I was so much wiser and older, so much more independent, with a bank account and clothes that I had bought for myself, that I was sure I had learned and earned the magic formula that would make me a part of the life my contemporaries led.

Not a bit of it. Within weeks, I realized that my schoolmates and I were on paths moving away from each other. They were concerned and excited over the approaching football games. They concentrated great interest on who was worthy of being student body president, and when the metal bands would be removed from their teeth, while I remembered conducting a streetcar in the uneven hours of the morning.

## Getting at Meaning

1. How does the story's war-time setting affect Maya's prospects for getting a job?

2. How does Maya react to her mother's announcement, "They don't accept black people on the streetcars"? How do her feelings change?

3. At first, Maya characterizes the receptionist as a "fellow victim of the same puppeteer." What does she mean? Why does she later describe her opinions as "comfortable lies"?

4. What contributes to the development of mutual admiration between Maya and her mother?

5. How does Maya's work experience affect her? How does it affect her relationships with her contemporaries at school?

## Developing Skills in Reading Literature

1. **Autobiography.** In this selection, what does the writer learn about the various ways of reacting to prejudice? What are the easy ways? What does she learn about herself when she rejects the easy ways?

2. **Theme.** The writer expresses surprise and disappointment at the dinginess of the Market Street Railway Company. What else does not meet her expectations? What insight about human beings and their expectations do her experiences provide?

3. **Character.** The writer offers no physical description of her mother, yet the reader develops a clear impression of this woman. What details in the selection combine to create a vivid impression of the writer's mother?

## Developing Vocabulary

**Latin Roots.** One of the words used in this selection is *conductor*. Its Latin root is *duc* or *duct*, which means "lead." Following is a list of Latin roots, along with their meanings and examples of English words based on the roots. For each root, give two more examples of English words.

| Root | Meaning | English Words |
|------|---------|---------------|
| duc, duct | lead | induce |
| capt | take, hold, seize | capture |
| cred | believe | creed |
| fac, fec | do, make | factory |
| dic, dict | speak, say, tell | dictate |

## Developing Writing Skills

**Writing About a Personal Experience.** In this selection, the writer recounts her first experience in applying for a job. Select one of your own experiences in a new situation; for example, your first day in high school or the first time you applied for a job. Using specific details and examples, describe your experience and your feelings and reactions to the experience. The finished composition should be five paragraphs long.

# *from* **Barrio Boy**     *Ernesto Galarza*

It was a short walk from the hotel to the house where we turned in, the tallest I had ever seen. A wide wooden stairway went up from the sidewalk to a porch on the second story, and above that another floor, and still higher a gable as wide as the house, decorated with carvings and fretwork. The porch balustrade was in the same gingerbread style of lattice work and the wooden imitation of a fringe between the round pillars. We walked up the stairway and the three of us waited while José went inside.

He came back with the landlady. She was certainly a *gringo*[1] lady—two heads taller than Gustavo, twice as wide as José, square-jawed, rosy-faced, a thin nose with a small bulge on the end and like all Americans, with rather large feet. She had a way of blinking when she smiled at us.

Standing as straight as the posts of the porch and holding her shoulders square and straight across, she seemed to me more like a general than a lady.

Mostly with blinks and hand motions and a great many ceremonial smiles, we were introduced to Mrs. Dodson, who led us into the house, down some narrow, dark stairs and to the back of the first floor where she left us in our new apartment.

We found the Americans as strange in their customs as they probably found us. Immediately we discovered that there were no *mercados*[2] and that when shopping you did not put the groceries in a *chiquihuite*.[3] Instead, everything was in cans or in cardboard boxes, or each item was put into a brown paper bag. There were neighborhood grocery stores at the corners and some big ones uptown, but no *mercado*. The grocers did not give children a *pilón*;[4] they did not stand at the door and coax you to come in and buy, as they did in Mazatlán.[5] The fruits and vegetables were displayed on counters instead of being piled up on the floor. The stores smelled of fly spray and oiled floors, not of fresh pineapple and limes.

Neither was there a plaza, only parks that had no bandstands, no concerts every Thursday, no Judases exploding on Holy Week, and no promenades of boys going one way and girls the other. There were no parks in the *barrio*;[6] and the ones uptown were cold and rainy in winter, and in summer there was no place to sit except on the grass. When there were celebrations, nobody set off rockets in the parks, much less on the street in front of your house to announce to the neighborhood that a wedding or a baptism was taking place. Sacramento did not have a *mercado* and a plaza with the cathedral to one side and the *Palacio de Gobierno*[7] on another to make it obvious that there and nowhere else was the center of the town.

---

1. **gringo** (griṇ' gō) *Mexican:* in Latin America, a foreigner, especially American or British.
2. **mercados** (mer kä' dōs) *Spanish:* markets.
3. **chiquihuite** (chē kē hwē' tä) *Mexican:* a willow basket.
4. **pilón** (pē lōn') *Spanish:* a loaf of sugar.
5. **Mazatlán** (mä sät län'): a seaport on the Pacific coast of Mexico.
6. **barrio** (bär' ē ō) *Spanish:* a district or suburb of a city.
7. **Palacio de Gobierno** (pä lä' sē ō  dä  gō bē er' nō) *Spanish:* Palace of Government.

In more personal ways we had to get used to the Americans. They did not listen if you did not speak loudly, as they always did. In the Mexican style, people would know that you were enjoying their jokes tremendously if you merely smiled and shook a little, as if you were trying to swallow your mirth. In the American style there was little difference between a laugh and a roar, and until you got used to them, you could hardly tell whether the boisterous Americans were roaring mad or roaring happy.

America was all around us, in and out of the *barrio*. Abruptly we had to forget the ways of shopping in a *mercado* and learn those of shopping in a corner grocery or in a department store. The Americans paid no attention to the Sixteenth of September,[8] but they made a great commotion about the Fourth of July. In Mazatlán, Don Salvador had told us, saluting and marching as he talked to our class, that the *Cinco de Mayo*[9] was the most glorious date in human history. The Americans had not even heard about it.

In Tucson, when I had asked my mother again if the Americans were having a revolution, the answer was, "No, but they have good schools, and you are going to one of them." We were by now settled at 418 L Street, and the time had come for me to exchange a revolution for an American education.

The two of us walked south on Fifth Street one morning to the corner of Q Street and turned right. Half of the block was occupied by the Lincoln School. It was a three-story wooden building, with two wings that gave it the shape of a double-T connected by a central hall. It was a new building, painted yellow, with a shingled roof that was not like the red tile of the school in Mazatlán. I noticed other differences, none of them very reassuring.

We walked up the wide staircase hand in hand and through the door, which closed by itself. A mechanical contraption screwed to the top shut it behind us quietly.

Up to this point, the adventure of enrolling me in the school had been carefully rehearsed. Mrs. Dodson had told us how to find it, and we had circled it several times on our walks. Friends in the *barrio* explained that the director was called a principal, and that it was a lady and not a man. They assured us that there was always a person at the school who could speak Spanish.

Exactly as we had been told, there was a sign on the door in both Spanish and English: "Principal." We crossed the hall and entered the office of Miss Nettie Hopley.

Miss Hopley was at a roll-top desk to one side, sitting in a swivel chair that moved on wheels. There was a sofa against the opposite wall, flanked by two windows and a door that opened on a small balcony. Chairs were set around a table, and framed pictures hung on the walls of a man with long white hair and another with a sad face and a black beard.

The principal half turned in the swivel chair to look at us over the pinch glasses that crossed the ridge of her nose. To do this she had to duck her head slightly as if she were about to step through a low doorway.

What Miss Hopley said to us we did not know, but we saw in her eyes a warm welcome; and when she took off her glasses and straightened up, she smiled wholeheartedly, like Mrs. Dodson. We were, of course, saying nothing, only catching the friendliness of her voice and the sparkle in her eyes while she said words we did not understand. She signaled us to the table. Almost tiptoeing across the office, I maneuvered myself to keep my mother between me and the *gringo* lady. In a matter of seconds I had to decide whether she

---

8. **Sixteenth of September:** Mexican Independence Day.
9. ***Cinco de Mayo*** (sēn′ kō dā mī′ ō) *Spanish:* Fifth of May, a Mexican national holiday to celebrate the defeat of French troops in 1862.

was a possible friend or a menace. We sat down.

Then Miss Hopley did a formidable thing. She stood up. Had she been standing when we entered, she would have seemed tall. But rising from her chair, she soared. And what she carried up and up with her was a buxom superstructure, firm shoulders, a straight sharp nose, full cheeks slightly molded by a curved line along the nostrils, thin lips that moved like steel springs, and a high forehead topped by hair gathered in a bun. Miss Hopley was not a giant in body, but when she mobilized it to a standing position, she seemed a match for giants. I decided I liked her.

She strode to a door in the far corner of the office, opened it, and called a name. A boy of about ten years appeared in the doorway. He sat down at one end of the table. He was brown like us, a plump kid with shiny black hair combed straight back, neat, cool, and faintly obnoxious.

Miss Hopley joined us with a large book and some papers in her hand. She, too, sat down and the questions and answers began by way of our interpreter. My name was Ernesto. My mother's name was Henriqueta. My birth certificate was in San Blas. Here was my last report card from the *Escuela Municipal Numero 3 para Varones*[10] of Mazatlán, and so forth. Miss Hopley put things down in the book and my mother signed a card.

As long as the questions continued, Doña[11] Henriqueta could stay and I was secure. Now that they were over, Miss Hopley saw her to the door, dismissed our interpreter, and without further ado took me by the hand and strode down the hall to Miss Ryan's first grade.

During the next few weeks Miss Ryan overcame my fears of tall, energetic teachers as she bent over my desk to help me with a word in the preprimer. Step by step, she loosened me and my classmates from the safe anchorage of the desks for recitations at the blackboard and consultations at her desk. Frequently she burst into happy announcements to the whole class. "Ito can read a sentence," and small Japanese Ito, squint-eyed and shy, slowly read aloud while the class listened in wonder: "Come, Skipper, come. Come and run." The Korean, Portuguese, Italian, and Polish first graders had similar moments of glory, no less shining than mine the day I conquered "butterfly," which I had been persistently pronouncing in standard Spanish as *boo-ter-flee.* "Children," Miss Ryan called for attention. "Ernesto has learned how to pronounce *butterfly!*" And I proved it with a perfect imitation of Miss Ryan. From that celebrated success, I was soon able to match Ito's progress as a sentence reader with "Come, butterfly, come fly with me."

Like Ito and several other first graders who did not know English, I received private lessons from Miss Ryan in the closet, a narrow hall off the classroom with a door at each end. Next to one of these doors Miss Ryan placed a large chair for herself and a small one for me. Keeping an eye on the class through the open door, she read with me about sheep in the meadow and a frightened chicken going to see the king, coaching me out of my phonetic ruts in words like *pasture, bow-wow-wow, hay,* and *pretty,* which to my Mexican ear and eye had so many unnecessary sounds and letters. She made me watch her lips and then close my eyes as she repeated words I found hard to read. When we came to know each other better, I tried interrupting to tell Miss Ryan how we said it in Spanish. It didn't work. She only said "oh" and went on with *pasture, bow-wow-wow,*

---

10. *Escuela Municipal Numero 3 para Varones* (es kōō ä' lä mōō nē sē päl' nōō mä rō träs pä' rä vä rō' näs) *Spanish:* Municipal School Number Three for Males.

11. **Doña** (dō' nyä) *Spanish:* Madam, a Spanish title of respect, used with a woman's name.

and *pretty*. It was as if in that closet we were both discovering together the secrets of the English language and grieving together over the tragedies of Bo-Peep. The main reason I was graduated with honors from the first grade was that I had fallen in love with Miss Ryan. Her radiant, no-nonsense character made us either afraid not to love her or love her so we would not be afraid; I am not sure which. It was not only that we sensed she was with it, but also that she was with us.

Like the first grade, the rest of the Lincoln School was a sampling of the lower part of town where many races made their home. My pals in the second grade were Kazushi, whose parents spoke only Japanese; Matti, a skinny Italian boy; and Manuel, a fat Portuguese who would never get into a fight but wrestled you to the ground and just sat on you. Our assortment of nationalities included Koreans, Yugoslavs, Poles, Irish, and home-grown Americans.

Miss Hopley and her teachers never let us forget why we were at Lincoln: for those who were alien, to become good Americans; for those who were so born, to accept the rest of us. Off the school grounds we traded the same insults we heard from our elders. On the playground we were sure to be marched up to the principal's office for calling someone a *wop*, a *chink*, a *dago*, or a *greaser*. The school was not so much a melting pot as a griddle, where Miss Hopley and her helpers warmed knowledge into us and roasted racial hatred out of us.

At Lincoln, making us into Americans did not mean scrubbing away what made us originally foreign. The teachers called us as our parents did, or as close as they could pronounce our names in Spanish or Japanese. No one was ever scolded or punished for speaking in his native tongue on the playground. Matti told the class about his mother's down quilt, which she had made in Italy with the fine feathers of a thousand geese. Encarnación

acted out how boys learned to fish in the Philippines. I astounded the third grade with the story of my travels on a stagecoach, which nobody else in the class had seen except in the museum at Sutter's Fort. After a visit to the Crocker Art Gallery and its collection of heroic paintings of the golden age of California, someone showed a silk scroll with a Chinese painting. Miss Hopley herself had a way of expressing wonder over these matters before a class, her eyes wide open until they popped slightly. It was easy for me to feel that becoming a proud American, as she said we should, did not mean feeling ashamed of being a Mexican.

The Americanization of Mexican me was no smooth matter. I had to fight one lout who made fun of my travels on the *diligencia*,[12] and my barbaric translation of the word into "diligence." He doubled up with laughter over the word until I straightened him out with a kick. In class I made points explaining that in Mexico roosters said "qui-qui-ri-qui" and not "cock-a-doodle-doo," but after school I had to put up with the taunts of a big Yugoslav who said Mexican roosters were crazy.

But it was Homer who gave me the most lasting lesson for a future American.

Homer was a chunky Irishman who dressed as if every day was Sunday. He slicked his hair between a crew cut and a pompadour. And Homer was smart, as he clearly showed when he and I ran for president of the third grade.

Everyone understood that this was to be a demonstration of how the American people vote for President. In an election, the teacher explained, the candidates could be generous and vote for each other. We cast our ballots in a shoe box and Homer won by two votes. I polled my supporters and came to the conclusion that I had voted for Homer and so

12. **diligencia** (dē lē hen' sē ə) *Spanish:* stagecoach.

had he. After class he didn't deny it, reminding me of what the teacher had said—we could vote for each other but didn't have to.

The lower part of town was a collage of nationalities in the middle of which Miss Nettie Hopley kept school with discipline and compassion. She called assemblies in the upper hall to introduce celebrities like the police sergeant or the fire chief, to lay down the law of the school, to present awards to our athletic champions, and to make important announcements. One of these was that I had been proposed by my school and accepted as a member of the newly formed Sacramento Boys' Band. "Now, isn't that a wonderful thing?" Miss Hopley asked the assembled school, all eyes on me. And everyone answered in a chorus, including myself, "Yes, Miss Hopley."

It was not only the parents who were summoned to her office and boys and girls who served sentences there who knew that Nettie Hopley meant business. The entire school witnessed her sizzling Americanism in its awful majesty one morning at flag salute.

All the grades, as usual, were lined up in the courtyard between the wings of the building, ready to march to classes after the opening bell. Miss Shand was on the balcony of the second floor of Miss Hopley's office, conducting us in our lusty singing of "My Country tiz-a-thee." Our principal, as always, stood there like us, at attention, her right hand over her heart, joining in the song.

Halfway through the second stanza she stepped forward, held up her arm in a sign of command, and called loud and clear, "Stop the singing." Miss Shand looked flabbergasted. We were frozen with shock.

Miss Hopley was now standing at the rail of the balcony, her eyes sparking, her voice low and resonant, the words coming down to us distinctly and loaded with indignation.

"There are two gentlemen walking on the school grounds with their hats on while we are singing," she said, sweeping our ranks with her eyes. "We will remain silent until the gentlemen come to attention and remove their hats." A minute of awful silence ended when Miss Hopley, her gaze fixed on something behind us, signaled Miss Shand, and we began once more the familiar hymn. That afternoon, when school was out, the word spread. The two gentlemen were the Superintendent of Schools and an important guest on an inspection.

I came back to the Lincoln School after every summer, moving up through the grades with Miss Campbell, Miss Beakey, Mrs. Wood, Miss Applegate, and Miss Delahunty. I sat in the classroom adjoining the principal's office and had my turn answering her telephone when she was about the building repeating the message to the teacher, who made a note of it. Miss Campbell read to us during the last period of the week about King Arthur, Columbus, Buffalo Bill, and Daniel Boone, who came to life in the reverie of the class through the magic of her voice. And it was Miss Campbell who introduced me to the public library on Eye Street, where I became a regular customer.

Lincoln School and the *barrio* cooperated to help me get further into *la lucha*.[13] I never had any homework. I took my books home to show off but never to prepare lessons. This meant that Miss Campbell or Miss Delahunty or Mrs. Wood did not interfere with my free working time after school or on Saturdays.

I worked up a small income as a part-time bellhop and house boy in the rooming house. Nobody at 418 L could scamper up and down the three stories or relay a laundry package to the alley and back as fast as I, or beat rugs with a stick on the laundry wire and hang blankets out to air. I wasn't paid in tips, but on Saturdays people flipped a nickel or a dime at me, and on holidays as much as a quarter.

---

13. **la lucha** (lä lōō′ chə) *Spanish:* the struggle or contest.

For me there was a smooth flow between these money-making employments and my tasks in our apartment—making my bed, sweeping the backyard, and checking the rat traps under the floor.

At about this time my mother remarried. To make room for a growing family, it was decided that we should move, and a house was found in Oak Park, on the far side of town where the open country began. The men raised the first installment for the bungalow on Seventh Avenue even after Mrs. Dodson explained that if we did not keep up the monthly payments we would lose the deposit as well as the house.

The real estate broker brought the sale contract to the apartment one evening. Myself included, we sat around the table in the living room, the *gringo* explaining at great length the small print of the document in a torrent of words none of us could make out. Now and then he would pause and throw in the only word he knew in Spanish: "Sabee?"[14] The men nodded slightly as if they had understood. Doña Henriqueta was holding firmly to the purse that contained the down payment, watching the broker's face, not listening to his words. She had only one question. Turning to me she said, "Ask him how long it will take to pay all of it." I translated, shocked by the answer: "Twenty years." There was a long pause around the table, broken by my stepfather. "What do you say?" Around the table the heads nodded agreement. The broker passed his fountain pen to him. He signed the contract and after him Gustavo and José. Doña Henriqueta opened the purse and counted out the greenbacks. The broker pocketed the money, gave us a copy of the document, and left.

Our new bungalow had five rooms, and porches front and back. In the way of furniture, what friends did not lend or Mrs. Dodson give us, we bought in the secondhand shops. The only new item was an elegant gas range, with a high oven and long, slender legs finished in enamel. Like the house, we would be paying for it in installments.

We could not have moved to a neighborhood less like the *barrio*. All the families around us were Americans. The grumpy retired farmer next door viewed us with alarm and never gave us the time of day, but the Harrisons across the street were cordial. Mr. Harrison loaned us his tools, and Roy, just my age but twice my weight, teamed up with me at once for an exchange of visits to his mother's kitchen and ours. I astounded him with my Mexican rice, and Mrs. Harrison baked my first waffle. Roy and I also found a common bond in the matter of sisters. He had an older one and by now I had two younger ones. It was a question between us whether they were worse as little nuisances or as big bosses. The answer didn't make much difference, but it was a relief to have another man to talk with.

Since Roy had a bicycle and could get away from his sister by pedaling off on long journeys, I persuaded my family to match my savings for a used one. Together we pushed beyond the boundaries of Oak Park miles out, nearly to Perkins and the Slough House. It was open country, where we could lean our wheels against a fence post and walk endlessly through carpets of golden poppies and blue lupin. With a bike I was able to sign on as a carrier of the *Sacramento Bee*, learning in due course the art of slapping folded newspapers against people's porches instead of into the bushes or on their roofs. Roy and I also became assistants to a neighbor who operated a bakery in his basement, taking our pay partly in dimes and partly in broken cookies for our families.

I transferred to the Bret Harte School, a

---

14. **Sabee:** mispronunciation of the Spanish word *sabe* (sä′ bā), meaning "understand."

gingerbread two-story building in which there was a notable absence of Japanese, Filipinos, Koreans, Italians, and the other nationalities of the Lincoln School. It was at Bret Harte that I learned how an English sentence could be cut up on the blackboard and the pieces placed on different lines connected by what the teacher called a diagram. The idea of operating on a sentence and rearranging its members as a skeleton of verbs, modifiers, subject, and prepositions set me off diagraming whatever I read, in Spanish and English. Spiderwebs, my mother called them, when I tried to teach her the art.

My bilingual library had grown with some copies of old magazines from Mexico, a used speller Gustavo had bought for me in Stockton, and the novels my mother discarded when she had read them. Blackstone[15] was still the anchor of my collection, and I now had a paperback dictionary called *El Inglés sin Maestro*.[16] By this time there was no problem of translating or interpreting for the family that I could not tackle with confidence.

It was Gustavo, in fact, who began to give my books a vague significance. He pointed out to me that with diagrams and dictionaries I could have a choice of becoming a lawyer or a doctor or an engineer or a professor. These, he said, were far better careers than growing up to be a *camello*, as he and José always would be. *Camellos*, I knew well enough, was what the *Chicanos* called themselves as the workers on every job who did the dirtiest work. And to give our home the professional touch he felt I should be acquiring, he had a telephone installed.

It came to the rest of us as a surprise. The company man arrived one day with our name and address on a card, a metal toolbox and a stand-up telephone wound with a cord. It was connected and set on the counter between the dining room and the parlor. There the black marvel sat until we were gathered for dinner that evening. It was clearly explained by Gustavo that the instrument was to provide me with a quick means of reaching the important people I knew at the Y.M.C.A., the boys' band, or the various public offices where I interpreted for *Chicanos* in distress. Sooner or later some of our friends in the *barrio* would also have telephones, and we could talk with them.

"Call somebody," my mother urged me.

With the whole family watching, I tried to think of some important person I could ring for a professional conversation. A name wouldn't come. I felt miserable and hardly like a budding engineer or lawyer or doctor or professor.

Gustavo understood my predicament and let me stew in it a moment. Then he said, "Mrs. Dodson." My pride saved by this ingenious suggestion, I thumbed through the directory, lifted the earpiece from the hook, and calmly asked central for the number. My sisters, one sitting on the floor and the other in my mother's arms, never looked less significant; but they, too, had their turn saying hello to the patient Señora Dodson on the other end of the line.

An epidemic erased the quiet life on 7th Avenue and the hopes we had brought with us.

I had been reading to the family stories in the *Bee* of the Spanish influenza. At first it was far off, like the war, in places such as New York and Texas. Then the stories told of people dying in California towns we knew, and finally the *Bee* began reporting the spread of the "flu" in our city.

One Sunday morning we saw Gustavo coming down the street with a suitcase in

---

15. **Blackstone:** *Commentaries on the Laws of England* by English jurist Sir William Blackstone.
16. ***El Inglés sin Maestro*** (el in glās′ sēn mä ēs′ trō) *Spanish:* English Without a Teacher.

his hand, walking slowly. I ran out to meet him. By the front gate, he dropped the suitcase, leaned on the fence, and fainted. He had been working as a sandhog on the American River, and had come home weak from fever.

Gustavo was put to bed in one of the front rooms. José set out to look for a doctor, who came the next day, weary and nearly sick himself. He ordered Gustavo to the hospital. Three days later I answered the telephone call from the hospital telling us he was dead. Only José went to Gustavo's funeral. The rest of us, except my stepfather, were sick in bed with the fever.

In the dining room, near the windows where the sunlight would warm her, my mother lay on a cot, a kerosene stove at her feet. The day Gustavo died she was delirious. José bicycled all over the city, looking for oranges, which the doctor said were the best medicine we could give her. I sweated out the fever, nursed by José, who brought me glasses of steaming lemonade and told me my mother was getting better. The children were quarantined in another room, lightly touched by the fever, more restless than sick.

Late one afternoon José came into my room, wrapped me in blankets, pulled a cap over my ears, and carried me to my mother's bedside. My stepfather was holding a hand mirror to her lips. It didn't fog. She had stopped breathing.

A month later I made a bundle of the family keepsakes my stepfather allowed me to have, including the butterfly serape, my books, and some family pictures. With the bundle tied to the bars of my bicycle, I pedaled to the basement room José had rented for the two of us on O Street near the corner of Fifth, on the edge of the *barrio*.

José had chosen our new home in the basement on O Street because it was close to the Hearkness Junior High School, to which I transferred from Bret Harte. As the *jefe de familia*,[17] he explained that I could help earn our living but that I was to study for a high school diploma. That being settled, my routine was clearly divided into schooltime and worktime, the second depending on when I was free from the first.

Few Mexicans of my age from the *barrio* were enrolled at the junior high school when I went there. At least, there were no other Mexican boys or girls in Mr. Everett's class in civics, or Miss Crowley's English composition, or Mrs. Stevenson's Spanish course. Mrs. Stevenson assigned me to read to the class and to recite poems by Amado Nervo, because the poet was from Tepic and I was, too. Miss Crowley accepted my compositions about Jalcocotán and the buried treasure of Acaponeta[18] while the others in the class were writing about Sir Patrick Spence and the Beautiful Lady without Mercy,[19] whom they had never met. For Mr. Everett's class, the last of the day, I clipped pieces from the *Sacramento Bee* about important events in Sacramento. From him I learned to use the ring binder in which I kept clippings to prepare oral reports. Occasionally he kept me after school to talk. He sat on his desk, one leg dangling over a corner, behind him the frame of a large window and the arching elms of the school yard, telling me he thought I could easily make the debating team at the high school next year, that Stanford University might be the place to go after graduation, and making other by-the-way comments that began to shape themselves into my future.

---

17. *jefe de familia* (hā' fā dā fä mē' lē ä) *Spanish:* head of the family.
18. **Jalcocotán . . . Acaponeta** (jäl kō kō tän', ä kä pō nyä' tä): towns in central Mexico.
19. **Sir Patrick Spence and the Beautiful Lady without Mercy:** fictional characters in British literature.

## Getting at Meaning

1. What American customs does Ernesto find particularly strange? What Mexican customs does he miss most?

2. Ernesto describes Miss Hopley as "a match for giants." What incident in this selection supports this description of the principal?

3. How does the approach taken by the teachers and principal at Lincoln School help Ernesto to become Americanized without giving up his Mexican heritage?

4. How does Ernesto's life change when the family moves to Oak Park? What forces him to move back to the barrio?

5. What effect might education have on the writer's future life? Explain.

## Developing Skills in Reading Literature

1. **Character.** The minor characters in an autobiography often are people who have had great influence on the writer's life. Select two such characters from this selection. What do you learn about each person? How have these people influenced the writer?

2. **Theme.** What is the theme of this selection? Reread the last sentence of the selection. How does the idea expressed in this sentence relate to the theme?

3. **Metaphor.** The writer says that Lincoln School was not so much "a melting pot as a griddle." Why does this seem an appropriate description for the school? Why does the writer believe that *griddle* is an appropriate term? Skim the paragraph that begins "During the next few weeks Miss Ryan . . ." (p. 292) What metaphor does the writer use to describe life in the classroom?

## Developing Vocabulary

1. **Prefixes.** The prefix *super-* has two common meanings, "over and above," as in *superman* and "very large," as in *supermarket*. Define each of the following words in terms of the prefix *super-*. Consult a dictionary if you need help.

superstructure    superannuated
superintendent    superimpose
supernatural    superstar

2. **Word Origins.** The word *gringo* came into English from Spanish. In Spanish it originally meant "gibberish or nonsensical talk." How do you think that *gringo* acquired its current meaning?

The word *barbarian* has a similar history. Research this word in a book of word origins and explain its original meaning.

## Developing Writing Skills

1. **Establishing Point of View.** Choose an American custom, such as eating popcorn at the movies or having cheerleaders at football games. Describe this custom from the point of view of a recent immigrant. Confine your description to a single well developed paragraph.

2. **Combining Description, Narration, and Exposition.** The writer of this selection says of one teacher, "She was with us." Decide what he means by that statement, and describe someone whom you feel is "with you." This person might be a parent, teacher, coach, or neighbor. Develop this idea in a five-paragraph composition. In the first paragraph, explain what being "with someone" means and identify the person whom you are describing. In the three body paragraphs, describe the person and give examples of incidents in which he or she was "with you." In the concluding paragraph, explain what you have learned from this person or comment on why he or she is special.

# Biography

# *from* Life Among the Savages        *Shirley Jackson*

Two days before his eighth birthday, Laurie rode his bike around a bend, directly into the path of a car. I can remember with extraordinary clarity that one of the people in the crowd that gathered handed me a lighted cigarette, I can remember saying reasonably that we all ought not to be standing in the middle of the road like this, I can remember the high step up into the ambulance. When they told us at the hospital, late that night, that everything was going to be all right, we came home and I finished drying the breakfast dishes. Laurie woke up in the hospital the next morning, with no memory of anything that had happened since breakfast two days before, and he was so upset by the thought that he had ridden in an ambulance and not known about it that the ambulance had to be engaged again to bring him home two weeks later, with the sirens screaming and an extremely proud Jannie sitting beside him and traffic separating on either side.

We put him, of course, into our bedroom; my mother always used to put sick children into the "big" bed, and I have still that half-remembered feeling that it is one of the signs of being *really* sick, sick enough to stay home from school. My mother, however, never had to cope with anything more complex than my brother's broken arm: I had under my wavering care this active patient with concussion, a broken hand, and various patched-up cuts and bruises; who was not, under doctor's orders, to excite himself, to move his arm; who was not, most particularly, to raise his head or try to turn over; and who was not, it was clearly evident, going to pay any attention to anything the doctor said.

"Now I'm home I can have whatever I want," Laurie announced immediately after I arrived in the room with the tray of orange juice, plain toast, and chicken soup that my mother before me believed was the proper basic treatment for an invalid; he cast a disapproving eye at the tray, and said, "Doc said I could have *real* food."

"The most important thing," I told him, "is for you to keep yourself quiet, and warm, and not excited. That dog, for instance."

Toby buried his huge head under the pillow and tried to pretend that he was invisible. "What dog?" said Laurie.

"And," I went on with great firmness, patting Toby absently on the shoulder, "you are absolutely not to lift your head and you are absolutely not to move without help and if you do—"

"I got to go back to the hospital," Laurie said. He wiggled comfortably into the hollow under Toby's chin. "It wasn't so bad there," he said. "*Food* was good, anyway."

"Jannie and Sally are not allowed in this room. No visitors at all for at least a week."

Shax moved softly into the doorway, looked at me and then speculatively at Laurie, and then walked sedately across the room and went up onto the bed, where he settled down without haste next to Laurie's feet, purring. Laurie grinned at me. "Jannie's already *been* here," he said. "She was telling me one of her stories while you were downstairs fixing that junk on the tray, and Sally brought me her teddy bear."

I sighed.

"It's under the covers somewhere," Laurie said. "Doc said you would tell me all about it, all about what happened."

"We won't think about it."

"Doc said I was hit by a car."

"So you were."

"I don't remember." Laurie was accusing. "Seems as though I'd remember *something* about it."

"I think it's just as well," I said. "Better to remember pleasant things than sad ones."

"What's so sad about *this?*"

"Keep your head down." I settled back in the armchair and took up my book. "You go to sleep; I'll sit right here."

Laurie closed his eyes obediently, but Toby wriggled and Laurie laughed. "Listen," he said, "tell me about it."

"There's nothing you don't already know," I said. "It's all over, after all."

"Was there a lot of blood?"

"Laurie, surely—"

"*Was* there?"

"There was some," I said reluctantly.

"On the road?"

"Yes. Keep your head down."

"Gee," Laurie said luxuriously. "And the cops—did the cops come? Doc said the cops called him."

"Officer Harrison was there, and he took charge of everything. It was Sunday and he was home cutting his lawn and he came right over when he heard—when it happened."

"When he heard the crash," Laurie said. "Gee, what a noise it must of made."

"Keep your *head* down."

"How many cops?"

"Officer Harrison, and Mr. Lanza, and two or three others I didn't know. I called the State police station and thanked them a few days ago. They were very happy to hear that you were so much better."

"Doc said you fainted."

"I did *not.*" I sat up indignantly.

"Did Daddy faint?"

"Certainly not."

"Did Jannie faint?"

"I sent Jannie and Sally down to the Olsons'," I said. "They don't know very much about it."

"I won't tell them," Laurie said reassuringly. "What about my bike—is it all right?"

"Well," I said, "no, it isn't. As a matter of fact, it's broken."

"I *bet* it is," said Laurie, with relish. "Boy, did that bike ever get smacked—I bet it's in a million pieces."

"Keep your head down."

"Hey, what about my clothes?" Laurie said, remembering. "I woke up in the hospital and I had on a nightgown; what about my clothes?"

"Since you're feeling so well," I said, remembering, "I might as well point out that even though I was quite worried about you, I was positively ashamed when they undressed you at the hospital. I distinctly remember telling you to put on clean clothes that morning, and whatever may be said for your shirt, your underwear—"

"They undressed me at the hospital? Who?"

"The nurse. And when I saw that underwear—"

"The *nurse? She* undressed me?"

"Keep your head *down.*"

"Oh, brother," said Laurie. He thought, while Toby, his head on the pillow, breathed heavily and happily, and Shax stirred, lifted his head, and curled up more comfortably. "Where are my clothes now?" Laurie asked finally.

"Your shoes are put neatly—*neatly*—under the chair in your room. That underwear has been sent to the laundry, and your socks and blue jeans, too." I hesitated. "Your shirt was thrown out," I said.

"Why?" Laurie demanded. "*Why* was my shirt thrown out?"

"It was torn," I said.

"Torn? You mean it was covered with blood or something?"

"No," I said. "It was torn. Cut."

"Cut?"

"Keep your head down. They cut it off you at the hospital."

"They did?" Laurie said, his eyes shining. "They had to *cut* it off?"

"Well, they *preferred* to."

"Where is it?"

"I told you it was thrown out. They gave me your clothes at the hospital and told me the shirt was thrown out."

Laurie asked accusingly, "You didn't keep that shirt? All covered with blood and you didn't *keep* it?"

"Why should I keep it?"

"Which one was it? The green checked one?"

"That was the one you took off in the morning. You put on the new shirt with the baseball picture."

"*That* one? My new one?"

"There are plenty of others," I said, making a mental note about never going near those baseball shirts again. "How about you go to sleep now?"

"That good baseball shirt? And you went and threw it out?"

"You couldn't have worn it again."

"Who wants to *wear* it?" said Laurie. "What else happened?"

"Well," I said, "Brooklyn lost the pennant that same afternoon."

"I heard the Series in the hospital," Laurie said. "What a robbery."

"Would you like to go to sleep now?"

"I bet Dad was nearly crazy," Laurie said.

"Not at all," I said, "he was—"

"Losing the last day like that. Gee," Laurie said, squeezing down between Toby and Shax, "it's not bad being home."

A month later, with satisfaction only secondary to Laurie's, I took him back to school to pick up his books so he could try to catch up on his work. "Remember," I told him in the car before we went into the school," "thank the teacher and the kids for the nice basket they sent you."

"Yeah," Laurie said. He had chosen ten in the morning as the ideal moment to present himself at school.

"And don't forget to thank the teacher for her flowers."

"Yeah."

"And tell her I'll help you at home with arithmetic."

"Come *on*," Laurie said.

We entered the classroom in triumph; Laurie threw open the door and stood for a moment in the doorway before advancing with a swagger Cyrano[1] might have envied. "I'm back," he said into the quiet of the spelling lesson.

"Thank you *so* much for the flowers," I told the teacher. "Laurie appreciated them *so* much."

Laurie sat on one of the front desks, holding his hand with the traction splint prominently displayed. All the third-grade girls gathered around him, and the boys sat on the floor and on nearby desks. "—And I guess there were five hundred people there," he was saying, "they came tearing in from all over. And the street—you oughta seen the street—*covered* with blood—"

"I'll go over his arithmetic with him," I told the teacher.

"He was doing splendidly," she said absently, her eyes on Laurie.

"—And my good shirt, they had to *cut* it off me, ten doctors, and there was so much blood on it they had to throw it away because it was all cut to pieces and bloody. And I

---

1. **Cyrano** (sir′ ə nō′): Cyrano de Bergerac (də bŭr′ zhə rak′), a French writer, soldier, and romantic hero.

went in an ambulance with the sireens and boy! did *we* travel. Boy!"

"And will he need to go over his reading?"

"Excuse me," said Laurie's teacher. Un- willingly, she moved closer to the spellbinder, her hand still reassuringly on my arm. "And my mother fainted," he was saying, "and my *father...*"

## Getting at Meaning

1. Why does Laurie's mother seem to remember only the little things about the accident?

2. In what ways is Laurie a typical eight-year-old? In what ways is his mother typical?

3. Referring to the torn shirt, Laurie says, "Who wants to *wear* it?" Why does he want it?

4. Why does Laurie choose ten o'clock in the morning to return to school? Is his timing right? Explain.

## Developing Skills in Reading Literature

1. **Biography.** A biography is the true story of a person's life written by someone else. Who is the subject of this biographical selection? Who is the writer? What is the relationship of the writer to the subject? How might this relationship affect the biography?

2. **Tone.** A writer's tone indicates how he or she feels about the events and people described in a selection. What is the tone of this selection? Support your answer with details from the selection.

3. **Allusion.** An allusion is a reference within a work of literature to a person, place, or event, either real or fictional. In this selection, the writer alludes to Cyrano de Bergerac: "Laurie threw open the door and stood for a moment in the doorway before advancing with a swagger Cyrano might have envied."

Using a biographical dictionary, a dictionary of fictional characters, or an encyclopedia, research this allusion. Who is Cyrano de Bergerac? Is he a real person or a fictional character? Why is he associated with a swaggering walk?

## Developing Vocabulary

1. **Prefixes.** The prefix *pro-* has two common meanings: "in favor of," as in *progovernment* and "forward or ahead," as in *proceed.* Decide which meaning of *pro-* applies in each of the following words:

| | |
|---|---|
| produce | project |
| prominent | proenvironment |
| prolabor | propel |

2. **Compound Words.** The writer refers to Laurie as a spellbinder. *Spellbinder* is a compound word, a word that is formed by joining two or more words. Some compounds are hyphenated, as *cease-fire.* Occasionally, a compound is written as two words, such as *ice cream.* These are called open compounds and are treated in dictionaries as single words.

Skim a dictionary and list five open compounds, five hyphenated compounds, and five closed compounds. For each compound, identify the part of speech of each component word. For example, *spellbinder* is a noun-noun compound; *cease-fire* is a verb-noun compound.

## Developing Writing Skills

**Establishing Tone.** Think of an incident in the life of a brother, sister, parent, classmate, or neighbor. The incident should be a potentially serious event with humorous aspects. Relate the incident in the third person, maintaining a light, humorous tone throughout. Use this selection as a guide.

# Harriet Tubman    *Henrietta Buckmaster*

Harriet Tubman was a black child, a slave, born to slave parents and owned by a Maryland master. She was born in 1821, the year of the great slave uprising in South Carolina led by a black man, Denmark Vesey. All through that year, and for many years to come, Vesey's name rang through the slave cabins. His exploit frightened some slaves because masters became harsher, but it excited others to hope. As a very small child, Harriet was taught to sing a song that Vesey had made popular:

> Go down, Moses,
> Way down to Egypt land!
> And tell old Pharaoh
> To let my people go!

It was a dangerous song to sing. It had to be sung under the breath even when no white man was around. But in the years to come, it became Harriet's song.

Harriet was a scrawny, bright little girl. At the age of six she was hired out to a woman who beat her, fed her scraps, and did not let her sleep enough. When the woman finally brought her back to the master as "not worth anything," Harriet's back was a mass of scars from her beatings.

The second time she was hired she was a little older and wiser. She worked in the fields, which she liked. Her father was hired out to the same person, and he taught her strange things—how to move silently through the woods so that no one could hear her, how to recognize edible berries and roots. It was as though he expected her to escape sometime, and he wanted her to be prepared.

Those runaways who did not succeed were punished terribly.

In the whisperings of the cabin Harriet had also learned that a mysterious system of help for those same runaways was called the Underground Railroad. It was really a long line of friends, white and black, stretching into the South, who passed fugitives from one hiding place to the next until they reached the North. It was very dangerous for both the fugitive and his friends if they were caught.

When Harriet was eleven, she put on a bandanna as a sign that she was grown up. A black girl of eleven was supposed to do a woman's work, although childhood was a luxury most had never known. Harriet began to think about the future in vague terms, mostly in terms of escape and freedom for her whole family. Some of her sisters had already been sold. Harriet had watched them, fastened together with chains, stumble down the road toward the Deep South. Her mother had not dared to weep, although she knew she would never see them again.

That year Virginia, a state practically next door to Maryland, shook to the sounds of another slave uprising led by Nat Turner. All over the South, controls tightened. Slaves, lying awake in their cabins, could hear the pounding of horses' hoofs night after night. "The patrol," they would whisper to each other, "out looking for runaway slaves."

One day when Harriet was working the field of her master, she realized that one of the slave men was edging closer and closer to the woods. Presently she knew that he was trying to make a break for freedom. The overseer realized it at the same time. Harriet moved quickly and succeeded in blocking the overseer for the moment it took the slave to get out of sight. In a rage, the overseer flung a metal weight after the man and struck Harriet in the forehead.

For hours she lay unconscious. The news that she had helped a slave escape spread through the plantation. Slaves crept in the dark to see her lying on a pallet tended by her fearful mother. A slave who had helped another escape had lost all value to his master. He was a liability who must be gotten rid of as quickly as possible, before he infected the other slaves.

While Harriet was still unconscious, her master tried to sell her. Buyers came to look at her, but when they saw the injured girl they laughed. Buy *her*? No man was such a fool.

For many months Harriet lay in a stupor. When she recovered and was able to work again, unconsciousness would come on her without warning. In the middle of a sentence, or as she was walking or working, her head would jerk forward and she would lose consciousness. When she opened her eyes she would finish her sentence or continue her action, but in the interval she was completely helpless.

Suddenly her master died. The heir was a child, and by the master's will the estate was to be held together until the child came of age.

Harriet was hired out because she was as strong as a man. One day as she was working in the field near the road, a white woman driving a wagon stopped. She watched Harriet for a few moments before she spoke to her. She seemed to understand the meaning of that terrible scar on Harriet's forehead. She said softly, "If you ever want any help, let me know."

That was all she said, and Harriet asked no questions. Within the year the heir to the plantation died. Immediately the rumors spread that all the slaves would be sold. Panic followed. When Harriet saw the white woman again, she mentioned her fear. The woman nodded and softly repeated what she had already said.

Two more of Harriet's sisters were sold, and Harriet knew that she could wait no longer. Escape—with this hole in her forehead and the constant danger of unconsciousness? She knew she would need help. One day as the waterboy gave her a dip of water in the field, he whispered that she had just been sold to a slave trader.

She had to move without delay. The trader would collect her the next morning as his gang moved from one plantation to another. She whispered, "Lord, I've got to hold steady on to You, and You've got to see me through."

That night she wrapped a little food in a handkerchief and started for the house where the white woman lived. It might be a trap, but she had to take the risk. Years later she wrote, "I had reasoned this out in my mind; there was one of two things I had the *right* to: liberty or death. If I could not have one I would have the other, for no man should take me alive. I should fight for my liberty as long as my strength lasted."

When she finally knocked on the door, the woman welcomed her without surprise. She wasted no words. She was a "conductor" on the Underground Railroad. She told Harriet exactly how to find the next "station," where friends would feed her and guide her on the next lap of the way north.

In the black of the night Harriet set out. She knew she had to reach that first station by morning, for the patrol would be looking for her the moment the alarm was raised. The scar on her forehead would be her worst enemy.

By dawn she had reached the first stop. Everything happened as the woman had said.

Another white woman fed her, then gave her a broom and told her to work in the yard. This was as good a disguise as any, for a working black would not cause any suspicion.

That night her new friend's husband hid her in a wagon and started off down the road. Harriet always marveled at her trust. He might be delivering her back to her master for all she knew, but somehow she felt these people were doing God's work and would not betray her.

Before dawn the man stopped his wagon. He told her to hurry along by the river until she reached the next station, which he described to her carefully. He warned her against all roads by daylight.

It took her nearly two weeks to travel the ninety miles into the free state of Pennsylvania. She had been hidden in a haystack, rowed up a river, hidden by free blacks in a potato hole, concealed in an attic, and at last delivered into freedom.

"I looked at my hands to see if I was the same person. There was such a glory over everything . . . that I felt like I was in heaven."

These were not grandiose words. Harriet, like many other great people, had a deep and simple faith that a spiritual power was controlling her movements.

She reached Philadelphia, which was a nerve center of the Underground Railroad. The "terminus" was found in a room in the Lebanon Seminary. William Still, a black, was in charge, aided and supported by several other blacks and Quakers of the city. They did business twenty-four hours a day.

Harriet had caught a vivid glimpse of the careful, accurate, almost infallible work of rescuing fugitives. She told herself that if the slaves in the South knew that running away need not be a hit-or-miss business, they would leave by the hundreds. Everyone had to be free! The imagination, the courage, the faith, that made freedom a living experience filled her heart with joy.

She found a job in a hotel and saved every penny she could. She was determined to return to Maryland and bring out her parents. But one day, when she was in the "terminus" office with William Still, she learned that a message had come from the "conductor" in Cambridge, Maryland. He needed a foolproof means of transporting "two large bales of wool and two small." He was especially worried about the last stage of the journey from Baltimore to Philadelphia because of the "two little bales."

Harriet understood that "bales of wool" referred to adults and children, but to her absolute astonishment she heard the name Bowley mentioned.

"That's my brother-in-law's name!" she cried, and her eager questions brought out the fact that "the bales of wool" were indeed her own family: one of her sisters, her sister's two children and her husband, a free black.

"I'll go!" Harriet said promptly. Mr. Still replied with an emphatic "No." Placards describing Harriet and offering rewards were still being circulated.

"The conductor who meets the family in Baltimore will have to lead them openly through the streets of the city."

But Harriet persisted. "I'm the one who's going to Baltimore," she said stubbornly. Mr. Still yielded. He gave her instructions and a disguise.

The Bowleys, exhausted and trembling, were brought into a warm, sweet-smelling kitchen in Baltimore. A black man got up from a chair and said, "Mary!"

Mary Bowley did not recognize this "man" as her sister Harriet until she took off her battered man's hat. Then there were tears and embraces.

The Bowleys and Harriet remained hidden in the house for a week till the hue and cry died down. There were endless talks about the inalienable right of freedom and how to make certain an escape did not fail. The Bowleys' escape had been extremely dramatic.

Mary and the two children had actually been in the possession of the slave auctioneer, locked in the slave pen, before John Bowley had discovered their danger.

John went in desperation to a Quaker friend, and they formed a daring plot.

John arrived at the office of the slave market with a large official envelope. He handed it to the guard. The guard read, "Send the woman and children to the inn. I have a buyer." It was signed with the auctioneer's name.

The auctioneer was a stranger to the guard, so he accepted Bowley's word that he was the auctioneer's servant and shoved out Mary and the two children.

John Bowley gave no sign of knowing his wife. He wanted to run with them, hide, but instead he led them at a careful walking pace. He was terrified that the auctioneer might appear at any moment.

His wife was in tears, believing that in some way John was betraying them. After a long agonizing walk during which he could give her no comfort, they came to a quiet street. He looked around carefully, opened a gate, and said, "Quick now! Run!" A side door of the house opened, and the four vanished from sight.

They remained hidden in their Quaker host's attic till dark. Late that night they were concealed in a wagon and driven to a river. John, who knew how to sail a boat, was given instructions. When he drew near Baltimore he was to watch for two lights, one blue, one yellow. At dawn he saw the lights faintly gleaming. A white woman was waiting for them. He gave the password, "A friend with friends." She hid them in her wagon and drove them to the other side of town. All day they stayed out of sight in a stable, and with

night they darted through the shadows into the kitchen and to reunion with Harriet.

At the end of the week Harriet brought them safely through Baltimore and up the secret road to Philadelphia. She was exhilarated. Freedom was such a living fact that she would never let it go. The road from Baltimore to Philadelphia was less than a hundred miles, and in the months that followed she became as familiar with it as with the streets of those cities.

But her exhilaration was cut short. The year was 1850 and the Fugitive Slave Law was passed by Congress. This law altered the entire picture. Everyone on the Underground Railroad, every abolitionist, was studying the law as though his life depended on it; and, in fact, this was the case.

It was a monstrous law, a concession made to the slave owners by Northern politicians who hoped in this way to bridge the widening gulf between the North and the South. With this law no black, whether born in the North or a fugitive, was really safe.

The identification of a black could be made on the affidavit of a slave catcher without any effort to prove his word. The black could offer no defense or testify for himself or herself. The fee of the commissioner who settled the case was ten dollars if he found for the master and only five dollars if he freed the black. If a federal agent in any way hampered the seizure of the black, he was fined one thousand dollars. If a fugitive escaped, with or without his aid, the federal agent was held responsible for the entire value claimed for the black. Bystanders were required to assist in the recapture of a fugitive. Anyone convicted of aiding an escaped slave was liable to a fine of a thousand dollars or imprisonment for six months. The fugitive could be shot without question or sent to the Deep South where he or she would have less chance of another escape.

Even free blacks, with identity papers,

were not really safe. As for fugitives like Harriet and the fifty thousand like her in the North, they could be seized at any moment. There was no true safety south of Canada.

Free blacks left northern towns by the hundreds, heading for Canada, although black leaders urged their people to stay and resist. The Underground Railroad became more active than ever. Passengers arrived day and night, and now the escape routes had to extend straight across the North. More and more people who had hitherto been aloof were lending a hand. The cruelty of the new law was so outrageous that many believed it their duty to disobey it.

Harriet's own danger increased of course—and also her eagerness. Her whole point of view broadened. Originally she had dreamed only of saving her family. Now anyone with a black skin had a claim on her courage.

In the spring of 1851 she went down the long dark road to Maryland and brought out three men. In the fall she collected a small group of slaves from the neighborhood of her old home and led them safely into Philadelphia, where they were turned over to other "conductors" for the journey north.

Both times she talked about freedom to every black she met. For those bold enough to strike out for themselves, she explained the route carefully. She had a strong, clear way of talking.

As her returns became more frequent, a legend grew up around her. She was called Moses. In the dark of the night the slaves waited to hear her low song, "Go down, Moses, and tell old Pharaoh to let my people go."

Not only had the slaves made her a legend but the white masters as well. Who was this Moses? What man dared to storm the fortress of slavery? Harriet chuckled. Let them think her a man and she would break a few more chains of slavery.

Harriet had convictions and insights that ran counter to practical good sense. She believed God talked to her. Almost all of Harriet's trips were made in response to what Harriet believed was a divine command: "So-and-so is in danger," or "So-and-so needs you." She always found this was true.

She required absolute obedience of those who came away with her—silence, promptness. She had the strength to lift a man in her arms and run with him if he did not move quickly enough when danger loomed. She had the sharp intelligence to meet every emergency, and proof of this lay in the fact that, in nineteen trips into Maryland, she never lost a single slave of the three hundred she led to freedom. She had the iron courage also to carry a pistol wherever she went and threaten to use it if any of her charges showed timidity.

The sound of a horse galloping in the dark meant a quick concealment by the side of the road. The sudden wail of a slave baby meant an extra dose of paregoric so that it lay quietly in its mother's arms. Invariably she had to dominate the fears of her charges and never let them see a moment's hesitation on her part.

Although she was often fearful and more often exhausted, she never let the frightened and weary fugitives see this. She had to be heroic, calm, in complete control, twenty-four hours a day. Mere bodily safety was only one part of her mission. She opened the eyes of the blacks to many new responsibilities they would face. As they traveled she instructed, comforted, sang, gave them an education in what it meant to be a free people—the hardships, the glories.

She usually chose a Saturday night for the escape because a day then intervened before an advertisement for the runaway could appear. Her routes varied. Sometimes she went west toward the mountains. Other times she went toward Wilmington where her good friend Thomas Garrett (who before he died had passed more than three thousand fugitives over the underground line) was always waiting for her.

She had to be prepared for any danger leaping out of a bush. Remember, this was the woman who, at any moment, at the peak of any crisis, might lose consciousness because of that old injury to her head. But she believed God guided and protected her, and her actions were always shaped by this faith and her lightning-quick wits.

Once, riding north on a train, she heard her name spoken. Frozen with caution, she looked under the edge of her sunbonnet and saw a tall man reading aloud an advertisement to a companion. A runaway slave named Harriet Tubman with a scar on her forehead was worth the incredible reward of five thousand dollars.

Harriet kept her head lowered until she reached the next station. There she took a train going south, knowing that a black woman going in that direction as fast as the wheels could turn would not be suspected. She made her way to the town near her old home and did not resume her journey north until the hue and cry had died down.

The reward for her finally reached $40,000.

To be a woman *and* a black were twin handicaps in those days, but Harriet's magnificence as a human being overcame obstacles and won her a host of loyal friends.

As the shadows of a civil war deepened, she sometimes found that a station was no longer open. Once she arrived with eleven fugitives at a trusted hiding place. But the "conductor," seeing twelve desperate and weary runaways, slammed the door in their faces. "Too many! Too many! My place was searched last week!"

She stayed with these eleven all the way to Canada. The trip took almost a month. In Canada she remained with them through the winter, helping them find jobs, build houses, meet the terrible onslaughts of a cold they had never known. A small community was established to which she could bring other runaways. In Canada blacks had legal rights. In Canada black men became county officials and members of school boards. Their children went to school.

For the next six years she went into Maryland every fall and spring and brought out bondmen. Each trip was in obedience to what she termed that "inner voice." At one point her dreams directed her to three of her brothers, Ben, John, and William Henry. She knew how difficult it would be to reach them, as they belonged to different masters. So she wrote the following letter to a free black friend in Maryland named Jacob Jackson:

Read my letter to the old folks and give my love to them, and tell my brothers to be always watching unto prayer, and when the good old ship of Zion comes along to be ready to step on board.

William Henry Jackson

Jacob Jackson had an adopted son, William Henry, who had moved legally to the North. But William Henry Jackson had neither brothers nor old folk, so Jacob Jackson had to read the letter for another meaning. He knew "Moses," he knew her brothers, he knew "the good ship Zion" meant escape. He interpreted the letter correctly, *"Warn my brothers to be ready to leave."*

However, Jacob Jackson was not able to read this letter in leisurely privacy. He had to read it swiftly under the eyes of a white postmaster who, as a matter of course, opened any letters addressed to free blacks. The postmaster also knew that William Henry Jackson had no kin except the free black, Jacob.

Jacob pretended great stupidity. "It can't be meant for me nohow!" Then he hurried as fast as he could to get word to Harriet's three brothers. All of them wondered how she knew of their danger; the three brothers had been sold to a trader who was to pick them up the day after Christmas.

Harriet came for them on December 23. On the 29th, William Still wrote in his record book, "Moses arrived with six passengers." She had brought not only her three brothers but a girl whom her brother William wished to marry and two other slave men.

Harriet's train was never derailed. She never lost a passenger. Many of her friends in the North tried to explain the reason for this—her courage, her resourcefulness, her experience. They seemed reluctant to give it the mysterious quality of faith that Harriet gave it. She believed that God was directing her and no one could make her believe differently. She believed that her instructions came in her vivid dreams. In June, 1857, her nights were filled with dreams of her parents, Rit and Ben. All day she lived with the picture she had seen in her dreams—her parents in danger, about to be sold.

For years she had wanted to bring Rit and Ben into freedom. But she had hesitated, for they were old, and the kind of travel she required—forced marches through the woods, chin-high wading through rivers—demanded youth and agility. How could she get them off safely? How?

But because she had faith she started south. She had no idea what she would do. She made her way at night to her parents' cabin. She had not seen them for five years.

Her mother welcomed her with tears and said that Ben was being questioned day and night about the escape of a slave. The white men did not let him alone. They threatened to get rid of him, for any slave suspected of aiding a fugitive was a danger to the whole plantation.

When her father returned to the cabin, Harriet took him aside. "Where can I find a horse?" she asked.

He pursed his lips. So many slaves had been escaping that horses were no longer be-ing left in pastures at night. But he remembered Dollie Mae, an old "critter" a mile down the road at the next plantation.

"I'll get her," Harriet whispered. "You get together food and be ready."

In the starlit night she found the old horse lying down asleep. She roused her, got her to her feet, talked sweetly to her, wondering whether the old horse would have the strength to carry the old people to safety.

She still needed a wagon and some sort of harness. She tied the horse in the woods and slipped quietly into the yard back of the old master's barn. Sure enough, there was the wagon she remembered—hardly ever used because it was too small and rickety. Still moving like a ghost in the dark of the stable, she found a harness. Just as she was leaving she had a terrible fright. A slave she had never seen before suddenly appeared in the doorway. He stared at her without a word. Harriet put her fingers to her lips, slipped past him, and melted into the night.

She still had to bring the horse to the wagon, harness them together. Would the unknown slave give an alarm? She had to trust. Perhaps he was watching from the dark. She did not know. She managed to get the horse harnessed and hitched, and no alarm was raised. Quietly, quietly, she drove to the woods again and went back on foot for her parents.

Her father would not be separated from his old broadax. Her mother would not leave without her feather tick. Rit, weeping with nerves, was hoisted into the wagon and made comfortable on the feather tick. Ben climbed up beside Harriet. With scarcely a sound they moved down the road, the slow old horse doing her best.

When day came, they slept, hidden in a deep woods. Three nights later Harriet had gotten them miraculously to Thomas Garrett's in Wilmington.

From Wilmington the journey was safer

and easier, for friends took charge. All the way to Canada loving hands passed them on.

When they reached Canada, Harriet knew that her own way of life would have to change. She was now responsible for these old people of hers. They would be helpless, alone, in the cold of Canada. Although the United States was filled with danger for young blacks, she believed that some town in upper New York State, settled and civilized but close to the border, would be safe for such old ones. She thought back over the stops on the underground line. The little town of Auburn came to mind again and again.

She borrowed money and bought a small house in Auburn and settled her parents in comfort and safety.

That same year she met John Brown. He told her of his intention to free as many slaves as he could reach. He called her "General Tubman," for he considered her one of the greatest warriors in the anti-slavery ranks. He wanted all the advice and help she could give. She instantly loved and admired a man with such a dream of freedom, but she was afraid for him. His plans were impractical in too many details. Yet she helped.

John Brown had made a great effort to talk to her because her fame had reached far and wide. The *National Antislavery Standard,* a well read newspaper, commented at this time on a convention of slave masters being held near Harriet's old home in Maryland.

The operations of the Underground Railroad on the Maryland border within the last few years have been so extensive that in some neighborhoods the whole slave population have made their escape, and the convention is the result of the general panic on the part of the owners.

Harriet's name was not mentioned, but every reader, white or black, mentally supplied it.

All over the North, antislavery meetings were attracting vast crowds. Harriet was a coveted speaker.

She did not like this public speaking but she saw it as part of her job. She needed money for her work. She knew that freedom had to be stirred in the hearts of people. Often she shared the platform with famous men, white and black. Harriet, short, muscular, black as night, dressed in a gray gown with lace at her throat and jet buttons down the bodice, was frequently the only woman. She told of her escapes, told them simply, undramatically, but her vivid language and her deep, beautiful voice made the dangerous journeys as real to these people as their own safe journeys home.

To Harriet the greatest miracle of all was the free men and women who endangered their lives and properties for the sake of the slaves. She told of being trapped once in a swamp by a posse of white men. She and her passengers did not know which way to turn. She said, "Lord, I'm going to hold steady on to You."

As dusk came and the patrol was still shouting in the distance, closing in on the swamp, she saw a man walking up and down the edge of the swamp. He was a stranger. He wore the broad-brimmed hat of the Quaker, but slave agents sometimes disguised themselves as Quakers. Harriet crept as close as she could. She saw his lips moving, though he never turned in the direction of the swamp. She strained to hear. He was saying, "My wagon stands in the barnyard right across the way. The horse is in the stable. The harness hangs on a nail."

He repeated the words several times. Then he turned abruptly and disappeared. How had he known where to walk? How did he know she had heard?

After dark, Harriet crept out of the swamp and slithered her way to the yard. There was the wagon. She made sure no spy was concealed in it, for the traps devised by slave

masters were very ingenious. She found the horse, harness, and a bundle of food. She got her passengers safely through the cordon of the patrol.

That same year, 1859, John Brown led the insurrection at Harper's Ferry, failed, and was hanged. Harriet wept. Although she felt he had not used his means well, she marveled at his courage and his love of humanity. His death made her feel that she was not doing enough. It was all very well to lead runaways through the blackness of a southern night, but the North needed rousing as well.

She stopped one night in Troy, New York, on her way to Boston. A large crowd around the courthouse caught her attention. What was happening? A fugitive black had been seized, was being taken before the commissioner, and would be returned automatically to slavery.

Harriet did not pause for a moment. She saw the struggling young black in the grip of half a dozen police. She forced her way through the crowd until she stood beside him. Then she caught hold of a small boy and whispered urgently, "Go out in the street and holler 'Fire!' as loud as you can."

The child nodded and slipped away. She heard other voices, she heard the firebells begin to ring. The police were still holding on to their prisoner, waiting for the commissioner, when the new excitement made them loosen their grip. Harriet seized the young man's hand and with her muscular arm delivered a blow at the nearest policeman, knocking him down by this surprise attack. She and the young black fled down the steps, stumbled, fell.

In the excitement she forced her sunbonnet onto his head. When they regained their feet, the sunbonnet disguised him in the crowd. She got him safely away and into the hands of friends.

It was now 1860. Harriet made one more trip into Maryland, but her friends up and down the routes were fearful for her safety. When John Brown had been captured, lists of sympathizers had been seized with him. The danger was now sharpened and intensified.

But she continued to make her way safely. William Still in Philadelphia had hidden his record book, but on a loose sheet of paper he noted, "Arrived from Dorcester Co. 1860, Harriet Tubman's last trip to Maryland," and the names of her passengers.

Her friends hurried Harriet to Canada. They were convinced she was in extreme danger. Lincoln had just been elected, war was inevitable.

But Harriet could not stay in Canada. She knew too much to be idle. Her friend Governor Andrews of Massachusetts urgently recommended that the army use her as a scout, a spy, a nurse—wherever she was most needed.

The Union forces had taken the Sea Islands off the coast of Georgia. Slaves were spilling onto these islands claiming their freedom. Sick, desperate, starving, many bearing wounds inflicted by their owners as they fled—someone had to care for them.

In a dirty ramshackle room called a hospital, Harriet nursed them as best she could. Medical care in the army was practically unknown, despite the persistent efforts of Dorothea Dix[1] and Elizabeth Blackwell.[2]

Dysentery was sweeping the hospital. Harriet went into the woods and found the roots and herbs that cured dysentery. She brewed them, administered the brew, controlled the epidemic. Then she made pies and root beer to sell, and with the money bought food and supplies for her patients.

When the first black regiment, commanded by her old Boston friend, Thomas Wentworth Higginson, paraded into the town, she broke into tears. Men who had been slaves six weeks before now wore the uniform of Union soldiers and marched to the music of a white band playing the great antislavery song, "John Brown's Body."

She was asked to join the regiment as a scout. She went on several raiding missions that attacked enemy installations and brought out nearly eight hundred slaves.

For two years she served with the army, providing invaluable assistance. When the war came to an end, she was nursing once more at Fortress Monroe.

With the passage of the Thirteenth Amendment abolishing slavery, Harriet knew one phase of her life had ended and another begun. Women must have the vote!

She clamored for women's rights as cleverly as she had worked for black freedom. The freed slaves also concerned her; they must have education and jobs. She thought of a dozen ways to raise money for their schools.

She needed money for herself as well, for the Government had refused her a pension in spite of all the work she had done with the army. Her parents had died, her home in Auburn had become a way station for the poor and forsaken. The people of Auburn knew and admired her. Neighbors helped generously. An admirer wrote her biography and gave her the money from the royalties. She received twelve hundred dollars from the sales.

Harriet never became an "old woman," though she lived to be ninety-two. Her interest in and work for the sick, the poor, and

---

1. **Dorothea Dix:** an American reformer and Civil War nurse who crusaded to improve conditions in institutions during the 19th century.
2. **Elizabeth Blackwell:** America's first woman doctor, who tried to convince medical professionals of the need for sanitary conditions in hospitals.

the homeless kept her young and vital. A new generation heard the stories of her courage and exploits, the love that had led her to help the enslaved and abandoned.

When she died, the town of Auburn erected a monument in her honor. On the day that the bronze tablet was unveiled, the city's flags were flown at half-mast.

IN MEMORY OF HARRIET TUBMAN

• •

CALLED THE MOSES OF HER PEOPLE.
WITH RARE COURAGE SHE LED OVER
THREE HUNDRED NEGROES UP FROM
SLAVERY TO FREEDOM
AND RENDERED INVALUABLE SERVICE
AS NURSE AND SPY.
WITH IMPLICIT TRUST IN GOD
SHE OVERCAME EVERY OBSTACLE.

• •

THIS TABLET IS ERECTED
BY THE CITIZENS OF AUBURN.

## Getting at Meaning

1. Which incidents related in this selection illustrate the extreme hardships endured by many slaves?

2. When Harriet prevents the overseer from catching the fleeing slave, what does she reveal about her own character? What do the other slaves think of her actions?

3. Harriet's scar is her enemy, because it makes her identification easy. How does the scar help her to begin life as a free woman?

4. What character traits are possessed by the conductors and the passengers on the Underground Railroad?

5. Give two examples of incidents that demonstrate Harriet Tubman's ". . . deep and simple faith that a spiritual power was controlling her movements."

6. In the escapes of both Harriet Tubman and the Bowley family, how does racial prejudice actually make the escapes easier?

7. Describe the Fugitive Slave Law. What were its intended effects? In what sense did it backfire?

8. Why is Harriet such an effective conductor on the Underground Railroad?

9. How are the views of Harriet Tubman and John Brown different?

10. What makes Harriet Tubman particularly well qualified to be a nurse and a scout during the Civil War?


## Developing Skills in Reading Literature

1. **Biography.** The admiration felt by this biographer for her subject is evident in the statement, ". . . Harriet's magnificence as a human being overcame obstacles. . . ." Find four examples from the selection to illustrate the truth of this comment.

2. **Allusion.** Harriet's nickname is Moses; her song is "Go Down, Moses." Explain this Biblical allusion. Why is the allusion especially appropriate to Harriet Tubman and her work?

3. **Extended Metaphor.** An extended metaphor expands an initial comparison to related items. What comparison does the term Underground Railroad imply? How are the two things compared similar? How are they different? How do the terms conductor, station, and terminus extend the initial comparison?


## Developing Vocabulary

**Latin Roots.** Circulated and terminus are among the words in this selection that are derived from Latin. Both words belong to word families that share common Latin roots. Other members of the same word families are as follows:

| | |
|---|---|
| circulated | terminus |
| circle | terminate |
| circulation | terminal |

Add one word to each word family. Then list two words that share a common root with each of these words:

vision    import


## Developing Writing Skills

**Writing a Report.** Many people, even in recent history, have struggled to gain freedom, to start new lives, and to survive the hardships of economic failure. Interview your parents, grandparents, and neighbors to find one of these people. Then interview the individual, asking questions about motivation, dangers, personal sacrifices, and ultimate success or failure. Take notes during the interview and then use these notes to write a five-paragraph report.

# Nellie Bly—Woman Reporter

*Iris Noble*

In the summer of 1887 Nellie Bly was in New York, and the first three months were the worst of her life.

It was hot, the hottest summer the city had known. Every day brought new accounts of people sickening and dying of the terrible, stifling heat. Work must go on; somehow people dragged themselves out of their homes in the mornings, hurried into the slight protection of the buildings where they worked, sat sweltering until it was time to go home, drooping, panting, perspiring in the horse trolleys, or slowly walking the streets. They crowded the brownstone stoops or the fire escapes in the evenings and hoped in vain for a cool breeze that would let them sleep at night.

Even with this pall upon it, New York was still a shock of noise and rushing movement, crowds of people and a babel of different languages. Immigrants were pouring into the city from Europe. Strange tongues, strange costumes, strange foods and habits put their stamp of cosmopolitan life upon this great seaport. The streets were thronged with vehicles of every kind—from the huge wooden brewery carts drawn by ponderous, massive horses, four teams linked together, to the dainty broughams and carriages with their graceful, thoroughbred horses, to the push-carts pulled by human hands—all clattering noisily over the rough cobblestones and all raising clouds of dust for the eyes of the pedestrians. Over the general hubbub of wheels and human voices rang out the hawkers crying their wares: the vegetable women; the applecarts; the milkmen who poured their thick, cream-clotted liquid from huge vats directly into the jugs of the housemaids; the vendors of shoelaces and buttons, handkerchiefs and scarfs; the chimney sweeps; the men who trundled cakes of ice in wheelbarrows, chipping off bits of it for a penny; and lately—an innovation by the publishers of the *World*—newsboys yelling on the street corners.

The heat, the noise, the strangeness—none of these daunted Nellie. She was young and she was strong. In fact, the uproar of the great city stimulated and thrilled her. The great city, though, wanted nothing whatever to do with her. No one would hire her. No one would even take her seriously.

For weeks she had tramped the pavements and the cobblestones of New York, besieging the newspaper publishers. No editor in his right mind would give a woman a job on his paper; this was the verdict she got and she was made to feel it in every possible fashion —insultingly, patronizingly, kindly, fatherly, curtly, with unnecessary humiliation. The *Times*, the *Tribune*, the *Sun*, the *World*—at the *World* she had not been allowed to speak to anyone but a copy boy, and the others had been almost as bad.

She had even written to John Cockerill of the *World,* offering as a stunt to go up in the balloon ascension sponsored by the paper in St. Louis. Cockerill had answered the letter, expressing his interest—but also his regret. And now she could not even get in to see him.

The stout courage, the high hopes, slowly ebbed away. She was reaching desperation when one day the final blow fell. She was robbed of her purse while she sat on a bench in Central Park. All of her money was gone. She was penniless, stranded, jobless.

That night she cried in great, shaking sobs of despair.

This was the end. She would have to give up, go home, beg Madden to give her her job back. But strangely, even as she was at last admitting her failure, something in her rebelled. She sat up on her hard, lumpy boardinghouse bed, pushing her hair back from her tear-soaked face. How could she go back? There must be a way for her to stay here. Had she really fought hard enough? Had it been too easy for her before, walking into Madden's office that first day and walking out with an assignment?

The next day she determined to make her last try. If it failed, she would go home.

She got off the trolley at the corner of what was called "Park Row"—the row of newspapers and journals. She walked quickly past the *Day Book*, past the *Tribune* offices, past Baker and Godwin, Printers, past the Currier and Ives Building. She crossed the street to where the *Times* majestically occupied the whole triangle apex of two converging streets, but she gave it hardly a glance. She was on her way to the building with the gold dome.

Why a gold dome? The New York *World* had once belonged to Jay Gould, who had treated it not only as a newspaper but as a means to further his own financial schemes. It was nothing, without reputation or subscribers, when Joseph Pulitzer bought it. In a few short years he had transformed it into one of the country's foremost newspapers, and he had built a big gold dome over it that could be seen through most of the windows of New York—to flaunt his success in the eyes of the other Park Row publishers who

had once laughed at him.

Nellie walked up the broad steps into the small dark lobby and up to the low gate and railing that separated this lobby from the busy offices beyond.

"I want to see Mr. Cockerill," she told the guard.

"I'm sorry, miss. No one can see him today. That's orders."

She rested her gloved hands on the top of the gate. To the dismayed eyes of the guard it was as if she had taken a grip that only force would break.

"I intend to see Mr. Cockerill. If I have to stay here all day and all night and all day tomorrow—I mean to see him. This is a matter of life and death for me."

"Oh, come, miss. It can't be that serious. Please—come back some other day. We're right on deadline getting out the Sunday paper and everybody is up to their necks in work."

She was wearing a thin summer dress of gray lawn trimmed in coral braid and a gray straw hat with a white veil. In spite of the heat and the pounding fear and anger inside her, she managed to look coolly poised. "I repeat. If you don't tell Mr. Cockerill I am here, I will wait right at this gate all day long."

"She'll soon get tired of that game," the usher confided to a reporter who was passing by. The reporter carelessly agreed, then looked at Nellie. He looked a second time and was not quite so sure. He had never seen such determination in a human face.

At any rate, this promised a little fun and variety to the day. He told a friend about it. The word spread like a chuckle through the main floor corridor, into offices and up the stairs. Reporters grinned at each other; a man from the circulation department popped his head out of his door to ask what the joke was all about; office boys who had been dodging work under the big back staircase suddenly found all kinds of errands that would bring them into the front lobby. They wanted to see the fun, too.

An hour went by. Two hours. The guard returned and he was angry this time.

"Miss, you will just have to leave. You're blocking passage for everybody coming in and going out, and I am not going to disturb Mr. Cockerill for you. The managing editor is a busy man. Now, do I have to make trouble for you?"

She was tired. Her legs were trembling with the strain of standing so long in one position; her back muscles ached with the effort to stand straight and tall. It was horrible to be threatened this way, worse even than being laughed at—and she was well aware of the laughter and the ridicule that was being directed her way—by the grinning faces, the open stares, the whispers and the jokes, by the way more and more of the copy boys found impudent excuses to come out front to get a look at her. Nellie was heartsick. She wanted to run away. If it were not for the desperation that gripped her, frantic and reckless, she would have done so. But she *would not go*.

"What am I going to do with her, sir?" the guard appealed to the advertising manager.

"Don't be a fool, Peters. Tell her to go. She's disrupting the whole place. All right! *I'll* get rid of her."

In three minutes he, too, was back, defeat and frustration written clearly on his face. Now the matter was getting serious. Should they call the police? He gathered up the head of the city desk, a circulation man, several reporters—the group growing and growing as he moved through the offices. They collected in the main corridor, arguing among themselves as to the best method of getting rid of this girl.

"Call the police—she's probably off her head, anyway. . . ."

"Let her stay there. She'll get tired. . . ."

"But why does she want to see Cockerill? He hates women—that kind of woman. . . ."

"She claims she was a reporter in Pittsburgh. . . ." ". . . call the police . . . no, don't, the other newspapers would use it against us. . . ." "Well, what else can we do?" "Maybe, if we talked to her again. . . ."

Someone laughed. It was Bill Nye, the paper's famous humor columnist and one of the great wits of his time. They all turned and looked at him. What was so funny?

"While you're standing there arguing, gentlemen, I think the matter has already been solved for you. Look"—he pointed past them down the hall toward the stairs leading to the next floor—"do you see what I see? The young lady seems to have taken the initiative out of your hands."

They looked and gasped. With their backs turned, while their attention was on their argument, Nellie had quietly opened the gate and just as quietly walked down the corridor and past them—already going up the stairs.

"Here! You! You can't go up there!" The advertising manager moved to cut her off, but Bill Nye held him back.

"Oh, let her in. Anyone with that much determination deserves a break."

"But Cockerill—"

"Let Cockerill handle her. He'll send her packing. But if you want my opinion, I hope he doesn't. I admire that kind of courage."

The rest of them stared at him dumbfounded. But in spite of themselves, one or two had been impressed the same way; they were reluctant to admit it but once Nye said it, they could, too.

"Sure—let her see him." "He'll eat her alive. . . ." "Let her have a chance. . . ."

The city editor cut it short. "So help me—all right! But when he comes roaring down here looking for somebody to put the blame on, just remember it wasn't me that wanted it. Nye, you'll have to be the goat. If I had my way it would be the police for her. Here, boy!" he signaled to an avidly interested, eavesdropping copy boy. "Run upstairs and find her. Show her the way to Cockerill's office. Don't try to explain to him. Just let her do her own talking!"

Nellie saw the boy coming, rushing up to her on the stairs. She wanted to cry and she was angry at the same time, angry at herself for her weakness of tears and angry at these stupid people who were going to stop her when she was this close to her goal. Well, she was past caring for her dignity. If they were going to stop her they would have to send someone besides a boy, because they were going to have to haul her off those steps physically!

The boy didn't touch her. He passed her. He turned, slightly. "This way, miss. Follow me. I'll take you to Mr. Cockerill's office." The disdain and cheekiness in his voice failed to reach Nellie. She only heard the words: those unbelievable, undreamed-of words. She had made it! She had passed the barrier. The boy was her *escort*.

He led the way up the three flights to the big offices under the gold dome of the *World*. Nellie slowly followed. Now her knees were really shaking, both with the ordeal of her three hours of standing and with the reaction that set in now that she had won. She could hardly believe it.

In the torture of those three hours something had happened to her that was both good and bad. She had gained a strength she did not realize she possessed. In the core of her something had hardened and toughened, something that would stand her in good stead in the struggles she would face in the future. But she had lost, too—lost much of her youthful optimism, her buoyant expectancy, her trust in other people. A tiny seed was planted of self-will, of tough, egoistic self-preservation, and of suspicion that was always afterward to damage her relations with other people.

The top floor was quiet, its carpeted hall wide. The offices were big and few, and two of them bore the magical names in gold leaf: JOHN A. COCKERILL, MANAGING EDITOR, and the other adjoining it: JOSEPH PULITZER, PUBLISHER.

The boy knocked and opened the door—then fled.

A large desk occupied the center of the room. From behind it the managing editor got to his feet. He was a big man, dignified and reserved. His mustache usually made him look stern and forbidding, but right now surprise and astonishment robbed him of his dignity. His mouth gaped.

"What is this? Young lady, what are you doing here? I gave instructions I wasn't to be disturbed!"

"I know. Don't blame the men downstairs. They did their best to keep me out. I'm Nellie Bly, Mr. Cockerill. I had to see you and I was determined to see you. It's too important to me to waste time being polite about it. I've stood down there and fought for three hours to get to see you, and I wouldn't have done that if I hadn't thought it was just as important to you as it is to me!"

She moved to the desk and stood facing him. Even though her legs trembled, her voice rang with passionate sincerity because she was staking all on this: that she could convince him she was *necessary* to him, not that he was doing her a favor.

He pursed his lips. He was trying to remember the name. "Nellie Bly? Oh, yes, you sent me a letter. And then I had one from Madden in Pittsburgh. Good man, Madden. A good editor."

"Then you must respect his judgment. And *he* hired me—he didn't want me to leave *his* paper. I'm asking you for a job, Mr. Cockerill. I know"—raising a gloved hand to stop his protests—"you have all the good reporters you need, and if you did need more it wouldn't be a woman. To get this job I'd have to offer you something special, something different. Well, that's what I'm doing. I can give you stories that would be unusual, a kind you've never had in your paper before—no paper ever has!—for that matter. If Mr. Madden had faith in me to write what he called my sensational stories, can't you give me a chance? At least listen to me?"

"Sensational?" John Cockerill was cautious, but his alert newspaper sense came alive. He had been on the point of dismissing her, but the *World* was a booming, fast-growing newspaper coming up from nowhere to challenge the big, established press of the city, and to do so demanded new, fresh, out-of-the-ordinary approaches. "What do you mean by sensational?"

She had a small, thin book of clippings with her and she laid them on his desk. Then she sank into a chair. A horrible thing had happened. She found herself so weak she couldn't stand up, so wrought up her throat had choked to the point where she could hardly speak.

She tried to tell him of her work on the *Dispatch*, but it didn't sound capable; it sounded more like a child telling a grown man that she had behaved well in school that year. Cockerill put up a hand to stop her talking; he was completely absorbed in the clippings.

Slightly behind her, the connecting door between Cockerill's office and that of Pulitzer quietly opened. Nellie did not hear it. She wasn't aware that a tall, thin, powerfully built man with a large head had come noiselessly into the room. John Cockerill raised his head and saw, but the figure motioned him to silence.

Nellie swallowed. She began again to plead.

"That's the sort of thing I want to do here. I read every paper in New York every day. They all print the same things—yours is the only one that is different—but even you—

it's still stories about Tammany Hall,[1] stories about Mrs. Astor and Mr. Rockefeller, Jay Gould and President Cleveland and finance and legislation. I want to write about the *other* New York. Since I've been here I've gone into every corner of the city—the wharfs, the Bowery,[2] the tenements, the shops and factories—I've looked everywhere —and everywhere there are stories for you."

Cockerill studied her. He had lost his first anger at her bursting in on him; but even though he was beginning to listen seriously, he was still unwilling to accept what she said. "You're right about one thing. We do want those stories. But we make our own efforts to get them. The *World* has a reputation for being interested in the lives of the people of this city; in fact, we've been accused of bad journalism because we poke our noses in where they aren't wanted. What do you have to offer that is so different?"

She took a deep breath. This was the moment. If she could sell him now!—"I can give you *real* stories. From the inside. My idea is to actually work in the shops and then give you the story of what goes on inside them. I won't be just interviewing people; I'll share their experiences, put myself in their place. Think of the possibilities, Mr. Cockerill! Don't you want to know what a servant in a home really thinks, what the work is really like? You see people going into employment agencies—the *World* can have a reporter who actually goes in and applies for a job and finds out what it is like! Do you want to know what it is to be a sick person in a charity hospital, what kind of treatment he's getting? I'll *be* that sick person. Do you want an idea of what it feels like to be a prisoner in a jail or someone asking for relief from a social agency? You have good reporters. They give you their eyes and their ears to get the facts—but they can't get them all and they can't give you the emotion, the feeling, the distress and the suffering—be-cause they don't live through it themselves. That's what I can give you. I'll go behind the scenes, and people will talk to me as they won't to an outsider. And my stories won't be just what someone else is willing to tell me; they will be *my own*, they will be about Nellie Bly working as a servant, or lying sick in a hospital or . . ."

"Turn around."

The deep voice, with its thick German gutturals, coming so unexpectedly behind her so startled Nellie that she flung herself around, out of her chair, her back to the desk.

The man who came slowly up to her and peered at her through unusually thick lenses with eyes that were almost blind was a stranger to her. Yet she knew him. His hand went out and touched her shoulder, and she knew that hand. Even in that slight impersonal touch she felt a nervous, potent strength that almost communicated words to her. A power emanated from him. A short, luxuriant Vandyke beard pointed up his thin, rough-carved face with haughtiness, impressiveness. Otherwise it was an ugly face.

She knew the face immediately. This was Joseph Pulitzer.

Not more than forty years old, he seemed an awesome sight to her eyes. This was the man who had emigrated to America a penniless youngster, an Austrian who spoke no English—yet this fabulous man now owned two of the country's largest newspapers, had been elected to the Missouri legislature, fought a duel, been responsible as no other man had for the fact that the Statue of Liberty stood in New York's harbor, and had been credited with electing a president of the United States. To his admirers he was a gen-

---

1. **Tammany Hall** (tam′ə nē): a powerful Democratic political organization of New York City.
2. **the Bowery** (bou′ ər ē): a street in New York City characterized by flophouses and saloons.

ius; to his enemies, a devil they regarded with superstitious awe.

His hand dropped from her shoulder. Courteously he motioned her to a seat, then took one himself. One arm rested on the desk, the other on the arm of his chair while his long, tapering fingers caressed the blue-veined temple of his forehead.

"Talk some more, please. I was interested. *What* shop? *What* hospital do you plan to go into? How? Can you fool some doctor into thinking you are sick?"

The thick *d* and *t*, the strongly accented vowels, were the heritage of his European background.

"Yes, I can if I have to." She named hospitals, orphan asylums, factories that hired women. "I can put on a shabby dress and pretend that I need charity and spend the night at The Home for Needy Women—I caught a glimpse of it the other day, and I think if I were down and out I'd rather sleep in the streets than go there. I know where women rent sewing machines and take them home to sew dresses or what they call 'piece-work.' The men who give them the materials are called 'sweaters' because that's just what they do—sweat those poor women for a few pennies a day. Then I talked to a woman yesterday who had a sister taken away to Black-well's Island for the Insane. She was crying. She had heard terrible stories about that island."

"*You* could get onto that island?"

"Yes." She said it without pause, although this had not occurred to her before.

"How? I suppose you think you could pretend to be insane?" Pulitzer's voice was insulting, heavy with scorn.

If she said she could do it and then she failed—but she *wouldn't* fail! "I will pretend to be insane. I will get on that island and no one will ever suspect that I am a reporter. Isn't that a challenge, Mr. Pulitzer? If I could do that. . . ."

"If you could—if rabbits could fly." Then suddenly his whole face seemed to change, to become very still. There was a long pause, and silence. Seconds passed. Both Nellie and Cockerill stared at the motionless figure of the great publisher, caught in a breathless kind of tenseness that seemed to emanate from him. He was unaware of them, rubbing the back of one hand with the other in an unconscious but troubled manner.

When he spoke again it was with such a harsh, impetuous manner that it startled both of them. "Yes! I think you could," he said. "I am just crazy enough to think you could." Behind his thick lenses his eyes glinted. He nodded his head rapidly. "I like you. You don't think anything is impossible. When I came first to this country, everyone told me *no*. No, you cannot do this. No, you cannot do that. But I did it. They laughed because I ran, ran, ran—all the time. But I got the story and the others did not. I did not think anything was impossible. You are like that. You are so young and so eager and so sure, and that is a good thing for a reporter to be. But aren't you afraid? The police wouldn't like it if you tried to fool them. And aren't you afraid of being locked up with crazy people, shut up on the island with them?"

He had, purposely she knew, picked out the toughest job to test her on.

"I've never been afraid of anything," she declared stoutly. It was not true; she had been afraid downstairs and she had been afraid in this very room, only a few minutes ago. But it wouldn't do to tell them that.

Pulitzer suddenly winced. He put a hand in front of his eyes to shield them. "Pull the shades, will you please, John?" he asked Cockerill. The editor hastened to obey, feeling guilty that he had forgotten one of the basic rules of the office—there must never be a crack of sunlight in a room when the publisher was there. Light was excruciatingly painful to his eyes, just as noise was unbearable to his nerves.

"Please, try me out on that story—if that is the one you want," Nellie found herself almost whispering. "I'm so sure of myself I will gamble with you. If I can get onto Blackwell's Island and get a story for you on the treatment of the insane, get in there by pretending to be insane myself, will you give me a job—as a reporter on the *World?*"

"If you can do that . . ." he left it dangling there. He was very thoughtful. "But why do you want so much to do this? You want to go out and do crazy stunts because they are a thrill? *Nein,*" [3] he said, answering his own question. "It's more than that, isn't it? You care about what happens to those people. I, too, care about them." To the other two in the room it was as if he had gone away from them in his thoughts and was brooding alone. "I believe in democracy." The way he said it, the word democracy was a precious thing. "When I bought this paper in '83, I ran the first issue on May 10th—and I put in it a statement. It said the *World* was a '. . . journal dedicated to the cause of the people rather than that of the purse potentates . . . that will expose all fraud and sham, fight all public evils and abuses—that will serve and battle for the people with earnest simplicity.' That is what I said. We have done that, too, eh, John?"

Though he looked at Cockerill, Nellie knew he was talking to her. She caught her breath, in hope and in dread. What did he mean to do about her? Would he take her up on her gamble?

"From every bit of information we've been able to receive, Blackwell's is not a very nice place—not for a young lady," Cockerill said.

But Pulitzer shook his head. "We will gamble with her, John. I think she will come to no harm. But," he added, turning to her, "you must stay there at least a week. You must not tell anyone you are a newspaper-

woman. And you must do this all alone. We will not help you, not with the doctors or the wardens or with anyone. If you get a good story, then you will have a job here. I promise it."

Nellie's excitement blazed out of her eyes. She tried to thank them both at the same time, but she was incoherent and could only stammer. Quick tears came into her eyes.

Cockerill ushered her to the door. "You go home now and wait, Miss Bly. You'll be sent word when to try this stunt of yours. I'll need time to clear space for the story and check with our legal department on the risks—it may be a week or more before you hear from us. Leave your address at the desk downstairs as you go out."

She turned to go. Again Joseph Pulitzer did an unprecedented thing. Something from his own terrible, poverty-stricken youth—the times when he lived on a bowl of soup as a whole day's meal—came to his mind. "Have you any money? Can you wait those few days or perhaps a week?"

"Oh!" she gasped. "I forgot!" She told them the story of her lost purse. "I can't even pay my rent!"

Pulitzer fumbled in his pocket and drew out a shabby old cloth purse. He fumbled with the clasp, opened it, tried to see the coins inside. His half-blind eyes could not distinguish one from the other, however, and he gave up. "Give her a voucher, John. Give her twenty-five dollars." Then, to Nellie: "We will call you. This money, this is not a loan, it is an advance on your salary. I feel it, *surely,* that you are going to bring us a fine story. And then you will work for me."

She didn't walk downstairs, she floated.

If it was not to her credit that she enjoyed her revenge, at least it was very human. She walked up to the guard. "You are to write down my name and address for Mr. Cockerill,

---

3. **Nein** (nīn) *German:* no.

so that he can get in touch with me." The guard was not impressed. "And you will please direct me to the cashier's office. I want to get this voucher cashed. It is an advance on my salary."

The guard's face remained impassive, but at the sight of Pulitzer's signature on the voucher his eyes were like marbles.

"Yes, miss. Come *right* this way, miss."

## Getting at Meaning

1. How does Nellie react to the noise and clamor of the city? What change occurs in Nellie as she fails to find a job?

2. What forces drive Nellie to stand for three hours at the gate in the newspaper office? What positive effects do those three hours have on her character? What negative effects do they have?

3. The *World* has a reputation as an innovative newspaper. What new manner of selling papers have they recently introduced?

4. What unique talents does Nellie offer the *World*?

5. Why does Pulitzer change his mind about Nellie?

## Developing Skills in Reading Literature

1. **Character.** Make a list of Nellie's character traits. Then make a list of Pulitzer's traits. Compare the lists. What is Nellie's one big disadvantage in finding a job as a reporter?

What was Pulitzer's disadvantage when he first arrived in America?

2. **Biography.** A skilled biographer presents a balanced view of his or her subject. The reader learns not only the subject's strengths, but also that person's weaknesses and less desirable qualities. Does the writer of this selection succeed in giving a balanced view of Nellie Bly? Support your answer with details from the story.

## Developing Vocabulary

**Word Origins.** The word *brougham,* which appears in the third paragraph of this selection, is derived from Lord Brougham, a nineteenth century British statesman. The following words also are related to proper names. Look up each in a dictionary and write the name of the person or place from which the word is derived.

| | |
|---|---|
| ritzy | cologne |
| chartreuse | silhouette |
| diesel | bedlam |

Choose three of the above words and research their origins in a book of word origins. Explain in detail the connection between the person or place and the word.

## Developing Writing Skills

1. **Writing Dialogue.** When she applies for a job as a reporter, Nellie is rejected *insultingly, patronizingly, kindly, fatherly,* and *curtly.* Write a passage of dialogue for each of these rejections. For example, write several insulting statements that an editor might have used to reject Nellie. Consult a dictionary if you need help with the meanings of these words.

2. **Writing a Report.** Nellie Bly was the pen name of Elizabeth Cochrane Seaman. Do some additional research on this woman's life and prepare a five-paragraph report on what you learn. Try to find out whether Nellie did get into the insane asylum, whether she got the job with the *World,* and what she accomplished in her life.

shedding his skin. Snakes are irritable and nervous while shedding, and the hamadryad had trouble sloughing off the thin membrane covering his eyes. Grace wrote in her diary, "I stroked his head and then pulled off the eyelids with eyebrow forceps. He flinched a little but was unafraid. He put out his tongue in such a knowing manner! I mounted the eyelids and they looked just like pearls. What a pity that there have been nothing but unfriendly, aggressive accounts about this sweet snake. Really, the intelligence of these creatures is unbelievable."

The King of Kings was so heavy that Grace was unable to lift him by herself. Jule offered to help her carry the snake outside for a picture. While Jule and Grace were staggering out the door with the monster reptile between them, the king suddenly reared and rapped Jule several times on her forehead with his closed mouth. "He's trying to tell you something!" exclaimed Grace. He was indeed. I saw that the Chinese crocodile had rushed out from under a table and had grabbed the hamadryad by the tail. Jule relaxed her grip, and the king dropped his head and gave a single hiss. The croc promptly let go, and the women bore the cobra out into the sunlight. I was the only person who seemed upset by the incident.

Out of curiosity, I asked Grace if she ever used music in taming her snakes. She laughed and told me what I already knew: all snakes are deaf. Grace assured me that the Hindu fakir[1] uses his flute only to attract a crowd, and by swaying his own body back and forth the fakir keeps the snake swaying as the cobra is feinting to strike. The man times his music to correspond to the snake's movements, and it appears to dance to the tune. The fakir naturally keeps well outside the cobra's striking range. Years later when I was in India, I discovered that this is exactly what happens. I never saw any snake charmer even approximate Grace's marvelous power over reptiles.

Grace's main source of income was to exhibit her snakes to tourists, although she was occasionally able to rent a snake to a movie studio (she always went along to make sure the reptile wasn't frightened or injured), and sometimes she bought ailing snakes from dealers, cured them, and resold them for a small profit to zoos. While I was with her, a dusty car stopped and discharged a plump couple with three noisy children who had seen her modest sign GRACE RILEY—REPTILES. Grace explained that she would show them her collection, handle the poisonous snakes, call over the tame alligators, and let the children play with Rocky, an eighteen-foot Indian rock python that she had raised from a baby. The charge was twenty-five cents. "That's too much," the woman said to her husband, and they went back to the car. Grace sighed. "No one seems interested in my snakes. No one really cares about them. And they're so wonderful."

One day Grace telephoned me to say that she had gotten a new shipment of snakes, including some Indian cobras from Siam. "One of them has markings that form a complete *G* on the back of his hood," she told me. "Isn't it curious that the snake and I have the same initial! I call him My Snake." We laughed about this, and then Jule and I went out to Cypress to take a last set of pictures of Grace and her snakes for an article I was doing about this remarkable woman.

We took several pictures, and then I asked Grace to let me get a picture of the cobra with the *G* on the hood. "I didn't look very well in those other pictures," said Grace anxiously. "I'll comb my hair and put on another blouse." She was back in a few minutes. Jule and I had set up our cameras in the yard be-

---

1. **fakir** (fə kir'): a beggar who claims to perform miracles.

hind the barn. I wanted a shot of the cobra with spread hood, and Grace brought him out cradled in her arms. Before allowing me to take the picture, she removed her glasses as she felt that she looked better without them. The cobra refused to spread, and Grace put him down on the ground and extended her flat palm toward him to make him rear —something I had often seen her do before, but never without her glasses.

I was watching through the finder of my camera. I saw the cobra spread and strike as I clicked the shutter. As the image disappeared from the ground glass of my Graflex, I looked up and saw that the snake had seized Grace by the middle finger. She said in her usual quiet voice, "Oh, he's bitten me."

I dropped the camera and ran toward her, feeling an almost paralyzing sense of shock, for I knew that Grace Wiley was a dead woman. At the same time I thought, "It's just like the book," for the cobra was behaving exactly as textbooks on cobras say they behave. He was deliberately chewing on the wound to make the venom run out of his glands. It was a terrible sight.

Quietly and expertly, Grace took hold of the snake and gently forced his mouth open. I knew that her only chance for life was to put a tourniquet around the finger instantly and slash open the wound to allow the venom to run out. Seconds counted. I reached out my hand to take the snake above the hood so she could immediately start squeezing out the venom, but Grace motioned me away. She stood up, still holding the cobra, and walked into the barn. Carefully, she put the snake into his cage and closed the door.

This must have taken a couple of minutes, and I knew that the venom was spreading through her system each moment. "Jule," said Grace, "call Wesley Dickinson. He's a herpetologist and a friend of mine. He'll know what to do." Calmly and distinctly she gave Jule the telephone number and Jule ran

to the phone. Then Grace turned to me. Suddenly she said, "He didn't really bite me, did he?" It was the only emotion I saw her show. I could only say, "Grace, where's your snakebite kit?" We both knew that nothing except immediate amputation of her arm could save her, but anything was worth a chance.

She pointed to a cabinet. There was a tremendous collection of the surgical aids used for snake bite, but I don't believe any of the stuff had been touched for twenty years. I pulled out a rubber tourniquet and tried to twist it around her finger. The old rubber snapped in my hands. Grace didn't seem to notice. I pulled out my handkerchief and tried that. It was too thick to go around her finger, and I twisted it around her wrist. "I'll faint in a few minutes," said Grace. "I want to show you where everything is before I lose consciousness."

Cobra venom, unlike rattlesnake venom, affects the nervous system. In a few minutes the victim becomes paralyzed and the heart stops beating. I knew Grace was thinking of this. She said, "You must give me strychnine injections to keep my heart going when I begin to pass out. "I'll show you where the strychnine is kept. You may have to give me caffeine also."

She walked to the other end of the room and I ran alongside trying to keep the tourniquet in place. She got out the tiny glass vials of strychnine and caffeine and also a hypodermic syringe with several needles. I saw some razor blades with the outfit and picked one up, intending to make a deep incision to let out as much of the venom as possible. Grace shook her head. "That won't do any good," she told me. Cobra venom travels along the nerves, so making the wound bleed wouldn't be very effective, but it was all I could think of to do.

Jule came back with a Mr. Tanner, Grace's cousin who lived next door. Tanner immediately got out his jackknife, intending to cut open the wound, but Grace stopped him. "Wait until Wesley comes," she said. Tanner told me afterward that he was convinced that if he had amputated the finger, Grace might have lived. This is doubtful. Probably nothing except amputation of her arm would have saved her then, and we had nothing but a jackknife. She probably would have died of shock and loss of blood.

Grace lay on the floor to keep as quiet as possible and slow the absorption of the venom. "You'd better give me the strychnine now, dear," she told Jule. Jule snapped off the tip of one of the glass vials, but the cylinder broke in her hands. She opened another tube and tried to fill the syringe; the needle was rusted shut. Jule selected another needle, tested it, and filled the syringe. "I'm afraid it will hurt," she told Grace. "Now don't worry, dear," said Grace comfortingly. "I know you'll do it very well."

After the injection, Grace asked Jule to put a newspaper under her head to keep her hair from getting dirty. A few minutes later, the ambulance arrived, with Wesley Dickinson following in his own car. Wesley had telephoned the hospital and arranged for blood transfusions and an iron lung. As Grace was lifted into the ambulance, she called back to Tanner, "Remember to cut up the meat for my frogs very fine and take good care of my snakes." That was the last we ever saw of her.

Grace died in the hospital half an hour later. She lived about ninety minutes after being bitten. In the hospital, Wesley directed the doctors to drain the blood out of her arm and pump in fresh blood. When her heart began to fail, she was put into the lung. She had become unconscious. Then her heart stopped. Stimulants were given. The slow beating began again but grew steadily weaker. Each time stimulants were given, the heart responded less strongly and finally stopped forever.

We waited with Mr. and Mrs. Tanner at the snake barn, calling the hospital at intervals. When we heard that Grace was dead, Mrs. Tanner burst into tears. "Grace was such a beautiful young girl—and so talented," she moaned. "There wasn't anything she couldn't do. Why did she ever want to mess around with those awful snakes?"

"I guess that's something none of us will ever understand," said her husband sadly.

Grace was born in Kansas in 1884. She studied entomology at the University of Kansas, and during field trips to collect insects it was a great joke among Grace's fellow students that she was terrified of even harmless garter snakes. Later, however, after her marriage failed, Grace turned with a passionate interest to the creatures she had so long feared. In 1923 she became curator of the Museum of Natural History at the Minneapolis Public Library, but quarreled with the directors, who felt that her reckless handling of poisonous snakes endangered not only her own life but that of others. She went to the Brookfield Zoo in Chicago; here the same difficulty arose. Finally Grace moved to California where she could work with reptiles as she wished.

An attempt was made by several of Grace's friends to keep her collection together for a Grace Wiley Memorial Reptile House, but this failed. The snakes were auctioned off, and the snake that had killed Grace was purchased by a roadside zoo in Arizona. Huge signboard's bearing an artist's conception of the incident were erected for miles along the highways.

So passed one of the most remarkable people I have ever known.

## Getting at Meaning

1. Why does the writer repeatedly stress Grace Wiley's height and size?

2. Describe Grace Wiley's attitude and behavior toward her snakes.

3. Why is Grace Wiley able to handle cobras successfully? Why does she refuse to pose as a woman with supernatural power?

4. The writer comments that Grace ". . . could tell by tiny, subtle indications what the reptile would probably do next." How do later events in the selection show that this ability is essential to her survival?

5. Why is the fact that Grace is able to touch her king cobras four days after their arrival so impressive?

6. As Jule and Grace carry him outside, how does King of Kings, the male king cobra, demonstrate the intelligence possessed by cobras?

7. What is phony or fake about a snake charmer's performance? What actually causes a snake to appear charmed?

8. What fatal mistake does Grace make while handling My Snake?

9. What is remarkable, almost astonishing, about Grace Wiley's behavior after My Snake bites her? In contrast, how do the people who try to help Grace behave?

10. Why are the efforts to save Grace at the snake barn and in the hospital essentially hopeless?

## Developing Skills in Reading Literature

1. **Biography.** The writer of this selection admires Grace Wiley as a truly remarkable person. Choose three incidents from the selection and identify the outstanding, and admirable, quality revealed by each.

2. **Suspense.** What is the attitude of the writer toward the events that he witnesses? How does this attitude increase the suspense of the selection? How does the writer use his knowledge of cobras to develop suspense? At what point in the selection does the suspense increase dramatically? How do the factors of time, the condition of the snake-bite kit, and the nature of cobra venom combine to intensify the suspense?

3. **Irony.** What is ironic about the name that Grace Wiley chooses for the cobra with a complete G on the back of his hood? What is even more ironic about the use of this snake by the Arizona roadside zoo?

## Developing Vocabulary

**Words from Greek.** The word *hypodermic* is formed by joining the prefix *hypo-* meaning "below or beneath" and the word *derma* meaning "skin." Both the prefix and the word are derived from Greek. Use a dictionary to find the meanings of the following Greek prefixes and then use each prefix to form three English words. If possible, establish the origins of the root words to which the prefixes are added.

hypno-    auto-    hyper-

## Developing Writing Skills

**Using Contrasts.** To impress upon the reader the incredible danger of cobras, the writer contrasts them with tigers, elephants, and rattlesnakes. Choose an animal whose power, beauty, grace, or deadliness impresses you. Write a paragraph in which you clearly describe one aspect of the animal through contrast with other animals.

# Gift from a Son Who Died

*Doris Herold Lund*

It's not the way I thought it would be. I thought the sun and the moon would go out. I thought joy itself would die when Eric died. He had given so much to all of us—his family, his friends. And yet his death is not the end of joy after all. It's somehow another beginning.

Eric died at twenty-two, after a four-and-a-half-year struggle with leukemia. While he left us with the deep bruises of grief, he left us so much more. So much to celebrate! There's a victory here that I'm still trying to understand. Why do I, even in loss, feel stronger? Why does life on this untidy, dangerous planet seem more wonderfully precious? I am conscious now of the value of each good moment, the importance of wasting nothing.

These things are Eric's gifts to me. They weren't easily bought or quickly accepted. And not all came tied with ribbons; many were delivered with blows. In addition to leukemia, Eric was suffering from adolescence. And there were times when this condition took more out of us than his other one. A seventeen-year-old boy who may not live to become a man is suddenly in a great hurry. Like a militant new nation, he wants instant independence and no compromises. After the first few weeks, Eric quickly took charge of his illness. I was no longer to talk to the doctors. In fact—the message came through early—I was no longer to talk at all unless I could avoid sounding like a worried mother.

Perhaps it would have been different if we'd had a chance to prepare for what was coming, but it was a thunderbolt from a cloudless sky.

We live in a small Connecticut town, just a block from the beach. This had been a summer like many others. The front hall was, as usual, full of sand and kicked-off sneakers, mysterious towels that didn't belong to us, an assortment of swimming fins, and soccer balls. By September, I, like many mothers, was half-longing for school to start and half-dreading it. Our twenty-year-old daughter had married, and now Eric was packed and ready to go off for his freshman year at the University of Connecticut. But ten-year-old Lisa and fourteen-year-old Mark would still be at home. I kept telling myself how lucky I'd be to have less laundry and fewer cookie crumbs to contend with. But I didn't exactly believe it.

One afternoon Eric and I both wanted the car at the same moment. "I've got to run at the track, Mom." He was wearing his soccer shorts and running shoes. "I've only got two more days before school starts, and I'm not in shape."

I knew how much he wanted to make the freshman soccer team when he got to college, but I had work to do. "I have to go to the printer," I said. "But I'll drop you off at the field and pick you up later."

"Okay." He scowled a bit at the compromise. As we drove off together, I noticed something on his leg—an ugly red sore, big and round as a silver dollar. There was another farther down. And another on his other leg.

"Eric. What have you got on your legs?"

"Dunno. Little infection maybe."

"It doesn't look little to me," I protested. "Impetigo is what it looks like. We'd better go right over to the doctor's office."

"Mom!" He was furious.

"Eric," I said. "Impetigo spreads like mad. If that's what it is, they aren't even going to let you into the locker room. We've got two days before you go. Let's get the doctor to clear it up now."

"All right," he said dully.

The sores did not look like impetigo to our doctor. He told his secretary to call the hospital and arrange to have Eric admitted next morning for tests. "Be there at eight, Eric," he said.

"What tests?" I turned to the doctor. Eric had had a complete physical required for all freshmen, only twelve days before. Blood tests, too. He'd passed with flying colors.

"I want them to rerun some of the blood tests," said the doctor. "I've also ordered a bone marrow——"

I blanked out the words "bone marrow" as if I'd never heard them. After all, I thought as we drove home, he'd just had that perfect physical.

Yet the next afternoon when the phone rang and the doctor was saying, "I'd like to talk to you and your husband together——" I knew at once. "You don't have to tell me," I said. "I know. Eric has leukemia."

I was once in a house struck by lightning. The sensation, the scene, even the strange electrical smell returned at that moment. A powerful bolt seemed to enter the top of my skull as I got the message. Eric had leukemia.

He'd always been a fine athlete, a competitor, a runner. Now fate had tripped him; he stumbled and fell. Yet how quickly he tried to get up and join the race again! Left at home that fall, very ill, with his friends scattering to schools and jobs, he still was determined to go to college later, study hard, make the soccer team, eventually make all-American. To these goals he soon added one more—to stay alive.

We both knew that tremendous ordeals lay ahead. Leukemia, cancer of the blood, had always been a swift killer. When Eric developed the disease in 1968, doctors had just found ways to slow it down by using powerful drugs to suppress symptoms and produce periods of remission. They did not know how to cure it.

There was hope, though, in the fact that Eric had a type of childhood leukemia that was especially responsive to drug therapy. (By now, a few youngsters are actually being cured of it.) But Eric, at seventeen, was beyond the age of most effective treatment. Soon we discovered that his body overreacted to many of the best drugs and that the recommended high dosage needed to destroy diseased cells, tended too quickly to wipe out healthy ones.

There were times during those first months when I saw him shaken, fighting for control. After all, it hadn't been too long since he was a small boy who could throw himself in my arms for comfort. Part of him must have been crying, "Please save me! Don't let me die!" I couldn't save him, but I could show him my own best courage. I learned to hide my concern, my tenderness, and I saw he was strengthened by my calm. He had to run free to be a man. I wanted that. If there were to be no other alternative, eventually I would help him die like a man.

We learned to be casual with danger, to live with death just around the corner. Whenever Eric was discharged from the hospital after transfusions (first they would give him two, then five, then seven), he would fly down the steps swinging a duffel bag, as if he were just back from a great weekend. I'd hand him the keys to the car, slide over, and he would pick up his life as if nothing had happened. But there were always drugs, always bouts of nausea.

I remember once starting up the stairs to bring him a cup of weak tea. He passed me on the way down wearing his swim trunks and carrying a spear gun. Ignoring the tea, he said, "Maybe I'll get you a fish for supper." He played pick-up soccer, weekend football, and basketball with a hemoglobin so low it left him short of breath, occasionally faint. On the basketball court, his teammates, galloping for a goal at the other end of the gym, would shout, "Just stay there, Eric—we'll be right back."

It was always more than a game he played. His life was on the line. "Exercise, Attitude, Desire" were the chalked words on his blackboard. These three words would bring him through. "You don't die of leuk, you know," he said once to me. "Something else goes. Your heart. Or your kidneys. I'm going to be ready for it when it comes for me. I'm going to win."

But he was not confused about the nature of his enemy—at least not by the time he'd spent some weeks on the eighth floor of Memorial Hospital's Ewing Pavillion in New York.

Ewing patients talk a lot about remissions, of course. "Remission"—that seductive word! Hope, with the end-to-hope implied. Eric's remissions encouraged us. Once he got an eleven-month stay of execution with the drug Methotrexate. I remember looking at him that summer as he ran the beach with friends. All of them tan, glowing, happy, all with the same powerful shoulders, the same strong, brown legs. What could there be in the bones of one that differed from the others? The next day Memorial phoned. Eric's most recent tests had shown that his remission was at an end. Even as I watched him, wild cells had been springing up in his marrow like dragon's teeth. More and then more. Always more than could be slain.

Eric endured and survived many crises. He learned to live on the edge of the ledge and not look down. Whenever he had to be in the hospital, Memorial's doctors gave him passes to escape the horror. He'd slip off his hospital bracelet (which was forbidden) and rush out to plunge into the life of the city. Crowds, shop windows, cut-rate records. Restaurants in Chinatown. Concerts in the park. Summer parties on rooftops. He listened a lot but never told his own story. "Where you from?" His answer was always, "I've got my own pad on First Avenue, between 67th and 68th. Nice neighborhood—handy to everything." (Some way to describe your bed on Ewing Eight!)

Even more than exploring the city, he loved working out, trying to get back his strength on these brief passes. Once he went out waving goodbye to less fortunate inmates on the floor, only to return an hour later waving from the ambulance stretcher. There was no living without risks and so he took them. (This is one of his special gifts to me. Dare! Take life, dangers and all.)

The disease gained on him. To prevent infection he was finally put in a windowless, isolated chamber, the laminar air-flow room. Sterile air, sterile everything, sterile masks, caps, gowns, gloves for anyone entering his room. He joked, played to the eager audience peering through his glass-windowed door. And then sudden severe hemorrhages. Six days of unconsciousness, soaring fevers. His white count was dangerously low. Platelet count zero! Hemoglobin hardly worth mentioning. Sure, I thought, this is the end. But friends came, literally by busloads, to give blood for transfusions. During that crisis, it took more than thirty-two blood donors a day just to keep him alive.

I watched the doctors and nurses jabbing for veins, taping both needled arms to boards, packing the hemorrhages, shaking him to rouse him from stupor, and I thought, Enough! Let him die in peace! Why bring him back for more? He's proved himself—and beyond. He's had two good years of college. He made the soccer team and even made the dean's list. No more! Let him go!

But I had more to learn about my son's strength and resources. There was still much good life to be lived at the edge of the dark place. Eric came back. He had to remain in the laminar air-flow room, off and on, for nearly four months. Yet within weeks he was running from twelve to fifteen miles a day. That spring he didn't get back to college, but in his absence they named him captain of the soccer team; he received the award for The Most Improved Player, and finally was listed among the All-New England All-Stars. Proud honors, justly won. And there were others. We have a bookcase full of plaques and medals.

But I treasure even more the things they don't give medals for; his irreverent humor; the warmth and love and consideration he gave his friends, especially his comrades in the War on the Eighth Floor. For these last he was a jaunty hero, survivor of epic battles. Yet he was always one of them; hopefully, the Golden Warrior who would lead them all to victory—or at least escape.

He and a fellow inmate almost managed it once. Hiding themselves in laundry carts under dirty linen, they rode down nine floors on the service elevator and out to the sidewalk. Just short of being loaded with the laundry on a truck, they decided to give themselves up and go back to bone marrow, intravenous bottles, and the rest of it. There was, after all, no real way out.

As a variation on the theme of escape, Eric invented Ralph the Camel, a melancholy dromedary who, although hospitalized for "humpomeia," somehow managed to survive all the witless treatments his doctors could devise, including daily injections of pineapple juice. Ralph starred in a series of underground comic books known as *The Adventures of Ewing 8*, which featured Memorial's top doctors, nurses, technicians, and other notables, all drawn by Eric in merciless caricature. As Dr. Bayard Clarkson put it, "Eric spared no one, but we could hardly wait for the next *Adventure*." When they asked for more, his price was simple, "Get me in remission."

One of his exploits became a legend. Ten important doctors made Grand Rounds together every week. This particular Monday they stopped by the bed of their liveliest patient, to find him huddled under blankets looking unusually bleak.

"Eric! How do you feel?" asked Dr. Dowling, concerned.

"Scaly," was the mumbled reply.

Only then was the doctor's eye caught by the live goldfish swimming around in Eric's intravenous bottle. The plastic tube running down under the covers wasn't, of course, hooked up, but it looked convincing. The doctors broke up. The ward cheered! For the moment, humor had death on the run.

The eighth floor was a bad place to make friends. As one crusty old patient put it, "Make 'em and you'll lose 'em." But for Eric, there was no way to stay uninvolved. In the beginning he looked for the secrets of survival in the most spirited people around him. "That Eileen is so great," he told me. "She's beaten this thing for five years!" Or, "Look at that old guy, Mr. Miller. They just took out his spleen, but he's hanging in there!"

Then, as the months of his treatments

lengthened into years, he began to see them go. The good, the brave, the beautiful, the weak, the whining, the passive. They were all going the same way . . . Eileen, Mr. Miller, and so many more. When he was at home during one his last remissions, he chalked up new words on his blackboard. "We are all in the same boat in a stormy sea and we owe each other a terrible loyalty" (G. K. Chesterton). Eric would not desert or fault his companions. He would play his heart out while the game might still be won, but he was beginning to think of the unthinkable. The casualty lists on the eighth floor were long.

At the end, Eric finally accepted his own death. This acceptance was his last, most precious gift to me—what made my own acceptance possible. There was no bitterness. He said, simply, "There comes a time when you say: 'Well, that's it. We gave it a try.'"

I remember one afternoon in Memorial a few days before he died. He wanted to talk of all the good things: the way he felt about his sisters; the wild, wonderful times he'd had with his brother, Mark. Suddenly he closed his eyes and said, "Running. That was so great—running on a beach for miles and miles!" He smiled, eyes still closed. "And snow! Snow was fun—" He was summing it up, living it, feeling it all again while there was still time.

He talked on quietly, gently, in the past tense, telling me, without telling me, to be ready, to be strong.

Once, thinking the light was hurting his eyes, I started to lower the window blind. "No, no!" he stopped me. "I want all the sky." He couldn't move (too many tubes), but he looked at that bright blue square with such love. "The sun," he said. "It was so good—"

It grew dark. He grew tired. Then he whispered, "Do something for me? Leave a little early tonight. Don't run for the bus. Walk a few blocks and look at the sky. Walk in the world for me."

And so I do, and so I will. Loving life that much, Eric gave it to me—new, strong, beautiful!—even as he was dying. That was his victory. In a way it is also mine. And I think perhaps it is a victory for all of us everywhere when human beings succeed in giving such gifts to each other.

## Getting at Meaning

1. Reread the opening paragraph. What does the writer mean when she says, "It's not the way I thought it would be"? To what does *it* refer? Explain the line, "It's somehow another beginning."

2. In what way does Eric suffer from adolescence? Find examples of this "suffering" in the selection.

3. Eric and his fellow patient almost escape from the hospital in the laundry carts, but they decide to turn themselves in because there is "no real way out." What is meant by this phrase?

4. Near the end of the selection, Eric begins to speak in the past tense, "Running. That was so great. . . . Snow was fun. . . ." What is he "summing up"? What change has occurred in Eric?

5. The writer refers several times to the gifts that she receives from Eric. Make a list of these gifts.

## Developing Skills in Reading Literature

1. **Biography.** Some people write biographies to glorify personal heroes, to discredit enemies, or to

make money by writing about popular figures. When one of these purposes motivates a writer, facts tend to be distorted and the balance necessary in a biography is upset.

What do you think was the motivation behind this biography? Does the writer succeed in giving the reader a balanced view of Eric? Support your answer with details from this selection.

2. **Character.** How is Eric's sense of humor a source of strength for him? How is Eric's humor important to his family? his doctors? the other patients?

3. **Theme.** What is the theme of this selection? Relate the first and last paragraphs to the theme.

4. **Extended Metaphor.** What metaphor does the writer use to describe how she feels when the doctor confirms Eric's leukemia? Is this an effective metaphor? Why, or why not?

## Developing Vocabulary

**Prefixes.** The prefix *trans-* has two common meanings: "across," as in *transcontinental*, and "beyond," as in *transnational*.

For each of the following sentences, write the correct word beginning with the prefix *trans-* on a separate sheet of paper.

1. When blood from a donor is given to a recipient, the process is called a _____.

2. When a person achieves beyond apparent limits, the person is said to have _____ expectations.

3. If you wish to send a message from one town to another, you will _____ it.

4. In writing, if you want to carry a thought from one sentence or paragraph to another, you use a _____.

5. If a person crosses legal limits and violates a law, that person commits a _____.

6. You can see through a window because glass is _____.

## Developing Writing Skills

**Explaining an Idea.** The writer of this selection describes the gifts that she receives from Eric. These are not concrete, tangible gifts but are abstract, intangible gifts. Think of a similar gift that someone has given you, such as a better understanding of yourself, an enjoyment of a sport or a subject, or a feeling of being needed. Describe the gift in one paragraph.

# Nature

# Old Times on the Mississippi

*Mark Twain*

During the afternoon watch, Mr. Bixby asked me if I knew how to run the next few miles. I said,

"Go inside the first snag above the point, outside the next one, start out from the lower end of Higgins's wood-yard, make a square crossing, and"—

"That's all right. I'll be back before you close up on the next point."

But he wasn't. He was still below when I rounded it and entered upon a piece of the river that I had some misgivings about. I did not know that he was hiding behind a chimney to see how I would perform. I went merrily along, getting prouder and prouder, for he had never left the boat in my sole charge such a length of time before. I even got to "setting" her and letting the wheel go, entirely, while I vaingloriously turned my back and inspected the stern marks and hummed a tune, a sort of easy indifference that I had prodigiously admired in Bixby and other great pilots. Once I inspected rather long, and when I faced to the front again my heart flew into my mouth so suddenly that if I hadn't clapped my teeth together I should have lost it. One of those frightful bluff reefs was stretching its deadly length right across our bows! My head was gone in a moment; I did not know which end I stood on; I gasped and could not get my breath; I spun the wheel down with such rapidity that it wove itself together like a spider's web; the boat answered and turned square away from the reef, but the reef followed her! I fled, but still it followed still it kept—right across my bows! I never looked to see where I was going, I only fled. The awful crash was imminent. Why didn't that villain come? If I committed the crime of ringing a bell, I might get thrown overboard. But better that than kill the boat. So in blind desperation I started such a rattling "shivaree" down below as never had astounded an engineer in this world before, I fancy. Amidst the frenzy of the bells the engines began to back and fill in a furious way, and my reason forsook its throne—we were about to crash into the woods on the other side of the river. Just then Mr. Bixby stepped calmly into view on the hurricane deck. My soul went out to him in gratitude. My distress vanished; I would have felt safe on the brink of Niagara, with Mr. Bixby on the hurricane deck. He blandly and sweetly took his toothpick out of his mouth between his fingers, as if it were a cigar—we were just in the act of climbing an overhanging big tree, and the passengers were scudding astern like rats—and lifted up these commands to me ever so gently:

"Stop the starboard. Stop the larboard. Set her back on both."

The boat hesitated, halted, pressed her nose among the boughs a critical instant, then reluctantly began to back away.

"Stop the larboard. Come ahead on it. Stop the starboard. Come ahead on it. Point her for the bar."

I sailed away as serenely as a summer's morning. Mr. Bixby came in and said, with mock simplicity,

"When you have a hail, my boy, you ought to tap the big bell three times before you land, so that the engineers can get ready."

I blushed under the sarcasm, and said I hadn't had any hail.

"Ah! Then it was for wood, I suppose. The officer of the watch will tell you when he wants to wood up."

I went on consuming, and said I wasn't after wood.

"Indeed? Why, what could you want over here in the bend, then? Did you ever know of a boat following a bend up-stream at this stage of the river?"

"No, sir,—and I wasn't trying to follow it. I was getting away from a bluff reef."

"No, it wasn't a bluff reef; there isn't one within three miles of where you were."

"But I saw it. It was as bluff as that one yonder."

"Just about. Run over it!"

"Do you give it as an order?"

"Yes. Run over it!"

"If I don't, I wish I may die."

"All right; I am taking the responsibility."

I was just as anxious to kill the boat, now, as I had been to save it before. I impressed my orders upon my memory, to be used at the inquest, and made a straight break for the reef. As it disappeared under our bows I held my breath, but we slid over it like oil.

"Now, don't you see the difference? It wasn't anything but a *wind* reef. The wind does that."

"So I see. But it is exactly like a bluff reef. How am I ever going to tell them apart?"

"I can't tell you. It is an instinct. By and by you will just naturally *know* one from the other, but you never will be able to explain why or how you know them apart."

It turned out to be true. The face of the water, in time, became a wonderful book— a book that was a dead language to the uneducated passenger, but which told its mind to me without reserve, delivering its most cherished secrets as clearly as if it uttered them with a voice. And it was not a book to be read once and thrown aside, for it had a new story to tell every day. Throughout the long twelve hundred miles there was never a page that was void of interest, never one that you could leave unread without loss, never one that you would want to skip, thinking you could find higher enjoyment in some other thing. There never was so wonderful a book written by man; never one whose interest was so absorbing, so unflagging, so sparklingly renewed with every reperusal. The passenger who could not read it was charmed with a peculiar sort of faint dimple on its surface (on the rare occasions when he did not overlook it altogether), but to the pilot that was an *italicized* passage; indeed, it was more than that; it was a legend of the largest capitals, with a string of shouting exclamation points at the end of it; for it meant that a wreck or a rock was buried there that could tear the life out of the strongest vessel that ever floated. It is the faintest and simplest expression the water ever makes, and the most hideous to a pilot's eye. In truth, the passenger who could not read this book saw nothing but all manner of pretty pictures in it, painted by the sun and shaded by the clouds; whereas to the trained eye these were not pictures at all, but the grimmest and most dead-earnest of reading-matter.

Now when I had mastered the language of this water and had come to know every trifling feature that bordered the great river as familiarly as I knew the letters of the alphabet, I had made a valuable acquisition. But I had lost something, too. I had lost something that could never be restored to me while I lived. All the grace, the beauty, the poetry, had gone out of the majestic river! I still keep in mind a certain wonderful sunset that I witnessed when steamboating was new to me. A broad expanse of the river was turned to blood; in the middle distance the red hue brightened into gold, through which a solitary log came floating, black and conspicuous; in one place a long, slanting mark lay sparkling upon the water; in another the surface was broken by boiling, tumbling rings that were as many-tinted as an opal; where the ruddy flush was faintest, was a smooth spot that was covered with graceful circles and radiating lines, ever so delicately traced. The shore on our left was densely wooded, and the somber shadow that fell from this forest was broken in one place by a long ruffled trail that shone like silver; and high above the forest wall a clean-stemmed dead tree waved a single leafy bough that glowed like a flame in the unobstructed splendor that was flowing from the sun. There were graceful curves, reflected images, woody heights, soft distances; and over the whole scene, far and near, the dissolving lights drifted steadily, enriching it, every passing moment, with new marvels of coloring.

I stood like one bewitched. I drank it in, in a speechless rapture. The world was new to me, and I had never seen anything like this at home. But as I have said, a day came when I began to cease from noting the glories and the charms that the moon and the sun and the twilight wrought upon the river's face; another day came when I ceased altogether to note them. Then, if that sunset scene had been repeated, I should have looked upon it without rapture, and should have commented upon it, inwardly, after this fashion: This sun means that we are going to have wind to-morrow; that floating log means that the river is rising, small

thanks to it; that slanting mark on the water refers to a bluff reef that is going to kill somebody's steamboat one of these nights if it keeps on stretching out like that; those tumbling "boils" show a dissolving bar and a changing channel there; the lines and circles in the slick water over yonder are a warning that that troublesome place is shoaling up dangerously; that silver streak in the shadow of the forest is the "break" from a new snag, and he has located himself in the very best place he could have found to fish for steamboats; that tall dead tree, with a single living branch, is not going to last long, and then how is a body ever going to get through this blind place at night without the friendly old landmark?

No, the romance and beauty were all gone from the river. All the value any feature of it had for me now was the amount of usefulness it could furnish toward compassing the safe piloting of a steamboat. Since those days, I have pitied doctors from my heart. What does the lovely flush in a beauty's cheek mean to a doctor but a "break" that ripples above some deadly disease? Are not all her visible charms sown thick with what are to him the signs and symbols of hidden decay? Does he ever see her beauty at all, or doesn't he simply view her professionally, and comment upon her unwholesome condition all to himself? And doesn't he sometimes wonder whether he has gained most or lost most by learning his trade?

## Getting at Meaning

1. What is Mr. Bixby's job? What is his relationship to the writer?

2. What does the writer mean when he says that the surface of the river is "dead language to the uneducated passenger"? Contrast the way that the average passenger views the river with the way that a riverboat pilot sees it.

3. What does the writer gain from his education as a riverboat pilot? What does he lose?

## Developing Skills in Reading Literature

1. **Essay.** An essay is a short piece of nonfiction writing in which the writer presents a point of view on a subject. Some essays are formal and impersonal, and the major argument is developed in a systematic way. Other essays are informal and personal and are less rigidly organized. The informal essay often includes anecdotes and humor.

Is this selection a formal or an informal essay? Support your answer with details from the selection.

In what way is this essay similar to an autobiography?

2. **Analogy.** An analogy is a point-by-point comparison between essentially dissimilar things, written for the purpose of clarifying or explaining the less familiar of the two subjects. The writer of this selection develops an analogy between the Mississippi River and a book. Identify at least three ways that the river resembles a book.

3. **Style.** The use of contrast is a stylistic device. The writer of this selection contrasts his view of the river before and after his training as a pilot. Reread the passage that begins, "I still keep in mind a certain wonderful sunset. . . ." (p. 342) Choose three aspects of the scene, and note the contrasting descriptions of each aspect. How is the language in each description different? How are the details included different? What effect does the contrast have on the reader?

4. **Theme.** Reread the last line of this essay. What comment does the writer make about knowledge? What is the theme of this essay? Do you agree or disagree with this theme? Explain.

## Developing Vocabulary

**Finding the Appropriate Meaning.** Read each of the following sentences from this selection. Look up the italicized word in a dictionary and copy the definition that corresponds with the way that the word is used in the sentence.

1. "Mr. Bixby asked me if I knew how to *run* the next few miles."

2. "When you have a *hail*, my boy, you ought to tap the big bell three times before you land. . . ."

3. "The *face* of the water, in time, became a wonderful book. . . ."

4. ". . . how is a body ever going to get through this *blind* place at night . . .?"

## Developing Writing Skills

**Description: Using Different Points of View.** To a child, a large rock may seem enormous and impossible to climb. Imagination may turn the rock into a mountain or a castle wall. An adult may see the same rock as merely a hunk of granite and climb it without a second thought.

Choose an object or a place and write two paragraphs of description. In the first paragraph, describe the object or place as an imaginative child might see it. In the second paragraph, describe the object or place as an adult might see it.

# Nightmare Spring

*Olive A. Fredrickson*

The moose track led off into scrubby spruce, away from the Slave River.[1] We had found it at dark the night before when we drove our two gaunt dogs in at the end of a heartbreaking trip twenty-three miles up the Slave and twenty-three miles back again in a futile attempt to get out to Fort Smith before we died of hunger at our remote trapline camp. We failed to reach Fort Smith, but Bert Bennett, a trapper we found living in a cabin on the river, had sold us some food.

When we got back after resting at Bennett's, we found that the moose had walked within two hundred feet of our cabin. If Walter could kill it, it meant meat for most of the remaining weeks of winter, and the bones and leavings would be urgently needed food for the dogs. Walter poked shells into my old .25/35 Winchester carbine, the best rifle we had, and took the track right after breakfast. My husband had a rifle of his own, a .303 Savage, but it was in bad condition, hardly safe for shooting, and he had very little ammunition for it.

He followed the moose all that day without catching sight of it, made a fire and camped under a spruce tree in below-zero cold that night, and took the trail again at daylight the next morning. But the moose was traveling through and kept going. By early afternoon Walter had to give up. His homemade snowshoes were wearing out, and he was getting so far from our camp that he did not dare to keep on. He trudged in after dark, tired and sick with disappointment, and I felt as bad as he did. That was

the only moose track we had seen, and the closest we had come to killing fresh meat, through the whole winter.

We did not see or hear a living thing except each other, the dogs, and three foxes that Walter trapped, until the end of March. It seemed as if all the game, even rabbits, had died off or left the country. Neither of us had ever seen a winter wilderness so lifeless and still as that country along the Slave.

We fed the three fox carcasses to the dogs, and they were starved enough to gulp them down with relish. The beans and flour Bert Bennett had sold us were running low, and we were eating less than half of what we wanted.

Toward the first of April, we decided to start our mink and muskrat trapping, even though the lakes and marshes were still covered with three or four feet of iron-hard ice. It wasn't so much that we wanted fur. We needed the muskrats as food for ourselves and the dogs. Things had reached a point where I hated to eat because we had almost nothing for the dogs. None of us would last much longer without meat.

We made a trip to the nearest lake where we had trapped before freeze-up, taking little Olive on the toboggan. We found the shallow, swampy lake frozen solid to the bottom. Not a muskrat was left alive. We went on to two or three other lakes farther away, and the situation was the same. When we turned the

---

1. **Slave River:** a river in southwest Canada between Lake Athabaska and Great Slave Lake.

dogs back toward camp that afternoon, Walter and I were about as disheartened and worried as two people could get.

A few days after that we packed up the little food we had left, took our tent, bedding, and traps, and went eight miles west to some bigger lakes that Walter had found earlier while tracking that moose.

We put up the tent at the first lake, found water under the ice, cut into muskrat houses, and caught a few rats. They eased the pinch of our hunger, but we were not taking enough for ourselves and the dogs.

At last Walter made the unhappy announcement that the dogs would have to be destroyed. I realized that was kinder than letting them starve, but the idea of it almost broke my heart, and I coaxed him to wait a few more days in the hope the weather would turn warmer and our trapping would pick up.

Instead, it turned bitterly cold and stayed that way for eight days. Before the end of the cold spell the dogs were so hungry they whined and howled for food almost continuously, and finally Walter shot them. It had to be done, but I cried until I was sick.

Less than a week after that the weather broke in our favor. The sun came out warm and bright, the snow started to melt, and the lakes opened up around the shores. We began trapping and shooting muskrats by the dozens. If the night was cold and ice formed, our luck fell off. Some days we took only five or six pelts, but one day before the fur spree was over we took seventy. Walter followed the trapline from daylight to dark, and I was kept busy every minute skinning rats and stretching the pelts. I made the stretchers by bending willow sticks.

We were living on muskrat meat, and for the first time that winter we had enough to eat. I boiled it and gave Olive the broth in her bottle. She thrived on it.

When spring comes to the North it comes with a rush. Suddenly it is sunny day after day, and the days are long and warm. But the short dark hours of the spring nights are often cold, and it was hard to keep warm in our tent, even with a fire in the tiny stove. That stove was to cause the worst disaster of all.

We were wet most of the time from wading out into the icy water to retrieve rats we shot, and our clothing didn't dry thoroughly overnight. But we were taking a rich harvest of pelts and saw no reason to complain. After the hunger and hardships of the winter, that spring was a welcome season indeed.

We continued trapping while the snow melted and the creeks rose and became treacherous little rivers. Walter and I agreed that we'd stay camped at the lake until May 10. Then we'd hike back to our cabin, go up the Slave to Bert Bennett's place in our rowboat and there catch the first steamer of the season to Fort Smith. But things don't always go as people plan them.

On the morning of May 2, I was in the tent baking bannock in the little stovepipe oven. I stepped outside to look for Walter and saw him coming a quarter-mile up the lake. I took Olive by the hand and walked to meet him. She was toddling all over by then.

There were muskrats swimming in the open water along the shore, and we kept back far enough not to frighten them. Every now and then, Walter would stop and pick off one with his Remington .22. When we met, I took part of his load of fresh pelts and the three of us started back.

All of a sudden we heard ammunition exploding at a terrible rate, and then smoke and flames rolled up around the tent. Walter dropped his sack of fur and ran, and I grabbed Olive and hurried after him as fast as I could. When I got to the tent my husband was dragging out charred foodstuffs and burning pieces of blankets. I grabbed the things as he pulled them out and doused them in the lake.

It was all over in ten minutes. A tent burns fast.

What we had saved would have made a very small bundle. There were two or three half burned pieces of blanket, the few matches in our pockets and in a waterproof container. Walter's .22 that he had been shooting rats with was safe, of course, and my .25/35 had been standing outside the tent. There were four shells in its magazine, and Walter had a box of .22's in his pocket. The rest of our ammunition was gone. We also pulled a scorched .22 Stevens of mine out of the burned tent. It was damaged, but it looked as though it could be fired. We didn't even have a piece of canvas big enough to wrap the baby in if rain came.

Most of the rat pelts had been hanging in a tree outside the tent and were safe. We had lost only ten or twelve that were inside to dry. But one of the possessions I loved most was gone—the violin my brother Lea had given me for my sixteenth birthday. That birthday seemed a long time ago, somehow.

Of our food, we had salvaged about four cups of flour, wet and mixed with cinders, a pound or so of beans, and a little bannock. For Olive, luckily, there were a few undamaged cans of condensed milk.

With muskrat meat, that handful of supplies would have to see us through until we could reach Bennett's cabin. That meant a hard hike of eight or ten miles without dogs through flooded and difficult country, and then twenty-three miles by rowboat against the spring current of the mighty Slave. Worst of all, we knew we could not make the trip upriver until the Slave broke up, and we had no idea when that would happen. We knew the ice went out of the Athabasca around the middle of May, but we asked each other hopelessly when the break-up was due on the Slave.

Things looked pretty grim. I was expecting a second baby in less than two months, and we knew we had a very rough time ahead. But there was no use sitting beside the ruins of our tent and worrying. The thing was to get started.

We hung our traps in trees where we would be able to find them the following fall, ate our bannock and a good meal of muskrat we had roasted earlier, rolled Olive in the patches of bedding, and lay down under a tree to rest for a few hours. We did not dare to use a match for a fire. We had to hoard them for times of genuine need.

When we awoke, we made up our loads and were ready to start. I wrapped Olive in the blanket pieces and tied her in with babiche. I'd carry her on my back, Indian style. She was so thin she wasn't very heavy. I rolled one cooking pot, knives, forks, spoons, a cup, and the baby bottle in a scorched scrap of blanket and tied it all on my back behind her. We tied the two .22's and the .25/35 together in one bundle. I'd carry that like a suitcase.

Walter's load consisted of the dry muskrat pelts, about 250 in all, our stove—it weighed only about ten pounds—and three lengths of stovepipe. He had fashioned a roomy pack-sack from a gunny sack and rope. By shoving in the rat skins nose down and then tele-scoping more and more inside those below, we managed to pack our total catch in the packsack. A fur buyer back at Tomato Creek had showed me that trick years before.

We left our burned-out camp with me carrying all I could handle and Walter packing a load of about 110 pounds. We had traveled eight miles in coming to that lake from our cabin during the late winter. Now we covered somewhere between sixteen and twenty going back. Every creek was roaring full and was two or three times as wide as usual. We detoured miles to find places where we could wade across and then had to follow the streams back to our blazed trail to avoid getting lost. Many times Walter had to make three trips through the swollen and icy creeks, one with his pack, one with Olive and my load, and a third to help me across.

It took two days of the hardest kind of travel to get back to our cabin. At the end of the first day we stopped and made a shelterless camp under a clump of spruces. We roasted a muskrat we had brought along Near that place we had earlier cached several rat carcasses on a high rack of poles. We had hung them high so they would dry, against some future need. After supper Walter went to get them.

He came back looking pretty glum. A wolverine had raided the cache, and there wasn't a rat left. We went without breakfast and our noon meal the second day, but in the middle of the afternoon, I shot a small muskrat in a slough. It wasn't big enough to make a good meal for one hungry person, let alone three, but we stopped and cooked it on the spot and divided it up.

It was midnight when we trudged up to our cabin. We were tired, discouraged, and hungry, but at least we had a roof over our heads again and four walls to keep out the cold at night. We didn't mind too much going to bed without supper.

When daylight came, I got up and picked out all the dried beans I could find from the place where I had discarded the culls during the winter. I also scraped each empty flour sack for the little flour that remained in it. I cooked the beans and baked a bannock from the flour, dirt and all.

One look at the Slave that morning confirmed our worst fears. Water was running between the ice and shore. We couldn't get out on the river. We wouldn't have dared. There was no hope of following the shore up to Bennett's place either, because of the many large creeks that flowed into the river. We had no choice but to wait for the ice to go out.

Walter started to caulk the rowboat and cover the seams with pitch. I put in the time hunting for muskrats, ducks, squirrels, or even small birds—anything edible. My total kill during the next five days consisted of three red squirrels. That wasn't much, but it helped.

They say trouble comes in bundles and I guess it's true. On May 10, with ice still solid in the river, Walter and I split up to hunt. He took Olive piggyback and went in one direction while I went in the other. He was carrying his Remington .22, and I had the fire-damaged Stevens we had salvaged from the burned tent. We had only enough am-

WOLVERINE, 1843. *John Woodhouse Audubon. Courtesy of American Museum of Natural History.*

munition for the .22's.

I scared up a flock of mallards, but they flushed out of range. Then, at the edge of a small muskeg half a mile north of camp, I saw a rabbit hunched under a clump of brush—the first one I had seen since fall. I've never wanted game more than I wanted that rabbit. I rested the .22 against a small tree and pulled the trigger. All I remember is fire in my face, blinding light, and then a numbness in my nose and eyes.

I don't know how long I leaned against that tree. I couldn't see, my ears rang, and there was terrible pain in the bridge of my nose, in my right eye, and clear around to my ear. Slowly the weakness went out of my legs, and I stamped the ground in agony. I couldn't get my eye wiped dry, and the more I wiped it the worse it hurt.

At first I didn't know what had happened. Then I remembered I had tried to shoot a rabbit. I felt around on the ground and found my gun. Next I looked for the rabbit, but there was nothing under the bush. Then I started to wonder if I'd be able to find my way home, half blinded as I was.

I knew I was straight north of our cabin, so I started walking in the direction I thought was south, stumbling along, blundering into trees, and falling over rough places. I could see enough with my left eye to know that my right hand was red with blood, and each time I wiped my cheek and chin, it got bloodier. Once I heard ducks quack nearby, and foolishly stopped to see whether I could make them out enough for a shot, not realizing that in all likelihood my rifle was beyond firing. But I couldn't see farther than I could reach my arms out in front of me, so I stumbled on. And by some stroke of luck that I still wonder about, I found the cabin.

Olive came running to meet me. Walter was picking a duck he had killed, and then I heard him cry, "Oh, my God, what happened to you?"

I let him ease me down, and then for the first time I was aware of severe pain in my right hand. I held it up to him and he looked quickly and mumbled, "Pieces of .22 shell. It's full of .22 shell. Your gun must have blown back."

He picked fragments of shell out of that hand and out of my nose for the next two days. Luckily my eye had escaped with nothing worse than powder burns. He kept washing it out with clean water, and I groped my way around the cabin with the sight of the other eye. The injured eye healed, but I have never regained full sight in it.

The eleven days between May 10, when I had my accident with the gun, and the time when the ice finally went out of the Slave were a lagging nightmare of hunger and worry—mostly hunger.

Because we were so short of matches, we kept plenty of wood on hand and fed the fire at intervals. We never let it go out.

I found a roll of wire and set snares for ducks, rabbits, muskrats—anything. In all, I snared two red squirrels and a blackbird. We peeled trees and scraped off and ate the juicy inner bark. We pulled up dead slough grass along the edge of the water and ate the tender yellow shoots below. One day I saw a fool hen—a spruce grouse—perched on a low branch of a tree. I hurried to rig a snare on a pole, reached up and dropped it over her head and jerked her to the ground. That was the best meal we had all that time. For once poor little Olive got all the broth she wanted.

Hunger cramps kept us awake at night, and when we slept we dreamed troubled dreams of food. In my own case, being seven months pregnant didn't make things any better. Right then I needed to eat for two. Each night we slept less. Each day we got weaker. The baby's whimpering for food tore us apart. Walter cursed himself over and over for bringing Olive and me down the Slave.

He vowed that if we got out alive he was through with the North for good, but somehow I doubted that.

If we had brought a few traps back from our tent camp, we could have caught muskrats or ducks. But we'd been counting on the cache of dried rat carcasses that the wolverine had robbed, and we had left all the traps behind.

We were down to two shells now, and they were for my .25/35. Our .22 ammunition was gone. Before that happened, Walter had thrown my .22 away to make sure I wouldn't be tempted into firing it again.

For three days our only food was what we called spruce tea. I stripped green needles off and boiled them, and we drank a few spoonfuls every couple of hours. It eased the hunger cramps and seemed to give us some strength, but a few times it also nauseated us.

Olive was no longer running around the cabin. She sat quiet and played listlessly with whatever was at hand. There was no color in her lips and cheeks, and her eyes looked hollow and dull. I can't put into words how worried and afraid Walter and I were.

We had left our fishhooks at our cabin on the east side of the Slave when we moved the previous fall, but we made crude hooks by bending safety pins, and tried fishing in the open water along the shore of the river, using pieces of red yarn for bait. Our catch totaled one very small jackfish.

On May 17 Walter killed a big drake mallard with the last shell for the .25/35, and we feasted. We even cleaned and washed the entrails, cooked them, and saved them for the next day. We set aside all of the broth for Olive, and she had her first good meal in many days.

The day after that I tapped a small birch tree (they were few and far between in that area) for sap. It tasted good, but we had only a half cup to divide among the three of us.

At last, at ten o'clock on the morning of May 21, the ice in the Slave began to move. By midnight it was gone, and the water was rolling past our door. At three in the morning of the twenty-second we shoved our little boat into the river and were on our way to Bennett's.

It was dangerous to try traveling so soon after the ice went out, even though it was light all night, for chunks of stranded ice weighing many tons kept sliding off the banks and drifting down with the current, but we had no choice.

Walter rowed, and I sat in the stern and paddled and steered us away from the floating ice. In our condition it was killing work, and to avoid the worst of the ice we had to stay well out from the bank and buck the current.

Our closest call came that first day. Rowing close to shore, we saw a huge block of ice come sliding off a pile forty feet high. It crashed into the water almost alongside us. The force of it literally lifted our rowboat into the air and sent it flying. We wound up 150 feet out in the swiftest part of the current, right side up only because we had happened to be pointed in the right direction when the ice thundered down.

Olive had the last of the duck broth that day. Walter and I drank spruce tea and gathered and ate slough-grass roots. We also drank water often because it seemed to ease our hunger, and we just kept rowing until we gave out. Then we'd rest, and then we'd row some more.

It took us six days to make the twenty-three mile trip up the Slave to Bert Bennett's cabin, and they were as dreadful as any days I can remember. We pulled up to shore at his place at midnight on May 27—dirty, ragged, starving, and burned so black by wind and sun that we hardly knew our own reflections when we looked in a mirror. In those six days Walter and I had eaten nothing but spruce tea, grass roots, and the inner bark of trees.

A Mr. and Mrs. King from Fort Smith were at Bennett's. They had come down on the ice in March. She gave us each half a biscuit and a couple of spoonfuls of stewed apricots, but the food was too much for our stomachs. We awakened three hours later with dreadful cramps and were miserably sick for the next twelve hours. It was four days before I was well enough to be out of bed, but Mrs. King fed me a few spoonfuls of canned soup and cream every hour, and at the end of that time I felt fine. By then Walter and Olive had bounced back too.

Bennett and the Kings fixed us up with some clothing, and we waited out a comfortable and happy month until the Miss Mackenzie came up the Slave on her first trip of the year. We boarded her near the end of June, and the trip to Fort Smith was lovely.

We sold our furs in Fort Smith. We had 560 muskrat pelts, 27 mink, 3 red foxes, 4 skunks, and a few weasels. The fox pelts brought $25 each, the mink $10. The Northwest Territories Store had grub-staked us when we left for our trapline the previous August. We paid off our debt and had $1,060 left in cash. We had never had money that came harder.

## Getting at Meaning

1. During the late winter, why does the situation at the Fredrickson's trapline camp become desperate? Why must they destroy the dogs?

2. This selection includes the statement ". . . things don't always go as people plan them." What have the Fredricksons planned? What events upset their plans?

3. What does Olive Fredrickson reveal about herself and her husband when she comments ". . . there was no use sitting beside the ruins of our tent and worrying"?

4. Describe the Fredricksons' return trip to their cabin. What elements of nature make this trip extremely difficult?

5. How does the destruction of their tent continue to plague the Fredricksons even after their return to the cabin?

6. How do the descriptions of young Olive throughout the selection clearly reveal the desperation of the family's situation? Support your answer with examples from the selection.

## Developing Skills in Reading Literature

1. **Nonfiction.** Nonfiction often presents detailed descriptions of worlds and events unfamiliar to the reader. In this selection, what does the reader learn about the dangers of life in the wilderness? What information does the reader gain about methods of survival?

2. **Setting.** The Fredricksons struggle to survive in a natural environment. How do their goals and problems affect the writer's presentation of the setting? In describing her surroundings, on what details does the writer focus?

3. **Conflict.** A conflict found in both fiction and nonfiction is the human being against nature. In this selection, which of the Fredricksons' problems are caused by nature? Which problems are caused by their own mistakes and limitations?

## Developing Vocabulary

**Suffixes.** The writer of this selection uses the word *direction,* a noun formed by adding the suffix -*tion* to the verb *direct.* Create a noun from each of the following verbs by adding the suffix -*tion.* Write the definitions of the nouns; use a dictionary to check definitions and spellings.

| | | |
|---|---|---|
| select | deviate | rotate |
| correct | invent | impose |

# Once More to the Lake
*E. B. White*

*August, 1941*

**O**ne summer, along about 1904, my father rented a camp on a lake in Maine and took us all there for the month of August. We all got ringworm from some kittens and had to rub Pond's Extract on our arms and legs night and morning, and my father rolled over in a canoe with all his clothes on; but outside of that the vacation was a success, and from then on none of us ever thought there was any place in the world like that lake in Maine. We returned summer after summer—always on August 1 for one month. I have since become a salt-water man, but sometimes in summer there are days when the restlessness of the tides and the fearful cold of the sea water and the incessant wind that blows across the afternoon and into the evening make me wish for the placidity of a lake in the woods. A few weeks ago this feeling got so strong I bought myself a couple of bass hooks and a spinner and returned to the lake where we used to go, for a week's fishing and to revisit old haunts.

I took along my son, who had never had any fresh water up his nose and who had seen lily pads only from train windows. On the journey over to the lake I began to wonder what it would be like. I wondered how time would have marred this unique, this holy spot—the coves and streams, the hills that the sun set behind, the camps and the paths behind the camps. I was sure that the tarred road would have found it out, and I wondered in what other ways it would be desolated. It is strange how much you can remember about places like that once you allow your mind to return into the grooves that lead back. You remember one thing, and that suddenly reminds you of another thing. I guess I remembered clearest of all the early mornings, when the lake was cool and motionless, remembered how the bedroom smelled of the lumber it was made of and of the wet woods whose scent entered through the screen. The partitions in the camp were thin and did not extend clear to the top of the rooms, and as I was always the first up I would dress softly so as not to wake the others, and sneak out into the sweet outdoors and start out in the canoe, keeping close along the shore in the long shadows of the pines. I remembered being very careful never to rub my paddle against the gunwale for fear of disturbing the stillness of the cathedral.

The lake had never been what you would call a wild lake. There were cottages sprinkled around the shores, and it was in farming country although the shores of the lake were quite heavily wooded. Some of the cottages were owned by nearby farmers, and you would live at the shore and eat your meals at the farmhouse. That's what our family did. But although it wasn't wild, it was a fairly large and undisturbed lake, and there were places in it that, to a child at least, seemed infinitely remote and primeval.

I was right about the tar; it led to within half a mile of the shore. But when I got back there, with my boy, and we settled into a camp near a farmhouse and into the kind of summertime I had known, I could tell that it was going to be pretty much the same as it had been before—I knew it, lying in bed the first morning, smelling the bedroom and hearing the boy sneak quietly out and go off along the shore in a boat. I began to sustain the illusion that he was I, and therefore, by simple transposition, that I was my father. This sensation persisted, kept cropping up all the time we were there. It was not an entirely new feeling, but in this setting it grew much stronger. I seemed to be living a dual existence. I would be in the middle of some simple act. I would be picking up a bait box or laying down a table fork, or I would be saying something, and suddenly it would be not I but my father who was saying the words or making the gesture. It gave me a creepy sensation.

We went fishing the first morning. I felt the same damp moss covering the worms in the bait can, and saw the dragonfly alight on the tip of my rod as it hovered a few inches from the surface of the water. It was the arrival of this fly that convinced me beyond any doubt that everything was as it always had been, that the years were a mirage and that there had been no years. The small waves were the same, chucking the rowboat under the chin as we fished at anchor, and the boat was the same boat, the same color green and the ribs broken in the same places; and under the floorboards the same freshwater leavings and débris—the dead helgramite, the wisps of moss, the rusty discarded fishhook, the dried blood from yesterday's catch. We stared silently at the tips of our rods, at the dragonflies that came and went. I lowered the tip of mine into the water, tentatively, pensively dislodging the fly, which darted two feet away, poised, darted two feet back, and came to rest again a little farther up the rod. There had been no years between the ducking of this dragonfly and the other one—the one that was part of memory. I looked at the boy, who was si-

lently watching his fly, and it was my hands that held his rod, my eyes watching. I felt dizzy and didn't know which rod I was at the end of.

We caught two bass, hauling them in briskly as though they were mackerel, pulling them over the side of the boat in a businesslike manner without any landing net, and stunning them with a blow on the back of the head. When we got back for a swim before lunch, the lake was exactly where we had left it, the same number of inches from the dock, and there was only the merest suggestion of a breeze. This seemed an utterly enchanted sea, this lake you could leave to its own devices for a few hours and come back to, and find that it had not stirred, this constant and trustworthy body of water. In the shallows, the dark, water-soaked sticks and twigs, smooth and old, were undulating in clusters on the bottom against the clean ribbed sand, and the track of the mussel was plain. A school of minnows swam by, each minnow with its small individual shadow, doubling the attendance, so clear and sharp in the sunlight. Some of the other campers were in swimming, along the shore, one of them with a cake of soap, and the water felt thin and clear and unsubstantial. Over the years there had been this person with the cake of soap, this cultist, and here he was. There had been no years.

Up to the farmhouse to dinner through the teeming, dusty field, the road under our sneakers was only a two-track road. The middle track was missing, the one with the marks of the hooves and the splotches of dried, flaky manure. There had always been three tracks to choose from in choosing which track to walk in; now the choice was narrowed down to two. For a moment I missed terribly the middle alternative. But the way led past the tennis court, and something about the way it lay there in the sun reassured me; the tape had loosened along the backline, the alleys were green with plantains and other weeds, and the net (installed in June and removed in September) sagged in the dry noon; and the whole place steamed with midday heat and hunger and emptiness. There was a choice of pie for dessert, and one was blueberry and one was apple, and the waitresses were the same country girls, there having been no passage of time, only the illusion of it as in a dropped curtain—the waitresses were still fifteen; their hair had been washed, that was the only difference—they had been to the movies and seen the pretty girls with the clean hair.

Summertime, oh, summertime, pattern of life indelible, the fade-proof lake, the woods unshatterable, the pasture with the sweetfern and the juniper forever and ever, summer without end; this was the background, and the life along the shore was the design, the cottagers with their innocent and tranquil design, their tiny docks with the flagpole and the American flag floating against the white clouds in the blue sky, the little paths over the roots of the trees leading from camp to camp and the paths leading back to the outhouses and the can of lime for sprinkling, and at the souvenir counters at the store the miniature birch-bark canoes and the postcards that showed things looking a little better than they looked. This was the American family at play, escaping the city heat, wondering whether the newcomers in the camp at the head of the cove were "common" or "nice," wondering whether it was true that the people who drove up for Sunday dinner at the farmhouse were turned away because there wasn't enough chicken.

It seemed to me, as I kept remembering all this, that those times and those summers had been infinitely precious and worth saving. There had been jollity and peace and goodness. The arriving (at the beginning of August) had been so big a business in itself, at the railway station the farm wagon drawn up, the first smell of the pine-laden air, the first glimpse of the smiling farmer, and the great importance of the trunks and your father's enormous authority in such matters, and the feel of the wagon under you for the long ten-mile haul, and at the top of the last long hill catching the first view of the lake after eleven months of not seeing this cherished body of water. The shouts and cries of the other campers when they saw you, and the trunks to be unpacked, to give up their rich burden. (Arriving was less exciting nowadays, when you sneaked up in your car and parked it under a tree near the camp and took out the bags and in five minutes it was all over, no fuss, no loud wonderful fuss about trunks.)

Peace and goodness and jollity. The only thing that was wrong now, really, was the sound of the place, an unfamiliar nervous sound of the outboard motors. This was the note that jarred, the one thing that would sometimes break the illusion and set the years moving. In those other summertimes all motors were inboard; and when they were at a little distance, the noise they made was a sedative, an ingredient of summer sleep. They were one-cylinder and two-cylinder engines, and some were make-and-break and some were jump-spark, but they all made a sleepy sound across the lake. The one-lungers throbbed and fluttered, and the twin-cylinder ones purred and purred, and that was a quiet sound, too. But now the campers all had outboards. In the daytime, in the hot mornings, these motors made a petulant, irritable sound; at night, in the still evening when the afterglow lit the water, they whined about one's ears like mosquitoes. My boy loved our rented outboard, and his great desire was to achieve single-handed mastery over it, and authority, and he soon learned the trick of choking it a little (but not too much), and the adjustment of the needle valve. Watching him I would remember the things you could do with the old one-cylinder engine with the heavy flywheel, how you could have it eating out of your hand if you got really close to it spiritually. Motorboats in those days didn't have clutches, and you would make a landing by shutting off the motor at the proper time and coasting in with a dead rudder. But there was a way of reversing them, if you learned the trick, by cutting the switch and putting it on again exactly on the final dying revolution of the flywheel, so that it would kick back against compression and begin reversing. Approaching a dock in a strong following breeze, it was difficult to slow up sufficiently by the ordinary coasting method, and if a boy felt he had complete mastery over his motor, he was tempted to keep it running beyond its time and then reverse it a few feet from the dock. It took a cool nerve, because if you threw the switch a twentieth of a second too soon you would catch the flywheel when it still had speed enough to go up past center, and the boat would leap ahead, charging bull-fashion at the dock.

We had a good week at the camp. The bass were biting well and the sun shone endlessly, day after day. We would be tired at night and lie down in the accumulated heat of the little bedrooms after the long hot day and the breeze would stir almost imperceptibly outside and the smell of the swamp drift in through the rusty screens. Sleep would come easily and in the morning the red squirrel would be on the roof, tapping out his merry routine. I kept remembering everything, lying in bed in the mornings—the small steamboat that had a long rounded stern like the lip of a Ubangi,[1] and how quietly she ran on the moonlight sails, when the older boys played their mandolins and the girls sang and we ate doughnuts dipped in sugar, and how sweet the music was on the water in the shining night, and what it had felt like to think about girls then. After breakfast we would

go up to the store and the things were in the same place—the minnows in a bottle, the plugs and spinners disarranged and pawed over by the youngsters from the boys' camp, the Fig Newtons and the Beeman's gum. Outside, the road was tarred and cars stood in front of the store. Inside, all was just as it had always been, except there was more Coca-Cola and not so much Moxie and root beer and birch beer and sarsaparilla. We would walk out with the bottle of pop apiece and sometimes the pop would backfire up our noses and hurt. We explored the streams, quietly, where the turtles slid off the sunny logs and dug their way into the soft bottom; and we lay on the town wharf and fed worms to the tame bass. Everywhere we went I had trouble making out which was I, the one walking at my side, the one walking in my pants.

One afternoon while we were there at that lake a thunderstorm came up. It was like the revival of an old melodrama that I had seen long ago with childish awe. The second-act climax of the drama of the electrical disturbance over a lake in America had not changed in any important respect. This was the big scene, still the big scene. The whole thing was so familiar, the first feeling of oppression and heat and a general air around camp of not wanting to go very far away. In mid-afternoon (it was all the same) a curious darkening of the sky, and a lull in everything that had made life tick; and then the way the boats suddenly swung the other way at their moorings with the coming of a breeze out of the new quarter, and the premonitory rumble. Then the kettle drum, then the snare, then the bass drum and cymbals, then crackling light against the dark, and the gods grinning and licking their chops in the hills.

1. **Ubangi** ($\overline{oo}$ baŋ′ gē): nickname for people living near the Ubangi River in Africa, with pierced lips enlarged by saucerlike disks.

Afterward the calm, the rain steadily rustling in the calm lake, the return of light and hope and spirits, and the campers running out in joy and relief to go swimming in the rain, their bright cries perpetuating the deathless joke about how they were getting simply drenched, and the children screaming with delight at the new sensation of bathing in the rain, and the joke about getting drenched linking the generations in a strong indestructible chain. And the comedian who waded in carrying an umbrella.

When the others went swimming, my son said he was going in, too. He pulled his dripping trunks from the line where they had hung all through the shower and wrung them out. Languidly, and with no thought of going in, I watched him, his hard little body, skinny and bare, saw him wince slightly as he pulled up around his vitals the small, soggy, icy garment. As he buckled the swollen belt, suddenly my groin felt the chill of death.

## Getting at Meaning

1. What motivates the writer to return to the lake? Is his son part of that motivation? Explain.
2. How has the lake changed? In what ways is it the same?
3. What "transposition" occurs in the writer's mind? What brings on the transposition? At what later points in the selection does the writer touch upon this idea?
4. Why does the writer describe the thunderstorm as if it were a play?
5. Explain the last line of the essay.

## Developing Skills in Reading Literature

1. **Essay.** The writer of an essay can attempt to persuade the reader to see something in a new or different way. What view of father-son relationships does the writer present? What has the writer learned from his experiences? What does he want the reader to learn?
2. **Style.** Richly descriptive language characterizes the style of this essayist. Be prepared to identify passages that appeal to at least four senses.

## Developing Vocabulary

**Jargon.** Every sport and profession has its own specialized vocabulary. This language, spoken by the "insiders," is called jargon. The writer of this essay shows a familiarity with the jargon of fishing. What are some of the terms that he uses?

Choose another sport and list several examples of its specialized vocabulary.

Ask your parents to tell you some of the jargon associated with their work. Keep a list of these words.

List some of the jargon unique to your school, such as place names and scheduling terms.

## Developing Writing Skills

**Writing About a Personal Experience.** In a five-paragraph composition, describe an experience that you shared with one or both of your parents. Be sure to include the answers to these questions: What made the experience special? Would you like to repeat the experience? Why, or why not?

# Time Is Short and the Water Rises

## John Walsh with Robert Gannon

*Operation Gwamba began when ISPA (the International Society for the Protection of Animals) learned that thousands of forest creatures were trapped by the spreading artificial lake behind the new Afobaka Dam in Surinam—formerly Dutch Guiana. To Surinam, ISPA sent John Walsh, a young man trained in rescue techniques by the Massachusetts SPCA. What followed was one of this century's most extraordinary true adventures of man and animal—the story of the rescue of 10,000 animals from certain death in a South American rain forest.*

**W**hen my tranquilizer guns—three rifles and a pistol—arrived in customs shortly after the project started, they posed a problem for the Surinam authorities. How were they to be classified? Were they really guns? Were they "traps," as are nets? Or would the classification fall under "medical equipment," because of the syringes, needles, and drugs?

Customs officials, typical of the genre, settled the problem by moving the equipment to a side room, hoping that we would forget about it. Official explanation for the delay was "We're working on it; just a couple more days," and it stood that way for weeks. Finally I threw the problem in Commissioner Michel's lap. Then, because a commissioner's authority is virtually boundless, the guns were released in only another three weeks.

Ten years ago hardly anyone had heard of tranquilizer guns. Newly introduced at that time and barely understood, they were used mainly to pacify zoo animals. A shot of the drug Sparine would tranquilize a tiger, for instance, so he could be examined without the vet fearing loss of an arm. The tiger wouldn't be out, just tranquil. Soon zookeepers and others began employing larger charges and stronger drugs to knock out the animals, and today tranquilizer guns are widely used by humane groups, dogcatchers, zoologists, ranchers, and conservationists. (Actually, they're "immobilizer guns," but nobody calls them that but the manufacturer.)

Essentially, a tranquilizer rifle works this way: Two small cylinders of compressed carbon dioxide—the same as used in air pistols—are snapped under the barrel, and gas pressure builds up behind the projectile, basically an aluminum hypodermic needle. The gun goes off with a "pffft" instead of a bang. The rifle is accurate to thirty-five yards or so, the pistol to only about ten.

When the syringe hits, the needle penetrates the skin, and a plunger drives forward to inject the knockout substance—primarily a nicotine alkaloid. Early models used a mixture of acetic acid and sodium bicarbonate or carbide and water to shove the plunger forward. The shock of firing would jar the chemical loose from little containers and mix them, causing bubbling. By the time the projectile hit, the effervescence would have started slowly to slide the plunger, to inject the charge under the skin.

There were two troubles, though. Sometimes the bubbling worked so well that all the drug had squirted out en route. Other times, when the animal was struck, it wouldn't stand still long enough. A monkey, for instance, would reach back, pull out the missile, and trot off not even sleepy. Today syringes are activated explosively. When the projectile hits, an internal spring-loaded 22-caliber power charge fires, driving the plunger forward and injecting the knockout substance in a fraction of a second.

Some weeks earlier I had told the men I had a gun in Boston that puts animals to sleep. They all laughed and joked and thought it was a good story. When the equipment was released, I told nobody about it other than Robb, and only he knew what I had in mind when we set off for an island some twenty miles south of the dam. It had been underwater for a few weeks now. Before it submerged, we had swept it clean of all terrestrial animals; then, after many of the leaves had died and fallen, we removed most of the arboreal creatures. The only species left that we knew about was the red howler monkey, a monkey huge by South American standards (including the tail, it's more than a yard long), and his name comes from his most impressive voice.

The island of Gran Pati (meaning "big split") always had been an island. The Surinam River split around it, isolating a piece of land five miles long, two wide. Water now had killed most of the trees, and was submerging even the tops of those originally growing at the island's periphery. Actually, though, the time was somewhat early to go after red howlers. There was too much room left for them to move in, and miripa seeds—

howler food—were still plentiful. But I was anxious to try out the gun, to see if it was at all practical for jungle use.

We paddled, pushed, and pulled the boats through the trees for a while, then high above us, maybe seventy-five feet, we saw the troupe, ten or fifteen howlers chattering and watching us and swinging through the branches. I opened the tranquilizer gun case. "This is the gun that puts animals to sleep," I dramatically announced to the men. "I'll shoot the king, and in a few minutes he'll fall asleep." They were laughing now. Even Robb asked me under his breath if I were sure it would work.

A red howler troupe always has a king, a leader. I picked him out, waited until he was in the clear, and shot. Earlier I had set up the gun with the howler in mind, carefully measuring my guess of the correct dose (about 1½ cubic centimeters), preparing three syringes, just in case I missed.

I did. The missile streaked upward, pinged off a branch, and was never seen again. I reloaded and shot, sensing that shooting in a rain forest is not as easy as in a Massachusetts field. This one hit the limb under the monkey, stuck fast, and, squeezing knockout solution forward, strove to put the branch to sleep.

Then the third projectile. Success; it hit the monk smack in the left rear leg and stuck there. He stopped short, turned around and looked at it, pulled it out, and threw it down into the water. Then he went skipping off through the trees again.

The Bushblacks laughed and hooted and rocked back and forth in the boats and shouted at each other. They thought the monkey had showed me up. But I motioned to Sime to stay with the king, because I knew the syringe had injected a big enough dose.

Soon the king halted, out on the end of a branch about thirty feet up. He began to rock back and forth, and the men went "wooooo-ooo-ooo" and stopped laughing. The monkey swayed, tried to hold his balance, then slowly slid around to the underside of the branch. He let go with his arms and legs, and like a pendulum swung gently to and fro, hanging by his tail. I hopped to the back of the boat, grabbed one of the long-handled nets, and held it under the branch. "Now he's going to fall," I said—and sure enough, he did, right into the net. What a production.

"Oh, you killed him, boss," said Sime, and I was a little surprised to hear that his voice was pensive.

I rolled my subject out on the dugout bottom and looked at his furriness. His long, thick coat, predominantly dark red, looked actually metallic close up, with glowing shimmers of gold, copper, and bronze. The top of his tail was heavily furred, but its underside was bald—the better to grip branches with. "Tonight when it gets dark, he'll be waking up," I announced.

On our way back to camp, we passed an island that once had been two miles across, but by now had shrunk to just a spot. We'd covered it twice already, once to capture the larger ground-living animals—deer, mostly—then later, when it had dwindled to a hundred yards across, to scoop up the smaller beasts: agoutis, pacas, armadillos.

I signaled Sime to turn the boat and to idle down so we barely moved. We picked our way first through the treetops at the outer edge, then through the trunks as the water became shallower, then through the newly submerged ferns, still green—but a brownish green—as they fountained from the water. Ahead was the only remaining spot of solid land—a hilltop now six feet across. If anything at all is left, I thought, it will be here.

I expected to see turtles, perhaps, or rats, or maybe snakes. What we did find were toads, scores of them—some in the water, bobbing in the waves made by our boat, the rest squeezed onto the little plot of ground, two, three deep. These were the giant *Bufo marinus*, called neotropical toads, common throughout northern South America and Central America, occasionally seen in Mexico and even Texas. But nowhere do these, the largest tailless amphibians in the world, grow as large as in the Guianas. Most of these had a diameter of maybe six inches, but a few were as large as LP records, ten, twelve inches—larger than any I had ever read about. The biggest ones all were females, and each had a male rider clinging piggyback, his forefeet grabbing little fingerholds handily located just back of her ears, waiting for her to just try to lay eggs without his participation.

We stepped overboard into the shallow water and started scooping the dozens of flaccid amphibians into the boat. Most were extremely skinny, sluggish, and weak from lack of food; but when I tried to pull a male from the back of his beloved, his foreleg muscles seemed to be made of steel.

The whole bottom of the boat was a warty, hopping mass a half foot deep when we set out again. The drugged howler monkey, fortunately, remained unconscious. He'd be unhappy if he came to. He was half submerged in toads.

Along the lakeside, on the way back to camp, we stopped four times to scoop out the giant toads, who, like great mounds of animated lichen, went plopping off into the forest.

It was after we returned to camp that I began worrying about the monkey. He should be waking now, I figured, but instead he was comatose, dangerously so, I felt. His heart was barely pumping, his breathing, shallow and plodding, was slowing even more. I must have given him an overdose.

Then his breathing stopped altogether, and his gums and tongue began to turn blue from lack of oxygen. I pulled the sprawling 25-pound body onto my lap and began squeezing his upper chest rhythmically, wondering how fast a monkey's respiration rate is supposed to be. I squeezed and squeezed and soon he began breathing again. Then he stopped, turned blue, and I squeezed again. The sequence continued, and finally I settled myself in a chair with the monkey on my lap and a book propped up in front of me and spent the next two and a half hours squeezing until he began breathing, then letting him go on his own until he stopped, then squeezing again. My hands got tired, then numb, as the ache worked its way up my arms into my shoulders. Finally the periods during which the monkey breathed by himself lengthened. The respiration became regular, the heart strong, and finally I could relax. Now every once in a while his eyelids fluttered.

I left him lying there, sprawled out on the box in the middle of camp. Every so often the men gathered around him would feel his beating heart or watch his eyes twitch, reassuring themselves that he actually was still alive. Then around seven o'clock he began to raise his head, look around and drop again, and each time he did his audience would exclaim and comment and laugh. Soon he sat up, and we slid him into a cage (we planned to hold him at camp until we captured the rest of his troupe, then release them all together), and he contented himself by spending the rest of the evening scowling at whoever looked his way.

The men called the tranquilizer rifle *doemi goeni*—sleep gun—and word of its magic quickly spread up the river. Throughout my stay, whenever I'd go into a strange village, the captain casually would mention that he had heard the story—undoubtedly a fabrication—that I had a *doemi goeni*, some device that would put animals to sleep. I'd

verify that it was so, but I could tell he still didn't quite believe it, not unless one of my men was with me, another Bushblack that the captain could really trust.

In many situations the guns were a blessing, but we quickly learned that they were no panacea. Shooting a hypodermic syringe through a rain-forest canopy is extremely difficult. Any little leaf or twig in the flight path will cause it to miss the target, and deflected needles rarely can be found. They're expensive, too; each needle costs from two to five dollars, depending on size. And maintenance was a problem. The guns were always being thrown hurriedly into the bottom of the boat as we took off after animals, there to be stepped upon or flooded with water.

The biggest problem, though, was deciding how much drug each kind of animal should get. We had two choices of the nicotine solution: One was fast-acting with a narrow margin of safety, a bigger chance of overdosing and killing the animal. The other was slow-acting, and if an overdose was accidentally given, the animal simply would sleep longer. Usually, when shooting a new kind of animal, we'd guess the amount needed, then use the slow-acting, high-safety solution a few times. When we were sure of the amount, we'd switch to the other concentration.

The slow-acting material was less desirable, mainly because being struck with an exploding hypodermic syringe panics many animals, and if the drug acts too slowly, the animal may escape, only to become dazed and collapse later, vulnerable to predators.

Our general yardstick was based on North American animals, a certain ratio of solution to body weight (cubic centimeters per pound), depending on species and solution concentration. But the trouble was, things didn't work out in nice, parallel steps. A tapir might weigh four times as much as a man, but will need ten times as much drug to achieve the same effect. Large, hoofed animals—North American cattle and deer, for instance—require about one cubic centimeter per one hundred pounds. But if you use that ratio on small animals, like foxes or raccoons, they are hardly fazed. You have to step up the ratio to one cubic centimeter per twenty-five pounds—a fourfold relative increase.

We never did find what some animals require. The giant armadillo, for instance. Giant armadillos are relatively rare in Surinam, or at least in the area we worked, for in the whole eighteen months of the project we caught only seven of them in the 650-square-mile area. We tranquilized our first *Priodontes giganteus* on an island a mile long and half mile wide, a former hilltop ten miles upriver from the dam.

The morning was half gone when Robb and I arrived. Bally, Deo, and the dogs were hollering and crashing through the brush, herding whatever was on the island to men waiting in the boats. We paddled up just as the dogs began to bark frantically, a somewhat different kind of bark than I had heard before.

We beached and ran toward the sound, as usual crashing through the foliage like madmen, stickers and thorns and vines bouncing off us. Then we broke into a sort of clearing, and stopped. Still. Like something out of a Tertiary[1] fantasy, the giant armadillo stood swaying and slowly turning its hundred-pound massiveness. Its shell was a yard long; add another yard for its bony snout and its scaly tail. Three dogs were facing it, yelping their fool heads off, while the animal stood at bay. One of the dogs dashed for the armadillo's tail. The quarry spun with astonishing speed, whipping his forefoot around toward the dog. He missed, and it's good he did. An armadillo's middle finger on the forefoot is equipped with a four-inch claw, sickle-shaped and vicious. This is the implement he uses to rip apart termite nests to get at his favorite food.

Deo rushed up and called the dogs away from the *graman kapasie*. It stood there looking at us, we looked at it, and both wondered what next.

The armadillo came to a decision first. He took off—straight through a patch of *baboenefi* (named for a Hindustani knife), and that was my first experience with *that* stuff, too. This is the famed razor grass or saw grass of tropical and semi-tropical America. It thrives wherever the jungle has been cleared, a harmless-looking, tall, wide-

---

1. **Tertiary** (tûr′ shē er′ ē): the geological period following the Mesozoic Era when the dinosaurs lived.

bladed grass growing in patches as innocent-appearing as northern cattail swamps. But each blade sports minute, razory teeth running along the edges.

The giant armadillo scurried massively into the patch, into an overgrown plot of cleared jungle, obviously an old cassava *gron*.[2] Not having had experience with the stuff before, I plunged after him into what looked like an eight- or nine-foot wall of thick grass. The men, I noticed about three seconds later, had stopped. I stopped, too. Quickly. My face and arms were cut as though I had run into a batch of razor blades dangling from strings. In dozens of crimson slivers, blood began oozing from my skin. I stood statuelike as the guys came in, hacking their way with machetes, making a tunnel through the razor grass. Blood was running down into my eyes now, and I noticed my ankles leaking into my tennis shoes. In some places the grass had sliced through my shirt and pants, and little slashings of blood were soaking through. I sent one of the guys back to my boat for the first-aid kit, then washed my face and arms in alcohol. It stung briefly, then was all over; the cuts were so thin they seemed to heal almost immediately—after ten minutes or so, hardly bothering me.

Meanwhile, some of the men and dogs had gone around the *gron*, heading the armadillo off, then surrounding him. By the time I got there, they were at an impasse again. And again the armadillo acted. He started digging, scooping the soft, red lateritic sand away with his snout and with his forefeet, flinging it to the sides in pink splashes. I grabbed onto his long, carrot-shaped tail, but my hands, sore from the *baboenefi*, slipped off. I doubt I could have held anyway, though, so strong was the creature.

*"Tjari* [Get the] *doemi goeni,"* I told Sime, who was watching with fascination. I planned to inject tranquilizer into the beast

directly. But the armadillo was disappearing from view, going down at about a forty-five degree angle. I yelled to Sime to bring back a couple of shovels, too.

By the time he returned—not more than five minutes—all we could see of our mammoth friend was that silly oatmeal-colored tail and a sliver of shell. With gusto, the men began digging in front of him, some twelve feet away. By the time I got the syringe loaded, he had disappeared. Hopefully, they would reach a spot in front of him, and he would break through into the open, where I could nab him with a hypo. I sent Sime back for two more shovels.

Part of the idea worked. We got there first, and the armadillo broke through. But he only poked his snout through, then hastily backed up, and began digging away at a different angle. With increased fury, the four shovelers attacked again at two different points. A half hour later, the snout broke through again, disappeared, and the whole digging process began once more. We dug for that animal until two-thirty in the afternoon, nearly four hours in all. At that time he changed tactics; he began burrowing straight down. We gave up.

Every few days through the next several weeks, I stopped off to check on my gross challenger. The island shriveled, food got sparse, and I knew he was getting hungry, probably becoming weak from the beginnings of starvation. No termites were left, and his substitute diet items—insects, lizards, grubs, certain roots, decaying vegetation—were also getting scarce.

One day four months later the island was only a hundred yards across, and no spot was more than six feet above the water—which meant that the armadillo couldn't dig down

---

2. **cassava gron** (kə sä' və grön): an area set aside to grow cassava, certain plants having edible starchy roots.

very far. With shovels and syringes at the ready, four of us stormed the island. We caught him above ground, snorting and scuffling along looking for food. While the three others grabbed him by the tail and the back of the shell—trying to hold him still but succeeding only in impeding his progress—I plunged the hypodermic into his rear leg muscle, just under the shell. I used the fast-acting solution, shooting in 1½ cubic centimeters. Then I helped hold him back. It should have knocked him cold in five or ten minutes.

A half hour later we were still being dragged around the forest floor. Every so often the beast would start to dig, and we'd flip him over on his back, dodging his built-in cleavers. Then he'd right himself and walk off, the four of us slipping and sliding behind. With forty-five minutes gone, I decided to give him another injection. I stepped up the dose and shot enough in him to stop a horse. Half an hour later we were still skiing. Whenever we let go, he would begin to dig down, and though he could burrow only six feet, I was afraid he might dig to the water-table line, there to relax, sleep, and drown.

Finally, he began hauling us with less enthusiasm. He was, in fact, staggering a bit. Then he stumbled, began falling every few steps, and two men could pretty well control him. We led him like a drunken bear to the boat, flipped his hundredweight into it, and three of us sat on him while Wimpy piloted us home. We tried to tie those mean forefeet together, but every time we got close, he'd start slinging them around.

Fortunately the trip to camp was short. There, we called for fresh troops, and by alternately pushing and leading the groggy beast, we guided him to the holding area. He was almost unconscious now; he didn't fight or try to dig but he did continue to walk, round and round, in thirty-foot circles as though sleepwalking. We placed an animal trap in front of him. He walked in, hit the bars on the other end, hooked his claws in them, bent and ripped them apart, and walked out the other side to continue his circular pacing. We led and pushed him to the storage hut. He walked in easily enough, and came out the other end, having battered through the wooden planks.

We couldn't hold him. Despite the fact that night was coming, we decided we had better get him to shore while we could still control him a little. Into the boat again, and under three guys went the armadillo, who should have been asleep hours ago. We headed for the nearest *gwamba loesoe pasi*, the boat path where we had cut trails from the lake back through the treetops to the shore for animal release. He seemed to be coming out of it by then—at least he was becoming more aggressive, slinging those forefeet at us with increased vigor.

Finally, as dusk closed in and we felt he was safe to leave alone, we turned him loose and set off for camp again. We could hear him tipsily stumbling and crashing through the undergrowth as we paddled out through the trees.

We never could seem to be able to give giant armadillos enough of the drug to knock them out. With some of the other animals, though, we had just the opposite trouble. One little peccary, for instance, I remember well, a fellow we found on the same island where we got the giant armadillo. All the peccaries we caught during the operation were of the white-collared variety (*Tayassu tajacu*), the same piglike creature found in the extreme southern United States and all the way south to the bottom of South America. Collared peccaries (also called javalina) once roamed as far north as Arkansas, but American sportsmen have succeeded in wiping them out everywhere except along the southern borders of Texas, New Mexico, and Arizona.

The little peccary on the armadillo island,

clad in long, stiff fur of grizzly-gray with a white collar around his neck—sort of like a skinny, long-legged Hampshire hog—was chased by Bally's dogs down into a hole. By the time Deo blocked up the other entrance so the animal couldn't run out, the rest of us had arrived. The guys cleared some brush away from the hole, then with shovels dug down about four feet. The little pig felt his rear end exposed to the world, so he turned around and clacked his tusks at us—two uppers pointing down, two lowers pointing up. When cornered, as this one was, peccaries can be vicious. So rather than try to haul him out full of fight, I fitted my tranquilizer pistol with a low charge of dope—enough to stun him, but not put him out for long.

I aimed at his shoulder and fired. He clacked his tusks a couple more times, then, in less than a minute, flopped down. Wimpy had the Ketch-all pole with the slipknot on the end, and he lowered it down and looped it over the pig's neck, then gently pulled him upward, out of the hole.

I knew something was wrong. The peccary was out cold, hardly moving. I pulled back his lips; his tongue and gums were that awful blue color from lack of oxygen. He wasn't breathing. Stretching the two-foot animal on the ground, I started giving him artificial respiration, pushing on his chest in about the same way I did the monkey. But I saw I was too late. His heart had stopped. He was dead.

The tranquilizer needle was still sticking in him, in his chest. I withdrew it, and only then noticed that instead of using the small-animal, ⅝-inch needle, I had inadvertently used the 2½-inch size, the largest one, to be used only for the biggest creatures. If I had hit him where I had aimed, though—the shoulder—probably no permanent damage would have been done. But I missed. Instead, I struck him in the forward rib cage, probably piercing either his lung or heart. We buried him where we found him.

I was so careful with the next peccary I didn't even use a tranquilizer. We came upon this one a few days later, on an island near the other, and because this peccary was a young one—only a foot high and a foot and a half long—three of us were able to chase her, surround her, and grab her. She was cute. And I felt so bad about killing the other one I decided to keep her for a pet. We named her Meena, after one of the men's wives.

Meena was rather slim for a pig (actually peccaries belong to a different family than U.S. pigs), and certainly behaved much better than the pigs I knew back in Massachusetts. When she walked on her thin, delicate legs tipped with shiny little hooves, it was most ladylike. When running—considerably faster than I could—her legs moved in a stiff-legged blur, and when she came trotting across the hard-pan center of the camp, her hooves sounded like a dozen tiny horses.

One of her two favorite activities was grub hunting. Her head tapered conelike to a flat, moist, turned-up nose, the nozzle flattened to the size of the bottom of a glass. This was her shovel. She'd snort and shuffle around camp, digging little ditches and piling up mounds here and there, head down, tiny tail up.

When you'd walk by, she'd look up at you pig-eyed with a terribly dirty nose and want you to pick her up. And that was her other favorite activity, riding around in someone's arms. If you'd do the ultimate—turn her over on her back like a baby and scratch her belly —she'd show her ecstasy by closing her eyes and grinding those teeth-tusks of hers like castanets.

When I was away for a few hours, or even a few minutes, Meena would come trotting up on my return, clacking her tusks, squeaking, snorting with delight, sighing mightily while she poked at my leg with her ridiculous nose. I'd try to walk away, and she'd step between my legs. In order to save myself from falling, I'd have to pick her up.

Early one morning I awakened to find an ice-cold, very wet, rubbery nose snuffling and pushing into my cheek through the mosquito netting. I opened my eyes and there was Meena, somehow having clambered up on the table. She gargled a greeting and indicated that we should bundle. So I lifted the netting and she galomphed in. I was sorry I had given in. She danced up and down on me on those stiletto heels of hers, nuzzling with her nozzle, occasionally fluffing her pillow—me—with her sharp baby tusks. Snort and chatter her tusks as much as she wanted, that was the last time we shared a bed.

Whenever we left in the morning for the day's hunt, she knew she would be lonely for hours, so she'd try to come along. She was extremely intelligent, as are all peccaries, and she'd try to outwit us. She'd watch for signs that we were leaving, then run down to the boats, climb into one of them, and stand very still in hopes that no one would notice her. We'd pick her up and put her on shore, pull away, and she would swim out to us. Then we'd have to back up again, put her on shore, get really angry in our scolding, and maybe she'd stay there.

After we captured Meena, barely tranquilized, we found that the easiest and most practical method of drugging peccaries was with just the needle, no gun. I'd dig down a burrow until I'd come to the clacking tusks, then, holding the animal tight with a Ketch-all pole, I'd pull him forward, grab him with animal gloves, then zip the needle into his shoulder. Afterward, I'd give the peccary a broad-spectrum antibiotic before letting him go, for prevention of possible infection developing at the point where the tranquilizer needle punctured the skin—for it was impossible to keep the needles sterile. We also used the tropical antiseptic Furacin on animals with superficial wounds. Most of the deer we caught, for example, had one or more sub-surface worms, usually embedded in the rib cage. We'd slit the wound, squeeze the grub out, then, with a pliable plastic bottle with a long snout on it, we'd squirt some Furacin into the hole. (And sometimes the Bush-blacks would daub the drug on their foreheads for headaches—logical; look how it healed the animals.)

The drugs were carried along with me in the boat, in what I called my bag of tricks—an old BWIA flight bag. Also inside was a first-aid kit (including boxes of antivenin), a can of beans (invariably rusty), malaria pills, pliers, a plastic raincoat, old cassava, waterproof matches, three fishhooks, and a line in case I got stranded, and extra tranquilizer gun parts.

Probably the most dramatic use of the gun came not long after we had got it, on an island just about to go underwater. We had just taken two deer, half a dozen agoutis and pacas, and a few sloths from the land, using eight boats, with two or three men to a boat. We were putputting through a pass cut with machetes from the island to the main river course, headed for an animal release point some six miles to the west, when suddenly a cry rang out to the side: "Tigre-katie! tigre-katie" (ocelot).

Motors roared as we headed in the direction of the yelling, the boats crashing through the thick growth. When we neared, we could see the ocelot in the branches—maybe thirty feet up—running from tree to tree as easily as though on land. I loaded by tranquilizer gun, but didn't even try to shoot; the branches were much too thick.

With Wimpy yelling instructions, the men formed a crescent with their dugouts, forcing the cat to flee through the trees toward the open water. Finally she reached a large tree standing rather by itself on the island's edge. The men paddled up behind her, and, with machetes flailing, dropped the adjacent trees into the water, isolating her.

Still sleek and in good, healthy condition—obviously well fed, probably from eating weakened smaller animals—the ocelot hunched snarling at the men as they began cutting the branches from her tree so I could get a clean shot. Suddenly she leaped at one of them. His partner was watching, and while the ocelot was in midair, he spun the boat with his paddle. She splashed into the water on one side of the boat while her intended victim plunged in on the other. Later he claimed he fell.

Each boat had a cat pole in it, but not a single one was fitted together; no one expected the cat to jump. I couldn't see to fire because the action was on the far side of the tree, and if I didn't smack the trunk with the needle, I'd get one of the men. So by the time cat poles were fitted together, the ocelot, wet, dripping, skinny-looking, and twice as mad as before, had climbed back into the tree.

The guys resumed their branch-cutting then—watchfully—and I took a shot, missed, tried again, missed again, both times because of twigs in the way. Then the cat changed branches. I shot a third round, and the needle hit her in the haunches. She hissed, reached back and swatted the needle away, but it was too late; the drug began to affect her almost immediately. She sat down, then lay down, and with a pitiful mew, lowered her head to the branch and went to sleep, her legs dangling on either side. She stayed there, wafting in the breeze like a stole.

Someone *could* go up after her, but because the tree was of softwood, the men decided to cut it down. Again the clang of machetes rang through the area, and soon the tree leaned, cracked, and fell.

As soon as the cat touched the water, she became a splashing, clawing, thrashing mill. She started swimming toward my boat, and, as she approached, I dived into the water, came up beside her, and caught her around the back. It was the first time I had ever grabbed an ocelot, but in the water it was easy; she seemed like a yard-long, quite-heavy house cat. But I knew enough to beware of those claws.

At the side of the boat, while I was trying to decide what to do with her, she passed out again. Treading water, I lifted her up to Sime, who grabbed her by the scruff of the neck and the tail. He laid her, unconscious, in the boat.

Before sliding her into a carrying bag, we inspected her closely. She was beautiful, about two or three years old, in her prime. She had not a mark on her—no ticks in her soft fur of black, ringlike fused spots against a buff background, no signs of worms.

She opened an eye, and quickly, before she

knew what was happening, I slipped her into a bag. Then she started struggling. To quiet her, I gave her another injection, right through the canvas. Otherwise she would have ripped the bag, maybe even herself.

When we touched land, we found a log and rested one end on the shore, the other on the side of the boat. Then we slid the ocelot out onto the seat. She lay there like a house cat sunning herself, her tail twitching slightly and her eyelids moving, dreaming. Then, in ten minutes or so, she awoke, slowly sat up, regarded us gravely, and slunk slowly along the log, still groggy. Soon as she touched land, though, all grogginess seemed to disappear. Like an alley cat pursued by a pack of hounds, she bounded off into the jungle, off to where food would be considerably harder to get, but where she would have a good chance for a long life.

## Getting at Meaning

1. What problems arise when Walsh's tranquilizer guns arrive in Surinam?

2. Contrast the conditions under which Walsh learned to use a tranquilizer gun and the conditions under which he now must put his training into practice.

3. How do the captures of the following animals illustrate Walsh's problems in using tranquilizer guns: the howler monkey, the giant armadillo, the peccary?

4. How do the actions of the giant armadillo and of Meena, the pet peccary, demonstrate the intelligence of these animals?

5. The writer describes both the ocelot and the howler monkey. What details can be included in these descriptions only because the animals are tranquilized?

6. The writer describes the reactions of both humans and animals to unfamiliar situations and unexpected events. Contrast, in general terms, the behavior of the two groups.

## Developing Skills in Reading Literature

1. **Nonfiction.** What insights into life in the natural world does this writer provide? List at least ten facts included in the selection.

2. **Setting.** The setting of this selection is a changing natural environment. What aspects of the environment are in transition? What problems do the changes cause for both the men and the animals? What is the writer's attitude toward the natural world? What is the reader's impression of this setting? How does the writer create this impression?

## Developing Vocabulary

**Latin Roots.** The Latin word *terra* means "land"; the Latin word *arbor* means "tree." These two Latin roots are the basis for the following groups of words. Write a definition for each word, using only your knowledge of its Latin root. Then check your definitions in a dictionary.

| | |
|---|---|
| terrestrial | arboreal |
| terrain | arboretum |
| terrarium | arboriculture |

## Developing Writing Skills

**Explaining a Process.** The writer of this selection explains in detail the process of using a tranquilizer gun. He covers the loading of the gun and the discharge of tranquilizing solution and describes modern improvements upon outdated methods. Choose a familiar piece of equipment, such as a bicycle or a bow and arrow. In one paragraph, explain the process of preparing and using the item.

# Flood     *Annie Dillard*

The creek's up. When the rain stopped to-day, I walked across the road to the downed log by the steer crossing. The steers were across the creek, a black clot on a distant hill. High water had touched my log, the log I sit on, and dumped a smooth slope of muck in its lee. The water itself was an opaque pale green, like pulverized jade, still high and very fast, lightless, like no earthly water. A dog I've never seen before, thin as death, was flushing rabbits.

A knot of yellow, fleshy somethings had grown up by the log. They didn't seem to have either proper stems or proper flowers, but instead only blind, featureless growth, like etiolated potato sprouts in a root cellar. I tried to dig one up from the crumbly soil, but they all apparently grew from a single, well rooted corm, so I let them go.

Still, the day had an air of menace. A broken bottle by the log, the brown tip of a snake's tail disappearing between two rocks on the hill at my back, the rabbit the dog nearly caught, the rabies I knew was in the county, the bees who kept unaccountably fumbling at my forehead with their furred feet.

I headed over to the new woods by the creek, the motorbike woods. They were strangely empty. The air was so steamy I could barely see. The ravine separating the woods from the field had filled during high water, and a dead tan mud clogged it now. The ragged orange roots of one tree on the ravine's jagged bank had been stripped of soil; now the roots hung, an empty net in the air, clutching an incongruous light bulb stranded by receding waters. For the entire time that I walked in the woods, four jays flew around me very slowly, acting generally odd, and screaming on two held notes. There wasn't a breath of wind.

Coming out of the woods, I heard loud shots; they reverberated ominously in the damp air. But when I walked up the road, I saw what it was, and the dread quality of the whole afternoon vanished at once. It was a couple of garbage trucks, huge trash com-pacters humped like armadillos, and they were making their engines backfire to im-press my neighbors' pretty daughters, high school girls who had just been let off the school bus. The long-haired girls strayed into giggling clumps at the corner of the road; the garbage trucks sped away gloriously, as if they had been the Tarleton twins on thor-oughbreds cantering away from the gates of Tara.[1] In the distance a white vapor was ris-ing from the waters of Carvin's Cove and catching in trailing tufts in the mountains' sides. I stood on my own porch, exhilarated, unwilling to go indoors.

It was just this time last year that we had the flood. It was Hurricane Agnes, really, but by the time it got here, the weather bureau had demoted it to a tropical storm. I see by a clipping I saved that the day was June twenty-first, the solstice, midsummer's night,

---

1. **Tarleton twins . . . Tara:** two gentlemen suitors of Scarlett O'Hara at Tara, her Georgia plantation, in the novel *Gone with the Wind.*

creek and is roving frantically to escape, big and ugly, like a blacksnake caught in a kitchen drawer. The color is foul, a rusty cream. Water that has picked up clay soils looks worse than other muddy waters, because the particles of clay are so fine; they spread out and cloud the water so that you can't see light through even an inch of it in a drinking glass.

Everything looks different. Where my eye is used to depth, I see the flat water, near, too near. I see trees I never noticed before, the black verticals of their rain-soaked trunks standing out of the pale water like pilings for a rotted dock. The stillness of grassy banks and stony ledges is gone; I see rushing, a wild sweep and hurry in one direction, as swift and compelling as a waterfall. The Atkins kids are out in their tiny rain gear, staring at the monster creek. It's risen up to their gates; the neighbors are gathering; I go out.

I hear a roar, a high windy sound more like air than like water, like the run-together whaps of a helicopter's propeller after the engine is off, a high million rushings. The air smells damp and acrid, like fuel oil, or insecticide. It's raining.

I'm in no danger; my house is high. I hurry down the road to the bridge. Neighbors who have barely seen each other all winter are there, shaking their heads. Few have ever seen it before: the water is *over* the bridge. Even when I see the bridge now, which I do every day, I still can't believe it: the water was *over* the bridge, a foot or two over the bridge, which at normal times is eleven feet above the surface of the creek.

Now the water is receding slightly; someone has produced empty metal drums, which we roll to the bridge and set up in a square to keep cars from trying to cross. It takes a bit of nerve even to stand on the bridge; the flood

the longest daylight of the year; but I didn't notice it at the time. Everything was so exciting, and so very dark.

All it did was rain. It rained, and the creek started to rise. The creek, naturally, rises every time it rains; this didn't seem any different. But it kept raining, and, that morning of the twenty-first, the creek kept rising.

That morning I'm standing at my kitchen window. Tinker Creek[2] is out of its four-foot banks, way out, and it's still coming. The high creek doesn't look like our creek. Our creek splashes transparently over a jumble of rocks; the high creek obliterates everything in flat opacity. It looks like somebody else's creek that has usurped or eaten our

---

2. **Tinker Creek:** a creek in Virginia.

has ripped away a wedge of concrete that buttressed the bridge on the bank. Now one corner of the bridge hangs apparently unsupported while water hurls in an arch just inches below.

It's hard to take it all in, it's all so new. I look at the creek at my feet. It smashes under the bridge like a fist, but there is no end to its force; it hurtles down as far as I can see till it lurches round the bend, filling the valley, flattening, mashing, pushed, wider and faster, till it fills my brain.

It's like a dragon. Maybe it's because the bridge we are on is chancy, but I notice that no one can help imagining himself washed overboard, and gauging his chances for survival. You couldn't live. Mark Spitz[3] couldn't live. The water arches where the bridge's supports at the banks prevent its enormous volume from going wide, forcing it to go high; that arch drives down like a diving whale, and would butt you on the bottom. "You'd never know what hit you," one of the men says. But if you survived that part and managed to surface . . . ? How fast can you live? You'd need a windshield. You couldn't keep your head up; the water under the surface is fastest. You'd spin around like a sock in a clothes dryer. You couldn't grab onto a tree trunk without leaving that arm behind. No, you couldn't live. And if they ever found you, your gut would be solid red clay.

It's all I can do to stand. I feel dizzy, drawn, mauled. Below me the floodwater roils to a violent froth that looks like dirty lace, a lace that continuously explodes before my eyes. If I look away, the earth moves backwards, rises and swells, from the fixing of my eyes at one spot against the motion of the flood. All the familiar land looks as though it were not solid and real at all, but painted on a scroll like a backdrop, and that unrolled scroll has been shaken, so the earth sways and the air roars.

Everything imaginable is zipping by, almost too fast to see. If I stand on the bridge and look downstream, I get dizzy; but if I look upstream, I feel as though I am looking up the business end of an avalanche. There are dolls, split wood and kindling, dead fledgling songbirds, bottles, whole bushes and trees, rakes and garden gloves. Wooden, rough-hewn railroad ties charge by faster than any express. Lattice fencing bobs along, and a wooden picket gate. There are so many white plastic gallon milk jugs that when the flood ultimately recedes, they are left on the grassy banks looking from a distance like a flock of white geese.

I expect to see anything at all. In this way, the creek is more like itself when it floods than at any other time: mediating, bringing things down. I wouldn't be at all surprised to see John Paul Jones coming round the bend, standing on the deck of the *Bon Homme Richard*, or Amelia Earhart waving gaily from the cockpit of her floating Lockheed. Why not a cello, a basket of breadfruit, a casket of antique coins? Here comes the Franklin expedition[4] on snowshoes, and the three magi, plus camels, afloat on a canopied barge!

The whole world is in flood, the land as well as the water. Water streams down the trunks of trees, drips from hat-brims, courses across roads. The whole earth seems to slide like sand down a chute; water pouring over the least slope leaves the grass flattened, silver side up, pointing downstream. Everywhere windfall and flotsam twigs and leafy boughs, wood from woodpiles, bottles, and saturated straw spatter the ground or streak it in curving windrows. Tomatoes in flat gardens are literally floating in mud; they look as though they have been dropped

---

3. **Mark Spitz:** champion Olympic swimmer.
4. **Franklin expedition:** the expedition of Sir John Franklin, English arctic explorer.

whole into a boiling, brown-gravy stew. The level of the water table is at the top of the toe of my shoes. Pale muddy water lies on the flat so that it all but drowns the grass; it looks like a hideous parody of a light snow on the field, with only the dark tips of the grass blades visible.

When I look across the street, I can't believe my eyes. Right behind the road's shoulder are waves, waves whipped in rhythmically peaking scallops, racing downstream. The hill where I watched the praying mantis lay her eggs is a waterfall that splashes into a brown ocean. I can't even remember where the creek usually runs—it is everywhere now. My log is gone for sure, I think—but in fact, I discover later, it holds, rammed between growing trees. Only the cable suspending the steers' fence is visible, and not the fence itself; the steers' pasture is entirely in flood, a brown river. The river leaps its banks and smashes into the woods where the motorbikes go, devastating all but the sturdiest trees. The water is so deep and wide it seems as though you could navigate the *Queen Mary* in it, clear to Tinker Mountain.

What do animals do in these floods? I see a drowned muskrat go by like he's flying, but they all couldn't die; the water rises after every hard rain, and the creek is still full of muskrats. This flood is higher than their raised sleeping platforms in the banks; they must just race for high ground and hold on. Where do the fish go, and what do they do? Presumably their gills can filter oxygen out of this muck, but I don't know how. They must hide from the current behind any barriers they can find, and fast for a few days. They must. Otherwise we'd have no fish; they'd all be in the Atlantic Ocean. What about herons and kingfishers, say? They can't see to eat. It usually seems to me that when I see any animal, its business is urgent enough that it couldn't easily be suspended for forty-eight hours. Crayfish, frogs, snails,

rotifers? Most things must simply die. They couldn't live. Then I suppose that when the water goes down and clears, the survivors have a field day with no competition. But you'd think the bottom would be knocked out of the food chain—the whole pyramid would have no base plankton, and it would crumble, or crash with a thud. Maybe enough spores and larvae and eggs are constantly being borne down from slower upstream waters to repopulate. I don't know.

Some little children have discovered a snapping turtle as big as a tray. It's hard to believe that this creek could support a predator that size: its shell is a foot and a half across, and its head extends a good seven inches beyond the shell. When the children —in the company of a shrunken terrier— approach it on the bank, the snapper rears up on its thick front legs and hisses very impressively. I had read earlier that since turtles' shells are rigid, they don't have bellows lungs; they have to gulp for air. And, also since their shells are rigid, there's only room for so much inside, so when they are frightened and planning a retreat, they have to expel air from their lungs to make room for head and feet—hence the malevolent hiss.

The next time I look, I see that the children have somehow maneuvered the snapper into a washtub. They're waving a broom handle at it in hopes that it will snap the wood like a matchstick, but the creature will not deign to oblige. The kids are crushed; all their lives they've heard that this is the one thing you do with a snapping turtle— you shove a broom handle near it, and it "snaps it like a matchstick." It's nature's way; it's sure-fire. But the turtle is having none of it. It avoids the broom handle with an air of patiently repressed rage. They let it go, and it beelines down the bank, dives unhesitatingly into the swirling floodwater, and that's the last we see of it.

A cheer comes up from the crowd on the

plate, erupting overnight mysteriously in the Bings' living room—from the back of an upholstered couch, say, or from a still-damp rug under an armchair.

Alas, the story as I had fixed it in my mind proved to be only partly true. The Bings often cook wild mushrooms, and they know what they're doing. This particular mushroom had grown outside, under a syca-more, on high ground that the flood hadn't touched. So the flood had nothing to do with it. But it's still a good story, and I like to think that the flood left them a gift, a consolation prize, so that for years to come they will be finding edible mushrooms here and there about the house, dinner on the bookshelf, hors d'oeuvres in the piano. It would have been nice.

## Getting at Meaning

1. At the beginning of this selection, the writer describes a sense of menace in the air. What factors contribute to her uneasiness? To answer this question, choose details from at least two different paragraphs. Why does the day remind the writer of the flood?

2. How does the flood bring neighbors together? How do the children react to the flood?

3. The writer says, ". . . the creek is more like itself when it floods than at any other time. . . ." What does she mean? Give examples to support your answer.

4. Why does the writer wish that the Bings' mushroom had been left by the flood? What does this reveal about her attitude toward the flood?

## Developing Skills in Reading Literature

1. **Mood.** What is the mood of the opening four paragraphs? Identify words and phrases that help to create this mood. What event alters the mood? Why has the event had this effect? Explain how the remainder of this selection follows the same pattern of mood change.

2. **Allusion.** Research the following allusions from this selection, and be prepared to explain their meanings.

the Tarleton twins riding away from Tara (p. 367)

Mark Spitz (p. 369)

John Paul Jones on the *Bon Homme Richard* (p. 369)

Amelia Earhart (p. 369)

the Franklin expedition on snow shoes (p. 369)

3. **Style.** The use of flashback is one of many stylistic devices available to the writer. Most of this selection is a flashback. Where does the flashback begin? Why didn't the writer begin the selection here? What do the opening four paragraphs add to the piece?

## Developing Vocabulary

**Suffixes.** The suffix *-ity* indicates a state or an abstract quality; for example, the flood water has the quality of *opacity.*

The following adjectives all appear in this selection. Make each into a noun by adding the suffix *-ity,* and then use each noun in a sentence of your own. If you are unsure of the meaning or spelling of a word, consult a dictionary.

| | | |
|---|---|---|
| incongruous | enormous | curious |
| odd | entire | impossible |
| acrid | rigid | |

## Developing Writing Skills

**Using Comparison and Contrast.** "Nightmare Spring," "Time Is Short and the Water Rises," and "Flood" all deal with the subject of floods. In a five-paragraph composition, compare and contrast the way that the writers of these selections view their subject. What are the similarities? the differences?

# Social Commentary

# Pagan Spain
### Richard Wright

The matador was Chamaco. The bull now stood in the center of the ring, winded, his head down, his eyes balefully watching the vague movements of the men at the barrier. Across the red sand came a slender figure carrying a *muleta*[1] and a sword under his left arm. The sun glinted softly on his "suit of lights" and his step was solemn, slow. With his chin almost on his chest, he walked towards the presidential box, stopped, looked up, bowed, then, following tradition, tossed his black hat to the red sand, and turned. He strode slowly along the barrier, his assistants following at a respectful distance.

Many people stood to get a full view of him. There was some handclapping. He gave a swift, enigmatic glance at the circular wall of faces, and I was stupefied to see how young he really was; the contours of adolescence were still upon his dark, brooding face. Impulsively, I turned to the man who sat on my left and asked him in French,

"*Quel age a-t-il?*"[2]

"*Dix-neuf,*"[3] he said.

"*C'est un enfant,*"[4] I said.

"*Oui. Mais il est brave,*"[5] the man said. He smiled at me. "That boy comes from a poor section of Spain, a town called Huelva, in Andalusia. He has a large family, many brothers and sisters. Two years ago he was starving; now he is almost rich."

I resumed watching Chamaco, who was now strolling with downcast head towards the bull. The bull turned and faced him, eyeing him, immobile. I had seen the boy Chamaco rushing about the ring with the others;

I had even noticed that he wore a "suit of lights," but I had refused to believe that one so young was a full-fledged bullfighter. (In fact, technically speaking, Chamaco was not a full-fledged bullfighter. He was what was called a *novillero*, that is, a fighter of young bulls. But he had been fighting full-grown bulls for a long time now and he was slated to take his *alternativa*, that is, his formal inauguration as a regular bullfighter, in the ring in Madrid.)

He strode across the bloody sand and stopped at a spot about ten yards from the bull who regarded him tensely, not moving. Then, without once glancing at the bull, Chamaco unfolded his *muleta* and took out his sword, as though he were at home pulling off his hat and coat to hang them up. He put the end of the spread *muleta* between his thighs, like a boy straddling a broomstick, making believe that it was a horse. The other end of the *muleta* now extended out, about a yard from his knees, the red folds dangling. His right hand held the sword which he now inserted under the cloth so that the tip of the sword terminated at the point where the *muleta* ended and fell towards the sand. Un-

---

1. ***muleta*** (moo̅ lāt′ ə) *Spanish:* a red cloth draped over a stick and manipulated by a matador.
2. ***Quel age a-t-il?*** (kel äzh′ ä t′ēl′) *French:* How old is he?
3. ***Dix-neuf*** (dēs nöf′) *French:* nineteen.
4. ***C'est un enfant*** (set àn àn fàn) *French:* He's a baby.
5. ***Oui. Mais il est brave.*** (wē′ mā ēl′ ā bräv′) *French:* Yes. But he is brave.

til that moment he had been facing the bull; now he turned his left side to the bull and stared straight ahead, acting as though the bull did not exist.

The thousands of onlookers were profoundly quiet, watching. The bull advanced a step, lifting his head imperceptibly, studying the new phenomenon. Then, for the first time, Chamaco looked at the bull, his chin still on his chest. The bull trotted closer, looking, watching for a movement. Chamaco's right hand now jiggled the sword ever so lightly and the outer fringes of the *muleta* fluttered a bit.

The bull was at Chamaco's left. Chamaco was fronting the crowded stands, his slight figure draped in an attitude of indifference. Once more he twitched the far end of the *muleta* with the sword, making the folds in the cloth tremble. Chamaco was sighting the bull's left eye, and was so gauging and calculating the bull's angle of attack that he knew exactly where the bull's right horn would pass and how deadly close.

The bull charged ahead full tilt. As he thundered forward, Chamaco moved the far end of the *muleta* slowly, slightly, lifting it, and the bull's right horn swept past, within inches of Chamaco's chest, his body rearing, and, as the *muleta* continued to float upward into the air, the bull finished his wild lunge with his head high, horns pointing skyward, both of his front legs extended, slanting upwards in mid-air, and his entire mass was one vast ensemble of taut black muscle covered with bristling hair. Other than the lifting of his arms to raise the *muleta*, Chamaco had not moved.

As with one voice, thirty thousand throats sang out in a soft slow burst,

"Olé!"[6]

The bull's wild leap finished and he settled to earth, turned; he now stood to Chamaco's right. Chamaco, without moving from his tracks, held the *muleta* in his right hand,

waist high, about two feet from him, and the bull, without ceasing to move, came in for another charge, his horns this time sweeping past Chamaco's stomach and, following the *muleta*, the bull rose the height of Chamaco's shoulder, the force of the beast's effort making his forelegs shoot into the air while the *muleta* floated above his head.

"Olé!" the crowd sang with bated breath.

Man and beast had now become fused into one plastic, slow-moving, terrible, delicate dance of death, the outcome of which hung upon the breadth of a split second. The bull, now to Chamaco's left again, was turning, his tail swishing, readying himself to resume attack. Chamaco, still rooted to the spot, lowered the *muleta* till it dragged in the sand, the handle of the stick of the *muleta* being held close to his thigh. He held the *muleta* this time in his right hand and, as the bull came in, he swept it gently, slowly backwards, round to his side. The bull, head down, hypnotized by the cloth, followed, hooking his horns past Chamaco's kneecaps. While the bull was in this low charge, Chamaco, pivoting slowly, advancing his left foot and pulling back his right, turned, still moving the *muleta* ahead of the bull's nose, luring the beast around him so that, when he whipped the *muleta* out of range of the bull's vision, the bull's horns were almost touching his knees, the beast having made a full circle around the man.

"Olé!" the mass chanted with fearful glee.

There was a dramatic pause. Chamaco hid the *muleta* behind him; he was now two feet from the bull, looking directly down at the bull not moving, his right hand lifted high into the air. The bull stared, baffled, outwitted.

Chamaco now stepped aside, disclosing the *muleta* that he now held in his left hand. The bull lowered his head, then looked at

---

6. **Olé** (ô lā′) *Spanish:* a shout of approval or joy.

Chamaco, then at the cloth, at Chamaco, then at the cloth.

The stadium filled with murmurs. Everyone knew that the bull was now trying to choose between the man and the cloth. Had the beast learned the difference so quickly? Then the bull hurled himself at the cloth and a sigh went up. Chamaco swept the cloth gently around him until he was facing the middle of the bull's body, while the bull rushed until his horns were in the back of the man. Chamaco shifted the cloth from his left to his right hand, and the bull was bound to his waist, still whirling, and at last his horns were almost scraping the back of Chamaco's calves.

"*Olé!*" the crowd whispered its reaction, waiting.

Two feet out of line with the bull, Chamaco now stood with his back to the bull's horns. The *muleta* was held in his right hand, about a foot from his body. The bull moved. The cloth moved. Head and horns lifted violently, viciously, sweeping under Chamaco's elbow and into the air.

"*Olé!*" rolled from the tiers of jammed seats.

Chamaco now draped the cloth over the bull's nose and lured the beast toward his feet, then, as the bull, head down, followed, the cloth moved to the side and then to the rear of Chamaco. Chamaco's left hand now reached behind him, taking the cloth from his right hand, keeping it moving all the while, and the bull circled him once more, his head and horns at Chamaco's feet.

"*Olé!*" It was barely heard now.

With the *muleta* still in his left hand, Chamaco drew the bull round past him, floating the cloth, his back leaning backward over the bull's back. The bull's horns, ever seeking the cloth, now thrust past the retreating cloth and into the blinding sun, rushing past Chamaco's chest and his lifted arm—the beast's forelegs kicking skyward

and his eyes round pools of frustrated fury.

"*Olé!*" It came crisp now; the crowd was sure that the man had mastered the bull.

Chamaco faced the bull, planted his feet in the sand, holding the *muleta* at his left side. The bull brushed past his left hip, his lunging head and horns lifting the *muleta*, his forelegs pawing the air.

"*Olé!*" The crowd sang.

The bull turned, always charging. Chamaco now extended his right arm behind his body so that the *muleta* jutted out from his left side. The bull leaped at it again, its horns grazing Chamaco's left side, rising in the air past Chamaco's shoulder, and the man stood gazing calmly at the madly lashing tail of the bull that was now directly under his eyes.

"*Olé!*" The voices now sounded like a prolonged sob.

Man and beast confronted each other. Chamaco, holding the *muleta* in his right hand, began a kind of slow, creeping movement with his feet, standing upright all the while, one foot thrusting out before the other, then the other. Standing still, the bull turned his head, his eyes following the ever-elusive cloth. Chamaco, shuffling one foot ahead of the other, completed half a circle about the bull, and his back was now to the barrier. Had the bull charged, he would have been killed, for he could not have escaped.

A sigh swept the stands. Men closed their eyes and moaned:

"*Bravo hombre . . .!*"[7]

On and on Chamaco turned, shuffling his feet in the sand; and the bull's eyes followed the cloth, his massive black and bleeding body turning. Chamaco returned to the original spot from which he had begun his creeping movement. The bull was mastered.

Soft handclapping swept the stands.

The bull now stood facing Chamaco, his eyes dazed, his four feet directly in line with

---

7. **Bravo hombre** (brä' vō ōm' brä) *Spanish:* brave man.

his vast, heaving body, his head down. Chamaco was about six feet away. Suddenly you knew that the moment for the kill had come.

Chamaco's left hand now grasped the *muleta* firmly; he turned away from the bull, looking at him sideways, letting the red cloth drop below his left knee. He now lifted his gleaming sword chin-high and sighted along the length of it, pointing its sharp, steel tip at the tormented and bloody mound of wounds on the bull's back. Chamaco's left hand twitched the cloth, sighting the bull. The bull saw it and charged. Chamaco charged, meeting the bull. But, as he moved towards the bull, his left hand swung the *muleta* farther leftwards and his feet moved sharply to the right. The bull's horns rushed past his stomach as Chamaco tiptoed, leaning in and over the driving horns, and sent the sword to its hilt into the correct spot in the bull's body.

The bull halted, swayed. Chamaco stood watching him, gazing gently, sadly it seemed, into the bull's glazed and shocked eyes.

An uproar broke out in the stands. Almost everybody stood up, pulled out white pocket handkerchiefs and waved them, making the looming, circular stadium resemble a ripe cotton field being whipped by wind.

I watched the bull. He sagged, his eyes on his tormentor. He took an uncertain, hesitant step forward, and then was still. Chamaco lifted his right hand high above the bull's dying head; it was a gesture that had in it a mixture of triumph and compassion. The bull now advanced a few feet more on tottering legs, then his back legs folded and his hind part sank to the sand, his forelegs bent at the knees. And you saw the split second when death gripped him, for his head nodded violently and dropped forward, still. A heave shook his body as he gave up his breath and his eyes went blank. He slid slowly forward, resting on his stomach in the sand, his legs stretching straight out. He rolled over on his back; his four legs, already stiffening in death, shot up into the air.

But what is this mysterious "spiritual exercise" of which Juan Belmonte, perhaps the most intelligent, courageous, and perceptive of all the men who ever entered a ring to kill a bull, speaks? Is there something hidden here? If there is something hidden, why are bullfights enacted out in the open, before thousands of spectators? The answer is so simple that it is not often recognized, even when one is directly confronted with it. It is the conquering of fear, the making of a religion of the conquering of fear. Any man with enough courage to stand perfectly still in front of a bull will not be attacked or killed by that bull. It has been known for a man to sit in the bullring in a chair reading a newspaper in front of the bull pen gate. The gate was thrown open; the bull thundered out, stopped, gazed at the seated man, and trotted away. But to remain immobile when a beast of more than a thousand pounds is hurtling towards you is usually beyond human capacity.

And that was why I had heard the phrase, *bravo hombre,* so often on the lips of the spectators in the stadium. They knew well that the ability to master one's feelings of fear in the presence of that which immediately and dramatically threatened one's life was the cardinal quality that made the bullfight the gripping emotional spectacle that it was. As an American, a man from a world that valued and eulogized intelligence, responsibility, industrial processes, social-mindedness, property, etc., it was indeed odd to hear personal bravery extolled so highly. But Spain was another world with other values.

## Getting at Meaning

1. Why is the writer shocked by the matador's age? As the story progresses, what effect does knowing Chamaco's age have on the reader?

2. Before a matador kills a bull, he must show that he has completely mastered the animal. How does Chamaco exhibit mastery of the bull? What is the most dangerous move that Chamaco makes?

3. Chamaco watches the bull die "sadly" and with a "mixture of triumph and compassion." What does his attitude reveal about the matador's character?

4. In what way is bullfighting a "spiritual exercise"?

## Developing Skills in Reading Literature

1. **Essay.** According to the writer, what is the point of bullfighting? Why is it difficult for the writer to appreciate this point? What commentary does the writer make about America in the final paragraph of the selection? What commentary does he make about Spain?

2. **Conflict.** Identify at least two possible conflicts within Chamaco.

3. **Description.** In this selection, the writer describes carefully even the slightest movements of bull and matador. Choose one paragraph of at least five lines and read it slowly, noting the details that describe action. Now, write a single sentence that simply states the action. Compare the original paragraph with your sentence. What is lost by eliminating descriptive detail?

## Developing Vocabulary

**Words from Spanish.** The Spanish words *bravo* and *hombre* can be found in an English dictionary. Other Spanish words, however, are found only in a Spanish dictionary or in a Spanish-English dictionary. What Spanish words in this selection would you not expect to find in an English dictionary? What seems to determine which words are included in an English dictionary and which are excluded?

## Developing Writing Skills

1. **Describing Action.** Choose a simple task that involves some movement; for example, slicing a carrot or throwing a Frisbee. In one paragraph, describe the action in detail for a reader who has never seen the task performed.

2. **Supporting an Opinion.** This writer suggests that for Spaniards, personal bravery is a cardinal virtue, a greatly admired quality. In one paragraph, explain what trait you consider to be a cardinal virtue. Begin your paragraph by identifying the quality, and then go on to explain why it is so important to you.

# The Hidden Songs of a Secret Soul

*Bob Greene*

Lenny was the loneliest of dreamers. No one knew; we wouldn't have known, either, except for the fact that the afternoons got long, and the only way to make it through was to talk. After a time we even talked to Lenny.

He worked in the shipping room of a bottling plant. It manufactured soda pop. Lenny was a thin, slight man in his middle forties with a stammer and a sad face. We worked at long tables. Lenny was the only full-timer at our table; the rest of us were in school, and we came in whatever afternoons we could spare and picked up pocket money for the weekends. For us, the job was a dreary way to kill time. For Lenny, it was his sustenance.

The other full-timers in the room liked to kid Lenny. Most of them were in their twenties, and they passed the day with talk of women and late-night intrigue. Lenny had no wife or family, and he never spoke of a woman. So when the full-timers became bored with their own talk, they would call over to our table and rag Lenny some. They would ask him about his romances, and when he would become embarrassed and turn away and try not to answer, they would not let up until they became bored with bothering him. They didn't mean anything by it.

He never said much, and for awhile we didn't say much to him. We would come in after classes, nod hello to him, and start loading boxes. Lenny had spent most of his life being invisible; we sensed that without really thinking about it. He just seemed happy that we didn't rag him like the others did.

One afternoon, though, he started to talk. He didn't slow up what he was doing, but as he worked he began to ask us about the classes we took in school, the courses we were studying. He asked if any of us were studying English as a major; he wanted to know if any of us were studying the great poets.

None of us thought much about the questions at first; I know I didn't. But after that, a couple of times every week, he would ask the same things. It was always about the poets. On the way back home in the evenings, we would talk about it, and wonder what he meant. One night we determined that we would find out.

So the next day, at break time, we asked Lenny to sit down for coffee with us. We had never had coffee with Lenny before; usually he would disappear on his break. One of us asked him about the poets.

"I just wondered," Lenny said. But we pressed.

He avoided it, and so we dropped it and finished our cups. Just before we were due back at our table, Lenny said, "Sometimes I write poems."

We went back to work and tried to make him tell us more. It was so unlikely, the idea of Lenny who seldom had the nerve to speak, and had trouble when he did, spending time committing his thoughts to paper. When we attempted to question him further, he became uncomfortable and flushed.

"Don't talk so loud," he pleaded. "The others will hear."

We asked him that day if he would let us

see his poems, and he said no. We kept it up, though; we wanted to see. Finally he said that he would like to let us see them, but that he was afraid that if he brought them in, the others would find out and make fun of him.

We told him we would go with him to see the poems. He said he would think about it, and we did not let him forget. One day he said that we could come home with him if we wished.

After work we rode the el. He lived in one room. There were not enough places for us to sit. He brought out a large scrapbrook. The poems were inside.

They were written all in longhand, with a fountain pen. Even before we started to read them, they looked elegant. Lenny's hand moved with strokes full of flourish and style, confident and strong while Lenny was timid and quiet. And when we did begin to read, the poems were beautiful. The verses were long, and rich with imagery and detail. They told of love, and of spiritual triumphs, and of life in faraway places. They were music. We must have sat and read for an hour, saying nothing. When we finished and looked up, there was Lenny, in his rented room, staring away from us.

"Please never say anything to the others," he said.

We tried to tell him how good the poems were, how he should be proud of what he had done, and not ashamed to let anyone know, but he cut us off.

"Please," he said. "I have to work there."

We went home, and the next day Lenny let us know, without a word, that we were not to talk about the poems again. For a few months we continued to work, and Lenny continued to take the joking from the other full-timers. Then school ended for the summer, and we left the job, and Lenny. We never went back.

The reason I am thinking about this is that I saw him the other day. There was no mistake; it was he. It was on a crowded street, and there was Lenny. I motioned to him, and called his name, and started walking toward him. He saw me; I know he did. He turned around very quickly and walked away, and I knew that I was not supposed to follow.

## Getting at Meaning

1. What evidence does the selection offer that Lenny is lonely?

2. In what sense is Lenny "invisible"?

3. Why doesn't Lenny want the other full-timers to know that he writes poetry? What does he mean when he says, "I have to work there"?

4. Why does Lenny avoid the writer when they see each other on the street?

## Developing Skills in Reading Literature

1. **Essay.** An essay presents factual information from the writer's point of view. What information does the reader gain from this selection about the full-time and part-time employees in the bottling plant? From what point of view does the writer describe the actions of each group?

2. **Tone.** Reread the first two paragraphs of the essay. What is the writer's attitude toward Lenny? Which words and phrases are especially important in developing this tone? How do subsequent events and descriptions reinforce the tone? Does the tone change at any point in the selection? Explain your answer.

# There Is No News from Auschwitz

*A. M. Rosenthal*

BRZEZINKA, Poland.

The most terrible thing of all, somehow, was that at Brzezinka the sun was bright and warm, the rows of graceful poplars were lovely to look upon, and on the grass near the gates children played.

It all seemed frighteningly wrong, as in a nightmare, that at Brzezinka the sun should ever shine or that there should be light and greenness and the sound of young laughter. It would be fitting if at Brzezinka the sun never shone and the grass withered, because this is a place of unutterable terror.

And yet, every day, from all over the world, people come to Brzezinka, quite possibly the most grisly tourist center on earth. They come for a variety of reasons—to see if it could really have been true, to remind themselves not to forget, to pay homage to the dead by the simple act of looking upon their place of suffering.

Brzezinka is a couple of miles from the better-known southern Polish town of Oswiecim. Oswiecim has about 12,000 inhabitants, is situated about 171 miles from Warsaw, and lies in a damp, marshy area at the eastern end of the pass called the Moravian Gate. Brzezinka and Oswiecim together formed part of that minutely organized factory of torture and death that the Nazis called Konzentrationslager[1] Auschwitz.

By now, fourteen years[2] after the last batch of prisoners was herded naked into the gas chambers by dogs and guards, the story of Auschwitz has been told a great many times. Some of the inmates have written of those memories of which sane men cannot conceive. Rudolf Franz Ferdinand Hoess, the superintendent of the camp, before he was executed wrote his detailed memoirs of mass exterminations and the experiments on living bodies. Four million people died here, the Poles say.

And so there is no news to report about Auschwitz. There is merely the compulsion to write something about it, a compulsion that grows out of a restless feeling that to have visited Auschwitz and then turned away without having said or written anything would somehow be a most grievous act of discourtesy to those who died here.

Brzezinka and Oswiecim are very quiet places now; the screams can no longer be heard. The tourist walks silently, quickly at first to get it over with and then, as his mind peoples the barracks and the chambers and the dungeons and flogging posts, he walks

---

1. **Konzentrationslager** (kən tse trat si ion' släg ər) *German:* concentration camp.
2. **fourteen years:** Allied troops reached the concentration camps in 1945. This report was written in 1959.

draggingly. The guide does not say much either, because there is nothing much for him to say after he has pointed.

For every visitor, there is one particular bit of horror that he knows he will never forget. For some it is seeing the rebuilt gas chamber at Oswiecim and being told that this is the "small one." For others, it is the fact that at Brzezinka, in the ruins of the gas chambers, and the crematoria the Germans blew up when they retreated, there are daisies growing.

There are visitors who gaze blankly at the gas chambers and the furnaces because their minds simply cannot encompass them, but stand shivering before the great mounds of human hair behind the plate glass window or the piles of babies' shoes or the brick cells where men sentenced to death by suffocation were walled up.

One visitor opened his mouth in a silent scream simply at the sight of boxes—great stretches of three-tiered wooden boxes in the women's barracks. They were about six feet wide, about three feet high, and into them from five to ten prisoners were shoved for the night. The guide walks quickly through the barracks. Nothing more to see here.

A brick building where sterilization experiments were carried out on women prisoners. The guide tries the door—it's locked. The visitor is grateful that he does not have to go in, and then flushes with shame.

A long corridor where rows of faces stare from the walls. Thousands of pictures, the photographs of prisoners. They are all dead now, the men and women who stood before the cameras, and they all knew they were to die.

They all stare blank-faced, but one picture, in the middle of a row, seizes the eye and wrenches the mind. A girl, 22 years old, plumply pretty, blonde. She is smiling gently, as at a sweet, treasured thought. What was

the thought that passed through her young mind and is now her memorial on the wall of the dead at Auschwitz?

Into the suffocation dungeons the visitor is taken for a moment and feels himself strangling. Another visitor goes in, stumbles out and crosses herself. There is no place to pray at Auschwitz.

The visitors look pleadingly at each other and say to the guide, "Enough."

There is nothing new to report about Auschwitz. It was a sunny day and the trees were green and at the gates the children played.

## Getting at Meaning

1. Why do sunshine and laughter seem "terrible" at Brzezinka?

2. What does the phrase "minutely organized factory" imply about the type of torture and death that took place at Auschwitz?

3. The prisoners at Auschwitz were herded naked into gas chambers. What does this description imply about the attitude of captors toward their prisoners?

4. What causes the tourists to walk draggingly? Why is commentary by the tour guide unnecessary?

5. One visitor feels grateful to remain outside the sterilization building. Why does this person flush with shame?

6. Why is the photograph of the young, smiling girl particularly thought-provoking?

## Developing Skills in Reading Literature

1. **Essay.** What is the primary purpose of this essay? What information does the reader gain about the past horror of Auschwitz? about the present horror?

2. **Connotation.** Connotation is the emotional response that a word creates. The writer uses the following words to recreate the impact of a visit to Auschwitz: *grisly, draggingly, blankly, shivering, scream, wrenches, strangling,* and *pleadingly*. What emotional responses do these words elicit in the reader?

3. **Understatement.** The writer of this essay makes the following understatement: ". . . it is seeing the rebuilt gas chamber at Oswiecim and being told that this is the 'small one'." What horrors are suggested by this comment? Why is it more effective to imply these horrors than to describe them directly? Find another example of understatement in the essay, and explain its implications.

# *from* **The Right Stuff** *Tom Wolfe*

A young man might go into military flight training believing that he was entering some sort of technical school in which he was simply going to acquire a certain set of skills. Instead, he found himself all at once enclosed in a fraternity. And in this fraternity, even though it was military, men were not rated by their outward rank as ensigns, lieutenants, commanders, or whatever. No, herein the world was divided into those who had it and those who did not. This quality, this *it*, was never named, however, nor was it talked about in any way.

As to just what this ineffable quality was . . . well, it obviously involved bravery. But it was not bravery in the simple sense of being willing to risk your life. The idea seemed to be that any fool could do that, if that was all that was required, just as any fool could throw away his life in the process. No, the idea here (in the all-enclosing fraternity) seemed to be that a man should have the ability to go up in a hurtling piece of machinery and put his hide on the line and then have the moxie, the reflexes, the experience, the coolness, to pull it back in the last yawning moment—and then to go up again *the next day,* and the next day, and every next day, even if the series should prove infinite— and, ultimately, in its best expression, do so in a cause that means something to thousands, to a people, a nation, to humanity, to God. Nor was there *a test* to show whether or not a pilot had this righteous quality. There was, instead, a seemingly infinite series of tests. A career in flying was like climbing one of those ancient Babylonian pyramids made up of a dizzy progression of steps and ledges, a ziggurat, a pyramid extraordinarily high and steep; and the idea was to prove at every foot of the way up that pyramid that you were one of the elected and anointed ones who had *the right stuff* and could move higher and higher and even—ultimately, God willing, one day—that you might be able to join that special few at the very top, that elite who had the capacity to bring tears to men's eyes, the very Brotherhood of the Right Stuff itself.

None of this was to be mentioned, and yet it was acted out in a way that a young man could not fail to understand. When a new flight (i.e., a class) of trainees arrived at Pensacola,[1] they were brought into an auditorium for a little lecture. An officer would tell them, "Take a look at the man on either side of you." Quite a few actually swiveled their heads this way and that, in the interest of appearing diligent. Then the officer would say, "One of the three of you is not going to make it!"—meaning, not get his wings. That was the opening theme, the *motif* of primary training. We already know that one-third of you do not have the right stuff—it only remains to find out who.

Furthermore, that was the way it turned out. At every level in one's progress up that

---

1. **Pensacola** (pen sə kō' lə): Pensacola Naval Air Station in Florida.

staggeringly high pyramid, the world was once more divided into those men who had the right stuff to continue the climb and those who had to be *left behind* in the most obvious way. Some were eliminated in the course of the opening classroom work, as either not smart enough or not hardworking enough, and were left behind. Then came the basic flight instruction, in single-engine, propeller-driven trainers, and a few more—even though the military tried to make this stage easy—were washed out and left behind. Then came more demanding levels, one after the other, formation flying, instrument flying, jet training, all-weather flying, gunnery, and at each level more were washed out and left behind. By this point easily a third of the original candidates had been, indeed, eliminated . . . from the ranks of those who might prove to have the right stuff.

In the Navy, in addition to the stages that Air Force trainees went through, the neophyte always had waiting for him, out in the ocean, a certain grim gray slab; namely, the deck of an aircraft carrier; and with it perhaps the most difficult routine in military flying, carrier landings. He was shown films about it, he heard lectures about it, and he knew that carrier landings were hazardous. He first practiced touching down on the

shape of a flight deck painted on an airfield. He was instructed to touch down and gun right off. This was safe enough—the shape didn't move, at least— but it could do terrible things to, let us say, the gyroscope of the soul. *That shape!—it's so small!* And more candidates were washed out and left behind. Then came the day, without warning, when those who remained were sent out over the ocean for the first of many days of reckoning with the slab. The first day was always a clear day with little wind and a calm sea. The carrier was so steady that it seemed, from up there in the air, to be resting on pilings; and the candidate usually made his first carrier landing successfully, with relief and even *élan*. Many young candidates looked like terrific aviators up to that very point—and it was not until they were actually standing on the carrier deck that they first began to wonder if they had the proper stuff, after all. In the training film the flight deck was a grand piece of gray geometry, perilous, to be sure, but an amazing abstract shape as one looks down upon it on the screen. And yet once the newcomer's two feet were on it . . . *Geometry*—man, this is a . . . *skillet!* It *heaved*, it moved up and down underneath his feet, it pitched up, it pitched down, it rolled to port (this great beast *rolled!*) and it rolled to starboard, as the ship moved into the wind and, therefore, into the waves, and the wind kept sweeping across, sixty feet up in the air out in the open sea, and there were no railings whatsoever. This was a *skillet!*—a frying pan! —a short-order grill!—not gray but black, smeared with skid marks from one end to the other and glistening with pools of hydraulic fluid and the occasional jet-fuel slick, all of it still hot, sticky, greasy, runny, virulent from God knows what traumas—still ablaze!—consumed in detonations, explosions, flames, combustion, roars, shrieks, whines, blasts, horrible shudders, fracturing impacts, as little men in screaming red and yellow and purple and green shirts with black Mickey Mouse helmets over their ears skittered about on the surface as if for their very lives (you've said it now!), hooking fighter planes onto the catapult shuttles so that they can explode their afterburners and be slung off the deck in a red-mad fury with a *kaboom!* that pounds through the entire deck—a procedure that seems absolutely controlled, orderly, sublime, however, compared to what he is about to watch as aircraft return to the ship for what is known in the military as "recovery and arrest." To say that an F-4 was coming back onto this heaving barbecue from out of the sky at a speed of 135 knots . . . that might have been the truth in the training lecture, but it did not begin to get across the idea of what the newcomer saw from the deck itself, because it created the notion that perhaps the plane was gliding in. On the deck one knew differently! As the aircraft came closer and the carrier heaved on into the waves and the plane's speed did not diminish and the deck did not grow steady—indeed, it pitched up and down five or ten feet per greasy heave—one experienced a neural alarm that no lecture could have prepared him for: This is not an *airplane* coming toward me, it is a brick with some poor sucker riding it (*someone much like myself!*), and it is not *gliding*, it is *falling*, a fifty-thousand-pound brick, headed not for a stripe on the deck but for *me*—and with a horrible *smash!* it hits the skillet, and with a blur of momentum as big as a freight train's it hurtles toward the far end of the deck—another blinding storm!—another roar as the pilot pushes the throttle up to full military power and another smear of rubber screams out over the skillet—and this is nominal!—quite okay!—for a wire streched across the deck has grabbed the hook on the end of the plane as it hit the deck tail down, and the smash was the rest of the fifteen-ton brute slamming onto the deck, as it tripped up, so that it is now straining against the wire at full throttle, in case it hadn't held and the plane had "boltered" off the end of the deck and had to struggle up into the air again. And already the Mickey Mouse helmets are running toward the fiery monster . . .

And the candidate, looking on, begins to *feel* that great heaving sun-blazing death-board of a deck wallowing in his own system —and suddenly he finds himself backed up against his own limits. He ends up going to the flight surgeon with so-called conversion symptoms. Overnight he develops blurred vision or numbness in his hands and feet or sinusitis so severe that he cannot tolerate changes in altitude. On one level the symptom is real. He really cannot see too well or use his fingers or stand the pain. But somewhere in his subconscious he knows it is a plea and a beg-off; he shows not the slightest concern (the flight surgeon notes) that the condition might be permanent and affect him in whatever life awaits him outside the arena of the right stuff.

## Getting at Meaning

1. How does military flight school differ from other technical schools?

2. What qualities are exhibited by a pilot with the right stuff?

3. How does standing on the deck of an aircraft carrier change a young pilot's attitude toward the carrier? What new fears does the pilot experience? What does the writer mean when he says that the pilot "finds himself backed up against his own limits"?

4. Why are the illnesses that some pilots develop called "conversion symptoms"? What "conversion" occurs? What causes the pilots' symptoms?

## Developing Skills in Reading Literature

1. **Conflict.** What conflicts does the writer discuss in this selection? Are they internal or external? How are some of the conflicts resolved?

2. **Metaphor.** The writer uses several vivid metaphors to communicate the quality and intensity of a pilot's thoughts. Identify and explain three of these metaphors.

3. **Style.** Identify at least two stylistic devices used by this writer. What makes his style of writing unique?

## Developing Vocabulary

**Word Origins.** The word *moxie* means "the ability to face difficulty with spirit." Before passing into use as a common noun, Moxie was the name of a popular soft drink. Other brand names, too, have been converted to common nouns.

Look up the following brand names in a dictionary. Which appear with small letters, indicating that the words have become common nouns?

| | |
|---|---|
| Escalator | Kleenex |
| Aspirin | Jello |
| Thermos | Zipper |

## Developing Writing Skills

**Using Figures of Speech: Simile and Metaphor.** In one paragraph, describe a skill that you have found to be frustrating or extremely difficult. Begin your description with a sentence that establishes a comparison; for example, "Learning to hit a baseball is like trying to swat a fly with a toothpick." Carry this comparison throughout the paragraph, using at least two more similes or metaphors.

# Aging in the Land of the Young

*Sharon Curtin*

Old men, old women, almost twenty million of them. They constitute ten percent of the total population, and the percentage is steadily growing. Some of them, like conspirators, walk all bent over, as if hiding some precious secret, filled with self-protection. The body seems to gather itself around those vital parts, folding shoulders, arms, pelvis, like a fading rose. Watch and you see how fragile old people come to think they are.

Aging paints every action gray, lies heavy on every movement, imprisons every thought. It governs each decision with a ruthless and single-minded perversity. To age is to learn the feeling of no longer growing, of struggling to do old tasks, to remember familiar actions. The cells of the brain are destroyed with thousands of unfelt tiny strokes, little pockets of clotted blood wiping out memories and abilities without warning. The body seems slowly to give up, randomly stopping, sometimes starting again as if to torture and tease with the memory of lost strength. Hands become clumsy, frail transparencies, held together with knotted blue veins.

Sometimes it seems as if the distance between your feet and the floor were constantly changing, as if you were walking on shifting and not quite solid ground. One foot down, slowly, carefully force the other foot forward. Sometimes you are a shuffler, not daring to lift your feet from the uncertain earth but forced to slide hesitantly forward in little whispering movements. Sometimes you are able to "step out," but this effort—in fact the pure exhilaration of easy movement—soon exhausts you.

The world becomes narrower as friends and family die or move away. To climb stairs, to ride in a car, to walk to the corner, to talk on the telephone; each action seems to take away from the energy needed to stay alive. Everything is limited by the strength you hoard greedily. Your needs decrease, you require less food, less sleep, and finally less human contact; yet this little bit becomes more and more difficult. You fear that one day you will be reduced to the simple acts of breathing and taking nourishment. This is the ultimate stage you dread, the period of helplessness and hopelessness, when independence will be over.

There is nothing to prepare you for the experience of growing old. Living is a process, an irreversible progression toward old age and eventual death. You see men of eighty still vital and straight as oaks; you see men of fifty reduced to gray shadows in the human landscape. The cellular clock differs for each one of us, and is profoundly affected by our own life experiences, our heredity, and perhaps most important, by the concepts of aging encountered in society and in oneself.

The aged live with enforced leisure, on fixed incomes, subject to many chronic illnesses, and most of their money goes to keep

a roof over their heads. They also live in a culture that worships youth.

A kind of cultural attitude makes me bigoted against old people; it makes me think young is best; it makes me treat old people like outcasts.

Hate that gray? Wash it away!
Wrinkle cream.
Monkey glands.
Face-lifting.
Look like a bride again.
Don't trust anyone over thirty.
I fear growing old.
Feel Young Again!

I am afraid to grow old—we're all afraid. In fact, the fear of growing old is so great that every aged person is an insult and a threat to the society. They remind us of our own death, that our body won't always remain smooth and responsive, but will someday betray us by aging, faltering, failing. The ideal way to age would be to grow slowly invisible, gradually disappearing, without causing worry or discomfort to the young. In some ways that does happen. Sitting in a small park across from a nursing home one day, I noticed that the young mothers and their children gathered on one side, and the old people from the home on the other. Whenever a youngster would run over to the "wrong" side, chasing a ball or just trying to cover all the available space, the old people would lean forward and smile. But before any communication could be established, the mother would come over, murmuring embarrassed apologies, and take her child back to the "young" side.

Now, it seemed to me that the children didn't feel any particular fear, and the old people didn't seem to be threatened by the children. The division of space was drawn by the mothers. And the mothers never looked at the old people who lined the other side of the park like so many pigeons perched on the benches. These well dressed young matrons had a way of sliding their eyes over, around, through the old people; they never looked at them directly. The old people may as well have been invisible; they had no reality for the youngsters, who were not permitted to speak to them, and they offended the aesthetic eye of the mothers.

My early experiences were somewhat different; since I grew up in a small town, my childhood had more of a nineteenth-century flavor. I knew a lot of old people, and considered some of them friends. There was no culturally defined way for me to "relate" to old people, except the rules of courtesy that applied to all adults. My grandparents were an integral and important part of the family and of the community. I sometimes have a dreadful fear that mine will be the last generation to know old people as friends, to have a sense of what growing old means, to respect and understand man's mortality and his courage in the face of death. Mine may be the last generation to have a sense of living history, of stories passed from generation to generation, of identity established by family history.

## Getting at Meaning

1. How do the physical problems of aging combine to destroy a person's independence?

2. Why is the aging process unpredictable on an individual basis?

3. How does society promote the idea that "young is best"? Why does society promote this idea?

4. Reread the description of the old people in the park. Why do the young mothers prevent their children from interacting with the old people?

5. According to the writer, if old people are forced out of the mainstream of society, what will be lost?

## Developing Skills in Reading Literature

1. **Essay.** An essay can be a direct expression of a writer's opinions on a subject. What does this writer think about aging? What does she think about old people? Of whom or what does she seem to be most critical?

2. **Description.** The writer's description of the aging process is particularly detailed and vivid. Select one example of description from the first four paragraphs and be prepared to explain what this description contributes to your understanding of aging.

3. **Irony.** Why is the behavior of the young mothers in the park ironic in terms of the ideas presented in this essay?

## Developing Vocabulary

**Using a Glossary.** Find each of the following words in the selection. Then look up the word in the Glossary. Write the definition, and use the word in a sentence of your own.

| | |
|---|---|
| conspirators | chronic |
| perversity | aesthetic |
| exhilaration | transparencies |
| integral | |

*from* **Travels with Charley**     *John Steinbeck*

From the beginning of my journey, I had avoided the great high-speed slashes of concrete and tar called "thruways," or "superhighways." Various states have different names for them, but I had dawdled in New England, the winter grew apace, and I had visions of being snowbound in North Dakota. I sought out U.S. 90, a wide gash of a superhighway, multiple-lane carrier of the nation's goods. Rocinante[1] bucketed along. The minimum speed on this road was greater than any I had previously driven. I drove into a wind quartering in from my starboard bow and felt the buffeting, sometimes staggering blows of the gale I helped to make. I could hear the sough of it on the square surfaces of my camper top. Instructions screamed at me from the road once: "Do not stop! No stopping. Maintain speed." Trucks as long as freighters went roaring by, delivering a wind like the blow of a fist. These great roads are wonderful for moving goods but not for inspection of a countryside. You are bound to the wheel and your eyes to the car ahead and to the rear-view mirror for the car behind and the side mirror for the car or truck about to pass, and at the same time you must read all the signs for fear you may miss some instructions or orders. No roadside stands selling squash juice, no antique stores, no farm products or factory outlets. When we get these thruways across the whole country, as we will and must, it will be possible to drive from New York to California without seeing a single thing.

At intervals there are places of rest and recreation, food, fuel and oil, postcards, steam-table food, picnic tables, garbage cans all fresh and newly painted, rest rooms and lavatories so spotless, so incensed with deodorants and with detergents that it takes a time to get your sense of smell back. For deodorants are not quite correctly named; they substitute one smell for another, and the substitute must be much stronger and more penetrating than the odor it conquers. I had neglected my own country too long. Civilization had made great strides in my absence. I remember when a coin in a slot would get you a stick of gum or a candy bar, but in these dining palaces were vending machines where various coins could deliver handkerchiefs, comb-and-nail-file sets, hair conditioners and cosmetics, first-aid kits, minor drugs such as aspirin, mild physics, pills to keep you awake. I found myself entranced with these gadgets. Suppose you want a soft drink; you pick your kind—Sungrape or Cooly Cola—press a button, insert the coin, and stand back. A paper cup drops into place, the drink pours out and stops a quarter of an inch from the brim—a cold, refreshing drink guaranteed synthetic. Coffee is even more interesting, for when the hot black fluid has ceased, a squirt of milk comes down and an envelope of sugar drops beside the cup. But of all, the hot-soup machine is the tri-

---

1. **Rocinante** (rō sē nän' tä): Steinbeck's vehicle; the Spanish word means "a miserable hack or workhorse."

umph. Choose among ten—pea, chicken noodle, beef and veg., insert the coin. A rumbling hum comes from the giant and a sign lights up that reads "Heating." After a minute a red light flashes on and off until you open a little door and remove the paper cup of boiling-hot soup.

It is life at a peak of some kind of civilization. The restaurant accommodations, great scallops of counters with simulated leather stools, are as spotless as and not unlike the lavatories. Everything that can be captured and held down is sealed in clear plastic. The food is oven-fresh, spotless, and tasteless; untouched by human hands. I remembered with an ache certain dishes in France and Italy touched by innumerable human hands.

These centers for rest, food, and replenishment are kept beautiful with lawns and flowers. At the front, nearest the highway, are parking places for passenger automobiles together with regiments of gasoline pumps. At the rear the trucks draw up, and there they have their services—the huge overland caravans. Being technically a truck, Rocinante took her place in the rear, and I soon made acquaintance with the truckers. They are a breed set apart from the life around them, the long-distance truckers. In some town or city somewhere, their wives and children live while the husbands traverse the nation carrying every kind of food and product and machine. They are clannish and they stick together, speaking a specialized language. And although I was a small craft among monsters of transportation, they were kind to me and helpful.

I learned that in the truck parks there are showers and soap and towels—that I could park and sleep the night if I wished. The men had little commerce with local people, but being avid radio listeners they could report news and politics from all parts of the nation. The food and fuel centers on the parkways or thruways are leased by the various states, but on other highways private enterprise has truckers' stations that offer discounts on fuel, beds, baths, and places to sit and shoot the breeze. But being a specialized group, leading special lives, associating only with their own kind, they would have made it possible for me to cross the country without talking to a local town-bound man. For the truckers cruise over the surface of the nation without being a part of it. Of course, in the towns where their families live, they have whatever roots are possible—clubs, dances, love affairs, and murders.

I liked the truckers very much, as I always like specialists. By listening to them talk I accumulated a vocabulary of the road, of tires and springs, of overweight. The truckers over long distances have stations along their routes where they know the service men and the waitresses behind the counters, and where occasionally they meet their opposite numbers in other trucks. The great get-together symbol is the cup of coffee. I found I often stopped for coffee, not because I wanted it but for a rest and a change from the unrolling highway. It takes strength and attention to drive a truck long distances, no matter how much the effort is made easier by air brakes and power-assisted steering. It would be interesting to know and easy to establish with modern testing methods how much energy in foot pounds is expended in driving a truck for six hours.

Quite often I sat with these men and listened to their talk and now and then asked questions. I soon learned not to expect knowledge of the country they passed through. Except for the truck stops, they had no contact with it. And this is why, on my journey that was designed for observation, I stayed as much as possible on secondary roads where there was much to see and hear and smell, and avoided the great wide traffic slashes that promote the self by fostering daydreams. I drove this wide, eventless way

*from TRAVELS WITH CHARLEY*  393

called U.S. 90 that bypassed Buffalo and Erie to Madison, Ohio, and then found the equally wide and fast U.S. 20 past Cleveland and Toledo, and so into Michigan.

On these roads out of the manufacturing centers there moved many mobile homes, pulled by specially designed trucks, and since these mobile homes comprise one of my generalities, I may as well get to them now. Early in my travels I had become aware of these new things under the sun, of their great numbers; and since they occur in increasing numbers all over the nation, observation of them and perhaps some speculation is in order. They are not trailers to be pulled by one's own car but shining cars long as pullmans. From the beginning of my travels I had noticed the sale lots where they were sold and traded, but then I began to be aware of the parks where they sit down in uneasy permanence. In Maine I took to stopping the night in these parks, talking to the managers and to the dwellers in this new kind of housing, for they gather in groups of like to like.

They are wonderfully built homes, aluminum skins, double-walled, with insulation, and often paneled with veneer of hardwood. Sometimes as much as forty feet long, they have two to five rooms, and are complete with air-conditioners, toilets, baths, and invariably television. The parks where they sit are sometimes landscaped and equipped with every facility. I talked with the park men, who were enthusiastic. A mobile home is drawn to the trailer park and installed on a ramp, a heavy rubber sewer pipe is bolted underneath, water and electric power connected, the television antenna raised, and the family is in residence. Several park managers agreed that last year one in four new housing units in the whole country was a mobile home. The park men charge a small ground rent plus fees for water and electricity. Telephones are connected in nearly all of them simply by plugging in a jack. Sometimes the park has a general store for supplies, but if not, the supermarkets that dot the countryside are available. Parking difficulties in the towns have caused these markets to move to the open country where they are immune from town taxes. This is also true of the trailer parks. The fact that these homes can be moved does not mean that they do move. Sometimes their owners stay for years in one place, plant gardens, build little walls of cinder blocks, put out awnings and garden furniture. It is a whole way of life that was new to me. These homes are never cheap and often are quite expensive and lavish. I have seen some that cost $20,000 and contained all the thousand appliances we live by—dishwashers, automatic clothes washers and driers, refrigerators and deep freezes.

The owners were not only willing but glad and proud to show their homes to me. The rooms, while small, were well proportioned. Every conceivable unit was built in. Wide windows, some even called picture windows, destroyed any sense of being closed in; the bedrooms and beds were spacious and the storage space unbelievable. It seemed to me a revolution in living and on a rapid increase. Why did a family choose to live in such a home? Well, it was comfortable, compact, easy to keep clean, easy to heat.

In Maine: "I'm tired of living in a cold barn with the wind whistling through, tired of the torment of little taxes and payments for this and that. It's warm and cozy and in the summer the air-conditioner keeps us cool."

"What is the usual income bracket of the mobiles?"

"That is variable, but a goodly number are in the ten-thousand- to twenty-thousand-dollar class."

"Has job uncertainty anything to do with the rapid increase of these units?"

"Well perhaps there may be some of that. Who knows what is in store tomorrow? Mechanics, plant engineers, architects, accountants, and even here and there a doctor or a dentist live in the mobile. If a plant or a factory closes down, you're not trapped with property you can't sell. Suppose the husband has a job and is buying a house and there's a layoff. The value goes out of his house. But if he has a mobile home he rents a trucking service and moves on, and he hasn't lost anything. He may never have to do it, but the fact that he can is a comfort to him."

"How are they purchased?"

"On time, just like an automobile. It's like paying rent."

And then I discovered the greatest selling appeal of all—one that crawls through nearly all American life. Improvements are made on these mobile homes every year. If you are doing well you turn yours in on a new model just as you do with an automobile if you can possibly afford to. There's status to that. And the turn-in value is higher than that of automobiles because there's a ready market for used homes. And after a few years the once expensive home may have a poorer family. They are easy to maintain, need no paint since they are usually of aluminum, and are not tied to fluctuating land values.

"How about schools?"

The school buses pick the children up right at the park and bring them back. The family car takes the head of the house to work and the family to a drive-in movie at night. It's a healthy life out in the country air. The payments, even if high and festooned with interest, are no worse than renting an apartment and fighting the owner for heat. And where could you rent such a comfortable ground-floor apartment with a place for your car outside the door? Where else could the kids have a dog? Nearly every mobile home has a dog, as Charley[2] discovered to his delight. Twice I was invited to dinner in a mobile home and several times watched a football game on television. A manager told me that one of the first considerations in his business was to find and buy a place where television reception is good. Since I did not require any facilities, sewer, water, or electricity, the price to me for stopping the night was one dollar.

The first impression forced on me was that permanence is neither achieved nor desired by mobile people. They do not buy for the generations, but only until a new model they can afford comes out. The mobile units are by no means limited to the park communities. Hundreds of them will be found sitting beside a farm house, and this was explained to me. There was a time when, on the occasion of a son's marriage and the addition of a wife and later of children to the farm, it was customary to add a wing or at least a lean-to on the home place. Now in many cases a mobile unit takes the place of additional building. A farmer from whom I bought eggs and home-smoked bacon told me of the advantages. Each family has a privacy it never had before. The old folks are not irritated by crying babies. The mother-in-law problem is abated because the new daughter has a privacy she never had and a place of her own in which to build the structure of a family. When they move away, and nearly all Americans move away, or want to, they do not leave unused and therefore useless rooms. Relations between the generations are greatly improved. The son is a guest when he visits the parents' house, and the parents are guests in the son's house.

Then there are the loners, and I have talked with them also. Driving along, you see high on a hill a single mobile home placed to command a great view. Others nestle under trees fringing a river or a lake. These loners have rented a tiny piece of land from the owner. They need only enough for the unit and the right of passage to get to it.

2. **Charley:** Steinbeck's dog.

Sometimes the loner digs a well and a cess-pool, and plants a small garden, but others transport their water in fifty-gallon oil drums. Enormous ingenuity is apparent with some of the loners in placing the water supply higher than the unit and connecting it with plastic pipe so that a gravity flow is insured.

One of the dinners that I shared in a mobile home was cooked in an immaculate kitchen, walled in plastic tile, with stainless-steel sinks and ovens and stoves flush with the wall. The fuel is butane or some other bottled gas that can be picked up anywhere. We ate in a dining alcove paneled in mahogany veneer. I've never had a better or a more comfortable dinner. I had brought a bottle of whisky as my contribution, and afterward we sat in deep comfortable chairs cushioned in foam rubber. This family liked the way they lived and wouldn't think of going back to the old way. The husband worked as a garage mechanic about four miles away and made good pay. Two children walked to the highway every morning and were picked up by a yellow school bus.

Sipping a highball after dinner, hearing the rushing of water in the electric dishwasher in the kitchen, I brought up a question that had puzzled me. These were good, thoughtful, intelligent people. I said, "One of our most treasured feelings concerns roots, growing up rooted in some soil or some community." How did they feel about raising their children without roots? Was it good or bad? Would they miss it or not?

The father, a good-looking, fair-skinned man with dark eyes, answered me. "How many people today have what you are talking about? What roots are there in an apartment twelve floors up? What roots are in a housing development of hundreds and thousands of small dwellings almost exactly alike? My father came from Italy," he said. "He grew up in Tuscany in a house where his family had lived maybe a thousand years.

That's roots for you, no running water, no toilet, and they cooked with charcoal or vine clippings. They had just two rooms, a kitchen and a bedroom where everybody slept, grandpa, father, and all the kids, no place to read, no place to be alone, and never had had. Was that better? I bet if you gave my old man the choice he'd cut his roots and live like this." He waved his hands at the comfortable room. "Fact is, he cut his roots away and came to America. Then he lived in a tenement in New York—just one room, walk-up, cold water, and no heat. That's where I was born, and I lived in the streets as a kid until my old man got a job upstate in New York in the grape country. You see, he knew about vines, that's about all he knew. Now you take my wife. She's Irish descent. Her people had roots too."

"In a peat bog," the wife said. "And lived on potatoes." She gazed fondly through the door at her fine kitchen.

"Don't you miss some kind of permanence?"

"Who's got permanence? Factory closes down, you move on. Good times and things opening up, you move on where it's better. You got roots you sit and starve. You take the pioneers in the history books. They were movers. Take up land, sell it, move on. I read in a book how Lincoln's family came to Illinois on a raft. They had some barrels of whisky for a bank account. How many kids in America stay in the place where they were born, if they can get out?"

"You've thought about it a lot."

"Don't have to think about it. There it is. I've got a good trade. Long as there's automobiles I can get work, but suppose the place I work goes broke. I got to move where there's a job. I get to my job in three minutes. You want I should drive twenty miles because I got roots?"

Later they showed me magazines designed exclusively for mobile dwellers, stories and poems and hints for successful mobile living. How to stop a leak. How to choose a place for sun or coolness. And there were advertisements for gadgets, fascinating things, for cooking, cleaning, washing clothes, furniture and beds and cribs. Also there were full-page pictures of new models, each one grander and more shiny than the next.

"There's thousands of them," said the father, "and there's going to be millions."

"Joe's quite a dreamer," the wife said. "He's always figuring something out. Tell him your ideas, Joe."

"Maybe he wouldn't be interested."

"Sure I would."

"Well, it's not a dream like she said, it's for real, and I'm going to do it pretty soon now. Take a little capital, but it would pay off. I been looking around the used lots for the unit I want at the price I want to pay. Going to rip out the guts and set it up for a repair shop. I got enough tools nearly already, and I'll stock little things like windshield wipers and fan belts and cylinder rings and inner tubes, stuff like that. You take these courts are getting bigger and bigger. Some of the mobile people got two cars. I'll rent me a hundred feet of ground right near and I'll be in business. There's one thing you can say about cars; there's nearly always something wrong with them that's got to be fixed. And I'll have my house, this here one right beside my shop. That way I would have a bell and give twenty-four-hour service."

"Sounds like a good deal," I said. And it does.

"Best thing about it," Joe went on, "if business fell off, why, I'd just move on where it was good."

His wife said, "Joe's got it all worked out on paper where everything's going to go, every wrench and drill, even an electric welder. Joe's a wonderful welder."

I said, "I take back what I said, Joe. I guess you've got your roots in a grease pit."

"You could do worse. I even worked that out. And you know, when the kids grow up, we could even work our way south in the winter and north in the summer."

"Joe does good work," said his wife. "He's got his own steady customers where he works. Some men come fifty miles to get Joe to work on their cars because he does good work."

"I'm a real good mechanic," said Joe.

Driving the big highway near Toledo I had a conversation with Charley on the subject of roots. He listened but he didn't reply. In the pattern-thinking about roots I and most other people have left two things out of consideration. Could it be that Americans are a restless people, a mobile people, never satisfied with where they are as a matter of selection? The pioneers, the immigrants who peopled the continent, were the restless ones in Europe. The steady rooted ones stayed home and are still there. But every one of us, except the blacks forced here as slaves, are descended from the restless ones, the wayward ones who were not content to stay at home. Wouldn't it be unusual if we had not inherited this tendency? And the fact is that we have. But that's the short view. What are roots and how long have we had them? If our species has existed for a couple of million years, what is its history? Our remote ancestors followed the game, moved with the food supply, and fled from evil weather, from ice and the changing seasons. Then, after millennia beyond thinking, they domesticated some animals so that they lived with their food supply. Then of necessity they followed the grass that fed their flocks in endless wanderings. Only when agriculture came into practice—and that's not very long ago in terms of the whole history—did a place achieve meaning and value and permanence. But land is a tangible, and tangibles have a way of getting into few hands. Thus it was that one man wanted ownership of land and at the same time wanted servitude because someone had to work it. Roots were in ownership of land, in tangible and immovable possessions. In this view we are a restless species with a very short history of roots, and those not widely distributed. Perhaps we have overrated roots as a psychic need. Maybe the greater the urge, the deeper and more ancient is the need, the will, the hunger to be somewhere else.

## Getting at Meaning

1. Why has the writer avoided superhighways on this trip? Although he enjoys truckers, he also avoids spending all of his time at truck stops. Why? What is the purpose of this trip? How do you know?

2. Identify some of the reasons that people choose to live in mobile homes. Why is the word *mobile* ironic in some cases?

3. Explain the meaning of the word *roots* as it is used in this selection. According to the mechanic, do modern Americans have roots? What proof does he offer to support his opinion? What does he mean when he says, "You got roots you sit and starve"?

4. Reread the last paragraph. How has the writer's concept of roots changed? What reasoning does he offer to support his new view of roots?

## Developing Skills in Reading Literature

1. **Setting.** The setting of this essay changes as the writer moves across the country. How does this change affect the selection?

2. **Tone.** Just as the setting changes, so does the writer's attitude toward his subject. What is the tone of the opening paragraphs, which describe superhighways, rest rooms, and food "untouched by human hands"? How does the writer's comment about French and Italian food "touched by innumerable human hands" reinforce this tone?

What is the writer's tone when he writes about the truckers? What is his tone when he shifts to a discussion of mobile homes?

3. **Symbol.** What does the mobile home symbolize? Does it symbolize the same thing for the writer as it does for people like the mechanic? Explain.

4. **Theme.** What is the theme of this selection?

## Developing Vocabulary

**Inferring Meaning from Context.** Find each of the following statements in the selection and study the context in which it appears. Then determine the meanings of the italicized words, and think of a synonym for each.

1. These homes are never cheap and often are quite expensive and *lavish*. (p. 394)

2. The husbands *traverse* the nation. (p. 393)

3. They are *clannish* and they stick together. (p. 393)

4. I found myself *entranced* with these gadgets. (p. 392)

5. The mother-in-law problem is *abated*. (p. 395)

## Developing Writing Skills

**Explaining an Idea.** Do you have roots? You may have moved many times, and yet you may still feel that you have roots in your community. On the other hand, you may have lived in the same place all your life and still feel rootless.

In a five-paragraph composition, discuss the concept of "having roots," the process of developing roots, and your own situation in regard to roots. You may also wish to discuss the advantages and disadvantages of having roots.

# Unit Review   *Nonfiction*

## Understanding the Unit

1. A major external conflict in literature is the struggle of the individual against society. Which autobiographies and biographies in this unit deal with this conflict? Name the specific conflict portrayed in each selection.

2. The writers of both *Fifth Chinese Daughter* and *Barrio Boy* describe their struggles to become Americans without losing their own cultural identities. In what ways are their struggles similar? How are they different?

3. A biographer often relies on his or her imagination to recreate dialogue and to reconstruct the subject's thoughts and feelings. Which of the biographers represented in this unit rely most heavily on such reconstructed detail?

4. The selections from *Policewoman, Act One,* and *I Know Why the Caged Bird Sings* each deal with one specific event in the writer's life. What does each selection reveal about the writer's character and personality? How does each selection illustrate the major conflicts faced by the writer?

5. Choose two autobiographical selections and explain how each selection would be different if it were a biography. What details might be different? Why? What additional information might the writer include? Why?

6. Each of the essays on nature deals with the writer's relationship to water. In which essays are the writers in conflict with the water? How are these conflicts different? How are they similar? In which essays do the writers describe the beauty of the water? Which essays include both conflict and descriptions of beauty?

7. Essays can be divided into three types: narrative, descriptive, and expository. Which essays on nature rely most heavily on narration? on description? Which of the social commentaries explain an idea or issue, relying heavily on exposition?

8. Writers of essays use many of the same literary devices as writers of short stories. Which of the essays in this unit develop characters? Identify the characters and assess their importance to the essays.

Which essays follow a plot structure of rising action, climax, and falling action? What does this structure add to the essays?

9. The writers of some essays attempt to persuade their readers to adopt a certain opinion. Which of the social commentaries in this unit obviously are designed to change the reader's opinion? Which simply make comments about society and allow the reader to form his or her own opinion?

## Writing

1. Many of the subjects of the autobiographical and biographical selections in this unit had to combat some kind of prejudice. Choose three of these subjects and, in a five-paragraph composition, describe the prejudice that each had to overcome and explain how the struggle shaped his or her life.

2. Style is a writer's unique way of expressing ideas. Word choice, sentence structure, the use of flashback, descriptive language, comparison and contrast, suspense, the choice of point of view, and tone all contribute to a writer's style. Choose one of the following selections, and analyze the writer's style in a five-paragraph composition.

| | |
|---|---|
| Fair and Circus Days | Nightmare Spring |
| Policewoman | There Is No News |
| Woman Without Fear | from Auschwitz |
| | Aging in the Land |
| | of the Young |

3. In general, a biography presents a series of incidents that reveal how one person deals with conflict and learns from his or her experiences. Think of an incident that involves an internal or external conflict faced by a member of your family. In a five-paragraph composition, relate this incident and explain what the family member learned from the experience.

**ORGAN GRINDER WITH BOY, 1905.** *Pablo Picasso.*
*Kunsthaus, Zürich.*

# Unit 3

# Poetry

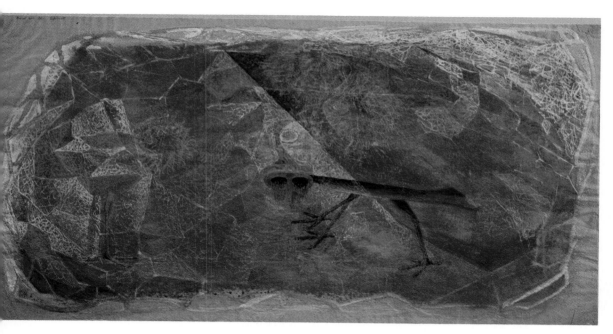

BIRD IN THE SPIRIT, 1940–41. *Morris Graves.*
*Collection of Whitney Museum of American Art.*

# Introduction to the Unit

"The chief work of poetry," wrote the poet Wallace Stevens, "is not to teach anything, nor to explain anything—though it may both teach and explain—it is to intensify life." The ability to "intensify life," to bring life into sharper focus for the reader, is one of poetry's chief attractions. Like all writers, poets attempt to re-create emotions and experiences. A poet, however, distills a subject to its essentials. It is this quality of compression that sets poetry apart from other types of writing.

Poetry is the most condensed form of literature. The poet selects words carefully, keeping in mind their suggestive power as well as their precise definitions. In a well wrought poem, each word is significant, and, because such a poem is so tightly packed, it takes work on the part of the reader to unpack its meaning.

The arrangement of a poem on a page may provide a key to meaning. In some poems, the form mirrors or expands the content. In other poems, the placement of a word or the isolation of a phrase directs attention to an important point.

Patterns of rhythm, rhyme, and repetition also can emphasize ideas in a poem. Sound patterns can be simple or complex, obvious or subtle. They can be based on the recurrence of a single letter or syllable or on the sounds of words and phrases. Recognizing that a poem is a fusion of sound and sense, a careful reader will read a poem aloud as a necessary step to understanding.

Finally, poems depend on unique presentations of words and ideas. A poet may create startling comparisons, ironic contrasts, and vivid sensory images. Through these devices, the poet challenges the reader to view life from a new perspective and to make uncommon connections. In this unit, for example, one poet connects growing up and running through a junkyard; another finds similarities between a passenger on a commuter train and the pilot of a downed fighter plane.

Once you have wrestled with the language and sounds of poetry and with the intricacies of structure and ideas, perhaps you will begin to appreciate how poetry can "intensify life" for the diligent reader.

# Rhythm and Rhyme

THE VIOLIN PLAYER, 1947. *Ben Shahn.*
*Collection, The Museum of Modern Art, New York.*
*Sam A. Lewisohn Bequest.*

# O What Is That Sound
*W. H. Auden*

O what is that sound which so thrills the ear
    Down in the valley drumming, drumming?
Only the scarlet soldiers, dear,
    The soldiers coming.

O what is that light I see flashing so clear 5
    Over the distance brightly, brightly?
Only the sun on their weapons, dear,
    As they step lightly.

O what are they doing with all that gear,
    What are they doing this morning, this morning? 10
Only the usual maneuvers, dear,
    Or perhaps a warning.

O why have they left the road down there,
    Why are they suddenly wheeling, wheeling?
Perhaps a change in the orders, dear. 15
    Why are you kneeling?

O haven't they stopped for the doctor's care,
    Haven't they reined their horses, their horses?
Why, they are none of them wounded, dear,
    None of these forces. 20

O is it the parson they want, with white hair,
    Is it the parson, is it, is it?
No, they are passing his gateway, dear,
    Without a visit.

O it must be the farmer who lives so near. 25
    It must be the farmer so cunning, so cunning?
They have passed the farmyard already, dear,
    And now they are running.

O where are you going? Stay with me here!
   Were the vows you swore deceiving, deceiving?     30
No, I promised to love you, dear,
   But I must be leaving.

O it's broken the lock and splintered the door,
   O it's the gate where they're turning, turning;
Their boots are heavy on the floor     35
   And their eyes are burning.

## Getting at Meaning

1. How many voices speak in each stanza? What is the relationship between them?

2. What is the first speaker's initial reaction to the sound of the soldiers? How does this reaction change as the poem progresses? What is the first speaker's reaction to the soldiers in the last stanza?

3. Explain line 16. Who is kneeling? Why?

4. For whom have the soldiers come?

## Developing Skills in Reading Literature

1. **Poetry.** Reduced to its simplest terms, poetry is language arranged in special ways; a poem looks like a poem. Poetry also evidences devices of sound and sense; a poem sounds like a poem.

If a section of an autobiography and a poem were placed side by side, would you recognize the poem? Why? In what ways does "O What Is That Sound" look like a poem? In what ways does it sound like a poem?

2. **Speaker.** The speaker of a poem is the voice that "speaks" the poem. Although a speaker might present the ideas of the poet, speaker and poet must be treated as distinct entities. This poem has two speakers. Describe each one on the basis of what you learn about them from the poem.

3. **Stanza.** A stanza of poetry is roughly comparable to a paragraph in prose. Technically, a stanza is a division of a poem, which is based on either the ideas presented or the pattern of rhyme in the poem. How many stanzas make up this poem? Are the stanzas divided by idea, by rhyme pattern, or by both?

4. **Rhyme.** Rhyme is the similarity of sound between two words. Words rhyme when their accented vowels, and all succeeding sounds, are identical. For true rhyme, the consonant that precedes the accented vowel must be different in each word. *Fun, run,* and *sun,* for example, fit the requirements of true rhyme. *Running,* and *sunning* are also true rhymes because the syllables follow-

ing the rhymed sounds are identical.

Rhymed words that appear at the ends of lines are called end rhyme. List the end rhymes in the first and second stanzas of this poem. Do the consonants that precede each vowel sound different?

5. **Quatrain.** A quatrain is a stanza or poem of four lines. Often, quatrains have a regular pattern of end rhyme. Do the quatrains in this poem have a regularly repeating pattern of rhyme?

6. **Rhyme Scheme.** The pattern of rhyme in a poem is called its rhyme scheme. A poem's rhyme scheme is charted by assigning a letter of the alphabet to each line. The last word in the first line of the poem is assigned the letter a. End words that rhyme with this word are also assigned the letter a. The next new sound to appear at the end of a line is given the letter b. This pattern is followed to the end of the poem.

The rhyme scheme for the first quatrain of "O What Is That Sound" is a b a b.

| . . . ear | a |
| . . . drumming? | b |
| . . . dear, | a |
| . . . coming. | b |

Now look at the second quatrain. Clear and dear have the same sound as ear and dear in the first quatrain, so these lines are assigned the letter a. The words brightly and lightly are new sounds, so they are assigned the letter c. The rhyme scheme for the second quatrain then is a c a c.

Chart the rhyme scheme for the remaining quatrains.

7. **Repetition.** Repetition is the repeated appearance of a word or phrase within a poem. In which line of each stanza does the poet use repetition? What effect does this repetition create? Which speaker uses repetition? What does this reveal about the speaker?

8. **Rhythm.** Rhythm is similar to the beat of a musical composition. A poet uses rhythm to emphasize the musical qualities of the language or to help create the mood of the poem. Rhythm is measured in unaccented and accented syllables. The symbol used to show an accented syllable is $/$ ; the symbol used to show an unaccented syllable is $\smile$ .

Copy the first three stanzas of this poem and mark the stressed and unstressed syllables of all words that contain two or more syllables. Read the three stanzas aloud, emphasizing the accented syllables. Does the rhythm remind you at all of marching? Why might the poet be striving for such an effect?

### Developing Vocabulary

**Latin Roots.** In poetry, a four-line stanza is called a quatrain. Quatra is the Latin word for "four." What other words can you think of that share this Latin root? Consult your dictionary for help.

Other common stanza lengths are named after Latin numbers. How many lines does each of the following stanzas have?

| triplet | sestet | octave |
| quintet | septet | |

Check each word in a dictionary and write out the Latin root for the word.

# The Puritan's Ballad   *Elinor Wylie*

My love came up from Barnegat,[1]
  The sea was in his eyes;
He trod as softly as a cat
  And told me terrible lies.

His hair was yellow as new-cut pine         5
  In shavings curled and feathered;
I thought how silver it would shine
  By cruel winters weathered.

But he was in his twentieth year,
  This time I'm speaking of;         10
We were head over heels in love with fear
  And half a-feared of love.

His feet were used to treading a gale
  And balancing thereon;
His face was brown as a foreign sail         15
  Threadbare against the sun.

His arms were thick as hickory logs
  Whittled to little wrists;
Strong as the teeth of terrier dogs
  Were the fingers of his fists.         20

Within his arms I feared to sink
  Where lions shook their manes,
And dragons drawn in azure ink
  Leapt quickened by his veins.

Dreadful his strength and length of limb         25
  As the sea to foundering ships;
I dipped my hands in love for him
  No deeper than their tips.

---

1. **Barnegat** (bär′ nē gat′): a bay off the New Jersey coast.

But our palms were welded by a flame
  The moment we came to part,
And on his knuckles I read my name
  Enscrolled within a heart.                    30

And something made our wills to bend
  As wild as trees blown over;
We were no longer friend and friend,           35
  But only lover and lover.

"In seven weeks or seventy years—
  God grant it may be sooner!—
I'll make a handkerchief for your tears
  From the sails of my captain's schooner.      40

"We'll wear our loves like wedding rings
  Long polished to our touch;
We shall be busy with other things
  And they cannot bother us much.

"When you are skimming the wrinkled cream       45
  And your ring clinks on the pan,
You'll say to yourself in a pensive dream,
  'How wonderful a man!'

"When I am slitting a fish's head
  And my ring clanks on the knife,              50
I'll say with thanks, as a prayer is said,
  'How beautiful a wife!'

"And I shall fold my decorous paws
  In velvet smooth and deep,
Like a kitten that covers up its claws          55
  To sleep and sleep and sleep.

"Like a little blue pigeon you shall bow
  Your bright alarming crest;
In the crook of my arm you'll lay your brow
  To rest and rest and rest."                   60

*Will he never come back from Barnegat*
  *With thunder in his eyes,*
*Treading as soft as a tiger cat,*
  *To tell me terrible lies?*

## Getting at Meaning

1. Who is the speaker? How do you know? What does the title of the poem reveal about the speaker?

2. What does the speaker mean when she says, "We were . . . in love with fear"? (line 11)

3. Explain the reference to lions and dragons in the sixth stanza. What are they? Where are they?

4. What does the speaker mean when she says, "I dipped my hands in love for him/No deeper than their tips"? (lines 27–28) What change occurs in the speaker when the couple parts? (lines 29–36)

5. Whom does the speaker quote in lines 37 through 60? What does this person promise? Are these promises kept? How does the speaker view these promises?

## Developing Skills in Reading Literature

1. **Ballad.** A ballad is a song that tells a story. Traditional folk ballads once were passed by word of mouth from singer to singer, from one generation to the next. Eventually, the words to some of these ballads were written down as narrative poems.

A folk ballad usually focuses on a single dramatic incident. It includes dialogue and repetition and evidences regular rhythm. A ballad also suggests more to the reader than it explains outright. "The Puritan's Ballad" is a twentieth century ballad that imitates the traditional form of the folk ballad. What characteristics of the folk ballad are illustrated by this poem? How does the speaker suggest more than she tells the reader?

2. **Rhyme Scheme.** Traditional ballads are written in quatrains with regular rhyme schemes. What is the rhyme scheme of this poem? Is the pattern consistent throughout the poem? What effect does the pattern of rhyme have on the reader? How does rhyme add emphasis to certain ideas in the poem?

3. **Meter.** The meter of a poem is the regular pattern of rhythmic units. Meter is determined by the pattern of stressed and unstressed syllables in a line of poetry. Read the first two lines of this poem, stressing the accented syllables:

My love came up from Barnegat,
The sea was in his eyes;

A unit of meter is called a foot. Each foot in this poem is made up of an unstressed syllable followed by a stressed syllable ( / ). This type of metrical foot is called an iamb; the repetition of this metrical unit is called iambic meter.

How many iambic feet are in the first line of the poem? In the second line of the poem?

Marking the meter of a poem is called scanning. Write out the second stanza of "The Puritan's Ballad" and scan it by marking unstressed (ᴗ) and stressed (/) syllables. Do not simply concentrate on the normal stressed and unstressed syllables of each word. Consider also the importance of the word in the poem and the metrical pattern established by the poet. For this poem, you may occasionally have to slur two syllables together to make the words fit the iambic meter. The word *yellow*, for example, should be scanned as if it were one syllable, *yellow*.

4. **Similes.** The poet uses many similes to describe the sailor and his relationship with the speaker. Quote three of these similes and explain what each adds to the reader's understanding of the poem.

## Developing Writing Skills

**Imitating a Poetic Form.** Following are the beginnings of three ballad quatrains. Complete each by writing two more lines. You may follow the traditional pattern in which the first and the third lines do not rhyme or the rhyming pattern used in "The Puritan's Ballad."

1. Said mother to her daughter dear,
   "Why are you home so late?"
2. "No game is lost," the coach declared,
   "Until the final out!"
3. He gazed at her across the room
   Her face was _____ _____ _____ (complete this line with a simile).

# Counting-Out Rhyme

*Edna St. Vincent Millay*

Silver bark of beech, and sallow
Bark of yellow birch and yellow
   Twig of willow.

Stripe of green in moosewood maple,
Colour seen in leaf of apple,      5
   Bark of popple.

Wood of popple pale as moonbeam,
Wood of oak for yoke and barn-beam,
   Wood of hornbeam.

Silver bark of beech, and hollow
Stem of elder, tall and yellow
   Twig of willow.

## Getting at Meaning

1. What does the speaker describe in this poem? Is anything described more than once?

2. What does *sallow* in line 1 describe? Why might the poet have placed this word at the end of line 1 instead of at the beginning of line 2?

3. Read the poem aloud several times. Are you more aware of the content of the poem or of the sounds of the words?

## Developing Skills in Reading Literature

1. **Rhyme.** What is the rhyme scheme of this poem? How does the end rhyme unify each stanza? How does it unify the poem?

Internal rhyme is rhyme within a line of poetry. Find an example of internal rhyme in the third stanza. What effect does this rhyme have on the reader's perception of these two words?

2. **Alliteration.** Rhyme is not the only sound device used in this poem. The poet also uses alliteration, which is the repetition of initial consonant sounds. For example, in the phrase "Peter Piper picked a peck of pickled peppers," the initial consonant *p* begins six words. This is an extreme example of alliteration. More often a consonant will be repeated only once or twice.

Identify two examples of alliteration in the first line of this poem. Which example is repeated in the second line? Find two other instances of alliteration in the poem. How does the poet's use of alliteration unify phrases and stanzas?

3. **Consonance.** Consonance is the repetition of consonant sounds. Unlike alliteration, consonance is not limited to the initial letter of a word. In the word *bubble,* for example, the three *b*'s are consonance; in the phrase *short and sweet* the *s*'s are alliteration while the final *t*'s are consonance.

What is the consonance in the words *beech* and *birch?* Find another example of consonance.

4. **Repetition.** Where does the poet use repetition? What is the effect of the repetition? Does repetition contribute to the sound of a poem? Explain.

5. **Meter.** The meter of this poem is a way of "counting out" the rhythm. Read the first stanza aloud, emphasizing the stressed syllables. Now write out the first stanza and scan it; that is, mark the meter, using the symbols for stressed and unstressed syllables.

The meter of this poem is trochaic; each foot is made up of a stressed syllable followed by an unstressed syllable ($/\cup$). Check your scanning of the first stanza to make certain that you have marked regular trochaic meter.

The meter of a poetic line is named also according to the number of feet in the line. The most common lines are these:

monometer: one metrical foot
dimeter: two metrical feet
trimeter: three metrical feet
tetrameter: four metrical feet
pentameter: five metrical feet
hexameter: six metrical feet
heptameter: seven metrical feet
octometer: eight metrical feet

To identify a line of poetry, you name the type of meter (iambic or trochaic, for example) and the number of feet (monometer or dimeter, for example). A line of poetry with two trochaic feet per line would be called trochaic dimeter.

How many trochaic feet make up the first line of this poem? the second line? the third line? What is the correct name for each line?

## Developing Vocabulary

**Using a Dictionary.** In a dictionary entry, the pronunciation of a word appears in parentheses after the word. Phonetic symbols are used to indicate the sound of the word. The key to these symbols usually is found at the bottom of every other dictionary page.

Look up each of the following words in a dictionary. Sound out the pronunciation and then copy the phonetic respelling. Be prepared to pronounce the words correctly.

| | | |
|---|---|---|
| monometer | tetrameter | heptameter |
| dimeter | pentameter | octometer |
| trimeter | hexameter | |

# Fast Run in the Junkyard

*Jeannette Nichols*

That junkyard fell down the side of the hill
like a river: baby buggy, black leather
cracked car back seat, sofa wind-siphoned
by a clutch of tangled wire hangers hanging on
like spiders. We stood and fell as momentum told us          5
toward somebody's sodden Sealey[1] dying of galloping miasma,[2]
jumped on bedsprings sprung to pogos, and leaped
for king-of-the-mountain where boxes and cans fountained
up the hill's other side. Sailing saucers, we rode
back down, flinging hat racks, burlap sacks, chairs cropped    10
of backs and flotsam crockery, breezed in league boots
back out of everybody's past hazards, up to the road
to break tar bubbles all-the-way-home where things
were wearing out as fast as we were growing up.

---

1. **Sealey:** a brand of mattress.
2. **miasma** (mī az′ mə): an unwholesome or foggy atmosphere.

## Getting at Meaning

1. Who are the people running in the junkyard? How do you know?

2. Why does the speaker call the junk "everybody's past hazards"?

3. Reread the last two lines. What connection is suggested between a junkyard and the process of growing up?

## Developing Skills in Reading Literature

1. **Speaker.** Describe the speaker of this poem. Is the speaker relating a recent event? Explain.

2. **Alliteration.** In this poem, sound devices, such as alliteration, carry the reader rapidly through the junkyard. What alliteration can you find in lines 2, 3, and 4? How do these sounds reinforce the action mentioned in the opening line? Find two other examples of alliteration and explain how each reinforces the action of the poem.

3. **Diction.** Diction refers to a writer's choice of words. Why is *sodden* an appropriate word to describe the mattress? Think of a synonym for *sodden*. What would be lost if the poet had used this synonym?

What does the word *fountained* in line 8 imply? Why is it an effective word? Find at least two more examples of precise diction and explain why each choice is effective.

## Developing Writing Skills

**Describing Action.** Using the description of action in this poem as a model, describe an action that you see around your home daily. You might describe your cat stretching, a person vacuuming, or children running through the house. Select precise words and use alliteration and other sound devices to reinforce the action. Write this description as either a paragraph or a poem.

# The Choice     *Dorothy Parker*

He'd have given me rolling lands,
   Houses of marble, and billowing farms,
Pearls, to trickle between my hands,
   Smoldering rubies, to circle my arms.
You—you'd only a lilting song,                                  5
   Only a melody, happy and high,
You were sudden and swift and strong—
   Never a thought for another had I.

He'd have given me laces rare,
   Dresses that glimmered with frosty sheen,     10
Shining ribbons to wrap my hair,
   Horses to draw me, as fine as a queen.
You—you'd only to whistle low,
   Gayly I followed wherever you led.
I took you, and I let him go—                                   15
   Somebody ought to examine my head!

## Getting at Meaning

1. What choice is presented to the speaker? What choice does she make? Why?

2. Up to the last line, how do you think the speaker feels about her choice?

## Developing Skills in Reading Literature

1. **Irony.** One type of irony, you will recall, arises from the contrast between what is expected and what actually happens. What is ironic about the ending of this poem? How does the speaker "set you up"?

2. **Rhythm.** Read the poem aloud several times, paying particular attention to its rhythm. Listen for the words that are stressed. What words are emphasized in line 7? How does this emphasis help to convey the speaker's feelings toward her love?

3. **Meter.** This poem has an intricate pattern of metrical feet. Lines 1, 3, 5, and 7 are scanned like this:

$$/ \smile \quad / \smile \smile \quad / \smile \quad /$$
He'd have given me rolling lands,

Lines 2, 4, 6, and 8 are scanned like this:

$$/ \smile \smile \quad / \smile \quad \smile \quad / \smile \smile \quad /$$
Houses of marble, and billowing farms,

The metrical foot used here is called dactylic. A dactylic foot consists of three syllables, a strongly stressed syllable followed by two unstressed syllables ($/ \smile \smile$). Words like *Saturday, beautiful,* and *billowing* are dactylic.

Write out the first stanza of the poem and scan it according to the patterns for odd numbered and even numbered lines. Note that every line ends with a stressed syllable. How many dactylic feet make up the even numbered lines? (Do not count the extra stress at the end of each line.)

4. **Rhyme Scheme.** What is the rhyme scheme of this poem? How does this rhyme scheme reinforce the division of ideas within the poem? What other sound device does the poet use?

## Developing Vocabulary

**Finding the Appropriate Meaning.** Look up each of the following italicized words in a dictionary and find the appropriate definition for the word as it is used in this poem. Copy the definition and then use the word in the same sense in a sentence of your own.

> *rolling* lands
> *billowing* farms
> *smoldering* rubies
> dresses that *glimmered*
> *shining* ribbons

PORTRAIT OF A COURT LADY, c. 1570. François Clouet. Courtesy of The Art Institute of Chicago.

# Quail Walk     *Heather Ross Miller*

Every afternoon at four,
The quail pass our door in quietness.
Black-crested,
Soft, and neat,
They put their feet down to earth          5
In care,
Prudently attentive to fear and anger there.

The open road blankly bares.
They pause;
Then break,                                10
One after one after one,
And none dare to look.

If a brother lies broken,
Brown feathers in a sack,
The spaniels circling;                     15
What use is it?

Home, home to the brushy nest,
In a line exact and discreet,
Black-crested,
Soft, and neat.                            20

## Getting at Meaning

1. Describe the way the quail walk. What words and phrases in the poem help you to picture their walk?

2. What is it that none of the quail dare look at?

3. What has happened to the "brother" quail? How do the quail react? Why?

4. What is the speaker's attitude toward the quail? Support your answer with examples from the poem.

## Developing Skills in Reading Literature

1. **Rhythm.** This poem does not have regular rhythm. If you read it aloud, however, you will sense a choppy, sharp beat alternating with a smoother, more continuous beat. Why has the poet chosen this rhythmic pattern?

2. **Rhyme.** This poem does not have a regular rhyme pattern, but it does include several rhymes that effectively emphasize important points. Find three examples of rhyme and explain what point is emphasized.

3. **Free Verse.** Free verse is poetry that lacks regular patterns of rhythm and rhyme.

4. **Denotation and Connotation.** The denotative meaning of a word is the exact, literal meaning as it is given in a dictionary definition. What is the denotative meaning of *broken* in line 13?

The connotative meanings of a word, as you know, are the suggestions, associations, and feelings that surround the word. What are the connotations of *broken?*

Does the poet want the reader to respond to the denotative meaning of *broken,* to the connotative meanings, or to a combination of meanings? Explain.

## Developing Writing Skills

**Writing a Poem.** In three or four sentences, describe the way that a person or animal walks. You might describe a baby toddling or a lion stalking. Select words that have the correct denotative and connotative meanings to describe your subject. After you have written the sentences, take out all the unnecessary words and rearrange what is left into a poem. Try to make the presentation of the lines match the pattern of the walk.

# Kansas Boy    *Ruth Lechlitner*

This Kansas boy who never saw the sea
Walks through the young corn rippling at his knee
As sailors walk; and when the grain grows higher
Watches the dark waves leap with greener fire
Than ever oceans hold. He follows ships,                    5
Tasting the bitter spray upon his lips,
For in his blood up-stirs the salty ghost
Of one who sailed a storm-bound English coast.
Across wide fields he hears the sea winds crying,
Shouts at the crows—and dreams of white gulls flying.    10

## Getting at Meaning

1. The speaker compares the boy's walk to a sailor's walk. Describe a sailor's walk.

2. What does the boy see when he looks at the tall grain?

3. Explain lines 7 and 8. Where does the boy's love of the sea originate?

4. What is ironic about a boy from Kansas being in love with the sea?

## Developing Skills in Reading Literature

1. **Meter.** This poem is written in iambic pentameter, the most common form of meter in English poetry. How many feet make up each regular line of iambic pentameter?

Copy the first four lines of this poem and scan the meter. What irregularities do you notice? Irregularities in meter are not mistakes by a poet. Instead, they prevent the poem from becoming too fixed or rigid. Sometimes irregularities help to emphasize a word or idea. In this poem, what word in line 4 is emphasized by the break in meter?

2. **Heroic Couplet.** A couplet is two lines of rhymed verse. If the lines are written in iambic pentameter, the couplet is called an heroic couplet. This poem is written in heroic couplets. What is the rhyme scheme of the poem?

3. **Imagery.** Words and phrases that appeal to the senses are called images. In line 4, what sense is appealed to with the phrase "greener fire"? What is unusual about this image? Is it appropriate? Explain.

To what other senses does the poem appeal? Give examples to support your answer.

## Developing Writing Skills

**Writing Heroic Couplets.** Write an heroic couplet on each of the following topics: people, animals, and sports. Here is a possible first line for the couplet on animals:

The lion looked at him with eyes on fire

# Form and Meaning

PORTRAIT NO. 1, 1938. *Joan Miro.*
*The Baltimore Museum of Art. Bequest of Saidie A. May.*

# Poem

*Philip G. Tannenbaum*

```
I d o
n t l
i k e
t e l
e p h
o n e
b o o
t h s
```

## Getting at Meaning

What does the speaker dislike? Why?

## Developing Skills in Reading Literature

**Concrete Poem.** A concrete poem is one in which the shape of the poem is directly related to its meaning. Form and meaning are inseparable in a concrete poem. Without the unique shape, or form, the poem loses its meaning.

Write "Poem" out as a prose sentence. Can you tell from the sentence why the poet dislikes tele-phone booths? What does the arrangement of letters into a rectangle add to the poem?

## Developing Writing Skills

**Writing a Concrete Poem.** Write a sentence in which you express a strong emotion. For example, "Younger brothers are a pain!" Then arrange the sentence into a concrete poem in which the form helps to explain the reasons behind the expressed emotion. The sample sentence, for instance, might be presented in the shape of a mouth.

# Letter Slot      *John Updike*

Once each day this broad mouth spews

Apologies,

bills,

rags,

and news.

**Getting at Meaning**

What apologies might come in the mail? What rags? What news?

**Developing Skills in Reading Literature**

1. **Concrete Poem.** How are form and meaning related in "Letter Slot"?
2. **Personification.** Where does the poet use personification in this poem? Why is this personification appropriate for the content and meaning of the poem?

**Developing Vocabulary**

**Slang.** Look up the word *rag* in a dictionary. Find a slang meaning of the word that fits the way the word is used in this poem. Can you think of other slang expressions for various kinds of mail?

# Pendulum

*John Updike*

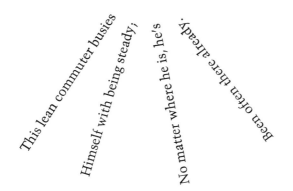

This lean commuter busies
Himself with being steady;
No matter where he is, he's
Been often there already.

## Getting at Meaning

Who or what is the "lean commuter" mentioned in the first line? Why lean? Why commuter?

## Developing Skills in Reading Literature

1. **Concrete Poem.** How are form and content related in this poem?

2. **Rhyme.** Although it is arranged differently, this poem is really a quatrain. What is the rhyme scheme? How does the rhyme relate to the content of the poem?

3. **Meter.** Identify the regular meter of this poem.

## Developing Vocabulary

**Clipping and Backformation.** Clipping is the process by which long words are shortened, or clipped. *Fan* is a clipping of *fanatic; bike* is a clipping of *bicycle*. When a clip results in a new part of speech, the process is called backformation. *Commute*, which means "to travel to and from work," is a clipping of *commuter*. Because the part of speech is changed from a noun to a verb, this is also an example of backformation.

From what longer words are the following words clipped? Consult a dictionary, if necessary.

| | |
|---|---|
| zoo | perk |
| prefab | dorm |
| ammo | ump |
| alum | comfy |
| champ | televise |

Which of these clips are backformations? List at least five other clips that you use in daily conversation.

# Foul Shot    *Edwin A. Hoey*

With two 60's stuck on the scoreboard
And two seconds hanging on the clock,
The solemn boy in the center of eyes,
Squeezed by silence,
Seeks out the line with his feet,                    5
Soothes his hands along his uniform,
Gently drums the ball against the floor,
Then measures the waiting net,
Raises the ball on his right hand,
Balances it with his left,                           10
Calms it with fingertips,
Breathes,
Crouches,
Waits,
And then through a stretching of stillness,          15
Nudges it upward.

The ball
Slides up and out,
Lands,
Leans,                                               20
Wobbles,
Wavers,
Hesitates,
Exasperates,
Plays it coy                                         25
Until every face begs with unsounding screams—
And then

        And then

          And then,

Right before ROAR-UP,                                30
Dives down and through.

## Getting at Meaning

1. What game does the poem describe? At what point in the game does the action occur?

2. Why is the boy solemn? Whose silence squeezes the boy? What movements of the ball are described? Where is the ball when these movements occur?

3. What verbs describe the actions of the boy? What verbs describe the movements of the ball?

4. Why does ROAR-UP occur?

## Developing Skills in Reading Literature

1. **Structure.** The physical arrangement of this poem emphasizes its content. For example, the line "And then through a stretching of stillness" is longer, more stretched out, than the lines immediately before and after it. Find two other lines or groups of lines in which the presentation of the words emphasizes content.

2. **Personification.** Find three words and phrases used by the poet to personify the ball.

3. **Consonance.** Throughout most of the poem, the writer repeats words that emphasize a particular consonant sound. What is that consonant? What effect does the repetition of the sound create? What does the writer accomplish by eliminating this sound from the last two lines of the poem?

## Developing Writing Skills

1. **Describing Action.** Choose a crucial moment from a sporting event. In one paragraph, describe the sequence of actions surrounding that moment. Use verbs and adjectives that vividly portray both actions and feelings.

2. **Writing a Poem.** Look again at the paragraph that you developed for the first writing exercise. Eliminate all unnecessary words; then arrange the remaining words and phrases into lines that emphasize or mirror the action described.

# Speaker and Tone

BAUHAUS STAIRWAY, 1932. *Oskar Schlemmer.*
*Collection, The Museum of Modern Art, New York. Gift of Philip Johnson.*

# The Secret     *Denise Levertov*

Two girls discover
the secret of life
in a sudden line of
poetry.

I who don't know the                    5
secret wrote
the line. They
told me

(through a third person)
they had found it                        10
but not what it was
not even

what line it was. No doubt
by now, more than a week
later, they have forgotten               15
the secret,

the line, the name of
the poem. I love them
for finding what
I can't find,                            20

and for loving me
for the line I wrote,
and for forgetting it
so that

a thousand times, till death             25
finds them, they may
discover it again, in other
lines

in other
happenings. And for                      30
wanting to know it,
for

assuming there is
such a secret, yes,
for that                                 35
most of all.

## Getting at Meaning

1. Why is the line of poetry "sudden" to the girls who read it?

2. Why doesn't the speaker know the secret that the girls have discovered?

3. Why is it likely that the girls have forgotten the secret? Why doesn't this idea upset the speaker?

4. What does the assumption that a secret of life exists imply about the girls? Why does the speaker love them for their belief?

## Developing Skills in Reading Literature

1. **Speaker.** In this poem, who is the speaker? In the poem that the girls read, who is the speaker? Is it possible for a reader to discover meanings in a poem that were not intended by the poet? Explain your answer.

2. **Tone.** What is the speaker's attitude toward the girls and their discovery?

## Developing Writing Skills

**Writing an Explanation.** Choose a line from a favorite poem. Then, in one paragraph, explain what the line means to you and describe the insight into life that the line offers.

# Forever  *Eve Merriam*

My father tells me
that when he was a boy
he once crashed a ball
through a neighbor's window.

He does not mean to,                          5
but he lies.

I know that aeons ago
the world was ice
and mud
and fish climbed out of the sea      10
to reptiles on land
to dinosaurs and mammals;

and I know also
that archeologists have found
remains of ancient times              15
when men lived in caves
and worshiped weather.

Nonetheless I know
that my father,
a grown man,                                   20
coming home at night
with work-lines in his face
and love for me hidden behind
the newspaper in his hand,
has always been so                           25
since the world began.

### Getting at Meaning

1. What does the word *tells* in line 1 imply about the speaker's attitude toward the father's story?

2. What does the speaker's description of evolution and of prehistoric humans imply about human beings?

3. What image of the father is held by the speaker? Why can't the speaker imagine the father as any different?

### Developing Skills in Reading Literature

1. **Speaker.** Who is the speaker in this poem? How old might the speaker be? Explain your answer.

2. **Tone.** What attitude toward the father does the speaker convey in the lines "He does not mean to,/but he lies"? Which lines develop further the speaker's attitude toward the father? Describe their relationship.

3. **Title.** How might the speaker in this poem define the word *forever*?

### Developing Writing Skills

1. **Combining Description and Exposition.** Choose a character trait possessed by an adult that you know well. In one paragraph, specifically describe the trait and explain why you are convinced that the person has always exhibited this trait.

2. **Describing a Person.** Write one paragraph in which you use specific details to describe the kind of boy or girl that you think your father or mother once was. Base your description on the characteristics of the adult you now know.

# The Writer    *Richard Wilbur*

In her room at the prow of the house
Where light breaks, and the windows are tossed with linden,
My daughter is writing a story.

I pause in the stairwell, hearing
From her shut door a commotion of typewriter-keys          5
Like a chain hauled over a gunwale.

Young as she is, the stuff
Of her life is a great cargo, and some of it heavy:
I wish her a lucky passage.

But now it is she who pauses,                               10
As if to reject my thought and its easy figure.
A stillness greatens, in which

The whole house seems to be thinking,
And then she is at it again with a bunched clamor
Of strokes, and again is silent.                           15

I remember the dazed starling
Which was trapped in that very room, two years ago;
How we stole in, lifted a sash

And retreated, not to affright it;
And how for a helpless hour, through the crack of the door,  20
We watched the sleek, wild, dark

And iridescent creature
Batter against the brilliance, drop like a glove
To the hard floor, or the desk-top,

And wait then, humped and bloody,                          25
For the wits to try it again; and how our spirits
Rose when, suddenly sure,

It lifted off from a chair-back,
Beating a smooth course for the right window
And clearing the sill of the world.                            30

It is always a matter, my darling,
Of life or death, as I had forgotten. I wish
What I wished you before, but harder.

## Getting at Meaning

1. With what are the words *prow, gunwale, cargo, tossed,* and *passage* usually associated?

2. Although the speaker's daughter is young, in what sense might the stuff of her life be a great cargo? How is the speaker's wish for a lucky passage related to the daughter's activity as a writer?

3. What "easy figure" does the daughter's pause seem to reject?

4. Why does the daughter's writing activity remind the speaker of the dazed starling? How is the young writer trapped?

5. Who (or what) experiences the helpless hour noted in line 20? Explain your answer.

6. What is the brilliance that the starling batters itself against? How is this action similar to the young writer's experience?

7. Explain how, after failing, both the starling and the young writer must wait "For the wits to try it again."

8. When the starling escapes from the room, how does it clear "the sill of the world"? How might a writer do the same thing?

9. What is a matter of life or death? Why does the speaker reaffirm the original wish?

## Developing Skills in Reading Literature

1. **Speaker and Tone.** Who is the speaker in this poem? How does the speaker feel about the young girl's experience as a writer? What do the descriptions of the starling as *sleek, wild, dark,* and *iridescent* reveal about the speaker's attitude toward the young writer? What does the comment "our spirits rose" in reference to the starling's escape reveal about the speaker's hopes for the young writer? How are the speaker's attempts to describe the young writer's experience similar to the experience itself?

2. **Metaphor and Extended Metaphor.** In the first three stanzas of the poem, find a clear metaphor that states that one thing is another. What two things are compared? How are they different yet similar? Now find the extended metaphor that is implied throughout the first three stanzas. Be prepared to evaluate the effectiveness of the extended metaphor.

## Developing Vocabulary

**Suffixes.** Using the following suffixes, create five words for each suffix and then use three of the words from each list in sentences.

-able, -ible    -less
-most           -like

# Plucking the Rushes

*Anonymous*

*A boy and girl are sent to gather rushes for thatching.*
*(Fourth or Fifth Century)*

Green rushes with red shoots,
Long leaves bending to the wind—
You and I in the same boat
Plucking rushes at the Five Lakes.
We started at dawn from the orchid-island;          5
We rested under the elms till noon.
You and I plucking rushes
Had not plucked a handful when night came!

## Getting at Meaning

1. What does the speaker note about the rushes in the first two lines? Does this description relate to any practical use of the rushes?

2. Why does the speaker make the comment "You and I in the same boat"?

3. How much time do the boy and girl spend on their rush-gathering excursion? How much time do they actually devote to their task?

## Developing Skills in Reading Literature

1. **Speaker and Tone.** Who is the speaker in this poem? What is the speaker's attitude toward his or her surroundings? How do you know? How does the speaker feel about failing to pluck the rushes?

2. **Understatement.** What does the speaker tell the reader directly about the young couple's day? What does the speaker imply or understate about their day?

# Here—Hold My Hand     *Mari Evans*

Here
hold my hand
let me touch you
there is
nothing                                    5
we can
say . . . your
soul
eludes me
when I reach                               10
out
your eyes
resent
my need to know
you                                        15

here
hold my hand
since
there is nothing
we can                                     20
say

## Getting at Meaning

1. Why does the speaker wish to touch the "you" in the poem?

2. What is it that the speaker cannot reach in the other person? Explain your answer.

3. Describe the other person's feelings toward the speaker.

## Developing Skills in Reading Literature

1. **Speaker and Tone.** What might be the relationship between the speaker and the person addressed in the poem? What is the speaker's attitude toward the other person and toward their relationship? How would the speaker like the relationship to change? Is such a change possible according to the speaker? Explain your answer.

2. **Understatement.** What does the speaker imply about the relationship with the words "there is/nothing/we can/say"? What is implied about the speaker's feelings in the lines "Here/hold my hand"?

## Developing Writing Skills

1. **Writing an Explanation.** Many different circumstances and relationships could have inspired the poet to write "Here—Hold My Hand." Choose two characters, a parent and a young child, a grown child and an elderly parent, a young couple on a date, or a married couple. In one paragraph, explain what might happen between them to cause a breakdown in communication.

2. **Writing a Poem.** Using "Here—Hold My Hand" as a model, write a poem in which the speaker is the person addressed in the poem by Mari Evans. Be sure that your speaker reveals his or her feelings about communicating and sharing.

# Untitled  *Niki Paulzine*

i am the fire of time.
the endless pillar
that has withstood death.
the support of an invincible nation.
i am the stars that have guided          5
lost men.
i am the mother of ten thousand
dying children.
i am the fire of time.
i am an indian woman!                     10

MENOMINEE WOMAN. *George Catlin.*
*The Newberry Library, Chicago. Courtesy of the Edward E. Ayer Collection.*

### Getting at Meaning

1. What does the phrase "fire of time" imply? In what sense does time burn? How is such a fire endless?

2. What is the purpose of a pillar? What line alludes to the role of the Indian woman as a pillar?

3. How can a nation of lost men and dying children be invincible?

### Developing Skills in Reading Literature

1. **Poetry.** The rules of punctuation and capitalization are not always followed as strictly in poetry as they are in prose. What does the poet achieve by not capitalizing the pronoun *i*? What does she accomplish by placing periods at the ends of incomplete sentences in the third and fourth lines? What effect does she create by using an exclamation point at the end of the poem?

2. **Speaker and Metaphor.** The speaker in this poem identifies herself through the use of metaphors. Find two examples of these metaphors and explain what the speaker reveals about herself through each comparison.

3. **Tone.** What attitudes toward her subject does the speaker express? Explain your answer. Write one sentence that states what you think is the tone of the entire poem.

### Developing Vocabulary

**Prefixes.** The prefix *in-* as it is used in the word *invincible* means "not." However, the prefix *in*— and also *ir-*, *il-*, and *im*—can mean "in or into" and "very." Define each of the following words, using a dictionary as necessary, and indicate the meaning of the prefix.

| | |
|---|---|
| incomplete | incorrect |
| investigate | illuminate |
| impossible | input |
| illustrious | invaluable |
| irregular | inconsistent |

# Long Distance     *Carole Gregory*

That phone call, the one that you wait for
but never expect to come
was phoned today. And
that voice, the voice you ache for
but seldom expect to hear                    5
spoke today. And that
loneliness, the loneliness you hurt from
but always held inside,
flies out like thin stones across water.

## Getting at Meaning

1. What does the phrase "the voice you ache for" reveal about the relationship between the caller and the speaker?

2. What does the fact that the loneliness is "always held inside" reveal about the speaker?

## Developing Skills in Reading Literature

1. **Speaker and Tone.** Who might the speaker in this poem be? How does the speaker feel about the person who makes the phone call? What effect does the phone call have upon the speaker? What is the tone of this poem?

2. **Simile.** Identify the simile used in this poem. What two things are compared? How are these things similar? What does the comparison add to your understanding of the speaker's feelings?

## Developing Writing Skills

**Writing Dialogue.** Imagine that you listened in on the telephone conversation referred to in "Long Distance." Write the dialogue that might have been spoken by the speaker and the caller.

# Driving to Town Late To Mail a Letter

*Robert Bly*

It is a cold and snowy night. The main street is deserted.
The only things moving are swirls of snow.
As I lift the mailbox door, I feel its cold iron.
There is a privacy I love in this snowy night.
Driving around, I will waste more time.          5

## Getting at Meaning

1. What details does the speaker note about his or her surroundings?

2. What makes the snowy night private?

3. Is the speaker really wasting time? Explain your answer.

## Developing Skills in Reading Literature

**Speaker and Tone.** What do the details in the first three lines reveal about the speaker? How does the speaker feel about this particular night? What does the speaker's intention to drive around reveal about the speaker's attitude toward life?

# Fireworks    *Amy Lowell*

You hate me and I hate you,
And we are so polite, we two!

But whenever I see you, I burst apart
And scatter the sky with my blazing heart.
It spits and sparkles in stars and balls,    5
Buds into roses—and flares, and falls.

Scarlet buttons, and pale green disks,
Silver spirals and asterisks,
Shoot and tremble in a mist
Peppered with mauve and amethyst.    10

I shine in the windows and light up the trees,
And all because I hate you, if you please.

And when you meet me, you rend asunder
And go up in a flaming wonder
Of saffron cubes, and crimson moons,    15
And wheels all amaranths and maroons.

Golden lozenges and spades,
Arrows of malachites and jades,
Patens of copper, azure sheaves.
As you mount, you flash in the glossy leaves.    20

Such fireworks as we make, we two!
Because you hate me and I hate you.

## Getting at Meaning

1. The speaker and the person addressed in the poem are polite to each other. What effect does their behavior have upon their hatred?

2. When they meet each other, how do the two people lose control?

3. What do the verbs *spits, sparkles, shoot,* and *tremble* contribute to the description of the speaker's hatred?

4. Compare the reactions experienced by the hated person to those experienced by the speaker. Be specific.

## Developing Skills in Reading Literature

1. **Speaker and Tone.** The speaker states, "You hate me and I hate you." He or she then proceeds to describe feelings in terms of fireworks. Is the resulting tone one of hostility? Why or why not?

What do lines 11 and 12 add to the tone of the poem?

2. **Rhyme.** How does the use of end rhyme in this poem affect its tone?

3. **Irony.** What kinds of images are generally used to describe feelings of hatred? With what feelings are fireworks commonly associated? What is ironic about the use of fireworks images in this poem?

## Developing Writing Skills

**Using the Senses in Writing: The Sense of Sight.** Choose an emotion, such as love, hate, fear, or sorrow. In one paragraph, describe the emotion in terms of visual images connected with an animal, clouds, flowers, traffic, or an inanimate object. Be sure to include several vivid, specific descriptive phrases in your paragraph.

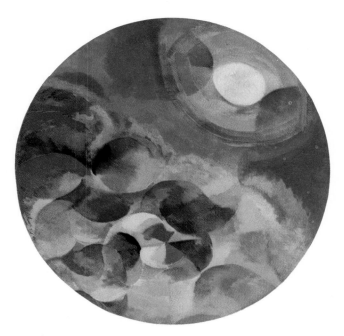

SIMULTANEOUS CONTRAST: SUN AND MOON, 1912. *Robert Delaunay. Collection, The Museum of Modern Art, New York. Mrs. Simon Guggenheim Fund.*

# Imagery

O THROUGH 9, 1961. *Jasper Johns.*
*Hirshhorn Museum and Sculpture Garden, Smithsonian Institution.*

# Haiku

## Untitled    *Basho*

> Old pond—
> and a frog jumps in:
> water-sound.

## The Peacock    *José Juan Tablada*

> Peacock, drawn out shimmer,
> you pass like a procession
> through the democratic henyard . . .

## Flying Fish    *José Juan Tablada*

> Struck by the sun's gold
> the pane of the sea bursts into splinters.

## Untitled    *W. H. Auden*

> Leaning out over
> The dreadful precipice,
> One contemptuous tree.

## Getting at Meaning

1. In the poem by Basho, how does the word *old* affect the reader's image of the pond? What is the mood of this poem?

2. In "The Peacock," why is *shimmer* an appropriate word to describe the way that a peacock walks? What is democratic about a henyard?

3. In "Flying Fish," what is "struck by the sun's gold": the fish? the sea? both?

4. In the poem by Auden, why is the tree "contemptuous"?

## Developing Skills in Reading Literature

1. **Haiku.** Haiku is a Japanese poetry form. When written in Japanese, a haiku has seventeen syllables arranged in three lines. The first line has five syllables, the second line seven syllables, and the third, five syllables. When a haiku is translated from Japanese into another language, however, it is impossible to maintain the syllable count. Translators instead try to capture the mood and imagery of the original. Poets writing haiku in languages other than Japanese also concentrate on the content of the poem rather than on syllable counts. All haiku exhibit four recognizable qualities:

Haiku depend on imagery.
Haiku are condensed; the poet leaves out all unnecessary words.
Haiku are concerned with emotions; nature is used to reflect these emotions.

Haiku rely heavily on the power of suggestion, or connotation.

Count the syllables in the poems presented here. How does the form of each poem vary from that of a traditional haiku? How does the poem illustrate the characteristics of haiku?

2. **Imagery.** To what senses does Basho appeal in his poem? Are the images in the poem specific, or do they allow the reader to complete the image in his or her mind? Explain.

How does the poem by Auden reflect human emotions? In what way is the image of the tree an image of a person?

3. **Connotation.** In "The Peacock," the bird's walk is compared to a procession. What are the connotations of *procession*? Contrast these connotations with the connotations of *democratic* in the next line. What point is made?

4. **Metaphor.** The poet uses a metaphor in the second line of "Flying Fish." What two things are compared? How is the comparison extended to the end of the line?

## Developing Writing Skills

**Writing Haiku.** Write two haiku, one in the 5-7-5 syllable count of the traditional form; the other in a more flexible form that need not follow the strict syllable count. Both poems should be condensed, use vivid images, rely on the connotative power of words, and focus on nature.

# Firefly Song    *Ojibwa Indian*

Flickering firefly
　　　　　give me light
　　　　　light
once more before I sleep

Dancing firefly　　　　　　　　　　　5
　　　　　wandering firefly
　　　　　light
once more before I sleep

White light sailing
　　　　　white light winking　　10
just once more before I sleep

## Getting at Meaning

Why is light so important to the speaker? What unexpressed fear does the speaker have? Explain.

## Developing Skills in Reading Literature

1. **Imagery.** What words does the speaker use to describe the intermittent appearance of the firefly's light? How do these words help the reader see the firefly from the speaker's point of view?

2. **Structure.** How does the arrangement of the words in this poem help to convey a picture of the firefly?

3. **Refrain.** A refrain is the repetition of one or more phrases or lines at intervals throughout a poem. What is the refrain in this poem?

4. **Symbol.** What does the firefly symbolize for the speaker?

## Developing Writing Skills

**Writing a Poem.** List any three things that move; for example, a bicycle, a baby, or a caterpillar. Then list five words to describe each movement. Choose one of the lists and expand it into a poem, using "Firefly Song" as a model.

# Words    *Pauli Murray*

We are spendthrifts with words,
We squander them,
Toss them like pennies in the air—
Arrogant words,
Angry words,                                                5
Cruel words,
Comradely words,
Shy words tiptoeing from mouth to ear.

But the slowly wrought words of love
And the thunderous words of heartbreak—    10
These we hoard.

## Getting at Meaning

1. Is this poem about single words or about groups of words, as in sentences?

2. In what way are words of love "slowly wrought"? How are words of heartbreak "thunderous"? Why might these words be hoarded and not spent freely?

## Developing Skills in Reading Literature

1. **Lyric.** A lyric is a short poem that expresses a personal emotion. What emotion is expressed in this lyric?

2. **Figurative Language.** Figurative language is richly suggestive language that is not meant to be interpreted literally. Specific kinds of figurative language include similes, metaphors, and personification. What simile is used in this poem? Where is personification used? What extended metaphor appears in the poem? How does each example of figurative language add to the reader's understanding of the poem?

3. **Structure.** What is the function of the stanza break after line 8? What change occurs in the second stanza?

## Developing Vocabulary

**Greek Roots.** This poem is about words that express one person's love for another person. Other words express love of a different type. Many of these words are derived from the Greek root *philein,* which means "to love." Look up the following words in a dictionary to find out what type of love each describes.

| | |
|---|---|
| philanthropy | Anglophile |
| philosophy | Francophile |
| philharmonic | Sinophile |
| bibliophile | |

If you cannot find the last two words in your dictionary, look up the prefixes *Franc-* and *Sino-*.

# First Ice
### *Andrei Voznesenski*

A girl in a phone box is freezing cold,
Retreating into her shivery coat.
Her face in too much make-up's smothered
With grubby tearstains and lipstick smudges.

Into her tender palms she's breathing.                    5
Fingers—ice lumps. In earlobes—earrings.

She goes back home, alone, alone,
Behind her the frozen telephone.

First ice. The very first time.
First ice of a telephone conversation.                    10

On her cheeks tear traces shine—
First ice of human humiliation.

## Getting at Meaning

1. Who might the girl have been talking to on the phone?

2. Why might the girl have been calling from a phone booth?

3. What does line 3 reveal about the reason for her call?

4. Why has the phone conversation been "icy"?

5. Which tends to be colder, a face to face conversation or a phone conversation? Why?

6. Explain the last line of the poem.

## Developing Skills in Reading Literature

1. **Imagery.** The poet creates a penetrating impression of cold in this poem. List all the words and phrases that create cold images. How do these images reinforce the reader's sense of the girl's isolation?

2. **Metaphor.** What is the one metaphor in this poem? What two things are compared? Rewrite the metaphor as a simile. Which is more effective? Why?

3. **Rhyme.** Find the couplet in this poem. What effect does the end rhyme have on the reader's perception of the telephone?

4. **Theme.** What two kinds of cold does the poet describe in this poem? How are they related? What comment is the poet making about human relations?

## Developing Writing Skills

**Writing Dialogue.** Write the dialogue for the phone conversation in "First Ice." Remember that this is a cold conversation that results in "human humiliation."

# Ex-Basketball Player     *John Updike*

Pearl Avenue runs past the high-school lot,
Bends with the trolley tracks, and stops, cut off
Before it has a chance to go two blocks,
At Colonel McComsky Plaza. Berth's Garage
Is on the corner facing west, and there,                           5
Most days, you'll find Flick Webb, who helps Berth out.

Flick stands tall among the idiot pumps—
Five on a side, the old bubble-head style,
Their rubber elbows hanging loose and low.
One's nostrils are two S's, and his eyes                          10
An E and O. And one is squat, without
A head at all—more of a football type.

Once Flick played for the high-school team, the Wizards.
He was good: in fact, the best. In '46
He bucketed three hundred ninety points,                          15
A county record still. The ball loved Flick.
I saw him rack-up thirty-eight or forty
In one home game. His hands were like wild birds.

He never learned a trade, he just sells gas,
Checks oil, and changes flats. Once in a while,                   20
As a gag, he dribbles an inner tube,
But most of us remember anyway.
His hands are fine and nervous on the lug wrench.
It makes no difference to the lug wrench, though.

Off work, he hangs around Mae's luncheonette.                     25
Grease-gray and kind of coiled, he plays pinball,
Smokes thin cigars, and nurses lemon phosphates.
Flick seldom says a word to Mae, just nods
Beyond her face toward bright applauding tiers
Of Necco Wafers, Nibs, and Juju Beads.                            30

## Getting at Meaning

1. Has Flick realized the expectations of his youth? Explain.

2. What are the "rubber elbows" on the pumps? Reread lines 10 and 11. What brand of gas does Berth sell?

3. What does Flick see in the tiers of candy behind the luncheonette counter?

4. Reread the opening stanza. How has Flick's life resembled Pearl Avenue?

## Developing Skills in Reading Literature

1. **Imagery.** One gas pump looks like a football player. What do the other pumps look like? What words and phrases help the reader to picture the gas pumps?

In the last stanza, what words and phrases help the reader to picture Flick? What do these visual images reveal about Flick's character and personality?

2. **Simile.** What simile describes Flick's hands? What is similar between the way that Flick handled a basketball and the way that he handles the lug wrench? What is the major difference?

3. **Personification.** Find two examples of personification in this poem. What objects are personified? How does the personification add to the reader's understanding of these objects?

4. **Tone.** What is the attitude of the poet toward Flick? Quote lines and phrases to support your answer. How does the title reflect the tone?

## Developing Writing Skills

**Writing Poetry.** Write an additional six-line stanza for this poem in which you describe what Flick sees, hears, and smells as he gazes at the racks of candy. Create several vivid images that communicate specific sensory impressions. End the stanza with a strong final line.

FOUR PINBALL MACHINES, 1962. Wayne Thiebaud. Courtesy of a Southern California Collector.

# Cavalry Crossing a Ford    *Walt Whitman*

A line in long array where they wind betwixt green islands,
They take a serpentine course, their arms flash in the sun—hark
    to the musical clank,
Behold the silvery river, in it the splashing horses loitering
    stop to drink,
Behold the brown-faced men, each group, each person a picture,
    the negligent rest on the saddles,
Some emerge on the opposite bank, others are just entering      5
    the ford—while,
Scarlet and blue and snowy white,
The guidon flags flutter gayly in the wind.

## Getting at Meaning

1. What are the "arms" that flash in the sun? Why do they "clank"?

2. How is the cavalry described in this poem different from the stereotype of the cavalry "riding to the rescue"?

## Developing Skills in Reading Literature

1. **Imagery.** To what senses does the poet appeal in this poem? Quote images from the poem to support your answer.

2. **Setting.** Describe the setting of this poem: the time, the place, and the weather. Cite images in the poem that help to create the setting.

3. **Mood.** What is the mood of this poem? What words and phrases help to create the mood?

4. **Onomatopoeia.** The use of words that imitate or reproduce sounds is called onomatopoeia. Identify examples of onomatopoeia in this poem. Then suggest onomatopoetic words to describe the sounds that might accompany the following: the horses drinking (line 3); the soldiers resting in the saddles (line 4); the flags fluttering in the wind (line 7).

## Developing Vocabulary

**Getting Word Meaning from Context.** Using the context clues in this poem, write definitions for the following words:

| | |
|---|---|
| serpentine | negligent |
| loitering | emerge |

Now write a brief paragraph that describes a group of people waiting in a long line. Use each of the listed words in the paragraph.

# A Narrow Fellow in the Grass

*Emily Dickinson*

A narrow Fellow in the Grass
Occasionally rides—
You may have met Him—did you not
His notice sudden is—

The Grass divides as with a Comb—                5
A spotted shaft is seen—
And then it closes at your feet
And opens further on—

He likes a Boggy Acre
A Floor too cool for Corn—                        10
Yet when a Boy, and Barefoot—
I more than once at Noon
Have passed, I thought, a Whip lash
Unbraiding in the Sun
When stopping to secure it                        15
It wrinkled, and was gone—

Several of Nature's People
I know, and they know me—
I feel for them a transport
Of cordiality—                                    20

But never met this Fellow
Attended, or alone
Without a tighter breathing
And Zero at the Bone—

## Getting at Meaning

1. Who or what is the narrow fellow described in this poem? In what way is his notice sudden? (line 4)

2. In the third stanza, the speaker points out two places where the narrow fellow can be found. What are these two places?

3. The speaker has mistaken the narrow fellow for a "Whip lash/Unbraiding in the Sun." What is a whip lash? How does it resemble the narrow fellow?

4. How does the speaker's attitude toward the narrow fellow differ from his attitude toward other creatures? Explain the last two lines of the poem.

## Developing Skills in Reading Literature

1. **Meter.** Write out, then scan the first stanza of this poem. What is the meter of lines 1 and 3? What is the meter of lines 2 and 4? (Name the type of metrical foot and the number of feet per line.)

What is unusual about the sentence structure in the first stanza? Why might the poet have used this sentence structure?

2. **Rhyme.** Find the one example of end rhyme in this poem. What is the effect of this rhyme?

What other sound devices can you find in this poem? Give examples and try to explain the purpose of each device.

3. **Imagery.** When an image describes the sight of something moving, it is said to be a kinetic image. Kinetic imagery is used in this poem to describe the narrow fellow. Quote one kinetic image.

When an image describes movement, or tension of bodily parts as felt through muscles, tendons, or joints, it is called a kinesthetic image. Quote a kinesthetic image from the last stanza of this poem.

## Developing Writing Skills

**Describing an Experience.** What animals or insects would you rather avoid? Choose one and, in a paragraph or poem, describe how the animal or insect makes itself known, how you try to avoid it, and what happens if you do encounter it. Try to imitate the style of "A Narrow Fellow in the Grass" by not naming the animal or insect.

# The Fifth Sense     *Patricia Beer*

*A 65-year-old Cypriot Greek shepherd, Nicolis Loizou, was wounded
by security forces early today. He was challenged twice; when he failed
to answer, troops opened fire. A subsequent hospital examination
showed that the man was deaf.* NEWS ITEM, 30th December, 1957

Lamps burn all the night
Here, where people must be watched and seen,
And I, a shepherd, Nicolis Loizou,
Wish for the dark, for I have been
Sure-footed in the dark, but now my sight     5
Stumbles among these beds, scattered white boulders,
As I lean towards my far slumbering house
With the night lying upon my shoulders.

My sight was always good,
Better than others. I could taste wine and bread     10
And name the field they spattered when the harvest
Broke. I could coil in the red
Scent of the fox out of a maze of wood
And grass. I could touch mist, I could touch breath.
But of my sharp senses I had only four.     15
The fifth one pinned me to my death.

The soldiers must have called
The word they needed: Halt. Not hearing it,
I was their failure, relaxed against the winter
Sky, the flag of their defeat.     20
With their five senses they could not have told
That I lacked one, and so they had to shoot.
They would fire at a rainbow if it had
A color less than they were taught.

Christ said that when one sheep
Was lost, the rest meant nothing any more.
Here in this hospital, where others' breathing
Swings like a lantern in the polished floor
And squeezes those who cannot sleep,
I see how precious each thing is, how dear,
For I may never touch, smell, taste, or see
Again, because I could not hear.

25

30

## Getting at Meaning

1. Who is the speaker? Why does the light in the hospital bother him?

2. Reread lines 10 and 11. What could the speaker tell about the grapes and the grain by tasting the wine and the bread?

3. What does the speaker mean when he says "I could coil in the red scent of the fox"?

4. Explain line 14. What kind of person can touch mist and breath?

5. What is the speaker's fifth sense? How has it pinned him to his death? (line 16)

6. Why would the sight of an old man "relaxed against the winter sky" anger the soldiers? How had the speaker defeated them?

7. Of what does the speaker accuse the soldiers in lines 23 and 24?

8. What feelings does the speaker express about his deafness in the last stanza? Is this a change of attitude? What does he now fear? Reread line 8. What "night" is lying on the speaker's shoulders?

## Developing Skills in Reading Literature

1. **Imagery.** To which of the five senses does the poet appeal in the first stanza? Quote two images from this stanza.

In the second stanza, why does the word *coil* appeal to the sense of smell? How does the word *spattered* help the reader to picture the fields at harvest time?

Considering the senses to which the images in this poem appeal, what is unusual about the simile in lines 27 and 28? Why is this an appropriate comparison from the point of view of the speaker?

To what sense does the image in line 29 appeal? Why is it an appropriate image for this stanza?

2. **Allusion.** What is the Biblical allusion in this poem? How does the allusion relate to the ideas expressed by the speaker?

3. **Rhyme.** The first, second, and fourth stanzas have intricate rhyme schemes. Which lines rhyme in these stanzas? How does the content of the third stanza differ from the content of the other stanzas? Does this difference account in part for the lack of rhyme in the third stanza? Explain.

4. **Theme.** What message does the poet convey in this poem?

## Developing Writing Skills

1. **Writing a Poem.** Select a brief newspaper article about an accident or a tragedy. Re-create the scene in your mind, and write a short poem from the point of view of one of the victims. The poem should center on the victim's feelings about the event.

2. **Poetry: Using the Senses in Writing.** Think of something that you enjoy touching, tasting, hearing, seeing, or smelling. Try to imagine the same experience after losing that one sense. For example, imagine what it would be like to pop a juicy strawberry into your mouth and not be able to taste it. Write a poem in which you show how the loss of one sense alters an enjoyable experience.

# November Day

*Eleanor Averitt*

Old haggard wind has
   plucked the trees
Like pheasants, held
   between her knees.
In rows she hangs them,     5
   bare and neat,
Their brilliant plumage at
   her feet.

## Getting at Meaning

1. Who plucks pheasants? What plucks the trees?
2. What part of the trees is the "brilliant plumage" mentioned in line 7?

## Developing Skills in Reading Literature

1. **Metaphor.** This entire poem is an extended metaphor. To whom is the wind compared? Go through the poem line by line and explain the specific comparisons that the speaker makes.
2. **Simile.** What simile is used in the middle of the extended metaphor? What two things are compared in the simile?
3. **Imagery.** What images in this poem paint a vivid picture of a November day?
4. **Meter.** Is this poem written in iambic or trochaic meter? Be prepared to explain your answer.
5. **Rhyme Scheme.** What is the rhyme scheme of this poem?

## Developing Writing Skills

**Poetry: Using Imagery.** This poem describes trees in late fall. Describe the same trees in spring or summer. Use precise images, and possibly a simile or a metaphor, to create a clear picture of the trees.

Condense your description to two sentences. Then arrange the sentences into a poem. Revise the poem so that you have either a pattern of end rhyme, a recognizable meter, or both.

# Figures of Speech

"THE TOBOGGAN," PLATE 20 FROM *JAZZ*, 1947. *Henri Matisse.*
*Collection, The Museum of Modern Art, New York. Gift of the artist.*

# Poetry Is a Tressel
## *Nikki Giovanni*

poetry is a tressel
spanning the distance between
what i feel
and what i say

like a locomotive                           5
i rush full speed ahead
trusting your strength
to carry me over

sometimes we share a poem
because people are near          10
and they would notice me
noticing you
so i write X and you write O
and we both win

sometimes we share a poem          15
because i'm washing the dishes
and you're looking at your news

or sometimes we make a poem
because it's Sunday and you want
ice cream while i want cookies          20

but always we share a poem
because belief predates action
and i believe
the most beautiful poem
ever heard is your heart          25
racing

## Getting at Meaning

1. What is the distance between what the speaker feels and what the speaker says? Can this distance be measured? Can it be overcome? Explain your answer.

2. In what way do both people win when they write *X* and *O*? Why do they choose to communicate in this manner?

3. Even though their interests and desires are different, what does poetry allow the two people to do?

4. In the final stanza, what is the belief that predates action? How does this idea relate to the idea in the first stanza?

## Developing Skills in Reading Literature

1. **Metaphor.** What two things does the writer compare in the first metaphor? How are these two things similar? How is the metaphor in the last stanza related to the comparison in the first stanza?

2. **Simile.** Find the one simile in this poem. What two things are compared? How are these things similar? How is the simile related to the metaphors in the poem? Explain your answer.

3. **Poetry.** Considering the metaphors and the simile in the poem, how does the poet's disregard for conventional punctuation enhance meaning? Why doesn't the poet capitalize the pronoun *I*? Explain your answer.

4. **Speaker and Tone.** Who is the speaker in this poem? What is the speaker's attitude toward the subject? How do you know?

## Developing Vocabulary

**Prefixes.** The prefix *pre-* in the word *predate* has only one meaning, which is "before." Listed here are five more prefixes of this type. Use a dictionary to find the one meaning of each prefix. Write four words that include each prefix and then write the definition of each word.

bene-    mis-    circum-
mal-     sub-

# Simile

### N. Scott Momaday

What did we say to each other
that now we are as the deer
who walk in single file
with heads high
with ears forward
with eyes watchful                                    5
with hooves always placed on firm ground
in whose limbs there is latent flight

## Getting at Meaning

1. What might have caused the change in the relationship described by the speaker?

2. What do the phrases "single file" and "eyes watchful" imply about the changed relationship? What does "latent flight" imply about the strength of the relationship?

3. What fear is implied by the line "with hooves always placed on firm ground"?

## Developing Skills in Reading Literature

1. **Simile.** This poem is based on a simile in which two people are compared to deer. What does the comparison reveal about the two people? Why is this comparison appropriate to the subject of the poem?

2. **Structure.** This poem is one continuous statement without punctuation or stanza breaks. How is this arrangement related to the content of the poem? What is particularly effective about the arrangement of lines 3, 4, 5, and 6? What does the absence of a punctuation mark at the end of the last line add to the meaning of the poem?

WILD DEER, 1815. Mori Tetsuzan. The Minneapolis Institute of Arts. Bequest of Richard P. Gale.

# Ebb

*Edna St. Vincent Millay*

I know what my heart is like
  Since your love died:
It is like a hollow ledge
Holding a little pool
    Left there by the tide,      5
    A little tepid pool,
Drying inward from the edge.

## Getting at Meaning

1. What has the speaker experienced recently?

2. What does the word *tide* imply about the love that the speaker once shared? How does this image contrast with the image of a tepid pool?

## Developing Skills in Reading Literature

1. **Simile.** Central to this poem is the comparison between the speaker's heart and a pool in a hollow ledge. What qualities of the speaker's heart are emphasized by describing the ledge as "hollow" and the pool as "little" and "tepid"?

2. **Speaker and Tone.** What do the words "left there" and "drying inward from the edge" reveal about the speaker's feelings? Describe the tone of this poem.

## Developing Writing Skills

**Establishing Tone.** The speaker in this poem uses words and phrases such as *hollow, little, left there, tepid,* and *drying inward* to express feelings of pain. Think about a strong emotion that you have experienced, such as joy, sorrow, or fear. List words, phrases, and comparisons that capture your feelings. Then write a poem or a paragraph that will communicate your feelings to a reader.

# March 1st    *Kathleen Spivack*

Coming out of the house on a fresh March morning,
I saw February still meandering around
like laundry caught in a Bendix.[1] Stray shreds
of cloud, like pillow slips, were rent from
her large endlessness. Outdated,      5
her decrepit body garlanded itself dis-
gracefully with powder. She luxuriated in old age.
Even her graying sheets were still there,
tattered, heaped carelessly on the street,
bearing the indentation of someone's huge body      10
and furred with a fine fringe of soot.
She had been plump, she had been heavy, sitting
on top of us since January. Winter, you
old clothes hamper, what mildew
still molders inside you before March      15
dribbles a bit, dries up, and is done for?

---

1. **Bendix:** a brand of washing-machine.

## Getting at Meaning

1. Describe the movement of laundry inside a washing machine. How does the speaker use this image in the poem?

2. What does the phrase "her large endlessness" describe?

3. What is the powder that garlands the decrepit body?

4. What are the graying sheets and why are they graying?

5. What is typical March weather in the region that is the setting for this poem? What effect does this weather have upon the remaining signs of winter?

## Developing Skills in Reading Literature

1. **Simile.** The first simile in this poem compares February to laundry in a washing machine. What comparison does the second simile make? How is the second simile related to the first? What does the second simile contribute to the visual image developed by the writer?

2. **Personification.** How does the speaker personify February within the first simile? What image of February is developed through personification in lines 5, 6, 7, 12, and 13?

3. **Metaphor.** Identify and explain the metaphor used to describe winter. Does the metaphor fit with the other figures of speech in the poem? Explain your answer.

## Developing Vocabulary

**Using Precise Verbs.** The images created in this poem succeed partly because of the writer's use of precise verbs. For example, February does not simply *walk*; it *meanders*. Find four other examples of precise verbs in the poem, and explain what each contributes to the image in which it appears.

# Corner     *Ralph Pomeroy*

THE cop slumps alertly on his motorcycle,
supported by one leg like a leather stork.
His glance accuses me of loitering.
I can see his eyes moving like fish
in the green depths of his green goggles.                    5

His ease is fake. I can tell.
My ease is fake. And he can tell.
The fingers armored by his gloves
splay and clench, itching to change something.

As if he were my enemy or my death,                          10
I just stand there watching.

I spit out my gum which has gone stale.
I knock out a new cigarette—
which is my bravery.
It is all imperceptible:                                     15
the way I shift my weight,
the way he creaks in his saddle.

The traffic is specific though constant.
The sun surrounds me, divides the street between us.
His crash helmet is whiter in the shade.                     20
It is like a bull ring as they say it is just before the fighting.
I cannot back down. I am there.

Everything holds me back.
I am in danger of disappearing into the sunny dust.
My levis bake and my T shirt sweats.                         25

My cigarette makes my eyes burn.
But I don't dare drop it.

Who made him my enemy?
Prince of coolness. King of fear.
Why do I lean here waiting?                                  30
Why does he lounge there watching?

I am becoming sunlight.
My hair is on fire. My boots run like tar.
I am hung-up by the bright air.

Something breaks through all of a sudden,                    35
and he blasts off, quick as a craver,
one with his power; watching me watch.

## Getting at Meaning

1. How does the speaker know that the cop is alert? What little signals indicate that the situation is tense?

2. What do the cop's leather jacket, goggles, and gloves provide for him? Why does the speaker take out a cigarette?

3. What would the cop or the speaker lose by backing down?

4. Why doesn't the speaker dare to drop the cigarette?

5. Why might the speaker question the cop's role as an enemy? How does the situation cause the speaker to feel?

6. How is the style of the cop's exit appropriate to the image of the cop throughout the poem?

## Developing Skills in Reading Literature

1. **Simile.** What image of the cop does the comparison to a stork create? What two things are compared in the second simile? How does the second simile change the initial image of the cop? Select one other simile from the poem. Explain what two things are compared and what the simile contributes to the poem.

2. **Speaker and Tone.** What does the cop represent to the speaker? What is the attitude of the speaker toward the cop? Explain your answer. What is the difference between the image that the speaker presents to the cop and the thoughts and feelings of the speaker about the situation? What is the attitude of the speaker toward himself or herself? Reread the last stanza. What is the major difference between the speaker and the cop?

3. **Free Verse.** Read a portion of the poem aloud. How does it sound? What does the poet accomplish by writing in free verse?

## Developing Writing Skills

**Describing an Event from a Different Point of View.** This poem presents the speaker's perception of a few minutes spent in the presence of a motorcycle cop. Write one paragraph that presents the same experience from the cop's point of view. Be sure to reveal the police officer's feelings as well as his perception of external reality.

# Metaphor    *Eve Merriam*

Morning is
a new sheet of paper
for you to write on.

Whatever you want to say,
all day,                                          5
until night
folds it up
and files it away.

The bright words and the dark words
are gone                                          10
until dawn
and a new day
to write on.

TURNSOLE, 1961. *Kenneth Noland. Collection, The Museum of Modern Art, New York. Blanchette Rockefeller Fund.*

## Getting at Meaning

1. What characteristics do morning and a blank sheet of paper share?

2. In what sense does night file away day?

3. What does the poem imply about the supply of new paper?

## Developing Skills in Reading Literature

1. **Extended Metaphor.** The basic metaphor of the poem is presented in the first stanza. How do the second and third stanzas further develop this metaphor?

2. **Structure.** How is the structure of the poem related to its content?

3. **Personification.** Find the example of personification in this poem. Explain what the use of personification contributes to the development of the basic metaphor.

## Developing Writing Skills

**Writing a Poem.** Choose a time of day, a day of the week, or a season of the year. Write a statement that compares the time, day, or season to an object that represents an impression of your subject. Then develop a poem based on this metaphor.

# First Lesson     *Philip Booth*

Lie back, daughter, let your head
be tipped back in the cup of my hand.
Gently, and I will hold you. Spread
your arms wide, lie out on the stream
and look high at the gulls. A dead-               5
man's-float is face down. You will dive
and swim soon enough where this tidewater
ebbs to the sea. Daughter, believe
me, when you tire on the long thrash
to your island, lie up, and survive.              10
As you float now, where I held you
and let go, remember when fear
cramps your heart what I told you:
lie gently and wide to the light-year
stars, lie back, and the sea will hold you.       15

CHILDREN BY THE SEA. *Edward Potthast.*
*Hirshhorn Museum and Sculpture Garden, Smithsonian Institution.*

## Getting at Meaning

1. In the first three lines of the poem, what does the speaker ask the daughter to do? Why?

2. Why does the speaker advise the girl to "look high at the gulls"?

3. What do the words "You will dive and swim soon enough" imply about the girl's age?

4. What might the island symbolize in the girl's future? Why might her journey to the island be tiring, a "long thrash"?

5. How are survival and the advice to "lie up" connected?

6. Once the speaker lets go of the young girl, what can she count on to support her? What must she do to gain this support?

## Developing Skills in Reading Literature

1. **Metaphor.** What is the central metaphor in this poem? How are these two things similar? Explain your answer.

2. **Speaker and Tone.** What is the speaker's attitude toward the daughter? Toward the lesson? Which specific words and phrases develop the tone of the poem?

3. **Understatement.** A light year is the distance that light travels in one year, or approximately 5.878 trillion miles. The light from some stars travels for many light years before reaching the earth. What might the reference to "light-year stars" be implying about the advice given to the daughter?

## Developing Writing Skills

**Supporting an Opinion.** What is your impression of the speaker's behavior as a parent? Do you think that the speaker's approach to educating the daughter about swimming and about life will be successful? Write one paragraph in which you present your opinion of the speaker as a parent. Be sure to support your opinion with references to the poem, as well as to your own experiences.

# Tenement Room: Chicago

*Frank Marshall Davis*

Bruised and battered
By the dark silent hammers of night,
The day creeps
Slowly
From the tired room.                                                5

Dirt and destitution
Lounge here in gaudy tatters
Through the bright hours,
Forever shouting
Its bony nakedness—                                                10
A crippled table, gray from greasy water;
Two drooping chairs, spiritless as wounded soldiers shoved
            into a prison hole;
A cringing bed, age-weary;
Corseted with wire, squats a flabby stove;
In this corner slumps a punished trunk;                            15
Through the lone window, broken-paned, light and weather
            spill on the dust-defeated and splintered floor.
Only night muffles
These visual cries
Of the despairing room.

The dusk                                                           20
Lays a soothing hand
On its whimpering poverty;
Even the solitary gas jet
Eases its quivering runners
Of chromium light                                                 25
Along quiet surfaces
As
Exhausted
The room sleeps dreamlessly. . . .

## Getting at Meaning

1. What do the first five lines imply about the strength of day against the darkness of night?

2. What do the bright hours reveal about the room?

3. How do its furnishings emphasize the despair that permeates the room?

4. Why does dusk have a soothing effect on the room?

5. Why does the room sleep dreamlessly? What might this description imply about the future of the room?

## Developing Skills in Reading Literature

1. **Personification.** In this poem, the speaker makes extensive use of personification. Find two examples that personify time. What does the personification of time add to the description of the room? Find three examples that personify the furniture in the room. Which human attributes are attributed to the furniture? What would a human being who possesses these attributes be like? Find two examples that personify the room itself. Are these personifications consistent with the others in the poem?

2. **Simile.** Find the one simile used in the poem and explain the comparison. What does the simile add to the reader's mental picture of the room?

3. **Speaker and Tone.** What is the speaker's attitude toward the subject? Which words and phrases are especially important in establishing this tone?

4. **Alliteration.** Find two lines in the poem that contain alliteration. Which sounds do these lines stress? Are the sounds harsh or gentle? What does this alliteration add to the description of the room?

## Developing Vocabulary

**Latin Roots.** The Latin root *tenere* means "to have or hold." A building designed to "hold" a large number of families is called a *tenement.* On a separate sheet of paper, complete the following sentences with words that have the Latin root *tenere.*

1. A renter who holds a house, apartment, or room is called a _____.

2. After working for several years, a teacher may be given a permanent hold on a position by the granting of _____.

3. In the army, a position that can be held is called a _____-able position.

4. If you are held down in school you are de-_____ and perhaps made to serve a de-_____.

5. Something that is held back is _____.

6. When someone holds on and won't let go, the person is described as _____-acious.

# Thoughts    *Sara Teasdale*

When I am all alone
  Envy me most,
Then my thoughts flutter round me
  In a glimmering host;

Some dressed in silver,      5
  Some dressed in white,
Each like a taper
  Blossoming light;

Most of them merry,
  Some of them grave,      10
Each of them lithe
  As willows that wave;

Some bearing violets,
  Some bearing bay,
One with a burning rose      15
  Hidden away—

When I am all alone
  Envy me then,
For I have better friends
  Than women and men.      20

## Getting at Meaning

1. What does the description of thoughts as blossoming lights imply about the quality or nature of the thoughts?

2. The speaker's thoughts are "lithe as willows." What does this imply about the speaker's mind and attitudes?

3. What do the references to violets, bay leaves, and a burning rose suggest about the variety of the speaker's thoughts?

4. Why might the speaker consider thoughts to be better friends than women and men?

## Developing Skills in Reading Literature

1. **Personification.** What human qualities does the speaker attribute to thoughts? What do the thoughts become for the speaker?

2. **Simile.** Find the two similes in the poem and explain the comparison in each.

3. **Theme.** The speaker values his or her own company above that of all others. What message does this suggest about solitude and friendship?

## Developing Writing Skills

**Writing a Poem.** If you were to personify your thoughts, what human attributes would you give them? Write a poem of six to ten lines, rhymed or unrhymed, in which the speaker personifies his or her thoughts. If possible, use a simile in your poem. Be sure that the tone is consistent throughout the poem.

# The Worker

### Richard Thomas

My father lies black and hushed
Beneath white hospital sheets
He collapsed at work
His iron left him
Slow and quiet he sank                               5
Meeting the wet concrete floor on his way
The wheels were still turning
They couldn't stop
Red and yellow lights flashing
Gloved hands twisting knobs                          10
They couldn't stop
And as they carried him out
The whirling and buzzing
And humming machines
Applauded him                                        15
Lapping up his dripping iron.

## Getting at Meaning

1. Why is the speaker's father "hushed"? Where is the speaker's father? What incidents that took place earlier are recalled by the speaker?

2. The speaker refers to his father's iron. What is this iron? What else named in the poem might also be described with the word *iron*?

3. The speaker repeats the line "they couldn't stop." To what does the pronoun *they* refer?

4. How do the machines present a contrast to the collapsed man?

5. What is the attitude of the machines toward the collapsed man? Explain your answer.

## Developing Skills in Reading Literature

1. **Personification.** How does the speaker personify the father's "iron"? Later, how does the speaker personify the machines? What might this suggest about the relationship between the father's iron and the machines? About the father as a worker?

2. **Speaker and Tone.** What is the speaker's attitude toward the father? Which words and phrases reveal the attitude?

# The Man in the Dead Machine

*Donald Hall*

High on a slope in New Guinea
the Grumman Hellcat[1]
lodges among bright vines
as thick as arms. In 1943,
the clenched hand of a pilot          5
glided it here
where no one has ever been.

In the cockpit, the helmeted
skeleton sits
upright, held                          10
by dry sinews at neck
and shoulder, and webbing
that straps the pelvic cross
to the cracked
leather of the seat, and the breastbone   15
to the canvas cover
of the parachute.

Or say that the shrapnel
missed him, he flew
back to the carrier, and every         20
morning takes the train, his pale
hands on his black case, and sits
upright, held
by the firm webbing.

---

1. **Grumman Hellcat:** a World War II fighter plane.

## Getting at Meaning

1. Describe the world situation in 1943. Why might the pilot have been in New Guinea? Why has the wreckage of the plane remained undiscovered?

2. What does the skeleton in the cockpit appear to be doing? What causes this appearance?

3. How is the appearance of the man described in the third stanza similar to that of the skeleton?

## Developing Skills in Reading Literature

1. **Simile.** Find the one simile in this poem. What two things are compared? How are these things similar? What does the simile contribute to the meaning of the poem?

2. **Structure.** This poem consists of three stanzas. What does the writer establish in the first stanza? How does the second stanza develop from the first stanza? Why does the third stanza begin with the word *or*? How is the third stanza related to, yet different from, the first two stanzas? Might the order of the stanzas have been different? Explain your answer.

3. **Pun.** A pun is a play on words. Sometimes a pun is based on different meanings of the same word. What two meanings of the word *firm* might fit the idea of the last line in the poem? How does this pun help to develop the meaning of the poem?

4. **Irony.** What is ironic about the fate of the man described in the third stanza? How do the first two stanzas help to develop this irony?

5. **Theme.** Through the description of the man in the third stanza, what comment does the writer make about the fate of some people in the business world?

## Developing Vocabulary

**Word Origins.** In this poem, the speaker uses the word *shrapnel,* which means "shell fragments from a high-explosive shell." The word comes from the name of its inventor, General Henry Shrapnel. The following words also are derived from people's names. Look up each word in a dictionary, and write the definitions and the derivation of the word.

| | |
|---|---|
| sandwich | leotard |
| teddy bear | sideburns |
| lynch | galvanize |

LA GRANDE FORÊT, 1927. Max Ernst. Kunstmuseum, Basel.

# Troubled Woman   *Langston Hughes*

She stands
In the quiet darkness,
This troubled woman
Bowed by
Weariness and pain          5
Like an
Autumn flower
In the frozen rain,
Like a
Wind-blown autumn flower    10
That never lifts its head
Again.

## Getting at Meaning

1. What does the woman's appearance suggest about her past?

2. How do the autumn weather conditions affect the flower?

## Developing Skills in Reading Literature

1. **Simile.** The speaker compares the woman and an autumn flower. Of what significance is the fact that it is an autumn flower? How are the woman's problems similar to the frozen rain and the wind that batter the flower?

2. **Repetition.** What does the speaker emphasize by repeating and expanding the simile?

3. **Structure.** This poem consists of one long sentence. How does the structure relate to the meaning of the poem? Why might the word *again* in line 12 stand alone?

# Lyric 17    *José Garcia Villa*

First, a poem must be magical,
Then musical as a sea-gull.
It must be a brightness moving
And hold secret a bird's flowering.
It must be slender as a bell,                    5
And it must hold fire as well.
It must have the wisdom of bows
And it must kneel like a rose.
It must be able to hear
The luminance of dove and deer.                 10
It must be able to hide
What it seeks, like a bride.
And over all I would like to hover
God, smiling from the poem's cover.

## Getting at Meaning

1. How is a poem musical? bright? secret? slender? fiery? wise? humble?
2. How is luminance usually noticed?
3. How does a poem hide what it seeks?
4. What does the image of a smiling God add to the reader's understanding of what a poem must be?

## Developing Skills in Reading Literature

1. **Simile and Metaphor.** This poem includes similes and metaphors that explain what a poem must be. Find one example of a metaphor and one of a simile. Explain what is compared in each and what the comparison adds to the meaning of the poem.

2. **Structure.** How many lines make up this poem? Why might the writer have decided to avoid breaking the poem into stanzas? What idea is reinforced by presenting the poem in one unit?

## Developing Vocabulary

**Suffixes.** The adjective suffixes listed here all mean "relating to" or "pertaining to." For each of the suffixes, create five words that mean relating to or pertaining to something. Then define each word; use a dictionary to check your definitions.

-al      -ant
-ical    -ic
-ish     -ative
-ive

# Idea

**FIRST STEPS**, 1943. *Pablo Picasso.*
*Yale University Art Gallery. Gift of Stephen C. Clark.*

# Dawn    *Eskimo*

I arise from rest
With the beat of a raven's wings.
I arise
To meet the day

My eyes turn from the night          5
To gaze at the dawn
Now whitening.

And I think over again
My small adventures
When with a shore wind I drifted out    10
In my kayak
And thought I was in danger.
My fears,
Those small ones
That I thought so big,               15
For all the vital things
I had to get and to reach.

And yet, there is only
One great thing,
The only thing:                      20
To live to see in huts and on journeys
The great day that dawns,
And the light that fills the world.

## Getting at Meaning

1. What activity is described in the first two stanzas? What is the attitude of the speaker toward this activity?

2. What color is a raven? How does the world whiten at dawn?

3. How has the speaker's attitude toward past experiences changed?

4. What is the "one great thing" referred to in the last stanza?

## Developing Skills in Reading Literature

1. **Speaker and Tone.** Who might be the speaker in this poem? What do you learn about the speaker's life? What are its dangers? its beauties? What is the speaker's attitude toward life? What has contributed to the development of this attitude?

2. **Theme.** The speaker explains that the fears that once seemed big now seem small. What message is implied concerning individual experience and the continuing cycle of the natural world?

## Developing Vocabulary

**Latin Roots.** The word *vital,* which is used in this poem, is derived from the Latin root *vita,* meaning "life." Listed here are words that belong to the same word family, along with three other Latin roots. Develop word families for each of the roots, by listing at least three related words.

| | |
|---|---|
| vita (life) | scribe, script (write) |
| vital | |
| vitality | spec (look, see) |
| vitalize | |
| vitals | vid, vis (see) |
| vitamin | |

*Stone-cut.* THE WOMAN WHO LIVES IN THE SUN, 1960, *Kenojuak.*

# Ballad of the Morning Streets

*Imamu Amiri Baraka*

The magic of the day is the morning
I want to say the day is morning high
and sweet, good
morning.

The ballad of the morning streets, sweet          5
voices turns
of cool warm weather
high around the early windows gray to blue
and down again amongst the kids and
broken signs, is pure love magic, sweet day        10
come into me, let me live with you
and dig your blazing

## Getting at Meaning

1. According to the speaker, why is the morning magic?

2. In the morning, how is the weather "cool warm"?

3. What changes the windows from gray to blue?

4. What is the "blazing" of the day?

## Developing Skills in Reading Literature

1. **Metaphor.** What two things does the metaphor in the first stanza compare? How are these things similar? What two things does the metaphor in the second stanza compare? How does the second metaphor expand the effect of the first metaphor?

2. **Speaker and Tone.** What is the speaker's attitude toward the subject? Which words are particularly important in developing this attitude?

3. **Theme.** What message is conveyed in the poem? Compare and contrast this theme with the theme of "Dawn."

## Developing Vocabulary

**Slang.** In the poem, the word *dig* means "to understand or to enjoy." This use of the word is considered slang, or nonstandard vocabulary. Use a dictionary to define the following slang terms, and then use each word in a sentence.

cool     hot
foxy     dough

# Nothing Gold Can Stay   *Robert Frost*

Nature's first green is gold,
Her hardest hue to hold.
Her early leaf's a flower;
But only so an hour.
Then leaf subsides to leaf.    5
So Eden sank to grief,
So dawn goes down to day.
Nothing gold can stay.

## Getting at Meaning

1. Why does nature's first green appear to be gold? Why is the hue so hard to hold?

2. When does a leaf look like a flower? What causes its appearance to change?

3. Explain the meaning of line 6.

4. How does the passage of time during a day parallel the development of the leaves?

## Developing Skills in Reading Literature

1. **Metaphor.** What two things are compared in line 3? How are these things similar? What does this metaphor contribute to the meaning of the poem?

2. **Allusion.** Why is the allusion to Eden appropriate to the subject of this poem? What does the allusion contribute to the meaning of the poem?

3. **Speaker and Tone.** What is the speaker's attitude toward the subject? Which words and phrases develop this attitude?

4. **Theme.** What point is made about natural life through the descriptions of nature in this poem? How does the theme of this poem compare to the themes of the two preceding selections?

## Developing Writing Skills

**Explaining an Idea.** The changes in nature described in this poem illustrate the idea that "Nothing gold can stay." Write one paragraph in which you use personal experiences or ideas from your reading to explain and illustrate the same idea.

# *from* **Ecclesiastes**   *The King James Bible*

To every thing there is a season,
And a time to every purpose under the heaven:
A time to be born, and a time to die;
A time to plant, and a time to pluck up that which is planted;
A time to kill, and a time to heal;                                   5
A time to break down, and a time to build up;
A time to weep, and a time to laugh;
A time to mourn, and a time to dance;
A time to cast away stones, and a time to gather stones together;
A time to embrace, and a time to refrain from embracing;              10
A time to get, and a time to lose;
A time to keep, and a time to cast away;
A time to rend, and a time to sew;
A time to keep silence, and a time to speak;
A time to love, and a time to hate;                                   15
A time of war, and a time of peace.

**Getting at Meaning**

How do the first two lines summarize the rest of
the poem?

**Developing Skills in Reading Literature**

1. **Repetition.** The phrase "a time to" is repeated
throughout the poem. How does this repetition
relate to the content of the poem?

2. **Theme.** What point does this selection make
about the changes a person may undergo in life?

# Was Worm

*May Swenson*

Was worm

swaddled in white
Now tiny queen
in sequin coat
peacockbright                              5

drinks the wind
and feeds
on sweat of the leaves

Is little chinks
of mosaic floating              10
a scatter
of colored beads

Alighting pokes
with her new black wire
the saffron yokes                   15

On silent hinges
openfolds her wings'
applauding hands
Weaned

from coddling white        20
to lakedeep air
to blue and green

Is queen

### Getting at Meaning

1. What kind of insect is the queen in this poem? What process is described in the poem?

2. In line 2, the worm is described as "swaddled in white." What is the white covering? Why is *swaddled* an appropriate word in this phrase?

3. What do the phrases "sequin coat," "chinks of mosaic," and "scatter of colored beads" indicate about the tiny queen?

4. What is the queen's "new black wire"? What are the "saffron yokes"? What is the queen doing?

5. How is the queen's transition to lakedeep air a weaning process?

### Developing Skills in Reading Literature

1. **Structure.** The poem begins with a one-line stanza about the queen's past and ends with a one-line stanza about her new status. What details of development are included in the six longer stanzas? How are the second and seventh stanzas similar? What does each emphasize about the queen's met-amorphosis? What is accomplished through this structure?

2. **Imagery.** This poem includes images that appeal strongly to the sense of sight. For instance, the queen wears a "sequin coat." List three other images from the poem that appeal to the sense of sight.

3. **Personification.** In describing the insect's transition from worm to queen, how does the speaker personify this creature?

### Developing Vocabulary

**Coined Words.** Poets often coin, or create, words for specific effects. In this poem, the speaker uses the coined word *peacockbright* to describe the queen's coat. What image is created through the use of this word? Why is the coined word more effective than a direct statement or a simile such as "the coat was as bright as a peacock"? Find two other coined words in the poem and explain what each contributes to the description of the queen.

TWO HUMMINGBIRDS AND TWO VARIETIES OF ORCHIDS. *Martin Johnson Heade.*

# Peter at Fourteen          *Constance Carrier*

What do you care for Caesar, who yourself
are in three parts divided, and must find,
past daydream and rebellion and bravado,
the final shape and substance of your mind?

What are the Belgae, the Helvetii,[1]                                    5
to you? I doubt that you will read in them
metaphor of your stand against dominion,
or see as yours their desperate stratagem.

They found their tribal rank, their feuds, their freedom,
obliterated, lost beyond return.                                        10
It took them years to see that law and order
could teach them things that they might care to learn.

As fiercely individual, as violent
as they, you clutch your values and your views,
fearful that self may not survive absorption.                           15
(Who said *to learn* at first is like *to lose*?)

Not courage, no, but nature will betray you.
You will stop fighting, finally, and your pride,
that fed so long upon your independence,
flourish on what convention can provide,                                20

till you may grow more Roman than the Romans,
contemptuous of pagan broils and brawls,
and even, mastering your mentors' knowledge,
go on to build cathedrals, like the Gauls.

---

1. **Belgae, Helvetii** (bel′ jē, hel vē′ shē ī′): tribes in ancient Gaul conquered by Julius Caesar.

## Getting at Meaning

1. What does the phrase "three parts divided" have to do with Julius Caesar? with Peter? with Peter's age?

2. What did the Belgae and the Helvetii resist that Peter also resists?

3. What in Peter's situation compares to the tribal rank, feuds, and freedom of the tribes in Gaul?

4. In order to learn, what might an individual initially have to lose?

5. How will nature betray Peter? If Peter is similar to the Gauls, who are the Romans in his life? What type of cathedrals might he build?

## Developing Skills in Reading Literature

1. **Metaphor.** The speaker doubts that Peter will see in the tribes of Gaul a metaphor of his own stand against dominion. The speaker, however, perceives the metaphor and develops it throughout the poem. What similarities between Peter and the Gallic tribes are noted?

2. **Speaker and Tone.** Who might be the speaker in this poem? What is the speaker's attitude toward Peter? Explain your answer.

3. **Theme.** The speaker says that nature will betray Peter and that he may go on to build cathedrals. What point might the writer be making about the nature of achievement or success? What point do both "Peter at Fourteen" and "Was Worm" seem to be making about the process of growth and change?

## Developing Vocabulary

**Context Clue: Definition.** In the poem, the word *obliterated* is followed by the definition "lost beyond return." Listed here are five other words from the poem. Use the Glossary to learn their definitions. Then write a sentence for each word in which you define the word immediately after its use.

bravado    flourish    mentors
stratagem    contemptuous

CONCENTRIC GROUP, 1925. *Oskar Schlemmer. Staatsgalerie, Stuttgart.*

# The Pioneers  *Charlotte Mortimer*

The Pioneers had
The best of this country
The boy said.
They grabbed all the
Adventure, Indian-fighting, danger    5
Since, it's been Dullsville.
And he rushed out to his car
And tore down the road
Doing sixty, maybe
And came around a curve    10
Behind an old Pontiac
Carrying two Barona Indians
Slow-moving, twenty thereabouts.
Overloaded from a scavenging
Trip to the dump.    15
And the fine pipe for fences
They were taking to the reservation
Pierced the boy's skull,
Removing a scalp-lock,[1] neatly
And they buried them both, the boy    20
Inside the stockaded Mem'ry Garden
And over the fence, in
Joe Booth's car dump
His faithful Mustang.

---

1. **scalp-lock:** a lock or tuft of hair left on a shaven head by certain North American Indian warriors.

## Getting at Meaning

1. Why does the boy envy the pioneers?

2. What dangers does the boy experience that the pioneers never imagined?

3. Why is the Indians' car moving so slowly? What unexpected encounter does the boy experience? How does this encounter tie in with the ideas expressed in the first five lines of the poem?

## Developing Skills in Reading Literature

1. **Irony.** Considering that the boy lacks a sense of danger, what is ironic about the way that he drives? What is ironic about the fact that the Indians are driving a Pontiac? About the fact that they have been scavenging? What is ironic about the way that the boy dies? About where he is buried? About the type of car that he drives?

2. **Theme.** What point might the writer be making about changes and about a person's ability to adapt to or understand changes?

## Developing Vocabulary

**Words from Indian Languages.** The two Indians drive a Pontiac, which is a model of car named after a famous Indian chief. Following are five other English words whose origins can be traced to Indian languages. Use a dictionary to check the original as well as the current definitions of these words.

| | |
|---|---|
| Manhattan | papoose |
| teepee | squash |
| squaw | |

# My Grandmother Would Rock Quietly and Hum

*Leonard Adamé*

in her house
she would rock quietly and hum
until her swelled hands
calmed

in summer                                        5
she wore thick stockings
sweaters
and gray braids

(when el cheque came
we went to Payless                               10
and I laughed greedily
when given a quarter)

mornings,
sunlight barely lit
the kitchen                                       15
and where
there were shadows
it was not cold

she quietly rolled
flour tortillas—                                  20
the papas[1]
cracking in hot lard
would wake me

she had lost her teeth
and when we ate                                   25
she had bread
soaked in café[2]

always her eyes
were clear
and she could see                                30
as I cannot yet see—
through her eyes
she gave me herself

she would sit
and talk                                          35
of her girlhood—
of things strange to me:
    México
    epidemics
    relatives shot                               40
    her father's hopes
    of this country—
how they sank
with cement dust
to his insides                                   45

now
when I go
to the old house
the worn spots
by the stove                                      50
echo of her shuffling
and
México
still hangs in her
fading                                            55
calendar pictures

---

1. **papas** (pä′ päs) *Spanish:* potatoes.
2. **café** (kä fä′) *Spanish:* coffee.

## Getting at Meaning

1. What do the descriptions of the grandmother's hands and clothing reveal about her age and health?

2. What is "el cheque"? What quality does the grandmother's giving the speaker a quarter reveal?

3. What does the speaker mean by these lines: "and she could see/as I cannot yet see—"?

4. Based upon her memories of the past, what kind of life has the grandmother had?

5. In what way does the speaker still find Mexico in the grandmother's house? When she gave herself, what else did the grandmother give to the speaker?

## Developing Skills in Reading Literature

1. **Speaker and Tone.** Who is the speaker in the poem? How old would you say the speaker is? When did the speaker experience most of what the poem describes? What is the speaker's attitude toward the grandmother? Which words and phrases are especially important in developing or revealing this attitude?

2. **Theme.** How is the speaker's life different because of the grandmother? How is the grandmother's life different from that of the speaker? What point might the writer be making about the relationship between generations in a family?

## Developing Writing Skills

**Describing a Person.** Select one of your grandparents, another relative, or a family friend who was important to you as a child. In a poem or a paragraph, present your memories of times shared with this person. Try to make the person come alive for your reader through the use of specific details and examples.

# Directions to the Armorer
*Elder Olson*

All right, armorer,
Make me a sword—
Not too sharp,
A bit hard to draw,
And of cardboard, preferably.     5
On second thought, stick
An eraser on the handle.
Somehow I always
Clobber the wrong guy.

Make me a shield with          10
Easy-to-change
Insignia. I'm often
A little vague
As to which side I'm on,
What battle I'm in.           15
And listen, make it
A trifle flimsy,
Not too hard to pierce.
I'm not absolutely sure
I want to win.               20

Make the armor itself
As tough as possible,
But on a reverse
Principle: don't
Worry about its              25
Saving my hide;
Just fix it to give me
Some sort of protection—
Any sort of protection—
From a possible enemy        30
Inside.

### Getting at Meaning

1. Whom is the speaker addressing?
2. The speaker wants the armor made on a "reverse principle." What does the speaker mean?
3. What does the speaker mean by "a possible enemy inside"? What kind of enemy? Inside where?
4. For what is the speaker of the poem searching?

### Developing Skills in Reading Literature

1. **Tone.** What is the tone of this poem? Support your answer with words and phrases from the poem.
2. **Irony.** How are the directions given to the armorer in this poem different from the directions that an armorer might expect to be given? Explain the irony.

### Developing Writing Skills

**Describing a Person.** Describe the speaker of this poem in detail. Identify the person's strengths and weaknesses and explain whether you would want this person as a friend or as a comrade in battle. Confine your description to a single paragraph.

# To Be of Use     *Marge Piercy*

The people I love the best
jump into work head first
without dallying in the shadows
and swim off with sure strokes almost out of sight.
They seem to become natives of that element,                    5
the black sleek heads of seals
bouncing like half-submerged balls.

I love people who harness themselves, an ox to a heavy cart,
who pull like water buffalo, with massive patience,
who strain in the mud and the muck to move things forward,     10
who do what has to be done, again and again.

I want to be with people who submerge
in the task, who go into the fields to harvest
and work in a row and pass the bags along,
who stand in the line and haul in their places,                15
who are not parlor generals and field deserters
but move in a common rhythm
when the food must come in or the fire be put out.

The work of the world is common as mud.
Botched, it smears the hands, crumbles to dust.                20
But the thing worth doing well done
has a shape that satisfies, clean and evident.
Greek amphoras[1] for wine or oil,
Hopi[2] vases that held corn, are put in museums
but you know they were made to be used.                        25
The pitcher cries for water to carry
and a person for work that is real.

---

1. **amphora** (am′ fər ə): a tall jar with a narrow neck and two
handles, used by the ancient Greeks.
2. **Hopi** (hō′ pē): a Pueblo tribe of Indians in Arizona.

## Getting at Meaning

1. How is a person like a pitcher? (lines 26 and 27) How does this comparison illustrate the title of the poem?

2. Explain line 19. What does the word *common* mean as it is used in this line?

3. What kind of work do you think that the speaker would define as "real"? Explain.

4. For what does the speaker seem to be searching?

## Developing Skills in Reading Literature

**Figurative Language.** Select two examples of figurative language from the similes, metaphors, and personifications in this poem. Explain how each helps to convey the meaning of the poem.

The final stanza of this poem is an extended metaphor. Reread this stanza. Of what material is a pitcher made? What happens to a pitcher if it is made poorly? Explain the extended metaphor.

## Developing Vocabulary

**Understanding Changes in Language.** The word *botch* originally meant "to repair." Over the years, it came to mean "to repair clumsily" and finally "to spoil by poor work."

Look up each of the following words in an unabridged dictionary or in a dictionary of word origins, and explain in your own words how its meaning has evolved.

| | |
|---|---|
| artful | pedant |
| egregious | pious |
| officious | propaganda |

BASKET DECORATED WITH BEADWORK. *Museum of the American Indian.*

# Fifteen    *William Stafford*

South of the Bridge on Seventeenth
I found back of the willows one summer
day a motorcycle with engine running
as it lay on its side, ticking over
slowly in the high grass. I was fifteen.                          5

I admired all that pulsing gleam, the
shiny flanks, the demure headlights
fringed where it lay; I led it gently
to the road and stood with that
companion, ready and friendly. I was fifteen.                    10

We could find the end of a road, meet
the sky on out Seventeenth. I thought about
hills, and patting the handle got back a
confident opinion. On the bridge we indulged
a forward feeling, a tremble. I was fifteen.                     15

Thinking, back farther in the grass I found
the owner, just coming to, where he had flipped
over the rail. He had blood on his hand, was pale—
I helped him walk to his machine. He ran his hand
over it, called me good man, roared away.                        20

I stood there, fifteen.

## Getting at Meaning

1. What does the speaker want to do with the motorcycle?

2. Reread lines 12–14. What feeling does the thought of hills arouse in the speaker? What is his source of confidence?

3. How is "a forward feeling, a tremble" similar to being fifteen?

4. How does the speaker feel as he watches the motorcycle roar away?

## Developing Skills in Reading Literature

1. **Symbol.** What does the motorcycle symbolize for the speaker?

2. **Refrain.** What refrain recurs in this poem? What effect does this refrain have on the poem? What effect does it have on the reader?

3. **Imagery.** Reread the second stanza. What images help you to see the motorcycle as the speaker sees it? In line 8, the speaker describes the headlights as "fringed." Where is the motorcycle? With what are the headlights fringed?

## Developing Writing Skills

**Writing an Explanation.** In one paragraph, explain what it means to be fifteen (or fourteen). How is this age unique? How is it frustrating? Use a comparison and examples in your paragraph.

# Oysters    *Anne Sexton*

Oysters we ate,
sweet blue babies,
twelve eyes looked up at me,
running with lemon and Tabasco.
I was afraid to eat this father-food          5
and Father laughed
and drank down his martini,
clear as tears.
It was a soft medicine
that came from the sea into my mouth,         10
moist and plump.
I swallowed.
It went down like a large pudding.
Then I ate one o'clock and two o'clock.
Then I laughed and then we laughed            15
and let me take note—
there was a death,
the death of childhood
there at the Union Oyster House
for I was fifteen                             20
and eating oysters
and the child was defeated.
The woman won.

## Getting at Meaning

1. Why does the speaker describe oysters as "father-food"? Is she more child or woman at this point in the poem?

2. Explain line 14 in terms of how the oysters are arranged on the plate.

3. What change occurs in the speaker after eating the oysters? Is this a change desired by the speaker? Why does eating oysters have this effect?

## Developing Skills in Reading Literature

**Imagery.** Why does the poet describe the oysters as "soft medicine"? What are the connotations of *soft*? What are the connotations of *medicine*? What is unusual about the joining of these two words? To what sense does this image appeal?

Select another image from the poem. Explain its sense appeal and the reason for its effectiveness.

## Developing Writing Skills

**Describing an Event.** A rite of passage is an event that signals the end of one stage in a person's life and the beginning of another. Graduations are rites of passage. For the speaker in "Oysters," the experience of eating oysters is a rite of passage.

Can you recall an event in your life that has marked an end and a beginning? The event may be a major public ceremony or a simple, private experience. In a five-paragraph theme, describe this event in detail. Explain what stage in your life ended, what new stage began, and how you felt as a result of the experience.

# The Children of the Poor
*Gwendolyn Brooks*

Life for my child is simple, and is good.
He knows his wish. Yes, but that is not all.
Because I know mine too.
And we both want joy of undeep and unabiding things,
Like kicking over a chair or throwing blocks out of a window
Or tipping over an icebox pan
Or snatching down curtains or fingering an electric outlet
Or a journey or a friend or an illegal kiss.
No. There is more to it than that.
It is that he has never been afraid.
Rather, he reaches out and lo the chair falls with a beautiful crash,
And the blocks fall, down on the people's heads,
And the water comes slooshing sloppily out across the floor.
And so forth.
Not that success, for him, is sure, infallible.
But never has he been afraid to reach.
His lesions are legion.
But reaching is his rule.

## Getting at Meaning

1. Identify the qualities of the speaker's child described in this poem. Which one of these qualities does the speaker share?

2. What is the literal meaning of the last line? What is the figurative meaning?

## Developing Skills in Reading Literature

1. **Structure.** Although this poem is written in only one stanza, it has a definite content break. Where is this content break? How is the content of the poem after the break different from the content before the break?

2. **Alliteration.** Where does alliteration occur in this poem? What is the effect of this sound device?

3. **Title.** Relate the title of this poem to the content.

## Developing Vocabulary

**Affixing.** In line 4 of this poem are two coined words, which were created by affixing the prefix *un-* to the root words *deep* and *abiding.*

The following coined words were created in the same way. What does each word mean?

unperson     unsalt     uncharming

Use the prefix *un-* or other prefixes to coin some interesting new words. Define each of the words. Check the dictionary to make sure that your words haven't already been coined.

# Sometimes Running    *John Ciardi*

Sometimes running
to yes nothing and
too fast to look
where and at what
I stand and there     5
are trees sunning
themselves long a
brook going and
jays and jewelry
in all leafages     10
because I pause.

WHITE PINE. *Thomas Cole.*
*Courtesy, Museum of Fine Arts, Boston. M. and M. Karolik Collection.*

### Getting at Meaning

1. Is the speaker running to a specific destination? Is the speaker running as a physical exercise or as a way of hurrying? Explain.

2. How does standing still change the scenery? What does the speaker realize?

### Developing Skills in Reading Literature

**Sound and Meaning.** How does the poet create a feeling of rapid movement in this poem? Which line sounds the slowest?

### Developing Writing Skills

**Writing a Poem.** Using "Sometimes Running" as a model, write a poem about some rapid activity that is suddenly interrupted. Your poem may be humorous or serious.

Begin with the word *sometimes* and the name of an activity; for example, sometimes dancing, sometimes knitting, or sometimes gargling. Limit your poem to fifteen lines and use no more than four words in a line. The movement of the words should mirror the movement of the action.

# The River   *Dabney Stuart*

The lifeguard's whistle organized our swimming
Around the anchored raft at summer camp,
Saving us from the tricky channel current.
When he blew it, we gave in to the system,
Each raising his buddy's hand in the sudden quiet          5
To be reckoned, officially, among the living.
Half a pair meant someone might have drowned
Or, more likely, not checking out, gone back
To his cabin where no one made him buddy,
Where, if he wished, he could desert the raft,          10
The restricting whistle, all practiced safety,
And, dreaming the channel's bottom, sound
That deep cut, the rock's dark hollows, and the cold.

I have been back once, when no one was there,
And poked around in the empty cabins          15
Boarded against vandals as if something valuable
Were left to steal, where no one was dreaming.
Yet, as if in a dream, I saw a name
The same as mine printed in fading chalk
On a wall, and I took a dented canteen          20
With a torn case from a nail rusted with rain.

It lay on the beach with my clothes while I went swimming
Where the channel cuts deep across from the steady raft,
Without a buddy. In over my head,
I finned to the bottom, expelling breath          25
Until the cold pressure cracked in my ears,
Then fought that pressure upwards with my arms
And shot, like a dolphin, high
Into the weightless air
Over and over again, each time higher,          30
Until I could use the bottom as a springboard.
However high I went, there was always bottom.

After, I took the canteen to the springs
Which feed the river, and filled it.
It hangs now on a nail in my room,                                    35
And when the season's dry and the city liquid
Tastes too much of metal and the system
That pumps it to my taps,
I drink that water, and find it cool and clear.

## Getting at Meaning

1. Why do the lifeguards keep the campers away from the channel? What is the only way that a camper can explore the channel bottom?

2. According to the speaker, what are the most valuable contents of the cabins?

3. What "camp rules" does the speaker break on returning to the camp? Why is this experience important to the speaker? What does the speaker mean by the comment "there was always bottom"? (line 32)

4. Why is the water in the canteen important to the speaker? What insights does the speaker gain by returning to the camp?

## Developing Skills in Reading Literature

1. **Symbol.** What does the channel bottom symbolize for the speaker? What does the canteen and its water symbolize?

2. **Imagery.** Kinesthetic imagery, as you know, creates the sensation of movement, pressure, or tension as it is felt within the body. What images in the third stanza are kinesthetic? Kinetic imagery creates a picture of movement. What images in the third stanza are kinetic?

## Developing Vocabulary

**Multiple Meanings of Words.** The word *sound* has several different meanings. Look up *sound* in a dictionary and write the correct definition for the word as it is used in line 12 of the poem.

Study all the various meanings of *sound*, and then write five original sentences using the word as (1) a noun derived from the Latin root *sonus*, (2) a noun derived from the Old Norse root *sund*, (3) an adjective, (4) an intransitive verb, and (5) a transitive verb.

# Gracious Goodness    *Marge Piercy*

On the beach where we had been idly
telling the shell coins
cat's paw, cross-barred Venus, china cockle,
we both saw at once
the sea bird fall to the sand                                    5
and flap grotesquely.
He had taken a great barbed hook
out through the cheek and fixed
in the big wing.
He was pinned to himself to die,                                10
a royal tern with a black crest blown back
as if he flew in his own private wind.
He felt good in my hands, not fragile
but muscular and glossy and strong,
the beak that could have split my hand                          15
opening only to cry
as we yanked on the barbs.
We borrowed a clippers, cut and drew out the hook.
Then the royal tern took off, wavering,
lurched twice,                                                  20
then acrobat returned to his element, dipped,
zoomed, and sailed out to dive for a fish.
Virtue: what a sunrise in the belly.
Why is there nothing
I have ever done with anybody                                   25
that seems to me so obviously right?

## Getting at Meaning

1. What is the speaker doing before the tern falls?

2. How does the speaker feel after freeing the tern? Why does this deed stand out in the speaker's life as "so obviously right"?

## Developing Skills in Reading Literature

1. **Imagery.** What images help the reader to picture the appearance of the tern? What images help the reader to picture the movements of the tern?

2. **Metaphor.** Why is virtue a sunrise in the belly? How does this metaphor help the reader to understand the feelings of the speaker?

## Developing Writing Skills

**Describing a Personal Experience.** Like most people, you probably have difficulty at times deciding on the "right" course of action. If, for example, you see someone cheating on a test, you may wonder what action, if any, to take. Think of an incident in your life in which the "right" course of action was clear to you. In a single paragraph, describe the situation, what you did and why, and your feelings afterwards.

# The Burden
### Francesca Yetunde Pereira

Tell me no secret, friend,
My heart will not sustain
Its load, too heavily
On my mind to weigh

Involve me not, friend,    5
Make not of me a mute.
Like a labyrinth
The road from my heart
Winds round and round,
Yet leads to an avenue—    10
The boulevard of speech.

Tell me no secret, friend,
To you I'll still be true.
For you I'll fight
No matter where—    15
But make not a mute of me.

## Getting at Meaning

1. Why will knowing a secret make the speaker mute?

2. Explain the title of the poem.

3. What does the speaker mean by the comment, "The road from my heart . . . leads to . . . the boulevard of speech"? What does this comment reveal about the speaker's knowledge of himself or herself?

## Developing Vocabulary

**Words from Greek Mythology.** The word *labyrinth* comes from the Greek story of Theseus and the Minotaur. Research this myth in a reference book on mythology and be prepared to explain the origin of the word and the plot of the myth.

The word *clue,* which means "a fact or object that helps solve a problem or puzzle," is related to the same myth. Look up the words *clue* and *clew* and try to trace the meaning of the word to the story of Theseus.

# Business
### *Victor Hernandez Cruz*

Don Arturo says:
There was a man
who sold puppets and whistles
for a living
He also played guitar          5
He used to go
to the shopping areas
and draw huge crowds
They bought his whistles
and puppets                    10
They threw money into
his guitar
This was against the law
So he was arrested at
least three times a week       15
When his turn came up
in the courtroom
He took a puppet out
and put a show on
All the detectives             20
and court clerks
rolled on the floor
When he finished
they all bought puppets
and whistles from him          25
The judge got angry
and yelled:
What kind of business
is this
And the man said               30
I am the monkey man
and the
Monkey man sells
Monkey business.

## Getting at Meaning

1. Why does the peddler call himself the "monkey man"? What are the connotations of the word *monkey*?

2. What insight about business does the monkey man express?

## Developing Skills in Reading Literature

**Poetry.** How does this poem fit your idea of poetry? Does it look like a poem? Does it sound like a poem? Explain.

## Developing Writing Skills

**Writing a Poem.** Select a short article from a magazine or newspaper. Rearrange the sentences so that the article looks like a poem. Add dialogue, if possible, and revise the wording so that, in the final draft, the article sounds like a poem. Attach the original article to the finished poem.

# Miss Rosie — *Lucille Clifton*

When I watch you
wrapped up like garbage
sitting, surrounded by the smell
of too old potato peels
or                                                                        5
when I watch you
in your old man's shoes
with the little toe cut out
sitting, waiting for your mind
like next week's grocery                                                  10
I say
when I watch you
you wet brown bag of a woman
who used to be the best looking gal in Georgia
used to be called the Georgia Rose                                        15
I stand up
through your destruction
I stand up

## Getting at Meaning

1. What has happened to Miss Rosie?
2. Reread the last three lines of the poem. Is the speaker simply saying, "I won't let what happened to you, happen to me"? If not, what does the speaker mean by the lines, "through your destruction/ I stand up"?

## Developing Skills in Reading Literature

**Figurative Language.** The poet uses simile and metaphor to paint a vivid picture of Miss Rosie. Identify each of the following as a simile or a metaphor and describe exactly the picture that each example creates in your mind. Then explain how each example adds to your understanding of Miss Rosie.

wrapped up like garbage
waiting for your mind like next week's
    grocery
you wet brown bag of a woman

## Developing Writing Skills

**Using Figures of Speech.** In a poem or a paragraph, describe an older person that you know or at least see regularly. Use figurative language to create a vivid picture of the way that this person looks, walks, talks, sits, and dresses. At the end of the description, explain what insight about life you gain from knowing or simply looking at this person.

# Grandpa     *W. M. Ransom*

Grandpa he was a man
he taught me the things that
       mattered
how to eat oxtail soup before
fishing on Saturday morning to       5
keep you warm how to
cast a line into a
streamful of angered anglers and
be the only one to
come home with anything worth       10
bragging about how to
set teeth in any saw and
dovetail a joint in a
chair leg and roof a
house and weld a       15
straight seam on a
kitchen pipe and make a
home out of a
workshop out of a
two-car garage and       20
smoke Granger's tobacco and
love work and kids and
fishing for "a Man's
life is his work and
his work is his life" and       25
once you take away his work
you pull the plug of his life
and it takes too long
for it to drain silently away.
One day they came and       30
told him to go home and
rest old man it's time
that you retire he begged
them "let me stay" but
they of course knew best for       35
everyone knows at sixty-five

all men are old and useless and
must be cast off to
rot so he came home and
tried to fish and                                    40
couldn't and tried to joke and
couldn't and tried to live and
couldn't. Every morning he was
up at four and cooked breakfast
              for                                     45
grandma and warmed up the house
              and
went to the workshop and
filed saws for neighbors but
they told him to stop that too               50
so he put all his tools away and
cleaned up the workshop and
came into the house for his
daily afternoon nap and
died. They didn't know                        55
what I knew because he
didn't tell them but
he showed them
Grandpa he was a man.

## Getting at Meaning

1. Why is Grandpa unable to fish, joke, or live after his retirement? What is missing?

2. Explain the idea expressed in lines 26–29. How does this idea relate to what Grandpa "showed them"? (line 58)

3. This poem begins and ends with the line "Grandpa he was a man." How would the speaker define what it means to be a man?

## Developing Skills in Reading Literature

1. **Irony.** Where does the speaker use verbal irony? What effect does this irony have on the poem?

2. **Poetry.** What devices make this poem sound like a poem? What does each device do for the content of the poem?

3. **Tone.** What is the tone of this poem? Support your answer with words and phrases from the poem.

## Developing Writing Skills

**Writing a Poem.** Relate an experience that you shared with a grandparent. Focus on a specific event and reveal through the poem what your grandparent has meant to you.

If you have not known a grandparent, you may write about another relative.

# Generations     *Amy Lowell*

You are like the stem
Of a young beech-tree,
Straight and swaying,
Breaking out in golden leaves.
Your walk is like the blowing of a beech-tree          5
On a hill.
Your voice is like leaves
Softly struck upon by a South wind.
Your shadow is no shadow, but a scattered sunshine;
And at night you pull the sky down to you          10
And hood yourself in stars.

But I am like a great oak under a cloudy sky,
Watching a stripling beech grow up at my feet.

## Getting at Meaning

1. Who is the speaker? To whom is this person speaking? What are their relative ages? What is their relationship?

2. Explain lines 10 and 11.

3. In what way is the speaker "under a cloudy sky"?

## Developing Skills in Reading Literature

**Figurative Language.** Reread line 9. Explain the literal meaning of this line as it relates to a tree. What is the figurative meaning of the line?

What extended metaphor is used in this poem? What similes are used to develop the metaphor? What aspect of the central comparison does each specific simile develop?

## Developing Vocabulary

**Synonyms.** A stripling is a youth or a young person. The English language has many other nouns and adjectives that describe people at various stages of their lives. Using a thesaurus or a dictionary of synonyms, list as many different words as you can to describe a child, an adolescent, an adult, and an old person.

# "Out, Out—" *Robert Frost*

The buzz saw snarled and rattled in the yard
And made dust and dropped stove-length sticks of wood,
Sweet-scented stuff when the breeze drew across it.
And from there those that lifted eyes could count
Five mountain ranges one behind the other       5
Under the sunset far into Vermont.
And the saw snarled and rattled, snarled and rattled,
As it ran light, or had to bear a load.
And nothing happened: day was all but done.
Call it a day, I wish they might have said       10
To please the boy by giving him the half hour
That a boy counts so much when saved from work.
His sister stood beside them in her apron
To tell them "Supper." At the word, the saw,
As if to prove saws knew what supper meant,       15
Leaped out at the boy's hand, or seemed to leap—
He must have given the hand. However it was,
Neither refused the meeting. But the hand!
The boy's first outcry was a rueful laugh,
As he swung toward them holding up the hand       20
Half in appeal, but half as if to keep
The life from spilling. Then the boy saw all—
Since he was old enough to know, big boy
Doing a man's work, though a child at heart—
He saw all spoiled. "Don't let him cut my hand off—       25
The doctor, when he comes. Don't let him, sister!"
So. But the hand was gone already.
The doctor put him in the dark of ether.
He lay and puffed his lips out with his breath.
And then—the watcher at his pulse took fright.       30
No one believed. They listened at his heart.
Little—less—nothing!—and that ended it.
No one to build on there. And they, since they
Were not the one dead, turned to their affairs.

## Getting at Meaning

1. What words in the opening description make the saw seem threatening or dangerous? How is this image developed later in the poem?

2. The phrase "those that lifted eyes" refers to the wood cutters. What does the phrase imply about their concerns and concentration?

3. What note of regret is introduced by the speaker in line 10?

4. Why does the speaker seem uncertain about how the accident happens? What does the speaker imply about the nature of accidents?

5. What does the phrase "to keep/The life from spilling" imply about the seriousness of the accident?

6. What does the boy see that is "all spoiled"? Explain your answer.

7. Describe the reaction to the boy's death.

## Developing Skills in Reading Literature

1. **Personification.** Find two lines in the poem in which the speaker personifies the saw.

2. **Theme.** What does the speaker imply about the value of life through the boy's reaction to the accident? Through the reaction of others to the boy's death?

3. **Allusion.** The title of this poem is an allusion to a speech from Shakespeare's *Macbeth* (Act Five, Scene 5, lines 17–28). Find a copy of the play and read the speech. What do the ideas in the speech add to your understanding of this poem?

## Developing Vocabulary

**Echoic Words.** An echoic word imitates a sound; for example, the word *echo* recalls the sound of an echo. In this poem, the words *snarled* and *rattled* recreate the sounds made by the saw. Make a list of ten words that imitate the sounds made by other tools. Then use each word in a sentence.

# If There Be Sorrow     *Mari Evans*

If there be sorrow
let it be
for things undone
undreamed
    unrealized     5
        unattained

to these add one:
love withheld
  restrained

## Getting at Meaning

1. What causes the speaker to feel sorrow?

2. Would the speaker feel sorrow at someone's death? Under what circumstances? Explain.

3. This poem is filled with negative thoughts. Is it a negative poem? Explain.

## Developing Skills in Reading Literature

1. **Speaker.** On the basis of this short poem, what kind of person do you think that the speaker is? Would you want this speaker for a friend? Why, or why not?

2. **Rhyme.** Where does the poet use rhyme in this poem? What is the effect of the rhyme?

3. **Repetition.** What effect is created by the repetition of the prefix *un-?* What synonyms could the poet have used to avoid the repetition? Why did she choose not to use them?

## Developing Writing Skills

**Writing a Poem.** Using this poem as a model, write an original poem beginning with the words "If there be. . . ." Complete the line with a word such as joy, anger, friendship, or love. Your poem should go on to give the reader a clear idea of what your speaker believes is important in life.

# A Song of Nezahualcoyotl

*Aztec Indian*

the riches of this world are only lent to us

the things that are so good to enjoy we do not own

the sun pours down gold
fountains pour out green water
colors touch us like fingers                                    5
of green quetzal wings

none of this can we own for more than a day

none of these beautiful things can we keep for more than an hour

one thing alone we can own forever
the memory of the just                                        10
the remembrance of a good act
the good remembrance of a just man

this one thing alone will never be taken away from us

will never die

## Getting at Meaning

1. What is it about the beauties of nature that make them temporary?

2. Is the speaker suggesting that natural beauty should be ignored? Explain.

3. What in life does the speaker consider lasting?

## Developing Skills in Reading Literature

1. **Poetry.** What idea is expressed in the first eight lines of this poem? What poetic devices are used to convey this idea?

What idea is expressed in lines 9–14? What poetic devices are used to convey this idea?

2. **Theme.** What is the theme of this poem? How does the theme unify the poem?

## Developing Vocabulary

**Word Origins.** Look up *quetzal* in a dictionary. Define *quetzal* as it is used in this poem. In what language did the word originate? Where was that language spoken? What other definitions can you find for *quetzal*? What does this definition indicate about the importance of the quetzal in Central America?

# Unit Review  *Poetry*

## Understanding the Unit

1. In the poem "Nothing Gold Can Stay," both rhythm and rhyme enhance the presentation of ideas. Identify the meter and the rhyme scheme of the poem and explain the contribution of each to the development of meaning in the poem.

2. In the following poems, structure is especially important to the development of meaning: "Plucking the Rushes," "The Man in the Dead Machine," "Troubled Woman," "Was Worm." "Simile," "Firefly Song," and "Sometimes Running." Select three of these poems and explain how the structure of each poem reinforces meaning.

3. Identify two images in each of the following poems. Explain the contribution of each image to the development of the poem.

"Fast Run in the Junkyard"
"Peter at Fourteen"
"Gracious Goodness"
"O What Is That Sound"
"A Song of Nezahualcoyotl"
"Tenement Room: Chicago"

4. Both "Troubled Woman" and "Miss Rosie" have as subjects women who appear to be defeated by life. Describe the speaker's attitude toward the subject in each poem. How do the poems differ as a result of the difference in the attitudes of the speakers?

5. In "Ex-Baketball Player," "The Man in the Dead Machine," "November Day" and "Miss Rosie," each poet makes use of one simile. In each poem, how is the simile related to the subject of the poem? What effect does the comparison have upon the tone of the poem? In general, what do the poets accomplish through the use of similes?

6. Reread "Here—Hold My Hand," "Long Distance," and "Ebb." How are the subjects of these poems similar? How do the experiences of the three speakers relate to the theme of "If There Be Sorrow"? What might all four writers be implying about human relationships?

7. Both "First Lesson" and "The Writer" describe an experience of a parent with a maturing child. How are the experiences similar? How are they different? What point do both writers make about the responsibility of parents to their children? About the degree of control that parents have over their children?

8. Both "Foul Shot" and "Ex-Basketball Player" focus upon athletes. Describe the speaker's attitude toward the subject in each poem. Considering both poems, what conclusions might the reader draw about the value of high school athletics?

9. Several poems in this unit deal with poetry and with the creative process. Reread these poems. Then summarize the ideas about poetry that are presented in the poems.

## Writing

1. Reread your three favorite poems from the section titled "Imagery." Carefully examine each writer's use of imagery. Then select a subject that offers the possibility of detailed description, such as an animal, a season of the year, an athlete, or a particular setting. In a poem or a paragraph, describe your subject, using images that appeal to at least two senses.

2. Select a subject about which you have strong feelings. Then write a poem in which the speaker's attitude toward the subject reflects your feelings. Be sure that the speaker in your poem has an identity distinct from your own. For instance, if your subject is the treatment of elderly people in today's society, your speaker might be an elderly person, a son or daughter of an elderly parent, or a young child who observes older people in a park.

3. Select a poem from the section titled "Idea." Reread the poem and analyze its structure, imagery, rhythm, rhyme, tone, figures of speech, and theme. Then write a five-paragraph composition in which you discuss in detail the three devices that seem most important to the development of theme.

EVERYMAN, 1954. *Ben Shahn.*
*Collection of Whitney Museum of American Art.*

# Unit 4

# Drama

FIRST ROW ORCHESTRA, 1951. *Edward Hopper.*
*Hirshhorn Museum and Sculpture Garden, Smithsonian Institution.*

# Introduction to the Unit

Drama is literature written specifically for performance before an audience. Because the word *drama* sounds so formal, many people believe that it applies only to plays performed in theaters. Television programs and movies, however, are also forms of drama.

Whether drama is performed on a stage or in a television or film studio, certain fundamentals remain constant. Actors and actresses impersonate the characters of the drama and recite the dialogue written by the playwright. The audience watches the action, listens to the dialogue, and, if the drama is well written and well acted, becomes involved in the play. The process of becoming caught up in drama so that the viewer forgets to a degree the artificiality of what he or she is watching is called "suspension of disbelief." When an audience cheers for a hero, boos a villain, or cries at the death of a character, that audience has suspended disbelief. The action has become real, the characters human, the play no longer a mere imitation of life.

The elements of drama are much the same as those of other literature. Plot, character, setting, conflict, and theme, all are important to the development of a play. Plays that are written in poetry instead of in prose make use of rhythm, rhyme, imagery, and figurative language. The unique quality of drama is its reliance on dialogue. In most plays, there is no narrator to fill in background details, no exposition to interpret events and characters and to provide transitions between scenes. Instead, all information must be learned from what the characters say to one another.

The characters in plays exhibit human strengths and weaknesses. The forces that motivate characters are the same as those that motivate all human beings. This holds true whether a play was created last year or a thousand years ago. In this unit, for example, anger, greed, lust for power, love of country, and sorrow at the death of a loved one are sources of motivation. The reader can recognize and identify with these emotions, and thus can suspend disbelief and become involved in the dramas.

# The Rising of the Moon

## Lady Augusta Gregory

SCENE: *Side of a quay in a seaport town. Some posts and chains. A large barrel. Enter three policemen. Moonlight.*

SERGEANT, *who is older than the others, crosses the stage to right and looks down steps. The others put down a pastepot and unroll a bundle of placards.*

POLICEMAN B. I think this would be a good place to put up a notice. (*He points to barrel.*)

POLICEMAN X. Better ask him. (*Calls to* SERGEANT.) Will this be a good place for a placard?

(*No answer.*)

POLICEMAN B. Will we put up a notice here on the barrel?

(*No answer.*)

SERGEANT. There's a flight of steps here that leads to the water. This is a place that should be minded well. If he got down here, his friends might have a boat to meet him; they might send it in here from outside.

POLICEMAN B. Would the barrel be a good place to put a notice up?

SERGEANT. It might; you can put it there.

(*They paste the notice up.*)

SERGEANT (*reading it*). Dark hair—dark eyes, smooth face, height five feet five—there's not much to take hold of in that—It's a pity I had no chance of seeing him before he broke out of jail. They say he's a wonder, that it's he makes all the plans for the whole organization. There isn't another man in Ireland would have broken jail the way he did. He must have some friends among the jailers.

POLICEMAN B. A hundred pounds is little enough for the Government to offer for him. You may be sure any man in the force that takes him will get promotion.

SERGEANT. I'll mind this place myself. I wouldn't wonder at all if he came this way. He might come slipping along there (*points to side of quay*), and his friends might be waiting for him there (*points down steps*), and once he got away it's little chance we'd have of finding him; it's maybe under a load of kelp he'd be in a fishing boat, and not one to help a married man that wants it to the reward.

POLICEMAN X. And if we get him itself, nothing but abuse on our heads for it from the people, and maybe from our own relations.

SERGEANT. Well, we have to do our duty in the force. Haven't we the whole country depending on us to keep law and order? It's those that are down would be up and those that are up would be down, if it wasn't for us. Well, hurry on, you have plenty of other places to placard yet, and come back here then to me. You can take the lantern. Don't be too long now. It's very lonesome here with nothing but the moon.

POLICEMAN B. It's a pity we can't stop with you. The Government should have brought more police into the town, with *him* in jail, and at assize[1] time too. Well, good luck to your watch. *(They go out.)*

SERGEANT *(walks up and down once or twice and looks at placard).* A hundred pounds and promotion sure. There must be a great deal of spending in a hundred pounds. It's a pity some honest man not to be the better of that.

*(A ragged man appears at left and tries to slip past.* SERGEANT *suddenly turns.)*

SERGEANT. Where are you going?

MAN. I'm a poor ballad-singer, your honor. I thought to sell some of these *(holds out bundle of ballads)* to the sailors. *(He goes on.)*

SERGEANT. Stop! Didn't I tell you to stop? You can't go on there.

MAN. Oh, very well. It's a hard thing to be poor. All the world's against the poor!

SERGEANT. Who are you?

MAN. You'd be as wise as myself if I told you, but I don't mind. I'm one Jimmy Walsh, a ballad-singer.

SERGEANT. Jimmy Walsh? I don't know that name.

MAN. Ah, sure, they know it well enough in Ennis.[2] Were you ever in Ennis, Sergeant?

SERGEANT. What brought you here?

MAN. Sure, it's to the assizes I came, thinking I might make a few shillings here or there. It's in the one train with the judges I came.

SERGEANT. Well, if you came so far, you may as well go farther, for you'll walk out of this.

MAN. I will, I will; I'll just go on where I was going. *(Goes toward steps.)*

SERGEANT. Come back from those steps; no one has leave to pass down them tonight.

MAN. I'll just sit on the top of the steps till I see will some sailor buy a ballad off me that would give me my supper. They do be late going back to the ship. It's often I saw them in Cork[3] carried down the quay in a hand-cart.

SERGEANT. Move on, I tell you. I won't have any one lingering about the quay tonight.

MAN. Well, I'll go. It's the poor have the hard life! Maybe yourself might like one, Sergeant. Here's a good sheet now. *(Turns one over)* "Content and a Pipe"—that's not much. "The Peeler and the Goat"—you wouldn't like that. "Johnny Hart"—that's a lovely song.

SERGEANT. Move on.

MAN. Ah, wait till you hear it. *(Sings.)*
There was a rich farmer's daughter lived near the town of Ross;
She courted a Highland soldier, his name was Johnny Hart;
Says the mother to her daughter, "I'll go distracted mad
If you marry that Highland soldier dressed up in Highland plaid."

SERGEANT. Stop that noise.

*(MAN wraps up his ballads and shuffles toward the steps.)*

SERGEANT. Where are you going?

MAN. Sure you told me to be going, and I am going.

SERGEANT. Don't be a fool. I didn't tell you to go that way; I told you to go back to the town.

MAN. Back to the town, is it?

SERGEANT *(taking him by the shoulder and shoving him before him).* Here, I'll show you the way. Be off with you. What are you stopping for?

MAN *(who has been keeping his eye on the notice, points to it).* I think I know what you're waiting for, Sergeant.

---

1. **assize** (ə sīz′): court sessions held periodically in each county of England to try criminal and civil cases.
2. **Ennis:** a town in County Clare, a county in western Ireland.
3. **Cork:** a county on the southern coast of Ireland.

SERGEANT. What's that to you?

MAN. And I know well the man you're waiting for—I know him well—I'll be going. *(He shuffles on.)*

SERGEANT. You know him? Come back here. What sort is he?

MAN. Come back is it, Sergeant? Do you want to have me killed?

SERGEANT. Why do you say that?

MAN. Never mind. I'm going. I wouldn't be in your shoes if the reward was ten times as much. *(Goes on off stage to left.)* Not if it was ten times as much.

SERGEANT *(rushing after him)*. Come back here, come back. *(Drags him back.)* What sort is he? Where did you see him?

MAN. I saw him in my own place, in the County Clare. I tell you you wouldn't like to be looking at him. You'd be afraid to be in the one place with him. There isn't a weapon he doesn't know the use of, and as to strength, his muscles are as hard as that board. *(Slaps barrel.)*

SERGEANT. Is he as bad as that?

MAN. He is then.

SERGEANT. Do you tell me so?

MAN. There was a poor man in our place, a sergeant from Ballyvaughan[4]—It was with a lump of stone he did it.

SERGEANT. I never heard of that.

MAN. And you wouldn't, Sergeant. It's not everything that happens gets into the papers. And there was a policeman in plain clothes, too . . . It is in Limerick he was. . . . It was after the time of the attack on the police barrack at Kilmallock.[5] . . . Moonlight . . . just like this . . . waterside. . . . Nothing was known for certain.

SERGEANT. Do you say so? It's a terrible county to belong to.

MAN. That's so, indeed! You might be standing there, looking out that way, thinking you saw him coming up this side of the quay *(points)*, and he might be coming up this other side *(points)*, and he'd be on you before you knew where you were.

SERGEANT. It's a whole troop of police they ought to put here to stop a man like that.

MAN. But if you'd like me to stop with you, I could be looking down this side. I could be sitting up here on this barrel.

SERGEANT. And you know him well, too?

MAN. I'd know him a mile off, Sergeant.

SERGEANT. But you wouldn't want to share the reward?

MAN. Is it a poor man like me, that has to be going the roads and singing in fairs, to have the name on him that he took a reward? But you don't want me. I'll be safer in the town.

SERGEANT. Well, you can stop.

MAN *(getting up on barrel)*. All right, Sergeant. I wonder, now, you're not tired out, Sergeant, walking up and down the way you are.

SERGEANT. If I'm tired I'm used to it.

MAN. You might have hard work before you tonight yet. Take it easy while you can. There's plenty of room up here on the barrel, and you see farther when you're higher up.

SERGEANT. Maybe so. *(Gets up beside him on barrel, facing right. They sit back to back, looking different ways.)* You made me feel a bit queer with the way you talked.

MAN. Give me a match, Sergeant *(he gives it and MAN lights pipe)*; take a draw yourself? It'll quiet you. Wait now till I give you a light, but you needn't turn round. Don't take your eye off the quay for the life of you.

SERGEANT. Never fear, I won't. *(Lights pipe. They both smoke.)* Indeed it's a hard thing to be in the force, out at night and no thanks for it, for all the danger we're in. And it's little we get but abuse from the

---

4. **Ballyvaughan:** another town in County Clare.
5. **Limerick . . . Kilmallock:** Limerick is a county in southwest Ireland, and Kilmallock is a town in Limerick.

people, and no choice but to obey our orders, and never asked when a man is sent into danger, if you are a married man with a family.

MAN (sings).
> As through the hills I walked to view the hills and shamrock plain,
> I stood awhile where nature smiles to view the rocks and streams,
> On a matron fair I fixed my eyes beneath a fertile vale,
> As she sang her song it was on the wrong of poor old Granuaile.

SERGEANT. Stop that; that's no song to be singing in these times.

MAN. Ah, Sergeant, I was only singing to keep my heart up. It sinks when I think of him. To think of us two sitting here, and he creeping up the quay, maybe, to get to us.

SERGEANT. Are you keeping a good lookout?

MAN. I am; and for no reward too. Amn't I the foolish man? But when I saw a man in trouble, I never could help trying to get him out of it. What's that? Did something hit me? (Rubs his heart.)

SERGEANT (patting him on the shoulder). You will get your reward in heaven.

MAN. I know that, I know that, Sergeant, but life is precious.

SERGEANT. Well, you can sing if it gives you more courage.

MAN (sings).
> Her head was bare, her hands and feet with iron bands were bound,
> Her pensive strain and plaintive wail mingles with the evening gale,
> And the song she sang with mournful air, I am old Granuaile.
> Her lips so sweet that monarchs kissed . . .

SERGEANT. That's not it. . . . "Her gown she wore was stained with gore." . . . That's it —you missed that.

MAN. You're right, Sergeant, so it is; I missed it. (Repeats line.) But to think of a man like you knowing a song like that.

SERGEANT. There's many a thing a man might know and might not have any wish for.

MAN. Now, I daresay, Sergeant, in your youth, you used to be sitting up on a wall, the way you are sitting up on this barrel now, and the other lads beside you, and you singing "Granuaile"? . . .

SERGEANT. I did then.

MAN. And the "Shan Bhean Bhocht"? . . .

SERGEANT. I did then.

MAN. And the "Green on the Cape"?

SERGEANT. That was one of them.

MAN. And maybe the man you are watching for tonight used to be sitting on the wall, when he was young, and singing those same songs. . . . It's a queer world.

SERGEANT. Whisht! . . . I think I see something coming. . . . It's only a dog.

MAN. And isn't it a queer world? . . . Maybe it's one of the boys you used to be singing with that time you will be arresting today or tomorrow, and sending into the dock.

SERGEANT. That's true indeed.

MAN. And maybe one night, after you had been singing, if the other boys had told you some plan they had, some plan to free the country, you might have joined with them . . . and maybe it is you might be in trouble now.

SERGEANT. Well, who knows but I might? I had a great spirit in those days.

MAN. It's a queer world, Sergeant, and it's little any mother knows when she sees her child creeping on the floor what might happen to it before it has gone through its life, or who will be who in the end.

SERGEANT. That's a queer thought now, and a true thought. Wait now till I think it out. . . . If it wasn't for the sense I have, and for my wife and family, and for me joining the force the time I did, it might be myself now would be after breaking jail and hiding in the dark, and it might be him that's hiding in the dark and that got out of jail would be sitting up where I am on this barrel. . . . And it might be myself would be creeping up trying to make my escape from himself, and it might be himself would be keeping the law, and myself would be breaking it, and myself would be trying maybe to put a bullet in his head, or to take up a lump of a stone the way you said he did . . . no, that myself did. . . . Oh! *(Gasps. After a pause.)* What's that? *(Grasps* MAN'S *arm.)*

MAN *(jumps off barrel and listens, looking out over water).* It's nothing, Sergeant.

SERGEANT. I thought it might be a boat. I had a notion there might be friends of his coming about the quays with a boat.

MAN. Sergeant, I am thinking it was with the people you were, and not with the law you were, when you were a young man.

SERGEANT. Well, if I was foolish then, that time's gone.

MAN. Maybe, Sergeant, it comes into your head sometimes, in spite of your belt and your tunic, that it might have been as well for you to have followed Granuaile.

SERGEANT. It's no business of yours what I think.

MAN. Maybe, Sergeant, you'll be on the side of the country yet.

SERGEANT *(gets off barrel).* Don't talk to me like that. I have my duties and I know them. *(Looks round.)* That was a boat; I hear the oars. *(Goes to the steps and looks down.)*

MAN *(sings).*

> O, then, tell me, Shawn O'Farrell,
> Where the gathering is to be.
> In the old spot by the river
> Right well known to you and me!

SERGEANT. Stop that! Stop that, I tell you!

MAN *(sings louder).*

> One word more, for signal token,
> Whistle up the marching tune,
> With your pike upon your shoulder,
> At the Rising of the Moon.

SERGEANT. If you don't stop that, I'll arrest you.

*(A whistle from below answers, repeating the air.)*

SERGEANT. That's a signal. *(Stands between him and steps.)* You must not pass this way. . . . Step farther back . . . Who are you? You are no ballad-singer.

MAN. You needn't ask who I am; that placard will tell you. *(Points to placard.)*

SERGEANT. You are the man I am looking for.

MAN *(takes off hat and wig.* SERGEANT *seizes them).* I am. There's a hundred pounds on my head. There is a friend of mine below in a boat. He knows a safe place to bring me to.

SERGEANT *(looking still at hat and wig).* It's a pity! It's a pity. You deceived me well. You deceived me well.

MAN. I am a friend of Granuaile. There is a hundred pounds on my head.

SERGEANT. It's a pity, it's a pity!

MAN. Will you let me pass, or must I make you let me?

SERGEANT. I am in the force. I will not let you pass.

MAN. I thought to do it with my tongue. *(Puts hand in breast.)* What is that?

*(Voice of* POLICEMAN X *outside.)* Here, this is where we left him.

SERGEANT. It's my comrades coming.

MAN. You won't betray me . . . the friend of Granuaile. *(Slips behind barrel.)*

*(Voice of* POLICEMAN B.*)* That was the last of the placards.

POLICEMAN X *(as they come in).* If he makes his escape it won't be unknown he'll make it.

*(*SERGEANT *puts hat and wig behind his back.)*

POLICEMAN B. Did any one come this way?

SERGEANT *(after a pause).* No one.

POLICEMAN B. No one at all?

SERGEANT. No one at all.

POLICEMAN B. We had no orders to go back to the station; we can stop along with you.

SERGEANT. I don't want you. There is nothing for you to do here.

POLICEMAN B. You bade us to come back here and keep watch with you.

SERGEANT. I'd sooner be alone. Would any man come this way and you making all that talk? It is better the place to be quiet.

POLICEMAN B. Well, we'll leave you the lantern anyhow. (Hands it to him.)

SERGEANT. I don't want it. Bring it with you.

POLICEMAN B. You might want it. There are clouds coming up and you have the darkness of the night before you yet. I'll leave it over here on the barrel. (Goes to barrel.)

SERGEANT. Bring it with you I tell you. No more talk.

POLICEMAN B. Well, I thought it might be a comfort to you. I often think when I have it in my hand and can be flashing it about into every dark corner (doing so) that it's the same as being beside the fire at home, and the bits of bogwood blazing up now and again. (Flashes it about, now on the barrel, now on SERGEANT.)

SERGEANT (furious). Be off the two of you, yourselves and your lantern! (They go out. MAN comes from behind barrel. He and SERGEANT stand looking at one another.)

SERGEANT. What are you waiting for?

MAN. For my hat, of course, and my wig. You wouldn't wish me to get my death of cold? (SERGEANT gives them.)

MAN (going toward steps). Well, good night, comrade, and thank you. You did me a good turn tonight, and I'm obliged to you. Maybe I'll be able to do as much for you when the small rise up and the big fall down . . . when we all change places at the Rising (waves his hand and disappears) of the Moon.

SERGEANT (turning his back to audience and reading placard). A hundred pounds reward! A hundred pounds! (Turns toward audience.) I wonder, now, am I as great a fool as I think I am?

## Getting at Meaning

1. Who is the man for whom the police are searching? What kind of criminal is he?

2. One of the policemen says that, even if they catch the man, they'll get "nothing but abuse" from the people. What does this reveal about the nature of the man's crimes?

3. Why is the disguise of a ballad singer appropriate for the criminal?

4. Is the ballad singer trying to frighten the sergeant with stories of the criminal's exploits or is he just teasing him? Explain.

5. The ballad singer says, "Is it a poor man like me, that has to be going the roads and singing in fairs, to have the name on him that he took a reward?" What does he mean? What does this reaction reveal about the relationship between the people and the authorities?

6. The sergeant is visibly upset when the ballad singer starts to sing "Granuaile"; when the ballad singer reveals his identity to the sergeant, the singer calls himself a "friend of Granuaile." From these and other clues in the play, what conclusions can you draw about the "Ballad of Granuaile"? What other ballads are mentioned in this play? Which of these might have the same political connotations as "Granuaile"?

7. The sergeant supplies a line to "Granuaile." Does the ballad singer skip this line on purpose? If so, why? What information does the ballad singer gain from this incident?

8. Explain this comment made by the sergeant: "There's many a thing a man might know and might not have any wish for."

9. Just before the other two policemen return, the ballad singer says, "I thought to do it with my tongue." What does he mean? What is he going to try next?

10. What change has occurred in the sergeant by the end of the play? How does the ballad singer effect this change?

## Developing Skills in Reading Literature

1. **Drama.** Drama is literature written to be performed by actors and actresses who impersonate the characters, perform the action, and recite the dialogue. Plays, as dramas are commonly called, are divided into acts and scenes. Generally, each act within a play builds to a suspenseful conclusion. A scene is a division of an act; no break in time or change of place occurs within a scene.

How many acts are in "The Rising of the Moon"? How many scenes? Do the time and place remain constant throughout the scene or scenes?

2. **Stage Directions.** Stage directions are statements, usually printed in italics, that help the reader to imagine the action and sound effects of a play the way that the dialogue is spoken. What information is provided by the stage directions at the beginning of this play? What kind of information is given in the stage directions within the play?

3. **Conflict.** Identify the conflicts in this play. Which are internal? Which are external? What is the central conflict?

## Developing Vocabulary

**Understanding Dialect.** This play takes place in Ireland; the characters, therefore, speak an Irish dialect. Find four examples of this dialect in the play. For each example, explain whether it differs from Standard English in vocabulary, sentence structure, or grammar, or in a combination of these.

## Developing Writing Skills

**Writing an Editorial.** Read several editorials in a newspaper to get an idea of the editorial approach. Then, write two editorials dealing with the escape from jail of the man described in "The Rising of the Moon." One editorial should be written for a newspaper controlled by the "authorities," the other for a newspaper run by the "people." Your editorials should reflect the two views of this man: the criminal and the hero.

# Orpheus     *Ted Hughes*

## CHARACTERS

NARRATOR                  PLUTO
ORPHEUS                   PERSEPHONE
EURYDICE                  VOICE
FRIEND ONE                TREES
FRIEND TWO                STONES
FRIEND THREE

NARRATOR. This is the story
    Of Orpheus[1] the Magician, whose magic was music.

*(Music—guitar—Pop)*

    This is the dance of the trees.
    His music is so magic, he makes the trees dance.
    The oaks unknot; they toss their limbs
    And the willows whirl in a ring.
    This is the dance of the trees.

*(Music stops. Giant sigh from all trees)*

    And this is the dance of the stones.

*(Music for stones—still Pop)*

    His music is so magic the stones dance.
    The rocks uproot and caper in their places,
    The pebbles skip like mice,
    The ordinary stones bounce like footballs.
    This is the dance of the stones.

*(Music stops. Sigh from all stones)*

    His music reaches out to the bears in the forest.

*(Bear music—still Pop)*

    It reaches up to the deer in the wrinkles of the hills.

*(Deer music)*

    It reaches down to the salmon in the pools below the falls.

---

1. **Orpheus** (ôr′ fē əs): in Greek mythology, a poet-musician with magical
powers who tries to lead his wife back from the dead.

*(Salmon music)*

And wherever his music is heard, the dancing begins.

*(Music)*

His music has a name. Its name is happiness.
Every living thing loves Orpheus
Because his music is happiness.

*(Eurydice becomes visible.)*

And this is the cause of Orpheus' happiness:
This is his wife; for her he makes his music.
ORPHEUS. Why shouldn't I be happy?
The world is beautiful.
Day after day the huge gift of the world
Is beautiful as ever.
More beautiful than the whole world is my wife
Eurydice.[2]
This is the secret of my music.
It is all for Eurydice, my happiness.

*(Music)*

NARRATOR. Nevertheless, there keeps coming a voice
To Orpheus—a voice which he does not like.
VOICE. Beware, Orpheus, beware.
NARRATOR. He dare not listen to the voice. He plays louder.

*(Music louder, to drown out the voice)*

NARRATOR. Is it the voice of a bird? Or a spider? Or a serpent?
VOICE *(very loud)*. Beware, Orpheus, beware.

*(Music stops.)*

VOICE *(very soft)*. Beware, beware, beware.
ORPHEUS. What should I beware of? Why should I beware?
VOICE. In the world of the trees,
In the world of the stones,
In the world of the frog, of the vole, of the linnet—
Every song has to be paid for.
ORPHEUS. Nonsense!
The world is a gift.
The brave take it with thanks and greet it with song.
Only the fearful peer at it with suspicion,
Thinking about the payment.

---

2. **Eurydice** (yoo rid′ ə sē′): in Greek mythology, the wife of Orpheus.

VOICE. Beware, Orpheus, beware.

(ORPHEUS *drowns the voice with a storm of his music.*)

NARRATOR. Orpheus hammers his guitar nevertheless.
  And the trees dance once again
  And the stones dance.
  The deer on the hills, and the salmon in the weirs
  And the bears in the holes of the forest
  And the travelers out on the roads
  Dance, dance when they hear it.
  The world dances with happiness.
  But suddenly—

*(Music falters and stops.)*

ORPHEUS. My hand! Something has happened to my hand.
NARRATOR. Orpheus' hand suddenly becomes numb.

*(Sudden terrible cry in distance; voice coming nearer; a friend bringing the news)*

FRIEND. Orpheus! *(Nearer)* Orpheus!
ORPHEUS. Who is that?
FRIEND *(nearer).* Orpheus!
ORPHEUS. Here.
FRIEND *(very close, entering).* Orpheus!
ORPHEUS. Your face is terrifying. So is your voice. What is your news?
FRIEND. Eurydice is dead.

*(Magnified crash of strings, as if instruments smashed light effects—sudden darkening)*

NARRATOR. Eurydice lies dead in the orchard, bitten by a snake.
  Her soul has left her body. Her body is cold.
  Her voice has been carried away to the land of the dead.
ORPHEUS. Eurydice!

*(He lies prostrate. His music—now erratic and discordant—struggles to tormented climax and again collapses as if all instruments smashed. Light effects)*

NARRATOR. Orpheus mourns for a month and his music is silent.
  The trees droop their boughs; they weep leaves.
  The stones in the wall weep.
  The river runs silent with sorrow under its willows.
  The birds sit mourning in silence on the ridge of the house.
  Orpheus lies silent and face downwards.
  His friends try to rouse him.
FRIEND. Orpheus, you are mourning too long. The dead are dead.
  Remember the living. Let your own music heal your sorrow.
  Play for us.

NARRATOR. The trees know better.

TREES. We shall never dance again. Eurydice is dead. Now we return to the ancient sadness of the forest.

NARRATOR. And the stones know better.

STONES. We are the stones, older than life. We have stood by many graves. We know grief to the bottom. We danced for a while because Orpheus was happy. Eurydice is dead. Now we return to the ancient sadness of the hills.

NARRATOR. But still his friends try to rouse him.

FRIENDS ONE, TWO, and THREE. Eurydice did not want you to grieve so long, Orpheus. Play your music again. Deceive your grief. Defeat evil fortunes. The dead belong to the dead, the living to the living. Play for us.

NARRATOR. Have they succeeded?

At last! Orpheus reaches for the magic strings.

*(One note, repeated, gathering volume and impetus—insane)*

FRIENDS ONE, TWO, and THREE. Horrible! Is this music? He has forgotten how to play. Grief has damaged his brain. This is not music.

ORPHEUS. I am going down to the underworld.

To find Eurydice.

FRIENDS. Mad! He is mad! Orpheus has gone mad!

ORPHEUS. I am going to the bottom of the underworld.

I am going to bring Eurydice back.

FRIEND ONE. Nobody ever came back from the land of the dead.

ORPHEUS. I am going. And I shall come back.

With Eurydice.

FRIENDS. Mad! He is mad! Orpheus has gone mad!

Nobody ever returns from the land of the dead.

*(Their voices fade. His crazy note strengthens, modulating into electronic infernal accompaniments. Major light effects through what follows)*

NARRATOR *(speaking with greatly magnified voice over the music—not declaiming so much as a giant whisper).*

Where is the land of the dead? Is it everywhere? Or nowhere?

How deep is the grave?

What is the geography of death?

What are its frontiers?

Perhaps it is a spider's web. Perhaps it is a single grain of dirt.

A million million souls can sit in an atom.

Is that the land of the dead?

A billion billion ghosts in the prison of an atom

Waiting for eternity to pass.

*(*ORPHEUS *music louder. Light effects)*

Orpheus beats his guitar. He is no longer making music. He is making a road of sound. He is making a road through the sky.

A road to Eurydice.

ORPHEUS. Eurydice! Eurydice! Eurydice!
NARRATOR. He flies on his guitar. His guitar is carrying him. It has lifted him off the earth. It lifts him over the treetops.

*(Music continuing, the monotonous note like a drum note insistent)*

FRIENDS. Orpheus, come back! Orpheus, come back!
ORPHEUS. Eurydice!
NARRATOR. It carries him into a cloud.

*(Light and sound effects through what follows, his music continuing throughout)*

Through the thunder he flies. Through the lightning.
It carries him
Through the storm of cries,
The last cries of all who have died on earth,
The jealous, screaming laments
Of all who have died on earth and cannot come back.

*(Storm of cries)*

ORPHEUS. Eurydice!
NARRATOR. He lays his road of sound across the heavens.
His guitar carries him.
Into the storm of blood,
The electrical storm of all the blood of all who have died on earth.
He is whirled into the summit of the storm.
Lightnings strike through him, he falls—
ORPHEUS. Eurydice!
NARRATOR. He falls into the mouth of the earth.
He falls through the throat of the earth; he recovers.
He rides his serpent of sound through the belly of the earth.
He drives his spear of sound through the bowels of the earth.
Mountains under the earth fall on him; he dodges.
He flies through walls of burning rock and ashes.
His guitar carries him.

*(Music continuing monotonous and insane)*

He hurtles towards the centermost atom of the earth.
He aims his beam of sound at the last atom.
ORPHEUS. Eurydice!
NARRATOR. He smashes through the wall of the last atom.
He falls
He falls
At the feet of Pluto, king of the kingdom of the dead.

*(Silence. Appropriate light effects)*

PLUTO. So you have arrived. At first I thought it was a fly. Then I thought it was a meteorite. But now I see—it is a man. A living man, in the land of the dead. Stand. I am Pluto,[3] king of the underworld. And you, I think, are Orpheus.

NARRATOR. Orpheus stands on the floor of the hall of judgment, like a mouse on the floor of a cathedral. Pluto's face, vast on his vast throne, is made of black iron, and it is the face of a spider. The face of Persephone,[4] his wife and queen, vast on her vast throne, beside him, is made of white ivory, and it is the pointed, eyeless face of a maggot.

PLUTO. Orpheus! I have heard of you. What is it, Orpheus, brings you alive to the land of the dead?

ORPHEUS. You took away my wife Eurydice.

PLUTO. That is true.

ORPHEUS. What can I do to get her back?

PLUTO. Get her back? (Laughs—Plutonic laughter in hell)
Alas, your wife has gone into the vaults of the dead.
You cannot have her back.

ORPHEUS. Release her. You are a god. You can do as you like.

PLUTO. Some things are not in my power, Orpheus. Here is my wife, for instance, Persephone. Perhaps you have heard about her. Six months she spends with me, here in the underworld. Six months she is up on earth, in the woods and meadows, with her mother. That is the arrangement. Up on the earth she is a flower-face, she laughs and sings; everybody adores her. But now you see her. Here in the underworld she is quite different. She never makes a sound. Never speaks, never sings. And you see her face? It is the peaked face of a maggot. Yet it is not a maggot. It is the white beak of the first sprout of a flower. I have never seen it open. Here in the underworld it is closed—white, pointed, and closed—the face of a maggot.
Here is something I cannot alter.
There is another thing, Orpheus. Here in the underworld, the accounting is strict. A payment was due from you.

ORPHEUS. Payment?

PLUTO. Nothing is free. Everything has to be paid for. For every profit in one thing—payment in some other thing. For every life—a death. Even your music—of which we have heard so much—that had to be paid for. Your wife was the payment for your music. Hell is now satisfied.

ORPHEUS. You took my wife—

PLUTO. To pay for your music.

ORPHEUS. But I had my music from birth. I was born with it.

PLUTO. You had it on credit. You were living in debt.
Now you have paid, and the music is yours.

ORPHEUS. Then take back my music. Give me my wife.

PLUTO. Too late.

---

3. **Pluto** (plo͞ot′ ō): in Greek mythology, the god who rules over the lower world.
4. **Persephone** (pər sef′ ə nē): in Greek mythology, the daughter of Zeus and Demeter kidnapped by Pluto to be his wife in the lower world.

ORPHEUS. What good is my music without my wife?
     What can I do to make you give me my wife.
PLUTO. Nothing can open Hell.

(ORPHEUS *strikes a chord—no longer Pop—solemn Handel, Bach, Vivaldi, or earlier. Light effects*)

     Now what are you doing?
     Your music is even more marvelous in Hell
     Than ever on earth. But it cannot help you.

*(Music)*

ORPHEUS. Look at your wife, Pluto. Look at Persephone, your queen.

*(Music)*

PLUTO. Her face is opening.
ORPHEUS. A wife for a wife, Pluto. Shall I continue to play?
PLUTO. Keep playing. Keep playing.

*(Music stops.)*

     Keep playing. Why have you stopped?
ORPHEUS. It is in my power to release the flower
     In your wife's face and awake her. Release my wife.
PLUTO. Play.
ORPHEUS. A wife for a wife.
PLUTO. Whatever you wish. Only play. You can have your wife.

*(Music)*

PLUTO. Beautiful as the day I plucked her off the earth!

*(Music stops.)*

ORPHEUS. You have your wife, Pluto.
PERSEPHONE. Keep your promise to Orpheus. Give him his wife.
PLUTO. I cannot.
ORPHEUS. Cannot? A god cannot break his promise.
     A god's promise is stronger than the god.
PLUTO. I cannot. Your wife's body is crumbling to dust.
PERSEPHONE. Give him her soul.
PLUTO. I can only give you her soul.
ORPHEUS. Let it be so. Let my wife's soul come with me.

*(Light effects. Dance and mime through what follows)*

PLUTO. You who have awakened the queen of Hell,
     Return to the world. Your wife's soul will be with you.

*(Orpheus' new music very soft)*

NARRATOR. Orpheus returns to the earth. It is not far. It is only a step.
     A step, a step, and a step,
     A step—and he turns. He looks for his wife. The air is empty.

ORPHEUS, PAINTED AFTER 1913. *Odilon Redon. The Cleveland Museum of Art. Gift from J. H. Wade.*

*(Music stops.)*

ORPHEUS. Eurydice?

EURYDICE. I am here.

ORPHEUS. Eurydice, where are you? Eurydice?

EURYDICE. Here at your side, Orpheus.

NARRATOR. He cannot see her. He cannot touch her. He can only hear her.
He listens.

EURYDICE. Play for me, Orpheus.

*(Orpheus plays his new music.)*

NARRATOR. Orpheus' friends come running. They listen to his music.
It is no longer the same music.

FRIEND ONE. This won't make anybody dance.

FRIEND TWO. This is queer music. He's gone to the dogs. This is dreary.

FRIEND THREE. Play as you used to play, Orpheus.
Make us dance.

*(Music continues.)*

NARRATOR. The trees did not dance. But the trees listened.
The music was not the music of dancing
But of growing and withering,
Of the root in the earth and the leaf in the light,
The music of birth and of death.
And the stones did not dance. But the stones listened.
The music was not the music of happiness
But of everlasting, and the wearing away of the hills,
The music of the stillness of stones,
Of stones under frost, and stones under rain, and stones in the sun,
The music of the seabed drinking at the stones of the hills.
The music of the floating weight of the earth.
And the bears in their forest holes
Heard the music of bears in their forest holes,
The music of bones in the starlight,
The music of many a valley trodden by bears,
The music of bears listening on the earth for bears.
And the deer on the high hills heard the crying of wolves,
And the salmon in the deep pools heard the whisper of the snows,
And the traveler on the road
Heard the music of love coming and love going
And love lost forever,
The music of birth and of death.
The music of the earth, swaddled in heaven, kissed by its cloud
and watched by its ray.
And the ears that heard it were also of leaf and of stone.
The faces that listened were flesh of cliff and of river.
The hands that played it were fingers of snakes and a tangle of flowers.

## Getting at Meaning

1. Why does the narrator describe Orpheus as a magician? What magic powers does he have?

2. Reread Orpheus's speech, "The world is a gift. . . ." (pp. 517–518) What does this speech reveal about his character at this point in the play?

3. How does Orpheus respond to the death of Eurydice? How is the response reflected in his music?

4. What metaphor does the narrator use to describe Pluto's face? Persephone's face?

5. Jazz musicians use the expression "paying your dues" to describe the suffering that a musician must experience before making good music. What "dues" does Orpheus pay?

6. Why has the experience in the underworld changed Orpheus's music? What is the difference between dancing music and listening music?

## Developing Skills in Reading Literature

1. **Dialogue.** Much of the dialogue in this play is written in poetry. What does the poetry add to the play? Select a speech written in prose and one written in poetry; compare and contrast these speeches. Which appeals more to the senses? Which seems more matter of fact and down to earth?

2. **Stage Directions.** What does music add to this play? How does the music reflect Orpheus's character and moods?

3. **Narrator.** What purpose does the narrator serve in this play? What would be lost if the narrator's role were eliminated? Why do most plays not have narrators?

4. **Myth.** A myth is a traditional story that attempts to explain why the world is the way it is. This play is based on two myths, the myth of Orpheus and the myth of Pluto and Persephone. Using a book of Greek myths or some other reference book, find the answers to these questions about the two myths.

a. How is this play different from the traditional myth of Orpheus? Why do you think that the playwright made these changes?

b. Pluto is the god of the underworld in Roman mythology. What is Pluto's name in Greek mythology?

c. Why does Persephone never speak when she is in the underworld with Pluto?

d. How did Pluto get Persephone for his bride?

e. What natural occurrence does the myth of Pluto and Persephone explain?

5. **Setting.** The stage directions for this play do not describe the setting. How might the playwright intend the setting to be established? What scenery do you think would be required for this play?

## Developing Vocabulary

**Using Reference Books.** The following italicized words appear in the stage directions of this play. Using a dictionary as well as other reference books, define these words. Be as specific as possible in your definitions. For example, do not simply define *pop* as a kind of music. Use a musical reference book to establish the exact nature of *pop*.

*Pop* music
His music is *erratic* and *discordant*
One note, gathering volume and *impetus*
His crazy note strengthens, *modulating* into electronic infernal accompaniments
Not *declaiming* so much as a giant whisper
*Plutonic* laughter

## Developing Writing Skills

**Using Contrast.** When do you listen to music? When you are tired? angry? happy? How does the music reflect your mood? In one paragraph, describe a mood and the type of music that you might listen to when in that mood. Show how the music reflects the mood. In a second paragraph, describe a different, contrasting mood and some related music. Again, show how the music reflects the mood.

# A Raisin in the Sun    *Lorraine Hansberry*

What happens to a dream deferred?
Does it dry up
Like a raisin in the sun?
Or fester like a sore—
And then run?
Does it stink like rotten meat?
Or crust and sugar over—
Like a syrupy sweet?

Maybe it just sags
Like a heavy load.

*Or does it explode?*

—Langston Hughes

## CHARACTERS

RUTH YOUNGER          JOSEPH ASAGAI

TRAVIS YOUNGER        GEORGE MURCHISON

WALTER LEE YOUNGER    KARL LINDNER

BENEATHA YOUNGER      BOBO

LENA YOUNGER          MOVING MEN

TIME: *Sometime between World War II and the present.*

PLACE: *Chicago's Southside.*

The YOUNGER *living room would be a comfortable and wellordered room if it were not for a number of indestructible contradictions to this state of being. Its furnishings are typical and undistinguished, and their primary feature now is that they have clearly had to accommodate the living of too many people for too many years—and they are tired. Still, we can see that at some time, a time probably no longer remembered by the family (except perhaps for* MAMA) *the furnishings of.this room were actually selected with care and love and even hope—and brought to this apartment and arranged with taste and pride.*

*That was a long time ago. Now the once loved pattern of the couch upholstery has to fight to show itself from under acres of crocheted doilies and couch covers that have themselves finally come to be more important than the upholstery. And here a table or a chair has been moved to disguise the worn places in the carpet; but the carpet has fought back by showing its weariness, with depressing uniformity, elsewhere on its surface.*

*Weariness has, in fact, won in this room. Everything has been polished, washed, sat on, used, scrubbed too often. All pretenses but living itself have long since vanished from the very atmosphere of this room.*

*Moreover, a section of this room, for it is not really a room unto itself, though the landlord's lease would make it seem so, slopes backward to provide a small kitchen area, where the family prepares the meals that are eaten in the living room proper, which must also serve as dining room. The single window that has been provided for these "two" rooms is located in this kitchen area. The sole natural light the family may enjoy in the course of a day is only that which fights its way through this little window.*

*At left, a door leads to a bedroom that is shared by* MAMA *and her daughter,* BE-NEATHA. *At right, opposite, is a second room (which in the beginning of the life of this apartment was probably a breakfast room) that serves as a bedroom for* WALTER *and his wife,* RUTH.

ACT I

Scene 1. *Friday morning.*

*It is morning dark in the living room.* TRAVIS *is asleep on the make-down bed at center. An alarm clock sounds from within the bedroom at right, and presently* RUTH *enters from that room and closes the door behind her. She crosses sleepily toward the window. As she passes her sleeping son she reaches down and shakes him a little. At the window she raises the shade and a dusky Southside morning light comes in feebly. She fills a pot with water and puts it on to boil. She calls to the boy, between yawns, in a slightly muffled voice.*

RUTH *is about thirty. We can see that she was a pretty girl, even exceptionally so, but now it is apparent that life has been little that she expected, and disappointment has already begun to hang in her face. In a few years, before thirty-five even, she will be known among her people as a "settled woman."*

*She crosses to her son and gives him a good, final, rousing shake.*

RUTH. Come on now, boy, it's seven-thirty! *(Her son sits up at last, in a stupor of sleepiness.)* I say hurry up, Travis! You ain't the only person in the world got to use a bathroom! *(The child, a sturdy, handsome little boy of ten or eleven, drags himself out of the bed and almost blindly takes his towels and "today's clothes" from drawers and a closet and goes out to the bathroom, which is in an outside hall and which is shared by another family or families on the same floor.* RUTH *crosses to the bedroom door at right and opens it and calls in to her husband.)* Walter Lee! . . . It's after seven-thirty! Lemme see you do some waking up in there now! *(She waits.)* You better get up from there, man! It's after seven-thirty I tell you. *(She waits again.)* All right, you just go ahead and lay there and next thing you know Travis be finished and Mr. Johnson'll be in there and you'll be fussing and cussing round here like a mad man! And be late too! *(She waits, at the end of patience.)* Walter Lee —it's time for you to get up!

*(She waits another second and then starts to go into the bedroom, but is apparently satisfied that her husband has begun to get up. She stops, pulls the door to, and returns to the kitchen area. She wipes her face with a moist cloth and runs her fingers through her sleep-disheveled hair in a vain effort and ties*

*an apron around her housecoat. The bedroom door at right opens and her husband stands in the doorway in his pajamas, which are rumpled and mismated. He is a lean, intense young man in his middle thirties, inclined to quick nervous movements and erratic speech habits—and always in his voice there is a quality of indictment.)*

WALTER. Is he out yet?

RUTH. What you mean *out*? He ain't hardly got in there good yet.

WALTER *(Wandering in, still more oriented to sleep than to a new day).* Well, what was you doing all that yelling for if I can't even get in there yet? *(Stopping and thinking.)* Check coming today?

RUTH. They *said* Saturday and this is just Friday and I hopes to God you ain't going to get up here first thing this morning and start talking to me 'bout no money— 'cause I 'bout don't want to hear it.

WALTER. Something the matter with you this morning?

RUTH. No—I'm just sleepy as the devil. What kind of eggs you want?

WALTER. Not scrambled. *(RUTH starts to scramble eggs.)* Paper come? *(RUTH points impatiently to the rolled up Tribune on the table, and he gets it and spreads it out and vaguely reads the front page.)* Set off another bomb yesterday.

RUTH *(Maximum indifference).* Did they?

WALTER *(Looking up).* What's the matter with you?

RUTH. Ain't nothing the matter with me. And don't keep asking me that this morning.

WALTER. Ain't nobody bothering you. *(Reading the news of the day absently again.)* Say Colonel McCormick[1] is sick.

RUTH *(Affecting tea-party interest).* Is he now? Poor thing.

WALTER *(Sighing and looking at his watch).* Oh, me. *(He waits.)* Now what is that boy doing in that bathroom all this time? He just going to have to start getting up earlier. I can't be being late to work on account of him fooling around in there.

RUTH *(Turning on him).* Oh, no, he ain't going to be getting up no earlier no such thing! It ain't his fault that he can't get to bed no earlier nights 'cause he got a bunch of crazy good-for-nothing clowns sitting up running their mouths in what is supposed to be his bedroom after ten o'clock at night . . .

WALTER. That's what you mad about, ain't it? The things I want to talk about with my friends just couldn't be important in your mind, could they?

*(He rises and finds a cigarette in her handbag on the table and crosses to the little window and looks out, smoking and deeply enjoying this first one.)*

RUTH *(Almost matter of factly, a complaint too automatic to deserve emphasis).* Why you always got to smoke before you eat in the morning?

WALTER *(At the window).* Just look at 'em down there . . . Running and racing to work . . . *(He turns and faces his wife and watches her a moment at the stove, and then, suddenly.)* You look young this morning, baby.

RUTH *(Indifferently).* Yeah?

WALTER. Just for a second—stirring them eggs. It's gone now—just for a second it was—you looked real young again. *(Then, drily.)* It's gone now—you look like yourself again.

RUTH. Man, if you don't shut up and leave me alone.

WALTER *(Looking out to the street again).* First thing a man ought to learn in life is not to make love to no black woman first

---

1. **Colonel McCormick:** publisher of the *Chicago Tribune* newspaper.

thing in the morning. You all some evil people at eight o'clock in the morning.

(TRAVIS *appears in the hall doorway, almost fully dressed and quite wide awake now, his towels and pajamas across his shoulders. He opens the door and signals for his father to make the bathroom in a hurry.*)

TRAVIS (*Watching the bathroom*). Daddy, come on!

(WALTER *gets his bathroom utensils and flies out to the bathroom.*)

RUTH. Sit down and have your breakfast, Travis.

TRAVIS. Mama, this is Friday. (*Gleefully.*) Check coming tomorrow, huh?

RUTH. You get your mind off money and eat your breakfast.

TRAVIS (*Eating*). This is the morning we supposed to bring the fifty cents to school.

RUTH. Well, I ain't got no fifty cents this morning.

TRAVIS. Teacher say we have to.

RUTH. I don't care what teacher say. I ain't got it. Eat your breakfast, Travis.

TRAVIS. I *am* eating.

RUTH. Hush up now and just eat!

(*The boy gives her an exasperated look for her lack of understanding, and eats grudgingly.*)

TRAVIS. You think Grandmama would have it?

RUTH. No! And I want you to stop asking your grandmother for money, you hear me?

TRAVIS (*Outraged*). Gaaaleee! I don't ask her, she just gimme it sometimes!

RUTH. Travis Willard Younger—I got too much on me this morning to be—

TRAVIS. Maybe Daddy—

RUTH. *Travis!*

(*The boy hushes abruptly. They are both quiet and tense for several seconds.*)

TRAVIS (*Presently*). Could I maybe go carry some groceries in front of the supermarket for a little while after school then?

RUTH. Just hush, I said. (*Travis jabs his spoon into his cereal bowl viciously, and rests his head in anger upon his fists.*) If you through eating, you can get over there and make up your bed.

(*The boy obeys stiffly and crosses the room, almost mechanically, to the bed and more or less carefully folds the covering. He carries the bedding into his mother's room and returns with his books and cap.*)

TRAVIS (*Sulking and standing apart from her unnaturally*). I'm gone.

RUTH (*Looking up from the stove to inspect him automatically*). Come here. (*He crosses to her and she studies his head.*) If you don't take this comb and fix this here head, you better! (TRAVIS *puts down his books with a great sigh of oppression, and crosses to the mirror. His mother mutters under her breath about his "slubbornness."*) 'Bout to march out of here with that head looking just like chickens slept in it! I just don't know where you get your slubborn ways . . . And get your jacket, too. Looks chilly out this morning.

TRAVIS (*With conspicuously brushed hair and jacket*). I'm gone.

RUTH. Get carfare and milk money—(*Waving one finger*)—and not a single penny for no caps, you hear me?

TRAVIS (*With sullen politeness*). Yes'm.

(*He turns in outrage to leave. His mother watches after him as in his frustration he approaches the door almost comically. When she speaks to him, her voice has become a very gentle tease.*)

RUTH (*Mocking; as she thinks he would say it*). Oh, Mama makes me so mad sometimes, I don't know what to do! (*She waits and continues to his back as he stands stock-still in front of the door.*) I wouldn't kiss that woman goodbye for nothing in this world this morning! (*The boy finally turns around and rolls his eyes at her, knowing the mood has changed and he is vindicated; he does not, however, move toward her yet.*) Not for nothing in this world! (*She finally laughs aloud at him and holds out her arms to him, and we see that it is a way between them, very old and practiced. He crosses to her and allows her to embrace him warmly but keeps his face fixed with masculine rigidity. She holds him back from her presently and looks at him and runs her fingers over the features of his face. With utter gentleness—*) Now—whose little old angry man are you?

TRAVIS (*The masculinity and gruffness start to fade at last*). Aw gaalee—Mama . . .

RUTH (*Mimicking*). Aw—gaaaaalleeeee, Mama! (*She pushes him, with rough playfulness and finality, toward the door.*) Get on out of here or you going to be late.

TRAVIS (*In the face of love, new aggressiveness*). Mama, could I *please* go carry groceries?

RUTH. Honey, it's starting to get so cold evenings.

WALTER (*Coming in from the bathroom and drawing a make-believe gun from a make-believe holster and shooting at his son*). What is it he wants to do?

RUTH. Go carry groceries after school at the supermarket.

WALTER. Well, let him go . . .

TRAVIS (*Quickly, to the ally*). I have to—she won't gimme the fifty cents . . .

WALTER (*To his wife only*). Why not?

RUTH (*Simply, and with flavor*). 'Cause we don't have it.

WALTER (*To* RUTH *only*). What you tell the boy things like that for? (*Reaching down into his pants with a rather important gesture.*) Here, son—

(*He hands the boy the coin, but his eyes are directed to his wife's.* TRAVIS *takes the money happily.*)

TRAVIS. Thanks, Daddy.

(*He starts out.* RUTH *watches both of them with murder in her eyes.* WALTER *stands and stares back at her with defiance, and suddenly reaches into his pocket again on an afterthought.*)

WALTER (*Without even looking at his son, still staring hard at his wife*). In fact, here's another fifty cents . . . Buy yourself some fruit today—or take a taxicab to school or something!

TRAVIS. Whoopee—

(*He leaps up and clasps his father around the middle with his legs, and they face each other in mutual appreciation; slowly* WALTER LEE *peeks around the boy to catch the violent rays from his wife's eyes and draws his head back as if shot.*)

WALTER. You better get down now—and get to school, man.

TRAVIS (*At the door*). OK. Goodbye.

(*He exits.*)

WALTER (*After him, pointing with pride*). That's my boy. (*She looks at him in disgust and turns back to her work.*) You know what I was thinking 'bout in the bathroom this morning?

RUTH. No.

WALTER. How come you always try to be so pleasant!

RUTH. What is there to be pleasant 'bout!

WALTER. You want to know what I was thinking 'bout in the bathroom or not!

RUTH. I know what you thinking 'bout.

WALTER (*Ignoring her*). 'Bout what me and Willy Harris was talking about last night.

RUTH (*Immediately—a refrain*). Willy Harris is a good-for-nothing loud mouth.

WALTER. Anybody who talks to me has got to be a good-for-nothing loud mouth, ain't he? And what you know about who is just a good-for-nothing loud mouth? Charlie Atkins was just a "good-for-nothing loud mouth" too, wasn't he! When he wanted me to go in the dry-cleaning business with him. And now—he's grossing a hundred thousand a year. A hundred thousand dollars a year! You still call *him* a loud mouth!

RUTH (*Bitterly*). Oh, Walter Lee . . .

(*She folds her head on her arms over the table.*)

WALTER (*Rising and coming to her and standing over her*). You tired, ain't you? Tired of everything. Me, the boy, the way we live—this beat-up hole—everything. Ain't you? (*She doesn't look up, doesn't answer.*) So tired—moaning and groaning all the time, but you wouldn't do nothing to help, would you? You couldn't be on my side that long for nothing, could you?

RUTH. Walter, please leave me alone.

WALTER. A man needs for a woman to back him up . . .

RUTH. Walter—

WALTER. Mama would listen to you. You know she listen to you more than she do me and Bennie. She think more of you. All you have to do is just sit down with her when you drinking your coffee one morning and talking 'bout things like you do and—(*He sits down beside her and demonstrates graphically what he thinks her methods and tone should be.*)—you just sip your coffee, see, and say easy like that you been thinking 'bout that deal Walter Lee is so interested in, 'bout the store and all, and sip some more coffee, like what you saying ain't really that important to you— And the next thing you know, she be listening good and asking you questions and when I come home—I can tell her the details. This ain't no fly-by-night proposition, baby. I mean we figured it out, me and Willy and Bobo.

RUTH (*With a frown*). Bobo?

WALTER. Yeah. You see, this little liquor store we got in mind cost seventy-five thousand, and we figured the initial investment on the place be 'bout thirty thousand, see. That be ten thousand each. Course, there's a couple of hundred you got to pay so's you don't spend your life just waiting for them clowns to let your license get approved—

RUTH. You mean graft?

WALTER (*Frowning impatiently*). Don't call it that. See there, that just goes to show you what women understand about the world. Baby, don't *nothing* happen for you in this world 'less you pay *somebody* off!

RUTH. Walter, leave me alone! (*She raises her head and stares at him vigorously—then says, more quietly.*) Eat your eggs, they gonna be cold.

WALTER (*Straightening up from her and looking off*). That's it. There you are. Man say to his woman: I got me a dream. His woman say: Eat your eggs. (*Sadly, but gaining in power.*) Man say: I got to take hold of this here world, baby! And a woman will say: Eat your eggs and go to work. (*Passionately now.*) Man say: I got to change my life, I'm choking to death, baby! And his woman say—(*In utter anguish as he brings his fists down on his thighs*)—Your eggs is getting cold!

RUTH (*Softly*). Walter, that ain't none of our money.

WALTER (*Not listening at all or even looking at her*). This morning, I was lookin' in the mirror and thinking about it . . . I'm thirty-five years old; I been married eleven years and I got a boy who sleeps in the living room—(*Very, very quietly*)—and all I got to give him is stories about how rich white people live . . .

RUTH. Eat your eggs, Walter.

WALTER. *Forget my eggs . . . forget all the eggs that ever was!*

RUTH. Then go to work.

WALTER (*Looking up at her*). See—I'm trying to talk to you 'bout myself—(*Shaking his head with the repetition*)—and all you can say is eat them eggs and go to work.

RUTH (*Wearily*). Honey, you never say nothing new. I listen to you every day, every night and every morning, and you never say nothing new. (*Shrugging.*) So you would rather *be* Mr. Arnold than be his chauffeur. So—I would *rather* be living in Buckingham Palace.

WALTER. That is just what is wrong with the black woman in this world . . . Don't understand about building their men up and making 'em feel like they somebody. Like they can do something.

RUTH (*Drily, but to hurt*). There *are* black men who do things.

WALTER. No thanks to the black woman.

RUTH. Well, being a black woman, I guess I can't help myself none.

(*She rises and gets the ironing board and sets it up and attacks a huge pile of rough-dried clothes, sprinkling them in preparation for the ironing and then rolling them into tight fat balls.*)

WALTER (*Mumbling*). We one group of men tied to a race of women with small minds.

(*His sister* BENEATHA *enters. She is about twenty, as slim and intense as her brother. She is not as pretty as her sister-in-law, but her lean, almost intellectual face has a handsomeness of its own. She wears a bright-red flannel nightie, and her thick hair stands wildly about her head. Her speech is a mixture of many things; it is different from the rest of the family's insofar as education has permeated her sense of English—and perhaps the Midwest rather than the South has finally —at last—won out in her inflection; but not altogether, because over all of it is a soft slurring and transformed use of vowels that is the decided influence of the Southside. She passes through the room without looking at either* RUTH *or* WALTER *and goes to the outside door and looks, a little blindly, out to the bathroom. She sees that it has been lost to the Johnsons. She closes the door with a sleepy vengeance and crosses to the table and sits down a little defeated.*)

BENEATHA. I am going to start timing those people.

WALTER. You should get up earlier.

BENEATHA (*Her face in her hands. She is still fighting the urge to go back to bed*). Really —would you suggest dawn? Where's the paper?

WALTER (*Pushing the paper across the table to her as he studies her almost clinically, as though he has never seen her before*). You a horrible-looking chick at this hour.

BENEATHA (*Drily*). Good morning, everybody.

WALTER (*Senselessly*). How is school coming?

BENEATHA (*In the same spirit*). Lovely. Lovely. And you know, biology is the greatest. (*Looking up at him.*) I dissected something that looked just like you yesterday.

WALTER. I just wondered if you've made up your mind and everything.

BENEATHA (*Gaining in sharpness and impatience*). And what did I answer yesterday morning—and the day before that?

RUTH (*From the ironing board, like someone disinterested and old*). Don't be so nasty, Bennie.

BENEATHA (*Still to her brother*). And the day before that and the day before that!

WALTER (*Defensively*). I'm interested in you. Something wrong with that? Ain't many girls who decide—

WALTER *and* BENEATHA *(In unison).* —"to be a doctor." *(Silence.)*

WALTER. Have we figured out yet just exactly how much medical school is going to cost?

RUTH. Walter Lee, why don't you leave that girl alone and get out of here to work?

BENEATHA *(Exits to the bathroom and bangs on the door).* Come on out of there, please!

*(She comes back into the room.)*

WALTER *(Looking at his sister intently).* You know the check is coming tomorrow.

BENEATHA *(Turning on him with a sharpness all her own).* That money belongs to Mama, Walter, and it's for her to decide how she wants to use it. I don't care if she wants to buy a house or a rocket ship or just nail it up somewhere and look at it. It's hers. Not ours—*hers.*

WALTER *(Bitterly).* Now ain't that fine! You just got your mother's interest at heart, ain't you, girl? You such a nice girl—but if Mama got that money she can always take a few thousand and help you through school too—can't she?

BENEATHA. I have never asked anyone around here to do anything for me!

WALTER. No! And the line between asking and just accepting when the time comes is big and wide—ain't it!

BENEATHA *(With fury).* What do you want from me, Brother—that I quit school or just drop dead, which!

WALTER. I don't want nothing but for you to stop acting holy 'round here. Me and Ruth done made some sacrifices for you—why can't you do something for the family?

RUTH. Walter, don't be dragging me in it.

WALTER. You are in it—Don't you get up and go to work in somebody's kitchen for the last three years to help put clothes on her back?

RUTH. Oh, Walter—that's not fair . . .

WALTER. It ain't that nobody expects you to get on your knees and say thank you, Brother; thank you, Ruth; thank you, Mama—and thank you, Travis, for wearing the same pair of shoes for two semesters—

BENEATHA *(Dropping to her knees).* Well—I do—all right?—thank everybody . . . and forgive me for ever wanting to be anything at all . . . forgive me, forgive me!

RUTH. Please stop it! Your mama'll hear you.

WALTER. Who told you you had to be a doctor? If you so crazy 'bout messing 'round with sick people—then go be a nurse like other women—or just get married and be quiet . . .

BENEATHA. Well—you finally got it said . . . It took you three years but you finally got it said. Walter, give up; leave me alone—it's Mama's money.

WALTER. *He was my father, too!*

BENEATHA. So what? He was mine, too—and Travis' grandfather—but the insurance money belongs to Mama. Picking on me is not going to make her give it to you to invest in any liquor stores—*(Underbreath, dropping into a chair)*—and I for one say, God bless Mama for that!

WALTER *(To* RUTH*).* See—did you hear? Did you hear!

RUTH. Honey, please go to work.

WALTER. Nobody in this house is ever going to understand me.

BENEATHA. Because you're a nut.

WALTER. Who's a nut?

BENEATHA. You—you are a nut. Thee is mad, boy.

WALTER *(Looking at his wife and his sister from the door, very sadly).* The world's most backward race of people, and that's a fact.

BENEATHA *(Turning slowly in her chair).* And then there are all those prophets who would lead us out of the wilderness—*(WALTER slams out of the house)*—into the swamps!

RUTH. Bennie, why you always gotta be pickin' on your brother? Can't you be a little sweeter sometimes? (*Door opens.* WALTER *walks in.*)

WALTER (*To Ruth*). I need some money for carfare.

RUTH (*Looks at him, then warms; teasing, but tenderly*). Fifty cents? (*She goes to her bag and gets money.*) Here, take a taxi.

(WALTER *exits.* MAMA *enters. She is a woman in her early sixties, full-bodied and strong. She is one of those women of a certain grace and beauty who wear it so unobtrusively that it takes a while to notice. Her dark-brown face is surrounded by the total whiteness of her hair, and, being a woman who has adjusted to many things in life and overcome many more, her face is full of strength. She has, we can see, wit and faith of a kind that keep her eyes lit and full of interest and expectancy. She is, in a word, a beautiful woman. Her bearing is perhaps most like the noble bearing of the women of the Hereros of Southwest Africa—rather as if she imagines that as she walks she still bears a basket or a vessel upon her head. Her speech, on the other hand, is as careless as her carriage is precise—she is inclined to slur everything— but her voice is perhaps not so much quiet as simply soft.*)

MAMA. Who that 'round here slamming doors at this hour?

(*She crosses through the room, goes to the window, opens it, and brings in a feeble little plant growing doggedly in a small pot on the window sill. She feels the dirt and puts it back out.*)

RUTH. That was Walter Lee. He and Bennie was at it again.

MAMA. My children and they tempers. Lord, if this little old plant don't get more sun than it's been getting it ain't never going to see spring again. (*She turns from the window.*) What's the matter with you this morning, Ruth? You looks right peaked. You aiming to iron all them things? Leave some for me. I'll get to 'em this afternoon. Bennie honey, it's too drafty for you to be sitting 'round half dressed. Where's your robe?

BENEATHA. In the cleaners.

MAMA. Well, go get mine and put it on.

BENEATHA. I'm not cold, Mama, honest.

MAMA. I know—but you so thin . . .

BENEATHA (*Irritably*). Mama, I'm not cold.

MAMA (*Seeing the make-down bed as* TRAVIS *has left it*). Lord have mercy, look at that poor bed. Bless his heart—he tries, don't he?

(*She moves to the bed* TRAVIS *has sloppily made up.*)

RUTH. No—he don't half try at all 'cause he knows you going to come along behind him and fix everything. That's just how come he don't know how to do nothing right now—you done spoiled that boy so.

MAMA. Well—he's a little boy. Ain't supposed to know 'bout housekeeping. My baby, that's what he is. What you fix for his breakfast this morning?

RUTH (*Angrily*). I feed my son, Lena!

MAMA. I ain't meddling—(*Underbreath; busy-bodyish.*) I just noticed all last week he had cold cereal, and when it starts getting this chilly in the fall a child ought to have some hot grits or something when he goes out in the cold—

RUTH (*Furious*). I gave him hot oats—is that all right!

MAMA. I ain't meddling. (*Pause.*) Put a lot of nice butter on it? (RUTH *shoots her an angry look and does not reply.*) He likes lots of butter.

RUTH (*Exasperated*). Lena—

MAMA (*To* BENEATHA. MAMA *is inclined to wander conversationally sometimes.*)

What was you and your brother fussing 'bout this morning?

BENEATHA. It's not important, Mama.

*(She gets up and goes to look out at the bathroom, which is apparently free, and she picks up her towels and rushes out.)*

MAMA. What was they fighting about?

RUTH. Now you know as well as I do.

MAMA *(Shaking her head)*. Brother still worrying hisself sick about that money?

RUTH. You know he is.

MAMA. You had breakfast?

RUTH. Some coffee.

MAMA. Girl, you better start eating and looking after yourself better. You almost thin as Travis.

RUTH. Lena—

MAMA. Un-hunh?

RUTH. What are you going to do with it?

MAMA. Now don't you start, child. It's too early in the morning to be talking about money. It ain't Christian.

RUTH. It's just that he got his heart set on that store—

MAMA. You mean that liquor store that Willy Harris want him to invest in?

RUTH. Yes—

MAMA. We ain't no business people, Ruth. We just plain working folks.

RUTH. Ain't nobody business people till they go into business. Walter Lee say black people ain't never going to start getting ahead till they start gambling on some different kinds of things in the world—investments and things.

MAMA. What done got into you, girl? Walter Lee done finally sold you on investing.

RUTH. No. Mama, something is happening between Walter and me. I don't know what it is—but he needs something— something I can't give him any more. He needs this chance, Lena.

MAMA *(Frowning deeply)*. But liquor, honey—

RUTH. Well—like Walter say—I spec people going to always be drinking themselves some liquor.

MAMA. Well—whether they drinks it or not ain't none of my business. But whether I go into business selling it to 'em *is*, and I don't want that on my ledger this late in life. *(Stopping suddenly and studying her daughter-in-law.)* Ruth Younger, what's the matter with you today? You look like you could fall over right there.

RUTH. I'm tired.

MAMA. Then you better stay home from work today.

RUTH. I can't stay home. She'd be calling up the agency and screaming at them, "My girl didn't come in today—send me somebody! My girl didn't come in!" Oh, she just have a fit . . .

MAMA. Well, let her have it. I'll just call her up and say you got the flu—

RUTH *(Laughing)*. Why the flu?

MAMA. 'Cause it sounds respectable to 'em. Something white people get, too. They know 'bout the flu. Otherwise they think you been cut up or something when you tell 'em you sick.

RUTH. I got to go in. We need the money.

MAMA. Somebody would of thought my children done all but starved to death the way they talk about money here late. Child, we got a great big old check coming tomorrow.

RUTH *(Sincerely, but also self-righteously)*. Now that's your money. It ain't got nothing to do with me. We all feel like that— Walter and Bennie and me—even Travis.

MAMA *(Thoughtfully, and suddenly very far away)*. Ten thousand dollars—

RUTH. Sure is wonderful.

MAMA. Ten thousand dollars.

RUTH. You know what you should do, Miss

Lena? You should take yourself a trip somewhere. To Europe or South America or someplace—

MAMA (*Throwing up her hands at the thought*). Oh, child!

RUTH. I'm serious. Just pack up and leave! Go on away and enjoy yourself some. Forget about the family and have yourself a ball for once in your life—

MAMA (*Drily*). You sound like I'm just about ready to die. Who'd go with me? What I look like wandering 'round Europe by myself?

RUTH. Shoot—these here rich white women do it all the time. They don't think nothing of packing up they suitcases and piling on one of them big steamships and—swoosh!—they gone, child.

MAMA. Something always told me I wasn't no rich white woman.

RUTH. Well—what are you going to do with it then?

MAMA. I ain't rightly decided. (*Thinking. She speaks now with emphasis.*) Some of it got to be put away for Beneatha and her schoolin'—and ain't nothing going to touch that part of it. Nothing. (*She waits several seconds, trying to make up her mind about something, and looks at* RUTH *a little tentatively before going on.*) Been thinking that we maybe could meet the notes on a little old two-story somewhere, with a yard where Travis could play in the summertime, if we use part of the insurance for a down payment and everybody kind of pitch in. I could maybe take on a little day work again, few days a week—

RUTH *(Studying her mother-in-law furtively and concentrating on her ironing, anxious to encourage without seeming to).* Well, Lord knows, we've put enough rent into this here rat trap to pay for four houses by now . . .

MAMA *(Looking up at the words "rat trap" and then looking around and leaning back and sighing—in a suddenly reflective mood—).* "Rat trap"—yes, that's all it is. *(Smiling.)* I remember just as well the day me and Big Walter moved in here. Hadn't been married but two weeks and wasn't planning on living here no more than a year. *(She shakes her head at the dissolved dream.)* We was going to set away, little by little, don't you know, and buy a little place out in Morgan Park.[2] We had even picked out the house. *(Chuckling a little.)* Looks right dumpy today. But Lord, child, you should know all the dreams I had 'bout buying that house and fixing it up and making me a little garden in the back —*(She waits and stops smiling.)* And didn't none of it happen.

*(Dropping her hands in a futile gesture.)*

RUTH *(Keeps her head down, ironing).* Yes, life can be a barrel of disappointments, sometimes.

MAMA. Honey, Big Walter would come in here some nights back then and slump down on that couch there and just look at the rug, and look at me and look at the rug and then back at me—and I'd know he was down then . . . really down. *(After a second very long and thoughtful pause; she is seeing back to times that only she can see.)* And then, Lord, when I lost that baby—little Claude—I almost thought I was going to lose Big Walter too. Oh, that man grieved hisself! He was one man to love his children.

RUTH. Ain't nothin' can tear at you like losin' your baby.

MAMA. I guess that's how come that man finally worked hisself to death like he done. Like he was fighting his own war with this here world that took his baby from him.

RUTH. He sure was a fine man, all right. I always liked Mr. Younger.

MAMA. Crazy 'bout his children! God knows there was plenty wrong with Walter Younger—hard-headed, mean, kind of wild with women—plenty wrong with him. But he sure loved his children. Always wanted them to have something— be something. That's where Brother gets all these notions, I reckon. Big Walter used to say, he'd get right wet in the eyes sometimes, lean his head back with the water standing in his eyes and say, "Seem like God didn't see fit to give the black man nothing but dreams—but He did give us children to make them dreams seem worth while." *(She smiles.)* He could talk like that, don't you know.

RUTH. Yes, he sure could. He was a good man, Mr. Younger.

MAMA. Yes, a fine man—just couldn't never catch up with his dreams, that's all.

*(BENEATHA comes in, brushing her hair and looking up to the ceiling, where the sound of a vacuum cleaner has started up.)*

BENEATHA. What could be so dirty on that woman's rugs that she has to vacuum them every single day?

RUTH. I wish certain young women 'round here who I could name would take inspiration about certain rugs in a certain apartment I could also mention.

---

2. **Morgan Park:** an area on the south side of Chicago.

BENEATHA (Shrugging). How much cleaning can a house need?

MAMA. Bennie!

RUTH. Just listen to her—just listen!

BENEATHA. Oh, God!

MAMA. If you use the Lord's name just one more time—

BENEATHA (A bit of a whine). Oh, Mama—

RUTH. Fresh—just fresh as salt, this girl!

BENEATHA (Drily). Well—if the salt loses its savor—

MAMA. Now that will do. I just ain't going to have you 'round here reciting the scriptures in vain—you hear me?

BENEATHA. How did I manage to get on everybody's wrong side by just walking into a room?

RUTH. If you weren't so fresh—

BENEATHA. Ruth, I'm twenty years old.

MAMA. What time you be home from school today?

BENEATHA. Kind of late. (With enthusiasm.) Madeline is going to start my guitar lessons today.

(MAMA and RUTH look up with the same expression.)

MAMA. Your what kind of lessons?

BENEATHA. Guitar.

RUTH. Oh, Father!

MAMA. How come you done taken it in your mind to learn to play the guitar?

BENEATHA. I just want to, that's all.

MAMA (Smiling). Lord, child, don't you know what to do with yourself? How long it going to be before you get tired of this now—like you got tired of that little play-acting group you joined last year? (Looking at Ruth.) And what was it the year before that?

RUTH. The horseback-riding club for which she bought that fifty-five-dollar riding habit that's been hanging in the closet ever since!

MAMA (To BENEATHA). Why you got to flit so from one thing to another, baby?

BENEATHA (Sharply). I just want to learn to play the guitar. Is there anything wrong with that?

MAMA. Ain't nobody trying to stop you. I just wonders sometimes why you has to flit so from one thing to another all the time. You ain't never done nothing with all that camera equipment you brought home—

BENEATHA. I don't flit! I—I experiment with different forms of expression—

RUTH. Like riding a horse?

BENEATHA. —People have to express themselves one way or another.

MAMA. What is it you want to express?

BENEATHA (Angrily). Me! (MAMA and RUTH look at each other and burst into raucous laughter.) Don't worry—I don't expect you to understand.

MAMA (To change the subject). Who you going out with tomorrow night?

BENEATHA (With displeasure). George Murchison again.

MAMA (Pleased). Oh—you getting a little sweet on him?

RUTH. You ask me, this child ain't sweet on nobody but herself—(Underbreath.) Express herself!

(They laugh.)

BENEATHA. Oh—I like George all right, Mama. I mean I like him enough to go out with him and stuff, but—

RUTH (For devilment). What does and stuff mean?

BENEATHA. Mind your own business.

MAMA. Stop picking at her now, Ruth. (A thoughtful pause, and then a suspicious sudden look at her daughter as she turns in her chair for emphasis). What does it mean?

BENEATHA (Wearily). Oh, I just mean I couldn't ever really be serious about George. He's—he's so shallow.

RUTH. Shallow—what do you mean he's shallow? He's *Rich!*

MAMA. Hush, Ruth.

BENEATHA. I know he's rich. He knows he's rich, too.

RUTH. Well—what other qualities a man got to have to satisfy you, little girl?

BENEATHA. You wouldn't even begin to understand. Anybody who married Walter could not possibly understand.

MAMA (Outraged). What kind of way is that to talk about your brother?

BENEATHA. Brother is a flip—let's face it.

MAMA (To RUTH, helplessly). What's a flip?

RUTH (Glad to add kindling). She's saying he's crazy.

BENEATHA. Not crazy. Brother isn't really crazy yet—he—he's an elaborate neurotic.

MAMA. Hush your mouth!

BENEATHA. As for George. Well. George looks good—he's got a beautiful car and he takes me to nice places and, as my sister-in-law says, he is probably the richest boy I will ever get to know and I even like him sometimes—but if the Youngers are sitting around waiting to see if their little Bennie is going to tie up the family with the Murchisons, they are wasting their time.

RUTH. You mean you wouldn't marry George Murchison if he asked you someday? That pretty, rich thing? Honey, I knew you was odd—

BENEATHA. No I would not marry him if all I felt for him was what I feel now. Besides, George's family wouldn't really like it.

MAMA. Why not?

BENEATHA. Oh, Mama—The Murchisons are honest-to-God-real-*live*-rich black people, and the only people in the world who are more snobbish than rich white people are rich black people. I thought everybody knew that. I've met Mrs. Murchison. She's a scene!

MAMA. You must not dislike people 'cause they well off, honey.

BENEATHA. Why not? It makes just as much sense as disliking people 'cause they are poor, and lots of people do that.

RUTH (A wisdom-of-the-ages manner. To MAMA). Well, she'll get over some of this—

BENEATHA. Get over it? What are you talking about, Ruth? Listen, I'm going to be a doctor. I'm not worried about who I'm going to marry yet—if I ever get married.

MAMA and RUTH. If!

MAMA. Now, Bennie—

BENEATHA. Oh, I probably will . . . but first I'm going to be a doctor, and George, for one, still thinks that's pretty funny. I couldn't be bothered with that. I am going to be a doctor and everybody around here better understand that!

MAMA (Kindly). 'Course you going to be a doctor, honey, God willing.

BENEATHA (Drily). God hasn't got a thing to do with it.

MAMA. Beneatha—that just wasn't necessary.

BENEATHA. Well—neither is God. I get sick of hearing about God.

MAMA. Beneatha!

BENEATHA. I mean it! I'm just tired of hearing about God all the time. What has He got to do with anything? Does he pay tuition?

MAMA. You 'bout to get your fresh little jaw slapped!

RUTH. That's just what she needs, all right!

BENEATHA. Why? Why can't I say what I want to around here, like everybody else?

MAMA. It don't sound nice for a young girl to say things like that—you wasn't brought up that way. Me and your father went to trouble to get you and Brother to church every Sunday.

BENEATHA. Mama, you don't understand. It's all a matter of ideas, and God is just one idea I don't accept. It's not important. I am not going out and be immoral or commit crimes because I don't believe in God. I don't even think about it. It's just that I get tired of Him getting credit for all the things the human race achieves through its own stubborn effort. There simply is no God—there is only man and it is he who makes miracles!

(MAMA *absorbs this speech, studies her daughter and rises slowly and crosses to* BENEATHA *and slaps her powerfully across the face. After, there is only silence and the daughter drops her eyes from her mother's face, and* MAMA *is very tall before her.*)

MAMA. Now—you say after me, in my mother's house there is still God. (*There is a long pause and* BENEATHA *stares at the floor wordlessly.* MAMA *repeats the phrase with precision and cool emotion.*) In my mother's house there is still God.

BENEATHA. In my mother's house there is still God.

(*A long pause.*)

MAMA (*Walking away from* BENEATHA, *too disturbed for triumphant posture. Stopping and turning back to her daughter*). There are some ideas we ain't going to have in this house. Not long as I am at the head of this family.

BENEATHA. Yes, ma'am.

(MAMA *walks out of the room.*)

RUTH (*Almost gently, with profound understanding*). You think you a woman, Bennie—but you still a little girl. What you did was childish—so you got treated like a child.

BENEATHA. I see. (*Quietly.*) I also see that everybody thinks it's all right for Mama to be a tyrant. But all the tyranny in the world will never put a God in the heavens!

(*She picks up her books and goes out.*)

RUTH (*Goes to* MAMA's *door*). She said she was sorry.

MAMA (*Coming out, going to her plant*). They frightens me, Ruth. My children.

RUTH. You got good children, Lena. They just a little off sometimes—but they're good.

MAMA. No—there's something come down between me and them that don't let us understand each other, and I don't know what it is. One done almost lost his mind thinking 'bout money all the time, and the other done commence to talk about things I can't seem to understand in no form or fashion. What is it that's changing, Ruth?

RUTH (*Soothingly, older than her years*). Now . . . you taking it all too seriously. You just got strong-willed children and it takes a strong woman like you to keep 'em in hand.

MAMA (*Looking at her plant and sprinkling a little water on it*). They spirited all right, my children. Got to admit they got spirit —Bennie and Walter. Like this little old plant that ain't never had enough sunshine or nothing—and look at it . . .

(*She has her back to* RUTH, *who has had to stop ironing and lean against something and put the back of her hand to her forehead.*)

RUTH (*Trying to keep* MAMA *from noticing*). You . . . sure . . . loves that little old thing, don't you? . . .

MAMA. Well, I always wanted me a garden like I used to see sometimes at the back of the houses down home. This plant is close as I ever got to having one. (*She looks out of the window as she replaces the plant.*) Lord, ain't nothing as dreary as the view from this window on a dreary day, is there? Why ain't you singing this morning, Ruth? Sing that "No Ways Tired."

That song always lifts me up so—*(She turns at last to see that* RUTH *has slipped quietly into a chair, in a state of semiconsciousness.)* Ruth! Ruth honey—what's the matter with you . . . Ruth!

## Scene 2

*It is the following morning, a Saturday morning, and house cleaning is in progress at the* YOUNGERS. *Furniture has been shoved hither and yon, and* MAMA *is giving the kitchen-area walls a washing down.* BENEATHA, *in dungarees, with a handkerchief tied around her face, is spraying insecticide into the cracks in the walls. As they work, the radio is on and a Southside disk-jockey program is inappropriately filling the house with a rather exotic saxophone blues.* TRAVIS, *the sole idle one, is leaning on his arms, looking out of the window.*

TRAVIS. Grandmama, that stuff Bennie is using smells awful. Can I go downstairs, please?

MAMA. Did you get all them chores done already? I ain't seen you doing much.

TRAVIS. Yes'm—finished early. Where did Mama go this morning?

MAMA *(Looking at* BENEATHA*)*. She had to go on a little errand.

TRAVIS. Where?

MAMA. To tend to her business.

TRAVIS. Can I go outside then?

MAMA. Oh, I guess so. You better stay right in front of the house, though . . . and keep a good lookout for the postman.

TRAVIS. Yes'm. *(He starts out and decides to give his* AUNT BENEATHA *a good swat on the legs as he passes her.)* Leave them poor little old cockroaches alone, they ain't bothering you none.

*(He runs as she swings the spray gun at him both viciously and playfully.* WALTER *enters from the bedroom and goes to the phone.)*

MAMA. Look out there, girl, before you be spilling some of that stuff on that child!

TRAVIS *(Teasing)*. That's right—look out now!

*(He exits.)*

BENEATHA *(Drily)*. I can't imagine that it would hurt him—it has never hurt the roaches.

MAMA. Well, little boys' hides ain't as tough as Southside roaches.

WALTER *(Into phone)*. Hello—Let me talk to Willy Harris.

MAMA. You better get over there behind the bureau. I seen one marching out of there like Napoleon yesterday.

WALTER. Hello, Willy? It ain't come yet. It'll be here in a few minutes. Did the lawyer give you the papers?

BENEATHA. There's really only one way to get rid of them, Mama—

MAMA. How?

BENEATHA. Set fire to this building.

WALTER. Good. Good. I'll be right over.

BENEATHA. Where did Ruth go, Walter?

WALTER. I don't know.

*(He exits abruptly.)*

BENEATHA. Mama, where did Ruth go?

MAMA *(Looking at her with meaning)*. To the doctor, I think.

BENEATHA. The doctor? What's the matter? *(They exchange glances.)* You don't think—

MAMA *(With her sense of drama).* Now I ain't saying what I think. But I ain't never been wrong 'bout a woman neither.

*(The phone rings.)*

BENEATHA *(At the phone).* Hay-lo . . . *(Pause, and a moment of recognition.)* Well—when did you get back! . . . And how was it? . . . Of course I've missed you—in my way . . . This morning? No . . . house cleaning and all that and Mama hates it if I let people come over when the house is like this . . . You *have?* Well, that's different . . . What is it— Oh, what the heck, come on over . . . Right, see you then.

*(She hangs up.)*

MAMA *(Who has listened vigorously, as is her habit).* Who is that you inviting over here with this house looking like this? You ain't got the pride you was born with!

BENEATHA. Asagai doesn't care how houses look, Mama—he's an intellectual.

MAMA. *Who?*

BENEATHA. Asagai—Joseph Asagai. He's an African boy I met on campus. He's been studying in Canada all summer.

MAMA. What's his name?

BENEATHA. Asagai, Joseph. As-sah-guy . . . He's from Nigeria.

MAMA. Oh, that's the little country that was founded by slaves way back . . .

BENEATHA. No, Mama—that's Liberia.

MAMA. I don't think I never met no African before.

BENEATHA. Well, do me a favor and don't ask him a whole lot of ignorant questions about Africans. I mean, do they wear clothes and all that—

MAMA. Well, now, I guess if you think we so ignorant 'round here maybe you shouldn't bring your friends here—

BENEATHA. It's just that people ask such crazy things. All anyone seems to know about when it comes to Africa is Tarzan—

MAMA *(Indignantly).* Why should I know anything about Africa?

BENEATHA. Why do you give money at church for the missionary work?

MAMA. Well, that's to help save people.

BENEATHA. You mean save them from heathenism—

MAMA *(Innocently).* Yes.

BENEATHA. I'm afraid they need more salvation from the British and the French.

*(RUTH comes in forlornly and pulls off her coat with dejection. They both turn to look at her.)*

RUTH *(Dispiritedly).* Well, I guess from all the happy faces—everybody knows.

BENEATHA. You pregnant?

MAMA. Lord have mercy, I sure hope it's a little old girl. Travis ought to have a sister.

*(BENEATHA and RUTH give her a hopeless look for this grandmotherly enthusiasm.)*

BENEATHA. How far along are you?

RUTH. Two months.

BENEATHA. Did you mean to? I mean did you plan it or was it an accident?

MAMA. What do you know about planning or not planning?

BENEATHA. Oh, Mama.

RUTH *(Wearily).* She's twenty years old, Lena.

BENEATHA. Did you plan it, Ruth?

RUTH. Mind your own business.

BENEATHA. It is my business—where is he going to live, on the *roof?* *(There is silence following the remark as the three women react to the sense of it.)* Gee—I didn't mean that, Ruth, honest. Gee, I don't feel like that at all. I—I think it is wonderful.

RUTH *(Dully).* Wonderful.

BENEATHA. Yes—really.

MAMA *(Looking at RUTH, worried).* Doctor say everything going to be all right?

RUTH (Far away). Yes—she says everything is going to be fine . . .

MAMA (Immediately suspicious). "She"— What doctor you went to?

(RUTH folds over, near hysteria.)

MAMA (Worriedly hovering over RUTH). Ruth honey—what's the matter with you —you sick?

(RUTH has her fists clenched on her thighs and is fighting hard to suppress a scream that seems to be rising in her.)

BENEATHA. What's the matter with her, Mama?

MAMA (Working her fingers in RUTH's shoulder to relax her). She be all right. Women gets right depressed sometimes when they get her way. (Speaking softly, expertly, rapidly.) Now you just relax. That's right . . . just lean back, don't think 'bout nothing at all . . . nothing at all—

RUTH. I'm all right . . .

(The glassy-eyed look melts and then she collapses into a fit of heavy sobbing. The bell rings.)

BENEATHA. Oh—that must be Asagai.

MAMA (To RUTH). Come on now, honey. You need to lie down and rest awhile . . . then have some nice hot food.

(They exit, RUTH's weight on her mother-in-law. BENEATHA, herself profoundly disturbed, opens the door to admit a rather dramatic-looking young man with a large package.)

ASAGAI. Hello, Alaiyo—

BENEATHA (Holding the door open and regarding him with pleasure). Hello . . . (Long pause.) Well—come in. And please excuse everything. My mother was very upset about my letting anyone come here with the place like this.

ASAGAI (Coming into the room). You look disturbed too . . . Is something wrong?

BENEATHA (Still at the door, absently). Yes . . . we've all got acute ghetto-itus. (She smiles and comes toward him, finding a cigarette and sitting.) So—sit down! How was Canada?

ASAGAI (A sophisticate). Canadian.

BENEATHA (Looking at him). I'm very glad you are back.

ASAGAI (Looking back at her in turn). Are you really?

BENEATHA. Yes—very.

ASAGAI. Why—you were quite glad when I went away. What happened?

BENEATHA. You went away.

ASAGAI. Ahhhhhhhh.

BENEATHA. Before—you wanted to be so serious before there was time.

ASAGAI. How much time must there be before one knows what one feels?

BENEATHA (Stalling this particular conversation. Her hands pressed together, in a deliberately childish gesture.) What did you bring me?

ASAGAI (Handing her the package). Open it and see.

BENEATHA (Eagerly opening the package and drawing out some records and the colorful robes of a Nigerian woman). Oh, Asagai! . . . You got them for me! . . . How beautiful . . . and the records too! (She lifts out the robes and runs to the mirror with them and holds the drapery up in front of herself.)

ASAGAI (Coming to her at the mirror). I shall have to teach you how to drape it properly. (He flings the material about her for the moment and stands back to look at her.) Ah—Oh-pay-gay-day, oh-gbah-mu-shay. (A Yoruba exclamation for admiration.) You wear it well . . . very well . . . mutilated hair and all.

BENEATHA *(Turning suddenly).* My hair—what's wrong with my hair?

ASAGAI *(Shrugging).* Were you born with it like that?

BENEATHA *(Reaching up to touch it).* No . . . of course not.

*(She looks back to the mirror, disturbed.)*

ASAGAI *(Smiling).* How then?

BENEATHA. You know perfectly well how . . . as crinkly as yours . . . that's how.

ASAGAI. And it is ugly to you that way?

BENEATHA *(Quickly).* Oh, no—not ugly . . . *(More slowly, apologetically.)* But it's so hard to manage when it's, well—raw.

ASAGAI. And so to accommodate that—you mutilate it every week?

BENEATHA. It's not mutilation!

ASAGAI *(Laughing aloud at her seriousness).* Oh . . . please! I am only teasing you because you are so very serious about these things. *(He stands back from her and folds his arms across his chest as he watches her pulling at her hair and frowning in the mirror.)* Do you remember the first time you met me at school? . . . *(He laughs.)* You came up to me and you said—and I thought you were the most serious little thing I had ever seen—you said: *(He imitates her.)* "Mr. Asagai—I want very much to talk with you. About Africa. You see, Mr. Asagai, I am looking for my *identity!*"

*(He laughs.)*

BENEATHA *(Turning to him, not laughing).* Yes—

*(Her face is quizzical, profoundly disturbed.)*

ASAGAI. *(Still teasing and reaching out and taking her face in his hands and turning her profile to him).* Well . . . it is true that this is not so much a profile of a Hollywood queen as perhaps a queen of the Nile—*(A mock dismissal of the importance of the question.)* But what does it matter? Assimilationism is so popular in your country.

BENEATHA *(Wheeling, passionately, sharply).* I am not an assimilationist!

ASAGAI *(The protest hangs in the room for a moment and* ASAGAI *studies her, his laughter fading).* Such a serious one. *(There is a pause.)* So—you like the robes? You must take excellent care of them—they are from my sister's personal wardrobe.

BENEATHA *(With incredulity).* You—you sent all the way home—for me?

ASAGAI *(With charm).* For you—I would do much more . . . Well, that is what I came for. I must go.

BENEATHA. Will you call me Monday?

ASAGAI. Yes . . . We have a great deal to talk about. I mean about identity and time and all that.

BENEATHA. Time?

ASAGAI. Yes. About how much time one needs to know what one feels.

BENEATHA. You never understood that there is more than one kind of feeling which can exist between a man and a woman—or, at least, there should be.

ASAGAI *(Shaking his head negatively but gently).* No. Between a man and a woman there need be only one kind of feeling. I have that for you . . . Now even . . . right this moment . . .

BENEATHA. I know—and by itself—it won't do. I can find that anywhere.

ASAGAI. For a woman it should be enough.

BENEATHA. I know—because that's what it says in all the novels that men write. But it isn't. Go ahead and laugh—but I'm not interested in being someone's little episode in America or—*(With feminine vengeance)*—one of them! *(*ASAGAI *has burst into laughter again.)* That's funny, huh!

ASAGAI. It's just that every American girl I have known has said that to me. White—black—in this you are all the same. And the same speech, too!

BENEATHA (Angrily). Yuk, yuk, yuk!

ASAGAI. It's how you can be sure that the world's most liberated women are not liberated at all. You all talk about it too much!

(MAMA enters and is immediately all social charm because of the presence of a guest.)

BENEATHA. Oh—Mama—this is Mr. Asagai.

MAMA. How do you do?

ASAGAI (Total politeness to an elder). How do you do, Mrs. Younger. Please forgive me for coming at such an outrageous hour on a Saturday.

MAMA. Well, you are quite welcome. I just hope you understand that our house don't always look like this. (Chatterish.) You must come again. I would love to hear all about—(Not sure of the name)—your country. I think it's so sad the way our American Negroes don't know nothing about Africa 'cept Tarzan and all that. And all that money they pour into these churches when they ought to be helping you people over there drive out them French and Englishmen done taken away your land.

(The mother flashes a slightly superior look at her daughter upon completion of the recitation.)

ASAGAI (Taken aback by this sudden and acutely unrelated expression of sympathy). Yes . . . yes . . .

MAMA (Smiling at him suddenly and relaxing and looking him over). How many miles is it from here to where you come from?

ASAGAI. Many thousands.

MAMA (Looking at him as she would WALTER). I bet you don't half look after yourself, being away from your mama, either. I spec you better come 'round here from time to time and get yourself some decent home-cooked meals . . .

ASAGAI (Moved). Thank you. Thank you very much. (They are all quiet, then—) Well . . . I must go. I will call you Monday, Alaiyo.

MAMA. What's that he call you?

ASAGAI. Oh—"Alaiyo." I hope you don't mind. It is what you would call a nickname, I think. It is a Yoruba word. I am a Yoruba.

MAMA. (Looking at BENEATHA). I—I thought he was from—

ASAGAI (Understanding). Nigeria is my country. Yoruba is my tribal origin—

BENEATHA. You didn't tell us what Alaiyo means . . . for all I know, you might be calling me Little Idiot or something . . .

ASAGAI. Well . . . let me see . . . I do not know how just to explain it . . . The sense of a thing can be so different when it changes languages.

BENEATHA. You're evading.

ASAGAI. No—really it is difficult . . . (Thinking.) It means . . . it means One for Whom Bread—Food—Is Not Enough. (He looks at her.) Is that all right?

BENEATHA (Understanding, softly). Thank you.

MAMA (Looking from one to the other and not understanding any of it). Well . . . that's nice . . . You must come see us again—Mr.—

ASAGAI. Ah-sah-guy . . .

MAMA. Yes . . . Do come again.

ASAGAI. Goodbye.

(He exits.)

MAMA (After him). Lord, that's a pretty thing just went out here! (Insinuatingly, to her daughter.) Yes, I guess I see why we done commence to get so interested in Africa 'round here. Missionaries my aunt Jenny!

*(She exits.)*

BENEATHA. Oh, Mama!...

*(She picks up the Nigerian dress and holds it up to her in front of the mirror again. She sets the headdress on haphazardly and then notices her hair again and clutches at it and then replaces the headdress and frowns at herself. Then she starts to wriggle in front of the mirror as she thinks a Nigerian woman might. TRAVIS enters and regards her.)*

TRAVIS. You cracking up?

BENEATHA. Shut up.

*(She pulls the headdress off and looks at herself in the mirror and clutches at her hair again and squinches her eyes as if trying to imagine something. Then, suddenly, she gets her raincoat and kerchief and hurriedly prepares for going out.)*

MAMA *(Coming back into the room).* She's resting now. Travis, baby, run next door and ask Miss Johnson to please let me have a little kitchen cleanser. This here can is empty as Jacob's kettle.

TRAVIS. I just came in.

MAMA. Do as you told. *(He exits and she looks at her daughter.)* Where you going?

BENEATHA *(Halting at the door).* To become a queen of the Nile!

*(She exits in a breathless blaze of glory. RUTH appears in the bedroom doorway.)*

MAMA. Who told you to get up?

RUTH. Ain't nothing wrong with me to be lying in no bed for. Where did Bennie go?

MAMA *(Drumming her fingers).* Far as I could make out—to Egypt. *(RUTH just looks at her.)* What time is it getting to?

RUTH. Ten-twenty. And the mailman going to ring that bell this morning just like he done every morning for the last umpteen years.

*(TRAVIS comes in with the cleanser can.)*

TRAVIS. She say to tell you that she don't have much.

MAMA *(Angrily).* Lord, some people I could name sure is tight-fisted! *(Directing her grandson.)* Mark two cans of cleanser down on the list there. If she that hard up for kitchen cleanser, I sure don't want to forget to get her none!

RUTH. Lena—maybe the woman is just short on cleanser—

MAMA *(Not listening).* —Much baking powder as she done borrowed from me all these years, she could of done gone into the baking business!

*(The bell sounds suddenly and sharply, and all three are stunned—serious and silent—mid-speech. In spite of all the other conversations and distractions of the morning, this is what they have been waiting for, even TRAVIS, who looks helplessly from his mother to his grandmother. RUTH is the first to come to life again.)*

RUTH *(To TRAVIS).* Get down them steps, boy!

*(TRAVIS snaps to life and flies out to get the mail.)*

MAMA *(Her eyes wide, her hand to her breast).* You mean it done really come?

RUTH *(Excited).* Oh, Miss Lena!

MAMA *(Collecting herself).* Well . . . I don't know what we all so excited about 'round here for. We known it was coming for months.

RUTH. That's a whole lot different from having it come and being able to hold it in your hands . . . a piece of paper worth ten thousand dollars . . . *(TRAVIS bursts back into the room. He holds the envelope high above his head, like a little dancer, his face is radiant and he is breathless. He moves to his grandmother with sudden*

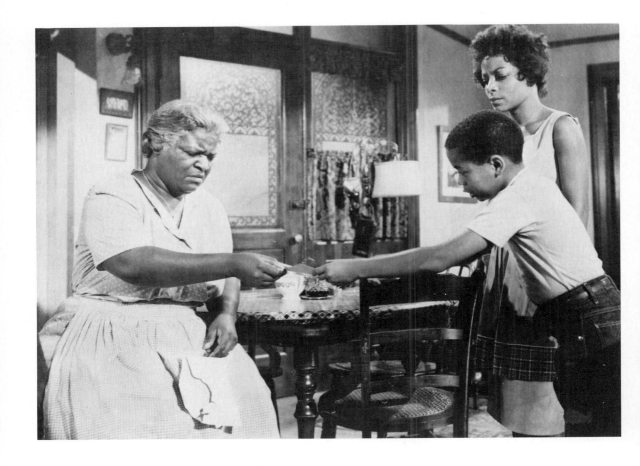

slow ceremony and puts the envelope into her hands. She accepts it, and then merely holds it and looks at it.) Come on! Open it . . . Lord have mercy, I wish Walter Lee was here!

TRAVIS. Open it, Grandmama!

MAMA (Staring at it). Now you all be quiet. It's just a check.

RUTH. Open it . . .

MAMA (Still staring at it). Now don't act silly . . . We ain't never been no people to act silly 'bout no money—

RUTH (Swiftly). We ain't never had none before—open it!

(MAMA finally makes a good strong tear and pulls out the thin blue slice of paper and inspects it closely. The boy and his mother study it raptly over MAMA's shoulders.)

MAMA. Travis! (She is counting off with doubt.) Is that the right number of zeros?

TRAVIS. Yes'm . . . ten thousand dollars. Gaalee, Grandmama, you rich.

MAMA (She holds the check away from her, still looking at it. Slowly her face sobers into a mask of unhappiness). Ten thousand dollars. (She hands it to RUTH.) Put it away somewhere, Ruth. (She does not look at RUTH; her eyes seem to be seeing something somewhere very far off.) Ten thousand dollars.

TRAVIS (*To his mother, sincerely*). What's the matter with Grandmama—don't she want to be rich?

RUTH (*Distractedly*). You go on out and play now, baby. (*TRAVIS exits. MAMA starts wiping dishes absently, humming intently to herself. RUTH turns to her, with kind exasperation.*) You've gone and got yourself upset.

MAMA (*Not looking at her*). I spec if it wasn't for you all . . . I would just put that money away or give it to the church or something.

RUTH. Now what kind of talk is that. Mr. Younger would just be plain mad if he could hear you talking foolish like that.

MAMA (*Stopping and staring off*). Yes . . . he sure would. (*Sighing.*) We got enough to do with that money, all right. (*She halts then, and turns and looks at her daughter-in-law hard; RUTH avoids her eyes and MAMA wipes her hands with finality and starts to speak firmly to RUTH.*) Where did you go today, girl?

RUTH. To the doctor.

MAMA (*Impatiently*). Now, Ruth . . . you know better than that. Old Doctor Jones is strange enough in his way but there ain't nothing 'bout him make somebody slip and call him "she"—like you done this morning.

RUTH. Well, that's what happened—my tongue slipped.

MAMA. You went to see that woman, didn't you?

RUTH (*Defensively, giving herself away*). What woman you talking about?

MAMA (*Angrily*). That woman who—

(*WALTER enters in great excitement.*)

WALTER. Did it come?

MAMA (*Quietly*). Can't you give people a Christian greeting before you start asking about money?

WALTER (*To RUTH*). Did it come? (*RUTH unfolds the check and lays it quietly before him, watching him intently with thoughts of her own. WALTER sits down and grasps it close and counts off the zeros.*) Ten thousand dollars—(*He turns suddenly, frantically to his mother and draws some papers out of his breast pocket.*) Mama—look. Old Willy Harris put everything on paper—

MAMA. Son—I think you ought to talk to your wife . . . I'll go on out and leave you alone if you want—

WALTER. I can talk to her later— Mama, look—

MAMA. Son—

WALTER. WILL SOMEBODY PLEASE LISTEN TO ME TODAY!

MAMA (*Quietly*). I don't 'low no yellin' in this house, Walter Lee, and you know it— (*WALTER stares at them in frustration and starts to speak several times.*) And there ain't going to be no investing in no liquor stores. I don't aim to have to speak on that again.

(*A long pause.*)

WALTER. Oh—so you don't aim to have to speak on that again? So *you* have decided . . . (*Crumpling his papers.*) Well, *you* tell that to my boy tonight when you put him to sleep on the living-room couch . . . (*Turning to MAMA and speaking directly to her.*) Yeah—and tell it to my wife, Mama, tomorrow when she has to go out of here to look after somebody else's kids. And tell it to *me*, Mama, every time we need a new pair of curtains, and I have to watch *you* go out and work in somebody's kitchen. Yeah, you tell me then!

(*WALTER starts out.*)

RUTH. Where you going?

WALTER. I'm going out!

RUTH. Where?

WALTER. Just out of this house somewhere—

RUTH (*Getting her coat*). I'll come too.

WALTER. I don't want you to come!

RUTH. I got something to talk to you about, Walter.

WALTER. That's too bad.

MAMA (*Still quietly*). Walter Lee—(*She waits and he finally turns and looks at her.*) Sit down.

WALTER. I'm a grown man, Mama.

MAMA. Ain't nobody said you wasn't grown. But you still in my house and my presence. And as long as you are—you'll talk to your wife civil. Now sit down.

RUTH (*Suddenly*). Oh, let him go on out and drink himself to death! He makes me sick to my stomach! (*She flings her coat against him.*)

WALTER (*Violently*). And you turn mine too, baby! (RUTH *goes into their bedroom and slams the door behind her.*) That was my greatest mistake—

MAMA (*Still quietly*). Walter, what is the matter with you?

WALTER. Matter with me? Ain't nothing the matter with *me*!

MAMA. Yes there is. Something eating you up like a crazy man. Something more than me not giving you this money. The past few years I been watching it happen to you. You get all nervous acting and kind of wild in the eyes—(WALTER *jumps up impatiently at her words.*) I said sit there now, I'm talking to you!

WALTER. Mama—I don't need no nagging at me today.

MAMA. Seem like you getting to a place where you always tied up in some kind of knot about something. But if anybody ask you 'bout it you just yell at 'em and bust out the house and go out and drink somewheres. Walter Lee, people can't live with that. Ruth's a good, patient girl in her way —but you getting to be too much. Boy, don't make the mistake of driving that girl away from you.

WALTER. Why—what she do for me?

MAMA. She loves you.

WALTER. Mama—I'm going out. I want to go off somewhere and be by myself for a while.

MAMA. I'm sorry 'bout your liquor store, son. It just wasn't the thing for us to do. That's what I want to tell you about—

WALTER. I got to go out, Mama—

(*He rises.*)

MAMA. It's dangerous, son.

WALTER. What's dangerous?

MAMA. When a man goes outside his home to look for peace.

WALTER (*Beseechingly*). Then why can't there never be no peace in this house then?

MAMA. You done found it in some other house?

WALTER. No—there ain't no woman! Why do women always think there's a woman somewhere when a man gets restless. (*Coming to her.*) Mama—Mama—I want so many things . . .

MAMA. Yes, son—

WALTER. I want so many things that they are driving me kind of crazy . . . Mama—look at me.

MAMA. I'm looking at you. You a good-looking boy. You got a job, a nice wife, a fine boy and—

WALTER. A job. (*Looks at her.*) Mama, a job? I open and close car doors all day long. I drive a man around in his limousine and I say, "Yes, sir; no, sir; very good, sir; shall I take the Drive, sir?" Mama, that ain't no kind of job . . . that ain't nothing at all. (*Very quietly.*) Mama, I don't know if I can make you understand.

MAMA. Understand what, baby?

WALTER (*Quietly*). Sometimes it's like I can see the future stretched out in front of me—just plain as day. The future, Mama. Hanging over there at the edge of my days.

Just waiting for me—a big, looming blank space—full of *nothing*. Just waiting for *me. (Pause.)* Mama—sometimes when I'm downtown and I pass them cool, quiet-looking restaurants where them white boys are sitting back and talking 'bout things . . . sitting there turning deals worth millions of dollars . . . sometimes I see guys don't look much older than me—

MAMA. Son—how come you talk so much 'bout money?

WALTER *(With immense passion).* Because it is life, Mama!

MAMA *(Quietly).* Oh—*(Very quietly).* So now it's life. Money is life. Once upon a time freedom used to be life—now it's money. I guess the world really do change . . .

WALTER. No—it was always money, Mama. We just didn't know about it.

MAMA. No . . . something has changed. *(She looks at him.)* You something new, boy. In my time we was worried about not being lynched and getting to the North if we could and how to stay alive and still have a pinch of dignity too . . . Now here come you and Beneatha—talking 'bout things we ain't never even thought about hardly, me and your daddy. You ain't satisfied or proud of nothing we done. I mean that you had a home; that we kept you out of trouble till you was grown; that you don't have to ride to work on the back of nobody's streetcar— You my children—but how different we done become.

WALTER. You just don't understand, Mama, you just don't understand.

MAMA. Son—do you know your wife is expecting another baby? (WALTER *stands, stunned, and absorbs what his mother has said.*) That's what she wanted to talk to you about. (WALTER *sinks down into a chair.*) This ain't for me to be telling—but you ought to know. (*She waits.*) I think Ruth is thinking 'bout getting rid of that child.

WALTER (*Slowly understanding*). No—no— Ruth wouldn't do that.

MAMA. When the world gets ugly enough— a woman will do anything for her family. *The part that's already living.*

WALTER. You don't know Ruth, Mama, if you think she would do that.

(RUTH *opens the bedroom door and stands there a little limp.*)

RUTH (*Beaten*). Yes I would too, Walter. (*Pause.*) I gave her a five-dollar down payment.

(*There is total silence as the man stares at his wife and the mother stares at her son.*)

MAMA (*Presently*). Well— (*Tightly.*) Well— son, I'm waiting to hear you say something . . . I'm waiting to hear how you be your father's son. Be the man he was . . . (*Pause.*) Your wife say she going to destroy your child. And I'm waiting to hear you talk like him and say we a people who give children life, not who destroys them— (*She rises.*) I'm waiting to see you stand up and look like your daddy and say we done give up one baby to poverty and that we ain't going to give up nary another one . . . I'm waiting.

WALTER. Ruth—

MAMA. If you a son of mine, tell her! (WALTER *turns, looks at her and can say nothing. She continues, bitterly.*) You . . . you are a disgrace to your father's memory. Somebody get me my hat.

## Act I

### Getting at Meaning

1. Walter says that women in his family don't understand him, that they "don't understand about building their men up and making 'em feel like they somebody." Have the women in his family failed Walter? How has Walter failed them?

2. Why is it so important to Walter that Travis look up to him? What need does Travis satisfy for Walter?

3. Why is Mama so set against Walter's investing in a liquor store?

4. Who is the head of the Younger family? Why is this a source of conflict in the home?

5. What dreams have been deferred in this family?

6. Why is there such a difference in the qualities that Ruth and Beneatha admire in men?

7. Mama says that something has come between her and her children. Is it simply a generation gap that has split this family or is it more serious? Explain.

8. What does Beneatha mean when she says, "We've all got acute ghetto-itus"?

9. How has Beneatha been searching for her identity? Why is Asagai important to her search? Why does she react so violently when Asagai implies that she is an assimilationist?

10. Is Alaiyo an appropriate name for Beneatha? Why? What does Asagai seem to understand about Beneatha that her family does not?

11. When Mama finally holds the insurance check in her hands, "her face sobers into a mask of unhappiness" and she says, "Ten thousand dollars they give you. Ten thousand dollars." Why does the money make her so unhappy? What would she rather have?

12. What is ailing Ruth? What does she plan to do? Why is Walter unable to "be his father's son" and tell her not to go through with her plan?

### Developing Skills in Reading Literature

1. **Setting.** What is the setting of this play?

2. **Stage Directions.** On the basis of the stage directions given at the beginning of this play, draw a floor plan of the Younger apartment.

3. **Conflict.** The first act of this play introduces the conflicts that will be developed as the play progresses. Identify the conflicts between these characters: Ruth and Walter, Walter and Beneatha, Walter and Mama, Mama and Beneatha, Ruth and Mama. Do these conflicts have common sources?

4. **Dialect.** The Youngers' dialect is characteristic of the south side of Chicago. Why is Beneatha's dialect somewhat different from her family's dialect? How does her line to Walter, "Thee is mad, boy," reflect the forces at work in shaping her speech?

5. **Symbol.** What does Mama's plant symbolize for her?

6. **Mood.** What is the mood at the conclusion of this act?

### Developing Writing Skills

**Analyzing a Character.** Reread Walter's speeches to Mama beginning, "I want so many things that they are driving me kind of crazy . . ." (p. 550) and continuing to his line "Because it is life, Mama!" In a single paragraph, explain why Walter is dissatisfied with his life and what he believes will cure his dissatisfaction.

ACT II

Scene 1. *Later the same day.*

RUTH *is ironing again. She has the radio going. Presently* BENEATHA's *bedroom door opens and* RUTH's *mouth falls and she puts down the iron in fascination.*

RUTH. What have we got on tonight!
BENEATHA *(Emerging grandly from the doorway so that we can see her thoroughly robed in the costume Asagai brought).* You are looking at what a well dressed Nigerian woman wears—*(She parades for* RUTH, *her hair completely hidden by the headdress; she is coquettishly fanning herself with an ornate oriental fan, mistakenly more like Butterfly³ than any Nigerian that ever was.)* Isn't it beautiful? *(She promenades to the radio and, with an arrogant flourish, turns off the good loud blues that is playing.)* Enough of this assimilationist junk! *(RUTH follows her with her eyes as she goes to the phonograph and puts on a record and turns and waits ceremoniously for the music to come up. Then, with a shout—)* OCOMOGOSIAY!

*(RUTH jumps. The music comes up, a lovely Nigerian melody.* BENEATHA *listens, enraptured, her eyes far away—"back to the past." She begins to dance.* RUTH *is dumbfounded.)*

RUTH. What kind of dance is that?
BENEATHA. A folk dance.
RUTH *(Pearl Bailey).* What kind of folks do that, honey?
BENEATHA. It's from Nigeria. It's a dance of welcome.
RUTH. Who you welcoming?
BENEATHA. The men back to the village.
RUTH. Where they been?
BENEATHA. How should I know—out hunting or something. Anyway, they are coming back now . . .

RUTH. Well, that's good.
BENEATHA *(With the record).*
    Alundi, alundi
    Alundi alunya
    Jop pu a jeepua
    Ang gu soooooooooo
    Ai yai yae . . .
    Ayehaye—alundi . . .

*(WALTER comes in during this performance; he has obviously been drinking. He leans against the door heavily and watches his sister, at first with distaste. Then his eyes look off—"back to the past"—as he lifts both his fists to the roof, screaming.)*

WALTER. YEAH . . . AND ETHIOPIA STRETCH FORTH HER HANDS AGAIN!
    . . .
RUTH *(Drily, looking at him).* Yes—and Africa sure is claiming her own tonight. *(She gives them both up and starts ironing again.)*
WALTER *(All in a dramatic shout).* Shut up! . . . I'm digging them drums . . . them drums move me! . . . (He makes his way to his wife's face and leans in close to her.) In my *heart of hearts*—(He thumps his chest.)—I am much warrior!
RUTH *(Without even looking up).* In your heart of hearts you are much drunkard.
WALTER *(Coming away from her and starting to wander around the room, shouting).* Me and Jomo⁴ . . . (Intently, in his sister's face. She has stopped dancing to watch him in this unknown mood.) That's my man, Kenyatta. (Shouting and thumping his chest). FLAMING SPEAR! (He is suddenly in possession of an imaginary spear and actively spearing enemies all over the room.) OCOMOGOSIAY . . . THE LION

---

3. **Butterfly:** Madame Butterfly, main character in *Madame Butterfly,* an opera set in Japan.
4. **Jomo:** Jomo Kenyatta (jō' mō ken yät' ə), African political leader and first president of independent Kenya from 1964–78.

IS WAKING . . . OWIMOWEH! *(He pulls his shirt open and leaps up on a table and gestures with his spear. The bell rings.* RUTH *goes to answer.)*

BENEATHA *(To encourage* WALTER, *thoroughly caught up with this side of him).* OCOMOGOSIAY, FLAMING SPEAR!

WALTER *(On the table, very far gone, his eyes pure glass sheets. He sees what we cannot, that he is a leader of his people, a great chief, a descendant of Chaka,[5] and that the hour to march has come).* Listen, my black brothers—

BENEATHA. OCOMOGOSIAY!

WALTER. —Do you hear the waters rushing against the shores of the coastlands—

BENEATHA. OCOMOGOSIAY!

WALTER. —Do you hear the screeching of the cocks in yonder hills beyond where the chiefs meet in council for the coming of the mighty war—

BENEATHA. OCOMOGOSIAY!

WALTER. —Do you hear the beating of the wings of the birds flying low over the mountains and the low places of our land—

*(RUTH opens the door. GEORGE MURCHISON enters.)*

BENEATHA. OCOMOGOSIAY!

WALTER. —Do you hear the singing of the women, singing the war songs of our fathers to the babies in the great houses . . . singing the sweet war songs? OH, DO YOU HEAR, MY BLACK BROTHERS!

BENEATHA *(Completely gone).* We hear you, Flaming Spear—

WALTER. Telling us to prepare for the greatness of the time—*(To* GEORGE.*)* Black Brother!

*(He extends his hand for the fraternal clasp.)*

GEORGE. Black Brother, my eye!

RUTH *(Having had enough, and embarrassed for the family).* Beneatha, you got company—what's the matter with you? Walter Lee Younger, get down off that table and stop acting like a fool . . .

*(WALTER comes down off the table suddenly and makes a quick exit to the bathroom.)*

RUTH. He's had a little to drink . . . I don't know what her excuse is.

GEORGE *(To* BENEATHA*).* Look honey, we're going to the theatre—we're not going to be in it . . . so go change, huh?

RUTH. You expect this boy to go out with you looking like that?

BENEATHA *(Looking at* GEORGE*).* That's up to George. If he's ashamed of his heritage—

GEORGE. Oh, don't be so proud of yourself, Bennie—just because you look eccentric.

BENEATHA. How can something that's natural be eccentric?

GEORGE. That's what being eccentric means —being natural. Get dressed.

BENEATHA. I don't like that, George.

RUTH. Why must you and your brother make an argument out of everything people say?

BENEATHA. Because I hate assimilationist Negroes!

RUTH. Will somebody please tell me what assimila-whoever means!

GEORGE. Oh, it's just a college girl's way of calling people Uncle Toms—but that isn't what it means at all.

RUTH. Well, what does it mean?

BENEATHA *(Cutting* GEORGE *off and staring at him as she replies to* RUTH*).* It means someone who is willing to give up his own culture and submerge himself completely in the dominant, and in this case, *oppressive* culture!

GEORGE. Oh, dear, dear, dear! Here we go! A lecture on the African past! On our Great West African Heritage! In one second we will hear all about the great

---

5. **Chaka** (cha' ka): a Zulu chief, the conqueror of most of southeast Africa, who lived from 1773 to 1823.

Ashanti empires; the great Songhay civilizations; and the great sculpture of Bénin —and then some poetry in the Bantu[6]— and the whole monologue will end with the word *heritage!* *(Nastily.)* Let's face it, baby, your heritage is nothing but a bunch of raggedy spirituals and some grass huts!

BENEATHA. *Grass huts!* (RUTH *crosses to her and forcibly pushes her toward the bedroom.*) See there . . . you are standing there in your splendid ignorance talking about people who were the first to smelt iron on the face of the earth! (RUTH *is pushing her through the door.*) The Ashanti were performing surgical operations when the English—(RUTH *pulls the door to, with* BENEATHA *on the other side, and smiles graciously at* GEORGE. BENEATHA *opens the door and shouts the end of the sentence defiantly at* GEORGE.)—were still tatooing themselves with blue dragons . . . *(She goes back inside.)*

RUTH. Have a seat, George. *(They both sit.* RUTH *folds her hands rather primly on her lap, determined to demonstrate the civilization of the family.)* Warm, ain't it? I mean for September. *(Pause.)* Just like they always say about Chicago weather: If it's too hot or cold for you, just wait a minute and it'll change. *(She smiles happily at this cliché of clichés.)* Everybody say it's got to do with them bombs and things they keep setting off. *(Pause.)* Would you like a nice cold beer?

GEORGE. No, thank you. I don't care for beer. *(He looks at his watch.)* I hope she hurries up.

RUTH. What time is the show?

GEORGE. It's an eight-thirty curtain. That's just Chicago, though. In New York standard curtain time is eight-forty.

*(He is rather proud of his knowledge.)*

RUTH *(Properly appreciating it).* You get to New York a lot?

GEORGE *(Offhand).* Few times a year.

RUTH. Oh—that's nice. I've never been to New York.

*(*WALTER *enters. We feel he has relieved himself, but the edge of unreality is still with him.)*

WALTER. New York ain't got nothing Chicago ain't. Just a bunch of hustling people all squeezed up together—being "Eastern."

*(He twists his face in displeasure.)*

GEORGE. Oh—you've been?

WALTER. *Plenty* of times.

RUTH *(Shocked at the lie).* Walter Lee Younger!

WALTER *(Staring her down).* Plenty! *(Pause.)* What we got to drink in this house? Why don't you offer this man some refreshment. *(To* GEORGE.)* They don't know how to entertain people in this house, man.

GEORGE. Thank you—I don't really care for anything.

WALTER *(Feeling his head; sobriety coming).* Where's Mama?

RUTH. She ain't come back yet.

WALTER *(Looking* MURCHISON *over from head to toe, scrutinizing his carefully casual tweed sports jacket over cashmere V-neck sweater over soft eyelet shirt and tie, and soft slacks, finished off with white buckskin shoes).* Why all you college boys wear them fairyish-looking white shoes?

RUTH. Walter Lee!

*(*GEORGE MURCHISON *ignores the remark.)*

WALTER *(To* RUTH).* Well, they look crazy— white shoes, cold as it is.

RUTH *(Crushed).* You have to excuse him—

WALTER. No he don't! Excuse me for what? What you always excusing me for! I'll excuse myself when I needs to be excused!

---

6. **Ashanti, Songhay, Bénin, Bantu** (ə shän′ tē, säng gī′, be′nēn, ban′ tōō): African peoples.

*(A pause.)* They look as funny as them black knee socks Beneatha wears out of here all the time.

RUTH. It's the college *style,* Walter.

WALTER. Style! She looks like she got burnt legs or something!

RUTH. Oh, Walter—

WALTER *(An irritable mimic).* Oh, Walter! Oh, Walter! *(To* MURCHISON.*)* How's your old man making out? I understand you all going to buy that big hotel on the Drive? *(He finds a beer in the refrigerator, wanders over to* MURCHISON, *sipping and wiping his lips with the back of his hand, and straddling a chair backwards to talk to the other man.)* Shrewd move. Your old man is all right, man. *(Tapping his head and half winking for emphasis.)* I mean he knows how to operate. I mean he thinks *big,* you know what I mean, I mean for a *home,* you know? But I think he's kind of running out of ideas now. I'd like to talk to him. Listen, man, I got some plans that could turn this city upside down. I mean I think like he does. *Big.* Invest big, gamble big, lose *big* if you have to, you know what I mean. It's hard to find a man on this whole Southside who understands my kind of thinking—you dig? *(He scrutinizes* MURCHISON *again, drinks his beer, squints his eyes and leans in close, confidential, man to man.)* Me and you ought to sit down and talk sometimes, man. Man, I got me some ideas . . .

MURCHISON *(With boredom).* Yeah—sometimes we'll have to do that, Walter.

WALTER *(Understanding the indifference, and offended).* Yeah—well, when you get the time, man. I know you a busy little boy.

RUTH. Walter, please—

WALTER *(Bitterly, hurt).* I know ain't nothing in this world as busy as you black college boys with your fraternity pins and white shoes . . .

RUTH *(Covering her face with humiliation).* Oh, Walter Lee—

WALTER. I see you all all the time—with the books tucked under your arms—going to your *(British A—a mimic.)* "clahsses." And for what! What you learning over there? Filling up your heads—*(Counting off on his fingers)*—with the sociology and the psychology—but they teaching you how to be a man? How to take over and run the world? They teaching you how to run a rubber plantation or a steel mill? Naw—just to talk proper and read books and wear white shoes . . .

GEORGE *(Looking at him with distaste, a little above it all).* You're all wacked up with bitterness, man.

WALTER *(Intently, almost quietly, between the teeth, glaring at the boy).* And you—ain't you bitter, man? Ain't you just about had it yet? Don't you see no stars gleaming that you can't reach out and grab? You happy?—you happy? You got it made? Bitter? Man, I'm a volcano. Bitter? Here I am a giant—surrounded by ants! Ants who can't even understand what it is the giant is talking about.

RUTH *(Passionately and suddenly).* Oh, Walter—ain't you with nobody!

WALTER *(Violently).* No! 'Cause ain't nobody with me! Not even my own mother!

RUTH. Walter, that's a terrible thing to say!

*(*BENEATHA *enters, dressed for the evening in a cocktail dress and earrings.)*

GEORGE. Well—hey, you look great.

BENEATHA. Let's go, George. See you all later.

RUTH. Have a nice time.

GEORGE. Thanks. Good night. *(To* WALTER, *sarcastically.)* Good night, *Prometheus.*[7]

*(*BENEATHA *and* GEORGE *exit.)*

---

7. **Prometheus** (prə mē′ thē əs): in Greek mythology, a Titan, or giant god.

WALTER (To RUTH). Who is Prometheus?

RUTH. I don't know. Don't worry about it.

WALTER (In fury, pointing after GEORGE). See there— they get to a point where they can't insult you man to man—they got to go talk about something ain't nobody never heard of!

RUTH. How do you know it was an insult? (To humor him.) Maybe Prometheus is a nice fellow.

WALTER. Prometheus! I bet there ain't even no such thing! I bet that simple-minded clown—

RUTH. Walter—

(She stops what she is doing and looks at him.)

WALTER (Yelling). Don't start!

RUTH. Start what?

WALTER. Your nagging! Where was I? Who was I with? How much money did I spend?

RUTH (Plaintively). Walter Lee—why don't we just try to talk about it . . .

WALTER (Not listening). I been out talking with people who understand me. People who care about the things I got on my mind.

RUTH (Wearily). I guess that means people like Willy Harris.

WALTER. Yes, people like Willy Harris.

RUTH (With a sudden flash of impatience). Why don't you all just hurry up and go into the banking business and stop talking about it!

WALTER. Why? You want to know why? 'Cause we all tied up in a race of people that don't know how to do nothing but moan, pray, and have babies!

(The line is too bitter even for him, and he looks at her and sits down.)

RUTH. Oh, Walter . . . (Softly.) Honey, why can't you stop fighting me?

WALTER (Without thinking). Who's fighting you? Who even cares about you?

(This line begins the retardation of his mood.)

RUTH. Well—(She waits a long time, and then with resignation starts to put away her things.) I guess I might as well go on to bed . . . (More or less to herself.) I don't know where we lost it . . . but we have . . . (Then, to him.) I—I'm sorry about this new baby, Walter. I guess maybe I better go on and do what I started . . . I guess I just didn't realize how bad things was with us . . . I guess I just didn't really realize—(She starts out to the bedroom and stops.) You want some hot milk?

WALTER. Hot milk?

RUTH. Yes—hot milk.

WALTER. Why hot milk?

RUTH. 'Cause after all that liquor you come home with, you ought to have something hot in your stomach.

WALTER. I don't want no milk.

RUTH. You want some coffee then?

WALTER. No, I don't want no coffee. I don't want nothing hot to drink. (Almost plaintively.) Why you always trying to give me something to eat?

RUTH (Standing and looking at him helplessly). What else can I give you, Walter Lee Younger?

(She stands and looks at him and presently turns to go out again. He lifts his head and watches her going away from him in a new mood that began to emerge when he asked her "Who cares about you?")

WALTER. It's been rough, ain't it, baby? (She hears and stops but does not turn around, and he continues to her back.) I guess between two people there ain't never as much understood as folks generally thinks there is. I mean like between me and you —(She turns to face him.) How we gets to the place where we scared to talk softness to each other. (He waits, thinking hard himself.) Why you think it got to be like that? (He is thoughtful, almost as a child *would be.)* Ruth, what is it gets into people ought to be close?

RUTH. I don't know, honey. I think about it a lot.

WALTER. On account of you and me, you mean? The way things are with us. The way something done come down between us.

RUTH. There ain't so much between us, Walter . . . Not when you come to me and try to talk to me. Try to be with me . . . a little even.

WALTER *(Total honesty).* Sometimes . . . sometimes . . . I don't even know how to try.

RUTH. Walter—

WALTER. Yes?

RUTH *(Coming to him, gently and with misgiving, but coming to him).* Honey . . . life don't have to be like this. I mean sometimes people can do things so that things are better . . . You remember how we used to talk when Travis was born . . . about the way we were going to live . . . the kind of house . . . *(She is stroking his head.)* Well, it's all starting to slip away from us . . .

*(MAMA enters, and WALTER jumps up and shouts at her.)*

WALTER. Mama, where have you been?

MAMA. My—them steps is longer than they used to be. Whew! *(She sits down and ignores him.)* How you feeling this evening, Ruth?

*(RUTH shrugs, disturbed some at having been prematurely interrupted and watching her husband knowingly.)*

WALTER. Mama, where have you been all day?

MAMA *(Still ignoring him and leaning on the table and changing to more comfortable shoes).* Where's Travis?

RUTH. I let him go out earlier and he ain't come back yet. Boy, is he going to get it!

WALTER. Mama!

MAMA *(As if she has heard him for the first time).* Yes, son?

WALTER. Where did you go this afternoon?

MAMA. I went downtown to tend to some business that I had to tend to.

WALTER. What kind of business?

MAMA. You know better than to question me like a child, Brother.

WALTER *(Rising and bending over the table).* Where were you, Mama? *(Bringing his fists down and shouting.)* Mama, you didn't go do something with that insurance money, something crazy?

*(The front door opens slowly, interrupting him, and TRAVIS peeks his head in, less than hopefully.)*

TRAVIS *(To his mother).* Mama, I—

RUTH. "Mama I" nothing! You're going to get it, boy! Get on in that bedroom and get yourself ready!

TRAVIS. But I—

MAMA. Why don't you all never let the child explain hisself.

RUTH. Keep out of it now, Lena.

*(MAMA clamps her lips together, and RUTH advances toward her son menacingly.)*

RUTH. A thousand times I have told you not to go off like that—

MAMA *(Holding out her arms to her grandson).* Well—at least let me tell him something. I want him to be the first one to hear . . . Come here, Travis. *(The boy obeys, gladly.)* Travis—*(She takes him by the shoulder and looks into his face.)*—you know that money we got in the mail this morning?

TRAVIS. Yes'm—

MAMA. Well—what you think your grandmama gone and done with that money?

TRAVIS. I don't know, Grandmama.

MAMA *(Putting her finger on his nose for emphasis).* She went out and she bought you a house! *(The explosion comes from*

WALTER *at the end of the revelation, and he jumps up and turns away from all of them in a fury.* MAMA *continues, to* TRAVIS.) You glad about the house? It's going to be yours when you get to be a man.

TRAVIS. Yeah—I always wanted to live in a house.

MAMA. All right, gimme some sugar then—(TRAVIS *puts his arms around her neck as she watches her son over the boy's shoulder. Then, to* TRAVIS, *after the embrace.)* Now when you say your prayers tonight, you thank God and your grandfather—'cause it was him who give you the house—in his way.

RUTH (*Taking the boy from* MAMA *and pushing him toward the bedroom*). Now you get out of here and get ready for your beating.

TRAVIS. Aw, Mama—

RUTH. Get on in there—(*Closing the door behind him and turning radiantly to her mother-in-law.*) So you went and did it!

MAMA (*Quietly, looking at her son with pain*). Yes, I did.

RUTH (*Raising both arms classically*). Praise God! (*Looks at* WALTER *a moment, who says nothing. She crosses rapidly to her husband.*) Please, honey—let me be glad . . . you be glad too. (*She has laid her hands on his shoulders, but he shakes himself free of her roughly, without turning to face her.*) Oh, Walter . . . a home . . . *a* home. (*She comes back to* MAMA.) Well—where is it? How big is it? How much it going to cost?

MAMA. Well—

RUTH. When we moving?

MAMA (*Smiling at her*). First of the month.

RUTH (*Throwing back her head with jubilance*). Praise God!

MAMA (*Tentatively, still looking at her son's back turned against her and* RUTH). It's—it's a nice house too . . . (*She cannot help speaking directly to him. An imploring*

quality in her voice, her manner, makes her almost like a girl now.) Three bedrooms—nice big one for you and Ruth. . . . Me and Beneatha still have to share our room, but Travis have one of his own—and (*With difficulty.*) I figure if the—new baby—is a boy, we could get one of them double-decker outfits . . . And there's a yard with a little patch of dirt where I could maybe get to grow me a few flowers . . . And a nice big basement . . .

RUTH. Walter honey, be glad—

MAMA (*Still to his back, fingering things on the table*). 'Course I don't want to make it sound fancier than it is . . . It's just a plain little old house—but it's made good and solid—and it will be *ours*. Walter Lee—it makes a difference in a man when he can walk on floors that belong to *him* . . .

RUTH. Where is it?

MAMA (*Frightened at this telling*). Well—well—it's out there in Clybourne Park—

(RUTH's *radiance fades abruptly, and* WALTER *finally turns slowly to face his mother with incredulity and hostility.*)

RUTH. Where?

MAMA (*Matter-of-factly*). Four o six Clybourne Street, Clybourne Park.

RUTH. Clybourne Park? Mama, there ain't no black people living in Clybourne Park.

MAMA (*Almost idiotically*). Well, I guess there's going to be some now.

WALTER (*Bitterly*). So that's the peace and comfort you went out and bought for us today!

MAMA (*Raising her eyes to meet his finally*). Son—I just tried to find the nicest place for the least amount of money for my family.

RUTH (*Trying to recover from the shock*). Well—well—'course I ain't one never been 'fraid of no crackers, mind you—but—well, wasn't there no other houses nowhere?

MAMA. Them houses they put up for blacks in them areas way out all seem to cost twice as much as other houses. I did the best I could.

RUTH (*Struck senseless with the news, in its various degrees of goodness and trouble, she sits a moment, her fists propping her chin in thought, and then she starts to rise, bringing her fists down with vigor, the radiance spreading from cheek to cheek again*). Well—well!—All I can say is—if this is my time in life—*my time*—to say goodbye—(*And she builds with momentum as she starts to circle the room with an exuberant, almost tearfully happy release*) —to these cracking walls!—(*She pounds the walls.*) —and these marching roaches! —(*She wipes at an imaginary army of marching roaches.*)—and this cramped little closet which ain't now or never was no kitchen! . . . then I say it loud and good, *Hallelujah! and goodbye misery . . . I don't never want to see your ugly face again!* (*She laughs joyously, having practically destroyed the apartment, and flings her arms up and lets them come down happily, slowly, reflectively, over her abdomen, aware for the first time perhaps that the life therein pulses with happiness and not despair.*) Lena?

MAMA (*Moved, watching her happiness*). Yes, honey?

RUTH (*Looking off*). Is there—is there a whole lot of sunlight?

MAMA (*Understanding*). Yes, child, there's a whole lot of sunlight.

(*Long pause.*)

RUTH. (*Collecting herself and going to the door of the room* TRAVIS *is in*). Well—I guess I better see 'bout Travis. (*To* MAMA.) Lord, I sure don't feel like whipping nobody today!

(*She exits.*)

MAMA (*The mother and son are left alone now and the mother waits a long time, considering deeply, before she speaks*). Son—you—you understand what I done, don't you? (WALTER *is silent and sullen.*) I—I just seen my family falling apart today . . . just falling to pieces in front of my eyes . . . We couldn't of gone on like we was today. We was going backwards 'stead of forwards—talking 'bout killing babies and wishing each other was dead . . . When it gets like that in life—you just got to do something different, push on out and do something bigger . . . (*She waits.*) I wish you say something, son . . . I wish you'd say how deep inside you you think I done the right thing—

WALTER (*Crossing slowly to his bedroom door and finally turning there and speaking measuredly*). What you need me to say you done right for? *You* the head of this family. You run our lives like you want to. It was your money and you did what you wanted with it. So what you need for me to say it was all right for? (*Bitterly, to hurt her as deeply as he knows is possible.*) So you butchered up a dream of mine—you—who always talking 'bout your children's dreams . . .

MAMA. Walter Lee—

(*He just closes the door behind him.* MAMA *sits alone, thinking heavily.*)

Scene 2

*Friday night. A few weeks later.*
*Packing crates mark the intention of the family to move.* BENEATHA *and* GEORGE *come in, presumably from an evening out again.*

GEORGE. OK. . . . OK, whatever you say . . . (*They both sit on the couch. He tries to kiss her. She moves away.)* Look, we've had a nice evening; let's not spoil it, huh? . . .

*(He again turns her head and tries to nuzzle in and she turns away from him, not with distaste but with momentary lack of interest; in a mood to pursue what they were talking about.)*

BENEATHA. I'm *trying* to talk to you.

GEORGE. We always talk.

BENEATHA. Yes—and I love to talk.

GEORGE *(Exasperated; rising).* I know it and I don't mind it sometimes . . . I want you to cut it out, see—The moody stuff, I mean. I don't like it. You're a nice-looking girl . . . all over. That's all you need, honey, forget the atmosphere. Guys aren't going to go for the atmosphere—they're going to go for what they see. Be glad for that. Drop the Garbo[8] routine. It doesn't go with you. As for myself, I want a nice— *(Groping.)*—simple *(Thoughtfully.)*—sophisticated girl . . . not a poet—OK?

*(She rebuffs him again and he starts to leave.)*

BENEATHA. Why are you angry?

GEORGE. Because this is stupid! I don't go out with you to discuss the nature of "quiet desperation" or to hear all about your thoughts—because the world will go on thinking what it thinks regardless—

BENEATHA. Then why read books? Why go to school?

GEORGE *(With artificial patience, counting on his fingers).* It's simple. You read books —to learn facts—to get grades—to pass the course—to get a degree. That's all—it has nothing to do with thoughts.

*(A long pause.)*

BENEATHA. I see. *(A longer pause as she looks at him.)* Good night, George.

*(GEORGE looks at her a little oddly, and starts to exit. He meets MAMA coming in.)*

GEORGE. Oh—hello, Mrs. Younger.

MAMA. Hello, George, how you feeling?

GEORGE. Fine—fine, how are you?

MAMA. Oh, a little tired. You know them steps can get you after a day's work. You all have a nice time tonight?

GEORGE. Yes—a fine time. Well, good night.

MAMA. Good night. *(He exits.* MAMA *closes the door behind her.)* Hello, honey. What you sitting like that for?

BENEATHA. I'm just sitting.

MAMA. Didn't you have a nice time?

BENEATHA. No.

MAMA. No? What's the matter?

BENEATHA. Mama, George is a fool—honest. *(She rises.)*

MAMA *(Hustling around unloading the packages she has entered with. She stops).* Is he, baby?

BENEATHA. Yes.

*(BENEATHA makes up TRAVIS' bed as she talks.)*

MAMA. You sure?

BENEATHA. Yes.

MAMA. Well—I guess you better not waste your time with no fools.

*(BENEATHA looks up at her mother, watching her put groceries in the refrigerator. Finally she gathers up her things and starts into the bedroom. At the door she stops and looks back at her mother.)*

BENEATHA. Mama—

MAMA. Yes, baby—

BENEATHA. Thank you.

MAMA. For what?

BENEATHA. For understanding me this time.

*(She exits quickly and the mother stands, smiling a little, looking at the place where* BENEATHA *just stood.* RUTH *enters.)*

RUTH. Now don't you fool with any of this stuff, Lena—

---

8. **Garbo:** Greta Garbo, a movie actress.

MAMA. Oh, I just thought I'd sort a few things out.

*(The phone rings.* RUTH *answers.)*

RUTH *(At the phone).* Hello—Just a minute. *(Goes to door.)* Walter, it's Mrs. Arnold. *(Waits. Goes back to the phone. Tense.)* Hello. Yes, this is his wife speaking . . . He's lying down now. Yes . . . well, he'll be in tomorrow. He's been very sick. Yes —I know we should have called, but we were so sure he'd be able to come in today. Yes—yes, I'm very sorry. Yes . . . Thank you very much. *(She hangs up.* WALTER *is standing in the doorway of the bedroom behind her.)* That was Mrs. Arnold.

WALTER *(Indifferently).* Was it?

RUTH. She said if you don't come in tomorrow that they are getting a new man . . .

WALTER. Ain't that sad—ain't that crying sad.

RUTH. She said Mr. Arnold has had to take a cab for three days . . . Walter, you ain't been to work for three days! *(This is a revelation to her.)* Where you been, Walter Lee Younger? *(WALTER looks at her and starts to laugh.)* You're going to lose your job.

WALTER. That's right . . .

RUTH. Oh, Walter, and with your mother working like a dog every day—

WALTER. That's sad too— Everything is sad.

MAMA. What you been doing for these three days, son?

WALTER. Mama—you don't know all the things a man what got leisure can find to do in this city . . . What's this—Friday night? Well—Wednesday I borrowed Willy Harris' car and I went for a drive . . . just me and myself and I drove and drove . . . Way out . . . way past South Chicago, and I parked the car and I sat and looked at the steel mills all day long. I just sat in the car and looked at them big black chimneys for hours. Then I drove back and I went to the Green Hat. *(Pause.)* And

Thursday—Thursday I borrowed the car again and I got in it and I pointed it the other way and I drove the other way—for hours—way, way up to Wisconsin, and I looked at the farms. I just drove and looked at the farms. Then I drove back and I went to the Green Hat. *(Pause.)* And today—today I didn't get the car. Today I just walked. All over the Southside. And I looked at the Negroes and they looked at me and finally I just sat down on the curb at Thirty-ninth and South Parkway and I just sat there and watched the Negroes go by. And then I went to the Green Hat. You all sad? You all depressed? And you know where I am going right now—

*(*RUTH *goes out quietly.)*

MAMA. Oh, Big Walter, is this the harvest of our days?

WALTER. You know what I like about the Green Hat? *(He turns the radio on and a steamy, deep blues pours into the room.)* I like this little cat they got there who blows a sax . . . He blows. He talks to me. He ain't but 'bout five feet tall and he's got a conked head and his eyes is always closed and he's all music—

MAMA *(Rising and getting some papers out of her handbag).* Walter—

WALTER. And there's this other guy who plays the piano . . . and they got a sound. I mean they can work on some music . . . They got the best little combo in the world in the Green Hat . . . You can just sit there and drink and listen to them three men play, and you realize that don't nothing matter, but just being there—

MAMA. I've helped do it to you, haven't I, son? Walter, I been wrong.

WALTER. Naw—you ain't never been wrong about nothing, Mama.

MAMA. Listen to me, now. I say I been wrong, son. That I been doing to you what the rest of the world been doing to you. *(She* stops and he looks up slowly at her and she meets his eyes pleadingly.) Walter—what you ain't never understood is that I ain't got nothing, don't own nothing, ain't never really wanted nothing that wasn't for you. There ain't nothing as precious to me . . . There ain't nothing worth holding on to, money, dreams, nothing else—if it means—if it means it's going to destroy my boy. (She puts her papers in front of him, and he watches her without speaking or moving.) I paid the man thirty-five hundred dollars down on the house. That leaves sixty-five hundred dollars. Monday morning I want you to take this money and take three thousand dollars and put it in a savings account for Beneatha's medical schooling. The rest you put in a checking account—with your name on it. And from now on any penny that come out of it or that go in it is for you to look after. For you to decide. (She drops her hands a little helplessly.) It ain't much, but it's all I got in the world, and I'm putting it in your hands. I'm telling you to be the head of this family from now on like you supposed to be.

WALTER (Stares at the money). You trust me like that, Mama?

MAMA. I ain't never stop trusting you. Like I ain't never stop loving you.

(She goes out, and WALTER sits looking at the money on the table as the music continues in its idiom, pulsing in the room. Finally, in a decisive gesture, he gets up, and, in mingled joy and desperation, picks up the money. At the same moment, TRAVIS enters for bed.)

TRAVIS. What's the matter, Daddy? You drunk?

WALTER. (Sweetly, more sweetly than we have ever known him). No, Daddy ain't drunk. Daddy ain't going to never be drunk again. . . .

TRAVIS. Well, good night, Daddy.

(The FATHER has come from behind the couch and leans over, embracing his son.)

WALTER. Son, I feel like talking to you tonight.

TRAVIS. About what?

WALTER. Oh, about a lot of things. About you and what kind of man you going to be when you grow up. . . . Son—son, what do you want to be when you grow up?

TRAVIS. A bus driver.

WALTER (Laughing a little). A what? Man, that ain't nothing to want to be!

TRAVIS. Why not?

WALTER. 'Cause, man—it ain't big enough—you know what I mean.

TRAVIS. I don't know then. I can't make up my mind. Sometimes Mama asks me that too. And sometimes when I tell her I just want to be like you—she says she don't want me to be like that and sometimes she says she does. . . .

WALTER (Gathering him up in his arms). You know what, Travis? In seven years you going to be seventeen years old. And things is going to be very different with us in seven years, Travis. . . . One day when you are seventeen I'll come home—home from my office downtown somewhere—

TRAVIS. You don't work in no office, Daddy.

WALTER. No—but after tonight. After what your daddy gonna do tonight, there's going to be offices—a whole lot of offices. . . .

TRAVIS. What you gonna do tonight, Daddy?

WALTER. You wouldn't understand yet, son, but your daddy's gonna make a transaction . . . a business transaction that's going to change our lives. . . . That's how come one day when you 'bout seventeen years old I'll come home and I'll be pretty tired, you know what I mean, after a day of conferences and secretaries getting things wrong the way they do . . . 'cause an executive's life is heavy, man—(The more he talks the farther away he gets.) And I'll pull the car up on the driveway . . . just a plain black Chrysler, I think, with white walls—no—black tires. More elegant. Rich people don't have to be flashy . . . though I'll have to get something a little sportier for Ruth—maybe a Cadillac convertible to do her shopping in. . . . And I'll come up the steps to the house and the gardener will be clipping away at the hedges and he'll say, "Good evening, Mr. Younger." And I'll say, "Hello, Jefferson, how are you this evening?" And I'll go inside and Ruth will come downstairs and meet me at the door and we'll kiss each other and she'll take my arm and we'll go up to your room to see you sitting on the floor with the catalogues of all the great schools in America around you. . . . All the great schools in the world! And—and I'll say, all right son—it's your seventeenth birthday, what is it you've decided? . . . Just tell me where you want to go to school and you'll go. Just tell me, what it is you want to be—and you'll *be* it. . . . Whatever you want to be—Yessir! *(He holds his arms open for* TRAVIS.) You just name it, son . . . *(*TRAVIS *leaps into them.)* and I hand you the world!

*(*WALTER'S *voice has risen in pitch and hysterical promise, and on the last line he lifts* TRAVIS *high.)*

Scene 3

*Saturday, moving day, one week later.*
*Before the curtain rises,* RUTH'S *voice, a strident, dramatic church alto, cuts through the silence.*

*It is, in the darkness, a triumphant surge, a penetrating statement of expectation: "Oh, Lord, I don't feel no ways tired! Children, oh, glory hallelujah!"*

*As the curtain rises we see that* RUTH *is alone in the living room, finishing up the family's packing. It is moving day. She is nailing crates and tying cartons.* BENEATHA *enters, carrying a guitar case, and watches her exuberant sister-in-law.*

RUTH. Hey!
BENEATHA *(Putting away the case).* Hi.
RUTH *(Pointing at a package).* Honey—look in that package there and see what I found on sale this morning at the South Center. *(*RUTH *gets up and moves to the package and draws out some curtains.)* Lookahere—hand-turned hems!
BENEATHA. How do you know the window size out there?
RUTH *(Who hadn't thought of that).* Oh—Well, they bound to fit something in the whole house. Anyhow, they was too good a bargain to pass up. *(*RUTH *slaps her head, suddenly remembering something.)* Oh, Bennie—I meant to put a special note on that carton over there. That's your mama's good china, and she wants 'em to be very careful with it.
BENEATHA. I'll do it.

*(*BENEATHA *finds a piece of paper and starts to draw large letters on it.)*

RUTH. You know what I'm going to do soon as I get in that new house?
BENEATHA. What?
RUTH. Honey—I'm going to run me a tub of water up to here . . . *(With her fingers practically up to her nostrils.)* And I'm going to get in it—and I am going to sit . . . and sit . . . and sit in that hot water and the first person who knocks to tell *me* to hurry up and come out—
BENEATHA. Gets shot at sunrise.
RUTH *(Laughing happily).* You said it, sister! *(Noticing how large* BENEATHA *is absent-mindedly making the note.)* Honey, they ain't going to read that from no airplane.

BENEATHA (*Laughing herself*). I guess I always think things have more emphasis if they are big, somehow.

RUTH (*Looking up at her and smiling*). You and your brother seem to have that as a philosophy of life. Lord, that man—done changed so 'round here. You know—you know what we did last night? Me and Walter Lee?

BENEATHA. What?

RUTH (*Smiling to herself*). We went to the movies. (*Looking at* BENEATHA *to see if she understands.*) We went to the movies. You know the last time me and Walter went to the movies together?

BENEATHA. No.

RUTH. Me neither. That's how long it been. (*Smiling again.*) But we went last night. The picture wasn't much good, but that didn't seem to matter. We went—and we held hands.

BENEATHA. Oh, Lord!

RUTH. We held hands—and you know what?

BENEATHA. What?

RUTH. When we come out of the show it was late and dark and all the stores and things was closed up . . . and it was kind of chilly and there wasn't many people on the streets . . . and we was still holding hands, me and Walter.

BENEATHA. You're killing me.

(WALTER *enters with a large package. His happiness is deep in him; he cannot keep still with his new-found exuberance. He is singing and wiggling and snapping his fingers. He puts his package in a corner and puts a phonograph record, which he has brought in with him, on the record player. As the music comes up, he dances over to* RUTH *and tries to get her to dance with him. She gives in at last to his raunchiness and in a fit of giggling allows herself to be drawn into his mood and together they deliberately burlesque an old social dance of their youth.*)

BENEATHA (*Regarding them a long time as they dance, then drawing in her breath for a deeply exaggerated comment which she does not particularly mean*). Talk about—olddddddddddd-fashionedddddddd—Negroes!

WALTER (*Stopping momentarily*). What kind of Negroes?

(*He says this in fun. He is not angry with her today, nor with anyone. He starts to dance with his wife again.*)

BENEATHA. Old-fashioned.

WALTER (*As he dances with* RUTH). You know, when these *New Negroes* have their convention—(*Pointing at his sister*)—that is going to be the chairman of the Committee on Unending Agitation. (*He goes on dancing, then stops.*) Race, race, race! . . . Girl, I do believe you are the first person in the history of the entire human race to successfully brainwash yourself. (BENEATHA *breaks up and he goes on dancing. He stops again, enjoying his tease.*) Even the N double A C P takes a holiday sometimes! (BENEATHA *and* RUTH *laugh. He dances with* RUTH *some more and starts to laugh and stops and pantomimes someone over an operating table.*) I can just see that chick someday looking down at some poor cat on an operating table before she starts to slice him, saying . . . (*Pulling his sleeves back maliciously.*) "By the way, what are your views on civil rights down there? . . ."

(*He laughs at her again and starts to dance happily. The bell sounds.*)

BENEATHA. Sticks and stones may break my bones but . . . words will never hurt me!

(BENEATHA *goes to the door and opens it as* WALTER *and* RUTH *go on with the clowning.* BENEATHA *is somewhat surprised to see a quiet-looking middle-aged white man in a business suit holding his hat and a briefcase in his hand and consulting a small piece of paper.)*

MAN. Uh—how do you do, miss. I am looking for a Mrs.—*(He looks at the slip of paper.)* Mrs. Lena Younger?

BENEATHA *(Smoothing her hair with slight embarrassment).* Oh—yes, that's my mother. Excuse me. *(She closes the door and turns to quiet the other two.)* Ruth! Brother! Somebody's here. *(Then she opens the door. The man casts a curious quick glance at all of them.)* Uh—come in please.

MAN *(Coming in).* Thank you.

BENEATHA. My mother isn't here just now. Is it business?

MAN. Yes . . . well, of a sort.

WALTER *(Freely, the Man of the House).* Have a seat. I'm Mrs. Younger's son. I look after most of her business matters.

*(RUTH and BENEATHA exchange amused glances.)*

MAN *(Regarding WALTER, and sitting).* Well— My name is Karl Lindner . . .

WALTER *(Stretching out his hand).* Walter Younger. This is my wife—*(RUTH nods politely.)*—and my sister.

LINDNER. How do you do.

WALTER *(Amiably, as he sits himself easily on a chair, leaning with interest forward on his knees and looking expectantly into the newcomer's face).* What can we do for you, Mr. Lindner!

LINDNER *(Some minor shuffling of the hat and briefcase on his knees).* Well—I am a representative of the Clybourne Park Improvement Association—

WALTER *(Pointing).* Why don't you sit your things on the floor?

LINDNER. Oh—yes. Thank you. *(He slides the briefcase and hat under the chair.)* And as I was saying—I am from the Clybourne Park Improvement Association, and we have had it brought to our attention at the last meeting that you people—or at least your mother—has bought a piece of residential property at—*(He digs for the slip of paper again.)*—four o six Clybourne Street . . .

WALTER. That's right. Care for something to drink? Ruth, get Mr. Lindner a beer.

LINDNER *(Upset for some reason).* Oh—no, really. I mean thank you very much, but no thank you.

RUTH *(Innocently).* Some coffee?

LINDNER. Thank you, nothing at all.

*(BENEATHA is watching the man carefully.)*

LINDNER. Well, I don't know how much you folks know about our organization. *(He is a gentle man; thoughtful and somewhat labored in his manner.)* It is one of these community organizations set up to look after—oh, you know, things like block upkeep and special projects, and we also have what we call our New Neighbors Orientation Committee . . .

BENEATHA *(Drily).* Yes—and what do they do?

LINDNER *(Turning a little to her and then returning the main force to WALTER).* Well —it's what you might call a sort of welcoming committee, I guess. I mean they, we, I'm the chairman of the committee— go around and see the new people who move into the neighborhood and sort of give them the lowdown on the way we do things out in Clybourne Park.

BENEATHA *(With appreciation of the two meanings, which escape RUTH and WALTER).* Un-huh.

LINDNER. And we also have the category of what the association calls—*(He looks elsewhere.)*—uh—special community problems . . .

BENEATHA. Yes—and what are some of those?

WALTER. Girl, let the man talk.

LINDNER *(With understated relief).* Thank you. I would sort of like to explain this thing in my own way. I mean I want to explain to you in a certain way.

WALTER. Go ahead.

LINDNER. Yes. Well. I'm going to try to get right to the point. I'm sure we'll all appreciate that in the long run.

BENEATHA. Yes.

WALTER. Be still now!

LINDNER. Well—

RUTH *(Still innocently)*. Would you like another chair—you don't look comfortable.

LINDNER *(More frustrated than annoyed)*. No, thank you very much. Please. Well—to get right to the point I—*(A great breath, and he is off at last.)* I am sure you people must be aware of some of the incidents that have happened in various parts of the city when black people have moved into certain areas—*(BENEATHA exhales heavily and starts tossing a piece of fruit up and down in the air.)* Well—because we have what I think is going to be a unique type of organization in American community life—not only do we deplore that kind of thing—but we are trying to do something about it. *(BENEATHA stops tossing and turns with a new and quizzical interest to the man.)* We feel—*(gaining confidence in his mission because of the interest in the faces of the people he is talking to)*—we feel that most of the trouble in this world, when you come right down to it—*(He hits his knee for emphasis.)*—most of the trouble exists because people just don't sit down and talk to each other.

RUTH *(Nodding as she might in church, pleased with the remark)*. You can say that again, mister.

LINDNER *(More encouraged by such affirmation)*. That we don't try hard enough in this world to understand the other fellow's problem. The other guy's point of view.

RUTH. Now that's right.

*(BENEATHA and WALTER merely watch and listen with genuine interest.)*

LINDNER. Yes—that's the way we feel out in Clybourne Park. And that's why I was elected to come here this afternoon and talk to you people. Friendly like, you know, the way people should talk to each other and see if we couldn't find some way to work this thing out. As I say, the whole business is a matter of *caring* about the other fellow. Anybody can see that you are a nice family of folks, hard working and honest I'm sure. *(BENEATHA frowns slightly, quizzically, her head tilted regarding him.)* Today everybody knows what it means to be on the outside of *something*. And of course, there is always somebody who is out to take the advantage of people who don't always understand.

WALTER. What do you mean?

LINDNER. Well—you see our community is made up of people who've worked hard as the dickens for years to build up that little community. They're not rich and fancy people; just hard-working, honest people who don't really have much but those little homes and a dream of the kind of community they want to raise their children in. Now, I don't say we are perfect, and there is a lot wrong in some of the things they want. But you've got to admit that a man, right or wrong, has the right to want to have the neighborhood he lives in a certain kind of way. And at the moment the overwhelming majority of our people out there feel that people get along better, take more of a common interest in the life of the community, when they share a common background. I want you to believe me when I tell you that race prejudice simply doesn't enter into it. It is a matter of the people of Clybourne Park believing, rightly or wrongly, as I say, that for the happiness of all concerned that our Negro families are happier when they live in their *own* communities.

BENEATHA *(With a grand and bitter gesture).* This, friends, is the Welcoming Committee!

WALTER *(Dumfounded, looking at LINDNER).* Is this what you came marching all the way over here to tell us?

LINDNER. Well, now we've been having a fine conversation. I hope you'll hear me all the way through.

WALTER *(Tightly).* Go ahead, man.

LINDNER. You see—in the face of all things I have said, we are prepared to make your family a very generous offer . . .

BENEATHA. Thirty pieces and not a coin less!

WALTER. Yeah?

LINDNER *(Putting on his glasses and drawing a form out of the briefcase).* Our association is prepared, through the collective effort of our people, to buy the house from you at a financial gain to your family.

RUTH. Lord have mercy, ain't this the living gall!

WALTER. All right, you through?

LINDNER. Well, I want to give you the exact terms of the financial arrangement—

WALTER. We don't want to hear no exact terms of no arrangements. I want to know if you got any more to tell us 'bout getting together?

LINDNER *(Taking off his glasses).* Well—I don't suppose that you feel . . .

WALTER. Never mind how I feel—you got any more to say 'bout how people ought to sit down and talk to each other? . . . Get out of my house, man.

*(He turns his back and walks to the door.)*

LINDNER *(Looking around at the hostile faces and reaching and assembling his hat and briefcase).* Well—I don't understand why you people are reacting this way. What do you think you are going to gain by moving into a neighborhood where you just aren't wanted and where some elements—well—people can get awful worked up when they feel that their whole way of life and everything they've ever worked for is threatened.

WALTER. Get out.

LINDNER *(At the door, holding a small card).* Well—I'm sorry it went like this.

WALTER. Get out.

LINDNER *(Almost sadly regarding WALTER).* You just can't force people to change their hearts, son.

*(He turns and puts his card on a table and exits. WALTER pushes the door to with stinging hatred, and stands looking at it. RUTH just sits and BENEATHA just stands. They say nothing. MAMA and TRAVIS enter.)*

MAMA. Well—this all the packing got done since I left out of here this morning. I testify before God that my children got all the energy of the dead. What time the moving men due?

BENEATHA. Four o'clock. You had a caller, Mama.

*(She is smiling, teasingly.)*

MAMA. Sure enough—who?

BENEATHA. *(Her arms folded saucily).* The Welcoming Committee.

*(WALTER and RUTH giggle.)*

MAMA *(Innocently).* Who?

BENEATHA. The Welcoming Committee. They said they're sure going to be glad to see you when you get there.

WALTER *(Devilishly).* Yeah, they said they can't hardly wait to see your face.

*(Laughter.)*

MAMA *(Sensing their facetiousness).* What's the matter with you all?

WALTER. Ain't nothing the matter with us. We just telling you 'bout the gentleman who came to see you this afternoon. From the Clybourne Park Improvement Association.

MAMA. What he want?

RUTH (*In the same mood as* BENEATHA *and* WALTER). To welcome you, honey.

WALTER. He said they can't hardly wait. He said the one thing they don't have, that they just *dying* to have out there is a fine family of black people! (*To* RUTH *and* BENEATHA.) Ain't that right!

RUTH *and* BENEATHA (*Mockingly*). Yeah! He left his card in case—

(*They indicate the card, and* MAMA *picks it up and throws it on the floor—understanding and looking off as she draws her chair up to the table on which she has put her plant and some sticks and some cord.*)

MAMA. Father, give us strength. (*Knowingly —and without fun.*) Did he threaten us?

BENEATHA. Oh—Mama—they don't do it like that any more. He talked Brotherhood. He said everybody ought to learn how to sit down and hate each other with good Christian fellowship.

(*She and* WALTER *shake hands to ridicule the remark.*)

MAMA (*Sadly*). Lord, protect us . . .

RUTH. You should hear the money those folks raised to buy the house from us. All we paid and then some.

BENEATHA. What they think we going to do —eat 'em?

RUTH. No, honey, marry 'em.

MAMA (*Shaking her head*). Lord, Lord, Lord . . .

RUTH. Well—that's the way the crackers crumble. Joke.

BENEATHA (*Laughingly noticing what her mother is doing*). Mama, what are you doing?

MAMA. Fixing my plant so it won't get hurt none on the way.

BENEATHA. Mama, you going to take *that* to the new house?

MAMA. Un-huh—

BENEATHA. That raggedy-looking old thing?

MAMA (*Stopping and looking at her*). It expresses *me*.

RUTH (*With delight, to* BENEATHA). So there, Miss Thing!

(WALTER *comes to* MAMA *suddenly and bends down behind her and squeezes her in his arms with all his strength. She is overwhelmed by the suddenness of it and, though delighted, her manner is like that of* RUTH *with* TRAVIS.)

MAMA. Look out now, boy! You make me mess up my thing here!

WALTER (*His face lit, he slips down on his knees beside her, his arms still about her*). Mama . . . you know what it means to climb up in the chariot?

MAMA (*Gruffly, very happy*). Get on away from me now . . .

RUTH (*Near the gift-wrapped package, trying to catch* WALTER's *eye*). Psst—

WALTER. What the old song say, Mama . . .

RUTH. Walter—Now?

(*She is pointing at the package.*)

WALTER (*Speaking the lines, sweetly, playfully, in his mother's face*).
   I got wings . . . you got wings . . .
   All God's Children got wings . . .

MAMA. Boy—get out of my face and do some work . . .

WALTER.
   When I get to heaven gonna put on my wings,
   Gonna fly all over God's heaven . . .

BENEATHA (*Teasingly, from across the room*). Everybody talking 'bout heaven ain't going there!

WALTER (*To* RUTH, *who is carrying the box across to them*). I don't know, you think we ought to give her that . . . Seems to me she ain't been very appreciative around here.

MAMA (*Eying the box, which is obviously a gift*). What is that?

WALTER (*Taking it from* RUTH *and putting it on the table in front of* MAMA). Well—what you all think? Should we give it to her?

RUTH. Oh—she was pretty good today.

MAMA. I'll good you—

(*She turns her eyes to the box again.*)

BENEATHA. Open it, Mama.

(*She stands up, looks at it, turns and looks at all of them, and then presses her hands together and does not open the package.*)

WALTER (*Sweetly*). Open it, Mama. It's for you. (MAMA *looks in his eyes. It is the first present in her life without its being Christmas. Slowly she opens her package and lifts out, one by one, a brand-new sparkling set of gardening tools.* WALTER *continues, prodding.*) Ruth made up the note —read it . . .

MAMA (*Picking up the card and adjusting her glasses*). "To our own Mrs. Miniver[9]—Love from Brother, Ruth, and Beneatha." Ain't that lovely . . .

TRAVIS (*Tugging at his father's sleeve*). Daddy, can I give her mine now?

WALTER. All right, son. (TRAVIS *flies to get his gift.*) Travis didn't want to go in with the rest of us, Mama. He got his own. (*Somewhat amused.*) We don't know what it is . . .

TRAVIS (*Racing back in the room with a large hatbox and putting it in front of his grandmother*). Here!

MAMA. Lord have mercy, baby. You done gone and bought your grandmother a hat?

TRAVIS (*Very proud*). Open it!

(*She does and lifts out an elaborate, but very elaborate, wide gardening hat, and all the adults break up at the sight of it.*)

---

9. **Mrs. Miniver:** the noble, brave heroine of a 1942 motion picture, *Mrs. Miniver.*

RUTH. Travis, honey, what is that?

TRAVIS (Who thinks it is beautiful and appropriate). It's a gardening hat! Like the ladies always have on in the magazines when they work in their gardens.

BENEATHA (Giggling fiercely). Travis—we were trying to make Mama Mrs. Miniver—not Scarlett O'Hara![10]

MAMA (Indignantly). What's the matter with you all! This here is a beautiful hat! (Absurdly). I always wanted me one just like it!

(She pops it on her head to prove it to her grandson, and the hat is ludicrous and considerably oversized.)

RUTH. Hot dog! Go, Mama!

WALTER (Doubled over with laughter). I'm sorry, Mama—but you look like you ready to go out and chop you some cotton sure enough!

(They all laugh except MAMA, out of deference to TRAVIS' feelings.)

MAMA (Gathering the boy up to her). Bless your heart—this is the prettiest hat I ever owned— (WALTER, RUTH, and BENEATHA chime in—noisily, festively and insincerely congratulating TRAVIS on his gift.) What are we all standing around here for? We ain't finished packin' yet. Bennie, you ain't packed one book.

(The bell rings.)

BENEATHA. That couldn't be the movers . . . it's not hardly two good yet—

(BENEATHA goes into her room. MAMA starts for door.)

WALTER (Turning, stiffening). Wait—wait—I'll get it.

(He stands and looks at the door.)

MAMA. You expecting company, son?

WALTER. (Just looking at the door). Yeah—yeah . . .

(MAMA looks at RUTH, and they exchange innocent and unfrightened glances.)

MAMA (Not understanding). Well, let them in, son.

BENEATHA (From her room). We need some more string.

MAMA. Travis—you run to the hardware and get me some string cord.

(MAMA goes out and WALTER turns and looks at RUTH. TRAVIS goes to a dish for money.)

RUTH. Why don't you answer the door, man?

WALTER (Suddenly bounding across the floor to her). 'Cause sometimes it hard to let the future begin! (Stooping down in her face.)
    I got wings! You got wings!
    All God's children got wings!
(He crosses to the door and throws it open. Standing there is a very slight little man in a not too prosperous business suit and with haunted frightened eyes and a hat pulled down tightly, brim up, around his forehead. TRAVIS passes between the men and exits. WALTER leans deep in the man's face, still in his jubilance.)
    When I get to heaven gonna put on my wings,
        Gonna fly all over God's heaven . . .
(The little man just stares at him.)
        Heaven—
(Suddenly he stops and looks past the little man into the empty hallway.) Where's Willy, man?

BOBO. He ain't with me.

WALTER (Not disturbed). Oh—come on in. You know my wife.

BOBO (Dumbly, taking off his hat). Yes—h'you, Miss Ruth.

RUTH (Quietly, a mood apart from her husband already, seeing BOBO). Hello, Bobo.

WALTER. You right on time today . . . Right on time. That's the way! (He slaps BOBO on his back.) Sit down . . . lemme hear.

10. **Scarlett O'Hara:** a Georgia belle in the novel *Gone with the Wind.*

(RUTH *stands stiffly and quietly in back of them, as though somehow she senses death, her eyes fixed on her husband.*)

BOBO (*His frightened eyes on the floor, his hat in his hands*). Could I please get a drink of water, before I tell you about it, Walter Lee?

(WALTER *does not take his eyes off the man.* RUTH *goes blindly to the tap and gets a glass of water and brings it to* BOBO.)

WALTER. There ain't nothing wrong, is there?

BOBO. Lemme tell you—

WALTER. Man—didn't nothing go wrong?

BOBO. Lemme tell you—Walter Lee. (*Looking at* RUTH *and talking to her more than to* WALTER.) You know how it was. I got to tell you how it was. I mean first I got to tell you how it was all the way . . . I mean about the money I put in, Walter Lee . . .

WALTER (*With taut agitation now*). What about the money you put in?

BOBO. Well—it wasn't much as we told you —me and Willy—(*He stops.*) I'm sorry, Walter. I got a bad feeling about it. I got a real bad feeling about it . . .

WALTER. Man, what you telling me about all this for? . . . Tell me what happened in Springfield . . .

BOBO. Springfield.

RUTH (*Like a dead woman*). What was supposed to happen in Springfield?

BOBO (*To her*). This deal that me and Walter went into with Willy— Me and Willy was going to go down to Springfield and spread some money 'round so's we wouldn't have to wait so long for the liquor license . . . That's what we were going to do. Everybody said that was the way you had to do, you understand, Miss Ruth?

WALTER. Man—what happened down there?

BOBO (*A pitiful man, near tears*). I'm trying to tell you, Walter.

WALTER (*Screaming at him suddenly*). THEN TELL ME . . . WHAT'S THE MATTER WITH YOU?

BOBO. Man . . . I didn't go to no Springfield, yesterday.

WALTER (*Halted, life hanging in the moment*). Why not?

BOBO (*The long way, the hard way to tell*). 'Cause I didn't have no reasons to . . .

WALTER. Man, what are you talking about!

BOBO. I'm talking about the fact that when I got to the train station yesterday morning —eight o'clock like we planned . . . Man —Willy didn't never show up.

WALTER. Why . . . where was he . . . where is he?

BOBO. That's what I'm trying to tell you . . . I don't know . . . I waited six hours . . . I called his house . . . and I waited . . . six hours . . . I waited in that train station six hours . . . (*Breaking into tears.*) That was all the extra money I had in the world . . . (*Looking up at* WALTER *with the tears running down his face.*) Man, Willy is gone.

WALTER. Gone, what you mean Willy is gone? Gone where? You mean he went by himself. You mean he went off to Springfield by himself—to take care of getting the license—(*Turns and looks anxiously at* RUTH.) You mean maybe he didn't want too many people in on the business down there? (*Looks to* RUTH *again, as before.*) You know Willy got his own ways. (*Looks back to* BOBO.) Maybe you was late yesterday and he just went on down there without you. Maybe—maybe—he's been callin' you at home tryin' to tell you what happened or something. Maybe—maybe —he just got sick. He's somewhere—he's got to be somewhere. We just got to find him—me and you got to find him. (*Grabs* BOBO *senselessly by the collar and starts to shake him.*) We got to!

BOBO (*In sudden angry, frightened agony*). What's the matter with you, Walter! When a cat take off with your money he don't leave you no maps!

WALTER (*Turning madly, as though he is looking for* WILLY *in the very room*). Willy! . . . Willy . . . don't do it . . . Please don't do it . . . Man, not with that money . . . Man, please, not with that money . . . Oh, God . . . Don't let it be true . . . (*He is wandering around, crying out for* WILLY *and looking for him or perhaps for help from God.*) Man . . . I trusted you . . . Man, I put my life in your hands . . . (*He starts to crumple down on the floor as* RUTH *just covers her face in horror.* MAMA *opens the door and comes into the room, with* BENEATHA *behind her.*) Man . . . (*He starts to pound the floor with his fists, sobbing wildly.*) That money is made out of my father's flesh . . .

BOBO (*Standing over him helplessly*). I'm sorry, Walter . . . (*Only* WALTER'S *sobs reply.* BOBO *puts on his hat.*) I had my life staked on this deal, too . . .

(*He exits.*)

MAMA *(To* WALTER). Son—*(She goes to him, bends down to him, talks to his bent head.)* Son . . . Is it gone? Son, I gave you sixty-five hundred dollars. Is it gone? All of it? Beneatha's money too?

WALTER *(Lifting his head slowly)*. Mama . . . I never . . . went to the bank at all . . .

MAMA *(Not wanting to believe him)*. You mean . . . your sister's school money . . . you used that too . . . Walter? . . .

WALTER Yessss! . . . All of it . . . It's all gone . . .

*(There is total silence.* RUTH *stands with her face covered with her hands;* BENEATHA *leans forlornly against a wall, fingering a piece of red ribbon from the mother's gift.* MAMA *stops and looks at her son without recognition and then, quite without thinking about it, starts to beat him senselessly in the face.* BENEATHA *goes to them and stops it.)*

BENEATHA. Mama!

*(*MAMA *stops and looks at both of her children and rises slowly and wanders vaguely, aimlessly away from them.)*

MAMA. I seen . . . him . . . night after night . . . come in . . . and look at that rug . . . and then look at me . . . the red showing in his eyes . . . the veins moving in his head . . . I seen him grow thin and old before he was forty . . . working and working and working like somebody's old horse . . . killing himself . . . and you—you give it all away in a day . . .

BENEATHA. Mama—

MAMA. Oh, God . . . *(She looks up to Him.)* Look down here—and show me the strength.

BENEATHA. Mama—

MAMA *(Folding over)*. Strength . . .

BENEATHA *(Plaintively)*. Mama . . .

MAMA. Strength!

## Act II

### Getting at Meaning

1. What does the Ocomogosiay episode at the beginning of this act reveal about Beneatha's view of Walter? What does it reveal about Walter? What does George Murchison's reaction to this episode reveal about his character? What makes this scene humorous?

2. After refusing the hot milk and coffee that Ruth offers him, Walter demands, "Why you always trying to give me something to eat?" (p. 559) What is Ruth's reply? What does her reply reveal about their marriage?

3. Why is Ruth so excited about the new house? How does she believe that life will be different for the family?

4. What reasons does Mama give Walter for purchasing the house? What problems does she hope that the house will solve?

5. What is ironic about Mama's comment, "Walter Lee—it makes a difference in a man when he can walk on floors that belong to *him* . . ."?

6. In Act 2, Scene 2, Mama shows that she is sensitive to her children's needs. How does she show this sensitivity to Beneatha? To Walter? What has caused this change?

7. Is Walter's speech to Travis at the end of Scene 2 realistic? Explain. In what way is this scene similar to the scene in which Walter gives Travis the fifty cents?

8. How is the relationship between Walter and Ruth changed in Act 2, Scene 3? What has caused this change?

9. What are Lindner's arguments against the Youngers' move into Clybourne Park? How might Lindner define *brotherhood*?

10. Mrs. Miniver is a character in a movie about World War II. She tends her garden despite the bombs falling nearby. Why does the family call Mama "our own Mrs. Miniver"?

11. What news does Bobo bring? Why is Walter unable to accept this news? Has Bobo lost as much money as Walter? Explain.

12. What does Walter mean when he says, "That money was made out of my father's flesh"?

13. Why does Beneatha cry "Mama" over and over at the end of Scene 3? How have Walter's actions affected her?

### Developing Skills in Reading Literature

1. **Setting.** How much time elapses between Act 2, Scene 1 and Act 2, Scene 2? Between Scene 2 and Scene 3?

2. **Mood.** Contrast the mood at the beginning of Act 2, Scene 3 with the mood at the end of the scene. How does the change in mood reflect the change in the family?

3. **Structure.** Act 2 contains some of the most depressing scenes in the play, as well as some of the most joyful scenes. How does the playwright move the action from one extreme to the other? List all the episodes in this act in the order in which they occur. Study the list and analyze the structure of the act. Do the scenes grow progressively more threatening or depressing? Does tension build? Does the confidence of the reader in the family increase? Try to diagram the emotional pattern of this act.

### Developing Writing Skills

**Writing an Explanation.** Beneatha continually looks for new ways to express herself. Mama says of her plant, "It expresses *me*." Choose an object that you feel expresses you. In one paragraph, describe this object and explain how it expresses you.

## ACT III

*An hour later.*
*There is a sullen light of gloom in the living room, gray light, not unlike that which began the first scene of Act I. At left we can see* WALTER *within his room, alone with himself. He is stretched out on the bed, his shirt out and open, his arms under his head. He does not smoke, he does not cry out, he merely lies there, looking up at the ceiling, much as if he were alone in the world.*

*In the living room* BENEATHA *sits at the table, still surrounded by the now almost ominous packing crates. She sits looking off. We feel that this is a mood struck perhaps an hour before, and it lingers now, full of the empty sound of profound disappointment. We see on a line from her brother's bedroom the sameness of their attitudes. Presently the bell rings and* BENEATHA *rises without ambition or interest in answering. It is* ASAGAI, *smiling broadly, striding into the room with energy and happy expectation and conversation.*

ASAGAI. I came over . . . I had some free time. I thought I might help with the packing. Ah, I like the look of packing crates! A household in preparation for a journey! It depresses some people . . . but for me . . . it is another feeling. Something full of the flow of life, do you understand? Movement, progress . . . It makes me think of Africa.

BENEATHA. Africa!

ASAGAI. What kind of a mood is this? Have I told you how deeply you move me?

BENEATHA. He gave away the money, Asagai . . .

ASAGAI. Who gave away what money?

BENEATHA. The insurance money. My brother gave it away.

ASAGAI. Gave it away?

BENEATHA. He made an investment! With a man even Travis wouldn't have trusted.

ASAGAI. And it's gone?

BENEATHA. Gone!

ASAGAI. I'm very sorry . . . And you, now?

BENEATHA. Me? . . . Me? . . . Me, I'm nothing . . . Me. When I was very small . . . we used to take our sleds out in the wintertime and the only hills we had were the ice-covered stone steps of some houses down the street. And we used to fill them in with snow and make them smooth and slide down them all day . . . and it was very dangerous you know . . . far too steep . . . and sure enough one day a kid named Rufus came down too fast and hit the sidewalk . . . and we saw his face just split open right there in front of us . . . And I remember standing there looking at his bloody open face thinking that was the end of Rufus. But the ambulance came and they took him to the hospital and they fixed the broken bones and they sewed it all up . . . and the next time I saw Rufus he just had a little line down the middle of his face . . . I never got over that . . .

*(*WALTER *sits up, listening on the bed. Throughout this scene it is important that we feel his reaction at all times, that he visibly respond to the words of his sister and* ASAGAI.*)*

ASAGAI. What?

BENEATHA. That that was what one person could do for another, fix him up—sew up the problem, make him all right again. That was the most marvelous thing in the world . . . I wanted to do that. I always thought it was the one concrete thing in the world that a human being could do. Fix up the sick, you know—and make them whole again. This was truly being God . . .

ASAGAI. You wanted to be God?

BENEATHA. No—I wanted to cure. It used to

be so important to me. I wanted to cure. It used to matter. I used to care. I mean about people and how their bodies hurt . . .

ASAGAI. And you've stopped caring?

BENEATHA. Yes—I think so.

ASAGAI. Why?

(WALTER *rises, goes to the door of his room and is about to open it, then stops and stands listening, leaning on the door jamb.*)

BENEATHA. Because it doesn't seem deep enough, close enough to what ails mankind—I mean this thing of sewing up bodies or administering drugs. Don't you understand? It was a child's reaction to the world. I thought that doctors had the secret to all the hurts. . . . That's the way a child sees things—or an idealist.

ASAGAI. Children see things very well sometimes—and idealists even better.

BENEATHA. I know that's what you think. Because you are still where I left off—you still care. This is what you see for the world, for Africa. You with the dreams of the future will patch up all Africa—you are going to cure the Great Sore of colonialism with Independence——

ASAGAI. Yes!

BENEATHA. Yes—and you think that one word is the penicillin of the human spirit: "Independence!" But then what?

ASAGAI. That will be the problem for another time. First we must get there.

BENEATHA. And where does it end?

ASAGAI. End? Who even spoke of an end? To life? To living?

BENEATHA. An end to misery!

ASAGAI (*Smiling*). You sound like a French intellectual.

BENEATHA. No! I sound like a human being who just had her future taken right out of her hands! While I was sleeping in my bed in there, things were happening in this world that directly concerned me—and nobody asked me, consulted me—

they just went out and did things—and changed my life. Don't you see there isn't any real progress, Asagai, there is only one large circle that we march in, around and around, each of us with our own little picture—in front of us—our own little mirage that we think is the future.

ASAGAI. That is the mistake.

BENEATHA. What?

ASAGAI. What you just said—about the circle. It isn't a circle—it is simply a long line—as in geometry, you know, one that reaches into infinity. And because we cannot see the end—we also cannot see how it changes. And it is very odd, but those who see the changes are called "idealists"—and those who cannot, or refuse to think, they are the "realists." It is very strange, and amusing too, I think.

BENEATHA. You—you are almost religious.

ASAGAI. Yes . . . I think I have the religion of doing what is necessary in the world—and of worshipping man—because he is so marvelous, you see.

BENEATHA. Man is foul! And the human race deserves its misery!

ASAGAI. You see: *you* have become the religious one in the old sense. Already, and after such a small defeat, you are worshipping despair.

BENEATHA. From now on, I worship the truth—and the truth is that people are puny, small and selfish. . . .

ASAGAI. Truth? Why is it that you despairing ones always think that only you have the truth? I never thought to see *you* like that. You! Your brother made a stupid, childish mistake—and you are grateful to him. So that now you can give up the ailing human race on account of it. You talk about what good is struggle; what good is anything? Where are we all going? And why are we bothering?

BENEATHA. *And you cannot answer it!* All your talk and dreams about Africa and

Independence. Independence and then what? What about all the crooks and petty thieves and just plain idiots who will come into power to steal and plunder the same as before——only now they will be black and do it in the name of the new Independence— You cannot answer that.

ASAGAI *(Shouting over her). I live the answer! (Pause.)* In my village at home it is the exceptional man who can even read a newspaper . . . or who ever *sees* a book at all. I will go home and much of what I will have to say will seem strange to the people of my village . . . But I will teach and work and things will happen, slowly and swiftly. At times it will seem that nothing changes at all . . . and then again . . . the sudden dramatic events that make history leap into the future. And then quiet again. Retrogression even. Guns, murder, revolution. And I even will have moments when I wonder if the quiet was not better than all that death and hatred. But I will look about my village at the illiteracy and disease and ignorance, and I will not wonder long. And perhaps . . . perhaps I will be a great man . . . I mean perhaps I will hold on to the substance of truth and find my way always with the right course . . . and perhaps for it I will be butchered in my bed some night by the servants of empire . . .

BENEATHA. *The martyr!*

ASAGAI. . . . or perhaps I shall live to be a very old man, respected and esteemed in my new nation . . . And perhaps I shall hold office, and this is what I'm trying to tell you, Alaiyo; perhaps the things I believe now for my country will be wrong and outmoded, and I will not understand and do terrible things to have things my way or merely to keep my power. Don't you see that there will be young men and women, not British soldiers then, but my own black countrymen . . . to step out of the shadows some evening and slit my then useless throat? Don't you see they have always been there . . . that they always will be. And that such a thing as my own death will be an advance? They who might kill me even . . . actually replenish me!

BENEATHA. Oh, Asagai, I know all that.

ASAGAI. Good! Then stop moaning and groaning and tell me what you plan to do.

BENEATHA. Do?

ASAGAI. I have a bit of a suggestion.

BENEATHA. What?

ASAGAI *(Rather quietly for him).* That when it is all over—that you come home with me—

BENEATHA *(Slapping herself on the forehead with exasperation born of misunderstanding).* Oh—Asagai—at this moment you decide to be romantic!

ASAGAI *(Quickly understanding the misunderstanding).* My dear, young creature of the New World—I do not mean across the city—I mean across the ocean; home—to Africa.

BENEATHA *(Slowly understanding and turning to him with murmured amazement).* To—to Nigeria?

ASAGAI. Yes! . . . *(Smiling and lifting his arms playfully).* Three hundred years later the African Prince rose up out of the seas and swept the maiden back across the middle passage over which her ancestors had come—

BENEATHA *(Unable to play).* Nigeria?

ASAGAI. Nigeria. Home. *(Coming to her with genuine romantic flippancy.)* I will show you our mountains and our stars; and give you cool drinks from gourds and teach you the old songs and the ways of our people —and, in time, we will pretend that— *(Very softly)*—you have only been away for a day—

*(She turns her back to him, thinking. He swings her around and takes her full in his*

*arms in a long embrace which proceeds to passion.)*

BENEATHA *(Pulling away).* You're getting me all mixed up—

ASAGAI. Why?

BENEATHA. Too many things—too many things have happened today. I must sit down and think. I don't know what I feel about anything right this minute.

*(She promptly sits down and props her chin on her fist.)*

ASAGAI *(Charmed).* All right, I shall leave you. No—don't get up. *(Touching her, gently, sweetly.)* Just sit awhile and think . . . Never be afraid to sit awhile and think. *(He goes to door and looks at her.)* How often I have looked at you and said, "Ah—so this is what the New World hath finally wrought . . ."

*(He exits.* BENEATHA *sits on alone. Presently* WALTER *enters from his room and starts to rummage through things, feverishly looking for something. She looks up and turns in her seat.)*

BENEATHA *(Hissingly).* Yes—just look at what the New World hath wrought! . . . Just look! *(She gestures with bitter disgust.)* There he is! *Monsieur le petit bourgeois noir*[11]—himself! There he is— Symbol of a Rising Class! Entrepreneur! Titan of the System! *(WALTER ignores her completely and continues frantically and destructively looking for something and hurling things to floor and tearing things out of their place in his search.* BENEATHA *ignores the eccentricity of his actions and goes on with the monologue of insult.)* Did you dream of yachts on Lake Michigan, Brother? Did you see yourself on that Great Day sitting down at the Conference Table, surrounded by all the mighty bald-headed men in America? All halted, waiting, breathless, waiting for your pronouncements on industry? Waiting for you—Chairman of the Board? *(WALTER finds what he is looking for—a small piece of white paper—and pushes it in his pocket and puts on his coat and rushes out without ever having looked at her. She shouts after him.)* I look at you and I see the final triumph of stupidity in the world!

*(The door slams and she returns to just sitting again.* RUTH *comes quickly out of* MAMA'S *room.)*

RUTH. Who was that?

BENEATHA. Your husband.

RUTH. Where did he go?

BENEATHA. Who knows—maybe he has an appointment at U.S. Steel.

RUTH *(Anxiously, with frightened eyes).* You didn't say nothing bad to him, did you?

BENEATHA. Bad? Say anything bad to him? No—I told him he was a sweet boy and full of dreams and everything is strictly peachy keen, as the ofay[12] kids say!

*(MAMA enters from her bedroom. She is lost, vague, trying to catch hold, to make some sense of her former command of the world, but it still eludes her. A sense of waste overwhelms her gait; a measure of apology rides on her shoulders. She goes to her plant, which has remained on the table, looks at it, picks it up and takes it to the window sill and sits it outside, and she stands and looks at it a long moment. Then she closes the window, straightens her body with effort and turns around to her children.)*

MAMA. Well—ain't it a mess in here, though? *(A false cheerfulness, a beginning of something.)* I guess we all better stop moping around and get some work done. All this unpacking and everything we got to do. *(RUTH raises her head slowly in response to the sense of the line; and BENEATHA in*

---

11. *Monsieur le petit bourgeois noir* (mə syö′ lə pə tē′ b<del>u</del>r zwä′ nwär) *French:* Mr. lower middle class black.
12. **ofay** *Slang:* a white person.

*similar manner turns very slowly to look at her mother.)* One of you all better call the moving people and tell 'em not to come.

RUTH. Tell 'em not to come?

MAMA. Of course, baby. Ain't no need in 'em coming all the way here and having to go back. They charges for that too. *(She sits down, fingers to her brow, thinking.)* Lord, ever since I was a little girl, I always remembers people saying, "Lena—Lena Eggleston, you aims too high all the time. You needs to slow down and see life a little more like it is. Just slow down some." That's what they always used to say down home—"Lord, that Lena Eggleston is a high-minded thing. She'll get her due one day!"

RUTH. No, Lena . . .

MAMA. Me and Big Walter just didn't never learn right.

RUTH. Lena, no! We gotta go. Bennie—tell her . . . *(She rises and crosses to* BENEATHA *with her arms outstretched.* BENEATHA *doesn't respond.)* Tell her we can still move . . . the notes ain't but a hundred and twenty-five a month. We got four grown people in this house—we can work . . .

MAMA *(To herself).* Just aimed too high all the time—

RUTH *(Turning and going to* MAMA *fast—the words pouring out with urgency and desperation).* Lena—I'll work . . . I'll work twenty hours a day in all the kitchens in Chicago . . . I'll strap my baby on my back if I have to and scrub all the floors in America and wash all the sheets in America if I have to—but we got to move . . . We got to get out of here . . .

*(*MAMA *reaches out absently and pats* RUTH's *hand.)*

MAMA. No—I sees things differently now. Been thinking 'bout some of the things we could do to fix this place up some. I seen a second-hand bureau over on Maxwell Street just the other day that could fit right there. *(She points to where the new furniture might go.* RUTH *wanders away from her.)* Would need some new handles on it and then a little varnish and then it look like something brand-new. And—we can put up them new curtains in the kitchen . . . Why this place be looking fine. Cheer us all up so that we forget trouble ever came . . . *(To* RUTH.*)* And you could get some nice screens to put up in your room round the baby's bassinet . . . *(She looks at both of them, pleadingly.)* Sometimes you just got to know when to give up some things . . . and hold on to what you got.

*(*WALTER *enters from the outside, looking spent and leaning against the door, his coat hanging from him.)*

MAMA. Where you been, son?

WALTER *(Breathing hard).* Made a call.

MAMA. To who, son?

WALTER. To The Man.

MAMA. What man, baby?

WALTER. The Man, Mama. Don't you know who The Man is?

RUTH. Walter Lee?

WALTER. *The Man.* Like the guys in the streets say—The Man. Captain Boss—Mistuh Charley . . . Old Captain Please Mr. Bossman . . .

BENEATHA *(Suddenly).* Lindner!

WALTER. That's right! That's good. I told him to come right over.

BENEATHA *(Fiercely, understanding).* For what? What do you want to see him for!

WALTER *(Looking at his sister).* We going to do business with him.

MAMA. What you talking 'bout, son?

WALTER. Talking 'bout life, Mama. You all always telling me to see life like it is. Well—I laid in there on my back today . . . and I figured it out. Life just like it is. Who gets and who don't get. *(He sits down with his coat on and laughs.)* Mama, you know it's all divided up. Life is. Sure enough. Between the takers and the "tooken." (He laughs.) I've figured it out finally. (He looks around at them.) Yeah. Some of us always getting "tooken." (He laughs.) People like Willy Harris, they don't never get "tooken." And you know why the rest of us do? 'Cause we all mixed up. Mixed up bad. We get to looking 'round for the right and the wrong; and we worry about it and cry about it and stay up nights trying to figure out 'bout the wrong and the right of things all the time . . . And all the time, man, them takers is out there operating, just taking and taking. Willy Harris? Shoot—Willy Harris don't even count. He don't even count in the big scheme of things. But I'll say one thing for old Willy Harris . . . he's taught me something. He's taught me to keep my eye on what counts in this world. Yeah—(Shouting out a little.) Thanks, Willy!

RUTH. What did you call that man for, Walter Lee?

WALTER. Called him to tell him to come on over to the show. Gonna put on a show for the man. Just what he wants to see. You see, Mama, the man came here today and he told us that them people out there where you want us to move—well they so upset they willing to pay us not to move out there. (He laughs again.) And—and oh, Mama—you would of been proud of the way me and Ruth and Bennie acted. We told him to get out . . . Lord have mercy! We told the man to get out. Oh, we was some proud folks this afternoon, yeah. (He lights a cigarette.) We were still full of that old-time stuff . . .

RUTH (Coming toward him slowly). You talking 'bout taking them people's money to keep us from moving in that house?

WALTER. I ain't just talking 'bout it, baby—I'm telling you that's what's going to happen.

BENEATHA. Oh, God! Where is the bottom! Where is the real honest-to-God bottom so he can't go any farther!

WALTER. See—that's the old stuff. You and that boy that was here today. You all want everybody to carry a flag and a spear and sing some marching songs, huh? You wanna spend your life looking into things and trying to find the right and the wrong part, huh? Yeah. You know what's going to happen to that boy someday—he'll find himself sitting in a dungeon, locked in forever—and the takers will have the key! Forget it, baby! There ain't no causes—there ain't nothing but taking in this world, and he who takes most is smartest—and it don't make a bit of difference how.

MAMA. You making something inside me cry, son. Some awful pain inside me.

WALTER. Don't cry, Mama. Understand. That white man is going to walk in that door able to write checks for more money than we ever had. It's important to him and I'm going to help him . . . I'm going to put on the show, Mama.

MAMA. Son—I come from five generations of people who was slaves and sharecroppers—but ain't nobody in my family never let nobody pay 'em no money that was a way of telling us we wasn't fit to walk the earth. We ain't never been that poor. (Raising her eyes and looking at him.) We ain't never been that dead inside.

BENEATHA. Well—we are dead now. All the talk about dreams and sunlight that goes on in this house. All dead.

WALTER. What's the matter with you all! I didn't make this world! It was give to me this way! Yes, I want me some yachts someday! Yes, I want to hang some real pearls 'round my wife's neck. Ain't she supposed to wear no pearls? Somebody tell me—tell me, who decides which women is suppose to wear pearls in this world. I tell you I am a *man*—and I think my wife should wear some pearls in this world!

*(This last line hangs a good while, and* WALTER *begins to move about the room. The word "Man" has penetrated his consciousness; he mumbles it to himself repeatedly between strange agitated pauses as he moves about.)*

MAMA. Baby, how you going to feel on the inside?

WALTER. Fine! . . . Going to feel fine . . . a man . . .

MAMA. You won't have nothing left then, Walter Lee.

WALTER. *(Coming to her).* I'm going to feel fine, Mama. I'm going to look The Man in the eyes and say—*(He falters.)*—and say, "All right, Mr. Lindner—*(He falters even more.)*—that's your neighborhood out there. You got the right to keep it like you want. You got the right to have it like you want. Just write the check and—the house is yours." And, and I am going to say—*(His voice almost breaks.)* And you—you people just put the money in my hand and you won't have to live next to this bunch of—*(He straightens up and moves away from his mother, walking around the room.)* Maybe—maybe I'll just get down on my black knees . . . *(He does so;* RUTH *and* BENNIE *and* MAMA *watch him in frozen horror.)* Captain, Mistuh, Bossman. *(He starts crying.)* A-hee-hee-hee! *(Wringing his hands in profoundly anguished imitation.)* Yassssssuh! Great White Father, just gi' ussen de money, fo' God's sake, and we's ain't gwine come out deh and dirty up yo' white folks neighborhood . . .

*(He breaks down completely, then gets up and goes into the bedroom.)*

BENEATHA. That is not a man. That is nothing but a toothless rat.

MAMA. Yes—death done come in this here house. *(She is nodding, slowly, reflec-*

*tively.)* Done come walking in my house. On the lips of my children. You what supposed to be my beginning again. You— what supposed to be my harvest. *(To* BENEATHA.*)* You—you mourning your brother?

BENEATHA. He's no brother of mine.

MAMA. What you say?

BENEATHA. I said that that individual in that room is no brother of mine.

MAMA. That's what I thought you said. You feeling like you better than he is today? *(*BENEATHA *does not answer.)* Yes? What you tell him a minute ago? That he wasn't a man? Yes? You give him up for me? You done wrote his epitaph too—like the rest of the world? Well, who give you the privilege?

BENEATHA. Be on my side for once! You saw what he just did, Mama! You saw him— down on his knees. Wasn't it you who taught me—to despise any man who would do that. Do what he's going to do.

MAMA. Yes—I taught you that. Me and your daddy. But I thought I taught you something else too . . . I thought I taught you to love him.

BENEATHA. Love him? There is nothing left to love.

MAMA. There is always something left to love. And if you ain't learned that, you ain't learned nothing. *(Looking at her.)* Have you cried for that boy today? I don't mean for yourself and for the family 'cause we lost the money. I mean for him; what he been through and what it done to him. Child, when do you think is the time to love somebody the most; when they done good and made things easy for everybody? Well then, you ain't through learning—because that ain't the time at all. It's when he's at his lowest and can't believe in hisself 'cause the world done whipped him so. When you starts measuring somebody, measure him right, child, measure

him right. Make sure you done taken into account what hills and valleys he come through before he got to wherever he is.

*(*TRAVIS *bursts into the room at the end of the speech, leaving the door open.)*

TRAVIS. Grandmama—the moving men are downstairs! The truck just pulled up.

MAMA. *(Turning and looking at him).* Are they, baby? They downstairs?

*(She sighs and sits.* LINDNER *appears in the doorway. He peers in and knocks lightly, to gain attention, and comes in. All turn to look at him.)*

LINDNER *(Hat and briefcase in hand).* Uh— hello . . .

*(*RUTH *crosses mechanically to the bedroom door and opens it and lets it swing open freely and slowly as the lights come up on* WALTER *within, still in his coat, sitting at the far corner of the room. He looks up and out through the room to* LINDNER.*)*

RUTH. He's here.

*(A long minute passes and* WALTER *slowly gets up.)*

LINDNER *(Coming to the table with efficiency, putting his briefcase on the table and starting to unfold papers and unscrew fountain pens).* Well, I certainly was glad to hear from you people. *(*WALTER *has begun the trek out of the room, slowly and awkwardly, rather like a small boy, passing the back of his sleeve across his mouth from time to time.)* Life can really be so much simpler than people let it be most of the time. Well—with whom do I negotiate? You, Mrs. Younger, or your son here? *(*MAMA *sits with her hands folded on her lap and her eyes closed as* WALTER *advances.* TRAVIS *goes close to* LINDNER *and looks at the papers curiously.)* Just some official papers, sonny.

RUTH. Travis, you go downstairs.

MAMA (*Opening her eyes and looking into* WALTER'S). No. Travis, you stay right here. And you make him understand what you doing, Walter Lee. You teach him good. Like Willy Harris taught you. You show where our five generations done come to. Go ahead, son—

WALTER (*Looks down into his boy's eyes.* TRAVIS *grins at him merrily, and* WALTER *draws him beside him with his arm lightly around his shoulders*). Well, Mr. Lindner. (BENEATHA *turns away.*) We called you— (*There is a profound, simple groping quality in his speech.*)—because, well, me and my family (*He looks around and shifts from one foot to the other.*) Well—we are very plain people . . .

LINDNER. Yes—

WALTER. I mean—I have worked as a chauffeur most of my life—and my wife here, she does domestic work in people's kitchens. So does my mother. I mean—we are plain people . . .

LINDNER. Yes, Mr. Younger—

WALTER (*Really like a small boy, looking down at his shoes and then up at the man*). And—uh—well, my father, well, he was a laborer most of his life.

LINDNER (*Absolutely confused*). Uh, yes—

WALTER (*Looking down at his toes once again*). My father almost beat a man to death once because this man called him a bad name or something, you know what I mean?

LINDNER. No, I'm afraid I don't.

WALTER (*Finally straightening up*). Well, what I mean is that we come from people who had a lot of pride. I mean—we are very proud people. And that's my sister over there and she's going to be a doctor— and we are very proud—

LINDNER. Well—I am sure that is very nice, but—

WALTER (*Starting to cry and facing the man eye to eye*). What I am telling you is that we called you over here to tell you that we are very proud and that this is—this is my son, who makes the sixth generation of our family in this country, and that we have all thought about your offer and we have decided to move into our house because my father—my father—he earned it. (MAMA *has her eyes closed and is rocking back and forth as though she were in church, with her head nodding the amen yes.*) We don't want to make no trouble for nobody or fight no causes—but we will try to be good neighbors. That's all we got to say. (*He looks the man absolutely in the eyes.*) We don't want your money.

(*He turns and walks away from the man.*)

LINDNER (*Looking around at all of them*). I take it then that you have decided to occupy.

BENEATHA. That's what the man said.

LINDNER (*To* MAMA *in her reverie*). Then I would like to appeal to you, Mrs. Younger. You are older and wiser and understand things better I am sure . . .

MAMA (*Rising*). I am afraid you don't understand. My son said we was going to move and there ain't nothing left for me to say. (*Shaking her head with double meaning.*) You know how these young folks is nowadays, mister. Can't do a thing with 'em. Goodbye.

LINDNER (*Folding up his materials*). Well—if you are that final about it . . . There is nothing left for me to say. (*He finishes. He is almost ignored by the family, who are concentrating on* WALTER LEE. *At the door* LINDNER *halts and looks around.*) I sure hope you people know what you're doing.

(*He shakes his head and exits.*)

RUTH (*Looking around and coming to life.*)

Well, for God's sake—if the moving men are here—LET'S GET OUT OF HERE!

MAMA (*Into action*). Ain't it the truth! Look at all this here mess. Ruth, put Travis' good jacket on him . . . Walter Lee, fix your tie and tuck your shirt in; you look just like somebody's hoodlum. Lord have mercy, where is my plant? (*She flies to get it amid the general bustling of the family, who are deliberately trying to ignore the nobility of the past moment.*) You all start on down . . . Travis child, don't go empty-handed . . . Ruth, where did I put that box with my skillets in it? I want to be in charge of it myself . . . I'm going to make us the biggest dinner we ever ate tonight . . . Beneatha, what's the matter with them stockings? Pull them things up, girl . . .

(*The family starts to file out as two moving men appear and begin to carry out the heavier pieces of furniture, bumping into the family as they move about.*)

BENEATHA. Mama, Asagai—asked me to marry him today and go to Africa—

MAMA (*In the middle of her getting-ready activity*). He did? You ain't old enough to marry nobody—(*Seeing the moving men lifting one of her chairs precariously.*) Darling, that ain't no bale of cotton, please handle it so we can sit in it again. I had that chair twenty-five years . . .

(*The movers sigh with exasperation and go on with their work.*)

BENEATHA (*Girlishly and unreasonably trying to pursue the conversation*). To go to Africa, Mama—be a doctor in Africa . . .

MAMA (*Distracted*). Yes, baby—

WALTER. Africa! What he want you to go to Africa for?

BENEATHA. To practice there . . .

WALTER. Girl, if you don't get all them silly ideas out your head! You better marry yourself a man with some loot . . .

BENEATHA (*Angrily, precisely as in the first scene of the play*). What have you got to do with who I marry!

WALTER. Plenty. Now I think George Murchison—

(*He and* BENEATHA *go out yelling at each other vigorously;* BENEATHA *is heard saying that she would not marry* GEORGE MURCHISON *if he were Adam and she were Eve, etc. The anger is loud and real till their voices diminish.* RUTH *stands at the door and turns to* MAMA *and smiles knowingly.*)

MAMA (*Fixing her hat at last*). Yeah—they something all right, my children . . .

RUTH. Yeah—they're something. Let's go, Lena.

MAMA (*Stalling, starting to look around at the house*). Yes—I'm coming. Ruth—

RUTH. Yes?

MAMA (*Quietly, woman to woman*). He finally come into his manhood today, didn't he? Kind of like a rainbow after the rain . . .

RUTH (*Biting her lip lest her own pride explode in front of* MAMA). Yes, Lena.

(WALTER'S *voice calls for them raucously.*)

MAMA (*Waving* RUTH *out vaguely*). All right, honey—go on down. I be down directly.

(RUTH *hesitates, then exits.* MAMA *stands, at last alone in the living room, her plant on the table before her as the lights start to come down. She looks around at all the walls and ceilings and suddenly, despite herself, while the children call below, a great heaving thing rises in her and she puts her fist to her mouth, takes a final desperate look, pulls her coat about her, pats her hat, and goes out. The lights dim down. The door opens and she comes back in, grabs her plant, and goes out for the last time.*)

## Act III

### Getting at Meaning

1. The stage directions on page 578 indicate that it is important for the audience to feel Walter's reactions to the scene between Beneatha and Asagai. Why?

2. What is an idealist? What is the difference between an idealist and a dreamer? Is Asagai an idealist or a dreamer? Which word describes Walter Lee?

3. Compare Beneatha's statement, "Man is foul! And the human race deserves its misery!" (p. 579) with the comment that she makes when Mama slaps her face. How has her attitude changed? Why has it changed?

4. What does Asagai mean when he says, "I live the answer!" (p. 580) What was the question?

5. What is the piece of paper for which Walter is searching?

6. What is the significance of Ruth's lines, "We got to move . . . We got to get out of here . . ."?

7. When Walter explains why he called Lindner and how he is going to "put on a show" for him, the rest of the family reacts with disgust and horror. How do their reactions affect Walter?

8. What effect does Travis's presence have on Walter's decision not to accept Lindner's money? Explain the reasons for this effect.

9. How does the halting manner in which Walter delivers his speech to Lindner help the reader to believe that Walter has undergone a change?

10. What is the significance of Beneatha's line, "That's what the man said"? (p. 586)

11. As Mama stands alone in the apartment at the end of the play, "a great heaving thing rises in her." What is troubling her? What is she thinking about? What is the significance of Mama's coming back into the apartment for her plant?

### Developing Skills in Reading Literature

1. **Climax.** Where does the climax of this play occur? Support your answer by explaining how the scene you have chosen fits the definition of *climax* as the turning point and the highest point of action in a play.

2. **Comic Relief.** Humorous speeches or scenes that relieve the tension of dramatic moments are called comic relief. Identify some humorous lines in the last few pages of the play and explain how they ease the tension of Walter's major confrontation with Lindner.

3. **Epigraph.** An epigraph in literature is a quotation that a writer puts at the beginning of a book or play. Reread the poem by Langston Hughes that appears at the beginning of Act 1. Why is the poem an appropriate epigraph for this play?

4. **Theme.** What is the theme of this play? Remember, when attempting to formulate the theme of a work of literature, the reader should think about the changes undergone by the central character, analyze the main conflicts, look at the title for a clue, and try to express the theme as a universal statement.

### Developing Writing Skills

1. **Analyzing Characters.** Mama says, "Sometimes you just got to know when to give up some things . . . and hold on to what you got." In a five-paragraph composition, explain how this statement relates to the action of the play as a whole and to the lives of any three major characters. What do the characters give up? What do they hold onto? How do they learn when to hold on and when to let go?

2. **Analyzing Theme.** In a five-paragraph composition, explain how the conflicts among the characters in this play contribute to the development of the theme. Identify the major conflicts and then show how each helps to develop the theme.

# Julius Caesar

BUST OF CAESAR. *Museo Pio-Clementino, Vatican, Rome.*

# The Life of William Shakespeare

WILLIAM SHAKESPEARE. Artist unknown.
By Courtesy of the National Portrait Gallery, London.

Why do readers and theater goers continue to enjoy the plays of William Shakespeare, nearly four hundred years after they were written? One answer lies in the beautiful lines and phrases that resound in the minds of all who experience his plays. No other writer, before or since, has developed the potential of the English language to such heights. Another answer lies in Shakespeare's brilliantly alive, memorable characters. His understanding of human psychology was profound, making his characters universal and timeless. Even in twentieth-century America, to understand Shakespeare's plays is to understand what is most important about human beings and about life.

William Shakespeare was born in the market town of Stratford-on-Avon in England in 1564. Although precise birth records were not kept in those days, scholars believe that Shakespeare was born on April 23, the day that has long been celebrated as his birthday. John Shakespeare, William's father, was a glover, or glove maker, and a respected middle-class citizen in Stratford. His wife, Mary Arden

Shakespeare, managed the household and took care of the seven children born to the couple.

William Shakespeare received a public education in Stratford, probably beginning grammar school at the age of seven. When he entered school, he would have known already how to read and write English, having learned these skills at home. Unlike grammar school today, grammar school in Shakespeare's time was chiefly the study of Latin— no history, geography, science, art, music, English instruction, or physical education. A typical school day went from seven to eleven o'clock in the morning, and from one to five o'clock in the afternoon. Students had only two half-days off a week and only forty days of vacation a year. Shakespeare probably remained in school until he was sixteen, supplementing his education all the while with a great deal of reading. Between the ages of sixteen and eighteen, he worked as a tutor. During these years, he continued to read classics and probably wrote poetry as well.

When he was eighteen, Shakespeare married Anne Hathaway, a Stratford woman of twenty-six. The couple had three children: a daughter, Susanna, and twins, Hamnet and Judith. Hamnet died as a boy, but the two daughters both married and survived Shakespeare, as did Anne.

In 1587 Shakespeare left Stratford for London, determined to make his living as an actor. Little is known of his first years in London, but by the early 1590's he was an acclaimed actor and an established playwright. In 1594 he joined Lord Chamberlain's Company, a prestigious acting company that often performed before the queen. Later, with several other members of the Company, Shakespeare commissioned the building of the Globe Theater, which was a successful venture, both financially and artistically.

During his London years, 1587–1611, Shakespeare wrote thirty-seven plays, as well as a number of sonnets and other poems. The plays are of three types: comedies, tragedies, and histories. A number of them, including *Julius Caesar*, were first performed at the Globe Theater.

In 1611 Shakespeare retired from London and returned to Stratford a wealthy and famous man. He lived there in comfort until his death in 1616, on April 23, probably his fifty-second birthday. The house where Shakespeare was born, the home that he bought for Anne Hathaway, and his grave are enormously popular tourist attractions, as is the beautiful theater in Stratford, where his plays are performed year round.

## Elizabethan Drama

Shakespeare was born during the reign of Elizabeth I of England. The daughter of Henry VIII and Anne Boleyn, "Good Queen Bess," the last of the Tudor monarchs, ruled from 1558 to 1603. Her reign, which came at the end of the European Renaissance, was a great period for England. In tribute to Elizabeth, the period is known as the Elizabethan Age.

By the Elizabethan Age, drama in England had evolved into a complicated and popular art form. In contrast to today's audiences, which represent only a small percentage of the population, audiences in Elizabethan London were large and enthusiastic. A substantial portion of the population, from members of the royal court to the commonest workers, regularly attended the theater.

The first actresses appeared on the stage in England in 1662. During Shakespeare's time, all female parts were played by males. When *Romeo and Juliet* was performed, for example, Juliet was played by a young male actor whose voice had not yet changed. Also characteristic of Elizabethan drama were minimal stage sets. Sets usually were confined to a few moveable props. Costumes, however, were elaborate, although generally not historically authentic. For performances of *Julius Caesar,* for example, the actors wore Elizabethan costumes, not the togas worn in the Rome of Caesar's day. Sometimes, special effects were quite realistic. Death scenes, for instance, were apt to be gory, for an actor who was to be stabbed usually wore a pig bladder filled with blood inside his costume.

## Shakespeare's Theater

A number of new theaters were built in London during Shakespeare's lifetime, among them the Globe, which was completed in 1599. Three stories high, the Globe was made of wood with a thatched roof. The theater was an octagon, with an open-air courtyard in the center, into which the stage protruded. The eight sides of the theater housed covered tiers of seats, where viewers sat for an admission fee of two or three pennies. Commoners paid one penny to sit in the courtyard in front of the stage, in this way earning themselves the name groundlings. Ironically, their one-penny admission bought the groundlings the best viewing position in the house (unless, of course, it rained). Audiences, especially the groundlings, participated actively in performances, cheering, booing, hissing, and sometimes even throwing rotten vegetables.

On performance days, a flag flew over the Globe Theater. Spectators crossed the Thames River from central London to the theater's location near the east bank of the river. Eventually, the Globe burned down, was rebuilt, and later burned down again. In London today a famous theater, the Old Vic, is located on the east bank of the Thames near where the Globe used to stand.

THE GLOBE THEATER, *Bankside, in the days of Shakespeare.*

## The Background of the Play

One of the first plays performed at the Globe Theater was *Julius Caesar*. Among Shakespeare's most famous plays, *Julius Caesar* is both a tragedy and a history.

Shakespeare's main source for *Julius Caesar* was a widely read book by Plutarch, a Greek biographer and essayist who died around A.D. 120. Plutarch's work, titled *Parallel Lives,* contains forty-six paired Greek and Roman biographies and four single biographies. The biography of the Roman ruler Julius Caesar is one of the best known selections in the *Lives.*

Julius Caesar, who died in Rome in 44 B.C., is a renowned military commander in world history. Born into a noble, or patrician, family, as a young man Caesar became a leading political figure in Rome. Later, he significantly extended the boundaries of the Roman Empire through his military campaigns. He conquered France, then called Gaul, and subsequently led his troops as far north as England, where remains of the Roman occupation still exist. Caesar's military campaigns took him as far south as Egypt, where he defeated his co-ruler Pompey. He pursued the remaining Pompeian forces to Africa and Spain, and after defeating them, he returned to Rome.

In Rome, dissatisfaction grew over Caesar's increasing power, resulting in the conspiracy to murder Caesar that is the subject of Shakespeare's play. On March 15 (the ides of March) in 44 B.C., Caesar was assassinated in the Roman Senate by a group of men who feared that he wanted to become king. The Romans feared and hated the power and office of king. They had expelled their last king, Tarquin, who took the throne by murder and held it by tyranny, and established a republican government.

Although he had been married three times, Caesar left no children. His will bequeathed most of his money and power to his grandnephew Octavius, who became Emperor Augustus after he and Mark Antony, another supporter of Caesar, had avenged Caesar's murder.

As the play opens, Caesar has just returned from his military triumphs, and the people are celebrating. There is a group of Romans, however, who envy Caesar and fear their own loss of power if he should become king.

# Julius Caesar　*William Shakespeare*

## CHARACTERS

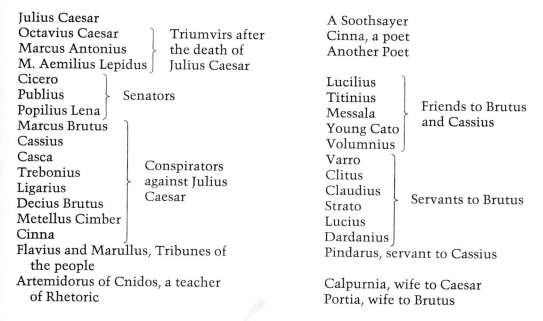

Julius Caesar
Octavius Caesar ⎫
Marcus Antonius ⎬ Triumvirs after the death of
M. Aemilius Lepidus ⎭ Julius Caesar

Cicero ⎫
Publius ⎬ Senators
Popilius Lena ⎭

Marcus Brutus ⎫
Cassius ⎪
Casca ⎪
Trebonius ⎬ Conspirators against Julius Caesar
Ligarius ⎪
Decius Brutus ⎪
Metellus Cimber ⎪
Cinna ⎭

Flavius and Marullus, Tribunes of the people
Artemidorus of Cnidos, a teacher of Rhetoric

A Soothsayer
Cinna, a poet
Another Poet

Lucilius ⎫
Titinius ⎪
Messala ⎬ Friends to Brutus and Cassius
Young Cato ⎪
Volumnius ⎭

Varro ⎫
Clitus ⎪
Claudius ⎬ Servants to Brutus
Strato ⎪
Lucius ⎪
Dardanius ⎭

Pindarus, servant to Cassius

Calpurnia, wife to Caesar
Portia, wife to Brutus

Senators, Citizens, Guards, Attendants, Servants, etc.

The Time: 44 B.C.
The Place: Rome; the camp near Sardis; the plains of Philippi.

# Act One

*Scene 1*

[*Julius Caesar has returned triumphantly from his conquest of Pompey, and the Roman people are celebrating his victory. Two of the tribunes, Flavius and Marullus, are afraid that Caesar's ambition for power will destroy their own power as leaders in Rome.*]

[*A street in Rome. It is the fifteenth of February. The people of Rome are celebrating* Caesar's *triumphant return from Spain and the Lupercalia, a festival of dancing, feasting, and public games.*
    *As the play opens,* Flavius *and* Marullus, *tribunes of the people, intercept a crowd of* Commoners *on their way to the Forum. They are angry at the people's enthusiasm over* Caesar's *return.*]

**Flavius.** Hence! home, you idle creatures, get you home!
   Is this a holiday? What, know you not,
   Being mechanical,[1] you ought not walk
   Upon a laboring day without the sign[2]
   Of your profession? Speak, what trade art thou?                    5
**First Commoner.** Why, sir, a carpenter.
**Marullus.** Where is thy leather apron and thy rule?
   What dost thou with thy best apparel on?
   You, sir, what trade are you?
**Second Commoner.** Truly sir, in respect of a fine workman[3] I am but, as    10
   you would say, a cobbler.[4]
**Marullus.** But what trade art thou? Answer me directly.[5]
**Second Commoner.** A trade, sir, that I hope I may use with a safe con-
   science, which is indeed, sir, a mender of bad soles.[6]
**Marullus.** What trade, thou knave? Thou naughty knave, what trade?       15
**Second Commoner.** Nay, I beseech you, sir, be not out[7] with me. Yet if you
   be out, sir, I can mend you.
**Marullus.** What mean'st thou by that? Mend me, thou saucy fellow?
**Second Commoner.** Why, sir, cobble you.
**Flavius.** Thou art a cobbler, art thou?                                  20

---

1. **mechanical:** workmen.  2. **sign:** tools and work clothes.  3. **in . . . workman:**  so far as fine work is concerned.
4. **cobbler:** shoemaker. In Shakespeare's time, the word also meant "bungler."  5. **directly:** without quibbling.
6. **soles:** pun on "sole" and "soul."  7. **out:** angry.

**Second Commoner.** Truly, sir, all that I live by is with the awl. I meddle
with no tradesman's matters nor women's matters, but with awl. I am
indeed, sir, a surgeon to old shoes. When they are in great danger, I recover them. As proper men as ever trod upon neat's leather[8] have gone
upon my handiwork. 25

**Flavius.** But wherefore art not in thy shop today?
Why dost thou lead these men about the streets?

**Second Commoner.** Truly, sir, to wear out their shoes, to get myself into
more work. But indeed, sir, we make holiday to see Caesar and to rejoice in his triumph.[9] 30

**Marullus.** Wherefore rejoice? What conquest brings he home?
What tributaries[10] follow him to Rome
To grace in captive bonds his chariot wheels?
You blocks, you stones, you worse than senseless things!
O you hard hearts, you cruel men of Rome! 35
Knew you not Pompey? Many a time and oft
Have you climbed up to walls and battlements,
To towers and windows, yea, to chimney tops,[11]
Your infants in your arms, and there have sat
The livelong day, with patient expectation, 40
To see great Pompey pass the streets of Rome.
And when you saw his chariot but appear,
Have you not made a universal shout,
That Tiber[12] trembled underneath her banks
To hear the replication[13] of your sounds 45
Made in her concave shores?
And do you now put on your best attire?
And do you now cull out[14] a holiday?
And do you now strew flowers in his way
That comes in triumph over Pompey's blood?[15] 50
Be gone!
Run to your houses, fall upon your knees,
Pray to the gods to intermit[16] the plague
That needs must light on this ingratitude.

**Flavius.** Go, go, good countrymen, and for this fault 55
Assemble all the poor men of your sort;
Draw them to Tiber banks, and weep your tears
Into the channel, till the lowest stream
Do kiss the most exalted shores of all.[17]  [*Exeunt all the* Commoners.]

---

8. **neat's leather:** oxhide.  9. **in his triumph:** after a victorious campaign, Roman generals entered Rome in a
triumphal procession. Caesar's triumph, however, is over another Roman, Pompey.  10. **tributaries:** captives.
11. **chimney tops:** Shakespeare is visualizing his own London, not Rome. This is an anachronism.  12. **Tiber:** the
river that flows through Rome.  13. **replication:** echo.  14. **cull out:** choose to take.  15. **Pompey's blood:** Caesar
had slain Pompey's two sons in Spain.  16. **intermit:** leave out.  17. **weep . . . all:** weep enough tears to bring the
lowest waterline up to the highest.

See, whether their basest metal[18] be not moved.　　　　　　　　60
They vanish tongue-tied in their guiltiness.
Go you down that way towards the Capitol;
This way will I. Disrobe the images[19]
If you do find them decked with ceremonies.[20]
**Marullus.** May we do so?　　　　　　　　　　　　　　　　65
You know it is the feast of Lupercal.[21]
**Flavius.** It is no matter. Let no images
Be hung with Caesar's trophies. I'll about
And drive away the vulgar[22] from the streets.
So do you too, where you perceive them thick.　　　　　　70
These growing feathers[23] plucked from Caesar's wing
Will make him fly an ordinary pitch,
Who else would soar above the view of men
And keep us all in servile fearfulness.

*[Exeunt.]*


*Scene 2*

[*While Caesar is attending the race that is traditionally
run at the Festival of Lupercalia, a soothsayer warns him
to beware the ides of March. Cassius speaks with Brutus,
his close friend, about Caesar's power and popularity.
Casca reveals that Mark Antony offered Caesar a crown
three times, and that Caesar refused it with greater
reluctance each time. Cassius and Brutus plan to meet
the next day, when Cassius hopes that Brutus may be
encouraged to strike out at Caesar.*]

[*A public place near the Forum. A flourish of trumpets announces
the approach of* Caesar. *A large crowd of* Commoners *has assembled;
a* Soothsayer *is among them. Enter* Caesar, *his wife,* Calpurnia, Portia,
Decius, Cicero, Brutus, Cassius, Casca, *and* Antony, *who is stripped
for running in the games.*]

---

18. **metal:** material, stuff of which they are made; "metal" and "mettle" were the same in Shakespeare's time.
19. **Disrobe . . . images:** strip the statues. 20. **ceremonies:** decorations. 21. **Lupercal:** Roman god of fertility.
22. **vulgar:** common people. 23. **growing feathers:** Caesar's followers. Without his followers, Caesar would not be
able to rise to such heights ("pitch"). Falconers often clipped the wings of falcons to prevent their soaring too high.

**Caesar.** Calpurnia!

**Casca.**             Peace, ho! Caesar speaks.

**Caesar.**                           Calpurnia!

**Calpurnia.** Here, my lord.

**Caesar.** Stand you directly in Antonius'[1] way             5
     When he doth run his course. Antonius!

**Antonius.** Caesar, my lord?

**Caesar.** Forget not in your speed, Antonius,
     To touch Calpurnia; for our elders say
     The barren, touchèd in this holy chase,             10
     Shake off their sterile curse.[2]

**Antonius.**                   I shall remember.
     When Caesar says "Do this," it is performed.

**Caesar.** Set on, and leave no ceremony out.

[*Flourish of trumpets.* Caesar *starts to leave.*]

**Soothsayer.** Caesar!                                 15

**Caesar.** Ha! Who calls?

**Casca.** Bid every noise be still. Peace yet again!

**Caesar.** Who is it in the press[3] that calls on me?
     I hear a tongue shriller than all the music
     Cry "Caesar!" Speak. Caesar is turned to hear.       20

**Soothsayer.** Beware the ides of March.[4]

**Caesar.**                           What man is that?

**Brutus.** A soothsayer bids you beware the ides of March.

**Caesar.** Set him before me; let me see his face.

**Cassius.** Fellow, come from the throng; look upon Caesar.    25

**Caesar.** What say'st thou to me now? Speak once again.

**Soothsayer.** Beware the ides of March.

**Caesar.** He is a dreamer; let us leave him. Pass.

[*Trumpets sound. Exeunt all but* Brutus *and* Cassius.]

**Cassius.** Will you go see the order of the course?

**Brutus.** Not I.                                         30

**Cassius.** I pray you do.

**Brutus.** I am not gamesome.[5] I do lack some part
     Of that quick spirit that is in Antony.
     Let me not hinder, Cassius, your desires.
     I'll leave you.                                      35

---

1. **Antonius:** Mark Antony is sometimes called Marcus Antonius.   2. **Calpurnia . . . curse:** Romans believed that women who are touched by the whip of goat's hide that racers carried will be able to bear children. Because Calpurnia has not been able to bear children, Caesar asks Antony to touch her as he goes by.   3. **press:** crowd.   4. **ides of March:** March 15.   5. **gamesome:** fond of games.

Marvin Blake as the Soothsayer, Len Cariou (Brutus), Nicholas Pennell (Cassius), Susan Wright (Portia), Elizabeth Leigh-Milne (Calpurnia), and Jack Medley (Caesar) in *Julius Caesar*, Stratford Festival, 1982.

**Cassius.** Brutus, I do observe you now of late;
    I have not from your eyes that gentleness
    And show of love as I was wont to have.
    You bear too stubborn and too strange a hand[6]
    Over your friend that loves you.                    40
**Brutus.**                           Cassius,
    Be not deceived. If I have veiled my look,
    I turn the trouble of my countenance
    Merely upon myself. Vexèd I am
    Of late with passions of some difference,[7]             45
    Conceptions only proper to myself,
    Which give some soil,[8] perhaps, to my behaviors.
    But let not therefore my good friends be grieved
    (Among which number, Cassius, be you one)
    Nor construe[9] any further my neglect               50
    Than that poor Brutus, with himself at war,
    Forgets the shows[10] of love to other men.
**Cassius.** Then, Brutus, I have much mistook your passion,
    By means whereof this breast of mine hath buried
    Thoughts of great value, worthy cogitations.          55
    Tell me, good Brutus, can you see your face?
**Brutus.** No, Cassius, for the eye sees not itself
    But by reflection, by some other things.
**Cassius.** 'Tis just.
    And it is very much lamented, Brutus,              60
    That you have no such mirrors as will turn[11]
    Your hidden worthiness into your eye,
    That you might see your shadow. I have heard
    Where many of the best respect in Rome
    (Except immortal Caesar),[12] speaking of Brutus       65
    And groaning underneath this age's yoke,[13]
    Have wished that noble Brutus had his eyes.
**Brutus.** Into what dangers would you lead me, Cassius,
    That you would have me seek into myself
    For that which is not in me?                  70
**Cassius.** Therefore, good Brutus, be prepared to hear;
    And since you know you cannot see yourself
    So well as by reflection, I, your glass,[14]
    Will modestly discover to yourself
    That of yourself which you yet know not of.         75
    And be not jealous on[15] me, gentle Brutus.

---

6. **bear . . . hand:** your behavior is too rough and unkind.   7. **passions . . . difference:** conflicting emotions.   8. **soil:** blemish.   9. **construe:** interpret.   10. **shows:** outward appearances.   11. **turn:** reflect.   12. **immortal Caesar:** spoken with great bitterness.   13. **age's yoke:** burdens of these times.   14. **glass:** mirror.   15. **jealous on:** suspicious of.

Were I a common laugher,[16] or did use
To stale[17] with ordinary oaths my love
To every new protester;[18] if you know
That I do fawn on men and hug them hard,                    80
And after scandal[19] them; or if you know
That I profess myself in banqueting
To all the rout,[20] then hold me dangerous.

[*Flourish and shout.*]

**Brutus.** What means this shouting? I do fear the people
Choose Caesar for their king.                               85
**Cassius.**                     Ay, do you fear it?
Then must I think you would not have it so.
**Brutus.** I would not, Cassius, yet I love him well.
But wherefore do you hold me here so long?
What is it that you would impart to me?                     90
If it be aught toward the general good,
Set honor in one eye and death i' the other,
And I will look on both indifferently;
For let the gods so speed[21] me as I love
The name of honor more than I fear death.                   95
**Cassius.** I know that virtue to be in you, Brutus,
As well as I do know your outward favor.[22]
Well, honor is the subject of my story.
I cannot tell what you and other men
Think of this life, but for my single self,                 100
I had as lief not be as live to be
In awe of such a thing as I myself.[23]
I was born free as Caesar, so were you;
We both have fed as well, and we can both
Endure the winter's cold as well as he.                     105
For once, upon a raw and gusty day,
The troubled Tiber chafing with her shores,
Caesar said to me, "Darest thou, Cassius, now
Leap in with me into this angry flood
And swim to yonder point?" Upon the word,                   110
Accoutered[24] as I was, I plunged in
And bade him follow. So indeed he did.
The torrent roared, and we did buffet it
With lusty sinews, throwing it aside

---

16. **laugher:** jester.   17. **stale:** make common.   18. **protester:** one who makes solemn protestations.   19. **scandal:** speak scandal of.   20. **rout:** rabble.   21. **speed:** give good fortune to.   22. **favor:** appearance.   23. **In . . . myself:** afraid of a mere mortal like myself.   24. **Accoutered:** fully armed.

And stemming it with hearts of controversy.[25]                          115
But ere we could arrive the point proposed,
Caesar cried, "Help me, Cassius, or I sink!"
I, as Aeneas,[26] our great ancestor,
Did from the flames of Troy upon his shoulder
The old Anchises bear, so from the waves of Tiber         120
Did I the tired Caesar. And this man
Is now become a god, and Cassius is
A wretched creature and must bend his body
If Caesar carelessly but nod on him.
He had a fever when he was in Spain,                             125
And when the fit was on him, I did mark
How he did shake. 'Tis true, this god did shake.
His coward lips did from their color fly,[27]
And that same eye whose bend[28] doth awe the world
Did lose his[29] luster. I did hear him groan.                    130
Ay, and that tongue of his that bade the Romans
Mark him and write his speeches in their books,
Alas, it cried, "Give me some drink, Titinius,"
As a sick girl! Ye gods! it doth amaze me
A man of such a feeble temper should                             135
So get the start[30] of the majestic world
And bear the palm[31] alone.

[Shout. Flourish.]

**Brutus.** Another general shout?
I do believe that these applauses are
For some new honors that are heaped on Caesar.         140
**Cassius.** Why, man, he doth bestride the narrow world
Like a Colossus,[32] and we petty men
Walk under his huge legs and peep about
To find ourselves dishonorable graves.
Men at some time are masters of their fates.              145
The fault, dear Brutus, is not in our stars,
But in ourselves, that we are underlings.
Brutus, and Caesar. What should be in that Caesar?
Why should that name be sounded more than yours?
Write them together: yours is as fair a name.            150
Sound them, it doth become the mouth as well.

---

25. **controversy:** competition. 26. **Aeneas:** one of the few Trojans who escaped the sack of Troy in Virgil's *Aeneid,* carrying his aged father Anchises on his back. According to legend, Aeneas was the founder of Rome. 27. **His . . . fly:** the color fled from his cowardly lips. 28. **bend:** look. 29. **his:** its. 30. **get the start:** become the leader. 31. **palm:** prize. 32. **Colossus:** The Colossus of Rhodes, one of the seven wonders of the ancient world, was a huge bronze statue of Apollo. It straddled the entrance to the harbor, and ships passed beneath it.

Weigh them, it is as heavy. Conjure[33] with 'em,
Brutus will start a spirit as soon as Caesar.
Now in the names of all the gods at once,
Upon what meat doth this our Caesar feed          155
That he is grown so great? Age, thou art shamed!
Rome, thou hast lost the breed of noble bloods!
When went there by an age since the great flood
But it was famed with more than with one man?
When could they say (till now) that talked of Rome     160
That her wide walls encompassed but one man?
Now is it Rome indeed, and room[34] enough,
When there is in it but one only man!
Oh, you and I have heard our fathers say
There was a Brutus[35] once that would have brooked[36]     165
The eternal devil to keep his state in Rome
As easily as a king.

**Brutus.** That you do love me I am nothing jealous.[37]
  What you would work me to, I have some aim.[38]
  How I have thought of this, and of these times,     170
  I shall recount hereafter. For this present,
  I would not (so with love I might entreat you)
  Be any further moved. What you have said
  I will consider; what you have to say
  I will with patience hear, and find a time     175
  Both meet[39] to hear and answer such high things.
  Till then, my noble friend, chew upon this:
  Brutus had rather be a villager
  Than to repute himself a son of Rome
  Under these hard conditions as this time     180
  Is like to lay upon us.

**Cassius.**           I am glad
  That my weak words have struck but thus much show
  Of fire from Brutus.

[*Voices and Music are heard approaching.*]

**Brutus.** The games are done, and Caesar is returning.     185
**Cassius.** As they pass by, pluck Casca by the sleeve,
  And he will (after his sour fashion) tell you
  What hath proceeded worthy note today.

[*Reenter* Caesar *and his train of followers.*]

---

33. **Conjure:** summon spirits. 34. **Rome . . . room:** a pun. Both words were pronounced and spelled alike in Shakespeare's day. 35. **Brutus:** Lucius Junius Brutus expelled Tarquin, the last king, from Rome. Marcus Brutus claimed descent from him. 36. **brooked:** permitted. 37. **am . . . jealous:** have no doubt. 38. **aim:** idea. 39. **meet:** suitable.

**Brutus.** I will do so. But look you, Cassius!
   The angry spot doth glow on Caesar's brow,
   And all the rest look like a chidden train.[40]        190
   Calpurnia's cheek is pale, and Cicero[41]
   Looks with such ferret[42] and such fiery eyes
   As we have seen him in the Capitol,
   Being crossed in conference[43] by some senators.      195
**Cassius.** Casca will tell us what the matter is.

[Caesar *looks at* Cassius *and turns to* Antony.]

**Caesar.** Antonius!
**Antonius.** Caesar?
**Caesar.** Let me have men about me that are fat,
   Sleek-headed men, and such as sleep o' nights.      200
   Yond Cassius has a lean and hungry look;
   He thinks too much, such men are dangerous.

---

40. **chidden train:** scolded followers.   41. **Cicero:** a Roman senator.   42. **ferret:** a weasel-like animal with nervous red eyes.   43. **crossed . . . conference:** opposed in debate.

**Antonius.** Fear him not, Caesar, he's not dangerous.
  He is a noble Roman, and well given.[44]

**Caesar.** Would he were fatter! But I fear him not.                                          205
  Yet if my name were liable to fear,
  I do not know the man I should avoid
  So soon as that spare Cassius. He reads much,
  He is a great observer, and he looks
  Quite through the deeds of men. He loves no plays                                            210
  As thou dost, Antony; he hears no music.
  Seldom he smiles, and smiles in such a sort
  As if he mocked himself and scorned his spirit
  That could be moved to smile at anything.
  Such men as he be never at heart's ease                                                      215
  Whiles they behold a greater than themselves,
  And therefore are they very dangerous.
  I rather tell thee what is to be feared
  Than what I fear, for always I am Caesar.
  Come on my right hand, for this ear is deaf,                                                 220
  And tell me truly what thou think'st of him.

[*Trumpets sound. Exeunt* Caesar *and all his train except* Casca,
*who stays behind.*]

**Casca.** You pulled me by the cloak. Would you speak with me?

**Brutus.** Ay, Casca. Tell us what hath chanced today
  That Caesar looks so sad.[45]

**Casca.** Why, you were with him, were you not?                                              225

**Brutus.** I should not then ask Casca what had chanced.

**Casca.** Why, there was a crown offered him; and being offered him, he put
  it by with the back of his hand, thus. And then the people fell a-shout-
  ing.

**Brutus.** What was the second noise for?                                                    230

**Casca.** Why, for that too.

**Cassius.** They shouted thrice. What was the last cry for?

**Casca.** Why, for that too.

**Brutus.** Was the crown offered him thrice?

**Casca.** Ay, marry,[46] was't! and he put it by thrice, every time gentler than            235
  other; and at every putting-by mine honest neighbors shouted.

**Cassius.** Who offered him the crown?

**Casca.** Why, Antony.

**Brutus.** Tell us the manner of it, gentle Casca.

---

44. **well given:** well disposed (toward Caesar).  45. **sad:** serious.  46. **marry:** Mary, by the Virgin.

**Casca.** I can as well be hanged as tell the manner of it. It was mere foolery; 240
I did not mark it. I saw Mark Antony offer him a crown—yet 'twas not
a crown neither, 'twas one of these coronets[47]—and, as I told you, he put
it by once. But for all that, to my thinking, he would fain[48] have had it.
Then he offered it to him again; then he put it by again; but to my
thinking, he was very loath to lay his fingers off it. And then he offered 245
it the third time. He put it the third time by; and still as he refused it,
the rabble-ment hooted, and clapped their chapped hands, and threw up
their sweaty nightcaps,[49] and uttered such a deal of stinking breath because Caesar refused the crown that it had, almost, choked Caesar; for
he swounded[50] and fell down at it. And for mine own part, I durst not 250
laugh, for fear of opening my lips and receiving the bad air.

**Cassius.** But soft,[51] I pray you. What, did Caesar swound?

**Casca.** He fell down in the market place and foamed at mouth and was
speechless.

**Brutus.** 'Tis very like. He hath the falling sickness.[52]

**Cassius.** No, Caesar hath it not; but you, and I, 255
And honest Casca, we have the falling sickness.

**Casca.** I know not what you mean by that, but I am sure Caesar fell down.
If the tag-rag people did not clap him and hiss him, according as he
pleased and displeased them, as they use to do the players in the theater, 260
I am no true man.

**Brutus.** What said he when he came unto himself?

**Casca.** Marry, before he fell down, when he perceived the common herd
was glad he refused the crown, he plucked me ope his doublet[53] and offered them his throat to cut. An I had been a man of any occupation,[54] if 265
I would not have taken him at a word, I would I might go to hell among
the rogues. And so he fell. When he came to himself again, he said if he
had done or said anything amiss, he desired their worships to think it
was his infirmity. Three or four wenches where I stood cried, "Alas,
good soul!" and forgave him with all their hearts. But there's no heed to 270
be taken of them. If Caesar had stabbed their mothers, they would have
done no less.

**Brutus.** And after that, he came thus sad away?

**Casca.** Ay.

**Cassius.** Did Cicero say anything?

**Casca.** Ay, he spoke Greek. 275

**Cassius.** To what effect?

**Casca.** Nay, an I tell you that, I'll ne'er look you i' the face again. But those
that understood him smiled at one another and shook their heads; but

---

47. **coronets**: little crowns worn by those of lesser rank than king. 48. **fain**: gladly. 49. **nightcaps**: close-fitting caps.
50. **swounded**: fainted. 51. **soft**: slowly. 52. **falling sickness**: epilepsy. (Cassius uses the term in a different
meaning.) 53. **ope . . . doublet**: open his short coat. (The actors wear Elizabethan costumes.) 54. **An . . . occupation**:
if I had been a tradesman with cutting tools.

for mine own part, it was Greek to me. I could tell you more news too.       280
Marullus and Flavius, for pulling scarfs[55] off Caesar's images, are put to
silence.[56] Fare you well. There was more foolery yet, if I could remember it.

**Cassius.** Will you sup with me tonight, Casca?

**Casca.** No, I am promised forth.       285

**Cassius.** Will you dine with me tomorrow?

**Casca.** Ay, if I be alive, and your mind hold, and your dinner worth eating.

**Cassius.** Good. I will expect you.

**Casca.** Do so. Farewell both.

                                                       [*Exit.*]

**Brutus.** What a blunt fellow is this grown to be!       290
He was quick mettle[57] when he went to school.

**Cassius.** So is he now in execution
Of any bold or noble enterprise,
However he puts on this tardy form.[58]
This rudeness is a sauce to his good wit,       295
Which gives men stomach to disgest his words
With better appetite.

**Brutus.** And so it is. For this time I will leave you.
Tomorrow, if you please to speak with me,
I will come home to you; or if you will,       300
Come home to me, and I will wait for you.

**Cassius.** I will do so. Till then, think of the world.

                                             [*Exit* Brutus.]

Well, Brutus, thou art noble; yet I see
Thy honorable mettle may be wrought
From that it is disposed.[59] Therefore it is meet       305
That noble minds keep ever with their likes;
For who so firm that cannot be seduced?
Caesar doth bear me hard;[60] but he loves Brutus.
If I were Brutus now and he were Cassius,
He should not humor[61] me. I will this night,       310
In several hands,[62] in at his windows throw,
As if they came from several citizens,
Writings, all tending to the great opinion
That Rome holds of his name, wherein obscurely
Caesar's ambition shall be glancèd[63] at.       315
And after this let Caesar seat him[64] sure,
For we will shake him, or worse days endure.

                                                    [*Exit.*]

---

55. **scarfs:** decorations.   56. **put to silence:** banished.   57. **mettle:** lively spirited.   58. **tardy form:** sluggish way.
59. **From . . . disposed:** from its natural inclinations.   60. **bear . . . hard:** dislike me.   61. **humor:** influence.
62. **several hands:** several handwritings.   63. **glancèd:** hinted.   64. **him:** himself.

# Scene 3

*[Cassius persuades Casca that Caesar's ambitions are not to be tolerated and that other important Romans feel the same way. They concoct a message that will provoke Brutus, and they send Cinna to place it where Brutus will find it. The conspirators plan to meet that night. Cassius and Casca hope to get Brutus' support for their plan to thwart Caesar.]*

*[A street. Thunder and lightning. Enter, from opposite sides, Casca, with his sword drawn, and Cicero. It is the night before the ides of March.]*

**Cicero.** Good even, Casca. Brought you Caesar home?
   Why are you breathless? and why stare you so?
**Casca.** Are not you moved when all the sway¹ of earth
   Shakes like a thing unfirm? O Cicero,
   I have seen tempests when the scolding winds          5
   Have rived² the knotty oaks, and I have seen
   The ambitious ocean swell and rage and foam
   To be exalted³ with the threatening clouds;
   But never till tonight, never till now,
   Did I go through a tempest dropping fire.          10
   Either there is a civil strife in heaven,
   Or else the world, too saucy with the gods,
   Incenses them to send destruction.
**Cicero.** Why, saw you anything more wonderful?
**Casca.** A common slave—you know him well by sight—     15
   Held up his left hand, which did flame and burn
   Like twenty torches joined; and yet his hand,
   Not sensible of fire, remained unscorched.
   Besides—I ha' not since put up my sword—
   Against the Capitol I met a lion,          20
   Who glared upon me, and went surly by
   Without annoying me. And there were drawn
   Upon a heap⁴ a hundred ghastly women,
   Transformèd with their fear, who swore they saw
   Men, all in fire, walk up and down the streets.     25
   And yesterday the bird of night⁵ did sit
   Even at noonday upon the market place,
   Hooting and shrieking. When these prodigies⁶
   Do so conjointly meet, let not men say,
   "These are their reasons, they are natural,"     30

---

1. **sway:** natural order. 2. **rived:** split. 3. **exalted:** lifted high. 4. **drawn . . . heap:** huddled together. 5. **bird of night:** screech owl. 6. **prodigies:** wonders.

For I believe they are portentous things
Unto the climate that they point upon.[7]
**Cicero.** Indeed it is a strange-disposèd time.
But men may construe things after their fashion,
Clean from the purpose[8] of the things themselves.    35
Comes Caesar to the Capitol tomorrow?
**Casca.** He doth, for he did bid Antonius
Send word to you he would be there tomorrow.
**Cicero.** God night then, Casca. This disturbèd sky
Is not to walk in.    40
**Casca.**                    Farewell, Cicero.

[*Exit* Cicero.]

[*Enter* Cassius.]

**Cassius.** Who's there?
**Casca.**                    A Roman.
**Cassius.**                              Casca, by your voice.
**Casca.** Your ear is good. Cassius, what night is this!    45
**Cassius.** A very pleasing night to honest men.
**Casca.** Who ever knew the heavens menace so?
**Cassius.** Those that have known the earth so full of faults.
For my part, I have walked about the streets,
Submitting me unto the perilous night,    50
And, thus unbraced,[9] Casca, as you see,
Have bared my bosom to the thunder stone.[10]
And when the cross[11] blue lightning seemed to open
The breast of heaven, I did present myself
Even in the aim and very flash of it.    55
**Casca.** But wherefore did you so much tempt the heavens?
It is the part of men to fear and tremble
When the most mighty gods by tokens send
Such dreadful heralds to astonish us.
**Cassius.** You are dull, Casca, and those sparks of life    60
That should be in a Roman you do want,[12]
Or else you use not. You look pale, and gaze,
And put on fear, and cast yourself in wonder,
To see the strange impatience of the heavens.
But if you would consider the true cause    65
Why all these fires, why all these gliding ghosts,
Why birds and beasts, from quality and kind;[13]
Why old men fool and children calculate;[14]

---

7. **portentous . . . upon:** omens of disaster for Rome.   8. **Clean . . . purpose:** opposite of the real meaning.
9. **unbraced:** with coat open.   10. **thunder stone:** thunderbolt.   11. **cross:** zigzag.   12. **want:** lack.   13. **from . . .**
**kind:** acting contrary to their natures.   14. **calculate:** prophesy.

Why all these things change from their ordinance,[15]
Their natures, and preformèd faculties,
To monstrous[16] quality, why, you shall find
That heaven hath infused them with these spirits
To make them instruments of fear and warning
Unto some monstrous state.
Now could I, Casca, name to thee a man
Most like this dreadful night
That thunders, lightens, opens graves, and roars
As doth the lion in the Capitol;
A man no mightier than thyself or me
In personal action, yet prodigious grown
And fearful, as these strange eruptions are.

**Casca.** 'Tis Caesar that you mean. Is it not, Cassius?

**Cassius.** Let it be who it is. For Romans now
Have thews[17] and limbs like to their ancestors.
But woe the while![18] our fathers' minds are dead,
And we are governed with our mothers' spirits,
Our yoke and sufferance[19] show us womanish.

**Casca.** Indeed, they say the senators tomorrow
Mean to establish Caesar as a king,
And he shall wear his crown by sea and land
In every place save here in Italy.

**Cassius.** I know where I will wear this dagger then;
Cassius from bondage will deliver Cassius.
Therein, ye gods, you make the weak most strong;
Therein, ye gods, you tyrants do defeat.
Nor stony tower, nor walls of beaten brass,
Nor airless dungeon, nor strong links of iron,
Can be retentive to the strength of spirit;
But life, being weary of these worldly bars,
Never lacks power to dismiss itself.
If I know this, know all the world besides,
That part of tyranny that I do bear
I can shake off at pleasure.

*[Thunder still.]*

**Casca.**                    So can I.
So every bondman in his own hand bears
The power to cancel his captivity.

**Cassius.** And why should Caesar be a tyrant then?
Poor man! I know he would not be a wolf
But that he sees the Romans are but sheep;

70
75
80
85
90
95
100
105

---

15. **ordinance:** natural order.  16. **monstrous:** unnatural.  17. **thews:** sinews.  18. **woe the while:** alas for our time.
19. **Our . . . sufferance:** our enduring this slavery.

He were no lion, were not Romans hinds.[20]                              110
Those that with haste will make a mighty fire
Begin it with weak straws. What trash is Rome,
What rubbish and what offal,[21] when it serves
For the base matter to illuminate[22]                                    115
So vile a thing as Caesar! But, O grief,
Where hast thou led me? I, perhaps, speak this
Before a willing bondman. Then I know
My answer must be made. But I am armed,
And dangers are to me indifferent.
**Casca.** You speak to Casca, and to such a man                         120
    That is no fleering[23] telltale. Hold, my hand.
    Be factious for redress of all these griefs,[24]
    And I will set this foot of mine as far
    As who goes farthest.
**Cassius.**                    There's a bargain made.                  125
    Now know you, Casca, I have moved already
    Some certain of the noblest-minded Romans
    To undergo with me an enterprise
    Of honorable-dangerous consequence;
    And I do know, by this they stay[25] for me                          130
    In Pompey's porch;[26] for now, this fearful night,
    There is no stir or walking in the streets,
    And the complexion of the element[27]
    In favor's[28] like the work we have in hand,
    Most bloody, fiery, and most terrible.                               135

        [*Enter* Cinna.]

**Casca.** Stand close[29] awhile, for here comes one in haste.
**Cassius.** 'Tis Cinna. I do know him by his gait.
    He is a friend. Cinna, where haste you so?
**Cinna.** To find out you. Who's that? Metellus Cimber?
**Cassius.** No, it is Casca, one incorporate                            140
    To our attempts.[30] Am I not stayed for, Cinna?
**Cinna.** I am glad on 't.[31] What a fearful night is this!
    There's two or three of us have seen strange sights.
**Cassius.** Am I not stayed for? Tell me.
**Cinna.**                              Yes, you are.                     145
    O Cassius, if you could
    But win the noble Brutus to our party—

---

20. **hinds:** female deer. 21. **offal:** garbage. 22. **base . . . illuminate:** the rubbish from which the light is kindled.
23. **fleering:** sneering. 24. **Be factious . . . griefs:** be a partisan with me in righting these wrongs. 25. **stay:** wait.
26. **Pompey's porch:** the covered porch, part of the theater Pompey had built. 27. **element:** sky. 28. **favor:**
appearance. 29. **close:** hidden. 30. **incorporate . . . attempts:** one of our conspiracy. 31. **on't:** of it.

**Cassius.** Be you content. Good Cinna, take this paper
    And look you lay it in the praetor's chair,³²
    Where Brutus may but find it, and throw this               150
    In at his window. Set this up with wax
    Upon old Brutus'³³ statue. All this done,
    Repair to Pompey's porch, where you shall find us.
    Is Decius Brutus and Trebonius there?
**Cinna.** All but Metellus Cimber, and he's gone          155
    To seek you at your house. Well, I will hie³⁴
    And so bestow these papers as you bade me.
**Cassius.** That done, repair to Pompey's theater.

                                        [*Exit* Cinna.]

    Come, Casca, you and I will yet ere day
    See Brutus at his house. Three parts of him        160
    Is ours already, and the man entire
    Upon the next encounter yields him ours.
**Casca.** O, he sits high in all the people's hearts,
    And that which would appear offense in us,
    His countenance, like richest alchemy,³⁵         165
    Will change to virtue and to worthiness.
**Cassius.** Him and his worth and our great need of him
    You have right well conceited.³⁶ Let us go,
    For it is after midnight, and ere day
    We will awake him and be sure of him.          170

                                        [*Exeunt.*]

---

32. **praetor's chair:** Brutus was a praetor, an official next in rank to Caesar's rank of consul.  33. **old Brutus:** Lucius Junius Brutus, Brutus' ancestor.  34. **hie:** hurry.  35. **alchemy:** an ancient science that tried to change baser metals into gold.  36. **conceited:** understood.

## Act One

### Getting at Meaning

*Scene 1*

1. Who are Marullus and Flavius? Why are they angry with the crowd of commoners? Find a line in which Marullus expresses his attitude toward the commoners.

2. Who was Pompey? What point does Marullus make through his reference to Pompey?

3. What does Flavius mean when he tells Marullus to "disrobe the images"? What attitude do the two apparently have toward Caesar?

*Scene 2*

4. What is Antony doing during the festival when he "doth run his course"? Why does Caesar tell Calpurnia to stand in Antony's way?

5. What is Cassius's complaint against Brutus?

How does Brutus explain himself? What does Cassius mean when he says that many people in Rome have been wishing "that noble Brutus had his eyes"? What is Cassius's intention when he offers to function as Brutus's "glass," or mirror?

6. What are Cassius's feelings about Caesar? What examples does he use to illustrate his views? Explain the meaning of these famous lines: "The fault, dear Brutus, is not in our stars,/But in ourselves, that we are underlings."

7. Why does Cassius speak of Brutus's ancestor? How does Brutus respond to Cassius's arguments?

8. What does Caesar mean when he says, "Yond Cassius has a lean and hungry look"? What are his fears about Cassius?

9. Why does Caesar look angry when he returns from the Forum? What happened when Antony offered Caesar the crown that would make him king?

10. Casca reports on the events in the market place. What does he report about the attitude of the commoners toward Caesar? Why didn't Casca understand Cicero's speech? What has happened to Marullus and Flavius?

*Scene 3*

11. How does Casca view Caesar? What does Cassius mean when he says to Casca, "Cassius from bondage will deliver Cassius"? What does he mean when he says of Caesar, ". . . I know he would not be a wolf/But that he sees the Romans are but sheep;/He were no lion, were not Romans hinds"?

12. What do the conspirators plan? How do they intend to convert Brutus to their views?

## Developing Skills in Reading Literature

1. **Pun.** A pun, you will remember, is a play on words. A pun may involve homonyms, words that sound alike, although they are spelled differently and have different meanings, or a word with two or more meanings.

Find an example of punning in Scene 1 of this act. What words are involved?

2. **Foreshadowing.** What is the function of the soothsayer in Act One? What effect does his warning "Beware the ides of March" have on Caesar? What effect does it have on the reader/viewer?

3. **Allusion.** Explain the allusion in these lines spoken by Cassius to Brutus:

I, as Aeneas, our great ancestor,
Did from the flames of Troy upon his shoulder
The old Anchises bear, so from the waves of Tiber
Did I the tired Caesar. And this man
Is now become a god . . .

Why is this particular allusion appropriate to the characters and circumstances of the play?

4. **Blank Verse.** Blank verse is poetry written in unrhymed iambic pentameter. The following three lines spoken by Cassius illustrate blank verse:

Brutus, I do observe you now of late;
I have not from your eyes that gentleness
And show of love as I was wont to have.

What other characters in Act One speak in blank verse?

5. **Character.** Cassius indicates a shrewd understanding of Brutus's character when he tries to persuade Brutus to his own view of Caesar. What argument does Cassius use to sway Brutus? To what character traits in Brutus does he appeal? What generalizations can you make about Cassius from his discourse?

The character Casca is presented in Act One as a cynic, or one who tends to doubt the goodness of human motives, often displaying this attitude through sarcasm and sneers. Find lines that suggest Casca's cynicism. How do Brutus and Cassius sum up Casca's character? What does Cassius mean when he says of Casca, "This rudeness is a sauce to his good wit,/Which gives men stomach to digest his words/With better appetite"? Why does Shakespeare have Casca speak prose, and not blank verse?

6. **Pathetic Fallacy.** John Ruskin, a nineteenth-century English critic, coined the term *pathetic fallacy*, which means "the attachment of human traits and feelings to nature." The term combines

the word *pathetic,* meaning "pertaining to the feelings," and the word *fallacy,* meaning "false notion," for in real life nature acts independently, without human feelings and without reference to human affairs.

Shakespeare employs the pathetic fallacy in Scene 3.

What is unusual about the storm that Casca describes? What other bizarre events happen in nature on this night? In what sense does the tumult in nature reflect what is happening in human affairs?

**Developing Vocabulary**

**Latin Roots.** The word *fallacy* is derived from the Latin verb *fallere,* meaning "to deceive." The words in this exercise are also derived from this verb. Look up each word in a dictionary, record its meaning, and explain its relationship to the Latin root. Then use each word in a sentence, making sure that you use it as the correct part of speech.

| | | |
|---|---|---|
| fallacious | fallible | falsification |
| fallibility | infallible | falsify |
| fallibilism | falsehood | |

# Act Two

*Scene 1*

[*Brutus is faced with two wrongs: to live under the tyranny of Caesar or to kill Caesar. While considering the problem, he receives Cassius' letter. Shortly after, Cassius and the conspirators visit him, and they agree to assassinate Caesar that same day.*]

[*Rome. Brutus' orchard.*]

**Brutus.** What, Lucius, ho!
  I cannot by the progress of the stars
  Give guess how near to day. Lucius, I say!
  I would it were my fault to sleep so soundly.
  When, Lucius, when? Awake, I say! What, Lucius!          5

[*Enter* Lucius *from the house.*]

**Lucius.** Called you, my lord?
**Brutus.** Get me a taper[1] in my study, Lucius.
    When it is lighted, come and call me here.
**Lucius.** I will, my lord.

                                         [*Exit.*]

   [Brutus *returns to his brooding.*]

**Brutus.** It must be by his[2] death; and for my part,     10
    I know no personal cause to spurn at him,
    But for the general.[3] He would be crowned.
    How that might change his nature, there's the question.
    It is the bright day that brings forth the adder,[4]
    And that craves[5] wary walking. Crown him that,     15
    And then I grant we put a sting in him
    That at his will he may do danger with.
    The abuse of greatness is when it disjoins
    Remorse[6] from power. And to speak truth of Caesar,
    I have not known when his affections swayed[7]     20
    More than his reason. But 'tis a common proof[8]
    That lowliness is young ambition's ladder,
    Whereto the climber-upward turns his face;
    But when he once attains the upmost round,[9]
    He then unto the ladder turns his back,     25
    Looks in the clouds, scorning the base degrees[10]
    By which he did ascend. So Caesar may.
    Then lest he may, prevent.[11] And since the quarrel
    Will bear no color[12] for the thing he is,
    Fashion it thus: that what he is, augmented,     30
    Would run to these and these extremities;
    And therefore think him as a serpent's egg,
    Which, hatched, would as his kind grow mischievous,
    And kill him in the shell.

   [*Reenter* Lucius *with a letter.*]

**Lucius.** The taper burneth in your closet,[13] sir.     35
    Searching the window for a flint, I found
    This paper, thus sealed up, and I am sure
    It did not lie there when I went to bed.

                      [*Gives him the letter.*]

---

1. **taper:** candle.  2. **his:** Caesar's.  3. **general:** general good.  4. **adder:** poisonous snake.  5. **craves:** demands.
6. **Remorse:** pity.  7. **affections swayed:** feelings ruled.  8. **proof:** experience.  9. **round:** rung.  10. **degrees:** steps.
11. **prevent:** he must be stopped.  12. **bear . . . color:** cannot be justified.  13. **closet:** small private room.

Len Cariou (Brutus) in *Julius Caesar*, Stratford Festival, 1982.

**Brutus.** Get you to bed again; it is not day.
　Is not tomorrow, boy, the ides of March? 40
**Lucius.** I know not, sir.
**Brutus.** Look in the calendar and bring me word.
**Lucius.** I will, sir.

　　　　　　　　　　　　　　　　　　　　　　　　　[*Exit.*]

**Brutus.** The exhalations,[14] whizzing in the air,
　Give so much light that I may read by them. 45

　　　　　　　　　　　　　　　[*Opens the letter and reads.*]
　"Brutus, thou sleep'st. Awake, and see thyself!
　Shall Rome, etc.[15] Speak, strike, redress!"[16]
　"Brutus, thou sleep'st. Awake!"
　Such instigations have been often dropped
　Where I have took them up. 50
　"Shall Rome, etc." Thus must I piece it out:

---

14. **exhalations:** meteors.　15. **Rome, etc:** Because the actor would have the complete letter, Shakespeare did not include it in the manuscript.　16. **redress:** right a wrong.

Shall Rome stand under one man's awe? What, Rome?
My ancestors did from the streets of Rome
The Tarquin[17] drive when he was called a king.
"Speak, strike, redress!" Am I entreated                              55
To speak and strike? O Rome, I make thee promise,
If the redress will follow, thou receivest
Thy full petition at the hand of Brutus!

    [*Reenter* Lucius.]

**Lucius.** Sir, March is wasted fifteen days.

                                   [*Knocking within.*]
**Brutus.** 'Tis good. Go to the gate, somebody knocks.              60
                                   [*Exit* Lucius.]

    Since Cassius first did whet me against Caesar,
    I have not slept.
    Between the acting of a dreadful thing
    And the first motion, all the interim is
    Like a phantasma or a hideous dream.[18]                         65
    The Genius and the mortal instruments[19]
    Are then in council,[20] and the state of man,
    Like to a little kingdom, suffers then
    The nature of an insurrection.

    [*Reenter* Lucius.]

**Lucius.** Sir, 'tis your brother[21] Cassius at the door,          70
    Who doth desire to see you.
**Brutus.**                            Is he alone?
**Lucius.** No, sir, there are more with him.
**Brutus.**                                      Do you know them?
**Lucius.** No, sir. Their hats[22] are plucked about their ears     75
    And half their faces buried in their cloaks,
    That by no means I may discover them
    By any mark of favor.[23]
**Brutus.**                            Let 'em enter.
                                   [*Exit* Lucius.]

    They are the faction.[24] O conspiracy,                          80
    Sham'st thou to show thy dang'rous brow by night,
    When evils are most free? O, then by day
    Where wilt thou find a cavern dark enough

---

17. **Tarquin:** Tarquinias Superbus, the last king of Rome.  18. **Between . . . dream:** the time between the first idea and the dreadful deed is like a hideous nightmare.  19. **The Genius . . . instruments:** the mind and the body.  20. **in council:** a state of war.  21. **brother:** brother-in-law. Cassius was married to Brutus' sister.  22. **hats:** Elizabethan costumes. An anachronism.  23. **favor:** appearance.  24. **faction:** members of the party.

To mask thy monstrous visage? Seek none, conspiracy,
Hide it in smiles and affability!
For if thou path, thy native semblance on,[25]                                      85
Not Erebus[26] itself were dim enough
To hide thee from prevention.[27]


[*Enter the conspirators,* Cassius, Casca, Decius, Cinna,
Metellus Cimber, *and* Trebonius.]

**Cassius.** I think we are too bold upon your rest.
    Good morrow, Brutus. Do we trouble you?                                      90
**Brutus.** I have been up this hour, awake all night.
    Know I these men that come along with you?
**Cassius.** Yes, every man of them; and no man here
    But honors you; and every one doth wish
    You had but that opinion of yourself                                      95
    Which every noble Roman bears of you.
    This is Trebonius.
**Brutus.**                He is welcome hither.
**Cassius.** This, Decius Brutus.
**Brutus.**                   He is welcome too.                                      100
**Cassius.** This, Casca; this, Cinna; and this, Metellus Cimber.
**Brutus.** They are all welcome.
    What watchful cares do interpose themselves
    Betwixt your eyes and night?
**Cassius.** Shall I entreat a word?                                      105

                              [*They whisper.*]

**Decius.** Here lies the east. Doth not the day break here?
**Casca.** No.
**Cinna.** O, pardon, sir, it doth; and yon grey lines
    That fret[28] the clouds are messengers of day.
**Casca.** You shall confess that you are both deceived.                                      110
    Here, as I point my sword, the sun arises,
    Which is a great way growing on the south,
    Weighing[29] the youthful season of the year.
    Some two months hence, up higher toward the north
    He first presents his fire; and the high east                                      115
    Stands as the Capitol, directly here.

[Brutus *and* Cassius *rejoin the others.*]

**Brutus.** Give me your hands all over, one by one.

---

25. **path . . . on:** walk openly in your usual manner.   26. **Erebus:** in Greek mythology, a dark region of the
underworld.   27. **prevention:** discovery.   28. **fret:** ornament.   29. **Weighing:** considering.

**Cassius.** And let us swear our resolution.
**Brutus.** No, not an oath. If not the face of men,
    The sufferance of our souls, the time's abuse—             120
    If these be motives weak, break off betimes,[30]
    And every man hence to his idle bed.
    So let high-sighted[31] tyranny range on
    Till each man drop by lottery.[32] But if these
    (As I am sure they do) bear fire enough                 125
    To kindle cowards and to steel with valor
    The melting spirits of women, then, countrymen,
    What need we any spur but our own cause
    To prick us to redress? what other bond
    Than secret Romans that have spoke the word       130
    And will not palter?[33] and what other oath
    Than honesty to honesty engaged
    That this shall be, or we will fall for it?
    Swear priests and cowards and men cautelous,[34]
    Old feeble carrions[35] and such suffering souls       135
    That welcome wrongs; unto bad causes swear
    Such creatures as men doubt; but do not stain
    The even virtue of our enterprise,
    Nor the insuppressive mettle of our spirits,
    To think that or our cause or[36] our performance     140
    Did need an oath when every drop of blood
    That every Roman bears, and nobly bears,
    Is guilty of a several bastardy[37]
    If he do break the smallest particle
    Of any promise that hath passed from him.         145
**Cassius.** But what of Cicero? Shall we sound him?
    I think he will stand very strong with us.
**Casca.** Let us not leave him out.
**Cinna.**                        No, by no means.
**Metellus.** O, let us have him! for his silver hairs     150
    Will purchase us a good opinion
    And buy men's voices to commend our deeds.
    It shall be said his judgment ruled our hands;
    Our youths and wildness shall no whit appear,
    But all be buried in his gravity.                155
**Brutus.** O, name him not! Let us not break with him,[38]
    For he will never follow anything
    That other men begin.

---

30. **betimes:** now.   31. **high-sighted:** proud-eyed.   32. **lottery:** turn.   33. **palter:** play false.   34. **cautelous:** crafty.
35. **carrions:** carcasses.   36. **or . . . or:** either . . . or.   37. **several bastardy:** individual betrayal.   38. **break with him:**
reveal our conspiracy to him.

**Cassius.**                   Then leave him out.

**Casca.** Indeed he is not fit.                                      160

**Decius.** Shall no man else be touched but only Caesar?

**Cassius.** Decius, well urged. I think it is not meet
    Mark Antony, so well beloved of Caesar,
    Should outlive Caesar. We shall find of him
    A shrewd contriver;[39] and you know, his means,                165
    If he improve them, may well stretch so far
    As to annoy[40] us all; which to prevent,
    Let Antony and Caesar fall together.

**Brutus.** Our course will seem too bloody, Caius Cassius,
    To cut the head off and then hack the limbs,                  170
    Like wrath in death and envy[41] afterwards;
    For Antony is but a limb of Caesar.
    Let us be sacrificers, but not butchers, Caius.
    We all stand up against the spirit of Caesar,
    And in the spirit of men there is no blood.                    175
    O that we then could come by Caesar's spirit
    And not dismember Caesar! But, alas,
    Caesar must bleed for it! And, gentle[42] friends,
    Let's kill him boldly, but not wrathfully;
    Let's carve him as a dish fit for the gods,                    180
    Not hew him as a carcass fit for hounds.
    And let our hearts, as subtle masters do,
    Stir up their servants to an act of rage
    And after seem to chide 'em. This shall make
    Our purpose necessary, and not envious;[43]                    185
    Which so appearing to the common eyes,
    We shall be called purgers, not murderers.
    And for Mark Antony, think not of him;
    For he can do no more than Caesar's arm
    When Caesar's head is off.                                     190

**Cassius.**                   Yet I fear him,
    For in the ingrafted love he bears to Caesar—

**Brutus.** Alas, good Cassius, do not think of him!
    If he love Caesar, all that he can do
    Is to himself—take thought, and die for Caesar.               195
    And that were much he should; for he is given
    To sports, to wildness, and much company.

**Trebonius.** There is no fear[44] in him. Let him not die,
    For he will live and laugh at this hereafter.          *[Clock strikes.]*

---

39. **shrewd contriver:** cunning plotter.  40. **annoy:** harm.  41. **envy:** hatred.  42. **gentle:** noble.  43. **envious:** full of malice.  44. **fear:** cause for fear.

**Brutus.** Peace! Count the clock.⁴⁵ 200

**Cassius.** The clock hath stricken three.

**Trebonius.** 'Tis time to part.

**Cassius.** But it is doubtful yet
　　Whether Caesar will come forth today or no;
　　For he is superstitious grown of late, 205
　　Quite from the main opinion he held once
　　Of fantasy, of dreams, and ceremonies.⁴⁶
　　It may be these apparent prodigies,⁴⁷
　　The unaccustomed terror of this night,
　　And the persuasion of his augurers⁴⁸ 210
　　May hold him from the Capitol today.

**Decius.** Never fear that. If he be so resolved,
　　I can o'ersway him; for he loves to hear
　　That unicorns may be betrayed with trees
　　And bears with glasses, elephants with holes, 215
　　Lions with toils,⁴⁹ and men with flatterers;
　　But when I tell him he hates flatterers,
　　He says he does, being then most flattered.
　　Let me work,
　　For I can give his humor the true bent,⁵⁰ 220
　　And I will bring him to the Capitol.

**Cassius.** Nay, we will all of us be there to fetch him.

**Brutus.** By the eighth hour.⁵¹ Is that the uttermost?⁵²

**Cinna.** Be that the uttermost, and fail not then.

**Metellus.** Caius Ligarius doth bear Caesar hard, 225
　　Who rated⁵³ him for speaking well of Pompey.
　　I wonder none of you have thought of him.

**Brutus.** Now, good Metellus, go along by him.
　　He loves me well, and I have given him reasons.
　　Send him but hither, and I'll fashion⁵⁴ him. 230

**Cassius.** The morning comes upon's. We'll leave you, Brutus.
　　And, friends, disperse yourselves; but all remember
　　What you have said and show yourselves true Romans.

**Brutus.** Good gentlemen, look fresh and merrily.
　　Let not our looks put on our purposes, 235
　　But bear it as our Roman actors do,

---

45. **clock:** There were no striking clocks in Caesar's day. An anachronism.　46. **ceremonies:** supernatural happenings.　47. **prodigies:** omens.　48. **augurers:** professionals who interpreted omens.　49. **unicorns . . . toils:** It was believed that unicorns could be trapped by trickery. A hunter, standing in front of a tree, provoked a unicorn to charge and stepped aside at the last moment. The unicorn, with his horn driven firmly into the tree, could not escape. Bears were thought to be vain and easily trapped with mirrors. Elephants were trapped in deep pits, and lions were immobilized with nets.　50. **humor . . . bent:** put him in a good mood.　51. **eighth hour:** the usual starting time for business in Shakespeare's day.　52. **uttermost:** latest.　53. **rated:** rebuked.　54. **fashion:** mold.

With untired spirits and formal constancy.[55]
And so good morrow to you every one.

[*Exeunt all but* Brutus.]

Boy! Lucius! Fast asleep? It is no matter.
Enjoy the honey-heavy dew of slumber.                                    240
Thou hast no figures[56] nor no fantasies
Which busy care draws in the brains of men;
Therefore thou sleep'st so sound.

[*Enter* Portia, Brutus' *wife.*]

**Portia.**                          Brutus, my lord!
**Brutus.** Portia! What mean you? Wherefore rise you now?               245
    It is not for your health thus to commit
    Your weak condition to the raw cold morning.
**Portia.** Nor for yours neither. You've ungently, Brutus,
    Stole from my bed. And yesternight at supper
    You suddenly arose and walked about,                                    250
    Musing and sighing with your arms across;
    And when I asked you what the matter was,
    You stared upon me with ungentle looks.
    I urged you further, then you scratched your head
    And too impatiently stamped with your foot.                              255
    Yet I insisted, yet you answered not,
    But with an angry wafture[57] of your hand
    Gave sign for me to leave you. So I did,
    Fearing to strengthen that impatience
    Which seemed too much enkindled, and withal                              260
    Hoping it was but an effect of humor,[58]
    Which sometime hath his hour with every man.
    It will not let you eat nor talk nor sleep,
    And could it work so much upon your shape
    As it hath much prevailed on your condition,                             265
    I should not know you Brutus. Dear my lord,
    Make me acquainted with your cause of grief.
**Brutus.** I am not well in health, and that is all.
**Portia.** Brutus is wise and, were he not in health,
    He would embrace the means to come by it.                                270
**Brutus.** Why, so I do. Good Portia, go to bed.
**Portia.** Is Brutus sick, and is it physical[59]
    To walk unbraced and suck up the humors[60]

---

55. **formal constancy:** steadfast appearance. 56. **figures:** fearful dreams. 57. **wafture:** wave. 58. **humor:** moodiness. 59. **physical:** good for your health. 60. **humors:** mists. Damp air was thought to cause illness.

Susan Wright (Portia) and Len Cariou (Brutus) in *Julius Caesar*, Stratford Festival, 1982.

Of the dank morning? What, is Brutus sick,
And will he steal out of his wholesome bed     275
To dare the vile contagion of the night,
And tempt the rheumy and unpurgèd[61] air,
To add unto his sickness? No, my Brutus.
You have some sick offense within your mind,
Which by the right and virtue of my place     280
I ought to know of; and upon my knees
I charm[62] you, by my once commended beauty,
By all your vows of love, and that great vow
Which did incorporate and make us one,
That you unfold to me, yourself,[63] your half,     285
Why you are heavy, and what men tonight
Have had resort to you; for here have been
Some six or seven, who did hide their faces
Even from darkness.
**Brutus.**                    Kneel not, gentle Portia.     290

---

61. **unpurged:** unpurified (by the sun).   62. **charm:** solemnly entreat.   63. **yourself:** part of you (by marriage).

**Portia.** I should not need if you were gentle Brutus.
    Within the bond of marriage, tell me, Brutus,
    Is it excepted I should know no secrets
    That appertain to you? Am I yourself
    But,[64] as it were, in sort or limitation?          295
    To keep with you at meals, comfort your bed,
    And talk to you sometimes? Dwell I but in the suburbs
    Of your good pleasure? If it be no more,
    Portia is Brutus' harlot, not his wife.
**Brutus.** You are my true and honorable wife,      300
    As dear to me as are the ruddy drops[65]
    That visit my sad heart.
**Portia.** If this were true, then should I know this secret.
    I grant I am a woman, but withal
    A woman that Lord Brutus took to wife.      305
    I grant I am a woman, but withal
    A woman well reputed, Cato's daughter.[66]
    Think you I am no stronger than my sex,
    Being so fathered and so husbanded?
    Tell me your counsels; I will not disclose 'em.      310
    I have made strong proof of my constancy,
    Giving myself a voluntary wound
    Here, in the thigh. Can I bear that with patience,
    And not my husband's secrets?
**Brutus.**                    O ye gods,      315
    Render me worthy of this noble wife!

                                  *[Knocking within.]*

    Hark, hark! one knocks. Portia, go in awhile,
    And by-and-by thy bosom shall partake
    The secrets of my heart.
    All my engagements I will construe[67] to thee,      320
    All the charactery[68] of my sad brows.
    Leave me with haste.

                                    *[Exit Portia.]*

    Lucius, who's that knocks?

    *[Reenter Lucius with Ligarius.]*

**Lucius.** Here is a sick man that would speak with you.
**Brutus.** Caius Ligarius, that Metellus spake of.      325
    Boy, stand aside. Caius Ligarius, how?

---

64. **But:** only.  65. **ruddy drops:** blood.  66. **Cato's daughter:** Marcus Porcius Cato, a man of rare political honesty, had strongly opposed Caesar. When Caesar defeated Pompey, Cato killed himself rather than live under a tyrant.
67. **construe:** explain.  68. **charactery:** what is written in my face.

**Ligarius.** Vouchsafe[69] good morrow from a feeble tongue.
**Brutus.** O, what a time have you chose out, brave Caius,
　　To wear a kerchief![70] Would you were not sick!
**Ligarius.** I am not sick if Brutus have in hand　　　　　　　330
　　Any exploit worthy the name of honor.
**Brutus.** Such an exploit have I in hand, Ligarius,
　　Had you a healthful ear to hear of it.
**Ligarius.** By all the gods that Romans bow before,
　　I here discard my sickness! Soul of Rome!　　　　　　　335
　　Brave son, derived from honorable loins!
　　Thou like an exorcist[71] hast conjured up
　　My mortified spirit. Now bid me run,
　　And I will strive with things impossible;
　　Yea, get the better of them. What's to do?　　　　　　　340
**Brutus.** A piece of work that will make sick men whole.
**Ligarius.** But are not some whole that we must make sick?
**Brutus.** That must we also. What it is, my Caius,
　　I shall unfold to thee as we are going
　　To whom it must be done.　　　　　　　　　　　　　　345
**Ligarius.**　　　　　　　　　　Set on your foot,
　　And with a heart new-fired I follow you,
　　To do I know not what; but it sufficeth
　　That Brutus leads me on.

　　　　　　　　　　　　　　　　　　　　　　*[Thunder.]*

**Brutus.**　　　　　　　　Follow me then.　　　　　　　　350

　　　　　　　　　　　　　　　　　　　　　　*[Exeunt.]*


*Scene 2*　　　　　*[Because of many threatening omens taking place in*
　　　　　　　　　*Rome, Calpurnia, Caesar's wife, insists that Caesar not go*
　　　　　　　　　*to the Capitol. Decius Brutus, one of the conspirators,*
　　　　　　　　　*comes to take him there, and insists that the omens are*
　　　　　　　　　*good ones and that Caesar's position may be weakened*
　　　　　　　　　*if he stays home because his wife is superstitious. Brutus*
　　　　　　　　　*and the rest of the conspirators also arrive to accompany*
　　　　　　　　　*Caesar, as does Mark Antony.]*

---

69. **Vouchsafe:** please accept.　70. **kerchief:** a muffler, worn by someone ill.　71. **exorcist:** one who summons the spirits of the dead ("mortified").

[Caesar's *house. Thunder and lightning. Enter* Caesar *in his nightgown.*¹]

**Caesar.** Nor heaven nor earth have been at peace tonight.
Thrice hath Calpurnia in her sleep cried out
"Help, ho! They murder Caesar!" Who's within?

[*Enter a* Servant.]

**Servant.** My lord?
**Caesar.** Go bid the priests do present² sacrifice,          5
And bring me their opinions of success.
**Servant.** I will, my lord.

                                                  [*Exit.*]

[*Enter* Caesar's *wife* Calpurnia, *alarmed.*]

**Calpurnia.** What mean you, Caesar? Think you to walk forth?
You shall not stir out of your house today.
**Caesar.** Caesar shall forth. The things that threatened me          10
Ne'er looked but on my back. When they shall see
The face of Caesar, they are vanished.
**Calpurnia.** Caesar, I never stood on ceremonies,³
Yet now they fright me. There is one within,
Besides the things that we have heard and seen,          15
Recounts most horrid sights seen by the watch.⁴
A lioness hath whelpèd⁵ in the streets,
And graves have yawned and yielded up their dead.
Fierce fiery warriors fought upon the clouds
In ranks and squadrons and right form of war,          20
Which drizzled blood upon the Capitol.
The noise of battle hurtled in the air,
Horses did neigh, and dying men did groan,
And ghosts did shriek and squeal about the streets.
O Caesar, these things are beyond all use,⁶          25
And I do fear them!
**Caesar.**               What can be avoided
Whose end is purposed by the mighty gods?
Yet Caesar shall go forth, for these predictions
Are to the world in general as to Caesar.          30

---

1. **nightgown:** dressing gown.  2. **present:** immediate.  3. **stood . . . ceremonies:** paid much attention to omens.
4. **watch:** night watchmen.  5. **whelpèd:** given birth.  6. **use:** custom.

**Calpurnia.** When beggars die there are no comets⁷ seen;
   The heavens themselves blaze forth the death of princes.
**Caesar.** Cowards die many times before their deaths;
   The valiant never taste of death but once.
   Of all the wonders that I yet have heard,                                   35
   It seems to me most strange that men should fear,
   Seeing that death, a necessary end,
   Will come when it will come.

   [*Reenter* Servant.]

                                             What say the augurers?
**Servant.** They would not have you to stir forth today.              40
   Plucking the entrails of an offering⁸ forth,
   They could not find a heart within the beast.
**Caesar.** The gods do this in shame of cowardice.
   Caesar should be a beast without a heart
   If he should stay at home today for fear.                                   45
   No, Caesar shall not. Danger knows full well
   That Caesar is more dangerous than he.
   We are two lions littered⁹ in one day,
   And I the elder and more terrible,
   And Caesar shall go forth.                                                       50
**Calpurnia.**                             Alas, my lord!
   Your wisdom is consumed in confidence.¹⁰
   Do not go forth today. Call it my fear
   That keeps you in the house and not your own.
   We'll send Mark Antony to the Senate House,                           55
   And he shall say you are not well today.
   Let me upon my knee prevail in this.
**Caesar.** Mark Antony shall say I am not well,
   And for thy humor¹¹ I will stay at home.

   [*Enter* Decius.]

   Here's Decius Brutus, he shall tell them so.                             60
**Decius.** Caesar, all hail! Good morrow, worthy Caesar!
   I come to fetch you to the Senate House.
**Caesar.** And you are come in very happy time
   To bear my greeting to the senators
   And tell them that I will not come today.                                  65

---

7. **comets:** comets were always portents of great disaster.  8. **offering:** sacrifice. Augurers divined the future by examining the entrails of sacrificed animals. Anything abnormal was thought to be highly significant.  9. **littered:** born.  10. **confidence:** overconfidence.  11. **humor:** whim.

Cannot, is false; and that I dare not, falser.
I will not come today. Tell them so, Decius.
**Calpurnia.** Say he is sick.
**Caesar.**                          Shall Caesar send a lie?
Have I in conquest stretched mine arm so far                70
To be afeard to tell greybeards the truth?
Decius, go tell them Caesar will not come.
**Decius.** Most mighty Caesar, let me know some cause,
Lest I be laughed at when I tell them so.
**Caesar.** The cause is in my will: I will not come.          75
That is enough to satisfy the Senate;
But for your private satisfaction,
Because I love you, I will let you know.
Calpurnia here, my wife, stays me at home.
She dreamt tonight she saw my statue,                      80
Which, like a fountain with an hundred spouts,
Did run pure blood, and many lusty Romans
Came smiling and did bathe their hands in it.
And these does she apply for warnings and portents
And evils imminent, and on her knee                        85
Hath begged that I will stay at home today.
**Decius.** This dream is all amiss interpreted;
It was a vision fair and fortunate.
Your statue spouting blood in many pipes,
In which so many smiling Romans bathed,                    90
Signifies that from you great Rome shall suck
Reviving blood, and that great men shall press
For tinctures, stains, relics, and cognizance.[12]
This by Calpurnia's dream is signified.
**Caesar.** And this way have you well expounded[13] it.      95
**Decius.** I have, when you have heard what I can say:
And know it now, the Senate have concluded
To give this day a crown to mighty Caesar.
If you shall send them word you will not come,
Their minds may change. Besides, it were a mock[14]         100
Apt to be rendered, for some one to say
"Break up the Senate till another time,
When Caesar's wife shall meet with better dreams."
If Caesar hide himself, shall they not whisper
"Lo, Caesar is afraid"?                                     105
Pardon me, Caesar, for my dear dear love

---

12. **tinctures ... cognizance:** tokens of your greatness.  13. **expounded:** explained.  14. **mock:** jibe.

To your proceeding bids me tell you this,
And reason to my love is liable.[15]

**Caesar.** How foolish do your fears seem now, Calpurnia!

I am ashamed I did yield to them.            110

Give me my robe, for I will go.

[*Enter* Brutus, Ligarius, Metellus, Casca, Trebonius, Cinna, *and* Publius.]

And look where Publius is come to fetch me.

**Publius.** Good morrow, Caesar.

**Caesar.**                           Welcome, Publius.

What, Brutus, are you stirred so early too?      115

Good morrow, Casca. Caius Ligarius,

Caesar was ne'er so much your enemy[16]

As that same ague[17] which hath made you lean.

What is't o'clock?

**Brutus.**                 Caesar, 'tis strucken eight.      120

**Caesar.** I thank you for your pains and courtesy.

[*Enter* Antony.]

See! Antony, that revels long o' nights,

Is notwithstanding up. Good morrow, Antony.

**Antony.** So to most noble Caesar.

**Caesar.**                       Bid them prepare within.      125

I am to blame to be thus waited for.

Now, Cinna, now, Metellus. What, Trebonius!

I have an hour's talk in store for you;

Remember that you call on me today;

Be near me, that I may remember you.      130

**Trebonius.** Caesar, I will. [*Aside*] And so near will I be

That your best friends shall wish I had been further.

**Caesar.** Good friends, go in and taste some wine with me,

And we (like friends) will straightway go together.

**Brutus.** [*Aside*] That every like is not the same, O Caesar,      135

The heart of Brutus yearns[18] to think upon.

                                              [*Exeunt.*]

---

15. **reason . . . liable:** my love forces me to tell you the truth.    16. **Caesar . . . enemy:** Ligarius was on Pompey's side during the civil war.    17. **ague:** fever, with chills.    18. **yearns:** grieves.

## Scene 3

[Artemidorus has heard about the conspiracy. He writes a letter of warning to Caesar and plans to give it to him as he is on his way to the Capitol.]

[A street near the Capitol. Enter Artemidorus, reading a paper.]

**Artemidorus.** "Caesar, beware of Brutus; take heed of Cassius; come not near Casca; have an eye to Cinna; trust not Trebonius; mark well Metellus Cimber; Decius Brutus loves thee not; thou hast wronged Caius Ligarius. There is but one mind in all these men, and it is bent against Caesar. If thou beest not immortal, look about you. Security[1] 5 gives way to conspiracy. The mighty gods defend thee!

                              "Thy lover,[2]
                              "ARTEMIDORUS."

Here will I stand till Caesar pass along
And as a suitor[3] will I give him this. 10
My heart laments that virtue cannot live
Out of the teeth of emulation.[4]
If thou read this, O Caesar, thou mayst live;
If not, the Fates with traitors do contrive.[5]

                                        [Exit.]

## Scene 4

[Brutus' wife, Portia, knows about the conspirators' plan and is anxious about the outcome. She meets a soothsayer who is on his way to warn Caesar again but who knows nothing of the conspirators' plan.]

[Another part of the same street, before the house of Brutus. Enter Portia and Lucius.]

---

1. **Security:** carelessness.  2. **lover:** friend.  3. **suitor:** petitioner.  4. **emulation:** envy.  5. **contrive:** plot.

**Portia.** I prithee,¹ boy, run to the Senate House.
    Stay not to answer me, but get thee gone!
    Why dost thou stay?
**Lucius.**             To know my errand, madam.
**Portia.** I would have had thee there and here again       5
    Ere I can tell thee what thou shouldst do there.
    O constancy, be strong upon my side,
    Set a huge mountain 'tween my heart and tongue!
    I have a man's mind, but a woman's might.
    How hard it is for women to keep counsel!       10
    Art thou here yet?
**Lucius.**            Madam, what should I do?
    Run to the Capitol and nothing else?
    And so return to you and nothing else?
**Portia.** Yes, bring me word, boy, if thy lord look well,     15
    For he went sickly forth; and take good note
    What Caesar doth, what suitors press to him.
    Hark, boy! What noise is that?
**Lucius.** I hear none, madam.
**Portia.**            Prithee, listen well.     20
    I heard a bustling rumor like a fray,²
    And the wind brings it from the Capitol.
**Lucius.** Sooth,³ madam, I hear nothing.

    [*Enter the* Soothsayer.]

**Portia.** Come hither, fellow. Which way hast thou been?
**Soothsayer.** At mine own house, good lady.     25
**Portia.** What is't o'clock?
**Soothsayer.**           About the ninth hour, lady.
**Portia.** Is Caesar yet gone to the Capitol?
**Soothsayer.** Madam, not yet. I go to take my stand,
    To see him pass on to the Capitol.     30
**Portia.** Thou hast some suit to Caesar, hast thou not?
**Soothsayer.** That I have, lady. If it will please Caesar
    To be so good to Caesar as to hear me,
    I shall beseech him to befriend himself.
**Portia.** Why, know'st thou any harm's intended towards him?     35
**Soothsayer.** None that I know will be, much that I fear may chance.
    Good morrow to you. Here the street is narrow.
    The throng that follows Caesar at the heels,

---

1. **prithee:** pray thee. 2. **rumor . . . fray:** noise like fighting. 3. **Sooth:** truly.

Of senators, of praetors, common suitors,
Will crowd a feeble man almost to death.
I'll get me to a place more void[4] and there                    40
Speak to great Caesar as he comes along.                         [*Exit.*]
**Portia.** I must go in. Ay me, how weak a thing
The heart of woman is! O Brutus,
The heavens speed thee in thine enterprise—                      45
Sure the boy heard me.—Brutus hath a suit
That Caesar will not grant.—O, I grow faint.—
Run, Lucius, and commend me to my lord;
Say I am merry. Come to me again
And bring me word what he doth say to thee.                      50
                                                    [*Exeunt severally.*][5]

---

4. **void:** empty.   5. **severally:** by different exits.

## Act Two

### Getting at Meaning

*Scene 1*

1. What are Brutus's thoughts about Caesar as he broods during the night? What does Brutus mean by the remark, "It is the bright day that brings forth the adder,/And that craves wary walking"?

2. How does the letter thrown in through the window affect Brutus? Explain the message, "Speak, strike, redress!"?

3. What does Brutus mean about the conspiracy when he says:

> O conspiracy,
> Sham'st thou to show thy dang'rous brow by
>    night,
> When evils are most free? O, then by day
> Where wilt thou find a cavern dark enough
> To mask thy monstrous visage?

4. What arguments does Brutus advance against the suggestion that the conspirators sign an oath?

5. Why do the conspirators want Cicero to be one of their party? Why does Brutus think that Cicero will not join them?

6. What are Brutus's reasons for not wanting to kill Mark Antony? What does Brutus mean when he says of Caesar, "Let's carve him as a dish fit for the gods,/Not hew him as a carcass fit for hounds"?

7. What does Portia beg of her husband? What arguments does she use to persuade Brutus to "unfold to me, yourself"? What has Portia done to prove her constancy?

*Scene 2*

8. What arguments does Calpurnia use to deter Caesar from going to the Forum? How does Caesar counter her arguments? What does he mean when he says, "Cowards die many times before their deaths;/The valiant never taste of death but once"?

9. Why does Caesar finally resolve to stay home from the Senate? How does Decius break down his resolve? How does Decius interpret Calpurnia's dream?

*Scene 3*

10. What is the content of the letter written by Artemidorus? When does he plan to give it to Caesar?

*Scene 4*

11. What is Portia's state of mind as she waits for Brutus?

## Developing Skills in Reading Literature

1. **Soliloquy.** When a character speaks directly to the audience rather than to another character, the speech is called a soliloquy. The soliloquy provides a way for a playwright to reveal a character's thoughts to the audience. Find two examples of soliloquy in Act Two.

2. **Simile and Metaphor.** Act Two contains a number of vivid similes and metaphors. For example, in Scene 1, thinking about the conspiracy to murder Caesar, Brutus says, "Between the acting of a dreadful thing/And the first motion, all the interim is/Like a phantasma or a hideous dream." What is the exact comparison in this simile? What does the simile indicate about Brutus's state of mind?

In Scene 1, Brutus creates an extended metaphor of lengthy dramatic parallels when he compares Caesar to an adder. What are the various parts to his comparison? What line of reasoning leads Brutus to conclude, "And therefore think of him as a serpent's egg,/Which, hatched, would as his kind grow mischievous,/And kill him in the shell"?

3. **Character.** An idealist is a person who sees things as they might be or as they should be, rather than as they are. A realist, on the other hand, tends to view things as they really are, even when it is uncomfortable or painful to do so.

Analyze the conversation among the conspirators in Scene 1. What evidence do you find that Brutus is an idealist? What evidence suggests that Cassius is a realist? Which character do you appreciate more at this point in the play?

Caesar is, of course, the subject of the conspiracy. What generalizations can you make about Caesar's character based on his behavior in Scene 2? What traits does Decius manipulate to convince Caesar to come to the Forum?

4. **Pathetic Fallacy.** At the beginning of Scene 3, Calpurnia alludes to strange happenings during the night. What are these strange happenings? How do they suggest that nature is mirroring the tumult of human affairs? What effect do the happenings have on Calpurnia?

## Developing Vocabulary

**Words from Greek.** A person can be described as cynical, stoical, or epicurean. All three words are derived from ancient Greek philosophies, Cynicism, Stoicism, and Epicureanism respectively.

Look up these three philosophies in an encyclopedia, and explain the meanings of the words *cynic*, *stoic,* and *epicurean*.

As already noted, Casca in *Julius Caesar* might be called a cynic. Which characters might be described as stoical? Is there a character who could fairly be called an epicurean?

# Act Three

## Scene 1

[*Artemidorus tries to give Caesar his letter of warning, but Caesar rejects him. In the Capitol, the conspirators surround Caesar and stab him to death. Brutus persuades them not to harm Antony and says that he himself will explain Caesar's death to the people. Antony will be allowed to speak at Caesar's funeral. While Antony pretends to be sympathetic to the assassination, he plans to avenge Caesar's death with help from Octavius Caesar, who is on his way to Rome.*]

[*Rome. A great crowd before the Capitol. The Senate sits on a higher level, waiting for* Caesar *to appear.* Artemidorus *and the* Soothsayer *are among the crowd.*

*A flourish of trumpets. Enter* Caesar, Brutus, Cassius, Casca, Decius, Metellus, Trebonius, Cinna, Antony, Lepidus, Popilius, *and others.* Caesar *stops in front of the* Soothsayer.]

**Caesar.** The ides of March are come.
**Soothsayer.** Ay, Caesar, but not gone.

[Artemidorus *steps up to* Caesar *with his warning.*]

**Artemidorus.** Hail, Caesar! Read this schedule.¹

[Decius *steps up quickly with another paper.*]

**Decius.** Trebonius doth desire you to o'erread
    (At your best leisure) this his humble suit.
**Artemidorus.** O Caesar, read mine first, for mine's a suit           5
    That touches Caesar nearer. Read it, great Caesar!
**Caesar.** What touches us ourself shall be last served.

[Caesar *pushes the paper aside and turns away.*]

**Artemidorus.** Delay not, Caesar! Read it instantly!
**Caesar.** What, is the fellow mad?
**Publius.**                    Sirrah,² give place.           10

[Publius *and other conspirators force* Artemidorus *away from* Caesar.]

---

1. **schedule:** paper.  2. **Sirrah:** way of addressing an inferior.

**Cassius.** What, urge you your petitions in the street?
    Come to the Capitol.

[Caesar *goes into the Senate House, the rest following.*
Popilius *speaks to* Cassius *in a low voice.*]

**Popilius.** I wish your enterprise today may thrive.
**Cassius.** What enterprise, Popilius?                 15
**Popilius.**                Fare you well.

                         [*Advances to* Caesar.]

**Brutus.** What said Popilius Lena?
**Cassius.** He wished today our enterprise might thrive.
    I fear our purpose is discovered.
**Brutus.** Look how he makes to³ Caesar. Mark him.       20
**Cassius.** Casca, be sudden, for we fear prevention.
    Brutus, what shall be done? If this be known,
    Cassius or Caesar never shall turn back,
    For I will slay myself.
**Brutus.**               Cassius, be constant.       25
    Popilius Lena speaks not of our purposes,
    For look, he smiles, and Caesar doth not change.
**Cassius.** Trebonius knows his time, for look you, Brutus,
    He draws Mark Antony out of the way.

                [*Exeunt* Antony *and* Trebonius.]

**Decius.** Where is Metellus Cimber? Let him go       30
    And presently prefer his suit to Caesar.
**Brutus.** He is addressed.⁴ Press near and second him.
**Cinna.** Casca, you are the first that rears your hand.

[Caesar *seats himself in his high Senate chair.*]

**Caesar.** Are we all ready? What is now amiss
    That Caesar and his Senate must redress?       35
**Metellus.** Most high, most mighty, and most puissant⁵ Caesar,
    Metellus Cimber throws before thy seat
    An humble heart.                      [*Kneeling.*]
**Caesar.**             I must prevent thee, Cimber.
    These couchings⁶ and these lowly courtesies       40
    Might fire the blood of ordinary men
    And turn preordinance and first decree
    Into the law of children.⁷ Be not fond⁸
    To think that Caesar bears such rebel blood
    That will be thawed from the true quality       45

---

3. **makes to:** goes toward.   4. **addressed:** ready.   5. **puissant:** powerful.   6. **couchings:** low bowings.   7. **And . . . children:** and turn established laws and penalties into laws and rules that change like the will of a child.   8. **fond:** foolish.

With that which melteth fools—I mean, sweet words,
Low-crookèd[9] curtsies, and base spaniel fawning.
Thy brother by decree is banished.
If thou dost bend and pray and fawn for him,
I spurn thee like a cur out of my way.                                     50
Know, Caesar doth not wrong, nor without cause
Will he be satisfied.
**Metellus.** Is there no voice more worthy than my own,
To sound more sweetly in great Caesar's ear
For the repealing of my banished brother?                                  55
**Brutus.** I kiss thy hand, but not in flattery, Caesar,
Desiring thee that Publius Cimber may
Have an immediate freedom of repeal.
**Caesar.** What, Brutus?
**Cassius.**                    Pardon, Caesar! Caesar, pardon!             60
As low as to thy foot doth Cassius fall
To beg enfranchisement[10] for Publius Cimber.

---

9. **Low-crookèd:** bending low.   10. **enfranchisement:** release.

**Caesar.** I could be well moved, if I were as you;
    If I could pray to move, prayers would move me;
    But I am constant as the Northern Star, 65
    Of whose true-fixed and resting quality
    There is no fellow in the firmament.[11]
    The skies are painted with unnumbered sparks,
    They are all fire, and every one doth shine;
    But there's but one in all doth hold his place. 70
    So in the world: 'tis furnished well with men,
    And men are flesh and blood, and apprehensive;[12]
    Yet in the number I do know but one
    That unassailable holds on his rank,
    Unshaked of motion; and that I am he, 75
    Let me a little show it, even in this,
    That I was constant Cimber should be banished
    And constant do remain to keep him so.
**Cinna.** O Caesar!
**Caesar.**        Hence! Wilt thou lift up Olympus?[13] 80
**Decius.** Great Caesar!
**Caesar.**       Doth not Brutus bootless[14] kneel?
**Casca.** Speak hands for me!

[*They stab* Caesar. Casca, *the others in turn, then* Brutus.]

**Caesar.** *Et tu, Brute?*[15]—Then fall Caesar!           [*Dies.*]
**Cinna.** Liberty! Freedom! Tyranny is dead! 85
    Run hence, proclaim, cry it about the streets!
**Cassius.** Some to the common pulpits and cry out
    "Liberty, freedom, and enfranchisement!"
**Brutus.** People and Senators, be not affrighted.
    Fly not; stand still. Ambition's debt is paid. 90
**Casca.** Go to the pulpit, Brutus.
**Decius.**              And Cassius too.
**Brutus.** Where's Publius?[16]
**Cinna.** Here, quite confounded[17] with this mutiny.
**Metellus.** Stand fast together, lest some friend of Caesar's 95
    Should chance—
**Brutus.** Talk not of standing! Publius, good cheer.
    There is no harm intended to your person
    Nor to no Roman else. So tell them, Publius.
**Cassius.** And leave us, Publius, lest that the people, 100
    Rushing on us, should do your age some mischief.

---

11. **no . . . firmament:** no equal in the heavens. 12. **apprehensive:** quick-witted. 13. **Olympus:** a mountain in Greece, legendary home of the gods. 14. **bootless:** in vain. 15. **Et tu, Brute:** Latin for "And you, too, Brutus!" 16. **Publius:** an elderly senator; not the exiled Publius Cimber. 17. **confounded:** confused.

**Brutus.** Do so, and let no man abide[18] this deed
    But we the doers.

    [*Reenter* Trebonius.]

**Cassius.**             Where is Antony?
**Trebonius.** Fled to his house amazed.                  105
    Men, wives, and children stare, cry out, and run,
    As it were doomsday.
**Brutus.**              Fates, we will know your pleasures.
    That we shall die, we know, 'tis but the time,
    And drawing days out, that men stand upon.[19]       110
**Cassius.** Why, he that cuts off twenty years of life
    Cuts off so many years of fearing death.
**Brutus.** Grant that, and then is death a benefit.
    So are we Caesar's friends, that have abridged
    His time of fearing death. Stoop, Romans, stoop,     115
    And let us bathe our hands in Caesar's blood
    Up to the elbows and besmear our swords.
    Then walk we forth, even to the market place,
    And waving our red weapons o'er our heads,
    Let's all cry, "Peace, freedom, and liberty!"       120
**Cassius.** Stoop then and wash. How many ages hence
    Shall this our lofty scene be acted over
    In states unborn and accents yet unknown!
**Brutus.** How many times shall Caesar bleed in sport,[20]
    That now on Pompey's basis lies along[21]         125
    No worthier than the dust!
**Cassius.**               So oft as that shall be,
    So often shall the knot of us be called
    The men that gave their country liberty.
**Decius.** What, shall we forth?                   130
**Cassius.**              Ay, every man away.
    Brutus shall lead, and we will grace his heels
    With the most boldest and best hearts of Rome.

    [*Enter a* Servant.]

**Brutus.** Soft! who comes here? A friend of Antony's.
**Servant.** Thus, Brutus, did my master bid me kneel;     135
    Thus did Mark Antony bid me fall down;
    And being prostrate, thus he bade me say:

---

18. **abide:** suffer for.   19. **stand upon:** worry about.   20. **sport:** dramas.   21. **Pompey's . . . along:** lies stretched out
on the base of Pompey's statue.

Brutus is noble, wise, valiant, and honest;
Caesar was mighty, bold, royal, and loving.
Say I love Brutus and I honor him;                              140
Say I feared Caesar, honored him, and loved him.
If Brutus will vouchsafe²² that Antony
May safely come to him and be resolved²³
How Caesar hath deserved to lie in death,
Mark Antony shall not love Caesar dead                          145
So well as Brutus living, but will follow
The fortunes and affairs of noble Brutus
Thorough the hazards of this untrod state²⁴
With all true faith. So says my master Antony.
**Brutus.** Thy master is a wise and valiant Roman.            150
I never thought him worse.
Tell him, so please him come unto this place,
He shall be satisfied and, by my honor,
Depart untouched.
**Servant.**                    I'll fetch him presently.²⁵     155

                                                    [*Exit.*]

**Brutus.** I know that we shall have him well to friend.²⁶
**Cassius.** I wish we may. But yet have I a mind
That fears him much; and my misgiving still
Falls shrewdly to the purpose.²⁷

        [*Reenter* Antony.]

**Brutus.** But here comes Antony. Welcome, Mark Antony.       160
**Antony.** O mighty Caesar! Dost thou lie so low?
Are all thy conquests, glories, triumphs, spoils,
Shrunk to this little measure? Fare thee well.
I know not, gentlemen, what you intend,
Who else must be let blood, who else is rank.²⁸               165
If I myself, there is no hour so fit
As Caesar's death's hour; nor no instrument
Of half that worth as those your swords, made rich
With the most noble blood of all this world.
I do beseech ye, if you bear me hard,                          170
Now, whilst your purpled hands do reek²⁹ and smoke,
Fulfil your pleasure. Live a thousand years,
I shall not find myself so apt to die;
No place will please me so, no mean³⁰ of death,

---

22. **vouchsafe:** permit.  23. **resolved:** convinced.  24. **untrod state:** uncertain future.  25. **presently:** immediately.
26. **well . . . friend:** as a good friend.  27. **Falls . . . purpose:** I am greatly disturbed at your proposal.  28. **rank:**
medical term, meaning in need of bleeding as a remedy for illness.  29. **reek:** steam.  30. **mean:** means.

As here by Caesar, and by you cut off, 175
The choice and master spirits of this age.
**Brutus.** O Antony, beg not your death of us!
Though now we must appear bloody and cruel,
As by our hands and this our present act
You see we do, yet see you but our hands 180
And this the bleeding business they have done.
Our hearts you see not. They are pitiful;
And pity to the general wrong of Rome
(As fire drives out fire, so pity pity)
Hath done this deed on Caesar. For your part, 185
To you our swords have leaden[31] points, Mark Antony.
Our arms in strength of malice,[32] and our hearts
Of brothers' temper, do receive you in
With all kind love, good thoughts, and reverence.
**Cassius.** Your voice shall be as strong as any man's 190
In the disposing of new dignities.[33]
**Brutus.** Only be patient till we have appeased
The multitude, beside themselves with fear,
And then we will deliver you the cause
Why I, that did love Caesar when I struck him, 195
Have thus proceeded.
**Antony.**                    I doubt not of your wisdom.
Let each man render me his bloody hand.
First, Marcus Brutus, will I shake with you;
Next, Caius Cassius, do I take your hand; 200
Now, Decius Brutus, yours; now yours, Metellus;
Yours, Cinna; and, my valiant Casca, yours.
Though last, not least in love, yours, good Trebonius.
Gentlemen all—Alas, what shall I say?
My credit[34] now stands on such slippery ground 205
That one of two bad ways you must conceit[35] me,
Either a coward or a flatterer.
That I did love thee, Caesar, O, 'tis true!
If then thy spirit look upon us now,
Shall it not grieve thee dearer than thy death 210
To see thy Antony making his peace,
Shaking the bloody fingers of thy foes,
Most noble! in the presence of thy corse?[36]
Had I as many eyes as thou hast wounds,
Weeping as fast as they stream forth thy blood, 215
It would become me better than to close

---

31. **leaden:** blunt.  32. **in . . . malice:** having the power to harm.  33. **disposing . . . dignities:** making decisions
about political power.  34. **credit:** reputation.  35. **conceit:** consider.  36. **corse:** corpse.

In terms of friendship with thine enemies.
Pardon me, Julius! Here wast thou bayed,[37] brave hart;
Here didst thou fall; and here thy hunters stand,
Signed in thy spoil,[38] and crimsoned in thy lethe.[39]          220
O world, thou wast the forest to this hart;
And this indeed, O world, the heart of thee!
How like a deer, strucken by many princes,
Dost thou here lie!

**Cassius.** Mark Antony—                                          225

**Antony.**                    Pardon me, Caius Cassius.
The enemies of Caesar shall say this;
Then, in a friend, it is cold modesty.

**Cassius.** I blame you not for praising Caesar so;
But what compact mean you to have with us?                        230
Will you be pricked in number[40] of our friends,
Or shall we on, and not depend on you?

**Antony.** Therefore I took your hands; but was indeed
Swayed from the point by looking down on Caesar.
Friends am I with you all, and love you all,                      235
Upon this hope, that you shall give me reasons
Why and wherein Caesar was dangerous.

**Brutus.** Or else were this a savage spectacle.
Our reasons are so full of good regard
That were you, Antony, the son of Caesar,                         240
You should be satisfied.

**Antony.**                    That's all I seek;
And am moreover suitor that I may
Produce his body to the market place
And in the pulpit, as becomes a friend,                          245
Speak in the order of his funeral.

**Brutus.** You shall, Mark Antony.

**Cassius.**                    Brutus, a word with you. [*Aside to* Brutus]
You know not what you do. Do not consent
That Antony speak in his funeral.                                 250
Know you how much the people may be moved
By that which he will utter?

**Brutus.** [*Aside to* Cassius]     By your pardon,
I will myself into the pulpit first
And show the reason of our Caesar's death.                       255
What Antony shall speak, I will protest
He speaks by leave and by permission,
And that we are contented Caesar shall

---

37. **bayed:** brought to bay, surrounded by hounds.  38. **Signed . . . spoil:** stained with your slaughter.  39. **lethe:**
blood.  40. **pricked . . . number:** marked in the list.

Have all true rites and lawful ceremonies.
It shall advantage more than do us wrong. 260
**Cassius.** [*Aside to* Brutus] I know not what may fall. I like it not.
**Brutus.** Mark Antony, here, take you Caesar's body.
You shall not in your funeral speech blame us,
But speak all good you can devise of Caesar,
And say you do't by our permission. 265
Else shall you not have any hand at all
About his funeral. And you shall speak
In the same pulpit whereto I am going,
After my speech is ended.
**Antony.**                    Be it so. 270
I do desire no more.
**Brutus.** Prepare the body then, and follow us.

[*Exeunt all but* Antony, *who looks down at* Caesar's *body.*]

**Antony.** O, pardon me, thou bleeding piece of earth,
That I am meek and gentle with these butchers!
Thou art the ruins of the noblest man 275
That ever lived in the tide of times.
Woe to the hand that shed this costly blood!
Over thy wounds now do I prophesy
(Which, like dumb mouths, do ope their ruby lips
To beg the voice and utterance of my tongue), 280
A curse shall light upon the limbs of men;
Domestic fury and fierce civil strife
Shall cumber[41] all the parts of Italy;
Blood and destruction shall be so in use
And dreadful objects so familiar 285
That mothers shall but smile when they behold
Their infants quartered[42] with the hands of war,
All pity choked with custom of fell[43] deeds;
And Caesar's spirit, ranging for revenge,
With Até[44] by his side come hot from hell, 290
Shall in these confines with a monarch's voice
Cry "Havoc!"[45] and let slip the dogs of war,
That this foul deed shall smell above the earth
With carrion men, groaning for burial.

[*Enter* Octavius' Servant.]

You serve Octavius Caesar,[46] do you not? 295

---

41. **cumber:** weigh down.   42. **quartered:** cut in pieces.   43. **fell:** cruel.   44. **Até:** Greek goddess of vengeance and strife.   45. **"Havoc":** no quarter!—no prisoners will be taken.   46. **Octavius Caesar:** the grandson of Julius Caesar's sister Julia, adopted by Caesar as his heir.

**Servant.** I do, Mark Antony.

**Antony.** Caesar did write for him to come to Rome.

**Servant.** He did receive his letters and is coming,
    And bid me say to you by word of mouth—
    O Caesar! 300

**Antony.** Thy heart is big. Get thee apart and weep.
    Passion, I see, is catching, for mine eyes,
    Seeing those beads of sorrow stand in thine,
    Began to water. Is thy master coming?

**Servant.** He lies tonight within seven leagues of Rome. 305

**Antony.** Post[47] back with speed and tell him what hath chanced.
    Here is a mourning Rome, a dangerous Rome,
    No Rome of safety for Octavius yet.
    Hie hence and tell him so. Yet stay awhile.
    Thou shalt not back till I have borne this corse 310
    Into the market place .There shall I try[48]
    In my oration how the people take
    The cruel issue[49] of these bloody men,
    According to the which thou shalt discourse
    To young Octavius of the state of things. 315
    Lend me your hand.

                             *[Exeunt with Caesar's body.]*

## Scene 2

*[Brutus briefly explains to the people why Caesar had to be slain for the good of Rome, and the people cheer him. Antony, a far better judge of human nature, manages to turn the crowd against the conspirators by telling them of Caesar's good works and his concern for the people, as shown by his will. He has left all his wealth to them. As Antony stirs the people to pursue the assassins and kill them, he learns that Octavius has arrived in Rome and Brutus and Cassius have left the city.]*

*[The Forum. Enter Brutus and Cassius and a throng of Citizens, disturbed by the death of Caesar.]*

---

47. **Post:** ride.  48. **try:** test.  49. **issue:** action.

**Citizens.** We will be satisfied! Let us be satisfied!

**Brutus.** Then follow me and give me audience, friends.
Cassius, go you into the other street
And part the numbers.[1]
Those that will hear me speak, let 'em stay here;          5
Those that will follow Cassius, go with him;
And public reasons shall be rendered
Of Caesar's death.

**First Citizen.**          I will hear Brutus speak.

**Second Citizen.** I will hear Cassius, and compare their reasons when sev-     10
erally[2] we hear them rendered.

[*Exit* Cassius, *with some of the* Citizens. Brutus *goes into the pulpit.*]

**Third Citizen.** The noble Brutus is ascended. Silence!

**Brutus.** Be patient till the last.
Romans, countrymen, and lovers, hear me for my cause, and be silent,
that you may hear. Believe me for mine honor, and have respect to     15
mine honor, that you may believe. Censure[3] me in your wisdom, and
awake your senses, that you may the better judge. If there be any in
this assembly, any dear friend of Caesar's, to him I say that Brutus' love
to Caesar was no less than his. If then that friend demand why Brutus
rose against Caesar, this is my answer: Not that I loved Caesar less, but     20
that I loved Rome more. Had you rather Caesar were living, and die all
slaves, than that Caesar were dead, to live all freemen? As Caesar loved
me, I weep for him; as he was fortunate, I rejoice at it; as he was valiant, I
honor him; but—as he was ambitious, I slew him. There is tears for his
love; joy for his fortune; honor for his valor; and death for his ambition.     25
Who is here so base that would be a bondman?[4] If any, speak, for him
have I offended. Who is here so rude[5] that would not be a Roman? If
any, speak, for him have I offended. Who is here so vile that will not
love his country? If any, speak, for him have I offended. I pause for a
reply.     30

**All.** None, Brutus, none!

**Brutus.** Then none have I offended. I have done no more to Caesar than
you shall do to Brutus. The question of his death is enrolled[6] in the
Capitol; his glory not extenuated,[7] wherein he was worthy, nor his
offenses enforced,[8] for which he suffered death.     35

[*Enter* Antony *and others, with* Caesar's *body.*]

Here comes his body, mourned by Mark Antony, who, though he had
no hand in his death, shall receive the benefit of his dying, a place in

---

1. **part . . . numbers:** divide the crowd.  2. **severally:** separately.  3. **Censure:** judge.  4. **bondman:** slave.  5. **rude:**
uncivilized.  6. **enrolled:** preserved in the records.  7. **extenuated:** underrated.  8. **enforced:** stressed.

the commonwealth, as which of you shall not? With this I depart, that, as I slew my best lover for the good of Rome, I have the same dagger for myself when it shall please my country to need my death. 40

**All.** Live, Brutus! live, live!

**First Citizen.** Bring him with triumph home unto his house.

**Second Citizen.** Give him a statue with his ancestors.

**Third Citizen.** Let him be Caesar.

**Fourth Citizen.**                     Caesar's better parts 45
    Shall be crowned in Brutus.

**First Citizen.** We'll bring him to his house with shouts and clamors.

**Brutus.** My countrymen—

**Second Citizen.**                     Peace! silence! Brutus speaks.

**First Citizen.** Peace, ho! 50

**Brutus.** Good countrymen, let me depart alone,
    And, for my sake, stay here with Antony.
    Do grace to Caesar's corpse, and grace his speech
    Tending to Caesar's glories which Mark Antony,
    By our permission, is allowed to make. 55
    I do entreat you, not a man depart,
    Save I alone, till Antony have spoke                    [*Exit.*]

R. H. Thompson (Antony), Len Cariou (Brutus) in *Julius Caesar*, Stratford Festival, 1982.

**First Citizen.** Stay, ho! and let us hear Mark Antony.

**Third Citizen.** Let him go up into the public chair.
We'll hear him. Noble Antony, go up. 60

**Antony.** For Brutus' sake I am beholding[9] to you.

*[Goes into the pulpit.]*

**Fourth Citizen.** What does he say of Brutus?

**Third Citizen.** He says for Brutus' sake
He finds himself beholding to us all.

**Fourth Citizen.** 'Twere best he speak no harm of Brutus here! 65

**First Citizen.** This Caesar was a tyrant.

**Third Citizen.** Nay, that's certain.
We are blest that Rome is rid of him.

**Second Citizen.** Peace! Let us hear what Antony can say.

**Antony.** You gentle Romans— 70

**All.** Peace, ho! Let us hear him.

**Antony.** Friends, Romans, countrymen, lend me your ears;
I come to bury Caesar, not to praise him.
The evil that men do lives after them;
The good is oft interrèd[10] with their bones. 75
So let it be with Caesar. The noble Brutus
Hath told you Caesar was ambitious.
If it were so, it was a grievous fault,
And grievously hath Caesar answered it.
Here, under leave of Brutus and the rest 80
(For Brutus is an honorable man;
So are they all, all honorable men),
Come I to speak in Caesar's funeral.
He was my friend, faithful and just to me;
But Brutus says he was ambitious, 85
And Brutus is an honorable man.
He hath brought many captives home to Rome,
Whose ransoms did the general coffers[11] fill.
Did this in Caesar seem ambitious?
When that the poor have cried, Caesar hath wept; 90
Ambition should be made of sterner stuff.
Yet Brutus says he was ambitious;
And Brutus is an honorable man.
You all did see that on the Lupercal
I thrice presented him a kingly crown, 95
Which he did thrice refuse. Was this ambition?
Yet Brutus says he was ambitious;
And sure he is an honorable man.

---

9. **beholding:** indebted.  10. **interrèd:** buried.  11. **general coffers:** public treasury.

I speak not to disprove what Brutus spoke,
But here I am to speak what I do know.                                     100
You all did love him once, not without cause.
What cause withholds you then to mourn for him?
O judgment, thou art fled to brutish beasts,
And men have lost their reason! Bear with me,[12]
My heart is in the coffin there with Caesar,                               105
And I must pause till it come back to me.

**First Citizen.** Methinks there is much reason in his sayings.

**Second Citizen.** If thou consider rightly of the matter,
Caesar has had great wrong.

**Third Citizen.**                                  Has he, masters?       110
I fear there will a worse come in his place.

**Fourth Citizen.** Marked ye his words? He would not take the crown;
Therefore 'tis certain he was not ambitious.

**First Citizen.** If it be found so, some will dear abide it.[13]

**Second Citizen.** Poor soul! his eyes are red as fire with weeping.      115

**Third Citizen.** There's not a nobler man in Rome than Antony.

**Fourth Citizen.** Now mark him. He begins again to speak.

**Antony.** But yesterday the word of Caesar might
Have stood against the world. Now lies he there,
And none so poor to do him reverence.[14]                                  120
O masters! If I were disposed to stir
Your hearts and minds to mutiny and rage,
I should do Brutus wrong, and Cassius wrong,
Who, you all know, are honorable men.
I will not do them wrong. I rather choose                                  125
To wrong the dead, to wrong myself and you,
Than I will wrong such honorable men.
But here's a parchment with the seal of Caesar.
I found it in his closet; 'tis his will.
Let but the commons[15] hear this testament,                               130
Which (pardon me) I do not mean to read,
And they would go and kiss dead Caesar's wounds
And dip their napkins[16] in his sacred blood;
Yea, beg a hair of him for memory,
And dying, mention it within their wills,                                  135
Bequeathing it as a rich legacy
Unto their issue.[17]

**Fourth Citizen.** We'll hear the will! Read it, Mark Antony.

**All.** The will, the will! We will hear Caesar's will!

---

12. **Bear . . . me:** be patient with me. 13. **dear . . . it:** pay dearly for it. 14. **And . . . reverence:** and you think that honoring Caesar is beneath your dignity. 15. **commons:** common people. 16. **napkins:** handkerchiefs. 17. **issue:** children.

**Antony.** Have patience, gentle friends, I must not read it. 140
    It is not meet you know how Caesar loved you.
    You are not wood, you are not stones, but men;
    And being men, hearing the will of Caesar,
    It will inflame you, it will make you mad.
    'Tis good you know not that you are his heirs, 145
    For if you should, O, what would come of it?
**Fourth Citizen.** Read the will! We'll hear it, Antony!
    You shall read us the will, Caesar's will!
**Antony.** Will you be patient? Will you stay awhile?
    I have o'ershot myself to tell you of it. 150
    I fear I wrong the honorable men
    Whose daggers have stabbed Caesar; I do fear it.
**Fourth Citizen.** They were traitors. Honorable men!
**All.** The will! the testament!
**Second Citizen.** They were villains, murderers! The will! Read the will! 155
**Antony.** You will compel me then to read the will?
    Then make a ring about the corpse of Caesar
    And let me show you him that made the will.
    Shall I descend? and will you give me leave?

R. H. Thompson (Antony) in *Julius Caesar*, Stratford Festival, 1982.

**All.** Come down.

**Second Citizen.** Descend.

**Third Citizen.** You shall have leave. 160

[Antony *comes down.*]

**Fourth Citizen.** A ring! Stand round.

**First Citizen.** Stand from the hearse! Stand from the body!

**Second Citizen.** Room for Antony, most noble Antony! 165

**Antony.** Nay, press not so upon me. Stand far off.

**All.** Stand back! Room! Bear back!

**Antony.** If you have tears, prepare to shed them now.
You all do know this mantle. I remember
The first time ever Caesar put it on. 170
'Twas on a summer's evening in his tent,
That day he overcame the Nervii.[18]
Look, in this place ran Cassius' dagger through.
See what a rent the envious Casca made.
Through this the well-belovèd Brutus stabbed; 175
And as he plucked his cursèd steel away,
Mark how the blood of Caesar followed it,
As rushing out of doors to be resolved
If Brutus so unkindly knocked or no;
For Brutus, as you know, was Caesar's angel. 180
Judge, O you gods, how dearly Caesar loved him!
This was the most unkindest cut of all;
For when the noble Caesar saw him stab,
Ingratitude, more strong than traitors' arms,
Quite vanquished him. Then burst his mighty heart; 185
And in his mantle muffling up his face,
Even at the base of Pompey's statue
(Which all the while ran blood) great Caesar fell.
O, what a fall was there, my countrymen!
Then I, and you, and all of us fell down, 190
Whilst bloody treason flourished over us.
O, now you weep, and I perceive you feel
The dint[19] of pity. These are gracious drops.
Kind souls, what, weep you when you but behold
Our Caesar's vesture wounded?[20] Look you here! 195
Here is himself, marred, as you see, with traitors.

[*He pulls the cloak off* Caesar's *body.*]

**First Citizen.** O piteous spectacle!

**Second Citizen.** O noble Caesar!

**Third Citizen.** O woeful day!

---

18. **Nervii:** a fierce tribe in Belgium, conquered in 57 B. C.   19. **dint:** stroke.   20. **vesture wounded:** clothing torn.

**Fourth Citizen.** O traitors, villains! 200

**First Citizen.** O most bloody sight!

**Second Citizen.** We will be revenged.

**All.** Revenge! About! Seek! Burn! Fire! Kill! Slay! Let not a traitor live!

**Antony.** Stay, countrymen.

**First Citizen.** Peace there! Hear the noble Antony. 205

**Second Citizen.** We'll hear him, we'll follow him, we'll die with him!

**Antony.** Good friends, sweet friends, let me not stir you up
To such a sudden flood of mutiny.
They that have done this deed are honorable.
What private griefs they have, alas, I know not, 210
That made them do it. They are wise and honorable,
And will no doubt with reasons answer you.
I come not, friends, to steal away your hearts.
I am no orator, as Brutus is,
But (as you know me all) a plain blunt man 215
That love my friend; and that they know full well
That gave me public leave to speak of him.
For I have neither wit, nor words, nor worth,

R. H. Thompson (Antony) in *Julius Caesar*, Stratford Festival, 1982.

Action, nor utterance, nor the power of speech
To stir men's blood. I only speak right on.                                        220
I tell you that which you yourselves do know,
Show you sweet Caesar's wounds, poor poor dumb mouths,
And bid them speak for me. But were I Brutus,
And Brutus Antony, there were an Antony
Would ruffle up your spirits, and put a tongue                                     225
In every wound of Caesar that should move
The stones of Rome to rise and mutiny.

**All.** We'll mutiny.

**First Citizen.**       We'll burn the house of Brutus.

**Third Citizen.** Away then! Come, seek the conspirators.                          230

**Antony.** Yet hear me, countrymen. Yet hear me speak.

**All.** Peace, ho! Hear Antony, most noble Antony!

**Antony.** Why, friends, you go to do you know not what.
Wherein hath Caesar thus deserved your loves?
Alas, you know not! I must tell you then.                                          235
You have forgot the will I told you of.

**All.** Most true! The will! Let's stay and hear the will.

**Antony.** Here is the will, under Caesar's seal.
To every Roman citizen he gives,
To every several[21] man, seventy-five drachmas.[22]                               240

**Second Citizen.** Most noble Caesar! We'll revenge his death!

**Third Citizen.** O royal Caesar!

**Antony.** Hear me with patience.

**All.** Peace, ho!

**Antony.** Moreover, he hath left you all his walks,                              245
His private arbors, and new-planted orchards,
On this side Tiber; he hath left them you,
And to your heirs for ever—common pleasures,
To walk abroad and recreate yourselves.
Here was a Caesar! When comes such another?                                        250

**First Citizen.** Never, never! Come, away, away!
We'll burn his body in the holy place
And with the brands fire the traitors' houses.
Take up the body.

**Second Citizen.** Go fetch fire!                                                 255

**Third Citizen.** Pluck down benches!

**Fourth Citizen.** Pluck down forms, windows,[23] anything!

                                            [*Exeunt* Citizens *with the body.*]

---

21. **several:** individual.   22. **drachmas:** Greek silver coins.   23. **forms, windows:** benches, shutters.

**Antony.** Now let it work. Mischief, thou art afoot,
    Take thou what course thou wilt.

    [*Enter a* Servant.]            How now, fellow?        260

**Servant.** Sir, Octavius is already come to Rome.
**Antony.** Where is he?
**Servant.** He and Lepidus[24] are at Caesar's house.
**Antony.** And thither will I straight to visit him.
    He comes upon a wish.[25] Fortune is merry,        265
    And in this mood will give us anything.
**Servant.** I heard him say Brutus and Cassius
    Are rid like madmen through the gates of Rome.
**Antony.** Belike[26] they had some notice of the people,
    How I had moved them. Bring me to Octavius.        270

                            [*Exeunt.*]

## Scene 3

[*The enraged people meet Cinna the poet in the street and kill him because he has the same name as one of the conspirators. They then continue to search for the assassins.*]

[*A street. Enter* Cinna, *the* Poet, *and after him the* Citizens, *armed with sticks, spears, and swords.*]

**Cinna.** I dreamt tonight that I did feast with Caesar,
    And things unluckily charge my fantasy.[1]
    I have no will to wander forth of doors,
    Yet something leads me forth.
**First Citizen.** What is your name?        5
**Second Citizen.** Whither are you going?

---

24. **Lepidus:** later one of the Big Three, with Antony and Octavius.  25. **He . . . wish:** just when I wanted him.
26. **Belike:** probably.
  1. **unluckily . . . fantasy:** bad omens fill my imagination.

**Third Citizen.** Where do you dwell?

**Fourth Citizen.** Are you a married man or a bachelor?

**Second Citizen.** Answer every man directly.

**First Citizen.** Ay, and briefly. 10

**Fourth Citizen.** Ay, and wisely.

**Third Citizen.** Ay, and truly, you were best.

**Cinna.** What is my name? Whither am I going? Where do I dwell? Am I a married man or a bachelor? Then, to answer every man directly and briefly, wisely and truly: wisely I say, I am a bachelor. 15

**Second Citizen.** That's as much as to say they are fools that marry. You'll bear me a bang² for that, I fear. Proceed—directly.

**Cinna.** Directly I am going to Caesar's funeral.

**First Citizen.** As a friend or an enemy?

**Cinna.** As a friend. 20

**Second Citizen.** That matter is answered directly.

**Fourth Citizen.** For your dwelling—briefly.

**Cinna.** Briefly, I dwell by the Capitol.

**Third Citizen.** Your name, sir, truly.

**Cinna.** Truly, my name is Cinna. 25

**First Citizen.** Tear him to pieces! He's a conspirator.

**Cinna.** I am Cinna the poet! Cinna the poet!

**Fourth Citizen.** Tear him for his bad verses! Tear him for his bad verses!

**Cinna.** I am not Cinna the conspirator.

**Fourth Citizen.** It is no matter; his name's Cinna! Pluck but his name out 30 of his heart, and turn him going.

**Third Citizen.** Tear him, tear him! Come, brands, ho! firebrands! To Brutus', to Cassius'! Burn all! Some to Decius' house and some to Casca's; some to Ligarius'! Away, go!

[*Exeunt.*]

---

2. **bear . . . bang:** I'll hit you.

## Act Three

### Getting at Meaning

*Scene 1*

1. What explanation does Caesar give for not reading the letter from Artemidorus?

2. What does Metellus petition of Caesar? What is Caesar's response? What other characters endorse the petition of Metellus?

3. Explain Caesar's lines:

I could be well moved, if I were as you;
If I could pray to move, prayers would move me;
But I am constant as the Northern Star,
Of whose true-fixed and resting quality
There is no fellow in the firmament.

4. What does Caesar realize when he utters the famous line, *"Et tu, Brute?—Then fall Caesar!"*?

5. What is Antony's first response to the death of Caesar? How does he gain favor with the conspirators? Why does he shake hands with them, while still praising Caesar? Why does Brutus want Antony to speak at Caesar's funeral?

6. What is Antony's true attitude toward the conspirators? What does he foresee for Rome?

7. Who is Octavius? What is Antony's message to him?

*Scene 2*

8. Describe Brutus's funeral speech to the crowds. How does he explain Caesar's death?

9. What remarks and actions of Antony sway the masses against the conspirators? Specifically, why does he show Caesar's body to the crowds? Why does he read the will? How does he fire up the crowd's desire to hear the will?

*Scene 3*

10. Why does the crowd kill Cinna the poet? Why might Shakespeare have included this short scene in the play?

### Developing Skills in Reading Literature

1. **Soliloquy.** This act contains one famous soliloquy. Locate the soliloquy and explain why it is important for a reader/viewer to learn the character's thoughts at this point in the play.

2. **Simile and Metaphor.** In Scene 1, Antony creates a metaphor as he talks to the conspirators over the body of Caesar. What is his comparison? What does he call the conspirators in his metaphor?

When Antony is alone with the body, what is his simile for Caesar's wounds? Why does he speak of "ruby lips"?

3. **Parallelism.** When a writer or speaker expresses ideas of equal worth with the same grammatical form, the result is called parallel construction. The following sentence from Brutus's funeral oration is an example of parallel construction: "As Caesar loved me, I weep for him; as he was fortunate, I rejoice at it; as he was valiant, I honor him; but—as he was ambitious, I slew him." In this sentence, Brutus expresses four equal thoughts in identical, or parallel grammatical form. As written, each thought is separated from the next by a semicolon.

Find two other examples of parallel construction in Brutus's speech. Why are parallel constructions effective? What makes Brutus's lines memorable?

4. **Rhetorical Question.** A question that is designed to produce an emotional effect and not an answer is called a rhetorical question. Find examples of rhetorical questions in the funeral orations of both Brutus and Antony.

5. **Irony.** Antony's funeral address is full of ever-increasing irony. When Antony first speaks to the crowd, he says of the conspirators, "For Brutus is an honorable man;/So are they all, all honorable men." He repeats the line "And Brutus is an honorable man" during his speech, and each time he says it, his tone shifts subtly. What causes the line to become ironic, so that when Antony alludes to Brutus's honor a final time, the crowd is ready to rip Brutus apart as a butcher? What other ironic touches do you find in Antony's speech? What is ironic in his lines, "I come not, friends, to steal away your hearts./I am no orator, as Brutus is,/But (as you know me all) a plain blunt man"?

6. **Blank Verse.** Pick four random lines from Antony's funeral oration and scan them, noting that

each line consists of five iambs. Why has Shakespeare written Antony's speech in blank verse while the funeral oration of Brutus is in prose? What makes the blank verse in many ways more powerful than the prose?

7. **Character.** In this act, Shakespeare presents a lesson in mass psychology. Notice the response of various individuals after Brutus has finished his funeral speech. What do they want to do with Brutus at this point? Notice the comments made by members of the crowd as Antony is speaking. What do they want to do with Brutus when Antony has finished? How would you characterize the crowd?

8. **Rising Action, Climax, Falling Action.** Gustav Freitag, a nineteenth-century German critic, presented an analysis of tragedy that is often applied to Shakespeare's plays. Freitag wrote that the five acts of a tragedy can be divided into three parts:

a. Rising Action. This is usually the first two acts of the play, which develop the characters and the conflict and show the ascending fortunes of the protagonists (heroes).

b. Climax. This is the highest point of the rising action, usually coming in the third act. It is the point at which the fortunes of the protagonists reach the height of their development.

c. Falling Action. This begins with the point in the action, at which the fortunes of the protagonists begin to fall. From this point on, everything is downhill for the heroes, with death at the end of the play the usual conclusion.

What are the chief events in the rising action of *Julius Caesar?* What would you label as the climax, the point at which the fortunes of the conspirators are at their peak? What events in Act Three indicate that things are beginning to go against the protagonists?

## Developing Writing Skills

1. **Developing an Argument.** What does Shakespeare demonstrate about crowd behavior in Act Three of *Julius Caesar?* Can you think of modern situations that illustrate or contradict his points? Write a short essay in which you either endorse or refute Shakespeare's ideas on this subject. Support your points with examples drawn from history and from your own experience.

2. **Analyzing a Character.** Just as Brutus may be called an idealist and Cassius a realist, Mark Antony may be called an opportunist. An opportunist is a person who takes advantage of opportunities, adapting behavior to circumstances and often sacrificing principles in the process. In a five-paragraph composition, analyze Antony's behavior in Act Three. In what ways is he an opportunist? What are his outstanding character traits? Use direct evidence from the play to support your points.

# Act Four

## Scene 1

*[Antony, Octavius, and Lepidus plan to kill their enemies. Lepidus is sent to procure Caesar's will. Antony and Octavius realize that they must gather an army to fight Brutus and Cassius.]*

*[Antony's house in Rome. Antony, Octavius, and Lepidus, seated at a table.]*

**Antony.** These many, then, shall die; their names are pricked.[1]
**Octavius.** Your brother too must die. Consent you, Lepidus?
**Lepidus.** I do consent.
**Octavius.**                   Prick him down, Antony.
**Lepidus.** Upon condition Publius shall not live,                5
    Who is your sister's son, Mark Antony.
**Antony.** He shall not live. Look, with a spot I damn him.
    But, Lepidus, go you to Caesar's house.
    Fetch the will hither, and we shall determine
    How to cut off some charge in legacies.[2]                10
**Lepidus.** What? shall I find you here?
**Octavius.** Or here or at the Capitol.

                                    *[Exit Lepidus.]*

**Antony.** This is a slight unmeritable man,
    Meet to be sent on errands. Is it fit,
    The threefold world divided, he should stand                15
    One of the three to share it?
**Octavius.**                               So you thought him,
    And took his voice who should be pricked to die
    In our black sentence[3] and proscription.[4]
**Antony.** Octavius, I have seen more days than you;                20
    And though we lay these honors on this man
    To ease ourselves of divers slanderous loads,
    He shall but bear them as the ass bears gold,
    To groan and sweat under the business,
    Either led or driven as we point the way;                25
    And having brought our treasure where we will,

---

1. **pricked:** marked by punching a hole next to the names on a wax tablet.   2. **cut . . . legacies:** avoid paying some of the bequests.   3. **black sentence:** sentence of death.   4. **proscription:** published lists of those who could be killed as public enemies.

Then take we down his load, and turn him off
(Like to the empty ass) to shake his ears
And graze in commons.⁵

**Octavius.**                     You may do your will;                         30
  But he's a tried and valiant soldier.
**Antony.** So is my horse, Octavius, and for that
  I do appoint him store of provender.⁶
  It is a creature that I teach to fight,
  To wind,⁷ to stop, to run directly on,                                        35
  His corporal⁸ motion governed by my spirit.
  And, in some taste,⁹ is Lepidus but so.
  He must be taught, and trained, and bid go forth:
  A barren-spirited fellow; one that feeds
  On abjects, orts,¹⁰ and imitations                                            40
  Which, out of use and staled by other men,
  Begin his fashion. Do not talk of him,
  But as a property.¹¹ And now, Octavius,
  Listen great things. Brutus and Cassius
  Are levying powers.¹² We must straight make head.¹³                           45
  Therefore let our alliance be combined,
  Our best friends made, and our best means stretched out;
  And let us presently go sit in council
  How covert matters may be best disclosed
  And open perils surest answered.                                             50
**Octavius.** Let us do so; for we are at the stake¹⁴
  And bayed about with many enemies;
  And some that smile have in their hearts, I fear,
  Millions of mischiefs.

                                                        [*Exeunt.*]

## Scene 2

[*Brutus and Cassius are not getting along well, and
Cassius has become unfriendly. They meet in Brutus' tent
to discuss their problems.*]

---

5. **in commons:** on public grazing ground.  6. **provender:** food.  7. **wind:** turn.  8. **corporal:** bodily.  9. **in . . . taste:** in some measure.  10. **abjects, orts:** worthless things, scraps.  11. **property:** an object for our use.  12. **levying powers:** assembling armies.  13. **make head:** gather forces.  14. **at . . . stake:** like a bear tied to a stake and surrounded by baying hounds.

*[The camp near Sardis. Before* Brutus' *tent. Sound of drums. Enter*
Brutus, Lucilius, Lucius, *and* Soldiers. Titinius *and* Pindarus,
*from* Cassius' *army, meet them.]*

**Brutus.** Stand ho!
**Lucilius.** Give the word, ho! and stand!
**Brutus.** What now, Lucilius? Is Cassius near?
**Lucilius.** He is at hand, and Pindarus is come
    To do you salutation from his master.                   5
**Brutus.** He greets me well.[1] Your master, Pindarus,
    In his own change, or by ill officers,[2]
    Hath given me some worthy cause to wish
    Things done undone; but if he be at hand,
    I shall be satisfied.[3]                        10
**Pindarus.**             I do not doubt
    But that my noble master will appear
    Such as he is, full of regard[4] and honor.
**Brutus.** He is not doubted. A word, Lucilius,
    How he received you. Let me be resolved.         15
**Lucilius.** With courtesy and with respect enough,
    But not with such familiar instances[5]
    Nor with such free and friendly conference
    As he hath used of old.
**Brutus.**              Thou hast described     20
    A hot friend cooling. Ever note, Lucilius,
    When love begins to sicken and decay
    It useth an enforcèd ceremony.
    There are no tricks in plain and simple faith;
    But hollow men, like horses hot at hand,[6]     25
    Make gallant show and promise of their mettle;

                            *[Low march within.]*

    But when they should endure the bloody spur,
    They fall their crests,[7] and like deceitful jades[8]
    Sink in the trial. Comes his army on?
**Lucilius.** They mean this night in Sardis to be quartered.     30
    The greater part, the horse in general,[9]
    Are come with Cassius.
**Brutus.**              Hark! He is arrived.
    March gently on to meet him.

---

1. **He . . . well:** it's good news that Cassius has sent his greetings.  2. **In . . . officers:** either as a result of a change in
himself or because of the actions of unworthy subordinates.  3. **be satisfied:** learn the truth.  4. **full . . . regard:**
worthy of respect.  5. **familiar instances:** friendly behavior.  6. **hot at hand:** restless when checked.  7. **fall . . .
crests:** become spiritless.  8. **jades:** poor-spirited nags.  9. **horse . . . general:** all the cavalry.

[*Enter* Cassius *and his army*.]

**Cassius.** Stand, ho!     35
**Brutus.** Stand, ho! Speak the word along.
**First Soldier.** Stand!
**Second Soldier.** Stand!
**Third Soldier.** Stand!
**Cassius.** Most noble brother, you have done me wrong.     40
**Brutus.** Judge me, you gods! wrong I mine enemies?
    And if not so, how should I wrong a brother?
**Cassius.** Brutus, this sober[10] form of yours hides wrongs,
    And when you do them—
**Brutus.**                   Cassius, be content.     45
    Speak your griefs[11] softly. I do know you well.
    Before the eyes of both our armies here
    (Which should perceive nothing but love from us)
    Let us not wrangle. Bid them move away.
    Then in my tent, Cassius, enlarge your griefs,     50
    And I will give you audience.
**Cassius.**                   Pindarus,
    Bid our commanders lead their charges off
    A little from this ground.
**Brutus.** Lucilius, do you the like, and let no man     55
    Come to our tent till we have done our conference.
    Let Lucius and Titinius guard our door.         [*Exeunt.*]

## Scene 3

[*Brutus accuses Cassius of corruption and greed, and they
argue bitterly. Cassius relents and they resolve their
differences. Brutus informs Cassius that Portia is dead.
Titinius and Messala arrive to discuss military plans.
Brutus decides to send their forces to Philippi to engage
Antony and Octavius, although Cassius objects. As
Brutus is reading in his tent that evening, he is visited by
the ghost of Caesar, who warns him that he will see him
again at Philippi.*]

[*Inside* Brutus' *tent. Enter* Brutus *and* Cassius.]

---

10. **sober:** composed.   11. **griefs:** grievances.

**Cassius.** That you have wronged me doth appear in this:
    You have condemned and noted[1] Lucius Pella
    For taking bribes here of the Sardians;
    Wherein my letters, praying on his side,
    Because I knew the man, were slighted off.        5
**Brutus.** You wronged yourself to write in such a case.
**Cassius.** In such a time as this it is not meet
    That every nice offense should bear his comment.[2]
**Brutus.** Let me tell you, Cassius, you yourself
    Are much condemned to have an itching palm,       10
    To sell and mart your offices[3] for gold
    To undeservers.
**Cassius.**          I an itching palm?
    You know that you are Brutus that speaks this,
    Or, by the gods, this speech were else your last!       15
**Brutus.** The name of Cassius honors this corruption,
    And chastisement doth therefore hide his head.
**Cassius.** Chastisement?
**Brutus.** Remember March; the ides of March remember.
    Did not great Julius bleed for justice' sake?       20
    What villain touched his body that did stab
    And not for justice? What, shall one of us,
    That struck the foremost man of all this world
    But for supporting robbers—shall we now
    Contaminate our fingers with base bribes,       25
    And sell the mighty space of our large honors
    For so much trash as may be graspèd thus?
    I had rather be a dog and bay the moon
    Than such a Roman.
**Cassius.**          Brutus, bait[4] not me!       30
    I'll not endure it. You forget yourself
    To hedge me in. I am a soldier, I,
    Older in practice, abler than yourself
    To make conditions.[5]
**Brutus.**          Go to! You are not, Cassius.       35
**Cassius.** I am.
**Brutus.** I say you are not.
**Cassius.** Urge me no more! I shall forget myself.
    Have mind upon your health, tempt me no farther.
**Brutus.** Away, slight man!       40
**Cassius.** Is't possible?

---

1. **noted:** censured.  2. **not . . . comment:** not necessary that every petty offense be carefully noted.  3. **mart . . . offices:** trade your services.  4. **bait:** antagonize.  5. **conditions:** rules.

**Brutus.**                    Hear me, for I will speak.
  Must I give way and room to your rash choler?[6]
  Shall I be frighted when a madman stares?
**Cassius.** O ye gods, ye gods! Must I endure all this?                    45
**Brutus.** All this? Ay, more! Fret till your proud heart break.
  Go show your slaves how choleric you are
  And make your bondmen tremble. Must I budge?
  Must I observe you? Must I stand and crouch
  Under your testy humor?[7] By the gods,                    50
  You shall digest the venom of your spleen,[8]
  Though it do split you; for from this day forth
  I'll use you for my mirth, yea, for my laughter,
  When you are waspish.
**Cassius.**                    Is it come to this?                    55
**Brutus.** You say you are a better soldier;
  Let it appear so. Make your vaunting[9] true,
  And it shall please me well. For mine own part,
  I shall be glad to learn of noble men.
**Cassius.** You wrong me every way! You wrong me, Brutus!                    60
  I said an elder soldier, not a better.
  Did I say "better"?
**Brutus.**                    If you did, I care not.
**Cassius.** When Caesar lived he durst not thus have moved me.
**Brutus.** Peace, peace! You durst not so have tempted him.                    65
**Cassius.** I durst not?
**Brutus.** No.
**Cassius.** What, durst not tempt him?
**Brutus.**                              For your life you durst not.
**Cassius.** Do not presume too much upon my love.                    70
  I may do that I shall be sorry for.
**Brutus.** You have done that you should be sorry for.
  There is no terror, Cassius, in your threats;
  For I am armed so strong in honesty
  That they pass by me as the idle wind,                    75
  Which I respect not. I did send to you
  For certain sums of gold, which you denied me,
  For I can raise no money by vile means—
  By heaven, I had rather coin my heart
  And drop my blood for drachmas than to wring                    80
  From the hard hands of peasants their vile trash
  By any indirection.[10] I did send
  To you for gold to pay my legions,

---

6. **choler:** anger.  7. **testy humor:** bad temper.  8. **spleen:** rage.  9. **vaunting:** boasting.  10. **indirection:** crooked
means.

Which you denied me. Was that done like Cassius?
Should I have answered Caius Cassius so?                          85
When Marcus Brutus grows so covetous
To lock such rascal counters[11] from his friends,
Be ready, gods, with all your thunderbolts,
Dash him to pieces!
**Cassius.**              I denied you not.                       90
**Brutus.** You did.
**Cassius.** I did not. He was but a fool that brought
    My answer back. Brutus hath rived[12] my heart.
    A friend should bear his friend's infirmities,
    But Brutus makes mine greater than they are.                 95
**Brutus.** I do not, till you practice them on me.
**Cassius.** You love me not.
**Brutus.**                    I do not like your faults.
**Cassius.** A friendly eye could never see such faults.
**Brutus.** A flatterer's would not, though they do appear       100
    As huge as high Olympus.
**Cassius.** Come, Antony, and young Octavius, come!
    Revenge yourselves alone[13] on Cassius.
    For Cassius is aweary of the world:
    Hated by one he loves; braved[14] by his brother;            105
    Checked like a bondman,[15] all his faults observed,
    Set in a notebook, learned and conned by rote[16]
    To cast into my teeth. O, I could weep
    My spirit from mine eyes! There is my dagger,
    And here my naked breast; within, a heart                    110
    Dearer than Pluto's[17] mine, richer than gold:
    If that thou be'st a Roman, take it forth.
    I, that denied thee gold, will give my heart.
    Strike as thou didst at Caesar; for I know,
    When thou didst hate him worst, thou lov'dst him better      115
    Than ever thou lovedst Cassius.
**Brutus.**                        Sheathe your dagger.
    Be angry when you will; it shall have scope.[18]
    Do what you will; dishonor shall be humor.[19]
    O Cassius, you are yokèd with a lamb                          120
    That carries anger as the flint bears fire;
    Who, much enforcèd, shows a hasty spark,
    And straight is cold again.

---

11. **rascal counters:** wretched tokens.  12. **rived:** split.  13. **alone:** only.  14. **braved:** taunted.  15. **Checked . . . bondman:** scolded like a slave.  16. **conned . . . rote:** learned by heart.  17. **Pluto:** the Greek god of riches.
18. **scope:** free range.  19. **dishonor . . . humor:** dishonorable conduct shall be regarded as just a mood, or whim.

**Cassius.**                      Hath Cassius lived
  To be but mirth and laughter to his Brutus                                    125
  When grief and blood ill-tempered vexeth him?
**Brutus.** When I spoke that, I was ill-tempered too.
**Cassius.** Do you confess so much? Give me your hand.
**Brutus.** And my heart too.
**Cassius.**                      O Brutus!                                              130
**Brutus.**                                What's the matter?
**Cassius.** Have you not love enough to bear with me
  When that rash humor which my mother gave me
  Makes me forgetful?
**Brutus.**                      Yes, Cassius, and from henceforth,                       135
  When you are over-earnest with your Brutus,
  He'll think your mother chides, and leave you so.

    [*Enter a* Poet *followed by* Lucilius, Titinius, *and* Lucius.]

**Poet.** Let me go in to see the generals!
  There is some grudge between 'em. 'Tis not meet
  They be alone.                                                                   140
**Lucilius.** You shall not come to them.
**Poet.** Nothing but death shall stay me.
**Cassius.** How now? What's the matter?
**Poet.** For shame, you generals! What do you mean?
  Love and be friends, as two such men should be,                                  145
  For I have seen more years, I'm sure, than ye.
**Cassius.** Ha, ha! How vilely doth this cynic[20] rhyme!
**Brutus.** Get you hence, sirrah! Saucy fellow, hence!
**Cassius.** Bear with him, Brutus. 'Tis his fashion.
**Brutus.** I'll know his humor when he knows his time.[21]                              150
  What should the wars do with these jigging fools?
  Companion,[22] hence!
**Cassius.**                      Away, away, be gone!
                             [*Exit* Poet.]

**Brutus.** Lucilius and Titinius, bid the commanders
  Prepare to lodge their companies tonight.                                        155
**Cassius.** And come yourselves, and bring Messala with you
  Immediately to us.
               [*Exeunt* Lucilius *and* Titinius.]
**Brutus.**                      Lucius, a bowl of wine.
                             [*Exit* Lucius.]

---

20. **cynic:** rude fellow.  21. **I'll . . . time:** I'll be patient with his whims if he displays them at the proper time.
22. **Companion:** fellow, used with contempt.

Len Cariou (Brutus), Simon Bradbury (Lucius), Nicholas Pennell (Cassius) in *Julius Caesar*, Stratford Festival, 1982.

**Cassius.** I did not think you could have been so angry.
**Brutus.** O Cassius, I am sick of many griefs.                                     160
**Cassius.** Of your philosophy you make no use
    If you give place to accidental evils.
**Brutus.** No man bears sorrow better. Portia is dead.
**Cassius.** Ha! Portia?
**Brutus.** She is dead.                                                165
**Cassius.** How scaped I killing when I crossed you so?
    O insupportable and touching loss!
    Upon what sickness?
**Brutus.**                        Impatient of my absence,
    And grief that young Octavius with Mark Antony
    Have made themselves so strong—for with her death        170
    That tidings came—with this she fell distract,[23]
    And (her attendants absent) swallowed fire.
**Cassius.** And died so?
**Brutus.**               Even so.                                     175
**Cassius.**                  O ye immortal gods!

    [*Reenter* Lucius, *with wine and tapers.*]

---

23. **distract:** distraught.

**Brutus.** Speak no more of her. Give me a bowl of wine.
    In this I bury all unkindness, Cassius.            *[Drinks.]*
**Cassius.** My heart is thirsty for that noble pledge.
    Fill, Lucius, till the wine o'erswell the cup.         180
    I cannot drink too much of Brutus' love.

                       *[Drinks. Exit* Lucius.]


       [*Reenter* Titinius, *with* Messala.]

**Brutus.** Come in, Titinius! Welcome, good Messala.
    Now sit we close about this taper here
    And call in question our necessities.[24]
**Cassius.** Portia, art thou gone?                 185
**Brutus.**                No more, I pray you.
    Messala, I have here received letters
    That young Octavius and Mark Antony
    Come down upon us with a mighty power,
    Bending their expedition toward Philippi.[25]       190
**Messala.** Myself have letters of the selfsame tenure.
**Brutus.** With what addition?
**Messala.** That by proscription and bills of outlawry
    Octavius, Antony, and Lepidus
    Have put to death an hundred senators.        195
**Brutus.** Therein our letters do not well agree.
    Mine speak of seventy senators that died
    By their proscriptions, Cicero being one.
**Cassius.** Cicero one?
**Messala.**            Cicero is dead,          200
    And by that order of proscription.
    Had you your letters from your wife, my lord?
**Brutus.** No, Messala.
**Messala.** Nor nothing in your letters writ of her?
**Brutus.** Nothing, Messala.                   205
**Messala.**              That methinks is strange.
**Brutus.** Why ask you? Hear you aught of her in yours?
**Messala.** No, my lord.
**Brutus.** Now as you are a Roman, tell me true.
**Messala.** Then like a Roman bear the truth I tell,     210
    For certain she is dead, and by strange manner.
**Brutus.** Why, farewell, Portia. We must die, Messala.
    With meditating that she must die once,
    I have the patience to endure it now.

---

24. **call . . . necessities:** consider what we must do.   25. **Philippi:** city in northern Greece.

**Messala.** Even so great men great losses should endure. 215
**Cassius.** I have as much of this in art[26] as you,
    But yet my nature could not bear it so.
**Brutus.** Well, to our work alive. What do you think
    Of marching to Philippi presently?
**Cassius.** I do not think it good. 220
**Brutus.**                    Your reason?
**Cassius.**                        This it is:
    'Tis better that the enemy seek us.
    So shall he waste his means, weary his soldiers,
    Doing himself offense, whilst we, lying still, 225
    Are full of rest, defense, and nimbleness.
**Brutus.** Good reasons must of force give place to better.
    The people 'twixt Philippi and this ground
    Do stand but in a forced affection,
    For they have grudged us contribution. 230
    The enemy, marching along by them,
    By them shall make a fuller number up,
    Come on refreshed, new-added, and encouraged;
    From which advantage shall we cut him off
    If at Philippi we do face him there, 235
    These people at our back.
**Cassius.**                   Hear me, good brother.
**Brutus.** Under your pardon. You must note beside
    That we have tried the utmost of our friends,
    Our legions are brimful, our cause is ripe. 240
    The enemy increaseth every day;
    We, at the height, are ready to decline.
    There is a tide in the affairs of men
    Which, taken at the flood, leads on to fortune;
    Omitted,[27] all the voyage of their life 245
    Is bound in shallows and in miseries.
    On such a full sea are we now afloat,
    And we must take the current when it serves
    Or lose our ventures.
**Cassius.**              Then, with your will, go on. 250
    We'll along ourselves and meet them at Philippi.
**Brutus.** The deep of night is crept upon our talk
    And nature must obey necessity,
    Which we will niggard[28] with a little rest.
    There is no more to say? 255

---

26. **art:** philosophical belief.   27. **Omitted:** neglected.   28. **niggard:** satisfy grudgingly.

**Cassius.**                    No more. Good night.
　　Early tomorrow will we rise and hence.
**Brutus.** Lucius! [*Reenter* Lucius.] My gown.

                                            [*Exit* Lucius.]

　　　Farewell, good Messala.
　　Good night, Titinius. Noble, noble Cassius,                    260
　　Good night and good repose!
**Cassius.**                    O my dear brother,
　　This was an ill beginning of the night!
　　Never come such division 'tween our souls!
　　Let it not, Brutus.                                            265

　　　[*Reenter* Lucius, *with the gown.*]

**Brutus.**                    Everything is well.
**Cassius.** Good night, my lord.
**Brutus.**                    Good night, good brother.
**Titinius and Messala.** Good night, Lord Brutus.
**Brutus.**                                Farewell every one.    270
                        [*Exeunt all but* Brutus *and* Lucius.]

　　Give me the gown. Where is thy instrument?
**Lucius.** Here in the tent.
**Brutus.**                    What, thou speak'st drowsily?
　　Poor knave,[29] I blame thee not, thou art o'erwatched.[30]
　　Call Claudius and some other of my men;                        275
　　I'll have them sleep on cushions in my tent.
**Lucius.** Varro and Claudius!

　　　[*Enter* Varro *and* Claudius.]

**Varro.** Calls my lord?
**Brutus.** I pray you, sirs, lie in my tent and sleep.
　　It may be I shall raise you by-and-by                          280
　　On business to my brother Cassius.
**Varro.** So please you, we will stand and watch your pleasure.[31]
**Brutus.** I will not have it so. Lie down, good sirs.
　　It may be I shall otherwise bethink me.
                            [Varro *and* Claudius *lie down.*]
　　Look, Lucius, here's the book I sought for so;                 285
　　I put it in the pocket of my gown.

---

29. **knave:** servant boy.　30. **o'erwatched:** weary with too much watchfulness.　31. **watch . . . pleasure:** await your command.

**Lucius.** I was sure your lordship did not give it me.
**Brutus.** Bear with me, good boy, I am much forgetful.
    Canst thou hold up thy heavy eyes awhile,
    And touch thy instrument a strain or two?          290
**Lucius.** Ay, my lord, an 't please you.
**Brutus.**                   It does, my boy.
    I trouble thee too much, but thou art willing.
**Lucius.** It is my duty, sir.
**Brutus.** I should not urge thy duty past thy might.       295
    I know young bloods look for a time of rest.
**Lucius.** I have slept, my lord, already.
**Brutus.** It was well done; and thou shalt sleep again;
    I will not hold thee long. If I do live,
    I will be good to thee.                  300

             *[Music, and a song. Lucius falls asleep as he sings.]*
    This is a sleepy tune. O murd'rous slumber!
    Layest thou thy leaden mace[32] upon my boy,
    That plays thee music? Gentle knave, good night.
    I will not do thee so much wrong to wake thee.
    If thou dost nod, thou break'st thy instrument;     305
    I'll take it from thee; and, good boy, good night.
    Let me see, let me see. Is not the leaf turned down
    Where I left reading? Here it is, I think.        *[Sits.]*

    *[Enter the* Ghost of Caesar.]

    How ill this taper burns! Ha! Who comes here?
    I think it is the weakness of mine eyes         310
    That shapes this monstrous apparition.
    It comes upon me. Art thou anything?
    Art thou some god, some angel, or some devil,
    That mak'st my blood cold and my hair to stare?[33]
    Speak to me what thou art.                315
**Ghost.** Thy evil spirit, Brutus.
**Brutus.**                 Why comest thou?
**Ghost.** To tell thee thou shalt see me at Philippi.
**Brutus.** Well; then I shall see thee again?
**Ghost.** Ay, at Philippi.                     320
**Brutus.** Why, I will see thee at Philippi then.

                         *[Exit Ghost.]*

    Now I have taken heart thou vanishest.

---

32. **mace:** both a weapon and an instrument of office; slumber is pictured as taking Lucius in charge, as though it
were a human official.  33. **stare:** stand up.

Ill spirit, I would hold more talk with thee.
Boy! Lucius! Varro! Claudius! Sirs! Awake!
Claudius!                                                    325
**Lucius.** The strings, my lord, are false.
**Brutus.** He thinks he still is at his instrument.
    Lucius, awake!
**Lucius.** My lord?
**Brutus.** Didst thou dream, Lucius, that thou so criedst out?     330
**Lucius.** My lord, I do not know that I did cry.
**Brutus.** Yes, that thou didst. Didst thou see anything?
**Lucius.** Nothing, my lord.
**Brutus.** Sleep again, Lucius. Sirrah Claudius!
    [*To* Varro] Fellow thou, awake!                       335
**Varro.** My lord?
**Claudius.** My lord?
**Brutus.** Why did you so cry out, sirs, in your sleep?
**Both.** Did we, my lord?
**Brutus.**                Ay. Saw you anything?            340
**Varro.** No, my lord, I saw nothing.
**Claudius.**               Nor I, my lord.
**Brutus.** Go and commend me to my brother Cassius.
    Bid him set on his powers betimes before,[34]
    And we will follow.                                     345
**Both.**              It shall be done, my lord.

                              [*Exeunt.*]

---

34. **set . . . before:** lead on his army ahead of ours promptly.

## Act Four

### Getting at Meaning

*Scene 1*

1. Antony, Octavius, and Lepidus are now the ruling triumvirate of Rome. In what activities are they engaged? Cite specific lines that reveal Antony's view of Lepidus.

2. What has happened to Brutus and Cassius? What plans do Antony and Octavius make?

*Scene 2*

3. What has happened between Brutus and Cassius? Explain what Brutus means when he says, "When love begins to sicken and decay/It useth an enforced ceremony."

4. Why does Brutus insist that he and Cassius speak together inside the tent?

*Scene 3*

5. Of what is Brutus complaining when he says to Cassius, ". . . you yourself/Are much condemned to have an itching palm"? What other complaints does Brutus make against Cassius? Of what does Cassius accuse Brutus?

6. To what is Cassius referring when he says to Brutus, "Of your philosophy you make no use/If you give place to accidental evils"?

7. How has Portia died? How does Brutus take her death? Quote lines that illustrate his philosophical approach.

8. Why does Cassius believe that Antony and Octavius should seek out the conspirators? What are Brutus's arguments for advancing to meet the enemy?

9. Explain the ghost. What does the ghost tell Brutus?

### Developing Skills in Reading Literature

1. **Simile and Metaphor.** Explain Antony's simile for Lepidus in Scene 1:

And though we lay honors on this man
To ease ourselves of divers slanderous loads,
He shall but bear them as the ass bears gold,
To groan and sweat under the business,
Either led or driven as we point the way;
And having brought our treasure where we will,
Then take we down his load, and turn him off
(Like to the empty ass) to shake his ears
And graze in commons.

In Scene 3, Brutus comments on human action as follows:

There is a tide in the affairs of men
Which, taken at the flood, leads on to fortune;
Omitted, all the voyage of their life
Is bound in shallows and in miseries.
On such a full sea are we now afloat,
And we must take the current when it serves
Or lose our ventures.

What are the points of comparison in this metaphor? What do these lines mean?

2. **Irony.** For what reasons do the conspirators murder Caesar? Ironically, what are the effects of their act? What ironies do you perceive in the relationship between Brutus and Cassius? In Antony's triumvirate?

### Developing Vocabulary

**Words from Latin.** A number of Latin words and phrases, commonly used in ancient Rome, have been incorporated into modern English. Look up the following Latin phrases in a dictionary and record their meanings. Use each phrase in a sentence that reveals the meaning of the phrase.

| | |
|---|---|
| caveat emptor | prima facie |
| rara avis | reductio ad absurdum |
| de facto | mirabile dictu |

# Act Five

*Scene 1*     [*The armies of Brutus and Antony meet in Philippi. Before they begin battle, they hurl scornful remarks* at *each other.*]

[*The plains of Philippi, in Greece. Enter* Octavius, Antony, *and their Army.*]

**Octavius.** Now, Antony, our hopes are answered.
    You said the enemy would not come down
    But keep the hills and upper regions.
    It proves not so, their battles[1] are at hand.
    They mean to warn[2] us at Philippi here,                                5
    Answering before we do demand of them.
**Antony.** Tut! I am in their bosoms[3] and I know
    Wherefore they do it. They could be content
    To visit other places,[4] and come down
    With fearful bravery,[5] thinking by this face                          10
    To fasten in our thoughts that they have courage.
    But 'tis not so.

        [*Enter a* Messenger.]

**Messenger.**        Prepare you, generals,
    The enemy comes on in gallant show;
    Their bloody sign of battle[6] is hung out,                             15
    And something to be done immediately.
**Antony.** Octavius, lead your battle softly[7] on
    Upon the left hand of the even field.
**Octavius.** Upon the right hand I. Keep thou the left.
**Antony.** Why do you cross me in this exigent?[8]                         20
**Octavius.** I do not cross you; but I will do so.

                                                    [*March.*]

[*Drum. Enter* Brutus, Cassius, *and their Army;* Lucilius, Titinius, Messala, *and others.*]

---

1. **battles:** battle forces.  2. **warn:** challenge.  3. **bosoms:** in the secrets of their hearts.  4. **They . . . places:** they would prefer to be anywhere but here.  5. **fearful bravery:** a show of defiance that hides their real fear.  6. **bloody . . . battle:** red flag.  7. **softly:** slowly.  8. **exigent:** critical moment.

**Brutus.** They stand and would have parley.
**Cassius.** Stand fast, Titinius. We must out and talk.
**Octavius.** Mark Antony, shall we give sign of battle?
**Antony.** No, Caesar, we will answer on their charge.
    Make forth. The generals would have some words.        25
**Octavius.** Stir not until the signal.

[Brutus, Cassius, Octavius, *and* Antony *meet in the center of the stage.*]

**Brutus.** Words before blows. Is it so, countrymen?
**Octavius.** Not that we love words better, as you do.
**Brutus.** Good words are better than bad strokes, Octavius.       30
**Antony.** In your bad strokes, Brutus, you give good words;
    Witness the hole you made in Caesar's heart,
    Crying "Long live! Hail, Caesar!"
**Cassius.**                  Antony,
    The posture of your blows are yet unknown;       35
    But for your words, they rob the Hybla[9] bees,
    And leave them honeyless.
**Antony.**              Not stingless too.
**Brutus.** O yes, and soundless too!
    For you have stol'n their buzzing, Antony,       40
    And very wisely threat before you sting.
**Antony.** Villains! you did not so when your vile daggers
    Hacked one another in the sides of Caesar.
    You showed your teeth like apes, and fawned like hounds,
    And bowed like bondmen, kissing Caesar's feet;      45
    Whilst damnèd Casca, like a cur, behind
    Struck Caesar on the neck. O you flatterers!
**Cassius.** Flatterers? Now, Brutus, thank yourself!
    This tongue had not offended so today
    If Cassius might have ruled.[10]       50
**Octavius.** Come, come, the cause! If arguing make us sweat,
    The proof of it will turn to redder drops.
    Look,
    I draw a sword against conspirators.
    When think you that the sword goes up[11] again?      55
    Never, till Caesar's three-and-thirty wounds
    Be well avenged, or till another Caesar
    Have added slaughter to the sword of traitors.
**Brutus.** Caesar, thou canst not die by traitors' hands
    Unless thou bring'st them with thee.      60

---

9. **Hybla:** Mount Hybla in Sicily was famous for its honey.  10. **ruled:** Cassius had wanted Antony slain.  11. **up:** returns to the scabbard.

Ian Deakin (Octavius), R. H. Thompson (Antony), Nicholas Pennell (Cassius), Len Cariou (Brutus) with members of the Stratford Festival Acting Company in *Julius Caesar*, Stratford Festival, 1982.

**Octavius.**                              So I hope.
　　I was not born to die on Brutus' sword.
**Brutus.** Oh, if thou wert the noblest of thy strain,
　　Young man, thou couldst not die more honorable.
**Cassius.** A peevish schoolboy, worthless of such honor,　　　　　65
　　Joined with a masker[12] and a reveller!
**Antony.** Old Cassius still.
**Octavius.**                    Come, Antony, Away!
　　Defiance, traitors, hurl we in your teeth.
　　If you dare fight today, come to the field;　　　　　70
　　If not, when you have stomachs.[13]

> [*Exeunt* Octavius, Antony, *and their Army.*]

**Cassius.** Why, now blow wind, swell billow, and swim bark![14]
　　The storm is up, and all is on the hazard.[15]
**Brutus.** Ho, Lucilius! Hark, a word with you.

> [Lucilius *and* Messala *stand forth.*]

**Lucilius.**                       My lord?　　　　　75

> [Brutus *and* Lucilius *converse apart.*]

**Cassius.** Messala.
**Messala.**        What says my general?
**Cassius.**                          Messala,
　　This is my birthday; as this very day
　　Was Cassius born. Give me thy hand, Messala.　　　　　80
　　Be thou my witness that against my will
　　(As Pompey was) am I compelled to set
　　Upon one battle all our liberties.
　　You know that I held Epicurus[16] strong
　　And his opinion. Now I change my mind　　　　　85
　　And partly credit things that do presage.[17]
　　Coming from Sardis, on our former ensign[18]
　　Two mighty eagles fell, and there they perched,
　　Gorging and feeding from our soldiers' hands,
　　Who to Philippi here consorted[19] us.　　　　　90
　　This morning are they fled away and gone,
　　And in their steads do ravens, crows, and kites[20]
　　Fly o'er our heads and downward look on us
　　As we were sickly prey. Their shadows seem
　　A canopy most fatal, under which　　　　　95
　　Our army lies, ready to give up the ghost.
**Messala.** Believe not so.

---

12. **masker:** actor.  13. **stomachs:** appetites.  14. **bark:** ship.  15. **on . . . hazard:** at stake.  16. **Epicurus:** Greek philosopher who denied supernatural interference, with consequent disbelief in omens.  17. **presage:** foretell as omens. 18. **former ensign:** foremost battle flag.  19. **consorted:** accompanied.  20. **kites:** hawks.

**Cassius.**                    I but believe it partly,
  For I am fresh of spirit and resolved
  To meet all perils very constantly.                                    100

                    [Brutus *and* Lucilius *end their conversation.*]

**Brutus.** Even so, Lucilius.
**Cassius.**                    Now, most noble Brutus,
  The gods today stand friendly, that we may,
  Lovers in peace, lead on our days to age!
  But since the affairs of men rest still incertain,                     105
  Let's reason with the worst that may befall.
  If we do lose this battle, then is this
  The very last time we shall speak together.
  What are you then determinèd to do?
**Brutus.** Even by the rule of that philosophy                          110
  By which I did blame Cato for the death
  Which he did give himself—I know not how,
  But I do find it cowardly and vile,
  For fear of what might fall, so to prevent
  The time of life[21]—arming myself with patience                      115
  To stay[22] the providence of some high powers
  That govern us below.
**Cassius.**                    Then, if we lose this battle,
  You are contented to be led in triumph
  Through the streets of Rome.                                           120
**Brutus.** No, Cassius, no. Think not, thou noble Roman,
  That ever Brutus will go bound to Rome.
  He bears too great a mind. But this same day
  Must end that work the ides of March begun,
  And whether we shall meet again I know not.                            125
  Therefore our everlasting farewell take.
  For ever and for ever farewell, Cassius!
  If we do meet again, why, we shall smile;
  If not, why then this parting was well made.
**Cassius.** For ever and for ever farewell, Brutus!                    130
  If we do meet again, we'll smile indeed;
  If not, 'tis true this parting was well made.
**Brutus.** Why then, lead on. O that a man might know
  The end of this day's business ere it come!
  But it sufficeth that the day will end,                                135
  And then the end is known. Come, ho! Away!

                                                        [*Exeunt.*]

---

21. **prevent . . . life:** forestall the natural end of life.  22. **stay:** await.

## Scene 2

[*Brutus sends Messala with instructions to his forces.*]

[*The field of battle. Alarum. Enter* Brutus *and* Messala.]

**Brutus.** Ride, ride, Messala, ride, and give these bills[1]
Unto the legions on the other side.

[*Loud alarum.*[2]]

Let them set on at once; for I perceive
But cold demeanor[3] in Octavius' wing,
And sudden push gives them the overthrow.                5
Ride, ride, Messala! Let them all come down.

[*Exeunt.*]

## Scene 3

[*Cassius receives false news that Titinius has been
captured. He orders Pindarus to kill him with the same
sword he used to kill Caesar. Titinius, finding Cassius
dead, kills himself with Cassius' sword.*]

[*Another part of the field. Alarums. Enter* Cassius *and* Titinius.]

**Cassius.** O, look, Titinius, look! The villains fly!
Myself have to mine own turned enemy.[1]
This ensign[2] here of mine was turning back;
I slew the coward and did take it from him.
**Titinius.** O Cassius, Brutus gave the word too early,        5
Who, having some advantage on Octavius,
Took it too eagerly. His soldiers fell to spoil,[3]
Whilst we by Antony are all enclosed.

[*Enter* Pindarus.]

---

1. **bills:** orders.  2. **alarum:** drum or trumpet call to arms.  3. **cold demeanor:** lack of offensive spirit.
1. **Myself . . . enemy:** I am now the enemy of my own men because they have become cowards.  2. **ensign:** flag bearer.  3. **spoil:** looting.

**Pindarus.** Fly further off, my lord! fly further off!
    Mark Antony is in your tents, my lord.            10
    Fly, therefore, noble Cassius, fly far off!
**Cassius.** This hill is far enough. Look, look, Titinius!
    Are those my tents where I perceive the fire?
**Titinius.** They are, my lord.
**Cassius.**                Titinius, if thou lovest me,     15
    Mount thou my horse and hide thy spurs in him
    Till he have brought thee up to yonder troops
    And here again, that I may rest assured
    Whether yond troops are friend or enemy.
**Titinius.** I will be here again even with[4] a thought.         *[Exit.]*   20
**Cassius.** Go, Pindarus, get higher on that hill.
    My sight was ever thick.[5] Regard Titinius,
    And tell me what thou notest about the field.
                         *[Pindarus ascends the hill.]*

    This day I breathèd first. Time is come round,
    And where I did begin, there shall I end.         25
    My life is run his compass. Sirrah, what news?
**Pindarus.** *[Above]* O my lord!
**Cassius.** What news?
**Pindarus.** *[Above]* Titinius is enclosèd round about
    With horsemen that make to him on the spur.     30
    Yet he spurs on. Now they are almost on him.
    Now, Titinius!
    Now some light.[6] O, he lights too! He's ta'en. *[Shout.]* And hark!
    They shout for joy.
**Cassius.**               Come down; behold no more.     35
    O coward that I am to live so long
    To see my best friend ta'en before my face!

    *[Enter Pindarus from above.]*

    Come hither, sirrah.
    In Parthia[7] did I take thee prisoner,
    And then I swore thee, saving of thy life,     40
    That whatsoever I did bid thee do,
    Thou shouldst attempt it. Come now, keep thine oath.
    Now be a freeman, and with this good sword,
    That ran through Caesar's bowels, search this bosom.
    Stand not to answer. Here, take thou the hilts,     45

---

4. **even with:** as quickly as.   5. **thick:** short.   6. **light:** dismount.   7. **Parthia:** ancient land in Asia.

And when my face is covered, as 'tis now,
Guide thou the sword. [Pindarus *stabs him*.]—Caesar, thou art revenged
Even with the sword that killed thee.                [*Dies*.]
**Pindarus.** So, I am free, yet would not so have been,
Durst I have done my will. O Cassius!                           50
Far from this country Pindarus shall run,
Where never Roman shall take note of him.          [*Exit*.]

[*Reenter* Titinius *with* Messala.]

**Messala.** It is but change,[8] Titinius; for Octavius
Is overthrown by noble Brutus' power,
As Cassius' legions are by Antony.                                 55
**Titinius.** These tidings will well comfort Cassius.
**Messala.** Where did you leave him?
**Titinius.**                                  All disconsolate,
With Pindarus his bondman, on this hill.
**Messala.** Is not that he that lies upon the ground?            60
**Titinius.** He lies not like the living. O my heart!
**Messala.** Is not that he?
**Titinius.**                              No, this was he, Messala,
But Cassius is no more. O setting sun,
As in thy red rays thou dost sink to night,
So in his red blood Cassius' day is set!                          65
The sun of Rome is set. Our day is gone;
Clouds, dews, and dangers come; our deeds are done!
Mistrust of my success hath done this deed.
**Messala.** Mistrust of good success hath done this deed.       70
O hateful Error, Melancholy's child,
Why dost thou show to the apt[9] thoughts of men
The things that are not? O Error, soon conceived,
Thou never comest unto a happy birth,
But kill'st the mother that engendered[10] thee!                 75
**Titinius.** What, Pindarus! Where art thou, Pindarus?
**Messala.** Seek him, Titinius, whilst I go to meet
The noble Brutus, thrusting this report
Into his ears. I may say "thrusting" it;
For piercing steel and darts envenomèd                           80
Shall be as welcome to the ears of Brutus
As tidings of this sight.

---

8. **change:** exchange.   9. **apt:** ready to be deceived.   10. **engendered:** conceived.

**Titinius.**              Hie you, Messala,
  And I will seek for Pindarus the while.

[*Exit* Messala.]

[Titinius *looks at* Cassius.]

  Why didst thou send me forth, brave Cassius?                    85
  Did I not meet thy friends, and did not they
  Put on my brows this wreath of victory
  And bid me give it thee? Didst thou not hear their shouts?
  Alas, thou hast misconstrued[11] everything!
  But hold thee, take this garland on thy brow.                    90
  Thy Brutus bid me give it thee, and I
  Will do his bidding. Brutus, come apace
  And see how I regarded Caius Cassius.
  By your leave, gods. This is a Roman's part.
  Come, Cassius' sword, and find Titinius' heart.      [*Dies.*]   95

  [*Alarum. Enter* Brutus, Messala, young Cato, Strato,
  Volumnius, *and* Lucilius.]

**Brutus.** Where, where, Messala, doth his body lie?
**Messala.** Lo, yonder, and Titinius mourning it.
**Brutus.** Titinius' face is upward.
**Cato.**              He is slain.
**Brutus.** O Julius Caesar, thou art mighty yet!                 100
  Thy spirit walks abroad and turns our swords
  In our own proper entrails.            [*Low alarums.*]
**Cato.**              Brave Titinius!
  Look whether he have not crowned dead Cassius.
**Brutus.** Are yet two Romans living such as these?              105
  The last of all the Romans, fare thee well!
  It is impossible that ever Rome
  Should breed thy fellow. Friends, I owe more tears
  To this dead man than you shall see me pay.
  I shall find time, Cassius; I shall find time.                  110
  Come therefore, and to Thasos[12] send his body.
  His funerals shall not be in our camp,
  Lest it discomfort[13] us. Lucilius, come;
  And come, young Cato. Let us to the field.
  Labeo and Flavius set our battles on.                           115
  'Tis three o'clock; and, Romans, yet ere night
  We shall try fortune in a second fight.

[*Exeunt.*]

---

11. **misconstrued:** misinterpreted.  12. **Thasos:** Greek island in the Aegean Sea.  13. **discomfort:** weaken our purpose.

## Scene 4

[*The battle is turning against Brutus' forces. Lucilius is captured, and he tells Antony that he will never capture Brutus alive.*]

[*Another part of the field. Alarum. Enter* Brutus, Messala, young Cato, Lucilius, *and* Flavius.]

**Brutus.** Yet, countrymen, O, yet hold up your heads!
**Cato.** What fellow doth not? Who will go with me?
   I will proclaim my name about the field.
   I am the son of Marcus Cato, ho!
   A foe to tyrants, and my country's friend.         5
   I am the son of Marcus Cato, ho!

   [*Enter* Soldiers *and fight.*]

**Brutus.** And I am Brutus, Marcus Brutus I!
   Brutus, my country's friend! Know me for Brutus!      [*Exit*]

                      [young Cato *falls.*]

**Lucilius.** O young and noble Cato, art thou down?
   Why, now thou diest as bravely as Titinius,      10
   And mayst be honored, being Cato's son.
**First Soldier.** Yield, or thou diest.
**Lucilius.**                Only I yield to die.
   [*Offering money*] There is so much that thou wilt kill me straight.
   Kill Brutus, and be honored in his death.      15
**First Soldier.** We must not. A noble prisoner!

   [*Enter* Antony.]

**Second Soldier.** Room ho! Tell Antony Brutus is ta'en.
**First Soldier.** I'll tell the news. Here comes the general.
   Brutus is ta'en! Brutus is ta'en, my lord!
**Antony.** Where is he?      20
**Lucilius.** Safe, Antony; Brutus is safe enough.
   I dare assure thee that no enemy
   Shall ever take alive the noble Brutus.
   The gods defend him from so great a shame!
   When you do find him, or alive or dead,      25
   He will be found like Brutus, like himself.

**Antony.** This is not Brutus, friend; but, I assure you,
    A prize no less in worth. Keep this man safe;
    Give him all kindness. I had rather have
    Such men my friends than enemies. Go on,     30
    And see whether Brutus be alive or dead;
    And bring us word unto Octavius' tent
    How every thing is chanced.

                                *[Exeunt.]*


## Scene 5

*[Knowing his army faces defeat, Brutus kills himself. Antony and Octavius praise Brutus' idealism and promise respectful and honorable burial rites for this noble Roman.]*

*[Another part of the field. Enter Brutus, Dardanius, Clitus, Strato, and Volumnius.]*

**Brutus.** Come, poor remains of friends, rest on this rock.
**Clitus.** Statilius showed the torchlight[1] but, my lord,
    He came not back. He is or ta'en or slain.
**Brutus.** Sit thee down, Clitus. Slaying is the word.
    It is a deed in fashion. Hark thee, Clitus.     *[Whispers.]*   5
**Clitus.** What, I, my lord? No, not for all the world!
**Brutus.** Peace then. No words.
**Clitus.**                 I'll rather kill myself.
**Brutus.** Hark thee, Dardanius.

                                  *[Whispers.]*

**Dardanius.**              Shall I do such a deed?     10
**Clitus.** O Dardanius!
**Dardanius.** O Clitus!
**Clitus.** What ill request did Brutus make to thee?
**Dardanius.** To kill him, Clitus. Look, he meditates.
**Clitus.** Now is that noble vessel full of grief,     15
    That it runs over even at his eyes.

---

1. **showed the torchlight:** gave the signal.

682    *JULIUS CAESAR*

**Brutus.** Come hither, good Volumnius. List² a word.

**Volumnius.** What says my lord?

**Brutus.**                         Why this, Volumnius.
The ghost of Caesar hath appeared to me                                    20
Two several³ times by night—at Sardis once,
And this last night here in Philippi fields.
I know my hour is come.

**Volumnius.**                         Not so, my lord.

**Brutus.** Nay, I am sure it is, Volumnius.                               25
Thou seest the world, Volumnius, how it goes.
Our enemies have beat us to the pit.⁴

                                                    [*Low alarums.*]

It is more worthy to leap in ourselves
Than tarry till they push us. Good Volumnius,
Thou know'st that we two went to school together.                         30
Even for that our love of old, I prithee
Hold thou my sword-hilts whilst I run on it.

**Volumnius.** That's not an office for a friend, my lord.

                                                    [*Alarum still.*]

**Clitus.** Fly, fly, my lord! There is no tarrying here.

**Brutus.** Farewell to you; and you; and you, Volumnius.                  35
Strato, thou hast been all this while asleep.
Farewell to thee too, Strato. Countrymen,
My heart doth joy that yet in all my life
I found no man but he was true to me.
I shall have glory by this losing day                                     40
More than Octavius and Mark Antony
By this vile conquest shall attain unto.
So fare you well at once, for Brutus' tongue
Hath almost ended his life's history.
Night hangs upon mine eyes; my bones would rest,                          45
That have but labored to attain this hour.

                    [*Alarum. Cry within:* "Fly, fly, fly!"]

**Clitus.** Fly, my lord, fly!

**Brutus.**                         Hence! I will follow.

                    [*Exeunt* Clitus, Dardanius, *and* Volumnius.]
I prithee, Strato, stay thou by thy lord.
Thou art a fellow of a good respect;⁵                                     50
Thy life hath had some smatch⁶ of honor in it.
Hold then my sword, and turn away thy face
While I do run upon it. Wilt thou, Strato?

---

2. **List:** listen to.  3. **several:** separate.  4. **Our . . . pit:** reference to hunters encircling and driving their prey into a
pit.  5. **of . . . respect:** worthy of respect.  6. **smatch:** taste.

**Strato.** Give me your hand first. Fare you well, my lord.
**Brutus.** Farewell, good Strato. Caesar, now be still.                    55
  I killed not thee with half so good a will.

                                                                    [*Dies.*]


[*Alarum. Retreat. Enter* Octavius, Antony, Messala, Lucilius,
*and the Army.*]

**Octavius.** What man is that?
**Messala.** My master's man. Strato, where is thy master?
**Strato.** Free from the bondage you are in, Messala.
  The conquerors can but make a fire of him;                       60
  For Brutus only overcame himself,
  And no man else hath honor by his death.
**Lucilius.** So Brutus should be found. I thank thee, Brutus,
  That thou hast proved Lucilius' saying true.
**Octavius.** All that served Brutus, I will entertain[7] them.     65
  Fellow, wilt thou bestow thy time with me?
**Strato.** Ay, if Messala will prefer[8] me to you.
**Octavius.** Do so, good Messala.
**Messala.** How died my master, Strato?
**Strato.** I held the sword, and he did run on it.                 70
**Messala.** Octavius, then take him to follow thee,
  That did the latest[9] service to my master.
**Antony.** This was the noblest Roman of them all.
  All the conspirators save only he
  Did that they did in envy of great Caesar;                       75
  He, only in a general honest thought
  And common good to all, made one of them.
  His life was gentle, and the elements
  So mixed in him[10] that Nature might stand up
  And say to all the world, "This was a man!"                      80
**Octavius.** According to his virtue let us use[11] him,
  With all respect and rites of burial.
  Within my tent his bones tonight shall lie,
  Most like a soldier, ordered[12] honorably.
  So call the field to rest, and let's away                        85
  To part[13] the glories of this happy day.

                                                                [*Exeunt.*]

---

7. **entertain:** take them into my service.   8. **prefer:** recommend.   9. **latest:** last.   10. **elements . . . him:** he was a
man perfectly balanced.   11. **use:** treat.   12. **ordered:** treated.   13. **part:** share.

## Act Five

### Getting at Meaning

*Scene 1*

1. The conspirators have made a tactical error that will cost them the battle. What is it?

2. Brutus, Cassius, Antony, and Octavius trade insults when they meet on the battlefield. What are some of these insults?

3. What does Cassius mean when he says to Messala, "You know that I held Epicurus strong/ And his opinion. Now I change my mind/And partly credit things that do presage"?

4. What evil omens does Cassius see on the morning of the battle?

*Scene 3*

5. What events in battle lead to the suicide of Cassius? Why does he kill himself? How does he kill himself?

6. Why does Titinius commit suicide?

7. Explain the meaning of these lines spoken by Brutus: "O Julius Caesar, thou art mighty yet!/ Thy spirit walks abroad and turns our swords/In our own proper entrails."

8. Describe the reaction of Brutus to the death of Cassius.

*Scene 4*

9. Why is the enemy pleased to capture Lucilius?

*Scene 5*

10. What is Brutus's rationale for killing himself? What does he say about mankind as he dies?

11. Antony pronounces some well known lines over the body of Brutus. What does he recognize about Brutus? Why does he call him "the noblest Roman of them all"?

### Developing Skills in Reading Literature

1. **Pun.** The insults between the opposing forces at the beginning of Act Five involve punning. Identify the puns and the words on which the puns are based.

2. **Tragedy.** The ancient Greek philosopher Aristotle, in a work of literary analysis called *The Poetics,* identified the main characteristics of tragedy. He explained that tragedy is a representation of serious actions that turn out disastrously for the main character or characters; usually, the actions are presented in poetic, dramatic form.

Aristotle wrote that all true tragedies arouse pity and fear in an audience: pity, because the audience feels sorry for the tragic characters and hates to see them suffer; and fear, because the viewers realize that, if circumstances were different, they, too, could be caught up in a web of tragic events. According to Aristotle, a tragedy purges an audience of pity and fear, a process that he called catharsis.

Do any scenes in *Julius Caesar* inspire pity and fear in you? Do you feel emotionally purged at the end of the play? Do you feel depressed because of the waste of human life, or perhaps relieved that the tension has ended and order has been restored? Look up the word *catharsis* in a dictionary and notice how the meaning of Aristotle's term has been extended. What is the adjective form of *catharsis?*

3. **Tragic Hero.** Aristotle taught that every tragedy involves a central character or characters with whom the audience identifies. Tragic heroes generally have four main qualities:

a. Goodness: Only characters who are good can arouse pity.

b. Superiority: Only characters who are somehow superior or elevated seem tragic in their destruction.

c. Tragic flaw: Tragic heroes make fatal errors in judgment that contribute to their downfall; often the flaw is a traditionally admirable quality carried to excess.

d. Tragic realization: Tragic characters perceive, before their fall, how they have contributed to their own destruction.

Brutus often is viewed as a tragic hero. Is Brutus

good? Is he superior? If so, in what ways? Would you say that Brutus has a tragic flaw? If so, what is it? Does Brutus realize, at the end of the play, that his errors in judgment have led to his downfall?

4. **Structure.** A. C. Bradley, a British Shakespearean scholar, has suggested in his book *Shakespearean Tragedy* that Shakespeare's tragedies may be viewed in three parts:

a. Exposition. This is usually all or most of Act One. The exposition introduces the characters, their positions and circumstances. Shakespeare usually begins a play with a short scene, often full of life and activity. Then, having captured our attention, he proceeds to conversations at a lower pitch, accompanied by little action but conveying much information. The characters often talk about the central character before he or she appears.

b. Conflict. This concerns the clash of opposing forces, the external conflict that is of primary importance. However, the internal struggle of the protagonist also is extremely significant. While the conflict builds, tension rises and falls, until a critical point at which the two opposing forces change places. After this point, the fortunes of the protagonist decline. In Act Four, Shakespeare often introduces a new kind of emotion, a quiet, pathetic emotion that is usually painful.

c. Catastrophe. This is generally all or most of Act Five. It involves a total reversal of the protagonist's fortunes. In Shakespeare's plays the reversal always results in the death of the character.

What are the opposing forces in *Julius Caesar*? How many of Bradley's points about structure can you apply to the play? Identify specific scenes or episodes in the play that illustrate each of his points.

5. **Theme.** Do you find a political message in *Julius Caesar*? Which of the political figures have your sympathy? Why? Which of the political figures do you admire? Why?

### Developing Writing Skills

1. **Analyzing Characters.** As noted previously, Brutus is an idealist, Cassius a realist. Find three major episodes in which these two characters have major differences of opinion, and analyze each episode in a five-paragraph composition. What does Brutus argue in each of the disagreements? What does Cassius argue? What can you conclude about each man's character from his views? Why does Cassius always concede to Brutus?

2. **Developing an Argument.** Cassius, when he is trying to win Brutus over to his cause in Act One, says of human beings that there are "none so firm that cannot be seduced." Do you agree with Cassius that everyone has a price? In a five-paragraph composition, argue the truth or falsity of Cassius's statement, drawing examples from the play and from your own knowledge of modern history and politics.

# Unit Review   *Drama*

## Understanding the Unit

1. Both *Julius Caesar* and "Orpheus" contain supernatural elements. What is the function of the supernatural in each play? In which play does the supernatural seem most believable? Why?

2. In *Julius Caesar,* Mark Antony uses his ability as an actor and public speaker to sway the crowd. The ballad singer in "The Rising of the Moon" uses the same skills to sway the sergeant. What acting techniques does each character use? What tricks of argument or persuasion does each use? Are there any other similarities between these two characters?

3. The ballad singer in "The Rising of the Moon" looks forward to the time "when the small shall rise up and the big fall down." What characters in *A Raisin in the Sun* share these sentiments? Explain.

4. "Orpheus" and *Julius Caesar* both have dialogue that is written in poetry instead of prose. What poetic devices do both playwrights use? What additional poetic devices does Shakespeare use that Hughes does not use in "Orpheus"? How does the poetic dialogue of each play fit the subject matter of the play? Does the poetry of "Orpheus" sound more modern? Why, or why not?

5. Each of the plays in this unit portrays characters who are faced with internal conflicts. Select one character from each play, and explain the internal conflict that this character must resolve.

6. *Julius Caesar* was written at the end of the sixteenth century; *A Raisin in the Sun* was written in the mid-twentieth century. On the basis of these two plays, what conclusions can you draw about how drama has changed in 350 years?

7. Many new theaters are designed with a stage that resembles the stage on which Shakespeare's plays were performed. This type of stage is often called a thrust stage because it projects, or "thrusts," into the audience. Because the audience sits on three sides of the stage, this design presents some problems for directors. What are some of these problems? Which of the plays in this unit would be most easily adapted to a thrust stage?

## Writing

1. What is honor? How does a person achieve honor? How does a person lose honor? Brutus, Walter Lee Younger, and the sergeant in "The Rising of the Moon" all struggle to retain their honor. In a five-paragraph composition, discuss how each of these characters defines honor, how each resolves his struggle and either loses or maintains his honor, and what these struggles teach you about honor.

2. Imagine that you are hosting a dinner party at a local restaurant. You may invite one character from each play to dinner. Unfortunately, seating in the restaurant is limited to tables with two immovable chairs. You must arrange your dinner party to suit this seating. You may sit with one character; two other characters may sit together; one character must sit alone. In a five-paragraph composition identify the four characters whom you will invite, and explain your seating arrangement and the reasons behind your decisions.

ENTER THE LAW. *E. F. Ward.*
*Thomas Gilcrease Institute, Tulsa, Oklahoma.*

# Unit 5
# The Novel

# Introduction to the Unit

The novel, as a form of literature, was introduced in the United States in the late nineteenth century. By definition, a novel is a lengthy work of fiction characterized by fully drawn characters, credible settings, and one or more major conflicts and themes. Novelists, unlike the writers of short stories, have the opportunity to explore in depth the intricacies of human personality and the infinite variety of life patterns. They do so within structured plots that may present several parallel stories or a tangled web of intersecting story lines. In the traditional novel, the plots and subplots eventually are resolved, leaving the reader with a sense of completion and some insight into the complexities of the human situation.

Hard-boiled detective thrillers, Gothic romances, biting satires, sentimental melodramas, sophisticated psychological portraits, science fiction adventures all are represented within the broad scope of the novel, as is the western, a genre unique to the American literary tradition. Generations of readers have been captivated by tales of the settlers and drifters who once inhabited the vast territory west of the Mississippi River. The cowboy, the gunslinger, the Indian scout, the marshal are American folk heroes whose triumphs and tragedies are the basic subject matter of the western.

Many western novels provide little more than stereotyped characters and broad descriptions of bold action. Others —such as *Shane*—present the reader with complex, universal characters who must reconcile personal and societal values.

As you read *Shane*, examine the literary techniques used by the novelist, particularly in developing the characters and conflicts. As you read, immerse yourself in the excitement and drama of the Old West.

# Shane    *Jack Schaefer*

## 1

We rode into our valley in the summer of '89. I was a kid then, barely topping the backboard of father's old chuck-wagon. I was on the upper rail of our small corral, soaking in the late afternoon sun, when I saw him far down the road where it swung into the valley from the open plain beyond.

In that clear Wyoming air I could see him plainly, though he was still several miles away. There seemed nothing remarkable about him, just another stray horseman riding up the road toward the cluster of frame buildings that was our town. Then I saw a pair of cowhands, loping past him, stop and stare after him with a curious intentness.

He came steadily on, straight through the town without slackening pace, until he reached the fork a half-mile below our place. One branch turned left across the river ford and on to Luke Fletcher's big spread. The other bore ahead along the right bank where we homesteaders[1] had pegged our claims in a row up the valley. He hesitated briefly, studying the choice, and moved again steadily on our side.

As he came near, what impressed me first was his clothes. He wore dark trousers of some serge material tucked into tall boots and held at the waist by a wide belt, both of a soft black leather tooled in intricate design. A coat of the same dark material as the trousers was neatly folded and strapped to his saddle-roll. His shirt was finespun linen, rich brown in color. The handkerchief knotted loosely around his throat was black silk. His hat was not the familiar Stetson, not the familiar gray or muddy tan. It was plain black, soft in texture, unlike any hat I had ever seen, with a creased crown and a wide curling brim swept down in front to shield the face.

All trace of newness was long since gone from these things. The dust of distance was beaten into them. They were worn and stained, and several neat patches showed on the shirt. Yet a kind of magnificence remained and with it a hint of men and manners alien to my limited boy's experience.

Then I forgot the clothes in the impact of the man himself. He was not much above medium height, almost slight in build. He would have looked frail alongside father's square, solid bulk. But even I could read the endurance in the lines of that dark figure and the quiet power in its effortless, unthinking adjustment to every movement of the tired horse.

He was clean-shaven, and his face was lean and hard and burned from high forehead to firm, tapering chin. His eyes seemed hooded in the shadow of the hat's brim. He came closer, and I could see that this was because the brows were drawn in a frown of fixed and habitual alertness. Beneath them the eyes were endlessly searching from side to side and forward, checking off every item in view, missing nothing. As I noticed this,

---

1. **homesteaders:** settlers who hold tracts of public land granted by the U.S. government to be developed as farms, under the Homestead Act of 1862.

MOUNTED TRAPPER. *Albert Bierstadt. Thomas Gilcrease Institute, Tulsa, Oklahoma.*

a sudden chill, I could not have told why, struck through me there in the warm and open sun.

He rode easily, relaxed in the saddle, leaning his weight lazily into the stirrups. Yet even in this easiness was a suggestion of tension. It was the easiness of a coiled spring, of a trap set.

He drew rein not twenty feet from me. His glance hit me, dismissed me, flicked over our place. This was not much, if you were thinking in terms of size and scope. But what there was was good. You could trust father for that. The corral, big enough for about thirty head if you crowded them in, was railed right to true sunk posts. The pasture behind, taking in nearly half of our claim, was fenced tight. The barn was small, but it was solid, and we were raising a loft at one end for the alfalfa growing green in the north forty. We had a fair-sized field in potatoes that year, and father was trying a new corn he had sent all the way to Washington for and they were showing properly in weedless rows.

Behind the house, mother's kitchen garden was a brave sight. The house itself was three rooms—two really, the big kitchen where we spent most of our time indoors and the bedroom beside it. My little lean-to room was added back of the kitchen. Father was planning, when he could get around to it, to build mother the parlor she wanted.

We had wooden floors and a nice porch across the front. The house was painted too, white with green trim, rare thing in all that region, to remind her, mother said when she made father do it, of her native New England. Even rarer, the roof was shingled. I knew what that meant. I had helped father split those shingles. Few places so spruce and well worked could be found so deep in the Territory in those days.

The stranger took it all in, sitting there easily in the saddle. I saw his eyes slow on the flowers mother had planted by the porch steps, then come to rest on our shiny new pump and the trough beside it. They shifted back to me, and again, without knowing why, I felt that sudden chill. But his voice was gentle, and he spoke like a man schooled in patience.

"I'd appreciate a chance at the pump for myself and the horse."

I was trying to frame a reply and choking on it, when I realized that he was not speaking to me but past me. Father had come up behind me and was leaning against the gate to the corral.

"Use all the water you want, stranger."

Father and I watched him dismount in a single flowing tilt of his body and lead the horse over to the trough. He pumped it almost full and let the horse sink its nose in the cool water before he picked up the dipper for himself.

He took off his hat and slapped the dust out of it and hung it on a corner of the trough. With his hands he brushed the dust from his clothes. With a piece of rag pulled from his saddle-roll he carefully wiped his boots. He untied the handkerchief from around his neck and rolled his sleeves and dipped his arms in the trough, rubbing thoroughly and splashing water over his face. He shook his hands dry and used the handkerchief to remove the last drops from his face. Taking a comb from his shirt pocket, he smoothed back his long dark hair. All his movements were deft and sure, and with a quick precision he flipped down his sleeves, reknotted the handkerchief, and picked up his hat.

Then, holding it in his hand, he spun about and strode directly toward the house. He bent low and snapped the stem of one of mother's petunias and tucked this into the hatband.

In another moment the hat was on his head, brim swept down in swift, unconscious gesture, and he was swinging gracefully into the saddle and starting toward the road.

I was fascinated. None of the men I knew were proud like that about their appearance. In that short time the kind of magnificence I had noticed had emerged into plainer view. It was in the very air of him. Everything about him showed the effects of long use and hard use, but showed too the strength of quality and competence. There was no chill on me now. Already I was imagining myself in hat and belt and boots like those.

He stopped the horse and looked down at us. He was refreshed, and I would have sworn the tiny wrinkles around his eyes were what with him would be a smile. His eyes were not restless when he looked at you like this. They were still and steady, and you knew the man's whole attention was concentrated on you even in the casual glance.

"Thank you," he said in his gentle voice and was turning into the road, back to us, before father spoke in his slow, deliberate way.

"Don't be in such a hurry, stranger."

I had to hold tight to the rail or I would have fallen backwards into the corral. At the first sound of father's voice, the man and the horse, like a single being, had wheeled to face us, the man's eyes boring at father, bright and deep in the shadow of the hat's brim. I was shivering, struck through once more. Something intangible and cold and terrifying was there in the air between us.

I stared in wonder as father and the stranger looked at each other a long moment, measuring each other in an unspoken fraternity of adult knowledge beyond my reach. Then the warm sunlight was flooding over us, for father was smiling, and he was speaking with the drawling emphasis that meant he had made up his mind.

"I said don't be in such a hurry, stranger.

Food will be on the table soon and you can bed down here tonight."

The stranger nodded quietly as if he too had made up his mind. "That's mighty thoughtful of you," he said and swung down and came toward us, leading his horse. Father slipped into step beside him and we all headed for the barn.

"My name's Starrett," said father. "Joe Starrett. This here," waving at me, "is Robert MacPherson Starrett. Too much name for a boy. I make it Bob."

The stranger nodded again. "Call me Shane," he said. Then to me, "Bob it is. You were watching me for quite a spell coming up the road."

It was not a question. It was a simple statement. "Yes . . ." I stammered. "Yes. I was."

"Right," he said. "I like that. A man who watches what's going on around him will make his mark."

A man who watches . . . For all his dark appearance and lean, hard look, this Shane knew what would please a boy. The glow of it held me as he took care of his horse, and I fussed around, hanging up his saddle, forking over some hay, getting in his way and my own in my eagerness. He let me slip the bridle off, and the horse, bigger and more powerful than I had thought now that I was close beside it, put its head down patiently for me and stood quietly while I helped him curry away the caked dust. Only once did he stop me. That was when I reached for his saddle roll to put it to one side. In the instant my fingers touched it, he was taking it from me, and he put it on a shelf with a finality that indicated no interference.

When the three of us went up to the house, mother was waiting and four places were set at the table. "I saw you through the window," she said and came to shake our visitor's hand. She was a slender, lively woman with a fair complexion even our weather never seemed to affect and a mass of light brown hair she wore piled high to bring her, she used to say, closer to father's size.

"Marian," father said, "I'd like you to meet Mr. Shane."

"Good evening, ma'am," said our visitor. He took her hand and bowed over it. Mother stepped back and, to my surprise, dropped in a dainty curtsy. I had never seen her do that before. She was an unpredictable woman. Father and I would have painted the house three times over and in rainbow colors to please her.

"And a good evening to you, Mr. Shane. If Joe hadn't called you back, I would have done it myself. You'd never find a decent meal up the valley."

She was proud of her cooking, was mother. That was one thing she learned back home, she would often say, that was of some use out in this raw land. As long as she could still prepare a proper dinner, she would tell father when things were not going right, she knew she was still civilized, and there was hope of getting ahead. Then she would tighten her lips and whisk together her special most delicious biscuits, and father would watch her bustling about and eat them to the last little crumb and stand up and wipe his eyes and stretch his big frame and stomp out to his always unfinished work like daring anything to stop him now.

We sat down to supper and a good one. Mother's eyes sparkled as our visitor kept pace with father and me. Then we all leaned back, and while I listened, the talk ran on almost like old friends around a familiar table. But I could sense that it was following a pattern. Father was trying, with mother helping and both of them avoiding direct questions, to get hold of facts about this Shane, and he was dodging at every turn. He was aware of their purpose and not in the least annoyed by it. He was mild and courteous and spoke readily enough. But always he put them off with words that gave no real information.

He must have been riding many days, for he was full of news from towns along his back trail as far as Cheyenne and even Dodge City and others beyond I had never heard of before. But he had no news about himself. His past was fenced as tightly as our pasture. All they could learn was that he was riding through, taking each day as it came, with nothing particular in mind except maybe seeing a part of the country he had not been in before.

Afterwards mother washed the dishes and I dried and the two men sat on the porch, their voices carrying through the open door. Our visitor was guiding the conversation now, and in no time at all he had father talking about his own plans. That was no trick. Father was ever one to argue his ideas whenever he could find a listener. This time he was going strong.

"Yes, Shane, the boys I used to ride with don't see it yet. They will some day. The open range can't last forever. The fence lines are closing in. Running cattle in big lots is good business only for the top ranchers, and it's really a poor business at that. Poor in terms of the resources going into it. Too much space for too little results. It's certain to be crowded out."

"Well, now," said Shane, "that's mighty interesting. I've been hearing the same quite a lot lately and from men with pretty clear heads. Maybe there's something to it."

"By Godfrey, there's plenty to it. Listen to me, Shane. The thing to do is pick your spot, get your land, your own land. Put in enough crops to carry you and make your money play with a small herd, not all horns and bone, but bred for meat and fenced in and fed right. I haven't been at it long, but already I've raised stock that averages three hundred pounds more than that long-legged stuff Fletcher runs on the other side of the river and it's better beef, and that's only a beginning.

"Sure, his outfit sprawls over most of this valley and it looks big. But he's got range rights on a lot more acres than he has cows, and he won't even have those acres as more homesteaders move in. His way is wasteful. Too much land for what he gets out of it. He can't see that. He thinks we small fellows are nothing but nuisances."

"You are," said Shane mildly. "From his point of view, you are."

"Yes, I guess you're right. I'll have to admit that. Those of us here now would make it tough for him if he wanted to use the range behind us on this side of the river as he used to. Altogether we cut some pretty good slices out of it. Worse still, we block off part of the river, shut the range off from the water. He's been grumbling about that off and on ever since we've been here. He's worried that more of us will keep coming and settle on the other side too, and then he will be in a fix."

The dishes were done and I was edging to the door. Mother nailed me as she usually did and shunted me off to bed. After she had left me in my little back room and went to join the men on the porch, I tried to catch more of the words. The voices were too low. Then I must have dozed, for with a start I realized that father and mother were again in the kitchen. By now, I gathered, our visitor was out in the barn in the bunk father had built there for the hired man who had been with us for a few weeks in the spring.

"Wasn't it peculiar," I heard mother say, "how he wouldn't talk about himself?"

"Peculiar?" said father. "Well, yes. In a way."

"Everything about him is peculiar." Mother sounded as if she was stirred up and interested. "I never saw a man quite like him before."

"You wouldn't have. Not where you come from. He's a special brand we sometimes get out here in the grass country. I've come across a few. A bad one's poison. A good one's straight grain clear through."

"How can you be so sure about him? Why, he wouldn't even tell where he was raised."

"Born back east a ways would be my guess. And pretty far south. Tennessee maybe. But he's been around plenty."

"I like him." Mother's voice was serious. "He's so nice and polite and sort of gentle. Not like most men I've met out here. But there's something about him. Something underneath the gentleness . . . Something . . ." Her voice trailed away.

"Mysterious?" suggested father.

"Yes, of course. Mysterious. But more than that. Dangerous."

"He's dangerous all right." Father said it in a musing way. Then he chuckled. "But not to us, my dear." And then he said what seemed to me a curious thing. "In fact, I don't think you ever had a safer man in your house."

# 2

In the morning I slept late and stumbled into the kitchen to find father and our visitor working their way through piles of mother's flapjacks. She smiled at me from over by the stove. Father slapped my rump by way of greeting. Our visitor nodded at me gravely over his heaped-up plate.

"Good morning, Bob. You'd better dig in fast or I'll do away with your share too. There's magic in your mother's cooking. Eat enough of these flannel cakes and you'll grow a bigger man than your father."

"Flannel cakes! Did you hear that, Joe?" Mother came whisking over to tousle father's hair. "You must be right. Tennessee or some such place. I've never heard them called that out here."

Our visitor looked up at her. "A good guess, ma'am. Mighty close to the mark. But you had a husband to help you. My folks came out of Mississippi and settled in Arkansas. Me, though—I was fiddle-footed[2] and left home at fifteen. Haven't had anything worth being called a real flannel cake since." He put his hands on the table edge and leaned back, and the little wrinkles at the corners of his eyes were plainer and deeper. "That is, ma'am, till now."

Mother gave what in a girl I would have called a giggle. "If I'm any judge of men," she said, "that means more." And she whisked back to the stove.

That was how it was often in our house, kind of jolly and warm with good feeling. It needed to be this morning because there was a cool grayness in the air, and before I had even begun to slow on my second plate of flapjacks, the wind was rushing down the valley with the rain of one of our sudden summer storms following fast.

Our visitor had finished his breakfast. He had eaten so many flapjacks that I had begun to wonder whether he really would cut into my share. Now he turned to look out the window and his lips tightened. But he pushed back from the table and started to rise. Mother's voice held him to his chair.

"You'll not be traveling in any such weather. Wait a bit and it'll clear. These rains don't last long. I've another pot of coffee on the stove."

Father was getting his pipe going. He kept his eyes carefully on the smoke drifting upward. "Marian's right. Only she doesn't go far enough. These rains are short. But they sure mess up the road. It's new. Hasn't settled much yet. Mighty soggy when wet. Won't be fit for traveling till it drains. You better stay over till tomorrow."

Our visitor stared down at his empty plate as if it was the most important object in the whole room. You could see he liked the idea. Yet he seemed somehow worried about it.

"Yes," said father. "That's the sensible dodge. That horse of yours was pretty much beat last night. If I was a horse doctor now, I'd order a day's rest right off. Darned if I don't think the same prescription would do me good too. You stick here the day and I'll follow it. I'd like to take you around, show you what I'm doing with the place."

He looked pleadingly at mother. She was surprised and for good reason. Father was usually so set on working every possible minute to catch up on his plans that she would have a tussle making him ease some once a week out of respect for the Sabbath. In bad weather like this he usually would fidget and stomp about the house as if he thought it was a personal insult to him, a trick to keep him from being out and doing things. And here he was talking of a whole day's rest. She was puzzled. But she played right up.

"You'd be doing us a favor, Mr. Shane. We don't get many visitors from outside the valley. It'd be real nice to have you stay. And besides—" She crinkled her nose at him the way she did when she would be teasing father into some new scheme of hers. "And besides—I've been waiting for an excuse to try a deep-dish apple pie I've heard tell of. It would just be wasted on these other two. They eat everything in sight and don't rightly know good from poor."

He was looking up, straight at her. She shook a finger at him. "And another thing. I'm fair bubbling with questions about what the women are wearing back in civilization. You know, hats and such. You're the kind of man would notice them. You're not getting away till you've told me."

Shane sat back in his chair. A faint quizzical expression softened the lean ridges of his face. "Ma'am, I'm not positive I appreci-

---

2. **fiddle-footed** *Western slang:* having a tendency to be a drifter.

ate how you've pegged me. No one else ever wrote me down as an expert on ladies' millinery." He reached out and pushed his cup across the table toward her. "You said something about more coffee. But I draw the line on more flannel cakes. I'm plumb full. I'm starting in to conserve space for that pie."

"You'd better!" Father was mighty pleased about something. "When Marian puts her mind to cooking, she makes a man forget he's got any limits to his appetite. Only don't you go giving her fancy notions of new hats so she'll be sending off to the mail-order house and throwing my money away on silly frippery. She's got a hat."

Mother did not even notice that. She knew father was just talking. She knew that whenever she wanted anything real much and said so, father would bust himself trying to get it for her. She whisked over to the table with the coffee pot, poured a fresh round, then set it down within easy reach and sat down herself.

I thought that business about hats was only a joke she made up to help father persuade our visitor to stay. But she began almost at once, pestering him to describe the ladies he had seen in Cheyenne and other towns where the new styles might be. He sat there, easy and friendly, telling her how they were wearing wide floppy-brimmed bonnets with lots of flowers in front on top and slits in the brims for scarves to come through and be tied in bows under their chins.

Talk like that seemed foolish to me to be coming from a grown man. Yet this Shane was not bothered at all. And father listened as if he thought it was all right, only not very interesting. He watched them most of the time in a good-natured quiet, trying every so often to break in with his own talk about crops and steers and giving up and trying again and giving up again with a smiling shake of his head at those two. And the rain

outside was a far distance away and meaningless because the friendly feeling in our kitchen was enough to warm all our world.

Then Shane was telling about the annual stock show at Dodge City and father was interested and excited, and it was mother who said, "Look, the sun's shining."

It was, so clear and sweet you wanted to run out and breathe the brilliant freshness. Father must have felt that way because he jumped up and fairly shouted, "Come on, Shane. I'll show you what this hop-scotch climate does to my alfalfa. You can almost see the stuff growing."

Shane was only a step behind him, but I beat them to the door. Mother followed and stood watching awhile on the porch as we three started out, picking our path around the puddles and the taller clumps of grass, bright with the raindrops. We covered the whole place pretty thoroughly, father talking all the time, more enthusiastic about his plans than he had been for many weeks. He really hit his stride when we were behind the barn where we could have a good view of our little herd spreading out through the pasture. Then he stopped short. He had noticed that Shane was not paying much attention. He was quiet as could be for a moment when he saw that Shane was looking at the stump.

That was the one bad spot on our place. It stuck out like an old scarred sore in the cleared space back of the barn—a big old stump, all jagged across the top, the legacy of some great tree that must have died long before we came into the valley and finally been snapped by a heavy windstorm. It was big enough, I used to think, so that if it was smooth on top you could have served supper to a good-sized family on it.

But you could not have done that because you could not have got them close around it. The huge old roots humped out in every direction, some as big about as my waist, pushing out and twisting down into the ground like they would hold there to eternity and past.

Father had been working at it off and on, gnawing at the roots with an axe, ever since he finished poling the corral. The going was slow, even for him. The wood was so hard that he could not sink the blade much more than a quarter inch at a time. I guess it had been an old burr oak. Not many of those grew that far up in the Territory, but the ones that did grew big and hard. Ironwood we called it.

Father had tried burning brushpiles against it. That old stump just jeered at fire. The scorching seemed to make the wood harder than ever. So he was fighting his way around root by root. He never thought he had much time to spare on it. The rare occasions he was real mad about something he would stomp out there and chew into another root.

He went over to the stump now and kicked the nearest root, a smart kick, the way he did every time he passed it. "Yes," he said. "That's the millstone round my neck. That's the one fool thing about this place I haven't licked yet. But I will. There's no wood ever grew can stand up to a man that's got the strength and the will to keep hammering at it."

He stared at the stump like it might be a person sprouting in front of him. "You know, Shane, I've been feuding with this thing so long I've worked up a spot of affection for it. It's tough. I can admire toughness. The right kind."

He was running on again, full of words and sort of happy to be letting them out, when he noticed again that Shane was not paying much attention, was listening to some sound in the distance. Sure enough, a horse was coming up the road.

Father and I turned with him to look toward town. In a moment we saw it as it cleared the grove of trees and tall bushes about a quarter-mile away, a high-necked sorrel drawing a light buckboard wagon. The mud was splattering from its hooves, but not bad, and it was stepping free and easy. Shane glanced sideways at father.

"Not fit for traveling," he said softly. "Starrett, you're poor shakes as a liar." Then his attention was on the wagon and he was tense and alert, studying the man upright on the swaying seat.

Father simply chuckled at Shane's remark. "That's Jake Ledyard's outfit," he said, taking the lead toward our lane. "I thought maybe he'd get up this way this week. Hope he has that cultivator I've been wanting."

Ledyard was a small, thin-featured man, a peddler or trader who came through every couple of months with things you could not get at the general store in town. He would pack in his stock on a mule-team freighter driven by an old, white-haired black man who acted like he was afraid even to speak without permission. Ledyard would make deliveries in his buckboard, claiming a hard bargain always and picking up orders for articles to bring on the next trip. I did not like him, and not just because he said nice things about me he did not mean for father's benefit. He smiled too much, and there was no real friendliness in it.

By the time we were beside the porch, he had swung the horse into our lane and was pulling it to a stop. He jumped down, calling greetings. Father went to meet him. Shane stayed by the porch, leaning against the end post.

"It's here," said Ledyard. "The beauty I told you about." He yanked away the canvas covering from the body of the wagon, and the sun was bright on a shiny new seven-pronged cultivator lying on its side on the floor boards. "That's the best buy I've toted this haul."

"Hm-m-m-m," said father. "You've hit it right. That's what I've been wanting. But when you start chattering about a best buy that always means big money. What's the tariff?"

"Well, now." Ledyard was slow with his reply. "It cost me more than I figured when we was talking last time. You might think it a bit steep. I don't. Not for a new beauty like that there. You'll make up the difference in no time with the work you'll save with that. Handles so easy even the boy here will be using it before long."

"Pin it down," said father. "I've asked you a question."

Ledyard was quick now. "Tell you what, I'll shave the price, take a loss to please a good customer. I'll let you have it for a hundred and ten."

I was startled to hear Shane's voice cutting in, quiet and even and plain. "Let you have it? I reckon he will. There was one like that in a store in Cheyenne. List price sixty dollars."

Ledyard shifted part way around. For the first time he looked closely at our visitor. The surface smile left his face. His voice held an ugly undertone. "Did anyone ask you to push in on this?"

"No," said Shane, quietly and evenly as before. "I reckon no one did." He was still leaning against the post. He did not move and he did not say anything more. Ledyard turned to father, speaking rapidly.

"Forget what he says, Starrett. I've spotted him now. Heard of him half a dozen times along the road up here. No one knows him. No one can figure him. I think I can. Just a stray wandering through, probably chased out of some town and hunting cover. I'm surprised you'd let him hang around."

"You might be surprised at a lot of things," said father, beginning to bite off his words. "Now give it to me straight on the price."

"It's what I said. A hundred and ten. Heck, I'll be out money on the deal anyway, so I'll shave it to a hundred if that'll make you feel any better." Ledyard hesitated, watching father. "Maybe he did see something in

Cheyenne. But he's mixed up. Must have been one of those little makes—flimsy and barely half the size. That might match his price."

Father did not say anything. He was looking at Ledyard in a steady, unwavering way. He had not even glanced at Shane. You might have believed he had not even heard what Shane had said. But his lips were folding in to a tight line like he was thinking what was not pleasant to think. Ledyard waited and father did not say anything and the climbing anger in Ledyard broke free.

"Starrett! Are you going to stand there and let that—that tramp nobody knows about call me a liar? Are you going to take his word over mine? Look at him! Look at his clothes! He's just a cheap, tinhorn—"

Ledyard stopped, choking on whatever it was he had meant to say. He fell back a step with a sudden fear showing in his face. I knew why even as I turned my head to see Shane. That same chill I had felt the day before, intangible and terrifying, was in the air again. Shane was no longer leaning against the porch post. He was standing erect, his hands clenched at his sides, his eyes boring at Ledyard, his whole body alert and alive in the leaping instant.

You felt without knowing how that each teetering second could bring a burst of indescribable deadliness. Then the tension passed, fading in the empty silence. Shane's eyes lost their sharp focus on Ledyard, and it seemed to me that reflected in them was some pain deep within him.

Father had pivoted so that he could see the two of them in the one sweep. He swung back to Ledyard alone.

"Yes, Ledyard, I'm taking his word. He's my guest. He's here at my invitation. But that's not the reason." Father straightened a little and his head went up and he gazed into the distance beyond the river. "I can figure men for myself. I'll take his word on anything he wants to say any day of God's whole year."

Father's head came down, and his voice was flat and final. "Sixty is the price. Add ten for a fair profit, even though you probably got it wholesale. Another ten for hauling it here. That tallies to eighty. Take that or leave that. Whatever you do, snap to it and get off my land."

Ledyard stared down at his hands, rubbing them together as if he were cold. "Where's your money?" he said.

Father went into the house, into the bedroom where he kept our money in a little leather bag on the closet shelf. He came back with the crumpled bills. All this while Shane stood there, not moving, his face hard, his eyes following father with a strange wildness in them that I could not understand.

Ledyard helped father heave the cultivator to the ground, then jumped to the wagon seat and drove off like he was glad to get away from our place. Father and I turned from watching him into the road. We looked around for Shane and he was not in sight. Father shook his head in wonderment. "Now where do you suppose—" he was saying, when we saw Shane coming out of the barn.

He was carrying an axe, the one father used for heavy kindling. He went directly around the corner of the building. We stared after him and we were still staring when we heard it, the clear ringing sound of steel biting into wood.

I never could have explained what that sound did to me. It struck through me as no single sound had ever done before. With it ran a warmth that erased at once and forever the feeling of sudden chill terror that our visitor had evoked in me. There were sharp hidden hardnesses in him. But these were not for us. He was dangerous as mother had said. But not to us as father too had said. And he was no longer a stranger. He was a man like father in whom a boy could believe in, the simple knowing that what was beyond comprehension was still clean and solid and right.

I looked up at father to try to see what he was thinking, but he was starting toward the barn with strides so long that I had to run to stay close behind him. We went around the far corner, and there was Shane squared away at the biggest uncut root of that big old stump. He was swinging the axe in steady rhythm. He was chewing into that root with bites almost as deep as father could drive.

Father halted, legs wide, hands on hips. "Now lookahere," he began, "there's no call for you—"

Shane broke his rhythm just long enough to level a straight look at us. "A man has to pay his debts," he said, and was again swinging the axe. He was really slicing into that root.

He seemed so desperate in his determination that I had to speak. "You don't owe us anything," I said. "Lots of times we have folks in for meals and—"

Father's hand was on my shoulder. "No, Bob. He doesn't mean meals." Father was smiling, but he was having to blink several times together, and I would have sworn that his eyes were misty. He stood in silence now, not moving, watching Shane.

It was something worth seeing. When father worked on that old stump, that was worth seeing too. He could handle an axe mighty well, and what impressed you was the strength and will of him making it behave and fight for him against the tough old wood. This was different. What impressed you as Shane found what he was up against and settled to it was the easy way the power in him poured smoothly into each stroke. The man and the axe seemed to be partners in the work. The blade would sink into the parallel grooves almost as if it knew itself what to do, and the chips from between would come out in firm and thin little blocks.

Father watched him and I watched the two of them and time passed over us, and then the axe sliced through the last strip and the root was cut. I was sure that Shane would stop. But he stepped right around to the next root and squared away again, and the blade sank in once more.

As it hit this second root, father winced like it had hit him. Then he stiffened and looked away from Shane and stared at the old stump. He began to fidget, throwing his weight from one foot to the other. In a short while more he was walking around inspecting the stump from different angles as if it was something he had never seen before. Finally he gave the nearest root a kick and hurried away. In a moment he was back with the other axe, the big double-bladed one that I could hardly heft from the ground.

He picked a root on the opposite side from Shane. He was not angry the way he usually was when he confronted one of those roots. There was a kind of serene and contented look on his face. He whirled that big axe as if it was only a kid's tool. The striking blade sank in maybe a whole half-inch. At the sound Shane straightened on his side. Their eyes met over the top of the stump and held and neither one of them said a word. Then they swung up their axes, and both of them said plenty to that old stump.

# 3

It was exciting at first watching them. They were hitting a fast pace, making the chips dance. I thought maybe each one would cut through a root now and stop. But Shane finished his and looked over at father working steadily away, and with a grim little smile pulling at his mouth he moved on to another root. A few moments later father smashed through his with a blow that sent the axe head into the ground beneath. He wrestled with the handle to yank the head loose, and he too tackled another root without even waiting to wipe off the dirt. This began to look like a long session, so I started to wander away. Just as I headed around the corner of the barn, mother came past the corner.

She was the freshest, prettiest thing I had ever seen. She had taken her hat and stripped the old ribbon from it and fixed it as Shane had told her. Some of the flowers by the house were in a small bouquet in front. She had cut slits in the brim and the sash from her best dress came around the crown and through the slits and was tied in a perky bow under her chin. She was stepping along daintily, mighty proud of herself.

She went up close to the stump. Those two choppers were so busy and intent that even if they were aware she was there, they did not really notice her.

"Well," she said, "aren't you going to look at me?"

They both stopped and they both stared at her.

"Have I got it right?" she asked Shane. "Is this the way they do it?"

"Yes, ma'am," he said. "About like that. Only their brims are wider." And he swung back to his root.

"Joe Starrett," said mother, "aren't you at least going to tell me whether you like me in this hat?"

"Lookahere, Marian," said father, "you know darn well that whether you have a hat on or whether you don't have a hat on, you're the nicest thing to me that ever happened on God's green earth. Now stop bothering us. Can't you see we're busy?" And he swung back to his root.

Mother's face was a deep pink. She pulled the bow out and the hat from her head. She held it swinging from her hand by the sash ends. Her hair was mussed, and she was really mad.

"Humph," she said. "This is a funny kind of resting you're doing today."

Father set the axe head on the ground and leaned on the handle. "Maybe it seems funny to you, Marian. But this is the best resting I've had for about as long as I can remember."

"Humph," said mother again. "You'll have to quit your resting for a while anyhow and do what I suppose you'll call work. Dinner's hot on the stove and waiting to be served."

She flounced around and went straight back to the house. We all tagged her in and to an uncomfortable meal. Mother always believed you should be decent and polite at mealtime, particularly with company. She was polite enough now. She was being special sweet, talking enough for the whole table of us without once saying a word about her hat lying where she had thrown it on the chair by the stove. The trouble was that she was too polite. She was trying too hard to be sweet.

As far as you could tell, though, the two men were not worried by her at all. They listened absently to her talk, chiming in when she asked them direct questions, but otherwise keeping quiet. Their minds were on that old stump and whatever it was that old stump had come to mean to them, and they were in a hurry to get at it again.

After they had gone out and I had been helping mother with the dishes awhile, she began humming low under her breath and I knew she was not mad any more. She was too curious and puzzled to have room for anything else.

"What went on out there, Bob?" she asked me. "What got into those two?"

I did not rightly know. All I could do was try to tell her about Ledyard and how our visitor had called him on the cultivator. I must have used the wrong words, because, when I told her about Ledyard talking mean and the way Shane acted, she got all flushed and excited.

WOOD HAWK. *O. C. Seltzer.*
*Thomas Gilcrease Institute, Tulsa, Oklahoma.*

"What do you say, Bob? You were afraid of him? He frightened you? Your father would never let him do that."

"I wasn't frightened of him," I said, struggling to make her see the difference. "I was—well, I was just frightened. I was scared of whatever it was that might happen."

She reached out and rumpled my hair. "I think I understand," she said softly. "He's made me feel a little that way too." She went to the window and stared toward the barn. The steady rhythm of double blows, so together they sounded almost as one, was faint yet clear in the kitchen. "I hope Joe knows what he's doing," she murmured to herself. Then she turned to me. "Skip along out, Bob. I'll finish myself."

It was no fun watching them now. They had eased down to a slow, dogged pace. Father sent me once for the hone, so they could sharpen the blades, and again for a spade so he could clear the dirt away from the lowest roots, and I realized he might keep me running as long as I was handy. I slipped off by myself to see how mother's garden was doing after the rain and maybe add to the population in the box of worms I was collecting for when I would go fishing with the boys in town.

I took my time about it. I played pretty far afield. But no matter where I went, always I could hear that chopping in the distance. You could not help beginning to feel tired just to hear it, to think how they were working and staying at it.

Along the middle of the afternoon, I wandered into the barn. There was mother by the rear stall, up on a box peering through the little window above it. She hopped down as soon as she heard me and put a finger to her lips.

"I declare," she whispered. "In some ways those two aren't even as old as you are, Bob. Just the same—" She frowned at me in such a funny, confiding manner that I felt all warm inside. "Don't you dare tell them I said so. But there's something splendid in the battle they're giving that old monster." She went past me and toward the house with such a brisk air that I followed to see what she was going to do.

She whisked about the kitchen, and in almost no time at all she had a pan of biscuits in the oven. While they were baking, she took her hat and carefully sewed the old ribbon into its old place. "Humph," she said, more to herself than to me. "You'd think I'd learn. This isn't Dodge City. This isn't even a whistle stop. It's Joe Starrett's farm. It's where I'm proud to be."

Out came the biscuits. She piled as many as she could on a plate, popping one of the leftovers into her mouth and giving me the rest. She picked up the plate and marched with it out behind the barn. She stepped over the cut roots and set the plate on a fairly smooth spot on top of the stump. She looked at the two men, first one and then the other. "You're a pair of fools," she said. "But there's no law against me being a fool too." Without looking at either of them again, she marched away, her head high, back toward the house.

The two of them stared after her till she was out of sight. They turned to stare at the biscuits. Father gave a deep sigh, so deep it seemed to come all the way from his heavy work shoes. There was nothing sad or sorrowful about it. There was just something in him too big to be held tight in comfort. He let his axe fall to the ground. He leaned forward and separated the biscuits into two piles beside the plate, counting them even. One was left on the plate. He set this by itself on the stump. He took up his axe and reached it out and let it drop gently on the lone biscuit exactly in the middle. He rested the axe against the stump and took the two halves of the biscuit and put one on each pile.

He did not say a word to Shane. He pitched

into one pile and Shane pitched into the other, and the two of them faced each other over the last uncut roots, munching at those biscuits as if eating them was the most serious business they had ever done.

Father finished his pile and dabbled his fingers on the plate for the last crumbs. He straightened and stretched his arms high and wide. He seemed to stretch and stretch until he was a tremendous tower of strength reaching up into the late afternoon sun. He swooped suddenly to grab the plate and toss it to me. Still in the same movement he seized the axe and swung it in a great arc into the root he was working on. Quick as he was, Shane was right with him, and together they were talking again to that old stump.

I took the plate in to mother. She was peeling apples in the kitchen, humming gaily to herself. "The woodbox, Bob," she said, and went on humming. I carried in stovelengths till the box would not hold any more. Then I slipped out before she might think of more chores.

I tried to keep myself busy down by the river, skipping flat stones across the current all muddy still from the rain. I was able to for a while. But that steady chopping had a peculiar fascination. It was always pulling me toward the barn. I simply could not grasp how they could stick at it hour after hour. It made no sense to me, why they should work so when routing out that old stump was not really so important. I was wavering in front of the barn, when I noticed that the chopping was different. Only one axe was working.

I hurried around back. Shane was still swinging, cutting into the last root. Father was using the spade, was digging under one side of the stump, bringing the dirt out between the cut roots. As I watched, he laid the spade aside and put his shoulder to the stump. He heaved against it. Sweat started to pour down his face. There was a little sucking sound and the stump moved ever so slightly.

That did it. Of a sudden I was so excited that I could hear my own blood pounding past my eardrums. I wanted to dash to that stump and push it and feel it move. Only I knew father would think I was in the way.

Shane finished the root and came to help him. Together they heaved against the stump. It angled up nearly a whole inch. You could begin to see an open space in the dirt where it was ripping loose. But as soon as they released the pressure, it fell back.

Again and again they heaved at it. Each time it would angle up a bit farther. Each time it would fall back. They had it up once about a foot and a half, and that was the limit. They could not get past it.

They stopped, breathing hard, mighty streaked now from the sweat rivulets down their faces. Father peered underneath as best he could. "Must be a taproot," he said. That was the one time either of them had spoken to the other, as far as I knew, the whole afternoon through. Father did not say anything more. And Shane said nothing. He just picked up his axe and looked at father and waited.

Father began to shake his head. There was some unspoken thought between them that bothered him. He looked down at his own big hands, and slowly the fingers curled until they were clenched into big fists. Then his head stopped shaking and he stood taller and he drew a deep breath. He turned and backed in between two cut root ends, pressing against the stump. He pushed his feet into the ground for firm footholds. He bent his knees and slid his shoulders down the stump and wrapped his big hands around the root ends. Slowly he began to straighten. Slowly that huge old stump began to rise. Up it came, inch by inch, until the side was all the way up to the limit they had reached before.

Shane stooped to peer under. He poked his axe into the opening and I heard it strike wood. But the only way he could get in position to swing the axe into the opening was to drop on his right knee and extend his left leg and thigh into the opening and lean his weight on them. Then he could bring the axe sweeping in at a low angle close to the ground.

He flashed one quick glance at father beside and behind him, eyes closed, muscles locked in that great sustained effort, and he dropped into position with the whole terrible weight of the stump poised above nearly half of his body and sent the axe sweeping under in swift, powerful strokes.

Suddenly father seemed to slip. Only he had not slipped. He had straightened even further. The stump had leaped up a few more inches. Shane jumped out and up and tossed his axe aside. He grabbed one of the root ends and helped father ease the stump down. They both were blowing like they had run a long way. But they would not stay more than a minute before they were heaving again at the stump. It came up more easily now, and the dirt was tearing loose all around it.

I ran to the house as fast as I could. I dashed into the kitchen and took hold of mother's hand. "Hurry!" I yelled. "You've got to come!" She did not seem to want to come at first and I pulled her. "You've got to see it! They're getting it out!" Then she was as excited as I was and was running right with me.

They had the stump way up at a high angle. They were down in the hole, one on each side of it, pushing up and forward with hands flat on the under part reared before them higher than their heads. You would have thought the stump was ready to topple over clear of its ancient foundation. But there it stuck. They could not quite push it the final inches.

Mother watched them battling with it.

"Joe," she called, "why don't you use some sense? Hitch up the team. Horses will have it out in no time at all."

Father braced himself to hold the stump still. He turned his head to look at her. "Horses!" he shouted. All the pent silence of the two of them that long afternoon through was being shattered in the one wonderful shout. "Horses! Great jumping Jehoshaphat! No! We started this with manpower and, by Godfrey, we'll finish it with manpower!"

He turned his head to face the stump once more and dropped it lower between his humped shoulders. Shane, opposite him, stiffened, and together they pushed in a fresh assault. The stump quivered and swayed a little—and hung fixed at its crazy high angle.

Father grunted in exasperation. You could see the strength building up in his legs and broad shoulders and big corded arms. His side of the upturned stump rocked forward and Shane's side moved back and the whole stump trembled like it would twist down and into the hole on them at a grotesque new angle.

I wanted to shout a warning. But I could not speak, for Shane had thrown his head in a quick sideways gesture to fling his hair from falling over his face, and I had caught a glimpse of his eyes. They were aflame with a concentrated cold fire. Not another separate discernible movement did he make. It was all of him, the whole man, pulsing in the one incredible surge of power. You could fairly feel the fierce energy suddenly burning in him, pouring through him in the single coordinated drive. His side of the stump rocked forward even with father's, and the whole mass of the stump tore loose from the last hold and toppled away to sprawl in ungainly defeat beyond them.

Father climbed slowly out of the hole. He walked to the stump and placed a hand on the rounded bole and patted it like it was an old friend and he was perhaps a little sorry for it. Shane was with him, across from him, laying a hand gently on the old hard wood. They both looked up, and their eyes met and held as they had so long ago in the morning hours.

The silence should have been complete. It was not, because someone was shouting, a high-pitched, wordless shout. I realized that the voice was mine, and I closed my mouth. The silence was clean and wholesome, and this was one of the things you could never forget, whatever time might do to you in the furrowing of the years, an old stump on its side with root ends making a strange pattern against the glow of the sun sinking behind the far mountains, and two men looking over it into each other's eyes.

I thought they should join the hands so close on the bole of the stump. I thought they should at least say something to each other. They stood quiet and motionless. At last father turned and came toward mother. He was so tired that the weariness showed in his walk. But there was no weariness in his voice. "Marian," he said, "I'm rested now. I don't believe any man since the world began was ever more rested."

Shane too was coming toward us. He too spoke only to mother. "Ma'am, I've learned something today. Being a farmer has more to it than I ever thought. Now I'm about ready for some of that pie."

Mother had been watching them in a wide-eyed wonder. At his last words she let out a positive wail. "Oh-h-h—you—you—men! You made me forget about it! It's probably all burned!" And she was running for the house so fast she was tripping over her skirt.

The pie was burned all right. We could smell it when we were in front of the house and the men were scrubbing themselves at the pump-trough. Mother had the door open to let the kitchen air out. The noises from inside sounded as if she might be throwing things around. Kettles were banging and dishes were clattering. When we went in, we saw why. She had the table set and was putting supper on it and she was grabbing the things from their places and putting them down on the table with solid thumps. She would not look at one of us.

We sat down and waited for her to join us. She put her back to us and stood by the low shelf near the stove, staring at her big pie-tin and the burned stuff in it. Finally father spoke kind of sharply. "Lookahere, Marian. Aren't you ever going to sit down?"

She whirled and glared at him. I thought maybe she had been crying. But there were no tears on her face. It was dry and pinched-looking and there was no color in it. Her voice was sharp like father's. "I was planning to have a deep-dish apple pie. Well, I will. None of your silly man foolishness is going to stop me."

She swept up the big tin and went out the door with it. We heard her on the steps, and a few seconds later the rattle of the cover of the garbage pail. We heard her on the steps again. She came in and went to the side bench where the dishpan was and began to scrub the pie tin. The way she acted, we might not have been in the room.

Father's face was getting red. He picked up his fork to begin eating and let it drop with a little clatter. He squirmed on his chair and kept taking quick side looks at her. She finished scrubbing the tin and went to the apple barrel and filled her wooden bowl with fat round ones. She sat by the stove and started peeling them. Father fished in a pocket and pulled out his old jackknife. He moved over to her, stepping softly. He reached out for an apple to help her.

She did not look up. But her voice caught him like she had flicked him with a whip.

"Joe Starrett, don't you dare touch a one of these apples."

He was sheepish as he returned to his chair. Then he was downright mad. He grabbed his knife and fork and dug into the food on his plate, taking big bites and chewing vigorously. There was nothing for our visitor and me to do but follow his example. Maybe it was a good supper. I could not tell. The food was only something to put in your mouth. And when we finished, there was nothing to do but wait because mother was sitting by the stove, arms folded, staring at the wall, waiting herself for her pie to bake.

We three watched her in a quiet so tight that it hurt. We could not help it. We would try to look away and always our eyes would turn back to her. She did not appear to notice us. You might have said she had forgotten we were there.

She had not forgotten because as soon as she sensed that the pie was done, she lifted it out, cut four wide pieces, and put them on plates. The first two she set in front of the two men. The third one she set down for me. The last one she laid at her own place and she sat down in her own chair at the table. Her voice was still sharp.

"I'm sorry to keep you men waiting so long. Your pie is ready now."

Father inspected his portion like he was afraid of it. He needed to make a real effort to take his fork and lift a piece. He chewed on it and swallowed and he flipped his eyes sidewise at mother and back again quickly to look across the table at Shane. "That's prime pie," he said.

Shane raised a piece on his fork. He considered it closely. He put it in his mouth and chewed on it gravely. "Yes," he said. The quizzical expression on his face was so plain you could not possibly miss it. "Yes. That's the best bit of stump I ever tasted."

What could a silly remark like that mean? I had no time to wonder, for father and mother were acting so queer. They both stared at Shane and their mouths were sagging open. Then father snapped his shut, and he chuckled and chuckled till he was swaying in his chair.

"By Godfrey, Marian, he's right. You've done it, too."

Mother stared from one to the other of them. Her pinched look faded and her cheeks were flushed and her eyes were soft and warm as they should be, and she was laughing so that the tears came. And all of us were pitching into that pie, and the one thing wrong in the whole world was that there was not enough of it.

# 4

The sun was already well up the sky when I awakened the next morning. I had been a long time getting to sleep because my mind was full of the day's excitement and shifting moods. I could not straighten out in my mind the way the grown folks had behaved, the way things that did not really matter so much had become so important to them.

I had lain in my bed thinking of our visitor out in the bunk in the barn. It scarce seemed possible that he was the same man I had first seen, stern and chilling in his dark solitude, riding up our road. Something in father, something not of words or of actions but of the essential substance of the human spirit, had reached out and spoken to him, and he had replied to it and had unlocked a part of himself to us. He was far off and unapproachable at times, even when he was right there with you. Yet somehow he was closer, too, than my uncle, mother's brother, had been when he visited us the summer before.

I had been thinking, too, of the effect he had on father and mother. They were more alive, more vibrant, like they wanted to show more what they were, when they were with him. I could appreciate that because I felt the same way myself. But it puzzled me that a man so deep and vital in his own being, so ready to respond to father, should be riding a lone trail out of a closed and guarded past.

I realized with a jolt how late it was. The door to my little room was closed. Mother must have closed it so I could sleep undisturbed. I was frantic that the others might have finished breakfast and that our visitor was gone and I had missed him. I pulled on my clothes, not even bothering with buttons, and ran to the door.

They were still at the table. Father was fussing with his pipe. Mother and Shane were working on a last round of coffee. All three of them were subdued and quiet. They stared at me as I burst out of my room.

"My heavens," said mother. "You came in here like something was after you. What's the matter?"

"I just thought," I blurted out, nodding at our visitor, "that maybe he had ridden off and forgotten me."

Shane shook his head slightly, looking straight at me. "I wouldn't forget you, Bob." He pulled himself up a little in his chair. He turned to mother and his voice took on a bantering tone. "And I wouldn't forget your cooking, ma'am. If you begin having a special lot of people passing by at mealtimes, that'll be because a grateful man has been boasting of your flannel cakes all along the road."

"Now there's an idea," struck in father as if he was glad to find something safe to talk about. "We'll turn this place into a boarding house. Marian'll fill folks full of her meals, and I'll fill my pockets full of their money. That hits me as a mighty convenient arrangement."

Mother sniffed at him. But she was pleased at their talk, and she was smiling as they kept on playing with the idea while she stirred me up my breakfast. She came right back at them, threatening to take father at his word and make him spend all his time peeling potatoes and washing dishes. They were enjoying themselves even though I could feel a bit of constraint behind the easy joshing. It was remarkable, too, how natural it was to have this Shane sitting there and joining in almost like he was a member of the family. There was none of the awkwardness some visitors always brought with them. You did feel you ought to be on your good behavior with him, a mite extra careful about your manners and your speech. But not stiffly so. Just quiet and friendly about it.

He stood up at last and I knew he was going to ride away from us, and I wanted desperately to stop him. Father did it for me.

"You certainly are a man for being in a hurry. Sit down, Shane. I've a question to ask you."

Father was suddenly very serious. Shane, standing there, was as suddenly withdrawn into a distant alertness. But he dropped back into his chair.

Father looked directly at him. "Are you running away from anything?"

Shane stared at the plate in front of him for a long moment. It seemed to me that a shade of sadness passed over him. Then he raised his eyes and looked directly at father.

"No. I'm not running away from anything. Not in the way you mean."

"Good." Father stooped forward and stabbed at the table with a forefinger for emphasis. "Look, Shane. I'm not a rancher. Now you've seen my place, you know that. I'm a farmer. Something of a stockman, maybe. But really a farmer. That's what I decided to be when I quit punching cattle for another man's money. That's what I want to be and I'm proud of it. I've made a fair start. This outfit isn't as big as I hope to have it some day. But there's more work here already than one man can handle if it's to be done right. The young fellow I had ran out on me after he tangled with a couple of Fletcher's boys in town one day." Father was talking fast, and he paused to draw breath.

Shane had been watching him intently. He moved his head to look out the window over the valley to the mountains marching along the horizon. "It's always the same," he murmured. He was sort of talking to himself. "The old ways die hard." He looked at mother and then at me, and as his eyes came back to father he seemed to have decided something that had been troubling him. "So Fletcher's crowding you," he said gently.

Father snorted. "I don't crowd easy. But I've got a job to do here, and it's too big for one man, even for me. And none of the strays that drift up this way are worth a darn."

"Yes?" Shane said. His eyes were crinkling again, and he was one of us again and waiting.

"Will you stick here awhile and help me get things in shape for the winter?"

Shane rose to his feet. He loomed up taller across the table than I had thought him. "I never figured to be a farmer, Starrett. I would have laughed at the notion a few days ago. All the same, you've hired yourself a hand." He and father were looking at each other in a way that showed they were saying things words could never cover. Shane snapped it by swinging toward mother. "And I'll rate your cooking, ma'am, wages enough."

Father slapped his hands on his knees. "You'll get good wages and you'll earn 'em. First off, now, why don't you drop into town and get some work clothes. Try Sam Grafton's store. Tell him to put it on my bill."

Shane was already at the door. "I'll buy my own," he said, and was gone.

Father was so pleased he could not sit still. He jumped up and whirled mother around. "Marian, the sun's shining mighty bright at last. We've got ourselves a man."

"But, Joe, are you sure what you're doing? What kind of work can a man like that do? Oh, I know he stood right up to you with that stump. But that was something special. He's been used to good living and plenty of money. You can tell that. He said himself he doesn't know anything about farming."

"Neither did I when I started here. What a man knows isn't important. It's what he is that counts. I'll bet you that one was a cow-puncher when he was younger and a top-hand too. Anything he does will be done right. You watch. In a week he'll be making even me hump or he'll be bossing the place."

"Perhaps."

"No perhapsing about it. Did you notice how he took it when I told him about Fletcher's boys and young Morley? That's what fetched him. He knows I'm in a spot, and he's not the man to leave me there. Nobody'll push him around or scare him away. He's my kind of a man."

"Why, Joe Starrett. He isn't like you at all. He's smaller and he looks different and his clothes are different and he talks different. I know he's lived different."

"Huh?" Father was surprised. "I wasn't talking about things like that."

Shane came back with a pair of dungaree pants, a flannel shirt, stout work shoes, and a good, serviceable Stetson. He disappeared into the barn and emerged a few moments later in his new clothes, leading his horse unsaddled. At the pasture gate he slipped off the halter, turned the horse in with a hearty slap, and tossed the halter to me.

"Take care of a horse, Bob, and it will take care of you. This one now has brought me better than a thousand miles in the last few weeks." And he was striding away to join father, who was ditching the field out past the growing corn where the ground was rich but marshy and would not be worth much till it was properly drained. I watched him swinging through the rows of young corn,

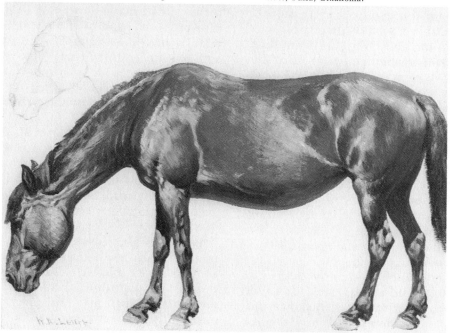

no longer a dark stranger but part of the place, a farmer like father and me.

Only he was not a farmer and never really could be. It was not three days before you saw that he could stay right beside father in any kind of work. Show him what needed to be done and he could do it, and like as not would figure out a better way of getting it done. He never shirked the meanest task. He was ever ready to take the hard end of any chore. Yet you always felt in some indefinable fashion that he was a man apart.

There were times when he would stop and look off at the mountains and then down at himself and any tool he happened to have in his hands as if in wry amusement at what he was doing. You had no impression that he thought himself too good for the work or did not like it. He was just different. He was shaped in some firm forging of past circumstance for other things.

For all his slim build he was plenty rugged. His slenderness could fool you at first. But when you saw him close in action, you saw that he was solid, compact, that there was no waste weight on his frame, just as there was no waste effort in his smooth, flowing motion. What he lacked alongside father in size and strength, he made up in quickness of movement, in instinctive coordination of mind and muscle, and in that sudden fierce energy that had burned in him when the old stump tried to topple back on him. Mostly this last slept in him, not needed while he went easily through the day's routine. But when a call came, it could flame forward with a driving intensity that never failed to frighten me.

I would be frightened, as I had tried to explain to mother, not at Shane himself, but at the suggestion it always gave me of things in the human equation beyond my comprehension. At such times there would be a concentration in him, a singleness of dedication to the instant need, that seemed to me at once wonderful and disturbing. And then he would be again the quiet, steady man who shared with father my boy's allegiance.

I was beginning to feel my oats about then, proud of myself for being able to lick Ollie Johnson at the next place down the road. Fighting, boy style, was much in my mind.

Once, when father and I were alone, I asked him, "Could you beat Shane? In a fight, I mean."

"Son, that's a tough question. If I had to, I might do it. But, by Godfrey, I'd hate to try it. Some men just plain have dynamite inside them, and he's one. I'll tell you, though, I've never met a man I'd rather have more on my side in any kind of trouble."

I could understand that and it satisfied me. But there were things about Shane I could not understand. When he came in to the first meal after he agreed to stay on with us, he went to the chair that had always been father's and stood beside it waiting for the rest of us to take the other places. Mother was surprised and somewhat annoyed. She started to say something. Father quieted her with a warning glance. He walked to the chair across from Shane and sat down like this was the right and natural spot for him, and afterwards he and Shane always used these same places.

I could not see any reason for the shift until the first time one of our homestead neighbors knocked on the door while we were eating and came straight on in as most of them usually did. Then I suddenly realized that Shane was sitting opposite the door where he could directly confront anyone coming through it. I could see that was the way he wanted it to be. But I could not understand why he wanted it that way.

In the evenings after supper when he was talking lazily with us, he would never sit by a window. Out on the porch he would always face the road. He liked to have a wall behind him and not just to lean against. No matter where he was, away from the table,

before sitting down he would swing his chair into position, back to the nearest wall, not making any show, simply putting it there and bending into it in one easy motion. He did not even seem to be aware that this was unusual. It was part of his fixed alertness. He always wanted to know everything happening around him.

This alertness could be noted, too, in the watch he kept, without appearing to make any special effort, on every approach to our place. He knew first when anyone was moving along the road, and he would stop whatever he was doing to study carefully any passing rider.

We often had company in the evenings, for the other homesteaders regarded father as their leader and would drop in to discuss their affairs with him. They were interesting men in their own fashions, a various assortment. But Shane was not anxious to meet people. He would share little in their talk. With us he spoke freely enough. We were, in some subtle way, his folks. Though we had taken him in, you had the feeling that he had adopted us. But with others he was reserved; courteous and softspoken, yet withdrawn beyond a line of his own making.

These things puzzled me and not me alone. The people in town and those who rode or drove in pretty regularly were all curious about him. It was a wonder how quickly everyone in the valley, and even on the ranches out in the open country, knew that he was working with father.

They were not sure they liked having him in their neighborhood. Ledyard had told some tall tale about what happened at our place that made them stare sharply at Shane whenever they had a chance. But they must have had their own measure of Ledyard, for they did not take his story too straight. They just could not really make up their minds about Shane, and it seemed to worry them.

More than once, when I was with Ollie

Johnson on the way to our favorite fishing hole the other side of town, I heard men arguing about him in front of Mr. Grafton's store. "He's like one of these here slow-burning fuses," I heard an old mule-skinner say one day. "Quiet and no sputtering. So quiet you forget it's burning. Then it sets off one heck of a blow-off of trouble when it touches powder. That's him. And there's been trouble brewing in this valley for a long spell now. Maybe it'll be good when it comes. Maybe it'll be bad. You just can't tell." And that puzzled me too.

What puzzled me most, though, was something it took me nearly two weeks to appreciate. And yet it was the most striking thing of all. Shane carried no gun.

In those days guns were as familiar all through the Territory as boots and saddles. They were not used much in the valley except for occasional hunting. But they were always in evidence. Most men did not feel fully dressed without one.

We homesteaders went in mostly for rifles and shotguns when we had any shooting to do. A pistol slapping on the hip was a nuisance for a farmer. Still, every man had his cartridge belt and holstered Colt to be worn when he was not working or loafing around the house. Father buckled his on whenever he rode off on any trip, even just into town, as much out of habit, I guess, as anything else.

But this Shane never carried a gun. And that was a peculiar thing because he had a gun.

I saw it once. I saw it when I was alone in the barn one day and I spotted his saddle roll lying on his bunk. Usually he kept it carefully put away underneath. He must have forgotten it this time, for it was there in the open by the pillow. I reached to sort of feel it—and I felt the gun inside. No one was near, so I unfastened the straps and un-rolled the blankets. There it was, the most beautiful-looking weapon I ever saw. Beautiful and deadly looking.

The holster and filled cartridge belt were of the same soft black leather as the boots tucked under the bunk, tooled in the same intricate design. I knew enough to know that the gun was a single-action Colt, the same model as the Regular Army issue that was the favorite of all men in those days and that oldtimers used to say was the finest pistol ever made.

This was the same model. But this was no Army gun. It was black, almost blue black, with the darkness not in any enamel but in the metal itself. The grip was clear on the outer curve, shaped to the fingers on the inner curve, and two ivory plates were set into it with exquisite skill, one on each side.

The smooth invitation of it tempted your grasp. I took hold and pulled the gun out of the holster. It came so easily that I could hardly believe it was there in my hand. Heavy like father's, it was somehow much easier to handle. You held it up to aiming level and it seemed to balance itself into your hand.

It was clean and polished and oiled. The empty cylinder, when I released the catch and flicked it, spun swiftly and noiselessly. I was surprised to see that the front sight was gone, the barrel smooth right down to the end, and that the hammer had been filed to a sharp point.

Why should a man do that to a gun? Why should a man with a gun like that refuse to wear it and show it off? And then, staring at that dark and deadly efficiency, I was again suddenly chilled, and I quickly put everything back exactly as before and hurried out into the sun.

The first chance I tried to tell father about it. "Father," I said, all excited, "do you know what Shane has rolled up in his blankets?"

"Probably a gun."

"But—but how did you know? Have you seen it?"

"No. That's what he would have."

I was all mixed up. "Well, why doesn't he ever carry it? Do you suppose maybe it's because he doesn't know how to use it very well?"

Father chuckled like I had made a joke. "Son, I wouldn't be surprised if he could take that gun and shoot the buttons off your shirt with you awearing it and all you'd feel would be a breeze."

"Gosh agorry! Why does he keep it hidden in the barn then?"

"I don't know. Not exactly."

"Why don't you ask him?"

Father looked straight at me, very serious. "That's one question I'll never ask him. And don't you ever say anything to him about it. There are some things you don't ask a man. Not if you respect him. He's entitled to stake his claim to what he considers private to himself alone. But you can take my word for it, Bob, that when a man like Shane doesn't want to tote a gun you can bet your shirt, buttons and all, he's got a mighty good reason."

That was that. I was still mixed up. But whenever father gave you his word on something, there was nothing more to be said. He never did that except when he knew he was right. I started to wander off.

"Bob."

"Yes, father."

"Listen to me, son. Don't get to liking Shane too much."

"Why not? Is there anything wrong with him?"

"No-o-o-o. There's nothing wrong about Shane. Nothing you could put that way. There's more right about him than most any man you're ever likely to meet. But—" Father was throwing around for what to say. "But he's fiddle-footed. Remember. He said so himself. He'll be moving on one of these days, and then you'll be all upset if you get to liking him too much."

That was not what father really meant. But that was what he wanted me to think. So I did not ask any more questions.

# 5

The weeks went rocking past, and soon it did not seem possible that there ever had been a time when Shane was not with us. He and father worked together more like partners than boss and hired man. The amount they could get through in a day was a marvel. The ditching father had reckoned would take him most of the summer was done in less than a month. The loft was finished and the first cutting of alfalfa stowed away.

We would have enough fodder to carry a few more young steers through the winter for fattening next summer, so father rode out of the valley and all the way to the ranch where he worked once and came back herding a half-dozen more. He was gone two days. He came back to find that Shane, while he was gone, had knocked out the end of the corral and posted a new section, making it half again as big.

"Now we can really get going next year," Shane said as father sat on his horse staring at the corral like he could not quite believe what he saw. "We ought to get enough hay off that new field to help us carry forty head."

"Oho!" said father. "So we can get going. And we ought to get enough hay." He was pleased as could be because he was scowling at Shane the way he did at me when he was tickled silly over something I had done and did not want to let on that he was. He jumped off his horse and hurried up to the house where mother was standing on the porch.

"Marian," he demanded right off, waving at the corral, "whose idea was that?"

"Well-l-l," she said, "Shane suggested it." Then she added slyly, "But I told him to go ahead."

"That's right." Shane had come up beside him. "She rode me like she had spurs to get it done by today. Kind of a present. It's your wedding anniversary."

"Well, I'll be darned," said father. "So it is." He stared foolishly at one and then the other of them. With Shane there watching, he hopped on the porch and gave mother a kiss. I was embarrassed for him and I turned away—and hopped about a foot myself.

"Hey! Those steers are running away!"

The grown folks had forgotten about them. All six were wandering up the road, straggling and separating. Shane, that soft-spoken man, let out a whoop you might have heard halfway to town and ran to father's horse, putting his hands on the saddle and vaulting into it. He fairly lifted the horse into a gallop in one leap, and that old cowpony of father's lit out after those steers like this was fun. By the time father reached the corral gate, Shane had the runaways in a compact bunch and padding back at a trot. He dropped them through the gateway neat as pie.

He was tall and straight in the saddle the few seconds it took father to close the gate. He and the horse were blowing a bit, and both of them were perky and proud.

"It's been ten years," he said, "since I did anything like that."

Father grinned at him. "Shane, if I didn't know better, I'd say you were a faker. There's still a lot of kid in you."

The first real smile I had seen yet flashed across Shane's face. "Maybe. Maybe there is at that."

I think that was the happiest summer of my life.

The only shadow over our valley, the recurrent trouble between Fletcher and us homesteaders, seemed to have faded away. Fletcher himself was gone most of those months. He had gone to Fort Bennett in Dakota and even on East to Washington, so we heard, trying to get a contract to supply beef to the Indian agent at Standing Rock, the big Sioux reservation over beyond the Black Hills. Except for his foreman, Morgan, and several surly older men, his hands were young, easy-going cowboys who made a lot of noise in town once in a while but rarely did any harm and even then only in high spirits. We liked them—when Fletcher was not there driving them into harassing us in constant shrewd ways. Now, with him away, they kept to the other side of the river and did not bother us. Sometimes, riding in sight on the other bank, they might even wave to us in their rollicking fashion.

Until Shane came, they had been my heroes. Father, of course, was special all to himself. There could never be anyone quite to match him. I wanted to be like him, just as he was. But first I wanted, as he had done, to ride the range, to have my own string of ponies and take part in an all-brand round-up and in a big cattle drive and dash into strange towns with just such a rollicking crew and with a season's pay jingling in my pockets.

Now I was not so sure. I wanted more and more to be like Shane, like the man I imagined he was in the past, fenced off so securely. I had to imagine most of it. He would never speak of it, not in any way at all. Even his name remained mysterious. Just Shane. Nothing else. We never knew whether that was his first name or last name or, indeed, any name that came from his family. "Call me Shane," he said, and that was all he ever said. But I conjured up all manner of adventures for him, not tied to any particular time or place, seeing him as a slim and dark and dashing figure, coolly passing through perils that would overcome a lesser man.

I would listen in what was closely akin to worship while my two men, father and Shane, argued long and amiably about the cattle business. They would wrangle over methods of feeding and bringing steers up to top weight. But they were agreed that controlled breeding was better than open range running and that improvement of stock was needed even if that meant spending big money on imported bulls. And they would speculate about the chances of a railroad spur ever reaching the valley, so you could ship direct without thinning good meat off your cattle driving them to market.

It was plain that Shane was beginning to enjoy living with us and working the place. Little by little the tension in him was fading out. He was still alert and watchful, instinct with that unfailing awareness of everything about him. I came to realize that this was inherent in him, not learned or acquired, simply a part of his natural being. But the sharp extra edge of conscious alertness, almost of expectancy of some unknown trouble always waiting, was wearing away.

Yet why was he sometimes so strange and stricken in his own secret bitterness? Like the time I was playing with a gun Mr. Grafton gave me, an old frontier model Colt with a cracked barrel someone had turned in at the store.

I had rigged a holster out of a torn chunk of oilcloth and a belt of rope. I was stalking around near the barn, whirling every few steps to pick off a skulking Indian, when I saw Shane watching me from the barn door. I stopped short, thinking of that beautiful gun under his bunk and afraid he would make fun of me and my sorry old broken pistol. Instead he looked gravely at me.

"How many you knocked over so far, Bob?"

Could I ever repay the man? My gun was a shining new weapon, my hand steady as a rock as I drew a bead on another one.

"That makes seven."

"Indians or timber wolves?"

"Indians. Big ones."

"Better leave a few for the other scouts," he said gently. "It wouldn't do to make them jealous. And look here, Bob. You're not doing that quite right."

He sat down on an upturned crate and beckoned me over. "Your holster's too low. Don't let it drag full arm's length. Have it just below the hip, so the grip is about halfway between your wrist and elbow when the arm's hanging limp. You can take the gun then as your hand's coming up and there's still room to clear the holster without having to lift the gun too high."

"Gosh agorry! Is that the way the real gunfighters do?"

A queer light flickered in his eyes and was gone. "No. Not all of them. Most have their own tricks. One likes a shoulder holster; another packs his gun in his pants belt. Some carry two guns, but that's a show-off stunt and a waste of weight. One's enough, if you know how to use it. I've even seen a man have a tight holster with an open end and fastened on a little swivel to the belt. He didn't have to pull the gun then. Just swung up the barrel and blazed away from the hip. That's mighty fast for close work and a big target. But it's not certain past ten or fifteen paces and no good at all for putting your shot right where you want it. The way I'm telling you is as good as any and better than most. And another thing—"

He reached and took the gun. Suddenly, as for the first time, I was aware of his hands. They were broad and strong, but not heavy and fleshy like father's. The fingers were long and square on the ends. It was funny how, touching the gun, the hands seemed to have an intelligence all their own, a sure movement that needed no guidance of thought.

His right hand closed around the grip and you knew at once it was doing what it had been created for. He hefted the old gun, letting it lie loosely in the hand. Then the fingers tightened and the thumb toyed with the hammer, testing the play of it.

While I gaped at him, he tossed it swiftly in the air and caught it in his left hand and in the instant of catching, it nestled snugly into this hand too. He tossed it again, high this time and spinning end over end, and as it came down, his right hand flicked forward and took it. The forefinger slipped through the trigger guard and the gun spun, coming up into firing position in the one unbroken motion. With him that old pistol seemed alive, not an inanimate and rusting metal object, but an extension of the man himself.

"If it's speed you're after, Bob, don't split the move into parts. Don't pull, cock, aim, and fire. Slip back the hammer as you bring the gun up and squeeze the trigger the second it's up level."

"How do you aim it, then? How do you get a sight on it?"

"No need to. Learn to hold it so the barrel's right in line with the fingers if they were out straight. You won't have to waste time bringing it high to take a sight. Just point it, low and quick and easy, like pointing a finger."

Like pointing a finger. As the words came, he was doing it. The old gun was bearing on some target over by the corral and the hammer was clicking at the empty cylinder. Then the hand around the gun whitened and the fingers slowly opened and the gun fell to the ground. The hand sank to his side, stiff and awkward. He raised his head and the mouth was a bitter gash in his face. His eyes were fastened on the mountains climbing in the distance.

"Shane! Shane! What's the matter?"

He did not hear me. He was back somewhere along the dark trail of the past.

He took a deep breath, and I could see the effort run through him as he dragged himself into the present and a realization of a boy staring at him. He beckoned to me to pick up the gun. When I did he leaned forward and spoke earnestly.

"Listen, Bob. A gun is just a tool. No better and no worse than any other tool, a shovel—or an axe or a saddle or a stove or anything. Think of it always that way. A gun is as good—and as bad—as the man who carries it. Remember that."

He stood up and strode off into the fields, and I knew he wanted to be alone. I remembered what he said all right, tucked away unforgettably in my mind. But in those days I remembered more the way he handled the gun and the advice he gave me about using it. I would practice with it and think of the time when I could have one that would really shoot.

And then the summer was over. School began again and the days were growing shorter and the first cutting edge of cold was creeping down from the mountains.

**Chapters 1–5**

**Getting at Meaning**

1. Why does Shane's appearance give Bob the impression of "a coiled spring, of a trap set"?

2. According to Joe Starrett, how are Luke Fletcher's ranching methods wasteful?

3. Joe Starrett agrees that there is something dangerous about Shane. Why then does he say, "I don't think you ever had a safer man in your house"?

4. Why does Marian Starrett assume that Shane is the kind of man who would notice women's fashions?

5. What debt is Shane paying when he attacks the old stump with an axe?

6. How does working on the stump together affect the relationship between Joe Starrett and Shane? When the stump has been defeated, why does Joe Starrett say, "I don't believe any man since the world began was ever more rested"?

7. Why does Shane describe Marian's pie as "the best bit of stump I ever tasted"?

8. Shane comments, "The old ways die hard." What does this comment reveal about his understanding of the conflict between Fletcher and Starrett? How do Shane's appearance and behavior as a farmer further illustrate his comment?

9. How does Shane indicate that he is constantly alert? What is unusual about Shane's gun?

10. Why does Joe Starrett tell Bob, "Don't get to liking Shane too much"?

11. What does Shane teach Bob about handling a gun? Shane tells Bob, "A gun is as good—and as bad—as the man who carries it." How might this comment relate to Shane's stricken behavior?

## Developing Skills in Reading Literature

1. **Characterization.** What does the description of Shane's physical appearance reveal about his character? How do the reactions of Bob and of Joe and Marian Starrett to Shane further develop this character? What does Ledyard's reaction to Shane add to the development of character? How does Shane's reluctance to say much about himself and his past affect the reader's impression of him? Select two examples of Shane's actions, and explain what each reveals about his character.

2. **Narrator.** How old is Bob Starrett when the story takes place? How old do you suppose he is as he narrates the story? How does the fact that the story is essentially a childhood memory affect the presentation of Shane's character?

3. **Conflict.** This story has two major conflicts, one external, the other internal. Describe the conflict between Joe Starrett and the other farmers and Luke Fletcher. Is this conflict external or internal? What type of conflict does Shane appear to experience when he decides to work for Starrett? When he advises Bob about the use of a gun?

4. **Symbol.** As the story begins, what does the fork in the road symbolize for Shane? What does his choice reveal about him? Describing the old stump, Joe Starrett says, "It's tough. I can admire toughness. The right kind." What does the stump symbolize for both men? After they have pulled up the stump, why does each man touch it gently?

## Developing Vocabulary

1. **Understanding Dialect.** The Starretts assume that Shane is from Tennessee because he uses the expression "flannel cakes." This is only one of many examples of dialect in the novel. Each of the following sentences contains another example. Read each sentence and explain the meaning of the italicized word or phrase.

a. "Starrett, you're *poor shakes* as a liar."

b. "Look at his clothes! He's just a cheap, *tinhorn*—"

c. "This isn't Dodge City. This isn't even a *whistle stop*."

d. "They were enjoying themselves even though I feel a bit of constraint behind the easy *joshing*."

e. "But they must have had their own measure of Ledyard, for they did not take his story *too straight*."

## Developing Writing Skills

1. **Analyzing a Character.** In the first third of the novel, Shane's character remains mysterious. How does the writer enhance this mysterious quality? In one paragraph analyze how Shane's behavior contributes to his air of mystery.

2. **Telling the Same Story from a Different Point of View.** Bob cannot understand why his father and Shane put so much effort into conquering the stump. To him, the stump does not seem important. How might Joe Starrett's feelings on the subject be different from his son's? In one paragraph, describe the battle against the stump from Joe Starrett's point of view.

# 6

More than the summer was over. The season of friendship in our valley was fading with the sun's warmth. Fletcher was back and he had his contract. He was talking in town that he would need the whole range again. The homesteaders would have to go.

He was a reasonable man, he was saying in his smooth way, and he would pay a fair price for any improvements they had put in. But we knew what Luke Fletcher would call a fair price. And we had no intention of leaving. The land was ours by right of settlement, guaranteed by the government. Only we knew, too, how faraway the government was from our valley way up there in the Territory.

The nearest marshal was a good hundred miles away. We did not even have a sheriff in our town. There never had been any reason for one. When folks had any lawing to do, they would head for Sheridan, nearly a full day's ride away. Our town was small, not even organized as a town. It was growing, but it was still not much more than a roadside settlement.

The first people there were three or four miners who had come prospecting after the blow-up of the Big Horn Mining Association about twenty years before, and had found gold traces leading to a moderate vein in the jutting rocks that partially closed off the valley where it edged into the plain. You could not have called it a strike, for others that followed were soon disappointed. Those first few, however, had done fairly well and had brought in their families and a number of helpers.

Then a stage and freighting line had picked the site for a relay post. That meant a place where you could get drinks as well as horses, and before long the cowboys from the ranches out on the plain and Fletcher's spread in the valley were drifting in of an evening. With us homesteaders coming now, one or two more almost every season, the town was taking shape. Already there were several stores, a harness and blacksmith shop, and nearly a dozen houses. Just the year before, the men had put together a one-room schoolhouse.

Sam Grafton's place was the biggest. He had a general store with several rooms for living quarters back of it in one half of his rambling building, a saloon with a long bar and tables for cards, and the like in the other half. Upstairs he had some rooms he rented to stray drummers[3] or anyone else stranded overnight. He acted as our postmaster, an elderly man, a close bargainer but honest in all his dealings. Sometimes he served as a sort of magistrate in minor disputes. His wife was dead. His daughter Jane kept house for him and was our schoolteacher when school was in session.

Even if we had had a sheriff, he would have been Fletcher's man. Fletcher was the power in the valley in those days. We homesteaders had been around only a few years, and the other people still thought of us as there by his sufferance. He had been running cattle through the whole valley at the time the miners arrived, having bought or bulldozed out the few small ranchers there ahead of him. A series of bad years working up to the dry summer and terrible winter of '86 had cut his herds about the time the first of the homesteaders moved in, and he had not objected too much. But now there were seven of us in all and the number rising each year.

It was a certain thing, father used to say, that the town would grow and swing our way. Mr. Grafton knew that too, I guess, but he was a careful man who never let thoughts about the future interfere with present business. The others were the kind to veer with the prevailing wind. Fletcher

---

3. **drummers:** traveling salesmen.

was the big man in the valley, so they looked up to him and tolerated us. Led to it, they probably would have helped him run us out. With him out of the way, they would just as willingly accept us. And Fletcher was back, with a contract in his pocket, wanting his full range again.

There was a hurried counsel in our house soon as the news was around. Our neighbor toward town, Lew Johnson, who heard it in Grafton's store, spread the word and arrived first. He was followed by Henry Shipstead, who had the place next to him, the closest to town. These two had been the original homesteaders, staking out their hundred and eighties[4] two years before the drought and riding out Fletcher's annoyance until the cut in his herds gave him other worries.

They were solid, dependable men, old-line farmers who had come West from Iowa.

You could not say quite as much for the rest, straggling in at intervals. James Lewis and Ed Howells were two middle-aged cowhands who had grown dissatisfied and tagged father into the valley, coming pretty much on his example. Lacking his energy and drive, they had not done too well and could be easily discouraged.

Frank Torrey from farther up the valley was a nervous, fidgety man with a querulous wife and a string of dirty kids growing longer every year. He was always talking about pulling up stakes and heading for California. But he had a stubborn streak in him, and he was always saying, too, that he'd be darned

---

4. **hundred and eighties:** the 180 acres of homesteads.

if he'd make tracks just because some big-hatted rancher wanted him to.

Ernie Wright, who had the last stand up the valley butting out into the range still used by Fletcher, was probably the weakest of the lot. Not in any physical way. He was a husky, likable man, so dark-complected that there were rumors he was part Indian. He was always singing and telling tall stories. But he would be off hunting when he should be working, and he had a quick temper that would trap him into doing fool things without taking thought.

He was as serious as the rest of them that night. Mr. Grafton had said that this time Fletcher meant business. His contract called for all the beef he could drive in the next five years, and he was determined to push the chance to the limit.

"But what can he do?" asked Frank Torrey. "The land's ours as long as we live on it, and we get title in three years. Some of you fellows have already proved up."

"He won't really make trouble," chimed in James Lewis. "Fletcher's never been the shooting kind. He's a good talker, but talk can't hurt us." Several of the others nodded. Johnson and Shipstead did not seem to be so sure. Father had not said anything yet, and they all looked at him.

"Jim's right," he admitted. "Fletcher hasn't ever let his boys get careless thataway. Not yet anyhow. That ain't saying he wouldn't, if there wasn't any other way. There's a hard streak in him. But he won't get real tough for a while. I don't figure he'll start moving cattle in now till spring. My guess is he'll try putting pressure on us this fall and winter, see if he can wear us down. He'll probably start right here. He doesn't like any of us. But he doesn't like me most."

"That's true." Ed Howells was expressing the unspoken verdict that father was their leader. "How do you figure he'll go about it?"

"My guess on that," father said—drawling now and smiling a grim little smile like he knew he was holding a good hole card in a tight game—"my guess on that is that he'll begin by trying to convince Shane here that it isn't healthy to be working with me."

"You mean the way he—" began Ernie Wright.

"Yes." Father cut him short. "I mean the way he did with young Morley."

I was peeping around the door of my little room. I saw Shane sitting off to one side, listening quietly as he had been right along. He did not seem the least bit surprised. He did not seem the least bit interested in finding out what had happened to young Morley. I knew what had. I had seen Morley come back from town, bruised and a beaten man, and gather his things and curse father for hiring him and ride away without once looking back.

Yet Shane sat there quietly as if what had happened to Morley had nothing to do with him. He simply did not care what it was. And then I understood why. It was because he was not Morley. He was Shane.

Father was right. In some strange fashion the feeling was abroad that Shane was a marked man. Attention was on him as a sort of symbol. By taking him on, father had accepted in a way a challenge from the big ranch across the river. What had happened to Morley had been a warning, and father had deliberately answered it. The long unpleasantness was sharpened now after the summer lull. The issue in our valley was plain and would in time have to be pushed to a showdown. If Shane could be driven out, there would be a break in the homestead ranks, a defeat going beyond the loss of a man into the realm of prestige and morale. It could be the crack in the dam that weakens the whole structure and finally lets through the flood.

The people in town were more curious than ever, not now so much about Shane's past as about what he might do if Fletcher tried any move against him. They would stop me and ask me questions when I was hurrying to and from school. I knew that father would not want me to say anything, and I pretended that I did not know what they were talking about. But I used to watch Shane closely myself and wonder how all the slow-climbing tenseness in our valley could be so focused on one man and he seem to be so indifferent to it.

For of course he was aware of it. He never missed anything. Yet he went about his work as usual, smiling frequently now at me, bantering mother at mealtimes in his courteous manner, arguing amiably as before with father on plans for next year. The only thing that was different was that there appeared to be a lot of new activity across the river. It was surprising how often Fletcher's cowboys were finding jobs to do within view of our place.

Then one afternoon, when we were stowing away the second and last cutting of hay, one fork of the big tongs we were using to haul it up to the loft broke loose. "Have to get it welded in town," father said in disgust and began to hitch up the team.

Shane stared over the river where a cowboy was riding lazily back and forth by a bunch of cattle. "I'll take it in," he said.

Father looked at Shane and he looked across the way and he grinned. "All right. It's as good a time as any." He slapped down the final buckle and started for the house. "Just a minute and I'll be ready."

"Take it easy, Joe." Shane's voice was gentle, but it stopped father in his tracks. "I said I'll take it in."

Father whirled to face him. "Darn it all, man. Do you think I'd let you go alone? Suppose they—" He bit down on his own words. He wiped a hand slowly across his face, and he said what I had never heard him say to any man. "I'm sorry," he said. "I should have known better." He stood there silently watching as Shane gathered up the reins and jumped to the wagon seat.

I was afraid father would stop me, so I waited till Shane was driving out of the lane. I ducked behind the barn, around the end of the corral, and hopped into the wagon going past. As I did, I saw the cowboy across the river spin his horse and ride rapidly off in the direction of the ranch house.

Shane saw it, too, and it seemed to give him a grim amusement. He reached backwards and hauled me over the seat and sat me beside him.

"You Starretts like to mix into things." For a moment I thought he might send me back. Instead he grinned at me. "I'll buy you a jackknife when we hit town."

He did, a dandy big one with two blades and a corkscrew. After we left the tongs with the blacksmith and found the welding would take nearly an hour, I squatted on the steps on the long porch across the front of Grafton's building, busy whittling, while Shane stepped into the saloon side and ordered a drink. Will Atkey, Grafton's thin, sad-faced clerk and bartender, was behind the bar and several other men were loafing at one of the tables.

It was only a few moments before two cowboys came galloping down the road. They slowed to a walk about fifty yards off and with a show of nonchalance, ambled the rest of the way to Grafton's, dismounting and looping their reins over the rail in front. One of them I had seen often, a young fellow everyone called Chris, who had worked with Fletcher several years and was known for a happy manner and reckless courage. The other was new to me, a sallow, pinch-cheek man, not much older, who looked like he had crowded a lot of hard living into his years. He must have been one of the new hands Fletcher had been bringing into the valley since he got his contract.

They paid no attention to me. They stepped softly up on the porch and to the window of the saloon part of the building. As they peered through, Chris nodded and jerked his head toward the inside. The new man stiffened. He leaned closer for a better look. Abruptly he turned clear about and came right down past me and went over to his horse.

Chris was startled and hurried after him. They were both so intent they did not realize I was there. The new man was lifting the reins back over his horse's head when Chris caught his arm.

"What the heck?"

"I'm leaving."

"Huh? I don't get it."

"I'm leaving. Now. For good."

"Hey, listen. Do you know that guy?"

"I didn't say that. There ain't nobody can claim I said that. I'm leaving, that's all. You can tell Fletcher. This is a heck of a country up here anyhow."

Chris was getting mad. "I might have known," he said. "Scared, eh. Yellow."

Color rushed into the new man's sallow face. But he climbed on his horse and swung out from the rail. "You can call it that," he said flatly and started down the road, out of town, out of the valley.

Chris was standing still by the rail, shaking his head in wonderment. "Heck," he said to himself, "I'll brace him myself." He stalked up on the porch, into the saloon.

I dashed into the store side, over to the opening between the two big rooms. I crouched on a box just inside the store where I could hear everything and see most of the other room. It was long and fairly wide. The bar curved out from the opening and ran all the way along the inner wall to the back wall, which closed off a room Grafton used as an office. There was a row of windows on the far side, too high for anyone to look in from outside. A small stairway behind them led up to a sort of balcony across the back with doors opening into several little rooms.

Shane was leaning easily with one arm on the bar, his drink in his other hand, when Chris came to perhaps six feet away and called for a whiskey bottle and a glass. Chris pretended he did not notice Shane at first and bobbed his head in greeting to the men at the table. They were a pair of mule-skinners who made regular trips into the valley freighting in goods for Grafton and the other shops. I could have sworn that Shane, studying Chris in his effortless way, was somehow disappointed.

Chris waited until he had his whiskey and had gulped a stiff shot. Then he deliberately looked Shane over like he had just spotted him.

"Hello, farmer," he said. He said it as if he did not like farmers.

Shane regarded him with grave attention. "Speaking to me?" he asked mildly and finished his drink.

"Heck, there ain't nobody else standing there. Here, have a drink of this." Chris shoved his bottle along the bar. Shane poured himself a generous slug and raised it to his lips.

"I'll be darned," flipped Chris. "So you drink whiskey."

Shane tossed off the rest in his glass and set it down. "I've had better," he said, as friendly as could be. "But this will do."

Chris slapped his leather chaps with a loud smack. He turned to take in the other men. "Did you hear that? This farmer drinks whiskey! I didn't think these plow-pushing dirtgrubbers drank anything stronger than soda pop!"

"Some of us do," said Shane, friendly as before. Then he was no longer friendly and his voice was like winter frost. "You've had your fun and it's mighty young fun. Now run home and tell Fletcher to send a grown-up man next time." He turned away and sang out to Will Atkey. "Do you have any soda pop? I'd like a bottle."

Will hesitated, looked kind of funny, and scuttled past me into the store room. He came back right away with a bottle of the pop Grafton kept there for us school kids. Chris was standing quiet, not so much mad, I would have said, as puzzled. It was as though they were playing some queer game and he was not sure of the next move. He sucked on his lower lip for a while. Then he snapped his mouth and began to look elaborately around the room, sniffing loudly.

"Hey, Will!" he called. "What's been happening in here? It smells. That ain't no clean cattleman smell. That's plain dirty barnyard." He stared at Shane. "You, farmer. What are you and Starrett raising out there? Pigs?"

Shane was just taking hold of the bottle Will had fetched him. His hand closed on it and the knuckles showed white. He moved slowly, almost unwillingly, to face Chris. Every line of his body was as taut as stretched whipcord, was alive and somehow rich with an immense eagerness. There was that fierce concentration in him, filling him, blazing in his eyes. In that moment there was nothing in the room for him but that mocking man only a few feet away.

The big room was so quiet the stillness fairly hurt. Chris stepped back involuntarily, one pace, two, then pulled up erect. And still nothing happened. The lean muscles along the sides of Shane's jaw were ridged like rock.

Then the breath, pent in him, broke the stillness with a soft sound as it left his lungs. He looked away from Chris, past him, over the tops of the swinging doors beyond, over the roof of the shed across the road, on into the distance where the mountains loomed in their own unending loneliness. Quietly he walked, the bottle forgotten in his hand, so close by Chris as almost to brush him yet apparently not even seeing him, through the doors and was gone.

I heard a sigh of relief near me. Mr. Grafton had come up from somewhere behind me. He was watching Chris with a strange, ironic quirk at his mouth corners. Chris was trying not to look pleased with himself. But he swaggered as he went to the doors and peered over them.

"You saw it, Will," he called over his shoulder. "He walked out on me." Chris pushed up his hat and rolled back on his heels and laughed. "With a bottle of soda pop too!" He was still laughing as he went out and we heard him ride away.

"That boy's a fool," Mr. Grafton muttered.

Will Atkey came sidling over to Mr. Grafton. "I never pegged Shane for a play like that," he said.

"He was afraid, Will."

"Yeah. That's what was so funny. I would've guessed he could take Chris."

Mr. Grafton looked at Will as he did often, like he was a little sorry for him. "No, Will. He wasn't afraid of Chris. He was afraid of himself." Mr. Grafton was thoughtful and perhaps sad, too. "There's trouble ahead, Will. The worst trouble we've ever had."

He noticed me, realizing my presence. "Better skip along, Bob, and find your friend. Do you think he got that bottle for himself?"

True enough, Shane had it waiting for me at the blacksmith shop. Cherry pop, the kind I favored most. But I could not enjoy it much. Shane was so silent and stern. He had slipped back into the dark mood that was on him when he first came riding up our road. I did not dare say anything. Only once did he speak to me, and I knew he did not expect me to understand or to answer.

"Why should a man be smashed because he has courage and does what he's told? Life's a dirty business, Bob. I could like that boy." And he turned inward again to his own thoughts and stayed the same until we had loaded the tongs in the wagon and were well started home. Then the closer we came, the more cheerful he was. By the time we swung in toward the barn, he was the way I wanted him again, crinkling his eyes at me and gravely joshing me about the Indians I would scalp with my new knife.

Father popped out the barn door so quick you could tell he had been itching for us to return. He was busting with curiosity, but he would not come straight out with a question to Shane. He tackled me instead.

"See any of your cowboy heroes in town?"

Shane cut in ahead of me. "One of Fletcher's crew chased us in to pay his respects."

"No," I said, proud of my information. "There was two of them."

"Two?" Shane said it. Father was the one who was not surprised. "What did the other one do?"

"He went up on the porch and looked in the window where you were and came right back down and rode off."

"Back to the ranch?"

"The other way. He said he was leaving for good."

Father and Shane looked at each other. Father was smiling. "One down and you didn't even know it. What did you do to the other?"

"Nothing. He passed a few remarks about farmers. I went back to the blacksmith shop."

Father repeated it, spacing the words like there might be meanings between them. "You—went—back—to—the—blacksmith—shop."

I was worried that he must be thinking what Will Atkey did. Then I knew nothing like that had even entered his head. He switched to me. "Who was it?"

"It was Chris."

Father was smiling again. He had not been there but he had the whole thing clear. "Fletcher was right to send two. Young ones like Chris need to hunt in pairs or they might get hurt." He chuckled in a sort of wry amusement. "Chris must have been considerable surprised when the other fellow skipped. And more when you walked out. It was too bad the other one didn't stick around."

"Yes," Shane said, "it was."

The way he said it sobered father. "I hadn't thought of that. Chris is just cocky enough to take it wrong. That can make things plenty unpleasant."

"Yes," Shane said again, "it can."

# 7

It was just as father and Shane had said. The story Chris told was common knowledge all through the valley before the sun set the next day, and the story grew in the telling. Fletcher had an advantage now and he was quick to push it. He and his foreman, Morgan, a broad slab of a man with flattened face and head small in proportion to great sloping shoulders, were shrewd at things like this, and they kept their men primed to rowel us homesteaders at every chance.

They took to using the upper ford, up above Ernie Wright's stand, and riding down the road past our places every time they had an excuse for going to town. They would go by slowly, looking everything over with in-

THE COWBOY, 1902. Frederic Remington. Courtesy Amon Carter Museum, Fort Worth, Texas.

solent interest and passing remarks for our benefit.

The same week, maybe three days later, a covey of them came riding by while father was putting a new hinge on the corral gate. They acted like they were too busy staring over our land to see him there close.

"Wonder where Starrett keeps the critters," said one of them. "I don't see a pig in sight."

"But I can smell 'em!" shouted another one. With that they all began to laugh and whoop and holler and went tearing off, kicking up a lot of dust and leaving father with a tightness around his mouth that was not there before.

They were impartial with attentions like that. They would hand them out anywhere along the line an opportunity offered. But they liked best to catch father within earshot and burn him with their sarcasm.

It was crude. It was coarse. I thought it silly for grown men to act that way. But it was effective. Shane, as self-sufficient as the mountains, could ignore it. Father, while it galled him, could keep it from getting him. The other homesteaders, though, could not help being irritated and showing they felt insulted. It roughed their nerves and made them angry and restless. They did not know Shane as father and I did. They were not sure there might not be some truth in the big talk Chris was making.

Things became so bad they could not go into Grafton's store without someone singing out for soda pop. And wherever they went, the conversation near by always snuck around somehow to pigs. You could sense the contempt building up in town, in people who used to be neutral, not taking sides.

The effect showed, too, in the attitude our neighbors now had toward Shane. They were constrained when they called to see father and Shane was there. They resented that he was linked to them. And as a result their opinion of father was changing.

That was what finally drove Shane. He did not mind what they thought of him. Since his session with Chris he seemed to have won a kind of inner peace. He was as alert and watchful as ever, but there was a serenity in him that had erased entirely the old tension. I think he did not care what anyone anywhere thought of him. Except us, his folks. And he knew that with us he was one of us, unchangeable and always.

But he did care what they thought of father. He was standing silently on the porch the night Ernie Wright and Henry Shipstead were arguing with father in the kitchen.

"I can't stomach much more," Ernie Wright was saying. "You know the trouble I've had with those blasted cowboys cutting my fence. Today a couple of them rode over and helped me repair a piece. Helped me, darn them! Waited till we were through, then said Fletcher didn't want any of my pigs getting loose and mixing with his cattle. My pigs! There ain't a pig in this whole valley and they know it. I'm sick of the word."

Father made it worse by chuckling. Grim, maybe, yet still a chuckle. "Sounds like one of Morgan's ideas. He's smart. Mean, but—"

Henry Shipstead would not let him finish. "This is nothing to laugh at, Joe. You least of all. Darn it, man, I'm beginning to doubt your judgment. None of us can keep our heads up around here any more. Just a while ago I was in Grafton's, and Chris was there blowing high about your Shane must be thirsty because he's so scared he hasn't been in town lately for his soda pop."

Both of them were hammering at father now. He was sitting back, saying nothing, his face clouding.

"You can't dodge it, Joe." This was Wright. "Your man's responsible. You can try explaining all night, but you can't change the facts. Chris braced him for a fight and he ducked out—and left us stuck with those stinking pigs."

"You know as well as I do what Fletcher's doing," growled Henry Shipstead. "He's pushing us with this, and he won't let up till one of us gets enough and makes a fool play and starts something so he can move in and finish it."

"Fool play or not," said Ernie Wright. "I've had all I can take. The next time one of those—"

Father stopped him with a hand up for silence. "Listen. What's that?"

It was a horse, picking up speed and tearing down our lane into the road. Father was at the door in a single jump, peering out.

The others were close behind him. "Shane?"

Father nodded. He was muttering under his breath. As I watched from the doorway of my little room, I could see that his eyes were bright and dancing. He was calling Shane names, cursing him, softly, fluently. He came back to his chair and grinned at the other two. "That's Shane," he told them and the words meant more than they seemed to say. "All we can do now is wait."

They were a silent crew, waiting. Mother got up from her sewing in the bedroom where she had been listening as she always did, and came into the kitchen and made up a pot of coffee, and they all sat there sipping at the hot stuff and waiting.

It could not have been much more than twenty minutes before we heard the horse again, coming swiftly and slewing around to make the lane without slowing. There were quick steps on the porch and Shane stood in the doorway. He was breathing strongly and his face was hard. His mouth was a thin line in the bleakness of his face, and his eyes were deep and dark. He looked at Shipstead and Wright, and he made no effort to hide the disgust in his voice.

"Your pigs are dead and buried."

As his gaze shifted to father, his face softened. But the voice was still bitter. "There's another one down. Chris won't be bothering anybody for quite a spell." He turned and disappeared, and we could hear him leading the horse into the barn.

In the quiet following, hoofbeats like an echo sounded in the distance. They swelled louder, and this second horse galloped into our lane and pulled to a stop. Ed Howells jumped to the porch and hurried in.

"Where's Shane?"

"Out in the barn," father said.

"Did he tell you what happened?"

"Not much," father said mildly. "Something about burying pigs."

Ed Howells slumped into a chair. He seemed a bit dazed. The words came out of him slowly at first as he tried to make the others grasp just how he felt. "I never saw anything like it," he said, and he told about it.

He had been in Grafton's store buying a few things, not caring about going into the saloon because Chris and Red Marlin, another of Fletcher's cowboys, had hands in the evening poker game, when he noticed how still the place was. He went over to sneak a look, and there was Shane just moving to the bar, cool and easy as if the room was empty and he the only one in it. Neither Chris nor Red Marlin was saying a word, though you might have thought this was a good chance for them to cut loose with some of their raw sarcasm. One look at Shane was enough to tell why. He was cool and easy, right enough. But there was a curious kind of smooth flow to his movements that made you realize without being conscious of thinking about it that being quiet was a mighty sensible way to be at the moment.

"Two bottles of soda pop," he called to Will Atkey. He leaned his back to the bar and looked the poker game over with what seemed a friendly interest while Will fetched the bottles from the store. Not another person even twitched a muscle. They were all watching him and wondering what the play was. He took the two bottles and walked to the table and set them down, reaching over to put one in front of Chris.

"The last time I was in here you bought me a drink. Now it's my turn."

The words sort of lingered in the stillness. He got the impression, Ed Howells said, that Shane meant just what the words said. He wanted to buy Chris a drink. He wanted Chris to take that bottle and grin at him and drink with him.

You could have heard a bug crawl, I guess, while Chris carefully laid down the cards in his right hand and stretched it to the bottle. He lifted it in a sudden jerk and flung it across the table at Shane.

So fast Shane moved, Ed Howells said, that the bottle was still in the air when he had dodged, lunged forward, grabbed Chris by the shirtfront and hauled him right out of his chair and over the table. As Chris struggled to get his feet under him, Shane let go the shirt and slapped him, sharp and stinging, three times, the hand flicking back and forth so quick you could hardly see it, the slaps sounding like pistol shots.

Shane stepped back and Chris stood swaying a little and shaking his head to clear it. He was a game one and mad down to his boots. He plunged in, fists smashing, and Shane let him come, slipping inside the flailing arms and jolting a powerful blow low into his stomach. As Chris gasped and his head came down, Shane brought his right hand up, open, and with the heel of it caught Chris full on the mouth, snapping his head back and raking up over the nose and eyes.

The force of it knocked Chris off balance and he staggered badly. His lips were crushed. Blood was dripping over them from his battered nose. His eyes were red and watery, and

he was having trouble seeing with them. His face, Ed Howells said, and shook a little as he said it, looked like a horse had stomped it. But he drove in again, swinging wildly.

Shane ducked under, caught one of the flying wrists, twisted the arm to lock it and keep it from bending, and swung his shoulder into the armpit. He yanked hard on the wrist and Chris went up and over him. As the body hurtled over, Shane kept hold of the arm and wrenched it sideways and let the weight bear on it and you could hear the bone crack as Chris crashed to the floor.

A long sobbing sigh came from Chris and that died away and there was not a sound in the room. Shane never looked at the crumpled figure. He was straight and deadly and still. Every line of him was alive and eager. But he stood motionless. Only his eyes shifted to search the faces of the others at the table. They stopped on Red Marlin and Red seemed to dwindle lower in his chair.

"Perhaps," Shane said softly, and the very softness of his voice sent shivers through Ed Howells, "perhaps you have something to say about soda pop or pigs."

Red Marlin sat quiet like he was trying not even to breathe. Tiny drops of sweat appeared on his forehead. He was frightened, maybe for the first time in his life, and the others knew it and he knew they knew and he did not care. And none of them blamed him at all.

Then, as they watched, the fire in Shane smouldered down and out. He seemed to withdraw back within himself. He forgot them all and turned toward Chris unconscious on the floor, and a sort of sadness, Ed Howells said, crept over him and held him. He bent and scooped the sprawling figure up in his arms and carried it to one of the other tables. Gently he set it down, the legs falling limp over the edge. He crossed to the bar and took the rag Will used to wipe it and returned to the table and tenderly cleared the blood from the face. He felt carefully along the broken arm and nodded to himself at what he felt.

All this while no one said a word. Not a one of them would have interfered with that man for a year's top wages. He spoke, and his voice rang across the room at Red Marlin. "You'd better tote him home and get that arm fixed. Take right good care of him. He has the makings of a good man." Then he forgot them all again and looked at Chris and went on speaking as if to that limp figure that could not hear him. "There's only one thing really wrong with you. You're young. That's the one thing time can always cure."

The thought hurt him, and he strode to the swinging doors and through them into the night. That was what Ed Howells told. "The whole business," he finished, "didn't take five minutes. It was maybe thirty seconds from the time he grabbed holt of Chris till Chris was out cold on the floor. In my opinion that Shane is the most dangerous man I've ever seen. I'm glad he's working for Joe here and not for Fletcher."

Father leveled a triumphant look at Henry Shipstead. "So I've made a mistake, have I?"

Before anyone else could push in a word, mother was speaking. I was surprised, because she was upset and her voice was a little shrill. "I wouldn't be too sure about that, Joe Starrett. I think you've made a bad mistake."

"Marian, what's got into you?"

"Look what you've done just because you got him to stay on here and get mixed up in this trouble with Fletcher!"

Father was edging toward being peeved himself. "Women never do understand these things. Lookahere, Marian. Chris will be all right. He's young and he's healthy. Soon as that arm is mended, he'll be in as good shape as he ever was."

"Oh, Joe, can't you see what I'm talking about? I don't mean what you've done to Chris. I mean what you've done to Shane."

# 8

This time mother was right. Shane was changed. He tried to keep things as they had been with us, and on the surface nothing was different. But he had lost the serenity that had seeped into him through the summer. He would no longer sit around and talk with us as much as he had. He was restless with some far hidden desperation.

At times, when it rode him worst, he would wander alone about our place, and this was the one thing that seemed to soothe him. I used to see him, when he thought no one was watching, run his hands along the rails of the corral he had fastened, test with a tug the posts he had set, pace out past the barn looking up at the bulging loft, and stride out where the tall corn was standing in big shocks to dig his hands in the loose soil and lift some of it and let it run through his fingers.

He would lean on the pasture fence and study our little herd like it meant more to him than lazy steers to be fattened for market. Sometimes he would whistle softly, and his horse, filled out now so you could see the quality of him and moving with a quiet sureness and power that made you think of Shane himself, would trot to the fence and nuzzle at him.

Often he would disappear from the house in the early evening after supper. More than once, the dishes done, when I managed to slip past mother, I found him far back in the pasture alone with the horse. He would be standing there, one arm on the smooth arch of the horse's neck, the fingers gently rubbing around the ears, and he would be looking out over our land where the last light of the sun, now out of sight, would be flaring up the far side of the mountains, capping them with a deep glow and leaving a mystic gloaming in the valley.

Some of the assurance that was in him when he came was gone now. He seemed to feel that he needed to justify himself, even to me, to a boy tagging his heels.

"Could you teach me," I asked him, "to throw somebody the way you threw Chris?"

He waited so long I thought he would not answer. "A man doesn't learn things like that," he said at last. "You know them and that's all." Then he was talking rapidly to me, as close to pleading as he could ever come. "I tried. You can see that, can't you, Bob? I let him ride me and I gave him his chance. A man can keep his self-respect without having to cram it down another man's throat. Surely you can see that, Bob?"

I could not see it. What he was trying to explain to me was beyond my comprehension then. And I could think of nothing to say.

"I left it up to him. He didn't have to jump me that second time. He could have called it off without crawling. He could have if he was man enough. Can't you see that, Bob?"

And still I could not. But I said I could. He was so earnest and he wanted me to so badly. It was a long, long time before I did see it, and then I was a man myself and Shane was not there for me to tell. . . .

I was not sure whether father and mother were aware of the change in him. They did not talk about it, not while I was around anyway. But one afternoon I overheard something that showed mother knew.

I had hurried home from school and put on my old clothes and started out to see what father and Shane were doing in the cornfield, when I thought of a trick that had worked several times. Mother was firm set against eating between meals. That was a silly notion. I had my mind set on the cookies she kept in a tin box on a shelf by the stove. She was settled on the porch with a batch of potatoes to peel, so I slipped up to the back of the house, through the window of my little room, and tiptoed into the kitchen. Just as I was carefully putting a chair under the shelf, I heard her call to Shane.

He must have come to the barn on some errand, for he was there by the porch in only a moment. I peered out the front window and saw him standing close in, his hat in his hand, his face tilted up slightly to look at her leaning forward in her chair.

"I've been wanting to talk to you when Joe wasn't around."

"Yes, Marian." He called her that the same as father did, familiar yet respectful, just as he always regarded her with a tenderness in his eyes he had for no one else.

"You've been worrying, haven't you, about what may happen in this Fletcher business? You thought it would just be a case of not letting him scare you away and of helping us through a hard time. You didn't know it would come to what it has. And now you're worried about what you might do if there's any more fighting."

"You're a discerning woman, Marian."

"You've been worrying about something else too."

"You're a mighty discerning woman, Marian."

"And you've been thinking that maybe you'll be moving on."

"And how did you know that?"

"Because it's what you ought to do. For your own sake. But I'm asking you not to." Mother was intense and serious, as lovely there with the light striking through her hair as I had ever seen her. "Don't go, Shane. Joe needs you. More than ever now. More than he would ever say."

"And you?" Shane's lips barely moved and I was not sure of the words.

Mother hesitated. Then her head went up. "Yes. It's only fair to say it. I need you too."

"So-o-o," he said softly, the words lingering on his lips. He considered her gravely. "Do you know what you're asking, Marian?"

"I know. And I know that you're the man to stand up to it. In some ways it would be easier for me, too, if you rode out of this valley and never came back. But we can't let Joe down. I'm counting on you not ever to make me do that. Because you've got to stay, Shane, no matter how hard it is for us. Joe can't keep this place without you. He can't buck Fletcher alone."

Shane was silent, and it seemed to me that he was troubled and hard pressed in his mind. Mother was talking straight to him, slow and feeling for the words, and her voice was beginning to tremble.

"It would just about kill Joe to lose this place. He's too old to start in again somewhere else. Oh, we would get along and might even do real well. After all, he's Joe Starrett. He's all man and he can do what has to be done. But he promised me this place when we were married. He had it in his mind for all the first years. He did two men's work to get the extra money for the things we would need. When Bob was big enough to walk and help some and he could leave us, he came on here and filed his claim and built this house with his own hands, and when he brought us here it was home. Nothing else would ever be the same."

Shane drew a deep breath and let it ease out slowly. He smiled at her and yet, somehow, as I watched him, my heart ached for him. "Joe should be proud of a wife like you. Don't fret any more, Marian. You'll not lose this place."

Mother dropped back in her chair. Her face, the side I could see from the window, was radiant. Then, woman like, she was talking against herself. "But that Fletcher is a mean and tricky man. Are you sure it will work out all right?"

Shane was already starting toward the barn. He stopped and turned to look at her again. "I said you won't lose this place." You knew he was right because of the way he said it and because he said it.

# 9

**A**nother period of peace had settled over our valley. Since the night Shane rode into town, Fletcher's cowboys had quit using the road past the homesteads. They were not annoying us at all, and only once in a while was there a rider in view across the river. They had a good excuse to let us be. They were busy fixing the ranch buildings and poling a big new corral in preparation for the spring drive of new cattle Fletcher was planning.

Just the same, I noticed that father was as watchful as Shane now. The two of them worked always together. They did not split any more to do separate jobs in different parts of the farm. They worked together, rode into town together when anything was needed. And father took to wearing his gun all the time, even in the fields. He strapped it on after breakfast the first morning following the fight with Chris, and I saw him catch Shane's eye with a questioning glance as he buckled the belt. But Shane shook his head and father nodded, accepting the decision, and they went out together without saying a word.

Those were beautiful fall days, clear and stirring, with the coolness in the air just enough to set one atingling, not yet mounting to the bitter cold that soon would come sweeping down out of the mountains. It did not seem possible that in such a harvest season, giving a lift to the spirit to match the well-being of the body, violence could flare so suddenly and swiftly.

Saturday evenings all of us would pile into the light work wagon, father and mother on the seat, Shane and I swinging legs at the rear, and go into town. It was the break in routine we looked forward to all week.

There was always a bustle in Grafton's store with people we knew coming and going. Mother would lay in her supplies for the week ahead, taking a long time about it and chatting with the womenfolk. She and the wives of the other homesteaders were great ones for swapping recipes, and this was their bartering ground. Father would give Mr. Grafton his order for what he wanted and go direct for the mail. He was always getting catalogues of farm equipment and pamphlets from Washington. He would flip through their pages and skim through any letters, then settle on a barrel and spread out his newspaper. But like as not he would soon be bogged down in an argument with almost any man handy about the best crops for the Territory, and it would be Shane who would really work his way into the newspaper.

I used to explore the store, filling myself with crackers from the open barrel at the end of the main counter, playing hide and seek with Mr. Grafton's big and knowing old cat that was a whiz of a mouser. Many a time, turning up boxes, I chased out fat furry ones for her to pounce on. If mother was in the right mood, I would have a bag of candy in my pocket.

This time we had a special reason for staying longer than usual, a reason I did not like. Our schoolteacher, Jane Grafton, had made me take a note home to mother asking her to stop in for a talk. About me. I never was too smart at formal schooling to begin with. Being all excited over the doings at the big ranch and what they might mean to us had not helped any. Miss Grafton, I guess, just sort of endured me under the best of conditions. But what tipped her into being downright annoyed and writing to mother was the weather. No one could expect a boy with any spirit in him to be shut up in a schoolroom in weather like we had been having. Twice that week I had persuaded Ollie Johnson to sneak away with me after the lunch hour to see if the fish were still biting in our favorite pool below town.

Mother finished the last item on her list, looked around at me, sighed a little, and stiffened her shoulders. I knew she was going to the living quarters behind the store and talk to Miss Grafton. I squirmed and pretended I did not notice her. Only a few people were left in the store, though the saloon in the adjoining big room was doing fair business. She went over to where father was leafing through a catalogue and tapped him.

"Come along, Joe. You should hear this, too. I declare, that boy is getting too big for me to handle."

Father glanced quickly over the store and paused, listening to the voices from the next room. We had not seen any of Fletcher's men all evening and he seemed satisfied. He looked at Shane, who was folding the newspaper.

"This won't take long. We'll be out in a moment."

As they passed through the door at the rear of the store, Shane strolled to the saloon opening. He took in the whole room in his easy, alert way and stepped inside. I followed. But I was supposed not ever to go in there, so I stopped at the entrance. Shane was at the bar, joshing Will Atkey with a grave face that he didn't think he'd have soda pop tonight. It was a scattered group in the room, most of them from around town and familiar to me by sight at least. Those close to Shane moved a little away, eyeing him curiously. He did not appear to notice.

He picked up his drink and savored it, one elbow on the bar, not shoving himself forward into the room's companionship and not withdrawing either, just ready to be friendly if anyone wanted that and unfriendly if anyone wanted that too.

I was letting my eyes wander about, trying to tag names to faces, when I saw that one of the swinging doors was partly open and Red Marlin was peeking in. Shane saw it too. But he could not see that more men were out on the porch, for they were close by the building wall and on the store side. I could sense them through the window near me, hulking shapes in the darkness. I was so frightened I could scarcely move.

But I had to. I had to go against mother's rule. I scrambled into the saloon and to Shane and I gasped, "Shane! There's a lot of them out front!"

I was too late. Red Marlin was inside, and the others were hurrying in and fanning out to close off the store opening. Morgan was one of them, his flat face sour and determined, his huge shoulders almost filling the doorway as he came through. Behind him was the cowboy they called Curly because of his shock of unruly hair. He was stupid and slow-moving, but he was thick and powerful, and he had worked in harness with Chris for several years. Two others followed them, new men to me, with the tough, experienced look of old herd hands.

There was still the back office with its outside door opening on a side stoop and the rear alley. My knees were shaking, and I tugged at Shane and tried to say something about it. He stopped me with a sharp gesture. His face was clear, his eyes bright. He was somehow happy, not in the pleased and laughing way, but happy that the waiting was over and what had been ahead was here and seen and realized and he was ready for it. He put one hand on my head and rocked it gently, the fingers feeling through my hair.

"Bobby boy, would you have me run away?"

Love for that man raced through me and the warmth ran down and stiffened my legs and I was so proud of being there with him that I could not keep the tears from my eyes. I could see the rightness of it and I was ready to do as he told me when he said, "Get out of here, Bob. This isn't going to be pretty."

But I would go no farther than my perch just inside the store where I could watch most of the big room. I was so bound in the moment that I did not even think of running for father.

Morgan was in the lead now, with his men spread out behind him. He came about half the way to Shane and stopped. The room was quiet except for the shuffling of feet as the men by the bar and the nearest tables hastened over to the far wall, and some of them ducked out the front doors. Neither Shane nor Morgan gave any attention to them. They had attention only for each other. They did not look aside even when Mr. Grafton, who could smell trouble in his place from any distance, stalked in from the store, planting his feet down firmly, and pushed past Will Atkey behind the bar. He had a resigned expression on his face and he reached under the counter, his hands reappearing with a short-barreled shotgun. He laid it before him on the bar and he said in a dry, disgusted voice, "There will be no gunplay, gentlemen. And all damages will be paid for."

Morgan nodded curtly, not taking his eyes from Shane. He came closer and stopped again little more than an arm's length away.

His head was thrust forward. His big fists were clenched at his sides.

"No one messes up one of my boys and gets away with it. We're riding you out of this valley on a rail, Shane. We're going to rough you a bit and ride you out and you'll stay out."

"So you have it all planned," Shane said softly. Even as he was speaking, he was moving. He flowed into action so swift you could hardly believe what was happening. He scooped up his half-filled glass from the bar, whipped it and its contents into Morgan's face, and when Morgan's hands came up reaching or striking for him, he grasped the wrists and flung himself backwards, dragging Morgan with him. His body rolled to meet the floor and his legs doubled and his feet, catching Morgan just below the belt, sent him flying on and over to fall flat in a grotesque spraddle and slide along the boards in a tangle of chairs and a table.

The other four were on Shane in a rush. As they came, he whirled to his hands and knees and leaped up and behind the nearest table, tipping it in a strong heave among them. They scattered, dodging, and he stepped, fast and light, around the end and drove into the tail man, one of the new men, now nearest to him. He took the blows at him straight on to get in close, and I saw his knee surge up and into the man's groin. A high scream was literally torn from the man, and he collapsed to the floor and dragged himself toward the doors.

Morgan was on his feet, wavering, rubbing a hand across his face, staring hard as if trying to focus again on the room about him. The other three were battering at Shane, seeking to box him between them. They were piling blows into him, crowding in. Through that blur of movement he was weaving, quick and confident. It was incredible, but they could not hurt him. You could see the blows hit, hear the solid chunk of knuckles on flesh. But they had no effect. They seemed only to feed that fierce energy. He moved like a flame among them. He would burst out of the melee and whirl and plunge back, the one man actually pressing the three. He had picked the second new man and was driving always directly at him.

Curly, slow and clumsy, grunting in exasperation, grabbed at Shane to grapple with him and hold down his arms. Shane dropped one shoulder and as Curly hugged tighter brought it up under his jaw with a jolt that knocked him loose and away.

They were wary now and none too eager to let him get close to any one of them. Then Red Marlin came at him from one side, forcing him to turn that way, and at the same time the second new man did a strange thing. He jumped high in the air, like a jack rabbit in a spry hop, and lashed out viciously with one boot at Shane's head. Shane saw it coming, but could not avoid it, so he rolled his head with the kick, taking it along the side. It shook him badly. But it did not block the instant response. His hands shot up and seized the foot and the man crashed down to land on the small of his back. As he hit, Shane twisted the whole leg and threw his weight on it. The man buckled on the floor like a snake when you hit it and groaned sharply and hitched himself away, the leg dragging, the fight gone out of him.

But the swing to bend down on the leg had put Shane's back to Curly and the big man was plowing at him. Curly's arms clamped around him, pinning his arms to his body. Red Marlin leaped to help and the two of them had Shane caught tight between them.

"Hold him!" That was Morgan, coming forward with the hate plain in his eyes. Even then, Shane would have broke away. He stomped one heavy work shoe, heel edged and with all the strength he could get in quick leverage, on Curly's near foot. As Curly winced and pulled it back and was unsteady, Shane strained with his whole body in a powerful arch and you could see their arms slipping and loosening. Morgan, circling in, saw it too. He swept a bottle off the bar and brought it smashing down from behind on Shane's head.

Shane slumped and would have fallen if they had not been holding him. Then, as Morgan stepped around in front of him and watched, the vitality pumped through him and his head came up.

"Hold him!" Morgan said again. He deliberately flung a huge fist to Shane's face. Shane tried to jerk aside and the fist missed the jaw, tearing along the cheek, the heavy ring on one finger slicing deep. Morgan pulled back for another blow. He never made it.

Nothing, I would have said, could have drawn my attention from those men. But I heard a kind of choking sob beside me and it was queer and yet familiar and it turned me instantly.

Father was there in the entranceway!

He was big and terrible, and he was looking across the overturned table and scattered chairs at Shane, at the dark purplish bruise along the side of Shane's head and the blood running down his cheek. I had never seen father like this. He was past anger. He was filled with a fury that was shaking him almost beyond endurance.

I never thought he could move so fast. He was on them before they even knew he was in the room. He hurtled into Morgan with ruthless force, sending that huge man reeling across the room. He reached out one broad hand and grabbed Curly by the shoulder, and you could see the fingers sink into the flesh. He took hold of Curly's belt with the other hand and ripped him loose from Shane, and

his own shirt shredded down the back and the great muscles there knotted and bulged as he lifted Curly right up over his head and hurled the threshing body from him. Curly spun through the air, his limbs waving wildly, and crashed on the top of a table way over by the wall. It cracked under him, collapsing in splintered pieces, and the man and the wreckage smacked against the wall. Curly tried to rise, pushing himself with hands on the floor, and fell back and was still.

Shane must have exploded into action the second father yanked Curly away, for now there was another noise. It was Red Marlin, his face contorted, flung against the bar and catching at it to keep himself from falling. He staggered and caught his balance and ran for the front doorway. His flight was frantic, headlong. He tore through the swinging doors without slowing to push them. They flapped with a swishing sound and my eyes shifted quickly to Shane, for he was laughing.

He was standing there, straight and superb, the blood on his face bright like a badge, and he was laughing.

It was a soft laugh, soft and gentle, not in amusement at Red Marlin or any single thing, but in the joy of being alive and released from long discipline and answering the urge in mind and body. The lithe power in him, so different from father's sheer strength, was singing in every fiber of him.

Morgan was in the rear corner, his face clouded and uncertain. Father, his fury eased by the mighty effort of throwing Curly, had looked around to watch Red Marlin's run and now was starting toward Morgan. Shane's voice stopped him.

"Wait, Joe. The man's mine." He was at father's side and he put a hand on father's arm. "You'd better get them out of here." He nodded in my direction and I noticed with surprise that mother was near and watching.

She must have followed father and have been there all this while. Her lips were parted. Her eyes were glowing, looking at the whole room, not at anyone or anything in particular, but at the whole room.

Father was disappointed. "Morgan's more my size," he said, grumbling fashion. He was not worried about Shane. He was thinking of an excuse to take Morgan himself. But he went no further. He looked at the men over by the wall. "This is Shane's play. If a one of you tries to interfere, he'll have me to reckon with." His tone showed that he was not mad at them, that he was not even really warning them. He was simply making the play plain. Then he came to us and looked down at mother. "You wait out at the wagon, Marian. Morgan's had this coming to him for quite a long time now, and it's not for a woman to see."

Mother shook her head without moving her eyes now from Shane. "No, Joe. He's one of us. I'll see this through." And the three of us stayed there together and that was right, for he was Shane.

He advanced toward Morgan, as flowing and graceful as the old mouser in the store. He had forgotten us and the battered men on the floor and those withdrawn by the wall and Mr. Grafton and Will Atkey crouched behind the bar. His whole being was concentrated on the big man before him.

Morgan was taller, half again as broad, with a long reputation as a bullying fighter in the valley. But he did not like this and he was desperate. He knew better than to wait. He rushed at Shane to overwhelm the smaller man with his weight. Shane faded from in front of him, and as Morgan went past hooked a sharp blow to his stomach and another to the side of his jaw. They were short and quick, flicking in so fast they were just a blur of movement. Yet each time at the in-stant of impact Morgan's big frame shook and halted in its rush for a fraction of a second before the momentum carried him forward. Again and again he rushed, driving his big fists ahead. Always Shane slipped away, sending in those swift hard punches.

Breathing heavily, Morgan stopped, grasping the futility of straight fighting. He plunged at Shane now, arms wide, trying to get hold of him and wrestle him down. Shane was ready and let him come without dodging, disregarding the arms stretching to encircle him. He brought up his right hand, open, just as Ed Howells had told us, and the force of Morgan's own lunge as the hand met the mouth and raked upwards snapped back his head and sent him staggering.

Morgan's face was puffy and red-mottled. He bellowed some insane sound and swung up a chair. Holding it in front of him, legs forward, he rushed again at Shane, who side-stepped neatly. Morgan was expecting this and halted suddenly, swinging the chair in a swift arc to strike Shane with it full on the side. The chair shattered and Shane faltered, and then, queerly for a man usually so sure on his feet, he seemed to slip and fall to the floor.

Forgetting all caution, Morgan dove at him —and Shane's legs bent and he caught Morgan on his heavy work shoes and sent him flying back and against the bar with a crash that shook the whole length of it.

Shane was up and leaping at Morgan as if there had been springs under him there on the floor. His left hand, palm out, smacked against Morgan's forehead, pushing the head back, and his right fist drove straight to Morgan's throat. You could see the agony twist the man's face and the fear widen his eyes. And Shane, using his right fist now like a club and lining his whole body behind it, struck him on the neck below the back of the ear. It made a sickening, dull sound and

Morgan's eyes rolled white and he went limp all over, sagging slowly and forward to the floor.

# 10

In the hush that followed Morgan's fall, the big barroom was so quiet again that the rustle of Will Atkey straightening from below the bar level was loud and clear and Will stopped moving, embarrassed and a little frightened.

Shane looked neither at him nor at any of the other men staring from the wall. He looked only at us, at father and mother and me, and it seemed to me that it hurt him to see us there.

He breathed deeply and his chest filled and he held it, held it long and achingly, and released it slowly and sighing. Suddenly you were impressed by the fact that he was quiet, that he was still. You saw how battered and bloody he was. In the moments before, you saw only the splendor of movement, the flowing brute beauty of line and power in action. The man, you felt, was tireless and indestructible. Now that he was still and the fire in him banked and subsided, you saw, and in the seeing remembered, that he had taken bitter punishment.

His shirt collar was dark and sodden. Blood was soaking into it, and this came only in part from the cut on his cheek. More was oozing from the matted hair where Morgan's bottle had hit. Unconsciously he put up one hand and it came away smeared and sticky. He regarded it grimly and wiped it clean on his shirt. He swayed slightly and when he started toward us, his feet dragged and he almost fell forward.

One of the townsmen, Mr. Weir, a friendly man who kept the stage post, pushed out from the wall, clucking sympathy, as though to help him. Shane pulled himself erect. His eyes blazed refusal. Straight and superb, not a tremor in him, he came to us and you knew that the spirit in him would sustain him thus alone for the farthest distance and forever.

But there was no need. The one man in our valley, the one man, I believe, in all the world whose help he would take, not to whom he would turn but whose help he would take, was there and ready. Father stepped to meet him and put out a big arm reaching for his shoulders. "All right, Joe," Shane said, so softly I doubt whether the others in the room heard. His eyes closed and he leaned against father's arm, his body relaxing and his head dropping sideways. Father bent and fitted his other arm under Shane's knees and picked him up like he did me when I stayed up too late and got all drowsy and had to be carried to bed.

Father held Shane in his arms and looked over him at Mr. Grafton. "I'd consider it a favor, Sam, if you'd figure the damage and put it on my bill."

For a man strict about bills and keen for a bargain, Mr. Grafton surprised me. "I'm marking this to Fletcher's account. I'm seeing that he pays."

Mr. Weir surprised me even more. He spoke promptly and he was emphatic about it. "Listen to me, Starrett. It's about time this town worked up a little pride. Maybe it's time, too, we got to be more neighborly with you homesteaders. I'll take a collection to cover this. I've been ashamed of myself ever since it started tonight, standing here and letting five of them jump that man of yours."

Father was pleased. But he knew what he wanted to do. "That's mighty nice of you, Weir. But this ain't your fight. I wouldn't worry, was I you, about keeping out of it." He looked down at Shane and the pride was plain busting out of him. "Matter of fact, I'd say the odds tonight, without me butting in, too, was mighty close to even." He looked again at Mr. Grafton. "Fletcher ain't getting in on this with a nickel. I'm paying." He tossed back his head. "No, by Godfrey! We're paying. Me and Shane."

He went to the swinging doors, turning sideways to push them open. Mother took my hand and we followed. She always knew when to talk and when not to talk, and she said no word while we watched father lift Shane to the wagon seat, climb beside him, hoist him to sitting position with one arm around him and take the reins in the other hand. Will Atkey trotted out with our things and stowed them away. Mother and I perched on the back of the wagon, father chirruped to the team, and we were started home.

There was not a sound for quite a stretch except the clop of hooves and the little creakings of the wheels. Then I heard a chuckle up front. It was Shane. The cool air was reviving him and he was sitting straight, swaying with the wagon's motion.

"What did you do with the thick one, Joe? I was busy with the redhead."

"Oh, I just kind of tucked him out of the way." Father wanted to let it go at that. Not mother.

"He picked him up like—like a bag of potatoes and threw him clear across the room." She did not say it to Shane, not to any person. She said it to the night, to the sweet darkness around us, and her eyes were shining in the starlight.

We turned in at our place, and father shooed the rest of us into the house while he unhitched the team. In the kitchen, mother set some water to heat on the stove and chased me to bed. Her back was barely to me after she tucked me in before I was peering around the door jamb. She got several clean rags, took the water from the stove, and went to work on Shane's head. She was tender as could be, crooning like to herself under her breath the while. It pained him plenty as the warm water soaked into the gash under the matted hair and as she washed the clotted blood from his cheek. But it seemed to pain her more, for her hand shook at the worst moments, and she was the one who flinched while he sat there quietly and smiled reassuringly at her.

Father came in and sat by the stove, watching them. He pulled out his pipe and made a very careful business of packing it and lighting it.

She finished. Shane would not let her try a bandage. "This air is the best medicine," he said. She had to be content with cleaning the cuts thoroughly and making certain all bleeding had stopped. Then it was father's turn.

"Get that shirt off, Joe. It's torn all down the back. Let me see what I can do with it." Before he could rise, she had changed her mind. "No. We'll keep it just like it is. To remember tonight by. You were magnificent, Joe, tearing that man away and—"

"Shucks," said father. "I was just peeved. Him holding Shane so Morgan could pound him."

"And you, Shane." Mother was in the middle of the kitchen, looking from one to the other. "You were magnificent, too. Morgan was so big and horrible and yet he didn't have even a chance. You were so cool and quick and—and dangerous and—"

"A woman shouldn't have to see things like that." Shane interrupted her, and he meant it. But she was talking right ahead.

"You think I shouldn't because it's brutal and nasty and not just fighting to see who is better at it, but mean and vicious and to win by any way, but to win. Of course it is. But you didn't start it. You didn't want to do it.

Not until they made you anyway. You did it because you had to."

Her voice was climbing and she was looking back and forth and losing control of herself. "Did ever a woman have two such men?" And she turned from them and reached out blindly for a chair and sank into it and dropped her face into her hands and the tears came.

The two men stared at her and then at each other in that adult knowledge beyond my understanding. Shane rose and stepped over by mother. He put a hand gently on her head and I felt again his fingers in my hair and the affection flooding through me. He walked quietly out the door and into the night.

Father drew on his pipe. It was out and absently he lit it. He rose and went to the door and out on the porch. I could see him there dimly in the darkness, gazing across the river.

Gradually mother's sobs died down. She raised her head and wiped away the tears. "Joe."

He turned and started in and waited then by the door. She stood up. She stretched her hands toward him and he was there and had her in his arms.

"Do you think I don't know, Marian?"

"But you don't. Not really. You can't. Because I don't know myself."

Father was staring over her head at the kitchen wall, not seeing anything there. "Don't fret yourself, Marian. I'm man enough to know a better when his trail meets mine. Whatever happens will be all right."

"Oh, Joe . . . Joe! Kiss me. Hold me tight and don't ever let go."

**Chapters 6–10**

**Getting at Meaning**

1. How does Fletcher's return with a contract end the "season of friendship"?

2. Describe the encounter between Chris and Shane at Grafton's place. How does Chris interpret the exchange? What actually happens?

3. Why do the sarcastic remarks made by Fletcher's men aggravate the other farmers when the same remarks do not bother Shane and Joe Starrett?

4. What does his treatment of Chris after the fight reveal about Shane?

5. Why does Marian Starrett feel that her husband's decisions have endangered Shane?

6. Following the fight with Chris, why does Shane lose the serenity that he has gained while living with the Starretts?

7. Why isn't Chris "man enough" to avoid the fight with Shane? What might be Shane's definition of a man?

8. In the fight with Morgan and his men, what does Shane demonstrate about his abilities as a fighter?

9. Why does the scene in Grafton's place fill Joe Starrett "with a fury that was shaking him"?

10. Why does Joe Starrett insist on paying for the damages at Grafton's place?

11. What does Joe Starrett realize about the relationship between Marian and Shane? What does he mean when he says, "Whatever happens will be all right"?

## Developing Skills in Reading Literature

1. **Characterization.** As the novel develops, the writer expands and refines the character of Shane. The narrator comments that Shane ". . . was not Morley. He was Shane." What does this observation contribute to the characterization? One of Fletcher's new men, after seeing Shane, abruptly leaves town. What effect does this incident have upon the narrator's and the reader's image of Shane? Shane says, "A man can keep his self-respect without having to cram it down another's throat." What does this remark reveal about his values? Three incidents involving Shane take place at Grafton's place. What does his behavior in each incident reveal about his character?

2. **Suspense.** Explain how each of the following contributes to the build-up of suspense in this part of the novel:

a. the vague comments about what happened to Morley

b. Grafton's comment that Shane is "afraid of himself"

c. the hints that Chris might possibly have misinterpreted his first encounter with Shane

3. **Conflict.** What specific developments in Chapters 6-10 deepen the conflict between the farmers and Luke Fletcher? What evidence does the story offer that the struggle between Fletcher and the farmers complicates Shane's internal conflict? How does his relationship with Marian Starrett further complicate the internal conflict?

4. **Setting.** Two familiar settings in Westerns are the general store and the town saloon. How does the combination of these two settings into Grafton's place affect the development of conflict and suspense in this novel?

## Developing Vocabulary

1. **Suffixes.** The narrator describes Frank Torrey's wife as *querulous* and the townspeople as *curious.* Each word ends with the suffix -*ous,* which means "full of." Three other adjective suffixes also mean "full of": -*ose, -acious,* and -*ful.* Form five words from each of these four adjective suffixes. Then use two words from each group in sentences.

2. **Slang.** The narrator says that Fletcher had "bulldozed" the small ranchers out of the valley. *Bulldozed* is a slang word meaning "bullied." Find five other examples of slang words or phrases in the novel. Look up the definition of each in a dictionary and write it next to the word or phrase.

## Developing Writing Skills

1. **Analyzing Plot.** The fight between Morgan and his men and Shane at Grafton's place is a key incident in the novel. In one paragraph, discuss the importance of this incident. Consider the effect of the incident on the major conflicts in the novel and the incident as a turning point in the story.

2. **Analyzing a Character.** Shane emerges victorious from each of the three incidents at Grafton's place. Why? What special qualities enable Shane to maintain his dignity? In one paragraph, describe Shane as he presents himself during the incidents at Grafton's place.

# 11

**W**hat happened in our kitchen that night was beyond me in those days. But it did not worry me because father had said it would be all right, and how could anyone, knowing him, doubt that he would make it so.

And we were not bothered by Fletcher's men any more at all. There might not have been a big ranch on the other side of the river, sprawling up the valley and over on our side above Ernie Wright's place, for all you could tell from our house. They left us strictly alone and were hardly ever seen now even in town. Fletcher himself, I heard from kids at school, was gone again. He went on the stage to Cheyenne and maybe farther, and nobody seemed to know why he went.

Yet father and Shane were more wary than they had been before. They stayed even closer together, and they spent no more time than they had to in the fields. There was no more talking on the porch in the evenings, though the nights were so cool and lovely they called you to be out and under the winking stars. We kept to the house, and father insisted on having the lamps well shaded; and he polished his rifle and hung it, ready loaded, on a couple of nails by the kitchen door.

All this caution failed to make sense to me. So at dinner about a week later I asked, "Is there something new that's wrong? That stuff about Fletcher is finished, isn't it?"

"Finished?" said Shane, looking at me over his coffee cup. "Bobby boy, it's only begun."

"That's right," said father. "Fletcher's gone too far to back out now. It's a case of now or never with him. If he can make us run, he'll be setting pretty for a long stretch. If he can't, it'll be only a matter o' time before he's shoved smack out of this valley. There's three or four of the men who looked through here last year ready right now to sharpen stakes and move in soon as they think it's safe. I'll bet Fletcher feels he got aholt of a bear by the tail and it'd be nice to be able to let go."

"Why doesn't he do something, then?" I asked. "Seems to me mighty quiet around here lately."

"Seems to you, eh?" said father. "Seems to me you're mighty young to be doing much seemsing. Don't you worry, son. Fletcher is fixing to do something. The grass that grows under his feet won't feed any cow. I'd be easier in my mind if I knew what he's up to."

"You see, Bob"—Shane was speaking to me the way I liked, as if maybe I was a man and could understand all he said—"by talking big and playing it rough, Fletcher has made this a straight win or lose deal. It's the same as if he'd kicked loose a stone that starts a rockslide, and all he can do is hope to ride it down and hit bottom safe. Maybe he doesn't realize that yet. I think he does. And don't let things being quiet fool you. When there's noise, you know where to look and what's happening. When things are quiet, you've got to be most careful."

Mother sighed. She was looking at Shane's cheek where the cut was healing into a scar like a thin line running back from near the mouth corner. "I suppose you two are right. But does there have to be any more fighting?"

"Like the other night?" asked father. "No, Marian, I don't think so. Fletcher knows better now."

"He knows better," Shane said, "because he knows it won't work. If he's the man I think he is, he's known that since the first time he sicced Chris on me. I doubt that was his move the other night. That was Morgan's. Fletcher'll be watching for some way that has more finesse—and will be more final."

"Hm-m-m," said father, a little surprised. "Some legal trick, eh?"

"Could be. If he can find one. If not—" Shane shrugged and gazed out the window. "There are other ways. You can't call a man like Fletcher on things like that. Depends on how far he's willing to go. But whatever he does, once he's ready, he'll do it speedy and sure."

"Hm-m-m," said father again. "Now you put it thataway, I see you're right. That's Fletcher's way. But you've bumped against someone like him before." When Shane did not answer, just kept staring out the window, he went on. "Wish I could be as patient about it as you. I don't like this waiting."

But we did not have to wait long. It was the next day, a Friday, when we were finishing supper, that Lew Johnson and Henry Shipstead brought us the news. Fletcher was back and he had not come back alone. There was another man with him.

Lew Johnson saw them as they got off the stage. He had a good chance to look the stranger over while they waited in front of the post for horses to be brought in from the ranch. Since it was beginning to get dark, he had not been able to make out the stranger's face too well. The light striking through the post window, however, was enough for him to see what kind of man he was.

He was tall, rather broad in the shoulders and slim in the waist. He carried himself with a sort of swagger. He had a mustache that he favored and his eyes, when Johnson saw them reflecting the light from the window, were cold and had a glitter that bothered Johnson.

This stranger was something of a dude about his clothes. Still, that did not mean anything. When he turned, the coat he wore matching his pants flapped open and Johnson could see what had been half-hidden before. He was carrying two guns, big capable forty-fives, in holsters hung fairly low and forward. Those holsters were pegged down at the tips with thin straps fastened around the man's legs. Johnson said he saw the tiny buckles when the light flashed on them.

Wilson was the man's name. That was what Fletcher called him when a cowboy rode up leading a couple of horses. A funny other name. Stark. Stark Wilson. And that was not all.

Lew Johnson was worried and went into Grafton's to find Will Atkey, who always knew more than anyone else about people apt to be coming along the road because he was constantly picking up information from the talk of men drifting in to the bar. Will would not believe it at first when Johnson told him the name. What would he be doing up here, Will kept saying. Then Will blurted out that this Wilson was a bad one, a killer. He was a gunfighter said to be just as good with either hand and as fast on the draw as the best of them. He came to Cheyenne from Kansas, Will claimed he had heard, with a reputation for killing three men there and nobody knew how many more down in the southwest territories where he used to be.

Lew Johnson was rattling on, adding details as he could think of them. Henry Shipstead was slumped in a chair by the stove. Father was frowning at his pipe, absently fishing in a pocket for a match. It was Shane who shut off Johnson with a suddenness that startled the rest of us. His voice was sharp and clear and it seemed to crackle in the air. You could feel him taking charge of that room and all of us in it.

"When did they hit town?"

"Last night."

"And you waited till now to tell it!" There was disgust in Shane's voice. "You're a farmer all right, Johnson. That's all you ever will be." He whirled on father. "Quick, Joe. Which one has the hottest head? Which one's the easiest to prod into being a fool? Torrey is it? Or Wright?"

"Ernie Wright," father said slowly.

"Get moving, Johnson. Get out there on your horse and make it to Wright's in a hurry. Bring him here. Pick up Torrey, too. But get Wright first."

"He'll have to go into town for that," Henry Shipstead said heavily. "We passed them both down the road riding in."

Shane jumped to his feet. Lew Johnson was shuffling reluctantly toward the door. Shane brushed him aside. He strode to the door himself, yanked it open, started out. He stopped, leaning forward and listening.

"Hey, man," Henry Shipstead was grumbling, "what's your hurry? We told them about Wilson. They'll stop here on their way back." His voice ceased. All of us could hear it now, a horse pounding up the road at full gallop.

Shane turned back into the room. "There's your answer," he said bitterly. He swung the nearest chair to the wall and sat down. The fire blazing in him a moment before was gone. He was withdrawn into his own thoughts, and they were dark and not pleasant.

We heard the horse sliding to a stop out front. The sound was so plain you could fairly see the forelegs bracing and the hooves digging into the ground. Frank Torrey burst into the doorway. His hat was gone, his hair blowing wild. His chest heaved like he had been running as hard as the horse. He put his hands on the doorposts to hold himself steady and his voice was a hoarse whisper, though he was trying to shout across the room at father.

"Ernie's shot! They've killed him!"

The words jerked us to our feet and we stood staring. All but Shane. He did not move. You might have thought he was not even interested in what Torrey had said.

Father was the one who took hold of the scene. "Come in, Frank," he said quietly. "I take it we're too late to help Ernie now. Sit down and talk and don't leave anything out." He led Frank Torrey to a chair and pushed him into it. He closed the door and returned to his own chair. He looked older and tired.

It took Frank Torrey quite a while to pull himself together and tell his story straight. He was frightened. The fear was bedded deep in him and he was ashamed of himself for it.

He and Ernie Wright, he told us, had been to the stage office asking for a parcel Ernie was expecting. They dropped into Grafton's for a freshener before starting back. Since things had been so quiet lately, they were not thinking of any trouble even though Fletcher and the new man, Stark Wilson, were in the poker game at the big table. But Fletcher and Wilson must have been watching for a chance like that. They chucked in their hands and came over to the bar.

Fletcher was nice and polite as could be, nodding to Torrey and singling out Ernie for talk. He said he was sorry about it, but he really needed the land Ernie had filed on. It was the right place to put up winter wind-shelters for the new herd he was bringing in soon. He knew Ernie had not proved up on it yet. Just the same, he was willing to pay a fair price.

"I'll give you three hundred dollars," he said, "and that's more than the lumber in your buildings will be worth to me."

Ernie had more than that of his money in the place already. He had turned Fletcher down three or four times before. He was mad, the way he always was when Fletcher started his smooth talk.

"No," he said shortly. "I'm not selling. Not now or ever."

Fletcher shrugged like he had done all he could and slipped a quick nod at Stark Wilson. This Wilson was half-smiling at Ernie. But his eyes, Frank Torrey said, had nothing like a smile in them.

"I'd change my mind if I were you," he said to Ernie. "That is, if you have a mind to change."

"Keep out of this," snapped Ernie. "It's none of your business."

"I see you haven't heard," Wilson said softly. "I'm Mr. Fletcher's new business agent. I'm handling his business affairs for him. His business with stubborn jackasses like you." Then he said what showed Fletcher had coaxed him to it. "You're a damn fool, Wright. But what can you expect from a breed?"

"That's a lie!" shouted Ernie. "My mother wasn't no Indian!"

"Why, you crossbred squatter," Wilson said, quick and sharp, "are you telling me I'm wrong?"

"I'm telling you you're a danged liar!"

The silence that shut down over the saloon was so complete, Frank Torrey told us, that he could hear the ticking of the old alarm clock on the shelf behind the bar. Even Ernie, in the second his voice stopped, saw what he had done. But he was mad clear through and he glared at Wilson, his eyes reckless.

"So-o-o-o," said Wilson, satisfied now and stretching out the word with ominous softness. He flipped back his coat on the right side in front and the holster there was free with the gun grip ready for his hand.

"You'll back that, Wright. Or you'll crawl out of here on your belly."

Ernie moved out a step from the bar, his arms stiff at his sides. The anger in him held him erect as he beat down the terror tearing at him. He knew what this meant, but he met it straight. His hand was firm on his gun and pulling up when Wilson's first bullet hit him and staggered him. The second spun him half-way around and a faint froth appeared

on his lips and all expression died from his face and he sagged to the floor.

While Frank Torrey was talking, Jim Lewis and a few minutes later Ed Howells had come in. Bad news travels fast, and they seemed to know something was wrong. Perhaps they had heard that frantic galloping, the sound carrying far in the still night air. They were all in our kitchen now, and they were more shaken and sober than I had ever seen them.

I was pressed close to mother, grateful for her arms around me. I noticed that she had little attention for the other men. She was watching Shane, bitter and silent across the room.

"So that's it," father said grimly. "We'll have to face it. We sell and at his price or he slips the leash on his hired killer. Did Wilson make a move toward you, Frank?"

"He looked at me." Simply recalling that made Torrey shiver through. "He looked at me and he said, 'Too bad, isn't it, mister, that Wright didn't change his mind?'"

"Then what?"

"I got out of there quick as I could and came here."

Jim Lewis had been fidgeting on his seat, more nervous every minute. Now he jumped up, almost shouting. "But darn it, Joe! A man can't just go around shooting people!"

"Shut up, Jim," growled Henry Shipstead. "Don't you see the setup? Wilson badgered Ernie into getting himself in a spot where he had to go for his gun. Wilson can claim he shot in self-defense. He'll try the same thing on each of us."

"That's right, Jim," put in Lew Johnson. "Even if we tried to get a marshal in here, he couldn't hold Wilson. It was an even break and the faster man won is the way most people will figure it, and plenty of them saw it. A marshal couldn't get here in time anyway."

"But we've got to stop it!" Lewis was really

shouting now. "What chance have any of us got against Wilson? We're not gunmen. We're just a bunch of old cowhands and farmers. Call it anything you want. I call it murder."

"Yes!"

The word sliced through the room. Shane was up, and his face was hard with the rock ridges running along his jaw. "Yes. It's murder. Trick it out as self-defense or with fancy words about an even break for a fair draw and it's still murder." He looked at father and the pain was deep in his eyes. But there was only contempt in his voice as he turned to the others.

"You five can crawl back in your burrows. You don't have to worry—yet. If the time comes, you can always sell and run. Fletcher won't bother with the likes of you now. He's going the limit and he knows the game. He picked Wright to make the play plain. That's done. Now he'll head straight for the one real man in this valley, the man who's held you here and will go on trying to hold you and keep for you what's yours as long as there's life in him. He's standing between you and Fletcher and Wilson this minute and you ought to be thankful that once in a while this country turns out a man like Joe Starrett."

And a man like Shane. . . . Were those words only in my mind or did I hear mother whisper them? She was looking at him and then at father and she was both frightened and proud at once. Father was fumbling with his pipe, packing it and making a fuss with it like it needed his whole attention.

The others stirred uneasily. They were reassured by what Shane said and yet shamed that they should be. And they did not like the way he said it.

"You seem to know a lot about that kind of dirty business," Ed Howells said, with maybe an edge of malice to his voice.

"I do."

Shane let the words lie there, plain and short and ugly. His face was stern, and behind the hard front of his features was a sadness that fought to break through. But he stared levelly at Howells, and it was the other man who dropped his eyes and turned away.

Father had his pipe going. "Maybe it's a lucky break for the rest of us," he said mildly, "that Shane here has been around a bit. He can call the cards for us plain. Ernie might still be alive, Johnson, if you had had the sense to tell us about Wilson right off. It's a good thing Ernie wasn't a family man." He turned to Shane. "How do you rate Fletcher now he's shown his hand?"

You could see that the chance to do something, even just to talk at the problem pressing us, eased the bitterness in Shane.

"He'll move in on Wright's place first thing tomorrow. He'll have a lot of men busy on this side of the river from now on, probably push some cattle around behind the homesteads, to keep the pressure plain on all of you. How quick he'll try you, Joe, depends on how he reads you. If he thinks you might crack, he'll wait and let knowing what happened to Wright work on you. If he really knows you, he'll not wait more than a day or two to make sure you've had time to think it over and then he'll grab the first chance to throw Wilson at you. He'll want it, like with Wright, in a public place where there'll be plenty of witnesses. If you don't give him a chance, he'll try to make one."

"Hm-m-m," father said soberly. "I was sure you'd give it to me straight, and that rings right." He pulled on his pipe for a moment. "I reckon, boys, this will be a matter of waiting for the next few days. There's no immediate danger right off anyway. Grafton will take care of Ernie's body tonight. We can meet in town in the morning to fix him a

funeral. After that, we'd better stay out of town and stick close to home as much as possible. I'd suggest you all study on this and drop in again tomorrow night. Maybe we can figure out something. I'd like to see how the town's taking it before I make up my mind on anything."

They were ready to leave it at that. They were ready to leave it to father. They were decent men and good neighbors. But not a one of them, were the decision his, would have stood up to Fletcher now. They would stay as long as father was there. With him gone, Fletcher would have things his way. That was how they felt as they muttered their goodnights and bunched out to scatter up and down the road.

Father stood in the doorway and watched them go. When he came back to his chair, he walked slowly, and he seemed haggard and worn. "Somebody will have to go to Ernie's place tomorrow," he said, "and gather up his things. He's got relatives somewhere in Iowa."

"No." There was finality in Shane's tone. "You'll not go near the place. Fletcher might be counting on that. Grafton can do it."

"But Ernie was my friend," father said simply.

"Ernie's past friendship. Your debt is to the living."

Father looked at Shane, and this brought him again into the immediate moment and cheered him. He nodded assent and turned to mother, who was hurrying to argue with him.

"Don't you see, Joe? If you can stay away from any place where you might meet Fletcher and—and that Wilson, things will work out. He can't keep a man like Wilson in this little valley forever."

She was talking rapidly and I knew why. She was not really trying to convince father as much as she was trying to convince herself. Father knew it, too.

"No, Marian. A man can't crawl into a hole somewhere and hide like a rabbit. Not if he has any pride."

"All right, then. But can't you keep quiet and not let him ride you and drive you into any fight?"

"That won't work either." Father was grim, but he was better and facing up to it. "A man can stand for a lot of pushing if he has to. 'Specially when he has his reasons." His glance shifted briefly to me. "But there are some things a man can't take. Not if he's to go on living with himself."

I was startled as Shane suddenly sucked in his breath with a long breaking intake. He was battling something within him, that old hidden desperation, and his eyes were dark and tormented against the paleness of his face. He seemed unable to look at us. He strode to the door and went out. We heard his footsteps fading toward the barn.

I was startled now at father. His breath, too, was coming in long, broken sweeps. He was up and pacing back and forth. When he swung on mother and his voice battered at her, almost fierce in its intensity, I realized that he knew about the change in Shane and that the knowing had been cankering in him all the past weeks.

"That's the one thing I can't stand, Marian. What we're doing to him. What happens to me doesn't matter too much. I talk big and I don't belittle myself. But my weight in any kind of a scale won't match his and I know it. If I understood him then as I do now, I'd never have got him to stay on here. But I didn't figure Fletcher would go this far. Shane won his fight before ever he came riding into this valley. It's been tough enough on him already. Should we let him lose just because of us? Fletcher can have his way. We'll sell out and move on."

I was not thinking. I was only feeling. For some strange reason I was feeling Shane's fingers in my hair, gently rocking my head. I could not help what I was saying, shouting across the room. "Father! Shane wouldn't run away! He wouldn't run away from anything!"

Father stopped pacing, his eyes narrowed in surprise. He stared at me without really seeing me. He was listening to mother.

"Bob's right, Joe. We can't let Shane down." It was queer, hearing her say the same thing to father she had said to Shane, the same thing with only the name different. "He'd never forgive us if we ran away from this. That's what we'd be doing. This isn't just a case of bucking Fletcher any more. It isn't just a case of keeping a piece of ground Fletcher wants for his range. We've got to be the kind of people Shane thinks we are. Bob's right. He wouldn't run away from anything like that. And that's the reason we can't."

"Lookahere, Marian, you don't think I want to do any running? No. You know me better than that. It'd go against everything in me. But what's my fool pride and this place and any plans we've had alongside of a man like that?"

"I know, Joe. But you don't see far enough." They were both talking earnestly, not breaking in, hearing each other out and sort of groping to put their meaning plain. "I can't really explain it, Joe. But I just know that we're bound up in something bigger than any one of us, and that running away is the one thing that would be worse than whatever might happen to us. There wouldn't be anything real ahead for us, any of us, maybe even for Bob, all the rest of our lives."

"Humph," said father. "Torrey could do it.

And Johnson. All the rest of them. And it wouldn't bother them too much."

"Joe! Joe Starrett! Are you trying to make me mad? I'm not talking about them. I'm talking about us."

"Hm-m-m," said father softly, musing like to himself. "The salt would be gone. There just wouldn't be any flavor. There wouldn't be much meaning left."

"Oh, Joe! Joe! That's what I've been trying to say. And I know this will work out some way. I don't know how. But it will, if we face it and stand up to it and have faith in each other. It'll work out. Because it's got to."

"That's a woman's reason, Marian. But you're part right anyway. We'll play this game through. It'll need careful watching and close figuring. But maybe we can wait Fletcher out and make him overplay his hand. The town won't take much to this Wilson deal. Men like that fellow Weir have minds of their own."

Father was more cheerful now that he was beginning to get his thoughts straightened out. He and mother talked low in the kitchen for a long time after they sent me to bed, and I lay in my little room and saw through the window the stars wheeling distantly in the far outer darkness until I fell asleep at last.

# 12

The morning sun brightened our house and everything in the world outside. We had a good breakfast, father and Shane taking their time because they had routed out early to get the chores done and were waiting to go to town. They saddled up presently and rode off, and I moped in front of the house, not able to settle to any kind of playing.

After she bustled through the dishes, mother saw me standing and staring down the road and called me to the porch. She got our tattered old parchesi board and she kept me humping to beat her. She was a grand one for games like that. She would be as excited as a kid, squealing at the big numbers and doubles and counting proudly out loud as she moved her markers ahead.

When I had won three games running, she put the board away and brought out two fat apples and my favorite of the books she had from the time she taught school. Munching on her apple, she read to me; and before I knew it the shadows were mighty short and she had to skip in to get dinner, and father and Shane were riding up to the barn.

They came in while she was putting the food on the table. We sat down and it was almost like a holiday, not just because it was not a work day, but because the grown folks were talking lightly, were determined not to let this Fletcher business spoil our good times. Father was pleased at what had happened in town.

"Yes, sir," he was saying as we were finishing dinner. "Ernie had a right good funeral. He would have appreciated it. Grafton made a nice speech and, by Godfrey, I believe he meant it. That fellow Weir had his clerk put together a really fine coffin. Wouldn't take a cent for it. And Sims over at the mine is knocking out a good stone. He wouldn't take a cent either. I was surprised at the crowd, too. Not a good word for Fletcher among them. And there must have been thirty people there."

"Thirty-four," said Shane. "I counted 'em. They weren't just paying their respects to Wright, Marian. That wouldn't have brought in some of those I checked. They were showing their opinion of a certain man named Starrett, who made a pretty fair speech himself. This husband of yours is becoming quite a respected citizen in these parts. Soon as the town gets grown up and organized, he's likely to start going places. Give him time and he'll be mayor."

Mother caught her breath with a little sob. "Give . . . him . . . time," she said slowly. She looked at Shane and there was panic in her eyes. The lightness was gone and before anyone could say more, we heard the horses turning into our yard.

I dashed to the window to peer out. It struck me strange that Shane, usually so alert, was not there ahead of me. Instead he pushed back his chair and spoke gently, still sitting in it. "That will be Fletcher, Joe. He's heard how the town is taking this and knows he has to move fast. You take it easy. He's playing against time now, but he won't push anything here."

Father nodded at Shane and went to the door. He had taken off his gunbelt when he came in and now passed it to lift the rifle from its nails on the wall. Holding it in his right hand, barrel down, he opened the door and stepped out on the porch, clear to the front edge. Shane followed quietly and leaned in the doorway, relaxed and watchful. Mother was beside me at the window, staring out, crumpling her apron in her hand.

There were four of them, Fletcher and Wilson in the lead, two cowboys tagging. They had pulled up about twenty feet from the porch. This was the first time I had seen Fletcher for nearly a year. He was a tall man who must once have been a handsome figure in the fine clothes he always wore and with his arrogant air and his finely chiseled face set off by his short-cropped black beard and brilliant eyes. Now a heaviness was setting in about his features and a fatty softness was beginning to show in his body. His face had a shrewd cast, and a kind of reckless determination was on him that I did not remember ever noticing before.

Stark Wilson, for all the dude look Frank Torrey had mentioned, seemed lean and fit. He was sitting idly in his saddle, but the pose did not fool you. He was wearing no coat and the two guns were swinging free. He was sure of himself, serene and deadly. The curl of his lip beneath his mustache was a combination of confidence in himself and contempt for us.

Fletcher was smiling and affable. He was certain he held the cards and was going to deal them as he wanted. "Sorry to bother you, Starrett, so soon after that unfortunate affair last night. I wish it could have been avoided. I really do. Shooting is so unnecessary in these things, if only people would show sense. But Wright never should have called Mr. Wilson here a liar. That was a mistake."

"It was," father said curtly. "But then Ernie always did believe in telling the truth." I could see Wilson stiffen and his lips tighten. Father did not look at him. "Speak your piece, Fletcher, and get off my land."

Fletcher was still smiling. "There's no call for us to quarrel, Starrett. What's done is done. Let's hope there's no need for anything like it to be done again. You've worked cattle on a big ranch and you can understand my position. I'll be wanting all the range I can get from now on. Even without that, I can't let a bunch of nesters keep coming in here and choke me off from my water rights."

"We've been over that before," father said. "You know where I stand. If you have more to say, speak up and be done with it."

"All right, Starrett. Here's my proposition. I like the way you do things. You've got some queer notions about the cattle business, but when you tackle a job, you take hold and do it thoroughly. You and that man of yours are a combination I could use. I want you on my side of the fence. I'm getting rid of Morgan and I want you to take over as foreman. From what I hear, your man would make one hell of a driving trail boss. The spot's his. Since you've proved up on this place, I'll buy it from you. If you want to go on living here, that can be arranged. If you want to play around with that little herd of yours, that can be arranged too. But I want you working for me."

Father was surprised. He had not expected anything quite like this. He spoke softly to Shane behind him. He did not turn or look away from Fletcher, but his voice carried clearly.

"Can I call the turn for you, Shane?"

"Yes, Joe." Shane's voice was just as soft, but it, too, carried clearly and there was a little note of pride in it.

Father stood taller there on the edge of the porch. He stared straight at Fletcher. "And the others," he said slowly. "Johnson, Shipstead, and the rest. What about them?"

"They'll have to go."

Father did not hesitate. "No."

"I'll give you a thousand dollars for this place as it stands and that's my top offer."

"No."

The fury in Fletcher broke over his face and he started to turn in the saddle toward Wilson. He caught himself and forced again that shrewd smile. "There's no percentage in being hasty, Starrett. I'll boost the ante to twelve hundred. That's a lot better than what might happen if you stick to being stubborn. I'll not take an answer now. I'll give you till tonight to think it over. I'll be waiting at Grafton's to hear you talk sense."

He swung his horse and started away. The two cowboys turned to join him by the road. Wilson did not follow at once. He leaned forward in his saddle and drove a sneering look at father.

"Yes, Starrett. Think it over. You wouldn't like someone else to be enjoying this place of yours—and that woman there in the window."

He was lifting his reins with one hand to pull his horse around and suddenly he dropped them and froze to attention. It must have been what he saw in father's face. We could not see it, mother and I, because father's back was to us. But we could see his hand tightening on the rifle at his side.

"Don't, Joe!"

Shane was beside father. He slipped past, moving smooth and steady, down the steps and over to one side to come at Wilson on his right hand and stop not six feet from him. Wilson was puzzled and his right hand twitched and then was still as Shane stopped and as he saw that Shane carried no gun.

Shane looked up at him and Shane's voice flicked in a whiplash of contempt. "You talk like a man because of that flashy hardware you're wearing. Strip it away and you'd shrivel down to boy size."

The very daring of it held Wilson motionless for an instant and father's voice cut into it. "Shane! Stop it!"

The blackness faded from Wilson's face. He smiled grimly at Shane. "You do need someone to look after you." He whirled his horse and put it to a run to join Fletcher and the others in the road.

It was only then that I realized mother was gripping my shoulders so that they hurt. She dropped on a chair and held me to her. We could hear father and Shane on the porch.

"He'd have drilled you, Joe, before you could have brought the gun up and pumped in a shell."

"But you, you crazy fool!" Father was covering his feelings with a show of exasperation. "You'd have made him plug you just so I'd have a chance to get him."

Mother jumped up. She pushed me aside. She flared at them from the doorway. "And both of you would have acted like fools just because he said that about me. I'll have you two know that if it's got to be done, I can take being insulted just as much as you can."

Peering around her, I saw them gaping at her in astonishment. "But, Marian," father objected mildly, coming to her. "What better reason could a man have?"

"Yes," said Shane gently. "What better reason?" He was not looking just at mother. He was looking at the two of them.

# 13

I do not know how long they would have stood there on the porch in the warmth of that moment. I shattered it by asking what seemed to me a simple question until after I had asked it and the significance hit me.

"Father, what are you going to tell Fletcher tonight?"

There was no answer. There was no need for one. I guess I was growing up. I knew what he would tell Fletcher. I knew what he would say. I knew, too, that because he was father he would have to go to Grafton's and say it. And I understood why they could no longer bear to look at one another, and the breeze blowing in from the sun-washed fields was suddenly so chill and cheerless.

They did not look at each other. They did not say a word to each other. Yet somehow I realized that they were closer together in the stillness there on the porch than they had ever been. They knew themselves and each of them knew that the other grasped the situation whole. They knew that Fletcher had dealt himself a winning hand, had caught father in the one play that he could not avoid because he would not avoid it. They knew that talk is meaningless when a common knowledge is already there. The silence bound them as no words ever could.

Father sat on the top porch step. He took out his pipe and drew on it as the match flamed, and fixed his eyes on the horizon, on the mountains far across the river. Shane took the chair I had used for the games with mother. He swung it to the house wall and bent into it in that familiar unconscious gesture and he, too, looked into the distance. Mother turned into the kitchen and went about clearing the table as if she was not really aware of what she was doing. I helped her with the dishes and the old joy of sharing with her in the work was gone and there was no sound in the kitchen except the drip of the water and the chink of dish on dish.

When we were done, she went to father. She sat beside him on the step, her hand on the wood between them, and his covered hers and the moments merged in the slow, dwindling procession of time.

Loneliness gripped me. I wandered through the house, finding nothing there to do, and out on the porch and past those three and to the barn. I searched around and found an old shovel handle and started to whittle me a play saber with my knife. I had been thinking of this for days. Now the idea held no interest. The wood curls dropped to the barn floor, and after a while I let the shovel handle drop among them. Everything that had happened before seemed far off, almost like another existence. All that mattered was the length of the shadows creeping across the yard as the sun drove down the afternoon sky.

I took a hoe and went into mother's garden where the ground was caked around the turnips, the only things left unharvested. But there was scant work in me. I kept at it for a couple of rows, then the hoe dropped and I let it lie. I went to the front of the house, and there they were sitting, just as before.

I sat on the step below father and mother, between them, and their legs on each side of me made it seem better. I felt father's hand on my head.

"This is kind of tough on you, Bob." He could talk to me because I was only a kid. He was really talking to himself.

"I can't see the full finish. But I can see this. Wilson down and there'll be an end to it. Fletcher'll be done. The town will see to that. I can't beat Wilson on the draw. But there's strength enough in this clumsy body of mine to keep me on my feet till I get him, too." Mother stirred and was still, and his voice went on. "Things could be worse. It helps a man to know that if anything happens to him, his family will be in better hands than his own."

There was a sharp sound behind us on the porch. Shane had risen so swiftly that his chair had knocked against the wall. His hands were clenched tightly and his arms were quivering. His face was pale with the effort shaking him. He was desperate with an inner torment, his eyes tortured by thoughts that he could not escape, and the marks were obvious on him and he did not care. He strode to the steps, down past us and around the corner of the house.

Mother was up and after him, running headlong. She stopped abruptly at the house corner, clutching at the wood, panting and irresolute. Slowly she came back, her hands outstretched as if to keep from falling. She sank again on the step, close against father, and he gathered her to him with one great arm.

The silence spread and filled the whole valley and the shadows crept across the yard. They touched the road and began to merge in the deeper shading that meant the sun was dipping below the mountains far behind the house. Mother straightened, and as she stood up, father rose, too. He took hold of her two arms and held her in front of him. "I'm counting on you, Marian, to help him win again. You can do it, if anyone can." He smiled a strange little sad smile and he loomed up there above me the biggest man in all the world. "No supper for me now, Marian. A cup of your coffee is all I want." They passed through the doorway together.

Where was Shane? I hurried toward the barn. I was almost to it when I saw him out by the pasture. He was staring over it and the grazing steers at the great lonely mountains tipped with the gold of the sun now rushing down behind them. As I watched, he stretched his arms up, the fingers reaching to their utmost limits, grasping and grasping, it seemed, at the glory glowing in the sky.

He whirled and came straight back, striding with long steady steps, his head held high. There was some subtle, new, unchangeable certainty in him. He came close, and I saw that his face was quiet and untroubled and that little lights danced in his eyes.

"Skip into the house, Bobby boy. Put on a smile. Everything is going to be all right." He was past me, without slowing, swinging into the barn.

But I could not go into the house. And I did not dare follow him, not after he had told me to go. A wild excitement was building up in me while I waited by the porch, watching the barn door.

The minutes ticked past and the twilight deepened and a patch of light sprang from the house as the lamp in the kitchen was lit. And still I waited. Then he was coming swiftly toward me and I stared and stared and broke and ran into the house with the blood pounding in my head.

"Father! Father! Shane's got his gun!"

He was close back of me. Father and mother barely had time to look up from the table before he was framed in the doorway. He was dressed as he was that first day when he rode into our lives, in that dark and worn magnificence, from the black hat with its wide curling brim to the soft black boots. But what caught your eye was the single

flash of white, the outer ivory plate on the grip of the gun, showing sharp and distinct against the dark material of the trousers. The tooled cartridge belt nestled around him, riding above the hip on the left, sweeping down on the right to hold the holster snug along the thigh, just as he had said, the gun handle about halfway between the wrist and elbow of his right arm hanging there relaxed and ready.

Belt and holster and gun . . . These were not things he was wearing or carrying. They were part of him, part of the man, of the full sum of the integrate force that was Shane. You could see now that for the first time this man who had been living with us, who was one of us, was complete, was himself in the final effect of his being.

Now that he was no longer in his crude work clothes, he seemed again slender, almost slight, as he did that first day. The change was more than that. What had been

seeming iron was again steel. The slenderness was that of a tempered blade, and a razor edge was there. Slim and dark in the doorway, he seemed somehow to fill the whole frame.

This was not our Shane. And yet it was. I remembered Ed Howells' saying that this was the most dangerous man he had ever seen. I remembered in the same rush that father had said he was the safest man we ever had in our house. I realized that both were right and that this, this at last, was Shane.

He was in the room now and he was speaking to them both in that bantering tone he used to have only for mother. "A fine pair of parents you are. Haven't even fed Bob yet. Stack him full of a good supper. Yourselves, too. I have a little business to tend to in town."

Father was looking fixedly at him. The sudden hope that had sprung in his face had as quickly gone. "No, Shane. It won't do.

Even your thinking of it is the finest thing any man ever did for me. But I won't let you. It's my stand. Fletcher's making his play against me. There's no dodging. It's my business."

"There's where you're wrong, Joe," Shane said gently. "This is my business. My kind of business. I've had fun being a farmer. You've shown me new meaning in the word, and I'm proud that for a while maybe I qualified. But there are a few things a farmer can't handle."

The strain of the long afternoon was telling on father. He pushed up from the table. "Darn it, Shane, be sensible. Don't make it harder for me. You can't do this."

Shane stepped near, to the side of the table, facing father across a corner. "Easy does it, Joe. I'm making this my business."

"No. I won't let you. Suppose you do put Wilson out of the way. That won't finish anything. It'll only even the score and swing things back worse than ever. Think what it'll mean to you. And where will it leave me? I couldn't hold my head up around here any more. They'd say I ducked and they'd be right. You can't do it and that's that."

"No?" Shane's voice was even more gentle, but it had a quiet, inflexible quality that had never been there before. "There's no man living can tell me what I can't do. Not even you, Joe. You forget there is still a way."

He was talking to hold father's attention. As he spoke the gun was in his hand, and before father could move he swung it, swift and sharp, so the barrel lined flush along the side of father's head, back of the temple, above the ear. Strength was in the blow and it thudded dully on the bone and father folded over the table, and as it tipped with his weight, slid toward the floor. Shane's arm was under him before he hit and Shane pivoted father's loose body up and into his chair and righted the table while the coffee cups rattled on the floor boards. Father's head lolled back and Shane caught it and eased it and the big shoulders forward till they rested on the table, the face down and cradled in the limp arms.

Shane stood erect and looked across the table at mother. She had not moved since he appeared in the doorway, not even when father fell and the table teetered under her hands on its edge. She was watching Shane, her throat curving in a lovely proud line, her eyes wide with a sweet warmth shining in them.

Darkness had shut down over the valley as they looked at each other across the table, and the only light now was from the lamp swinging ever so slightly above them, circling them with its steady glow. They were alone in a moment that was all their own. Yet, when they spoke, it was of father.

"I was afraid," Shane murmured, "that he would take it that way. He couldn't do otherwise and be Joe Starrett."

"I know."

"He'll rest easy and come out maybe a little groggy but all right. Tell him, Marian. Tell him no man need be ashamed of being beat by Shane."

The name sounded queer like that, the man speaking of himself. It was the closest he ever came to boasting. And then you understood that there was not the least hint of a boast. He was stating a fact, simple and elemental as the power that dwelled in him.

"I know," she said again. "I don't need to tell him. He knows, too." She was rising, earnest and intent. "But there is something else I must know. We have battered down words that might have been spoken between us and that was as it should be. But I have a right to know now. I am part of this, too. And what I do depends on what you tell me now. Are you doing this just for me?"

Shane hesitated for a long, long moment. "No, Marian." His gaze seemed to widen and encompass us all, mother and the still figure of father and me huddled on a chair by the window, and somehow the room and the house and the whole place. Then he was looking only at mother and she was all that he could see.

"No, Marian. Could I separate you in my mind and afterwards be a man?"

He pulled his eyes from her and stared into the night beyond the open door. His face hardened, his thoughts leaping to what lay ahead in town. So quiet and easy you were scarce aware that he was moving, he was gone into the outer darkness.

# 14

Nothing could have kept me there in the house that night. My mind held nothing but the driving desire to follow Shane. I waited, hardly daring to breathe, while mother watched him go. I waited until she turned to father, bending over him; then I slipped around the doorpost out to the porch. I thought for a moment she had noticed me, but I could not be sure and she did not call to me. I went softly down the steps and into the freedom of the night.

Shane was nowhere in sight. I stayed in the darker shadows, looking about, and at last I saw him emerging once more from the barn. The moon was rising low over the mountains, a clean, bright crescent. Its light was enough for me to see him plainly in outline. He was carrying his saddle, and a sudden pain stabbed through me as I saw that with it was his saddle roll. He went toward the pasture gate, not slow, not fast, just firm and steady. There was a catlike certainty in his every movement, a silent, inevitable deadliness. I heard him, there by the gate, give his low whistle, and the horse came out of the shadows at the far end of the pasture, its hooves making no noise in the deep grass, a dark and powerful shape etched in the moonlight drifting across the field straight to the man.

I knew what I would have to do. I crept along the corral fence, keeping tight to it, until I reached the road. As soon as I was around the corner of the corral, with it and the barn between me and the pasture, I started to run as rapidly as I could toward town, my feet plumping softly in the thick dust of the road. I walked this every school day and it had never seemed long before. Now the distance stretched ahead, lengthening in my mind as if to mock me.

I could not let him see me. I kept looking back over my shoulder as I ran. When I saw him swinging into the road, I was well past Johnson's, almost past Shipstead's, striking into the last open stretch to the edge of town. I scurried to the side of the road and behind a clump of bullberry bushes. Panting to get my breath, I crouched there and waited for him to pass. The hoofbeats swelled in my ears, mingled with the pounding beat of my own blood. In my imagination he was galloping furiously and I was positive he was already rushing past me. But when I parted the bushes and pushed forward to peer out, he was moving at a moderate pace and was only almost abreast of me.

He was tall and terrible there in the road, looming up gigantic in the mystic half-light. He was the man I saw that first day, a stranger, dark and forbidding, forging his lone way out of an unknown past in the utter loneliness of his own immovable and instinctive defiance. He was the symbol of all the dim, formless imaginings of danger and terror in the untested realm of human potentialities beyond my understanding. The impact of the menace that marked him was like a physical blow.

I could not help it. I cried out and stumbled and fell. He was off his horse and over me before I could right myself, picking me up, his grasp strong and reassuring. I looked at him, tearful and afraid, and the fear faded from me. He was no stranger. That was some trick of the shadows. He was Shane. He was shaking me gently and smiling at me.

"Bobby boy, this is no time for you to be out. Skip along home and help your mother. I told you everything would be all right."

He let go of me and turned slowly, gazing out across the far sweep of the valley silvered in the moon's glow. "Look at it, Bob. Hold it in your mind like this. It's a lovely land, Bob. A good place to be a boy and grow straight inside as a man should."

My gaze followed his, and I saw our valley as though for the first time and the emotion in me was more than I could stand. I choked and reached out for him and he was not there.

He was rising into the saddle and the two shapes, the man and the horse, became one and moved down the road toward the yellow squares that were the patches of light from the windows of Grafton's building a quarter of a mile away. I wavered a moment, but the call was too strong. I started after him, running frantically in the middle of the road.

Whether he heard me or not, he kept right on. There were several men on the long porch of the building by the saloon doors. Red Marlin's hair made him easy to spot. They were scanning the road intently. As Shane hit the panel of light from the near big front window, the store window, they stiffened to attention. Red Marlin, a startled expression on his face, dived quickly through the doors.

Shane stopped, not by the rail but by the steps on the store side. When he dismounted, he did not slip the reins over the horse's head as the cowboys always did. He left them looped over the pommel of the saddle and the horse seemed to know what this meant. It stood motionless, close by the steps, head up, waiting, ready for whatever swift need.

HORSE WRANGLER. *O. C. Seltzer.*
*Thomas Gilcrease Institute, Tulsa, Oklahoma.*

Shane went along the porch and halted briefly, fronting the two men still there.

"Where's Fletcher?"

They looked at each other and at Shane. One of them started to speak. "He doesn't want—" Shane's voice stopped him. It slapped at them, low and with an edge that cut right into your mind. "Where's Fletcher?"

One of them jerked a hand toward the doors and then, as they moved to shift out of his way, his voice caught them.

"Get inside. Go clear to the bar before you turn."

They stared at him and stirred uneasily and swung together to push through the doors. As the doors came back, Shane grabbed them, one with each hand, and pulled them out and wide open and he disappeared between them.

Clumsy and tripping in my haste, I scrambled up the steps and into the store. Sam Grafton and Mr. Weir were the only persons there, and they were both hurrying to the entrance to the saloon, so intent that they failed to notice me. They stopped in the opening. I crept behind them to my familiar perch on my box where I could see past them.

The big room was crowded. Almost everyone who could be seen regularly around town was there, everyone but our homestead neighbors. There were many others who were new to me. They were lined up elbow to elbow nearly the entire length of the bar. The tables were full and more men were lounging along the far wall. The big round poker table at the back between the stairway to the little balcony and the door to Grafton's office was littered with glasses and chips. It seemed strange, for all the men standing, that there should be an empty chair at the far curve of the table. Someone must have been in that chair, because chips were at the place and a half-smoked cigar, a wisp of smoke curling up from it, was by them on the table.

Red Marlin was leaning against the back

wall, behind the chair. As I looked, he saw the smoke and appeared to start a little. With a careful show of casualness he slid into the chair and picked up the cigar.

A haze of thinning smoke was by the ceiling over them all, floating in involved streamers around the hanging lamps. This was Grafton's saloon in the flush of a banner evening's business. But something was wrong, was missing. The hum of activity, the whirr of voices, that should have risen from the scene, been part of it, was stilled in a hush more impressive than any noise could be. The attention of everyone in the room, like a single sense, was centered on that dark figure just inside the swinging doors, back to them and touching them.

This was the Shane of the adventures I had dreamed for him, cool and competent, facing that room full of men in the simple solitude of his own invincible completeness.

His eyes searched the room. They halted on a man sitting at a small table in the front corner with his hat on low over his forehead. With a thump of surprise I recognized it was Stark Wilson, and he was studying Shane with a puzzled look on his face. Shane's eyes swept on, checking off each person. They stopped again on a figure over by the wall, and the beginnings of a smile showed in them and he nodded almost imperceptibly. It was Chris, tall and lanky, his arm in a sling, and as he caught the nod he flushed a little and shifted his weight from one foot to the other. Then he straightened his shoulders and over his face came a slow smile, warm and friendly, the smile of a man who knows his own mind at last.

But Shane's eyes were already moving on. They narrowed as they rested on Red Marlin. Then they jumped to Will Atkey trying to make himself small behind the bar.

"Where's Fletcher?"

Will fumbled with the cloth in his hands. "I—I don't know. He was here awhile ago."

Frightened at the sound of his own voice in the stillness, Will dropped the cloth, started to stoop for it, and checked himself, putting his hands to the inside rim of the bar to hold himself steady.

Shane tilted his head slightly so his eyes could clear his hatbrim. He was scanning the balcony across the rear of the room. It was empty and the doors there were closed. He stepped forward, disregarding the men by the bar, and walked quietly past them the long length of the room. He went through the doorway to Grafton's office and into the semi-darkness beyond.

And still the hush held. Then he was in the office doorway again and his eyes bored toward Red Marlin.

"Where's Fletcher?"

The silence was taut and unendurable. It had to break. The sound was that of Stark Wilson coming to his feet in the far front corner. His voice, lazy and insolent, floated down the room.

"Where's Starrett?"

While the words yet seemed to hang in the air, Shane was moving toward the front of the room. But Wilson was moving, too. He was crossing toward the swinging doors and he took his stand just to the left of them, a few feet out from the wall. The position gave him command of the wide aisle running back between the bar and the tables and Shane coming forward in it.

Shane stopped about three quarters of the way forward, about five yards from Wilson. He cocked his head for one quick sidewise glance again at the balcony and then he was looking only at Wilson. He did not like the setup. Wilson had the front wall and he was left in the open of the room. He understood the fact, assessed it, accepted it.

They faced each other in the aisle, and the men along the bar jostled one another in their hurry to get to the opposite side of the room. A reckless arrogance was on Wilson, certain of himself and his control of the situation. He was not one to miss the significance of the slim deadliness that was Shane. But even now, I think, he did not believe that anyone in our valley would deliberately stand up to him.

"Where's Starrett?" he said once more, still mocking Shane but making it this time a real question.

The words went past Shane as if they had not been spoken. "I had a few things to say to Fletcher," he said gently. "That can wait. You're a pushing man, Wilson, so I reckon I had better accommodate you."

Wilson's face sobered and his eyes glinted coldly. "I've no quarrel with you," he said flatly, "even if you are Starrett's man. Walk out of here without any fuss and I'll let you go. It's Starrett I want."

"What you want, Wilson, and what you'll get are two different things. Your killing days are done."

Wilson had it now. You could see him grasp the meaning. This quiet man was pushing him just as he had pushed Ernie Wright. As he measured Shane, it was not to his liking. Something that was not fear but a kind of wondering and baffled reluctance showed in his face. And then there was no escape, for that gentle voice was pegging him to the immediate and implacable moment.

"I'm waiting, Wilson. Do I have to crowd you into slapping leather?"

Time stopped and there was nothing in all the world but two men looking into eternity in each other's eyes. And the room rocked in the sudden blur of action indistinct in its incredible swiftness, and the roar of their guns was a single sustained blast. And Shane stood, solid on his feet as a rooted oak, and Wilson swayed, his right arm hanging useless, blood beginning to show in a small stream from under the sleeve over the hand, the gun slipping from the numbing fingers.

He backed against the wall, a bitter disbelief twisting his features. His left arm hooked and the second gun was showing and Shane's bullet smashed into his chest and his knees buckled, sliding him slowly down the wall till the lifeless weight of the body toppled it sideways to the floor.

Shane gazed across the space between and he seemed to have forgotten all else as he let his gun ease into the holster. "I gave him his chance," he murmured out of the depths of a great sadness. But the words had no meaning for me, because I noticed on the dark brown of his shirt, low and just above the belt to one side of the buckle, the darker spot gradually widening. Then others noticed, too, and there was a stir in the air and the room was coming to life.

Voices were starting, but no one focused on them. They were snapped short by the roar of a shot from the rear of the room. A wind seemed to whip Shane's shirt at the shoulder, and the glass of the front window beyond shattered near the bottom.

Then I saw it.

It was mine alone. The others were turning to stare at the back of the room. My eyes were fixed on Shane and I saw it. I saw the whole man move, all of him, in the single flashing instant. I saw the head lead and the body swing and the driving power of the legs beneath. I saw the arm leap and the hand take the gun in the lightning sweep. I saw the barrel line up like—like a finger pointing —and the flame spurt even as the man himself was still in motion.

And there on the balcony Fletcher, impaled in the act of aiming for a second shot, rocked on his heels and fell back into the open doorway behind him. He clawed at the jambs and pulled himself forward. He staggered to the rail and tried to raise the gun. But the strength was draining out of him and he collapsed over the rail, jarring it loose and falling with it.

Across the stunned and barren silence of the room Shane's voice seemed to come from a great distance. "I expect that finishes it," he said. Unconsciously, without looking down, he broke out the cylinder of his gun and reloaded it. The stain on his shirt was bigger now, spreading fanlike above the belt, but he did not appear to know or care. Only his movements were slow, retarded by an unutterable weariness. The hands were sure and steady, but they moved slowly and the gun dropped into the holster of its own weight.

He backed with dragging steps toward the swinging doors until his shoulders touched them. The light in his eyes was unsteady, like the flickering of a candle guttering toward darkness. And then, as he stood there, a strange thing happened.

How could one describe it, the change that came over him? Out of the mysterious resources of his will the vitality came. It came creeping, a tide of strength that crept through him and fought and shook off the weakness. It shone in his eyes and they were alive again and alert. It welled up in him, sending that familiar power surging through him again until it was singing again in every vibrant line of him.

He faced that room full of men and read them all with the one sweeping glance and spoke to them in that gentle voice with that quiet, inflexible quality.

"I'll be riding on now. And there's not a one of you that will follow."

He turned his back on them in the indifference of absolute knowledge they would do as he said. Straight and superb, he was silhouetted against the doors and the patch of night above them. The next moment they were closing with a soft swish of sound.

The room was crowded with action now. Men were clustering around the bodies of Wilson and Fletcher, pressing to the bar, talking excitedly. Not a one of them, though, approached too close to the doors. There was a cleared space by the doorway as if someone had drawn a line marking it off.

I did not care what they were doing or what they were saying. I had to get to Shane. I had to get to him in time. I had to know, and he was the only one who could ever tell me.

I dashed out the store door and I was in time. He was on his horse, already starting away from the steps.

"Shane," I whispered desperately, loud as I dared without the men inside hearing me. "Oh, Shane!"

He heard me and reined around and I hurried to him, standing by a stirrup and looking up.

"Bobby! Bobby boy! What are you doing here?"

"I've been here all along," I blurted out. "You've got to tell me. Was that Wilson—"

He knew what was troubling me. He always knew. "Wilson," he said, "was mighty fast. As fast as I've ever seen."

"I don't care," I said, the tears starting. "I don't care if he was the fastest that ever was. He'd never have been able to shoot you, would he? You'd have got him straight, wouldn't you—if you had been in practice?"

He hesitated a moment. He gazed down at me and into me and he knew. He knew what goes on in a boy's mind and what can help him stay clean inside through the muddled, dirtied years of growing up.

"Sure. Sure, Bob. He'd never even have cleared the holster."

He started to bend down toward me, his hand reaching for my head. But the pain struck him like a whiplash and the hand jumped to his shirt front by the belt, pressing hard, and he reeled a little in the saddle.

The ache in me was more than I could bear. I stared dumbly at him, and because I was just a boy and helpless I turned away and hid my face against the firm, warm flank of the horse.

"Bob."

"Yes, Shane."

"A man is what he is, Bob, and there's no breaking the mold. I tried that and I've lost. But I reckon it was in the cards from the moment I saw a freckled kid on a rail up the road there and a real man behind him, the kind that could back him for the chance another kid never had."

"But—but, Shane, you—"

"There's no going back from a killing, Bob. Right or wrong, the brand sticks and there's no going back. It's up to you now. Go home to your mother and father. Grow strong and straight and take care of them. Both of them."

"Yes, Shane."

"There's only one thing more I can do for them now."

I felt the horse move away from me. Shane was looking down the road and on to the open plain, and the horse was obeying the silent command of the reins. He was riding away, and I knew that no word or thought could hold him. The big horse, patient and powerful, was already settling into the steady pace that had brought him into our valley, and the two, the man and the horse, were a single dark shape in the road as they passed beyond the reach of the light from the windows.

I strained my eyes after him, and then in the moonlight I could make out the inalienable outline of his figure receding into the distance. Lost in my loneliness, I watched him go, out of town, far down the road where it curved out to the level country beyond the valley. There were men on the porch behind me, but I was aware only of that dark shape growing small and indistinct along the far reach of the road. A cloud passed over the moon and he merged into the general shadow and I could not see him and the cloud passed on and the road was a plain thin ribbon to the horizon and he was gone.

I stumbled back to fall on the steps, my head in my arms to hide the tears. The voices of the men around me were meaningless noises in a bleak and empty world. It was Mr. Weir who took me home.

# 15

Father and mother were in the kitchen, almost as I had left them. Mother had hitched her chair close to father's. He was sitting up, his face tired and haggard, the ugly red mark standing out plain along the side of his head. They did not come to meet us. They sat still and watched us move into the doorway.

They did not even scold me. Mother reached and pulled me to her and let me crawl into her lap as I had not done for three years or more. Father just stared at Mr. Weir. He could not trust himself to speak first.

"Your troubles are over, Starrett."

Father nodded. "You've come to tell me," he said wearily, "that he killed Wilson before they got him. I know. He was Shane."

"Wilson," said Mr. Weir. "And Fletcher."

Father started. "Fletcher, too? By Godfrey, yes. He would do it right." Then father sighed and ran a finger along the bruise on his head. "He let me know this was one thing he wanted to handle by himself. I can tell you, Weir, waiting here is the hardest job I ever had."

Mr. Weir looked at the bruise. "I thought so. Listen, Starrett. There's not a man in town doesn't know you didn't stay here of your own will. And there's damn few that aren't glad it was Shane came into the saloon tonight."

The words broke from me. "You should have seen him, father. He was—he was—" I could not find it at first. "He was—beautiful, father. And Wilson wouldn't even have hit him if he'd been in practice. He told me so."

"He told you!" The table was banging over as father drove to his feet. He grabbed Mr. Weir by the coat front. "My God, man! Why didn't you tell me? He's alive?"

"Yes," said Mr. Weir. "He's alive all right. Wilson got to him. But no bullet can kill that man." A puzzled, faraway sort of look flitted across Mr. Weir's face. "Sometimes I wonder whether anything ever could."

Father was shaking him. "Where is he?"

"He's gone," said Mr. Weir. "He's gone, alone and unfollowed as he wanted it. Out of the valley and no one knows where."

Father's hands dropped. He slumped again into his chair. He picked up his pipe and it broke in his fingers. He let the pieces fall and stared at them on the floor. He was still staring at them when new footsteps sounded on the porch and a man pushed into our kitchen.

It was Chris. His right arm was tight in the sling, his eyes unnaturally bright and the color high in his face. In his left hand he was carrying a bottle, a bottle of red cherry soda pop. He came straight in and righted the table with the hand holding the bottle. He smacked the bottle on the top boards and seemed startled at the noise he made. He was embarrassed, and he was having trouble with his voice. But he spoke up firmly.

"I brought that for Bob. I'm a darned poor substitute, Starrett. But as soon as this arm's healed, I'm asking you to let me work for you."

Father's face twisted and his lips moved, but no words came. Mother was the one who said it. "Shane would like that, Chris."

And still father said nothing. What Chris and Mr. Weir saw as they looked at him must have shown them that nothing they could do or say would help at all. They turned and went out together, walking with long, quick steps.

Mother and I sat there watching father. There was nothing we could do either. This was something he had to wrestle alone. He was so still that he seemed even to have stopped breathing. Then a sudden restlessness hit him and he was up and pacing aimlessly about. He glared at the walls as if they stifled him and strode out the door into the yard. We heard his steps around the house and heading into the fields and then we could hear nothing.

I do not know how long we sat there. I know that the wick in the lamp burned low and sputtered awhile and went out and the darkness was a relief and a comfort. At last mother rose, still holding me, the big boy bulk of me, in her arms. I was surprised at the strength in her. She was holding me tightly to her and she carried me into my little room and helped me undress in the dim shadows of the moonlight through the window. She tucked me in and sat on the edge of the bed, and then, only then, she whispered to me: "Now, Bob. Tell me everything. Just as you saw it happen."

I told her, and when I was done, all she said in a soft little murmur was "Thank you." She looked out the window and murmured the words again and they were not for me, and she was still looking out over the land to the great gray mountains when finally I fell asleep.

She must have been there the whole night through, for when I woke with a start, the first streaks of dawn were showing through the window and the bed was warm where she had been. The movement of her leaving must have wakened me. I crept out of bed and peeked into the kitchen. She was standing in the open outside doorway.

I fumbled into my clothes and tiptoed

through the kitchen to her. She took my hand and I clung to hers and it was right that we should be together and that together we should go find father.

We found him out by the corral, by the far end where Shane had added to it. The sun was beginning to rise through the cleft in the mountains across the river, not the brilliant glory of midday but the fresh and renewed reddish radiance of early morning. Father's arms were folded on the top rail, his head bowed on them. When he turned to face us, he leaned back against the rail as if he needed the support. His eyes were rimmed and a little wild.

"Marian, I'm sick of the sight of this valley and all that's in it. If I tried to stay here now, my heart wouldn't be in it any more. I know it's hard on you and the boy, but we'll have to pull up stakes and move on. Montana, maybe. I've heard there's good land for the claiming up that way."

Mother heard him through. She had let go my hand and stood erect, so angry that her eyes snapped and her chin quivered. But she heard him through.

"Joe! Joe Starrett!" Her voice fairly crackled and was rich with emotion that was more than anger. "So you'd run out on Shane just when he's really here to stay?"

"But, Marian. You don't understand. He's gone."

"He's not gone. He's here, in this place, in this place he gave us. He's all around us and in us, and he always will be."

She ran to the tall corner post, to the one Shane had set. She beat at it with her hands. "Here, Joe. Quick. Take hold. Pull it down."

Father stared at her in amazement. But he did as she said. No one could have denied her in that moment. He took hold of the post and pulled at it. He shook his head and braced his feet and strained at it with all his strength. The big muscles of his shoulders and back knotted and bulged till I thought this shirt, too, would shred. Creakings ran along the rails and the post moved ever so slightly and the ground at the base showed little cracks fanning out. But the rails held and the post stood.

Father turned from it, beads of sweat breaking on his face, a light creeping up his drawn cheeks.

"See, Joe. See what I mean. We have roots here now that we can never tear loose."

And the morning was in father's face, shining in his eyes, giving him new color and hope and understanding.

# 16

I guess that is all there is to tell. The folks in town and the kids at school liked to talk about Shane, to spin tales and speculate about him. I never did. Those nights at Grafton's became legends in the valley, and countless details were added as they grew and spread just as the town, too, grew and spread up the river banks. But I never bothered, no matter how strange the tales became in the constant retelling. He belonged to me, to father and mother and me, and nothing could ever spoil that.

For mother was right. He was there. He was there in our place and in us. Whenever I needed him, he was there. I could close my eyes and he would be with me and I would see him plain and hear again that gentle voice.

I would think of him in each of the moments that revealed him to me. I would think of him most vividly in that single flashing instant when he whirled to shoot Fletcher on the balcony at Grafton's saloon. I would see again the power and grace of a coordinate force beautiful beyond comprehension. I would see the man and the weapon wedded in the one indivisible deadliness. I would see the man and the tool, a good man and a good tool, doing what had to be done.

And always my mind would go back at the last to that moment when I saw him from the bushes by the roadside just on the edge of town. I would see him there in the road, tall and terrible in the moonlight, going down to kill or be killed, and stopping to help a stumbling boy and to look out over the land, the lovely land, where that boy had a chance to live out his boyhood and grow straight inside as a man should.

And when I would hear the men in town talking among themselves and trying to pin him down to a definite past, I would smile quietly to myself. For a time they inclined to the notion, spurred by the talk of a passing stranger, that he was a certain Shannon who was famous as a gunman and gambler way down in Arkansas and Texas and dropped from sight without anyone knowing why or where. When that notion dwindled, others followed, pieced together in turn from scraps of information gleaned from stray travelers. But when they talked like that, I simply smiled because I knew he could have been none of these.

He was the man who rode into our little valley out of the heart of the great glowing West, and when his work was done rode back whence he had come and he was Shane.

## Getting at Meaning

1. Why does Shane become angry with Lew Johnson? What does Shane anticipate about Stark Wilson that Johnson doesn't even understand?

2. What does the shooting of Ernie Wright reveal about the character of Stark Wilson?

3. What does Joe Starrett mean when he says, "Shane won his fight before ever he came riding into this valley"? Why is Joe Starrett more concerned about Shane than he is about himself? Explain your answer.

4. Why does the reaction of the townspeople to Ernie Wright's death give Joe Starrett and Shane confidence?

5. How is Stark Wilson's comment about Marian Starrett similar to his insulting remarks about Ernie Wright? What are the comments intended to accomplish? What do the comments reveal about Wilson's knowledge of people?

6. Joe Starrett knows that he faces certain death at the hands of Stark Wilson. What comfort does he draw from his predicament?

7. When Bob sees Shane with a gun, he says, ". . . this at last, was Shane." How has Shane changed?

8. When Shane arrives at Grafton's place, he sees an empty chair at the poker table. Why is the empty chair significant?

9. How is Wilson betrayed by his own character?

10. Of whom is Shane speaking when he says, ". . . for the chance another kid never had"?

11. Why does Chris offer to work for Joe Starrett? Why does he bring the soda pop for Bob?

12. Why does Joe Starrett want to move to Montana? How does Marian convince him to stay?

13. Why is Bob unwilling to accept the various theories regarding Shane's identity?

## Developing Skills in Reading Literature

1. **Characterization.** What motivates Shane to go to Grafton's place for the showdown with Luke Fletcher and Stark Wilson? How does this motivation relate to the earlier comment, "A gun is as good—and as bad—as the man who carries it"? Bob comments repeatedly on Shane's unique energy and alertness. How does Shane's behavior at Grafton's place illustrate the importance of these two qualities? Why does Shane leave the valley? What does his departure reveal about his character? What qualities cause the townspeople to make Shane a legend?

2. **Climax.** How does the shootout at Grafton's place provide a climax for the conflict between Fletcher and the farmers? Which earlier incident is the climax of Shane's personal struggle? How does the shootout at Grafton's place relate to this struggle?

3. **Foil.** A foil is a character who, through contrast, enhances certain characteristics of a main character. In what ways is Stark Wilson a foil for Shane?

4. **Theme.** Consider Shane's reactions to Chris and his comments about growing up "straight" and about the use of a gun. What might the writer be saying about the sources and development of goodness and strength in people? About violence in the Old West?

## Developing Vocabulary

1. **Synonyms.** List one or more synonyms for each of the following words from the novel. Then use each word in a sentence.

| | |
|---|---|
| insolent | malice |
| wary | inanimate |
| assurance | irresolute |
| discerning | exasperation |
| serenity | |

2. **Using Precise Verbs.** The tension in the final section of the novel is enhanced by the use of precise verbs. Wilson *swaggers,* Wilson's bullet *staggered* Ernie Wright, and Shane *whirls* on Joe Starrett. Select ten other examples of precise verbs from this part of the novel, and explain what each contributes to the description in which it appears.

**Developing Writing Skills**

1. **Description: Selecting Specific Details.** Reread the descriptions of Fletcher and Wilson in Chapter 12. Notice how the writer uses a few well selected details to create an image of each man. Choose a person whose personality and physical appearance are familiar to you. In one paragraph, create a clear image of this person through the use of specific details.

2. **Analyzing a Character.** Shane's past arouses curiosity, seems to be a source of personal anguish, and finally causes him to say that ". . . there's no breaking the mold." Throughout the novel, how does Shane illustrate the idea that a person cannot escape his or her past? In a five-paragraph composition, discuss incidents and behavior that demonstrate that Shane is trapped by his past.

# Handbook of Literary Terms

**Alliteration.** Alliteration is the repetition of initial consonant sounds. Alliteration occurs in everyday speech and in all forms of literature. Poets, in particular, use alliteration to emphasize certain words, to create mood, to underscore meaning, and to enhance rhythm. Read the following lines, and notice how the writers relate the alliterated sounds to the other elements in the poem.

> Its quick soft silver bell beating, beating,
> And down the dark one ruby flare
> Pulsing out red light like an artery,
> KARL SHAPIRO<br>"Auto Wreck"

> Passing through huddled and ugly walls,
> By doorways when women haggard
> Looked from their hunger-deep eyes,
> Haunted with shadows of hunger-hands,
> Out from the huddled and ugly walls,
> I came sudden, at the city's edge,
> On a blue burst of lake—
> Long lake waves breaking under the sun
> On a spray-flung curve of shore;
> And a fluttering storm of gulls,
> Masses of great gray wings
> And flying white bellies
> Veering and wheeling free in the open.
> CARL SANDBURG<br>"The Harbor"

**Allusion.** An allusion is a reference to an historical or literary person, place, or event with which the reader is assumed to be familiar. The title of the poem "Out, Out—" is an allusion to a famous speech from Shakespeare's *Macbeth*. Understanding this allusion enriches the reader's appreciation and understanding of the poem. Similarly, familiarity with the Garden of Eden story in the Bible enhances the reader's appreciation of "A Narrow Fellow in the Grass" and "Nothing Gold Can Stay," poems included in this text. In the following selection, the poet alludes to Greek mythological figures.

> *He stood still by her bed*
> *Watching his daughter breathe,*
> *The dark and silver head,*
> *The fingers curled beneath,*
> *And thought:* Though she may have
> Intelligence and charm
> And luck, they will not save
> Her life from every harm.

> The lives of children are
> Dangerous to their parents
> With fire, water, air,
> And other accidents;
> And some, for a child's sake,
> Anticipating doom,
> Empty the world to make
> The world safe as a room.

> Who could endure the pain
> That was Laocoön's?
> Twisting, he saw again
> In the same coil his sons.
> Plumed in his father's skill,
> Young Icarus flew higher
> Toward the sun, until
> He fell in rings of fire.

A man who cannot stand
Children's perilous play,
With lifted voice and hand
Drives the children away.
Out of sight, out of reach,
The tumbling children pass;
He sits on an empty beach,
Holding an empty glass.

Who said that tenderness
Will turn the heart to stone?
May I endure her weakness
As I endure my own.
Better to say goodnight
To breathing flesh and blood
Each night as though the night
Were always only good.

LOUIS SIMPSON<br>
"The Goodnight"

**Analogy.** An analogy is a point by point comparison between two dissimilar things for the purpose of clarifying the less familiar of the two subjects. The analogy is distinct in structure and intent from figures of speech such as simile, metaphor, and personification, which also are types of comparisons.

In the following paragraph, the author draws an analogy between preparing for war and getting ready to go sailing. On the surface, these two activities seem totally dissimilar, but the analogy makes an effective point about war.

> Preparation for fighting a war is like preparation for taking a cruise in a small sailing boat— there is no end to it. It is possible to get so absorbed in the details of preparation as to lose sight of the trip. Anyone who has ever had the experience will know what I mean. If you were to wait until both you and the boat were really ready to put to sea, the summer would pass and the autumn would find you still at your home mooring. No boat is ever entirely ready to put to sea, no country is ever fully prepared to go to war; always there remain things that should be attended to, contingencies that should be pro-

vided for. But there comes a moment when you have to forget about preparations and think about the stars and the sea and the lengthening nights. You know that if you don't go now you will never go. So you drop off your mooring and shape your course to the wind. From then on things begin to move, you may not be ready in every particular, but you are under way.

E. B. WHITE

**Antagonist.** The antagonist of a short story or novel is the character or force against which the protagonist is pitted. The antagonist may be another character, a force of nature, a group of people, or even some aspect of the protagonist's personality or psyche. When the antagonist is internal, the central conflict takes place within the protagonist.

See *Protagonist*.

**Assonance.** Assonance is the repetition of a vowel sound within words. "Helter-skelter," "sweet dreams," and "high and mighty" are examples of assonance. Writers of both poetry and prose use assonance to give their work a musical quality and to unify stanzas and passages. Notice the effect created by the repetition of vowel sounds in the final three stanzas of "Annabel Lee," a poem by Edgar Allan Poe.

The angels, not half so happy in Heaven,
    Went envying her and me:—
Yes!—that was the reason (as all men know,
    In this kingdom by the sea)
That the wind came out of the cloud by night,
    Chilling and killing my Annabel Lee.

But our love it was stronger by far than the love
    Of those who were older than we—
    Of many far wiser than we—
And neither the angels in Heaven above,
    Nor the demons down under the sea,
Can ever dissever my soul from the soul
    Of the beautiful Annabel Lee:—

For the moon never beams, without bringing me
   dreams
  Of the beautiful Annabel Lee;
And the stars never rise, but I feel the bright
   eyes
  Of the beautiful Annabel Lee:
And so, all the night-tide, I lie down by the side
Of my darling—my darling—my life and my
   bride,
In the sepulchre there by the sea—
In her tomb by the sounding sea.

See *Consonance.*

**Autobiography.** An autobiography is the story of a person's life written by that person. "Fair and Circus Days" and the selections from *Act One* and *I Know Why the Caged Bird Sings* are examples of autobiography. In each autobiographical selection, the writer focuses upon events that are particularly significant in his or her life. Autobiographies, which are almost always told from the first-person point of view, offer the reader unique opportunities to share and understand the experiences of other individuals.

See *Biography.*

**Ballad.** A ballad is a narrative poem that was originally meant to be sung. Ballads usually begin abruptly, focus on a single tragic incident, contain dialogue and repetition, and imply more than they actually tell. Traditional ballads are written in four-line stanzas with regular rhythm and rhyme. The rhythm often alternates between four-stress and three-stress lines, and the rhyme scheme usually is a b c b or a a b b.

Folk ballads were composed anonymously and handed down by word of mouth. The music to most of these ballads has been lost. The literary ballad is a poem written by a contemporary poet who imitates the form and content of the folk ballad.

The following ballad was popular in both the North and the South during the Civil War. Each line has four stresses and the rhyme scheme is a b c b.

"Mother, is the battle over?
  Thousands have been slain, they say.
Is my father come? and tell me,
  Has the army gained the day?

"Is he well, or is he wounded?
  Mother, do you think he's slain?
If he is, pray will you tell me,
  Will my father come again?

"Mother, I see you always sighing
  Since that paper last you read;
Tell me why you are crying:
  Is my dearest father dead?"

"Yes, my boy, your noble father
  Is one numbered with the slain;
Though he loves me very dearly,
  Ne'er on earth we'll meet again."
               ANONYMOUS
         "Mother, Is the Battle Over?"

**Biography.** A biography is the story of a person's life written by another person. "Harriet Tubman," "Nellie Bly—Woman Reporter" and "Woman Without Fear" are three examples of biography included in this text. In these selections, the writers focus on remarkable and admirable aspects of their subjects. Although a biographer, by necessity and by inclination, presents a subject from a certain point of view, a skilled biographer strives for a balanced treatment, highlighting weaknesses as well as strengths, failures as well as achievements.

See *Autobiography.*

**Blank Verse.** Blank verse is unrhymed poetry written in iambic pentameter. Each line has five metrical feet, and each foot has an unstressed syllable followed by a stressed syllable.

Tennyson's poem "The Passing of Arthur" is written in blank verse. The following lines from the poem describe the famous scene in which, at King Arthur's request, his sword Excaliber is thrown into the water. Note the iambic pentameter meter and the lack of end rhyme.

So flash'd/and fell/the brand/Excal/ibur:
But ere/he dipt/the sur/face, rose/an arm
Clothed in/white sam/ite, mys/tic,
 won/derful,
And caught/him by/the hilt,/and bran/dish'd him
Three times,/and drew/him un/der in/the mere.

**Character.** Characters are the people and sometimes the animals who participate in the action of a literary work. Characters may be major or minor, depending on the degree of their development and on their role in the narrative. Creating believable, interesting characters whose actions and emotions provide insights into everyday life is the goal of writers of short stories, novels, plays, and narrative poems.

See *Characterization*.

**Characterization.** Characterization refers to the techniques employed by writers to develop characters. There are five basic types of characterization.

1. The writer may use physical description. In "The Heyday of the Blood," gran'ther is described as ". . . the little, shriveled cripple, his face shining with perspiring animation. . . ." This statement not only points out gran'ther's age and physical handicaps but also stresses his zest for life.

2. Descriptions of actions may be used. When gran'ther disobeys his son and coerces his grandson into accompanying him to the county fair, the reader learns that gran'ther is rebellious and independent.

3. Dialogue spoken by the character and by other characters is another means of characterization. When gran'ther tells Joey his motto "Live while you live, and then die and be done with it!," the reader realizes that his fierce independence results from his love of life.

4. Direct comments from the narrator can be used to develop a character. Describing the encounter with the fat lady, the narrator states, "My admiration for gran'ther's daredevil qualities rose to infinity when he entered into free-and-easy talk with her. . . ."

5. A narrator may describe the reactions of other characters to a particular character. The fat lady's response to gran'ther emphasizes his humanity:

She laughed a great deal at us, but she was evidently touched by his human interest, for she confided to him that it was not velvet at all, but furniture covering; and when we went away she pressed on us a bag of peanuts.

**Climax.** In dramatic or narrative literature, the climax is the turning point of action, the moment when interest and intensity reach their peak. In "By the Waters of Babylon," John's discovery of the dead "god" is the climax of the story. The climax of a story determines the direction or nature of the remaining events. In *Shane*, Shane's decision to reassume his former identity clearly indicates the events that the reader may expect as the novel draws to a conclusion.

See *Conflict, Falling Action, Plot, Rising Action*.

**Comic Relief.** Comic relief refers to humorous scenes or speeches that alleviate the tension that has built up during the development of the conflicts. The term comic relief nearly always is used in connection with drama, especially tragedy. The practice of including comic relief developed during Shakespeare's time as a means of allowing the audience to relax, laugh, and consider the consequences of the developing tragedy.

**Concrete Poem.** A concrete poem visually presents something important about the poem's meaning. In concrete poetry, a direct and often obvious relationship exists between form and meaning. The following poem illustrates this relationship.

silencio silencio silencio
silencio silencio silencio
silencio            silencio
silencio silencio silencio
silencio silencio silencio
EUGEN GOMRINGER
"Silencio"

**Conflict.** Conflict is the struggle between opposing forces that is the basis of plot in dramatic and narrative literature. Various types of conflict occur in literature. Often two characters struggle against one another, as do Todd Lander and the foreman in "The Breed of 'Em." Sometimes conflict occurs between a character and society, as in "Prelude," in which the characters struggle against prejudice. Conflict also may be within an individual character, between opposing tendencies in the character's mind, as in "Of Missing Persons." Sometimes conflict occurs when a character clashes with nature, as in "Corvus the Crow."

Longer works of fiction may develop several conflicts. In *Shane*, for instance, the farmers are in conflict with Luke Fletcher, and Shane experiences a conflict between his desire to help Joe Starrett and his need to reject the past.

See *Climax, Falling Action, Plot, Rising Action.*

**Connotation.** Connotation is the emotional response evoked by a word. *Kitten*, for example, is defined as "a young cat." However, the word also conveys images of softness, warmth, and playfulness. These suggested meanings are the connotations of the word.

See *Denotation.*

**Consonance.** Consonance is the repetition of consonant sounds within and at the ends of words. "Last but not least" and a "stroke of luck" contain examples of consonance. Consonance, assonance, alliteration, and rhyme give writing a musical quality and may be used to unify poems and passages of prose writing. Notice the repetition of internal and final consonants in the following lines.

Season of mists and mellow fruitfulness,
    Close bosom-friend of the maturing sun;
Conspiring with him how to load and bless
    With fruit the vines that round the
        thatch-eves run;
To bend with apples the mossed cottage-trees,
    And fill all fruit with ripeness to the core;
    To swell the gourd, and plump the hazel
        shells
With a sweet kernel; to set budding more,
    And still more, later flowers for the bees,
    Until they think warm days will never cease,
    For summer has o'er-brimmed their
        clammy cells.
JOHN KEATS
"To Autumn"

See *Assonance.*

**Couplet.** See *Heroic Couplet.*

**Denotation.** Denotation refers to the dictionary definition of a word.

See *Connotation.*

**Description.** Description is writing that appeals to the senses. Good descriptive writing helps the reader to see, hear, touch, taste, and/or smell the subject of the description. For effectiveness, description usually relies on precise adjectives, adverbs, nouns, and verbs, as well as on vivid, original phrases. Figurative language, such as similes, metaphors, and personification, is also an important tool in description.

The following passage illustrates the use of vividly detailed descriptive language.

> We crossed the singing stream: on either bank great bushes of blackthorn—last native flower of the season—put forth their wealth of magnificent creamy bloom, its rich perfume floating far on the hot summer air. How the sunlight blazed and danced and flickered on the familiar and dearly loved landscape! Over a rise, and the house was lost to view, then goodbye to the crystal creek. The trees of Five-Bob Downs came within eye-range far away on our left. What merry nights I had spent there amid music, flowers, youth, light, love, and summer warmth, when the tide of life seemed full! . . . It was all over! My pleasant life at Caddagat was going into the past, fading as the hills that surrounded it were melting into a hazy line of blue.
> MILES FRANKLIN
> *My Brilliant Career*

**Dialect.** A dialect is the particular variety of language spoken in a definite place by a distinct group of people. Dialects vary in pronunciation, vocabulary, colloquial expressions, and grammatical constructions. Writers use dialect to establish setting, to provide local color, and to develop characters.

The following selection is from *Tom Sawyer* by Mark Twain. Twain effectively reproduces a dialect spoken in the Mississippi River town of Hannibal, Missouri, in about the middle of the nineteenth century.

> Hang the boy, can't I never learn anything? Ain't he played me tricks enough like that for me to be looking out for him by this time? But old fools is the biggest fools there is. Can't learn an old dog new tricks, as the saying is. But my goodness, he never plays them alike, two days,

and how is a body to know what's coming? He 'pears to know just how long he can torment me before I get my dander up. . . .

**Dialogue.** Dialogue is written conversation between two or more characters. Dialogue is used in most forms of prose writing and also in narrative poetry. In drama, the dialogue carries the story line. In scripts for plays, dialogue is indicated by the placement of words next to a character's name and by the appearance of the type in which the dialogue is printed.

Realistic, well placed dialogue enlivens narrative, descriptive, and expository prose and provides the reader with insights into characters and their personalities. In prose writing, dialogue is set apart according to special rules for punctuation, capitalization, and paragraphing; for example:

> Here the Red Queen began again. "Can you answer useful questions?" she said. "How is bread made?"
> "I know *that!*" Alice cried eagerly. "You take some flour—"
> "Where do you pick the flower?" the White Queen asked. "In a garden or in the hedges?"
> "Well, it isn't *picked* at all," Alice explained. "It's *ground*—"
> "How many acres of ground?" said the White Queen. "You musn't leave out so many things."
> "Fan her head!" the Red Queen anxiously interrupted. "She'll be feverish after so much thinking." So they set to work and fanned her with bunches of leaves, till she had to beg them to leave off, it blew her hair about so.
> "She's all right again now," said the Red Queen. "Do you know Languages? What's the French for fiddle-de-dee?"
> "Fiddle-de-dee's not English," Alice replied gravely.
> "Who ever said it was?" said the Red Queen.
> LEWIS CARROLL
> *Through the Looking Glass*

**Diction.** Diction is a writer's choice of words. The diction of a poem or passage of prose can be analyzed by examining the denotative and connotative meanings of the words and by identifying the vocabulary as formal or informal, abstract or concrete, technical or common, literal or figurative.

The writer of a scientific essay on weather, for example, would use formal, technical words with precise denotative meanings. An essayist describing a lake after a summer storm, however, would rely more on the connotative power of words and on figurative language.

By choosing their words with care, writers achieve clear, effective writing and a unique writing style.

See *Style*.

**Drama.** Drama is literature that develops plot and character through dialogue and action; in other words, drama is literature in play form. Dramas are meant to be performed by actors and actresses who appear on a stage, before radio microphones, or in front of television or movie cameras.

Drama assumes an audience, as well as performers and a script. When an audience becomes caught up in a drama and forgets to a degree the artificiality of a play, the process is called the suspension of disbelief.

Most plays are divided into acts, with each act having an emotional peak, or climax, of its own. The acts sometimes are divided into scenes; each scene is limited to a single time and place. Shakespeare's plays all have five acts. Contemporary plays usually have two or three acts, although some have only one act. "The Rising of the Moon" and "Orpheus" are examples of one-act plays.

**Dramatic Irony.** See *Irony*.

**Epigraph.** An epigraph in literature is a motto or quotation that appears at the beginning of a book or play. An epigraph generally relates to the theme of the book or play, and the reader can gain insight into the theme by relating the epigraph to the work. Occasionally an epigraph includes a line that the writer has used as the title of the work. Lorraine Hansberry, for example, selected a line from a poem by Langston Hughes as the title of her play, *A Raisin in the Sun*. A portion of the poem is the epigraph for her play.

At one time, writers put epigraphs at the beginning of every chapter in a book, but this practice is seldom followed by contemporary authors.

**Essay.** The essay is one of the most flexible of literary forms. It is a brief, nonfiction composition that offers an opinion on a subject. Frequently the essayist tries to persuade the reader to accept a particular point of view. Some essays are formal and impersonal, and the major argument is developed systematically. Other essays are informal, personal, and less rigidly organized. The informal essay often includes anecdotes and humor.

Essays are classified as descriptive, narrative, or expository. Few essays, however, rely exclusively on a single writing technique. The essay "Once More to the Lake," for example, is primarily a descriptive essay, but the writer includes some narration and exposition to make his point about father-son relationships.

**Exposition.** Exposition is a detailed statement or explanation which often comes at the beginning of a work of literature to lay the groundwork for the narrative and to provide necessary background information. In *Romeo and Juliet*, in order to understand the events of the play it is necessary to know about the feud between the Montagues and the Capulets, the families of the two lovers. Shakespeare provides this exposition in the Prologue to the play and through the dialogue and action of the servants in the opening scene of the play.

Similarly, in *Julius Caesar* it is important to know something of Caesar's history and why important Romans might wish to assassinate him. Shakespeare provides this exposition through the conversation between Marullus and Flavius in the opening scene of the play and, a short while later, in the first discussion between Brutus and Cassius.

In the short story and the novel, exposition appears most commonly as the opening paragraphs of a selection or a chapter or as a flashback within the narrative. At the beginning of "Point of Departure," for example, the narrator describes the unsettled behavior of the main character that precedes her pivotal encounter with the teenage boy, thus intensifying and explaining the significance of the episode. In "Sweet Potato Pie," the narrator recalls his childhood, information that enables the reader to comprehend the deep love for his older brother expressed at the beginning of the story.

**Extended Metaphor.** In an extended metaphor, two unlike things are compared in several ways. Sometimes the comparison is carried throughout a paragraph, a stanza, or an entire selection, as in the following poem.

What syrup, what unusual sweet,
  Sticky and sharp and strong,
Wafting its poison through the street,
  Has lured this buzzing throng
That swarms along the counters there
  Where bargain bait is dangled—
Clustered like flies in honey snare,
  Shrill, cross, and well entangled?
                PHYLLIS MCGINLEY
                "Sale Today"

In this poem, the poet draws a comparison between shoppers searching for bargains at a sale and flies swarming around something sticky and sweet. The comparison is clarified by the simile in the next to the last line, which states what has up to that point only been implied.

See *Figurative Language, Metaphor.*

**Falling Action.** In a dramatic or narrative work, the falling action occurs after the climax, or high point of intensity or interest. The falling action shows the results of the major events and resolves loose ends in the plot. In *Shane,* the final shootout at Grafton's place and Shane's departure from the valley result from Shane's decision to reassume his role as a gunfighter in order to help Joe Starrett.

See *Climax, Conflict, Plot, Rising Action.*

**Fiction.** Fiction refers to imaginative works of prose, including the novel and the short story. Fiction often is inspired by actual events and by real people, but a work of fiction also may be entirely imaginative. Writers of fiction treat their subjects in a variety of ways. Some write light, humorous pieces the main purpose of which is to entertain the reader. Others criticize, interpret, and comment on behavior and situations in order to deepen the reader's understanding of the human experience.

The basic elements of fiction are plot, character, setting, and theme.

See *Character, Nonfiction, Novel, Plot, Setting, Short Story, Theme.*

**Figurative Language.** Language that communicates ideas beyond the ordinary meanings of the words is called figurative language. The words in a figurative expression are not literally true, but rather they stimulate vivid pictures and concepts in the mind of the reader. Note the difference between the literal and the figurative meanings of the words in the following excerpt.

Bowed by the weight of centuries he leans
Upon his hoe and gazes on the ground,
The emptiness of ages in his face,
And on his back the burden of the world.

EDWIN MARKHAM
"The Man with the Hoe"

Centuries do not literally have weight, ages cannot be empty, and the world does not have a burden that a person could assume. The poet relies instead on the figurative meanings of the words to convey a sense of extreme age and weariness.

Figurative language appears in poetry and prose, as well as in spoken language. The general term figurative language includes specific figures of speech. The most common are simile, metaphor, personification, and hyperbole.

See *Hyperbole, Metaphor, Personification, Simile.*

**First-Person Narration.** See *Point of View.*

**Flashback.** A flashback is a conversation, a scene, or an event that happened before the beginning of a story, or at an earlier point in the narrative. Usually, a plot moves forward chronologically, beginning at one point in time and proceeding until the conclusion. When a flashback is included, it is generally because a writer believes that information from the past is necessary if the reader is to understand the present situation of a character or characters. For example, the novel *The Go-Between,* by L. P. Hartley, is set in the year 1952. However, the narrator begins the novel with the sentences, "The past is a foreign country: they do things differently there. When I came upon the diary it was lying at the bottom of a rather battered red cardboard collar-box . . . ." This opening prepares the reader for the story, which is a flashback to the year 1900. The flashback is triggered by the narrator's finding his diary for that year.

Much of the famous novel *Wuthering Heights,* by Emily Brontë, is a flashback narrated by an old servant. As she describes to a newcomer, Mr. Lockwood, events from the childhood of Mr. Heathcliff, her employer, Mr. Lockwood gains a fuller understanding of Heathcliff and of others whose lives Heathcliff has touched.

**Foil.** A foil is a character who provides a striking contrast to another character. A writer may use a foil to call attention to certain characteristics possessed by a main character or to emphasize the importance of those characteristics. In *Shane,* Stark Wilson functions as a foil to Shane. Although both men are expert gunfighters, Wilson's total lack of moral standards makes Shane's behavior seem more impressive to the reader.

**Foreshadowing.** To foreshadow is to show beforehand, or to foretell. Thus, in literature, foreshadowing is a writer's use of hints or clues to indicate events that will occur later in the narrative. The usual reason for the use of this technique is to create tension and to excite curiosity about further complications of plot.

In *The Great Gatsby*, F. Scott Fitzgerald foreshadows the violent death of one of his characters in an automobile accident by referring to two minor accidents early in the novel. The two accidents that are mentioned involve front wheels, as does the major accident that is the climax of Fitzgerald's novel.

In the Russian novel *Crime and Punishment,* by Fyodor Dostoevsky, Raskolnikov, the central character, murders an old pawnbroker with an ax. Later, he feels great guilt. The murder and Raskolnikov's subsequent guilt are both foreshadowed early in the novel by a dream in which Raskolnikov witnesses the senseless murder of a horse. In the dream, Raskolnikov feels pain over the murder and sympathy for the horse.

**Free Verse.** Poetry written without regular patterns of rhyme and meter is known as free verse. Like most poetry, free verse is usually more rhythmic than ordinary language. Much of the poetry written in the twentieth century is free verse.

An example of free verse is the following poem by Walt Whitman, the nineteenth-century American poet generally credited with originating this type of poetry.

> Facing west from California's shores,
> Inquiring, tireless, seeking what is yet unfound,
> I, a child, very old, over waves, towards the
>     house of maternity, the land migrations, look
>     afar,
> Look off the shores of my Western sea, the
>     circle almost circled;
> For starting westward from Hindustan, from the
>     vales of Kashmere,
> From Asia, from the north, from the God, the
>     sage, and the hero,
> From the south, from the flowery peninsulas
>     and the spice islands,
> Long having wander'd since, round the earth
>     having wander'd,
> Now I face home again, very pleas'd and
>     joyous,
> (But where is what I started for so long ago?
> And why is it yet unfound?)
>                 "Facing West from California's
>                 Shores"

**Haiku.** Haiku is a Japanese poetry form. When written in Japanese, the haiku has seventeen syllables arranged in three lines. The first line has five syllables, the second line has seven syllables, and the third line has five syllables. When haiku are translated from Japanese into other languages, however, it is difficult, if not impossible, to maintain the syllable count while conveying the appropriate meaning. Translators therefore concentrate on capturing the mood and imagery of the original. Poets writing haiku in languages other than Japanese tend to emphasize content rather than syllable count.

All haiku have four recognizable qualities:

1. Haiku depend on imagery.
2. Haiku are condensed; the poet leaves out all unnecessary words.
3. Haiku are concerned with emotions; nature reflects these emotions.
4. Haiku rely heavily on the power of suggestion, or connotation.

The following haiku are translations from the Japanese.

> There a beggar goes!
> Heaven and earth he's wearing
> For his summer clothes.
>             KIKAKU (1661–1707)

> A trout leaps high—
> Below him in the river bottom,
> Clouds flow by.
>             ONITSURA (1660–1738)

**Hero.** See *Tragic Hero.*

**Heroic Couplet.** A heroic couplet is two consecutive lines of poetry that rhyme and that are written in iambic pentameter. A line of iambic pentameter consists of five metrical feet; each foot is made up of an unstressed syllable followed by a stressed syllable. Heroic couplets can function alone as units of meaning or can be combined into longer poems.

The following lines are heroic couplets.

> Whoever thinks a faultless piece to see,
> Thinks what ne're was, nor is, nor e're shall be.
> In ev'ry work regard the writer's end,
> Since none can compass more than they intend;
> And if the means be just, the conduct true,
> Applause, in spite of trivial faults, is due.
>             ALEXANDER POPE
>           "An Essay on Criticism"

**Hyperbole.** Hyperbole is a figure of speech in which the truth is exaggerated for emphasis. The expression, "I'm so hungry I could eat a horse" is an example of hyperbole.

Hyperbole is common in expressions of love. Notice the use of hyperbole in these three stanzas.

> O, my luve is like a red, red rose,
>     That's newly sprung in June.
> O, my luve is like the melodie,
>     That's sweetly play'd in tune.
>
> As fair art thou, my bonie lass,
>     So deep in luve am I;
> And I will luve thee still, my dear,
>     Till a' the seas gang dry.
>
> Till a' the seas gang dry, my dear,
>     And the rocks melt wi' the sun!
> And I will luve thee still, my dear,
>     While the sands o' life shall run.
>
> And fare thee weel, my only luve,
>     And fare thee weel a while!
> And I will come again, my luve,
>     Tho' it were ten thousand mile!
>                     ROBERT BURNS
>                 "O, My Luve Is Like a Red,
>                     Red Rose"

Hyperbole can create a humorous effect. In the selection from "Life Among the Savages," Laurie gives this exaggerated account of his accident: "—And I guess there were five hundred people there. They came tearing in from all over. And the street—you oughta seen the street—*covered* with blood —"

See *Figurative Language*.

**Imagery.** Imagery describes words and phrases that re-create vivid sensory experiences for the reader. Because sight is the most highly developed sense, the majority of images are visual. Imagery may also appeal to the senses of smell, hearing, taste, and touch. Special types of images are given specific names. Images that re-create heat are called thermal; images that re-create movement are called kinetic; and images that re-create ten-

sion felt through muscles, tendons, or joints within the body are called kinesthetic.

The images in the following poem enable the reader to "see" and "hear" the garbage truck as it moves through the empty streets.

> It rolls
> upon the hush of morning
> ignoring delicate embroidered forms
> born of bright beams, descending:
> spreading a gauze glazing net,
> veiling the bald street.
>
> Its giant grey hulk whines
> gears grind their metallic chorus
> bemoaning a slow advance
> before rows of three-story houses
> (at whose windows, sun beckons!)
>
> Two sullen figures, trailing,
> gather rusted containers;
> two silent keepers
> of a whining machine,
> whose rotating mouth
> tumbles village dross.
>                     JAMES W. THOMPSON
>                     "Thursday's Collection"

**Indeterminate Ending.** When a work of literature ends with no definite conclusion or resolution, the ending is called indeterminate. In such a work, the conflicts are not resolved in favor of either the protagonist or the antagonist. While this type of ending may not be satisfying for the reader who would like everything tied up in a neat package, it may be the most realistic and appropriate ending for a particular short story, play, or novel.

**Internal Rhyme.** See *Rhyme*.

**Irony.** Irony is a contrast between appearance and actuality. There are three basic types of irony. When people say one thing but in actuality mean something quite different, they are using verbal irony. In *Julius*

*Caesar,* Marc Antony uses verbal irony in his funeral oration when he says that Brutus is honorable, but in fact he means just the opposite.

Irony of situation occurs when a character or the reader expects one thing to happen but something entirely different occurs. In "The Cask of Amontillado," Fortunato expects to be led to a barrel of wine; instead, he is led to his tomb.

Dramatic irony occurs when the reader or viewer is aware of information of which the characters are unaware. In *A Raisin in the Sun,* when Asagai enters the Younger apartment, he says, "Ah, I like the look of packing crates! A household in preparation for a journey!" Because the audience knows that the Youngers' plans have abruptly changed, Asagai's joyful words at this time of despair create a moment of dramatic irony.

**Lyric.** In ancient Greece, the lyre was a musical instrument, and the lyric became the name for a song accompanied by music. In common speech, the words of songs are still called lyrics.

In literature, a lyric is any short poem that presents a single speaker who expresses thoughts and feelings. In a love lyric, a speaker expresses romantic love. In other lyrics, a speaker may meditate on nature or seek to resolve an emotional crisis.

The short lyric that follows is by William Wordsworth, a famous English poet.

> My heart leaps up when I behold
>   A rainbow in the sky;
> So was it when my life began;
> So is it now I am a man;
> So be it when I shall grow old.
>   Or let me die!
> The Child is father of the Man;
> And I could wish my days to be
> Bound each to each by natural piety.
>                 "My Heart Leaps Up. . . ."

**Metaphor.** A metaphor is a figure of speech that implies a comparison between two unlike things that have something in common. Unlike similes, metaphors do not use the words *like* or *as;* the comparisons are suggested rather than directly expressed.

The following lines are from Sonnet 73 by William Shakespeare.

> That time of year thou mayst in me behold
> When yellow leaves, or none, or few, do hang
> Upon those boughs which shake against the cold

The poet draws a comparison between old age and approaching winter. This metaphor helps the reader to perceive the similarity between a person approaching the cold of death and a tree enduring the cold of winter. Here is another metaphor that describes old age.

> Old age is
> a flight of small
> cheeping birds
> skimming
> bare trees
> above a snow glaze.
>                 WILLIAM CARLOS WILLIAMS
>                 "To Waken an Old Lady"

In the following metaphor, the poet draws a comparison between life and a boat.

> But life without meaning is the torture
> Of restlessness and vague desire—
> It is a boat longing for the sea and yet afraid.
>                 EDGAR LEE MASTERS
>                 "George Gray"

See *Extended Metaphor, Figurative Language, Simile.*

**Meter.** Meter is the repetition of a regular rhythmic unit in a line of poetry. The meter of a poem emphasizes the musical quality of the language and often relates directly to the subject matter of the poem.

Each unit of meter is known as a foot, with each foot having one stressed and one or two unstressed syllables. The four basic types of metrical feet are the iamb, an unstressed syllable followed by a stressed syllable (⌣/); the trochee, a stressed syllable followed by an unstressed syllable (/⌣); the anapest, two unstressed syllables followed by a stressed syllable (⌣⌣/); and the dactyl, a stressed syllable followed by two unstressed syllables (/⌣⌣).

A line of poetry is named not only for the type of meter but also for the number of feet in the line. The most common metrical names are monometer, a one-foot line; dimeter, a two-foot line; trimeter, a three-foot line; tetrameter, a four-foot line; pentameter, a five-foot line; hexameter, a six-foot line; heptameter, a seven-foot line; and octometer, an eight-foot line.

The following is an example of iambic pentameter, the most common form of meter in English poetry.

> 1   2   3   4   5
> ⌣ / ⌣ / ⌣ / ⌣ / ⌣ /
> Shall I/compare/thee to/a sum/mer's day?
> ⌣ / ⌣ / ⌣ / ⌣ / ⌣ /
> Thou art/more love/ly and/more tem/perate:
> ⌣ / ⌣ / ⌣ / ⌣ / ⌣
> Rough winds/do shake/the dar/ling buds/of
>   /
> May,
> ⌣ / ⌣ / ⌣ / ⌣ / ⌣ /
> And sum/mer's lease/hath all/too short/a date;
>
> WILLIAM SHAKESPEARE
> "Sonnet 18"

This next selection is an example of trochaic tetrameter.

> 1   2   3   4
> / ⌣ / ⌣ / ⌣ / ⌣
> There he/sang of/Hia/watha,
> / ⌣ / ⌣ / ⌣ / ⌣
> Sang the/Song of/Hia/watha,
> / ⌣ / ⌣ / ⌣ / ⌣
> Sang his/wondrous/birth and/being,
> / ⌣ / ⌣ / ⌣ / ⌣
> How he /prayed and/how he /fasted,
> / ⌣ / ⌣ / ⌣ / ⌣
> How he /lived, and/toiled, and/suffered,
> / ⌣ / ⌣ / ⌣ / ⌣
> That the /tribes of/men might/prosper,
> / ⌣ / ⌣ / ⌣ / ⌣
> That he /might ad/vance his/people!
>
> HENRY WADSWORTH
> LONGFELLOW
> *The Song of Hiawatha*

Most poems are not written in exact meters but in a combination of meters. An iambic line may end with an anapestic foot, for example, or lines of iambic tetrameter may alternate with lines of iambic trimeter. Such variations are not mistakes but conscious choices made by the poets to achieve desired effects.

**Mood.** Mood is the atmosphere, or feeling, that the writer creates for the reader. The writer's use of connotation, imagery, and figurative language, as well as sound and rhythm, develop the mood of a selection.

Notice how Ray Bradbury gradually builds a feeling of terror in this passage from *The Martian Chronicles*.

> And here we all are tonight, in various houses, in various beds, with no weapons to protect us, and the rocket lies in the moonlight, empty. And wouldn't it be horrible and terrifying to discover that all of this was part of some great clever plan by the Martians to divide and conquer us, and kill us? Sometime during the night, perhaps, my brother here on this bed will change form, melt, shift, and become another thing, a terrible thing, a Martian. It would be very simple for him just to turn over in bed and put a knife into my heart. And in all those other houses down the street, a dozen other brothers or fathers suddenly melting away and taking knives and doing things to the unsuspecting, sleeping men of Earth. . . .
>
> His hands were shaking under the covers. His body was cold. Suddenly it was not a theory. Suddenly he was very afraid.

**Myth.** A myth is a traditional story, usually concerning some superhuman being or unlikely event, that was once widely believed to be true. Frequently, myths attempt to explain natural phenomena, such as solar and lunar eclipses and the cycle of the seasons. For earlier peoples, myths were both a kind of crude science and a religion. In addition, myths served as literature and entertainment, just as they do for modern-day audiences.

The most famous myths, such as the stories of Theseus and Hercules, originated among the ancient Greeks and Romans. Norse mythology, consisting of myths from Scandinavia and Germany, is also important classical literature. Indian tribes throughout North America have produced fascinating myths of various kinds, as have the peoples of Africa and South America.

**Narration.** See *Point of View.*

**Narrative Poem.** A narrative poem tells a story. The ballad is a specific type of narrative poem, often intended to be sung. Following is an old Chinese narrative poem, entitled "The River-Merchant's Wife: A Letter," translated by poet Ezra Pound.

While my hair was still cut straight across my
  forehead
Played I about the front gate, pulling flowers.
You came by on bamboo stilts, playing horse,
You walked about my seat, playing with blue
  plums.
And we went on living in the village of Chokan:
Two small people, without dislike or suspicion.

At fourteen I married My Lord you.
I never laughed, being bashful.
Lowering my head, I looked at the wall.
Called to, a thousand times, I never looked back.

At fifteen I stopped scowling,
I desired my dust to be mingled with yours
Forever and forever and forever.
Why should I climb the look out?

At sixteen you departed,
You went into far Ku-to-yen, by the river of
  swirling eddies,
And you have been gone five months.
The monkeys make sorrowful noise overhead.

You dragged your feet when you went out.
By the gate now, the moss is grown, the different
  mosses,
Too deep to clear them away!
The leaves fall early this autumn, in wind.
The paired butterflies are already yellow with
  August
Over the grass in the West garden;
They hurt me. I grow older.
If you are coming down through the narrows of
  the river Kiang,
Please let me know beforehand,
And I will come out to meet you
                    As far as Cho-fu-Sa.

See *Ballad.*

**Narrator.** The narrator is the person from whose point of view a story is told. The narrator of a short story, novel, or nonfiction selection may be the writer, a character within the selection, or someone outside the action.

See *Point of View.*

**Nonfiction.** Nonfiction is prose writing that is about real people, places, and events. Unlike fiction, which is inspired by a writer's imagination, nonfiction is based on factual information and on real events and subjects. Biographies, autobiographies, histories, editorials, essays, journals, and news articles are all examples of nonfiction.

See *Autobiography, Biography, Essay, Fiction.*

**Novel.** The novel is an extended work of prose fiction. Like the short story, a novel is essentially the product of a writer's imagination. The most obvious difference between a novel and a short story is length. Because the novel is considerably longer, a novelist can develop a wider range of characters and a more complex plot.

The four main elements of a short story—setting, character, plot, and theme—are also the chief elements of a novel. Additional techniques of fiction, such as symbolism, irony, and foreshadowing, are frequently important in the novel. *Shane* represents the western novel, which is only one of many types of novels.

**Onomatopoeia.** The word *onomatopoeia* literally means "name-making." It is the process of creating or using words that imitate sounds. The *buzz* of the bee, the *honk* of the car horn, the *peep* of the chick are all onomatopoetic words. One theory of the origin of language is that the first words were imitations of the sounds in nature.

Onomatopoeia as a literary technique goes beyond the use of simple echoic words. Writers, particularly poets, choose words whose sounds suggest their denotative and connotative meanings; for example, *whisper*, *kick*, *gargle*, *gnash*, and *clatter*.

In the following poem, the writer's combination of echoic words, suggestive words, and newly coined words demonstrates the rich possibilities of onomatopoeia.

> The rusty spigot
> sputters,
> utters
> a splutter,
> spatters a smattering of drops,
> gashes wider;
> slash,
> splatters,
> scatters,
> spurts,
> finally stops sputtering
> and plash!
> gushes rushes splashes
> clear water dashes.
>
> Eve Merriam<br>"Onomatopoeia"

**Parallelism.** When a writer or speaker expresses ideas of equal worth with the same grammatical form, the technique is called parallelism, or parallel construction.

Julius Caesar's famous Latin sentence, "Veni, vidi, vici," which in English means "I came, I saw, I conquered," is an example of effective parallelism. Caesar economically expresses three ideas of equal weight with the same construction: the subject *I* followed by a simple verb in the past tense.

A more modern example of the skillful use of parallelism appears in the prologue to *The Autobiography of Bertrand Russell*, the celebrated twentieth-century philosopher. Russell begins his life story with the sentence, "Three passions, simple but overwhelmingly strong, have governed my life: the longing for love, the search for knowledge, and unbearable pity for the suffering of mankind." Because the three passions have had equal importance in Russell's life, he presents them in parallel grammatical form: a noun followed by a prepositional phrase beginning with the preposition *for*.

Attention to parallelism generally makes both spoken and written expression more concise and powerful.

**Pathetic Fallacy.** Coined by the nineteenth-century English writer John Ruskin, the term pathetic fallacy refers to the attachment of human traits and feelings to nature. Ruskin chose the word *pathetic*, meaning "pertaining to the feelings," because the term describes a situation in which nature "feels" with human beings. He chose the word *fallacy*, meaning "false notion," because nature does not feel with human beings but acts independently, without reference to human affairs.

Writers often use the pathetic fallacy to emphasize human emotions and actions. For example, in the American novel *The Scarlet Letter*, Nathaniel Hawthorne uses the pathetic fallacy to elicit sympathy for his heroine, Hester Prynne, who rebels against the harsh punishment inflicted by society. At the moment when Hester decides to run away from her restrictive Puritan village with the man she loves the following happens.

All at once, as with a sudden smile of heaven, forth burst the sunshine, pouring a very flood into the obscure forest, gladdening each green leaf, transmuting the yellow fallen ones to gold, and gleaming adown the gray trunks of the solemn trees. The objects that had made a shadow hitherto, embodied the brightness now. The course of the little brook might be traced by its merry gleam afar into the wood's heart of mystery, which had become a mystery of joy.

Such was the sympathy of Nature—that wild, heathen Nature of the forest, never subjugated by human law, nor illumined by higher truth— with the bliss of these two spirits!

**Personification.** Personification is a figure of speech in which human qualities are attributed to an object, an animal, or an idea. Writers use personification to concretize, and therefore to clarify, images and feelings for the reader.

In the following poem, the writer uses personification to present vividly his unique view of an ordinary, everyday experience.

A silver-scaled Dragon with jaws flaming red
Sits at my elbow and toasts my bread.
I hand him fat slices, and then, one by one,
He hands them back when he sees they are
    done.

WILLIAM JAY SMITH
"The Toaster"

See *Figurative Language.*

**Plot.** Plot refers to the actions and events that take place in a dramatic or narrative work. The characters participate in the plot and in the conflict, which may be between characters, within one character's mind, or between a character and nature or society. The conflict almost always builds to a climax, or turning point.

Long literary works frequently have subplots as well as a main plot. In *Shane*, for instance, the main plot focuses upon the struggle between the farmers and the rancher, Luke Fletcher. A subplot in the novel involves Shane and Chris, one of Fletcher's ranchhands.

See *Climax, Conflict, Falling Action, Rising Action.*

**Poetry.** Poetry is language arranged in lines. Like other forms of literature, poetry attempts to re-create emotions and experiences. Poetry, however, is usually more condensed and suggestive than prose. Because poetry frequently does not include the kind of detail and explanation common to the short story or the novel, poetry tends to leave more to the reader's imagination. Poetry also may require more work on the part of the reader to unlock meaning.

Poems often are divided into stanzas, or paragraphlike groups of lines. The stanzas in a poem may contain the same number of lines or they may vary in length. Some poems have definite patterns of meter and rhyme. Others rely more on the sounds of words and less on fixed rhythms and rhyme schemes. The use of figurative language is also characteristic of poetry, with some poems depending more heavily on imaginative language than others.

A poem looks and sounds like a poem, but more importantly, the form and content of a poem combine to convey meaning. The way that a poem is arranged on the page, the impact of the images, the sounds of the words and phrases, and all the other details that make up a poem, work together to help the reader grasp its central idea.

**Point of View.** Point of view refers to the narrative method used in a short story, novel, or nonfiction selection. The two basic points of view are first-person and third-person.

When a character within a selection describes the action as a participant, in his or her own words, the writer is using the first-person point of view. A first-person narrator tends to involve the reader in the story and to communicate a sense of immediacy and personal concern. "The Scarlet Ibis" and "The Heyday of the Blood" are examples of the first-person point of view.

When a narrator outside the action describes events and characters, the point of view is third-person. A third-person narrator may be omniscient; that is, the narrator may describe the action and also the thoughts and feelings of the characters. The use of a third-person narrator gives the writer tremendous flexibility and provides the reader with access to all the characters and to events that may be occurring simultaneously. "The Sentimentality of William Tavener," The Breed of 'Em," and "A White Heron" are told from the third-person omniscient point of view.

In the third-person limited point of view, events are related through the eyes of one character, who describes only his or her own feelings and the events that he or she witnesses. "Corvus the Crow," "Act of a Hero," and "The Magic Shop" are examples of the third-person limited point of view.

**Protagonist.** The central character in a short story or novel is called the protagonist. The protagonist always is involved in the central conflict of the story and often changes after the central conflict reaches the climax. In short stories that are written in the first person, the narrator often is the protagonist. Sometimes more than one character appears to be the protagonist of a story. In the short story "Prelude," for example, it is possible to view both the narrator and his sister Syl as protagonists.

See *Antagonist*.

**Pun.** A pun is a play on words. Frequently a pun involves homonyms, words that sound alike but are spelled differently and have different meanings. A pun also can involve playing with two or more dissimilar meanings for the same word.

When the American forefathers signed the Declaration of Independence, Benjamin Franklin is reported to have said, "Now we must all hang together or we will surely hang separately." Franklin's pun on the two meanings of the word *hang* dramatized his awareness that, if the revolutionaries did not remain united, their individual lives would be in danger.

Samuel Johnson, the celebrated eighteenth-century writer and wit, made no secret of his dislike for puns. When Boswell, his friend and biographer, suggested that Dr. Johnson's negative view of puns sprang from his own inability to play upon words, Johnson replied, "Sir, if I were *pun*ish-ed for every pun I shed, there would not be left a *pun*y shred of my *pun*nish head."

**Quatrain.** A quatrain is a four-line stanza, or unit of poetry. The most common stanza in English poetry, the quatrain evidences a variety of meters and rhyme schemes. The ballad stanza is one of the most common quatrains.

Below are two quatrains from a poem by Robert Frost.

A tree's leaves may be ever so good,
So may its bark, so may its wood;
But unless you put the right thing to its root
It never will show much flower or fruit.

But I may be one who does not care
Ever to have tree bloom or bear.
Leaves for smooth and bark for rough,
Leaves and bark may be tree enough.
                    "Leaves Compared with Flowers"

**Refrain.** In poetry, a refrain consists of one or more lines or phrases that are repeated at the ends of succeeding stanzas. Sometimes the refrain will be slightly altered in each stanza. Most ballads contain some kind of refrain.

The following stanzas from a narrative poem illustrate the use of the refrain.

Half a league, half a league,
  Half a league onward,
All in the valley of Death
  Rode the six hundred.
"Forward the Light Brigade!
Charge for the guns!" he said:
Into the valley of Death
  Rode the six hundred.

"Forward the Light Brigade!"
Was there a man dismay'd?
Not tho' the soldier knew
  Some one had blunder'd:
Theirs not to make reply,
Theirs not to reason why,
Theirs but to do and die:
Into the valley of Death
  Rode the six hundred.

ALFRED, LORD TENNYSON
"The Charge of the Light Brigade"

**Repetition.** Repetition is a literary technique in which a word or a phrase is repeated for emphasis. Note the use of repetition in the following stanzas, which are taken from a long poem written in the nineteenth century to protest the working conditions of seamstresses.

With fingers weary and worn,
  With eyelids heavy and red,
A woman sat, in unwomanly rags,
  Plying her needle and thread,—
    Stitch—stitch—stitch!
In poverty, hunger, and dirt;
  And still with a voice of dolorous pitch
She sang the "Song of the Shirt!"

"Work—work—work
  Till the brain begins to swim!
Work—work—work
  Till the eyes are heavy and dim!
Seam, and gusset, and band,
  Band, and gusset, and seam,—
Till over the buttons I fall asleep,
  And sew them on in a dream!

"O men with sisters dear!
  O men with mothers and wives!
It is not linen you're wearing out,
  But human creatures' lives!
    Stitch—stitch—stitch,
  In poverty, hunger, and dirt,—
Sewing at once, with a double thread
  A shroud as well as a shirt!

"Work—work—work
  From weary chime to chime!
Work—work—work
  As prisoners work for crime!
Band, and gusset, and seam,
  Seam, and gusset, and band,
Till the heart is sick and the brain benumbed,
  As well as the weary hand."

THOMAS HOOD
"The Song of the Shirt"

By repeating the words *stitch* and *work*, the poet emphasizes the unending drudgery of the seamstresses' task. The repetition of "seam, and gusset, and band," all parts of a shirt, points out the monotonous quality of the sewing. The repetition of the line "In poverty, hunger, and dirt" reminds the reader of how poorly these women were paid.

**Rhetorical Question.** A question that is designed to produce an effect, usually emotional, and not an answer, is called a rhetorical question. For example, in Shakespeare's play *Henry IV* (Part I), the character Falstaff addresses a famous speech about honor to Prince Hal, later to become Henry IV of England. When Falstaff says, "What is in that word honour? what is that honour? air. A trim reckoning! Who hath it?" he does not expect answers to his questions. The questions are simply designed to give emotional power to his sentiments.

In the English play *The Tragedy of Doctor Faustus*, by Christopher Marlowe, the character Faustus sells his soul to the devil in exchange for infinite knowledge. One of the things that Faustus requests is the most beautiful woman in the world, Helen of Troy. When he first sees Helen, Faustus exclaims, "Was this the face that launched a thousand ships/And burnt the topless towers of Ilium?" He does not expect an answer to his question. He merely wishes to pay tribute to Helen's beauty and to note that her beauty caused the ancient Greeks to sail for Ilium, or Troy, and to destroy that city.

**Rhyme.** Rhyme is the similarity of sound between two words. Words rhyme when the sound of their accented vowels, and all succeeding sounds, are identical. For true rhyme, the consonants that precede the vowels must be different. When rhyme comes at the end of a line of poetry, it is called end rhyme, as in this example.

> An angel, robed in spotless white,
> Bent down and kissed the sleeping Night.
> Night woke to blush; the sprite was gone.
> Men saw the blush and called it Dawn.
> PAUL LAURENCE DUNBAR
> "Dawn"

Rhyme that occurs within a single line, as in the following example, is called internal rhyme.

> Once upon a midnight *dreary*, while I pondered weak and *weary*,
> Over many a quaint and curious volume of forgotten lore,
> While I nodded, nearly *napping*, suddenly there came a *tapping*,
> As of someone gently *rapping*, *rapping* at my chamber door.
> EDGAR ALLAN POE
> "The Raven"

See *Rhyme Scheme.*

**Rhyme Scheme.** A rhyme scheme is the pattern of end rhyme in a poem. The pattern is charted by assigning a letter of the alphabet, beginning with the letter *a*, to each line. Lines that rhyme are given the same letter.

The rhyme scheme for the following poem is identified to the right of the poem.

> I wear them. They help me. But I     a
> Don't care for them. Two birds, steel hinges     b
> Haunt each an edge of the small sky     a
> My green eyes make. Rim-horn impinges     b
> Upon my vision's furry fringes;     b
> Faint dust collects upon the dry,     a
> Unblinking shield behind which cringes     b
> My naked, deprecated eye.     a
>
> My gaze feels aimed. It is as if     c
> Two manufactured beams had been     d
> Lodged in my sockets—hollow, stiff,     c
> And gray, like mailing tubes—and when     d
> I pivot, vases topple down     e
> From tabletops, and women frown.     e
> JOHN UPDIKE
> "Glasses"

See *Rhyme.*

**Rhythm.** Rhythm refers to the pattern or beat of stressed and unstressed syllables in a line of poetry. Poets use rhythm to bring out the musical quality of language, to emphasize ideas, to create mood, and to reinforce content.

See *Meter.*

**Rising Action.** Rising action refers to the events that build to the climax, or highest point of interest and intensity, in a plot. In *Shane,* the complications of plot that lead to Shane's decision to reassume his former identity constitute the rising action.

See *Climax, Conflict, Falling Action, Plot.*

**Science Fiction.** Science fiction is prose writing that presents the possibilities of the past or the future, using known scientific data and theories as well as the creative imagination of the writer. "By the Waters of Babylon" and "There Will Come Soft Rains" are science fiction stories that describe life in the future as seen by the writers. Among the best known science fiction novels are *The Time*

Machine and *The War of the Worlds* by H. G. Wells, *2001: A Space Odyssey* by Arthur C. Clarke, and *Foundation* by Isaac Asimov.

**Setting.** Setting is the time and place of the action of a story. The importance of setting varies. In some works of literature, setting is of little importance, whereas in others it is of primary importance. In *Julius Caesar,* for instance, it is vital to know that the action takes place in ancient Rome, in 44 B.C, the year of Caesar's death.

Time and place may be revealed gradually, or a writer may establish setting immediately, as Thomas Hardy does at the beginning of *The Return of the Native.*

> A Saturday afternoon in November was approaching the time of twilight, and the vast tract of unenclosed wild known as Egdon Heath embrowned itself moment by moment. Overhead the hollow stretch of whitish cloud shutting out the sky was as a tent that had the whole heath for its floor.

Often writers use setting to help create the mood for a story, and in narratives of this type, the setting can be almost as important as the characters and events. An example is Edgar Allan Poe's short story, "The Fall of the House of Usher," which opens with the following passage.

> During the whole of a dull, dark, and soundless day in the autumn of the year, when the clouds hung oppressively low in the heavens, I had been passing alone, on horseback, through a singularly dreary tract of country; and at length found myself, as the shades of the evening drew on, within view of the melancholy House of Usher. I know not how it was—but, with the first glimpse of the building, a sense of insufferable gloom pervaded my spirit. I say insufferable; for the feeling was unrelieved by any of that half-pleasurable, because poetic, sentiment, with which the mind usually receives even the sternest natural images of the desolate or terrible. I looked upon the scene before me—upon

the mere house, and the simple landscape features of the domain—upon the bleak walls—upon the vacant eye-like windows . . . with an utter depression of soul that I can compare to no earthly sensation. . . .

Weather is often a key element in setting, sometimes providing a necessary backdrop for events, sometimes emphasizing the mental states of characters or reinforcing suspense of a sense of impending doom. In the novel *The Great Gatsby,* for example, just before the emotional tensions among the characters surface in a catastrophic fashion, Fitzgerald describes the intense heat of the summer day.

> The next day was broiling, almost the last, certainly the warmest, of the summer. As my train emerged from the tunnel into sunlight, only the hot whistles of the National Biscuit Company broke the simmering hush at noon. The straw seats of the car hovered on the edge of combustion; the woman next to me perspired delicately for a while into her white shirtwaist, and then, as her newspaper dampened under her fingers, lapsed despairingly into deep heat with a desolate cry. . . .
>
> "Hot!" said the conductor to familiar faces. "Some weather! . . . Hot! . . . Hot! . . . Hot! . . . Is it hot enough for you? Is it hot? Is it . . . ?"
>
> F. SCOTT FITZGERALD

**Short Story.** A short story is a work of fiction that can be read in one sitting. Generally, a short story develops one major conflict. The four basic elements of a short story are setting, character, plot, and theme. The setting is the time and place of the action; the characters are the people or animals who carry out the action; the plot is the story line, or the working out of the conflict. The three elements of setting, character, and plot usually combine to reveal the theme, the central idea or message conveyed by the writer.

A short story must be unified; all the elements must work together to produce a total effect. This unity of effect is reinforced through an appropriate title and through the use of symbolism, irony, and other literary devices.

See *Character, Conflict, Plot, Setting, Theme*.

**Simile.** A simile is a stated comparison between two things that are actually unlike, but that have something in common. Like metaphors, similes are figures of speech, but whereas a metaphor implies a comparison, a simile expresses the comparison clearly by the use of the words *like* or *as*.

Writers use similes to give readers a fresh look at familiar things. Notice how the simile that begins this poem creates a new and vivid picture of a familiar animal.

> Like a small grey
> coffee-pot
> sits the squirrel.
> He is not
>
> all he should be,
> kills by dozens
> trees, and eats
> his red-brown cousins.
>
> The keeper, on the
> other hand
> ,who shot him, is
> a Christian, and
>
> loves his enemies,
> which shows
> the squirrel was not
> one of those.
>
> HUMBERT WOLFE<br>"The Grey Squirrel"

The following poems also illustrate the use of similes.

> You are beautiful and faded,
> Like an old opera tune
> Played upon a harpsichord;
> Or like the sun-flooded silks
> Of an eighteenth-century boudoir.
>
> AMY LOWELL<br>"A Lady"

> I found a dimpled spider, fat and white,
> On a white heal-all, holding up a moth
> Like a white piece of rigid satin cloth—
> Assorted characters of death and blight
> Mixed ready to begin the morning right,
> Like the ingredients of a witches' broth—
> A snow-drop spider, a flower like a froth,
> And dead wings carried like a paper kite.
>
> ROBERT FROST<br>"Design"

See *Figurative Language, Metaphor*.

**Soliloquy.** A soliloquy is a speech in a dramatic work in which a character speaks his or her thoughts aloud. The character is almost always on stage alone, and generally appears to be unaware of the presence of an audience. The plays of William Shakespeare frequently include soliloquys.

**Speaker.** The speaker in a poem is the voice that "talks" to the reader. Speaker and poet are not necessarily synonymous. Often, a poet creates a speaker with a distinct identity in order to achieve a particular effect.

In the following poem, the speaker is a young soldier who, prior to the war, was an average working man. The use of this speaker reinforces the central message of the poem.

> Had he and I but met
> By some old ancient inn,
> We should have sat us down to wet
> Right many a nipperkin!
>
> But ranged as infantry
> And staring face to face,
> I shot at him as he at me,
> And killed him in his place.
>
> I shot him dead because—
> Because he was my foe,
> Just so: my foe of course he was;
> That's clear enough; although
>
> He thought he'd 'list, perhaps
> Offhand-like—just as I—
> Was out of work—had sold his traps—
> No other reason why.

Yes; quaint and curious war is!
You shoot a fellow down
You'd treat if met where any bar is,
Or help to half-a-crown.
                    THOMAS HARDY
                    "The Man He Killed"


**Stage Directions.** In the script for a play, stage directions are the italicized instructions that help the reader to visualize those actions not described in the dialogue. Stage directions tell the actors how to move and how to read certain lines. They also might include suggestions for sound effects and music, as well as for the lighting and design of the stage set. While the stage directions for a modern play such as *A Raisin in the Sun* are quite complete, the stage directions for *Julius Caesar* are brief. The stage directions that do appear in this and other Shakespearean plays generally are restricted to those that announce the entrances and exits of characters. One of the most memorable of Shakespeare's stage directions appears in *The Winter's Tale*: *Exit, pursued by a bear.*


**Stanza.** A stanza is a group of lines that form a unit of poetry. The stanza is roughly comparable to the paragraph in prose. Stanzas usually are divided by the ideas presented in the poem or by the pattern of rhyme employed. Generally, the stanzas of a poem have the same number of lines, although contemporary poets experiment a great deal with stanza forms.

The following poem is made up of three stanzas, two quatrains and a couplet.

These buildings are too close to me.
I'd like to PUSH away.
I'd like to live in the country,
And spread my arms all day.

I'd like to spread my breath out, too—
As farmers' sons and daughters do.

I'd tend the cows and chickens.
I'd do the other chores.
Then, all the hours left I'd go
A-SPREADING out-of-doors.
                    GWENDOLYN BROOKS
                    "Rudolph Is Tired of the City"

**Stereotype.** In everyday speech and in literature the term stereotype refers to something that conforms to a fixed or general pattern, without individual distinguishing marks or qualities. Often a stereotype is a standardized mental picture, held in common by members of a group, which represents an oversimplified opinion, such as of a race or national group. In some foreign countries, for example, a widely held view is that all Americans are rich. Like most stereotypes, this one has some basis in fact, for Americans do have a high standard of living compared to many other countries, and most Americans who travel abroad are relatively wealthy.

Simplified, or stock characters in literature are often called stereotypes. A familiar stereotype from popular literature and melodrama is the villain who ties the innocent maiden to the railroad tracks; the innocent maiden too is a stereotype. Such characters do not usually demonstrate the complexities of real people.

**Structure.** Structure is the way that a work of literature is put together. In poetry, structure refers to the arrangement of words and lines to produce a desired effect. A common structural unit in poetry is the stanza, of which there are numerous types.

In prose, structure is the arrangement of larger units or parts of a selection. Paragraphs, for example, are a basic unit in prose, as are chapters in novels and acts in plays.

The structure of a poem, short story, novel, play, or nonfiction selection usually emphasizes certain important aspects of content. In *Julius Caesar*, for example, each of the five acts presents a different stage of the action and illustrates a different phase in the fortunes of each central character. In *Shane,* chapters that describe tense encounters between the farmers and the ranchers are separated by chapters that focus on the interactions between Shane and the Starrett family. Thus both the main plot and an important subplot develop simultaneously; both contribute to the characterization of Shane as a man in conflict.

**Style.** Style is the way that a play, poem, short story, novel, or nonfiction selection is written. Style refers not to what is said but to how it is said. Many elements contribute to a writer's characteristic style; for example, diction, descriptive language, tone, point of view, irony, and techniques of characterization. A literary style might be described as formal, conversational, impersonal, objective, wordy, obscure, flowery, or crisp. Every writer has a unique way of expressing ideas that constitutes a personal style. The styles of some writers, however, are so consistent and recognizable that their names become synonymous with the general characteristics of their styles; for example, Hemingway's style or Dickens's style.

The two passages below both describe highways. Notice the difference in the styles.

> Highway 66 is the main migrant road. 66—the long concrete path across the country, waving gently up and down on the map, from the Mississippi to Bakersfield—over the red lands and the gray lands, twisting up into the mountains, crossing the Divide and down into the bright and terrible desert, and across the desert to the mountains again, and into the rich California valleys.
>
> 66 is the path of a people in flight, refugees from dust and shrinking land, from the thunder of tractors and shrinking ownership, from the desert's slow northward invasion, from the twisting winds that howl up out of Texas, from the floods that bring no richness to the land and steal what little richness is there. From all of these the people are in flight, and they come into 66 from the tributary side roads, from the wagon tracks and the rutted country roads. 66 is the mother road, the road of flight.
>
> JOHN STEINBECK
> *The Grapes of Wrath*

> Mason City. To get there you follow Highway 58, going northeast out of the city, and it is a good highway and new. Or was new, that day we went up it. You look up the highway and it is straight for miles, coming at you, with the black line down the center coming at you and at you, black and slick and tarry-shining against the white of the slab, and the heat dazzles up from the white slab so that only the black line is clear, coming at you with the whine of the tires, and if you don't quit staring at that line and don't take a few deep breaths and slap yourself hard on the back of the neck you'll hypnotize yourself and you'll come to just at the moment when the right front wheel hooks over into the black dirt shoulder off the slab, and you'll try to jerk her back on but you can't because the slab is high like a curb, and maybe you'll try to reach to turn off the ignition just as she starts the dive. But you won't make it, of course.
>
> ROBERT PENN WARREN
> *All the King's Men*

**Surprise Ending.** A surprise ending is an unexpected twist in plot at the conclusion of a story. The death of the mother at the end of "The Tradition," for example, surprises the reader, as the events of the story point only to her child's death.

**Suspense.** Suspense is the tension or excitement felt by the reader as he or she becomes involved in a story and eager to know the outcome of the conflict. In "By the Waters of Babylon," the reader wants to know if John will survive his journey, what he will discover, and what understandings he will gain from his experiences. As the dangers increase, and the clues are presented, readers may find themselves responding to the building suspense by reading faster.

**Symbol.** A symbol is a person, place, object, or idea that represents something beyond itself. For instance, a star on a door represents fame; a star pinned to the shirt of a sheriff stands for authority and power. Symbols can succinctly communicate complicated, emotionally rich ideas. A flag, for example, can symbolize patriotism and a national heritage. A turkey can symbolize the traditions, values, and activities associated with the national holiday of Thanksgiving.

The use of symbols in literature is called symbolism.

**Theme.** The theme is the main idea in a work of literature. It is a writer's perception about life or humanity shared with the reader. Some stories and poems are pure entertainment and as such have no underlying message. In most serious writing, however, the writer makes one or more points about life or the human condition. These themes are seldom stated directly and may reveal themselves only through careful reading and thought.

One way to discover the theme of a work of literature is to think about what happens to the central character. The importance of that event, stated in terms that apply to all human beings, is the theme of the story, play, or nonfiction selection. In the short story "The Snob," for example, the central character, John Harcourt, is ashamed to introduce his girl friend to his father. As a result, he causes himself and his father great pain. The theme of this story might be stated, "Being dishonest in our relationships can cause great pain for us and for those we care about."

**Third-Person Narration.** See *Point of View*.

**Tone.** Tone is the attitude a writer takes toward a subject. All of the literary elements used by the writer contribute to the development of tone, which might be detached, critical, amused, bitter, cynical, or joyous. Unlike mood, which refers to the emotional response of the reader to a work, tone reflects the feelings of the writer.

"Harriet Tubman" and "Woman Without Fear" evidence admiration felt by the writers for their subjects. "Aging in the Land of the Young" conveys the frustration and anger of the essayist about the plight of the elderly in contemporary American society.

**Tragedy.** In broad terms, tragedy is literature, especially drama, in which actions and events turn out disastrously for the main character or characters. In tragedy, the main characters, and sometimes other involved characters and innocent bystanders as well, are destroyed. Usually the destruction is death, as in *Julius Caesar*. Some tragedies, however, end with the main characters alive but in a devastated condition. Tragic heroes evoke both pity and fear in readers or viewers: pity because they feel sorry for the characters, and fear because they realize that the problems and struggles faced by the characters are perhaps a necessary part of human life. At the end of a tragedy, a reader or viewer generally feels a sense of waste, because humans who were in some way superior have been destroyed.

See *Tragic Hero*.

**Tragic Hero.** A tragic hero or heroine is the central character in a tragedy, for whom events end disastrously. Brutus in *Julius Caesar* is one well known example of a tragic hero. Aristotle, the famous Greek philosopher and the first recorded literary critic, cited the following characteristics for tragic heroes:

1. Goodness. Characters who are not good would fail to arouse pity in the reader or viewer.

2. Superiority. Characters who are not somehow superior or elevated would seem less tragic in their destruction.
3. A tragic flaw. Tragic heroes make fatal errors in judgment that contribute to their downfall. Often the flaw is a traditionally admirable quality carried to excess.
4. A tragic realization. Tragic characters understand how they have helped to bring about their destruction.

Tragic heroes abound throughout classical literature, and their usual fate is death. The ancient Greeks wrote many plays centering on tragic heroes, as did Shakespeare and other Elizabethan playwrights.

See *Tragedy*.

**Understatement.** Understatement is the technique of creating emphasis by saying less than is actually or literally true. As such, it is the opposite of exaggeration, or hyperbole. If someone says of Babe Ruth, "He was not a bad ball player," the statement is a clear example of understatement, for it so obviously understates the truth.

Understatement can be a biting form of sarcasm, or verbal irony. Jonathan Swift, the eighteenth-century English writer best known for *Gulliver's Travels*, often used understatement as a satiric weapon. For example, Swift once wrote, "Last week I saw a woman flayed [skinned alive], and you will hardly believe how much it altered her appearance for the worse."

**Verbal Irony.** See *Irony*.

# Biographies of the Writers

**Peter Abrahams** (born 1919) grew up in South Africa, the son of an Ethiopian father and a French-African mother. His mixed heritage meant that he belonged to the "Colored" community, distinct from the Black Africans, but with no more opportunity for education. He was illiterate until age nine when he began attending school in between odd jobs, such as dishwasher, porter, and tinsmith's helper. He wrote his first story at age eleven. After failing in an attempt to establish a school for poor Africans, Abrahams signed on as a ship's stoker in order to reach England, where he settled in 1941. He worked as a newspaper correspondent and published several books. His novel, *Song of the City,* was the first novel by a non-white South African to appear in fifteen years. Abrahams moved to France and Ghana while continuing to write novels, short stories, poems, travel books, essays, and an autobiography. In 1956, he traveled to Jamaica on commission from the British government. He was to have stayed only long enough to write a travel book but decided to make the island his home. Along with writing, he does editing and radio news commentary. Among his many noteworthy books are a novel, *A Wreath for Udomo;* a short story collection, *Dark Testament;* an autobiography, *Tell Freedom;* and a book of poetry, *A Blackman Speaks of Freedom.*

**Leonard Adamé** (born 1947) grew up in California's San Joaquin Valley where he worked part time in his father's restaurant and on his uncle's farm. Adamé admits that high school studies were not his favorite activity, but he persevered long enough to gain his diploma. More to his liking were the three years he spent touring the United States with a rock group. Adamé, now a writer, is married and has three daughters.

**Joan Aiken** (born 1924) always wanted to be a writer and still has the first pad of paper she bought at age five. It is filled with poems and stories, all indicative of the richly imaginative books she would later publish. Aiken was born in Sussex, England, the daughter of American poet, Conrad Aiken. She worked as an editor and copywriter before retiring to a domestic life. Widowhood at thirty and the necessity of providing for two young children forced her to resume writing in earnest. She chose to devote much of her effort to children's literature, creating worlds of fantasy, mystery, and humor. "What I would have liked to read as a child," she says. *Black Hearts in Battersea* and *The Wolves of Willoughby Chase* are two of her most popular titles.

**Maya Angelou** (born 1928) is a multi-talented and successful individual, best known for two autobiographical books, *I Know Why the Caged Bird Sings* and *Gather Together in My Name.* As a writer, she also has crafted poems, stage and screen plays, television specials, short stories, and magazine articles. Angelou has directed plays, studied dance with Martha Graham, toured twenty-two countries in a production of *Porgy and Bess,* acted in off-Broadway shows, and served as a television narrator and interviewer. She has made two recordings, written songs, and composed musical scores for her screen plays. When time has permitted, Angelou has toured the country as a lecturer and visiting professor to various colleges and universities. She worked with Dr. Martin

Luther King, Jr. as a coordinator for the Southern Christian Leadership Conference and was appointed to the Bicentennial Council by President Ford. Angelou is fluent in Arabic, Spanish, French, and Italian and has done newspaper work in Egypt and Ghana.

**W. H. Auden** (1907–1973), by the age of forty, was recognized as one of the most influential and original poets of the English language. He was born in England and in 1946 became a citizen of the United States. Auden's creative energy produced an outpouring of not only poetry, but also drama, translations, fiction, criticism, and essays. Quality did not appear to be affected by quantity, as Auden's work received almost every important literary prize in existence on both sides of the Atlantic. Auden also found time for travel and for a thirty-year academic career. He taught at American colleges, such as Swarthmore, Bryn Mawr, Bennington, Barnard, Smith, and the University of Michigan, and at Oxford University in England.

**Toni Cade Bambara** (born 1939) is known for her stories, essays, and articles on black Americans and, in particular, on black women. Much of her writing is aimed at young audiences. She urges them to read everything they can find and to listen intently, especially to the stories of family elders. Bambara says, "It's a funny thing about the living history you hear in the family kitchen—it doesn't always match what you are supposed to learn from books." Bambara was born in New York City; she spent her childhood in various locations including the Harlem area of New York City, New Jersey, and the South. She studied in New York, Italy, and Paris and has done social work, college teaching, and educational consulting.

**Imamu Amiri Baraka** (Leroi Jones) (born 1934) is generally considered a poet, but he also has achieved success as a dramatist, music critic, and theatrical producer. He studied religion and medicine and received his degree in English at the age of nineteen. During the next decade, his activities ranged widely. After three years in the Air Force, he established himself as a respected music critic, studied philosophy at Columbia University, edited literary journals, taught poetry, and published the first volume of his own verse. The collections that followed established him firmly in the forefront of contemporary poets. His interest, however, gradually turned to drama. He wrote several successful plays including *Dutchman,* which won an Obie Award. In 1964, he founded and directed the Black Arts Repertory Theatre in Harlem, New York City. The move to Harlem was a turning point for Baraka, who became increasingly critical of white cultural influences. He adopted an African name and became a political activist, encouraging the development of black talent and pushing for social change. Baraka has received Whitney and Guggenheim fellowships and a grant from the National Endowment for the Arts. His major collections of poetry include *Preface to a Twenty Volume Suicide Note* and *The Dead Lecturer.*

**Matsuo Basho** (1644–1694) has been called the Shakespeare of Japanese haiku verse because of his important contributions to the development of the form. He was born in the Iga province of Japan and, as a boy, played and studied with the son of his feudal lord in Kyoto. It was here that he first became familiar with haiku. Before Basho, construction of the three-line poems was considered a parlor game or hobby for the amusement of the rich. Basho, with his subdued, elegant verse, raised haiku to the level of true literature.

**Patricia Beer** (born 1924) is a poet and scholar from Devonshire, England. She studied at the universities of Exeter and London and at Oxford University before moving to Italy where she taught English literature for several years. She returned to London and continued teaching until 1968 when she became a full time writer. Beer has published six volumes of verse and has edited several anthologies of poetry.

**Steven Vincent Benét** (1898–1943) was the most famous member of a writing family that included a brother, William, and a sister, Laura. As a boy, Benét was frail, studious, and nearsighted. His main companions were the books in the family library. A love of poetry came naturally. His father continuously read it aloud and would often discuss form and content with the children. Benét studied literature at Yale University and eventually wrote in almost every form. He authored numerous novels, poems, short stories, and radio and film scripts and sometimes collaborated with his wife, Rosemary. Benét was deeply patriotic and much of his writing is based on American history and folklore. His most famous work includes the short story "The Devil and Daniel Webster" and the long ballad poem "John Brown's Body" for which he won a Pulitzer Prize. A second Pulitzer was awarded for the first part of "Western Star," a narrative poem that was unfinished at the time of his death.

**Algernon Blackwood** (1869–1951) lived a life as fascinating as the strange, supernatural stories for which he is famous. He was born in Kent, England, the son of strictly religious parents who forbade worldly pastimes such as dancing, drinking alcohol, attending the theater, and playing cards. At age twenty, Blackwood escaped the confines of family life by moving to Canada. Within one year, he managed to lose his entire inheritance. A dairy farm failed within six months, and his second investment, a small hotel, was equally unsuccessful. Blackwood lived on the fringes of starvation between

jobs as a reporter, artist's model, actor, and soap maker. He tried prospecting for gold and then spent a brief but comfortable period as private secretary to a millionaire banker before returning to England at age thirty. Blackwood felt no desire to write and, despite some newspaper work, believed that he had little talent. He was, however, consumed by three passions that dominated his spare hours and that eventually compelled him to put ideas on paper. First, he was a voracious reader of books in French, German, and English. Next, he was deeply involved with nature, escaping whenever possible into the woods. Finally, he was fascinated with the idea of psychic powers and was convinced that all humans possess limitless and powerful untapped mental abilities. At thirty-six, to amuse himself, Blackwood began to express his thoughts in story form. He had no intention of publishing the stories, but without his knowledge, a friend submitted them to a publisher. The stories were put into print and became the first of more than thirty books written by Blackwood.

**Robert Bly** (born 1926) has a three-faceted career in poetry, being a translator, a writer, and a publisher. After receiving degrees from Harvard University and the University of Iowa, Bly founded his own poetry magazine titled *The Fifties*. (The title changes with each passing decade to *The Sixties, The Seventies,* and so forth.) The publication was designed to introduce American readers to works by poets of other nations, with Bly doing many of the translations. He also has published separate volumes of translated works from Swedish, German, and Spanish poets. Bly's own collections of poetry include *Silence in the Snowy Fields* and *The Light Around the Body* for which he won the 1967 National Book Award.

**Philip Booth** (born 1925) was raised in New Hampshire and Maine and has had strong ties with New England throughout his life. He has been referred to as "the poet of the Maine coast" and, not surprisingly, the sea is a presence in most of his works. Booth received a degree from Dartmouth College, where he realized a childhood dream by becoming a member of the school's ski team. He did graduate work at Columbia University and served in the Air Force. His first book of poetry, *Letter from a Distant Land*, was awarded the 1957 Lamont Prize, and he has received two Guggenheim fellowships. Booth divides his time each year between university teaching and solitary months on the Maine coast during which he writes.

**Kay Boyle** (born 1903) was destined to become a writer, although she studied violin and architecture in college. She has been writing stories for as long as she can remember. Of her early years she says, "My sister and I had the idea that you made books for your family—for birthdays and for Christmas. I don't know where we got it. But I still have some of those old books around that I made when I was ten." Boyle has lived in England, Austria, France, and Germany and was a foreign correspondent for *The New Yorker* magazine from 1946 to 1953. In recent years, she has been on the English faculty of San Francisco University. Boyle has been a productive writer of novels, poems, and above all, short stories. The underlying theme of most of her work is the human need for love. Among the many awards that she has received are two Guggenheim fellowships and two O. Henry awards for best short story of the year.

**Ray Bradbury** (born 1920) is America's best known writer of science fiction. At an early age, he listened in breathless fascination to the stories of Edgar Allan Poe. He devoured comic strips and adventure books, spent Saturdays at the movies, and sent for every secret code ring available. Of these

years Bradbury writes, "I was in love with everything I did. I did not warm toward a subject, I boiled over." Bradbury received a toy typewriter for his twelfth Christmas and began to write. He sold his first story in 1940 and has written over a thousand stories since then, in addition to novels, plays, and scripts for movies and television programs. Two of his most popular books are *The Martian Chronicles* and *Dandelion Wine*. Bradbury creates his wildly imaginative visions of the future as entertainment, but he also has a more serious purpose. He is concerned about the future and prods the reader into thinking about what could happen to the freedom and relative tranquillity and comfort enjoyed today. For someone who writes of outer space and rocketships, Bradbury lives a remarkably cautious life. He has never learned to drive a car and has never ridden in an airplane.

**Gwendolyn Brooks** (born 1917) was born in Topeka, Kansas, but has spent most of her life in Chicago. Although her background is middle-class, she identifies deeply with ghetto dwellers and often makes them the subject of her poems and short stories. Brooks graduated from Wilson Junior College and has taught at several colleges and universities in the Chicago area. From the beginning, her poetry won praise for its simplicity and depth of feeling. *Annie Allen*, her second book, won the 1950 Pulitzer Prize. While Brooks's verse makes use of her personal experiences as a black, her work deals with universal themes. In 1969 she was named poet laureate of Illinois.

**Heywood Broun** (1888–1939) had a long career as a journalist with New York City's leading newspapers. At various times, he was a sports reporter, drama critic, foreign correspondent, editor, and columnist. Broun was a liberal, and his outspoken commentary frequently cost him his job. For a short time, he was a member of the Socialist Party, and he ran unsuccessfully for Congress on the Socialist ticket. In 1933 he founded the American Newspaper Guild, a union that still represents journalists in labor negotiations. During his middle years, Broun took up painting and had several exhibitions of his work. Along with journalistic writing, Broun authored novels, short stories, biographies, and essays. Two collections of essays, *Seeing Things at Night* and *Pieces of Hate,* are among his best.

**Henrietta Buckmaster** (born 1909) is a compassionate person whose concern for people has prompted the writing of her books. "I was young when I wrote *Let My People Go,*" she says, "and each day became an extraordinary revelation of the horrors and injustices endured by the black people." The research for this book, which is a history of the Underground Railroad, provided material for five more books, both fiction and nonfiction. Buckmaster also has written novels based on the lives of historical figures such as Paul the Apostle and Shakespeare.

**Morley Callaghan** (born 1903), after graduating from college, worked as a reporter for the Toronto *Daily Star* and wrote stories in his spare hours. While working at the newspaper, he met Ernest Hemingway, a chance encounter that was to have great influence on his later life and writing. Callaghan returned to law school and earned a law degree but did not pursue a career in the field. Instead, with Hemingway's encouragement, he went to Paris to write. He became part of what was later called the "Lost Generation," a group of expatriate writers and artists who lived in France during the 1920's and who sought new ways to express their ideas. Callaghan's writing style is reminiscent of Hemingway's—straightforward, clipped, and stark.

**Dorothy Canfield** [Fisher] (1879–1958) led an unusually varied life for a woman of her time. She successfully combined scholarship, travel, creativity, and domesticity. At age ten, she left her Kansas home for a year's schooling in France where she became fluent in the language. She continued language studies, both in the United States and abroad, eventually receiving a Ph.D. from Columbia University. In 1912, while traveling in Italy, she became enthusiastic about the educational philosophy of Dr. Maria Montessori and later wrote several books about the Montessori approach to teaching and learning. Canfield returned to Europe during World War I and spent three years doing relief work. When she and her husband returned to the United States, they settled in a Vermont farmhouse that had once belonged to Dorothy's pioneer ancestors. Here they farmed and quietly blended into the New England community. Amidst farm and family duties, Canfield found time to write more than thirty-five books including novels, short stories, and translations from French into English. She is best known for her realistic and sympathetic portrayals of rural life, its people, and their values.

**Constance Carrier** (born 1908) is a poet and Latin scholar. She taught high school Latin for thirty-eight years and also conducted workshops for Latin teachers at Tufts University. Carrier has published several translations of Roman poets and dramatists. Her own award-winning verse has been collected in two volumes, *The Middle Voice* and *The Angled Road.* Individual poems and articles have appeared in periodicals such as *Harper's, Atlantic Monthly, The New Yorker,* and *American Scholar.*

**Willa Cather** (1873–1947) was born in Virginia, yet she will always be associated with the West where she spent her childhood. Nebraska was still pioneer country when Cather's family emigrated there in 1881. Her early education was provided by grandmothers who taught her the classics in English, Latin, and Greek and by foreign-born neighbors who coached her in German and French. A local music teacher spent countless hours with her, instilling a life-long love of music and opera. Cather worked her way through the University of Nebraska, then found a newspaper job in Pittsburgh. She switched to teaching and began writing poetry and short stories. In 1906, she moved to New York where she was managing editor of *McClure's Magazine* for six years, until the success of her own books allowed her to concentrate on writing. Although she has written about musicians, city dwellers, and religious figures, Cather's most popular books are those that deal with the West and the immigrant farmers she knew as a child. *O Pioneers!* and *My Antonia* are the most famous of this group.

**John Ciardi** (born 1916) claims to be "an expert on bad poetry." As poetry editor for the *Saturday Review,* he reads about 1,000 poems a week and is highly critical of anything he considers mediocre. His own poems, including those written for children, are strong and active and demonstrate his belief that poetry should not be "written by a sponge dipped in warm milk and sprinkled with sugar." *The Man Who Sang the Sillies* and *I Met a Man* are two of his books for young people. Ciardi was born in Boston, Massachusetts. He attended Bates College, graduated with honors from Tufts College, and received a master's degree from the University of Michigan. Before joining the *Saturday Review*, he taught at the University of Kansas, Harvard, and Rutgers.

**Lucille Clifton** (born 1936) writes with love, warmth, and humor about the vitality of black life. Her simple, straightforward poetry and prose have earned many awards and prizes, including a grant from the National Endowment for the Arts. She is particularly effective in her writings for young

people. A series of poetry books featuring a young boy named Everett Anderson is popular with children and educators alike. She is also the co-author of *Free To Be You and Me,* a television program that won a 1974 Emmy Award. Clifton grew up in DePew, New York, and attended Howard University and Fredonia State Teachers College.

**Eugenia Collier** (born 1928) has been teaching college literature since 1955, but she did not begin her writing career until 1969. She received what she describes as a "conventional, western-type education" and did not experience her black culture and heritage until many years later. The discovery of her roots, combined with her educational background, sparked a creativity that has been explosive. One of her first efforts, "Marigolds," won the 1969 Gwendolyn Brooks fiction award. She has contributed essays on black writers to several nonfiction books, and her poetry and short stories have appeared in magazines, anthologies, and educational journals. Currently, Collier is working on a collection of poems, more stories, and a history of Black American writing. She holds degrees from Howard and Columbia universities and is a professor of English at the Community College of Baltimore.

**Hector Hernandez Cruz** (born 1949), a native of Aguas Buenas, Puerto Rico, grew up in Spanish Harlem in New York City. Cruz describes his childhood as "full of music, guitars, and conga drums, maracas and songs. My mother sang songs. Even when it was five below zero she sang warm tropical ballads." His poetry often combines the two dominant features of his life—a driving musical rhythm and memories of the bitter, sometimes violent life of the ghetto. Cruz has published three books of verse: *Snaps, Mainland,* and *Tropicalization.* He has also been a guest lecturer at the University of California, Berkeley.

**Sharon Curtin** grew up in a small Wyoming town where her grandparents were a close and important part of her life. She entered the field of nursing, moved to various parts of the country, and met old people both as friends and as patients. Her frustration with society's lack of concern for the aged eventually evolved into her first book, *Nobody Ever Died of Old Age*. In it, she offers vivid portraits of the old people she met—brilliant mathematicians, bag ladies, wealthy matrons. Curtin's book makes two demands: that we treat old people as "human beings with a future as well as a past"; and that old people themselves must "rise up angry" to effect a change in their situation.

**Frank Marshall Davis** (born 1905) has had a distinguished career in journalism. He helped to found the Atlanta *Daily World*, one of the few black daily papers in the United States, and later became editor of Chicago's *Associated Negro Press*. Journalism allowed Davis certain room for expression, but his deeper feelings about black life and the role of black artists were expressed in poetry. *Black Man's Verse, I Am the American Negro,* and *47th Street* were written in the 1930's and 40's, yet the poems in these collections are surprisingly modern.

**Emily Dickinson** (1830–1886), one of the finest poets of American literature, never sought the experiences, popularity, and readership that many poets crave. As a result, her life and personality are a mystery that intrigues readers to this day. Dickinson was born and raised in Amherst, Massachusetts. Her early years appear to have been typical of an upper-class young woman in provincial New England. She traveled, went away to school, had friends, and attended parties. Suddenly, however, at age twenty-six, Emily abruptly ended her public life. Most biographers assume that an unhappy love affair caused the dramatic change in her personality. For whatever reason, she retired to her father's Amherst home and was rarely seen outside its walls again. Emily spent long hours in her room, secretly writing poetry on envelopes, book margins, and other scraps of paper. More than 1,700 poems were discovered after her death, along with a note requesting that they be destroyed. Dickinson's poems are brief but full of intense feeling. With simple language, she creates strong, original images about human life, love, and nature, her most common subjects. A key to understanding Dickinson's writing might be found in her own definition of poetry: "If I feel physically as if the top of my head were taken off, I know that is poetry."

**Annie Dillard** (born 1945) is one of a handful of writers whose first published prose has received critical acclaim. Even fewer first books have won a Pulitzer Prize, as did Dillard's *Pilgrim at Tinker Creek* in 1974. The book is a nonfiction recollection of time spent in Virginia's Roanoke Valley. Dillard is the author of a poetry collection, *Tickets for a Prayer Wheel,* and a contributor to many magazines and journals. She has taught poetry and creative writing at Western Washington State University and Wesleyan University and is quick to emphasize the difficulty of writing. She explains that the writing of *Pilgrim at Tinker Creek* took eight months, seven days a week, fifteen hours a day working in a library from hundreds of index cards. Dillard says, "It's all hard, conscious, terrible frustrating work! But this never occurs to people. They think that you just sit on a tree stump and take dictation from some little chipmunk!"

**Arthur Conan Doyle** (1859–1930) is the creator of Sherlock Holmes, the world's most famous literary crime solver. Doyle was born in Edinburgh, Scotland. His formal education included five years as a medical student at Edinburgh University. He received his medical degree in 1881 and spent the next three and a half years as a ship's doctor. The impressions and experiences he gained during these years appeared many times over in his later writings. Upon returning to England, Doyle set up an unsuccessful practice as an oculist. Needing money, he began to write during office hours while waiting for patients who never appeared. He invented detective Sherlock Holmes, who was based on a former medical professor named Dr. Joseph Bell, and wrote his first detective story, *A Study in Scarlet*. The growing popularity of the Sherlock Holmes tales allowed Doyle to give up medicine permanently to concentrate on writing. Doyle was also the author of more scholarly works. *The Great Boer War*, a defense of the British cause, earned him knighthood and the title of "Sir." Doyle would have preferred to establish his reputation on the basis of his serious books. The creation of Sherlock Holmes, however, earned him a place in literary history.

**Walter D. Edmonds** (born 1903) is a regional novelist who uses upstate New York and the Erie Canal as settings for his work. His portraits of American frontier life have been cited for their realism and honesty. Edmonds does not glamorize the early settlers. His heroes are quiet, determined people who face good times and bad with equal calmness. Edmonds has written novels for children and adults, winning acclaim in both areas. *The Matchlock Gun* was awarded the 1942 Newbery Medal for children's literature and *Bert Breen's Barn* received the National Book Award in 1976. *Drums Along the Mohawk* is his most popular novel.

**Mari Evans,** according to critics, writes poetry that is a powerful, authentic voice expressing both the dignity and the frustration of the black experience in contemporary society. Evans is a widely read poet, with an appeal partly based on her use of simple, precise language to convey her message. Her work has been published in over 200 anthologies and textbooks, as well as in many magazines. A collection of verse, *I Am a Black Woman*, has won several awards, and she has written many books for younger readers, such as *Singing Black*. Evans, born and educated in Ohio, has been a professor of black literature; has produced, directed, and written a weekly television program, "The Black Experience"; and has served as a consultant for the National Endowment for the Arts.

**Jack Finney** (born 1911) worked as an advertising copywriter until the publication of his first story at age thirty-five. As a fiction writer, Finney has achieved success both in and out of the science fiction field. Three of his novels, *Five Against the House, Good Neighbor Sam*, and *The Invasion of the Body Snatchers*, have been made into movies. His short stories have appeared in leading magazines and have been translated into many foreign languages. Finney was born in Milwaukee, Wisconsin, and graduated from Knox College in Galesburg, Illinois.

**Olive A. Fredrickson** (born 1901) is a gentle, self-educated woman who enjoys animals, flowers, and a quiet life far from big city crowds and noises. Most of her time has been devoted to the duties of wife, mother, farmer, and ranch hand. In 1960, however, she began to write, and in 1972 her first book, *The Silence of the North*, was published. This book depicts the incredible hardships that she and her family suffered during their years as trappers in the Canadian wilderness.

**Robert Frost** (1874–1963) was born in San Francisco, although for eight generations his ancestors had been New Englanders. When Frost was ten, his family moved back to Massachusetts. As a young adult, he married and worked at many odd jobs—mill hand, shoe salesman, farmer—to support his family. At thirty-eight his New Hampshire farm failed, and he moved his family to England where he concentrated on writing poetry. Frost had been producing poems since age fifteen with no success whatsoever, but suddenly his work began to receive critical recognition. His first two collections were praised on both sides of the Atlantic, and he returned to the United States. His stature grew with each succeeding volume, and long before his death he was considered one of the most important modern poets of the English language. He was issued a special congressional medal in 1960 and is the only American poet to win four Pulitzer Prizes. In 1961 he was asked to read his work at the inauguration of President John F. Kennedy. Most of Frost's poetry is set in New England. He creates realistic word pictures of the area and its people, using an easy-going, conversational, and deceptively simple style. Frost once commented that poetry is "saying one thing and meaning another."

**Ernesto Galarza** (born 1905) began life in a remote Mexican mountain village called Jalcocotán. The violent Mexican Revolution caused the family to flee to the United States where they settled in Sacramento, California. Galarza became an American citizen and partook fully of the American educational system, eventually earning a Ph.D. at Columbia University. He has been a teacher and lecturer as well as a writer. Most famous of his books is *Barrio Boy*, the autobiographical story of his early years. He is also the author of *Zoo Risa* and *Spiders in the House and Workers in the Field*.

**Robert Gannon** (born 1931) worked in the fields of public relations and television production before deciding to combine his two major interests, writing and a love for animals, into a career. Since 1960, he has published books for both adults and children on animal care, dog training, tropical fish, and ecology. His nonfiction articles appear with regularity in *Reader's Digest, Popular Mechanics, True,* and *Family Circle.* He is a contributing editor for *Popular Science* magazine and teaches nonfiction writing at Pennsylvania State University.

**Hugh Garner** (born 1913) spent his first three years in England before moving to Canada where he now resides. Garner saw several years of military duty, first with the International Brigade in Spain, then two years with the Canadian Army, and finally, five years with the Canadian Navy. He worked briefly in the public relations field before turning to writing in 1952. Since then, he has produced novels and short story collections as well as television scripts, and newspaper columns. His work also has appeared in anthologies and magazines.

**Nikki Giovanni** (born 1943) grew up in Tennessee and Ohio. Many of her poems, particularly those for young readers, mirror her happy childhood. They are filled with joy, innocence, and imagination. Giovanni's essays and poems for adult audiences generally take more skeptical look at the world. Her formal education includes work at Fisk and Columbia universities and the University of Pennsylvania. She has taught at various colleges and has founded a publishing business. Giovanni has published several poetry collections, including *Black Feeling, Black Talk, Black Judgment,* and *Re: Creation.* "Truth Is on Its Way," a record, combines Giovanni's poetry with gospel music. Her books for children include *Spin a Soft Black Song* and *Ego Tripping.*

**Bob Greene** (born 1947) has been writing for newspapers since his high school days in Ohio when he spent summer vacations as a reporter for the *Columbus Citizen-Journal.* After attending Northwestern University, Greene joined the *Chicago Sun-Times* as a reporter and columnist. In 1978, he moved to the *Chicago Tribune*. His award-winning column appears in more than 150 papers in the United States and Canada, and he is also the author of several books and numerous magazine articles. Greene pens a monthly column, "American Beat," for *Esquire* magazine and is a contributing correspondent for "ABC News Nightline."

**Lady Augusta Gregory** (1852–1932). The pastoral life of a titled young Irish gentlewoman seems far removed from Isabella Gregory's eventual achievements as a dramatist, Irish partisan, and "godmother" to Dublin's Abbey Theatre. The death of her husband in 1892 indirectly led to her writing career. As she edited his autobiography, she discovered a need to know more about Irish history and folklore. Her studies brought about an ardent Irish nationalism, and a chance meeting with poet William Butler Yeats convinced her to participate in the literary revival taking place in Ireland. She helped found the Abbey Theatre, which is still in existence, and did whatever work was necessary to keep it viable. This sometimes included managing productions, selling tickets, arranging tours, and writing plays. Her door was always open to actors, playwrights, and poets who needed encouragement and a place to sleep. Her own work included popular English translations of Gaelic folk stories and adaptations of the works of the French dramatist Molière. Of her original plays, *The Workhouse Ward* and *The Rising of the Moon* are best known.

**Carole Gregory** (born 1945), a native of Youngstown, Ohio, graduated from Youngstown State University with a degree in English. Her poetry has been published in anthologies, such as *The New Black Poetry*, *Nine Black Poets*, and *To Gwen with Love*. Gregory also has worked for *Look* magazine and in the field of educational television.

**Donald Hall** (born 1928) began writing poetry as a teenager on the chance that it might improve his relationships with the opposite sex. The poetry was successful and Hall has refrained from commenting on any additional benefits. He was born in Connecticut and, after studying at Harvard University and Oxford University in England, joined the faculty of the University of Michigan. He has written several volumes of poems, including *Exiles and Marriages*, *The Dark Houses*, and *Kicking the Leaves*. He has published children's books, an autobiography, *String Too Short To Be Saved*, and has edited several poetry anthologies.

**Albert Halper** (born 1904) is a native Chicagoan with over ten novels and many short stories to his credit. He attended Northwestern University and was the recipient of a Guggenheim fellowship in 1934. Among his titles are *Sons of the Fathers*, *Only an Inch from Glory*, and *On the Shore*. His stories and articles have appeared in *The New Yorker*, *Harper's*, *Atlantic Monthly*, and *Holiday*.

**Lorraine Hansberry** (1930–1965) was the first black woman to achieve success on Broadway. Her first completed play, *A Raisin in the Sun*, opened in 1959 with a cast that included Sidney Poitier, Louis Gossett, Ruby Dee, and Claudia McNeil. For this play, Hansberry won the Drama Critics Circle Award, the youngest person ever to receive it. In a letter to her mother, she described the play as one ". . . that tells the truth about people, blacks, and life, and I think it will help a lot of people to understand how we are just as complicated as they are—and just as mixed up—but above all, that we have among our miserable and downtrodden ranks, people who are the very essence of human dignity." Hansberry was born in Chicago to a wealthy family. In 1938 her father bought a home in an all-white neighborhood and had to fight to the Supreme Court to stay there. Hansberry left home to study stage design and painting, but found neither satisfying. In 1950 she moved to New York, where she worked at odd jobs while writing stories and plays. She began *Raisin in the Sun* after becoming enraged at the way that blacks were being portrayed on Broadway. Her second production, *The Sign in Sidney Brustein's Window*, received mixed reviews and closed upon Hansberry's death at the age of thirty-five.

**Moss Hart** (1904–1961) was a partner in one of the most famous of all American playwriting teams. Hart and George S. Kaufman wrote a series of successful comedies that dominated the Broadway stage during the 1930's. Hart claimed that his interest in theater was fostered by his eccentric Aunt Kate, one of the many relatives who lived in his parents' crowded Bronx apartment. Despite severe financial difficulty, Hart and his aunt managed to attend Saturday matinees at the theater with devoted frequency. Hart left school after the seventh grade and worked at jobs on the fringes of his beloved theatrical world. Eventually, he had a yearly routine that involved directing amateur theater groups, coordinating social activities at a summer resort, and writing plays. His first serious dramas met with such unqualified failure that he decided to try a comedy. A rough draft of *Once in a Lifetime* attracted the attention of Kaufman, who suggested co-operating on a revision of the play. The rave reviews after opening night cemented a partnership that lasted for ten years and that included the creation of plays such as *The Man Who Came to Dinner*, *Merrily We Roll Along*, and *You Can't Take It with You*, which won a Pulitzer Prize. During his career, Hart also collaborated with Irving Berlin, Cole Porter, and Richard Rogers. He wrote screen plays and later a widely read autobiography, *Act One*. He was also a suc-cessful director, winning the 1956 Tony Award for his staging of *My Fair Lady*.

**Ernest Hemingway** (1899–1961) is one of America's most famous writers. His stark, simple, and bluntly realistic style has influenced scores of modern and contemporary writers. Hemingway's personal life was legendary, and the public followed his adventurous exploits as eagerly as they read his books. Hemingway was born in Oak Park, Illinois, and spent much of his youth in northern Michigan. Shortly after high school, in the early years of World War I, he set out for Europe where he volunteered as an ambulance driver and was seriously wounded. During the 1920's, he lived in Paris, the central figure of an expatriate gathering of writers and artists known as the "Lost Generation." F. Scott Fitzgerald, Gertrude Stein, Pablo Picasso, and Ezra Pound were among the group. Hemingway craved adventure and seemed happiest in situations that provided danger and the possibility of sudden death. He fought in and reported on wars, hunted big game in Africa, and cheered the bull-fights in Spain. He was involved in several near-fatal accidents during his life. Hemingway's standards of courage, honor, and endurance in the face of danger and defeat are major themes in his work. He was a disciplined writer who produced a large number of short stories and novels. Among them are *The Sun Also Rises*, *A Farewell to Arms*, and *For Whom the Bell Tolls*. In 1953 *The Old Man and the Sea* won the Pulitzer Prize, and in 1954 Hemingway was awarded the Nobel Prize for Literature.

**Edwin A. Hoey** (born 1930) attended Swarthmore College, served in the Army, then worked for a publishing company. In spare moments, he tried his hand at writing, eventually finding a market for his poems and articles. His work has appeared in magazines, journals, and textbooks.

**Langston Hughes** (1903–1967) lived in six different cities before age twelve. By the time his first book was published, he had been a farmer, cook, waiter, sailor, and doorman and had worked his way through more than eight countries. Although he wrote novels, short stories, plays, song lyrics, and radio scripts, Hughes is best known for his poetry. He was the first black American to earn his living solely from writing and spent much time encouraging other young blacks to write. His first recognition as a poet came when he was a hotel busboy. He left some of his poems at the table where poet Vachel Lindsay was dining. Lindsay was so impressed that he incorporated Hughes's work into his poetry readings. In his writings, Hughes described the common people of Harlem. He used their dialect and the rhythms of their blues music and explored the topics of racial prejudice and the struggle for equality.

**Ted Hughes** (born 1930) is a native of Mytholmroyd, Yorkshire, an area of England that abounds with mystical lore and magical tales recounting the adventures of mythical heroes and supernatural animals. This folklore often filters through the background of this writer's imaginative stories, poems, and plays. After service in the Royal Air Force, Hughes studied at Cambridge University, married American poet Sylvia Plath, and worked at a succession of odd jobs, such as rose gardener and night watchman, until he could turn to full-time writing. His first book of poems, *The Hawk in the Rain,* was published in 1957. The book won praise in both England and the United States. The following year, Hughes received a Guggenheim fellowship. Since then he has published over twenty-five volumes of poetry and a dozen or more plays and has edited many books of verse by other poets. Nearly half of Hughes's work is written specifically for children.

**James Hurst** (born 1922) left the North Carolina farm where he was raised to study chemical engineering. In a short time, he gave in to his love of music and began voice lessons at the Julliard School of Music. Hoping for an operatic career, Hurst went to Rome for additional study, but he soon realized that he had little chance for success in this field. He returned to the United States where he worked as a bank clerk and wrote in his spare time. His first real recognition came in 1960 with the publication of "The Scarlet Ibis" in the *Atlantic Monthly.*

**Shirley Jackson** (1919–1965) claimed that she wrote because "it's the only chance I get to sit down." This statement is typical of her humorous books and stories about the turmoil of ordinary family life. *And Baby Makes Three* and *Life Among the Savages* are two examples of these entertaining writings. Readers who enjoy her domestic humor often are surprised to learn that she also wrote particularly chilling tales of horror. These include her widely anthologized story "The Lottery" and the novels *We Have Always Lived in the Castle* and *The Haunting of Hill House.* Many of her stories have been adapted for stage, film, and television.

**Will James** (1892–1942) was a writer and illustrator known for his books about the American West. He wrote from experience about cowboy life, using the simple language that he heard spoken around him. "What I've wrote," he said, "is without the help of the dictionary or any course in story writing. Good english is all right, but when I want to say *something,* I believe in hitting straight to the point without fishing for decorated language." James was born in Montana, orphaned at age four, and adopted by a French-Canadian trapper and prospector. He began work as a cowboy at thirteen and, a few years later, took up rodeo riding. James enjoyed sketching in free moments and sold his first drawing in 1919. After a long spell with no buyers for his sketches, a friend suggested that he send a story along with them. Its acceptance signaled the beginning of James's writing career. His first novel was published the following year, and, three years later, he won the Newbery Medal for *Smoky*.

**Sarah Orne Jewett** (1849–1909) was born, raised, and died in South Berwick, Maine, a town she loved and often wrote about. She spent a quiet, happy childhood traveling through the country with her physician father and educating herself in his extensive library. She was extremely close to an assortment of elderly relatives and considered them her friends and playmates. At fourteen, she began writing poetry and short stories. In a bold and secret move, she sent some of her work to a children's magazine under an assumed name. The acceptance of a story marked the beginning of a writing career that included hundreds of short stories and several novels. In later years, Jewett was saddened by the changing landscape near her home, with its deserted farms and ravaged forests. Her writing was often an attempt to re-create the life and scenery that she had loved as a child, as if to preserve it both for herself and others.

**William Melvin Kelley** (born 1937) is an award-winning author whose work focuses on the rights and freedoms of the individual. He writes about blacks, not as a cultural group, but as separate and unique human beings. In this same spirit, Kelley resents critics who try to bunch all black writers into what he calls the "Negro literary ghetto." People who read black authors, says Kelley, immediately begin to search for profound comments on the relationship between black and white Americans. He does not want his work to be thought of as propaganda for a particular cause, but rather as something that will have continuing value and meaning.

Kelley's articles and short stories have been widely published in magazines, anthologies, and textbooks. His novels include *A Different Drummer, dem,* and *Dunford Travels Everywhere.*

**Ruth Lechlitner** was born in Wakarusa, Indiana, and received degrees from the universities of Michigan and Iowa. She has written two books of poems, *Tomorrow's Phoenix* and *Only the Years,* and has reviewed poetry for the *New York Herald Tribune.*

**Denise Levertov** (born 1923) grew up in England in a strangely spiritual atmosphere. Her father, a converted Russian Jew, was an Anglican minister who filled the house with thousands of books and dozens of temporary refugees, artists, and literary exiles. Her mother, a descendant of a mystical Welsh preacher, read classics to the family and provided all of Levertov's education. When she was twelve, Levertov sent some of her poems to T. S. Eliot who thought them worthy enough to merit a long letter of advice. Her first collection was published in 1946. Her second did not not appear until ten years later, after she had married an American soldier, moved to New York, and immersed herself in American culture. Levertov's many books include *Here and Now, The Sorrow Dance,* and *Footprints.* The poems in these books are characterized by fine craftsmanship and richly evocative language.

**Amy Lowell** (1874–1925) was born into a wealthy and distinguished family from New England. This provided her the luxury of extensive travel and time to think about a future career. She shunned the expected volunteer work and social life of her class and finally, at age twenty-eight, decided that poetry would be her life's work. For ten years, she studied, practiced, and wrote and finally published her first book—a little-read volume that echoed the work of earlier romantic poets. Two years later, a second book, *Sword Blades and Poppy-Seeds*, demonstrated a striking contrast. The poems were bold, radical, and a definite break with established forms and patterns. From this moment on, Lowell was a vehement voice for the New Poetry movement. She wrote numerous articles and gave many outspoken lectures in which she demanded that the poet's freedom of choice in form, style, and subject matter be recognized. During the last ten years of her life, her voice and pen were seldom stilled. The many volumes of verse produced at this time are notable for their vigor and variety. A posthumous collection, *What's O'Clock*, won the 1925 Pulitzer Prize.

**Doris Herold Lund** (born 1919) worked as a copywriter for two New York advertising agencies before becoming a freelance writer and cartoonist. She has written several books for children and has published poems and cartoons in magazines such as *Look* and *Ladies' Home Journal*. She is best known, however, for *Eric*, the story of the losing battle with leukemia fought by her oldest son for four and a half years. The book was chosen as an alternate selection by several book clubs and has been translated into fifteen languages. The television version, starring Patricia Neal, was aired in 1975.

**Daniel P. Mannix** (born 1911) began his own backyard zoo as a child; his collection included an alligator, lizards, tarantulas, and a vulture, as well as the more common skunks, foxes, and owls. Later, while studying writing at the University of Pennsylvania, he sold stories about the zoo to *The Saturday Evening Post*. College was interrupted for three years when Mannix decided to join a carnival. He was fascinated with side-show feats, such as sword-swallowing and fire-eating, and eventually developed his own act, billing hmself as "The Great Zadma." Marriage did nothing to dim Man-

nix's desire for travel and excitement. He and his wife Jule have explored and hunted the world over, and he has used these experiences as background for articles, film scripts, lectures, and television specials. His books include *Step Right Up*, *The Fox and the Hound*, and *The Outcasts*. When not traveling, the Mannix family lives on a farm with, of course, a backyard zoo.

**Durango Mendoza** (born 1945) is a descendant of American Indians of the Creek tribe. He grew up in Oklahoma, a shy child whose sensitive observations of the world were later translated into his writing. Mendoza attended the University of Missouri and the Art Institute of Chicago. His work has been published in magazines, anthologies, and textbooks.

**Eve Merriam** (born 1916) says, "I am fortunate in that my work is my main pleasure, and, while I find all forms of writing absorbing, I like poetry as the most immediate and richest form of communication." Merriam's enjoyment of writing is evidenced by her large body of work, which includes advertising copy, television scripts and documentaries, fashion commentary, song lyrics, plays, and magazine articles. She also has published more than thirty books, including the following poetry collections: *Family Circle*, *The Trouble with Love*, and *It Doesn't Always Have To Rhyme*. She frequently has addressed the issue of women's rights in books such as *After Nora Slammed the Door* and *Growing Up Female in America*. When not writing, Merriam teaches creative writing, travels, haunts second-hand book stores, swims, and bicycles.

**Elliott Merrick** (born 1905) wrote several novels about the two years that he spent in Labrador traveling with backwoods trappers. *Frost and Fire* is the most widely read of these novels. "Without Words," a chapter from this book, has been widely anthologized and translated into many languages. In commenting about the story, Merrick points out the contrasting philosophies between nomad Indian hunters and white trappers. "My story shows, I hope, that we highly civilized ones have almost as much to learn from the primitives as they have to learn from us."

**Edna St. Vincent Millay** (1892–1950) while still in Camden, Maine, at age nineteen, wrote "Renascence," a lyric poem that quickly attracted the attention of literary critics. This poem, still considered one of her best, was the first of a body of work that eventually included plays, stories, and twenty volumes of poetry. One of these collections, *The Harp-Weaver,* was awarded the 1923 Pulitzer Prize for poetry. Millay was part of the rebellious movement of the twenties, which was led by young artists and writers, eager to throw off both social and artistic confinements. In her daring and dramatic works, Millay attacked conventional views of femininity. While her messages were bold, even shocking to the older generation, many were expressed in traditional verse forms such as the sonnet and the ballad. Millay's poetry is noted for its musical quality. It deals with serious topics without being overly solemn; it is joyful without being foolish.

**Heather Ross Miller** (born 1939), an award-winning novelist, poet, and short story writer, claims that her "biggest contribution will be in teaching others to write." She has taught at several colleges in her native North Carolina and is currently at work on a creative writing textbook. Her fiction titles include *The Edge of the Woods* and *Confessions of a Champeen Fire-Baton Twirler.* Her poetry, collected in *The Wind Southerly* and *Horse Horse, Tyger Tyger,* has been influenced by "poet-friend-teacher" Randall Jarrell.

**N. Scott Momaday** (born 1934), a full-blooded Kiowa Indian, was born in Oklahoma and grew up on reservations in the Southwest. Culture flourished in his family, for his parents' combined professions included teaching, painting, and writing. Momaday was an ambitious student, focusing his talents on writing and eventually receiving a Ph.D. from Stanford University where he joined the faculty in 1973. His writing, which includes poetry, folktales, and novels, has thus far dealt exclusively with his Indian heritage. With emotion and sensitivity, he describes the historical and contemporary experience of growing up Indian in America. Momaday has received a Guggenheim fellowship, and in 1969, though considered a relative unknown in literary circles, he won the Pulitzer Prize for the novel *House Made of Dawn.*

**Don Moser** (born 1932) spent twelve years as a reporter, correspondent, and assistant editor for *Life* magazine before becoming a full time freelance writer. His books reflect his interest in wildlife and wilderness areas and include *The Peninsula, The Snake River Country,* and *A Heart to the Hawks.* Moser is a native of Cleveland, Ohio, and has studied at the University of Ohio and Stanford University. A Fulbright Scholarship allowed him to complete additional graduate work at the University of Sydney, Australia.

**Hector Hugh Munro** (Saki) (1870–1916) is a Scottish novelist and short story writer. He was born in Burma where his father was serving as inspector-general of the Burmese Police. Before age two, Munro's mother died, and he was sent to England to be raised under the watchful eyes of two aunts. After completing his education, Munro traveled with his father who eventually arranged work for him in Burma. Seven bouts of malaria in thirteen months convinced Munro to return to England. He began a career as a journalist, which lasted for many years and which saw him employed by several newspapers. Humor, wit, and imagination were his strengths, both as a journalist and as a writer of short stories and novels, published under the name "Saki," a character in a twelfth-century Persian poem. At the beginning of World War I, Munro signed up as a private, refusing offers of a commission. He died during an attack on Beaumont-Hamil, France.

**Pauli Murray** (born 1910) was an activist for civil and women's rights long before they became popular causes. She protested the segregation of buses by becoming a "freedom rider" in the 1940's and used her skills as a lawyer to sue universities that refused to accept women in their graduate programs. Murray's poetry has appeared in periodicals and in a collection titled *Dark Testament. Proud Shoes* is a history of her family. Murray has been a member of the bar in New York and California and has taught law in Ghana and at Brandeis University.

**Iris Noble** (born 1922) is a prolific writer who has concentrated her writing talents on biography. She has produced at least one new title each year since she began in 1955 with *Nellie Bly: Woman Reporter.* Her subjects include scientists, writers, physicians, politicians, royalty, artists, and religious figures from all ages and all parts of the world. If a prejudice exists in her choice of topics, it is towards courageous women in history. Noble also has written several popular novels for younger readers, such as *One Golden Summer* and *Megan.*

**Elder Olson** (born 1909) is a distinguished literary scholar and poet from Chicago where he was born, educated, and now resides. Olson received B.A., M.A., and Ph.D. degrees from the University of Chicago and has continued there as a professor of English. He spent one year at the University of the Philip-

pines as a Rockefeller Visiting Professor. Olson's poetry collections—*Thing of Sorrow* and *The Scarecrow Christ*—have received many awards. He also is recognized for his texts on poetry, drama, and criticism.

**Dorothy Parker** (1893–1967) is remembered best for her sarcastically witty poems and short stories. Readers delight in her ability to find humor in any situation, no matter how tragic. Parker's work appeared in many magazines, but she was most closely associated with *The New Yorker,* to which she contributed regularly for over thirty years. She also spent several years in Hollywood as a screen writer. Parker's tongue-in-cheek writing style was matched by her mastery of the witty retort. When asked what inspired her to write, she replied, "Need of money, dear. I'd like to have money. And I'd like to be a good writer. These two can come together and I hope they will, but if that's all too adorable, I'd rather have money." Despite such comments, Parker was a great champion of liberal causes and left the bulk of her estate to Dr. Martin Luther King, Jr. and the NAACP.

**Harry Mark Petrakis** (born 1923) has achieved a special place in the literary world by writing about the Greek immigrant experience in America. His novels and short stories are fictionalized accounts of the people he met and the events he experienced while growing up in Chicago's Greek community. Adding to his storehouse of background material are the recollections of his own family life. Petrakis was born in St. Louis to Greek-American parents. His father was an Eastern Orthodox priest. Petrakis worked at several occupations—steelworker, real estate salesman, speechwriter—until the publication of his first book in 1959. Many books have followed, including two National Book Award nominees, *Pericles on 31st Street* and *A Dream of Kings.* He has adapted several of his stories for movie and television productions and has taught writing workshops at universities and colleges.

**Marge Piercy** (born 1936) was "raised in a working class neighborhood of little wooden houses in Detroit." She attended the University of Michigan and Northwestern University and then spent fourteen years writing and moving between Chicago, Paris, Boston, San Francisco, and New York, before settling in Cape Cod. As a writer, Piercy has found success with both fiction and poetry. She has published seven novels, including *Small Changes* and *Vida*, and an equal number of poetry collections, which include *Breaking Camp, Living in the Open*, and *The Moon Is Always Female*. A political activist, Piercy has been involved with the civil rights, antiwar, and women's movements.

**Edgar Allan Poe** (1809–1849) was born in Boston, the son of traveling actors. The desertion of his father and the death of his mother when he was only two years old marked the beginning of a tragic and unhappy life. The orphaned Poe was taken in by Mr. and Mrs. John Allan of Virginia, whose name he adopted, but constant disagreements with his stepfather made the arrangement difficult. After brief studies at the University of Virginia and a self-engineered dismissal from West Point, Poe sought work as a journalist and editor. He received recognition for his biting, sarcastic literary reviews. Nevertheless, money was scarce and Poe was often without funds for even food and heat. Poverty intensified his despair over the lingering illness and eventual death of his beloved wife, Virginia. Deeply depressed, Poe often sought escape in alcohol. Despite, or perhaps because of, his tragic life, he produced a body of work that continues to be both unique and popular. He was an innovator in the composition of the modern short story, and many critics also credit him with the invention of the detective story. His classic horror tales, such as "The Pit and the Pendulum" and "The Cask of Amontillado," have never been equalled in their mastery of unified mood and unrelenting terror. Poe also wrote haunting poetry, such as "The Raven" and "Annabel Lee."

**Ralph Pomeroy** (born 1926) grew up in Winnetka, Illinois, and attended the Art Institute of Chicago and the universities of Illinois and Chicago. He has lived and traveled extensively in Europe while pursuing a dual career in poetry and painting. At various times, he has helped to support himself by working as a magazine editor, art gallery director, stage manager, bartender, and candy salesman at Radio City Music Hall. He has published a book of poetry, *Stills & Movies*, and has had several one-man showings of his paintings.

**Conrad Richter** (1890–1968) is a novelist and short story writer best known for his portraits of American pioneer life. He was raised in Pennsylvania and by age fifteen was on his own, working as a teamster, farmhand, bank teller, and lumberman. Four years later, he landed a job with the Patton, Pennsylvania, *Courier*. It was the first of his many newspaper positions. In 1928, Richter sold the small business that he had established and moved west where he began collecting material for his books on early America. In 1951, he received the Pulitzer Prize for *The Town*. In 1961, *The Waters of Kronos* won the National Book Award.

**A. M. Rosenthal** (born 1922) is one of America's most distinguished journalists. Born in Canada, he moved to the United States at age four and is now a naturalized citizen. After studies at City College in New York, Rosenthal was hired by the *New York Times* as a United Nations correspondent. He has been with the newspaper ever since, serving for nine years as a foreign correspondent in India, Poland, Switzerland, and Japan. In 1967, he was promoted to assistant managing editor. Rosenthal's numerous awards for journalism include the 1960 Pulitzer Prize for international reporting. He is the author of magazine articles and several nonfiction books, including *Thirty-Eight Witnesses* and *The Night the Lights Went Out.*

**Franklin Russell** (born 1926), a New Zealand born writer, had visited Peking, Warsaw, Canada, Singapore, and Buenos Aires by the age of five. His parents finally settled in Australia just in time for Russell to begin school. His education continued in New Zealand when the family moved to a farm in the back country. This place stirred Russell's interest in natural history and created a focus for his writing career. For many years, he has worked as a freelance writer, constantly traveling and writing about animals and the natural world. He often transforms factual information and situations involving animals into fictional stories. The response to his writing pleases him, as shown by this comment: "At last people are beginning to realize what I have known for many years: We cannot live on this planet, despite our technology, without conforming to most of the laws of natural history."

**Saki.** See **Hector Hugh Munro.**

**Carl Sandburg** (1878–1967) was born in Illinois to Swedish immigrant parents. His father was illiterate and "suspicious of books," but his mother encouraged young Sandburg to write, and saved wrapping paper for his scribblings. He left school at age fourteen to help support the family. Before he was twenty, he had worked as a truck driver, dishwasher, farmhand, janitor, and potter's apprentice. He served in the Spanish American War, studied briefly at Lombard College, then launched a career in journalism. While working in Chicago, he published *Chicago Poems* and quickly found himself both famous and controversial. Critics both praised and criticized his powerful free verse and his use of slang and street language. In 1950 his *Complete Poems* won a Pulitzer Prize. A second Pulitzer was awarded for his four-volume biography of Abraham Lincoln. When Sandburg felt the urge to travel, he would shoulder his guitar and set out across the country. During his travels, he collected native American folksongs, which eventually were published.

**William Saroyan** (1908–1981) grew up in Fresno, California, the son of Armenian immigrants. After eighth grade, he left school to help support his family. He worked at a succession of odd jobs until his first book was published in 1933. Saroyan was a prolific writer who produced an incredibly large body of work. In one six-year period, he turned out over 500 stories. His most widely read work is the novel, *The Human Comedy.* A play, *The Time of Your Life,* received a Pulitzer Prize. In typical fashion, he refused the award, stating that art should be supported by common people, not by the wealthy. Much of Saroyan's writing describes in simple language, the ordinary, working-class people he knew as a boy, and praises their ability to endure life's difficulties with dignity. He wrote quickly and rarely revised his work. Some critics have suggested that his writing could have used more polishing, but Saroyan replied that he wanted readers to see him as a human being, not as a piece of machinery.

**Jack Schaefer** (born 1907) was a newspaper writer for nearly twenty years before turning to freelance fiction writing. His first novel, *Shane,* is still his most popular, and the movie version, filmed in 1953, is now considered a classic western. Without exception, Schaefer's many short stories and novels are set in the Old West. They bear titles such as *The Plainsmen, The Pioneers,* and *Old Ramon.* A native of Cleveland, Ohio, Schaefer now resides in Albuquerque, New Mexico.

**Anne Sexton** (1928–1974) received many grants and awards during her literary career, yet she continually questioned her abilities as a poet. She began writing in high school but soon stopped and did not find the courage to start again until she was twenty-eight. Encouraged by her mentor, poet Robert Lowell, she allowed her first collection of poems to be published in 1960. The book, *To Bedlam and Part Way Back,* describes in poignant detail, her battle with mental illness. All of her work is of a confessional nature, dealing with her personal, often painful feelings about life, death, motherhood, insanity, and love. Her books include *Live or Die,* which won the 1966 Pulitzer Prize. Her poems have appeared in numerous anthologies and magazines, and she has also collaborated with poet Maxine Kumin on three books of children's verse.

**William Shakespeare** (1564–1616) was the third of eight children born to a glovemaker in Stratford-on-Avon, a small English town. Despite his modest background and education, Shakespeare became the greatest and most popular English playwright in the world. His work continues to touch the hearts and minds of modern audiences, just as it did those who crowded into the Globe Theater almost four hundred years ago. (For a complete biography of William Shakespeare, see page 590.)

**Kathleen Spivack** (born 1938) taught poetry workshops in Massachusetts while working on the collections of verse titled *Flying Island* and *The Jane Poems.* She is a native of Bronxville, New York, and received degrees from Oberlin College and Boston University. She is also the recipient of a Radcliffe fellowship in poetry writing. Spivack currently resides in Watertown, Massachusetts, where she is working on another collection of poetry.

**William Stafford** (born 1914) grew up in Kansas in a family that enjoyed the outdoor life and evenings devoted to reading and conversation. This early appreciation of literature stayed with him, and he eventually earned a Ph.D. in English from the University of Iowa. When his studies were interrupted during World War II, Stafford worked in civilian public service camps as a conscientious objector. He also served as education secretary for the Church World Service, a relief organization. Stafford's first book of poetry, *West of Your City,* was published in 1960, followed by *Traveling Through the Dark,* which won the 1963 National Book Award. His poetry style has been described as simple, conversational, and highly readable. While pursuing an academic career, Stafford also has written textbooks and autobiographies.

**John Steinbeck** (1902–1968) was an American novelist who often used his books to point out injustice in society and to voice his concern for the oppressed. *The Grapes of Wrath,* a story of migrant workers during the Depression, received the 1939 Pulitzer Prize. Before his books became popular, Steinbeck worked at a variety of odd jobs. He was, among other things, a hod-carrier, fruit picker, and painter. The people whom he met and the things that he experienced during this time appeared in his later writing. Steinbeck eventually found work as a reporter and war correspondent, jobs that took him to Africa, Europe, and Asia. In addition to novels, he also wrote short stories, plays, and movie scripts. In 1962, Steinbeck was awarded the Nobel Prize for a body of work that includes books such as *Tortilla Flat, Of Mice and Men, East of Eden,* and *Cannary Row.* Steinbeck was born in Salinas, California, the setting for many of his stories.

**Dabney Stuart** (born 1937) received degrees from Davidson College and Harvard University before embarking on an academic career. He has been associated with the English department of Washington and Lee University for many years. Stuart has published several poetry collections including *The Diving Bell* and *The Other Hand.* He has also served as poetry editor of *Shenandoah,* a literary journal.

**May Swenson** (born 1919) writes that poetry is "based in a craving to get through the curtains of things as they *appear,* to things as they *are,* and then into the larger, wilder space of things as they are *becoming.*" In order to reach this point, Swenson encourages readers to use all five senses in experiencing a poem. To this end, she likes to create new forms for her work, often shaping her words into typed pictures. Despite her experimental tendencies, critics regard her as a serious writer with a gift for expressing ordinary ideas in new and unusual ways. Swenson has received many awards for her books, which include *Poems To Solve, To Mix with Time,* and *New and Selected Things Taking Place.*

**José Juan Tablada** (1871–1945) was born in Mexico City where he became a respected poet, art critic, and journalist with over 10,000 newspaper articles to his credit. In 1900, Tablada visited Japan and was fascinated with the Japanese verse form of haiku. He was the first Latin American poet to experiment with haiku and to modify the form for the Spanish language. Tablada spent four years in New York as an exile during the Mexican Revolution. He returned to Mexico in 1918 as a member of the diplomatic corps but resigned after two years and lived in the United States for the remainder of his life.

**Sara Teasdale** (1884–1933) is one of the more elusive figures in American literature. Her collections of poetry were widely read and well received, but her achievements did not provide the happiness and peace she constantly sought. Teasdale was a tall, slender woman, privately educated and wealthy enough to travel freely. Her choice of filmy dresses and her masses of fine hair accentuated her frailty, a result of many real and imagined illnesses. She frequently visited Chicago, mingling with that city's young literary crowd. Here she met poet Vachel Lindsay, a man who was a part of her life for many years, until she abruptly married someone else. The marriage was not successful and Teasdale became increasingly withdrawn. Friends offered invitations but she usually refused, preferring the solitude of her New York apartment. During her life, Teasdale published six volumes of poetry. *Love Songs* received the 1918 Poetry Society award, an honor later known as the Pulitzer Prize.

**Richard Thomas** (born 1939) has had his poems published in periodicals and anthologies, including *Black Fire* and *A Galaxy of Black Writing.* After a tour with the United States Marines, Thomas received B.A. and M.A. degrees in history from Michigan State University. He has been an instructor at the Center for Urban Affairs at that university.

**Theodore L. Thomas** (born 1920) writes his science fiction stories as a hobby. He was a chemical engineer with a degree from the Massachusetts Institute of Technology before deciding to study law. He received a law degree from Georgetown University in 1953 and has been a practicing patent attorney ever since. Along with his science fiction stories and novels, such as *The Clone,* Thomas has written a newspaper column on scientific topics and a series on patent attorneys.

**James Thurber** (1894–1961) was an American humorist and cartoonist known for his witty essays, stories, and sketches. Thurber created his own special world of small, frightened adults and innocent looking, wide-eyed dogs who bow under the social and mechanical problems of modern life. He frequently illustrated his writings with his own drawings. Much of Thurber's work first appeared in *The New Yorker*. He served as the magazine's managing editor for a short time and continued to be a regular contributor throughout his life. Thurber is from Ohio and attended Ohio State University. After college, he worked as a newspaper reporter for several years before turning to the humorous writing that made him famous. Some of his most popular selections are "The Secret Life of Walter Mitty," *The Thurber Carnival,* and the semi-autobiographical *My Life and Hard Times.*

**Mark Twain** (1835–1910) was the pen name of Samuel Clemens, one of America's best and most loved humorists. Critics agree that, as adventure stories, Twain's work would stand alone, but the addition of his great gift of humor has made them true classics. Twain grew up in Hannibal, Missouri, on the Mississippi River. He loved the water and lived a wild and joyous boyhood, fishing, rafting, and often being pulled out of the river's depths. These experiences were the basis for his most popular books, *The Adventures of Tom Sawyer* and *The Adventures of Huckleberry Finn.* When his father died, Twain was allowed to leave school, which he did with great enthusiasm. He worked as a printer and then as a riverboat pilot—a career that he assumed would be his for life. The Civil War, however, closed the river to travel, and Twain headed west where he was a prospector, adventurer, and eventually a journalist. At this time, he first used his pen name, a riverboat term that means "the water marks the measuring twine at two fathoms." In San Francisco, Twain began to gain recognition for his humorous writing, and, in 1866, he embarked on a series of witty public lectures that continued to be enthusiastically received throughout his life.

**Dorothy Uhnak** (born 1933) spent fourteen years as a policewoman and detective in New York City, a background that provided ample material for the mystery and crime books she began writing in 1967. Her novels, such as *Policewoman, Law and Order,* and *The Investigation,* have been praised for their authenticity and realism. Many critics label them semi-autobiographical, but Uhnak prefers to call them "fictionalized fact." The heroine of three of these novels, Christy Opara, was the basis for a television series, "Get Christy Love." Uhnak has received awards for outstanding police work and for achievements in the field of mystery writing. In 1955, she was given the Police Duty Medal for disarming an attacker who was holding a gun to her forehead; in 1968, she won an Edgar from the Mystery Writers of America for her first novel, *The Bait.*

**John Updike** (born 1932) began writing after visions of an art career had dimmed and after two years with *The New Yorker* had proved unsatisfactory. His move to a small Massachusetts town in 1958 seems to have been beneficial. Since then, he has produced twenty-five volumes of fiction, poetry, and criticism. His first two books, *Poorhouse Fair* and *Rabbit, Run,* were best-sellers, followed by *The Centaur,* which won the 1964 National Book Award. Approximately every ten years, Updike pens another book about the character Rabbit Angstrom. After *Rabbit, Run* came *Rabbit Redoux* and, in 1981, *Rabbit Is Rich.* The latter captured the Pulitzer Prize, The Critic's Circle Award, and the National Book Award. The trilogy (and Updike hints at a fourth Rabbit book) chronicles one man's attempt to understand and to cope with modern middle class society. This theme, common throughout Updike's work, is handled with a light, witty style.

**José Garcia Villa** (born 1914) is a native of the Philippine Islands and was elected National Artist of that country in 1973. He came to the United States, where he currently resides, in 1930 to attend the University of New Mexico. While still a student, he began to write short stories and received almost instant recognition. Despite success with this form, Villa decided that poetry was a more satisfactory way to express himself. His collections include *Have Come, Am Here, Volume Two,* and *The Portable Villa.* His work is original and often experimental. He enjoys the manipulation of rhyme schemes and sometimes creates typographical pictures with words and letters. Villa has taught at universities and served as cultural adviser to the Philippine government.

**Andrei Voznesenski** (born 1933) is a Russian poet, controversial within his own country, but highly regarded in other areas of the world. He grew up in Moscow where his mother surrounded him with great books and read poetry aloud. He graduated from architecture college but immediately turned to writing. He was influenced by poet Boris Pasternak who was, says Voznesenski, "my god, my father, and for a long time, my university." Eventually Voznesenski found his own style, one that delighted Russian audiences of the 1960's. They were tired of the repetitive, restricted poetry of the Stalin era and eager to hear the bold, radically different work of young poets, such as Voznesenski and his colleague, Yevgeny Yevtushenko. Crowds for poetry readings numbered as many as 14,000, and books were often sold out an hour after reaching the stores. Voznesenski's popularity remains strong in Russia, but he has periodically been harassed and criticized by government officials who accuse him of being politically immature and unnecessarily obscure. Despite these conflicts, he professes a deep love for his country. Voznesenski has a large international following, although readers sometimes find his poetry difficult to understand. He defends his work by saying, "The poet is not the one to supply the answers for mankind. All he can do is pose the questions. And if the poems are complicated . . . why then so is life."

**John Walsh** graduated from Boston University with a major in biology. He later attended Northeastern University School of Law Enforcement and became a prosecuting officer with power of arrest throughout the state of Massachusetts. He is currently the regional director for the World Society for the Protection of Animals, an organization with headquarters in London and offices throughout the world, which deals with problems of animal protection and wildlife conservation at government level. Because of his knowledge of wildlife and his experience with the tranquilizer gun, he was asked to undertake Operation Guwamba in Surinam (Dutch Guiana) in 1964–65, where he successfully directed the rescue of 9,737 jungle animals whose lives were threatened by a flood caused by the creation of a hydroelectric dam. "Time Is Short and the Water Rises" is a selection from his book about these rescue operations. He has a series of programs on PBS called "Walsh's Animals."

**H. G. Wells** (1866–1946) was a prominent British historian, science writer, social critic, and novelist who published hundreds of books in these various fields. During his life, he traveled widely and associated with other prominent writers, such as George Bernard Shaw, Henry James, and Joseph Conrad. Wells was born in Kent, the son of a professional cricket player and a housemaid. He served two brief and unwilling apprenticeships to a draper and a druggist before enrolling at London University where he received a degree (with honors) in science. Wells made use of his science background when he wrote a four-volume text on biology titled *The Science of Life.* Another well known book was *Outline of History,* which traces the development of the human race. However, with all the literary success he experienced in other fields, he is most widely known for his highly imaginative science fiction novels, such as *The War of the Worlds* and *The Time Machine.* In his fantasy writing, he described airplanes, submarines, and trips to the moon long before anyone dreamed such things might actually come to pass.

**E. B. White** (born 1899) is a well known essayist, poet, and humorist, but his most popular books have been for young people. *Stuart Little, Charlotte's Web,* and *The Trumpet of the Swan* are all considered classics in the field of children's literature. White was born in Mount Vernon, New York, and educated at Cornell University. He spent a brief time as a newspaper reporter and advertising copywriter before joining the staff of *The New Yorker* magazine. In his collections of essays, White deals with a variety of serious and light-hearted topics, using the informal, personal style for which he is famous. In 1963 he was awarded the Presidential Medal of Freedom.

**Walt Whitman** (1819–1892) is known as the "good, gray poet," one of America's most loved and original writers. He was a large, powerful man whose greatest pleasure was to be among people. He loved crowds and surrounded himself with friends, especially from the laboring class. He traveled extensively, dressed in gray work clothes, and took any job available to support himself. He seemed determined to see and to experience everything that America had to offer. This joyful celebration of life was evidenced in his first book of poetry, *Leaves of Grass.* Because no publisher was interested in this strange new poetry with its free form, rhymeless verse, Whitman paid for the printing of the book. The few critics who read it were unanimous in their condemnation. One suggested that instead of *Leaves of Grass,* the title should be *Weeds.* Undaunted, Whitman continued writing and expanding on the original version. During the Civil War, he volunteered to nurse wounded soldiers in Washington, D.C. With great dedication, he tended the sick and dying until the end of the war. It was later estimated that he had personally aided over 50,000 soldiers. The experience moved him deeply and inspired some of his finest poetry. In 1873, Whitman was struck by paralysis and spent the rest of his life in Camden, New Jersey. He continued to write and was frequently visited by friends and admirers. Although there was little recognition of Whitman's poetry during his life, his new verse forms and stubborn refusal to follow traditional poetic standards opened the door to a new literary freedom for future poets.

**Richard Wilbur** (born 1921) is best known as a poet whose collections have won prestigious awards such as the Pulitzer Prize and The National Book Award. He has, however, other scholarly credits that include translations of works by the French playwright Molière and several successful children's books. He is regarded as an expert on the works of Edgar Allan Poe and has recorded his own poetry for the Library of Congress. Wilbur has taught at Harvard and Wesleyan universities and, in 1961, traveled to Russia as an American specialist for the Department of State. Two of his most popular poetry collections are *Things of this World* and *The Beautiful Changes.* Critics have called his work elegant and imaginative. His writings often focus on nature, a fact that he says stems from a rural New England boyhood filled with woods, cornfields, horses, and haywagons.

**Tom Wolfe** (born 1931) is difficult to categorize as a writer, but critics and readers alike agree that he possesses a unique talent. Wolfe attempts to combine the excitement of fiction, the intellectual stimulation of essays, and the factuality of newspaper reporting. He has created his own unconventional style, which is characterized by the use of italics, exclamation points, and the repetition of letters. Wolfe first attracted attention in the 1960's with his colorful articles on popular culture. Collections of these short pieces were gathered into the widely read volumes, *The Kandy-Kolored Tangerine-Flake Streamline Baby* and *The Pumphouse Gang*. His latest book, *The Right Stuff*, is an account of the first U.S. astronauts. Wolfe is a native of Virginia and graduated with honors from Washington and Lee University where he helped to found a literary journal and pitched on the baseball team. When a tryout with the New York Giants failed, he returned to school, eventually earning a Ph.D. from Yale University. He has been employed by several newspapers and has contributed to magazines, winning awards in both fields. At times, Wolfe has gained notoriety for his outspoken comments and flamboyant manner of dress.

**Jade Snow Wong** (born 1922) was one of the first Chinese-American women to be a published author. Her autobiography, *Fifth Chinese Daughter*, which appeared in 1950, was highly successful and has been translated into several languages. Wong's book detailed her struggle to establish a balance between her father's unbending strictness and the more relaxed customs of American society. Twenty-five years later, Wong wrote *No Chinese Stranger*, a continuation of her life story. Although her writing has been successful, Wong's primary interest has been pottery and ceramics.

**Richard Wright** (1908–1960). Richard Wright's childhood was an unhappy kaleidoscope of poverty, illness, orphanages, and foster homes. By fifteen, he was on his own, working at odd jobs, reading, writing, and moving from place to place. In 1935 he was able to get work with the government-sponsored Federal Writers' Project. Three years later, he published a collection of stories, *Uncle Tom's Children*, and the following year he received a Guggenheim fellowship. *Native Son*, his first novel, was published in 1940. It won both national and international praise as did the autobiographical *Black Boy*, which appeared in 1945. Wright spent the last sixteen years of his life in Paris where he continued to write. The second half of his life story, *American Hunger*, was published posthumously.

**Elinor Wylie** (1885–1928) was the daughter of a prominent social and political family. She spent her youth in Washington, D.C. where her father served in both the McKinley and Theodore Roosevelt administrations. Elinor, considered a prodigy by her teachers, studied painting at the Corcoran Museum. In secret, she composed poetry, a hobby that soon replaced art as a career. After a broken engagement and a hasty but unhappy marriage, Wylie eloped to England with her second husband, Horace Wylie. She spent several years working on her writing with great determination. When she returned to the United States in 1916, her poems were already beginning to find an audience. Within eight years, she was well known, the author of a novel and two successful volumes of poetry. Wylie and her third husband, poet William Rose Benét, were active members of New York's exclusive literary circle.

# Glossary

The glossary is an alphabetical listing of words from the selections, along with their meanings. If you are not familiar with a word as you read, look it up in the glossary.

**The glossary gives the following information:**

1. **The pronunciation of each word.** For example, **turbulent** (tʉr′byə lənt). If there is more than one way to pronounce a word, the most common pronunciation is listed first. For example, **status** (stā′təs, stat′əs).

    **A primary accent** ′ is placed after the syllable that is stressed the most when the word is spoken. A **secondary accent** ′ is placed after a syllable that has a lighter stress. For example, **imitation** (im′ə tā′shən). The Pronunciation Key below shows the symbols for the sounds of letters, and key words that contain those sounds. Also, there is a short pronunciation key at the bottom of each right-hand page in the glossary.

2. **The part of speech of the word.** The following abbreviations are used:
    *adj.* adjective   *conj.* conjunction   *pro.* pronoun
    *adv.* adverb   *n.* noun   *v.* verb

3. **The meaning of the word.** The definitions listed in the glossary are the ones that apply to the way a word is used in these selections.

4. **Related forms.** Words with suffixes such as *-ing, -ed, -ness,* and *-ly* are listed under the base word. For example, **decisive** *adj.* . . . **decisively** *adv.,* **decisiveness** *n.*

## Pronunciation Key

| Symbol | Key Words | Symbol | Key Words | Symbol | Key Words | Symbol | Key Words |
|---|---|---|---|---|---|---|---|
| a | ask, fat, parrot | oi | oil, point, toy | b | bed, fable, dub | t | top, cattle, hat |
| ā | ape, date, play | ou | out, crowd, plow | d | dip, beadle, had | v | vat, hovel, have |
| ä | ah, car, father | u | up, cut, color | f | fall, after, off | w | will, always, swear |
| | | ʉr | urn, fur, deter | g | get, haggle, dog | y | yet, onion, yard |
| e | elf, ten, berry | | | h | he, ahead, hotel | z | zebra, dazzle, haze |
| ē | even, meet, money | ə | a in ago | j | joy, agile, badge | | |
| i | is, hit, mirror | | e in agent | k | kill, tackle, bake | ch | chin, catcher, arch |
| ī | ice, bite, high | | i in sanity | l | let, yellow, ball | sh | she, cushion, dash |
| | | | o in comply | m | met, camel, trim | th | thin, nothing, truth |
| ō | open, tone, go | | u in focus | n | not, flannel, ton | *th* | then, father, lathe |
| ô | all, horn, law | | | p | put, apple, tap | zh | azure, leisure |
| o͞o | ooze, tool, crew | ər | perhaps, murder | r | red, port, dear | ŋ | ring, anger, drink |
| oo | look, pull, moor | | | s | sell, castle, pass | ′ | able (ā′b'l) |
| yo͞o | use, cute, few | | | | | | |
| yoo | united, cure, globule | | | | | | |

This pronunciation key is from *Webster's New World Dictionary, Students Edition.*
Copyright © 1981, 1976 by Simon & Schuster. Used by permission.

# A

**abate** (ə bāt′) *v.* To make less.

**aberration** (ab′ər ā′shən) *n.* A turning aside from what is right or normal.

**abeyance** (ə bā′əns) *n.* Temporary suspension.

**abide** (ə bīd′) *v.* To put up with.

**abolitionist** (ab′ə lish′ən ist) *n.* One in favor of putting an end to slavery in the U.S.

**abrupt** (ə brupt′) *adj.* Happening suddenly or unexpectedly.—**abruptly** *adv.*

**absorption** (əb zôrp′shən) *n.* A taking in and incorporating.

**abut** (ə but′) *v.* To border on.

**abyss** (ə bis′) *n.* A bottomless gulf or pit.

**accolade** (ak′ə lād) *n.* Anything done as a sign of great respect and appreciation.

**acknowledgment** (ək näl′ij mənt) *n.* Something done to recognize or thank.—**acknowledge** *v.*

**acquisition** (ak′wə zish′ən) *n.* A getting by one's efforts.

**acrid** (ak′rid) *adj.* Sharp, bitter.

**acute** (ə kyōot′) *adj.* Sensitive, sharp.

**adobe** (ə dō′bē) *n.* Unburnt, sun-dried brick.

**aeon** (ē′ən) *n.* An extremely long period of time.

**aesthetic** (es thet′ik) *adj.* Aware of beauty.

**affability** (af′ə bil′ə tē) *n.* Friendliness; gentle kindliness.—**affable** *adj.*

**affidavit** (af′ə dā′vit) *n.* A written statement sworn to be true.

**affirmation** (af′ər mā′shən) *n.* A confirming; a positive declaration.

**affluence** (af′lōo wəns) *n.* Wealth, riches.

**affright** (ə frīt′) *v.* To frighten, terrify.

**afterburner** (af′tər bur′nər) *n.* A device on the tailpipe of some jet engines for obtaining additional thrust by using the hot exhaust gases to burn extra fuel.

**agitation** (aj′ə tā′shən) *n.* Emotional disturbance.

**akimbo** (ə kim′bō) *adj.* With hands on hips and elbows bent outward.

**allegiance** (ə lē′jəns) *n.* Loyalty or devotion.

**alluring** (ə loor′iŋ) *adj.* Tempting with something desirable.

**aloof** (ə lōof′) *adj.* Distant in sympathy or interest.

**amaranth** (am′ə ranth′) *n.* A dark, purplish red.

**ambiance** (am′bē ans) *n.* An environment or its distinct atmosphere.

**ambrosial** (am brō′zhə əl) *adj.* Delicious.

**amethyst** (am′ə thist) *n.* Purple or violet.

**anatomical** (an′ə täm′i k'l) *adj.* Structural.

**ancestral** (an ses′trəl) *adj.* Of people from whom one is descended.

**anchorage** (aŋ′kər ij) *n.* A secure place to hold on to.

**anemia** (ə nē′mē ə) *n.* Lack of vigor; lifelessness.

**anguish** (aŋ′gwish) *n.* Great suffering.

**animation** (an′ə mā′shən) *n.* Liveliness, spirit.— **animate** *v.*

**anonymity** (an′ə nim′ə tē) *n.* The fact of being without distinctive features.

**antiquity** (an tik′wə tē) *n.* The early period of history.

**antivenin** (an′ti ven′ən) *n.* An antibody to act against venom.

**apace** (ə pās′) *adv.* Swiftly.

**aperture** (ap′ər chər) *n.* An opening or hole.

**apex** (ā′peks) *n.* The highest point.

**aphorism** (af′ə riz′m) *n.* A short sentence expressing a wise observation.

**apprehension** (ap′rə hen′shən) *n.* An anxious feeling or dread.

**aqueduct** (ak′wə dukt′) *n.* A bridgelike structure for carrying a canal across a river.

**arboreal** (är bôr′ē əl) *adj.* Living in trees.

**archeologist** (är′kē äl′ə jist) *n.* One who studies ancient cultures, as by digging up remains.

**arduous** (är′joo wəs) *adj.* Strenuous; using much energy.

**armada** (är mä′də) *n.* A fleet.

**array** (ə rā′) *n.* An orderly grouping.

**arrogant** (ar′ə gənt) *adj.* Proud, overbearing; full of self-importance.

**articulate** (är tik′yə lāt′) *v.* To express clearly.

**ascertain** (as′ər tān′) *v.* To find out or learn.

**askew** (ə skyōo′) *adv.* To one side.

**assail** (ə sāl′) *v.* To attack or have a forceful effect on.

**assay** (as′ā) *v.* To test or analyze.

**assemblage** (ə sem′blij) *n.* A group of persons gathered together.

**assent** (ə sent′) *v.* To agree.

**assimilationism** (ə sim′ə lā′shən iz′m) *n.* The process of a group being absorbed into the main culture.—**assimilationist** *n.*

**astern** (ə sturn′) *adv.* Toward the back of a ship.

**astuteness** (ə stōot′nəs) *n.* Cleverness, keenness, shrewdness.

**audaciously** (ô dā′shəs lē) *adv.* Boldly; in a brazen way.

**audible** (ô′də b′l) *adj.* Loud enough to be heard.

**avenge** (ə venj′) *v.* To get revenge; to punish in a desire for justice.—**avenger** *n.*

**avert** (ə vʉrt′) *v.* To turn away.

**avidly** (av′id lē) *adv.* Greedily and eagerly.

**awestruck** (ô′struk′) *adj.* Filled with deep respect mixed with fear and wonder.

**azure** (azh′ər) *adj.* Sky-blue.

## B

**babel** (bā′b′l) *n.* A confusion of languages.

**babiche** (bä bēsh′) *n.* Thongs or lacings as of rawhide.

**balefully** (bāl′fə lē) *adv.* In an evil, sinister way.

**balustrade** (bal′ə strād′) *n.* A railing held up by small posts.

**bange** (banj) *v.* To gather or lounge about in groups.

**banish** (ban′ish) *v.* To get rid of or send away.

**bannock** (ban′ək) *n.* A flat cake of oatmeal or barley meal.

**bay** (bā) *adj.* Reddish-brown.

**bedeck** (bi dek′) *v.* To cover with decorations.

**beguilingly** (bi gīl′iŋ lē) *adv.* Charmingly, delightfully.

**benefactor** (ben′ə fak′tər) *n.* A person who has given help.

**benevolently** (bə nev′ə lənt lē) *adv.* Kindly.

**benign** (bi nīn′) *adj.* Good-natured, kindly.

**berth** (bʉrth) *n.* A position or job.

**beseechingly** (bi sēch′iŋ lē) *adv.* In a begging tone.

**betray** (bi trā′) *v.* To break faith with or lead astray.

**bewilderment** (bi wil′dər mənt) *n.* Hopeless confusion.

**bewitch** (bi wich′) *v.* To cast a spell over.

**bilingual** (bī liŋ′gwəl) *adj.* Of two languages.

**billet** (bil′it) *n.* A position or job.

**birthright** (bʉrth rīt′) *n.* The rights that a person has from birth.

**blench** (blench) *v.* To shrink back, as in fear.

**blight** (blīt) *n.* Anything that destroys or prevents growth.

**blunder** (blun′dər) *v.* To move clumsily or carelessly.

**bog** (bäg) *n.* Wet, spongy ground; a small swamp.—**boggy** *adj.*

**boisterous** (bois′tər əs) *adj.* Noisy and unruly.

**bole** (bōl) *n.* A tree trunk.

**bounty** (boun′tē) *n.* A reward.

**brackish** (brak′ish) *adj.* Having an unpleasant taste.

**brandish** (bran′dish) *v.* To wave or shake in a showy way.

**bravado** (brə vä′dō) *n.* A pretending to be brave when one is really afraid.

**breeching** (brich′iŋ) *n.* A harness strap around a horse's hindquarters.

**brockle** (bräk′′l) *adj.* Likely to break.

**brougham** (broֿoֿm) *n.* A closed carriage with the driver's seat outside.

**brusqueness** (brusk′nəs) *n.* A manner that is rough, short, and rude.

**buckboard** (buk′bôrd′) *n.* A four-wheeled, open carriage.

**buckeye** (buk′ī′) *n.* The seed of a chestnut tree.

**buffet** (buf′it) *v.* To thrust about.

**bullion** (bool′yən) *n.* Gold and silver as raw material.

**buoyant** (boi′ənt) *adj.* **1.** Having the tendency to rise in air. **2.** Cheerful in spirit.

**burlesque** (bər lesk′) *v.* To parody or imitate comically.

**burly** (bʉr′lē) *adj.* Big and strong.

**burrow** (bʉr′ō) *v.* To make a tunnel in the ground.

**burthen** (bʉr′thən) *n.* Archaic word for *burden*; responsibility.

**buxom** (buk′səm) *adj.* Healthy, attractive, plump, jolly.

## C

**cache** (kash) *n.* Anything hidden in a safe place.

**calabash** (kal′ə bash′) *n.* A large gourd.

**calliope** (kə lī′ə pē) *n.* A keyboard instrument like an organ, having a series of steam whistles.

**candidly** (kan′did lē) *adv.* Very honestly or frankly.

**canker** (kaŋ′kər) *v.* To become infected with a sore.

**canopy** (kan′ə pē) *n.* A covering.

**caper** (kā′pər) *v.* To skip about.

**cardinal** (kärd′′n əl) *adj.* Of main importance.

**cassock** (kas′ək) *n.* A long, closefitting garment.

---

fat, āpe, cär; ten, ēven; is, bīte; gō, hôrn;
tooֿl, look; oil, out; up, fʉr; get; joy; yet;
chin; she; thin, *th*en; zh, leisure; ŋ, ring;
ə for *a* in *ago*, *e* in *agent*, *i* in *sanity*,
*o* in *comply*, *u* in *focus*; ′ as in *able* (ā′b′l)

**casualty** (kazh′əl tē) n. Anyone hurt or killed in an accident.

**catacombs** (kat′ə kōmz′) n. A series of galleries in an underground burial vault.

**catapult** (kat′ə pult′) n. A mechanism for launching an airplane or rocket.

**ceremonial** (ser′ə mō′nē əl) adj. Ritual, formal.

**ceremoniously** (ser′ə mō′nē əs lē) adv. Politely, formally.

**cessation** (se sā′shən) n. A ceasing or stopping.

**chagrin** (shə grin′) n. A feeling of embarrassment and annoyance because one has been disappointed.

**charade** (shə rād′) n. An action that is easily seen as false.

**cheekiness** (chēk′ē nis) n. Bold rudeness.

**chesty** (ches′tē) adj. Boastful, proud, or conceited.

**chink** (chiŋk) n. A crack.

**chirrup** (chɥr′əp) v. To chirp repeatedly.

**chromium** (krō′mē əm) n. A hard, steel-gray metal.

**chronic** (krän′ik) adj. Lasting a long time.

**chronicle** (krän′i k′l) v. To write the story of.

**cipher** (sī′fər) n. A code.

**circumscribe** (sɥr′kəm skrīb′) v. To encircle or bound.

**clamor** (klam′ər) **1.** v. To cry out, complain, or demand noisily. **2.** n. A loud noise.

**clannish** (klan′ish) adj. Sticking closely to one's own group.

**clematis** (klem′ə tis) n. A plant or woody vine with bright flowers.

**cliché** (klē shā′) n. An expression that has become stale from too much use.

**clinically** (klin′i kə lē) adv. Objectively in a scientific way.

**clove** (klōv) n. Split, separation.

**coddle** (käd′′l) v. To treat tenderly; pamper.

**collage** (kə läzh′) n. A composition made of bits of objects.

**colonialism** (kə lō′nē əl iz′m) n. The policy by which a country holds onto foreign colonies.

**comatose** (kō′mə tōs′) adj. In a coma; unconscious.

**comber** (kōm′ər) n. A large wave.

**combustion** (kəm bus′chən) n. The act of burning.

**commence** (kə mens′) v. To begin.

**commerce** (käm′ərs) n. Dealings or relations of any kind.

**commiserate** (kə miz′ə rāt′) v. To sympathize or show sorrow for another's troubles.

**compass** (kum′pəs) v. To achieve or understand.

**compassion** (kəm pash′ən) n. Sorrow for the sufferings of another; pity.

**compulsion** (kəm pul′shən) n. A driving force.

**compunction** (kəm puŋk′shən) n. A sharp feeling of uneasiness brought on by guilt.

**comradely** (käm′rad lē) adj. Friendly.

**concession** (kən sesh′ən) n. A giving in.

**confederate** (kən fed′ər it) n. A person united with another for a common purpose; an ally.

**conical** (kän′i k′l) adj. Shaped like a cone.

**conjurer** (kän′jər ər) n. A magician.

**consolation** (kän′sə lā′shən) n. A thing that consoles or comforts.

**conspirator** (kən spir′ə tər) n. A person who takes part in a plot.

**conspiratorial** (kən spir′ə tôr′ē əl) adj. Showing that one is taking part in a plot.

**consternation** (kän′stər nä′shən) n. Great fear or shock that makes one feel helpless.

**constraint** (kən strānt′) n. Forced, unnatural manner.—**constrain** v.

**contemplative** (kən tem′plə tiv) adj. Given to thoughtful study.

**contemptuously** (kən temp′choo wəs lē) adv. With contempt or scorn.—**contemptuous** adj.

**contort** (kən tôrt′) v. To twist out of its usual form.

**contradiction** (kän′trə dik′shən) n. Something in opposition; a going against.

**contrarily** (kän′trer ə lē) adv. In stubborn opposition.

**conundrum** (kə nun′drəm) n. A puzzling question or problem.

**convalescent** (kän və les′′nt) adj. Getting back health after illness.

**converge** (kən vɥrj′) v. To come together at a point.

**conveyance** (kən vā′əns) n. A vehicle.

**coquettishly** (kō ket′ish lē) adv. Flirtaciously.

**cordiality** (kôr′jē al′ə tē) n. Warm, friendly feeling.

**cordon** (kôr′d′n) n. A circle or line of guards around an area.

**corm** (kôrm) n. The fleshy underground stem of certain plants.

**cornice** (kôr′nis) n. A horizontal molding projecting along the top of a wall.

**corroboration** (kə räb′ə rā′shən) n. Proof, support, confirmation.

**cosmopolitan** (käz′mə päl′ə t′n) adj. Representative of all the world.

**coster** (käs'tər) *n.* A person who sells fruit or vegetables from a cart.

**counsel** (koun's'l) *v.* To urge acceptance.

**countenance** (koun'tə nəns) *n.* Face or facial features.

**covey** (kuv'ē) *n.* A small flock of birds.

**craftily** (kraf'tə lē) *adv.* Slyly, shrewdly.

**craver** (krāv'ər) *n.* One who has a strong desire or longing.

**credential** (kri den'shəl) *n.* Something showing a right to a certain authority.

**crematorium** (krē'mə tôr'e əm) *n.* A building with a furnace for burning dead bodies to ashes.

**crevice** (krev'is) *n.* A narrow opening caused by a crack or split.

**crockery** (kräk'ər ē) *n.* Earthenware pots and dishes.

**cruse** (krōōz) *n.* A small container.

**crypt** (kript) *n.* An underground chamber, especially a burial vault.

**culminate** (kul'mə nāt') *v.* To reach its highest point.

**cultist** (kult'ist) *n.* One who has great devotion to something.

**culvert** (kul'vərt) *n.* A drain or waterway passing under a road.

**curate** (kyoor'it) *n.* A clergyperson.

**curator** (kyoo rāt'ər) *n.* A person in charge of a museum.

**curry** (kur'ē) *v.* To rub down and clean the coat of.

**curt** (kurt) *adj.* So short or abrupt as to seem rude.—**curtly** *adv.*

**cynicism** (sin'ə siz'm) *n.* A doubting remark or idea; the attitude of doubting people's motives or the value of living.

**D**

**dally** (dal'ē) *v.* To waste time.

**daunt** (dônt) *v.* To make afraid or discouraged.

**dauntless** (dônt'lis) *adj.* Fearless; that cannot be frightened or discouraged.

**debauch** (di bôch') *n.* Orgy; wild merrymaking.

**debunk** (di buŋk') *v.* To expose the false claims of.

**deception** (di sep'shən) *n.* Something that misleads, as an illusion.—**deceptive** *adj.* **deceptively** *adv.*

**declaim** (di klām') *v.* To speak in a loud and showy way.

**decorous** (dek'ər əs) *adj.* Showing dignity; behaving well.

**decrepit** (di krep'it) *adj.* Broken down or worn out by old age.

**defensively** (di fen'siv lē) *adv.* With the feeling that one is under attack and needs to justify one's actions.

**defer** (di fur') *v.* To put off, postpone.

**deference** (def'ər əns) *n.* Courteous regard or respect for the opinions of others.

**defiantly** (di fī'ənt lē) *adv.* With open, bold resistance.—**defiance** *n.*

**deft** (deft) *adj.* Skillful in a quick, sure way.—**deftly** *adv.*

**deign** (dān) *v.* To stoop.

**dejection** (di jek'shən) *n.* A being sad; depression.

**delirium** (di lir'ē əm) *n.* A temporary state of extreme mental excitement.—**deliriously** *adv.*

**delusion** (di lōō'zhən) *n.* A false belief or opinion.

**demure** (di myoor') *adj.* Modest, reserved, shy.

**deplore** (di plôr') *v.* To be sorry about.

**deprave** (di prāv') *v.* To corrupt.

**deprecatingly** (dep'rə kāt'iŋ lē) *adv.* In a belittling way.

**deride** (di rīd') *v.* To ridicule.

**derision** (di rizh'ən) *n.* Contempt, ridicule; a making fun of.

**desolate** (des'ə lit) **1.** *adj.* Lonely; ruined or destroyed. **2.** *v.* To destroy or lay waste.

**destitution** (des'tə tōō'shən) *n.* The state of utter poverty.

**detonation** (det'ə nā'shən) *n.* Explosion.

**devastate** (dev'ə stāt') *v.* **1.** To overwhelm, make helpless. **2.** To destroy.

**devilment** (dev''l mənt) *n.* Mischief.

**dexterous** (dek'strəs) *adj.* Having or showing skill in the use of the hands.—**dexterously** *adv.* **dexterity** *n.*

**diffidence** (dif'ə dəns) *n.* Lack of confidence; shyness.

**dilatory** (dil'ə tôr ē) *adj.* Slow, inclined to delay.

**diligent** (dil'ə jənt) *adj.* Hard-working, industrious.

**disarray** (dis'ə rā') *n.* An untidy condition.

---

fat, āpe, cär; ten, ēven; is, bīte; gō, hôrn, tōōl, look; oil, out; up, fur; get; joy; yet; chin; she; thin, then; zh, leisure; ŋ, ring; ə for a in ago, e in agent, i in sanity, o in comply, u in focus; ' as in able (ā'b'l)

**discernible** (di surn′ə b′l) *adj.* Able to be recognized or made out.

**discerning** (di surn′iŋ) *adj.* Having good judgment or understanding.

**disconcerting** (dis′kən surt′iŋ) *adj.* Upsetting, frustrating.

**discord** (dis′kord) *n.* A harsh, clashing noise.—**discordant** *adj*

**discreet** (dis krēt′) *adj.* Careful about what one says or does.—**discreetly** *adv.*

**disdain** (dis dān′) *n.* Contempt or scorn.

**disengage** (dis in gāj′) *v.* To release itself.

**dishearten** (dis här′t′n) *v.* To discourage, depress.

**dishevel** (di shev′′l) *v.* To cause to become mussed or untidy.

**disjointedly** (dis joint′id lē) *adv.* In a disconnected way.

**dispiritedly** (di′spir′it id lē) *adv.* Sadly.

**disquieting** (dis kwī′ət iŋ) *adj.* Disturbing; causing anxiety.

**disreputable** (dis rep′yoo tə b′l) *adj.* Not fit to be seen.

**divan** (dī′vən) *n.* A large sofa.

**divine** (də vīn′) *v.* To guess or predict.

**doggedly** (dôg′id lē) *adv.* Stubbornly, without giving in.—**doggedness** *n.* **dogged** *adj.*

**doldrums** (däl′drəmz) *n.* Equatorial ocean regions known for dead calms.

**domestic** (də mes′tik) *adj.* Of the home or family.

**domesticate** (də mes′tə kāt′) *v.* To tame.

**dominion** (də min′yən) *n.* Rule or control.

**dour** (door) *adj.* Gloomy, forbidding.

**dovetail** (duv′tāl) *v.* To join together by means of fan-shaped projections.

**draught** (draft) *n.* British spelling of *draft*, referring to an animal used for pulling heavy loads.

**dray** (drā) *n.* A low, sturdy cart for heavy loads.


**E**

**earnestness** (ur′nist nis) *n.* Seriousness, sincerity.—**earnest** *adj.*

**eccentricity** (ek′sen tris′ə tē) *n.* The state of being odd or unusual.

**eddy** (ed′ē) *n.* A little whirlwind or whirlpool.

**edifice** (ed′ə fis) *n.* A building.

**effervescence** (ef′ər ves′əns) *n.* A bubbling.

**egoistic** (ē′gō is′tik) *adj.* Thinking only about one's own interests.

**egotist** (ē′gə tist) *n.* One who thinks too much about oneself.

**ejaculate** (i jak′yə lāt′) *v.* To exclaim or say suddenly.

**élan** (ā län′) *n.* Much spirit or enthusiasm.

**elemental** (el′ə men′t′l) *adj.* Basic and powerful.

**eloquent** (el′ə kwent) *adj.* Expressing much feeling.

**elude** (i lood′) *v.* To evade or escape from by quickness or cunning.

**elusive** (i loo′siv) *adj.* Hard to catch or discover.

**emanate** (em′ə nāt′) *v.* To come forth.

**embellish** (im bel′ish) *v.* To improve by adding details, often fictitious ones.

**emigrate** (em′ə grāt′) *v.* To leave one country to settle in another.

**emphatically** (im fat′i kə lē) *adv.* Forcefully; with emphasis.—**emphatic** *adj.*

**enchantment** (in chant′mənt) *n.* A magic spell or charm.

**enigmatic** (en′ig mat′ik) *adj.* Puzzling, mysterious.

**ennui** (än′wē) *n.* Boredom.

**enrapture** (in rap′chər) *v.* To fill with great pleasure or delight.

**entomology** (en′tə mäl′ə jē) *n.* The branch of zoology that deals with insects.

**entrails** (en′trālz) *n.* The inner organs.

**entrepreneur** (än′trə prə nur′) *n.* A person who organizes and manages a business undertaking.

**epidemic** (ep′ə dem′ik) *n.* A contagious disease affecting many people.

**epitaph** (ep′ə taf′) *n.* An inscription, as on a tomb.

**epithet** (ep′ə thet′) *n.* A descriptive name.

**erratic** (i rat′ik) *adj.* Having no fixed course.

**etiolate** (ēt′ē ə lāt′) *v.* To bleach by depriving of sunlight.

**eulogize** (yoo′lə jīz′) *v.* To praise.

**exasperation** (ig zas′pə rā′shən) *n.* Anger, irritation, annoyance.—**exasperate** *v.*

**excruciatingly** (iks kroo′shē āt′iŋ lē) *adv.* Intensely; with great suffering or agony.

**executive** (ig zek′yə tiv) *adj.* Concerned with managing affairs.

**exhilarate** (ig zil′ə rāt′) *v.* To invigorate or stimulate.

**exhilaration** (ig zil′ə rā′shən) *n.* A merry, lively feeling; high spirits.

**explicit** (ik splis′it) *adj.* Clearly stated; definite.

**exposition** (eks′pə zish′ən) *n.* A large public exhibition or show.

**extol** (ik stōl´) *v*. To praise highly.

**extravagant** (ik strav´ə gent) *adj*. Going beyond reasonable limits.

**exuberant** (ig zoo´bər ənt) *adj*. Full of life, vitality, or high spirits.—**exuberance** *n*.

**exultation** (eg´zəl tā´shən) *n*. Rejoicing; triumph.—**exultant** *adj*. **exultantly** *adv*.

## F

**fabrication** (fab´rə kā´shən) *n*. Something made up.

**facetiousness** (fə sē´shəs nis) *n*. Humor; a joke.

**facilitate** (fə sil´ə tāt) *v*. To make easier.

**falteringly** (fôl´tər iŋ lē) *adv*. Unsteadily; showing hesitation or uncertainty.

**fandango** (fan daŋ´gō) *n*. A lively Spanish dance.

**feeder** (fēd´ər) *n*. A branch transportation line or channel that leads into something else.

**feint** (fānt) *v*. To deliver a pretended blow.

**fester** (fes´tər) *v*. To cause irritation; fill with pus.

**festoon** (fes toon´) *v*. To decorate.

**feverishly** (fē´vər ish lē) *adv*. Nervously, excitedly.

**fichu** (fish´oo) *n*. A three-cornered lace or muslin cape.

**finesse** (fi nes´) *n*. Skillfulness and delicacy of performance.

**flaccid** (flak´sid) *adj*. Soft and limp; weak.

**flagon** (flag´ən) *n*. A container for liquids.

**flippancy** (flip´ən sē) *n*. A joking or trying to be funny.

**floe** (flō) *n*. A piece of floating sea ice.

**florid** (flôr´id) *adj*. Flushed with red.

**flotsam** (flät´səm) *n*. Odds and ends.

**flourish** (flur´ish) **1.** *v*. To wave in the air. **2.** *n*. A sweeping movement; decorative lines.

**foolscap** (foolz´kap´) *n*. A size of writing paper.

**foppish** (fäp´ish) *adj*. Vain, affected; paying too much attention to appearance.

**forlorn** (fər lôrn´) *adj*. Pitiful, miserable.—**forlornly** *adv*.

**formidable** (fôr´mə də b'l) *adj*. Causing dread; awe-inspiring.

**forsaken** (fər sā´kən) *adj*. Abandoned.

**founder** (foun´dər) *v*. To fill with water and sink.

**fraternity** (frə tur´nə tē) *n*. The relationship or feeling between brothers.

**freshet** (fresh´it) *n*. A rush of fresh water flowing into the sea.

**fretfully** (fret´fə lē) *adv*. With annoyance or worry.

**fretwork** (fret´wurk) *n*. Decorative openwork.

**frippery** (frip´ər ē) *n*. Cheap, gaudy clothes.

**frontage** (frunt´ij) *n*. The front part of a building.

**fugitive** (fyoo´jə tiv) *n*. A person who flees from danger.

**funereally** (fyoo nir´ē ə lē) *adv*. Sadly, solemnly, gloomily.

**furrow** (fur´ō) *v*. To plow or make grooves.

**furtively** (fur´tiv lē) *adv*. In a sly, sneaky way.

**futile** (fyoot´'l) *adj*. Useless, hopeless, ineffective.—**futilely** *adv*.

## G

**gall** (gôl) *n*. Rude boldness.

**gamely** (gām´lē) *adv*. Bravely; having spirit.

**garish** (ger´ish) *adj*. Too bright or gaudy.

**garland** (gär´lənd) *v*. To decorate with a wreath.

**garrulous** (gar´ə ləs) *adj*. Talking too much.

**gaunt** (gônt) *adj*. Thin, bony, and hollow-eyed.

**gauntlet** (gônt´lit) *n*. Attack from both sides.

**genoa** (jen´ə wə) *n*. A large forward sail used on a racing yacht.

**genre** (zhän´rə) *n*. A kind or type.

**genteel** (jen tēl´) *adj*. Formerly, elegant or fashionable.

**gesticulation** (jes tik´yə lā´shən) *n*. A gesture.

**gilt** (gilt) *adj*. Overlaid with a gold substance.

**gingerly** (jin´jər lē) *adv*. Very carefully; cautiously.

**gloaming** (glō´miŋ) *n*. Evening dusk; twilight.

**graft** (graft) *n*. A dishonest use of one's position to get money.

**grandiose** (gran´dē ōs´) *adj*. Trying to seem important.

**graphically** (graf´i kə lē) *adv*. In realistic detail.

**gravity** (grav´ə tē) *n*. Solemn calmness.

**grievous** (grē´vəs) *adj*. Very bad; atrocious.

**grimace** (gri mās´) *v*. To twist the face in a look of pain or disgust.

**grisly** (griz´lē) *adj*. Very frightening and horrible.

**grudgingly** (gruj´iŋ lē) *adv*. Unwillingly.

---

fat, āpe, cär; ten, ēven; is, bīte; gō, hôrn,
tool, look; oil, out; up, fur; get; joy; yet;
chin; she; thin, *th*en; zh, leisure; ŋ, ring;
ə for *a* in *ago, e* in *agent, i* in *sanity,
o* in *comply, u* in *focus;* ' as in *able* (ā´b'l)

**gruffness** (gruf′nis) *n.* Roughness, unfriendliness.

**guerrilla** (gə ril′ə) *n.* Any member of a small defensive force of soldiers, not part of a regular army.

**guidon** (gīd′'n) *n.* The identification flag of a military unit.

**gunnel** (gun′'l) *n.* The upper edge of the side of a boat.

**gutter** (gut′ər) *v.* To melt rapidly so that the wax runs down the side in channels.

**guttural** (gut′ər əl) *adj.* Produced in the throat.

**gyroscope** (jī′rō skōp′) *n.* A wheel mounted in a ring so that the shaft on which it spins is free to turn in any direction.

## H

**haggard** (hag′ərd) *adj.* Having a wild, wasted, worn look.

**hallmark** (hôl′märk′) *n.* A mark of genuineness.

**halyard** (hal′yərd) *n.* A rope for raising or lowering a sail.

**hamper** (ham′pər) *v.* To keep from acting freely.

**harass** (hə ras′) *v.* To trouble, worry, or torment.

**haughtiness** (hôt′ē nis) *n.* Great pride in oneself and contempt for others.

**haven** (hā′vən) *n.* A sheltered, safe place; a refuge.

**hearken** (här′kən) *v.* To listen carefully.

**heathenism** (hē′thən izm) *n.* The state of not worshipping God, regarded as irreligious and uncivilized.

**hemoglobin** (hē′mə glō′bin) *n.* The red matter in blood cells that carries oxygen to the tissues.

**hemorrhage** (hem′ər ij) *n.* Heavy bleeding.

**herald** (her′əld) *v.* To announce, publicize.

**heresy** (her′ə sē) *n.* An opinion opposed to established doctrines.

**hermitage** (hur′mit ij) *n.* A retreat; a place where a person can live apart from others.

**herpetologist** (hur′pə täl′ə jist) *n.* One who studies reptiles.

**heyday** (hā′dā′) *n.* The time of greatest health, vigor, and success.

**hippodrome** (hip′ə drōm′) *n.* An oval course for horse and chariot races.

**homage** (häm′ij) *n.* Anything done to honor or show respect.

**hornbeam** (hôrn′bēm′) *n.* A tree with hard white wood.

**hue** (hyōō) *n.* Color.

**hunker** (hun′kər) *v.* To squat or crouch.

**hypocrisy** (hi päk′rə sē) *n.* A pretending to be what one is not.

**hysteria** (his tir′ē ə) *n.* An outbreak of wild, uncontrolled excitement.—**hysterical** *adj.*

## I

**ibis** (ī′bis) *n.* A large wading bird related to the herons.

**idealist** (ī dē′əl ist) *n.* One who sees things in ideal form.

**ignoble** (ig nō′b'l) *adj.* Shameful, dishonorable.

**illimitable** (i lim′it ə b'l) *adj.* Without limit or bounds.

**illusion** (i lōō′zhən) *n.* A false idea or mistaken belief.

**imminent** (im′ə nənt) *adj.* About to take place.

**impasse** (im′pas) *n.* A difficulty that cannot be solved.

**impassive** (im pas′iv) *adj.* Not showing emotion.

**impede** (im pēd′) *v.* To hinder, obstruct, or delay.

**impend** (im pend′) *v.* To be about to happen.

**impenetrable** (im pen′i trə b'l) *adj.* That cannot be passed through; not open to new ideas.

**imperative** (im per′ə tiv) *adj.* Absolutely necessary.

**imperceptibly** (im′pər sep′tə blē) *adv.* So slightly that it is barely noticed.—**imperceptible** *adj.*

**imperil** (im per′əl) *v.* To endanger.

**imperiously** (im pir′ē əs lē) *adv.* Arrogantly; in a domineering way.

**impetuously** (im pech′ōō wəs lē) *adv.* Violently, rashly, impulsively.—**impetuous** *adj.*

**impetus** (im′pə təs) *n.* The force with which something moves.

**implacable** (im plak′ə b'l) *adj.* That cannot be made calm.

**implore** (im plôr′) *v.* To beg to do something.

**imposture** (im päs′chər) *n.* Fraud; the practice of an impostor.

**improvise** (im′prə vīz′) *v.* To compose and perform at the same time without any preparation.—**improvisation** *n.*

**impudent** (im′pyōō dənt) *adj.* Shamelessly bold; disrespectful.

**impulsively** (im pul′siv lē) *adv.* On a sudden impulse.

**impunity** (im pyōō′nə tē) *n.* Freedom from punishment or harm.

**inaccessible** (in'ək ses'ə b'l) *adj.* Difficult to reach.

**inalienable** (in āl'yən ə b'l) *adj.* That may not be taken away.

**inanimate** (in an'ə mit) *adj.* Without life.

**inaudible** (in ô'də b'l) *adj.* That cannot be heard.—**inaudibly** *adv.*

**inauspicious** (in'ô spish'əs) *adj.* Unfavorable, unlucky.

**incalculable** (in kal'kyə lə b'l) *adj.* Too great to be counted.

**incessant** (in ses''nt) *adj.* Constant; never ceasing.—**incessantly** *adv.*

**incite** (in sīt') *v.* To urge to action.

**incoherent** (in'kō hir'ənt) *adj.* Not using speech that makes sense.

**incongruous** (in käŋ'groo wəs) *adj.* Not fitting; unsuitable.

**incredulously** (in krej'oo ləs lē) *adv.* With doubt or disbelief.—**incredulity** *n.*

**indelible** (in del'ə b'l) *adj.* That cannot be erased.

**india rubber** *n.* Crude natural rubber that comes from latex.

**indictment** (in dīt'mənt) *n.* An accusing or charging with a crime.

**indifference** (in dif'ər əns) *n.* A lack of concern or interest.

**indignation** (in'dig nā'shən) *n.* Anger at something that seems unjust.—**indignantly** *adv.*

**indiscriminately** (in'dis krim'ə nit lē) *adv.* Done in a random, careless way.

**indisputably** (in'dis pyoot'ə blē) *adv.* Certainly; without doubt.

**indomitable** (in däm'it ə b'l) *adj.* Unyielding; not easily discouraged.—**indomitably** *adv.*

**indubitably** (in doo'bi tə blē) *adv.* Undoubtedly, unquestionably.

**indulgence** (in dul'jəns) *n.* A kind yielding; lack of strictness.—**indulgently** *adv.*

**ineffable** (in ef'ə b'l) *adj.* Too overwhelming to be expressed.

**infallible** (in fal'ə b'l) *adj.* Incapable of error; not liable to fail.

**inference** (in'fər əns) *n.* Conclusion or opinion arrived at by reasoning.

**infernal** (in fur'n'l) *adj.* Hellish; fiendish.

**infirmities** (in fur'mə tēz) *n.* Physical weaknesses or defects.

**inflection** (in flek'shən) *n.* A change in tone or pitch of the voice.

**ingenious** (in jēn'yəs) *adj.* Cleverly made.

**inherent** (in hir'ənt) *adj.* Inborn, natural.

**inscrutable** (in skroot'ə b'l) *adj.* That cannot be easily understood; mysterious.

**insinuatingly** (in sin'yoo wāt'iŋ lē) *adv.* Slyly, by hinting.

**insolent** (in'sə lənt) *adj.* Boldly disrespectful, rude.

**insufferably** (in suf'ər ə blē) *adv.* Unbearably.

**insurrection** (in'sə rek'shən) *n.* A revolt.

**integral** (in'tə grəl) *adj.* Essential.

**integrity** (in teg'rə tē) *n.* Uprightness, honesty.

**intelligible** (in tel'i jə b'l) *adj.* That can be understood; clear.

**interminably** (in tur'mi nə blē) *adv.* Endlessly.

**interpose** (in'tər pōz') *v.* To place between.

**intimate** (in'tə māt') *v.* To hint or suggest.

**intravenous** (in'trə vē'nəs) *adj.* Into a vein.

**introspective** (in'trə spek'tiv) *adj.* Given to looking into one's own mind or feelings.—**introspect** *v.*

**intuition** (in'too wish'ən) *n.* Instant understanding.

**inundate** (in'ən dāt') *v.* To cover as with a flood.

**invincible** (in vin'sə b'l) *adj.* That cannot be defeated or conquered.

**invulnerable** (in vul'nər ə b'l) *adj.* Able to resist attack.

**iridescent** (ir'ə des''nt) *adj.* Showing a play of rainbowlike colors.

**irresolute** (i rez'ə loot') *adj.* Not able to decide; hesitating.

**irreverent** (i rev'ər ənt) *adj.* Showing lack of respect.

**irreversible** (ir'i vur'sə b'l) *adj.* That cannot be undone.

## J

**jaded** (jā'did) *adj.* Tired, worn-out.

**jaunty** (jôn'tē) *adj.* Happy and carefree.

**jetty** (jet'ē) *n.* A landing pier.

**jib** (jib) *n.* A triangular sail projecting ahead of the foremast.

---

fat, āpe, cär; ten, ēven; is, bīte; gō, hôrn,
tool, look; oil, out; up, fur; get; joy; yet;
chin; she; thin, *th*en; zh, leisure; ŋ, ring;
ə for *a* in *ago, e* in *agent, i* in *sanity,*
*o* in *comply, u* in *focus;* **'** as in *able* (ā'b'l)

**jibe** (jīb) *v.* To shift from one side of a boat to another, as a sail.

**joust** (joust) *v.* To engage in combat with lances between two knights on horseback.

**jubilance** (jōō'b'l əns) *n.* Joy, triumph.

**judicially** (jōō dish'ə lē) *adv.* Fairly and carefully; like a judge.

## K

**keel** (kēl) *n.* The chief wooden or steel piece along the entire bottom of a boat.

**keening** (kēn'iŋ) *n.* A wailing for the dead.

**ketch** (kech) *n.* A kind of fore-and-aft rigged sailing vessel.

**kilo** (kē'lō) *n.* A kilogram, 2.2 pounds.

## L

**labyrinth** (lab'ə rinth) *n.* A maze or network of winding passages.

**lament** (lə ment') *n.* An outward expression of sorrow; a wail.

**languid** (laŋ'gwid) *adj.* Sluggish, slow, listless.— **languor** *n.* **languidly** *adv.*

**larboard** (lär'bərd) *n.* The left-hand side of a ship as one faces forward.

**latent** (lāt''nt) *adj.* Lying hidden and undeveloped.

**lateritic** (lat'ə rit'ik) *adj.* Of a red soil formed by the decomposition of rocks.

**latticework** (lat'is wʉrk') *n.* An openwork structure of crossed strips of wood.

**lee** (lē) *n.* Shelter, protection.

**leer** (lir) *n.* A sly, sidelong look together with a wicked smile.

**leeward** (lē'wərd) *adj.* In the direction toward which the wind blows.

**legacy** (leg'ə sē) *n.* Anything handed down, as from an ancestor.

**legion** (lē'jən) *n.* A large number.

**lesion** (lē'zhən) *n.* An injury or hurt.

**liability** (lī'ə bil'ə tē) *n.* Something that works against one.

**liberation** (lib'ə rā'shən) *n.* A being released.

**lichen** (lī'kən) *n.* Any of a group of small plants composed of a fungus and an alga.

**linden** (lin'dən) *n.* A tree with heart-shaped leaves.

**linnet** (lin'it) *n.* A small bird, a finch.

**listlessly** (list'lis lē) *adv.* With no interest, as because of illness or weariness.

**literal** (lit'ər əl) *adj.* Real, strict, not going beyond the actual facts.

**lithe** (līth) *adj.* Limber, bending easily.

**livery** (liv'ər ē) *n.* A stable that keeps horses.

**livid** (liv'id) *adj.* Pale, grayish-blue.

**loiter** (loit'ər) *v.* To move slowly and lazily.

**lollop** (läl'əp) *v.* To move in a clumsy way, bobbing up and down.

**longevity** (län jev'ə tē) *n.* A long life.

**loom** (lōōm) *v.* To take shape indistinctly.

**lozenge** (läz''nj) *n.* A diamond shape.

**ludicrous** (lōō'di krəs) *adj.* Causing laughter because absurd or ridiculous.

**lumber** (lum'bər) *v.* To move heavily, clumsily, and noisily.

**luminance** (lōō'mə nəns) *n.* The state of being bright, shining, or full of light.

**lurid** (loor'id) *adj.* Glowing through a haze.

**luxuriant** (lug zhoor'ē ənt) *adj.* Growing thick and full.

**luxuriate** (lug zhoor'ē āt) *v.* To take great pleasure.

**lynch** (linch) *v.* To murder by action of a mob.

## M

**machete** (mə shet'ē) *n.* A large, heavy-bladed knife.

**mackintosh** (mak'in täsh') *n.* A raincoat.

**maggot** (mag'ət) *n.* A wormlike insect larva.

**magistrate** (maj'is trāt') *n.* A minor official with some powers to judge.

**magnate** (mag'nāt) *n.* An important, powerful person in business.

**malachite** (mal'ə kīt') *n.* Green.

**malevolent** (mə lev'ə lənt) *adj.* Showing ill will; evil.

**malice** (mal'is) *n.* Ill will; desire to harm another.—**malicious** *adj.* **maliciously** *adv.*

**mandolin** (man'd'l in') *n.* A musical instrument with four or five pairs of strings and a deep, round soundbox.

**manic** (man'ik) *adj.* Like a mental disorder that is wild or violent.

**manifest** (man'ə fest') *v.* To appear to the senses.

**marina** (mə rē'nə) *n.* A small harbor for docking and supplying small pleasure craft.

**marquisette** (mär'ki zet') *adj.* Of a thin meshlike fabric.

**martyrdom** (mär′tər dəm) *n.* The suffering of great pain or misery for a long time.

**meander** (mē an′dər) *v.* To wander aimlessly.

**measuredly** (mezh′ərd lē) *adv.* Carefully; in a planned way.

**mediate** (mē′dē āt′) *v.* To be in an intermediate position.

**meditative** (med′ə tāt′iv) *adj.* Showing quiet thought or deep reflection.

**melancholy** (mel′ən käl′ē) *adj.* Sad, gloomy.

**mêlée** (mā′lā) *n.* A noisy, confused hand-to-hand fight.

**melodrama** (mel′ə drä′mə) *n.* A play in which there is much suspense and strong feeling.

**melodramatic** (mel′ə drə mat′ik) *adj.* Sensational; excessively emotional.—**melodramatically** *adv.*

**menace** (men′is) *n.* Anything threatening harm.

**menacingly** (men′is iŋ′lē) *adv.* In a threatening way.

**mentor** (men′tər) *n.* A wise adviser or teacher.

**mesa** (mā′sə) *n.* A small, high plateau or flat tableland with steep sides.

**metaphor** (met′ə fôr′) *n.* A figure of speech that suggests a likeness by speaking of one thing as if it were a different thing.

**mettle** (met′′l) *n.* Quality of character; spirit.

**mettlesome** (met′′l səm) *adj.* Brave; full of spirit.

**midway** (mid′wā′) *n.* That part of a fair where rides, shows, games, and food stands are located.

**milennium** (mi len′ē əm) *n.* A period of 1,000 years.

**mirage** (mi räzh′) *n.* Something that seems to be real but is not.

**mirthful** (murth′fəl) *adj.* Merry, joyful.—**mirth** *n.*

**misgiving** (mis giv′iŋ) *n.* A disturbed feeling of fear, doubt, or worry.

**mismate** (mis māt′) *v.* To join badly as a pair.

**mizzen** (miz′′n) *n.* A fore-and-aft sail.

**modulate** (mäj′ə lāt′) *v.* To shift the key.

**monologue** (män′ə lôg′) *n.* A long speech.

**moorings** (moor′iŋz) *n.* A place where a boat is secured, usually by chains or cables.

**mortality** (môr tal′ə tē) *n.* The condition of being sure to die.

**mosaic** (mō zā′ik) *n.* A design made by laying bits of colored stone in mortar.

**motif** (mō tēf′) *n.* A main idea or theme that is repeated.

**motley** (mät′lē) *n.* A garment of various colors, worn by a jester.

**mottled** (mät′əld) *adj.* Marked with blotches or streaks.

**muskeg** (mus′keg) *n.* A kind of marsh containing thick layers of decaying vegetable matter.

**mutilate** (myoot′′l āt′) *v.* To damage or make imperfect.—**mutilation** *n.*

**myriad** (mir′ē əd) *adj.* Countless, innumerable.

**mystic** (mis′tik) *adj.* Mysterious, awe-inspiring.

**mythic** (mith′ik) *adj.* Having the nature of an old story handed down; imaginary.

## N

**napoleon** (nə pō′lē ən) *n.* A former gold coin of France.

**negligent** (neg′li jənt) *adj.* Careless, lax.

**neural** (noor′əl) *adj.* Of the nervous system.

**neurotic** (noo rät′ik) *n.* A person who has a mental disorder.

**nocturnal** (näk tur′n′l) *adj.* Happening in the night.

**nominal** (näm′i n′l) *adj.* Very small.

**nonchalance** (nän′shə läns′) *n.* The state of being cool, casual, and unconcerned.

**nondescript** (nän′di skript′) *n.* A person or thing without distinctive features.

**nuance** (noo′äns) *n.* Shade of difference.

## O

**obliterate** (ə blit′ə rāt′) *v.* To blot out.

**oblivious** (ə bliv′ē əs) *adj.* Not noticing.

**obscure** (əb skyoor′) **1.** *adj.* Vague, not easily understood; hidden. **2.** *v.* To hide or conceal.—**obscurity** *n.*

**obstinate** (äb′stə nit) *adj.* Stubborn, determined.

**officious** (ə fish′əs) *adj.* Giving unwanted advice or services.

**omen** (ō′mən) *n.* A thing that is supposed to foretell a future event.

**ominous** (äm′ə nəs) *adj.* Threatening, sinister; serving as an evil omen.—**ominously** *adv.*

---

fat, āpe, cär; ten, ēven; is, bīte; gō, hôrn, tool, look; oil; out; up, fur; get; joy; yet; chin; she; thin, *th*en; zh, leisure; ŋ, ring; ə for *a* in *ago*, *e* in *agent*, *i* in *sanity*, *o* in *comply*, *u* in *focus*; ′ as in *able* (ā′b′l)

**opacity** (ō pas'ə tē) *n.* The state of not letting light through.

**opaque** (ō pāk') *adj.* Not letting light through.

**oppressive** (ə pres'iv) *adj.* **1.** Weighing heavily on the mind. **2.** Cruel, unjust, harsh.—**oppressively** *adv.* **oppression** *n.*

**opulence** (äp'yə ləns) *n.* Wealth, abundance.

**or** (ôr) *adj.* Gold or yellow in color.

**ornithologist** (ôr'nə thäl'ə jist) *n.* One who studies birds.

## P

**pacify** (pas'ə fī') *v.* To make peaceful or calm.

**palaver** (pə lav'ər) *n.* Talk, especially idle chatter.

**palazzo** (pä lät'sô) *n.* A palace or palacelike mansion.

**pall** (pôl) *n.* A dark or gloomy covering.

**pallet** (pal'it) *n.* A small crude bed or a mattress used on the floor.

**pallid** (pal'id) *adj.* Lacking in normal color.

**panacea** (pan'ə sē'ə) *n.* A cure-all.

**papier-mâché** (pā'pər mə shā') *n.* A material made of paper pulp mixed with glue that is easily molded when moist and dries strong and hard.

**paragon** (par'ə gän') *n.* A model of perfection or excellence.

**paramount** (par'ə mount') *adj.* Chief, supreme, most important.

**paranoia** (par'ə noi'ə) *n.* A mental disorder in which one thinks others are persecuting him or her.

**paregoric** (par'ə gôr'ik) *n.* A certain medicine containing opium.

**pariah** (pə rī'ə) *n.* An outcast.

**passivity** (pa siv'ə tē) *n.* Inactivity.

**paten** (pat''n) *n.* A metal plate.

**patronage** (pā'trən ij) *n.* The regular business of customers.

**patronizingly** (pā'trə nīz'iŋ lē) *adv.* Kindly but snobbishly.

**peaked** (pē'kid) *adj.* Weak and pale.

**penicillin** (pen'ə sil'in) *n.* An antibiotic used to treat diseases.

**pensively** (pen'siv lē) *adv.* In deep thought; dreamily.—**pensive** *adj.*

**penury** (pen'yə rē) *n.* Lack of money; poverty.

**peril** (per'əl) *n.* Danger.

**perpetuate** (pər pech'oo wāt') *v.* To cause to continue.

**perusal** (pə rōō'z'l) *n.* The act of reading.

**perversity** (pər vur'sə tē) *n.* A being stubborn.

**petrol** (pet'rəl) *n.* British term for gasoline.

**pettishly** (pet'ish lē) *adv.* Crossly, peevishly.

**petulant** (pech'oo lənt) *adj.* Showing anger or annoyance.

**phonetic** (fə net'ik) *adj.* Of speech sounds.

**phosphorescence** (fas'fə res''ns) *n.* Light given off without heat.

**physic** (fiz'ik) *n.* A medicine.

**piazza** (pē az'ə) *n.* A large, covered porch.

**piecemeal** (pēs'mēl') *adv.* In small degrees.

**pike** (pīk) *n.* A weapon with a metal spearhead on a long shaft.

**pilaster** (pi las'tər) *n.* A rectangular support sticking out partially from a wall and treated architecturally as a column.

**pinion** (pin'yən) **1.** *n.* A bird's wing. **2.** *v.* To keep from moving by binding.

**pip** (pip) *n.* Any of the figures or spots on playing cards.

**pirouette** (pir'oo wet') *n.* A whirling around on one foot.

**placidity** (plə sid'ə tē) *n.* Calmness.

**plaguy** (plā'gē) *adj.* Annoying, disagreeable.

**plaintive** (plān'tiv) *adj.* Mournful, sad, sorrowful.—**plaintively** *adv.*

**plait** (plāt) *n.* A braid of hair.

**plankton** (plaŋk'tən) *n.* The microscopic animal and plant life in water, used as food by fish.

**platelet** (plāt'lit) *n.* Certain disks in the blood associated with clotting.

**plausibility** (plô'zə bil'ə tē) *n.* The state of seeming true or acceptable.

**plumage** (plōō'mij) *n.* A bird's feathers.

**plunder** (plun'dər) *v.* To rob by force.

**pompadour** (päm'pə dôr') *n.* A hairdo in which the hair is swept up high from the forehead.

**ponderous** (pän'dər əs) *adj.* Very heavy and bulky.

**popple** (päp''l) *n.* A poplar, a tree of the willow family.

**populace** (päp'yə lis) *n.* Population.

**portage** (pôr'tij) *n.* A carrying of boats and supplies overland.

**portly** (pôrt'lē) *adj.* Large and heavy.

**potentate** (pōt''n tāt) *n.* A person having great power.

**precariously** (pri ker'ē əs lē) *adv.* Unsafely, insecurely, dangerously.

**precedence** (pres′ə dəns) *n.* The act or right of coming before.

**precedent** (pres′ə dənt) *n.* An act that serves as an example or rule.

**precept** (prē′sept) *n.* A rule of conduct.

**precipice** (pres′ə pis) *n.* A steep cliff.

**preclude** (pri klōōd′) *v.* To prevent, make impossible.

**predate** (prē dāt′) *v.* To come before in time.

**predator** (pred′ə tər) *n.* An animal that lives by killing and feeding on other animals.

**predecessor** (pred′ə ses′ər) *n.* A thing replaced by another thing.

**predominate** (pri däm′ə nāt′) *v.* To have controlling influence.—**predominantly** *adv.*

**prelude** (prel′yōōd) *n.* A part that comes before or leads up to what follows.

**premonition** (prē′mə nish′ən) *n.* A warning in advance.—**premonitory** *adj.*

**preoccupy** (prē äk′yə pī′) *v.* To absorb or completely occupy the thoughts of.—**preoccupation** *n.*

**presumably** (pri zōōm′ə blē) *adv.* Probably.

**pretense** (pri tens′) *n.* A false show.

**pretension** (pri ten′shən) *n.* A pretending to be more grand than one really is.

**primeval** (prī mē′v′l) *adj.* Of the earliest times.

**prodigiously** (prə dij′əs lē) *adv.* Hugely, enormously, greatly.

**proffer** (präf′ər) *v.* To offer.

**profusely** (prə fyōōs′lē) *adv.* Freely, abundantly.

**projectile** (prə jek′t′l) *n.* An object made to be shot with force through the air.

**promenade** (präm′ə nād) *n.* A leisurely walk; a parade.

**promiscuously** (prə mis′kyoo wəs lē) *adv.* In a mixture without sorting; in an unplanned way, casually.

**prophetic** (prə fet′ik) *adj.* That predicts.

**propitiation** (prə pish′ē ā′shən) *n.* A thing to appease or regain good will.

**proprietary** (prə prī′ə ter′ē) *adj.* Of an owner.

**propriety** (prə prī′ə tē) *n.* The quality of being proper or fitting.

**prostrate** (präs′trāt) *adj.* Lying flat.

**protestation** (prät′is tā′shən) *n.* A protest or objection.

**protract** (prō trakt′) *v.* To draw out in time.

**provisional** (prə vizh′ən′l) *adj.* Temporary.

**provisions** (prə vizh′ənz) *n.* Something provided for the future.

**provocation** (präv′ə kā′shən) *n.* A cause of anger or irritation.

**prowess** (prou′is) *n.* Superior ability or skill.

**prudently** (prōōd′′nt lē) *adv.* Cautiously, sensibly.

**psychic** (sī′kik) *adj.* Of the mind or soul.

**psychopathic** (sī′kə path′ik) *adj.* Mentally ill.

**pullet** (pool′it) *n.* A young hen.

**pullman** (pool′mən) *n.* A railroad car with small private rooms.

**pulverize** (pul′və rīz′) *v.* To crush or grind.

**pummel** (pum′′l) *v.* To beat or hit with repeated blows.

**puncheon** (pun′chən) *n.* A large cask.

**pungent** (pun′jənt) *adj.* Producing a sharp sensation of smell.

**purgative** (pur′gə tiv) *n.* A substance that purges.

**Q**

**quarry** (kwôr′ē) *n.* An animal that is being hunted.

**quarter** (kwôr′tər) *v.* To blow on the after part of a ship's side.

**quay** (kē) *n.* A wharf for loading ships.

**querulous** (kwer′ə ləs) *adj.* Always complaining; impatient.

**quizzical** (kwiz′i k′l) *adj.* Perplexed, questioning.—**quizzically** *adv.*

**R**

**rampant** (ram′pənt) *adj.* Standing up on its tail.

**rampart** (ram′pärt) *n.* A defensive embankment.

**rank** (raŋk) *adj.* Too vigorous and coarse.

**rapier** (rā′pē ər) *n.* A light sword.

**rapt** (rapt) *adj.* Completely absorbed.—**raptly** *adv.*

**rapture** (rap′chər) *n.* The state of being carried away with love or joy.

**raunchiness** (rôn′chē nis) *n.* Sloppiness.

**ravenous** (rav′ə nəs) *adj.* Greedily hungry.

**reactionary** (rē ak′shə ner′ē) *adj.* Showing movement backward.

---

fat, āpe, cär; ten, ēven; is, bīte; gō, hôrn, tōōl, look; oil, out; up, fur; get; joy; yet; chin; she; thin, **th**en; zh, leisure; ŋ, ring; ə for *a* in *ago*, *e* in *agent*, *i* in *sanity*, *o* in *comply*, *u* in *focus*; ′ as in *able* (ā′b′l)

**rebuff** (ri buf') *v.* To refuse bluntly; snub.

**rebuke** (ri byo͞ok') *v.* To blame or scold in a sharp way.

**reckon** (rek'ən) *v.* To count.

**recoil** (ri koil') *v.* To draw back, as in fear or disgust.

**recommence** (rē'kə mens') *v.* To begin again.

**recurrent** (ri kur'ənt) *adj.* Appearing from time to time.

**redresser** (ri dres'ər) *n.* One who sets right, as by making up for.

**reflective** (ri flek'tiv) *adj.* Thoughtful.

**refrain** (ri frān') *n.* A phrase repeated from time to time.

**refuge** (ref'yo͞oj) *n.* Shelter or protection.

**regale** (ri gāl') *v.* To delight with something amusing.

**relentless** (ri lent'lis) *adj.* Persistent, not softening.

**remission** (ri mish'ən) *n.* A lessening or disappearance of symptoms.

**remit** (ri mit') *v.* To free someone from.

**rend** (rend) *v.* To tear or part with violence.

**replenishment** (ri plen'ish mənt) *n.* The act of supplying or making complete again.—**replenish** *v.*

**reproach** (ri prōch') *v.* To accuse of and blame for a fault.

**resignation** (rez'ig nā'shən) *n.* Patient acceptance of something.—**resigned** *adj.*

**resolute** (rez'ə lo͞ot') *adj.* Determined; having a fixed, firm purpose.—**resolutely** *adv.*

**resonance** (rez'ə nəns) *n.* A resounding or reechoing.

**restive** (res'tiv) *adj.* Unruly, restless.

**resurrect** (rez'ə rekt') *v.* To bring back into notice.

**retardation** (rē'tär dā'shən) *n.* A slowing the advancement of.

**reticent** (ret'ə s'nt) *adj.* Reserved; not willing to say much.

**retribution** (ret'rə byo͞o'shən) *n.* Punishment for a wrong done.

**retrogression** (ret'rə gres'shən) *n.* A movement backward.

**revel** (rev''l) *v.* To take much pleasure.

**revelation** (rev'ə lā'shən) *n.* A revealing or making known.

**reverberate** (ri vur'bə rāt') *v.* To echo back.

**reverie** (rev'ər ē) *n.* Daydreaming.

**rheum** (ro͞om) *n.* A watery discharge; a cold.

**righteous** (rī'chəs) *adj.* Doing what is right and just.

**roil** (roil) *v.* To stir up or agitate.

**rollicking** (räl'ik iŋ) *adj.* Playful, happy, carefree.

**rowel** (rou'əl) *v.* To spur.

**rudimentary** (ro͞o'də men'tər ē) *adj.* Not fully developed.

**ruefully** (ro͞o'fə lē) *adv.* Sorrowfully; with regret.—**rueful** *adj.*

**ruminate** (ro͞o'mə nāt') *v.* To turn something over in the mind.

**ruthless** (ro͞oth'lis) *adj.* Cruel; without pity.

## S

**saffron** (saf'rən) *adj.* Orange-yellow.

**sage** (sāj) *adj.* Having wisdom or good judgment.—**sagely** *adv.* **sagest** *adj.*

**sallow** (sal'ō) *adj.* Having an unhealthy, pale-yellow look.

**salvation** (sal vā'shən) *n.* A being saved.

**sandhog** (sand'hôg') *n.* A person who works on underwater construction projects under compressed air.

**sanitarium** (san'ə ter'ē əm) *n.* An institution for the care of invalids or those recovering from an illness.

**sapid** (sap'id) *adj.* Having a pleasing taste.

**sarape** (sə rä'pē) *n.* A woolen blanket used as an outer garment by men in Spanish-American countries.

**sarcastic** (sär kas'tik) *adj.* Mocking, sneering.—**sarcasm** *n.* **sarcastically** *adv.*

**sardonic** (sär dän'ik) *adj.* Scornfully or bitterly sneering.

**saturnalia** (sat'ər nā'lē ə) *n.* Any period of uncontrolled merrymaking.

**saucily** (sô'sə lē) *adv.* Boldly, with liveliness.

**savor** (sā'vər) *n.* Taste, flavor.

**savvy** (sav'ē) *v.* To understand.

**scallop** (skäl'əp) *n.* A curve, like a shell.

**scavenge** (skav'inj) *v.* **1.** To look for food. **2.** To collect material.

**sconce** (skäns) *n.* A bracket attached to a wall for holding a candle.

**scrutiny** (skro͞ot''n ē) *n.* A lengthy, searching look.—**scrutinize** *v.*

**scud** (skud) *v.* To move swiftly.

**scullery** (skul'ər ē) *n.* A room adjoining the kitchen where dirty kitchen work is done.

**sedative** (sed'ə tiv) *n.* A medicine that calms or quiets.

**seductive** (si duk′tiv) *adj.* Very tempting or attractive.

**self-righteously** (self rī′chəs lē) *adv.* In a way that shows one thinks of oneself as more moral than others.

**semblance** (sem′bləns) *n.* Outward appearance.

**sepulchre** (sep′′l kər) *n.* British spelling of *sepulcher*, a tomb.

**serpentine** (sur′pən tēn′) *adj.* Twisted or winding, like a serpent.

**serried** (ser′ēd) *adj.* Placed close together.

**servitude** (sur′və tood′) *n.* Slavery.

**settee** (se tē′) *n.* A small sofa.

**sextant** (seks′tənt) *n.* An instrument used by navigators in finding the position of a ship.

**shanty** (shan′tē) *n.* A shack or small, shabby dwelling.

**sharecropper** (sher′kräp′ər) *n.* A farmer who works for a share of the crop.

**shiftlessness** (shift′lis nis) *n.* Laziness, carelessness.

**shivaree** (shiv′ə rē′) *n.* A mock serenade.

**shoal** (shōl) *adj.* Shallow.

**shroud** (shroud) *v.* To hide, cover, or screen.

**sibilant** (sib′′l ənt) *adj.* Having a hissing sound.

**sidle** (sī′d′l) *v.* To move sideways, especially in a shy way.

**simile** (sim′ə lē) *n.* A figure of speech in which one thing is compared to a different thing by using the word *like* or *as.*

**sinew** (sin′yoo) *n.* A tendon.

**sinister** (sin′is tər) *adj.* Evil; unfortunate, disastrous.

**siphon** (sī′fən) *v.* To draw off, as through a bent tube.

**skittish** (skit′ish) *adj.* Nervous, easily frightened.

**skulk** (skulk) *v.* To move about in a sneaky way.

**slew** (sloo) *v.* To turn or swing around a fixed point.

**slipway** (slip′wā) *n.* A place between piers where ships can dock.

**sluice** (sloos) *n.* An artificial channel for water.

**slur** (slur) *n.* A remark that is belittling or harmful to one's reputation.

**snag** (snag) *n.* An underwater tree stump that is dangerous to ships.

**snigger** (snig′ər) *n.* A snickering laugh.

**sodden** (säd′′n) *adj.* Soaked.

**solicitude** (sə lis′ə tood′) *n.* Concern or care.

**solstice** (säl′stis) *n.* Either of two points at which the sun is farthest north or farthest south of the equator.

**sorrel** (sôr′əl) *adj.* A light reddish-brown color.

**sough** (sou) *n.* A soft sighing or rustling sound.

**sovereign** (säv′rən) *n.* A former British gold coin.

**spasmodic** (spaz mäd′ik) *adj.* Sudden, sharp, and irregular.

**speakeasy** (spēk′ē′zē) *n.* A place selling alcoholic drinks illegally.

**speculate** (spek′yə lāt′) *v.* To ponder, make guesses.—**speculatively** *adv.*

**spendthrift** (spend′thrift′) *n.* A person who spends money carelessly.

**spinnaker** (spin′ə kər) *n.* A large, triangular forward sail used on some racing yachts.

**splay** (splā) *v.* To spread apart.

**spoor** (spoor) *n.* The track or trail of a wild animal.

**spore** (spôr) *n.* A seed, germ, or cell that can develop into a new individual.

**squall** (skwôl) *n.* A brief, violent windstorm.

**squalor** (skwäl′ər) *n.* Filth and wretchedness.—**squalid** *adj.*

**squander** (skwän′dər) *v.* To use wastefully.

**stalactite** (stə lak′tīt) *n.* An icicle-shaped deposit hanging from the roof of a cave.

**starboard** (stär′bord) *n.* The right-hand side of a ship, as one faces forward.

**stealthily** (stelth′ə lē) *adv.* Quietly, secretly.

**stereopticon** (ster′ē äp′ti kən) *n.* A kind of slide projector.

**stiletto** (sti let′ō) *n.* A small dagger with a slender blade.

**stoicism** (stō′i siz′m) *n.* Calm and unbothered behavior.

**stratagem** (strat′ə jəm) *n.* A plan or scheme for deceiving an enemy.

**strategist** (strat′ə jist) *n.* One skilled in strategy or planning.—**strategic** *adj.*

**stricken** (strik′′n) *adj.* Suffering, as from pain or trouble.

**strident** (strīd′′nt) *adj.* Harsh-sounding, shrill.

---

fat, āpe, cär; ten, ēven; is, bīte; gō, hôrn,
tool, look; oil, out; up, fur; get; joy; yet;
chin; she; thin, *th*en; zh, leisure; ŋ, ring;
ə for *a* in *ago*, *e* in *agent*, *i* in *sanity*,
*o* in *comply*, *u* in *focus*; ′ as in *able* (ā′b′l)

**stripling** (strip′liŋ) *n.* A youth or grown boy.

**stupefy** (stoo′pə fī′) *v.* To stun or astound.

**stupor** (stoo′pər) *n.* A state in which the mind and senses are dulled.

**suavity** (swä′və tē) *n.* Graciousness or politeness of a smooth kind.

**sublime** (sə blīm′) *adj.* Of the highest kind; great.

**subterfuge** (sub′tər fyooj) *n.* Any action used to hide one's true purpose.

**subterranean** (sub′tə rā′nē ən) *adj.* Underground.

**sufferance** (suf′ər əns) *n.* Permission implied by not stopping.

**sulky** (sul′kē) *n.* A light two-wheeled carriage.

**sullen** (sul′ən) *adj.* Silent and keeping to oneself because one feels angry or hurt.

**sultry** (sul′trē) *adj.* Uncomfortably hot and moist.

**supercilious** (soo′pər sil′ē əs) *adj.* Proud, scornful; looking down on others.—**superciliously** *adv.*

**superlative** (sə pur′lə tiv) *n.* Something supreme or of the highest kind.

**supple** (sup′'l) *adj.* Limber, flexible.

**surly** (sur′lē) *adj.* Bad-tempered, rude, unfriendly.

**sustenance** (sus′ti nəns) *n.* One's means of livelihood or support.

**swaddle** (swäd′'l) *v.* To wrap or bind as in bandages.

**swathe** (swā*th*) *n.* A wrapping.

**symmetry** (sim′ə trē) *n.* Similarity of form on either side of a dividing line.

## T

**tandem** (tan′dəm) *adj.* Having two parts, one behind the other.

**tangible** (tan′jə b'l) *adj.* Having actual form and substance.

**taper** (tā′pər) *n.* A wax candle.

**tariff** (tar′if) *n.* A list of prices.

**tauten** (tôt′ən) *v.* To become tightly stretched.

**teeming** (tēm iŋ) *adj.* Full, abounding.

**tenacious** (tə nā′shəs) *adj.* Persistent, tough.

**tentatively** (ten′tə tiv lē) *adv.* Done as a test; not done definitely.—**tentative** *adj.*

**tepid** (tep′id) *adj.* Slightly warm.

**termination** (tur′mə nā′shən) *n.* The end or limit.

**terminus** (tur′mə nəs) *n.* An end or final point.

**terse** (turs) *adj.* Using no more words than are needed.

**theoretical** (thē′ə ret′i k'l) *adj.* Limited to theory; not practical.

**timorously** (tim′ər əs lē) *adv.* Timidly, fearfully.

**titanic** (tī tan′ik) *adj.* Of great strength or power.—**titan** *n.*

**torrid** (tôr′id) *adj.* Intensely hot.

**tourniquet** (toor′nə kit) *n.* A device for pressing on a blood vessel.

**transfusion** (trans fyoo′zhən) *n.* A transferring, especially of blood.

**transparency** (trans per′ən sē) *n.* Something so fine as to be seen through.

**transposition** (trans pə zish′ən) *n.* A change of positions.

**traverse** (tra vurs′) *v.* To pass across or through.

**treacherous** (trech′ər əs) *adj.* Seeming safe but not really so.

**tremulous** (trem′yoo ləs) *adj.* Trembling, quivering.

**tule** (too′lē) *n.* A large bulrush found in lakes and marshes.

**tump-line** (tump′līn) *n.* A broad band passed across the forehead and over the shoulders to support a pack on the back.

**tumult** (too′mult) *n.* A confused or disturbed condition.

**tumultuous** (too mul′choo wəs) *adj.* Wild, noisy, and uproarious.

**tunic** (too′nik) *n.* A short coat forming part of a policeman's uniform.

**turbulent** (tur′byə lənt) *adj.* Full of uproar or wild disorder.

## U

**ubiquitous** (yoo bik′wə təs) *adj.* Present, or seeming to be present, everywhere.

**unaffectedly** (un ə fek′tid lē) *adv.* Sincerely, naturally.

**unapproachable** (un′ə prōch′ə b'l) *adj.* Distant; hard to be friendly with.

**unavailing** (un′ə vā′liŋ) *adj.* Useless, ineffective.

**uncanny** (un kan′ē) *adj.* Strange, weird.

**unceremoniously** (un′ser ə mō′nē əs lē) *adv.* So quickly or suddenly as to be rude.

**uncongenial** (un′kən jēn yəl) *adj.* Disagreeable, unsuitable.

**unconscionable** (un kän′shən ə b'l) *adj.* Unreasonable, excessive.

**undulate** (un′joo lāt′) *v.* To move in waves.

**unendurable** (un′in door′ə b'l) *adj.* Unbearable.

**unfeigned** (un fānd') *adj.* Genuine, real, sincere.

**unfilial** (un fil'ē əl) *adj.* Not suitable to or expected from a son or daughter.

**unflagging** (un flag'iŋ) *adj.* Not weakening or drooping.

**unflinching** (un flin'chiŋ) *adj.* Steadfast, unyielding.

**ungainly** (un gān'lē) *adj.* Awkward, clumsy.

**unhinged** (un hinj'd') *adj.* Upset; thrown into confusion.

**unobtrusively** (un'əb trōō'siv lē) *adv.* In an understated, subtle way.

**unprecedented** (un pres'ə den'tid) *adj.* Unheard-of; not done before.

**unredressed** (un ri dres'd') *adj.* Not set right.

**unsubstantial** (un'səb stan'shəl) *adj.* Having no substance; light.

**unutterable** (un ut'ər ə b'l) *adj.* That cannot be described.

**unwary** (un wer'ē) *adj.* Not watchful, not alert to danger.

**usurer** (yōō'zhoo rər) *n.* A person who lends money at interest.

**usurp** (yōō surp') *v.* To take and hold by force.


## V

**vagrant** (vā'grənt) **1.** *adj.* Random. **2.** *n.* One who wanders.

**vaingloriously** (vān'glôr'ē əs lē) *adv.* With boastful conceit and pride.

**valedictory** (val'ə dik'tər ē) *adj.* Spoken as a farewell statement.

**valet** (val'it) *n.* A man's personal manservant.

**veneer** (və nir') *n.* A thin layer used to cover something.

**venerable** (ven'ər ə b'l) *adj.* Worthy of respect or reverence.

**vengeance** (ven'jəns) *n.* Great force or fury.

**verdant** (vur'd'nt) *adj.* Fresh and green.

**vermilion** (vər mil'yən) *adj.* Bright red.

**vermin** (vur'min) *n.* An insect or small animal regarded as a pest.

**vex** (veks) *v.* To disturb, annoy, irritate.

**vigil** (vij'əl) *n.* A time of staying awake during the usual hours of sleep in order to keep watch.

**vindicate** (vin'də kāt') *v.* To clear from blame.

**virtuoso** (vur'choo wō'sō) *adj.* Of a person with highly cultivated artistic tastes.

**virulent** (vir'yoo lənt) *adj.* Extremely poisonous or harmful; deadly.

**vole** (vōl) *n.* A small rodent.

**voluble** (väl'yoo b'l) *adj.* Talking very much.

**voucher** (vou'chər) *n.* A paper attesting to the payment of money.

**vouchsafe** (vouch sāf') *v.* To be kind enough to give.

**vulnerable** (vul'nər ə b'l) *adj.* Open to attack.


## W

**wane** (wān) *v.* To approach the end.

**warrant** (wôr'ənt) *v.* To guarantee.

**wary** (wer'ē) *adj.* Cautious.

**wayfarer** (wā'fer'ər) *n.* A person who travels, especially from place to place on foot.

**wean** (wēn) *v.* To get a young animal used to food other than its mother's milk.

**whimsical** (hwim'zi k'l) *adj.* Having odd notions; unpredictable.

**wile** (wīl) *n.* A sly or clever trick to fool someone.

**wince** (wins) *v.* To draw back slightly, twisting the face in pain.

**wistfully** (wist'fə lē) *adv.* With vague yearnings or longings.

**withers** (with'ərz) *n.* The highest part of the back of a horse.

**wizened** (wiz''nd) *adj.* Withered or dried up.

**wont** (wōnt) *n.* Habit, usual practice.

**wrangle** (raŋ'g'l) *v.* To argue, quarrel.

**wrath** (rath) *n.* Intense anger; rage.

**writhe** (rīth) *v.* To twist, turn, or squirm.

**wryly** (rī'lē) *adv.* In a way that is bent to one side.

---

fat, āpe, cär; ten, ēven; is, bīte; gō, hôrn,
tōōl, look; oil, out; up, fur; get; joy; yet;
chin; she; thin, *th*en; zh, leisure; ŋ, ring;
ə for *a* in *ago*, *e* in *agent*, *i* in *sanity*,
*o* in *comply*, *u* in *focus*; ' as in *able* (ā'b'l)

# Index of Titles and Authors

# Index of Fine Art

**The Museum of Modern Art**

*The Wing*, 1958. Odilon Redon.
Lithograph, printed in black. Composition: 12-1/2 x 9-5/8".

*The Blind Swimmer*, 1943. Max Ernst.
Oil on Canvas, 36-3/8 x 29".

*Self-Portrait*, 1929. John Kane.
Oil on canvas over composition board, 36-1/8 x 27-1/8".

*The Violin Player*, 1947. Ben Shahn.
Tempera on plywood, 40 x 26".

*Bauhaus Stairway*, 1932. Oskar Schlemmer.
Oil on canvas, 63-7/8 x 45".

*Simultaneous Contrast: Sun and Moon*, 1912. Robert Delaunay.
Oil on canvas, 53" diameter.

"The Toboggan," Plate 20 from *Jazz*, 1947. Henri Matisse.
Pochoir, printed in color 13 x 11-7/8".

*Turnsole*, 1961. Kenneth Noland.
Synthetic polymer paint on canvas, 7'10-1/8" x 7'10-1/8".

# Index of Skills

## Reading and Literary Skills

# Vocabulary and Language Skills

# Writing Skills

# Art Credits

## Cover

*Hommage à Blériot,* 1914. Robert Delaunay. Kunstmuseum, Basel.

## Photographs

Hans Hinz, cover, 467; Lee Stalsworth, xii, 455, 460, 507; Brown Brothers, 312, 319; Geoffrey Clements, 401; John Tennant, 62, 436; Joseph Szaszfai, 470; Sotheby Parke-Bernet/Editorial Photocolor Archives, 477; The Museum of Modern Art/Film Stills Archive, 534–584; Editorial Photocolor Archives/Scala, 589; The Bettmann Archive, 593; Robert C. Ragsdale/Photos Courtesy of the Stratford Festival, 600–674.

Photo Researchers: Russ Kinne, 32, 235; Farrell Grehan, 230; Carl Frank, 256; Richard Hutchings, 257; Susan McCartney, 259; Katrina Thomas, 273; Lynn McLaren, 281; Peter Miller, 299; E. Hanumantha Rao, 326; S. Nagendra, 328; Noelle Bloom, 339; Paul Crum, 360; Tom McHugh, 363; Michael P. Gadomski, 368; Norman R. Lightfoot, 371; Ronny Jaques, 374; Mike Coggins, 386; F.B. Grunzweig, 390.

## Illustrations

Steven Schindler, 22, 429, 439; Robert Masheris, 44, 77, 204; Alan Daniel, 86–87, 101, 487; Robert Korta, 95; James Watling, 111, 433, 449, 468, 492; Ben Otero, 121, 215, 249, 422, 423; Phill Renaud, 167, 241; Larry Raymond, 182; George Armstrong, 188; Jean Helmer, 225, 410, 474; Debbie Chabrian, 482; Karen Lidbeck, 494, 502.

# Acknowledgments    *Continued from copyright page*

Letter," from *Silence In the Snowy Fields*, Wesleyan University Press, 1962; copyright © 1962 by Robert Bly, reprinted with his permission. Brandt & Brandt Literary Agents, Inc.: For "Searching for Summer" by Joan Aiken, from *The Green Flash and Other Tales of Horror;* copyright © 1958 by Joan Aiken. For "By the Waters of Babylon" by Stephen Vincent Benét, from *The Selected Works of Stephen Vincent Benét*, Holt, Rinehart & Winston, Inc.; copyright 1937, by Stephen Vincent Benét, copyright renewed © 1964 by Thomas C. Benét, Stephanie B. Mahin, and Rachel Benét Lewis. Constance Carrier: For "Peter at Fourteen" by Constance Carrier, from *The Middle Voice*. John Ciardi: For "Sometimes Running" by John Ciardi, from *In Fact;* copyright 1962 by Rutgers University, reprinted by permission of John Ciardi. Bill Cooper Associates Agency, Inc., Heywood Hale Broun and Patricia Broun: For "The Fifty-First Dragon" by Heywood Broun, from *With a Merry Heart.* Crown Publishers, Inc.: For material adapted from *The Silence of the North* by Olive A. Fredrickson with Ben East; copyright © 1972 by Olive A. Fredrickson and Ben East. Doubleday & Company, Inc.: For "A Visit to Grandmother" by William Melvin Kelley, from *Dancers on the Shore;* copyright © 1964 by William Melvin Kelley. Norma Millay Ellis: For "Ebb" and "Counting-Out Rhyme" by Edna St. Vincent Millay, from *Collected Poems*, Harper & Row; copyright 1921, 1928, 1948, 1955 by Edna St. Vincent Millay and Norma Millay Ellis. Mari Evans: For "If There Be Sorrow" and "Here — Hold My Hand" by Mari Evans, from *I Am a Black Woman*, published by Wm. Morrow & Company, 1970, by permission of the author. Farrar, Straus & Giroux, Inc.: For excerpts from *Life Among the Savages* by Shirley Jackson; copyright 1945, 1948, 1949, 1950, 1951, 1952, 1953 by Shirley Jackson, copyright renewed © 1973, 1976, 1977, 1978, 1979, 1980, 1981 by Laurence Hyman, Barry Hyman, Mrs. Sarah Webster, and Mrs. Joanne Schnurer. For excerpts from *The Right Stuff* by Tom Wolfe; copyright © 1979 by Tom Wolfe. For "First Ice" by Andrei Voznesensky, from *Voznesensky: Selected Poems*, translated by Herbert Marshall; copyright © 1966 by Herbert Marshall, reprinted by permission of Hill and Wang, a division of Farrar, Straus and Giroux, Inc. Field Newspaper Syndicate: For "The Hidden Songs of a Secret Soul" by Bob Greene, in *The Chicago Sun-Times*, March 3, 1975; © 1975 Field Enterprises, Inc. Barthold Fles, Literary Agent: For excerpts from *Nellie Bly: First Woman Reporter* by Iris Noble; copyright © 1956 by Iris Noble. Donald Hall: For "The Man in the Dead Machine," from *The Alligator Bride* by Donald Hall. Harcourt Brace Jovanovich, Inc.: For "Fair and Circus Days" by Carl Sandburg, from *Prairie Town Boy* and from *Always the Young Strangers;* copyright 1952, 1953 by Carl Sandburg, copyright renewed 1980, 1981 by Margaret Sandburg, Janet Sandburg, and Helga Sandburg Crile. For "The Writer" by Richard Wilbur, from *The Mind Reader: New Poems;* copyright © 1971 by Richard Wilbur. For "Quail Walk" by Heather Ross Miller, from *The Wind Southerly;* copyright © 1967 by Heather Ross Miller. Harper & Row, Publishers, Inc.: For "Fifteen," from *Stories That Could Be True* by William Stafford; copyright © 1964 by William E. Stafford. For an abridgment from pp. 121–132 in *Fifth Chinese Daughter* by Jade Snow Wong; copyright 1950 by Jade Snow Wong. For specified excerpts (under the title "Old Times on the Mississippi") from *Life On the Mississippi* by Mark Twain. For "Tenement Room: Chicago" (pp. 136–137) by Frank Marshall Davis, from *Golden Slippers*, compiled by Arna Bontemps; copyright 1941. For "Once More to the Lake" (pp. 197–202), from *Essays of E. B. White* by E. B. White; copyright 1941 by E. B. White. For excerpts from "Flood" (pp. 148–158) in *Pilgrim at Tinker Creek* by Annie Dillard; copyright © 1974 by Annie Dillard. For "My Grandmother Would Rock Quietly and Hum" by Leonard Adamé (pp. 108–109), from *From the Barrio: A Chicano Anthology*, edited by Luis Omar Salinas and Lillian Faderman; copyright © 1973 by Luis Omar Salinas and Lillian Faderman. For "The Children of the Poor" (pp. 99–103), from *The World of Gwendolyn Brooks* by Gwendolyn Brooks; copyright 1949, by Gwendolyn Brooks Blakely. For an abridgment and adaptation from *Eric* by Doris Lund (J. B. Lippincott, Publishers—as it appeared in *Good Housekeeping* under the title "Gift from a Son Who Died"); copyright © 1974 by Doris Lund. Harvard University Press: For "A Narrow Fellow in the Grass" by Emily Dickinson, reprinted by permission of the publishers and the Trustees of Amherst College, from *The Poems of Emily Dickinson*, edited by Thomas H. Johnson, Cambridge, Mass.: The Belknap Press of Harvard University Press, copyright 1951, © 1955, 1979 by the President and Fellows of Harvard College. Ronald Hobbs Literary Agency: For "The Worker" by Richard Thomas, from *Black Fire;* copyright 1968. Holt, Rinehart and Winston, Publishers: For "Out, Out—" and "Nothing Gold Can Stay" by Robert Frost, from *The Poetry of Robert Frost*, edited by Edward Connery Lathem; copyright 1916, 1923, © 1969 by Holt, Rinehart and Winston; copyright 1944, 1951 by Robert Frost. For "The Heyday of the Blood," from *Hillsboro People* by Dorothy Canfield Fisher; copyright 1915 by Holt, Rinehart and Winston; copyright 1943 by Dorothy Canfield Fisher. Houghton Mifflin Company: For "Fireworks" and "Generations," from *The Complete Poetical Works of Amy Lowell;* copyright © 1955 by Houghton Mifflin Company. For "Oysters," from *The Book of Folly* by Anne Sexton; copyright 1972 by Anne Sexton. For *Shane* by Jack Schaefer; copyright 1949 and © renewed 1976 by Jack Schaefer. James Hurst: For "The Scarlet Ibis" by James Hurst; copyright 1960 by The Atlantic Monthly Company. Indiana University Press: For "The Burden" by Francesca Yetunde Pereira, from *Poems from Black Africa*, edited by Langston Hughes, published by Indiana University Press. Johnson Publishing Company, Inc. and Eugenia Collier: For "Sweet Potato Pie" by Eugenia Collier; copyright © August, 1982 by Johnson Publishing Company, Inc. Alfred A. Knopf, Inc.: For "To Be of Use" by Marge Piercy, from *Circles on the Water;* copyright © 1982 by Marge Piercy. Ruth Lechlitner: For "Kansas Boy" by Ruth Lechlitner, from *Poetry Magazine*, November, 1931. Lenniger Literary Agency, Inc.: For "The Cub" by Lois Dykeman Kleihauer, reprinted by permission of the author and her agents, Lenniger Literary Agency, 104 East 40th Street, New York, N. Y. 10016. Little, Brown and Company in association with the Atlantic Monthly Press: For excerpts from "Aging in the Land of the Young" by Sharon Curtin; copyright © 1972 by Sharon R. Curtin, first appeared in *The Atlantic*, from *Nobody Ever Died of Old Age.* For "Was Worm" by May Swenson, from *New & Selected Things Taking Place;* copyright © 1958 by May Swenson. The Sterling Lord Agency, Inc.: For "Ballad of the Morning Streets" by Leroi Jones, from *Black Magic Poetry, 1961–1967;* copyright 1969 by Leroi Jones. Manna Lowenfels-Perpelitt: For "Untitled" by Niki Paulzine, from *From the Belly of the Shark*, edited by Walter Lowenfels; copyright © 1973 by Walter Lowenfels, published by Vintage Books, a Division of Random House, reprinted by permission of Manna Lowenfels-Perpelitt Literary Executrix. McGraw-Hill Ryerson Limited: For "Act of a Hero" by Hugh Garner, from *Violation of the Virgins;* copyright © Hugh Garner, 1971. Macmillan Publishing Co., Inc.: For "Harriet Tubman" by Henrietta Buckmaster, from *Women Who Shaped History;* copyright © 1966 by Macmillan Publishing Co., Inc. For "Thoughts" by Sara Teasdale, from *Collected*

*Poems;* copyright 1915 by Macmillan Publishing Co., Inc., renewed 1943 by Marie T. Wheless. For "Haikus" by José Juan Tablada, from *The Yellow Canary Whose Eye Is So Black,* edited and translated by Cheli Durán; copyright © 1977 Cheli Durán Ryan. Harold Matson Company, Inc.: For "Woman Without Fear" by Daniel P. Mannix; copyright © 1963 by Daniel P. Mannix. For "The Snob" by Morley Callaghan; copyright © 1959 by Morley Callaghan. For "Of Missing Persons" by Jack Finney; copyright © 1957 by Jack Finney. For "There Will Come Soft Rains" by Ray Bradbury, from chapter "August 2026," pp. 214–221; copyright © 1950 by Ray Bradbury, copyright © renewed 1978. Durango Mendoza: For "The Passing" by Durango Mendoza; copyright 1981, used by permission of the author. Elliott Merrick: For "Without Words" by Elliott Merrick, from *Frost and Fire.* N. Scott Momaday: For "Simile" by N. Scott Momaday, from *Angle of Geese and Other Poems,* David R. Godine, publisher. William Morrow & Company, Inc.: For "Nahuatl: A Song of Nezahualcoyotl," adapted from *Ancient Nahuatl Poetry,* from *The Magic World,* selected and edited by William Brandon; copyright © 1971 by William Brandon. For "Poetry Is a Tressel," from *The Women and the Men* by Nikki Giovanni; copyright © 1970, 1974, 1975 by Nikki Giovanni. Don Moser: For "Evening Flight" by Don Moser; copyright © 1957 by *Harper's Magazine.* University of Nebraska Press: For "The Sentimentality of William Tavener," from *Willa Cather's Collected Short Fiction, 1892–1912* (Rev. Ed.) with introduction by Mildred R. Bennett; edited by Virginia Faulker by permission of University of Nebraska Press; copyright © 1965, 1970 by the University of Nebraska Press. New Directions Publishing Corporation: For "The Secret" by Denise Levertov, from *O Taste and See;* copyright © 1964 by Denise Levertov Goodman. The New York Times: For "There Is No News from Auschwitz" by A. M. Rosenthal, April 16, 1981 *Magazine;* copyright © 1981 by The New York Times Company. *The New Yorker:* For "March 1st" by Kathleen Spivack, from March 6, 1965 issue; copyright © 1965 The New Yorker Magazine, Inc. For "Directions to the Armorer" by Elder Olson, from *The New Yorker,* Nov. 14, 1959; copyright © 1959 The New Yorker Magazine, Inc. University of Notre Dame Press: For excerpts from *Barrio Boy* by Ernesto Galarza; copyright 1971, University of Notre Dame Press, Notre Dame, IN 46556. Ralph Pomeroy: For "Corner" by Ralph Pomeroy, from *In the Financial District;* copyright © 1968 Ralph Pomeroy. Random House, Inc.: For *A Raisin in the Sun* by Lorraine Hansberry; copyright © 1958, 1959 by Robert Nemiroff as the Executor of the Estate of Lorraine Hansberry; reprinted by permission of Random House, Inc. For "Blues Ain't No Mockin' Bird," from *Gorilla, My Love* by Toni Cade Bambara; copyright © 1972 by Toni Cade Bambara. For excerpts from *I Know Why the Caged Bird Sings* by Maya Angelou; copyright © 1969 by Maya Angelou. For excerpts from *Act One* by Moss Hart; copyright © 1959 by Catherine Carlisle Hart and Joseph M. Hyman. For "O What Is That Sound" by W. H. Auden, from *W. H. Auden: Collected Poems;* copyright 1937 and renewed 1965 by W. H. Auden. For "The Puritan's Ballad," from *Collected Poems of Elinor Wylie* by Elinor Wylie; copyright 1928 by Alfred A. Knopf, Inc. and renewed 1965 by Edwina C. Rubinstein, by permission of Alfred A. Knopf, Inc. For "Plucking the Rushes," from *Translations from the Chinese,* translated by Arthur Waley; copyright 1919, 1941 by Alfred A. Knopf, Inc. and renewed 1947 by Arthur Waley, by permission of Alfred A. Knopf, Inc. For "Troubled Woman" by Langston Hughes, from *Selected Poems of Langston Hughes;* copyright 1926 by Alfred A. Knopf, Inc. and renewed 1954 by Langston Hughes, by permission of Alfred A. Knopf, Inc. For "Business," from *Mainland* by Victor Hernandez Cruz; copyright © 1973 by Victor Hernandez Cruz. For "Gracious Goodness," from *Living in the Open* by Marge Piercy; copyright © 1976 by Marge Piercy, by permission of Alfred A. Knopf, Inc. For "Miss Rosie," from *Good Times* by Lucille Clifton; copyright © 1969 by Lucille Clifton. For an excerpt from "Symmetries and Asymmetries," from *W. H. Auden Collected Poems* by W. H. Auden; copyright © 1959 by W. H. Auden. For excerpts from *Tell Freedom* by Peter Abrahams; copyright 1954 by Peter Abrahams, reprinted by permission of Alfred A. Knopf, Inc. For "Letter Slot" and "Pendulum," from *Telephone Poles and Other Poems* by John Updike; copyright © 1958, 1959, 1960, 1961, 1962, 1963, by John Updike, reprinted by permission of Alfred A. Knopf, Inc. For "Ex-Basketball Player" and "Glasses" from *The Carpentered Hen and Other Tame Creatures* by John Updike; copyright © 1957, 1982 by John Updike, by permission of Alfred A. Knopf, Inc. Bill Ransom: For "Grandpa" by W. M. Ransom, from *From the Belly of the Shark.* Paul R. Reynolds, Inc.: For "Early Marriage" by Conrad Richter, from *Early Americana and Other Stories;* copyright © 1934, 1935, 1936 by The Curtis Publishing Company. For excerpts from *Pagan Spain* by Richard Wright; copyright © 1957 by Richard Wright. Rutgers University Press: For "Fast Run in the Junkyard," from *Mostly People* by Jeannette Nichols; copyright © 1966 by Rutgers, The State University. *The Saturday Evening Post:* For "November Day" by Eleanor Averitt; copyright © 1958 The Curtis Publishing Company. Scholastic, Inc.: For "The Carnival" by Michael W. Fedo, from *Practical English,* Oct. 18, 1968—a Scholastic Magazine. For material from *Corvus the Crow* by Franklin Russell; copyright © 1972 by Franklin Russell, reprinted by permission of Four Winds Press, a division of Scholastic, Inc. Charles Scribner's Sons: For "A Day's Wait," in *Winner Take Nothing* by Ernest Hemingway; copyright 1933 Charles Scribner's Sons; copyright renewed 1961 Mary Hemingway. For "The Breed of 'Em" by Will James, from *Cow Country;* copyright 1927 Charles Scribner's Sons; copyright renewed 1955 by August Dufault. Silvermine Publishers, Inc.: For "Words" by Pauli Murray. Simon & Schuster, a Division of Gulf & Western Corporation: For material from *Policewoman* by Dorothy Uhnak; copyright © 1963 by Dorothy Uhnak. Toni Strassman, Agent: For "The Wooing of Ariadne," from *Pericles on 31st Street* by Harry Mark Petrakis; copyright 1965 by Harry Mark Petrakis, published by Quadrangle Press in 1965. Dabney Stuart: For "The River," from *The Diving Bell;* copyright 1966 by Dabney Stuart, used by permission of the author. Theodore L. Thomas: For "The Test" by Theodore L. Thomas, from *The Magazine of Fantasy and Science Fiction.* Mrs. James Thurber: For "Snapshot of a Dog" by James Thurber, from *The Middle-Aged Man on the Flying Trapeze;* copyright © 1935 by James Thurber, copyright © 1963 by Helen W. Thurber and Rosemary T. Sauers, published by Harper & Row. Viking Penguin, Inc.: For "The Choice" by Dorothy Parker, from *The Portable Dorothy Parker,* revised and enlarged edition, edited by Brendan Gill; copyright renewed 1954 by Dorothy Parker. For "The Open Window," from *The Complete Short Stories of Saki* by H. H. Munro; copyright 1930 by The Viking Press, Inc. For an excerpt from *Travels with Charley* by John Steinbeck; copyright © 1961, 1962 by The Curtis Publishing Co., Inc.; copyright © 1962 by John Steinbeck. For "First Lesson," from *Letter from a Distant Place* by Philip Booth; copyright © 1957 by Philip Booth. For "Orpheus" by Ted Hughes, from *Tiger's Bones and Other Plays for Children* by Ted Hughes; copyright © 1970 by Ted Hughes. For "Sale Today," from *Times Three* by Phyllis McGinley; copyright renewed 1968 by Phyllis McGinley. José Garcia Villa: For "Lyric 17," from *Selected Poems and New* by José Garcia Villa; copyright © 1958. A. Watkins, Inc.: For "Winter Night" by Kay Boyle, from *The New Yorker* issue dated Jan. 19, 1946. John Walsh and World Society for the Protection of Animals: For a selection from *Time Is Short and the Water Rises* by John Walsh and Robert Gannon;

## Staff Credits

Editorial Director: Joy Littell
Managing Editor: Kathleen Laya
Associate Editor: Zana Courser
Rights and Permissions: Irma Rosenberg
Director of Design: Allen Carr
Associate Designer: Marcia Vecchione

Editor-in-Chief: Joseph F. Littell